Handbook of

North American Indians

Handbook of North American Indians

WILLIAM C. STURTEVANT
General Editor

VOLUME 7

Northwest Coast

WAYNE SUTTLES
Volume Editor

SMITHSONIAN INSTITUTION

WASHINGTON

1990

For sale by the Superintendent of Documents,
U.S. Government Printing Office, Washington, D.C. 20402.

Library of Congress Cataloging in Publication Data

Handbook of North American Indians.

    Bibliography.
    Includes index.
    CONTENTS:

                v. 7. Northwest Coast.

    1. Indians of North America.
I. Sturtevant, William C.

E77.H25   970′.004′97   77–17162

Contents

This map is a diagrammatic guide to the coverage of this volume; it is not an authoritative depiction of territories for several reasons. Sharp boundaries have been drawn and no area is unassigned. The groups mapped are in some cases arbitrarily defined, subdivisions are not indicated, no joint or disputed occupations are shown, and different kinds of land use are not distinguished. Since the map depicts the situation at the earliest periods for which evidence is available, the ranges mapped for different groups often refer to different periods, and there may have been intervening movements, extinctions, and changes in range. Not shown are groups that came into separate existence later than the map period for their areas. The simplified ranges shown are a generalization of the situation in the early 19th century, with those of the Kwakiutl and Northern Coast Salish for the mid-19th century. For more specific information see the maps and text in the appropriate chapters.

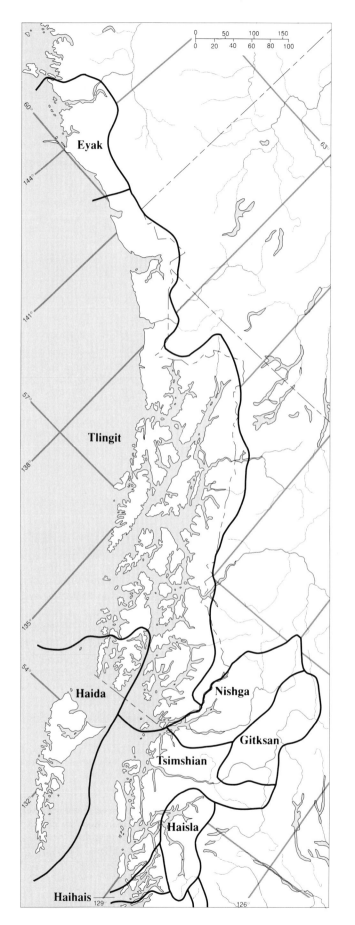
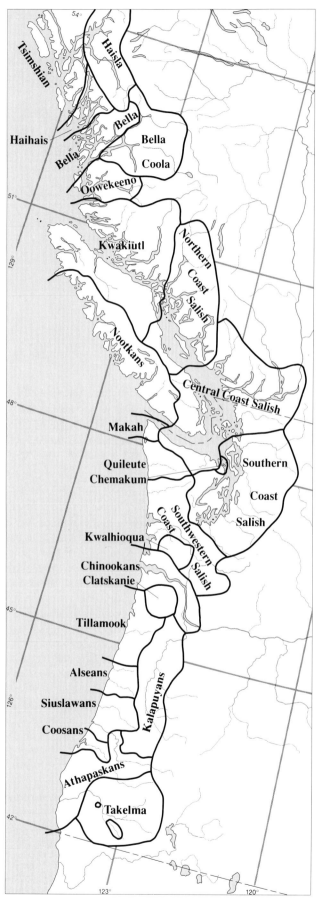

ix

Technical Alphabet

Consonants

		bilabial	labiodental	dental	alveolar	alveopalatal	velar	back velar	glottal
stop	vl	p		t	t		k	q	ʔ
	vd	b		d	d		g	ġ	
affricate	vl			θ̂	c	č			
	vd			δ̂	ʒ	ǯ			
fricative	vl	φ	f	θ	s	š	x	x̣	h
	vd	β	v	δ	z	ž	γ	γ̇	
nasal	vl	M			N		N		
	vd	m			n		ŋ	ŋ̇	
lateral	vl				ɫ				
	vd				l				
semivowel	vl	W				Y			
	vd	w				y			

vl=voiceless; vd=voiced

Other symbols include: λ (voiced lateral affricate), ƛ (voiceless lateral affricate), ˀ (pharyngeal stop), ḥ (voiceless pharyngeal fricative), r (medial flap, trill, or retroflex approximant), ẏ or ÿ (unrounded velar glide).

Vowels

	front	central	back
high	i (ü)	ɨ	u (ɨ)
	I		U
mid	e (ö)	ə	o
	ε		ɔ
			Λ
low	æ	a	a

Unparenthesized vowels are unrounded if front or central, and rounded if back; *ü* and *ö* are rounded; *i* is unrounded. The special symbols for lax vowels (I, U, ε, ɔ) are generally used only where it is necessary to differentiate between tense and lax high or mid vowels. *i* and *a* are used for both central and back vowels, as the two values seldom contrast in a given language.

Modifications indicated for consonants are: glottalization (*t̓*, *k̓*, etc.), fronting (*x̱*, etc.), retroflexion (*ʈ*), palatalization (*tʸ*, *kʸ*, *nʸ*, * lʸ*), labialization (*kʷ*), aspiration (*tʰ*), length (*t·*). For vowels: length (*a·*), three-mora length (*a:*), nasalization (*ą*), voicelessness (*A*). The commonest prosodic markings are, for stress: *á* (primary) and *à* (secondary), and for pitch: *á* (high), *à* (low), *â* (falling), and *ǎ* (rising); however, the details of prosodic systems and the uses of accents differ widely from language to language.

Words in Indian languages cited in italics in this volume are, with one set of exceptions, in phonemic transcription. That is, the letters and symbols are used in specific values defined for them by the structure of the sound system of the particular language. However, as far as possible, these phonemic transcriptions use letters and symbols in generally consistent values, as specified by the standard technical alphabet of the *Handbook*, displayed on this page. Deviations from these standard values as well as specific details of the phonology of each language (or references to where they may be found) are given in an orthographic footnote in each tribal chapter. One deviation from the standard values that is found in the transcriptions of Athapaskan-Eyak, Tlingit, and Northern Wakashan (except Kwakiutl) is the use of the voiceless stop and affricate symbols for voiceless aspirates, and of the voiced symbols for the corresponding plain (unaspirated) stops and affricates. For example, in these languages *t* represents phonetic [tʰ] and *d* represents [t]. Exceptionally, italics are used for Chinook Jargon words, which appear in the conventional English-based spellings of the sources. Phonetic transcriptions, even if available, would be variable, and a unified phonemic transcription impossible, since speakers of Chinook Jargon tended to pronounce it using the sounds of their respective languages.

No italicized Indian word is broken at a line end except when a hyphen would be present anyway as part of the word. Words in italicized phonemic transcription are never capitalized. Pronunciations or phonetic values given in the standard technical alphabet without regard to phonemic analysis are put in square brackets rather than in italics. The glosses, or conventionalized translations, of Indian words are enclosed in single quotation marks.

Indian words recorded by nonspecialists or before the phonemic systems of their languages had been analyzed are often not written accurately enough to allow respelling in phonemic transcription. Where phonemic retranscription has been possible the citation of source has been modified by the label "phonemicized" or "from." A few words that could not be phonemicized have been "normalized"—rewritten by mechanical substitution of the symbols of the standard technical alphabet. Others have been rationalized by eliminating redundant or potentially misleading diacritics and substituting nontechnical symbols. Words that do not use the standard technical alphabet occasionally contain some letters used according to the values of other technical alphabets or traditional orthographies. The most common of these are g for the *Handbook* [ġ]; g· for [gʸ] and k· for [kʸ] (but for [ġ] and [q], respectively, in some late-nineteenth-century sources); H for [x]; kq for [kʷ]; L for [ƛ] and Ḻ for [λ]; q for [x] or [x̣]; c for [š] and tc for [č]; x for [x]; χ for [x]; ' for [h]; ' and ˀ for [ʔ]; ! for glottalization (e.g., t! for [t̓]); ä for [æ]; â for [ɔ·]; ᴇ for [ə]; î, ɪ (or I), and ɩ for short [i]; ô for [ɔ]; ᴜ (or U) for short [u]; and ᵘ for ʷ.

All nonphonemic transcriptions give only incomplete, and sometimes imprecise, approximations of the correct pronunciation.

Nontechnical Equivalents

Correct pronunciation, as with any foreign language, requires extensive training and practice, but simplified (incorrect) pronunciations may be obtained by ignoring the diacritics and reading the vowels as in Italian or Spanish and the consonants as in English. For a closer approximation to the pronunciation or to rewrite into a nontechnical transcription the substitutions indicated in the following table may be made. The orthographic footnote for some languages contains a practical alphabet that may be used as an alternative by substituting the letters and letter groups for their correspondents in the list of technical symbols in the same footnote.

technical	nontechnical	technical	nontechnical	technical	nontechnical
æ	ae	M	mh	Y	yh
β	bh	N	nh	ž	zh
c	ts	ŋ	ng	ʒ	dz
č	ch	$\mathbf{N}$	ngh	ǯ	j
δ	dh	ɔ	o	ʔ	'
ɛ	e	θ	th	ǩ, p̌, ť, etc.	k', p', t', etc.
γ	gh	φ	ph	a·, e·, k·, s·, etc.	aa, ee, kk, ss, etc.
ɫ	lh	š	sh	ą, ę, etc.	an, en, etc.
λ	dl	W	wh	k^y, t^y, etc.	ky, ty, etc.
ƛ	tlh	x	kh	k^w	kw

Transliteration of Russian Cyrillic

А	а	a	I	i [a]	ī	С	с	s	Ъ	ъ [b]	"
Б	б	b	И	й	ĭ	Т	т	t	Ы	ы	y
В	в	v	К	к	k	У	у	u	Ь	ь	'
Г	г	g	Л	л	l	Ф	ф	f	Ѣ	ѣ [a]	ie
Д	д	d	М	м	m	Х	х	kh	Э	э	ė
Е	е	e	Н	н	n	Ц	ц	ts	Ю	ю	iu
Ё	ё	ë	О	о	o	Ч	ч	ch	Я	я	ia
Ж	ж	zh	П	п	p	Ш	ш	sh	Ѳ	ѳ [a]	f
З	з	z	Р	р	r	Щ	щ	shch	Ѵ	ѵ [a]	ẏ
И	и	i									

[a] Not in the alphabet adopted in 1918.
[b] Disregarded in final position.

The transcription from Russian Cyrillic script is not entirely consistent. The Library of Congress transliteration displayed here has been used in the titles of items in the bibliography and in names and words that were available in Cyrillic, but the names of some authors appear in a simplified version. The names of historical personages and place-names are generally in the spellings used in the most available English sources or translations. The older alphabet has been followed when the sources use it.

English Pronunciations

The English pronunciations of the names of tribes and a few other words are indicated parenthetically in a dictionary-style orthography in which most letters have their usual English pronunciation. Special symbols are listed below, with sample words to be pronounced as in nonregional United States English. Approximate phonetic values are given in parentheses in the standard technical alphabet.

ŋ: thing (ŋ)
θ: thin (θ)
ð: this (ð)
zh: vision (ž)

ă: bat (æ)
ä: father (a)
ā: bait (ey)
e: bet (ɛ)
ē: beat (iy)

ə: about, gallop (ə)
ĭ: bit (ɪ)
ī: bite (ay)
ô: bought (ɔ)

ō: boat (ow)
oo: book (ʊ)
oo: boot (uw)
u: but (ʌ)

'(primary stress), ˌ(secondary stress): elevator ('eləˌvātər) (élǝvèytǝr)

Conventions for Illustrations

Map Symbol

- • Native settlement
- ○ Abandoned settlement
- ■ Non-native or mixed settlement
- □ Abandoned settlement
- · Archeological or other site
- ▲ Modern reservation or reserve
- Estimated tribal territory
- Body of water
- River or creek
- National boundary
- Province or state boundary

Haisla Tribe

Portland Settlement, fort, site

Stephens Passage Geographical feature

Settlements on maps reflect their status in 1989.

Credits and Captions

Credit lines give the source of the illustrations or the collections where the artifacts shown are located. The numbers that follow are the catalog or inventory numbers of that repository. When the photographer mentioned in the caption is the source of the print reproduced, no credit line appears. "After" means that the *Handbook* illustrators have redrawn, rearranged, or abstracted the illustration from the one in the cited source. All maps and drawings not otherwise credited are by the *Handbook* illustrators. Measurements in captions are to the nearest millimeter if available; "about" indicates an estimate or a measurement converted from inches to centimeters. The following abbreviations are used in credit lines:

Amer.	American	Ind.	Indian
Anthr.	Anthropology, Anthropological	Inst.	Institute
	ical	Instn.	Institution
Arch.	Archives	Lib.	Library
Arch(a)eol.	Arch(a)eology,	Mus.	Museum
	Arch(a)eological	NAA	National Anthropological
Assoc.	Association		Archives
Co.	County	Nat.	Natural
Coll.	Collection(s)	Natl.	National
Dept.	Department	opp.	opposite
Div.	Division	pl(s).	plate(s)
Ethnol.	Ethnology, Ethnological	Prov.	Provincial
fol.	folio	Res.	Reservation (U.S.)
Ft.	Fort		Reserve (Canada)
Hist.	History	Soc.	Society
Histl.	Historical	U.	University

Metric Equivalents

10 mm = 1 cm	10 cm = 3.937 in.	1 km = .62 mi.	1 in = 2.54 mi.	25 ft. = 7.62 m
100 cm = 1 m	1 m = 39.37 in.	5 km = 3.1 mi.	1 ft. = 30.48 cm	1 mi. = 1.60 km
1,000 m = 1 km	10 m = 32.81 ft.	10 km = 6.2 mi.	1 yd. = 91.44 cm	5 mi. = 8.02 km

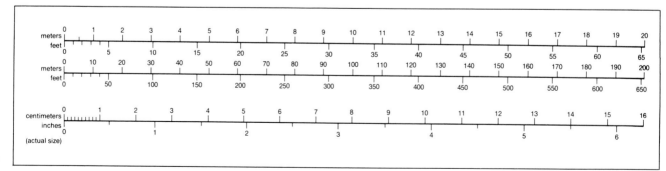

Preface

This is the ninth volume to be published of a 20-volume set planned to give an encyclopedic summary of what is known about the prehistory, history, and cultures of the aboriginal peoples of North America north of the urban civilizations of central Mexico. Volumes 5–6 and 8–15 treat the other major culture areas of the continent.

Some topics relevant to the Northwest Coast area are excluded from this volume because they are more appropriately discussed on a continent-wide basis. Readers should refer to volume 1, Introduction, for general descriptions of anthropological and historical methods and sources and for summaries for the whole continent of certain topics regarding social and political organization, religion, and the performing arts. Volume 2 contains detailed accounts of the different kinds of Indian and Eskimo communities in the twentieth century, especially during the second half, and describes their relations with one another and with the surrounding non-Indian societies and nations. Volume 3 gives the environmental and biological backgrounds within which Native American societies developed, summarizes the early and late human biology or physical anthropology of Indians and Eskimos, and surveys the earliest prehistoric cultures. (Therefore the Paleo-Indian or Early Man period in the Northwest Coast receives major treatment in volume 3 rather than in this volume.) Volume 4 contains details on the history of the relations between Whites and Native American societies. Volume 16 is a continent-wide survey of technology and the visual arts—of material cultures broadly defined. Volume 17 surveys the Native languages of North America, their characteristics and historical relationships. Volumes 18 and 19 are a biographical dictionary; included in the listing are many Northwest Coast Indians. Volume 20 contains an index to the whole, which will serve to locate materials on Northwest Coast Indians in other volumes as well as in this one; it also includes a list of errata found in all preceding volumes.

Preliminary discussions on the feasibility of a new encyclopedic *Handbook of North American Indians* and alternatives for producing it began in 1965 in what was then the Smithsonian's Office of Anthropology. By 1971 funds were available and plans had advanced to the point where the details of the Northwest Coast volume could be worked out. Accordingly, a specially selected Planning Committee (listed on p. *v*) met with the General Editor and the Volume Editor in Portland, Oregon, on February 27–28, 1971. That meeting soon resulted in a list of 70 chapters by 38 authors. Each author was sent instructions that included a brief description of the desired contents of the chapter, prepared by the Volume Editor, and a "Guide for Contributors" prepared by the General Editor, which described the general aims and methods of the *Handbook* and the editorial conventions. One convention has been to avoid the present tense, where possible, in historical and cultural descriptions. Thus a statement in the past tense, with a recent date or approximate date, may also hold true for the time of writing.

As they were received, the manuscripts were reviewed by the Volume Editor, the General Editor, and usually one or more referees, who frequently included a member of the Planning Committee and often authors of other chapters. Suggestions for changes and additions often resulted. The published versions frequently reflect more editorial intervention than is customary for academic writings, since the encyclopedic aims and format of the *Handbook* made it necessary to attempt to eliminate duplication, avoid gaps in coverage, prevent contradictions, impose some standardization of organization and terminology, and keep within strict constraints on length. Where the evidence seemed so scanty or obscure as to allow different authorities to come to differing conclusions, authors have been encouraged to elaborate their own views, although the editors have endeavored to draw attention to alternative interpretations published elsewhere.

During the 1970s a few draft chapters were received, the first arriving on May 1, 1972. The outline and the list of authors were occasionally revised, until it became necessary about 1977 to change the publication schedules for the *Handbook* volumes. Editorial attention then focused on one after another of the eight volumes that were published first (see the list on p. *i*). In June 1985 intensive work to complete the *Northwest Coast* volume began. At that time, all authors of manuscripts then on hand were asked to revise and bring them up to date, and many new assignments were made. The 58 chapter titles in the final volume include about 45 of the 70 chapters that were listed in 1971. However, of the 59 authors in this volume, only 17 appeared on the original outline. Thus the contents of this volume reflect the state of knowledge in the late 1980s rather than in the early 1970s. The first editorial acceptance of an author's manuscript was on

June 21, 1985, and the last on April 27, 1989. Edited manuscripts were sent from the Washington office to authors for their final approval between June 24, 1986, and April 28, 1989. These dates for all chapters are given in the list of Contributors.

Linguistic Editing

As far as possible, all cited words in Native languages were referred to consultants with expert knowledge of the respective languages and rewritten by them in the appropriate technical orthography. In some cases a chapter author served as the linguistic consultant. The consultants and the spelling systems are identified in the orthographic footnotes, drafted by the Linguistic Editor, Ives Goddard.

Statements about the genetic relationships of Northwest Coast languages have also been checked with linguist consultants, to ensure conformity with recent findings and terminology in comparative linguistics and to avoid conflicting statements within the *Handbook*. In general, only the less remote genetic relationships are mentioned in the individual chapters. The chapter "Languages" discusses the wider relationships of those languages.

The Linguistic Editor served as coordinator and editor of these efforts by linguist consultants. A special debt is owed to these consultants, who provided advice and assistance without compensation and, in many cases, took time from their own research in order to check words with native speakers. The Linguistic Editor is especially grateful to John A. Dunn, Barbara Efrat and John Thomas, John Enrico, Victor Golla, M. Dale Kinkade, Michael E. Krauss, Jeff Leer, Neville J. Lincoln, John C. Rath and D. Stevenson, and Bruce Rigsby.

In the case of words that could not be respelled in a technical orthography, an attempt has been made to rationalize the transcriptions used in earlier anthropological writings in order to eliminate phonetic symbols that are obsolete and diacritics that might convey a false impression of phonetic accuracy.

Synonymies

Toward the end of ethnological chapters is a section called Synonymy. This describes the various names that have been applied to the groups and subgroups treated in that chapter, giving the principal variant spellings used in English and sometimes in Russian, self-designations, and often the names applied to the groups in neighboring Indian languages. For the major group names, an attempt has been made to cite the earliest attestations in English.

Many synonymies have been expanded or reworked by the Linguistic Editor, who has added names and analyses from the literature and as provided by linguist consult-

ants. Where a synonymy is wholly or substantially the work of the Linguistic Editor, a footnote specifying authorship is given.

These sections should assist in the identification of groups mentioned in the earlier historical and anthropological literature. They should also be examined for evidence on changes in the identifications and affiliations of groups, as seen by their own members as well as by neighbors and by outside observers.

Radiocarbon Dates

Authors were instructed to convert radiocarbon dates into dates in the Christian calendar. Such conversions normally have been made from the dates as originally published, without taking account of changes that may be required by developing research on revisions on the half-life of carbon 14, long-term changes in the amount of carbon 14 in the atmosphere, and other factors that may require modifications of absolute dates based on radiocarbon determinations.

Bibliography

All references cited by contributors have been unified in a single list at the end of the volume. Citations within the text by author, date, and often page identify the works in this unified list. Wherever possible the *Handbook* Bibliographer, Lorraine H. Jacoby, has resolved conflicts between citations of different editions, corrected inaccuracies and omissions, and checked direct quotations against the originals. The bibliographic information has been verified by examination of the original work or from standard reliable library catalogs (especially the National Union Catalog and the published catalog of the Harvard Peabody Museum Library). The unified bibliography lists all and only the sources cited in the text of the volume, except personal communications. In the text "personal communications" to an author are distinguished from personal "communications to editors." The sections headed Sources at the ends of most chapters provide general guidance to the most important sources of information on the topics covered.

Illustrations

Authors were requested to submit suggestions for illustrations: photographs, maps, drawings, and lists and locations of objects that might be illustrated. To varying degrees they complied with this request. Yet considerations of space, balance, reproducibility, and availability required modifications in what was submitted. In addition much original material was provided by staff members from research they conducted in museums and other repositories, in the published literature, and from correspondence. Locating suitable photographs and earlier drawings and paintings was the responsibility of the Illustrations Researcher, Joanna Cohan Scherer, who used some materials collected by Laura J. Greenberg. Artifacts in museum collections suitable for photographing or drawing were selected by the Artifact Researcher, Ernest S. Lohse. All uncredited drawings are by the Scientific Illustrator, Karen B. Ackoff, with contributions from John Michael Yanson.

Many individuals, including professional photographers, have generously provided photographs free or at cost. Victor Krantz of the Smithsonian Photographic Laboratory photographed the artifacts illustrated from the Smithsonian collections, and most of those illustrated from the collections of the American Museum of Natural History and the Museum of the American Indian, New York, and the Peabody Museum of Harvard University.

All maps were drawn by the *Handbook* Cartographer, Daniel G. Cole, who redrew some submitted by authors and compiled many new ones using information from the chapter manuscripts, from their authors, and from other sources. The base maps for all are authoritative standard ones, especially sheet maps produced by the U.S. Geological Survey and the Department of Energy, Mines and Resources, Canada. Anachronistic political boundaries have occasionally been added, to aid in orientation, on maps of past eras. The tribal territories as mapped normally do not indicate regions shared with adjacent tribes; comparison with the territories shown in other chapters will usually reveal such cases.

Final layout and design of the illustrations have been the responsibility of the Scientific Illustrators Jo Ann Moore (until 1986) and Karen B. Ackoff (1987–). Captions for illustrations were usually composed by Scherer, Lohse, and Ackoff, and for maps by Cole. However, all illustrations, including maps and drawings, and all captions, have been approved and sometimes revised by the General Editor or Managing Editor, the Volume Editor, and the authors of the chapters in which they appear.

The list of Illustrations was compiled by Frances Sundt and Joanna Cohan Scherer.

Acknowledgements

During the first few years of this project, the *Handbook* editorial staff in Washington worked on materials for all volumes of the series. Since intensive preparation of this volume began in 1985, especially important contributions were provided by the Editorial Assistant, Paula Cardwell; the Production Manager and Manuscript Editor, Diane Della-Loggia; the Bibliographer, Lorraine H. Jacoby; the Researcher, Cesare Marino; the Scientific Illustrators, Jo Ann Moore (through 1986) and Karen B. Ackoff (1987–); the Cartographer, Daniel G. Cole; the Cartographic Technician, Amy Ahner; the Illustrations Researcher, Joanna Cohan Scherer; the Assistant Illustrations Researcher, Frances Sundt (through 1988); the Artifact Researcher, Ernest S. Lohse; the Administrative Specialist, Melvina Jackson; and the Secretaries Tujuanna L. Evans, Lorretta Williams, Vivian Cobb, and Janna Marchione. Lottie Katz and Eleanor Peterson served as volunteer assistants for the Bibliographer, while the Scientific Illustrator was assisted by Robin Ann Davidson and Scott Rawlins as summer interns, and for some of the production by Britt Griswold. The index was compiled by Editorial Experts, Inc.

From January 1985 to January 1989 Ives Goddard served as Managing Editor in addition to his other *Handbook* responsibilities as Linguistic Editor and advisor to the General Editor. He replaced the General Editor during the latter's absence abroad for the year beginning in September 1986 and in most respects after his return. After January 1989, he served as Technical Editor. Karla E. Billups served as Managing Editor beginning in January 1989.

The Volume Editor would like to thank Ailsa Crawford for editorial and research assistance during the early years of the project, Phyllis Lancefield and Robert Boyd for research asssistance at different times, Roy Carlson for advice and guidance on archeological matters, Barbara Lane for advice and guidance on contemporary Indian affairs, Bill Holm for help on technology and art, Yvonne Hajda for help on southern coast ethnohistory, and most especially Shirley Suttles for constant patient counsel on writing.

Acknowledgement is due to the Department of Anthropology, Smithsonian Institution (and to its other curatorial staff), for releasing Sturtevant and Goddard from part of their curatorial and research responsibilities so that they could devote time to editing the *Handbook*. Suttles thanks the Department of Anthropology of Portland State University, Oregon, for a good many years of help and moral support.

Preparation and publication of this volume have been supported by federal appropriations made to the Smithsonian Institution, in part through its Bicentennial Programs.

August 8, 1989   William C. Sturtevant
                                  Wayne Suttles

Introduction

WAYNE SUTTLES

The Northwest Coast culture area as covered by this volume includes the north Pacific coast of North America from the Copper River delta on the Gulf of Alaska to the Winchuk River near the Oregon-California border, extending inland to the Chugach and Saint Elias ranges of Alaska, the Coast Mountains of British Columbia, and the Cascade Range of Washington and Oregon. It includes the territories of the Native peoples of the coast from the Eyak to the Chetco, together with those of all the inland peoples within this region except for a few groups in the western foothills of the Cascades—Sahaptins in Washington and the Molala and Shasta in Oregon.

This area is not precisely the same in extent as the Northwest Coast culture area as identified in other works on North American Indians or on this region. In the north it includes the Eyak, not always identified as a Northwest Coast tribe, and in the south it includes inland peoples of southwest Washington and western Oregon (the Cowlitz, Chinookans of the Portland Basin, Kalapuya, Upper Umpqua, and Takelma), sometimes placed in the Plateau culture area. On the other hand, it does not include several peoples who have sometimes been placed in the Northwest Coast—the Chinookans on the Columbia River above the Portland Basin and the Molala of the western foothills of the Cascade Range (described in vol. 12) and the Tolowa and other tribes of northwestern California (described in vol. 8). The boundaries between the areas covered by volumes 7, 8, and 12 were determined by the volume editors on the basis of a combination of cultural criteria and practical considerations. They do not reflect any new analysis.

The term "North-West Coast of America" has been in use since the late eighteenth century (Beresford 1789; Meares 1790) for the Pacific coast of the continent north of California, the last coast of North America except the western Arctic explored by Europeans. For these explorers the term had no northern limit (Wagner 1937:1), and it would be geographically accurate to apply it to the North American shores of both the Bering Sea and the Pacific Ocean; therefore, the term "North Pacific Coast" (Boas 1897:317; Wissler 1917; Drucker 1965; McFeat 1966) would be more appropriate for this region. However, Northwest Coast is firmly established in the literature of anthropology and will be used in this volume.

The term "Pacific Northwest" for the states of Washington and Oregon perhaps reflects a time when "the Northwest" meant the Upper Great Lakes and may still be useful, but the phrase "Pacific Northwest Coast" is redundant, because the northwestern coast of the continent is necessarily the Pacific coast, or perhaps self-contradictory, since it refers to the northeastern shore of the Pacific Ocean.

There can be no question that the Northwest Coast is a natural region. This strip of coast with its relatively mild climate, temperate rain forest, and rich marine life is sharply bounded on the inland side by mountain ranges, and it is radically different in climate, vegetation, and fauna from the regions beyond the mountains. Only at the northern and southern ends is there any shading into other natural regions ("Environment," this vol.).

The Native peoples of the area are not biologically greatly different from other American Indians, and they constituted neither a single population nor a series of discrete populations. There is evidence for gene flow throughout the area and beyond ("Human Biology," this vol.).

Linguistically the area is paradoxical. In the genetic relations that can be established among its languages, it is highly fragmented; its peoples speak, or once spoke, over 40 languages belonging to a dozen language families, only two of which have members outside the area. Postulated distant relationships tentatively link several families, both to one another and to families outside the area, but they still leave six unrelatable taxa. In spite of this apparent genetic diversity, features of phonology, morphology, syntax, and semantics are shared by members of different language families, making it possible to discern subareas within the Northwest Coast and characterize the whole area ("Languages," this vol.).

Culturally the Northwest Coast is as distinct as it is environmentally, as most of this volume will show.

Character of the Culture Area

The Northwest Coast has been identified as a culture area on the basis of features of several aspects of culture (Wissler 1917:213-215; Kroeber 1923; Drucker 1955:196; Driver 1961:15). Some of these features are also found

1

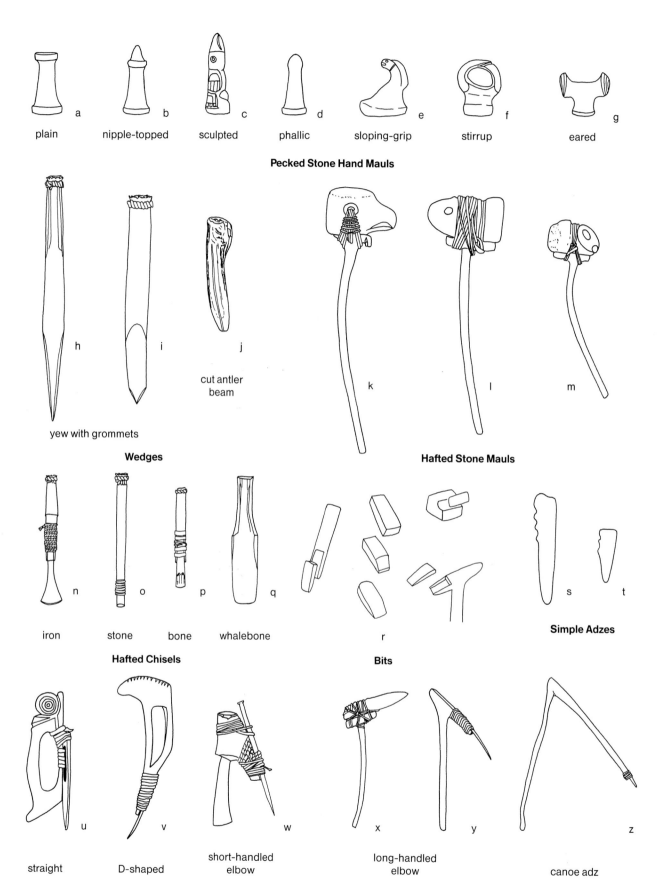

plain   nipple-topped   sculpted   phallic   sloping-grip   stirrup   eared

a   b   c   d   e   f   g

Pecked Stone Hand Mauls

h   i   j

cut antler
beam

yew with grommets

k   l   m

Wedges

Hafted Stone Mauls

n   o   p   q

iron   stone   bone   whalebone

r

s   t

Simple Adzes

Hafted Chisels

Bits

straight   D-shaped   short-handled elbow   long-handled elbow   canoe adz

u   v   w   x   y   z

Hafted Adzes

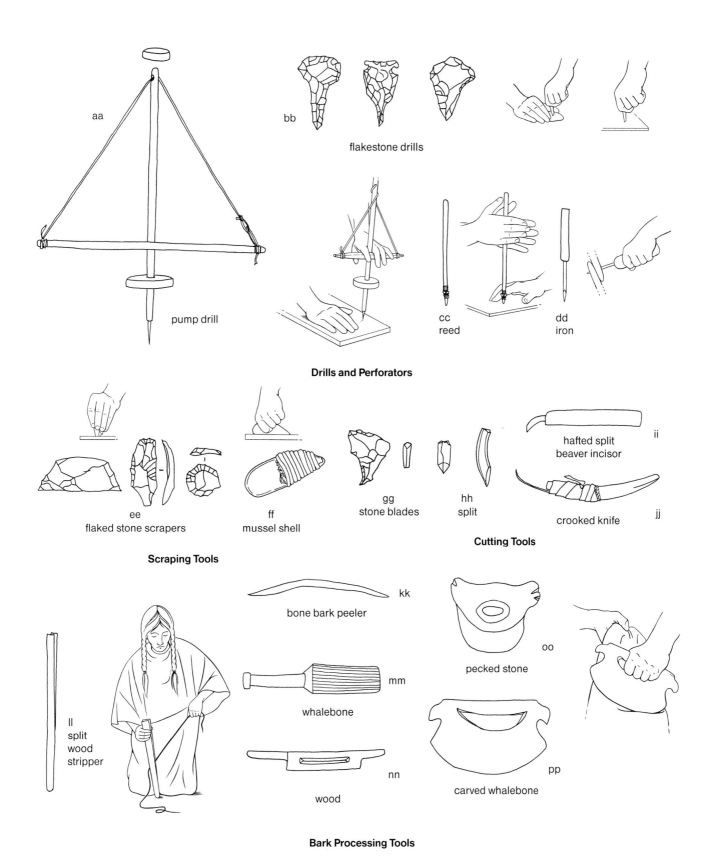

aa

pump drill

bb
flakestone drills

Drills and Perforators

cc
reed

dd
iron

ee
flaked stone scrapers

Scraping Tools

ff
mussel shell

gg
stone blades

hh
split

hafted split
beaver incisor

ii

crooked knife

jj

Cutting Tools

kk
bone bark peeler

ll
split
wood
stripper

mm
whalebone

nn
wood

oo
pecked stone

pp
carved whalebone

Bark Processing Tools

Smithsonian, Dept. of Anthr.: a, 130977; b, 16391; c, 67849; d, 206554; e, 378199; f, 23417; g, 75417; h, 74780; i, 206562; j, 20899; k, 88815; l, 20893; m, 19124; o, 20604; p, 336582; q, 127865; s, 74981; t, 74987; u, 74770; v, 127856; w, 23442; y, 20642; z, 20641; jj, 129977; kk, 130978; nn, 20609; oo, 23416; pp, 23371. Mus. of the Amer. Ind., Heye Foundation, New York: n, 5/24. Amer. Mus. of Nat. Hist., New York: x, E/2672; aa, E/449.

Fig. 1. Woodworking tools.

INTRODUCTION

outside the culture area however defined, and some are not found everywhere within the culture area, but collectively they give it a distinctive character.

In subsistence base the Northwest Coast belongs with the other nonhorticultural areas of northern and western North America. Its economies resemble those of most of the Plateau and adjacent parts of the Arctic, Subarctic, and California in depending heavily on fishing, especially for salmon, and they resemble those of the Arctic in the importance of sea mammals, especially as a source of oil. Where they may have differed is in the combination of fishing, hunting, and gathering of both shellfish and vegetable foods and in their methods of taking and preserving the great quantities periodically available to them.

Northwest Coast material culture is distinctive in its highly developed woodworking technology (fig. 1), capable of producing houses (fig. 2) and canoes (figs. 3–4) of remarkable size and in several forms, bowls, boxes, and other utensils, ceremonial paraphernalia, and monuments. It is notable for its twined basketry decorated with false embroidery or overlay, woolen and vegetable-fiber textiles, clothing consisting of robes, ponchos, tunics, and skirts, with basketry hats and a general absence of footgear.

Houses of planks were built from the western Arctic to northern California, dugout canoes were used nearly everywhere in the Plateau and southward into northern California, wooden dishes were made in the adjacent Arctic and elsewhere, and twined basketry was made from the Aleutian Islands to California, but in each case the Northwest Coast forms are characteristic of the whole or a part of this area.

The Northwest Coast peoples (with a few exceptions) had permanent villages or towns they occupied in winter, and many had permanent structures for other seasons. Social organization was notable for the existence of great differences in status based on a combination of birth and wealth. The people of a larger village or town usually consisted of a wealthy elite (the "chiefs" or "nobles"), their followers (the "commoners"), and their slaves. From the Nootkans and Kwakiutl northward the elite were individually ranked; from the Central Coast Salish southward individual ranking was less developed if at all. Usually a "chief" was simply the head of a kin group or local group whose influence came from his economic and ritual position, there being no formal councils or other political institutions giving him authority.

Along the coast there were regional differences in the principles of descent (matrilineal from the Eyak to the Haisla, bilateral elsewhere except for the patrilineal Southwestern Oregon Athapaskans) and residence that formed kin groups and local groups and in the kinds of privileges claimed by the elite. But everywhere the elite maintained their status through their wealth. From the

Copper River to Puget Sound, and by the mid-nineteenth century to the Columbia, claims to status had to be validated through formal gift-giving at occasions known as potlatches. South of the area of potlatching, wealth was still essential in matters such as arranging marriages and paying fines, and the poor were dependent upon the rich in these matters.

Over most of the area, slaves were acquired by capture or purchase, and they were the property of their masters, who could use them for any purpose, put them to death, or free them at will. Unless freed by their masters, their status was permanent and hereditary. The marriage of a free person with a slave was disgraceful, and for a free person any slave ancestry was a serious social handicap. From the Columbia River southward there was another source of slaves; free persons could be enslaved by their fellow tribesmen for debt and unless sold away might in time redeem themselves. Among the Central and Southern Kalapuyans and some of the Southwestern Oregon Athapaskans, debt slavery may have been the usual or only form.

Social stratification with hereditary slavery and the importance of wealth have been identified as the most distinctive features of the culture area and unusual if not unique among nonhorticultural peoples. But again they are not limited by the boundaries of the culture area. The usual Northwest Coast pattern was found among the Pacific Eskimo, while the southwestern Oregon pattern of debt slavery is that of northwestern California.

The belief that human beings could get power from individual entities in the nonhuman world underlay much of the belief system of the Northwest Coast, as in most of native North America. Throughout the area, shamans treated their patients with the help of guardian spirits obtained by their own efforts. From the Coast Salish southward, guardian-spirit power was in theory within reach of anyone of either sex. It was seen as the basis of skill and success in many endeavors, and in the winter spirit dance, during which each person sang and danced possessed by his or her tutelary.

This guardian-spirit complex seems to have been the basis of several developments within segments of the Northwest Coast, in the north of the crest system associated with kin groups, which had spread southward as far as the Kwakiutl, and among the Wakashans and Bella Coola of the "secret societies" of the winter ceremony.

Conceptually separate is power inherent in verbal formulae. The concept may have been widespread, but there seem to have been only two regions within the Northwest Coast where it had developed to the point where ritualists, professional users of verbal formulae, were as important as shamans—among the Central Coast Salish and the Southwestern Oregon Athapaskans. The latter group shared this with Northwest California.

Art has given the Northwest Coast wider recognition than perhaps any other feature of culture. It included carving, painting, and textiles. The northern two-dimensional style is most immediately recognizable, but there are two other styles of incised carving, one produced in the Central Coast Salish region, the other in the Chinookan region. There are also several sculptural styles, and two distinctly different textile traditions, one among the Tlingit and Tsimshian, the other among the Central Coast Salish and some of their neighbors.

External Relations

Kroeber (1923) identified the Northwest Coast as, after the Arctic, the most distinctive culture area of Native North America; it shared with the rest of the continent only traits and institutions coming from its most ancient heritage; it lacked features of Middle American culture—horticulture, pottery, political organization, temple mounds—that had diffused to other areas; and its distinctive features were either indigenous or had developed under Asian influence.

This degree of cultural isolation from the rest of the New World was not accepted by all. Olson (1929), Loeb (1929), and W.C. MacLeod (1929) suggested Mexican or South American origins for several Northwest Coast traits. Drucker (1936) saw the Arctic and the adjacent interior as sources of much of the material culture of the Northwest Coast but the Plains and Northeast as the source of social stratification and emphasis of wealth and elements of ritualism. Drucker later (1955a:61) decided that the lack of interest in wealth and rank in the Subarctic and Plateau made it unlikely that these features came through those regions.

Influences from East Asia are not impossible. There are a good many records of East Asian craft washing ashore on the Northwest Coast in historic times (Brooks 1876; J.G. Nelson 1962). But there are no known instances of the Natives acquiring any East Asian cultural traits from castaways (Kroeber 1948:561; Drucker 1955a:62).

Definitions of the Culture Area

Classification of the peoples, as distinct from the languages, of northwestern North America began in the 1840s with Scouler (1841, 1848), Hale (1846:197–199), and Gallatin (1848), all using a mixture of physical, cultural, and supposed intellectual and moral characteristics. Bancroft (1874–1876, 1) used a similar classification for a compendium of information on western North America. None of these classifications identified the Northwest Coast in anything like its presently recognized form or distinguished the coast from adjacent interior areas.

Classification based on culture alone and without judgments about intellect and morals began with Franz Boas and Otis T. Mason. Boas did not attempt a culture-area system but did distinguish a North Pacific Coast. He was flexible in his use of the term, in one work (Boas 1891c) including data from northern British Columbia to southwestern Oregon and in another (Boas 1897:317–321) defining the area as extending from Yakutat Bay to the Strait of Juan de Fuca, while identifying "the tribes comprising the North Pacific group" as including those as far south as the Columbia River.

Mason (1896, 1907) was the first to devise a continent-wide classification of culture areas or ethnic environments. His North Pacific Coast extended from Yakutat Bay to the mouth of the Columbia River. The lower Columbia Valley (presumably including the Willamette Valley) and the northern Oregon coast formed part of his Columbia-Fraser region—the Plateau of later scholars. Southwestern Oregon formed part of his California-Oregon region.

Since Boas and Mason, no one has challenged the view that there was an area of distinctive culture in a distinctive environment and that it included minimally all peoples along the coast from the Tlingit to the Coast Salish or the Chinook. There have been differences in how far beyond this minimal culture area the boundaries should be extended (fig. 5).

Wissler's (1914, 1917) North Pacific Coast was similar to Boas's in its broadest sense, except that his straight, arbitrary boundaries seemed to include a few interior tribes now placed in the Subarctic and Plateau. Kroeber (1904:87–88, 1925:903–911) had identified Northwest Coast traits in the culture of the Yurok and other tribes of northwestern California, and so on this basis he (Kroeber 1923a:337, 1939) extended the culture area southward to include the lower Klamath River region. Murdock and O'Leary (1975) identified a minimal Northwest Coast but added an Oregon Seaboard culture area, the two covering an area almost identical with Kroeber's Northwest Coast. Drucker (1955a) followed Kroeber in including the Lower Klamath region, but he did not include the inland-dwelling Kalapuya and Takelma in his Northwest Coast. Driver and Massey (1957) and Driver (1961) expanded Kroeber's Northwest Coast to the north to include the Eyak, who had been mistakenly identified as Eskimo, but in southwestern Washington and western Oregon, they restricted it to the narrow strip west of the Willapa Hills and Coast Range, giving the inland valleys to the Plateau culture area.

Until the 1970s, culture areas had been distinguished impressionistically on the basis of a relatively small number of conspicuous culture traits and complexes. In a departure from this tradition, Driver and Coffin (1975) defined culture areas based on a comparison of 392 culture traits among 245 tribes. They reduced Kroeber's Northwest Coast at both ends, placing the Eyak in the

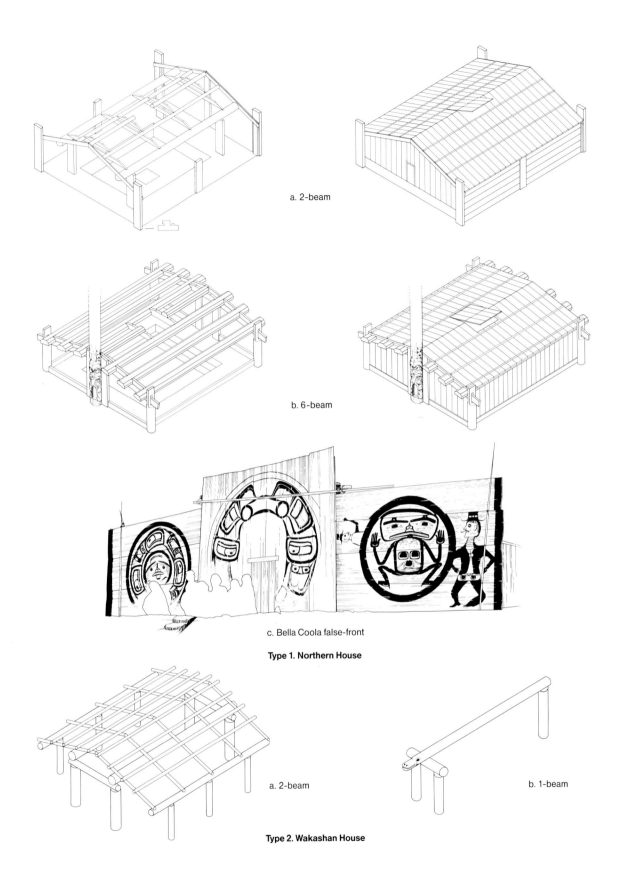

a. 2-beam

b. 6-beam

c. Bella Coola false-front

Type 1. Northern House

a. 2-beam

b. 1-beam

Type 2. Wakashan House

1a, based on Shotridge and Shotridge 1913:87; 1b, based on Duff and Kew 1958:c49 and on drawing by Gordon Miller, U. of B.C., Mus. of Anthr., Vancouver, B.C.; 1c, after Amer. Mus. of Nat. Hist., New York, N.Y.: 32951; 2a, based on photograph of Scow House at Guilford I., B.C., by Wayne Suttles; 2b, based on Smithsonian, NAA: 43220; 3, based on Boas 1891:figs. 1–2; 4, based on Waterman and Greiner 1921:pl. III; 5b, based on Swan 1857:110–111, 331, 339 and on oil painting by Paul Kane, Stark Mus. of Art, Orange, Tex: WOP 13; 5c, based on *Frank Leslie's Illustrated News*, April 24, 1858; 5a, based on Olson 1936:64.

6   Fig. 2. House types.

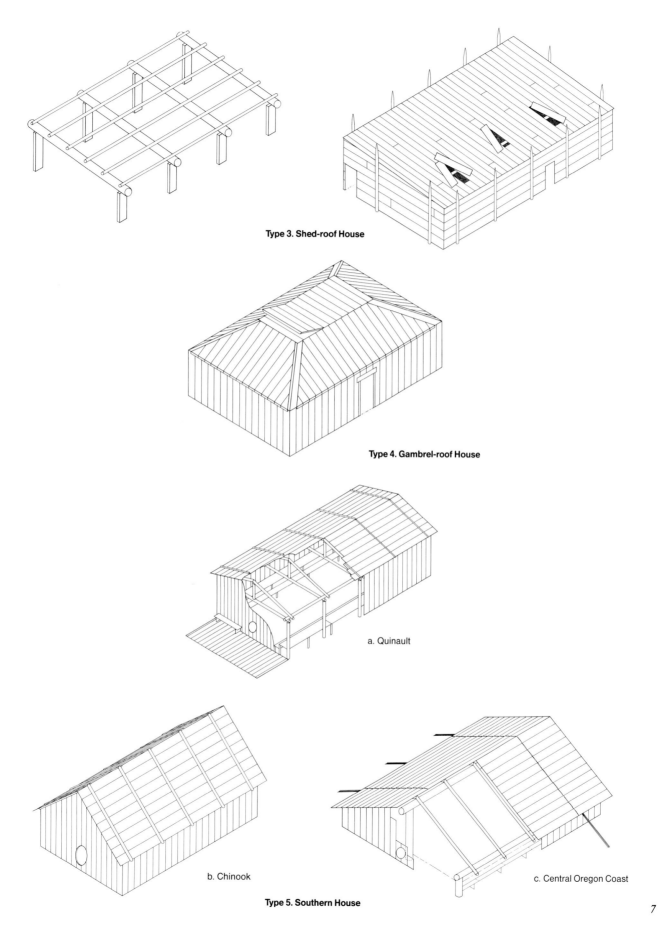

Type 3. Shed-roof House

Type 4. Gambrel-roof House

a. Quinault

b. Chinook

c. Central Oregon Coast

Type 5. Southern House

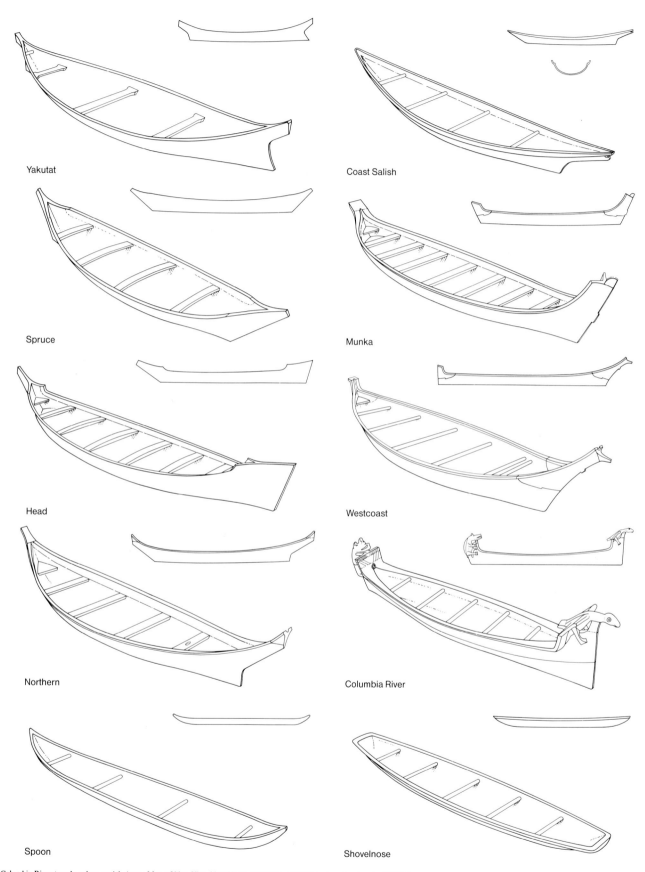

Yakutat

Coast Salish

Spruce

Munka

Head

Westcoast

Northern

Columbia River

Spoon

Shovelnose

Columbia River type based on model, Amer. Mus. of Nat. Hist., New York: 16.1/1786a; others based on drawings by Bill Holm.

Fig. 3. Canoe types.

Fig. 4. Drawings of totemic figures on canoes. left and center, Stern and bow of Northern type canoe. The two bears were said to be a male at the bow and a female at the stern, referring to the myth from which the Tlingit *na·nẏa·ʔa·ẏí* clan derived the Grizzly Bear crest (Holm 1987:192–197). The bear figures were attached to the canoe only for ceremonial purposes. Collected by George T. Emmons, Wrangell, Alaska, 1880s; length 18m. right, Stern (top) of model of Columbia River type canoe with bear figure and bow (bottom) with bird. Length 74 cm.

Arctic and the tribes south of the Tolowa in California. Jorgensen (1980) identified culture areas of western North America on the basis of a comparison of the tribes for which data were available for 292 variables in several aspects of culture. He defined (1980:93–94) the Northwest Coast as extending from the Tlingit to the Cahto, near Cape Mendocino, but indicated that northwestern California south of the Tolowa could as easily be considered part of the California culture area.

Subareas

Most of those who have identified a culture area have distinguished subareas or subgroupings of peoples within it. Wissler (1917) recognized three subareas (Northern, Central, and Southern), Kroeber (1939) seven (Northern Maritime, Central Maritime, Gulf of Georgia, Puget Sound, Lower Columbia, Willamette Valley, and Lower Klamath), and Drucker (1955a) four (Northern, Wakashan, Coast Salish-Chinook, and Northwest California).

These divisions reflect different views of cultural development. For Wissler the Northern subarea was "the type" that defined the culture area; the other areas differed in some material traits, but the "art, social, and ceremonial traits of the North all thin out as we move southward" (1917:215). Presumably the area was historically a unit with influences radiating from its northern center.

Kroeber distinguished his subareas by a combination of environmental and cultural features and found them unequal in "cultural intensity." In his view (Kroeber 1923, 1939:30–31) the history of the Northwest Coast was one of increasing adaptation of a riverine culture to a maritime environment, with the "climax" of the area shifting from the mouth of the Fraser River to the Bella Bella and their neighbors, who worked out the Cannibal ceremony, to the Northern Maritime tribes, whom he recognized as the latest climax by "their aggressiveness and the vigor of their art." In this development, the Lower Columbia was blocked by environmental limitations, Puget Sound was a "backwash," the Willamette Valley a "pocket" of inland modification, and Northwest California a riverine subclimax.

Drucker (1955a) rejected an inland origin for Northwest Coast culture. The Wakashans, he believed, were earliest on the coast and were in contact with the Eskimo and Aleut, from whom they acquired whaling and other maritime traits. Later this contact was broken by movements to the coast by ancestors of the Tlingit, Haida, and Tsimshian in the north and the Coast Salish and Chinookans in the south. To different degrees, these newcomers to the coast retained features of their interior cultures and acquired the maritime adaptations of the Wakashans, who constituted the culture climax of the area. Thus while Wissler's and Kroeber's subareas had different statuses within a developmental sequence, Drucker's reflect diverse origins and diffusion from a Wakashan center.

The Northern subarea of Wissler and Drucker and Northern Maritime of Kroeber were nearly identical. All included the Tlingit, Haida, and Tsimshian; Kroeber and Drucker added the Haisla, probably because they share the matrilineal kinship system of the other three, a fact that was not clearly understood when Wissler constructed

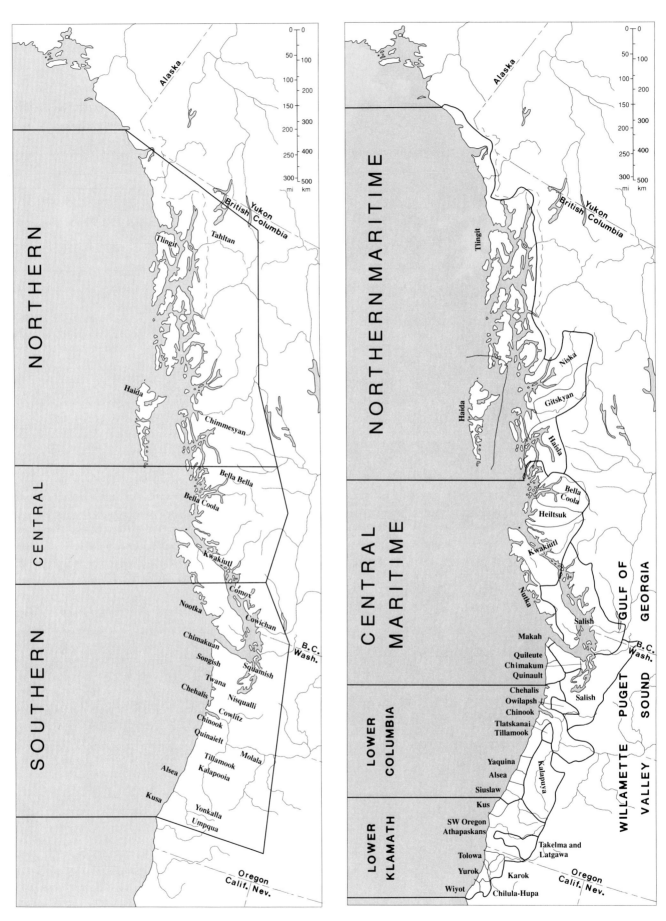

10

NORTHERN

CENTRAL

SOUTHERN

Alaska

Yukon
British Columbia

Tlingit

Tahltan

Haida

Chimmesyan

Bella Bella
Bella Coola

Kwakiutl

Comox

Nootka

Cowichan

Chimakuan

Songish

Squamish

Twana

Chehalis

Nisqualli

Cowlitz

Chinook

Quinaielt

Tillamook

Molala

Alsea

Kalapooia

Kusa

Yonkalla

Umpqua

B.C.
Wash.

Oregon
Calif. Nev.

NORTHERN MARITIME

CENTRAL MARITIME

LOWER COLUMBIA

LOWER KLAMATH

GULF OF GEORGIA

PUGET SOUND

WILLAMETTE VALLEY

Alaska

Yukon
British Columbia

Tlingit

Haida

Niska

Gitskyan

Haisla

Bella Coola

Heiltsuk

Kwakiutl

Nutka

Salish

Makah

Quileute
Chimakum
Quinault

Chehalis
Owilapsh
Chinook

Tlatskanai
Tillamook

Yaquina
Alsea
Siuslaw

Kus

SW Oregon
Athapaskans

Tolowa

Yurok

Wiyot

Salish

Kalapuya

Takelma and
Latgawa

Karok

Chilula-Hupa

B.C.
Wash.

Oregon
Calif. Nev.

SUTTLES

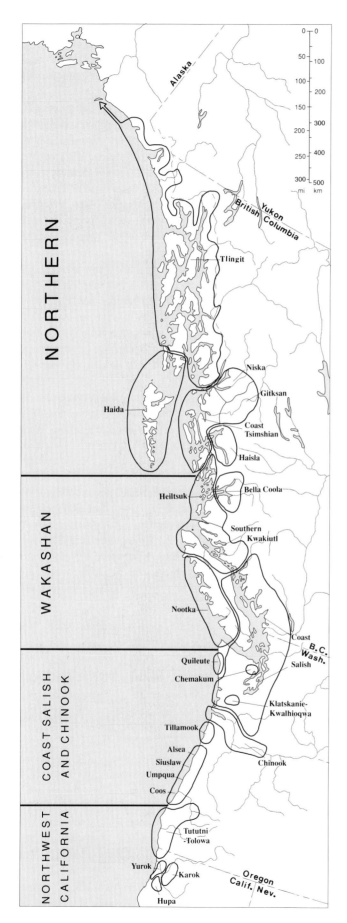

NORTHERN

WAKASHAN

COAST SALISH AND CHINOOK

NORTHWEST CALIFORNIA

Alaska

Yukon

British Columbia

Tlingit

Niska

Gitksan

Haida

Coast Tsimshian

Haisla

Bella Coola

Heiltsuk

Southern Kwakiutl

Nootka

Coast

Quileute

B.C.
Wash.

Chemakum

Salish

Klatskanie-Kwalhioqwa

Tillamook

Alsea

Siuslaw

Chinook

Umpqua

Coos

Tututni-Tolowa

Yurok

Karok

Oregon

Calif. Nev.

Hupa

Fig. 5. Previous portrayals of the Northwest Coast culture area. a, Wissler's (1914) version. He drew straight arbitrary lines throughout the region and placed the Songish (Songhees) in Wash. and the Quinaielt (Quinault) in Oreg., when they are actually in southern Vancouver I. and in Wash., respectively. b, Kroeber's (1939) version. He had 7 subregions that encompassed but excluded the Owilapsh (Kwalhioqua), Tlatskanai (Clatskanie), and Takelma and Latgawa (Latkawa). He also assigned the Chimakum (Chemakum) to both the Gulf of Georgia and Puget Sound subregions. c, Drucker's (1955) version. He left gaps between all the tribal boundaries and combined the Klatskanie (Clatskanie), who should be in Oreg., with the Kwalhiokwa (Kwalhioqua) in Wash.

his classification.

Wissler's Central subarea consisted of the Bella Coola and "Kwakiutl," presumably in the sense of Northern Wakashan (Haisla, Haihais, Bella Bella, Oowekeeno, and Kwakiutl proper). Kroeber's Central Maritime was somewhat greater, eliminating the Haisla but adding the Southern Wakashans (Nootkans of Vancouver Island and Makah), Quileute, and Quinault. Drucker's Wakashan culture province was restricted to the Bella Coola and the Wakashans minus the Haisla. Thus Kroeber and Drucker agreed in keeping the Wakashans (except for the Haisla) together. But Kroeber put the non-Wakashan tribes of the ocean shore of Washington into his Central Maritime subarea, largely on the basis of their secret societies but perhaps also their environment, while Drucker excluded them from his Wakashan province, perhaps on the basis of language.

Wissler's Southern subarea included all tribes from the Nootkans and Coast Salish south, tribes that Kroeber (1939) put into six of his seven subareas and Drucker into three of his four. Drucker's Coast Salish–Chinook province was the most diverse of his four provinces; it included Kroeber's Gulf of Georgia, Puget Sound, and Lower Columbia subareas, plus a bit of Kroeber's Central Maritime (the Quileute, Quinault, and Lower Chehalis) and a bit of his Northwestern California subarea (the Coosans).

In an earlier work on Washington and Oregon, Lewis (1906) distinguished three culture areas west of the Cascades: Columbian (embracing western Washington and northwestern Oregon, extending south on the Oregon coast to include the Alsea), Southwestern Oregon, and Willamette Valley. He found (1906:202–204) the Columbian and Plateau culture areas most distinct, Southwestern Oregon intermediate between the Columbian area and northwestern California, and the Willamette Valley possibly belonging to the Plateau. (Other classifications are discussed by Driver 1962:12–13.)

Thus there has been near agreement about a Northern subarea, less agreement about a Wakashan area, and great disagreement about everything south of Vancouver Island.

● VALUE JUDGMENTS The nineteenth-century view that the northern tribes were intellectually or racially superior to the southern tribes did not survive in scholarly work, largely because of Boas's consistent opposition to ethnocentrism and racism. Nevertheless, there has been a persisting popular image of a culturally superior "real" Northwest Coast in the north and an imitation one in the south, and this image may have been supported by the culture area concept with its attendant notions such as Wissler's "type" tribes and Kroeber's "culture climax."

True to his principles, Boas (1938:671) warned against the assumption that cultures identified as "marginal" within a culture area were inferior to the cultures identified as central. Some cultures are less institutionalized and their material possessions less complex. But it does not follow "that the cultural life of a people is poorer, because it is not so easy for the observer to formalize a culture permitting greater freedom to the individual." Or to put it another way: It does not follow that a culture with rules that make describing it easy for the anthropologist is therefore superior to one that gives the individual choices that make describing it harder. The more formal social structure, ceremonial structure, and art of the northern Northwest Coast may have created an image of cultural superiority. In the organization of this volume, an effort has been made to give adequate attention to all tribes of the culture area.

● CULTURE HISTORY Kroeber's (1939) and Drucker's (1955a) subarea systems were fashioned under the influence of reconstructions of culture history that did not suppose any great antiquity for Northwest Coast culture, and these have not been supported by more recent archeology. Drucker appears to have been correct in postulating an early maritime culture but incorrect in supposing there had been recent migrations out of the interior. As of the 1980s it appeared that the ancestors of most northwest peoples had entered the area by 3000 B.C. and had five millennia for in-situ cultural development ("Cultural Antecedents," this vol.).

● STATISTICALLY BASED GROUPINGS There is no more than a partial correspondence between the impressionistic divisions of Wissler (1917), Kroeber (1939), and Drucker (1955a) and the statistically based groupings of Driver and Coffin and Jorgensen. Driver and Coffin (1975:11–12) separate the Northwest Coast peoples into a northern group consisting of the Tlingit and Haida, a central group extending from the Tsimshian to the Southwestern Coast Salish, and a southern group extending from the Chinookans to the Tolowa. Jorgensen (1980:89, 94) gives a two-dimensional mapping and a tree diagram of 172 western North American tribes. In the first, as Adams (1981:363) points out, the Tlingit, Gitksan, and Tsimshian stand apart from the rest of the Northwest Coast, which appears to form a continuum with much of the rest of western North America. But in the tree diagram the Northwest Coast stands apart and branches first into two smaller trees, a northern tree including all tribes from the Tlingit to the Chinookans and a southern tree including the

Oregon Coast tribes from the Tillamook to the Tolowa. Within the northern tree, the first branching separates a northern branch, consisting of the Tlingit, Haida, and Tsimshian, from a southern branch, consisting of all tribes from the Haisla to the Chinookans.

Tree diagrams of this sort show simply the sharing of culture traits as recorded by the ethnographers, coded by the analyst, and all given equal weight. As measures of overall cultural similarities and differences they are an improvement over the earlier subjective definition of culture areas. However, they can be no better than the ethnographic reporting on which they are based, and that is probably never complete, sometimes inaccurate, and always a reflection of the experience and interests of the ethnographer.

Moreover, quantification of cultural distance is not a measure of social distance. For example, Jorgensen's tree diagram shows the Upper Stalo, Lower Fraser (Downriver Halkomelem), and Lummi separated from the West (Brentwood Bay) Saanich and Cowichan at a level of 80 percent of shared traits, a little more than the percentage shared by the Fort Rupert Kwakiutl and the Haisla. But in fact, the Upper Stalo, Lower Fraser, and Cowichan spoke dialects of the same language, were participants in the same social continuum, and to some extent seasonally shared resources, all equally true of the Lummi and West Saanich. On the other hand, the Kwakiutl and Haisla were not in direct contact and had very different social systems. Similarly, in Jorgensen's (1980) tree diagram the deepest cleavage on the Northwest Coast, indicating only about 56 percent of shared traits, separates the Chinook from the Tillamook, suggesting they are as different from one another as the Tlingit from the Tolowa; yet the Chinook and Tillamook had adjacent territories and were coparticipants in a Lower Columbia social network, while the Tlingit and Tolowa were at opposite ends of the culture area.

Regional Social Systems

While a good deal of attention has been paid to discerning culture areas and measuring cultural distances among peoples, less notice has been given to the social networks or regional social systems in which the peoples participated.

There is evidence for such networks in the observations of the early explorers and traders. From sources of 1792–1830 Hajda (1984:123–132) has mapped a Greater Lower Columbia in which marriages, visiting, shared access to resources, and trade in food linked tribes on the coast from the Makah to the Alsea with the upriver Chinookans, Southwestern Coast Salish Cowlitz, and Tualatin Kalapuya.

There is also evidence in collections of texts. Kwakiutl family histories (Boas 1921:836–1277) show a network of intermarriage and ceremonial relations extending from the Oowekeeno to the Comox (Northern Coast Salish). Nootka texts (Sapir and Swadesh 1955:299–306) describe one mid-nineteenth-century potlatch attended by Nitinaht, Makah, Songhees, and Clallam and another attended by Northern Nootkans and Kwakiutl.

Ethnographic work by Elmendorf (1960:298–305) shows that during the middle of the nineteenth century the elite of the Twana (Southern Coast Salish) village of Skokomish had ties of intermarriage with a circle of villages that included speakers of three other Coast Salish languages as well as Chemakum. People of this village participated in three kinds of intervillage activities within circles of different extent. Two of them overlapped at Skokomish only; some Skokomish participated in intervillage eating contests with people from villages to the south, including the Satsop (Southwestern Coast Salish), while some Skokomish participated in secret-society initiations with people from villages to the north, including the Makah and the Songhees. The Satsop presumably had only a hearsay knowledge of the secret society, as the Makah had of the eating contests; the two were linked by a social network but were by no means culturally identical. Genealogies collected among the Lummi and Musqueam (Central Coast Salish) show circles of intermarriage that overlap with one another and with the Skokomish circle, extending the social network into the Strait of Georgia to include tribes who differed from the Skokomish in beliefs, ceremonies, and art (Suttles 1987c).

Although such networks of intermarriage included tribes who were linguistically and to some extent culturally different, they presumably required some shared understandings about social status and the interfamilial obligations that marriage involved. It should be possible to identify indicators of such shared understandings.

Permanent modifications of the human body may be seen as markers of actual or potential participation in regional social systems. On the Northwest Coast there were three such modifications—pierced lips for labrets, modified head shape, and facial tattooing.

There was certainly a Northern Northwest Coast regional social system, in which marriageable women of quality wore labrets and people were in general agreement about the rules of marriage. The Tlingit, Haida, Tsimshian, and Haisla shared a system of matrilineal lineages, and although the names and crests of their larger units, the moieties or phratries, were different, they could be equated for purposes of intergroup marriage (Boas 1916: 519–523; Garfield 1939:230–231; J.A. Dunn 1984, 1984a). Other features of the matrilineal system were cross-cousin marriage, avunculocal residence, and joking and avoidance relationships among relatives.

Within the long central part of the coast, types of artificial head deformation (see "Human Biology," this vol.) suggest a division into four regions consisting of: (1),

the Bella Coola, Bella Bella, and Oowekeeno; (2), the Kwakiutl, Northern and Central Nootkans, and Northern Coast Salish (at least the Comox, possibly the others); (3), the Nitinaht, Makah, Quileute, Central Coast Salish, Chemakum, and Southern Coast Salish; and (4), the Chinookans and others of southwestern Washington and northwestern Oregon. In regions 1, 3, and 4 the practice was to flatten the forehead and occiput, in regions 1 and 3 to produce variations of Boas's (1891c) "Cowitchin" type and in region 4 the more extreme "Chinook" type. In region 2 the practice was to bind the head to produce an elongated head, the extreme version of which was Boas's "Koskimo" type found at the north end of Vancouver Island. (The distribution of these forms suggests that historically head flattening was once continuous, and that head lengthening was an innovation on northern Vancouver Island.) The function of head-flattening as a marker of membership in a regional social system was suggested by Lewis (1906:154–155), and Hajda's (1984) analysis of the Lower Columbia region tends to confirm it for that region. It is not inconsistent with ethnographic and historic data to suggest that these four groups of peoples constituted four regional social networks.

The whole area of head deformation was one in which kinship was reckoned bilaterally and usually close kin of any kind could not marry, though there were exceptions among the Bella Coola and Kwakiutl. The joking and avoidance relations of the northern region were quite foreign. Residence was usually patrilocal but not rigidly so, allowing for movement. Marriage involved relatively equal exchanges between the families of bride and groom. Regional systems within the larger region of head deformation may have been distinguishable by other markers. The Lower Columbia tribes made a distinction, not found elsewhere, between limited conflict with coparticipants in the regional social system and lethal conflict and slave raiding with outsiders.

Tattooing was practiced widely on the Northwest Coast. On the northern coast, men and women had crest designs tattooed on their chests, arms, and legs. On the central coast some women had geometric designs on their arms and legs and in a few areas on their chins. But it was the regular practice from the Central Kalapuya southward through the Southwestern Oregon Athapaskans and into northern California for women to have their chins tattooed (Kroeber 1925:905). This practice may have marked the participation in a social system with a more rigid rule of patrilocal residence and even patrilineal descent, great importance of bride price with half-married state for a man who could not afford it, a legal system with fines, wealth in dentalia and woodpecker scalps.

These regional social systems were neither sharply bounded nor stable. Peoples at the borders in some instances served as interfaces; the Haihais practiced both labret wearing and head flattening, so that women of these tribes were marriageable with men to both north and south. In historic times Plateau tribes adjacent to the Upper Chinookans flattened the heads of female babies (Lewis 1906:180), probably to make them marriageable downriver. In the first millennium B.C., both head flattening and labret wearing were practiced around the mouth of the Fraser (Keddie 1981:65; "Prehistory of the Coasts of Southern British Columbia and Northern Washington," this vol.). Identifying these regional systems and recovering their history is a major task for ethnology and archeology. Linguistics also contributes, not just through the discovery of more remote genetic relations among languages but also through the analysis of areal features, which give evidence of ancient and recent social ties.

Organization of the Volume

The initial section provides background on the Northwest Coast environment, the languages of the area, its human biology, and its early prehistory. The second describes the sources of information on the Native peoples from the observations of the early explorers and museum collections through research in the four subfields of anthropology. And the third presents the history of contact, consisting of chapters on the early period, the demographic consequences of contact, and the history as it relates to the Native peoples of each of the four politically separate segments of the coast—Alaska, British Columbia, Washington, and Oregon—from the time they were organized.

The fourth and largest section consists mainly of chapters on the peoples of the area, the ethnographic chapters, beginning at the northern end of the coast and proceeding southward. Interspersed are chapters on the prehistory of the segment of the area described in the chapters that follow. For two peoples there are separate chapters on recent developments, and there are two chapters on ceremonial systems. Finally, there are three chapters on special topics—mythology, art, and the Indian Shaker Church.

Selection, Balance, and Nomenclature

Inevitably, the ethnographic chapters cover groups of very different size and composition. Some relatively small groups have their own chapters, while some larger groups are subsumed under a more general heading. Ideally perhaps every linguistically distinct group should have been given its own entry. But because of the number of languages and the cultural similarity of the speakers of some groups of languages, this was not practical. Therefore, there are several chapters that describe the speakers of more than one language. The ethnographic chapters differ also in length, reflecting partly how much is known about the people described and partly their cultural distinctiveness and the space needed for adequate coverage.

Most English names for tribes are based on names the Indian peoples have used for themselves, such as Eyak, Tlingit, Haida, and Quileute, or names that were originally given by their Indian neighbors and have come into general use, such as Makah, Chemakum, and Tillamook. These names present no problems except for variations in spelling resulting from the fact that they are all attempts to cope with the profoundly different sound systems of the Indian languages. Each is an arbitrary English equivalent of the original Indian name. Their Native sources and alternatives are given under Synonymy in each chapter.

More serious problems arise out of the extension of names. On the Northwest Coast, as elsewhere, it has often happened that a name originally given to one group has been extended to its neighbors, or the name of a single village has become extended to a much larger group, to all the speakers of the same dialect, the same language, or group of related languages. A name may thus appear in a specific and a generic sense. *Handbook* practice has generally been to restrict names to the speakers of one language. If no other term is available for the larger group, a derivative with the suffix -an is used.

One exception to this is the name Tsimshian, in which the final -an is not a suffix but part of the root. In its Native form and in Native usage, it refers to the people of the lower Skeena River and coast, but in English it has been extended to include the Nishga of the Nass River and the Gitksan of the upper Skeena and thus to embrace the whole language family. *Handbook* usage is to identify the speakers of all the languages as the Tsimshian peoples and to refer to the Tsimshian proper as Coast Tsimshian.

The name Kwakiutl, based on the Native term for the group who settled at Fort Rupert, was extended to all the speakers of the language spoken at Fort Rupert and then to the speakers of the several languages that constitute the northern branch of the Wakashan family. In this volume, the name is restricted to the group to which it was first extended. Kwakiutl is used for the speakers of the one language only, while the speakers of the other languages (the Haisla, Haihais, Bella Bella, and Oowekeeno) are identified by their own distinctive names.

Nootka, mistakenly taken for a place-name by Capt. James Cook, was first applied to Nootka Sound and its people and then extended to other speakers of their language. Nootkan refers to the southern branch of the Wakashan family, consisting of Nootka, Nitinaht, and Makah. The speakers of Nootka and Nitinaht are described in a single chapter as the Nootkans of Vancouver Island.

The name Salish is from the name of a Plateau tribe of western Montana also known as the Flathead, the easternmost member of the Salishan language family. Coast Salish has been used since the late nineteenth century for the speakers of the 14 contiguous Salishan languages on the coast, sometimes extended to include the two isolated Salishan languages on the coast, Bella Coola and Tillamook. In this volume Coast Salish is restricted to the speakers of the contiguous Salishan languages. Several of these languages were spoken over relatively small areas, and their names are also used as tribal names to designate their speakers. But others, especially Halkomelem, Northern Straits, and Lushootseed, were spoken over wider areas, each by a number of groups with their own tribal names. Networks of intermarriage and cooperation in economic and ceremonial activities among neighboring tribes regardless of language made the whole Coast Salish region a kind of social continuum. At the same time there were considerable differences in aboriginal culture and post-contact experience within the region. The differences were not great enough to justify, within the limitations of this volume, a chapter on each language group, to say nothing of each named tribe. But at the same time the similarities are not enough to justify describing them all in a single chapter. A division into four subregions seemed the best compromise.

The name Chinook, in its Native form, was originally the name of a single village on the north shore of the mouth of the Columbia, but it was extended in time to the speakers of all Chinookan languages. Chinook, as a tribal name, is restricted to the speakers of Chinook language on the north side of the Columbia, and the rest of the family are called Chinookans. The chapter in this volume is Chinookans of the Lower Columbia, because the Chinookans of the region above the Cascades are described in volume 12. The pidgin or "trade language" that developed on the Lower Columbia, once commonly called simply Chinook, is always identified as Chinook Jargon.

During the 1970s, as part of the rising consciousness of Indian and tribal identity, at least three Native peoples in British Columbia made changes in their names. Representatives of the peoples known in the literature as Bella Coola, Kwakiutl, and Nootka have asked the non-Indian public to recognize them as Nuxalk, Kwakwaka'wakw, and Nuu-chah-nulth respectively (see synonymies in the appropriate chapters). The symbolic value of such acts is understandable, and there is a risk of giving offense by not complying. Nevertheless, the position taken in this volume is that Bella Coola, Kwakiutl, and Nootka are long-established English names and that to change them would create new problems in an already confusing nomenclature.

Environment

WAYNE SUTTLES

The Shape of the Land

The Northwest Coast as defined for this volume is a long narrow arc extending along the North Pacific Coast of North America from the delta of the Copper River on the Gulf of Alaska to the mouth of the Chetco River on the southern Oregon Coast, a distance of over 1,500 miles (fig. 1). Its inland boundary follows the crests of a series of mountain ranges—the Chugach and Saint Elias mountains of southern Alaska, the Coast Mountains of southeastern Alaska and British Columbia, and the Cascade Range of Washington and Oregon. The coastline runs roughly parallel to these ranges. The axis of the Chugach and Saint Elias mountains runs nearly west to east, that of the Coast Mountains northwest to southeast, and that of the Cascades north to south. The whole region is somewhat crescent-shaped, very thin at its northern end, thickening out in the center to a width of 200 or more miles, and thinning in the south to a width of about 100 miles.

Three segments of the region parallel the ranges that mark their inland boundaries. In the north, along the Gulf of Alaska coast, the mountains rise almost directly out of the sea. The habitable coast is narrow and further limited by glaciers coming down to the sea. There are a few bays; the estuary of the Copper River and Yakutat Bay are the biggest. But most of the coastline is straight and uninviting. The mountains are high and generally form a barrier between coast and interior. The Copper and Alsek are the only rivers flowing out of the interior. But there are many small streams, lakes, and lagoons. In the last 500 years there have been great changes in the extent of glaciation along this coast (De Laguna 1972:24–29; Fields 1975).

In the center, stretching for more than half the total length of the region, is the very complex coast of southeastern Alaska and British Columbia. To the west of the Coast Mountains and roughly parallel, another range rises out of the sea as the Alexander Archipelago, the Queen Charlotte Islands, and Vancouver Island. The Queen Charlottes are the most isolated part of the coast, separated from the Alexander Archipelago by Dixon Entrance and from the rest of British Columbia by Hecate Strait and the expanse of Queen Charlotte Sound. Vancouver Island lies closer to the mainland, separated from it by Queen Charlotte Strait, Johnstone Strait, and the Strait of Georgia (locally known as the Gulf of Georgia), and the Strait of Juan de Fuca. Puget Sound is a southern extension of this sheltered water, the whole of which is the "Inland Passage" to Alaska. Numerous smaller islands and inlets penetrating deep into the mainland give this segment of the region an actual shoreline of nearly 10,000 miles (Kroeber 1939:170). In many places the shoreline is rocky and beaches are rare. Two marine environments can be distinguished, an outer coast exposed to the ocean and an inner coast of sheltered salt water. Several large rivers flow into the sea in this segment, the most important being the Taku, Stikine, Nass, Skeena, Bella Coola, and Fraser. The Skeena has the largest drainage area that belongs to the Northwest Coast, but the Fraser drains a much greater area in the interior and is the second-largest Northwest Coast river.

From the Strait of Juan de Fuca southward, the straight coast of Washington and Oregon is broken only by the entrances to bays that are estuaries of rivers. The largest of these are Gray's Harbor and Willapa (formerly Shoalwater) Bay on the Washington Coast, the estuary of the Columbia, and Tillamook and Coos bays on the Oregon Coast. There are also many smaller bays and lagoons behind the ocean beaches, and altogether there is a good deal more sheltered salt water in this segment of the Northwest Coast than a small-scale map might suggest.

Between the coast and the Cascade Range there is a parallel series of outer ranges comprising the Olympic Mountains and Willapa Hills in Washington and the Coast Range in Oregon. The northern end of the intervening trough is partly filled by Puget Sound and Hood Canal. Southward is a series of inland valleys—the Cowlitz Corridor (the upper Chehalis and lower Cowlitz valleys), Portland Basin, Willamette Valley, and the valleys of the Umpqua and Rogue rivers in southwestern Oregon. The Cowlitz and Willamette rivers flow into the Columbia, which is the largest river of the region, draining an enormous area east of the Cascades. At the southern end of the Northwest Coast, the Klamath Mountains extend from the Cascades to the ocean shore, giving the Klamath-Siskiyou region a complex and difficult topography.

The mountain ranges that mark the inland boundary of the Northwest Coast include peaks that rise to great

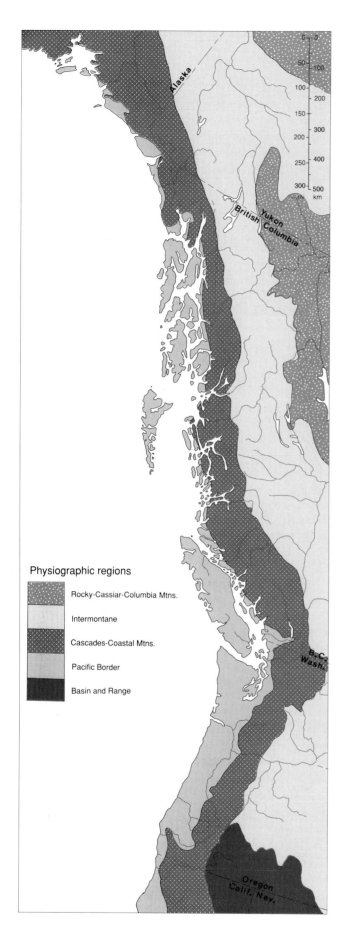

Physiographic regions

- Rocky-Cassiar-Columbia Mtns.
- Intermontane
- Cascades-Coastal Mtns.
- Pacific Border
- Basin and Range

Fig. 1. Physiographic regions of the Northwest Coast (Farley 1979; Hartman and Johnson 1984; Rosenfeld 1985).

heights, a number exceeding 10,000 feet and several over 12,000 feet. The highest, Mount Saint Elias and Mount Logan in the Saint Elias Range, are respectively 18,008 and 19,524 feet high. These ranges bar easy passage between coast and interior for much of the total distance, but the barrier is broken not only by the major rivers that flow through the mountains but also by a number of mountain passes.

In addition to the major rivers named above, there are a great many smaller rivers and streams in every part of the coast. There are a number of large lakes, especially on Vancouver Island and on the mainland from the Fraser Valley southward. From Vancouver Island and the Fraser Delta southward less of the shoreline is sheer rock; long sandy or gravelly beaches are usual.

Climate

The climate of the Northwest Coast (except perhaps for the inland valleys of western Oregon) is of the West Coast Marine type (E.B. Shaw 1965). Summers are cool and winters are wet and mild. This type of climate comes from having an ocean to the west and being in latitudes where the prevailing winds are westerly. The ocean cools the air in summer and warms it in winter. The climate of the Northwest Coast is therefore, latitude for latitude, more like that of western Europe than that of eastern North America or the Pacific shore of Asia.

Northwest Coast weather is primarily determined by seasonal shifts in position and strength of two great semipermanent atmospheric pressure cells, the North Pacific High and the Aleutian Low (R.E. Thomson 1981: 23–24). The North Pacific High lies off the California coast through the winter, widens during the spring, and covers most of the North Pacific during the summer. A clockwise circulation of air brings west winds to the Gulf of Alaska coast, northwest winds to the coasts of British Columbia and Washington, and more northerly winds to the coast of Oregon. During the summer the Aleutian Low is centered in the northern Bering Sea, but during the fall it strengthens, its center moves southward, and in winter it dominates the North Pacific, gradually receding in the spring. From fall to spring a counterclockwise circulation results in winds from the east and southeast on the Gulf of Alaska and southeast to southwest along the British Columbia and Washington coasts. Every few days cyclonic storms move in with much moisture. Local topography can greatly modify these general directions of winds. For the Native peoples, winds were generally predictable and taken into account in any travel.

Along most of the coast, because the moisture comes in from the west, it falls as rain most heavily on the western slopes of the outer ranges of mountains (the mountains of *17*

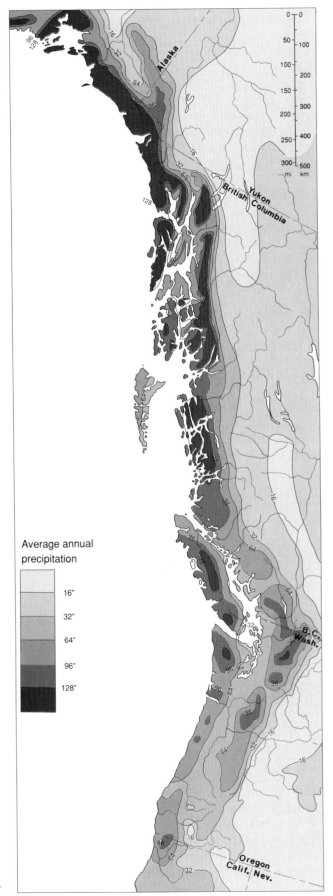

Average annual
precipitation

	16"
	32"
	64"
	96"
	128"

Fig. 2. Mean annual precipitation for the Northwest Coast (Hartman and Johnson 1984; P.L. Jackson 1985; Canada. Surveys and Mapping Branch. Geography Division 1974).

the Queen Charlottes, Vancouver Island, the Olympics, and the Coast Range of Oregon) and next on the western slopes of the Coast Mountains and Cascade Range. On the leeward (eastern or northeastern) sides of the outer ranges there are areas with greatly reduced precipitation (fig. 2). In southeastern Alaska, Baranof Island gets over 300 inches of rainfall annually, while western Admiralty Island, immediately to the east, gets as little as 40 inches. Areas of less rainfall include in varying degrees the northeastern Queen Charlottes, the Strait of Georgia–Puget Sound Basin, and the valleys of western Oregon. Perhaps the most conspicuous is an area around the eastern end of the Strait of Juan de Fuca, in the "rain shadow" of the Olympic Mountains, where annual precipitation is generally less than 30 inches and in places less than 20 inches. On the south shore of the Strait of Juan de Fuca the annual precipitation at Sequim is 17 inches, while at Clallam Bay, about 65 miles to the west, it is 83 inches; the westward rise in precipitation is over one inch per mile (Phillips 1960).

Mean temperature decreases not only from south to north but also, especially, from sea to shore. The outer coasts of the Queen Charlottes and Vancouver Island enjoy an average of over twice as many frost-free days as the heads of mainland inlets (fig. 3). There is an accompanying difference in the kind of precipitation experienced—rain on the outer coast, deep snow in some inlets. Up to 800 inches of snow falls yearly on the Coast Mountains of southeastern Alaska, feeding the extensive snowfields and glaciers of the region (Hartman and Johnson 1984).

Storms with strong winds are not uncommon, but rarely of destructive force. Summer thunderstorms are unusual. On rare occasions in winter, masses of extremely cold continental air may break out through the Coast Mountains and Cascade Range, bringing periods of up to 10 days of 0°F weather. In British Columbia such severe outbreaks have been recorded only at 10–18-year intervals (Canadian Hydrographic Service 1951:xli–xlii). In the Portland Basin, Arctic air pouring out the Columbia Gorge, if overridden by wet warm Pacific air, can result in an ice storm. But from southern British Columbia southward, at lower elevations, there are also occasionally winters without frost.

The Sea

For people whose lives are spent mainly on the shore, which means most of the Indians of the Northwest Coast, the tides are of great importance. There are three tidal cycles, a daily, a monthly, and a yearly cycle. The daily cycle is one of 24 hours, 50 minutes, the time between one

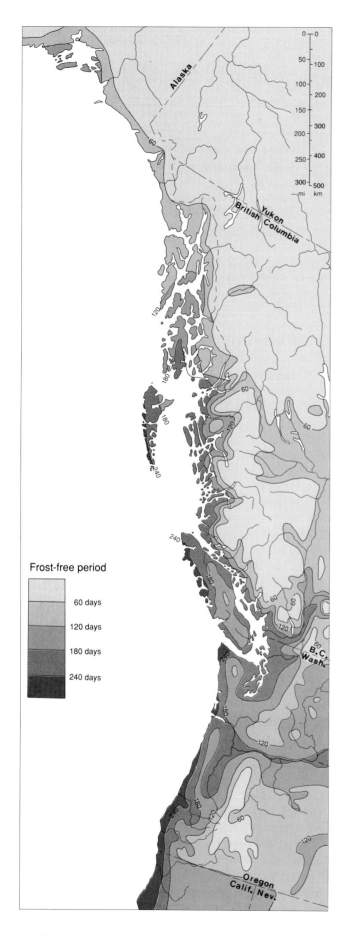

Fig. 3. Mean annual frost-free periods in the Northwest Coast (Farley 1979; P.L. Jackson 1985; U.S. Geological Survey 1970).

Frost-free period

60 days

120 days

180 days

240 days

high or low tide and the corresponding one the next day. On most parts of the coast the tide is of "mixed" type, semidiurnal, in that there are two highs and two lows in a day, but with marked inequality. In a few places, such as around the southeastern end of Vancouver Island, the inequality is so great that for a part of each month there is a diurnal tide, with only one high and one low in the day (R.E. Thomson 1981:49). The monthly cycle is related to the moon's phases. During each lunar month of 29.5 days, there is about a week during which the height of the tide gets progressively greater, followed by a week during which it becomes progressively less, followed by another period of rise and another of decline. The two periods of a few days each of greatest range, the spring tides, are around the new and full moon. During the month the tides move around the clock; on any day the low tide will be 50 minutes later than it was the day before. But in any month the lowest lows of the second period of spring tides will be only slightly later in the day than they were during the first period. During the year, however, the lower lows will move around the clock and also vary in range. The lowest lows of the year come in June and in December, around the winter and summer solstices. The time of day of the tide varies with location; in Puget Sound and the Strait of Georgia they are about six hours later than on the outer coast. On the outer coast the June low tides come at dawn and the December low tides at dusk, while on Puget Sound and the Strait of Georgia the June lows come around noon and the December lows around midnight.

These tidal cycles thus set limits and offer opportunities for the harvesting of intertidal resources. These resources are most easily taken for periods of a few days twice each month, at different hours of the day, depending on the season. The best times of all come twice each year, when the tides are lowest and the time longest during which the clambeds and other resources are exposed. The other side of the coin is that there are periods, twice a month, when the tide is not low enough to give access to most species.

The mean tidal range varies with the body of water, and the amount of foreshore uncovered by the tide also varies, of course, with its steepness. There are shores where the low tide exposes only a sheer face of rock, and others where it exposes a vast expanse of mud flats.

Narrow channels may have tidal currents of great force. Currents of six to eight knots are not uncommon, and these change directions with a change in the tide. The tide also affects the lower courses of many rivers. In the Fraser River, during the winter low-runoff period, a strong flood tide can reverse the flow of water as far upstream as Mission, British Columbia, and there is also a tide in Pitt Lake (R.E. Thomson 1981:167–168). In the Columbia the tide is perceptible as far upstream as the

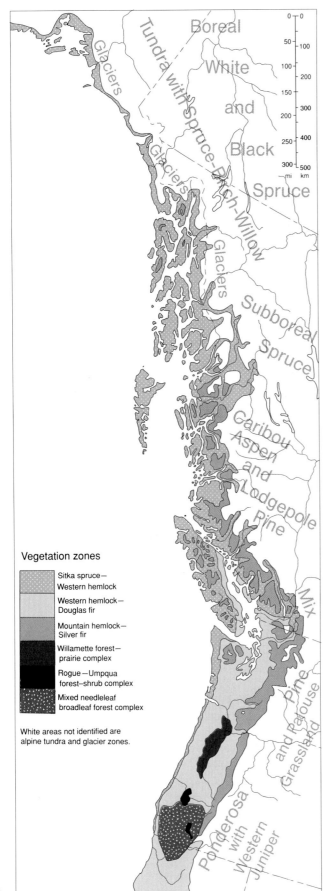

Vegetation zones

Sitka spruce—
Western hemlock

Western hemlock—
Douglas fir

Mountain hemlock—
Silver fir

Willamette forest—
prairie complex

Rogue—Umpqua
forest-shrub complex

Mixed needleleaf
broadleaf forest complex

White areas not identified are
alpine tundra and glacier zones.

Fig. 4. Potential natural vegetation throughout the Northwest Coast (Farley 1979; Frenkel 1985; U.S. Geological Survey 1970).

Cascades and in the Willamette to Willamette Falls. These facts affect travel. In a channel with a swift current, travelers will have to wait for the tide to change. At the mouth of a river, under the right conditions, they may catch the up-bound tide.

Salinity is a variable that relates to resources. Waters around river mouths may be poor in shellfish because of brackish water. Near the heads of deep inlets, water on the surface may be too brackish for shellfish, but deep water may be saline enough for saltwater fishes.

The temperature of the sea varies with location and season. In the ocean it decreases to the north, varying in winter from about 46°F off Vancouver Island to 43° off southeastern Alaska, in summer rising to as much as 68° on the surface off Vancouver Island to 59° off southeastern Alaska. In sheltered salt water the temperature may stay about the same the year round, as in Puget Sound at around 50°F, or it may rise in summer as high as 68°, as in a few favored locations in the Strait of Georgia (R.E. Thomson 1981:19–20). Low temperatures are productive of marine life, but dangerous for human beings. A person washed overboard in water of 43° to 48°F, as in southeastern Alaska, risks death from hypothermia after one-half to one hour; in water of 52° to 54°, as in Washington or Oregon, he may survive one to two hours. In periods of severe cold, ice from streams may cover the heads of inlets.

The widely held belief that the Japan Current warms the Northwest Coast is without foundation (R.E. Thomson 1981:231–234), but other currents do influence the region. In summer, the Subarctic Current flows east and splits offshore from Vancouver Island. From this division, the Alaskan Current flows north and the California Current south, bringing cold water along the coast. In winter, these currents are forced farther offshore by the warm north-flowing Davidson Current coming from off Baja California.

The upwelling of colder water offshore keeps the coast cooler in summer and, more important, nourishes the plankton that are the base of the food chain for the abundant fish, sea birds, and sea mammals of the region (R.E. Thomson 1981:83).

Vegetation Zones

The Northwest Coast culture area, as defined for this volume, lies almost wholly within two vegetation areas, one characterized by Sitka spruce and western hemlock, the other by western hemlock and Douglas fir. Exceptional areas are subalpine regions of mountain hemlock and silver fir and enclaves of other vegetation types within the hemlock–Douglas fir area and bordering it on the south (fig. 4). (U.S. Geological Survey 1970; Krajina 1969;

Farley 1979; Küchler 1964; Franklin and Dyrness 1973; Frenkel 1985).

Forests of Sitka spruce (*Picea sitchensis*) (fig. 5) and western hemlock (*Tsuga heterophylla*) extend along the Pacific Coast of North America from northeastern Kodiak Island in Alaska to the Chetco River on the southern Oregon Coast. Except for their extension into Pacific Eskimo territory, these species define the linear extent of the area covered in this volume. From the middle of the Alexander Archipelago southward, western red cedar (*Thuja plicata*) becomes the third species, along with spruce and hemlock, defining the coast forest. This forest type occupies a narrow belt along the coast at the northern end of its range, along the Gulf of Alaska coast, becomes a broad belt through southeastern Alaska and the northern coast of British Columbia, then becomes narrow again from Vancouver Island southward.

Yellow cedar (*Chamaecyparis nootkatensis*) grows along the coast in the spruce-hemlock forest from nearly its northern limit southward into southeastern Alaska; farther south it is generally restricted to higher elevations, while the closely related Port Orford cedar (*C. lawsoniana*) grows along the coast from Coos Bay south. Other trees found within the hemlock-spruce forest region include the black cottonwood (*Populus trichocarpa*) and Sitka willow (*Salix sitchensis*) throughout the region; shore pine (*Pinus contorta*), red alder (*Alnus rubra*), and Oregon crabapple (*Pyrus fusca*) from Yakutat south; Scouler willow (*Salix scouleriana*) and Douglas maple (*Acer glabrum*) from Lynn Canal south; western yew (*Taxus brevifolia*) and black hawthorn (*Crataegus douglasii*) from the southern end of the Alexander Archipelago south; bigleaf maple (*Acer macrophyllum*) from Dixon Entrance south; Pacific dogwood (*Cornus nuttallii*) and cascara (*Rhamnus purshiana*) from Bella Coola south; grand fir (*Abies grandis*, also called balsam or white fir), Pacific willow (*Salix lasiandra*), vine maple (*Acer circinatum*), and bitter cherry (*Prunus emarginata*) from Queen Charlotte Strait south. The western white birch (*Betula papyrifera*) grows in a few areas on the mainland between the Skeena and Fraser rivers, but not much farther south. At the southern end of the spruce-hemlock forest, on the Chetco River, are the northernmost stands of redwood (*Sequoia sempervirens*).

At the heads of some of the inlets on the central British Columbia coast there are stands of Douglas fir (*Pseudotsuga menziesii*). From around Johnstone Strait southward Douglas fir is the most common conifer species nearly everywhere except in the narrow strip of spruce-hemlock forest along the ocean shore and at higher elevations. Western hemlock and western red cedar grow with Douglas fir, in this forest type. The condition separating the spruce-hemlock forest from the hemlock–Douglas fir forest is moisture. Douglas fir is found where there is less than 70 inches of annual precipitation. The reason for this is that Douglas fir seedlings require sunlight, and mature stands of the species will not perpetuate themselves; without the periodic burning that has occurred in this drier region, Douglas firs would be replaced by the climax forest dominated by hemlock (Munger 1940).

Most trees of the spruce-hemlock forest are also found in the hemlock–Douglas fir forest. In addition, there are: madrona (*Arbutus menziesii*, called arbutus in British Columbia, madrona in Washington and Oregon, madrone in California) and Garry oak (*Quercus garryana*, also Oregon white oak) in drier areas from the northern end of the Strait of Georgia south; Oregon ash (*Fraxinus latifolia*) from Puget Sound south; and golden chinquapin (*Castanopsis chrysophylla*) from southwestern Washington south. Western white pine (*Pinus monticola*) grows from Vancouver Island south and ponderosa pine (*P. ponderosa*) from Puget Sound south.

A subalpine forest of mountain hemlock (*Tsuga mertensiana*), amabilis fir (*Abies amabilis*), and alpine fir (*Abies lasiocarpa*) extends south through the Coast Mountains and Cascade Range and at higher elevations in the Coast Mountains, Cascades, and Olympics.

Within the Douglas fir region there are, or once were, areas of semi-open parkland—on southeastern Vancouver Island, the Gulf Islands, San Juan Islands, and northern Whidbey Island; and on the mainland there were many small prairies from the Fraser River southward through the Puget Sound region. There were larger prairies in the Puyallup, Nisqually, and upper Chehalis valleys. The Willamette Valley was largely prairie with widely spaced old Garry oaks in hilly areas and ash and cottonwoods along stream banks (Habeck 1961; Thilenius 1968; Johannessen et al. 1971).

In southwestern Oregon there are several trees unknown farther north—incense cedar (*Calocedrus decurrens*), sugar pine (*Pinus lambertiana*), Oregon myrtle (*Umbellularia californica*), California black oak (*Quercus kelloggii*), and tanoak (*Lithocarpus densiflorus*). In the upper Umpqua and Rogue river valleys, in the rain shadow of the Siskiyous, there are areas of buckbrush (*Ceanothus cuneatus*) chaparral that are a northern extension of California vegetation (Detling 1961).

The prairies of western Washington, the Willamette Valley, and southwestern Oregon were maintained by the Native peoples through seasonal burning (Norton 1979; Habeck 1961; Boyd 1986).

Plants in Native Life

The Native peoples used plants as sources of food, materials used in technology, medicines, and fuel, and they were concerned about the total vegetation of their environment as it related to the abundance of useful plants and game animals.

top left, U. of Pa., U. Mus., Philadelphia: 14771; top right, Prov. of B. C., Vancouver; center left, U.S. Forest Service: 486770; bottom left, Royal B.C. Mus., Victoria: PN 10551; bottom right, Whatcom Mus. of Hist. and Art, Bellingham, Wash.: 3887.

Fig. 5. Selected Northwest Coast terrain. top left, Tlingit fishing platforms on the Chilkat River, Alaska, with Coast Mountains in the background. Photograph by Louis Shotridge, 1915–1917. top right, Moss-covered trees in rain forest in Naikoon Provincial Park, near Masset, Queen Charlotte Is., B.C., 1975. center left, Mendenhall Peninsula and Glacier, N. Tongass National Forest, Alaska. An area in the Sitka spruce forest was clear-cut. The mountains are part of the Juneau Snow Cap. Photograph by Leland J. Prater, July 1958. center right, Ocean shoreline at the entrance of the Umpqua River, Oreg. Photograph by Leonard Delano, 1957. bottom left, Fraser Canyon fishing grounds of the Central Coast Salish, above Yale, B.C. Drying racks dot the rocky banks. Photograph probably by Frederick Dally, 1867–1870. bottom right, Lummi Indian fishing camp, Wash. Areas once kept clear by browsing deer and by fires were later covered with blackberries and other introduced plants. Photograph by Charles H. Townsend, 1895.

SUTTLES

Foods of animal origin may have contributed more in volume and in calories to native diet, but vegetable foods must have been essential to a healthful diet.

Ferns with edible rhizomes include bracken (*Pteridium aquilinum*), the most widely eaten, the sword fern (*Polystichum munitum*), lady fern (*Athyrium felix-femina*), spiny wood fern (*Dryopteris carthusiana*), male fern (*D. felix-mas*), and licorice fern (*Polypodium glycyrrhiza*), the last used mainly for its flavor.

Lilies with edible bulbs or corms include two species of fritillary (*Fritillaria camschatcensis* and *F. lanceolata*), both called rice-root and chocolate lily; two of camas (*Camassia quamash* and *C. leichtlinii*); tiger lily (*Lilium columbianum*); two onions, nodding (*Allium cernuum*) and Hooker's (*A. acuminatum*); four fawn lilies, pink (*Erythronium revolutum*), yellow (*E. grandiflorum*), giant (*E. oregonum*), and alpine (*E. montanum*); two fool's onions, harvest lily (*Brodiaea coronaria*) and wild hyacinth (*B. hyacinthina*); and Tolmie's mariposa (*Calochortus tolmiei*). The corm of an orchid (*Calypso bulbosa*) was also eaten. Of these only rice-root and alpine fawn lily (also called avalanche lily) are available on the northern coast. Nodding onion, tiger lily, and pink fawn lily are available from the central coast of British Columbia southward. The others were formerly common in more open areas from the Strait of Georgia southward, except for the mariposa, which was confined to the inland valleys of southwestern Oregon. Rice-root and camas were the most important of these food plants (Turner and Kuhnlein 1983).

Other plants with edible roots or rhizomes include eelgrass (*Zostera marina*), Pacific cinquefoil or silverweed (*Potentilla pacifica*), springbank clover (*Trifolium wormskjoldii*), seashore lupine (*Lupinus littoralis*), blue lupine (*L. nootkatensis*), wild caraway (*Perideridia gairdneri*), spring gold (*Lomatum utriculatum*), and hemlock-parsley (*Conioselinum pacificum*), the last three all called wild carrot, yellow sandverbena (*Abronia latifolia*), cattail (*Typha latifolia*), and skunk cabbage (*Lysichitum americanum*). Most of these species were widely available, but wild caraway and spring gold were more common from Vancouver Island south.

The tuber of the wapato (*Sagittaria latifolia*), which was abundant in ponds in the lower Fraser and Columbia valleys, was perhaps as important as camas in the Native diet where it grew and in trade with neighboring regions.

Over 40 berries and fruits were available over some part of the area. Gooseberries and currants include the common gooseberry (*Ribes divaricatum*), swamp gooseberry (*R. lacustre*), sticky gooseberry (*R. lobbii*), stink currant (*R. bracteosum*), red-flowering currant (*R. sanguineum*), and white-flowered currant (*R. laxiflorum*). Members of the rose family with edible fruits include the salmonberry (*Rubus spectabilis*), thimbleberry (*R. parviflorus*), cloudberry (*R. chamaemorus*), nagoonberry (*R. acaulis*), trailing wild raspberry (*R. pedatus*), trailing wild blackberry (*R. ursinus*), blackcap (*R. leucodermis*), wild raspberry (*R. idaeus*), wild strawberry (*Fragaria chiloensis* and *F. vesca*), wild rose (*Rosa nutkana*, *R. piscocarpa*, and *R. gymnocarpa*), serviceberry or saskatoon (*Amelanchier alnifolia*), black hawthorn (*Crataegus douglasii*), Pacific crabapple (*Pyrus fusca*), Indian plum (*Oemleria cerasiformis*), Sitka mountain ash (*Sorbus sitchensis*), chokecherry (*Prunus virginiana*) and Klamath plum (*P. subcordata*). Members of the heath family include salal (*Gaultheria shallon*), evergreen huckleberry (*Vaccinium ovatum*), bog cranberry (*V. oxycoccos*), red huckleberry (*V. parvifolium*), oval-leaved huckleberry (*V. ovalifolium*), bog blueberry (*V. uliginosum*), mountain bilberry (*V. membranaceum*), Alaska blueberry (*V. alaskense*), lingenberry or low-bush cranberry (*V. vitis-idaea*), and kinnikinnick or bearberry (*Arctostaphylos uva-ursi*). Other fruit-bearing species include the red elderberry (*Sambucus racemosa*), blue elderberry (*S. cerulea*), bunchberry (*Cornus canadensis*), soapberry or soopolallie (*Shepherdia canadensis*), crowberry (*Empetrum nigrum*), wild lily-of-the-valley (*Maianthenum dilatatum*), false Solomon's seal (*Smilacina racemosa*), and star-flowered Solomon's seal (*S. stellata*).

A few plants provided shoots and greens, especially important in the spring after a winter diet of dried fish and oil. These include the common horsetail (*Equisetum arvense*) and giant horsetail (*E. telmateia*), bracken and lady ferns, salmonberry, thimbleberry, cow parsnip (*Heracleum lanatum*, often called Indian celery), water parsley (*Oenanthe sarmentosa*), western dock (*Rumex occidentalis*, called Indian rhubarb), fireweed (*Epilobium angustifolium*), stinging nettle (*Urtica dioica*), stonecrop (*Sedum divergens*), and surf grass (*Phyllospadix scouleri* and *P. torreyi*).

Several marine algae were eaten, especially on the northern and central coast. These include red laver and black seaweed (*Porphyra* spp.) and, perhaps on the Gulf of Alaska only, iridescent seaweed (*Iridaea* spp.), as well as giant kelp (*Macrocystis pyrifera*), bull kelp (*Nereocystis leutkeana*), and boa kelp (*Egregia menziesii*) when herring have deposited roe on them.

Edible cambium was scraped from the bark of the Sitka spruce, shore pine, western hemlock, red alder, and black cottonwood by peoples from the northern end of the area south to the Strait of Georgia.

Nut-bearing trees are absent in most of the spruce-hemlock forest. The hazelnut (*Corylus cornuta*) grows on the upper Skeena and on the coast from Vancouver Island south, and the nuts were used throughout its range. Acorns from the Garry oak were eaten throughout its range, but they were more important from the lower Columbia region southward, where there were better developed methods of removing the tannic acid. In the inland valleys of southwestern Oregon, the Native peoples also used the acorns of the California black oak and nuts of the golden chinquapin and sugar pine.

Seeds were almost wholly neglected except in the Willamette Valley and southward, where tarweed (*Madia sativa*, *M. glomerata*, and *M. elegans*) and wyethia (*Wyethia angustifolia*) were important resources.

Black tree lichen or bearded moss (*Bryoria fremontii*) was a source of food in the Skeena Valley and in southwestern Oregon (Turner 1977).

A number of edible mushrooms are native to the Northwest Coast, but no Indian use of any has been reported.

The food value of some of the plants used has been analyzed by Rivera (1949), Norton (1979a), Turner and Kuhnlein (1982), Keely et al. (1982), and Norton et al. (1984).

Plants Used in Technology

Western red cedar provided the preferred wood, wherever it was available, for house planks, posts, and beams, carved monuments, canoes, boxes, and a wide variety of implements and ceremonial paraphernalia. It is light and easily split yet strong and resistant to rot. Sitka spruce was used for houses and canoes in the northern end of the coast. Western hemlock and Douglas fir saplings were used for poles, as for weirs. Yellow cedar, big-leaf maple, and Oregon ash, where available, were preferred for canoe paddles. Red alder was the most widespread wood used for spoons, bowls, feast dishes, rattles, and masks, followed by big-leaf maple, Rocky mountain maple, and yellow cedar. The western yew was generally preferred for bows, wedges, clubs, and digging sticks. Vine maple, crabapple, and flowering dogwood are also hard, tough woods useful for small tools. From Vancouver Island south, ocean spray (*Holodiscus discolor*), commonly called ironwood, was the favorite wood for harpoon foreshafts, spear prongs, mat needles, and sticks for drying and roasting foods. Serviceberry, syringa or mock-orange (*Philadelphus lewisii*), and hardhack (*Spiraea douglasii*) had similar uses.

Western red cedar limbs were twisted into rope, the roots were split and used in baskets, the whole bark was used in some places for roofing material and makeshift canoes, and the inner bark was everywhere cut in strips for baskets and mats and shredded for skirts, capes, towels, babies' diapers, and many other uses. Yellow cedar bark was used in similar ways. Strips of bitter cherry bark were used for binding.

Other materials used for cordage were bull kelp stipes, cedar root, spruce root, willow bark, stinging nettle (*Urtica dioica*) fibers, and the fiber of Indian hemp (*Apocynum cannabinum*) obtained in trade from the interior. From the Strait of Georgia south the cattail and tule (*Scirpus acutus*) were used for mats. Other plants used in basketry included bear grass (*Xerophyllum tenax*), sedges (*Carex obnupta* and other species), cut-grass (*Scirpus microcarpus*), and dune grass (*Elymus mollis*).

Plants with Medicinal Uses

A great many plants were used medicinally or ritually. Devil's club (*Oplopanax horridum*, see Turner 1982) and Indian consumption plant or hogfennel (*Lomatium nudicaule*) were especially well known.

Domestication

Tobacco was grown in western Oregon, where it was smoked, and on the northern coast, where it was mixed with lime and chewed. The species was probably *Nicotiana quadrivalvis* (Turner and Taylor 1972; Meilleur 1979). Tobacco was the only truly domesticated plant. However, in some regions, beds of wild food plants were tended, and measures were taken to ensure their survival (Suttles 1951a; R. White 1980; Turner and Kuhnlein 1982).

Sources on the Native uses of plants are Brown (1868), Gill (1983, 1985), Gunther (1973), Jacobs and Jacobs (1982), Kennedy and Bouchard (1976), Norton (1981, 1985), Norton et al. (1984), Rollins (1972), Smith (1929a), Turner (1973, 1975, 1977, 1979, 1981), Turner and Bell (1973), Turner and Kuhnlein (1982, 1983), Turner and Efrat (1982), Turner et al. (1983), and Williams (1979), and on the identification of plants Hultén (1968), Hitchcock and Cronquist (1973), Franklin and Dyrness (1973), and Soil Conservation Service (1982).

Fauna

For the Native peoples the most important animal resources were fishes, larger mammals, waterfowl, and marine shellfish.

Fishes

The Northwest Coast was rich in saltwater and anadromous fishes, less so in freshwater fishes. Anadromous fishes include the Pacific salmons, steelhead and some other trouts, eulachon, sturgeons, and lampreys.

There are five species of Pacific salmon. All are hatched in fresh water, make their way to the sea to mature, and return to their native streams to spawn and die. They differ in migratory patterns and feeding habits, which relate to methods of fishing, and in size and qualities of flesh, which relate to methods of processing and preserving. The chinook salmon (*Oncorhynchus tshawytscha*, known in different regions as spring, king, tyee, or quinnat) is the largest, weighing up to 80 pounds.

It generally spawns in larger streams, and in some rivers there are two or more populations that spawn in different seasons, so there may be a spring run and a fall run. The coho (*O. kisutch*, silver or silverside), usually weighs 6 to 12 pounds but can weigh up to 31 pounds. It begins to run in early fall but may not spawn until late fall, usually in smaller streams but often a great distance from the sea. Unlike the other species, chinook and coho salmon have feeding habits that allow them to be taken by trolling in the salt water. The sockeye (*O. nerka*, red or blueback) is somewhat smaller but varies in weight from one river system to another. It is almost wholly limited to river systems that have lakes. Some lakes have populations of landlocked sockeye called kokanee. The pink (*O. gorbuscha*, humpback) weighs 3 to 10 pounds. It spawns in early fall in smaller streams, usually not far from the sea. The chum (*O. keta*, dog salmon), at 8 to 18 pounds, spawns in late fall in smaller streams generally close to the sea. The sockeye is the fattest species, which gives it value as food but makes it harder to keep. The chum is lean and valued because it can be smoked dry and hard so that it lasts through the winter.

Salmon of some species ran in nearly every stream, blocked only by waterfalls too high to jump. Many smaller streams were limited to one or two species that were present in abundance for a few days to a few weeks in the year. But in the great rivers, with many separate populations headed for different tributaries, salmon run in enormous numbers, and there may be some present for much of the year.

Patterns of salmon migration, fluctuations in abundance, loss of food value upriver, and estimates of aboriginal consumption have been explored by Hewes (1947, 1973), Kew (1976, 1988), Schalk (1977, 1986), and Romanoff (1985).

The steelhead (*Salmo gairdneri*) is a sea-run rainbow trout that weighs up to 36 pounds. Like the Atlantic salmon, to which it is closely related, it does not die after spawning but returns to the sea. Thus it can be taken either ascending or descending. It is often present through the winter, after the salmon have gone. In many streams there are much smaller nonmigratory races of rainbow trout. The coastal cutthroat trout (*Salmo clarki*) also exists in both sea-run and resident populations.

The eulachon (*Thaleichthys pacificus*), commonly called hooligan in British Columbia and also known as candlefish or Columbia River smelt, is a species of smelt that runs in a number of larger streams, generally in early spring. The eulachon is very important from the Kwakiutl northward as a source of oil (H.A. Collison 1941; Macnair 1971; Kuhnlein et al. 1982). Swan (1881) reported it was richer in oil farther north, but it was an important late winter resource on the Columbia (Boyd and Hajda 1987). The longfin smelt (*Spirinchus thaleichthys*) exists in both anadromous and landlocked populations.

Two species of sturgeon are present, the white (*Acipenser transmontanus*) and the green (*A. medirostris*). The white sturgeon is the larger, the record on the Fraser being 1,800 pounds, and is the more common. It was a major resource in the Fraser and Columbia rivers.

The Pacific lamprey (*Lampetra tridentata*) and river lamprey (*L. ayresi*) are most easily caught as they cling to rocks at a waterfall.

Among saltwater fishes, halibut, herring, smelts, and the true cods were especially important. The halibut (*Hippoglossus stenolepis*) was caught in water of 20–30 fathoms or more, generally in late spring and summer. Halibut rivaled salmon in importance for some of the tribes of the outer coast from the Tlingit to the Makah. The Pacific herring (*Clupea harengus*) spawns in shallow water in late winter or spring, and at that time it is most easily taken and the roe can be gathered. The surf or silver smelt (*Hypomesus pretiosus*), capelin (*Mallotus villosus*), and night smelt (*Spirinchus starksi*) all spawn along beaches during limited periods in different seasons. Herring were important everywhere, smelts perhaps especially on ocean shores of Washington and Oregon.

The term cod is commonly used for a variety of fishes not always distinguished in the ethnographic literature. There are four true cods, the Pacific cod (*Gadus macrocephalus*), Pacific hake (*Merluccius productus*), Pacific tomcod (*Microgadus proximus*), and walleye pollock (*Theragra chalcogramma*). There are also a number of species of rockfish (*Sebastes* spp., commonly called rock cod), the sablefish (*Anoplopoma fimbria*, commonly called black cod), the kelp greenling (*Hexagrammos decagrammus*, known as tommycod), and the lingcod (*Ophiodon elongatus*).

Also of some importance are the spiny dogfish (*Squalus acanthias*), big skate (*Raja binoculata*), and ratfish (*Hydrolagus colliei*); the plainfin midshipman (*Porichthys notatus*), or singing fish; perches, including the pile perch (*Rhacochilus vacca*) and striped sea perch (*Embiotoca lateralis*); a number of sculpins (Family Cottidae), also called bullheads, including the buffalo sculpin (*Enophrys bison*), cabezon (*Scorpaenichthys marmoratus*), Irish lord (*Hemilepidotus* spp.), and staghorn sculpin (*Leptocottus armatus*); and the starry flounder (*Platichthys stellatus*) and several other flatfish (Pleuronectidae) grouped together as sole.

There is archeological evidence (McMillan 1979) from the west coast of Vancouver Island for the use of two species of tuna, the bluefin tuna (*Thunnus thynnus*) and the albacore (*T. alalunga*), pelagic fishes present only when warmer water moves northward; their use is not reported ethnographically.

In the nineteenth century a number of tribes caught the dogfish in great numbers, because there was a demand among Whites for its oil. The Makah also took the basking shark (*Cetorhinus maximus*) for this reason. For anadromous and saltwater fishes see Hart (1973).

Freshwater species of possible economic importance and wide distribution include the mountain whitefish (*Prosopium williamsoni*), Dolly Varden char (*Salvelinus malma*), largescale sucker (*Catostomus macrocheilus*, longnose sucker (*C. catostomus*), white sucker (*C. commersoni*), northern squawfish (*Ptychocheilus oregonensis*), peamouth chub (*Mylocheilus caurinus*), redside shiner (*Richarsonius balteatus*), several species of dace (*Rhinichthys*), threespine stickleback (*Gasterosteus aculeatus*), prickly sculpin (*Cottus asper*), and Aleutian or coast-range sculpin (*C. aleuticus*). At the northern end of the coast the arctic grayling (*Thymallus arcticus*), lake trout (*Salvelinus namaycush*), and burbot (*Lota lota*) may have been available. The white sucker was confined to the Skeena, the chiselmouth (*Acrocheilus alutaceus*) to the Lower Columbia and Willamette, and the Umpqua squawfish (*Ptychocheilus umpquae*) and Klamath and Sacramento suckers (*Catostomus rimiculus* and *C. occidentalis*) to rivers of western Oregon (Carl, Clemens, and Lindsey 1959; McPhail and Lindsey 1986; Minckley, Hendrickson, and Bond 1986). Freshwater fishes probably nowhere rivaled the anadromous species, but in the lower Fraser and Columbia valleys the suckers, squawfish, and chub were of secondary importance (Saleeby 1983).

Mammals

The distinction between sea mammals and land mammals was basic for Native peoples.

The harbor or hair seal (*Phoca vitulina*) lives everywhere along the coast and enters many rivers, ascending the Skeena River for 200 miles, and is present in Harrison Lake in Fraser Valley the year round (H.D. Fisher 1952). In the Columbia the seals once went as far upstream as the Cascades and in the Willamette to Willamette Falls. The northern fur seal (*Callorhinus ursinus*) is almost wholly an offshore migrant. The Steller or northern sea lion (*Eumetopias jubatus*) ranges along most of the coast, frequenting both offshore islands and estuaries. It has a few rookeries where several thousand gather in summer. The smaller California sea lion (*Zalophus californianus*) ranges as far north as Vancouver Island, the northern elephant seal (*Mirounga angustirostris*) as far as Hecate Strait.

The harbor porpoise (*Phocoena phocoena*) is common inshore and in estuaries, the Pacific white-sided dolphin (*Lagenorhynchus obliquidens*) in the less sheltered water, and the Dall's porpoise (*Phocoenoides dalli*) along the outer coast. The orca or killer whale (*Orcinus orca*), once commonly called blackfish, is present all along the coast and abundant in inner waters from Alaska to Puget Sound. Pilot whales (*Globicephala* spp.), also called blackfish, are much less common; blackfish in the earlier anthropological literature probably refers to the orca.

Before commercial whaling the most common species of larger whales were the humpback (*Megaptera novaeangliae*), which often entered straits and sounds, and the gray whale (*Eschrichtius gibbosus*), which migrates seasonally just off the outer coast. Other whales present were the fin (*Balaenoptera physalus*), sei (*B. borealis*), minke (*B. acutorostrata*), blue (*B. musculus*), northern right (*Balaena glacialis*), and sperm (*Physeter catadon*). The humpback and California gray were the species most commonly hunted (Kool 1982; Inglis and Haggerty 1983; Huelsbeck 1988a). For some nonwhaling tribes, beached whales were an important resource.

The sea otter (*Enhyda lutris*) was once very common all along the outer coast; pelts were in use when first Europeans arrived and became the most sought-after product from 1780 until the near extinction of the animal.

Among land mammals the ungulates were the most important in most regions. The blacktail deer (*Odocoileus hemionus*) is native to the coast from southeast Alaska to western Oregon (except for the Queen Charlotte Islands), the Sitka subspecies north of the central coast of British Columbia and the Columbian to the south. It was introduced to the Yakutat area (De Laguna 1972) and the Queen Charlottes (Foster 1965). The whitetail deer (*Odocoileus virginiana*) is confined to the lower Columbia Valley and western Oregon south to the upper Rogue Valley. Deer are much more abundant in Douglas fir forests and parkland than in the spruce-hemlock forest (Cowan 1945). The elk or wapati (*Cervus elephus*) was once common from the northern end of Vancouver Island southward. The mountain goat (*Oreamnos americanus*) lives in open rocky terrain from the Gulf of Alaska through the Coast Mountains to the Cascade Range of Washington.

Several species have a peripheral distribution: the caribou (*Rangifer tarandus*) in tundra and alpine habitat surrounding the northern Northwest Coast and extending south as far as central British Columbia, with an isolated subspecies or species (*R. tarandus* var. *dawsoni*) confined to northwestern Graham Island in the Queen Charlottes (Foster 1965); the moose (*Alces alces*) in a more interior habitat extending south to southern British Columbia; two species of mountain sheep—the Dall sheep (*Ovis dalli*), ranging through the Saint Elias Mountains to the northern Coast Mountains, and the bighorn sheep (*O. canadensis*) from the southern Coast Mountains into the eastern slopes of the Cascade Range; and the pronghorn antelope (*Antilocapra americana*), whose range once extended from east of the Cascades into the upper Rogue River Valley.

The American black bear (*Ursus americanus*) is found everywhere except on a few islands. There are several regional subspecies, and a single subspecies can have different color phases. The grizzly bear (*U. arctos*) also had a range extending the length of the culture area but on the British Columbia mainland and in or near the Cascade

Range only. It too exists in several subspecies, including the big brown bear of Alaska.

Other carnivores include: the river otter (*Lutra candensis*), marten (*Martes americana*), and ermine (*Mustela erminea*), everywhere on the coast; the wolf (*Canis lupus*), wolverine (*Gulo gulo*), lynx (*Lynx canadensis*), and mink (*Mustela vision*), everywhere but the Queen Charlottes; the fisher (*Martes pennanti*) from the northern coast of British Columbia south; the cougar (*Felis concolor*) and raccoon (*Procyon lotor*), from the central coast of British Columbia south; and the bobcat (*Lynx rufus*), striped skunk (*Mephitis mephitis*), and spotted skunk (*Spilogale putorius*), from southern British Columbia south; the coyote (*Canis latrans*), in the Willamette Valley and southwestern Oregon; the red fox (*Vulpes vulpes*) and gray fox (*Urocyon cinereoargenteus*) in the mountains of western Oregon; and the ringtail (*Bassaroscus astutus*) in the upper Rogue Valley.

A few rodents and lagomorphs were of economic importance: the beaver (*Castor canadensis*), found everywhere except on the Queen Charlottes; the hoary or whistling marmot (*Marmota caligata*), in the mountains on the northern coast and elsewhere; the mountain beaver (*Aplodontia rufa*, from the Fraser Valley south to western Oregon; and the snowshoe hare (*Lepus americanus*), found everywhere on the mainland. There were other small mammals—rodents such as squirrels, woodrats, mice, and voles, as well as shrews and moles, and bats.

Sources on mammals are Cowan and Guiguet (1973), Dalquest (1948), Bailey (1936), Hall (1981), Ingles (1965), Pike and MacAskie (1969), and Banks, McDiarmid, and Gardner (1987).

Birds

For the Native peoples, birds were probably a more important resource than commonly supposed. Archeological work (Friedman 1976; Calvert 1980) has shown more species used than generally reported by ethnographers.

Waterfowl were vastly more important than land birds. Except for some of the birds of prey, waterfowl are generally larger than the birds encountered on land. Many species of waterfowl are migratory and were seasonally available in limited areas in huge numbers, while land birds are rarely concentrated at any time or place.

Pelagic species that breed elsewhere include the short-tailed and black-footed albatross (*Diomedea albatrus* and *D. nigripes*), sooty and slender-billed shearwater (*Puffinus griseus* and *P. tenuirostris*), and northern fulmar (*Fulmarus glacialis*). Although generally out in the ocean, some of these are occasionally available inshore. The black-footed albatross may enter the wider straits. Sooty shearwaters have come into Willapa Bay in enormous flocks, and fulmars are sometimes driven ashore by fall and winter storms (Jewett et al. 1953:69, 72).

Breeding colonies of seabirds were an important resource, seasonally providing nesting birds and eggs. The fork-tailed and Leach's storm-petrel (*Oceanodroma furcata* and *O. leucorhoa*), common murre (*Uria aalge*), pigeon guillemot (*Cepphus columba*), marbled murrelet (*Brachyramphus marmoratus*), ancient murrelet (*Synthliboramphus antiquus*), Cassin's auklet (*Ptychoramphus aleuticus*), rhinoceros auklet (*Cerorhinca monocerata*), and tufted puffin (*Fratercula cirrhata*), and the double-crested, Brandts's and pelagic cormorants or shags (*Phalacrocorax auritus, P. penicillatus,* and *P. pelagicus*) all breed from Alaska to Oregon. The horned puffin (*F. corniculata*) is restricted to the northern coast. The glaucus-winged gull (*Larus glaucescens*) breeds as far south as the Washington coast; the western gull (*L. occidentalis*) breeds on the Oregon coast. The murrelets nest inland and may have been safe from human predation. The other species generally nest in rocky islets, where some were harvested in great numbers.

Even more important in most regions were the Anatidae. This family includes the whistling swan (*Cygnus columbianus*) and trumpeter swan (*C. buccinator*), white-fronted goose (*Anser albifrons*), snow goose (*Chen caerulescens*), Canada goose (*Branta canadensis*), brant (*B. bernicla*), and at least 26 species of ducks, including the wood duck (*Aix sponsa*). Dabbling ducks include the mallard (*Anas platyrhynchos*), pintail or sprig (*A. acuta*), shoveller or spoonbill (*A. clypeata*), gadwall (*A. strepera*), widgeon or baldpate (*A. americana*), and green-winged, blue-winged, and cinnamon teals (*A. crecca, A. discors,* and *A. cyanoptera*). Diving ducks include the redhead (*Aythya americana*), canvasback (*A. valisineria*), ring-necked duck (*A. collaris*), greater and lesser scaups or bluebills (*A. marila* and *A. affinis*), American and Barrow's goldeneye (*Bucephala clangula* and *B. islandica*), bufflehead or butterball (*B. albeola*), oldsquaw (*Clangula hyemalis*), harlequin duck (*Histrionicus histrionicus*), black, white-wing, and surf scoters or black ducks (*Melanitta nigra, M. fusca,* and *M. perspicillata*), ruddy duck (*Oxyura jamaicensis*), and American, red-breasted, and hooded mergansers or sawbills (*Mergus merganser, M. serrator,* and *Lophodytes cucullatus*). A few of these (one variety of Canada goose, the mallard, shoveller, wood duck, American and hooded mergansers) are year-round residents. The rest breed elsewhere and winter on the Northwest Coast, several species mainly from Vancouver Island south. Swans, geese, and dabbling ducks were once abundant in winter in the wetlands of the Lower Fraser valley, Puget Sound, and Lower Columbia Valley, as were diving ducks in the adjacent salt water. Flocks of widgeons and scoters numbered in the tens of thousands (Jewitt et al. 1953:127–128, 148).

Other diving, wading, and shore birds include four species of loon (*Gavia immer, G. adamsii, G. arctica,* and

G. stellata), five grebes or divers (*Aechmorphorus occiden-talis, Podiceps auritus, P. nigricollis, P. grisegena,* and *Podilymbus podiceps*), the great blue heron (*Ardea herodias*), American bittern (*Botaurus lentiginosus*), sandhill crane (*Grus canadensis*), American coot (*Fulica americana*), black oyster catcher (*Haematopus bachmani*), killdeer (*Charadrius vociferus*), and a number of snipes and sandpipers. Most loons and grebes are only winter visitors. The heron (once commonly called crane) is a year-round resident, valued by the Indians for its flesh in winter and for the alarm it sounds at the approach of human visitors. The sandhill crane was once present in great numbers from the Fraser Delta southward through the summer. The coot and oyster catcher are present through the year.

There are a few upland game birds: the willow, rock, and white-tailed ptarmigan (*Lagopus lagopus, L. mutus,* and *L. leucurus*) in barer areas at the northern end of the coast, the last at higher elevations as far south as the northern Cascades; the spruce, blue, and ruffed grouse (*Dendragapus canadensis, D. obscurus,* and *Bonansa umbellus*) in forested areas from Alaska to Oregon, the spruce grouse at higher elevations in the south; the California quail (*Callipepla californica*) and mountain quail (*Oreortyx pictus*) in western Oregon; and the band-tailed pigeon (*Columba fasciata*) from the Skeena River south.

Birds of prey include the bald eagle (*Haliaeetus leucocephalus*), common all along the coast; the golden eagle (*Aquila chrysaetos*), in the mountains; 10 or more species of hawks and falcons, most of them widely distributed; and the turkey vulture or buzzard (*Cathartes aura*), from the Strait of Georgia south in dryer regions. The California condor (*Gymnogyps californianus*) also once ranged as far north as the lower Fraser Valley. Owls include the western screech owl (*Otus asio*) and great-horned owl (*Bubo virginianus*), both resident throughout the area; the snowy owl (*Nyctea scandiaca*), a winter visitor; and several other species. Members of the crow family include the raven (*Corvus corax*), American and northwestern crows (*C. brachyrhynchos* and *C. caurinus*), and Steller's jay (*Cyanocitta stelleri*), all present nearly everywhere, as well as a few of more restricted distribution. Woodpeckers include the northern flicker (*Colaptes auratus,* in yellow-shafted and red-shafted varieties), the pileated woodpecker (*Dryocopus pileatus*), and several smaller species. One species of hummingbird, the rufous (*Selasphorus rufus*), is present throughout the area. Probably none of these species was commonly used for food, but several were important as sources of feathers and in tradition. In addition, there are a great many species of smaller birds such as swallows, titmice, wrens, thrushes, warblers, and sparrows.

Sources on birds are Munro and Cowan (1947), Jewett et al. (1953), Gabrielson and Jewett (1970), Larisson (1981), Godfrey (1986), and Banks, McDiarmid, and Gardner (1987).

Reptiles and Amphibians

Few reptiles and amphibians are found throughout the Northwest Coast, although many inhabit the southern half of the region. None of the snakes, lizards, turtles, salamanders, frogs, and toads was of any economic importance to the Indians, who generally viewed these animals with some fear. Rattlesnakes were known on the Lower Fraser, because they sometimes rode down from the interior on rafts of vegetation. They were also present in a few areas in western Oregon. Otherwise there were no poisonous snakes in the area. Sources are Carl (1950, 1951), R.P. Hodge (1976), Nussbaum, Brodie, and Storm (1983), Green and Campbell (1984), and Gregory and Campbell (1984).

Marine Invertebrates

Marine invertebrates used by the Native peoples include mollusks, crustaceans, and echinoderms. They can be categorized by the kind of effort involved in collecting them.

Species exposed on rocks and beaches at low tide and simply collected or pried off rocks include the sea mussel (*Mytilus californianus*), bay mussel (*M. edulis*), purple-hinged rock scallop (*Hinnites multirugosus*), native or Olympia oyster (*Ostrea lurida*), basket cockle (*Cardium corbis*), northern abalone (*Haliotis kamtschatkana*), limpets (*Collisella pelta, Notoacmea scutum*), snail-like univalves (*Tegula funebralis, Astraea gibberosa, Littorina sitkana, Searlesia dira, Polinices lewisii,* and *Nucella lamellosa*), chitons (*Mopalia muscosa, Katharina tunicata,* and *Cryptochiton stelleri*), barnacles (*Balanus glandula* and *Mitella polymerus*), and green, red, and purple sea urchins (*Strongylocentrotus drobachiensis, S. franciscanus,* and *S. purpuratus*).

Species available at low tides but requiring digging include the butter clam (*Saxidomus giganteus*), littleneck clam (*Protothaca staminea*), horse clam (*Schizothaerus nuttalli, S. capax*), geoduck (*Panopea generosa*), thin-shelled clam (*Protothaca tenerrima*), and razor clam (*Siliqua patula*), the last available only on sandy ocean beaches.

Species available at low tides by wading or spearing from a canoe include the red rock crab (*Cancer productus*), Dungeness crab (*C. magister*), spider crab (*Pugettia producta*), Alaska king crab (*Paralithodes camtschatica*), sea cucumber (*Stichopus californicus*), and octopus (*Octopus appollyon*).

The dentalium (*Dentalium pretosium*) was collected from canoes on the west coast of Vancouver Island, from which the shells were traded over a large part of western North America to be used as ornaments and wealth. The weather-vane scallop (*Pecten caurinus*) lives at depths of 10 fathoms or more but was reportedly caught swimming. Their shells were used as rattles. Other nonfood uses include clam shells as dishes and for disk beads, Olivella shells as beads, and opercula of the red turban (*Astraea gibberosa*) as decorative elements on carvings. The abalone used for personal ornaments and on carvings is not the native species, the northern abalone (*Haliotis kamtschatkana*), but one imported from California by the early traders (Heizer 1940).

Sources on marine invertebrates are Quayle (1960), Griffith (1967), and Kozloff (1983), and on Indian uses Ellis and Swan (1981), Ellis and Wilson (1976), and Kennedy and Bouchard (1976a).

Freshwater and Land Invertebrates

The freshwater mussel (*Margaritifera margaritifera*) and the crayfish (*Astacus pacifastacus*) were widely available but reportedly eaten in western Oregon only, by the Kalapuya and Takelma. Land snails and slugs were common in wet forests, but not used. Insects were not eaten in most of the area; exceptions are yellow-jacket larvae, grasshoppers, and a species of tree caterpillar in the interior valleys of western Oregon.

Environmental Hazards

The Northwest Coast lies within a volcanic and seismically active region, and there are active volcanoes in the Saint Elias and Cascade ranges. Earthquakes occasionally occur and can cause tsunami of destructive force (R.E. Thomson 1981:129–135). The 1980 eruption of Mount Saint Helens resulted in a devastating flood and widespread deposition of ash that had a negative effect on food plants (Hunn and Norton 1984). Severe winds may have occasionally destroyed houses and damaged stores of food. Heavy rainfall can cause mudslides, such as the one that covered the prehistoric village at Ozette (see "Prehistory of the Ocean Coast of Washington," this vol.). Larger predators were probably rarely a hazard; some invertebrates were at least a nuisance. Fleas were common in houses, as noted by early explorers, and it has been suggested (Swan 1857:255; Bancroft 1874–1876, 1:231)

that they contributed to the pattern of seasonal movement. Lice were common. A mosquito vector for malaria (*Anopheles malculipennis*) was present in the Lower Columbia Valley and southward, one of the conditions permitting the epidemic of 1830 (Boyd 1975:144). In summer months in some areas the toxic marine organism known as red tide can make shellfish poisonous.

Post-Settlement Changes

In addition to the more obvious and better-known changes that have resulted from logging, dam-building, overfishing, and population growth, such as the destruction of old-growth forests, flooding of valleys, decline in fish runs, and loss of natural landscape to cities and highways, there are other, less obvious changes. In the more heavily settled part of the Northwest Coast, from the Strait of Georgia southward, there is not only less forest but also less of what was once open or semi-open land. The prohibition of seasonal burning of prairies resulted in new growth of tree cover, shrinkage of prairie land, and less room for native food plants, many of which in any case have been largely destroyed by livestock.

Introduced plants and animals have prospered at the expense of native species, especially in the more settled southern part of the area. Old World blackberries have covered streambanks and other open places with brambles and have spread northward to cover deserted Kwakiutl village sites (Bill Holm, personal communication 1988). Lakes have been stocked with fish not native to the region—bass, perch, catfish, and carp, the last destructive of native plants. There is one new anadromous fish, the shad. Two introduced birds, the house sparrows and European starling, have become abundant, and the ring-necked pheasant has prospered. In the more settled southern region the wolf and grizzly are extinct or nearly so. But the coyote has become common in southwestern British Columbia and western Washington, where it was absent before White settlement. Introduced mammals include the roof rat, Norway rat, house mouse, opossum, and nutria. In shellfish beds there are nonnative mollusks, Japanese oysters, and Japanese littleneck clams. Introduced invertebrates include European slugs, earthworms, and numerous insects (Carl and Guiguet 1958).

ENVIRONMENT

Languages

LAURENCE C. THOMPSON AND M. DALE KINKADE

Languages and Language Families

The Northwest Coast was the second most diverse linguistic area of aboriginal North America (after California). It involved 13 of Powell's (1891) linguistic families, represented in at least 45 distinct languages.

At the time of the first European contact, these linguistic families were distributed with some discontinuities that suggest earlier displacements (fig. 1). Languages are listed in table 1 in generally north to south order, but keeping families together. Phyla are groupings of language families hypothesized, but not proven, to be remotely related. Language families are groups of languages that can be shown to be genetically related, using techniques developed by comparative linguistics; branches are subdivisions of families. Dialects are different, but mutually intelligible, varieties of a single language, while languages are not mutually intelligible; the decision as to whether two communities speak different languages or only different dialects is sometimes difficult to make. Before 1930 the term "dialect" was often used to emphasize the fact of genetic linguistic relationship, so that the term sometimes is applied to what later would be called distinct languages.

Eyak-Athapaskan

Eyak is demonstrably related to the Athapaskan family but is coordinate with it, being just as far removed from neighboring Ahtna as from remote Navajo (Krauss 1973: 950). During the eighteenth and nineteenth centuries Eyak lost ground to Tlingit and gained from Pacific Eskimo.

Eyak and the Athapaskan languages share many of their general characteristics. They distinguish as major word classes nouns, verbs, and particles. They are primarily prefixing languages, using strings of short elements before the main root of verbs to mark subjects and objects, several tense-aspect categories, and—particulary characteristic—a special set of classifiers with complex functions (including various transitivity relations); derivational prefixes occur frequently to modify meanings in many ways. Suffixes are fewer in number, and are mostly aspectlike and derivational. Variation in stem shape between paradigms is common. Classificatory verbs are typical of Athapaskan, but vestigial in Eyak. The consonant systems typically have few labials, with only m in Eyak, and either m or b (and occasionally both) in Oregon Athapaskan (where w is classified as a prevelar). Eyak further has lost all labialized consonants except the two prevelars g^w and x^w (and w). A set of (secondary) nasalized vowels occurs throughout the family, and both oral and nasalized vowels may occur long. Both Eyak and Oregon Athapaskan, instead of developing tone like many Athapaskan languages, have kept glottal modification of the stem-vowel. For a brief sketch of Eyak structure, see Krauss (1965); for texts and dictionary, see Krauss (1963–1970, 1970, 1982).

The Tsetsaut were the only documented Northern Athapaskan group to reach the Pacific coast and penetrate the Northwest Coast culture area. Discussion of their language is found in volume 6:67–72, 83.

Pacific Coast Athapaskan is a main branch of the Athapaskan family that "is more divergent from the North than is Apachean, shows more internal divergence than does Apachean, and was probably never an undifferentiated linguistic community even if, as is historically somewhat improbable, it split off from the North as one group. Nevertheless, it is clear that Pacific Coast Athapaskan split off from a relatively restricted or linguistically homogeneous sector of the North, and that a number of important phonological and morphological innovations are unique to and universal in" Pacific Coast Athapaskan (Krauss 1973:919–920). Krauss (1973:943) emphasizes that the whole of Athapaskan must be viewed as a dialect complex with many shared and convergent developments; at the same time dialects are diverging in more conventionally recognized ways, on the basis of which genetic family trees are constructed. The complex of languages on the southern Oregon and northern California coast is itself affected by a number of convergent developments, for example, the loss of postvelar consonants, the loss of Proto-Athapaskan $*\lambda$ and $*\dot\lambda$, the falling together of $*s$ and $*z$ and of $*\check{s}$ and $*\check{z}$, and collapse of several stop-fricative oppositions of consonants into single consonants, either stop or fricative. However, divergent developments do seem to divide the complex into distinct Oregon and California groups, with internal relationships somewhat closer in the Oregon group. For example, Proto-Athapaskan *č remains *č in California but becomes a fricative in Oregon, each of the pairs *k and *x, *kʷ and *xʷ remains as a single consonant—either stop or fricative—in Oregon, but all four become a single consonant in California (Hoijer 1960). For further information see Krauss (1973, 1979) and volume 6:67–85.

The Oregon group is perhaps best characterized as comprising four languages: Upper Umpqua, Tututni, Galice-Applegate, and Tolowa. Upper Umpqua, northernmost of the group, was apparently a rather uniform language spoken by a small group on the upper Umpqua River (and is not to be confused with the Siuslaw dialect, Lower Umpqua). It is rather different from the other three languages, but, oddly enough, shares some features with the California group. Galice, of which the poorly documented Applegate (upstream from Galice) is likely only a slightly different variant, was well inland, and both dialects were isolated enclaves within the territory of the Takelma. Galice is very close to Tututni, of which it could be viewed as simply a very divergent detached dialect, as there was said to be a fair degree of mutual intelligibility. Tututni and Tolowa are chains of intergrading dialects. Most of the dialects of Tolowa, including that of Smith River, occupied territory in California; the Chetco dialect was spoken in Oregon. A grammatical sketch of the Tututni dialect is Golla (1976). For a brief grammatical sketch of Galice, see Hoijer (1966), for Chasta Costa Tututni, Sapir (1914a), and for the phonology of Smith River Tolowa, Bright (1964). For a Galice stem list see Hoijer (1973a) and for Galice and Tututni vocabulary see Landar (1977).

Lower Columbia Athapaskan seems to have been a single isolated language with two closely similar dialects, Kwalhioqua and Clatskanie; the Clatskanie group may have moved to its Oregon location from an area closer to the Kwalhioqua not long before White contact. It does not belong linguistically with the Pacific Coast subgroup of Athapaskan, at least phonologically; its "position by morphological and lexical criteria appears less clear, perhaps intermediate between the North" and Pacific Coast Athapaskan (Krauss 1973:919). The language was extinct by 1930 or so (Melville Jacobs, personal communication 1961) and is poorly documented. For vocabulary see Boas and Goddard (1924); for other sources of data, see Krauss (1973).

Tlingit

Tlingit is a rather homogeneous language with only mild dialect diversity (Swanton 1911), despite its large territory; this implies relatively recent expansion. There are perhaps four areas of differentiated speech: Gulf Coast, Inland, Northern, and Southern (De Laguna 1972:15ff.). The remoter relationships of Tlingit are still debated.

Tlingit closely resembles Athapaskan and Eyak in its prefixing structure and in the meaning of the tense-aspect and classificatory elements involved, and the preceding characterization of those languages applies largely to Tlingit as well. It differs in that objects are marked by preposed particles (rather than prefixes), and its classifiers include more truly classificatory functions than do the comparable elements in Eyak-Athapaskan. Its phonological structure is quite different from all other languages of the area in that it has a whole series of glottalized spirants; it has no labial consonants at all (except for some speakers who use m for w in certain positions). It has two sets of four vowels distinguished by a tense-lax opposition rather than by length, as is the case in neighboring languages. Vowels have tonal contrasts, except in the southernmost dialect, which has an apparently earlier system of nontonal glottal modifications. For grammatical information on Tlingit see Swanton (1911), Naish (1966), Story (1966), Story and Naish (1973), and H. Davis (1976); for dictionaries see Naish and Story (1963) and Story and Naish (1973); for texts see Swanton (1909) and Velten (1939, 1944), Williams and Williams (1978), and Dauenhauer and Dauenhauer (1987). Pinnow (1966) is a historical study of Tlingit phonology.

Haida

Haida has considerable dialectal diversity. There are two surviving major dialect clusters, Skidegate and Masset (the latter spoken by those groups who moved into Alaska since the eighteenth century as well as those remaining in the northern Queen Charlotte Islands). The extinct Ninstints, in the south of the islands, is considered to have been a variety of Skidegate.

In Haida, all inflections are suffixed; derivation may be by either prefixation or suffixation, and reduplication is absent. Verbal inflectional categories are aspect, number, and tense; person is marked by separate particles. Among the derivational affixes are over two dozen shape classifiers prefixed to both verbs and nouns, and several manner-instrument suffixes. The few labial consonants that occur are almost certainly recent, and rounded velars are lacking entirely. Some tonal-accent features present analytical difficulties but are clearly different from those of any other languages in the area. For grammar and texts see Swanton (1905a, 1908, 1911a), Levine (1977a), and Enrico (1980). Swanton's recordings of Haida are generally considered to be phonetically unreliable. For a dictionary see Lawrence (1977).

Tsimshian

Tsimshian is a close-knit family of two (perhaps three) languages, Nass-Gitksan and Coast Tsimshian, a divergent southern dialect of which may be considered a

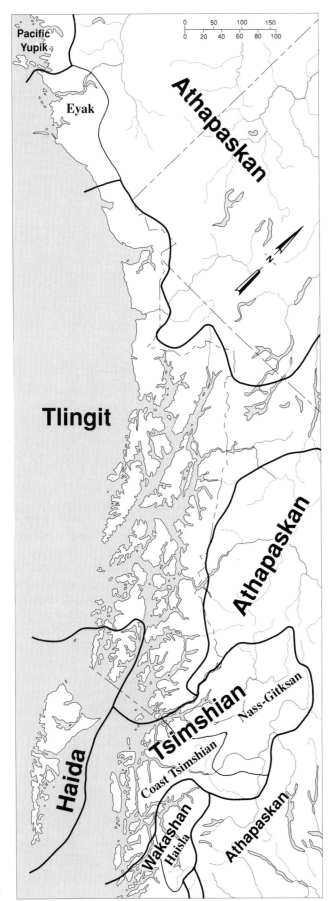
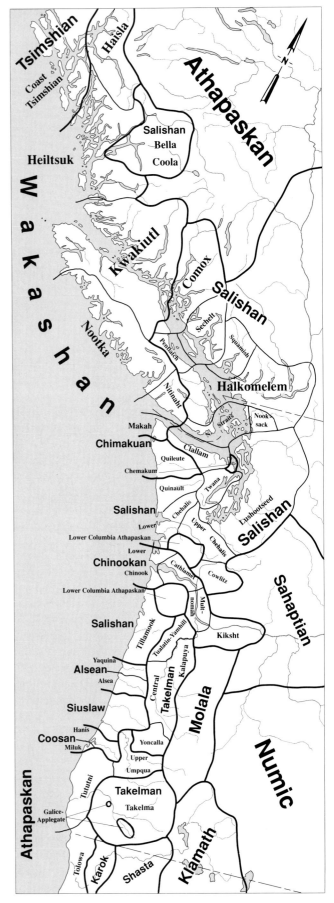

Pacific
Yupik

Eyak

Athapaskan

0   50   100   150
0 20 40 60 80 100

Tlingit

Athapaskan

Haida

Nass-Gitksan

Tsimshian

Coast Tsimshian

Wakashan
Haisla

Athapaskan

Tsimshian

Coast
Tsimshian

Haisla

Heiltsuk

Athapaskan

Salishan
Bella
Coola

Kwakiutl

Comox

Salishan

Nootka

Sechelt

Squamish

Pentlatch

Nitinaht

Halkomelem

Strait
W
a
k
a
s
h
a
n

Makah

Nook-
sack

Chimakuan

Clallam

Quileute

Chemakum

Quinault

Twana

Salishan

Chehalis

Upper
Chehalis

Dushootseed

Salishan

Lower
Lower Columbia Athapaskan

Lower
Chinook

Chinookan

Cathlamet

Cowlitz

Lower Columbia Athapaskan

Multi-
nomah

Salishan

Tillamook

Kiksht

Tualatin-Yamhill

Kalapuya

Sahaptian

Yaquina

Alsean

Alsea

Central

Takelman

Molala

Siuslaw

Hanis

Coosan
Miluk

Yoncalla

Upper

Umpqua

Numic

Athapaskan

Tututni

Takelman

Takelma

Galice-
Applegate

Tolowa

Karok

Shasta

Klamath

THOMPSON AND KINKADE

32

Fig. 1. Language families and languages of the Northwest Coast in the early 19th century, along with language families of adjacent areas (Kinkade and Suttles 1987; Suttles and Suttles 1985).

separate language, Southern Tsimshian (J.A. Dunn 1979a). Other coastal dialects present an intergrading spread. Nass-Gitksan divides into three dialects—Nishga spoken in the Nass River valley and Eastern and Western Gitksan (Hindle and Rigsby 1973:2).

Tsimshian languages are analytic to mildly synthetic, using many preposed particles, proclitics, and a small inventory of suffixes; compounding and initial reduplication are also extensively used. The preposed particles provide numerous adverbial contrasts of location, direction, position, manner, extent, and several tense distinctions. Some aspectual contrasts are made with independent intransitive lexical verbs that have sentential subjects. The syntax is thoroughly ergative, equating subjects of intransitives with objects of transitives in most cases. Independent transitive subject pronouns and possessive pronouns are suffixed, as also are subordinated transitive object and intransitive subject ones. Nouns are divided by possessive inflection into alienable and inalienable. The sound system opposes long and short vowels; among the consonants, rounded prevelars are distinct from unrounded, but there are no corresponding distinctive postvelars; the glottalized lateral affricate ƛ̓ is rare in Nass-Gitksan and lacking in Coast Tsimshian. For a grammar of Coast Tsimshian see Boas (1911b) and J.A. Dunn (1970); for a dictionary of Coast Tsimshian see Dunn (1978); for grammars of Nass-Gitksan see Boas (1911b), Rigsby (1975), and Tarpent (1983, 1989); for a dictionary, see Hindle and Rigsby (1973); for texts see Boas (1902, 1912) and Anonymous (1977).

Salishan

Salishan is a large, much ramified family of 23 languages, of which 16 were spoken in the Northwest Coast culture area; the other seven form a separate Interior Salish division, belonging to the Plateau culture area. The coastal part of Salishan consists of four divisions: the two enclaves Bella Coola and Tillamook, a long chain of closely related languages in the central group (here referred to as Central Salish), and the smaller Tsamosan (formerly Olympic) group. A number of innovations set apart each of the smaller groups, leaving the long complex of Central Salish in which some innovations have begun around the center but have not reached all the languages. Bella Coola is more divergent than all the rest; Tsamosan is less divergent than Bella Coola; Central Salish and Tillamook are somewhat more closely related (Elmendorf 1962). Swadesh (1950) classified the languages somewhat differently, according to glottochronological calculations based on early vocabulary collections; his names for certain

groups will be given as they are discussed later in this section because published sources have frequently used these terms. For comparative Salishan studies see Boas and Haeberlin (1927), Swadesh (1952), Reichard (1958–1960), Kuipers (1970, 1978, 1981, 1982) Kinkade and Thompson (1974), and S. Newman (1976, 1979, 1979a, 1980). Elmendorf (1961a) treats changes in portions of Salishan kinship systems. For a general discussion of Salishan see L.C. Thompson (1979).

Salishan languages are highly polysynthetic, employing numerous suffixes and reduplication patterns; prefixes and infixes are less numerous. Major grammatical categories required are aspect, transitivity, voice, control,* person, and gender (feminine and nonfeminine). Tense and number are optional categories. In all the languages transitive objects are suffixed, but in Central Salish and Tsamosan independent predicates use clitic particles to express both transitive and intransitive subjects. Everywhere except in Bella Coola possessive pronouns occur as a mixed set of prefixes and suffixes. Aspect markers take a variety of shapes, and contrast at least durative/nondurative and stative/active predication. Words also often include ("lexical") suffixes referring to concrete physical objects (such as body parts, objects in nature, or cultural objects; see Haeberlin 1974) or abstract extensions from them. All words, except for a limited number of grammatical particles, have primarily predicative function, and are only secondarily adapted for use in clauses to indicate subjects, objects, or instruments. A characterization of these languages as opposing nounlike words and verblike words thus appears inappropriate (see Kinkade 1983a;

*There is an all-encompassing opposition between, on the one hand, acts and states that are viewed as controlled by some person or entity (marked) and, on the other hand, those that are uncontrolled or controlled only to a limited extent (unmarked); systems sometimes provide also one or two marked formations emphasizing lack or limitation of control. Most of the lexical roots in the languages indicate actions, states, or entities with no indication of control or intervention by any agent. (A very few roots with meanings such as 'go', 'walk', and 'eat' do imply such control or intervention.) Most words in the languages then force a speaker to choose one or another of a set of forms that oppose control and limited control meanings; this is especially clear in transitive forms where one inflected form will mean, for example, 'I cut it accidentally' or '(It took a long time or great effort but) I managed to cut it' (limited control), while an opposing one means 'I cut it (intentionally, being in control of the situation)' (control); still other forms can emphasize the limitation of control ('I managed to cut it'—emphatic limited control). This sort of choice then is forced for nearly every situation the way the English speaker is forced to choose one tense of the verb over other tenses. The system intersects with more familiar transitive, voice, and mood oppositions, and with categories such as reflexive and stative, so that it cannot be understood as some sort of specialization of any of these. For a fuller discussion of control in Salishan see L.C. Thompson (1985).

Table 1. Language Classification

Phylum	Family	Subfamily	Branch	Language	Dialect
Na-Dene Phylum					
	Eyak-Athapaskan Family				
		Eyak			
		Athapaskan			
			Lower Columbia Athapaskan		
					Kwalhioqua
					Clatskanie
			Pacific Coast Athapaskan		
				Upper Umpqua	
				Tututni	
				Galice-Applegate	
				Tolowa	
	Tlingit Language Isolate				
					Gulf Coast
					Inland
					Northern Tlingit
					Southern Tlingit
Haida Language Isolate					
					Skidegate
					Masset
Tsimshian Language Family					
				Coast Tsimshian	
					Coast Tsimshian
					Southern Tsimshian
				Nass-Gitksan	
					Nishga
					Western Gitksan
					Eastern Gitksan
Wakashan Language Family					
			Kwakiutlan		
				Haisla	
				Heiltsuk-Oowekyala	
					Bella Bella
					Oowekeeno
				Kwakiutl	
			Nootkan		
				Nootka	
				Nitinaht	
				Makah	
Chimakuan Language Family					
				Chemakum	
				Quileute	
Salishan Language Family					
			Bella Coola		
					Bella Coola
					Kimsquit
					Tallio
			Central Salish		
				Comox	
					Island Comox
					Sliammon
				Pentlatch	
				Sechelt	

Table 1. Language Classification (Cont.)

Phylum	Family	Subfamily	Branch	Language	Dialect
Salishan Language Family (Cont.)			Central Salish (Cont.)		
				Squamish	
				Halkomelem	
					Chilliwack
					Musqueam
					Cowichan
				Nooksack	
				Northern Straits	
					Saanich
					Sooke
					Songhees
					Samish
					Lummi
					Semiahmoo
				Clallam	
				Lushootseed	
					Northern Lushootseed
					Southern Lushootseed
				Twana	
			Tsamosan		
				Quinault	
				Lower Chehalis	
				Upper Chehalis	
					Satsop
					Upper Chehalis 1
					Upper Chehalis 2
				Cowlitz	
			Tillamook		
					Tillamook
					Siletz
Penutian Phylum					
	Chinookan Family				
			Lower Chinook		
			Upper Chinook		
				Cathlamet	
				Multnomah	
				Kiksht	
	Takelman Family				
		Takelma			
		Kalapuyan			
				Tualatin-Yamhill	
				Central Kalapuyan	
				Yoncalla	
	Alsean Family				
				Alsea	
				Yaquina	
	Siuslaw Language Isolate				
					Siuslaw
					Lower Umpqua
	Coos Family				
				Hanis	
				Miluk	

van Eijk and Hess 1986).

Consonant systems are elaborate, but distinctive vowels are generally restricted to four or five, and vowel length is rarely distinctive. The obstruent and resonant systems show extensive matching of articulation positions, and there is considerable evidence of historical relationship between corresponding elements. Underlying vowels are frequently lost in unstressed syllables, leaving long clusters of consonants (4, 5, and 6 being common). Stress accent is generally strong; patterns of shifting word stress in various derivatives are important.

• BELLA COOLA Bella Coola is said to have had two (Boas 1892d:408) or three (McIlwraith 1948, 1:17–18) mildly different dialects: Bella Coola proper in the Bella Coola valley and on North Bentinck Arm, Kimsquit on the Dean and Kimsquit rivers and Dean Channel, and Tallio at the head of South Bentinck Arm. Bella Coola is set apart from the rest of Salishan in many ways. It retains the obstruents k, $\acute{k}$, and x (which all other coastal Salishan languages except Cowlitz and some Upper Chehalis have shifted to consonants produced farther forward in the mouth), and has dropped many vowels so that whole words may consist of nothing but strings of consonants. It suffixes or postposes all pronominal elements, whereas most other Salishan languages prefix at least first and second person singular possessive markers. It regularly brackets complements with deictic particles, whereas the common pattern in coastal Salishan languages is to prepose them only. It compounds lexical suffixes to a degree not found elsewhere in Salishan, incorporating, for example, both object and instrument concepts within a single predicate. Vocabulary differences between Bella Coola and other Salishan languages are greater than those between any of the other divisions of the family. For grammatical descriptions of Bella Coola see S. Newman (1947, 1969a, 1969, 1971), Davis and Saunders (1973, 1975a, 1975, 1976, 1978, 1984) and Saunders and Davis (1975a, 1975b, 1975); for a dictionary see Nater (1977); for texts see Davis and Saunders (1980).

• CENTRAL SALISH Central Salish comprises four of the branches that Swadesh (1950) included in his Coast Division: North Georgia Branch (Comox, Pentlatch, Sechelt), South Georgia Branch (Squamish, Nanaimo Group, Lkungen Group, Nooksack), Puget Sound Branch (Skagit-Snohomish-Nisqually), and Hood Canal Branch (Twana). (This grouping comprises all Coast Salish in this volume except Southwestern Coast Salish.) Swadesh's Nanaimo Group has been more often called Halkomelem, and his Lkungen Group is usually called Straits. This composite is what remains after recognition of shared innovations has set apart smaller subgroups of the family—Bella Coola, Interior Salish, Tsamosan, and Tillamook. In this long chain, apparently the surviving heart area of the original dialect continuum, each language shares a number of characteristics with its close

neighbors, but no clear independent innovations of the entire subgroup itself distinguish it from other subgroups.

Comox is the northernmost language of Central Salish. There are important differences of pronunciation and perhaps grammar between the speech on Vancouver Island and that of the Sliammon, the southernmost group on the mainland. Differences among the various mainland groups are apparently slight, but more material is necessary to determine surely that no other dialect divisions are indicated. It may be that the large number of speakers of the mainland form of the language in the mid-twentieth century represent an expansion of a southern dialect in recent times, while older distinctive dialects to the north have become extinct; Boas (1887a) and Barnett (1955:8) indicate that people living in the Homalco area were relative newcomers. Early in the nineteenth century Island Comox territory extended along Johnstone Strait as far as Kelsey Bay, but by the middle of the century the southernmost group of Kwakiutl speakers had pushed out or absorbed the Johnstone Strait people and established themselves on the Campbell River and at Cape Mudge (a number of place-names used by the Kwakiutl in this area are of Salishan origin; Boas 1887a; Taylor and Duff 1956); additional dialect divisions may have existed in this area. It is convenient to refer to the mainland dialect as Sliammon and to that on Vancouver Island as Island Comox. Since about 1950 the language as a whole has usually been referred to as Comox. Boas, whose considerable material on Comox remains in manuscript form in the American Philosophical Society Library in Philadelphia, consistently referred to the language as Çatlotlq (presumably $\theta \acute{a}\npreceq u \npreceq tx^w$ in phonemic orthography). This form suggests that his material represents mainland speech, because the island dialect lacks θ and $\dot{\theta}$, having rather s and $\check{c}$ (although these could also have been adopted through Kwakiutl influence). Sliammon is one of the few Salishan dialects to have θ (from *c) and $\dot{\theta}$ (from *$\check{c}$), the only others being Pentlatch, the dialects of Halkomelem, and the Saanich dialect of Northern Straits. $\check{j}$ and g occur as developments from Proto-Salishan *y and *w respectively, but y and w are reintroduced as developments from Proto-Salishan *l in specific environments. A number of Comox peculiarities seem to reflect the strong cultural influence of Kwakiutl: nondistinctive stress, stress having shifted to the first vowel of all words; elimination of all initial consonant clusters, and hence all nonreduplicative prefixes; presence of λ and k^y. For a study of reduplication in Island Comox, containing also phonetic indications, based on limited material taken from a Nootka informant who had learned the language from his Comox mother, see Sapir (1915). For grammars see Hagège (1981), and H.R. Harris (1977); for a dictionary see Timmers (1978); for place-names see Kennedy and Bouchard (1983).

Pentlatch was spoken by a presumably small community

in aboriginal times, and the language began to be replaced early by neighboring Comox, Halkomelem, and apparently Nootka (there are place-names of apparent Salishan origin in the territory west of the Pentlatch area occupied by the Opetchesaht band of Nootka as recorded in the lexicon of Sapir and Swadesh 1939). There is no clear indication of dialectal diversity, although Boas (1887a) refers to a slight dialect difference between Pentlatch proper and the groups immediately south of them. The language has apparently been extinct for some time, the last known speaker having been contacted by Barnett (1955:6–7) in the mid-1930s, although he collected no linguistic data. Boas left texts and an extensive vocabulary in manuscript (see Freeman 1966: 114, 317, 328).

Sechelt was spoken in a rather small territory on the east coast of the Strait of Georgia, and there are no indications of dialectal variations in earlier times. The phonology of Sechelt deviates from the common inventory of Central Salish only in having several instances of k^y, primarily in loanwords from Kwakiutl and Chinook Jargon. There is a teaching grammar of the language by Beaumont (1985), and it is also represented by Beaumont (1973) and by Hill-Tout (1904), which includes a brief grammar, several texts in Sechelt, and considerable vocabulary; for word lists see Timmers (1977, 1978a).

Squamish was also fairly confined in area, and there are no clear indications about dialect diversity; however, Kuipers (1970:48) speculates that the language of modern times may be a mixture of dialects in some of which earlier *l had developed to y, while remaining l in others, in order to account for competing forms with l and y. Beyond this, Squamish phonology does not deviate from the common phonemic inventory of Central Salish. For extensive grammar and dictionary with a few accompanying texts see Kuipers (1967–1969).

Halkomelem is a long continuum of intergrading dialects showing considerable diversity, but with mutual intelligibility throughout. Elmendorf and Suttles (1960) recognize a phonological-morphological break between speech forms upriver from the Matsqui village area in the Fraser valley and those below, and strong lexical differentiation between mainland and Vancouver Island dialects. Halkomelem phonology is notable in having developed θ

(from *c) and $\overset{\circ}{\theta}$ (from *ċ). The mainland dialects have retained x^y (the only Central Salish dialects to retain an unrounded prevelar fricative); the island dialects have shifted it to $\check{s}$. These sound changes are part of a general fronting of consonants in Halkomelem that has also shifted Proto-Salishan *k and *ḱ to c and ċ. This fronting is not as thorough in upriver dialects, which tend to use s and $\check{s}$ for downriver θ and s, respectively. The Upriver dialects, such as Chilliwack, have merged all instances of *n and *l to l. Certain Musqueam speakers (at the mouth of the Fraser River) merged *n and *l to n. Chilliwack has also developed a peculiar length phoneme and a pitch-accent system. For a discussion of Halkomelem phonology and dialect variation, as well as topically arranged word lists in three representative dialects (Cowichan on Vancouver Island, Musqueam for the lower Fraser River dialects, and Chilliwack for the upriver dialects) see Elmendorf and Suttles (1960). For studies of Halkomelem syntax see Gerdts (1988, 1984). For a grammar of Chilliwack see Galloway (1977). Grammatical information on the Kwantlen and Chilliwack dialects is contained in Hill-Tout (1903); it also contains a Chilliwack glossary and a few Kwantlen texts; for Chilliwack vocabulary see Galloway (1980a). For a grammar of Cowichan see Leslie (1979); for a Cowichan text see Hukari, Peter, and White (1977).

Nooksack was probably a rather homogeneous language spoken by a small group in aboriginal times. It shares with Squamish and Lushootseed, among other things, the patterning of apparently old root shapes of the type $C_1V_1C_2V_1$ in surface forms, whereas other Central Salish languages have eliminated these vocalic repetitions. By the 1940s it was all but replaced by adjacent Upriver Halkomelem, the northern dialect of Northern Lushootseed (Nuwhaha), or English. There are no published sources on Nooksack, although a fairly large amount of data on the language exists in manuscripts (fig. 2).

Straits consists of a spread of intergrading dialects, Northern Straits, and a separate language with little internal diversity, Clallam.

Northern Straits dialects fall into several groups: Sooke, Saanich, Songhees, Lummi, Samish, and Semiahmoo (little is known of these last two groups, and their proper classification is uncertain). Clallam shows only mild lexical differences among villages extending over a considerable area, suggesting a recent spread. The phonological differences among the various Northern Straits dialects and Clallam are summarized in table 2. In addition, both Songhees and Saanich retain many unstressed vowels that are lost in other dialects, and all the northern dialects have shifted stress in more cases and simplified original consonant clusters more drastically than Clallam. Characteristic of all Straits Salish is a velar nasal η, found nowhere else in Salishan (indeed phonemically elsewhere only in Haida on the whole Northwest

Table 2. Straits Phonological Developments

Proto-Salishan	*ú	*á	*ḱ	*ċ	*k	*c	*x	*s	*l
Lummi	ó	é ó	ċ	ċ	s	s	s	s	l
Samish	ó	é ó	ċ	ċ	c	c	s	s	l
Songhees	á	é á	ċ	ċ	s	s	s	s	l
Saanich	á	é á	$\overset{\circ}{\theta}$	$\overset{\circ}{\theta}$	s,θ	s,θ	s	s	l
Sooke	ó	é ó	ċ	ċ	s	s	s	s	y
Clallam	ú	á	ċ	ċ	c	c	s	s	y

Coast); these languages have a set of palatal and velar consonants (*č, č̓, ŋ, ŋ̓*) and a set of labial consonants (*p, ṗ, m, ṁ*) that correspond to a single labial series elsewhere in Salishan. Also, Straits has split **y* into *y* and *č, and *w* into *w* and k^w. Since a number of borrowings with *č* occur in Straits, this phoneme may have three origins. For a sketch of Clallam grammar see Thompson and Thompson (1971); for Northern Straits grammars see Efrat (1969) on Sooke, Montler (1986) on Saanich, and Raffo (1972) on Songhees; a comparative study of Straits Salish phonology is Thompson, Thompson, and Efrat (1974).

Lushootseed, called Puget (Sound) Salish in earlier writings, is a widespread group of mildly differentiated dialects that show a cleavage bordering on a language boundary between the northern and southern sets; but the dialects were all mutually intelligible and it seems more important to emphasize the unity than the divergence. Vocabulary, stress positioning, and a few grammatical features differ between the two sets of dialects. Lushootseed has developed a set of voiced stops and affricates larger than that found in any other Salishan language: *ʒ* and *ǯ* developed from **y*; *g* and g^w from **w*; and *b* and *d* from original nasals. Glottalized *ẏ* and *ẇ* were retained, and the original glottalized nasals are reflected in at least some positions by *b* and *d* with adjacent glottal stop. (The language also has numerous instances of *y* and *w*, and rare instances of *m* and *n*, especially in ceremonial and other special usages). On the syntactic side, Lushootseed developed three or four aspectual categories not treated as primary in other Salishan languages. For grammars of Lushootseed see Tweddell (1950), W.A. Snyder (1968), Hess (1967), and Hess and Hilbert (1980); for dictionaries see Gibbs (1877:285–361) on Nisqually and Hess (1976); and for published texts and dictionary see W.A. Snyder (1968a) and Hilbert and Hess (1977).

Twana is a less varied language than Lushootseed or Northern Straits; it was spoken aboriginally in a more confined area with apparently very mild dialectal differences. Slight dialectal variation presumably identified three clusters: (1) toward the mouth of Hood Canal; (2) near the mouth of the Skokomish River; and (3) at the head of the canal (Elmendorf 1960:280). Twana, like Lushootseed, has changed **m* to *b* and **n* to *d*, and it shows glottal stop quite consistently adjacent to *b* and *d* reflecting original glottalized nasals. It has developed a type of reduplication found otherwise in Coast Salishan languages only in Tillamook, that is, plurals are formed by prefixing the second consonant of the root to the root itself. A detailed generative phonological study of Twana (with some grammatical notes and extensive treatment of reduplication patterns) is Drachman (1969); much linguistic information is also contained in Elmendorf (1960, 1961); for a dictionary see N. Thompson (1979).

● TSAMOSAN The Tsamosan branch is divided into two subgroups of two closely related languages each: Quinault

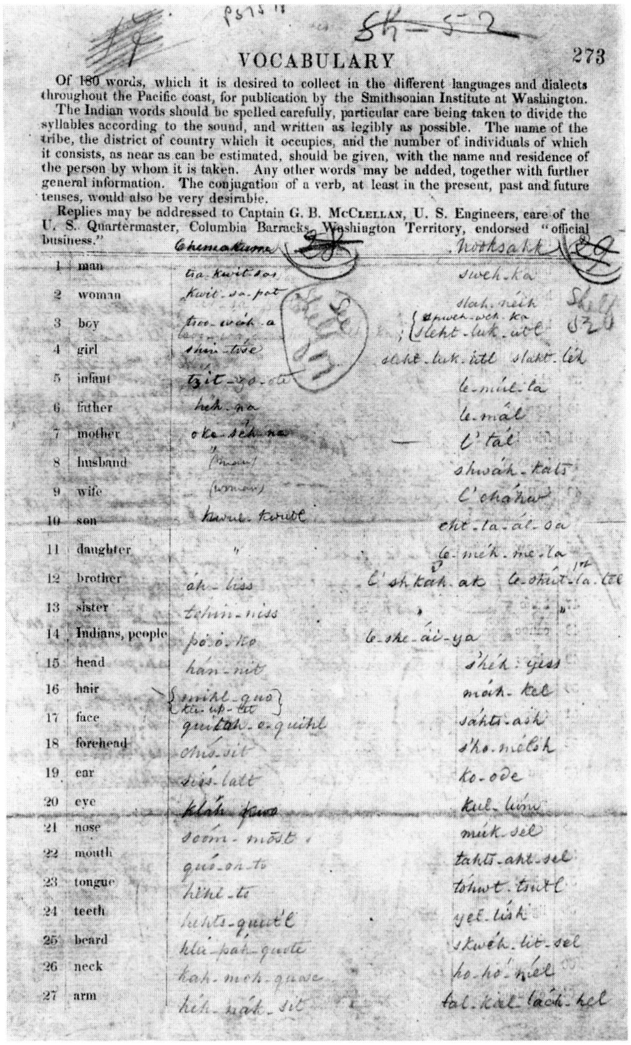
VOCABULARY 273

Of 180 words, which it is desired to collect in the different languages and dialects throughout the Pacific coast, for publication by the Smithsonian Institute at Washington.

The Indian words should be spelled carefully, particular care being taken to divide the syllables according to the sound, and written as legibly as possible. The name of the tribe, the district of country which it occupies, and the number of individuals of which it consists, as near as can be estimated, should be given, with the name and residence of the person by whom it is taken. Any other words may be added, together with further general information. The conjugation of a verb, at least in the present, past and future tenses, would also be very desirable.

Replies may be addressed to Captain G. B. McClellan, U. S. Engineers, care of the U. S. Quartermaster, Columbia Barracks, Washington Territory, endorsed "official business."

1 man
2 woman
3 boy
4 girl
5 infant
6 father
7 mother
8 husband
9 wife
10 son
11 daughter
12 brother
13 sister
14 Indians, people
15 head
16 hair
17 face
18 forehead
19 ear
20 eye
21 nose
22 mouth
23 tongue
24 teeth
25 beard
26 neck
27 arm

Smithsonian, NAA 273.

Fig. 2. Vocabulary of Chemakum of Port Townsend, and Nooksack of Nooksack River, Washington Terr., approximately 180 words collected 1853–1854 by George Gibbs for the Smithsonian. This printed vocabulary schedule was one of a series issued during the mid-19th century, from about 1851 to 1862. Such lists were some of the earliest systematic attempts to collect and compare native vocabularies. John Wesley Powell developed vocabulary schedules, based in part on Gibbs's lists, which were widely used in the late 19th century to gather words for use in linguistic classification (vol. 11: 101).

and Lower Chehalis on the Pacific coast, and Upper Chehalis and Cowlitz in the inland river valleys. Quinault has a slightly divergent northern dialect Queets. Lower Chehalis extends with minor local differences in a chain of dialects from south of Quinault as far as the northern half of Willapa Bay. Upper Chehalis spread over a considerable territory and had three dialects, of which Satsop, located adjacent to Lower Chehalis, was the most divergent; upriver beyond Grand Mound fronted *k k̓ x* were used, while *č č̓ š* are found in both downriver dialects. Boas and Haeberlin (1927) labeled the dialects Satsop, Upper Chehalis 1, and Upper Chehalis 2. Cowlitz is quite similar to Upper Chehalis, but not quite mutually intelligible with it, and there are important grammatical differences. Cowlitz occupied what seems to have been a small territory in aboriginal times, and, as explained by Jacobs (1937), the upriver communities had been gradually infiltrated and eventually taken over by Plateau neighbors, the Taitnapam. There is no information on dialect differences within Cowlitz.

Tsamosan languages show several minor phonological innovations. Quinault and the northern dialects of Lower Chehalis have shifted word-initial *y and *w to phonetic ǰ and g^w, without creating a contrast in the two pairs of sounds. Upper Chehalis and Cowlitz have unrounded several instances of *x^w, resulting in x and š in Cowlitz and š in Upper Chehalis. Upper Chehalis has lost *l in many environments, sometimes replacing it with vowel length. Vowel length is an important feature in all four languages, serving morphological functions; this makes for a vocalic pattern quite different from that of other Salishan languages. Cowlitz is unusual in having retained k, k̓, and x in most words, but shifts them to č, č̓, and š in others, and yet in other cases uses both in regular morphophonemic alternations. But it is grammatical developments that set the Tsamosan languages off most noticeably from other languages of the family. Upper Chehalis and Cowlitz have developed a rigorous system of modifications throughout predicate words whereby roots and suffixes are changed according to which of two aspectual sets is marked at the beginning of each predicate. Object and subject markers usually have completely different shapes for the two sets. One aspect is marked by articlelike deictic elements, and the predicates involve extensive vowel deletion. There are also several quite different ways of forming plurals; but reduplication, although common for other purposes, is not used for pluralization, as it is in all other Salishan languages. These two languages also have specific suffixes to mark a form as intransitive, and have another to detransitivize a usually transitive form. Cowlitz morphology is notably different even from the rest of Tsamosan in using a suffix -i to mark third person possessive instead of the -s found in all other Salishan languages. Little information is available on the grammatical structure of Quinault or Lower Chehalis, but many of these characteristics of the two inland languages appear to be relevant there too. For a grammar of Upper Chehalis see Kinkade (1963–1964); Boas (1934a) presents a text in Upper Chehalis with extensive grammatical notes; for other texts see Kinkade (1983, 1984, 1987).

● TILLAMOOK Tillamook, separated from the main body of Salishan languages by Chinookan and Athapaskan speakers, apparently had a southern dialect, Siletz, with moderate divergence, and probably an expanse of mildly distinguished intergrading dialects of Tillamook proper. Tillamook is notable in having lost all labial consonants: *p and *p̓ have become h, and *m has become w; rounding of velars and w is weak and is achieved by

some internal mechanism rather than by lip rounding. At the same time, unrounded velars often involve considerable lip-spreading. Original rounded velars have been unrounded before *i, re-establishing an unrounded prevelar series (k, k̓, x). An extra stop-affricate manner series has been developed, creating a contrast between plain voiceless and voiced (lenis) segments. Grammatically the language has many archaic features, as shown by correspondences to Interior Salish systems. However, it has done away with the enclitic intransitive subject pronouns found in all the other Salishan languages except Bella Coola, substituting subject suffixes from the transitive system so that all active predicates have pronominal affixation. It usually preposes deictic words to predicates as well as to complements, developing a concord system between the two types of elements. Before complements, there are two positions for such deictic words, of which the second usually involves words compounding two elements that occur elsewhere independently; this parallels the compounding of similar deictic elements in Tsamosan languages. Predicates are generally introduced by mode-aspect prefixes distinguishing unrealized from realized action or state; however, a durative aspect appears less prominent than in the other languages, secondary to realized/unrealized. Tillamook has the most complex kinship system of all the coastal Salishan languages, and cognacy of the words with various terms in other systems indicates that this complexity is inherited from Proto-Salishan (Elmendorf 1961a). For a description of Tillamook phonology see Thompson and Thompson (1966); for grammar see Edel (1939).

Wakashan

Wakashan is a family consisting of two subgroups, Kwakiutlan and Nootkan, each consisting of three languages: Haisla, Heiltsuk, and Kwakiutl in the first, and Nootka, Nitinaht, and Makah in the second. These languages are closely connected in each subgroup, but the relationship between the two subgroups is rather distant. There is no information on dialectal differentiation within Haisla, but slight differences are reported between Bella Bella and Oowekeeno dialects of Heiltsuk: the former has phonemic tonal contrasts lacking in the latter. Descriptions of the Kwakiutl dialectal situation are confusing and somewhat contradictory, but there seem to have been two dialect clusters—outer, on the ocean shore from Cape Cook to Smith Sound, and inner, within Queen Charlotte and Johnstone Straits. The northern language of the Nootkan subgroup, Nootka proper, extends in a long chain of intergrading dialects along the west coast of Vancouver Island. Nitinaht was spoken in aboriginal times by a small community with little dialectal variation; the same is true of Makah. Nootka, Nitinaht, and Makah are reported to be considered a single language by the

Indians, sometimes referred to as the Westcoast language, after the native expression; however, as they are not mutually intelligible, they are considered here to be three separate languages.

Wakashan languages are polysynthetic; incorporated are verbal subjects and objects, tense-aspect-mode markers, and lexical suffixes (about 300) designating familiar objects of the natural environment such as body parts, terrain features, cultural artifacts, and many more abstract notions. Reduplication is extensive, and some reduplicative elements precede word bases. Nearly all other affixes are suffixes. Morphological combinations show considerable irregularity and complex morphophonemic alternations, indicating a very old system. Except for particles all words can be marked for use as the heart of clause predicates so that (as in Salishan and Chimakuan) a noun-verb opposition seems misleading (cf. Jacobsen 1979c). The basic durative/nondurative aspect opposition has also extensive further subcategories; beyond aspectual stems inflectional endings distinguish numerous modal categories as well as subjects and objects.

Vowel systems usually oppose short and long vowels. Consonant clusters are usually prohibited at the beginning of words and seldom involve more than four consonants medially. Obstruents and resonants show considerable matching in articulation position and sounds corresponding in this way are extensively interchanged in grammatical formations.

There is considerable literature on Wakashan languages, but extensive grammatical treatment exists in print only for Kwakiutl and Nootka. Boas's writings on Kwakiutl constitute what is perhaps the largest corpus on a single indigenous North American language: two grammars (Boas 1911c, 1947), notes on vocabulary and suffixes (Boas 1931, 1924a), and text collections (Boas 1910, 1935–1943; Boas and Hunt 1902–1905, 1906). For treatment of Kwakiutl syntax see S.R. Anderson (1984) and Levine (1984). For dictionaries see Lincoln and Rath (1980) on Kwakiutlan, Grubb (1977) on Kwakiutl, Lincoln and Rath (1986) on Haisla, and Rath (1981) on Heiltsuk. For another Kwakiutl text see Levine (1977a); for Heiltsuk texts see Boas (1928, 1932). For Nootka, there is a grammar by Rose (1981) and grammatical sketch by Swadesh (1938), and grammatical notes and an extensive lexicon in Sapir and Swadesh (1939); besides the texts contained in the latter, published texts appear in Sapir (1924); important grammatical information is also found in Haas (1969a, 1972). Swadesh and Swadesh (1932) present a Nitinaht text; another is in Touchie (1977a). Densmore (1927) presents some Makah vocabulary. Important comparative studies of Wakashan are Boas (1891:604–632, 655–658), Sapir (1911), and Jacobsen (1969); some Wakashan linguistic history is recapitulated in Sapir (1938).

Chimakuan

Chimakuan is a small isolated family of two languages, Chemakum and Quileute, which occupied noncontiguous areas, separated by the Olympic Mountains and the territory of the Clallam. No broader genetic relationships for these languages has been demonstrated. Chemakum was apparently spoken by a very small community in aboriginal times; the Quileutes occupied a larger territory, but there are no indications of original dialect diversity for either language. Indications are that in 1890, when Boas recorded a small corpus of vocabulary and phrases, Chemakum had already largely been replaced by Clallam and (perhaps somewhat later) by Northern Lushootseed.

The Chimakuan languages lack prefixes and have only two or three dozen inflectional suffixes but make extensive use of lexical suffixes (about 250) designating familiar objects of the natural environment as well as abstract notions. These lexical suffixes may also attach to three empty bases that distinguish locative-partitive, existential, and substantive. Infixes are used to mark diminutives and some plurals. Subject, object, and aspect must be marked in each predicate; subject-nonsubject distinctions are made in articles as well as in pronominal suffixes. Feminine and nonfeminine genders are distinguished within the deictic/demonstrative system. Except for particles all words can be marked for use as the heart of clause predicates so that (as in Salishan and Wakashan) a noun-verb opposition seems misleading.

The consonant system is elaborate, as among other language families of the area; few vowel positions are distinguished, but vowel length is contrastive. A pitch-accent system has developed (at least in Quileute) in which pitch relates in complex ways to stress and vowel length.

Chemakum and Quileute differ in a number of respects. Quileute retains a series of prevelar obstruents that Chemakum has shifted to prepalatals, but Quileute has changed original nasals *m and *n to b and d. Chemakum seems to have retained original stress patterns, while Quileute shifts stress to the penultimate syllable. Quileute has added λ to its phonemic inventory through Makah influence. Grammatically, the two languages have different types of plural: it is distributive in Quileute, but collective in Chemakum (presumably from Clallam influence). Chemakum subject pronouns distinguish more details than the comparable Quileute forms. Little information about Chemakum is available in published form, but notes on the structure and usage of Chemakum are found in Boas (1892). For a grammar of Quileute see Andrade (1933); for a dictionary see Powell and Woodruff (1976); for texts see Andrade (1931). Andrade (1953) presents comparative information on the two languages; a general comparison is contained in J.V. Powell (1974).

Chinookan

Chinookan is a family with two branches, Lower (Coastal) Chinookan (Chinook proper) and Upper (River) Chinookan. Upper Chinookan is a chain of languages, including Cathlamet, Multnomah, and Kiksht. Lower Chinookan was spoken by the Clatsop on the south shore of the mouth of the Columbia River and Chinook proper on the north shore and northward. Cathlamet was spoken, evidently in a single dialect, along both banks of the Columbia from just above the mouth upstream as far as the Kalama River (except where Athapaskan and Salishan reached the Columbia). Both Lower Chinookan and Cathlamet probably became extinct in the 1930s with the death of Charles Cultee, whom Boas (1894:6) found, in the 1890s, to be the last person capable of dictating texts in these two languages. Kiksht consisted of a series of intergrading dialects including Clackamas, on the lower Willamette and Clackamas rivers; Cascades, around the Cascade Rapids; and Wasco-Wishram, from Hood River to The Dalles (for the relations of Cascades and Wasco-Wishram see vol. 12).

The Chinookan languages are highly inflected, using many prefixes and fewer suffixes. The roots are notable in that most of them consist of the same concise phonological forms (between one and 3–4 phonemes) as affixes; this produces compact words often the equivalent of sentences. Reduplication is confined to particles and a few terms for natural species. Nouns may be inflected for number and possession. Verbs must be inflected at least for aspect or tense, and one participant, and may also include subject, direct object, indirect object, and various modal, adverbial, and directional concepts. Lower Chinookan uses aspectual distinctions more prominently than tense distinctions; Kiksht has reversed this, developing four past tenses, while Cathlamet is intermediate in having a simpler tense system with aspectual implications. To a considerable extent, an intransitive subject and a direct object are treated alike, different from a transitive subject, making the language partially ergative. Other pronominal categories, which include singular-dual-plural and inclusive-exclusive distinctions, are identical in both types of subject, direct and indirect object, and possessive forms, the distinction being made by the position of the pronominal prefixes in the word. Three genders are distinguished in nouns and pronouns: masculine, feminine, and neuter. Chinookan languages have a complicated consonant system of the type found in neighboring languages, and only three or four vowels. For grammars of Lower Chinookan see Boas (1904, 1911b) and Swanton (1900); for texts see Boas (1894). For Cathlamet grammar see Hymes (1955); for texts see Boas (1901). Boas (1911a) includes notes by Sapir on Kiksht; for Kiksht texts see Sapir (1909a), Jacobs (1958–1959), and Hymes (1981a). A discussion of the development of Chinookan tense-aspect systems is found in Silverstein (1974), and of the inflectional syntax in Silverstein (1976a).

Lower Chinookan furnished a major component of Chinook Jargon, a trade language that spread rapidly over the greater Northwest; on the coast it seems to have been in use nearly to the California border to the south and to the Alaska panhandle in the north. It also has accretions of vocabulary from English and French, as well as from indigenous languages of the area. The Chinook Jargon should not be confused with the Chinookan languages, in comparison with which it is far simpler. It is disputed whether the Jargon existed before White contact; at least there is no indisputable evidence that it did. For further discussion of Chinook Jargon, including grammatical information, see Jacobs (1932), R.V. Grant (1945), Silverstein (1972), B.P. Harris (1983), Thomason (1983), Thomason and Kaufman (1988), and Zenk (1984); for texts see Jacobs (1936c). For a compilation and classification of over 100 Chinook Jargon dictionaries and vocabularies see Johnson (1978).

Takelman

Takelman is a family containing the small Kalapuyan branch of the Willamette valley in Oregon and the isolated language Takelma in a separate enclave to the south in the Rogue River drainage. Kalapuyan comprises three languages, Tualatin-Yamhill in the north, Central Kalapuyan in several very similar dialects extending over a large area in the center, and Yoncalla in a few dialects to the south of modern Eugene. The northern language presumably became extinct in 1937, and the southern language not long after; the central language survived until the mid-1950s.

Takelma may have been spoken in four or five dialects, the distribution of which is unknown. It was probably extinct by 1945 at the latest. For comparative Kalapuyan and Takelman see Swadesh (1965) and Shipley (1969, 1970).

The Kalapuyan languages make extensive use of suffixes and proclitics. Subject pronouns, interrogative pronouns, and independent adverbs occur as proclitics to verbs; possessive pronouns occur as proclitics to nouns. Object pronouns, modes, and tense-aspect categories are suffixed. A few instrumental suffixes ('hand', 'eye', 'voice', 'foot', 'ear', 'teeth') occur. Glottalized consonants are only mildly ejective and rather lenis, and glottal stop is similarly weakly articulated. The velar fricative x is common only in Tualatin-Yamhill but is infrequent in the other two languages, where only f ([f, ϕ]), ł, s, and h are the usual spirants; these are the only languages on the Northwest Coast to have a labial fricative. A prevelar-postvelar contrast is lacking. The languages are characterized by a pitch-accentuation system. For texts see Jacobs (1945); no grammar of Kalapuyan exists.

The Takelman verb is highly inflected; among the grammatical categories represented are locative, instrumental, aspect, transitive, temporal-modal, object, and subject. The 16 locative and 17 body-part instrumental markers are loosely preposed to the verb, but other inflections are suffixed. Several transitive and temporal-modal categories occur; aspects are frequentative, continuative, and usitative. The noun is inflected for possession; dual, plural, and exclusivity are expressed by suffixes distinct from the pronominal suffixes. Adjectives constitute a distinct word-class. The consonant system is relatively small by Northwest Coast standards; it lacks postvelar and lateral series (having only *l*) and has only three spirants (*s, x, h*). Vowel length is distinctive, and two syllable pitches are contrasted. For grammar see Sapir (1922), for texts see Sapir (1909). Kendall (1977) is a syntactic analysis based on the Sapir texts.

Alsean

The Alsean family (formerly Yakonan) comprised two closely related languages (or perhaps a single language with two dialects) spoken on the Oregon coast—Yaquina, around the present Newport, and Alsea, around the present Waldport. The last known record of Yaquina (and the only one of any extent) is a vocabulary collected by J. Owen Dorsey in 1884; when Frachtenberg recorded Alsea in 1910 he could find no more speakers of Yaquina. Alsea has presumably been extinct since the late 1930s.

Alsea has both prefixes and suffixes, but reduplication is rare and irregular. Aspect and person (both objects and subjects) are suffixed and are the major grammatical categories of the language; tense is usually unmarked (except future). The pronominal system distinguishes singular, dual, and plural, and contrasts inclusive and exclusive. Three cases are distinguished in nouns. Plural marking of nouns is optional; forms have collective force. Nonglottalized consonants are lenis, rather than fortis as in most other languages of the coast. Only three vowels are distinctive but they may occur nasalized or long. Complicated consonant clusters (up to 5 word-initially) are permitted. For texts see Frachtenberg (1917a, 1920b); the latter includes vocabularies and a list of formative elements covering all the items in the texts.

Siuslaw

Siuslaw had two dialects, Siuslaw proper, around the present Florence, and Lower Umpqua (not to be confused with Upper Umpqua, an Athapaskan language), around the present Reedsport. Brief samples of both dialects were recorded in 1884, but the major work available on the language (Frachtenberg 1922) deals primarily with Lower Umpqua. The language was presumed to be extinct by the 1970s.

The Siuslaw verb is heavily inflected for number, tense-aspect, mode, object, and subject. All are suffixed; only two prefixes occur in the language. Tense-aspect distinctions are elaborate; pronouns distinguish singular, dual, and plural numbers, and inclusive and exclusive. Nouns may be inflected for case and possession; four cases are distinguished. Word order is relatively free. The Siuslaw phonological system is in general much like those in other Northwest Coast languages; but it contrasts alveolar affricates and palatal affricate series with prevelar stops where most other languages of the area distinguish only two such series. For grammar see Frachtenberg (1922); Hymes (1966) uses field notes by himself and by Swadesh to reinterpret Frachtenberg's notation; for texts and vocabulary see Frachtenberg (1914).

Coosan

Coosan, on the Oregon coast south of Siuslaw, is a small family of two closely related languages, Hanis, around Coos Bay, and Miluk, on the lower Coquille River, with apparently mildly distinguished dialects in each.

The Coosan languages inflect verbs by affixation and reduplication for person, transitivity, aspect, mode, and voice (passive). Pronominal inflection distinguishes singular, dual, and plural, and exclusive and inclusive. First and second person transitive subjects are suffixed, but transitive objects and intransitive subjects are identical and loosely preposed; third person is unmarked. Aspects distinguish inchoative, frequentative, and transitional categories. Nouns are preceded by a definite article and may have adverbial, locative, and instrumental affixes. It is difficult to characterize Coosan phonology, although Pierce (1971) attempts to reinterpret earlier phonetic recordings; the consonant systems appear to be elaborate, and length is distinctive for vowels. For a grammar (primarily of Hanis) see Frachtenberg (1922a); for vocabulary see Frachtenberg (1913); for texts see Frachtenberg (1913) and Jacobs (1939, 1940). Frachtenberg (1914) contains a few pages comparing Hanis and Miluk.

Areal Features

A number of linguistic features occur over the Northwest Coast culture area and tend to define it as a distinct linguistic diffusion area. However, most of these features extend into the Plateau, California, or Subarctic culture areas. On the other hand, some features are found only in northwestern North America and are rare elsewhere in the world; the combination of a number of these features makes the overall region (as a whole) unique in the world. Other features cover only parts of the area, often cutting across language family boundaries, forming distinct sub-areas. Areal phonological features are easiest to recognize (Boas 1899a, 1911d, 1920a, 1929; Jacobs 1954; Haas 1969;

Sherzer 1973). Widespread grammatical and semantic features are more difficult to identify, largely because adequate descriptions of some languages are lacking or the studies treat categories in such different ways.

All the languages have richly developed consonantal systems (table 3). Unlike languages in many other parts of the world, sounds such as nasals, *l*, *w*, and *y* function as a single series of resonants, each resonant often corresponding to a point of articulation pertinent for the obstruent systems; there is frequently a grammatical interchange of related sounds (morphophonemics) between these obstruent and resonant systems. Tlingit is unique in the area in having glottalized spirants: *ś ł̓ x̣̓ x̣̓ x̓ʷ x̣̓ʷ*. In obstruent systems, all languages oppose a glottalized (ejective) series with an unglottalized series of stops and affricates. All utilize glottal stop as an important element parallel to other stops, although specialized uses are also common, as in aspect marking, creation of diminutives, and so on. Postvelar obstruents contrast with prevelars everywhere except in the Takelman and Oregon Athapaskan languages. All but universal in the area is the opposition of rounded (labialized) and unrounded velars; the rounded velars are absent only in Haida. In most languages of the area the labial set of consonants is less developed than sets of consonants produced farther back in the mouth; *w* generally belongs with the rounded velar category, rather than with labials. Two languages—Tlingit and Tillamook—lack labials entirely, and some others typically have only one labial—Eyak (with only *m*) and the Oregon Athapaskan languages (with either *m* or *b*). Both *m* and *b* occur in Galice Athapaskan and in Haida. Although all the languages of the area have extensive series of voiceless spirants, labial spirants are entirely lacking in the area except for Kalapuyan, in which *f* apparently developed from *x̣ʷ*. All languages have a set of affricates of either the *c* [tˢ] or *č* type, and they generally have both. All the languages of the area except Takelma have multiple laterals (usually at least *l*, *ł*, and *ƛ̓*). *l* is present everywhere except the Sooke dialect of Northern Straits, Clallam, Nootka, and Tlingit. The voiceless lateral spirant *ł* is present everywhere, although it occurs in Takelma only to characterize the speech of certain myth characters in tales (Hymes 1979a); Takelma, the Kalapuyan languages, and Coast Tsimshian lack the glottalized affricate *ƛ̓.*

In contrast to their elaborate consonant systems, these languages usually have relatively few distinctively different vowels. Throughout the area, only three or four vowel positions are usually contrasted. More occur in only four areas: Coast Tsimshian and Haisla; around the Strait of Juan de Fuca in Makah, and through late precontact developments in Northern Straits and Halkomelem; Twana; and in southwestern Oregon in Takelma and Tututni-Tolowa, and probably Lower Umpqua and Hanis Coos. Six is the maximum number of vowel position contrasts reported anywhere in the area.

The languages are predominantly polysynthetic—that is, they typically make up words with a number of elements, incorporating concepts such as subject, object, tense, aspect, and mode. Morphophonemic adjustments—changes of sounds in combination with each other in the derivation and inflection of words and in juxtaposition of words in phrases—are generally complex. Reduplication, often of several different kinds, is extensively used to signal grammatical and lexical distinctions but is absent in the three northernmost languages and in Athapaskan; it occurs but is not a productive process in Chinookan and Alsea. Among grammatical categories, aspectual distinctions are basic everywhere but in Cathlamet, Kiksht, Siuslaw, and Hanis Coos, and are usually more important than tense distinctions. Passivelike constructions are used everywhere but in

Table 3. Northwest Coast Consonants

	Labial	Interdental	Apical	Alveolar	Lateral	Palatal	Prevelar	Postvelar	Rounded Prevelar	Rounded Postvelar	Pharyngeal	Laryngeal
Voiceless or fortis, often aspirated	p		t	c	ƛ	č	k	q	kʷ	qʷ	(ˤ)	ʔ
Glottalized	ṗ	(θ̇)	ṫ	ċ	ƛ̓	č̓	k̓	q̓	k̓ʷ	q̓ʷ		
Voiced or lenis	b		d	ʒ	λ	ǯ	g	ġ	gʷ	ġʷ		
Spirants	(f)	(θ)		s	ł	š	x	x̣	xʷ	x̣ʷ	(ḥ)	h
Resonants	m		n		l	y	(γ)	(ŋ)	w			
Glottalized resonants	ṁ		ṅ		l̓	ẏ		(ŋ̇)	ẇ			

ª This symbol is used here for a pharyngealzied glottal stop.

Tlingit. An unexpectedly general feature of word order is that the negative (whether a predicate or a particle) regularly appears as the first element in a clause, regardless of the usual order of other elements (in Hanis adverbial elements sometimes precede).

Several subareas are defined along the Northwest Coast cutting across language family boundaries, and reflecting (at least in part) ancient diffusion, although the direction of diffusion cannot always be determined. One such subarea comprises the three northernmost languages—Eyak, Tlingit, and Haida. The features of these languages are also found in the neighboring Athapaskan languages and in Oregon Athapaskan, such as the presence typically of one or no labial consonants. Eyak and Tlingit but not Haida and languages immediately to the south have affricate sets of both the c and $č$ type. On the morphological side, Eyak, all the Athapaskan languages, and Tlingit have noun-classificatory systems; Haida has a similar system, marked by shape-prefixes. One feature of word order is common to Eyak, Tlingit, and Haida (also Takelma): the most usual position of a main verb is final in a sentence (after subject and object).

Other, partly overlapping, major subareas seem to be defined by the data: from Eyak to the northern part of the Strait of Georgia (table 4); from the Nass River to the Columbia River (excluding Kwalhioqua) (table 5); a greater Salishan area, including the Salishan and a few neighboring languages (table 6); a south-central area radiating from southern Puget Sound (table 7); and western Oregon (table 8). On these tables, Tillamook and Alsea are included on table 5, and Tsimshian is included with greater Salishan, because of the striking number of features they share with these noncontiguous groups. Kwalhioqua-Clatskanie, Yaquina, and Miluk are not included on the tables because of lack of sufficient data. The three Kalapuyan languages are treated together; no differences were noted in these three languages in any of the features considered here.

A few additional features that cross language family boundaries, or that occur in different branches of the same family, are worthy of note, although they apply to only a few languages each. (1) Tonal contrasts are distinctive in Tlingit, the Bella Bella dialect of Heiltsuk, Takelma, and Haida; something approaching distinctive tone also developed in Quileute and Upriver Halkomelem. In all these languages, tone probably developed as a concomitant glottal modification of vowels. (2) Regular full words (other than particles) without vowels occur commonly in both Bella Coola and Heiltsuk. (3) The interdental obstruents $θ$ and $θ̓$ have developed in Halkomelem, the Saanich dialect of Northern Straits (undoubtedly by diffusion from Halkomelem), and some dialects of Comox. Boas's recordings of Pentlatch show many instances of $θ$ but no clear cases of $θ̓$. Both [θ] and [θ̓] occur in one Chasta Costa dialect as the realization of Tututni s and $č̓$.

Table 4. Language Features on the Northern Coast

	1	2	3	4	5	6	7
Eyak	●	●		●	●	●	
Tlingit	●	●		●	●	●	●
Haida	●	●	●	●	●	●	●
Nass-Gitksan		●	●				●
Coast Tsimshian		●	●				●
Haisla	●		●	●	●	●	
Bella Coola		●	●				
Heiltsuk	●	●	●	●	●		
Kwakiutl	●	●	●	●	●	●	
Comox	( )	●		●		●	●

( ) = partial presence of the feature

Features

1. Three stop-affricate series (glottalized, fortis, and lenis); also Lushootseed and (with partial lenis series) Comox, Nitinaht, Makah, Quileute, Twana, Kwalhioqua-Clatskanie.

2. Fronted prevelar obstruent series [k^y, $k̓^y$, x^y], but at the phonetic level only; also Nitinaht, Sechelt (few), Lushootseed, and probably Nootka (Boas 1891); [x^y] only, in Musqueam and Chilliwack Halkomelem (which also has a few loans with [k^y].

3. A single alveolar or palatal affricate-spirant obstruent series (or both alternating nondistinctively); also mainland Halkomelem and Kwalhioqua-Clatskanie.

4. $λ$ contrasting with $λ̓$; also Nootka, Nitinaht, Makah, Quileute, Taitnapam, Lower Chinook, Cathlamet, Siuslaw, and probably Coosan.

5. $λ$ in addition to $λ̣$ and $λ̓$; also possibly Coosan.

6. Three (or more) primary aspectual categories are distinguished.

7. The language is at least partly ergative (intransitive subjects take the same form as transitive objects but are different from transitive subjects); also Taitnapam, Chinookan, Hanis, and Miluk.

(4) Halkomelem, Northern Straits, Clallam, Nitinaht, and Makah use several different devices for marking aspects (prefixation, suffixation, infixation, metathesis, reduplication, vowel lengthening), whereas other languages of the coast prefer only one or two of these. (5) In Northern Straits, Clallam, Makah, and Chemakum w has become k^w, and y has become $č$ in certain environments.

Prehistory

In the Na-Dene grouping the relationship between Eyak and Athapaskan is well established, but a postulated more distant relationship with Tlingit and Haida is heavily based on claims of a remarkable similarity in grammatical and semantic coverage of the various prefixes grouping in long strings in virtually the same order in the words of these languages (Sapir 1915; Hymes 1956). It has become increasingly clear as fuller data have been assembled in many areas of the world that unrelated and distantly related languages in contact tend to grow more and more like one another in many different ways, although it is less clear exactly how this comes about. As a matter of fact, Boas (1929:3) offers diffusion as an explanation for the similarities observed in the Na-Dene case. The classical sort of proof for genetic relationship—systematically related recurrent sound correspondences in a sizable number of words of diverse semantic and functional classes—has yet to be offered to connect other languages to Eyak-Athapaskan. Only a very small number of lexical items seem reconstructible for a possible common ancestor of Eyak-Athapaskan and Tlingit, but their grammars are very similar. Work on Haida dispels even the impression of typological similarity (Levine 1977, 1979). For a history and comprehensive study of the Na-Dene hypothesis see Pinnow (1976).

Penutian comparison presents enormous difficulties because of the great geographical spread and the number of very diverse languages involved; in many cases work is made still harder by the limited amount and the nature of the data on some of these languages. Still further relations of the stock have been proposed, including Zuni in the Southwest and some families in Mexico (for a survey of post-1929 proposals on Penutian, see Shipley 1973: 1052–1059 and Silverstein 1979). For western Oregon the basic material is especially difficult: except for a few languages where small collections could be made later, all the records of the languages were made prior to 1940, when the awkward nature of sound recording equipment precluded the making of anything but relatively poor quality audio recordings in small samples with considerable interfering noise. Grammatical sketches were published for Takelma, Hanis Coos, Siuslaw, and Chinook proper, but all are difficult to use for comparative purposes. Only for Alsea, Siuslaw, Hanis Coos, and Takelma are there printed word lists of any length; there are shorter lists of Lower Chinookan. For the Kalapuyan languages, Miluk Coos, and Upper Chinookan, the printed sources are primarily text collections, making systematic data on them largely inaccessible. However, most scholars agree that a genetic relationship will eventually be demonstrated for the languages of Oregon that have been called Penutian; on the inclusion of Tsimshian there is somewhat less unanimity.

Because so much remains to be done in the research on genetic and diffusional relations on the Northwest Coast it is rather difficult to say what the implications of language distribution are. The following statements are necessarily speculative.

The two stocks showing the greatest apparent antiquity in the area—Penutian and Salishan—presumably developed differently in the very different natural habitats that constituted their original homelands, although they may have occupied those homelands at around the same time. The Proto-Salishans settled in a rich, bountiful environment, probably around the delta of the Fraser River (cf.

Suttles and Elmendorf 1963; Suttles 1987b), where increasing numbers of people could be accommodated by the food supply in a relatively small area; the long stretch of similar lands to the north and south provided for still further expansion over a considerable period. What is more, the protected inland waterways that characterize this whole region made for easy transportation and continuing contact among the expanding peoples.xx

The Proto-Penutians, on the other hand, may well have settled in an inland region in the lower Willamette valley of western Oregon between the coastal mountains and the Cascades. (The great diversity and remoteness of relationships among the northern Penutian languages suggests Oregon as the most likely homeland.) Population pressure must have been a recurrent problem very early, and it is easy to understand that on repeated occasions groups of people moved considerable distances in search of lands to support their increased numbers. Because of the distances and the lack of easy transportation between them contact was rapidly lost in most cases. In this way one can see the peopling of the central California valleys at a very early time, presumably in successive migrations that separated an early continuum of Hokan there. If all these languages are really genetically related, then Proto-Penutian must antedate Proto-Salishan by several thousand years; there may have been an early Penutian spread covering much of the Pacific Northwest, later split up by arrival and spread of Salishan and other peoples, with subsequent assimilation of many original Penutian speakers by these later groups. A few early groups of these essentially inland peoples apparently made their way independently to the Oregon coast, establishing the communities of Coosan, Siuslaw, and Alsean speakers—independently because they suggest no period of separate common development. The ancestors of the Tsimshian, whether the only people out of an early Oregon–Washington–British Columbia continuum to retain their original Penutian speech or later fugitives from population pressures nearer the original homeland, came to occupy the lower and middle valley of the Skeena River and probably also inlets and islands along the coast to the south. Communication between the residents upriver from the canyon of the Skeena and the rest of the people on the coast was likely limited by that natural barrier, and the developing interior language (Nass-Gitksan) acquired further dialectal diversity on removal of a group from the middle Skeena to the lower Nass valley (Bruce Rigsby, personal communication 1977). The coastal people also developed different local dialects, of which a quite divergent southern type seems to border on a distinct language (J.A. Dunn 1979a).

The exploitation of the lower Columbia valley probably began quite early, expanding from the confluence of the Willamette, from which the Chinookans early moved down the Columbia to take up residence near the ocean. They later spread back up the Columbia valley eventually

Table 5. Language Features from the Nass River to the Columbia River

	1	2	3	4	5	6	7	8	9	10	11	12	13	14	15	16	17	18	19	20	21	22
Nass-Gitksan		●	●		●	●	●		●		●			●	●	●	●			●	●	
Coast Tsimshian		●	●		●	●	●		●		●			●	●	●	●	●		●	●	
Haisla						●	●	●	?	●	●	●	●	●	●	?	●	?	●	●	?	●	●
Bella Coola		●	●		●	●	●	?	●		●		●	●	●	●	●	●		F	●	
Heiltsuk			●			●	●	●	●	●	●	●	●		●	●	●	●	●	●		●
Kwakiutl			●		●	●	●	●	●	●	●	●	●		●	●	●	●	●	●		●
Comox	( )	H	●	●	●		●	●	●	●	●	●	●	●	●	●	●	●	●	●		●
Pentlatch		●	●	●			?	?	●	●	●	?	?	●	?	?	?	?	●	?	?	?
Sechelt		●	●	●		●	●	●	●	●	●	●	●	●	●	●	●	●	●	F		●
Squamish		●	●	●	( )	●	?	●			●	●	●	●	●	●		●		●		
Halkomelem	( )	●	●	●	( )	●	●	●	H		●	●	●	●	●	●	●	●	●			●
Nootka		●	●	●	●	●	?	●	?		●	●	●	●				?		●	●	●
Nitinaht	●	H	●	●	●	●	●	●	H		●	●	●	●	●			●	●	F	●	●
Makah	●	H	H		●	●	●	●	●		●	●	●	●					●	●	●	●
Nooksack		●	●	●		●	●	●	●	●	●	●	●		●		●	●	●		?	●
Northern Straits		●	●	●	( )	●	●	●	●	●	●	●	●	●	●	●	●	●	●			●
Clallam		●	●	●		●	●	●	●	●	●	●	●	●	●	●	●	●	●			●
Chemakum		●	H		●	●	●	?	?		●	●	●	●	●	●		?	●		●	●
Quileute	●	H	H	●	●	●	●	●			●	●	●	●	●	●	●	●	●			●
Lushootseed	●	H	●	●	( )		●	●	●		●	●	●	●	●	●	●	●	●			
Twana	●	H	●		●	●	●	●	●		●	●	●	●	●	●	●	●	●	●		
Quinault		●	?	●	●	●	●	●	●	●	●	●	●	?	●	?	●	?	●	?		
Lower Chehalis		●	●	●	●	●	●	●	?	●	●	●	●	●	●	●	●	?	●			?
Upper Chehalis		●	●	●	●	●	●	●	●	●	●	●	●	●	●	●	●	●	●			
Cowlitz		●	●	●	●	●	●	●	●	●	●	●	●	●	●	●	●	●	●			
Tillamook		H	●	●		●	●	?			●	●	●	●	●	●	●		●			
Alsea		●					?		●		●	●		●				?				●

( ) = partial presence of the feature   H = feature present historically; now lost

F = few instances of the feature; not systematic

Features

1. Nasals have become voiced stops (Thompson and Thompson 1972; Kinkade 1985), marginally in Island Comox and Upriver Halkomelem.

2. Two stop-affricate series (glottalized and voiceless); also Siuslaw.

3. Glottalized resonants contrast with plain resonants; also Masset Haida and underlyingly in Eyak.

4. Contrast between alveolar and palatal affricate-spirant positions, although sound shifts have sometimes eliminated one or two contrasts; in Halkomelem the contrast obtains only in Vancouver Island dialects; also Eyak, Tlingit.

5. A set of long vowels contrasts with the set of short vowels; also Eyak and Masset Haida.

6. Clusters of four or more consonants are allowed word-medially and word-finally; also Eyak, all Chinookan, Takelma, and Siuslaw.

7. Vowels may be drawn out for emphasis, especially in narratives; also Hydaburg Haida, Tlingit, all Chinookan, and Kalapuyan, and occasionally in Eyak.

8. 'Ripe' and 'cooked' are expressed by the same lexical item, or one is derived from the other; the same is sometimes true for 'unripe' and 'raw'; also Eyak, Hydaburg Haida, all Chinookan, and Coquille-Tolowa.

9. 'Yellow' and 'green' are expressed by a single lexical item, opposed to 'blue'; also Hydaburg Haida and Kwalhioqua-Clatskanie; the situation in Halkomelem is not clear.

10. Lexical suffixes (expressing concrete notions, but phonologically unlike independent roots expressing the same notions) are common.

11. Numeral classifiers (for counting various types of objects) are present; also Eyak, Tlingit, Haida, and a few in Kalapuyan.

12. Marking of plurality is largely optional; also Eyak, Haida, Takelma, Kwalhioqua-Clatskanie, and Coquille-Tolowa.

13. Tense is not a basic grammatical category and is not obligatorily marked; also Tlingit and Skidegate Haida.

14. The most usual position of a main predicate is initial in a sentence (it is not certain that Alsea belongs here); also all Chinookan, Siuslaw, and perhaps Hanis.

15. Deictic particles resembling definite articles are used; in Coast Tsimshian and Nass-Gitksan these are suffixes.

16. Concepts of space and time occur within the same deictic particle; also Tlingit, and in Chinookan verbal morphemes.

17. Visible-invisible (present-absent, or the like) contrast in the deictic system; also Lower Chinook and Coquille-Tolowa; superficial in Chemakum and Quileute.

18. Possessive constructions may be used as main predicates (e.g., 'my liking . . . '); also Hydaburg Haida and Chinookan.

19. All words (except for particles) can be marked for use as the heart of clause predicates so that a noun-verb opposition is not relevant.

20. There are no prefixes in the language (except reduplicative material); there are very few also in Haida, Kalapuyan, and Hanis.

21. Two primary aspectual categories are distinguished; also Lower Chinook and Kalapuyan.

22. Tense is marked by suffixes or postponed elements; also Haida.

as far as The Dalles; both the greater diversity in the lower valley and the apparent way the tense-aspect systems must have developed indicate this direction of expansion (Silverstein 1974). The remaining peoples in the Willamette valley, presumably the Proto-Takelmans, exported another group southward that settled in the Rogue valley, becoming historic Takelma; the three Kalapuyan languages developed in the original homeland from the remainder.

Salishan expansion, on the contrary, seems to have taken the shape of gradual occupation of more and more distant sites from the original homeland until the whole protected maritime environment had been exploited, from the southern end of Puget Sound and along Hood Canal to the northern part of Vancouver Island, settling both shores of this long inland passage. In fact, it may well have reached beyond to the location of the historic Bella Coola. Whether cut off by other peoples (which certainly eventually happened) or simply isolated by distance and the demise of intervening dialects, the Bella Coola were in any case early split from the continuum, throughout which innovations continued to travel from the center for some time. (Bella Coola shows a number of innovations in development that it shares with no other Salish language; a few others are shared with Comox, suggesting diffusion from Bella Coola while they were still in contact.) But there shortly developed other splits. The first isolated a group that either then or somewhat later crossed the Cascades and diversified in the Plateau, giving eventually the historic spread of seven Interior Salish languages (Elmendorf 1965). The other perhaps reflected a change in culture to exploit the prairie country of southern Washington; in any case it isolated Proto-Tsamosan speakers from the central body. Lexical similarities seem to indicate that Tsamosan languages, and, to a lesser extent, Twana were in contact with southern Interior Salish languages for a time. The ancestors of Tillamook may have moved beyond the southern end of Puget Sound and Hood Canal first to the Pacific shores of southern Washington, but they eventually made their way on beyond the Chinookan speakers (already occupying the whole lower Columbia valley) to settle in another area of waterways protected from the open ocean. Innovations shared by Tillamook and Central Salish suggest this was

the latest split; Tillamook subsequently developed several characteristics of its own. Central Salish remained essentially undivided but developed increasing differentiation among the various languages while still being affected by the spread of innovations throughout most of the area. The Tsamosan group meanwhile diversified and expanded to the Pacific coast; these languages share many specialized innovations. A few peculiarities shared with Tillamook suggest contact perhaps at the time the Tillamook may have been their neighbors to the west, before removing south of the Columbia. For further discussion of the spread of Salish see Suttles and Elmendorf (1963) and Suttles (1987b).

Probably by the time the initial Salishan expansion had reached to or near Bella Coola territory, the Proto-Wakashans had already settled on northern Vancouver Island, likely early contesting with the Salishan speakers the utilization of the western shores of Johnstone Strait. There was also fairly early a separation into two groups, Proto-Nootkans moving to the west coast of Vancouver Island, where, perhaps accompanying a shift in subsistence to whaling, contact declined with the eastern group. Kwakiutlan speakers expanded onto the adjacent mainland and northward perhaps absorbing or displacing the northern portion of the Salishan continuum, and in any case cutting off Bella Coola from the rest. The Haisla with their relatively little dialectal diversity probably moved last, beyond the already established Heiltsuk, who had occupied lands on both sides of Bella Coola. Kwakiutl proper represents the oldest settlement with its considerable dialectal diversity. Nootkan expanded down the west coast of Vancouver Island, leaving a long extent of intergrading dialects of Nootka proper; two very diverse dialects eventually assumed the status of separate languages—Nitinaht on the southwest coast of the island and Makah on Cape Flattery in Washington. In historic times, Kwakiutl speakers expanded on Vancouver Island at the expense of Comox Salish speakers (Boas 1887a; Taylor and Duff 1956).

Proto-Chimakuan speakers may well have occupied much of the northern Olympic Peninsula of Washington at a time when Nootkan and Central Salish were completing their separation into the historic languages. It is unclear where the Proto-Chimakuans came from, or *47*

Table 6. Language Features of Greater Salishan

	1	2	3	4	5	6
Nass-Gitksan	●		●		●	●
Coast Tsimshian			●		●	●
Bella Coola	●	H		●		●
Comox	H	H	●	●	●	●
Pentlatch	●	H	?	?	?	
Sechelt	●	H		●	●	●
Squamish	●	H	●	●	?	●
Halkomelem	●	●	●	●	●	●
Nooksack	●	H	●	●	?	●
Northern Straits	●	●	●	●	●	●
Clallam	●	●	●	●	●	●
Chemakum	●	H	●	●	?	?
Quileute	H		●	●		●
Lushootseed	●	H	●	●		●
Twana	●	H	?	●	?	●
Quinault	●	H	●	●	?	?
Lower Chehalis	●	H	?	●	?	●
Upper Chehalis	●	H	●	●	●	●
Cowlitz	●	H	●	●	●	●
Tillamook	●	H		●	●	?
Alsea	●	●			●	

H = feature present historically; now lost

Features

1. A glottalized lateral affricate ƛ̓ occurs, but a matching nonglottalized ƛ does not; also Oregon Athapaskan; ƛ in Comox and Quileute is a result of borrowings from Wakashan.

2. Metathesis is used as a regular grammatical process, or can be shown to have been a relatively common phenomenon historically.

3. Two tense categories are marked (although they are usually not obligatory); also Nitinaht, Lower Chinook, and perhaps Eyak.

4. Feminine and nonfeminine gender categories are distinguished; Chinookan languages distinguish two true genders and one gender-number (neuter-collective-abstract).

5. Predicates/verbs marked for plurality refer to a plural subject in intransitive forms, but a plural object in transitive forms (in Comox, for distributive plural only); also Eyak, Tlingit, Chinookan, and Hanis; Haida has 4 such verbs.

6. A negative is often followed by a subordinate construction.

Table 7. Language Features on the South-Central Coast

	1	2	3	4	5	6	7	8	9
Halkomelem	●		●	●		●	( )		
Northern Straits	●		●	●		●	( )		
Clallam	●		●	●		●	( )		
Lushootseed	●	●		●	●	●	●		
Twana	●	?	●		?	●	●	●	
Quinault		?	?	●	?	●	?		?
Lower Chehalis	●		?	●	?	●	●	?	?
Upper Chehalis	●	●	●	●	●	●	●	●	
Cowlitz	●		●	●	●	●	●	●	●
Taitnapam		●		●	●	●			
Lower Chinook	F	F	●		●		●		
Cathlamet	F	F	●		●			●	
Kiksht	F	●	●	●	●			●	
Tillamook	●	●	●		?	●	●	?	

( ) = partial presence of the feature
F = few instances of the feature; not systematic

Features

1. Clusters of four or more consonants are permitted word-initially; also Coast Tsimshian, Heiltsuk, and Alsea.

2. Consonant symbolism occurs (i.e., consonant changes may indicate diminutive, augmentative, etc.), although it seems to be common only in Chinookan; also Kwakiutl and Alsea.

3. Different roots are used for the singular and plural of various concepts (e.g., 'sit', 'stand', 'take'), although each member of such pairs is considered a distinct concept within the language, coded by a single stem; also Eyak, Tlingit, Nass-Gitksan, Coast Tsimshian, Kwalhio-qua-Clatskanie, Kalapuya, Alsea, Hanis, Tututni-Tolowa; rarely in Alaskan Haida; only one such pair is attested for Chemakum.

4. A special affix is used for basic color terms (and only these terms); also Halkomelem, Nooksack, and Takelma; Quinault uses a suffix, all others use a prefix; Siuslaw reduplicates color terms; 'white' is not so marked in Halkomelem, Northern Stratis, and Clallam.

5. Different formations are used for distributive and collective plurals; also Nass-Gitksan, Coast Tsimshian, Bella Coola, Comox, Sechelt, Nitinaht, Makah, and Tututni-Tolowa.

6. Three (or more) primary aspectual categories are distinguished; also Hanis and all Athapaskan; there seem to be more than 3 in Halkomelem, Northern Straits, Clallam, and Lushootseed.

7. Aspect is marked by prefixes or proclitics; also Eyak, Tlingit, Kalapuyan, and all Athapaskan; Halkomelem, Northern Straits, and Clallam use both prefixes and other devices.

8. Tense is marked by prefixes or proclitics; also Eyak, Nass-Gitksan, and Kalapuyan; Cathlamet and Kiksht use both prefixes and suffixes.

9. The language has a copula (linking predicate/verb like English *be*); also Takelma.

how. The split into Chemakum and Quileute probably reflected expansion of the latter to the Pacific littoral, subsequently cut off by Clallam Salishan speakers, spun off from the expanding Straits Salish dialect continuum.

Somewhat later, it would seem, Haida speakers settled the Queen Charlotte Islands, diversifying into two clusters of dialects. The spread of Masset speakers to the southern Alaska islands occurred in the eighteenth century.

If Tlingit is relatable to Eyak-Athapaskan, speakers of the original protolanguage must have arrived in North America rather late, and may well have settled somewhere in interior or southeastern Alaska, probably at roughly the time of Proto-Wakashan unity or somewhat earlier. On the other hand, the original split must have been early, moving Tlingit to (or leaving it in) its historic location; its dialects are only weakly differentiated, so that it must have expanded its territory as recently as the nineteenth

century. Eyak moved early to the southern coast of Alaska and became isolated there. Successive groups of Athapaskan speakers moved south and east out of the Alaska interior and on to what is now western Canada. One group must have split off and made its way overland to the southern Oregon–northern California coast, where it gradually diversified (Hoijer 1960) and spread to occupy lands adjacent to Penutian, Hokan, and Ritwan languages presumably already in residence. Another small group made its way, again overland, from somewhere in the

Table 8. Language Features in Central Oregon

	1	2	3	4	5	6	7	8	9	10	11	12	13	14	15	16	17
Lower Chinook		●	●				●		●				●	●			●
Cathlamet			●				◐			●		( )	●	●			●
Kiksht	●		●				●			●		( )	●	●			●
Kalapuyan	?			●	●	●	●	( )		●	●					●	
Takelma	?			●	●	●		?				●				●	
Tillamook	●	●	●					H								●	
Alsea		●		●			●	●		●	●	●	●	●	●		●
Siuslaw	?	●	●		●		●	●	●	●	●	●	●	●	●		●
Hanis	●	●	●				●	?	●	?	?	●	●	●		●	●
Upper Umpqua	●		●			●	?			●	?	●		?		?	
Tututni-Tolowa	●		●			●	?			●	●	●		●		●	

( ) = partial presence of the feature
H = feature present historically; now lost

Features

1. Three stop-affricate series (glottalized, fortis, and lenis); there is some question as to whether Kalapuyan, Takelma, and Siuslaw had 2 or 3 such series.

2. Fronted prevelar obstruent series [k^y, k'^y, x^y], but at the phonetic level only.

3. Contrast between alveolar and palatal affricate-spirant positions; *s* and *š* alternate in Chinookan to indicate augmentative-diminutive contrasts.

4. A single alveolar or palatal affricate-spirant obstruent series (or both alternating nondistinctively).

5. A set of long vowels contrasts with the set of short vowels.

6. Clusters of only two consonants are permitted word-initally; also Eyak (?), Sechelt, and Quinault.

7. 'Blue' and 'green' are expressed by a single lexical item, opposed to 'yellow'; also Quileute and Twana.

8. Metathesis is used as a regular grammatical process; it was relatively common historically in Tillamook; it is sporadic and infrequent in Kalapuyan.

9. Aspect is not a basic grammatical category and is not obligatorily marked.

10. Tense is a basic, obligatory grammatical category; also Eyak, Nass-Gitksan, Coast Tsimshian, Nitinaht, and Makah.

11. Three primary tense categories are distinguished; also Haida, Kwakiutl, Nootka, Nitinaht, Makah, and Sechelt; 6 are distinguished in Kiksht.

12. Tense is marked by suffixes or postposed elements; Cathlamet and Kiksht use both suffixes and prefixes.

13. The pronominal system distinguishes hearer-included and hearer-excluded in nonsingular first-person forms; also Kwakiutl.

14. A dual number category is marked in or with the pronominal system; also Miluk; dual is marked only with third-person subjects in Tututni-Tolowa.

15. Nouns are marked for case distinctions; also Quileute.

16. Deictic particles resembling definite articles are used.

17. Preferred word order is verb-object-subject.

north toward the mouth of the Columbia, where a very recent split left apparently nearly identical Kwalhioqua and Clatskanie on the two sides of Chinookan territory (Krauss 1973). There are no indications that either of these groups moved south from the Alaska coast by sea.

Survival of Languages

Most of the languages in the southern part of the region were extinct by the late twentieth century, and a large proportion of those farther north were on the verge of disappearing. Even where there were sizable numbers of speakers, they were generally adults, mostly middle-aged or older. However, with the renewal of pride in heritage that was apparent from the 1960s on, the languages took on a new significance, and there were many attempts to establish programs to encourage language learning (figs. 3–4). In all, programs were begun in fewer than 15 communities during the 1970s and 1980s, nearly all on reserves in British Columbia. None has had more than limited success in teaching the languages to children, and

numbers of speakers have continued to decline. Lushootseed was taught successfully at the University of Washington, Seattle, from 1972 to 1988, but classes consisted mostly of non-Indian students.

In 1972 the state of Alaska passed legislation (Bills No. SB 421 and SB 422) making it obligatory for elementary schools in which there are 15 or more students whose language is an Alaska native language to provide instruction in that language, with English taught as a foreign language in the predominantly native curriculum. To this end the Alaska Native Language Center, Fairbanks, was created.

In British Columbia the provincial government and the Union of British Columbia Indian Chiefs supported efforts to maintain and refurbish tribal traditions and practices. In this connection they sponsored the creation of writing systems for all languages of the province still spoken and encouraged the recording of traditional narratives and customs. Beginning in the 1960s researchers at universities in British Columbia, at the British Columbia Indian Language Project, Victoria, and at the

The symbol x̱ in Makah stands for a sound like an h in English but is made with the tongue raised in the middle.

xad?ak
woman

Makah practice words :

xutac (bucket)   xad?awišč (girl)

xutaqsix̱ (taking a drink)   wipaxbis (nuisance)

Makah Cultural and Research Center, Neah Bay, Wash.

Fig. 3. Page from the *Makah Alphabet Book* (Makah Cultural and Research Center 1979). This textbook was used in teaching the language classes sponsored by the Makah Cultural and Research Center, Neah Bay, Wash. The illustration depicts a woman with facial decorations wearing a woven basketry cap and a robe probably of cedar bark with fur trim. Illustration by Scott Tyler and Chris Walsh.

KWAK̓WALA ALPHABET

© U'mista Cultural Society, 1979   illustrations by Nola Johnston

Fig. 4. Kwakiutl language program. The Kwakiutl language, sometimes called Kwak'wala, was used in the 1980s in everyday conversations as well as in ceremonies, but only a small percentage of primary school children spoke or understood it. top, Poster illustrating the alphabet developed by the U'mista Cultural Society in Alert Bay, B.C. Drawn by Nola Johnston, 1979. bottom, A classroom at the U'mista Cultural Centre, Alert Bay, B.C., where Gloria Webster is teaching fundamentals of the language using the alphabet developed by U'mista. The children are, left to right, Adrienne Taylor, Josh Howes, and Shawn Matilpi. Photograph by Vicki Jensen, 1980.

Royal British Columbia Museum, Victoria, worked with Indians in various groups on the development of a nontechnical written notation of tribal traditions using this system, and they also made tape recordings of traditional narratives. In Washington and Oregon there have been several similar independent programs reflecting cooperation of Indians and university researchers.

The Native languages of the Northwest Coast have contributed a few words to the vocabulary of English. These include the names of three fishes, eulachon (from Chinook *u̓łxan*), coho (from Mainland Halkomelem *kʷóxʷəθ*), and sockeye (from Halkomelem *sθə́qəy̓* or Northern Straits *sə́qəy̓*), and a putative giant primate, sasquatch (from Mainland Halkomelem *sésq̓əc*). Their number is small, probably reflecting the phonological difficulty of the Indian languages and the very small number of non-Indians who learned to speak any of them.

Chinook Jargon, used by most fur traders, missionaries, and early settlers, contributed more words to regional English. These include potlatch 'give, ceremony at which gifts are given' (Jargon *páłač*, presumably from a Nootkan source), tyee 'chief' (Jargon *táyi*, from Nootka *ta·yi·*

'older brother, senior'), tillikum 'friend, people' (Jargon *tílxam*, from Chinook *télxam* 'people'), Siwash 'Indian' (Jargon *sawáš*, from French *sauvage*), and a few others. The Jargon *sawáš* was the ordinary word for 'Indian' as opposed to King-George for 'English' and Boston for 'American', but by the mid-nineteenth century the regional English term Siwash had become derogatory and offensive to Indians. Nevertheless, well into the twentieth century it was still assumed by many Whites to be a tribal name.

Human Biology

JEROME S. CYBULSKI

Physical anthropology studies human populations in terms of the physical features and biochemical makeup of living members and the skeletal and dental remains of forebears. The first part of this chapter focuses on morphological and biological elements concerned with the genetics, adaptations, and origins of Northwest Coast Indians. It includes data from both the living and the dead. The second part, paleopathology, principally involves skeletal remains. It treats patterns of health, disease, and injury during prehistory and the early historic period.

On both counts, it is impossible to provide definitive and comprehensive portraits. There are many gaps in the data that have been accumulated; inadequacies in the representation, identification, or sample sizes of local and regional populations; and comparative limits imposed by the specific methodological and technical applications of different investigators.

Physical Features, Population Biology, and Origins

Physical anthropology has attempted to investigate heterogeneity and homogeneity in physical and biological features. Such data may provide knowledge about the interrelationships of local and regional groups, their affinities with geographic and cultural neighbors, and, ultimately, their evolutionary histories and origins.

For the Northwest Coast, three kinds of data have accumulated; physical characteristics of people living at the time of contact and during the nineteenth century; blood group studies undertaken as early as the 1930s but particularly in the 1950s and 1960s; and skeletal features and characteristics of early historic and of prehistoric Indians.

Physical Features in the Living

The writings of the early explorers and observations by Franz Boas (1890, 1892d, 1895b) late in the nineteenth century indicated both homogeneity and heterogeneity in the physical characteristics of living Northwest Coast Indians. Head hair predominantly ranged in color from very dark brown to black; however, red hair was noted on rare occasions and mentioned in tales of the people themselves as a peculiar beauty in some women. In texture, the hair was coarse and smooth. In form, it was straight, though Boas reported that a few individuals of each group he examined had slightly wavy hair, and he observed even curly hair in some Coast Salish.

Body hair was sparse. Facial hair appeared abundant in men as moustaches and chin tufts, but it was plucked from the cheeks. Eyebrows were thick, "remarkably" wide on the outer sides, but trimmed. Eye color was predominantly dark brown. Boas noted frequent occurrences of the internal epicanthic fold, particularly among Haida and Tsimshian. The color of the skin appeared lighter in the groups of British Columbia—generally no darker than that of southern Europeans—than in those of more southerly Northwest Coast regions and in Indians east of the Rocky Mountains.

In head size, face width and height, and features of the nose, Boas found differences between Haida and Tsimshian on one hand and Bella Coola, Heiltsuk speakers, and Kwakiutl on the other. The former reportedly had larger heads, prominent foreheads, wide and moderately high faces, and concave or straight noses. Among the latter groups, whom Boas regarded as a "Kwakiutl type," faces were very high, noses were very high, narrow, and predominantly convex (hooked), and the forehead was flatter. Both the northern and Kwakiutl types were identified as having short pointed noses to contrast them with the longer noses of Interior Salish.

Differences in the forehead of British Columbia groups may have resulted from the practice of artificial head deformation. For the Northwest Coast as a whole, variations on the custom were distributed continuously from Bella Bella and Bella Coola in the north to the Alsea or Siuslaw in the south. Three distinctive types were recognized by Boas: a "Koskimo" type, epitomized by Kwakiutl groups of the northern end of Vancouver Island where the malleable heads of newborn infants were circumferentially bound with kelp; a "Chinook" type, evidently restricted to the Columbia River valley and marked by extreme flattening of the forehead and occiput ("Chinookans of the Lower Columbia," fig. 10, this vol.); a "Cowitchin" type, principally found in the Strait of Georgia region and on the coast of Washington, in which the back of the head was compressed at a higher level than in the Chinook and pressure was also applied to the forehead by means of cedar bark pads ("Southwestern Coast Salish," fig. 5, this vol.).

Variations or intermediate expressions of these extremes, also noted by Boas, have been confirmed by studies of early historic period skulls (Cybulski 1975, 1975a, 1978a). A less intense form of the Koskimo type, technically known as annular deformation or popularly as sugarloaf deformity, was practiced by Northern and Central Nootkans, Comox, and Kwakiutl between Fort Rupert and Campbell River ("Kwakiutl: Traditional Culture," fig. 4, this vol.). Modifications of the Cowitchin type, also referred to as anteroposterior deformation, prevailed among other groups including Bella Bella and Bella Coola, Oowekeeno, Coast Salish other than Comox, Nitinaht and Makah, and groups to the south.

The radical changes made during infancy persisted throughout the life of an individual, thus making it difficult to define head form accurately for biological description and comparison. Annular deformation, which produces an elongated and narrow head, mimics dolichocephaly, while anteroposterior deformation, including the extreme form practiced by the Chinook, results in a short and broad head, mimicking brachycephaly. Some data on the cephalic index, available for northern Northwest Coast groups who did not practice deformation, are presented in table 1. Although scant in number, they suggest that brachycephaly (roundheadedness) clearly outweighed dolichocephaly (longheadedness) in the area late in the nineteenth century.

In their general physique, Boas (1899) collectively characterized the coastal groups of British Columbia as having medium stature, short and broad trunks, long and powerfully developed arms, and less strongly developed lower limbs. His data indicated local variations in mean heights (table 2) and in other body dimensions (Hall and Macnair 1972). For example, Nishga, Gitksan, and Bella Coola men appeared taller than the mean (163.6 cm for the 10 groups of living men in table 2), while Nootka and Oowekeeno appeared shorter.

Boas also reported male averages as high as 173 centimeters for Tlingit, 169.5 for Haida, 169.3 for Tsimshian, 169.4 for a combined Cowichan and Clallam sample, and 169.1 for Chinook. These consistently high figures were primarily derived from the measurements of other investigators, and, unlike the data in table 2, the source locations of the individuals who contributed to the samples are unknown. The Haida and Tsimshian figures are particularly puzzling in light of those in table 2 calculated directly from Boas's published measurements. Possibly, the other samples were largely composed of men in Alaska and in the upper Skeena or Nass River regions respectively, where some of Boas's data indicated taller statures than in Haida of the Queen Charlotte Islands and in Coast Tsimshian.

Table 1. Cephalic Index in Northern Northwest Coast Men Living Late in the 19th Century

		Number of individuals		
Group	Average	Dolicho-cephalic	Meso-phalic	Brachy-cephalic
Nishga	83.0	0	8	11
Gitksan	81.3	2	3	4
Coast Tsimshian	79.9	1	1	1
Haida (Masset, Skidegate)	82.4	0	3	3

SOURCES: Individual measurements in Boas (1890, 1895b) and Boas and Farrand (1899). Individuals selected had village identification or both parents from the same group.

Multivariate statistical analysis of Boas's anthropometric data for British Columbia has tended to support his threefold classification of a coastal northern type, a Kwakiutl type, and a Thompson River interior type (Hall and Macnair 1972). However, this study also found that only those local groups that formed Boas's Thompson River type clustered distinctively. The local groups of the coast appeared different among themselves. To what extent these differences were influenced by genetics, environment, or past population history is unknown, but it is reasonable to conclude from these results that geographic propinquity greatly influenced physical differences, a hypothesis fostered by Boas.

Blood Groups

Blood grouping studies on the Northwest Coast have indicated the following patterns: a high frequency of type O blood, a variably high incidence of type M, a prevalence of Rh positive reaction, virtual absence of the AB phenotype, and only rare occurrences of type B. Type A blood could not be considered infrequent. It has been identified in 10 to 25 percent of individuals in eight of 22 samples and in 25 to 40 percent in seven groups. Type N blood has been found in less than 10 percent in 12 of 15 samples and less than 5 percent in nine of these.

Gene (allele) frequencies furnish a more exact measure of biological makeup than do phenotypic frequencies. The most comprehensive Northwest Coast data are available only for the ABO system, shown in table 3. Frequencies of the O allele are above .800 in 20 of these groups, and above .900 in eight. They are among the highest in the world with the exception of South America. Relatively high frequencies of the A allele have occurred in Tsimshian and Haisla, particularly at Klemtu and Kitimaat, and to some extent among Coast Salish. On the other hand, negligible occurrences have consistently been reported for Northern and Central Nootka, and for Kwakiutl at Smith Inlet.

Only four coastal groups have received extensive   53

testing for other allele systems. They include Sitka Tlingit (Corcoran et al. 1959), Masset and Skidegate Haida (Thomas et al. 1964), and Ahousaht Nootka (Alfred et al. 1969). The data these samples have produced, as well as those of a less extensively tested sample, the Swinomish Salish (Hulse 1957), are of special interest because they have figured prominently in studies of genetic distance among North American Indian and Eskimo groups, and, to some extent, Asian peoples (Spuhler 1979; Szathmary 1979; Szathmary and Ossenberg 1978). These studies have commonly identified the Nootka sample as most distinctive and unique relative to the other Northwest Coast groups and to neighboring Indian populations. The Tlingit and Haida samples have presented conflicting degrees of association, depending on whether the two Haida samples have been treated separately or combined, but have generally been considered to show close affinities to Athapaskan groups. The Swinomish Salish have shown close associations with Masset Haida, but not with Skidegate Haida, and with neighboring groups of the Plateau culture area. Insofar as northeast Asian populations are concerned, the Tlingit, Haida, and Nootka samples have appeared no closer than other Indian or Eskimo groups.

A major problem associated with reliance on blood groups for study of Native American affinities and origins is the high probability of European and Asian admixture in the gene pools of populations tested many generations after initial historic contacts. Indeed, the original investigators of the Haida groups used in the genetic distance studies estimated as much as one-third Caucasian admixture in their samples (Thomas et al. 1964).

A second problem involves the possible affects of genetic drift. Following European contact, the populations of the Northwest Coast were progressively and at times rapidly reduced in size, a factor that may have significantly altered the gene pools of some groups studied much later. This chance phenomenon, resulting in survivors not carrying alleles predominant in the ancestral population, may account for peculiar blood group patterns shown by the Ahousaht Nootka relative to other Northwest Coast groups. For example, in the 1950s, 234 Central Nootkans, including 14 Ahousahts, gave frequencies of .84 and .16 for the M and N alleles respectively (Hulse 1955). In the 1960s 198 Ahousahts produced frequencies of .399 and .601 (Alfred et al. 1969). The M allele frequencies for all other known tested Northwest Coast groups have ranged from .72 to .92. Other peculiarities of the Ahousaht, possibly attributable to genetic drift, have been discussed by the original investiga-

Table 2. Statures of British Columbia Coast Men

Group	Number	Mean	Standard deviation	Range
Late 19th Century—Living				
Nishga	19	165.76 cm	4.15cm	172.6 – 157.3cm
Gitksan	9	165.89	4.57	173.2 – 160.7
Coast Tsimshian	3	162.50	3.17	164.9 – 158.9
Haida (Masset, Skidegate)	6	162.47	4.91	168.5 – 154.2
Bella Coola	26	166.09	5.38	174.3 – 154.2
Bella Bella	5	163.74	5.83	172.5 – 156.8
Oowekeeno	7	160.66	5.20	166.6 – 150.0
Kwakiutl	49	163.31	5.20	174.9 – 154.0
Nootka	4	161.55	6.68	171.1 – 161.2
Halkomelem Salish	4	163.48	2.67	165.1 – 160.6
Early Historic—Skeletal				
Haida (Masset, Skidegate)	35	164.52	4.02	171.5 – 155.3
Oowekeeno	2	157.78	2.33	159.4 – 156.1
Kwakiutl	22	164.02	4.21	176.0 – 158.6
Nootka	25	160.94	3.91	170.9 – 155.6
Coast Salish	12	163.91	5.02	174.4 – 159.4
Prehistoric—Skeletal				
Blue Jackets Creek	6	162.43	4.44	167.7 – 157.1
Prince Rupert Harbour	65	163.20	3.72	171.4 – 155.5
Namu	7	164.00	4.76	171.3 – 156.7
Strait of Georgia	17	161.66	3.22	167.5 – 154.1

SOURCES: Data on the living compiled from, and means and standard deviations calculated from individual measurements in Boas (1890, 1892d, 1895b) and Boas and Farrand (1899). Individuals selected had village identification or both parents from the same group. All skeletal data were calculated from lower limb long-bone lengths using the male Mongoloid regression formulae of Trotter and Gleser (1958); long-bone lengths for Namu were furnished by A.J. Curtin (1984) and for 15 of the prehistoric Strait of Georgia individuals by Beattie (1980); those for Blue Jackets Creek were obtained from P.L. Murray (1981).

Table 3. Blood Allele A, B, and O Frequencies in Northwest Coast Samples

Sample	Number	O	A	B	Sources
Tlingit	120	0.871	0.129	0.000	V.E. Levine 1951
Sitka	79	0.893	0.079	0.032	Corcoran et al. 1959
Haida					
Masset	284	0.852	0.134	0.012	Thomas et al. 1964
Skidegate	153	0.946	0.050	0.003	Thomas et al. 1964
Tsimshian					
1930s	54	0.850	0.150	0.000	Gates and Darby 1934; Ride 1935
1950s	50	0.860	0.128	0.010	Hulse 1955
Tsimshian and Haihais (Klemtu)	41	0.796	0.188	0.012	Gates and Darby 1934; Ride 1935
Haisla (Kitamaat)	58	0.766	0.223	0.009	Gates and Darby 1934; Ride 1935
Kitamaat and Bella Bella	31	0.823	0.177	0.000	Hulse 1955
Bella Bella	94	0.962	0.038	0.000	Gates and Darby 1934
Oowekeeno (Rivers Inlet)	24	0.913	0.087	0.000	Gates and Darby 1934
Gwasilla Kwakiutl	30	1.000	0.000	0.000	Gates and Darby 1934
Nootkans					
Northern and Central	61	0.992	0.008	0.000	Gates and Darby 1934; Ride 1935
Central	234	0.981	0.019	0.000	Hulse 1955
Central (Ahousaht)	198	0.992	0.008	0.000	Alfred et al. 1969
Southern (Nitinaht)	107	0.922	0.078	0.000	Hulse 1955
Makah	112	0.945	0.050	0.004	Hulse 1955
Coast Salish					
Strait of Georgia	47	0.875	0.113	0.011	Hulse 1955
Swinomish	149	0.886	0.099	0.014	Hulse 1957
Port Madison Reservation, Wash.	86	0.807	0.172	0.042	Hulse 1955
Tulalip Reservation, Wash.	89	0.874	0.076	0.046	Hulse 1955
Muckleshoot Reservation, Wash.	82	0.834	0.166	0.012	Hulse 1955

NOTE: All but the Tlingit frequencies were recalculated from the published phenotype figures assuming Hardy-Weinberg equilibrium for each sample.

tors of this sample (Alfred et al. 1969). Blood group or other biochemical patterns of the 1950s and 1960s may not accurately reflect genetic patterns thousands or even hundreds of years earlier.

Skeletal Remains

Skeletal remains of the early historic and prehistoric periods are largely known from the British Columbia coast. The early historic period, in this context, spans the middle of the eighteenth to the middle of the nineteenth centuries. The period is represented by remains in museums that were collected late in the nineteenth or early in the twentieth centuries (for example, Cybulski 1975) and by remains excavated under controlled archeological conditions in the 1960s and 1970s (Cybulski 1973a, 1975a, 1978a).

Prehistoric skeletal remains are known from four regions, including Prince Rupert Harbour on the north mainland coast, the Queen Charlotte Islands, the central mainland coast, and the Strait of Georgia. The Prince Rupert Harbour remains, minimally representing 270 individuals from eight sites, have been dated by radiocarbon and relative stratigraphic techniques to between 1500 B.C. and A.D. 500. Likewise, the Strait of Georgia remains, numbering 272 individuals at 15 sites, can principally be assigned to this time-frame. The Queen Charlotte Islands and central coast are each represented by one site with human remains, Blue Jackets Creek and Namu. Radiocarbon dates have placed the Blue Jackets Creek remains, 25 individuals, at 2000 B.C. (P. Sutherland, personal communication 1988), while the Namu remains, numbering 42 people, date from 4000 B.C. to A.D. 1000 (Curtin 1984).

While skeletal remains are not available for all areas where Boas studied the living, those collections available suggest that there has been little change in physique. The mean heights of men appeared to have varied little for as much as 3,000 or 4,000 years (see table 2), and a classic coastal body build, like that described for late nineteenth-century living peoples, has been identified for prehistoric Prince Rupert Harbour (Cybulski et al. 1981).

In the southern British Columbia coast, cranial defor- 55

mation appears to have had a time-depth of at least 2,500 years. This cultural influence was primarily responsible for early archeologists' contentions that two distinct physical types, identified on the basis of head form, prehistorically inhabited the Strait of Georgia region (Smith 1903; Drucker 1943). Other measures of skeletal morphology have been insufficient to conclude that earlier inhabitants, associated with the Locarno Beach and earlier cultural phases, were biologically different from later prehistoric inhabitants of the region, largely defined by the Marpole culture phase (Beattie 1980).

There is, however, some evidence to conclude differences in head form among skeletal samples in northern British Columbia where artificial deformation is not known prehistorically (see fig. 1). Comparable to the brachycephalic condition among the later living peoples of this region, early historic Haida skulls show a tendency to roundheadedness. Skulls from Blue Jackets Creek and Prince Rupert Harbour show tendencies to longheadedness.

A trend toward increasing brachycephalization has been observed in various parts of the world, and the northern British Columbia coast may be no exception. The distributions in figure 1 might be expected in this context given the temporal positions of each sample.

Broad-based comparative temporal and regional studies to determine biological relationships, ancestral-descendant ties, and origins from skeletal remains have been limited. On the basis of dental characteristics, Northwest Coast groups have been claimed to be remarkably homogeneous relative to other Indian groups, closely associated with Subarctic Athapaskan peoples, and part of a second, post-Paleo-Indian migration to the New World, prior to the immigration of Eskimo-Aleut peoples (C.G. Turner 1983, 1986). Variability in nonmetric skull traits has shown considerable heterogeneity among linguistically identified Northwest Coast samples (Finnegan 1972) and, in some cases, close associations with Eskimo samples (Szathmary and Ossenberg 1978).

Synopsis

Considering all physical anthropological data that have accumulated, it is reasonable to conclude that the whole of the Northwest Coast did not comprise a single breeding population either historically or prehistorically. Viable population units were most probably formed locally, corresponding in large part to the physiographically oriented habitation centers distributed throughout the coast (Cybulski 1975). These units were probably stable for a long period of time, but they were not genetically closed systems. When people were close enough, they interbred, and sociocultural proscriptions also influenced gene flow. However, these elements were not strong enough to bring about a genetic uniformity of the

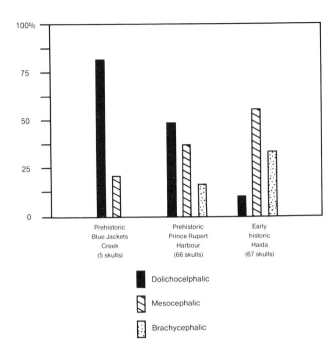

Fig. 1. Distributions by category of male cranial indices in northern B.C. coast skeletal remains. Indices for Blue Jackets Creek were calculated from absolute measurements in J.S. Murray (1981); all others were calculated from measurements by the author (collections in Field Museum of Natural History, Chicago, and Canadian Museum of Civilization, Ottawa).

Northwest Coast people or to have established discrete genetic boundaries between the neighboring local populations who collectively formed different cultural and language divisions.

Paleopathology

There are limits to the kinds and amount of information that can be obtained about health, disease, and injury in earlier populations solely from skeletal remains. The full range of environmental insults to which human beings may be subjected cannot be demonstrated; observation is restricted to those diseases and injuries that may affect bones or teeth. It is also impossible to know the true prevalence of a particular disease or injury in the sampled population. In part, this is a function of differential burial preservation or collection techniques. Not all parts of a person's skeleton may be available for study. For example, many Northwest Coast remains in museums are represented only by skulls, as early collectors tended to concentrate their efforts on that part of the anatomy for purposes of morphological analysis. Disease or injury may have been present in the limb skeletons or spinal columns of these people, in parts of excavated skeletons that have been lost to soil erosion or site disturbances, or in parts of skeletons that have been removed from burial grounds for ritual or other cultural purposes (for example, Cybulski 1978). For these reasons, it is seldom possible even to know the exact sample incidence

56

of a particular skeletal lesion.

Knowledge of true prevalence in a population is also influenced by the progress of disease and its variable manifestations in individuals. Many diseases that affect bone initially affect other body organs. A person may die before the bones become involved, and the archeological record of that disease is, therefore, lost. Bone fractures may heal to the point where visible signs are no longer present. For most manifested afflictions, therefore, any skeletal record can be presumed to reflect a minimal presence in the contributing population.

There is an important class of diseases that may never be known from skeletal remains. Historical records indicate that acute infections such as smallpox, measles, influenza, whooping cough, scarlet fever, and malaria reached epidemic proportions among Northwest Coast Indians soon after European contact. It is almost impossible to know whether such diseases existed prehistorically. Acute infections rarely implicate bone. It is only when infections become chronic that they are likely to leave skeletal signs.

Surveys of museum-collected and archeologically excavated Northwest Coast remains of the early historic period have revealed the presence of primary and secondary bone cancer, bone tuberculosis, pyogenic osteomyelitis, treponemal infection, and osteoarthritis. Primary bone cancer, in the form of multiple myeloma, a disease that develops in blood-forming elements of the marrow, and secondary bone cancer, cancer that may spread to bone from other body sites such as the lung, breast, or prostate, have been observed in skeletons from the Queen Charlotte Islands and Strait of Georgia region respectively (Cybulski and Pett 1981). No similar evidences have been observed in the prehistoric Northwest Coast record, but both malignancies have been identified elsewhere in precontact Indian remains (Steinbock 1976; Allison et al. 1980).

Tuberculous bone lesions, involving either the spinal column or limb joints, have been identified in Kwakiutl remains, in Nootka remains from Hesquiat Harbour, and in Songhees Salish remains. The bone lesions of treponematosis are best known from Songhees skeletal remains in the collections of the Field Museum of Natural History, Chicago.

Skeletal evidence for chronic tuberculosis and treponematosis might be expected in the historic period. Tuberculosis and venereal syphilis have been cited as contributing to the decline of the Indian population following European contact (Duff 1964; "Demographic History, 1774–1874," this vol.). Whether these diseases were entirely new to the Indians is difficult to say. Skeletal tuberculosis has not been identified in prehistoric remains from the coast, but there is evidence from two localities for the presence of treponemal infection, the Boardwalk site at Prince Rupert Harbour and the Duke Point site near Nanaimo, in the Strait of Georgia region.

One Boardwalk example is an adult female skeleton, directly radiocarbon-dated from bone collagen at 325 B.C. ± 90 years (S-1735), with cranial lesions like those of the *caries sicca* sequence of bone syphilis described by Hackett (1976). At Duke Point, 10 individuals, including a fetus, were buried together, and one of them has been directly dated at 1490 B.C. ± 125 years (S-2350). Four of the skeletons show distinct signs of treponematosis either in the limb bones or skull, and as many as six people, including the fetus, may have been affected (Cybulski 1983). Quite possibly, treponemal infection, perhaps in the form of endemic (nonvenereal) syphilis, was present at a constant low level in the native population but stimulated to higher levels following the influx of a foreign population and increased movements of the native people as a by-product of the fur trade.

Aside from the presence or absence of tuberculous and cancerous lesions, differences in kind cannot clearly be demonstrated in the skeletal manifestations of disease between the prehistoric and early historic Northwest Coast periods. One skeletal indicator of equivalent health status is *cribra orbitalia*, a porous lesion in the roof of the eye socket that has been related to iron-deficiency anemia. Overall, the lesion has been documented at 13–14 percent in both groups, a figure much lower than reported for Indian remains elsewhere (El-Najjar et al. 1976; P.L. Walker 1986). There are indications of regional variations in frequency for the British Columbia coast. Notably high frequencies occur in prehistoric Strait of Georgia remains and at Blue Jackets Creek on the Queen Charlotte Islands. Lower frequencies occur among early historic period skulls from these two regions (Haida and Coast Salish), but they are still somewhat higher than in other regions at the same time level (table 4).

The reasons for iron-deficiency anemia are varied, ranging from associations with nutritional deficiency, including iron-chelating agents in an otherwise adequate diet, to blood loss through injury, chronic infections, intestinal parasites, multiple childbirth in women, prolonged breast-feeding, weanling diarrhea, and possibly crowded living conditions serving as a vector for disease (Cybulski 1977; P.L. Walker 1986). It is difficult to cite any one of them to account for regional differences in the incidence of *cribra orbitalia* on the British Columbia coast, though variations in population density might have been a contributing factor.

Dental caries (cavities) were notably infrequent in earlier Northwest Coast populations. A sample of 6,264 teeth from prehistoric sites throughout the British Columbia coast shows a frequency of 0.34 percent, while 6,830 early historic period teeth show a frequency of 0.82 percent. These figures might be compared with an average of 26 percent for prehistoric and contact populations elsewhere in Canada who mainly subsisted on agriculture

57

Table 4. Distribution of *Cribra Orbitalia* in Prehistoric and Early Historic British Columbia Coast Groups

Group	Number of skulls	Percent affected
Prehistoric Period		
Blue Jackets Creek	21	28.6
Prince Rupert Harbour	157	6.4
Namu	25	8.0
Strait of Georgia	58	31.0
Total	261	13.8
Early Historic Period		
Haida (Skidegate, Masset)	113	14.2
Kwakiutl, Haisla, Hai-hais, Bella Bella, and Oowekeeno	174	9.8
Nootka	82	11.0
Coast Salish	98	19.4
Total	467	13.1

SOURCES: Observations by the author with the following exceptions: for Namu, Curtin (1984); for Strait of Georgia, Beattie (1980) and Gordon (1974, personal communication 1983).

(D.K. Patterson 1984), an indication of the influence of diet on dental disease. The staple fish and meat diet of Northwest Coast Indians, coupled with techniques of food preparation that introduced grit, led to rapid wear of the tooth cusps, reducing the opportunity for plaque formation and for bacteria to be harbored in the pits and fissures normally present in unworn or little worn teeth. The diet was low in carbohydrates (sugars, starches, and fats), important contributors to the formation of caries in agricultural groups.

Although cavities were rare, abscessed jaw sockets were common. Incidences of 2.95 percent have been found in a sample of 10,797 early historic period upper and lower jaw sockets of the permanent dentition and 9.16 percent in a sample of 6,305 prehistoric jaw sockets. Fully one-third of early historic period adults were affected by abscesses, while upward of 50 percent were affected in the prehistoric period.

A pertinent and likely related observation is a statistically higher frequency of abscesses in prehistoric jaws and a statistically lower frequency of dental caries. This inverse relationship may partly be explained by a greater degree of tooth wear in prehistoric jaws. Abscesses often develop from dead or dying pulp chambers in teeth exposed to bacteria either through crown cavities or through rapid and severe crown attrition. The rare occurrence of dental caries in Northwest Coast groups does not adequately explain the high incidence of abscesses, but some evidence indicates a high frequency of worn open pulp chambers in the prehistoric period (for example, Beattie 1980).

Nondietary factors may also have been responsible for abscesses in the prehistoric period. Evidence from Prince Rupert Harbour indicates that women used their teeth, particularly those of the lower jaw, as tools (Cybulski 1974), thus adding to the rapid wear of crowns. Also from these sites, there are frequent examples of head and facial fractures in men that suggest a high degree of actual or probable trauma to the upper jaws and teeth. Chronic trauma likely contributed to high frequencies of abscessed anterior tooth sites in the upper jaws of men.

In addition to head and facial fractures, the Prince Rupert Harbour sites have also revealed frequent occurrences of limb and spinal fractures. Close to 40 percent of individuals were affected in some way. A similarly high incidence of trauma has been reported for Namu, but in the Strait of Georgia region, only about 11 percent of individuals are known to have suffered skeletal injuries. These differences suggest markedly different circumstances, probably frequent intertribal warfare at Prince Rupert Harbour and Namu (Curtin 1984). For example, of those skeletons with injuries in the Prince Rupert Harbour sites, almost 60 percent manifested trauma plausibly attributable to episodes of interpersonal violence. Such trauma included depressed skull fractures from club blows, facial and anterior tooth fractures, defensive forearm "parry" fractures, defensive fractures of the outer hand, disarming fractures of the forearm and hand, and instances of decapitation. Similar findings have not been apparent for the Strait of Georgia region, or, for that matter, the Queen Charlotte Islands Blue Jackets Creek site.

The larger and, therefore, more statistically valid samples from Prince Rupert Harbour and the Strait of Georgia have also shown marked differences in the sex ratios of remains. At Prince Rupert Harbour, interred males outnumbered females by 1.8 to 1, while in the Strait of Georgia region, the sex ratio has been more nearly equal at 1.2 to 1 over a span of 2,000 years. These sex ratios more likely reflected population composition and socially selective mortuary practices than they did differential mortality. A possible explanation for Prince Rupert Harbour is that slaves cyclically made up a substantial portion of the adult female population and, because of their lack of social status, were not buried in the same sites as the other population. This explanation would accord with the evidence for frequent intertribal warfare in the area, perhaps motivated in part by a desire for women as an important resource (Adams 1973). The Strait of Georgia skeletal data provides little evidence for warfare and little evidence for selective burial practices; therefore, it probably contained a very dissimilar sociocultural construct.

Much of the above dental, trauma, sex ratio, and related data were compiled by the author based on his study of Prince Rupert Harbour materials in the Canadian Museum of Civilization, Ottawa, and early historic materials in the Field Museum of Natural History, Chicago, and the American Museum of Natural History, New York (Cybulski 1967–1986).

59

Cultural Antecedents

ROY L. CARLSON

Between 14,000 and 15,000 years ago the glacial ice covering the Northwest Coast began to melt, and by 12,000 years ago migrating peoples with the requisite technology could have reached Puget Sound from the north (Hopkins 1979; Fladmark 1983:25–26), spread to the coast from unglaciated regions to the south, or both. There are definite artifactual assemblages from Northwest Coast sites that date between 10,000 and 5,000 years ago, and other somewhat equivocal finds that may be 1,000–2,000 years earlier (fig. 1).

Archeological remains with a firm antiquity of greater than 5,000 years are not abundant on the Northwest Coast. In the few sites that are known, mollusk shells, whose alkaline content assists in the preservation of bone, are usually absent, so the faunal remains and bone tools that enrich the archeological record of later periods are poorly represented. With few exceptions only the stone tools and the debitage from stone tool production remain. Archeological knowledge is limited almost entirely to the forms and technology of these stone tools, to their specific context, and to the geographic locations and geological contexts of the sites in which they are found. Site geography is significant, as certain inferences concerning the way of life of the peoples who made these early tools can be drawn from this information. Some early assemblages are well dated whereas others are surface finds, and assignment to the period before 3000 B.C. is based on their similarities with dated assemblages. In this early period there were fewer identifiable cultures than later, and those that are found seem simpler in overall technology and more widespread in geographic extent.

In the period from about 8000 to 7000 B.C. in the Pacific Northwest there were four somewhat different technological complexes distributed over adjacent geographic regions. These complexes overlapped at their borders. These distributions suggest that there were four early cultural traditions each bearing a somewhat different technology (Carlson 1983c). Extending from Whidbey Island in Puget Sound south through the Puget lowlands to the Columbia River and then both east to the Plains and south to the Great Basin and California was the Fluted Point tradition. From the mouth of the Columbia River eastward to the Snake and then south through the Great Basin was the Stemmed Point tradition. Centered on the lower Fraser River, but extending north at least as far as the central coast of British Columbia and south to coastal Oregon was a pebble-tool and leaf-shaped-point complex called the Pebble Tool tradition. On the central and northern coasts and the Queen Charlotte Islands was the Microblade tradition with affinities north to the Subarctic and Siberia. The peoples bearing these traditions were all food collectors relying on hunting, fishing, gathering, or combinations thereof for sustenance. The different forms of projectile points associated with each tradition may indicate differences in weaponry. These differences suggest that each of these cultures had a somewhat different historical background. The different habitats also suggest differences in how these peoples made their living, but it seems better to define the cultures on the basis of their known artifactual forms rather than on the less well known subsistence systems.

The Fluted Point Tradition

The Fluted Point tradition, the most widespread of the early cultural traditions of North America, is only minimally represented on the Northwest Coast (Carlson 1983c: 83–86). Elsewhere on the continent, its hallmarks are fluted points frequently associated with elephant remains. A few mammoth and mastodon remains and 11 undated, isolated fluted points have been found in coastal regions, but none has been found in association with faunal remains or with other artifacts. There are surface finds of fluted points in western Oregon: Siltcoos Lake on the coast; on the Rogue drainage east of Ashland at 4,600 feet; in the Willamette drainage near Cottage Grove and in the Mohawk Valley east of Eugene; and on the north Umpqua (Minor 1985; Follansbee 1977). In Washington there are surface finds near Olympia and Chehalis (D. Osborne 1956) and from Whidbey Island in northern Puget Sound (Chatters 1985). Elsewhere in North America the earliest clear expression of this tradition, Clovis, is given an average age of 9500 B.C. (Haynes et al. 1984). Later forms of fluted points persist to at least 8500 B.C. in northeastern British Columbia (Fladmark, Alexander, and Driver 1984). On the Northwest Coast the only dated site within this time span is the Manis mastodon site near Sequim, Washington; and its cultural affiliation, if any, is uncertain.

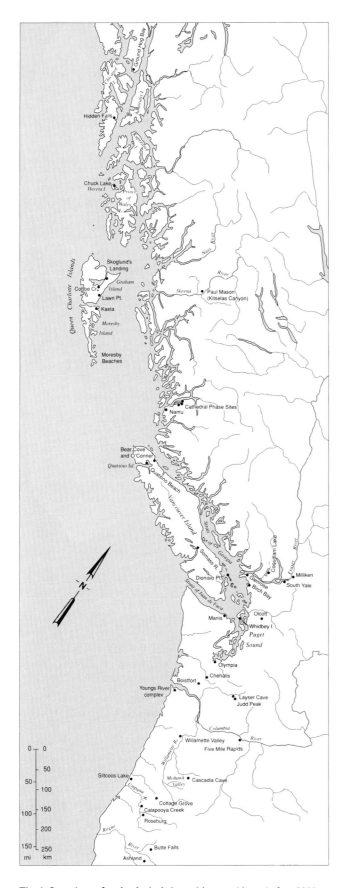

Fig. 1. Locations of archeological sites with assemblages before 3000 B.C.

The Manis site has evidence of at least 12 depositional levels between 10,000 and 4000 B.C. (Gustafson and Manis 1984). Bison bones and a partial mastodon skeleton with a pointed bone fragment embedded in a rib were recovered from a layer of brown colluvium radiocarbon dated to between 10,000 and 9000 B.C. Parts of a second elephant were found in an older stratum. No demonstrable stone artifacts were recovered from either of these layers, and the pointed bone fragment and some polishing and striations on other bones are not conclusive evidence of human presence. Whidbey Island, where a fluted point has been reported, is about 20 miles from Sequim. There are also mammoth remains without definitely associated artifacts from the Willamette Valley.

The question of antecedents of the Fluted Point tradition is much debated in American archeology. Because no fluted points have been found in Siberia or beyond, the place of origin of the points themselves, if not the way of life, would seem to be in the New World. Whatever the case, the place of origin was not the Northwest Coast, and the brief occurrence of this tradition there is probably late and derived from the Great Basin via the Columbia River and its tributaries. Strong evidence of continuity or transition between the Fluted Point tradition and later cultures of the Northwest Coast is lacking.

The Stemmed Point Tradition

The Stemmed Point tradition is primarily a culture of interior North America that spills over to the coast along the Columbia River waterway. It is typified by chipped stone crescents and points with long stems and by an emphasis on hunting. Other forms of points also occur, as well as bone needles, harpoons, and atlatl hooks, and shell beads and pendants. On the Northwest Coast–Plateau boundary area a small assemblage is found as the earliest (Initial Early) component at Five Mile Rapids (Rice 1972: 164; Cressman 1977:134) where it dates to 7835 B.C. ± 220 (Cressman et al. 1960:48). Upriver in the Plateau area, it is well dated to between 8800 and 6600 B.C. (Rice 1972). Down the Columbia, assemblages from undated sites grouped as the Youngs River complex (Minor 1984; "Prehistory of the Lower Columbia and Willamette Valley" this vol.) also appear to belong to this tradition, as do some of the projectile points from the Judd Peak Rockshelters in Lewis County, Washington (Daugherty, Flenniken, and Welch 1987).

This tradition is primarily interior in distribution, and its weak expression on the coast is poorly known. Before 3000 B.C. its subsistence system based on hunting was succeeded by one in which salmon became a staple and in which leaf-shaped points became important. This succession becomes later farther up the Columbia and its tributaries, where these later components are sometimes grouped as the Cascade phase. Upriver this tradition is found in the region occupied historically by Sahaptin-speaking peoples, and downriver it is found in the territory occupied by Chinookan speakers. The Stemmed Point tradition probably represents the ancestors of these peoples.

The Pebble Tool Tradition

The Pebble Tool tradition is defined on the basis of the co-occurrence of unifacial pebble choppers (fig. 2) and leaf-shaped bifaces in early assemblages, but it includes assemblages of pebble (or cobble) tools by themselves. Formerly pebble tool assemblages without bifaces were considered a very early part of the tradition and were referred to as the Pasika complex (Borden 1968). However, study of the assemblages from the type site, South Yale (DjRi7) at the mouth of the Fraser Canyon (Haley 1983), has demonstrated the presence of bifacial trimming flakes, and radiocarbon dates place the Pasika complex at the type site at 4000–2000 B.C. Such assemblages are contemporaneous with components in which leaf-shaped bifaces do occur and may well go back to 7000 or 8000 B.C., but there is no evidence that they are earlier. Pebble tools are found in assemblages belonging to other cultural traditions, but not with such abundance or regularity. The Pebble Tool tradition centers in the heartland of ethnographic Northwest Coast culture, the protected waterways of the Straits of Georgia and Juan de Fuca, Johnson Strait, Puget Sound, and the lower reaches of coastally flowing rivers teaming with salmon and eulachon.

U. of B.C., Mus. of Anthr., Vancouver: a, 5021; b, 1899; c, 4900; d, 4981; e, 1958; f, 2621; g, 2675; h, 2517.

Fig. 3. Artifacts from the earliest component (6200–3750 B.C.) at the Glenrose Cannery site (DgRr 6), B.C., assignable to the Pebble Tool tradition. a–e, Leaf-shaped bifaces; f, antler point; g, antler wedge; h, pebble tool. Length of a, 4.3 cm.

Various local names are in use for components or regional expressions of the Pebble Tool tradition (fig. 1). The Olcott complex is the conveniently vague term frequently used in western Washington. On the Lower Fraser, the Old Cordilleran component at the Glenrose Cannery site (Matson 1976), and in the Fraser Canyon, the Milliken and Mazama components at the Milliken site (Borden 1968) are included (figs. 3–4). On the Lower Columbia the early component from Cascadia Cave (T.M. Newman 1966) belongs, as does the later portion of the Youngs River complex and the earlier parts of the succeeding Seal Island phase, or at least to an interface with the Stemmed Point tradition. Farther south on the Oregon coast early leaf-shaped points may belong to this tradition. Bear Cove I (C. Carlson 1979a), O'Connor I (Chapman 1982), and beach assemblages from Quatsino Sound (Carlson and Hobler 1976) on northern Vancouver

U. of B.C., Laboratory of Archeol., Vancouver: Dj Ri 7.

Fig. 2. Unifacial pebble choppers of the Pasika complex, South Yale site (Dj Ri 7), Fraser River canyon, B.C. These woodworking tools are characteristic of the Pebble Tool tradition. lower right, 7 cm.

62

Island mark the northern end of the tradition, although some small, undated assemblages (leaf-shaped points lacking) from the Queen Charlotte Islands (Fladmark 1970a; Hobler 1978) constitute the northern aspect of this tradition. At Namu (Carlson 1979; Hester and Nelson 1978) and related Cathedral phase sites (Apland 1982) the early period assemblages after 6500 B.C. may be conceptualized as interfaces with the Microblade tradition.

The Olcott assemblages in western Washington fall in the period after the time of initial settlement (whenever that was) and before the appearance of shell middens or late artifact types (Butler 1961; Kidd 1964; Dancey 1969). Assemblages from both coastal localities such as Birch Bay (Gaston and Grabert 1975) and upriver locations have been found. There seems to be no single site in Washington that is both radiocarbon dated and contains a large sample of material. The best-dated assemblages are from the postmastodon levels of the Manis site, where 16 pebble spalls and a single point were found in contexts dating from about 8000 to 4000 B.C. (Gustafson and Manis 1984). The Olcott material seems to be a pale representation of the same culture known from the larger assemblages of the Milliken and Mazama phases (Borden 1968) and Old Cordilleran component (Matson 1976)

from the sites on the Fraser River just to the north.

The oldest component from the Glenrose Cannery site (Matson 1976, 1981) is the largest and best reported of those included in the Pebble Tool tradition. This site is situated at the edge of the uplands along the south arm of the Fraser River near its mouth. The oldest component dates between 3750 and 6200 B.C. Antler wedges indicating woodworking and one barbed antler point were found in addition to numerous leaf-shaped points, scrapers, pebble tools, and retouched flakes (fig. 3).

The earliest component at the Milliken site, about 100 miles upriver from Glenrose, is a little earlier with radiocarbon dates of 7050 B.C. ±15 (S-113) and 6200 B.C. ±310 (S-47) (Borden 1983:133). This site is in the steep canyon of the Fraser within the stretch of river that contained the main native fishery of the historic Upper Stalo Indians at the upriver end of the Central Coast Salish language distribution (fig. 4). The artifactual assemblage from the earliest component, the Milliken phase (fig. 5), consists of about a dozen leaf-shaped and single-shouldered bifaces, scrapers on thin flakes, burins and pointed flakes, pebble tools, fragments of polished soapstone, an obsidian fragment, and red ocher (Borden 1968:13). Hearths with charcoal and carbonized choke-

Fig. 4. The Milliken site (DjRi 3), B.C. left, Sheer, steep rim of granite that underlies the site and protects geological and archeological deposits from erosion by the Fraser River. Excavations in this sediment trap exposed 14 m of strata, with the earliest cultural complex at 6.5–8 m radiocarbon dated 7050 B.C. ±150 and 6200 B.C. ±130 (Borden 1975:61). right, Excavation carried to the sands holding the earliest cultural deposit, the Milliken phase component. Scattered hearths and charred wild cherry pits in these early levels indicate seasonal occupations exploiting the main runs of spring and sockeye salmon. Photographs by Roy and Maureen Carlson, 1958.

cherry pits suggest occupation in August, the time of the major salmon runs. No other organics were preserved. The succeeding Mazama phase component, separated from the earlier one by a layer of alluvial gravel, consists of a small assemblage with the same main artifact types. It is dated at 5240 to 5400 B.C. (Borden 1983:133). There would have been no reason for living in this steep canyon if it were not for the salmon runs.

The Bear Cove site (C. Carlson 1979a) is on Hardy Bay on the northeast side of Vancouver Island. The oldest component there dates between 6070 B.C. ±110 (WSU 2141) and 2230 B.C. ±90 (WSU 2140) and is contained within an early nonshell matrix underlying a shell midden. The artifacts consist of pebble tools, leaf-shaped bifaces, and flake tools. Numerous fish and sea mammal remains were found only in the upper levels of the earliest stratum. Nearby at the O'Conner site (Chapman 1982), a small

assemblage from the base of the midden is similar and part of the same tradition. Earlier dated samples from northern Vancouver Island sites have been found to contain coal (Capes 1977), which renders the dates far too old. At Namu (Hester and Nelson 1978; Carlson 1979) much the same artifactual assemblage—leaf-shaped bifaces, pebble tools, and scrapers—is present (figs. 6–7) in deposits (fig. 8) with a beginning date of 7770 B.C. ±140 (WAT 452).

Faunal remains have been studied at several sites, but analyses have so far failed to demonstrate clearly that the relative proportions of different species found in any single component or site indicate the relative importance of different subsistence strategies for the culture as a whole. Small sample size and problems of preservation are clear causes of this dilemma, and seasonal occurrence of both resources and human occupation is probably another. Blukis Onat (1984) has addressed this problem for Puget

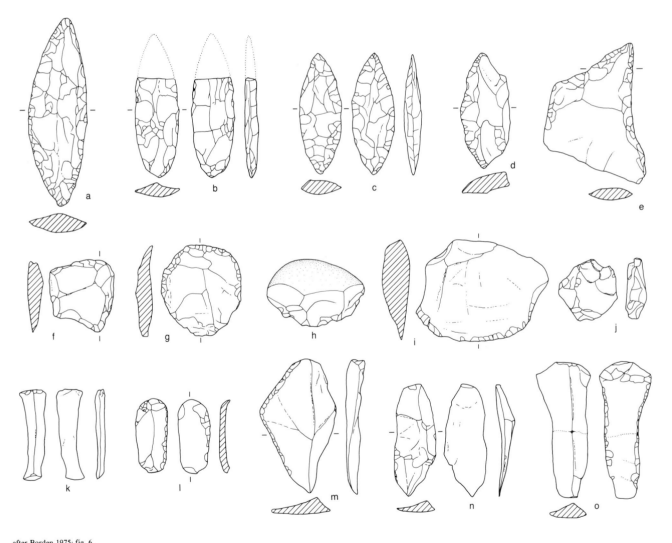

after Borden 1975: fig. 6.

Fig. 5. Milliken phase artifact assemblage, Milliken site (DjRi 3), B.C. a–c, Large, broad, asymmetrically foliate, bifacially flaked knives and laurel-leaf-shaped points. Scrapers include convex-shaped side scrapers on flakes or cortex spalls (d, i), straight- to concave-edged scrapers on bladelike flakes (o), keeled end scrapers (f), blade end scrapers (l), discoidal scrapers (g), angled scrapers (m), and a multi-edged scraper with a stout point that may have been a perforator (e). Bladelike flakes (k, n) are common. One stout angle burin was recovered (j). Hammerstones and anvils, pebble choppers (h), various other unifacially flaked pebble tools, pebble rasps, and utilized flakes fill out this early assemblage. Length of a, 11.5 cm.

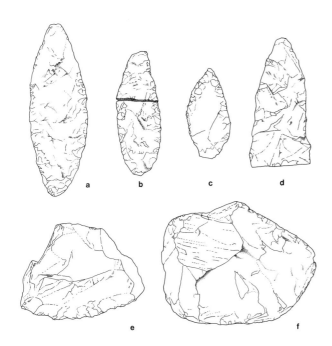

Simon Fraser U., Mus. of Archeol. and Ethnol., Burnaby, B.C.: a, ELSX1: 2096; b, ELSX1: 1262; c, ELSX1: 1780; d, ELSX1: 2082; e, ELSX1: 2121; f, ELSX1: 1996.

Fig. 6. Stone artifacts from Namu, B.C., dating 8000–6000 B.C. a–d, bifaces; e–f, scrapers. Length of a 9.6 cm; others to same scale.

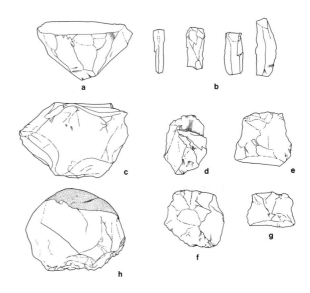

Simon Fraser U., Mus. of Archeol. and Ethnol., Burnaby, B.C.: a, ELSX1: 2189; b, ELSX1: 1937, ELSX1: 2085, ELSX1: 1868, ELSX1: 2191; c, ELSX1: 1754; d, ELSX1: 1375; e, ELSX1: 1869a; f, ELSX1: 1869b; g, ELSX1: 2281; h, ELSX1: 2165.

Fig. 7. Artifacts and debitage from the early component at Namu. a, Blade core; b, blades dating 4500–3000 B.C. c, Flake core; d–g, flakes; h, pebble tool, dating 8000–6000 B.C. Length of striking platform on blade core of a, 9 cm; others to same scale.

Sound sites, and Croes and Hackenberger for the Strait of Georgia.

Cervids (elk and deer) followed by either canids (probably dog) or phocids (mostly seal) dominate all mammalian faunal assemblages except Bear Cove, where 78 percent of the identified mammalian remains are sea mammal, and only 22 percent land mammal. At Bear Cove fish remains are about half as common as mammal bones, and the largest genus represented is rockfish, followed in frequency by small numbers of cod and other species including salmon (C. Carlson 1979a:188). This assemblage is very late in the sequence, probably about 3000 B.C. right at the time of transition to the shell midden period. At Glenrose Cannery (Matson 1976, 1981) salmon bones are abundant, but there are also sturgeon, flounder, eulachon, squawfish, and sticklebacks. Elk bones are common. Bay mussels may also have been very important in the diet.

At Namu (Cannon 1987, 1988) the earliest faunal assemblage belongs to the period between 4500 and 3000 B.C. Mollusk shells first occur at this time. All species found in later deposits at the site are present. The highest proportion of sea mammals occurs in this early period as is the case also at Bear Cove (C. Carlson 1979a). Salmon bones outnumber those of other species but constitute a much lower percentage of the faunal assemblage than in younger periods. At Five Mile Rapids the more than 125,000 salmon bones in the Full Early component outnumber everything else (Cressman et al. 1960). What is important in all these sites is the presence of these bones,

which indicates knowledge of the techniques necessary for taking these species. For the coast as a whole, adaptability and the presence of technology to exploit both marine and terrestrial resources are what should be stressed for this early period.

Relative importance of marine and terrestrial protein in the diet can be determined from stable carbon isotope analyses of human bone (Chisholm 1986). Two early period burials have been analyzed; both are close to 5,000 years in age. The earliest dated burial in the Strait of Georgia region is on Pender Island (DeRt 2, Burial 84-12) at 3220 B.C. ±220, and the earliest at Namu is 3640 B.C. ±100 (ElSx 1, Burial 1.11.B.1). Analysis indicates about 90 percent marine protein in the diet of both individuals. There is no sound reason to believe that the maritime adaptation indicated by this figure does not extend far backward in time to the beginning of human occupation in coastal regions north of the Strait of Juan de Fuca.

Several assemblages from the Queen Charlotte Islands can be grouped in the Pebble Tool tradition. All are small and none is radiometrically dated, but they do occur in circumstances indicating geological antiquity. At Skoglund's Landing on Graham Island a small collection of crude flaked stone artifacts including pebble tools was collected from an ancient raised beach gravel deposit estimated to be older than 7000 B.C. (Fladmark 1979). On Moresby Island several small assemblages of artifacts and flakes recovered from intertidal sites were estimated to date to 8000–6500 B.C., when sea level was lower than at present (Hobler 1978). There are additional isolated finds of pebble tools and large flakes from other sites in the

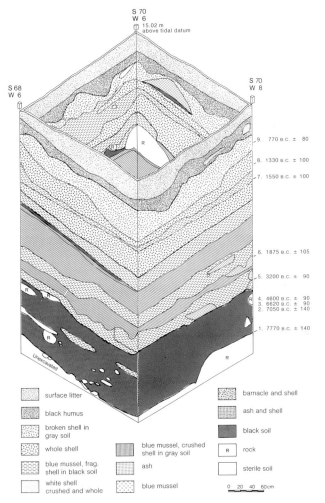

surface litter

black humus

broken shell in
gray soil

whole shell

blue mussel, frag.
shell in black soil

white shell
crushed and whole

barnacle and shell

ash and shell

black soil

blue mussel, crushed
shell in gray soil

ash

rock

sterile soil

blue mussel

0 20 40 60cm

S 70
W 6
15.02 m
above tidal datum

S 68
W 6

S 70
W 8

9. 770 B.C. ± 80

8. 1330 B.C. ± 100

7. 1550 B.C. ± 100

6. 1875 B.C. ± 105

5. 3200 B.C. ± 90

4. 4600 B.C. ± 90
3. 6620 B.C. ± 90
2. 7050 B.C. ± 140

1. 7770 B.C. ± 140

Unexcavated

Fig. 8. Excavations at Namu, B.C. top, Deep stratigraphic section in unit 68-70 S, 6-8 W. At bottom, a one-meter thick, black nonshell deposit held the early period remains, succeeded by 3 meters of shell midden. Photograph by Roy L. Carlson, 1979. bottom, Stratigraphic wall profiles for unit 68-70 S, 6-8 W. The sequence extends from 7770 B.C. ±140 to 770 B.C. ±80, the date of the last cultural deposit below the humus layer. Stratum 1 is sterile glacial till. Stratum 2 contains the early period materials seen in the top photograph as a black basal deposit. Shellfish remains first appear 4500–3000 B.C. Drawing by Barbara Hodgson.

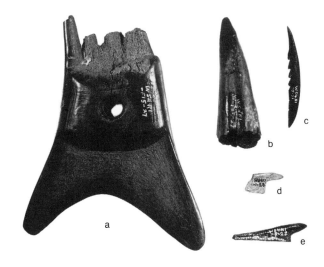

U. of Oreg., Oreg. State Mus. of Anthr., Eugene: a, WS4R1-F15-27; b, WS4R1-F13-37; c, WS4R1-4-5-31; d, Ws4R1-6-1-28; e, WS4R1-3-9-22.

Fig. 9. Bone and antler artifacts from the Full Early component at Five Mile Rapids, The Dalles, Oreg. a, Carved antler comb; b, antler-tine flaker; c, unilaterally barbed point for fishing gear; d–e, atlatl spurs. Similar artifacts were probably used throughout the Northwest Coast culture area around 6000 B.C. but have not been found because of poor preservation. Length of a 11.5 cm; others to same scale.

Queen Charlottes. Foliate bifaces are absent in all these assemblages.

At Five Mile Rapids on the Columbia (Cressman et al. 1960) the Full Early component seems to be an interface between the Pebble Tool tradition and the Stemmed Point tradition. It is from this component that there is the best evidence for both heavy salmon utilization and the presence of an extensive bone and antler industry (fig. 9). Atlatl hooks, wedges, small barbed leister parts, red ocher, and girdled bola stones or fish weights are found. This component dates to about 6000 B.C.

Overall, the distribution of the Pebble Tool tradition, the location of sites at major fisheries on both the Fraser and Columbia rivers, and site locations such as Bear Cove and Namu, which presuppose advanced water transport, suggest that fishing and sea mammal hunting played an important role in this culture at the very beginning. The Pebble Tool tradition was not an unspecialized cordilleran hunting and gathering culture that later adapted to marine resources (cf. Butler 1961; Matson 1976); it was originally a coastal culture that spread up the rivers and into the mountains and the interior. The pursuit of salmon was probably the moving force in this expansion as these anadromous fish spread to spawning grounds farther and farther up the rivers as part of the postglacial environmental adjustments.

A prototype for the Pebble Tool tradition should have pebble tools, leaf-shaped bifaces, be marine adapted, and lack microblade technology. This tradition may be a continuation of a pattern of adaptation to coastal and downriver resources such as has been proposed for the Aleut (Laughlin 1963; C.G. Turner 1984). If such is the case the antecedents are in Beringia, probably underwater, and comparisons must be made in Northeast Asia. The closest Asian parallel is probably Ushki VI in Kamchatka (Dikov 1979) with its salmon, leaf-shaped bifaces, riverine location, and radiocarbon dates of 10,000–9000 B.C., although weakly developed microblade technology is present. Across from Kamchatka on the northwest coast of the Sea of Okhotsk is a poorly known variant of the late Paleolithic Diuktai culture that has bifaces and lacks wedge-shaped microblade cores (Mochanov 1984:717). It is in this cultural milieu, around Kamchatka and the Sea of Okhotsk, that the antecedents of the Pebble Tool tradition may be found.

In later derivatives of the Pebble Tool tradition either contracting stemmed points or microblade technology or both are added to the cultural inventory. Undated sites on the Somass River on Vancouver Island (McMillan and St. Claire 1982) and at Coquitlam Lake (M. Wright 1988) have yielded such assemblages, which probably date between 5000 and 3000 B.C. Along the Fraser from Esilao Village near Yale to at least Helen Point in the Gulf Islands are a series of sites with cultural components referred to variously as the Charles, Mayne, St. Mungo, or Eayem phase or culture type, which begin before 3500 B.C. and persisted to about 1500 B.C. The changes in lithic technology, the appearance of large shell middens, and the appearance of ground stone woodworking tools, ground slate points and knives, art and sculpture, and labret use all begin in the late part of this period. By 1500 B.C. certain ritual and ceremonial aspects of ethnographic Northwest Coast culture—including masks and the memorial potlatch—are recognizable in the archeological record of the Strait of Georgia region (Carlson 1987). The record also indicates transition and continuity from the Pebble Tool tradition into these later phases and suggests that the bearers of the Pebble Tool tradition there were the ancestors of the Coast Salish.

The Microblade Tradition

Microblade technology offers a different solution to the problem of making stone cutting and piercing tools, a problem resolved in the other traditions by flaking bifacial projectile points and knives. In sites of the Microblade tradition small, parallel-sided blades and the cores from which they were struck are found. Segments of these blades were presumably inset into wooden hafts and points to form the cutting edges of cutting and piercing implements. Northwestern North America is at the forward edge of the distribution of this practice, which spread across northern Asia in the late Pleistocene. Between 8000 and 6000 B.C. the northern Northwest Coast was colonized by peoples bearing a marine-oriented, microblade-using culture.

Microblade technology is progressively more recent as

one moves south along the Northwest Coast (Borden 1969: fig. 1; Carlson 1983c; Mochanov 1984). This technology reached southwest Washington by 5000 B.C. (Daugherty, Flenniken, and Welch 1987). The earliest microblade sites on the Northwest Coast share a common feature, which is that human access and survival could only have been attained with superior water transport and knowledge of marine subsistence.

The earliest dated sites on the northern Northwest Coast all contain microblade technology that persists throughout the first 5,000 years of known prehistory in this region. In the Alaska panhandle are three sites—Ground Hog Bay 2 (Ackerman, Hamilton, and Stuckenrath 1979), Hidden Falls, and Locality 1 at Chuck Lake on Heceta Island (Ackerman et al. 1985). Ground Hog Bay 2 is situated high on a marine terrace, 10–15 meters above beach level. Its oldest component, dated between 8230 B.C. ±800 (WSU-412) and 7180 B.C. ±130 (I-6304), contains only two biface fragments, three flakes, and a water-rolled chert scraper (Ackerman 1974:3). The succeeding component, dated between 6930 B.C. ±125 (I-7057) and 2205 B.C. ±95 (I-7056) contains microcores of various types, microblades showing end and side use, macrocores, flakes, choppers, biface fragments, and waste flakes. Hidden Falls on Baranof Island has one date at the base of the microblade-bearing layer, 7110 B.C. ±230. Scrapers, pebble tools, and engraving tools are present in the small assemblage; there are no bifaces. At Chuck Lake a shell midden is associated with the microblade industry radiocarbon dated to 6200 B.C.

In the Queen Charlotte Islands microblade assemblages are known from two excavated sites, Lawn Point and Kasta (Fladmark 1988), from several beach finds (Hobler 1978), and from an inland midden on Graham Island (Ham 1988). At Lawn Point where the site is on an old marine terrace well above high tide, charcoal from two small hearth areas was dated to 5100 B.C. ±110 (Gak 3272) and 5450 B.C. ±140 (S-679). An underlying cultural level remains undated, but a younger one has a single date of 3800 B.C. ±110 (Gak 3271). Kasta yielded dates of 4060 B.C. ±95 (S-677) and 3470 B.C. ±100 (Gak 3511). Flakes, core fragments, hammerstones, microcores, and numerous microblades all made of chert and cherty argillite constitute the total assemblage. These microblade assemblages are named the Moresby tradition.

The earliest assemblage known from the Skeena Valley, the Bornite phase component at the Paul Mason site in Kitselas Canyon, lacks bifaces and is dominated by both pebble tools and microblades (Coupland 1985). It is dated at 3100 B.C. ±140.

At about 6000 B.C. microblade technology appears in the stratigraphic record at Namu and continues along with the earlier tool types until 3000 B.C. A few bone artifacts—barbs for composite fishhooks, and small unilaterally barbed harpoon heads—have also been preserved from the period between 4500 and 3000 B.C. and attest to the presence of fishing and sea mammal hunting.

On the Northwest Coast the distribution of microblade technology before 5000 B.C., except for Namu, is limited to that area occupied ethnographically by the Tlingit and Haida. Aleut, Eskimo, and Athapaskan territories in Alaska were also the homes of early microblade users, and the Microblade tradition may represent the ancestors of all these peoples. Between 5000 and 3000 B.C. microblade technology spread farther south, and assemblages of that time period from the southern coast of British Columbia contain both microblades and leaf-shaped and stemmed bifaces (fig. 10). At Layser Cave and the Judd Peak Rockshelters (Daugherty, Flenniken, and Welch 1987, 1987a) in southwest Washington microblades and cores occur as early as 4500 B.C. as part of the tool kit of early hunters who also used both leaf-shaped and large stemmed and side-notched points. The latter type indicates influence from the adjacent Columbia plateau, whereas the presence of microblades indicates influence from the north.

Borden (1975), Dumond (1969, 1974), and Carlson (1979) have suggested an association between microblades and the proposed but controversial Na-Dene language phylum and attributed their spread to the southward movement of Athapaskan speakers. If Tlingit and Eyak-Athapaskan prove to be related, the antiquity of this grouping might correspond to the separation of coast and interior microblade traditions in the north. However, the probable date of the movement that took the Athapaskan languages to the southern Northwest Coast (between 500 B.C. and A.D. 500) is much too late to account for microblades there (vol. 6:67–68).

While it is clear that microblade technology is Old World in origin, it is equally clear that it was adopted and used by many peoples as cultures diverged and expanded in time and space. There is no one-to-one correspondence between any of the microblade-using cultures to the north with the Microblade tradition of the Northwest Coast. This is not unusual in view of the nature of archeological sampling and the multiple variables affecting the content of archeological assemblages.

Summary

Early prehistoric remains on the Northwest Coast consist of assemblages of stone tools and lithic detritus that exhibit both typological distinctiveness and geographical patterning sufficient to indicate that the Northwest Coast was colonized following the retreat of ice of the last glaciation by peoples with diverse cultural backgrounds bearing at least four cultural traditions: the Fluted Point tradition, the Stemmed Point tradition, the Pebble Tool tradition, and the Microblade tradition.

These early cultures reached the Northwest Coast by two different routes at slightly different times. The Fluted Point and Stemmed Point traditions both spread down the Columbia River from interior North America between 9000 and 8000 B.C. They were probably derived from interior hunting cultures of Beringia that expanded south during the retreat of the last Wisconsinan glaciation, and their bearers are closely related historically to the Paleo-Indian peoples of the rest of North and South America. The other two traditions, which are not in evidence until 8000 to 7000 B.C., seem to have spread down the coast and up the river valleys. They may have been derived from earlier cultures occupying the coastal fringes and river valleys of Beringia, and their bearers are probably less closely related to the Paleo-Indian peoples of the remainder of the New World.

The pattern of external similarities of early Northwest Coast cultures resembles the overall pattern of relationships in human biology deduced by C.G. Turner (1983, 1984) from a comparative study of selected dental attributes of New World and Asian populations. In this study the greater Northwest Indian group (Northwest

a   b   c   d   e   f   g   h   i

Alberni Valley Mus., Port Alberni, B.C.: a–b, d–i, DhSf 32; c, DhSf 31.
Fig. 10. Microblades and microblade cores from Somass River sites, southern Vancouver I., B.C. Assemblages with both leaf-shaped points and microblades from southern Vancouver I. are estimated to date 5000–3000 B.C. a–c, microblade cores; d–i, microblades. Height of a 3 cm; others to same scale.

Coast plus all Athapaskan speakers) is intermediate in frequencies of these traits between Eskimo-Aleut on the one hand and all other New World Indians (including Paleo-Indians) on the other. While C.G. Turner (1984:65) prefers a model of biological hybridization in Siberia and subsequent migration to the New World of three groups bearing the gene frequencies for these dental traits, archeology would suggest that the equivalent cultural process, acculturation, was taking place on the Northwest Coast between interior American cultures (Fluted Point and Stemmed Point traditions) and those derived perhaps slightly later from coastal and riverine portions of Beringia (Pebble Tool and Microblade traditions). Between 8000 and 3000 B.C. differences among these early period cultures were being leveled through the processes of adaptation, population growth, and acculturation, bringing about greater similarity throughout the area.

The abundant and diverse flaked stone tool industries typical of the archeology of the pre-3000 B.C. period look quite different from the pecked and ground stone tools and other artifactual remains found in later prehistoric and early historic periods. Could these flaked stone tools have been used for many of the same purposes as the artifacts of later periods? It seems probable that the large core scrapers and pebble tools are woodworking implements, that this industry was widespread on the coast before 3000 B.C., and that the later ground stone chisels and adz blades were simply improvements that began a millennium later. Poor preservation of bone probably accounts for the early period scarcity of fishing and sea hunting implements, which are abundant in sites after 3000 B.C. Mere glimpses of these technologies are provided by the few surviving examples from Namu and Five Mile Rapids.

Distributional correlations noted between some of the early cultural traditions and the language groupings of the historic period suggest that these early cultural traditions were borne by the ancestors of the historic peoples and that there has been long continuity and in-place development of culture. The distribution of Coast Salish and to some extent Wakashan (early period remains are unknown in Nootkan territory) correlates with the early distribution of the Pebble Tool tradition. Assemblages of the Stemmed Point tradition are the most widespread cultural remains found in the areas occupied by historic Chinookan speakers and linguistically distantly related Sahaptian speakers. Microblade technology is typical of the early northern Northwest Coast and the adjacent Subarctic, regions occupied historically by speakers of Haida, Tlingit, and Eyak-Athapaskan languages, which make up the proposed Na-Dene linguistic phylum. Microblade technology seems to have been originally northeast Asian, then Alaskan and Yukon, and only finally Northwest Coast. Was it migration borne? If so, it could mark the separation of ancestral Haida, Tlingit, and Eyak-Athapaskan speakers.

The unknown factors in the early period of Northwest Coast prehistory are still considerable. Many are factors of culture content. What were the religious beliefs, clothing, houses, canoe types and other aspects of culture? What is the early prehistory in the Tsimshian and Nootkan regions? Is the scarcity of shellfish remains before 3000 B.C. the result of land and sea level changes that have destroyed the middens, or was a different subsistence system employed? How were fish and sea mammals actually taken at this time? What food storage and preservation techniques were known and used? In spite of the absence of substantive evidence for these particular factors much before 3000 B.C., it is clear that the early migrants to the Northwest Coast achieved a successful adaptation to the wealth of environmental resources and established a basis for the later development of a level of cultural achievement rarely found among food collecting peoples the world over.

History of Research: Early Sources

WAYNE SUTTLES*

Contact and Exploration

The date of the first European contact with Northwest Coast Indians is uncertain. The alleged discovery in 1592 by Juan de Fuca of the strait that now bears his name probably never happened (Wagner 1931; cf. W.L. Cook 1973:22–29). However, there is evidence for the wreck of a Manila galleon on the northern Oregon coast, possibly the *San Francisco Xavier*, lost in 1707, and for survivors of this or other wrecks who left descendants among the Tillamook and Chinook (W.L. Cook 1973:31–40).

The earliest recorded exploration of the region is that of Vitus Bering's second expedition for Russia in 1741 ("History of the Early Period," fig. 1, this vol.), during which Aleksei I. Chirikov lost two manned boats, possibly to hostile Tlingits, and Georg W. Steller (1988) visited a Native camp, possibly Eyak. This expedition discovered the sea otter and subsequently its value to the Chinese market, and the discovery led to the invasion of the Aleutian Islands by fur traders. During the next two decades the Russians expanded eastward and in the 1780s made contact with the Eyak and Tlingit.

News of the Russian expansion moved the Spanish to explore north of California. In 1774 Juan Pérez Hernández got as far as the vicinity of Dixon Entrance, making contact there with the Tlingit and Haida and, returning south, with the Nootka. In 1775 Bruno de Hezeta landed near Point Grenville, Washington, the first recorded European landing on the Northwest Coast. After losing men to hostile Quinault, he turned south and discovered the mouth of the Columbia River but was unable to enter it. Juan Francisco de la Bodega y Quadra, in a second ship, went on to southeastern Alaska. In 1779 an expedition led by Ignacio Arteaga spent a month at Bucareli Bay in southeastern Alaska.

British exploration began in 1778, when James Cook, on his third voyage of discovery, anchored for nearly a month in Nootka Sound and went on to the Gulf of Alaska. Cook's men, like Bering's, discovered the value of sea otter pelts on the Chinese market, and this time the news traveled internationally, with the result that mer-

chant ships of several nations soon entered the region in large numbers (vol. 4:380).

In 1786 a French expedition under Jean-François Galaup de LaPérouse visited the northern coast, spending some time at Lituya Bay.

After learning of the British and French expeditions and the development of the maritime fur trade, the Spaniards again became active. In 1788 Estéban José Martínez and Gonzalo López de Haro investigated the Russian expansion in the north, and in 1789 Martinez established a base on Vancouver Island at Nootka Sound. After trouble with British fur traders, Martínez abandoned the base, but it was soon reoccupied by Francisco de Eliza y Reventa and made the center of further exploration. In 1790 Salvador Fidalgo went north, where he met the Russians, still in Eskimo country, while Manuel Quimper went south to the entrance of the Strait of Juan de Fuca. In 1791 Eliza explored the Strait of Juan de Fuca and the southern end of the Strait of Georgia, and in that year the Spanish scientific expedition under Alejandro Malaspina reached the region, spending a few days at Port Mulgrave on Yakutat Bay.

The exploration of the inner coast, from Puget Sound to Lynn Canal, was essentially completed in 1792 and 1793 by the British expedition under George Vancouver and by the Spanish explorers Jacinto Caamaño, Dionisio Alcalá Galiano, and Cayento Valdés.

The first Americans in the region were the Boston traders John Kendrick and Robert Gray. In 1792 Gray rediscovered the mouth of the Columbia and was the first to enter its estuary.

In 1794 Spain and Britain concluded an agreement giving both countries equal rights in trade at Nootka Sound and neither the right to a base, and in 1795 Spanish activity north of California ceased.

In the north, Russian expansion culminated in the founding, by Aleksandr A. Baranov, of the Russian-American Company's fort at Sitka in 1799. The Tlingit destroyed the fort in 1802, but Baranov recaptured the site in 1804 with the help of a Russian naval vessel, commanded by IUriĭ Lisi͡anskiĭ, on the first of a series of Russian round-the-world expeditions. The fort was rebuilt as Novo-Arkhangel'sk, the first permanent European base on the Northwest Coast and the center of Russian activity

*This chapter was written using material prepared by Julia Averkieva, Erna Gunther, Douglas Cole, and Cesare Marino.

until the American purchase of Alaska in 1867.

The first approach to the Northwest Coast by land, and the first crossing of North America north of Mexico, occurred in 1792, when Alexander Mackenzie of the Montreal-based North West Company descended the Bella Coola River to the sea. The second crossing was that of the American expedition of Meriwether Lewis and William Clark, who descended the Columbia River in 1805, built winter quarters, Fort Clatsop, near the mouth of the Columbia, and went back across the continent in 1806. The third arrival by land was that of the North West Company fur trader Simon Fraser, who in 1808 descended the river later named for him.

In 1811 John Jacob Astor's American Fur Company arrived by sea and founded Fort Astoria in the estuary of the Columbia River. Later that year David Thompson of the North West Company arrived from the interior. In 1813 Fort Astoria was acquired by the North West Company and became Fort George. In 1821 the North West Company was obliged to unite with the Hudson's Bay Company, which then had a near monopoly of authority between the Russians in Alaska and the Spaniards in California.

Hudson's Bay Company authority was ended south of 49° north latitude in 1846 after the Treaty of Washington established the international boundary, but it persisted in British Columbia until the organization of colonial government in the 1850s.

Sources

Most of the explorers and many of the traders and missionaries left records of their observations. Few of the early observers were scholars, and very few learned more than a few words of an Indian language. Their observations vary in quality from excellent to nearly useless and must be examined critically and evaluated within the context of their authors and their time. Gunther (1972) reviews the ethnographic value of many of the eighteenth-century accounts. Henry (1984) surveys and reproduces works of the early artists. Wagner (1937) is indispensable for identifying place-names used by the early explorers. Strathern's (1970) annotated bibliography of works on exploration and early history includes Washington and Oregon as well as British Columbia.

Russian America

Polansky (1987) reviews the published sources on Russian America, including bibliographies, and R.A. Pierce (1987) reviews archival material outside the Soviet Union. R.A. Pierce (1972-) offers English translations of works previously available only in Russian and German. Other monographic series of translations from Russian sources include those of the Arctic Institute of North America

(1961–1974), the Oregon Historical Society (1972-), and the University of Alaska, Elmer E. Rasmuson Library (1985-). Useful reference works are M.W. Falk (1983, 1989) on cartography, Tebenkov's (1981) atlas, Ivashintsov's (1980) compilation of the Russian voyages, Wertsman's (1977) chronology and fact book, Carnahan's (1976) biographical sketches of authors, and R.A. Pierce's (1989) biographical dictionary. J.R. Gibson (1976) demonstrates the value of the Russian sources, and Black (1989) reviews the growing field of Russian-American studies. Modern Soviet contributions to the field are found in the journal *Sovietskaya Étnografiia*.

Useful ethnographic information was recorded by the round-the-world voyagers Lisiânskiĭ (1814), Georg H. von Langsdorf (1813–1814), Otto von Kotzebue (1967), Fëdor P. Litke (1987), and Vasiliĭ M. Golovnin (1979). With Golovnin was the artist Mikhail Tikhanov, whose works include portraits of Tlingits ("History of the Early Period," fig. 10, this vol.) (Shur and Pierce 1976; some reproductions in Fitzhugh and Crowell 1988). The scientist Ilia G. Voznesenskii (Alekseev 1987), who spent time in Russian America in the 1840s, made important collections (Lipshits 1950) and drawings (Blomkvist 1972; R.A. Pierce 1975). Other valuable ethnographic data were recorded by Ferdinand P. Wrangell (1980) and Kirill T. Khlebnikov (1976). Quite exceptional is Ivan E. Veniaminov's (1984) ethnographic work on the Tlingit, based on several years' service as a missionary and research on the Tlingit language. Exceptional in areal reference is Timofei Tarakanov's account (Owens 1985) of the experience of the survivors of the wrecked *Sv. Nikolai* among the Quileute and Makah in 1808–1810.

Spaniards

Gormly (1977) gives an evaluation of eighteenth-century Spanish sources on Northwest Coast Indians and an annotated bibliography. W.L. Cook (1973) is a full account of Spanish exploration with a bibliography listing both published and manuscript materials (see also Rey-Tejerina 1988). Officers of Spanish expeditions delivered their journals and log books to the viceroy of Mexico. Copies were made for the archives there and the originals were sent to Spain. The major manuscript repositories are the Archivo General de la Nación, Mexico City; the Archivo General de Indias, Seville; the Archivo Histórico National, Madrid; the Biblioteca de Palacio, Madrid; the Museo Naval, Madrid; and for visual material, the Museo de América, Madrid. The most important published work is an ethnography of the Nootka written in 1792 by José Marino Moziño (1970). The work of the artists Tomás de Suría, José Cardero, and Anastasio Echeverria, who were on the Malaspina expedition, is described and illustrated by Cutter (1963), Cutter and Palau (1977), Palau (1984), and Sotos (1982). Palau (1988) contains some excellent reproductions.

British

The account of Cook's third voyage prepared by his successor as commander of the expedition and edited by John Douglas (Cook 1784) has been superseded by Beaglehole (1967). Despite the prohibition of unofficial journals, four members of Cook's expedition (Ledyard 1964; Ellis 1782; Rickman 1781; Zimmermann 1930) published accounts, none of which is very good. The drawings of the artist John Webber, who accompanied Cook, are scattered; most are in the British Museum and the British Library, London; the Peabody Museum of Archaeology and Ethnology, Harvard University; and the Dixon Library, Sydney, Australia. A catalog of the complete graphic record of the Cook voyages was prepared by Joppien and Smith (1988).

Vancouver's account of his voyage, edited by his brother (Vancouver 1801), has been superseded by Lamb (1984). Portions of the journals of other members of the expedition include that of Archibald Menzies (1923) and Peter Puget (Anderson 1939).

French

The LaPérouse expedition was lost in the South Pacific in 1788 or 1789, but LaPérouse had sent journals and graphic records to Paris from Kamchatka and Australia (Inglis 1986), ensuring the publication of his work (LaPérouse 1797, 1798a; Dunmore and de Brossard 1985.) In 1791 the French trader Étienne Marchand visited the Queen Charlotte Islands and Sitka Sound (Fleurieu 1801).

Maritime Fur Traders

Howay (1973) gives a chronological list of trading vessels, to which Richard Pierce has added, in this edition, bibliographical and archival information. Among the more important for ethnographic content are the accounts of John Meares (1790), who was at Nootka Sound in the late 1780s; Robert Haswell, John Hoskins, and John Boit (Howay 1941), who were with Gray in the late 1780s and early 1780s; Charles Bishop (1967), who got acquainted with the Chinook a decade before Lewis and Clark; Alexander Walker (Fisher and Bumsted 1982), which includes an interview with John Mackay, who had been left at Nootka Sound for a year in the 1780s; and John R. Jewitt (1967), who was held captive at Nootka Sound from 1803 to 1805. Drawings of artists with the fur traders include those of Sigismund Bacstrom ("History of the Early Period," fig. 2, this vol.) (Cole 1980) and George Davidson, some of which are reproduced in Vaughan and Holm (1982).

Inland Explorers and Fur Traders

Mackenzie's journal (1801) gives a brief but valuable account of the Bella Coola. The journals of Lewis and Clark (Thwaites 1904–1905) contain a great deal of interest on the Chinookans and their neighbors. The letters of Lewis and Clark are edited by Jackson (1978) and the maps by Moulton (1983). Other members of the expedition who left journals are Patrick Gass (1958) and John Ordway (Quaife 1916). Fraser's journal (Lamb 1960) gives the earliest view of the Coast Salish of the lower Fraser River.

Accounts of Astorians and North West Company men on the lower Columbia River include those of Gabriel Franchère (1969), Alexander Henry (Coues 1897), Ross Cox (1957), Alexander Ross (1849), and David Thompson (Glover 1962). Irving (1951) is based on some of these and other, unidentified sources. The journal of the botanist David Douglas (1914) has information on western Oregon.

Several Hudson's Bay Company men left journals containing information on the Indian peoples of the 1820s to 1840s. They include John Work (1945a), John Scouler (1905), William Fraser Tolmie (1963), and George Simpson (Merk 1968; Simpson 1931, 1847). Material from John McLoughlin, chief factor at Forts George and Vancouver throughout the period, has been edited by E.E. Rich (1941, 1943, 1944). Much manuscript material relating to the company's activities on the coast remains unpublished. Some is in the British Columbia Archives and Records Service, Victoria, but the great repository is the Hudson's Bay Company Archives in Winnipeg, Manitoba. Microfilms of its records for this period are available at the Public Archives of Canada and the Public Records Office, Ottawa.

Records of missionaries associated with the Hudson's Bay Company include the letters of the Rev. Herbert Beaver (1959) and the letters of Fathers Modeste Demers and François N. Blanchet and others, originally published in Quebec and translated by Landerholm (1956), unfortunately without clear indication as to their exact source. Loewenberg (1976) gives sources on the mission of Jason Lee.

History of Research in Ethnology

WAYNE SUTTLES AND ALDONA JONAITIS

The history of ethnological research on the Northwest Coast seems best defined in relation to the work of its dominant figure, Franz Boas, who first went to the region in 1886, returned a number of times, and continued to work on Northwest Coast materials until his death in 1942. Meanwhile, he virtually defined the discipline of anthropology in North America, taught the majority of the anthropologists who came to occupy the first academic positions on this continent, and wielded considerable influence beyond anthropology.

Pre-Boasian Research, 1841–1886

With a few exceptions, such as José Mariano Moziño (1970) and Ivan E.P. Veniaminov (1984), the early accounts were essentially by-products of explorations and the fur trade. Professional ethnology began with Horatio Hale, philologist and ethnologist with the United States Exploring Expedition under Charles Wilkes, which visited the region from the Strait of Juan de Fuca southward in 1841. Wilkes's official narrative (1845) and diary (Meany 1925–1926) tell something of the condition of the Native peoples, especially Coast Salish and Chinookans. Hale collected, directly from Native speakers and from missionaries and other non-Indians, examples of a number of Native languages and Chinook Jargon and began a classification of languages and peoples (Hale 1846: 197–225; Gallatin 1848). Forty years later Hale directed some of Boas's early work and may have had an important influence on the development of Boas's theoretical orientation (Gruber 1967; Cole 1973).

In 1846–1847 the central coast was visited by the Canadian painter Paul Kane, whose writings (1857, 1859; Vaughan 1971) and sketches and paintings (Harper 1971) uniquely record features of Chinookan and Coast Salish life.

Some of the Hudson's Bay Company men, like William F. Tolmie, had already lived many years on the coast. Longer residence by Americans began with George Gibbs and James G. Swan (fig. 1). Gibbs was in the region from 1849 to 1860 (Beckham 1969), occupying various official positions including assisting Gov. Isaac I. Stevens of Washington Territory in negotiating treaties. His principal published ethnographic works are a report (1855) on the Indians of Washington Territory, a fuller account (1877) of the tribes of western Washington and northwestern Oregon, and a work (Clark 1955–1956) on the mythology and religion of the tribes of Washington and Oregon. (For Gibbs's work on the native languages, see "History of Research in Linguistics," this vol.)

Swan arrived in 1852 and, except for brief trips east, stayed in western Washington until his death in 1900. His popular book (Swan 1857) describing his life as an oyster farmer contains a good deal on the mixed Chinook-Chehalis people of Willapa Bay. He drew on his experiences as a teacher on the Makah Reservation to write a monograph on the Makah (Swan 1870), the first on a single Northwest Coast people. He wrote one short piece on the Haida (Swan 1876) based on work with Haida visitors at Port Townsend, Washington, before he went to the Queen Charlotte Islands as a collector. Short articles originally published in newspapers form another book (Swan 1971). His unpublished journals (in the University of Washington Archives, Seattle) have been drawn on by others (L. McDonald 1972; Doig 1980).

In British Columbia, Charles Wilson, employed by the International Boundary Commission, published (1866) on some of the Central Coast Salish; his journal (1970) has additional material. John Keast Lord (1866), a naturalist on the Boundary Commission, published information obtained from Tolmie as well as observations of his own. Gilbert Sproat established a settlement at Alberni in 1860 (Rickard 1937) and published an article (Sproat 1867) on the Nootkans of the region and a book (Sproat 1868) on his experiences. Robert Brown, a geographer and botanist and leader in 1864 of the first party to explore the interior of Vancouver Island, described (Brown 1868) the native use of plants in western North America, including some data from southeastern Vancouver Island. His compendium of world ethnography (Brown 1873–1876, 1:20–152) was sensationalized with irrelevant illustrations; nevertheless, it included a good deal of information on northwestern North America, mainly on the Coast Salish of Vancouver Island and the Alberni Nootka.

In 1850–1851, Finnish naturalist H.J. Holmberg collected information on the Tlingit for an ethnographic sketch (Holmberg 1985).

An American naturalist, William Healey Dall, was in

Alaska in 1865–1868 and published a general work on the region (1870), a work on tribal distribution and nomenclature (1877), and a study of masks and labrets (1884), all of which include some material on the Tlingit.

During the 1850s and 1860s several travelers wrote accounts containing some useful information—Mayne (1862) and Whymper (1868) in British Columbia, and Winthrop (1913) in Washington. Drawings by James Madison Alden (Stenzel 1975) made in the 1850s show Central Coast Salish houses and grave posts.

In late 1870s, the Canadian geologist George M. Dawson added anthropological observations to his geological work in British Columbia. His accounts of the Haida (Dawson 1880a) and of the Kwakiutl (Dawson 1888) are the first full accounts of these peoples. Dawson knew the natural setting, especially that of the Haida, probably better than any anthropologist for the next century, and, unlike many who followed, he did not ignore the historical record. His early death may have cut short the development of a Canadian school of anthropology (Cole 1973; Van West 1976).

In western Washington, from the 1870s to the end of the century, the most prolific writer on the Native people was the Congregational missionary Myron Eells. In 1874 he established a mission on the Skokomish Reservation and in 1875 received an ethnographic questionnaire drawn up by Otis T. Mason. Eells (1877) responded in detail, describing current practices as well as ones only remembered and noting which items were absent. He revised and expanded this work to include materials on other tribes in the region, but his data are best for the Twana and Clallam. Portions of the revision were published as a series of journal articles, and much of it as a monograph (Eells 1889), but an unabridged version did not appear until later (Eells 1985).

In 1877, John Wesley Powell of the U.S. Geographical and Geological Survey sent a philologist, Albert S. Gatschet, to Oregon. At Grand Ronde Reservation Gatschet collected linguistic and ethnographic material, especially Tualatin Kalapuya data, later reworked by Melville Jacobs (1945). Gatschet joined Powell at the Bureau of American Ethnology, organized under Powell's direction in 1879. In 1884 Powell sent the Rev. James Owen Dorsey to western Oregon to collect linguistic and other information on the tribes on the Siletz Reservation (Dorsey 1889, 1890).

In southeastern Alaska, the German geographer Aurel Krause spent the winter of 1881–1882 in the Tlingit village of Chilkat and published a fairly full account (1885, 1956). In 1882, George Thornton Emmons (fig. 1) an officer in the U.S. Navy, was stationed in Tlingit territory. Emmons developed an interest in the Tlingit that endured for a half-century and resulted in a number of publications on art and technology (Emmons 1903, 1907, 1914a, 1916, 1930, among others). He was impor-

tant as a collector (Low 1977) and as an advisor to President Theodore Roosevelt on the welfare of Alaska Natives (Conrad 1978). In 1882 another naval officer, Albert Parker Niblack, was sent to study collections in the U.S. National Museum and then to investigate the Indians of southeastern Alaska in the summers of 1885, 1886, and 1887; his survey (Niblack 1890) remains an important source on technology.

In 1881, Johan Adrian Jacobsen arrived on the Northwest Coast, collecting artifacts for an ethnological museum in Berlin. A narrative of Jacobsen's experiences soon appeared (Jacobsen 1884, 1977). In 1885 he returned to the Northwest Coast and with the aid of his brother Fillip, who was then living at Bella Coola, he enlisted a group of Bella Coola Indians to go to Germany to perform in an ethnic exhibition (Cole 1982a). Studying Jacobsen's collection in Berlin and meeting the Bella Coola moved Franz Boas to undertake a trip to the Northwest Coast in 1886. The Jacobsens published on the winter dances (Jacobsen 1891; F. Jacobsen 1895).

Overlapping with Boas temporally but uninfluenced by his work were several missionaries who wrote on the peoples they served among. The Russian Orthodox Archimandrite Anatolii Kamenskiĭ as at Sitka from 1895 to 1898 and published a fairly full account of the Tlingit (1985). The Anglican Rev. William H. Collison (1915) started work with the Haida in 1876. Others include Thomas Crosby (1907, 1914), Charles Harrison (1925), and L.F. Jones (1914).

Boasian Anthropology, 1886–1942

From his earliest fieldwork, Boas collected myths in Chinook Jargon and in the Indian languages, later getting them in written form from literate Native speakers. He used texts in the Indian languages as data for the analysis of the languages as well as for the understanding of the cultures, and some of his students followed him in this. For this period the history of ethnology is intimately related to the history of linguistics (see "History of Research in Linguistics," this vol.).

Boas and Coworkers

In 1886, on his first trip to the Northwest Coast, Boas spent two weeks in the isolated Kwakiutl village of Nahwitti, where he witnessed and participated in potlatching. During his three months in British Columbia, Boas also elicited ethnographic information and myths from Tsimshian, Bella Coola, and other Indians in Victoria, visited Northern and Central Coast Salish villages on Vancouver Island, and met local authorities, including William F. Tolmie, William Duncan, and Israel W. Powell (Rohner 1969:17–77). He wrote several articles based on this work, among them one on tribal distribution

top left, Smithsonian, NAA: 4101; Royal B.C. Mus., Victoria: top right, PN 1551; bottom right: PN 1165; bottom left, Natl. Mus. of Canada, Ottawa: 56872.

Fig. 1. Northwest Coast ethnographers in the field. top left, James G. Swan and Johnnie Kit Elswa, Haida interpreter. Photograph by A.P. Niblack, Port Townsend, Wash. Terr., 1886. top right, George T. Emmons examining a stone adz, baskets, canoe model, and other materials he was collecting from the Tlingit. Photographed in Sitka, Alaska, 1890. bottom left, Thomas P. McIlwraith (far left) and Bella Coolas. The men wear costumes used in the Kusiut and Sisaok dances (McIlwraith 1948), and the child holds a small copper, a symbol of wealth. Photograph by Harlan I. Smith, Indian reserve, Bella Coola River, B.C., 1922. bottom right, Erna Gunther taking notes on weaving while observing a Central Coast Salish woman. Photograph by William A. Newcombe, Esquimalt, B.C., 1930.

(Boas 1887a) with a map that has not been superseded. In 1887 Boas settled in the United States.

Between 1888 and 1897 Boas made six more trips to the Northwest Coast supported by the British Association for the Advancement of Science (whose spokesman was Horatio Hale); the American Museum of Natural History, New York; and the U.S. National Museum, Washington (fig. 2). During this period he worked with members of nearly every Indian group from the Tsimshian to the Tillamook. In his reports Boas (1890, 1891, 1892d, 1895b, 1896, 1899a) presented ethnographic, linguistic, and anthropometric data on all the major divisions of the coast and southern interior of British Columbia. Work on the Nass River resulted in a volume of Nishga texts (Boas 1902), and work in Washington and Oregon resulted, among other publications, in a volume each of texts in Chinook (Boas 1894) and Cathlamet (Boas 1901) and a collection of Tillamook traditions in English (Boas 1898a). Myths collected throughout the region appeared in German (Boas 1895).

The Kwakiutl were the people to whom Boas kept returning. In 1888 Boas had met George Hunt, who was to become a collaborator in research on the Kwakiutl for the next 40 years (fig. 2). Hunt was English-Tlingit in origin, but he had grown up at the Kwakiutl village of Fort Rupert, speaking Kwakiutl and participating in Kwakiutl life. (Johan A. Jacobsen had already found him an excellent interpreter of Kwakiutl culture, as E.S. Curtis did two decades later.) In 1893 both Hunt and Boas were involved in the World's Columbian Exposition at Chicago, Hunt as the organizer of a group of Kwakiutls on display and Boas as an assistant to Frederic Ward Putnam of Harvard, who was in charge of anthropology at the fair. Hunt was already writing the Kwakiutl language in an inadequate missionary orthography, and Boas took this opportunity to teach him the orthography that he was developing and urged him to record materials in Kwakiutl. Late in 1894 Boas spent three weeks with Hunt at Fort Rupert witnessing the winter ceremonies, in which Hunt's son David was a hamatsa initiate. For Boas, this experience was the culmination of

top left, Glenbow-Alberta Inst., Calgary, Alta.: NA-860-1; top right, Amer. Mus. of Nat. Hist., New York: 11604; Smithsonian NAA: bottom left: MNH 8304; bottom right, 77-10036.

Fig. 2. Franz Boas. top left, Three of the 9 Bella Coola men brought to Germany, who stimulated Boas's early interest in Northwest Coast studies. Photograph by E. Hattorff, Hamburg, Germany, 1885. top right, Demonstration of a Kwakiutl woman, wearing a native-made cloak, spinning yarn while rocking a cradle by means of a cord tied to her toe. Franz Boas (left) and George Hunt hold the backdrop. Boas was gathering artifacts and documentation for exhibits on Kwakiutl culture for the U.S. National Museum and the American Museum of Natural History (Jacknis 1984:6,55). George Hunt was an important collaborator of Boas, helping him acquire important Kwakiutl and Nootka objects (Jonaitis 1988:182–184). Photograph by Oregon C. Hastings, Ft. Rupert, B.C., Nov. 30, 1894. bottom left, Boas posing for an exhibit of a Kwakiutl novice hamatsa coming out of the secret room (Hinsley and Holm 1976). Photographed Jan.–Feb. 1895. bottom right, The Kwakiutl exhibit for which Boas posed, U.S. National Museum. bottom left and bottom right, Photographs probably by William Dinwiddie or Thomas W. Smillie, Washington, D.C., 1895.

work over the previous years with data elicited on mythology, ceremonies, art, and social organization, and the result was a major work (Boas 1897a).

In 1895 Boas was given a curatorial position at the American Museum of Natural History and in 1896 a teaching position at Columbia University, which became his academic base for the rest of his life. Boas's (1897a) analysis of Northwest Coast art was incorporated into his major work on primitive art (Boas 1927). In 1897, Morris K. Jesup, president of the American Museum, agreed to finance a six-year research project in northwestern North America and northeast Asia under Boas's direction. Boas returned to British Columbia in 1897 and in 1900 for this work.

The Jesup North Pacific Expedition involved work on both continents and in archeology, physical anthropology, and linguistics as well as ethnology. Boas's contributions were mainly on the Northwest Coast—a study of facial paintings (Boas 1898c) based on work with the Haida artist Charles Edenshaw; notes on native interpretations of Chilkat blanket designs, incorporated into a work by Emmons (1907); a collection of Bella Coola myths (Boas 1898); a volume on Kwakiutl technology (Boas 1909); and two volumes of texts done with Hunt (Boas and Hunt 1902–1905, 1906). For ethnological work on the Northwest Coast, Boas recruited John R. Swanton and Livingston Farrand as well as Emmons, and for archeological work he engaged Harlan I. Smith.

Swanton had studied linguistics with Boas and in 1900 had just been appointed ethnologist in the Bureau of American Ethnology. He produced a Haida ethnography (1905) and Haida texts (1905a, 1908), a Tlingit ethnography (1908a) and Tlingit texts (1909). Farrand, a colleague of Boas at Columbia, analyzed Salish basketry designs (Farrand 1900a) and collected Quinault myths (Farrand and Kahnweiler 1902), Quileute traditions (Farrand 1919), ethnographic information on the Alsea (Farrand 1901), and southwestern Oregon Athapaskan myths (Farrand and Frachtenberg 1915). Emmons was responsible for a study of Tlingit basketry (Emmons 1903) in addition to his study of the Chilkat blanket (Emmons 1907). Boas published interim reports (1900a, 1903, 1905) and a summary of the results of the Jesup Expedition (Boas 1910a), but he did not produce the final volume that the American Museum expected (Freed and Freed 1983).

From 1902 to 1914, Henry W. Tate, a Tsimshian who wrote his language in a missionary orthography, sent Boas myths in Coast Tsimshian, some of which Boas retranscribed with the aid of another Tsimshian, Archie Dundas, and published as a volume of texts (Boas 1912). The rest introduced a major comparative work (Boas 1916).

Boas made five more trips to British Columbia, in 1914, 1922, 1923, 1927, and 1930–1931 (Rohner 1969:271–301), on the last three working mainly on Kwakiutl and Bella Bella materials. On his last trip he was accompanied by the Russian anthropologist Julia Averkieva. The results of the Kwakiutl work were three major ethnographic works (Boas 1921, 1925, 1934), consisting of Kwakiutl texts and translations recorded by Hunt and edited by Boas, and including material such as recipes, family histories, dreams, practices associated with rank and property, and Hunt's account of how he became a shaman. Boas also published more on tales (1910, 1935–1943), place-names (1934), and Kwakiutl culture in mythology (1935). The Bella Bella work resulted in a volume of texts (1928), including ethnographic material, and a volume of tales in English (1932). A partly finished general work on the Kwakiutl (Boas 1966) left at his death was edited by Helen Codere. Much manuscript material is in the Library of the American Philosophical Society in Philadelphia (Voegelin and Harris 1945).

Boas's work has been the subject of a considerable literature, by his students (Kroeber et al. 1943; Goldschmidt 1959), his critics (White 1963, 1966), and historians of anthropology (Stocking 1974a; Jacknis 1984, 1985). Boas's letters from the field were edited by Rohner (1969). George Hunt's role is discussed by Cannizzo (1983).

Boas rejected the popular view that culture had evolved orthogenetically through a series of stages, each stage being characterized by particular forms of society, religion, art, and perhaps intellectual and moral development.

A form of this social evolutionism had been proposed by Lewis H. Morgan and to some degree accepted by the staff of the Bureau of American Ethnology. Boas argued that rather than speculating about the whole of human history, ethnology ought to attempt to reconstruct the history of limited areas like the Northwest Coast. In time he became increasingly committed to the study of the "mental life" (Benedict 1934:28) of a particular tribe, with language as the means to that end. By recording texts in the native language he was allowing the Indians to speak for themselves (Reichard 1943:55). His critics accused him of never pulling his data together and producing a coherent account, even of the Kwakiutl. His Kwakiutl material was indeed scattered and unintegrated; the only place where he presented Kwakiutl kinship terms was in an essay on the Tsimshian (Boas 1916:494–495). But perhaps his real objective was reached with *Kwakiutl Culture as Reflected in Mythology* (Boas 1935), which he once called his "main job" (Reichard 1943:53).

Boas's Students and Their Students

For a half-century after the Jesup Expedition, most work on the Northwest Coast that was not done by Boas himself was done by his students, their students, or persons influenced by them.

Boas's students who did ethnographic work in the region include Edward Sapir, Leo Frachtenberg, Hermann Haeberlin, T.T. Waterman, Erna Gunther, Melville Jacobs, Thelma Adamson, Frederica de Laguna, Viola Garfield, and Marian W. Smith. Of these, Sapir, Frachtenberg, and Jacobs combined linguistic and ethnographic work, and de Laguna combined ethnographic, archeological, and historical work, as did Smith to a lesser extent. Nearly all collected myths and folktales. Several of these taught or otherwise influenced others who worked in the area, as did two other students of Boas, Alfred Louis Kroeber at the University of California at Berkeley and Leslie Spier for a time at the University of Washington at Seattle and later with Sapir at Yale University.

Early in the century, while Boas was continuing work with Tsimshian and Kwakiutl materials, it seemed urgent that more work be done on the southern coast. In 1906 Sapir worked with the last speakers of Takelma; between 1909 and 1917 Frachtenberg worked with the Coos, Lower Umpqua, Alsea, and Kalapuya in Oregon and the Quileute in Washington; and in 1916–1917 Haeberlin worked with the Southern Coast Salish. Frachtenberg's Kalapuya texts were later reworked by Melville Jacobs and his Quileute texts by Manuel Andrade. Haeberlin died in 1918, and his ethnographic notes and collection of myths were edited by Erna Gunther.

In 1910 Sapir took a position in Ottawa with the Geological Survey of Canada and began work with the Nootkans, enlisting the help of a Nootkan Indian, Alex

Thomas. His Nootka texts were edited, much later, by his student Morris Swadesh. Sapir guided the development of anthropology at the National Museum of Canada until 1925 (Preston 1980). He was joined by three British-trained Canadian anthropologists, C. Marius Barbeau, Diamond Jenness, and, temporarily, Thomas F. McIlwraith.

Beginning in 1915, Barbeau did a great deal of work with the Tsimshian, especially in collaboration with William Beynon, collecting much material on social organization, analyzed much later by Marjorie Halpin. McIlwraith was sent by Sapir to work with the Bella Coola in 1922 (fig. 1) and 1923–1924. He directed his efforts toward myth, religion, and ceremonialism and had the extraordinary good luck to be able to participate in the winter ceremony himself (Barker 1987), and so his monograph (McIlwraith 1948) is especially full in this respect. Jenness's principal area of research was the Arctic, but during the 1930s he worked with several Central Coast Salish groups. McIlwraith and Jenness were influenced by Sapir; Barbeau seems not to have been.

During this period, anthropology was established at the University of Washington in Seattle. From 1918 to 1920, while teaching there, T.T. Waterman did important work on Makah and Southern Coast Salish technology. Waterman may also have been responsible for encouraging Arthur Ballard, a White neighbor of the Muckleshoot Indians, to collect Lushootseed folklore.

Waterman's successor was Leslie Spier, who was joined by Erna Gunther (fig. 1). In 1924 Gunther began work on Clallam ethnography and folklore and a few years later began work with the Makah. Between 1925 and 1927, Ronald Olson, a student of Spier's, worked with the Quinault. By the late 1930s the department consisted of Gunther, Melville Jacobs, Viola Garfield, and Verne F. Ray.

From 1928 to 1939, Jacobs spent part of each year in linguistic research in western Oregon, collecting Coosan, Kalapuya, and Clackamas Chinookan myth and ethnographic texts. His wife, Elizabeth Derr Jacobs, collected Tillamook folktales and ethnographic data as well as southwestern Oregon Athapaskan material. Jacobs may also have encouraged the sociologist Bernhard Stern to do ethnographic work in 1929–1930 with the Lummi. Garfield and Ray both began academic work at the University of Washington and did graduate work elsewhere—Garfield at Columbia, Ray at Yale. Garfield had become interested in the Tsimshian as a teacher at New Metlakatla in 1922, worked on Tsimshian social organization for her dissertation, and continued work on the northern coast. Ray's major field of research was the Plateau but between 1931 and 1936 worked with Lower Chinook survivors.

Boas's students continued to come to the region. In 1926 and 1927, Thelma Adamson collected folklore and ethnographic material among the Upper Chehalis and Cowlitz. In 1935–1936 Marian W. Smith worked with the Lushootseed of southern Puget Sound. In 1945 she supervised a summer field school in ethnography in the Fraser Valley; some of the work done by her students appears in the collection on the Coast Salish that she edited (M.W. Smith 1949).

Frederica de Laguna's first work on the Northwest Coast was an encounter on Prince William Sound in 1930 with two Eyaks and the rediscovery of the fact, known to the Russians, that this tribe was not Eskimo, as American anthropologists had supposed. In 1933 de Laguna joined the Danish anthropologist Kaj Birket-Smith in an archeological and ethnological expedition to the area, which resulted in a full Eyak ethnography (Birket-Smith and De Laguna 1938). Her ethnographic work on the Tlingit includes a study of the village of Angoon, combining ethnological with archeological and historical data (De Laguna 1960) and a monumental Yakutat ethnography (De Laguna 1972).

During the 1930s, the University of California at Berkeley became involved in Northwest Coast research. Ronald Olson did ethnographic work with the Haisla, Oowekeeno, Bella Bella, and Tlingit, and Kroeber extended his culture element distribution survey to include the area. Homer Barnett and Philip Drucker participated in this survey, Barnett on the Oregon coast and the Strait of Georgia, Drucker on the coast from the Nootka northward. Barnett also produced an ethnography of the Coast Salish of the Strait of Georgia and studies of the potlatch, the Indian Shaker Church, and Tsimshian acculturation.

Drucker did ethnographic work with southwestern Oregon Athapaskan and Alsea informants and published an ethnography of the Nootka. During the early 1950s he worked in southeastern Alaska and British Columbia, principally on contemporary Native organizations (Drucker 1958). He published an interpretation of Northwest Coast culture history (Drucker 1955a), two general works on the culture area (Drucker 1955, 1965), and a work on the Kwakiutl potlatch (Drucker and Heizer 1967).

William W. Elmendorf began work with the Twana in the 1930s, while a student at the University of Washington, and completed his Twana ethnography as a student of Kroeber at Berkeley. He also published a collection of myths, the only one of Kroeber's students to do so.

Boasian anthropology survived at the University of Washington during the late 1940s and early 1950s. Students of that period who worked on the Northwest Coast include Joyce Wike, June M. Collins, Wayne Suttles, Wilson Duff, Barbara Lane, Warren Snyder, Ram Raj Prasad Singh, Pamela Amoss, and Sally Snyder. Most at some point attempted ethnographic reconstruction in the Boasian tradition.

Meanwhile, other researchers in the area were conscious of the work of Boas and his students and used it as a model or reacted against it. Between 1896 and 1906, the English settler and teacher Charles Hill-Tout worked with most of the Salish of British Columbia, following Boas's example in getting texts in the native languages as well as myths and ethnographic data in English. Maud (1978) reprinted most of his work together with an appreciation of Hill-Tout himself.

The series of volumes produced by the Seattle photographer Edward S. Curtis (1907–1930) covers a number of Northwest Coast peoples, the Haida and Nootka (vol. 11), Kwakiutl (vol. 10), Coast Salish, Chemakum, Quileute, and Kwalhioqua (vol. 9), Chinookans (vol. 8), and Tututni (vol. 13), with much good ethnographic data. Holm and Quimby (1980) describe Curtis's making of a motion picture with a Kwakiutl cast and the help of George Hunt.

George Hunt, Henry Tate, and Alex Thomas were not the only Indian researchers. Louis Shotridge, a high-ranking Chilkat Tlingit from the village of Klukwan, became a collector for the University Museum, University of Pennsylvania (fig. 3) (Carpenter 1975; Cole 1985:

254–266). With his wife Florence he wrote on the Tlingit and Tsimshian (Shotridge and Shotridge 1913; F. Shotridge 1913; Shotridge 1919, 1919a, 1928, 1929).

William Beynon, the son of a Tsimshian mother and Welsh father, grew up in Victoria but in his late twenties assumed a place among his mother's people. After interpreting for Barbeau in 1915, he soon began working on his own, and over a period of many years he recorded Tsimshian mythology and ethnography, sending quantities of material to Barbeau, Boas, Drucker, and others (Halpin 1978).

Kalervo Oberg, a student at the University of Chicago with a background in economics, spent the winter of 1931–1932 in the Tlingit village of Klukwan and wrote his dissertation on Tlingit economy (Oberg 1973). George Peter Murdock, an anthropologist standing outside the Boasian tradition and with a more sociological background, undertook field research with the Haida in 1932, gathering data on kinship and the potlatch. Other works somewhat outside the Boasian tradition were Vincent A. Koppert's study of the Clayoquot Nootka, based on observations made in 1923 and research done in 1929, dealing mainly with material culture, and Ivan A. Lopatin's ethnography of the Haisla.

left, Amer. Mus. of Nat. Hist., New York: 333573; right, U. of Pa., U. Mus., Philadelphia: 101628.

Fig. 3. Indian informants and collectors. left, Dr. Atlieu (a Nootka shaman from Clayoquot), Charles Nowell (Kweeha Kwakiutl from Fort Rupert), Bob Harris (Kwakiutl from Fort Rupert), and unidentified man at the St. Louis World's Fair. Nowell was the Kwakiutl collaborator of Charles F. Newcombe beginning about 1899, and Bob Harris was a village associate. Both made and collected artifacts for museum display and performed at the World's Fair (MacNair 1982:3–9). Dr. Atlieu was an informant for Berlin ethnologist Karl von den Steinen in 1902 (Cole 1985:200). Photograph possibly by William H. Rau, 1904. right, Louis Shotridge, Chilkat Tlingit, wearing woven tunic, decorated hide leggings probably made by Athapaskans, Chilkat blanket, and crest hat. He holds a ceremonial knife. Shotridge worked for the University Museum, Philadelphia, collecting artifacts from 1905 to 1932. Photograph by William Witt, Philadelphia, 1912.

The Results

The ethnographers of this period aimed at reconstructing Native culture as it was before White influence, and so most worked with a small number of old persons and elicited "memory culture," often ignoring what was going on about them as well as historical records and the observations of missionaries, Indian agents, and even earlier ethnological work.

The focus on the remote past at the expense of the recent past and present was a product of the goal of salvage ethnography (Gruber 1970). The diversity of Indian cultures was disappearing, and it was urgent that it should be recorded and saved. Most of the Boasian ethnographers were new to the region, unfamiliar with its social and natural history, and perhaps unaware of the long involvement (Knight 1978) of the Indians in the larger economy. Some may have seen their task as simply recording and analyzing their informants' perceptions.

Insofar as they did focus on what was in their informants' minds, the Boasian ethnographers were emulating Boas, but mainly without Boas's means. Boas himself was not fluent enough in Kwakiutl to follow rapid oratory and conversation but could follow a recited narrative (Rohner 1969:293), and he could use his knowledge of the language to explore Kwakiutl concepts, as in his analysis of religious terminology (Boas 1927, 1940: 612–618). Boas's students who worked in the area as linguists had similar skills. But most of the ethnographers were not at all fluent in any Indian language. Indeed, few had enough linguistic training and skill to record native terms for native concepts with any accuracy, much less to get them in context, as Boas had done.

Post-Boasian Field Research

During the whole Boasian period nearly every field worker aimed at a full reconstruction of aboriginal culture. But as it became increasingly difficult to find informants with the knowledge needed and as new questions arose, the aims of fieldwork changed. The new questions concerned the relations between culture and the individual, processes of culture change, and the nature of contemporary Indian groups. One important development was the growing recognition that the Indians were not losing all their traditional culture but were retaining many features, modifying others, and developing new forms. Another was the growth in the number of institutions from which researchers came into the region.

Attention to the individual began with Sapir, who used a short life history of Tom Sayach'apis, his principal Nootkan informant, as a means of presenting a synopsis of the culture (Sapir 1921; Sapir and Swadesh 1939, 1955). The first book-length autobiography published was that of the Kwakiutl chief Charles Nowell (Ford 1941). Short autobiographies were elicted in Miluk Coosan by Jacobs (1939:104–114) and in Lushootseed by W.A. Snyder (1968a:97–123). Other life histories recorded in English include those of John Fornsby, an Upper Skagit shaman (J.M. Collins 1949); James Sewid, a Kwakiutl (Spradley 1969); and Florence Davidson, a Haida (Blackman 1981a, 1982).

Fieldwork directed toward contemporary life may have begun with Elizabeth Colson's (1953) study of the Makah. Others include Pettitt (1950) on the Quileute; Wolcott (1967), Rohner (1967), and Rohner and Rohner (1970) on the Kwakiutl; C. Lewis (1970) on the Cowichan; Adams (1973) on the Gitksan; and Stearns (1981) on the Masset Haida.

Tribal histories based on work with both the people themselves and the historical record include M.W. Smith (1940) on the Puyallup, Suttles (1954) on the Lummi, Codere (1961) on the Kwakiutl, and Van den Brink (1974) on the Haida. De Laguna (1972) combined traditional ethnography and history in a monumental work on the Yakutat Tlingit. Aspects of Tlingit acculturation are described by Tollefson (1982, 1984).

Recording traditional knowledge and uses of plants and animals as an aim apart from general ethnography began with Gunther (1936, 1945) and has been pursued most vigorously by Turner (1975, 1979) and Kennedy and Bouchard (1976a). Other traditional activities given special attention include gambling (Maranda 1984) and gambling music (Stuart 1972). Contemporary ceremonial activities have been described for nearly every group from the Coast Salish north.

The effects of missionary work have been studied among the Tlingit (Kan 1985, 1987), Tsimshian (Barnett 1942), and Northern Coast Salish (Lemert 1954).

Studies of the contemporary Indian economy and Indian involvement in the larger economy include Hawthorn, Belshaw, and Jamieson (1958), K.A. Mooney (1976, 1978), and McDonald (1984).

Much that has been written on the Northwest Coast has not been based on field research. Adams (1981) reviews the major works that appeared in the 1960s and 1970s.

Issues in Anthropology

Mythology

Boas used the mythology of northwestern North America to refute current theories of mythology (which were mainly linked to nineteenth-century social evolutionism), to reveal facts about the cultures of their narrators, and to support hypotheses about the movements of peoples.

Boas (1895) showed that stories with Raven as the leading character were most numerous on the northern coast and diminished toward the south; this distribution, he argued, could be explained best as the result of diffusion, contradicting the notion that peoples at the same stage of social evolution spontaneously produced similar stories. He also demonstrated that similar stories are told by different peoples to account for different things; the kidnapping of a girl by a monster was told to account for the Cannibal Dance among the Kwakiutl and to account for the culture hero among the Chinook. He concluded that even a people's basic myths are partly borrowed. Boas (1897) explored the relationship among myth, ceremony, and social organization, and found different myths linked to the same ceremony. In this work and in his work on Bella Coola mythology (1898:126) he concluded that the rituals were probably older than the myths told to account for them. Boas (1916) presented an extensive comparative and analytic study of the mythology of northwestern North America, demonstrating how plots, characters, and incidents have separate histories, freely separating and recombining. He concluded (1916: 879) that myths were not "a direct reflex of the contemplation of nature" and that "we have no reason to believe that the myth-forming processes of the last ten thousand years have differed materially from modern myth-making processes."

Boas also rejected the assumption that every people's mythology is an integrated system, perhaps unseen by the people themselves but discoverable by the analyst through a search for hidden meanings. Reviewing a work (Locher 1932) that identified the two-headed serpent as the integrating symbol in Kwakiutl mythology, Boas (1933, 1940:446–450) asserted that such attempts were based on a fundamental misunderstanding of the relations of people to their myths. Throughout the region people were constantly borrowing and embellishing myths to support claims of status, a practice that made a stable system of myths impossible.

Boas believed that in a people's myths and tales, references to daily life and the development of plots reflect real practices and values, and that a description based on this material would more accurately portray the culture as the people themselves see it than one based on usual field methods.

Boas supported two of his postulated migrations with the distributions of myths. He saw an early connection between the Northwest Coast and northeastern Siberia broken by a movement of the Eskimo from northern Canada into Alaska. The old connection, he argued, is shown by the distribution of Raven myths on both sides of the North Pacific. However, as Chowning (1962) has shown, this argument ignored the great development of Raven myths among the Alaska Eskimo. Boas also saw evidence that the Tsimshian had moved to the coast from the interior, a conclusion criticized by Barbeau (1917a) on the grounds that it was based on only the few family traditions Tate had collected; Beynon's much larger

collection pointed in other directions.

Boas's theoretical statements were mainly reprinted in his *Race, Language, and Culture* (1940). Spier (1931) used *Tsimshian Mythology* as the basis for an analysis of Boas's methods, and Jacobs (1959a) gives an appraisal of Boas's work on mythology.

Boas's contemporaries and students collected myths from nearly every group on the Northwest Coast. McIlwraith's (1948) work on the Bella Coola is especially notable for demonstrating the relationship of myth, ceremony, and social organization. It also curiously supports Boas against himself. Boas (1898:27) had reported that the Bella Coola cosmology was unusually systematized, having five superimposed worlds with deities assigned to each. However, McIlwraith (1948:25) discovered that the five-level system figured in the myths of only two families; other family myths described the world differently.

Some of Boas's students also used Northwest Coast materials in comparative works, notably Lowie (1908) on the test theme, Waterman (1914) on the explanatory element, and Gunther (1928) on the first-salmon ceremony and associated myths.

Of Boas's students only Melville Jacobs developed a new theoretical approach. Although he recorded myths in several languages, his major theoretical work (Jacobs 1959a, 1960) is based on material recorded from Victoria Howard in the Clackamas dialect of Kiksht (Jacobs 1958–1959, 1, 1959). In Jacobs's view a myth is a kind of drama with a cast of "precultural" people, for example, Coyote men and Bear women, who play roles that are not otherwise given expression. Jacobs saw evidence of repressed hostility between siblings, the sexes, and the old and young, and he drew inferences about humor, ethical values, and world view. His interpretation explained features of style. Because the audience knew the drama by heart and was interested primarily in the characters, the narration could be terse, with little description and participants in dialogs indicated by voice alone, the form polished by generations of retelling and discussion. For critical appraisal see Liljeblad (1962) and Hymes (1965). Sally Snyder (1964) analyzed Skagit (Southern Coast Salish) myths in similar fashion.

Approaches to the study of myth developed in the 1960s and after include those of Dell Hymes and Claude Levi-Strauss ("Mythology," this vol.). Maud (1982) has reviewed the history of myth-collecting in British Columbia.

Art

"Northwest Coast art" as a subject for analysis and theoretical discussion has generally meant the art of a region extending from the Tlingit southward at most as far as the Nootkan and Coast Salish tribes. If Chinookan or more southerly Northwest Coast art is treated at all, it may be under a heading other than Northwest Coast (as in Feder 1971a).

● BOAS Boas was the first to analyze Northwest Coast art systematically and from a theoretical perspective, in his earlier work addressing the question of evolution in art. He (1897a) argued against the position that art always developed from realism to abstraction, instead proposing that on the Northwest Coast conventionalization resulted from the artist's aim to depict on the surface at hand all the essential characteristics of the animal to be represented. The shape of the object being decorated might require the artist to abstract and distort the animal to make it fit the surface. One radical distortion was "split-representation," in which an artist rendered on a two-dimensional surface both profiles of a three-dimensional animal's face and body, split down the middle and flattened out. Boas (1898c) continued to address the question of the relation of abstraction to shape of the surface being decorated in his study of face painting. In his contribution to Emmons's (1907) monograph on the Chilkat blanket, Boas pointed to the inadequacy of any interpretation of highly conventionalized images, demonstrating that in many cases blanket designs were identified quite differently by different informants. Boas (1927) demonstrated the complexity of the artistic process, which involves skill, tradition, and creativity, and he reconstructed the history of the art of the region. He identified an older geometric style, like that found among the Coast Salish and Nootkans, and a complex symbolic style invented by the Tlingit, Haida, and Tsimshian and partly adopted in historic times by the Kwakiutl. Boas not only provided a key for recognizing the creatures portrayed in all but the most abstract ways, but he also provided alternatives to evolutionist theories of art development, described the psychological dimensions of artistic creativity, and proposed a reconstruction of art history on the Northwest Coast.

● FROM BOAS TO THE 1960S Several of Boas's students built on his work—Haeberlin (1918a), Waterman (1923), Garfield (1951, 1955b), and Gunther (1951, 1956, 1962, 1966). Gunther was particularly important as the curator of a number of exhibitions of Northwest Coast art and, with Garfield, as a teacher of students in the field, including Bill Holm, Wilson Duff, and Roy Carlson. She was also an influence on Inverarity (1941, 1946, 1950). Drucker (1955) and Duff (1967) followed Boas's lead in historic reconstruction.

Outside the Boasian tradition, Wingert, the first art historian to study Northwest Coast material, treated Coast Salish art (1949, 1949a) from a strictly formal perspective, offering little information on function. In an article on the larger region (1951), he described stylistic differences in sculpture, especially masks and totem poles, refining Boas's characterizations of tribal styles.

Barbeau compiled much information on totem poles (1929, 1950) and argillite carvings (1953, 1957, 1958). Unfortunately this work was flawed by a number of errors and by its historical perspective. Believing that mythology indicated recent migrations from Asia, Barbeau (1930a, 1945) argued that the crest system and totem poles developed in historic times. This view was strongly criticized by Drucker (1948) and Duff (1964a) and has been disproved by archeological work. Despite these shortcomings, Barbeau did a great deal to familiarize scholars and the public alike with Northwest Coast art.

Adam (1923, 1931, 1936) began describing Northwest Coast art in a rather Boasian fashion but then began pointing out stylistic similarities to early Chinese art. Adam remained cautious about the feasibility of trans-Pacific contact, but several other writers (Creel 1935; Hentze 1936; Schuster 1951; Covarrubias 1954; Badner 1966; Fraser 1968; Coe 1972; Davis and Davis 1974), with no evidence beyond perceived similarities, implied an ancient Chinese origin for the complex, highly symbolic art of the Northwest Coast.

Between 1930 and 1960, the only divergence from descriptive and diffusionist treatments of Northwest Coast art came from Surrealists and innovative American artists who became fascinated with what they felt to be profoundly mystic and mythical qualities in it (Jonaitis 1981). Surrealist spokesman Wolfgang Paalen (1943) wrote that this art reflected the early stages of human consciousness in which emotion, not reason, prevailed, and all dualisms were shattered in a universal communion in which all is one. Abstract expressionist Barnett Newman (1946, 1947) praised the other-worldly metaphysical qualities of Northwest Coast art. Claude Lévi-Strauss (1943) wrote about this art from a Surrealist perspective. Lévi-Strauss (1963-1976, 1) considered that split-representation was related to a hierarchical type of society.

From the 1930s on, two activities outside ethnology had an influence on research. One was a series of exhibitions of Northwest Coast art selected for its aesthetic qualities, giving it the status of art; the other was the development of museum- and government-supported projects for the restoration or recreation of "traditional" objects that the Indians had largely ceased producing ("History of Research: Museum Collections," this vol.).

● 1960S TO 1980S—ANALYSIS OF STYLE Bill Holm's (1965) stylistic analysis was a major advance beyond Boas's treatment. Holm rediscovered the manner in which the northern two-dimensional style was rendered—the formline system—making it possible to recreate Northwest Coast art in traditional fashion. Holm (1972) identified tribal styles of masks.

Bill Reid, an artist of Haida descent, was also involved in the rediscovery of the northern two-dimensional style. Reid's (1967) contribution to the "Arts of the Raven" show was a sensitive "appreciation" of Northwest Coast art. He wrote on Haida totem poles in an equally poetic fashion (1971). Holm and Reid (1975) offered aesthetic evaluations of individual pieces in a dialogue that Halpin (1978) identified as an expression of connoisseurship.

A mark of the increasing acceptance of Northwest Coast art as art, as well as a concern for style, was the literature that identified works by named artists. This literature elevated the Northwest Coast carver and painter from craftsman to fine artist in its usually tacit—but sometimes explicit—acknowledgement of personal expression, individuality, and artistic creativity. Barbeau (1957) had endeavored to identify individual Haida argillite carvers. The work of Kwakiutl artist Mungo Martin was described by Duff (1959), H.B. Hawthorn (1961), and Hawthorn (1964). Nuytten (1982) included Martin with the Kwakiutl carvers Charlie James and Ellen Neel. Studies of Haida artist Charles Edenshaw's work include Appleton (1970), Holm (1974a, 1981), S. J. Thomas (1967), and Hoover (1983). Other publications on individual artists are Gessler on Haida drawings (1971) and the Haida master Nunstins (Gessler 1981), Holm (1974, 1983b) on the Kwakiutl Willie Seaweed, Wright (1983) on several Haida argillite carvers, and Brown (1987) on an anonymous but very individualist Tlingit master.

From the 1960s on, an increasing number of publications dealt with the art of a single people or with a single art form. These include works on Tlingit art (Jonaitis 1981, 1986; Corey 1983), Haida totem poles (Smyly and Smyly 1975; Smith 1979; MacDonald 1983), Tsimshian art (MacDonald 1984; Laforet 1984), Bella Coola art (Stott 1975), Kwakiutl art (Mochon 1966; Hawthorn 1967, 1979), Central Coast Salish carving (Suttles 1982, 1983; Feder 1983), Coast Salish textiles (Gustafson 1980), masks (Malin 1978; King 1979), architecture (Vastokas 1966), totem poles (A. Chapman 1965; Halpin 1981b; Malin 1986), the copper (Widerspach-Thor 1981), northern textiles (Samuel 1982, 1987; Holm 1982), and frontlets (Holm 1986).

Argillite sculpture, all made for trade and so once assumed to be "decadent" (Paalen 1943:18), is the subject of serious study (Kaufman 1976; Wright 1979, 1980, 1982, 1983, 1986, 1987; Drew and Wilson 1986; Sheehan 1981; Macnair and Hoover 1984), most going beyond the value judgments inherent in works that question the authenticity of art made for tourists. Works on the effects of acculturation on art (J.M. Jones 1968; Blackman 1976a; Wyatt 1984) also assume a dynamic relationship between Whites and Indians. The enhanced position of Northwest Coast art as art and the expanded market for it resulted in guides for looking at and purchasing this art (Hall, Blackman, and Rickard 1981; Duffek 1983; H. Stewart 1977). Several publications describe the revivals of traditions ('Ksan 1972; Arima and Hunt 1975; Macnair,

Hoover, and Neary 1980; Steltzer 1984), while others focus on individual artists such as Robert Davidson (H. Stewart 1979), Bill Reid (Shadbolt 1986), and Art Thompson (Blackman and Hall 1986).

● INTERPRETATION Most work on Northwest Coast art is either in the anthropological tradition of describing imagery, meaning, and function or in the art-historical tradition of formal analysis, but since 1960 there have been some interpretive works. During the 1960s and 1970s some writers found shamanism a useful vehicle for interpretation (R. Johnson 1973; Jonaitis 1978, 1980). Waite (1966) proposed that Kwakiutl transformation masks originated with the shamanic experience of human-animal metamorphosis. Vastokas (1973) suggested that the totem pole was an elaboration of the shamanic tree of life. In MacDonald's view (1981), house fronts, Chilkat blankets, robed dancers, coppers, and images of eyes, ears, and tongues were all associated originally with shamanism. Carlson (1983b) wrote that the crest images usually associated with secular status evolved from spirit images. These works suggest that the origin of artistic motifs can be found in the shamanic experience. A modified but related position is one asserting that Northwest Coast crest art, commonly considered secular, is in fact profoundly spiritual (Walens 1981).

Another body of scholarship was influenced by structuralism, treating art as a cultural product that reflects the high intellectual level of its creators and expresses aspects of the society's structure, often in a dualistic fashion. Wilson Duff (1975) suggested that art mediates between dualities such as life and death, male and female, and human and animal. In an essay on meaning in Northwest Coast art Duff (1981a) concentrated on sexual imagery. McLaren (1978) identified the hawk as related to the salmon in an elaborate mythic complex and interpreted the history of the Haida argillite pipe according to Duff's framework. Halpin (1981a) analyzed the shamanic and chiefly elements of Tsimshian masking.

Other scholars interpreting Northwest Coast art from a structuralist perspective have sought relationships between art, social structure, and world view. Lévi-Strauss (1982) interprets several Kwakiutl and Coast Salish masks in the context of an elaborate mythic complex that involves marriage, nature, and wealth. MacDonald (1984) related Tsimshian house facades to frontlets, boxes, and coppers. For Jacknis (1974) art can serve as a mediating function between dualisms such as the biological act of eating and the cultural act of feasting. Vastokas (1978) identified cognitive aspects of Northwest Coast style in her assertion that in addition to dualistic representations, tripartite and quadripartite renderings exist as well. Jonaitis (1988) studied the structural relationships between the art of the shaman and that of the chief among the northern Tlingit.

Winter Ceremonies

Boas (1897:336–338, 662) supposed that both the Kwakiutl crest system and the winter ceremonies had developed through a reworking of widespread North American Indian beliefs and practices associated with guardian spirits. Numaym crests were "manitous" that had become hereditary (cf. Boas 1920:125–126); performances by the groups he called "secret societies" were dramatizations of ancestors' encounters with guardian spirits. Warfare provided many of the symbols used in these performances. The development of the winter ceremonies had occurred among the Kwakiutl and other Northern Wakashans, and they had spread to peoples to the north and south.

Essentially agreeing with Boas, Drucker (1965:97–98, 167) proposed a developmental sequence: (1), spirit dancing, in which each performer displays the song, dance, and perhaps feat of power given him in his own encounter with his guardian spirit; (2), crest dances, in which a performer displays the gift an ancestor received; and (3), dancing society (secret society) performances, in which the performers dramatize the ancestor's encounter as well as display the gift. He also (Drucker 1940) suggested that the dog-eating dance was the earliest form of secret society (he preferred "dancing society") and that shamanism as well as warfare had provided symbols and motifs.

In a comparative study Haekel (1954) saw similar connections. Müller (1955) suggested the Kwakiutl winter ceremonies were rooted in shamanism and rites symbolizing death and resurrection, pointing to parallels in the Northeast and California.

Assessments of the emotional quality of the Kwakiutl winter ceremonies have differed greatly. Benedict (1934) identified them as religious ceremonies in which the chief dancer strove for Dionysian ecstasy, a state in which he had lost control of himself and could commit terrible acts such as eating human flesh.

But those who had worked in the region saw this behavior as feigned—a "simulated supernatural experience" (Drucker 1940:202), a "hollow caricature" of spirit possession (Barnett 1938a:138). The ceremonies were "cycles of dramas," involving theatrical illusion and trickery, making it doubtful whether human flesh was actually ever consumed (Drucker 1955:148, 1965: 163–165).

Wike (1952:97) suggested that what had once been religious ceremonies had become secularized. They seemed to be "historical pageants dramatizing a period when men did, indeed, have supernatural powers" and "theatrical vehicles for the display of wealth and hereditary prerogatives." The earlier focus of ceremonies may have been the role of the dead in the affairs of the living. Codere (1961:473–478) suggested that this secularization began with the founding of Fort Rupert in 1849 and the subsequent growth of the Kwakiutl potlatch and shift from physical violence to "fighting with property."

Boas (1966:172) identified the winter ceremonies as "essentially religious in character," because of the belief in the presence during the winter of the spirits who possessed the dancers, but he found that because the ceremonies were "so intimately associated with non-religious activities, such as feasts and potlatches," it was hard to assess their religious value.

Boas had found no system in Kwakiutl mythology, and Drucker (1955:138–140) found no consistent system of beliefs about creation, cosmology, and deities anywhere on the central or northern coast. Nevertheless, with the development of symbolic anthropology there were new attempts at finding meanings. Goldman (1975) attempted an analysis and synthesis of Kwakiutl thought discoverable through metaphors and symbols in the Hunt-Boas texts. Starting with the assumptions that in traditional societies religion always has "total control" and that a religion is necessarily coherent and systematic, he predictably discovered that the Kwakiutl were deeply religious and that the winter ceremonies, the potlatch, and marriage rites were all primarily religious events serving to maintain the world order and the position of the elite. Scholars with a firsthand knowledge of the Kwakiutl were unconvinced (Drucker 1979; Holm 1976; Bill Holm, personal communication 1979). Following Goldman's lead, Walens (1981) found the Kwakiutl world view expressed especially in oral metaphors. The most important part of the winter ceremony, the Cannibal Dance, was a morality play demonstrating that humans can control the world through controlling its most important force—hunger. In a different fashion, S. Reid (1979) related the initiation of the Cannibal dancer to world view, individual psychology, and social structure.

Ceremonialism elsewhere in the region has not been neglected ("Central and Southern Coast Salish Ceremonies Since 1900," this vol.). Ernst (1952) traced the connections between the Wolf Dance of the Nootkans, Makah, and Quileute. Haekel (1958) examined the concept of a cosmic tree or pole in Bella Coola and other mythic and ceremonial systems. Halpin (1981b, 1984), Guédon (1984), and Seguin (1984) have done much to clarify the different ceremonial systems of the Tsimshian, Nishga, and Gitksan.

The Potlatch

Along the Northwest Coast from the Eyak to the Chinook and among many tribes in adjacent parts of the Arctic, Subarctic, and Plateau, hosts gave gifts of wealth to formally invited guests at ceremonies generally known by the Chinook Jargon term *potlatch* 'give'. To missionaries and officials, the quantities given and sometimes destroyed seemed wasteful and harmful, and the potlatch was long forbidden by Canadian law (LaViolette 1961). Among scholars perhaps no aspect of Northwest Coast culture has been the subject of more debate. Irvin (1977), Mauzé (1984:175–193), and Schulte-Tenckhoff (1986) trace the history of this debate.

Mainly on the basis of work with the Kwakiutl, Boas (1890:834–835, 1897:341–343, 1899a:681–682) identified the potlatch as a "method of acquiring rank" and an "interest-bearing investment." Potlatchers gave with the knowledge that the recipients would repay with interest; it was a kind of insurance for themselves and their children.

In the matter of interest, Boas seems to have confused two activities: accumulating the means to potlatch by making loans, which had to be repaid with high interest— as much as 100 percent, and giving potlatch gifts, which might be returned with some increment or might not be returned at all. This difference had already been noted by Dawson (1888), and it was later described by Curtis (1907–1930, 10:141–155), who insisted that potlatchers gave out of a feeling of pride not greed. However, Curtis's account was generally unnoticed, and for several decades the potlatch was usually pictured as a struggle between rivals trying to break each other through the rule of double return.

Mauss (1967) compared the potlatch with practices in Polynesia, Melanesia, and classical antiquity. He identified (1967:1–5, 36–37) the potlatch as a "total social phenomenon . . . religious, legal, moral, and economic," a struggle between nobles, on behalf of their clans, bound by the moral obligations to give, receive, and repay with sacred gifts. The potlatch, he concluded (1967:45), was a stage in the evolution of society between that of egalitarian kin groups united by exchanges of gifts and that of individual contract, money, and market. Mauss stressed the moral aspect of gift giving in traditional societies, but he saw the potlatch as an aberration, "the monster child of the gift system" (1967:41).

The Boas-Hunt texts do show that Kwakiutl nobles made self-glorifying speeches and tried to outdo each other in the giving and even destruction of property, and so Benedict (1934) chose the Northwest Coast as one of her examples of cultures dominated by a single idea, portraying the Kwakiutl as paranoid megalomaniacs. Potlatching was simply an expression of Kwakiutl character.

Murdock (1936) described several types of Haida potlatch and reported that potlatchers raised the status of their children but not their own. For Garfield (1939: 214–217) the Coast Tsimshian potlatch was "the foundation of the economic system," stimulating production and acquisition and playing a fundamental role in distribution. It was socially important in that it involved all members of the lineage while accentuating differences in rank. The Tlingit potlatch was described by Oberg (1973), the Nootka by Drucker (1951), and the Southern Coast Salish by M.W. Smith (1940).

Using Kwakiutl and Coast Salish data, Barnett (1938b, 1968) identified the potlatch as essentially a means of publicly making claims to status and expressing self-esteem and esteem for others. Guests were witnesses to the host's claims, and their acceptance and reciprocation validated the claims. Contrary to Boas, the potlatch was not an investment system. Nor was competition an essential feature.

In the first historical work on the potlatch, Codere (1950) documented an expansion of the Kwakiutl potlatch in quantity of goods given and scope of participation. She related this to demographic and economic changes and especially to the decline of warfare. Potlatching was a substitute for physical conflict; in the words of a Kwakiutl, it was "fighting with property." She accepted Boas's statement that potlatch gifts had to be returned two-fold and offered an ingenious explanation of why the system did not collapse—the destruction of coppers liquidated credit; but after fieldwork, she (1961:468) changed her position. Codere (1956) also described the "play potlatch" as a corrective to Benedict's view of the Kwakiutl as humorless paranoids.

It was generally assumed that the richness of Northwest Coast ceremonial life was made possible by the richness of the environment, and that potlatch exchanges had little or no relationship to problems of livelihood (Benedict 1934:190; Goldman 1937:180; Barnett 1938b: 352). The potlatch became an example of the workings of a prestige economy (Herskovits 1952:415). It was identified in some anthropology texts (for example, Linton 1955:52) as an example of values driving people to engage in wasteful and nonfunctional practices.

A reaction to this position came from researchers interested in ecological relations. Suttles (1960, 1962, 1968) stressed the variability of the environment of the Central Coast Salish and argued that their potlatch was a kind of safety valve in a system of exchange of food and wealth between affines in different villages, and that this system was adaptive in this environment. This interpretation challenged the view that the Northwest Coast environment presented no problems, that there were separate subsistence and prestige economies, and that the potlatch was simply the expression of values run wild. Vayda (1961) suggested extending this interpretation to the rest of the Northwest Coast. Piddocke (1965) offered an interpretation of the Kwakiutl potlatch that stressed the hazards of the Kwakiutl environment. This approach was criticized by Drucker and Heizer (1967), Schneider (1974), Orans (1975), and others.

Drucker and Heizer (1967) presented new data on the Kwakiutl potlatch and evaluated existing theories. They supported Barnett on the motives of the potlatcher, presented much evidence against the view that potlatch gifts were returned two-fold, and argued against the view that Kwakiutl potlatching was a substitute for warfare and against the view (attributed to the ecological approach) that the potlatch had been devised to alleviate hunger. For Drucker and Heizer (1967:8) the potlatch was "a formal procedure for social integration, its prime purpose being to identify publicly the membership of the group and to define the social status of this membership." Competitive potlatching occurred only when two persons claimed the same position. Destruction of property (the "rivalry gesture") occurred at potlatches, but was not a normal part of potlatching. The potlatch probably developed gradually through a fusion of practices and concepts such as "gift exchanges at marriage, leading to a continuing special relationship between affinal kin, a wealth system, the concept of inheritance rights associated with social status, and the formal presentation of the heir at the mortuary rites in honor of a deceased chief." Drucker (1983:93–94) suggested that during the nineteenth century changes in the potlatch played a role in the formation of the ceremonial aggregations of local groups.

Weinberg (1973) offered a systems-theory interpretation of the Kwakiutl potlatch accounting for changes in the system. Kobrinsky (1975) attributed the expansion of Kwakiutl potlatching to the chiefs' struggle to maintain their positions in the face of European power and the rise of commoners with the means to potlatch. Grumet (1975) considered economic and demographic stress in tracing the history of the Coast Tsimshian potlatch.

Adams (1973) presented evidence for flexibility in the northern matrilineal structure and argued that the potlatch served to redistribute people over the resource base.

The question of origins concerned Birket-Smith (1964, 1967), who showed how widely similar institutions existed outside the Northwest Coast and objected to any explanation based simply on Northwest Coast forms. He suggested that the origin of the potlatch lay in individual rank, hereditary property, and feasts for the dead, pointing to circum-Pacific connections.

Rubel and Rosman (1970, 1971) also compared the potlatch to similar institutions in Oceania, and they (Rosman and Rubel 1971, 1972) applied Levi-Strauss's models of kinship and marriage systems to the Northwest Coast to account for the different structural relations among potlatch participants that they saw among several Northwest Coast peoples. Questions about this analysis were raised by Vaughan (1976, 1984), Kasakoff (1974), Cove (1976), and Baugh (1978).

Structuralist-symbolist and psychological interpretations became popular in the 1970s. For Goldman (1975) and Walens (1981) the Kwakiutl potlatch was essentially a religious ceremony; in Walens's view the potlatch promoted the circulation of souls among humans, animals, and spirits, and the great increase in potlatching during the nineteenth century was an attempt to put more souls into circulation to compensate for the great population loss the Kwakiutl had experienced.

Snyder (1975) interpreted Skagit (Southern Coast Salish) potlatching as an unloading of the impurities associated with food and sex. Dundes (1979) offered a Freudian explanation of the symbols and metaphors of the Kwakiut potlatch; wealth is feces, and so potlatching is dumping feces on a rival or swallowing him and reducing him to feces. Fleisher (1981) offered a more Jungian view. Seguin (1984) rejected these views as applicable to the Coast Tsimshian, finding their potlatch concerned with the reincarnation of humans and animals.

Reviewing Northwest Coast warfare, Ferguson (1983, 1984) argued that, contrary to the ecological view, the advantage to participation in the potlatch system was political rather than economic. Warfare was everywhere a serious threat, and fear of warfare drove the system.

Descent

In his Northwest Coast materials, Boas believed he had evidence against the usual nineteenth-century view that human society had evolved through a sequence of matrilineal to patrilineal to bilateral stages. He had identified the Tlingit, Haida, and Tsimshian as matrilineal and the tribes south of them as patrilineal (Boas 1887c: 289, 1887b:422); he saw the Kwakiutl practice of transmitting some privileges to a son-in-law as "an adaptation of maternal laws by a tribe which was on a paternal stage" (Boas 1897:334–335; Reichard 1938:425); and he saw the Coast Salish as originally an interior people with a simple family organization who had moved to the coast and adopted a clan organization (Boas 1910a:15–16; Goldenweiser 1915:359–360; Lowie 1937:150).

Among Boas's students the Kwakiutl case was often cited as a case of a shift from patrilineal to matrilineal descent, though Sapir (1915a) saw difficulties, pointing out that the Nootka were not really patrilineal. On the other hand, the French (Moret and Davy 1970:87–89; Lévi-Strauss 1975:166) and Averkieva (1966:20, 1981) interpreted the facts to show that the Kwakiutl were shifting from matrilineal to patrilineal descent.

Boas (1920) identified the corporate group of Kwakiutl society as the numaym, an anglicization of the native term, dropping his earlier terms gens and clan on the grounds that they implied unilineal descent. It appeared that kinship was reckoned bilaterally, and the numaym was a nonexogamous group in which membership was optionally through father or mother and even marriage. But Boas (1924) again listed the Kwakiutl and Coast Salish as having patrilineal descent.

To set the record straight on the matter of sequence of forms of descent, Lowie (1948:261) and Murdock (1949: 190–191) pointed out that the Kwakiutl were essentially bilateral or nonunilineal. The practice Boas identified as matrilineal was not that; in a matrilineal system a man's heir is not his daughter's husband or daughter's son but his younger brother or sister's son. The Haisla (then called Northern Kwakiutl) do indeed appear to have shifted to a fully matrilineal system, but the shift was from bilateral not patrilineal descent.

The contradiction in Boas's statements may reflect a change in the composition of the numaym from an early period when membership was largely transmitted in the male line to a later period when, in response to population loss, members were recruited in every possible way (see "Kwakiutl: Traditional Culture," this vol.). Adams (1981: 367) reported evidence that would support this view. Lévi-Strauss (1982:163–187) compared the numaym and similar corporate groups in the region to the noble "house" of the Old World, which had alternate strategies for transmitting its title. Jenness (1934–1935:52) also identified the Central Coast Salish kin group with the "house" in this sense.

Boas's Coast Salish case against nineteenth-century social evolutionism was in fact no better than his Kwakiutl case; the Coast Salish did not have a clan system and were no more patrilineal than the Kwakiutl. Jorgensen (1980: 462–463) classified the Northwest Coast tribes from the Haihais to the Coosans as having bilateral descent and bilateral demes, though he also identified (1980:179) the Kwakiutl numaym as a patrideme.

The presence of matrilineal descent on the northern Northwest Coast and in the adjacent Subarctic is anomalous (Driver and Massey 1957:435) and has seemed to require an explanation. Swanton (1904) thought that it originated through intermarriage between the Haida and Tlingit across Hecate Strait; he barely suggested what the process might have been, but he might have endorsed Goodenough's (1976) model. Olson (1933), Birket-Smith and De Laguna (1938:527), Garfield (1951:19), Murdock (1955:86), and Driver and Massey (1957:435) thought an Old World origin more likely, while Suttles (1962), Inglis (1970), and Riches (1979) looked for conditions that might have led to an indigenous development on the Northwest Coast. Dyen and Aberle (1974) proposed a reconstruction of the proto-Athapaskan kinship system that implies matrilineal descent, and Rubel and Rosman (1983) identified an Athapaskan social structure as the prototype of structures they proposed for the coast.

Adams (1981:369, 385) has argued that concern for rules of descent may be an impediment to understanding, because differences in descent are superficial and the way Northwest Coast societies actually functioned was much the same.

Social Inequality

Until the 1930s it was generally agreed that Northwest Coast societies, perhaps excluding those south of the Columbia River, were divided into three classes—nobles, commoners, and slaves (Ray 1956). This view was challenged by Drucker (1939), who argued that the only sharp division was between freemen and slaves, the free consisting of a continuously ranked series.

The question of class or rank became contentious in the 1950s, when Ray (1955) asserted that Boas had been concerned with Kwakiutl nobility only and had neglected the commoners. Lowie (1956) used Drucker to defend Boas with the argument that there was no separate commoner class. Codere (1957) supported Drucker with an analysis of the social implications of 120 recipes recorded by Hunt. Suttles (1958) argued that the absence of ranked positions among the Central Coast Salish made it easier to distinguish classes. McFeat (1966) reprinted the whole exchange, but by then positions had changed; Drucker and Heizer (1967) freely used the terms "chiefs" and "commoners." Through the 1970s most writers argued for social classes (Adams 1981:370).

Fried (1967) had identified Northwest Coast societies as "rank societies" rather than "stratified societies," but to defend this position he had to argue (1967:218–223) that slaves on the Northwest Coast were merely war captives kept for their prestige value.

For many years the standard view of Northwest Coast slavery was that slaves were merely prestige goods; they lived as well as their masters (except when killed as a act of wealth-destruction) and probably cost more for their keep than they contributed. Exceptions were MacLeod (1925, 1929a), Averkieva (1966), and Garfield (1945). A renewed interest is seen in Ruyle (1973), Donald (1983), Mitchell (1984, 1983a, 1985b), and Mitchell and Donald (1985).

The question of how status differences arose had been addressed briefly by Jacobs and Stern (1947) and Wike (1958), but it became a major issue in the 1970s (Ruyle 1973; Donald and Mitchell 1975; Gleason, Fleisher, and Gamble 1979; Yesner 1980; Morgan 1981; Ames 1981, 1983; Cohen 1981; Richardson 1982; Testart 1982; De Laguna 1983; Drucker 1983; Mitchell 1983, 1983a; Burley 1983; Matson 1983, 1985; Donald 1985; Coupland 1985). These works involve the reinterpretation of ethnographic data, ethnohistorical data, or archeological data. A significant number are by archeologists who are familiar with the ethnographic data.

History of Research: Museum Collections

E.S. LOHSE AND FRANCES SUNDT

The first known collection of Northwest Coast Indian objects occurred on the voyage of Ensign Juan Pérez Hernández in 1774 (Crespí 1927; Cutter 1969). Several of these objects are in Muséo de America, Madrid (Cabello 1983:129–130). Capt. James Cook and his men made significant collections on his third voyage in 1778 (Beaglehole 1967; Fisher 1979). Cook's own collection was presented to the Leverian Museum (Force and Force 1968), which dissolved in 1806, the pieces eventually going to the British Museum, Museum of Mankind, London; the University Museum, Cambridge University; the Royal Albert Museum, Exeter; the Museum für Völkerkunde, Vienna; and the Museo Nazionale di Antropologia ed Etnologia, Florence (Kaeppler 1978: 73–74; Gunther 1972:Appendix 1; Giglioli 1978:75–85). Surgeon David Samwell's collection was sold at auction. Lt. James King's objects went to the Leverian and British Museums, and to Trinity College in Dublin, now the National Museum of Ireland (King 1981:23; Cole 1985:5). Some pieces, given to the Russian governor of Kamchatka, are in the Muzei Antropologii i Etnografii, Leningrad (Zolotarevskaja, Blomkvist, and Zibert 1958; Rozina 1978). The collection of John Webber, expedition artist, is intact in the Bernisches Historisches Museum, Bern, Switzerland (Kaeppler 1978:18–20; Henking 1978:29–30; Joppien and Smith 1985-1988).

Spain sent Capt. Alejandro Malaspina's scientific expedition to the Northwest Coast in 1791 (Weber 1976); 58 objects collected are held in the Museo de América, Madrid (Rüstow 1939; Gunther 1972:161–162; Feder 1977; Museum of New Mexico 1977). The drawings and journal of expedition artist Tomas de Suría are in the Museo Naval, Madrid, and the Museo de América (Wagner 1936; Palau de Iglesias 1980; Sotos Serrano 1982).

England sent Capt. George Vancouver to the coast in 1792 (Vancouver 1798; Menzies 1923; Bell 1914; Puget 1939). Collections from that expedition are in the British Museum (Read 1892; King 1981; Hewitt 1891; Dillon 1951:153–155; Menzies 1795).

The Curio Trade

Before, during, and after these expeditions, the coasts of Northwest America teemed with vessels employed in the maritime fur trade (vol. 4:380). Captains like Nathaniel Portlock (Portlock 1789), George Dixon (Beresford 1789; Howay 1969a), John Meares (Meares 1790; Howay 1969a), and James Magee (Howay 1930) left records. Most did not. New England maritime societies and early museums have objects brought back by these seamen. Particularly notable is the Peabody Museum of Salem, Massachusetts, inheritor of the collection of the East India Marine Society of Salem, an organization of shipmasters, factors, and supercargoes who were encouraged to collect information respecting other lands and cultures (Dodge 1945; Goodspeed 1945; Whitehill 1949). "Exotic" artifacts were displayed in the society's halls (Dodge and Copeland 1949; Malloy 1986).

After 1910, land-based fur traders proved the equal of the sea captains in passing curios home to repositories in England, Scotland, Ireland, and the eastern United States. Artifacts collected about 1819 by Roderic Mackenzie, chief trader of the North West Company, were acquired by the American Antiquarian Society, then in Boston, and in 1895 accessioned into the Peabody Museum of Archeology and Ethnology, Harvard University (fig. 1). This tiny collection contains some of the earliest and most significant Northwest Coast material in existence (Vaughan and Holm 1982:157). George Simpson, Hudson's Bay Company governor, had a sizable personal collection (S. Stewart 1982) and, at the urging of officials at the Royal Scottish Museum, Edinburgh, encouraged his traders to collect curiosities (Kerr 1953). The Hudson's Bay House, company headquarters in London, maintained a small museum (Kerr 1953; Cole 1985:6). William F. Tolmie, Hudson's Bay Company surgeon and factor, shipped lots to Inverness Museum, Inverness, Scotland, and sent carved argillite pipes and natural history specimens to Dr. John Scouler, who passed them on to the Musée du Trocadero, Paris, in the 1870s (Anonymous 1872; Tolmie 1963).

Russian-American Company fur traders also sent Indian curiosities home. The Imperial Academy's Cabinet of Curiosities benefited by presentations from F.P. Wrangell, K.T. Khlebnikov, and Aleksandr A. Baranov (Zolotarevskaja, Blomkvist, and Zibert 1958). By 1846 Adolph K. Etolin, governor of Russian America, and his contemporaries, Uno Cygnaeus, H.J. Holmgren, John Bartram, and E.H. Furuhjelm, had acquired over 800 pieces that were ultimately placed in the Suomen Kansallismuseo, Helsinki, most Aleut and Eskimo (Pirjo Varjola, personal communication 1985). Ilia G. Voznesenskiĭ, a preparator at the Russian imperial zoological museum, collected zoological, geological, and ethnological specimens over a five-year tour of the north Pacific coast of America (Blomkvist 1972). He also produced a fine set of drawings. All are held in the Muzei Antropologii i Etnografii, informally called the Kunstkammer.

The United States Exploring Expedition led by Capt. Charles Wilkes was on the coast in 1841 (Stanton 1975). Collected pieces, first placed with the National Institute for the Promotion of Science and displayed at the United States Patent Office in Washington, D.C., were transferred to the Smithsonian Institution in 1857 (Marr 1984).

The Quest for Specimens

In 1863 the Smithsonian Institution produced a circular that was distributed to western correspondents and institutions, emphasizing the need for collections of ethnological specimens (Gibbs 1863). Limited funds were available to dispatch collectors into the field and museums of the time had to rely on traders, customs officials, military officers, and other government agents to add to their collections (Deiss 1980). James G. Swan, a school teacher at Neah Bay, Washington Territory, who responded to the call, was instrumental in collecting for the Smithsonian on the Northwest Coast (McDonald 1972; Cole 1985:9–47). George Gibbs, a member of the 49th Parallel Boundary Survey of 1862–1863 and 1872 (Fitzhugh 1988:90), Dr. Thomas T. Minor, surgeon of the revenue steamer *Wayanda*, 1868, Lt. F.M. Ring, an artillery officer stationed in Alaska, and Dr. Alexander Hoff, chief army medical offier for Alaska—all produced valuable collections for the Smithsonian Institution (Fitzhugh and Selig 1981).

Swan was commissioned in 1875, with congressional funds, to acquire objects for the 1876 Centennial Exposition in Philadelphia (Perkes 1876; Miner 1972; Trennert 1974; Braun 1975; Rydell 1980, 1984). Using a network of local collectors, Swan obtained artifacts from Puget Sound to Sitka, notably a 60-foot-long Northern type canoe, a Tsimshian housefront ("Tsimshian Peoples: Southern Tsimshian, Coast Tsimshian, Nishga, and Gitksan," fig. 6, this vol.), and Haida totem poles (Swan 1875, 1876a). Exhibition of these three types of object was a first in the East (Braun 1975:51). The exposition drew over 10 million visitors (Maass 1976:21–22) and was the grandest display of North American Indian objects yet seen.

Assistant Secretary of the Smithsonian Spencer Baird (1875) realized that professional collectors, rather than traders and Indian agents, were more likely to provide

Harvard U., Peabody Mus., Cambridge, Mass.: top left, 95-20-10/48401; center left, 45-20-10/48405; bottom left, 95-20-10/48392; right, 95-20-10/48392.

Fig. 1. Items collected by Roderic Mackenzie about 1819. top left, Carved mountain sheep horn rattle, Coast Salish, lacking the wooden handle and wool fringe. center left, Mountain goat horn bracelet, Coast Salish, a rare item collected only in the 18th and 19th centuries. bottom left, Wooden comb carved in the Central Coast Salish two-dimensional style. Elements are those used on the abstract horn bracelets, but arranged in animal shapes: a wolf on one side, interlocking animal profiles on the other. right, Throwing stick, probably Tlingit. Throwing sticks are found only in early collections, and then rarely. They may have been ceremonial objects (De Laguna 1972, 1:369). Length of top left, 15 cm; bottom left to same scale. Length of center left, 8 cm. Length of right, 39 cm.

collections with documentation of their cultural contexts. Baird believed that Indian cultures were about to disappear and that museums had to act quickly (S.N. Clark 1877). The need for systematic collection had prompted Mason's (1875) instructions on collecting ethnological information and objects, which replaced Gibbs's (1863) guide. The Smithsonian Institution intended to use appropriations allocated for the 1876 Centennial to fill out its own collections (Baird 1876:60). Swan continued as an important collector into the late 1880s, while employed as a government agent at Neah Bay. Baird's insistence on representative specimens rather than curios, and their display in carefully planned exhibits, marks the beginning of professional anthropological research that was to prompt the large-scale systematic collections of the late nineteenth century.

The principal rival for the Smithsonian Institution in amassing Northwest Coast Indian specimens during this period was the American Museum of Natural History in New York (Osborn 1911). The American Museum acquired a large collection obtained by Indian Commis-

Fig. 2. Haida canoe collected by Israel W. Powell on display in the North Pacific Hall of the American Museum of Natural History, New York. Photograph by Thomas Lundt, 1911.

sioner for British Columbia Israel W. Powell, who acted for Heber R. Bishop, 1880–1885. A Haida canoe, acquired by Powell, that it took considerable trouble to transport to New York in 1884 has been on display since then. In 1911 manikins depicting a Chilkat entourage arriving at a potlatch were placed in the canoe under the direction of George T. Emmons (fig. 2) (Dickerson 1910; Neandross 1910).

In 1888 the American Museum's collection was greatly expanded by acquisition of 1,351 pieces, mostly Tlingit, collected by George T. Emmons from 1882 to 1887. The musuem paid $12,000 (Wardwell 1978:26). As officer aboard the *U.S.S. Adams* and later, the *U.S.S. Pinta*, Lieutenant Emmons was an exceptional collector, assembling carefully labeled and documented collections (Boas 1888b, 1889a; Low 1977; Conrad 1978). Between 1888 and 1893 Emmons sent over 4,000 pieces to the American Museum (Jonaitis 1988:87) ("History of Research in Ethnology," fig. 1, this vol.). He supplied detailed notes on meaning, function, and significance of pieces but omitted exact geographic provenience and informant names, lest competitors use these. His collections are particularly valuable for the hundreds of Tlingit shamanistic objects. Emmons exhibited another large collection at the 1893 World's Columbian Exposition in Chicago, where he had the attention of museum officials (Boas 1893; Starr 1893:621; Mason 1894, 1894a; Collier and Tschopik 1954:769; Ewers 1959:521; Dexter 1966). In fact, the interest of the exposition director, Frederic Ward Putnam, was in using exposition collections to establish what was to become the Field Museum of Natural History in Chicago. Under the threat of its rival buying Emmons's collection, the American Museum paid almost $30,000 for 3,067 specimens in 1894 (Wardwell 1978:27–28). Emmons was involved with the American Museum from 1896 to 1938, although by 1897, his free market tactics incurred

the ire of Franz Boas, and for the duration of Boas's tenure he was forced to look elsewhere to sell his collections. In 1900, the Smithsonian Institution commissioned Emmons to equip and install a Chilkat life group, one of 12 life groups planned by W.H. Holmes for the 1901 Pan-American Exposition in Buffalo (fig. 3) (Emmons 1900, 1900a; Mason 1901; Holmes 1903:pl. 26). In 1902, Emmons sold another large collection, this time to the Field Museum for $10,000 and exchanges (the Spuhn Collection), and followed with sale of mostly Tlingit baskets for $2,500 (Cole 1985:150–151). In 1905, Emmons was again peddling a large collection, but by then the market was becoming glutted. After exhibiting at the Alaska-Yukon-Pacific Exposition in Seattle in 1908, he arranged a sale to the Washington State Museum (Thomas Burke Memorial), Seattle (Cole 1985:221). Emmons continued to sell smaller collections to many museums, mostly small repositories, but met with less interest in the acquisition of Northwest Coast specimens.

The American Museum launched its own large-scale collecting program in 1897 with the Jesup North Pacific Expedition, which lasted six years under the direction of Boas (Freed, Freed, and Williamson 1988). Harlan I. Smith, who spent four years in ethnological and archeological fieldwork on the coast, collected from the Coast Salish (Wintemberg 1940). Livingston Farrand collected among the Quinault and Quileute. Boas assigned George Hunt, a half-Tlingit born at Fort Rupert, to collect among the Kwakiutl. B. Fillip Jacobsen obtained objects from the Nootka. Always, Boas emphasized the need for collecting commonplace as well as unique or unusual items. The opening of the American Museum's North Pacific Hall in 1899 attracted favorable popular attention (Jonaitis 1988: 211–212). George Dorsey of the Field Columbian Museum, Chicago, wrote that between 1895 and 1905, the American Museum anthropologists had surpassed all other institutions in acquiring comprehensive collections that were exceptionally well displayed (Dorsey 1907:584). Lowie (1910) published notes concerning these new collections. Jacknis (1985) assesses the impact of Boas on museum exhibits.

Dorsey and the Field Museum had been anything but lacking in initiative over the same period of time (Dorsey 1900, 1907). Dorsey commissioned Dr. Charles F. Newcombe of Victoria. Newcombe began his career as a collector with a four-fold commission in 1897 from the Bremen Museum, Germany, the premier of British Columbia, the director of the Canadian Geological Survey, Ottawa, and Franz Boas of the American Museum (Cole 1985:179–180). In 1901 he accepted a three-year contract with the Field Museum. Dorsey wanted principally Haida material, and the museum was willing to pay inflated prices. That Newcombe succeeded so well can be attributed to his hiring Charles Edenshaw, a Haida carver, as his informant and collaborator (Barbeau

1944; Appleton 1970; Holm 1981; Hoover 1983). Newcombe was also successful in obtaining Kwakiutl materials through the work of his collaborator Charlie Nowell, a high-ranking Kwakiutl.

The end of Newcombe's contract with the Field Museum marks the end of rivalry between the large American museums for Northwest Coast material (Cole 1982a, 1985:212). Declining interest was in part practical, as the major repositories could display only a fraction of their collections. However, there also had evolved a sophistication in anthropology that placed much less emphasis on material culture. Collecting did continue, but it was on a far smaller scale and addressed the needs of smaller museums and individuals. George T. Emmons, for instance, found a reliable buyer in George C. Heye well into the 1940s. Heye established the Museum of the American Indian, Heye Foundation, in New York in 1916. Pieces collected by Stewart S. Culin and by Newcombe went to Heye through the University Museum, University of Pennsylvania, Philadelphia. Leo J. Frachtenberg collected among the Quileute, Quinault, and Makah. T.T. Waterman collected for Heye from the Southern Coast Salish.

During this period Culin sought specimens for the Brooklyn Museum, New York, including material from Newcombe. Newcombe also found a buyer in the Canadian Geological Survey. The British Columbia Provincial Museum, Victoria, established in 1886, became interested in collecting about 1900 in response to foreign museums' collecting in the area (Newcombe 1909), and from 1911 to 1914, Newcombe gathered pieces for the museum (Newcombe 1914, 1915). Kermode (1916, 1917) produced an annotated list of collections.

The Peabody Museum of Harvard University had people working in the Northwest Coast in this period. The museum, which had collections from the Boston Marine Society, the American Antiquarian Society, and the Boston Society of Natural History (Vaughan and Holm 1982), had purchased a collection of Tlingit material in 1869 (Fast 1869) and engaged in exchanges with the Smithsonian Institution for pieces collected by Wilkes, Swan, and J.J. McLean. Additions were made by F.W. Rindge in the 1890s and by Lewis H. Farlow, both men of wealth. In particular, Farlow worked with Grace Nicholson of Pasadena, California, who through her network of buyers supplied Harvard with high-quality Northwest Coast baskets, 1902–1915 (Cole 1985:237; McLendon 1981). At C.C. Willoughby's direction, Newcombe and Nowell supplied the Peabody Museum of Harvard with a significant Kwakiutl collection in 1917.

After 1906, some collectors, convinced that little was to be had from Indian hands, resorted to obtaining old collections made by pioneers, early traders, and Victoria and Sitka dealers (Emmons 1913, 1914). However, Culin (1908) collected successfully from the Hesquiat and other

Smithsonian, Natl. Mus. of Nat. Hist.: top, 13702; center, 30238; bottom, MNH 037.
Fig. 3. Evolution of a display. top, Chilkat Tlingit family life group designed by W.H. Holmes for the 1901 Pan-American Exposition, Buffalo, N.Y. Manikins were used to "present in the most striking manner possible a synopsis of the Pan-American aborigines" (Holmes 1903:200). Creation of life groups allowed demonstration of idealized cultural and male-female roles. center, Chilkat Tlingit life group display at the Museum of Natural History, Smithsonian Institution, about 1920, using the same manikins, but with some new specimens and another manikin weaving a Chilkat blanket from a painted pattern board. Holmes's life groups were the central exhibits in the North American ethnology halls of the Museum of Natural History from 1911, when it opened, until 1957, when the halls were redesigned (Ewers 1959:522). bottom, Museum of Natural History display in 1988, using only the weaver and signs explaining the weaving process.

Nootkans and the Songhees. Occasionally collectors purchased caches of Indian ceremonial paraphernalia and favored heirlooms. Samuel A. Barrett of the Milwaukee Public Museum, Wisconsin, was successful in collecting 1914–1915. Hiring George Hunt at Fort Rupert, Barrett was amazed at the ease with which they gathered a large collection, attributing his success to the Pentecostal movement that prompted believers to abandon the old ways (Ritzenthaler and Parsons 1966:17). Equally important were Canadian government attempts to stop potlatching, officially banned since 1885. In December 1921, Kwakiutl Dan Cranmer held a six-day potlatch at Village Island, and shortly afterward the Royal Canadian Mounted Police arrested the participants (Codere 1961:470–471; Sewid-Smith 1979). Coppers, headdresses, masks, blankets, and all other potlatch materials were confiscated. Agent William M. Halliday intended to ship the pieces to Edward Sapir at the National Museum of Man, in Ottawa, but a delay enabled George Heye to buy a number of fine objects. The remainder did go to Ottawa, constituting an impressive array of valuable and rare pieces from an area thought denuded by collectors. A portion of the collection was entrusted to the Royal Ontario Museum, Toronto. The National Museum, after negotiations begun in the 1960s, returned the confiscated objects to the Alert Bay and Cape Mudge communities in 1979 and 1980. The Department of Indian Affairs recalled the objects from the Royal Ontario Museum in 1987, and the objects were divided between the U'Mista Cultural Centre at Alert Bay and the Kwagiulth Museum at Cape Mudge on January 30, 1988.

Following World War I, collectors concentrated on remote groups. Prominent during this period was Louis Shotridge, a Chilkat Tlingit of high-ranking family. Shotridge first entered museum records in 1905, when he sold a small Tlingit collection to the University Museum, University of Pennsylvania (Cole 1985:255; M.R. Harrington 1912). In 1911 he was hired as staff by that museum ("History of Research in Ethnology," fig. 3, this vol.), and from 1915 to 1932, Shotridge spent most of his time in the field, based usually at Haines and Sitka, Alaska. From 1922–1927 he assisted the Wanamaker Expedition. Shotridge sought prestige items rather than household and ceremonial objects (Shotridge 1919a, 1928, 1929a; Cole 1985:264, 353).

Another prominent collector began his career in the 1920s. C. Marius Barbeau, an Oxford-educated anthropologist with the National Museum of Canada, Ottawa, was an immensely productive fieldworker and author (Duff 1964a). Barbeau, who collected directly from the Indians for the most part, was a meticulous recorder of collection information (Halpin 1973:22). His noteworthy 1927 collection from the Gitksan and Nishga went to the Royal Ontario Museum. In 1929, he collected for both the National Museum of Canada and the Royal Ontario Museum. Spurred by public concern for protection of the remaining totem poles in British Columbia, Barbeau inventoried the Skeena River poles in 1924, work sponsored by the federal Department of Indian Affairs. The Department undertook restoration of the poles (Smith 1928), and the results were controversial. A positive aspect of the program was the Indian Act Amendment of 1926, which allowed Indian Affairs to veto any sale of poles on reserve land.

By the 1920s large-scale collecting was effectively over. Collection continued (fig. 4), but it was confined in large part to acquiring old pieces from collectors and dealers, de-accessioned museum pieces, repatriated items, or heirlooms. The Portland Art Museum, Oregon, obtained in 1948 pieces collected by Axel Rasmussen from the 1920s to 1940s when he was superintendent of schools at Wrangell and Skagway, Alaska (R.T. Davis 1949; Gunther 1966:175–183). The Museum of Anthropology of the University of British Columbia, Vancouver, benefited from acquisition of the collections of missionaries G.H. Raley, William H. Collison, and G.H. Darby. In the 1950s, that museum acquired Kwakiutl material through its association with Kwakiutl carver Mungo Martin (Duff 1959; De Laguna 1963; Hawthorn 1964; Borrelly 1971; Carter 1971). The Thomas Burke Memorial, Washington State Museum, University of Washington, Seattle, acquired the Walter Waters collection in 1953 and the Gerber collection in 1969, the latter strong in Kwakiutl ceremonial paraphernalia and Haida argillite carvings (Holm 1972). Other collections being assembled (Holm 1972a) did not come from Indians and lacked documentation.

Collecting Art

In the 1980s collection of Northwest Coast pieces was based on the perception of the objects as art. Recognition of Northwest Coast Indian art began in the nineteenth century (Boas 1897a; Haeberlin 1918a; Waterman 1923; Krieger 1926; Leechman 1928; Emmons 1930; Boas 1927). An important event that encouraged the perception of Northwest Coast productions as art rather than as artifacts was an exhibition at the Museum of Modern Art, New York, in 1941 (Douglas and d'Harnoncourt 1941; Jonaitis 1981a; Schrader 1983). The most influential group to promote Northwest Coast Indian art was the Surrealists, who aspired to produce elemental myth-oriented art, which in their view exuded the spiritual qualities common to man's development. Max Ernst, André Breton, Kurt Seligmann, and other Surrealists gravitated toward Northwest Coast art in the 1940s, collecting what they regarded as visual puns (Cowling 1978). In 1946 they staged an exhibition entitled "Northwest Coast Indian Painting" at the Betty Parsons Gallery, New York, which included their own pieces, some

Fig. 4. Henry Moody, Haida, and Charles F. Newcombe. Moody was one of many informants used by Newcombe to gather excellent collections of Northwest Coast artifacts. On this trip, Newcombe purchased a Haida totem pole for the Royal Ontario Museum, Toronto (Cole 1985:238–239). Photographed at Tanu, Queen Charlotte Is., B.C., 1923.

obtained from George Heye, and specimens borrowed from the American Museum of Natural History. Still, "until about 1955, this material had no more value than seashells or beetles" (Carpenter in Holm and Reid 1975: 17).

The Denver Art Museum, Colorado, established a department of Indian art in 1925. Since then the museum has been a pioneer in acquiring and displaying Northwest Coast Indian art, particularly through the efforts of Frederic Douglas, named curator in 1929 (Douglas and d'Harnoncourt 1941; Feder and Malin 1962; Hassrick and Bach 1960; Conn 1979).

A resurgence in collecting Northwest Coast pieces since the 1940s is attributable to three parallel developments: (1) frequent exhibitions, with illustrated catalogs, and scholarly publications that reach a broad audience (Garfield and Forrest 1948; Garfield and Wingert 1966; Gunther 1951, 1953, 1962, 1966, 1971; Hawthorn 1956, 1967, 1979; H. Stewart 1979a, 1984; Holm 1987; Jonaitis 1988); (2) restoration and recreation programs like the totem pole projects sponsored by the University of British Columbia and British Columbia Provincial Museum in Canada and by the United States Forest Service in cooperation with the Indian Civilian Conservation Corps in the United States (Duff 1954); and (3) the efforts of talented artists and artist-scholars in the region (for example, Holm 1965, 1972, 1972a; B. Reid 1967; Holm and Reid 1975; MacNair, Hoover, and Neary 1980).

Prior to 1930, most exhibitions of Northwest Coast Indian art objects occurred as a minor part of permanent ethnological exhibits. Major temporary exhibits that focused entirely on Northwest Coast Indian art began in the 1960s. Major exhibits and catalogs have been produced by these repositories: Seattle Art Museum (Gunther 1951, 1962; Holm 1983b), Denver Art Museum (Feder and Malin 1962), The Art Institute of Chicago (Wardwell 1964), Robert H. Lowie Museum of Anthropology (Harner and Elsasser 1965), Portland Art Museum (Gunther 1966), Vancouver Art Gallery (Duff 1967; Vancouver Art Gallery 1974), Princeton University Art Museum (1969), Société des Amis du Musée de l'Homme (1969), Thomas Burke Memorial Washington State Museum (Holm 1972a, 1987), National Gallery of Art (Collins et al. 1973), Renwick Gallery (1974), Sheldon Jackson Museum (1976), Museum für Völkerkunde, Hamburg (Haberland 1979), Oregon Historical Society (Vaughan and Holm 1982), University Museum, University of Pennsylvania (Kaplan and Barsness 1986), Glenbow Museum, and the American Museum of Natural History (Wardwell 1978; Jonaitis 1988).

In British Columbia alone from 1956 to 1980, 33 major exhibitions were produced in which Northwest Coast objects were displayed as art (M. Ames 1986:53–55, table 1). The first shows featured mostly early pieces with only a few objects by contemporary artists, but exhibitions in British Columbia in the 1980s showed a preponderance of work by living artists. As an example, the Royal British Columbia Museum commissioned the majority of pieces shown in its two "Legacy" exhibitions (A. Ames 1986:55). In 1976, permanent exhibits of Northwest Coast Indian art were installed in the University of British Columbia Museum of Anthropology, the Royal British Columbia Museum, and the National Museum of Canada, Ottawa. The University of British Columbia Museum of Anthropology and the Vancouver Centennial Museum have also acted as patrons for Indian artists since the 1960s.

With or without museum sponsorships, the production of Northwest Coast art never ceased. Indian artists like Kwakiutls Charlie James (Nuytten 1982), Willie Seaweed (Holm 1974a, 1983), and Mungo Martin (Duff 1959; H.B. Hawthorn 1961; Hawthorn 1964; Nuytten 1982) were producing traditional objects throughout the early and middle twentieth century. In 1947 Martin was invited to the University of British Columbia, Vancouver, to direct work on totem pole restoration and to carve new poles for Totem Park (Duff 1981b; Nuytten 1982). In his seventies, Martin moved to Victoria, to work at the British Columbia Provincial Museum as resident carver. He constructed a traditional Kwakiutl house there in 1953 and sponsored a potlatch in it, the government having lifted its ban three years before (J.K. Nesbitt 1954). Henry Hunt and his son Tony Hunt, both apprenticed to Martin, followed Martin as resident carvers at the British Columbia Provinical Museum. Bill Reid, an artist of Haida descent, and Doug Cranmer, Kwakiutl, constructed

left, U. of B.C., Mus. of Anthr., Vancouver; right, Field Mus., Chicago: Gen-83369.4.

Fig. 5. Contemporary Northwest Coast museum exhibits. left, Totem Park, University of British Columbia Museum of Anthropology, Vancouver, B.C. The houses and poles were carved by Bill Reid and Doug Cranmer, 1959–1963. Photograph by William McLennan, 1984. right, Raising a pole at the opening of the Maritime Peoples Hall, Field Museum, Chicago, Ill. The pole was carved by Norman Tait, a Tsimshian. Members of Tait's family, in button blankets, supervise the raising. Photograph by Ron Testa, April 1982.

houses and carved totem poles at the University of British Columbia (fig. 5) ("Art," fig. 23, this vol.).

Bill Holm wrote the definitive analysis of the style of traditional two-dimensional Northwest Coast art (Holm 1965). As curator emeritus of the Thomas Burke Memorial, Washington State Museum, Holm taught both artists and anthropologists. Holm's use of museum collections as a basis for the production of new work has expanded many Indian artists' perceptions of their art. Reference to collected masterworks has enabled these artists to reach and exceed traditional standards of excellence. Artists have produced pieces not only for sale but also for traditional community ceremonies (MacNair 1973–1974; Vancouver Art Gallery 1974; H. Stewart 1979; MacNair, Hoover, and Neary 1980; Blackman 1985; Duffek 1986; Shadbolt 1986). Bill Reid, Robert Davidson, and Henry, Tony, and Richard Hunt and others produced work for tribal communities, private collectors, and corporate sponsors ("Art," fig. 8 and "Mythology," fig. 1, this vol.).

Museums in the late twentieth century acted more as reference sources for artists and their public than as repositories to save rare items from extinct cultures. Museums also act to promote Indian artists, their work, and their culture. A number of Northwest Coast Indian bands and tribes operate their own museums, hire curators, and lobby for repatriation of tribal pieces (S. Inglis 1979). M. Ames (1986:56) suggests that a reversal of the traditional patron-client relationship between anthropologists and Indians has taken place, where the Indians may act as patrons and the anthropologists as clients. This is certainly the case in Indian-owned and -operated museums. Nevertheless, non-Indian museums have acted to preserve aspects of Indian cultures and have promoted the idea of Northwest Coast Indian art as fine art, a position that is responsible for public acceptance of that art and important in the vitality of Northwest Coast culture (Hawthorn, Belshaw, and Jamieson 1958: 265–267).

Museums still collect, but collection is highly selective in a high-priced and intensely competitive art market. Repositories like the Royal British Columbia Museum and the Canadian Museum of Civilization compete in international art markets to purchase and repatriate prized objects to Canada (M. Ames 1986). The Royal British Columbia Museum's practice of supplying objects to the Indian communities is innovative. Its Human History section employed museum carvers to produce pieces for potlatches and arranged for loans of items from the museum's collections to potlatch sponsors (Macfarlane 1978). It also supervised creation of a detailed record of contemporary Kwakiutl potlatching through taping and filming. The museum retains the films but the Indian families keep all copyright privileges, and anthropologists must obtain the owner's permission before use.

Selected Repository Collections[†]

Artifact collections listed here have documentation including location, collector, date of collection, and tribe. Exceptions are collections with unusual historical context. Documentation for photographs and artwork (paintings

---

[†] Information on the photographs and artwork in this section was collected by Joanna C. Scherer, and the compilation of the photographic sources section was a collaborative effort of Joanna C. Scherer and the authors.

and drawings) requires the name of the photographer or artist, approximate date of creation, and sometimes the tribal group. Dates for artifacts are the dates of collection and dates for photographs are their dates of creation. All dates given were obtained from the repository or from the cited sources. Date ranges are those for a specified collection and do not necessarily indicate the entire scope of collections in the repository. All collections are listed in chronological order. An asterisk next to a photographer's name indicates that the repository holds the original negatives. Tribes cited in entries are those identified as significant parts of the collection and do not necessarily represent the entire range of tribes within the collection.

Alaska State Museum and Historical Library, Juneau. Photographs: Tlingit and Haida, *Winter and Pond, 1891–1945; Tlingit, *V. Soboleff, 1896–1920; Tlingit, *Case and Draper, 1898–1920; Yakutat Tlingit, *F. Kayamori, 1912–1941 (De Laguna 1972).

Alberni Valley Museum, Port Alberni, British Columbia. Photographs: Nootka, E. Fleming, 1896, and F. Brand, 1898–1908.

American Museum of Natural History, New York. Artifacts: northern tribes, I.W. Powell, 1881–1882; Tlingit, G.T. Emmons, 1884–1914; Kwakiutl and Bella Coola, F. Boas and G. Hunt, 1894–1905; Coast Salish, H.I. Smith, 1897–1909; Quinault, L. Farrand, 1898; Haida, J.R. Swanton, 1900–1901, and C.F. Newcombe, 1901. Photographs: Tlingit and Haida, G.T. Emmons, 1880s–1890s; Bella Coola, Haida, and Tsimshian, E. Dossetter, 1881 (I.W. Powell survey); various, H.I. Smith, 1892–1902 (Jesup Expedition); Kwakiutl, *O.C. Hastings, 1894 and 1898; Kwakiutl, *G. Hunt, 1901–1920s, and F. Boas, 1930–1931; Kwakiutl and Tsimshian, P.E. Goddard, 1922.

Bancroft Library, University of California, Berkeley. Photographs: Tlingit and Coast Salish, E. Muybridge, 1868; various, *Case and Draper, 1898–1920.

Bernisches Historisches Museum, Bern, Switzerland. Artifacts: Nootka, J. Webber, 1778, Cook's third voyage (Henking 1978; Bandi 1958; J. Thompson 1977).

Brooklyn Museum, Brooklyn, New York. Artifacts: Haida, Kwakiutl, Nootka, and Coast Salish, S. Culin and C.F. Newcombe, 1905, 1908, 1911.

University of British Columbia, Museum of Anthropology, Vancouver. Artifacts: Haisla, Tsimshian, and Coast Salish, G.H. Raley; Haida, Nishga, and Tsimshian, W.H. Collison; Kwakiutl ceremonial gear collected after 1955 (Hawthorn 1967, 1979; University of British Columbia. Museum of Anthropology 1975, 1975a). Photographs: Coast Salish, E.W. Crocker, 1910–1936; Kwakiutl, W. Halliday, 1910, and W. Duff, 1958, Coast Salish and Nootka, H. Hawthorn, 1949–1951.

British Library, Department of Manuscripts, London. Artwork: Nootka sketches, J. Webber, 1778, Cook's third voyage (Joppien and Smith 1985–1988).

British Museum, Museum of Mankind, London. Artifacts: Nootka, 1778, from Cook's third voyage, and from Vancouver's 1790 voyage; western Oregon, S.C. Freer, 1900. Photographs: Tlingit, E. Muybridge, 1868; Haida, B.W. Leeson, 1898–1900.

Thomas Burke Memorial, Washington State Museum, Seattle. Artifacts: Haida, Makah, and Quinault, J.G. Swan and M. Eells, 1893; Tlingit and Haida, G.T. Emmons. Photographs: Tlingit, A.C. Pillsbury, 1898; Makah, E. Gunther, 1956.

California State Library, Sacramento. Photographs: Tlingit, E. Muybridge, 1860s.

Canadian Museum of Civilization, National Museums of Canada, Ottawa. Artifacts: Haida and Tsimshian, I.W. Powell, 1879; Haida and Kwakiutl, G.M. Dawson, 1885 and 1891; various, C.F. Newcombe, 1890–1904 and 1895–1901; Nootka, E. Sapir, 1910 and 1913–1915; Tsimshian, C.M. Barbeau, 1915–1932; various, H.I. Smith, 1919–1929; Tlingit, G.T. Emmons; various, A.C. Bossom, 1955. Photographs: Bella Coola and Haida, R. Maynard, 1873–1874 (I.W. Powell survey); Kwakiutl and Haida, G.M. Dawson, 1885 and 1888; various, *H.I. Smith, 1892–1902 (Jesup Expedition); Tsimshian, G.T. Emmons, 1910, and *C.M. Barbeau, 1920–1926; Kwakiutl, B.W. Leeson, 1912 and 1915.

Carnegie Museum, Pittsburgh, Pennsylvania. Artifacts: Tlingit, Haida, and Kwakiutl, F. Harvey.

Denver Art Museum, Denver, Colorado. Artifacts: northern tribes, A.L. Lindsay, 1879; Tlingit and Kwakiutl (Conn 1979).

Douglas County Museum, Roseburg, Oregon. Artwork: Rogue River Indians, Capt. A. Lyman, 1850–1851.

Field Museum of Natural History, Chicago. Artifacts: Tlingit and Haida, F. Boas, 1893, and J.A. Jacobsen, 1893; Haida totem poles and Bella Coola, Kwakiutl, and Nootka masks, G.A. Dorsey and C.F. Newcombe, 1899–1905. Photographs: Coast Salish, R. Maynard, 1872, and C.F. Newcombe, 1893; Tsimshian and Haida, *E.P. Allen, 1897 (Dorsey Expedition); Kwakiutl, C.F. Carpenter, 1904; various tribes, R. Testa, 1980.

Glenbow Museum, Calgary, Alberta. Photographs: Bella Coola, E. Hattorff, 1885.

Hydrographic Department, Ministry of Defense, Taunton, Somerset, England. Artwork: Kwakiutl and Coast Salish watercolors, H. Humphrys and J. Sykes, 1791–1795, Vancouver's voyage.

Hudson's Bay Company Archive, Provincial Archives of Manitoba, Winnipeg. Photographs: various, R. Maynard, 1860s–1890s; various, R. Harrington, 1940s–1960s.

Library of Congress, Prints and Photographs Division, Washington, D.C. Photographs: various, E.S. Curtis, 1890–1927; Makah, A. Curtis, 1911; Tlingit, 1935–1940.

Robert H. Lowie Museum of Anthropology, University of California, Berkeley. Artifacts: Tlingit and Haida baskets, Alaska Commercial Company, 1867–1898; Coos baskets, A.R. Sengstacken, as early as 1869.

McCord Museum, McGill University, Montreal. Artifacts: Haida, G.M. Dawson, 1878. Photographs: Coast Salish, B. Baltzly, 1871.

Makah Cultural and Research Center, Neah Bay, Washington. Artifacts: Ozette archeological collections, 1971–1980.

Milwaukee Public Museum, Wisconsin. Artifacts: Kwakiutl and Bella Coola, S.A. Barrett, 1915 (Ritzenthaler and Parsons 1966). Photographs: Kwakiutl, S.A. Barrett, 1915–1916.

Museo de América, Madrid. Artifacts: Tlingit and Nootka, A. Malaspina, 1789–1794. Artwork: Tlingit and Nootka paintings, J. Cardero and T. Suría, 1789–1794, Malaspina Expedition (Sotos Serrano 1982; Palau de Iglesias 1980).

Museo Naval, Madrid. Artwork: Tlingit, Kwakiutl, Nootka, Makah, and Coast Salish drawings and paintings, J. Cardero and T. Suría, 1789–1794, Malaspina Expedition (Sotoca 1970).

Museo Nazionale di Antropologia ed Etnologia, Florence. Artifacts: Nootka, 1778, Cook's third voyage (Giglioli 1978).

Museum of the American Indian, Heye Foundation, New York. Artifacts: various, D.F. Tozzier, 1891–1907, and G.T. Emmons, 1903, 1905, 1909; Kwakiutl potlatch material, G. Heye, 1921. Photographs: Central Coast Salish, R. Maynard, 1882, and W.A. Newcombe, 1934 and 1938.

Museum of History and Industry, Seattle, Washington. Photographs: Makah and Coast Salish, *A. Wilse, 1898–1903, and *J.G. McCurdy, 1900–1920.

Museum für Völkerkunde, Berlin. Artifacts: various, J.A. Jacobsen, 1881–1883 (Jacobsen 1884); Tlingit and Haida, P. Schulze, 1882; Kwakiutl and Bella Coola, F. Jacobsen, 1884 and 1906; Kwakiutl, Tsimshian, and Coast Salish, F. Boas, 1885–1886; Haida and Nootka, K. von den Steinen, 1897–1898.

Museum für Völkerkunde, Vienna. Artifacts: Nootka, L. von Fichtel, 1806 (including some from Cook's third voyage, 1778); various, J.G. Swan, 1873, J.A. Jacobsen and B.F. Jacobsen, 1893 and 1894.

Muzei Anthropologi i Étnografiĭ, Leningrad. Artifacts: cloaks from Cook's third voyage, 1778 (Siebert and Forman 1967); northern tribes, I. Lisiânskiĭ, 1804–1806, I.G. Vosnesenskii, 1839–1845, and G. Chudnovskii, 1890. Artwork: I.G. Vosnesenskii, 1839–1845.

National Archives, Still Pictures Branch, Washington, D.C. Photographs: Central Coast Salish, Tlingit and Kwakiutl, *C.H. Gilbert, *N.B. Miller, *C.H. Townsend, 1895–1897.

National Museum of Ireland, Dublin. Artifacts: Nootkan cedar bark blankets, J. King, 1778, Cook's third voyage.

96 Oregon Historical Society, Portland. Photographs:

Umpqua, L. Lorrain, 1857–1858. Artwork: paintings of Kwakiutl, G. Davidson, 1792; sketch of Chinook, J. Drayton, 1841.

University of Oregon Library, Special Collection, Eugene. Photographs: various, *L. Moorhouse, about 1900.

Peabody Museum of Archaeology and Ethnology, Harvard University, Cambridge. Artifacts: Nootka, J. Magee, 1790; Chinook, M. Lewis and W. Clark, 1804–1805; Coast Salish, R. Mackenzie, before 1819; Tlingit, E.G. Fast, 1867–1868. Photographs: Kwakiutl, E. Muybridge, 1862, and J.H. Graybill, 1893; Haida, R. Maynard, 1864–1893, and J.R. Swanton, 1901–1902; Kwakiutl and Nootka, C.F. Newcombe, 1899–1921 and 1911–1933; various, G. Nicholson, about 1905–1910. Artwork: drawings of Nootka Sound, J. Webber, 1778, Cook's third voyage.

Perth Museum and Art Gallery, Perth, Scotland. Artifacts: Coast Salish, J.M. Yale, 1833 (Idiens 1983, 1987).

Portland Art Museum, Portland, Oregon. Artifacts: Kwakiutl and Tlingit, A. Rasmussen (Davis 1949; Gunther 1966).

B.C. Archives and Records Service, Victoria. Photographs: Nootka, R. Maynard, 1864–1893, and E. Fleming and Fleming Brothers, 1887–1900; Coast Salish, *F. Dally, 1866 and 1868; Salish and Tlingit, E. Muybridge, 1868; Kwakiutl, Tsimshian, and Haida, O.C. Hastings, 1879; Bella Coola, E. Dossetter, 1880s; Haida, C.F. Newcombe, 1897–1901. Artwork: drawings of Haida and Tlingit, S. Bacstrom, 1793; watercolors of Salish, J.M. Alden, 1854 and 1858.

Public Archives of Canada, Ottawa. Artwork: sketch of Coast Salish, H.J. Warre, 1848; sketches of Umpqua and Kalapuya, E. de Giradin, 1856.

Royal Albert Museum, Exeter, England. Artifacts: Makah and Nootka, B. Gregory, 1871.

Royal British Columbia Museum, Victoria. Artifacts: Kwakiutl, Nootka, Makah, Coast Salish, Haida, and Tsimshian, N. Chittenden, J. Deans, C.F. and W.A. Newcombe, 1880s–1961. Photographs: Nootka, C. Gentile, 1864, and E. Fleming, 1896; Nootka and Coast Salish, F. Dally, 1868; Haida, Nootka, and Tlingit, R. Maynard, 1873–1874 and 1884 (I.W. Powell survey); Haida, Kwakiutl and Tlingit, C.F. Newcombe, 1888–1913; Tsimshian and Kwakiutl, W. Duff, 1949 and 1953.

Royal Ontario Museum, Toronto. Artwork: Central Coast Salish, Southwestern Coast Salish, Chinook and Nootka sketches and watercolors, P. Kane, 1846–1847 (Harper 1971).

Sheldon Jackson Museum, Sheldon Jackson College, Sitka, Alaska. Photographs: Tlingit, *E.W. Merrill, 1899–1929 (Chambers 1977).

Smithsonian Institution, Department of Anthropology and National Anthropological Archives, Washington,

D.C. Artifacts: various tribes, C. Wilkes, 1841, J.G. Swan, 1863, 1870, 1875–1876, 1878, and 1881–1885, J.J. McLean, 1881–1882 and 1884, and F. Boas, 1887, 1890, 1892–1893 and 1895–1896. Photographs: Tlingit, E. Muybridge, 1868; Nootka and Kwakiutl, R. Maynard, 1873 and 1880–1885; Central Coast Salish, J.G. Swan, 1873; Haida, R. Maynard or E. Dossetter, 1880–1885; various, A.P. Niblack, 1885–1886; Kwakiutl, *O.C. Hastings, 1894, and *T.W. Smiley, before 1895; Haida, Tsimshian, and Tlingit, G.T. Emmons, 1885–1886 and 1890s; Haida and Tlingit, Winter and Pond, 1895–1900; Nootka, W.A. Newcombe, 1896, and C.F. Newcombe, 1903; Tlingit, Case and Draper, 1906–1926; Southern Coast Salish, *D.W. Gill, 1907; Makah and Nootka, A. Curtis, 1909–1926; Central and Southern Coast Salish, E.S. Curtis, 1913; Kalapuya, L.J. Frachtenberg, 1915. Artwork: sketches of Chinook, H.J.K. Duncan, 1953; sketches of Makah, G. Gibbs, 1867; Tlingit, Haida, Tsimshian, and Makah, J.G. Swan, 1873–1874 and 1880–1883.

Stark Museum of Art, Orange, Texas. Artwork: sketches of Chinook, Central Coast Salish, and Southwestern Coast Salish, P. Kane, 1846–1847 (Harper 1971).

State Library of New South Wales, Dixson Library, Sydney, Australia. Artwork: watercolors of Nootka, J. Webber, 1778, Cook's third voyage (Joppien and Smith 1985-1988); Tsimshian, Haida, or Kwakiutl watercolors, Z. Mudge, 1792, Vancouver's voyage.

Suquamish Museum, Tribal Photographic Archives, Suquamish, Washington. Photographs: Southern Coast Salish, 1885–1988 (The Suquamish Museum 1985).

University of Toronto Archives, Ontario. Photographs: Bella Coola, T.F. McIlwraith, 1913–1950 (McIlwraith 1948).

University of Toronto, Thomas Fisher Rare Book Room, Ontario. Photographs: Tlingit, G.D. Goetze, 1889–1906.

Übersee Museum, Bremen, Federal Republic of Germany. Artifacts: Tlingit, A. Krause, 1881–1883.

University Museum, University of Cambridge, England. Artifacts: Nootka, Earl of Denbigh, 1778, Cook's third voyage; Nootka, S. Swaine, 1792, Vancouver's voyage.

University Museum, University of Pennsylvania, Philadelphia. Artifacts: Makah, S. Culin, 1900 (Wanamaker Expedition); Haida, C.F. Newcombe, 1900 (Wanamaker Expedition); Tlingit, Haida, and Salish, G. Gordon, before 1915; Tlingit and Tsimshian, L. Shotridge, 1915–1932; Tlingit, G.T. Emmons, 1916, 1918, 1929; Eyak, F. DeLaguna, 1933. Photographs: Kwakiutl, H. Maynard, 1888, and B.W. Leeson, 1912; Tlingit and Tsimshian, *L. Shotridge, 1915–1932 (Shotridge 1919a).

Vancouver City Archives, British Columbia. Photographs: Central Coast Salish, G. Hastings, 1860s; Northern Coast Salish, Bailey Brothers, about 1890; Kwakiutl, B.W. Leeson, about 1900.

Vancouver Public Library, British Columbia. Photographs: Northern Coast Salish, *Bailey Brothers, about 1890; Kwakiutl, *B.W. Leeson, 1894–1939.

Washington State Capitol Museum, Olympia, Photographs: Southern Coast Salish, J.E. Mitchell, 1885.

Washington State Historical Society, Tacoma. Photographs: Makah, Quileute, and Clallam, *S.G. Morse, 1890s–1907 (Marr, Colfax, and Monroe 1987); Makah, *A. Curtis, 1890s–1940s (Frederick 1980; Sucher 1973).

University of Washington, Suzzallo Library, Special Collections, Seattle. Photographs: Tlingit and Haida, *Winter and Brown and Winter and Pond, 1885–1900; Salish, Tlingit, and Tsimshian, *F. LaRoche, 1890–1895; various, E.S. Curtis, 1899–1927; Tsimshian at New Metlakatla, *E.A. Hegg, 1900–1905; Tlingit, Tsimshian, and Haida, *Case and Draper, 1903–1908; Tsimshian, *G.T. Emmons, 1905 and 1913, and A. Curtis, 1930; Tlingit, V. Garfield, 1930s–1940s.

Whatcom Museum of History and Art, Bellingham, Washington. Artifacts: basketry, Melville Jacobs. Photographs: Lummi, 1910–1920s.

History of Research in Linguistics

M. DALE KINKADE

Early Recording

The earliest written records of the languages of the Northwest Coast date from the eighteenth century when the first English, Spanish, and French explorers and fur traders visited the area. The first publication on any of these languages was a list of some hundred words of Nootka by William Ellis (1782, 1:224–229), who was assistant surgeon with Capt. James Cook on his first visit to Vancouver Island in 1778. Much of the information on early collection of language samples is derived from Pilling (1885, 1892, 1893a, 1893, 1894); see also Freeman (1966) and Catalogue to Manuscripts at the National Anthropological Archives (1975). A larger vocabulary, about 250 words, was collected by another surgeon with Cook, William Anderson (Cook 1784, 2:335–336, 3: 540–546). Cook's astronomer, William Bayly, also has 135 words of Nootka in his journal (Bayly 1778). The first Tlingit, the numbers 1–10 and five nouns, was collected in 1786 by Robert de Paul, chevalier de Lamanon, a naturalist with La Pérouse (1797, 2:210–213) on his explorations of the Pacific (see also Krauss 1964:127). Captains George Dixon and Nathaniel Portlock also collected the numbers one to 10 and 14 other items in Tlingit in 1787 (G. Dixon in Beresford 1789:241). Alexander Walker (1982:277-303) on the expedition of James Strange in 1785–1786 collected over 350 words and phrases of Nootka. The Spaniard Manuel Quimper collected 11 pages of Nootka vocabulary in 1790 (Pilling 1894:51), although at least part of this was copied from a lost manuscript of Joseph Ingraham, who wintered at Nootka in 1788–1789 (Bancroft 1886a,1:185–192, 202–209, 243). The first Haida words were collected in 1791 by Ingraham (Pilling 1885:988), John Box Hoskins (1941), and John Bartlett (1925). Later in 1791, Claude Roblet and Prosper Chanal collected a few dozen words of Tlingit and Haida (Fleurieu 1797–1800, 1:284–286, 361, 585–591). In the same year, Alejandro Malaspina (1885) collected 151 words of Tlingit. In 1799 William Sturgis also collected 150 words of Tlingit and Haida (Loring 1864; Pilling 1885:668).

In 1793, the first overland expedition (under Alexander Mackenzie) reached the north Pacific coast, and as a result the first Salishan language was recorded—25 words of Bella Coola (Mackenzie 1801:376). In 1804 I͡uriĭ Lisi͡anskiĭ (1812) collected a few hundred words of Tlingit, Gavriil Davydov (1812) collected 251 words of Tlingit in 1805, and about 1805 Nikolai Rezanov collected extensive vocabularies of Tlingit (1,200 items) and Eyak (1,175 items); his Eyak vocabulary was edited and published mainly by Radloff (1858); material from these various sources was assembled by Ivan Fedorovich Kruzenshtern (1813), cf. Krauss (1964:127–128).

Meriwether Lewis reported collecting a Chinook vocabulary in 1806 (Thwaites 1904–1905, 4:273), but this and other materials were lost (D. Jackson 1978, 2: 464–465). Otherwise Chinookan (apart from tribe and place-names) was not recorded until 1811 (and then only 46 words and 11 phrases), when Gabriel Franchère (1820: 204–205) arrived on the Tonquin. A much larger amount of Chinook (187 words and the numbers 1–33 and others up to 5,000) and some Chinook Jargon (28 words and two phrases) was recorded by Alexander Ross (1849:342–349) while at Fort Astor between 1810 and 1824. Chinook and Chinook Jargon subsequently received much attention, including material collected by Rev. Samuel Parker (1838: 333–338) on an exploring tour 1835–1837 (he also collected three pages of Kalapuya. In 1838–1839 the first dictionary and text collection (catechism, prayers, and hymns) of a Northwest Coast language (Chinook Jargon) were compiled by Demers (1871), a collection that went through several revised reprintings. For a study of many early Chinook Jargon dictionaries and their adaptations see Johnson (1978).

Systematic Collecting

The 1830s also saw the beginning of more systematic data collection, beginning with William F. Tolmie, and continuing with Horatio Hale in the 1840s, George Gibbs from the 1850s, and Alphonse Pinart in the 1870s. Tolmie arrived at Vancouver on the Columbia River in 1833, where he served as surgeon and clerk with the Hudson's Bay Company; from 1842 he was in charge of that company's posts on Puget Sound, and he became chief factor in 1855, moving to Vancouver Island in 1859. His diary (Tolmie 1963) notes in 1835 that he already had materials on several languages, although none appeared in

98

print until 1841 (Scouler 1841:230–247). Seventeen Northwest Coast languages are represented in the published lists of Tolmie's vocabularies (Tolmie and Dawson 1884). Tolmie's transcriptions are rather impressionistic and not entirely consistent; they use English spelling conventions insofar as they are applicable to Northwest Coast languages.

Hale, upon graduation from Harvard, was appointed in 1837 as linguist and ethnographer to the United States Exploring Expedition under Charles Wilkes, and for the next five years collected ethnographic and linguistic material around the world. In 1841 the expedition was on the Northwest Coast. While there Hale (1846:533–629) collected extensive vocabularies and some grammar on 14 languages (including two dialects of some); these lists also include several Plateau, California, and other languages. He also collected grammatical notes and vocabulary in Chinook Jargon (Hale 1846:635–650). Hale's transcriptions are consistent (he used orthographic conventions recommended by Pickering 1818) and are considerably better than those of Tolmie.

Gibbs was even more industrious than Tolmie or Hale. He lived for many years in Oregon and Washington territories (Beckham 1969) and spent considerable time accumulating data on native languages of western America. He held a variety of government and private posts while there (port collector at Astoria, geologist and botanist to the boundary survey commission, commissioner of another boundary survey, rancher, geologist for a railroad survey, surveyor of military roads), and spent the last years of his life working for the Smithsonian Institution. Although Gibbs himself collected material on several languages while in the Northwest, he also requested and received help in collecting vocabularies from a number of other people. Through his own (and his younger brother's) military connections, he had some Army officers who were active in southwestern Oregon (and involved in the Rogue River Wars) collect samples of languages and fill out 180-word lists. Among these were Tututni (Kautz 1855, 1855a), Applegate and Takelma (Hazen 1857), and Tolowa (Crook 1858). Dr. John J. Milhau (1856, 1856a, 1856b, 1856c), in the Army in the West until 1861, collected data in 1856 on Yaquina-Alsea, Lower Umpqua–Siuslaw, two dialects of Hanis Coos, and Upper Umpqua. Among others who collected vocabularies for Gibbs were G.H. Abbott (1858) on Upper Coquille Athapaskan; W.H. Barnhardt (1859) on Central Kalapuyan, Takelma (which he called Lower Rogue River), and Lower Umpqua; Alexander Caulfield Anderson (1854, 1854–1855, 1856, 1857, 1858) for comparative vocabularies in Clatskanie, Willapa, Lower Umpqua, Tututni, and Applegate; U.G. Warbass (1857–1858, 1858) on Cowlitz; and Alexander S. Hamilton (1856) for a Tolowa vocabulary. Gibbs himself collected vocabularies on Bella Bella (1859), Chinook Jargon (1850), Molala (1851), Yamhill Kalapuyan (1851a), Applegate (see Hazen

1857), Bella Coola (1859a), Haida (1854, 1857), Tlingit (1857a), Tsimshian (1857b, 1857c), and others. Gibbs published volumes only on Clallam and Lummi (1863a), Chinook (1863b), and Chinook Jargon (1863c) but was preparing a volume on American Indian languages for the Smithsonian Institution when he died, and much of this material appeared posthumously. Of the language samples that Gibbs accumulated, 27 were from the Northwest Coast. Gibbs (1863) issued specific instructions for collecting language material and for transcribing.

Alphonse Pinart, an Americanist from France, studied documents at Saint Petersburg pertaining to the Russians in America, from which he provided Hubert Howe Bancroft with information for his histories. In 1871–1872 he was in Alaska, and between 1874 and 1876 he traveled throughout western North America collecting large amounts of linguistic material (Parmenter 1966). The majority of this material appears to have been copied from other sources (Pinart 1849, 1876, 1880, 1880a, 1880b, 1880c). He reported to Pilling (1885:1043–1044) that he had material on a huge number of North American languages, including at least 23 on the Northwest Coast; his claims appear to be greatly exaggerated. The few manuscripts pertaining to his collection that are known are in the Bancroft Library, University of California, Berkeley (Morgan and Hammond 1963).

The word lists of Tolmie, Hale, and Gibbs were the most extensive available in the middle and later nineteenth century and proved invaluable to the numerous scholars in the eastern United States and in Europe who were interested in classifying the languages of America. The complex sounds of Northwest Coast languages were greatly underdifferentiated (a defect that continued until the end of the century), but this proved to be no hindrance to those attempting to classify languages. Indeed, the classification of the languages of this area was fairly well worked out by the early 1860s, even before Gibbs's data were available (see, for example, Latham 1862:388–407). The western Oregon and Chimakuan languages were still poorly known, but this did not affect classifications, inasmuch as Yaquina, Siuslawan, Coosan, and Chimakuan constitute separate families.

By the twentieth century, when more extensive data on these Northwest Coast languages became available, and transcriptions had been refined so that they reflected phonetic detail more accurately, the earlier vocabularies were largely ignored. Their crude transcriptions made them of little use to later scholars, and with limited exceptions, grammatical information was unavailable. At best, they were used to stimulate the memories of later speakers of these languages into recalling words that they had forgotten or that had become obsolescent (such as names of months, words for 'bow', 'arrow', or the like).

Tolmie, Hale, Gibbs, and Pinart were not, of course, the only persons collecting data on Indian languages in the

Northwest. Settlers sometimes collected data, and church missionaries often collected vocabularies and wrote grammars for their own purposes. Joel Palmer (1847) collected 200 words of Chinook Jargon in Oregon in 1845–1846. John Russell Bartlett reportedly collected a Makah vocabulary (Pilling 1894), probably in the early 1850s; with Gibbs, Albert Gallatin, and others he had cofounded the American Ethnological Society in 1842. Charles W. Wilson (1866), a British officer on the Boundary Commission in British Columbia, recorded a small amount of vocabulary in Halkomelem and Chinook Jargon. Other important contributions were being made at this time by the Russians in the north: grammar and vocabulary lists (over 1,100 items) in Tlingit by Ivan E. Veniaminov (1840, 3, 1846), and grammatical notes and a compendium of vocabulary of Kaigani Haida published by Leopold Radloff (1858a). Radloff also left Tlingit texts and vocabulary in manuscript and compared Haida, Tlingit, Eyak, and Athapaskan (1858a, 1858; see also Krauss 1964). The largest Tlingit dictionary of this time was by Henrik Johan von Holmberg (1873).

Both Protestant and Catholic missionaries were active among the Indians, even from the time of the earliest Spanish contacts. Many of these men collected material on the native languages, often translated religious materials into them, and occasionally wrote grammars. Father Eugene Casimir Chirouse worked at Tulalip from 1857 to 1878 (Sullivan 1932), preparing a grammar (Chirouse 1880) and translating religious materials into Snohomish. In Chinook Jargon, Reverend John Booth Good (1880) published a dictionary (although most of his work was on Thompson), Father Jean-Marie Raphael Le Jeune (1896a) published a vocabulary and lessons, and Charles M. Tate (1889) published a dictionary. Hymns, the Lord's Prayer, and the Ten Commandments were published in Chinook Jargon and Halkomelem (Crosby, Tate, and Barraclough 1898). In 1891 Le Jeune also began publishing the *Kamloops Wawa* (1891–1905), a periodical, mostly of Catholic religious materials, written in Chinook Jargon (and using the French Duployer shorthand as its orthography). He also published a primer (1892) and reading and religious materials (1896, 1896–1897, 1898; Durieu 1893, 1899). Rev. Myron Eells, an American Protestant missionary to the Twana and Clallam, published and left in manuscript large amounts of lexical, grammatical, and textual material on Chinook Jargon, Lower Chehalis, Twana, Lushootseed, Clallam, and Chemakum (1877, 1878a, 1878, 1886, 1889, 1893, 1894). One early missionary to the Kwakiutl was Rev. Alfred James Hall (1889), who published the first grammar of their language. Several missionaries active among the Nootkas and Nitinahts in the last third of the nineteenth century left noteworthy works on language. The first grammar and a vocabulary of Nootka (Knipe 1868) includes a little Nitinaht compared with Nootka; additional comparative vocabulary of Nitinaht, Makah, and several dialects of Nootka was unpublished. The Roman Catholics began missionary work on the west coast of Vancouver Island in 1874 and immediately began learning Nootka. Father Augustin J. Brabant, first missionary to the Hesquiat band, prepared a grammar and dictionary (Brabant 1911, 1911a, 1911b, 1911c) during his tenure there from 1875–1908, and other priests had compiled dictionaries of Nootka by 1890 (Nicolaye 1890; Lemmens 1888, 1889; Lemmens and Enssen 1888 see also Pilling 1894:42). Beginning in the last decade of the nineteenth century there was a flurry of accumulation of language materials, especially in the north. Among the Coast Tsimshian, William Duncan translated a considerable amount of religious material from 1859 onward (Krauss and McGary 1980:44–45) and published a church manual in Tsimshian (W. Duncan 1880); William Ridley also translated and published materials in Tsimshian (Krauss and McGary 1980:46–47) and prepared a grammar (Ridley 1895). Rev. James B. McCullagh (1897) did similar work among the Nishga. Rev. Charles Harrison, who worked among the Haida (Krauss and McGary 1980: 81–82), published a grammar (Harrison 1895) and prepared a large dictionary (Harrison 1900); Rev. J.H. Keen also worked among the Haida (Krauss and McGary 1980: 82) and published a grammar (J.H. Keen 1906). William A. Kelly and Frances H. Willard (1906) published a grammar of Tlingit, and Rev. George H. Raley (1904) compiled a dictionary of Haisla.

Two additional prominent figures were active studying languages in the Northwest in the 1870s and after. George M. Dawson, geologist and naturalist, published a small amount of Haida material (1880b) and collaborated with Tolmie on a combined vocabulary of several Northwest Coast languages (Tolmie and Dawson 1884). Albert S. Gatschet recorded languages all over the United States and in 1877 went to work for John Wesley Powell as ethnologist in the U.S. Geological Survey (Pilling 1893). That same year he spent six months in Oregon, where he collected vocabulary in Lower Chinook, Tillamook, Upper Umpqua, and Central Kalapuyan, as well as some Plateau languages and over 400 pages of Tualatin texts, grammatical notes, words, and sentences (Pilling 1885: 290–292; Gatschet 1877, 1877a, 1877b, 1877c, 1877d, 1877e, 1877f, 1877g, 1877h, 1877i). This remains one of only three large bodies of data on Kalapuyan languages, the others collected by Frachtenberg about 1914, and Jacobs between 1928 and 1936.

The Bureau of American Ethnology project to classify the languages of North America, under the leadership of John Wesley Powell, sent two of its members to Oregon in 1884 to fill out schedules. James Owen Dorsey, best known for his work on Siouan languages, completed schedules on 10 dialects of Tututni, Tolowa, and Upper Umpqua, and on Miluk Coos, Takelma, both dialects of

Siuslaw (Frachtenberg 1922), and Yakonan (J.O. Dorsey 1884). The project also had a schedule completed by Willis Eugene Everette on Tututni (1882), who also completed a manuscript comparing 1,000 words of Alsea and Klamath (1882a) and comparative vocabularies of Tlingit and Chinook Jargon (1884; Pilling 1885:941). Somewhat later, Franz Boas, who was already working on the Northwest Coast, was employed to provide information on classifying Salishan languages. The Powell committee had prepared lengthy schedules to be completed in the field and had provided careful instructions on transcription practice, hoping to acquire data that were more phonetically reliable and consistent than had previously been available. However, much remained to be learned about phonetics in North America, and these late nineteenth-century schedules are not entirely reliable. Boas soon became familiar with a large number of Northwest languages and realized that more accurate transcriptions were necessary; he developed a more detailed notation system to this end, and much of his work is indeed phonetically accurate. Furthermore, it set the standards to be followed thereafter by others in North America studying native languages.

Boas also stressed the collection of native texts, and set impressive examples in this endeavor. He published texts in Lower Chinook (1894), Cathlamet (1901), Coast Tsimshian (1912), Nass-Gitksan (1902), Bella Bella (1928), Kwakiutl (1910, 1935–1943, and with George Hunt 1902–1905, 1906), and Upper Chehalis (1934a), left more in manuscripts, and published texts in English and German for these and several other languages. He also wrote several grammars: Lower Chinook (1911a), Kwakiutl (1911c, 1947), and Tsimshian (1911b). Boas collected the last significant data on several extinct languages: Lower Chinook, Cathlamet, Chemakum, and Pentlatch. He trained many students, some of whom were active in the Northwest studying native languages. Boas's influence was widespread in America and Europe. A.C. von der Schulenburg (1894) wrote a grammar and dictionary of Tsimshian based on texts and other data provided him by Boas. Raoul de La Grasserie (1902) wrote grammatical sketches and vocabularies of Haida, Tlingit, Tsimshian, Kwakiutl, and Nootka based on published materials of Schulenburg, Boas, Tolmie and Dawson, and Harrison.

While he was working for the British Association for the Advancement of Science, Boas had some influence on Charles Hill-Tout, who collected linguistic data (as well as ethnographic data) on a number of languages: Sechelt (1904), Squamish (1897, 1900), Halkomelem (1903, 1904a, 1905, 1907a), and Northern Straits (1907a). John R. Swanton, a student of Boas in the employ of the Bureau of American Ethnology, accompanied Boas on the Jesup North Pacific Expedition, collecting data on Haida and Tlingit; he published texts in Haida (1905a, 1908), and Tlingit (1909) and grammars of both (1902, 1911a, 1911).

Another of Boas's students in the early 1900s was Edward Sapir, who collected materials on Takelma and Tututni at this time, and later on Nootka; he published a grammar of Takelma (1922) Takelma texts (1909), a sketch of Chasta Costa Tututni (1914a), and, with Morris Swadesh, texts in Nootka with a word list (1939). Harry Hull St. Clair, a student of Boas for a short time (Stocking 1974:460), collected a Wasco text (1901), Coosan grammatical notes and texts in 1903 (Frachtenberg 1922a), and Takelma data in 1904 (Sapir 1922). Livingston Farrand, a colleague of Boas's at Columbia University, was also a member of the Jesup Expedition; he collected texts (largely in English), grammatical data, and vocabulary in several languages but published only the texts: Bella Bella (1916), Quileute (1919), Quinault (1902), and Tututni (1915); he included Alsea kin terms in his ethnographic notes on that group (1901). James A. Teit was also influenced by Boas; he worked mostly on interior Salish but collected some Halkomelem data (a few texts were published in English in 1917), vocabulary and paradigms in several Tsamosan languages (1916–1917), and a word list of Kwalhioqua (Boas and Goddard 1924).

Boas also trained many students in all branches of anthropology, several of whom did important linguistic work in the Northwest. Most of these have been discussed adequately in L.C. Thompson (1973)—notably Manuel Andrade, May Edel, Leo Frachtenberg, Hermann Haeberlin, and Melville Jacobs (fig. 1).

Three other individuals collected extensive linguistic material in the first two decades of the twentieth century. One was Pliny Earle Goddard, the well-known Athapaskanist. He is best known for his work in other parts of North America but also collected a large amount of data (texts, paradigms, vocabulary) on Galice and southern dialects of Tolowa (1902–1903). The second was W.E. Myers, who traveled with and collected linguistic data for the photographer Edward S. Curtis (1907–1930, 9:xii). The third was J.P. Harrington, who collected data on 23 languages of the Northwest Coast, none of which has been published (see Mills 1981; Parr 1974; Krauss and McGary 1980).

Most subsequent study of Northwest Coast languages has been carried out by scholars from universities and museums. For the most part they follow in the traditions of Boas (Krauss 1973, 1979; L.C. Thompson 1973, 1979; Silverstein 1979; W.H. Jacobsen 1979a, 1979).

Special note must be made of various Northwest Coast Indians who became, in effect, ethnographers and collectors of linguistic material. Henry W. Tate, a Tsimshian, was not linguistically trained; he used the inadequate orthography of Ridley (1895). Between 1902 and 1914 he sent texts to Boas, who published the small part of them (1912) that he was able to correct with the help of a Tsimshian from New Metlakatla who was a student at Carlisle Indian School in Carlisle, Pennsylvania. William Beynon, another

Fig. 1. Melville Jacobs (b. 1902, d. 1971) and Annie Miner Peterson (Coos, d. 1939) with the locally made battery-powered disk-recording equipment he used in his fieldwork with her. Numerous sound recordings of folklore and music (mostly in Hanis and Miluk Coos) were made on this device by Peterson; these recordings are in the U. of Wash. Lib., Manuscripts and U. Arch. Division, Seattle. Photographed in Charleston, Oreg., July 1934.

Tsimshian, collected vast quantities of ethnographic and folkloristic data on Coast Tsimshian and Nass-Gitksan. He received some training from C. Marius Barbeau and sent Barbeau and other ethnographers (Sapir, Boas, Philip Drucker, and Viola Garfield) data from 1916 to 1955. In 1939, Boas sent Amelia Susman to work with Beynon, and she collected extensive grammatical and lexical material on Coast Tsimshian. Together they reworked Boas's (1911b) Tsimshian grammar. Beynon independently collected large amounts of vocabulary both before and after his work with Susman. George Hunt (fig. 2) was a speaker of Kwakiutl, trained by Boas, who furnished Boas with ethnographic information and texts (Boas and Hunt 1902–1905, 1906). Hunt also assisted Boas in collecting Bella Bella texts. Alex Thomas (fig. 3) was a Nootka, trained to write his language by Edward Sapir; beginning in 1914, he provided textual, lexical, and grammatical material (Sapir and Swadesh 1939). Thomas continued transcribing material in his 70s (Thomas and Arima 1970).

Objectives

The focus of interest in Northwest Coast languages has changed several times since the first records were published in 1782. Most of the interests have been persistent and cumulative, but varying needs at different times have affected the nature of the studies made. At first, short samples were collected by explorers as a part of the record of the exotic societies being encountered. As more became known in Europe and the eastern United States about Indian languages, interest shifted to classification. The prevailing method of determining language relationships during the nineteenth century was to compare vocabulary; this required reasonably long word lists, preferably with uniform vocabularies. The data provided by Tolmie, Hale, and Gibbs were particularly useful to comparatists, and the word lists compiled by Gibbs and those for the Smithsonian and the Bureau of American Ethnology in the 1880s were expressly for this purpose. The goal of the missionaries was

Fig. 2. George Hunt (b. 1854, d. 1933) and his second wife Francine. In addition to collecting information and objects for Franz Boas (vol. 4:551), Hunt was also the collector, translator, expedition leader and assistant for the German ethnographer Johan Adrian Jacobsen in 1881–1883 (Cannizzo 1983), for Edward S. Curtis in 1912–1914, and for Samuel Barrett in 1915. Hunt holds a single-headed hide drum used to accompany shaman's rituals. Francine Hunt was one of the artisans who made blankets, capes, aprons, and neck rings for Edward Curtis's 1914 film, *In the Land of the Head-Hunters*, the first full-length ethnographic motion picture of Native Americans (Holm and Quimby 1980:31–61). Photograph by J.B. Scott, Ft. Rupert, B.C., 1928–1933.

to convert the Indians to Christianity, and they prepared dictionaries and grammars to help in translating religious materials into the native languages and to assist the missionaries to learn the languages in order to preach and teach in them until the Indians had learned English.

With Boas, priorities changed sharply. Boas wanted three things for each language: a large text collection in the native language, a grammar, and a dictionary. These were intended for scholarly purposes, and later study of languages pursued these goals. Primary emphasis was on text collection from the 1890s until the 1930s or 1940s, and then it shifted to grammars and detailed grammatical and phonological studies. Boas also early thought about a volume of grammatical sketches of American Indian languages (Stocking 1974). He wanted these sketches to be "analytic"—to include information on phonetics, grammatical processes, and grammatical categories, which were to be "derived internally from an analysis of the language itself rather than imposed from without" (Stocking 1974:470). The result was the *Handbook of American Indian Languages*, which included five Northwest Coast languages in volume 1 (Swanton 1911, 1911a; Boas 1911, 1911a, 1911b) and three in volume 2 (Sapir 1922; Frachtenberg 1922, 1922a).

As it became clear that many of the languages were rapidly dying out, linguists realized that it was imperative to preserve whatever could be salvaged of them. Boas's

Fig. 3. Alex Thomas (b. 1895, d. 1971), Sheshaht Nootka, a recorder and translator of Nootka stories. Photograph by C.A. Davis, Ramsayville, Ont., May 1968.

objectives were not abandoned; different emphases have resulted from the increasing difficulty in collecting data (especially traditional texts), and from developments in linguistic theory that focused attention on phonology and syntax. Texts and dictionaries became increasingly difficult to publish, although recognition of their importance never decreased. Beginning in the 1960s, a new need arose as the Indians themselves became alarmed at the loss of their languages, and linguists began assisting in the preparation of teaching materials for use in local schools, and even in universities.

Results

Among the earliest efforts at devising a standard way of writing American Indian languages was John Pickering's (1818); Hale followed these conventions. Gibbs (1863) modified this system, and William Dwight Whitney developed the alphabet that was adopted by Powell (1877). Powell further modified this alphabet for use in collecting the word lists for the classification of North American languages (1891). Boas and others also adopted this system at first, but Boas in particular felt it (and all others available at the time) was still not adequate for refined and accurate transcriptions of American Indian languages. He therefore instituted a number of changes over the years so that in the second decade of the twentieth century the American Anthropological Association felt it necessary to set up a committee to recommend an alphabet to be the standard for use in North America (Boas et al. 1916). This remained in use until changes in the 1930s (Herzog et al. 1934); the system as revised in 1934 is still used by most linguists in North America. Additional discussion of these developments can be found in I. Goddard (1973).

The earliest classifications of Northwest Coast languages were often impressionistic, based more on geography than on linguistic similarities. A summary of these classifications can be found in Powell (1891:88–101) and Hoijer (1973). This was due in part to gaps in what was known about the languages, or even of which languages were documented. Another problem was with the phonetically inaccurate nature of recordings until the end of the nineteenth century; as long as important phonetic differences in sounds were not noted (as, for example, between plain and glottalized consonants) false comparisons could be, and were, made. All these languages turned out to be among the most phonologically complex on the continent.

The Powell (1891) classification listed 13 families with languages within the Northwest Coast culture area. Twelve of these are still considered Northwest Coast family units, except that Yakonan is now divided into Alsean and Siuslaw, and Kalapooian and Takilman are combined as Takelman (table 1). This was the standard classification of Northwest Coast languages until Sapir (1929) published his classification suggesting more remote relationships between language families. Evidence for much of his classification has never been adduced, and considerable rearrangement has occurred. Sapir's notion of grouping language families into larger units (now called phyla) has been continued, but it is accepted that some languages and families should not be so grouped and are to be considered isolates. Not only has Mosan been separated from Algonquian, but also it has been dismantled entirely, and its three members are considered to be isolates, not demonstrably relatable to any other groups, although J.V. Powell (1976a) attempted to show a relationship between Chimakuan and Wakashan. Haida has similarly been separated from Na-Dene (Levine 1979), and the possibility of a relationship between Tlingit and Athapaskan is not without serious problems. The Penutian phylum too has always been problematic but has not formally been changed as pertains to Northwest Coast languages except to combine Takelma and Kalapuyan in a single family. Swadesh dealt further with classification problems using his

Table 1. Northwest Coast Language Classifications

Powell 1891	Sapir 1929	1988
	Algonkin-Wakashan	
	Mosan (Wakashan-Salish)	
Wakashan	Wakashan (Kwakiutl-Nootka)	Wakashan Family
Chimakuan	Chimakuan	Chimakuan Family
Salishan	Salish	Salishan Family
	Nadene	
Skittegetan	Haida	Haida Language Isolate
	Continental Nadene	Na-Dene Phylum
Koluschan	Tlingit	Tlingit Language Isolate
Athapascan	Athapaskan	Eyak-Athapaskan Family
	Penutian	Penutian Phylum
	Oregon Penutian	
Takilman	Takelma	Takelman Family
		Takelma
		Kalapuyan Family
	Coast Oregon Penutian	
Kusan	Coos	Coosan Family
	Siuslaw	Siuslaw Language Isolate
Yakonan		
	Yakonan	Alsean Family
Kalapooian	Kalapuya	
Chinookan	Chinook	Chinookan Family
Chimmesyan	Tsimshian	Tsimshian Family

lexicostatistical techniques (Swadesh 1950, 1952, 1953a, 1953, 1956); he earlier supported the Mosan hypothesis (1953a) but later abandoned it (1971).

Swadesh (1950) presented a refined classification of Salishan languages, showing subdivisions down (at least) to the language level, and this has also been modified (table 2). (Other Northwest language families are smaller and have presented fewer problems of subclassification.)

Table 2. Salishan Family Classifications

Swadesh 1950	*1988*
Bella Coola	Bella Coola
Coast Division	Central Salish
North Georgia Branch	
Comox	Comox
Seshalt	Sechelt
Pentlatch	Pentlatch
South Georgia Branch	
Squamish	Squamish
	Nooksack
Nanaimo Group	Halkomelem
Fraser	Chilliwack
	Musqueam
Nanaimo	Cowichan
Lkungen Group	
Lummi	
Lkungen	Northern Straits
Clallam	Clallam
Nootsak	
Puget Sound Branch	Lushootseed
Skagit-Snohomish	Northern
Nisqualli	Southern
Hood Canal Branch	Twana
Twana	
Olympic Branch	Tsamosan
Satsop Group	Inland
Cowlitz	Cowlitz
Chehalis-Satsop	Upper Chehalis
	Upper Chehalis
	Satsop
	Maritime
Lower Chehalis	Lower Chehalis
Quinault	Quinault
Oregon Division	Tillamook
Tillamook	Tillamook
Siletz	Siletz
Interior Division	Interior Salish
	Northern
Lillooet	Lillooet
Thompson Group	
Thompson	Thompson
Shuswap	Shuswap
	Southeastern
Okanagon Group	
Okanagon-Colville-Sanpoil-Lake	Okanagan
Spokane-Kalispel-Pend d'Oreille	Kalispel
	Spokane
	Kalispel
	Flathead
Columbia	Columbian
Coeur d'Alène	Coeur d'Alene

Large quantities of data on these languages have been collected over the years, the majority in the twentieth century. A few languages ceased to be spoken before adequate records could be made (Pentlatch, Chemakum, Kwalhioqua-Clatskanie, Yaquina), but enough was collected even of these (except Yaquina) to make accurate classification possible. Boas's ideal of text collections in the native languages, grammars, and dictionaries has been met for fewer than half the languages, and teaching materials have been prepared for only a few languages.

Further information on research on Northwest Coast languages can be found in Krauss (1973, 1979), Pinnow (1977), and L.C. Thompson (1973, 1979). Sources for earlier publications on these languages are Pilling (1885, 1892, 1893a, 1893, 1894), Murdock (1960), Adler (1961), Parr (1974), and Krauss and McGary (1980). Much unpublished material is contained, in particular, in the Smithsonian Institution, National Anthropological Archives, and in the American Philosophical Society Library, Philadelphia.

History of Research in Archeology

ROY L. CARLSON

While the basis for the discipline of archeology is field research and discovery of substantive evidence of the human past, such research normally operates within a conceptual framework or model of the prehistory of a given area, a model based on many kinds of data, not all archeological. The history of archeological research on the Northwest Coast is both a history of finding and excavating sites and a history of ideas concerning the relationships of archeological data to models of the areal culture history generated for the most part initially from ethnological and linguistic information, and only later from archeological and paleoenvironmental data.

Prehistory or culture history—the formulation of cultural chronology and the reconstruction of the lifeways of past peoples—has been and continues to be the main goal of archeological research on the Northwest Coast. Since the beginnings of Northwest Coast archeology in the 1870s, there has been a considerable accumulation of archeological information, assisted by various techniques and interpreted through a variety of conceptual frameworks. These frameworks involve the migration of peoples, the spread or diffusion of innovations and ideas around the world, and the adaptation of peoples and cultures to the changing environments of the post-Pleistocene. Origins, both of the Northwest Coast peoples themselves and of their distinctive culture patterns, have figured prominently in these models.

The history of archeological research on the Northwest Coast may be divided by the discovery of radiocarbon dating about 1950, when it became possible to come close to the real age of most excavated archeological assemblages.

Before 1950

In Oregon, Paul Schumacher (1877, 1877a, 1874) undertook archeological work; in Washington James Wickersham (1896, 1896a, 1900) and Myron Eells (1886a) played much the same role; and in British Columbia, James Deans (1891, 1892) and Charles Hill-Tout (1895, 1932). To this may be added a few scientists trained in natural history such as George Dawson (1880), who described archeological remains in the course of geological surveys. Of these early pioneers, it was Hill-Tout who possibly exerted the most international influence by providing an influential migration model of population replacement.

Hill-Tout, a schoolmaster and farmer in British Columbia, practiced ethnology and archeology as avocations (Banks 1970). He worked particularly in the Central Coast Salish region (Maud 1978). He first investigated the Marpole site, near the mouth of the Fraser River, where he employed evidence from both tree growth and delta accumulation to date this site rather correctly at about 2,000 years ago (Hill-Tout 1895). He promoted the idea of "invasion of a hostile people," based on a presumed sequence of a broadheaded population succeeding a longheaded one, as the mechanism for change in this region. He hypothesized that this antecedent group was Eskimo (Hill-Tout 1895:112, 1932) but provided cranial indices on only two skulls without saying where they came from or how the measurements were made (Beattie 1985). This Eskimo theme surfaces again and again in the works of later scholars. Hill-Tout was in contact with the Jesup North Pacific Expedition, the first professional scientific effort to pursue archeological work on the Northwest Coast.

The Jesup Expedition was actually a series of field trips coordinated by Franz Boas and sponsored by Columbia University and the American Museum of Natural History, New York. It provided both the first data from controlled archeological excavations and the intellectual context in which most archeological research on the Northwest Coast is still pursued. Boas wrote that "before we seek for what is common to all culture, we must analyze each culture by careful and exact methods . . . . We must, so far as we can, reconstruct the actual history of mankind, before we can hope to discover the laws underlying that history" (Boas 1900a:4).

Reconstruction of the "actual history of mankind" was undertaken not only by archeological research but also with the aid of historical linguistics, physical anthropology, and historical ethnology. The past was reconstructed through distributional analysis of culture traits and complexes and various assessments of similarities and differences. Boas's students developed programs at other American universities and continued this tradition of researching culture history, an intellectual tradition sometimes referred to as the American historical school. One of Boas's students, Edward Sapir (1916a), provided the most

107

complete formulation of the cultural historical approach. Ethnographic work of the Jesup North Pacific Expedition provided much of the information still relied on by archeologists for analogy.

Harlan I. Smith, the archeologist with the Jesup group, conducted fieldwork on the coast in British Columbia and Washington between 1897 and 1903 (Smith 1903, 1907; Smith and Fowke 1901). He excavated at Port Hammond and Marpole on the lower Fraser and carefully recorded burial cairns and rock art sites in Puget Sound and the Strait of Georgia. As an archeologist with the Geological Survey of Canada after 1911, Smith undertook considerable coastal survey. Smith's published work is almost entirely descriptive, and he tended to operate without stratigraphic and taxonomic markers. Artifacts were described in relation to the lifeways of their makers rather than typologically. He did not take up Hill-Tout's population replacement model, but he did (1907:430–438) subscribe to migration from the interior as the mechanism for populating the British Columbia coast.

Another student of Boas, Alfred L. Kroeber, founded the department of anthropology at the University of California at Berkeley and continued the American historical school tradition. Kroeber (1939:28) suggested an adaptational model for Northwest Coast culture based on change from an interior riverine subsistence pattern to a fully marine one. Archeological data accumulated in the late 1960s have shown that much of the coast was populated initially by peoples who were already maritime adapted (Carlson 1983c:90; Ackerman et al. 1985).

In 1938 Philip Drucker undertook an archeological survey in Coast Tsimshian and Bella Bella territories and an examination of archeological collections in museums (Drucker 1943:23–24). He described his excavations and survey thoroughly and introduced both artifact typology and the McKern taxonomic system to this area. He defined cultural "aspects" within the Northwest Coast culture "pattern." The aspects correspond closely to the known ethnographic divisions outlined by Kroeber (1939). Neither his artifact types nor his aspects were widely adopted. His excavations yielded no cultural sequence (the remains recovered are all late), no evidence of one culture following another. Misreading Boas in Smith (1903:189–190), Drucker equated the narrow skull type reported at the Marpole site with skulls that Hill-Tout called dolichocephalic and seriated Smith's sites on this basis. This resulted in the perpetuation of Hill-Tout's (1895:112) migration model of a broadheaded population replacing a longheaded one, at least in the Puget Sound–Strait of Georgia region. Cranial indexes calculated on the skulls reported from Marpole (Smith 1903:189, 190) show that there was no dolichocephalic group there (Beattie 1985). A number of traits common to this region and to the Plateau led Drucker (1943:126–27) to propose a sequence consisting of an older coastal component over-laid by more recent culture of Plateau origin. Drucker (1955a) equated the coastal component with the "ice-hunting stratum," a construct proposed by Birket-Smith and De Laguna (1938:517) as the basal culture of the circumpolar region, and the Plateau culture with the ancestors of the Coast Salish. Later archeological work (Carlson 1983c) suggests that the situation is reversed; that the ancestors of the Salish spread up the rivers and into the interior from the coast, a model also supported by linguistic reconstructions (Suttles and Elmendorf 1963).

Modern archeological work in Oregon began in the upriver regions in the mid-1920s with the research by Strong, Schenck, and Steward (1930) in the Dalles-Deschutes region and was extended to the coast. Luther S. Cressman's archeological work in the 1930s also emphasized eastern Oregon. Strongly influenced by the Boasian tradition, Cressman's (1977) cultural-historical syntheses have carried through the principles outlined by Sapir (1916a) more than those of any other archeologist. Berreman (1935, 1944) and Leatherman and Krieger (1940) did site survey and shell midden excavation, and Laughlin (1941) undertook excavations and surveys in the Willamette Valley.

By the mid-1940s archeological research was also under development at the University of Washington under the guidance of the ethnologist, Erna Gunther. Archeology was taught at this time by another Columbia-trained ethnologist, Viola Garfield, with field trips to the Seattle city dump until Arden King joined the faculty and ran the Cattle Point research project in the San Juan Islands, 1946–1948. The excavations at the shell midden at Cattle Point constituted the first large-scale investigation of a single Northwest Coast site (A.R. King 1950) and were associated with an intensive survey of the San Juan archipelago and an ethnographic study designed to complement the archeological investigations (Suttles 1951).

A.R. King (1950) related the earliest phase at Cattle Point to life on land, compared it to the inland Archaic cultures of North America, and interpreted later phases as more maritime in adaptation. This interpretation followed Kroeber's line of thought, although King did recognize the later diffusion of "ice hunting" traits and "circumpacific drift." King's phase sequence has seen little use, partly because the components identified there have not been found as discrete units at other sites, and partly because it was suspected that there was great intrasite variability among his disconnected excavation units.

The first coastal sequence of archeological cultures to become widely used and withstand reinvestigation was that developed by Charles E. Borden based on excavations on the Fraser Delta and Point Roberts. Borden excavated at five sites between 1946 and 1950: Marpole, Locarno Beach, Point Grey, Musqueam, and the Whalen site at Point Roberts. Components were seriated into three horizons beginning with "Eskimoid cultures," followed by "interior cultures in a state of transition," and ending with the "Developed Southern aspect of the Northwest Coast culture" (Borden 1950, 1951). Hill-Tout, Drucker, and De Laguna (1947:12) had constructed similar models. Paradoxically, King's earliest phase at Cattle Point and Borden's at the Fraser Delta sites are quite similar in culture content even though one was presumably more closely related to interior North American cultures, and the other to Arctic cultures; similarities with both Arctic and interior cultures are indeed present. Both components date to much the same time period and are not the earliest cultures of the region.

By the close of the 1940s archeology was no longer subordinate to ethnology and linguistics in the task of reconstructing the past. Site surveys and a few excavations had shown that there were many sites and some deep ones with cultural stratigraphy and that site content was different and sites could be seriated chronologically. The replacement of historical ethnology by archeology as the primary source of new information on aboriginal culture had begun. The prevailing model of Northwest Coast prehistory toward the close of this period of research is summarized by Martin, Quimby, and Collier (1947: 469–470): "The archeological remains indicate an age of at least five or six centuries for the Northwest Coast pattern of culture. The earliest inhabitants, who were longheaded, mixed with and were absorbed by a later roundheaded people who may have come from the interior." By 1960 information from dated archeological sequences resulted in dramatic changes to this model.

After 1950

After 1950 archeology in North America continued to grow as a result of a number of factors: public interest in the past and the rise of tourism, the economic surplus of postwar North America, university expansion and government funding for both education and research, especially the National Science Foundation, the Inter-Agency Archeological Salvage Program of the National Park Service, and the Smithsonian Institution publication of the Bureau of American Ethnology River Basin surveys. Dam building on the Columbia River and its tributaries contributed to the growth of Northwest archeology in general, but the effect was to focus research on the interior rather than the coast since that was where the salvage was most pressing.

In 1950 W.F. Libby proclaimed the crucial ingredient to worldwide archeological expansion—radiocarbon dating—which more than any other single discovery increased archeologists' ability to reconstruct the past. Additional techniques from the physical sciences were introduced later, and innovations such as the archeology of waterlogged sites, direct involvement of Native peoples,

and systemic approaches to data gathering and interpretation all contributed to the growth of research.

Initially, research continued very much as before. Cressman instituted a formal research program on the prehistory of the Oregon coast that included a site survey, and in 1952 excavations began at the mouth of the Coquille River. The same year the pressing need for salvage in The Dalles Reservoir on the Columbia was recognized, and this coastal prehistory program was extended upriver to include important sites (35WS1, 35WS4) near Five Mile Rapids, Oregon. The model to be tested was "that population movements from the earlier occupied interior down the river valleys were responsible for the initial occupation of the Oregon coast" (Cressman et al. 1960:7). It is the same model developed by Smith (1907:438) for the British Columbia coast. Cressman had by this time demonstrated through radiocarbon dating that there were very early remains in interior Oregon that were not immediate post-Basketmaker as implied by Steward (1940) and A.D. Krieger (1944:358) but were indeed at least 9,000 years old. He had also by this time recognized and developed the concept of volcanic ash as a chronological tool in Northwest archeology. In 1956 excavations began in Tillamook territory and in 1964 at Cascadia Cave, Oregon (T.M. Newman 1959, 1966).

In Washington, Carlson (1954, 1960) related the San Juan Islands project to Borden's Fraser River delta sequence in nearby British Columbia, and Bryan (1955, 1963) undertook site surveys and excavations in northern Puget Sound. W.A. Snyder (1956a) continued the direct historic approach by excavating Old Man House, where Chief Seattle had once lived, and De Laguna (1960) used the same approach in investigating northern Tlingit prehistory. Charcoal samples from the lower parts of the Marpole site were dated by radiocarbon to 65 B.C. ± 168 and A.D. 70 ± 180 (Meighan 1956:446). These radiocarbon dates were the first on a Northwest Coast site. In 1956, while pursuing a site survey on the Lower Fraser, Borden recorded the Milliken site near Yale, British Columbia, and in 1959 an extended excavation program began there. By 1960 the chronological situation had changed dramatically with two long sequences established, both at the upriver edges of the Northwest Coast culture area, one at The Dalles on the Columbia and the other near Yale on the Fraser.

The Dalles sequence (Cressman et al. 1960) provided some startling new information. First, occupation began nearly 10,000 years ago, and by 7,500 years ago, if not earlier, the culture of the full Early stage at The Dalles was dependent on fish. The 125,000 salmon bones found associated with the cultural remains of this period established the great antiquity of the salmon area of Native North America. The early component at the Milliken site (Borden 1960) indicated the same thing, although the clue was site geography, since no bones were *109* preserved in the acid soil. Second, the Late stage at Five Mile Rapids began some 6,000 years ago and suggested continuity to the historic period. Cultural stability was beginning to look like the rule, and migrations the exception.

Willey and Phillips (1958) provided a classificatory scheme for time, space, and culture, as well as integrating concepts while defining the goal of archeology: cultural-historical synthesis. Borden and Carlson used the concepts of component and phase as defined by Willey and Phillips for Marpole and Locarno Beach and similar units of culture content (Carlson 1960), although they never accepted the social realities proposed for these taxa. The system has since been widely used on the Northwest Coast but is not without its faults and its critics (Abbott 1972). An era of building formal, local chronological sequences had begun.

Butler (1961:70) proposed what he called the Old Cordilleran culture, an early cultural tradition in North and South America characterized by a leaf-shaped point and blade complex, which on the Northwest Coast became a maritime tradition. This construct was the first attempt to define a named, basal cultural tradition for the Northwest Coast. Later models shifted from this concept of one basal tradition to two (Borden 1969, 1979) and finally to three or four (Carlson 1979a, 1983c). All these models are based on the correlations of isolatable technological complexes with (partly hypothetical) subsistence systems, and in Carlson's case with the distribution of linguistic stocks or phyla. Conceptually, they are little different from the idea of prehistoric culture areas. All these models have much the same epistomological basis, but they differ on whether there was one ancestral interior culture that diverged with one stream becoming later Northwest Coast cultures (Old Cordilleran), one early northern and one early southern culture that influenced each other (Early Boreal and Protowestern, Borden), or two early coastal cultures (Microblade tradition, Pebble Tool tradition) and two early interior cultures (Stemmed Point tradition, Fluted Point tradition) that through time became acculturated and little differentiated technologically. Data derived from fieldwork in the late 1960s and early 1970s plus the discovery of early cultural components actually on the salt water that were nearly as early as those in the interior were largely responsible for the progressive modifications in these grand syntheses.

The late 1960s and early 1970s was a period of extensive fieldwork in the Strait of Georgia, which had seen earlier excavation, and in remote, wet frontiers that could only be reached by a boat or airplane and had seen little or no previous excavation. In 1966, Richard Daugherty of Washington State University, Pullman, began the Ozette Project on the coast of Washington, which continued for the next 15 years. From that developed the Hoko River Project under Dale Croes (figs. 1–2). Also in

1966, the National Museums of Canada began, under George MacDonald, the North Coast Archeological Project in Tsimshian and Haida territory, which was continued by Knut Fladmark in the Queen Charlotte Islands (Fladmark 1970a; MacDonald and Inglis 1979). In 1968 Philip Hobler began the Central British Columbia Coast Project, which was coordinated with the Bella Bella Project in 1968–1970 (Hobler 1970a; Hester and Nelson 1978) and became the main research area of the Department of Archeology at Simon Fraser University, Burnaby, British Columbia, established in 1970. The Yuquot Project at Friendly Cove, Vancouver Island, which began excavations in 1966 to test historic-period fur-trade archeology, continued down into five meters of stratified prehistoric deposits (Dewhirst 1980). The Royal British Columbia Museum, Victoria, the University of Victoria, and Simon Fraser University all undertook excavations in the Gulf Islands in the late 1960s, which provided data for Mitchell's synthesis of Strait of Georgia prehistory (Carlson 1970a; Mitchell 1971). Robert Ackerman (1968) began excavations at Ground Hog Bay, Alaska, in 1966. The Hesquiat Project on the west coast of Vancouver Island, sponsored by the Royal British Columbia Museum, began in 1972, and in 1971 the University of British Columbia, Vancouver, began work at the Glenrose Cannery site near the mouth of the Lower Fraser (Matson 1976). By 1971 there was some chronological information for all major regions of the coast, and these data were reshaping ideas on the prehistory of the entire area.

Cultural sequences beginning 9,000–10,000 years ago were established by 1968 at Ground Hog Bay near the upper end of the Alaska panhandle (Ackerman 1968, 1974; Ackerman, Hamilton, and Stuckenrath 1979), and by 1971 at Namu on the central British Columbia coast (Hester and Nelson 1978). The outer margins of the Northwest Coast, the high maritime regions, demonstrated as much antiquity as the inner, upriver edges. It was becoming much more difficult to derive the ancestors of all early coastal populations from the continental interior, and Butler's (1961) Old Cordilleran model would no longer be accepted. In 1969 Borden proposed the two-culture model of Northwest Coast prehistory, the Early Boreal tradition that spread southward from the Subarctic along the coast, and the Protowestern that spread northward from south of the glaciated regions (Borden 1969, 1975). Sufficient data had accumulated to allow serious questioning of the model of the continental interior as the only route of early man. A few researchers had postulated early coastal migrations, but it was Fladmark (1975, 1979a) who first marshaled the geologic and archeologic evidence to demonstrate that the Northwest Coast was indeed a feasible major migration route from Beringia at an early time period. If there were peoples south of the ice sheets before the end of the last glaciation, how and when did they get there?

Fig. 1. Archeology of waterlogged sites. left, Waterlogged cultural deposits at the mouth of the Hoko River, Wash., during excavation by a field crew from Wash. State U., Pullman. Photograph by Ruth and Louis Kirk, 1977. top right, Excavation of Axeti, a site at the mouth of the Kwatna River, B.C., by a field school of Simon Fraser University, Burnaby, B.C. Photograph by Roy L. Carlson, 1972. bottom right, Excavation of House 1 at Ozette, Wash., by a Wash. State U. field crew. Photograph by Ruth and Louis Kirk, 1972.

Archeologists throughout North America during the 1960s were ever pursuing the search for preglacial "earlier" man. "Earlier" man was anything that preceded the mammoth-eating, fluted-point-using, Paleo-Indian cultures that were by then reasonably well dated. Even on the Northwest Coast, where the Fluted Point tradition is almost unknown except on the inland fringes, this quest for earlier man resulted in Borden's (1968b, 1969, 1975) identification of a large assemblage of unifacial pebble tools called the Pasika complex from a series of terracelike formations above the Fraser near Yale. This model was never widely adopted by other archeologists, and Borden always had some reservations about it himself. Research on the Pasika complex collections has shown that bifacial trimming flakes are present, and radiocarbon dates place the assemblage between 4,000 and 6,000 years ago, though they could well go back to 9,000 years ago (Haley 1983). Critics such as Browman and Munsell (1969:252), who felt that these assemblages indicated specialized resource use rather than great antiquity, are probably correct.

Publication of reports on Northwest Coast archeology increased greatly during the 1970s. Quantification of artifactual remains, faunal analysis, and a typological approach continued to be the norm. However, no uniform scheme of artifact typology or cultural taxonomy was adopted, and multiple names for the same taxons continued to be employed.

Chronology and culture content continued to be of interest in the late 1960s and early 1970s, but there was a much greater emphasis on paleoecology—the interaction of the cultural system with its environment. Kroeber (1939) had already laid the basis for the ecological approach. Interest in the abundant faunal remains and attempts at identification had been apparent since Drucker's (1943) survey, but by the late 1960s research proposals were being formulated in terms of paleoecological objectives. The most ambitious proposal of this sort was that of Hester (1969) for the Bella Bella region, which investigated reconstruction of prehistory on faunal evidence alone. Mitchell's (1971) areal subdivisions of the Strait of Georgia were primarily ecological in nature. This emphasis is also present in the many excellent reports emanating from the Ozette Project. Fladmark (1975:292) postulated a close relationship between development of the Northwest Coast village pattern and the late stabilization of the postglacial coastal environment only about 5,000 years ago. Whereas Hill-Tout and Smith had relied on migration hypotheses to which Drucker, King, and Borden had added concepts of diffusion, the emphasis in the 1970s changed to adaptation as the prime mover in cultural change, although the other two members of this trio—migration and diffusion—were never completely neglected.

The search for general laws that typified the "new archeology" of the 1960s in much of North America mostly bypassed the archeology of the Northwest Coast. Field archeologists did not take to the idea of general laws any more than did Boas in 1898. The intellectual challenge of comparing the archeological and ethnographic to arrive at cultural-historical conclusions remained the norm. L. Johnson (1972) wrote a masterful critique of the "new archeology."

Some changes also took place during the 1970s. Native peoples were becoming very interested in what archeologists were doing in respect to their past. Indian participation in archeological projects became mandatory in some regions. Part of this interest was related to the growing sophistication and level of education in Indian communities; part was related to land claims to which archeology could certainly contribute; and part was related to the overall quest for political power by Native peoples. The Ozette Project with the Makah, the Central British Columbia Coast Project with the Bella Bella and Bella Coola, and the Hesquiat Project all established excellent longstanding working relationships between Native peoples and archeologists (fig. 2). Uncompromising confrontation between archeologist and Indian peoples was very rare.

Waterlogged sites were also a new part of the archeology of this period. The adage that "the Northwest Coast has had one of the richest Indian cultures in North America—and the poorest archaeology" (Gunther 1972: xi) became no longer tenable. Excavations of waterlogged or "wet" sites began almost simultaneously at Ozette, Washington, in 1967–1968 and at Kwatna, British Columbia. At Ozette, what had started as a program of investigation of sea coast terrace occupations in 1966 turned into the recovery of a waterlogged village with exceptional arts and crafts covered by a mudslide (Daugherty and Friedman 1983). The work at Kwatna yielded hundreds of normally perishable artifacts of wood and basketry (Hobler 1970a; Carlson 1972). Remains at other sites have been dated to 1000 B.C. (Croes 1976; Croes and Blinman 1980).

The late 1970s and early 1980s also witnessed continued archaeological excavations and survey with an emphasis on conservation archeology and cultural resource management. American state and federal governments and Canadian provincial governments either added archeological expertise to those agencies concerned with parks and land or created new agencies concerned with heritage. Archeology added the applied science role of conserving the past to its traditional role as a theoretical science reconstructing and explaining the past. Cultural resource management seeks to manage and plan for archeological and heritage sites in the same manner that environmental resources are managed. The difference is that archeological sites are nonrenewable resources. Environmental consulting firms with archeological expertise multiplied, and it has become possible for archeologists to make a living independent of universities, museums, and government agencies. The impact of this revolution on research

Fig. 2. Archeologists and Indians working together. left, Simon Fraser U. graduate student Anja Streich Brown (third from left) working with Bella Bella high school students to restore grave poles near Bella Bella, B.C. Photograph by Philip M. Hobler, June 1983. right, Makahs examining artifacts from the Hoko River site, Wash., with Dale Croes at center. Photograph by Ruth and Louis Kirk, 1980.

CARLSON

has been both to provide data on marginal as well as core areas of past human habitation and to foster research in situations where research problems could be combined with required excavations before industrial expansion or other events destroy particular archeological sites (salvage archeology).

Computer technology has facilitated the storage and retrieval of archeological information, particularly site survey data (tables 1–2), and has permitted sophisticated quantitative and comparative studies of excavated material. Quantitative techniques beyond the calculation of simple graphs and percentages were added to the repertory of coastal archeologists with Matson's (1974) work on

Strait of Georgia sites. Quantitative techniques had been widely used in the historical ethnology of this area by Kroeber (1936), and to a certain extent by Cressman, but for the most part archeology had remained remarkably nonstatistical. Mathematical expressions of similarities and differences among archeological assemblages have become standard in archeological reports.

New physical science techniques have also contributed to reconstruction of the past. Energy-dispersive X-ray fluorescence studies of obsidian (Nelson, D'Auria, and Bennett 1975) have been perfected and used to document prehistoric trade (Carlson 1983:fig. 1:4; Toepel and Sappington 1982). Direct accelerator dating of minute

Table 1. Recorded Archeological Sites by Ethnolinguistic Group, Coastal B.C., 1988

Kwakiutl		971
Oowekeeno		129
Bella Bella		347
Haisla		30
Nootkans		
Northern Nootkans	257	
Southern Nootkans	18	
Total		275
Northern Coast Salish		
Comox	608	
Pentlatch	207	
Total		815
Central Coast Salish		
Halkomelem	1,165	
Northern Straits	815	
Squamish	79	
Total		2,059
Bella Coola		69
Tsimshian		
Nishga	67	
Coast Tsimshian	399	
Total		466
Haida		
Skidegate	235	
Masset	100	
Total		335
Total		5,496

SOURCE: John McMurdo, personal communication 1988.

HISTORY OF RESEARCH IN ARCHEOLOGY

Table 2. Site features by Ethnolinguistic Group, Coastal B.C.

Feature	Coast Salish	Nootkan	Kwakiutl	Oowekeeno, Bella Bella, Haisla	Bella Coola	Tsimshian	Haida
Shell midden	1,769	134	677	144	19	218	167
Burial	87	46	65	26	–	10	20
Fish trap	217	17	13	106	1	68	16
Pictograph	108	7	92	29	3	11	3
Petroglyph	47	9	27	6	9	27	3
Canoe run	4	6	3	2	–	9	–
Trench embankment	6	–	1	–	1	–	–
Architecture	248	18	8	50	–	39	46
Cave or Rock shelter burial	13	6	1	2	–	1	1
Totem Pole	1	–	–	–	–	1	–
Lithic scatter	48	–	1	6	12	3	6
Quarry	–	1	–	5	2	–	–
Historic component	17	10	3	12	–	12	3

SOURCE: John McMurdo, personal communication 1988.

organic samples as small as 0.1 milligram (Nelson, Korteling, and Stott 1977) permits multiple radiocarbon dates on single specimens, dates on specks of material adhering to disassociated artifacts, nondestructive direct dating of art objects, and generally increased rapidity of dating. The first accelerator date on a Northwest Coast site, obtained on a minute sample of charcoal from the McNaughton Island site, British Columbia (Carlson 1976; Pomeroy 1980), in 1984, gave a reading of A.D. 500 ± 120 years (RIDDL 36). Others have been run on bone samples from the Pender Canal site, British Columbia (Nelson, Vogel, and Southon 1985). Related to carbon-14 dating is stable-carbon isotopic analysis of human bone, which provides data on the relative amounts of terrestrial and marine protein in the diet. The results of using this technique (Chisholm, Nelson, and Schwarcz 1983:396) show a predominantly marine diet as far back as the age of the earliest skeletal material so far recovered, about 5,000 years.

Comparative study of human skeletal populations is still being undertaken ("Human Biology," this vol). Even the old idea of a prehistoric Eskimoid population on the Northwest Coast continues to surface. Turner's (1983) study of Asian and New World human dentition indicates that the Northwest aborigines are intermediate in dental attribute frequencies between the Eskimo-Aleut and the group containing all other New World peoples. The dental attribute frequencies of the prehistoric population at Namu are nearly identical to Turner's sample from Kodiak Island. These data suggest but do not prove that the Northwest Coast peoples are a hybrid population.

Biochemical techniques for analyzing bone may permit a more definite answer to this question.

In addition to the practical and technical bent of archeology in the late 1970s and 1980s with cultural resource management, computer technologies, and advanced quantitative and physical science techniques, there have been continued attempts at synthesis and explanation of particular patterns of Northwest Coast culture. A systemic approach based very much on the accumulation of a variety of data from known archeological contexts typifies research of this period. Sufficient archeological information has accumulated to permit a synthesis of a single prehistoric culture, Marpole, and to develop a systemic model of how the Marpole culture came into being (Burley 1979, 1980). This model of the interactive forces that produced the Marpole pattern could with some modification be more widely applied in explaining Northwest Coast cultural development. Other studies focused on settlement and subsistence (Pomeroy 1980), on art and belief (Carlson 1983), on social organization (Ames 1983; Coupland 1985), and on economies (Isaac 1988). Croes and Hackenberger (1988) have presented a provocative model of economic decisionmaking and population growth for the Strait of Georgia–Puget Sound region based on work at the Hoko River sites.

Conclusion

Northwest Coast archeology arose late in the nineteenth century in response to local interest in archeological remains and to the scientific goal of reconstructing the actual history of mankind. The techniques of archeological research on the Northwest Coast have become much more sophisticated since the time of the Jesup North Pacific Expedition, but the goals have varied only slightly. Throughout this span there have been two quests, one for more and more archeological data from both the field and the laboratory, and the second for both better and different kinds of frameworks to help understand and explain the past. Archeology has maintained its ties to both historical ethnology and linguistics, and to some aspects of physical anthropology, even while adding paleoecology and cultural resource management to its areas of interest. Culture history has remained the main framework and ethnographic analogy the main interpretative method, perhaps because of the quantity of available ethnological data to which the archeological remains of the last 5,000 years can be linked with a reasonable degree of probability. The ethnographic record is still being mined by archeologists as a basis for inference (Blukis Onat 1984) and used as a test of the archeological record. Huelsbeck (1988), for example, asks whether the surplus essential to cultural elaboration can really be identified archeologically.

Changes in emphasis within the cultural-historical paradigm have been related to both advances in technical analyses and data accumulation. The direct historical approach was still useful but no longer critical after the development of radiocarbon dating. Once cultural continuity was perceived, migration models could almost be discarded, except for the earliest period, and replaced by diffusional and adaptional or paleoecological emphases whereby peoples learned to take full advantage of their environment. The greater and more widespread the comparative data base, the better the definition of prehistoric cultures could become; conceptualization changed from one to four early basal cultures as information increased. Some excavation data is available from all periods in most regions. Chronological gaps in the Tsimshian and Nootkan areas remain to be filled, and fuller information is desirable everywhere, but the main outlines of Northwest Coast prehistory have been established.

115

History of Research in Physical Anthropology

JEROME S. CYBULSKI

Almost all the early explorers of the Northwest Coast commented, sometimes in detail, on physical features of the Indians they met. One summary of the early accounts can be found in Bancroft (1886b, 1:95–114, 153–250). Further observations were provided by Niblack (1890) and Hill-Tout (1907), as well as by other individuals who generally were untrained in the systematic procedures of physical anthropology. Although they were much depended upon by later interpreters of Northwest Coast racial history, the early descriptions were subjective, largely impressionistic, and at times contradictory. Nevertheless, these accounts provide the only information on living Indians at the time of contact.

The literature in physical anthropology might appear substantial, yet it does have restrictions. Most studies have centered on the Indians of British Columbia. There is less known about people in other parts of the Northwest Coast culture area. Knowledge about the different subfields of physical anthropology is unevenly distributed with respect to different ethnic groups and local populations, and for different periods in their histories. Thus, comparative and general inferences about microevolutionary and adaptive changes within the Northwest Coast have been limited.

The most widespread popular attention that has been given to inferences about physical variation involves studies conducted prior to 1950, and especially before 1925. Interpretations were largely formulated within the concept of "physical type," a prevalent theoretical framework of that time. The assumption was made that a group of people possessed a cluster of physical attributes that would serve to distinguish them from other groups. Physical traits were largely thought to be transmitted from generation to generation as unchanging unitary characteristics. In many instances, type identifications within a localized area were believed to reflect diverse genetic histories and, therefore, diverse origins of the people outside the area (for example, Drucker 1943, 1955). The potential for in situ change generally was not recognized.

Anthropometry and Anthroposcopy

Measurement of the living was first undertaken by Rudolf Virchow, who studied a group of Bella Coola in Berlin in 1885–1886 (see Boas 1890). More extensive and sustained

research was carried out by Franz Boas in the 1880s and 1890s. Boas measured close to 1,000 individuals of all ages and both sexes from throughout the Northwest Coast and in the adjacent Plateau culture area. Obtained measurements were published in detail (Boas 1890, 1892d, 1895b, 1896; Boas and Farrand 1899), and the data were supplemented by summary observations on pigmentation, hair form, nose form, and other qualitative features. Interpretations were advanced on the growth and development of children and with respect to variation in physical type among the adult samples of different regions (see also Boas 1891c, 1897, 1899a).

Little original work in anthropometry and the observation of qualitative features was accomplished after Boas's time. Ride (1935) studied palm print patterns, the occurrence of ear pits, and variations in hair whorl form among British Columbia coastal groups. Lee et al. (1971) collected anthropometric data among Ahousaht Nootka in conjunction with a study of nutrition (see also Birkbeck et al. 1971; Birkbeck and Lee 1973). Haggarty (1971) investigated dermatoglyphics among Nootka, Kwakiutl, and Tsimshian. Boas's typological conclusions were reevaluated by Codere (1949) and by Hall and Macnair (1972), and his published measurements were also used to investigate sexual differences in size (R.L. Hall 1978).

Boas's anthropometric studies led him to define three physical types in British Columbia: a Northern type, including Haida, Nishga, and Tsimshian; a Kwakiutl type, made up of Bella Coola and Kwakiutl; and a Thompson River type, encompassing Thompson and Lillooet Indians of the Plateau area. Additional data were limited, but Boas (1899a) recognized the possibility of a fourth type formed by groups of Harrison Lake and the Strait of Georgia.

Functional, adaptational, and evolutionary frameworks to explain physical variation were generally lacking in the early studies. It is fortunate that in some cases, such as in the anthropometry of Franz Boas, data were published in detail, affording opportunities for later evaluations and interpretations (for example, Hall and Macnair 1972; R.L. Hall 1978). In many instances, the original descriptive data were inadequate, especially in the early skeletal studies that attempted to define precontact population movements in southern British Columbia on the basis of remains recovered in the Strait of Georgia region (critically reviewed by E.W. Robinson 1976).

Osteology

Boas occasionally included measurements of several skulls, or other references to cranial morphology, to supplement his descriptions of the living (Boas 1889e). His main contribution in this area was to type artificial head shapes, which were prevalent among groups in the southern coast of British Columbia and in Washington and Oregon (see also Boas 1888a, 1889d, 1890f, 1891). The cultural techniques used to achieve the varied forms have been described by Boas (1921), Dingwall (1931), Drucker (1951), and Barnett (1955).

Collections of skeletal remains, acquired by museum expeditions late in the nineteenth and early in the twentieth centuries, have been the subjects of several studies. Dorsey (1897b, 1897c) described limb bones of Kwakiutl and Coast Salish, and Dorsey (1897a), Oetteking (1917, 1924, 1928a, 1928, 1930), and McNeil and Newton (1965) examined the effects of artificial head deformation on elements of cranial morphology. The work of Oetteking also provided the first comprehensive treatment of metric and nonmetric cranial variation in samples from different regions of the coast including British Columbia, Washington, and Oregon. These samples were grouped and compared on the basis of expressed differences in artificial head shape rather than on the basis of ethnic and local affiliations. Collections of museum skulls served as focal points for population identification and affinity studies by Finnegan (1972, 1974) and Cybulski (1973a, 1975).

Cranial variation analyses or descriptions of a worldwide or continental nature have included Northwest Coast remains collected by the early expeditions (Russell 1900; L.R. Sullivan 1922; Hrdlička 1924, 1927, 1944; Riesenfeld 1956; Berry and Berry 1967; Ossenberg 1969, 1981; Korey 1980; Costa 1986). Carbonell (1963) made reference to Northwest Coast crania in a study of dental morphology, Merbs (1974) investigated variations in the number of vertebrae in individual skeletons, and Hall and German (1975) and R.L. Hall (1976) studied dental pathology and occlusal tooth wear in a diverse assemblage of skulls from museums in British Columbia.

Most skeletal remains included in the above studies were poorly documented as to temporal provenience. Some may have been prehistoric but many probably represented populations of the protohistoric and early contact period. The osteology of known precontact remains has been reported for the north coast of British Columbia (Cybulski 1972, 1973b, 1974, 1978, 1979; J.S. Murray 1981), for the central coast of British Columbia (Finnegan 1972, 1974; Finnegan and Marcsik 1980; C.G. Turner 1983; Curtin 1984), for the Strait of Georgia

region (Hill-Tout 1895; Boas in Smith 1903, 1924b; G.E. Kidd 1930, 1933, 1946; Kidd and Darby 1933; Heglar 1958; Bork-Feltkamp 1960; Mitchell 1971; Gordon 1974; Beattie 1976, 1980; Styles 1976; Hall and Haggarty 1981), for Washington (Blukis Onat and Haversat 1977; Wolverton 1978; J.K. Lundy 1981), and for Oregon (Cressman and Larsell 1945). These studies have provided information on morphology and population identification, disease and injury, presumed skull surgery, tooth wear related to material culture, and ritual postmortem modifications of human bone. The possibility of skull surgery (trephination) has been explored in remains of uncertain provenience (Leechman 1944; T.D. Stewart 1958; Cybulski 1978b, 1980). Evidence for health, disease, and population relationships has also been studied in archeological samples from known postcontact sites of the British Columbia coast (Cybulski 1973, 1975a, 1977, 1978a, 1980a, 1985; Cybulski and Pett 1981).

Biochemical Variability

Blood group studies began early in the 1930s but did not become prominent until the 1950s and 1960s. The first were those of Gates and Darby (1934) and Ride (1935) who reported ABO frequencies in different samples of Tsimshian, Kwakiutl, Nootka, and Salish. Gates and Darby also included Haida. Hulse (1955, 1957) investigated the ABO, MN, and Rh blood types in populations of the British Columbia coast and northwestern Washington. Hulse and Firestone (1961) examined blood type frequencies among Quinault.

Data on at least nine separate blood group systems have been made available for Tlingit (V.E. Levine 1951; Corcoran et al. 1959), Masset and Skidegate Haida (Thomas et al. 1964), and Ahousaht Nootka (Alfred et al. 1969). Other original data for British Columbia Indians have appeared in the work of Mourant (1954).

Biochemical phenomena other than blood groups have received less attention. Polesky and Rokala (1967) included Tlingit in a study of serum albumin polymorphism, and Alfred et al. (1969) considered hemoglobin variants, phosphoglucomutase, and G6PD in their study of Ahousaht (see also Desai and Lee 1971). The frequency of dry type earwax, a prevalent genetic trait among North American Indians (Petrakis 1969), was also reported for Ahousaht.

Other Investigations

Medical surveys among native Northwest Coast groups have resulted in a number of publications directly or indirectly applicable to the problems of physical anthropology (Hrdlička 1909; Price 1934; Klatsky 1948; Robinson, Gofton, and Price 1963; Cambon, Galbraith, and Kong 1965; Gofton et al. 1966; Gofton, Robinson, and Trueman 1966; Thomas 1968; Galbraith et al. 1969; Hill and Robinson 1969; Hill and Walters 1969; Lowry and Renwick 1969; Lowry 1970a, 1970). In addition to Lee et al. (1971; see also Lee, Reyburn, and Carrow 1971), nutrition has been discussed by Rivera (1949), and diets in precontact times have been investigated by Chisholm, Nelson, and Schwarcz (1982, 1983) through chemical analysis of human bone.

History of the Early Period

DOUGLAS COLE AND DAVID DARLING

Northwest Coast Indians first came into contact with Europeans—Spaniards, Russians, British, and Americans—in the late eighteenth century. The Europeans initially arrived as explorers, but, with the realization of the profitability of trade in sea otter pelts to China, they soon came as traders. The early trade was conducted from vessels along the coast and, while this maritime trade continued well into the nineteenth century, permanent posts were soon established, initially by the Russians among the Tlingit in 1799 and by American traders on the lower Columbia River in 1811 (fig. 1) (vol. 4:375–390). After 1821 the Hudson's Bay Company gradually became dominant in the area south of Russian America to the point where it had, excepting some American-based independent fur traders, a near-monopoly on commerce with the Indians. The Russian-American Company had a similar monopoly to the north, part of which it assigned to the Hudson's Bay Company. Permanent agricultural settlement had little effect upon the native population until the 1830s, and that was restricted largely to the Willamette Valley. Missionary efforts among the Indians were of small account in the period before the establishment of territorially based American and British governments.

At the same time, Northwest Coast Indians were encountering non-Europeans—Chinese, Hawaiians, and Iroquois—in the course of trade. Exposure to these people was another aspect of culture contact in the late eighteenth century (Quimby 1948).

In considering the effect of the fur trade on native society, scholars tended to emphasize its disastrous consequences. Howay (1932:14) posited the complete destruction and degradation of coastal Indian society as a result of European contact: Natives were ravaged by disease; became dependent upon European tools, weapons, and even foodstuffs; and generally lost any semblance of their former economic, social, and political independence. In contrast, Drucker (1943:27) played down the disastrous nature of the contact and argued that, in general, the consequences of the fur trade were beneficial: Indian society was enriched culturally and materially from early European contact.

This enrichment thesis has had a strong influence on all subsequent studies of the effects of the fur trade on Northwest Coast Indian society. Wike (1951:106) argued

that, although native life was eventually shattered by White contact, its disruption was the result of White colonization and settlement. The fur trade, on the other hand, had been generally beneficial and stimulating in its effects. During the fur-trade period, Indian society had continued along pre-existing lines, intensifying traditional patterns and developments, rather than allowing impositions from outside to create significant breaks with the past. Coppock (1969:133) concluded that before 1840 Tlingit culture "although modified in some ways, went on much as before the arrival of foreigners."

Although the fur trade clearly brought change to Indian society, "it was change that the Indians directed and therefore their culture remained intact" (Fisher 1977: 47). This was an example of unforced alteration and adaptation (Linton 1940:501). Only with White settlement was the traditional culture of the Indians corroded and their position in the economy reduced from an integral to a peripheral role (Fisher 1977:210). Contact on the Lower Columbia prior to 1830 "stimulated, not just disrupted, processes already existing" (Hajda 1984:267).

The Maritime Fur Trade

To a great degree, Indians exercised control over the maritime fur trade. Trade required their good will and had to meet their demands, both for what was offered to them and the price at which it would be exchanged. Indeed, European merchantmen seem to have been considerably more dependent upon Indians than were Indians upon them.

Indians were accomplished traders, having long engaged in intergroup trade. The journals of the explorers and early traders contain many reports of the hard bargaining techniques of the natives. Of the Yakutat Tlingit, Jean-François de Galaup de La Pérouse observed in 1786 that they were "well accustomed" to trade and "bargained with as much skill as any tradesman of Europe" (De Laguna 1972,1:116). Meriwether Lewis described the Chinooks as "great hagglers in trade" who would spend a whole day bargaining for a handful of roots (Thwaites 1904–1905, 3:311).

One factor in the Indian advantage was that they had a large degree of choice over whether even to trade at all.

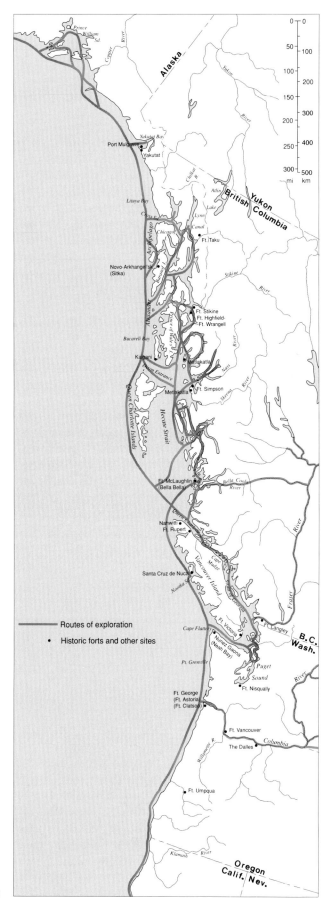

Routes of exploration
• Historic forts and other sites

Fig. 1. Selected sites of early Indian-White contact with routes of exploration. The Russians Vitus Bering and Aleksei Chirikov in 1741 and Gerasim G. Izmailov and Dimitrii Bocharov in 1788 explored the Alaska coastline as far south as Baranof Island. The Spanish explorer Salvador Fidalgo in 1790–1793 traversed the entire Northwest Coast beyond Prince William Sound north to Cook Inlet. Other Spanish explorers, Juan Pérez Hernández in 1774, Juan Francisco de la Bodega y Quadra in 1775, Francisco de Eliza y Reventa in 1790, Cayento Valdés and Dionisio Alcalá Galiano in 1792, and Jacinto Caamaño in 1792, ventured as far north as the Alexander Archipelago. The British, James Cook in 1778–1779 and George Vancouver in 1792–1794, traveled along the entire coast and far beyond to the north and south. Interior expeditions included: Alexander Mackenzie in 1793 crossing from the upper Fraser River to the coast; Simon Fraser in 1806–1808 exploring the Fraser River; and Meriwether Lewis and William Clark, 1806, and David Thompson, 1811, traversing the Columbia River (vol. 4:377; Ruggles 1987).

Although they might covet European trade goods, they were not dependent upon them. The Indians had existed without European goods before and, for the most part, could continue to do so. One prominent Indian of Nootka Sound, for example, spurned trade, telling the Spaniards that he did not admire European products; however, he did find gunpowder and sails and hemp rope for his canoes useful (Wagner 1936:276). Indian dependence upon European trade was conditional; European merchantmen's was less so. The Europeans were half-way round the world: the return of unsold trade cargoes was prohibitively expensive, and there were no storage facilities on the Northwest Coast. This meant that they had to trade, even if at terms more favorable to the Indians than to themselves. Thus Europeans found themselves adapting to the Indian custom of ceremonial gift-giving in order to initiate trade. They often had to allow Indians on board ship to trade despite the danger of attack that this might entail. They had to accommodate the native social hierarchy by trading with group leaders, since these were the ones who had access to most furs. Above all, they also had to recognize and accommodate Indian preferences in trade goods.

The principal items in demand by the natives during the fur trade period were iron and copper, firearms, cloth and blankets, ornaments and clothing (fig. 2), and food and liquor. The earliest demand was for metals—iron that could be used for chisels and knives (fig. 3) and copper that was used for decorative purposes. Iron had to be worked cold, preventing any great sophistication in its shaping, but soon after contact Indians themselves began limited forging of iron—the Tlingit by 1786 and the Haida by 1798 (Wike 1951:34). In the early 1790s the demand for iron declined. Copper, highly valued at the beginning of the trading period, also declined in demand as the coast became saturated. After 1800 it was of negligible value as a trade item.

Guns and ammunition were highly prized items from the start. By 1792 everyone at Nootka was reported to have had muskets (W.L. Cook 1973:341). Through the extensive network of intertribal trade, these items, like other trade goods, rapidly found their way into the hands

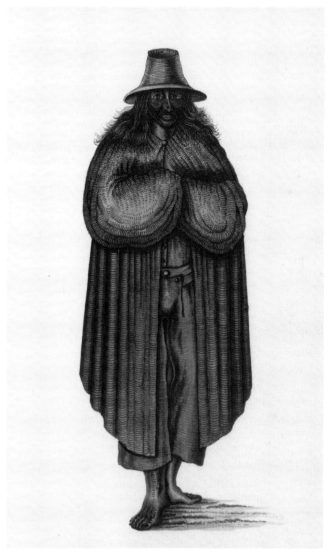

Fig. 2. Haida Indians using European trade goods. left, Cunnyha, a Haida chief of the Parry Passage area, from the village of Kiusta, wearing trade trousers and shirt with the native-made skin robe that was often a distinguishing mark of a chief (Cole 1980:70). His hat may be of Indian or European manufacture. right, Hangi, daughter of a Kaigani chief of Dall Island, Alaska, with native-made labret and copper bracelets and anklets that may be trade goods. Around her neck she wears a silver dining fork. Her trade cloth dress is decorated at the hem with buttons, the earliest evidence of button decoration on Northwest Coast clothing. These drawings are among the most realistic portraits from this period (Cole 1980:61). Watercolor sketches by Sigismund Bacstrom, 1793.

of tribes who had yet to make direct contact with Europeans. Archibald Menzies found the Kwakiutl already had guns before his arrival in 1792, the Kwakiutl chief Cheslakees alone possessing at least seven, and anxious to acquire more (Gunther 1972:99). George Vancouver (1798, 1:285) found the Skagit and Snohomish of Puget Sound with European weapons but concluded, from their curiosity at English skin color, that they had not met Whites before. In 1791 the Spanish commander Alejandro Malaspina (1885) reported no guns at Yakutat (fig. 4), yet when Vancouver's exploring party arrived in 1794 it was met by 200 Chilkat warriors, some of whom were armed with muskets and brass blunderbusses. By the beginning of the nineteenth century, virtually all Tlingits

had guns and Kotlean of the Sitkas possessed more than 20 of the best muskets (J.R. Gibson 1978:368). While spears and arrows were "almost wholly out of use" among the Tlingit by 1805 (Lisíanskiĭ 1814:239), the same was not true everywhere. Very few firearms were seen among Indians on Juan de Fuca Strait and the Strait of Georgia in 1825, and as late as 1838 a census of Puget Sound groups showed the highest incidence of gun ownership (among the Nisqually) to be only 10 percent (Scouler 1905:201; Taylor 1974:425). The Makah and the Athapaskans of Oregon, off the main line of European contact, continued to use traditional weapons throughout the period (Gibbs 1877:192; Beckham 1971:39).

The demand for cloth and blankets also remained fairly

The British Museum, Mus. of Mankind, London: top, NWC 67; bottom, NWC 88.

Fig. 3. Iron-bladed knives from southern B.C. in which the iron was heavily cold worked (Lang and Meeks 1981:103–106). top, Bone-handled knife made of wrought iron that had been heated and cooled many times before the final cold hammering, probably by an Indian smith. The wrought iron likely came from a ship's fitting or barrel hoop. bottom, Knife with wrought iron welded to steel for the blade. The blade was probably forged from a European cutting tool. Both were collected on Capt. James Cook's third voyage, 1778. top, Length 32 cm, right to same scale.

Food was more consistent as a trade item, and it was exchanged both ways. Maritime traders relied upon the Indians for fresh food, especially meat and fish, and land-based traders were, at least initially, even more dependent upon native food supplies. The Hudson's Bay Company attained a large measure of self-sufficiency by developing its farms at Fort Vancouver, Nisqually, and Fort Langley (fig. 1), but the Russians at Sitka remained much more dependent upon neighboring Indians for potatoes, berries, fish, and game (J.R. Gibson 1978). Molasses became popular among the Indians fairly early, but only in the later fur-trade period, when rice and bread had become adopted into native diet, did European foodstuffs become a significant reverse trade item. Alcohol, after a brief initial period of distaste, became and remained popular, with rum the preferred spirit. The Tlingit of Chatham Strait themselves began to distill rum from trade molasses (Wike 1951:49). The Hudson's Bay Company discouraged the trade, trading liquor only when competition forced its use.

Very much secondary in importance were variety items and novelties such as buttons, beads (except among the Chinook), and tobacco. There were other items in local demand such as camphorwood trunks from China. The explanation for the stable demand for blankets and muskets and the variable demand for many other items lies in the degree of uniformity in the articles themselves. Blankets, fathom lengths of beads, and muskets could be acquired in numbers beyond immediate need because they were standard, durable items that could be counted and compared. They became units of exchange in the fur trade, in intertribal trade, and in native cultural life, especially in potlatch distribution (Wike 1951:29; J.M. Collins 1974a; Fisher 1977:6).

The pattern in trade exchange indicates that the

stable, with only occasional variations in the preference of textile or color; blue was the favorite color of the early period (Wike 1951:45). As much as half the pelts supplied during the whole period of the maritime fur trade may have been exchanged for blankets (Wike 1951:29). Coins, especially the perforated Chinese ones that could be strung or sewn, were popular exchange goods (fig. 6). Blue beads were found to be extremely valuable on the lower Columbia, where they partially replaced dentalium shells as currency. European clothing found a ready use, both for ordinary and ceremonial wear. The Haida Cunnyha appeared before Jacinto Caamaño in 1792 wearing two frock coats, one worn over the other, ornamented with beads and Chinese coins. His breeches were also trimmed with coins (Caamaño 1938:219).

Muséo de America, Madrid: 178.

Fig. 4. Yakutat Tlingits from Port Mulgrave, appealing to members of Alejandro Malaspina's expedition for peace. Only the stern of the expedition schooner has been fully detailed in the drawing. The chief, standing in the canoe closest to the schooner, is holding up a pair of sailor's trousers, the theft of which had caused trouble between Malaspina and the Indians (W.L. Cook 1973:308–309). Individuals in the canoes and kayak wear bearskin cloaks, and some wear the traditional painted cone-shaped hat. Watercolor sketch by José Cardero, June 1791.

COLE AND DARLING

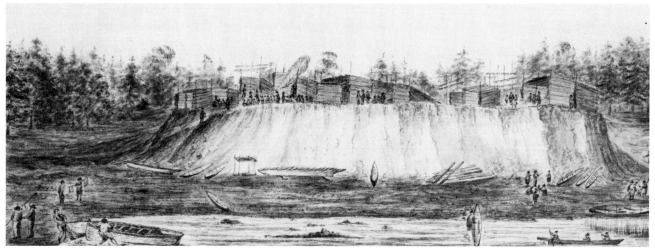

Hydrographer of the Navy, Taunton, England: 44.

Fig. 5. The Comox village on Cape Mudge, Strait of Georgia, in 1792. Fish racks stand between the shed-roof houses. In the foreground members of the George Vancouver expedition are pulling their small boat ashore. Gray watercolor by John Sykes, 1792.

Indians, like any set of consumers, exercised a strong discrimination in their selection of items. If traders could not offer the type or quality of articles Indians demanded, there could be no trade. The records of early traders are replete with complaints at Indian refusals to trade. Malaspina complained at an early stage that Nootkan chiefs were becoming very choosy (W.L. Cook 1973:312), and Capt. James Cook had already noted that the Nootka were selective even in what they stole. Maquinna was interested only in window panes, firearms, and blue cloth. The Haida became progressively more difficult to please in the 1790s when the market had become glutted with beads, iron, and copper (fig. 8), the items of their initial preference. They refused on one occasion to barter more than five skins because the items they wanted, woollen jackets and blankets, were not available (Gunther 1972: 128). Spanish traders reported that the Nimpkish Kwakiutl refused to trade for iron, demanding instead sheet copper and coarse blue cloth (Gunther 1972:100). On another occasion the Nimpkish refused to trade for anything other than powder and shot.

Traders were sometimes able to adapt to altered tastes. When Joseph Ingraham found his goods difficult to sell, he put a smith to work forging necklaces in twisted iron rods made in imitation of the copper ones he observed being worn by a woman alongside the *Hope* in Parry Passage in 1791. He found these were preferred to any other goods aboard his ship and would bring three of the best skins (Kaplanoff 1971:105). Rings and bracelets were similarly made. Such inventiveness was often of temporary duration and still subject to the whims of local taste. Following Ingraham by two years, Josiah Roberts found that iron neck pieces were out of fashion among the Haida (though he was able to trade them elsewhere). The demand was now for elkskins to be fashioned into tunics or cuirasses (Gunther 1972:136). He

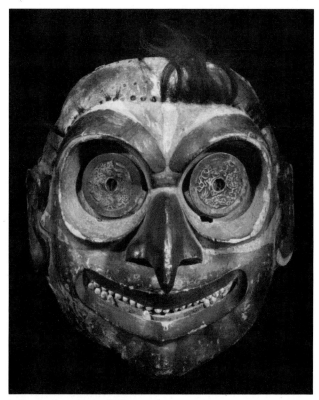

Smithsonian, Dept. of Anthr.: 76855.

Fig. 6. Chilkat Tlingit mask with Chinese temple coins as eyes. Representing an unspecified mythological being, this mask has tufts of human hair pegged along the brow, opercula for teeth, and is painted crimson on ears, lips, and chin; blue on eyes, eyebrows, and nose; and turquoise on cheeks, chin, and forehead. Collected at Sitka, Alaska, before 1886; height 24 cm.

met this new demand by acquiring the hides from Chinooks, who wanted copper.

With French, British, Spanish, and American traders in competition, Indians were quick to play one off against the other. In the maritime phase of the fur trade there was no

Fig. 7. Chinese man wearing coat and hat made of sea otter fur from the Northwest Coast of America. Portrait in embroidered silk by Wú Caixia of Chángshā, about 1790–1840.

Fig. 8. Metalworking. top, Bella Bella bracelet cold hammered from a nugget of native copper. Collected by James G. Swan at Bella Bella, B.C., 1876. center, Bracelet of twisted copper wire. Collected by George T. Emmons, Alaska, before 1891. bottom, Silver bracelet engraved by Haida artist "Geneskelos." Collected by James G. Swan in the Queen Charlotte Is., B.C., 1876. Indian artists did some cold hammering of native copper, but work in metals greatly expanded when copper and iron were supplied by 18th- and 19th-century White traders. By the mid-19th century, silver and gold ornaments were being produced from coins. Diameter of top, 9.1 cm, center to same scale; bottom, 6.3 cm.

monopoly anywhere along the coast. John Work noted that the Indians around Fort Simpson were not very keen to trade with the Hudson's Bay Company in 1835, "no doubt in expectation of the arrival of the American vessels, when they anticipate realising high prices" (Work 1945:18). Even in the north, where the Russian-American Company had land bases, it did not have complete control. The Tlingit were able to trade with visiting American interlopers who offered more for furs than the Russians, a subject of frequent complaint at Sitka. Effective monopoly did not occur until the 1840s on the central and northern coasts, at a time when it was lost in the south. Where there was competition, Indians could continue to exercise strong influence on the terms of trade.

Indians used their favorable position also to secure advantageous prices. From the beginning, they used their long trading experience to manipulate the exchange and force up prices. The *Ruby*, a British ship, found in 1795 that Indians, having seen its cargo, "began to set their own Price on the Skins which . . . was not moderate, we were Plagued the whole day to break trade on their own terms" (Elliott 1927:263).

Moreover, most of the period was characterized by an exchange rate that improved the Indians' position. The value of one prime sea otter pelt in 1801 was the equivalent of one piece of cloth or two or three muskets or a cask of powder; in 1812 one prime skin brought four blankets, four buckets of molasses, one bucket of rice, two dozen loaves of bread, and an ax as well as other items (Wike 1951:52). Certainly the picture that emerges from the traders' journals and from the secondary literature is that the Indians were a confident group, astute in their business dealings and more exploiting than exploited. At

124

least in the Nootka trade, if any group may be considered exploited, it is the European traders and their promoters, many of whom found Indian price manipulation ruinous (Fisher 1977:9).

Trade Patterns

In the early years of the trade, ships tended to anchor in the same few accessible harbors—the mouth of the Columbia, Nootka Sound, Kaigani, Kiusta, and Sitka. This allowed some coastal Indian groups to establish control of the trade as middlemen between Europeans and Indians at a distance from the frequented anchorages. The Mowachaht Nootka on the west coast of Vancouver Island, the Tsimshian on the Skeena River, and the Chinook on the Columbia quickly established themselves as intermediaries. As early as 1792 the few sea otter pelts available at Nootka Sound had come from neighboring groups (Moore 1977:353). Nootkans attempted to keep their middleman position: they gave Europeans incorrect directions and told them tales of sea monsters and hostile neighbors and resorted to force to prevent other Indian groups from reaching the Europeans (Wike 1951:17–18; Fisher 1977:11; W.L. Cook 1973:90). By the 1780s the Nootka and Haida were losing their status as middlemen, as Europeans began trading directly with the Coast Tsimshian. As middlemen between the coastal European traders and the interior fur producers, the Tsimshian enjoyed a trade monopoly until the early 1850s (Grumet 1975:301, 307).

Patterns changed only slightly as the fur trade shifted to land-based posts. The principals remained the same as did many of the conditions: Europeans were still interested primarily in furs, not land, and continued to depend upon the Indian to provide them, while the Indians still had considerable choice in their participation.

The main trade items remained blankets, guns, and cloth but included more foodstuffs as well as steel traps for use in hunting the beaver and other fur-bearing animals. Indian demands still had to be met before there could be trade. Journals at Nisqually House often record occasions when the Clallam and Skagit left with their skins rather than accept trade goods or prices they did not like (Bagley 1915–1916:69).

Indians were quick to exploit the opportunities that the establishment of forts presented. They settled around the posts as "home guards," seeking to benefit from strategic trade location. The Tsimshian were very quick to move to Fort Simpson in order to protect their trading interest. In the same way the Kwantlen Salish consolidated at Fort Langley, the Songhees at Fort Victoria, and four Kwakiutl groups moved to Fort Rupert to become "the Kwakiutl." Those who most benefited from middleman status in the land-based trade were the Chinook, Tlingit, Tsimshian, and Bella Coola, groups that controlled the coastal-interior exchange routes.

The Chinook were able to control commerce northward to Puget Sound as well as to the west and south. "The crafty Chinookes," wrote Alexander Ross at Fort Astoria, "fomented and nourished the misunderstanding between us and the distant tribes," thereby "monopolizing all the trade themselves" (Ross 1849:77). The Astorians countered this by trading directly with the Cowlitz, but Concomly's people later regained their monopoly position. In 1824 Gov. George Simpson of the Hudson's Bay Company found that nearly all the company furs at Fort George passed through Chinook hands. To other tribes "they represent us as Cannibals and every thing that is bad" and were "so tenacious" of their monopoly as to pillage and even murder to protect it (Merk 1968:98). The Chinook did little trapping themselves. "In short," wrote Simpson, "they are quite a Nation of Traders and not of Hunters" (Merk 1968:102). The Chinook position was considerably eroded by the opening of posts at Vancouver, Nisqually, and even Fort Langley.

Simpson's policy in establishing new posts along the coast was designed to make inroads into such middleman trade. Fort Simpson, for example, was an attempt to secure to the company direct access to the Nass River trade with the interior.

Indians considered the rewards to be gained as agents and dealers, rather than as hunters and trappers, so beneficial that they favored the establishment of posts among them. The establishment of Fort Simpson in 1831 was facilitated by the offer of property by the Tsimshian chief Legaik (whose daughter was married to a Hudson's Bay Company physician). The post became the new winter village for the Tsimshian who abandoned their site on the Metlakatla Channel 17 miles to the south (Darling 1955:24). From their new location, they were able to limit trade access by other native groups. The Gitksan of the upper Skeena were prevented by force from coming downriver to trade and the Haida were forced to trade much of their potatoes through the Tsimshian. Friction over access between the Haida and the Tsimshian "home guard" spilled over into occasional violence. One such "potato war" in 1841 left four dead. To protect their intermediary position further, the Tsimshian periodically plundered the fort's own potato garden (Grumet 1975: 308–309).

Besides soliciting the establishment of posts, Indians protected existing ones and resented their removal. The Songhees, for example, were prepared to protect Fort Victoria when it was threatened by attack by Makahs (Shankel 1945:30). When the Hudson's Bay Company moved Fort Simpson to the coast in 1834, it did so while the local Nishgas were away fishing, in order to avoid difficulty over their departure (Fisher 1977:30).

Far from reducing European dependence on the Indian, in many ways the advent of the land-based trade

125

increased it. To the dependence for furs was often added the dependence for food provisions. The journals of many coastal forts record the degree to which European needs were met by the local Indian population. By 1830 most of the food for Russian posts in Alaska was being supplied by the Tlingit, despite the poor relations that generally existed between the two (J.R. Gibson 1978:369). Fish, game, and potatoes were the largest items in this trade. The Queen Charlotte Islands Haida were supplying coastal forts of the Hudson's Bay Company with potatoes by 1835 (J.R. Gibson 1978:381).

Intergroup Hostilities

One of the remarkable features of the relations between Whites and Indians on the Northwest Coast in the period before settlement is the relative absence of major hostilities and even of very much overt violence. There were a number of isolated conflicts for specific local reasons during the fur trade period, but, excepting the hostility between Tlingits and Russians, the relationship between Natives and Europeans was characterized by surprising amicability. Many of the journals of the early explorers, British, French, and Spanish, remark upon the friendly reception of the newcomers by the natives, whether Nootka, Chinook, Coast Salish, or Kwakiutl, as well as on their eagerness to engage in trade. At the same time, Northwest Coast Indians were accustomed to raids upon vulnerable visitors, and they did not quickly abandon the practice when those visitors were outnumbered Europeans. Until the area Natives were all fully aware of the value of trade with the strangers, there was always a danger to small, vulnerable parties; and there are numerous incidents of unprovoked as well as retaliatory attacks (W.L. Cook 1973).

Maritime merchantmen had to be on guard against what they understandably regarded as Native treachery. Europeans, too, could be aggressive and treacherous. There is a dismal catalog of cruel and violent acts on both sides (Howay 1925). However, the developing trade came to be recognized by both sides as a beneficial relationship in which violence was counterproductive to the interests of both. With little interest in Indian land or in forcing radical changes to native society, European traders posed little overt threat. Indicative of the mutual absence of fear is the fact that hostage exchange was rarely considered necessary (De Laguna 1972, 1:116).

Undoubtedly the small number of Europeans in the area would help to account for the lack of threat perceived by the natives. Contact with the Whites was generally with only a few at a time and, until the establishment of permanent forts, tended to be brief. Europeans felt secure on their vessels and were usually cautious in limiting the number of natives allowed on them. On land, they were extremely vulnerable, notwithstanding the apparent supe-

Oreg. Histl. Soc., Portland: 59297.

Fig. 9. The *Columbia* attacked by Indians, probably Kwakiutl, on June 9, 1792, near Port Hardy in Queen Charlotte Strait. About 20 large war canoes with more than 30 men in each made up the attack, which was beaten back (Boit in Howay 1941:404). Painting by George Davidson.

riority of their weaponry. Several attacks on the *Columbia* were unsuccessful (fig. 9); only when a party was ashore could the crew be captured or killed.

Except when confronted by the floating armory of a ship, Indians were seldom overawed by European firearms. With 80 Tlingit canoes ominously approaching his ships in Bucareli Bay in 1779, Ignacio Arteaga reported that the natives were not frightened by his canonfire. Even after a canoe was struck by a canonball and one of its occupants killed, he noted that "the effect was only temporary" (Gormly 1971:159). Similarly, the Chinook, intent on preventing the Jonathan and Nathan Winship party from establishing a post upriver, boldly told the Americans that they were not afraid of them. The *Albatross* yielded to Indian superiority and left the lower Columbia (Ruby and Brown 1976:122).

Firearms were awesome, but they had distinct liabilities. The smooth-bore flintlock musket, the standard European gun on the Northwest Coast, was slow to load, had a very short range, and was neither accurate nor dependable, especially in a damp climate where it was prone to misfire. Most of the coast, with its impenetrable undergrowth and October-to-April dampness, was not conducive to powder and ball. Moreover, a gun's noise and flash at discharge might draw unwelcome attention to its operator (Fisher 1976:7–9). For speed of fire, accuracy, unobtrusiveness, and dependability, the Indian bow often had the edge as an offensive weapon. On the Columbia in 1811, "it was the natives' skill in their aboriginal weapons that concerned the outnumbered Astorians" (Ruby and Brown 1976:133).

In the hostilities that occurred between the two groups, the Indians did not seem to perceive themselves as being at a disadvantage. European possession of firearms in these instances neither deterred attack in the first place nor necessarily determined the outcome. Attacks on the *Boston* in 1803 and the *Tonquin* in 1811 were successful using traditional Indian weapons and tactics (see Howay 1922, 1926). With advance warning of an attack and time to make preparations to repel it, firearms could be a devastating asset against superior numbers; however, native methods of warfare emphasized deception and surprise. Fighting was usually at close quarters with hand-held weapons. The Nootka used these tactics in their attack on the *Boston*. Maquinna persuaded 10 of the crew to leave the ship to fish and, having thus divided his enemy, launched simultaneous surprise attacks on both the ship and the fishing party. With their greater experience in hand-to-hand fighting, the Nootkas held the advantage, and firearms played no significant role (Howay 1926). The surprise attack on the shore party of the *Sonora* during the 1775 Bruno de Hezeta–Juan Francisco de la Bodega y Quadra expedition on the Washington coast came so suddenly that the crewmen had no chance to use their guns, and those left on the ship could only look on in horror as the shore party was overwhelmed (W.L. Cook 1973:75; see also Wagner and Baker 1930).

In any case, the natives could secure their own muskets (though powder and ball were often in short supply), which frequently gave them an enviable superiority should they choose to exercise it. Europeans remained long fearful of the physical threat posed by Indian numbers and skills. Simpson forsaw that the establishment of a Nass River post would be "a Work of great danger, and great expense on account of the number and hostility of the Natives and of their powerful means of offense" (Merk 1968:300).

The forts that characterized the land-based fur trade were strongly fortified out of fear of Indian attack. Defense slackened considerably as peaceful relationships were cemented between the Hudson's Bay Company and their home guard. The company establishments at Nisqually and Cowlitz were practically defenseless. That no concerted attacks occurred outside Russian America is witness that the presence of a post was perceived by the Indians as presenting no serious threat. Indeed, they were seen as security against raids by other Indian groups, Fort Langley, for example, giving the Upper Stalo Salish protection against Cowichan and Lekwiltok raiders. Although there were isolated attacks on individual traders, none was directed against traders in general. During the period 1824 to 1845 when John McLoughlin was chief factor, the Hudson's Bay Company enjoyed very good relations with Indians. The records detail only four occasions when peace was severely disturbed (D.O. Johansen 1946:19). By contrast, conflict was general between local Indians and trapping parties of Whites and Iroquois (as opposed to traders) (Fisher 1977:39), who posed a direct economic threat.

Russian relations with the Tlingit were different. The

Institut Zhivopisi Skulpturi i Arkhitekturi im. I. E. Repina, Leningrad.

Fig. 10. The Tlingit leader Kotlean and his wife. He is wearing a Chilkat blanket, a Russian medal, Athapaskan caribou skin trousers, and a painted spruce root crest hat with potlatch rings. His wife (shown full face and profile) wears a labret and has tattoo marks on her hand. In the background is the new Russian post of Novo-Arkangel'sk, rebuilt after Kotlean attacked and destroyed it in 1802 (De Laguna 1972,1:170–173; Shur and Pierce 1976:40–49). Watercolor by Mikhail Tikhanov, the artist on the Vasilii M. Golovnin Expedition, 1818.

Russians established permanent posts at a time when other Europeans were still maritime rather than land-based (fig. 10)(vol. 4:124). Because the Russians occupied lands and attempted to seize hostages, they were regarded from the outset with a hostility that never entirely disappeared (Coppock 1969:97; J.R. Gibson 1978:368). The strength of the Tlingit made it impossible for the Russians to employ the same techniques of forced labor with the Tlingit that they had with the Aleuts and Koniag Eskimos. The Tlingit obtained firearms and ammunition from American traders (De Laguna 1972, 1:170) and, armed with not only pistols and muskets but also heavy cannons, they were able to take a decidedly more aggressive stand against those they regarded as intruders. The result was the destruction of Russian forts and settlements at Novo-Arkangel'sk in June 1802 and at Yakutat in August 1805, attacks that brought death to 47 Russians and 130 of their Aleut laborers. The Russians remained fearful of the Tlingit throughout most of the period, and they had little control immediately outside their forts. In 1829 Simpson described Novo-Arkangel'sk as having more the character of "a military Post, than that of a civil body," since the surrounding Tlingits were so formidable and well supplied with arms by American maritimers (Merk 1968:314).

Consequences of Contact

The nature of the contact and trade must be borne in mind when considering the consequences for Indian society. Early Europeans wanted furs. They had no interest in changing Indian society or in depriving Indians of their land. They were small in numbers and dependent upon the Indians to provide those furs. It was therefore very much in their interests to maintain a peaceful relationship with the Indians. Moreover, the European traders had little desire to disturb native society. They might wish to increase Indian demand for their trade goods, but anything that interfered with the Indians' ability to hunt, trap, and trade was clearly inimical.

While the European trader did not seek extensive alterations in native society, this did not mean that change did not take place. Change was inevitable in a contact process that introduced one society, possessing a cash economy, firearms, factory technology, agriculture, and formal political and religious organizations, to one that did not. The technology and increased wealth that the fur trade brought, as well as the way it was conducted, had significant effects on Indian societies, their economy, and culture. Most of these changes were unintentional, often representing an intensification and acceleration of pre-existing trends (Fisher 1977; Wike 1951; Codere 1956, 1966; Suttles 1951a, 1954).

Social Organization

Scholars are in agreement that the effect of contact and trade was to strengthen social stratification and the role of the leader. Northern groups might have their hereditary chiefs and southern groups their leader for specific functions, but neither possessed a formal political organization. There was no paramount tribal chief to direct activities. Contact changed that, at least to a degree. European explorers and traders needed to deal with some form of authority who might act as a spokesman for all the Indians in a particular area, someone who might authorize the use of local resources and who might mediate points of conflict. Indians, too, could benefit from leaders who could negotiate with the visitors, bringing trade benefits to their own group.

Native leaders competed for this position, offering–and often magnifying—their abilities, influence, and power. At Nootka Sound, Tlu-pana-nutl tried unsuccessfully to replace Maquinna (fig. 11) in European favor. He

welcomed Alejandro Malaspina with a strong speech aimed at discrediting Maquinna. He charged his rival with perfidy, then offered his own protection to the Spaniards, bragging "about the glories of his nation and his ancestors and . . . about his own feats and military exploits," as well as bringing fresh food and offering his canoe to the Spaniards (W.L. Cook 1973:273–376, 310–311, 335; Wagner 1936:273–276; Moziño 1970:80). Though Tlu-pana-nutl and Callicum (fig. 11) regarded themselves as equal to Maquinna and gave him no deference, Maquinna was, partly from his central location, partly from priority, given preference by Europeans. This, and his success in defending that preference, undoubtedly affected his position. Concomly rose from a secondary Chinook chief in 1795 to become by 1824 the most influential chief on the lower Columbia River (Hajda 1984:200). The European presence seems to have increased competition among Indian leaders for preeminence at the same time as it decreased their number. Increased wealth and prestige among successful ones may have driven out the less able or less ruthless. From formerly being simply a kind of "first among equals," the village chief often came to occupy a distinct position (Hajda 1984:268).

While European preferment was an element in the

Fig. 11. Callicum and Maquinna, Nootka leaders. They wear sea otterskin robes made of 2 skins sewed on one side and tied over the right shoulder by a leather thong. They have multiple ear decorations made of small thongs strung with porcupine quills or pieces of copper and ankle and wrist bracelets made of metal (Meares 1790:251–253). Engraving based on drawing by Thomas Stothard, 1788.

elevation of some to recognized preeminence, that position seems not to have been attained by any who had not indigenous claims to leadership status. The leaders who emerged during the contact period—Concomly, Casino, Legaik, Sebassa, Shakes, Maquinna, Wickaninnish, Koyah, Cunnyha, and Cow—came from the ranks of precontact leadership.

Although Drucker (1939a:63) suggested that the fur trade made it easy for anyone to become rich through hunting the sea otter, it is doubtful that the trade increased the opportunity for social mobility. It was not easy for the less privileged to climb upward since the rights to resource use were restricted, usually along family lines (Hajda 1984:202). Greater social mobility was only possible when ties between chiefs and people were broken and new, individual, economic opportunites arose. While this situation was not entirely lacking in the fur trade period, greater opportunities occurred with the beginning of White settlement and the introduction of wage labor.

The enhancement of leaders was especially true of those tribes who were fortunately placed to capitalize upon the new commerce and its ramifications. Concomly at the crossroads of Columbia River trade, Maquinna and Cunnyha at the entrepôts of Nootka Sound and Parry Passage, and Legaik on the Nass route were elevated far above the wealth and prestige of any who had preceded them. Though networks of intergroup trade had long existed on the coast, the fur trade brought peltry from great distances and distributed European goods widely. Some of the stimulated trade may have been in slaves, with some leaders like the Tsimshian Sebassa and some groups like the Lekwiltok augmenting their power by increasing their slaving activity.

Trade shifts, notably those from sea to land mammals and from ships to trading posts, altered native roles and preferments and brought reorderings of relative tribal positions or a reorientation of tribal activities. As local sea otter sources were depleted, the Nootka Sound Indians turned increasingly from hunting to regional trade (Moore 1977:352), but the decline of the sea otter and of maritime trade meant a corresponding decline in their position. By the early nineteenth century the trade had passed them by. In 1825 Nootka Sound Indians were living in poverty (Scouler 1905:195). The Haida of the Queen Charlotte Islands were similarly affected by the changes, but were able to develop new sources of income, such as potato cultivation and curio carving (fig. 12), to offset partially the loss of commerce in furs (Scouler 1841:219; Fisher 1977:44).

Trade competition, while sometimes intensifying intergroup tension, only occasionally led to war. Conflict disrupted trade and was discouraged by both fur traders and Indians. Some groups, notably the Puyallup and Nisqually (Southern Coast Salish) and Kwakiutl, subliminated warfare and raids into less violent meetings.

top, Joslyn Art Mus., Omaha, Nebr.: 1959.532; bottom, Suomen Kansallismuseo, Helsinki: VKL 8257 VK 39.

Fig. 12. Curio carvings. top, Haida mask reminiscent of a Euro-American sea captain. The finely carved wood may be an individual's portrait, exact in detail to the chin beard, sharp nose, and freckles of glass. Collected by George T. Emmons in 1919, but probably carved in the early 19th century; height 26.5 cm. bottom, Tlingit hardwood pipe carved with the visage of a seaman. The face is carved in traditional native style. Both the stem and bowl are capped with metal. Collected before 1839–1840; length 9 cm.

Potlatches substituted for conflict, though these retained some of the aggression and even the violence of war (Codere 1966). Puyallup and Nisqually potlatch guests approached the host village in war formation and mock battles might occur between host and guest groups (M.W. Smith 1940:108–109; Snyder 1975:153). Intertribal relations were generally peaceful, and increased trade facilitated intertribal acculturation and marriages, which served further to cement trade relations.

Postcontact trade also affected women and their roles. *129*

There is evidence, for example, that polygyny, practiced by those who could afford it among many Northwest Coast groups, increased as a result of the new wealth. Marriages were often economic and political alliances: wives, through their contacts with their kin and access to kin resources, made it possible for a ranking man to extend his area of influence and his access to profitable possibilities. This was one reason why Indians were anxious, especially on the lower Columbia, to marry their daughters to White traders (Hajda 1984:195). Daughters of Concomly were married to traders Duncan McDougall, Alexander Mackenzie, and Archibald McDonald and of the Tsimshian leader Legaik to John Kennedy, all within the traditional pattern of marrying offspring into groups that were trading partners. Fur companies welcomed these alliances for their own purposes, Governor Simpson regarding them as "the best security we can have of the goodwill of the Natives" (Van Kirk 1980:31).

Women assumed an increased economic value in other ways. Their labor was of use in preparing sea otter pelts during that phase of the trade and, among Chinooks, in curing of elk hide. Potato growing probably enhanced the economic position of women (Blackman 1981a:72). So, too, did prostitution.

Prostitution, it seems, was alien to native society (Fisher 1979:95). Capt. James Cook's men found the modest demeanor of Nootka women in 1778 disappointing. Yet Indians learned very early to exploit the economic value of women's sex. By the time of Vancouver's arrival at Nootka in 1792 women were offered openly and without embarrassment (Fisher 1977:19). When Malaspina visited Yakutat he and his men were offered women as prostitutes (W.L. Cook 1973:309). In 1806 Lewis and Clark found the lower Columbia natives quite willing to prostitute their wives and daughters "for a fishing hook or a strand of beads" (Thwaites 1904–1905, 3:315).

It is usually supposed that such women were slaves, but the evidence is often conjectural. Slave women certainly were prostituted. On the lower Columbia they were sold by their free mistresses, the Princess of Wales (Concomly's daughter and wife of Mackenzie) carrying on the traffic with 8 to 10 slaves (Merk 1968:101). On the other hand, according to Alexander Ross, "all classes, from the highest to the lowest, indulge in coarse sensuality and shameless profligacy," and even the chief would exchange his daughter for a toy or trifle (Ross 1849:93). Cunnyha, a Haida chief, offered his daughter for Caamaño's pleasure (Caamaño 1938:216–217).

Prostitution seems to have been a source of women's income. Chinook wives of White Fort George employees strongly opposed the Hudson's Bay Company's attempt to suppress the prostitution of their slaves, "as it deprived them of a very important source of Revenue" (Merk 1968: 101).

To the extent that the practice was limited to slaves or to high-born prerogative, the economic opportunity opened up by the trade would have consolidated the wealth and social status of those who already possessed both. There would be little increase in social mobility and hence little disturbance of Indian society.

With the establishment of permanent posts, fur traders often entered into more enduring relationships with Native women, called country marriages. Whatever the form of liaison, for almost the entire period Europeans were dependent upon Indians for their women, and the Indians often profited from the advantage.

Sexual contacts between Whites and Indians did have a significant impact upon the host society. The spread of venereal disease was soon an obvious consequence, though its effect, and that of prostitution, became more noticeable and more general in the settlement period. With settlement, prostitution became more important as a means of enhancing individual prestige and wealth.

Disease

Venereal disease was only one of a number of new diseases against which the Indians had no immunity. For most groups introduced disease was the most important, the most devastating, and the most long-term consequence of contact. Smallpox, venereal disease, measles, influenza, and other infectious diseases made their impact almost simultaneously with contact, perhaps indirectly even before. Smallpox seems first to have struck the Northwest Coast during the 1770s. Further outbreaks, probably less severe because of aquired immunities among survivors of the early pandemic, struck portions of the coast in 1801, 1836–1838, 1853, and 1862 ("Demographic History, 1774–1874," this vol.). In many areas the decline in Native numbers permitted White settlement in the deserted territories.

Economy

Economic life was significantly altered by contact. Furs, previously used only domestically, were now commercially marketable, and their acquisition assumed an increasingly high priority in the native economy. Precontact society had fished and hunted; now it hunted more. Maritime traders were interested almost exclusively in sea otter pelts, and so the Indian economy shifted more and more to hunting sea otter. This preoccupation meant less time and effort devoted to the fishery that was essential for the winter food supply. The result, at least among the Nootka, was periodic famine during the winter months of the 1790s (W.L. Cook 1973:313). Maritime tribes suffering famine or near famine were sometimes forced to fish halibut in mid-winter when the open sea was most hazardous (Wike 1951:62).

Although the demand for sea otter pelts might be

inexhaustible, the supply was not. The fur trade was, as elsewhere in North America, exploitative to the point of destruction. By the 1830s the animal was virtually extinct, its disappearance the result of continued commercial demand and the ability of the Indians to hunt the animal with increased efficiency.

Even before the depletion of the sea otter, the fur trade was shifting, particularly on the Columbia, to land mammals, especially the beaver. There, European technology—traps and guns—was of greater use. While coastal Indians engaged in hunting beaver and other land animals, their role was almost as often that of traders and agents for interior groups.

The fur trade changed the balance between trade and subsistence activities within the native economy: a predominantly food-gathering society became a fur-gathering society. There was, however, another change: the introduction of limited agricultural production. A gathering society became an agricultural one.

Precontact Northwest Coast Indians tended root vegetables, such as camas and wapato, but, with the possible exception of tobacco, did not engage in true agriculture. Wild roots, for example, were tended by Coast Salish women on plots of prairie land in the Puget Sound area using fire-hardened wooden sticks (J.M. Collins 1974a: 187). The sedentary nature of the Coast Salish allowed for regular plant care and for the development of a concept of ownership (Suttles 1951a:281). Postcontact horticultural developments, particularly the cultivation of the potato, fitted into this economic pattern. The same methods and tools were used for potato cultivation as in traditional root gathering. In fact, the potato was so like the wild roots that they had always used that the Coast Salish used the English term "Indian potatoes" for native tubers (J.M. Collins 1974a:186).

The Russians introduced the Tlingit to the potato some time between the late 1810s and the early 1820s (J.R. Gibson 1978:370). To the south vegetable gardens sprouted up around company posts so that by the early 1840s the Coast Salish were well acquainted with potato cultivation (Suttles 1951a:274). In 1841 Blanchet (1956:65) reported finding potato gardens in a meadow on Whidbey Island. By that time the Tlingit and the Haida were productive growers, able to supply the Russian-American Company and the Hudson's Bay Company on a regular basis. The Haida began selling their potatoes to the coastal forts of the Hudson's Bay Company in 1835 (Gibson 1978:381). In 1841 the Tlingit sold potatoes at the Sitka fair, inaugurated by the Russians that year to encourage Indian trade. In autumn 1845 between 160 and 250 Indian vessels arrived at Sitka with potatoes, many from as far as the Queen Charlotte Islands, some 300 miles distant. This trade in potatoes, which continued nearly every year until at least 1861 (J.R. Gibson 1978:370), became the major source of fresh vegetables for Sitka residents.

With minimal reorganization of the traditional economy, Indians successfully adopted the cultivation of a European crop, even becoming a major producer upon whom European trading settlements became dependent. For maritime groups like the Haida, bypassed by the decline of of the sea otter trade, potato cultivation almost certainly represented an attempt to adopt a new economic role. Faced with a declining standard of living, they used the new crop for trade advantage, finding in potatoes a replacement for pelts. The Nootka, isolated from fur-trade posts, were unable to find a similar substitute and declined in prosperity.

Technology

The nature of the trade relationship during the fur-trade period meant that Indians retained substantial autonomy and control of their land, their society, and their economic relations. Despite the extent and intensity of trade and of the native demand for some European goods, Northwest Coast Indians did not abandon their own material culture and become irrevocably habituated to Euro-American items.

Many of the commodities that the Indians sought and received in trade with the Europeans directly affected the native economy. In some cases the result was simply the substitution of readily available and uniform European articles for their native counterparts.

Such articles were not necessarily ones upon which Indian livelihood was dependent. Iron, firearms, and cloth were the most useful, but most items were desirable only for decorative or "luxury" consumption. Blue beads, blankets, copper, and much of the firearms demand fall into this category. There was some substitution of trade items for indigenous ones, but traditional tools and utensils were long preferred to European ones. In the mid-1820s along the lower Columbia, where the Chinook and their neighbors had been trading with Europeans and Americans for decades, Hudson's Bay Company Governor Simpson noted that "our Iron Works are not as yet come into general use among them." The Indians, he continued, had no use for Company hatchets, still used stone wedges to make their canoes, and continued to cook in baskets (Merk 1968:103). The Columbia River Indians retained their own counterparts for goods such as kettles, knives, and awls (Ruby and Brown 1976:174). The principal trade items in demand on the Columbia were trunks, blankets, duffel and fearnought woolens, scarlet and blue cloth, beads, muskets, powder and shot, and traps (Morrison 1927:124). Such trade items did not necessarily rob Indians of their independence. "Of articles bartered by the Company for peltry and other native produce," wrote Rev. Herbert Beaver at the end of the 1830s, "one half may be classified as useless, one quarter as pernicious, and the remainder of doubtful utility" *131*

(Ruby and Brown 1976:227). Although unsympathetic to uses to which Indians might put "useless" goods, Beaver's opinion allows some idea of the degree of dependence upon imported commodities among the Chinook, Indians long in close contact with the European fur trade.

Other groups might be even less interested in European goods. Athapaskans of southwest Oregon bartered for trinkets and metal, but continued to use bows, arrows, stone knives, and even bark and skin clothing throughout the first half of the century (Beckham 1971:39). The Makah remained equally remote from contact and consumption, seldom using any imported clothing except blankets (Wilkes 1845, 5:487; Gibbs 1877:219). While documentation on the point is thin, groups like the Nootka and the Kwakiutl of Nahwitti village, who lost easy access to European trade items with the decline and disappearance of the maritime trade, seem to have had no difficulty in returning to a condition very close to their precontact one.

Art and Ceremonies

European trade goods affected the ceremonial life and art of Northwest Coast Indians. Like most other changes in native life, fur-trade era alterations were evolutionary rather than revolutionary in nature. European metal tools, especially chisels, the most highly prized of early trade goods, made wood carving much easier, especially on large sculptures. The early European explorers and traders found various kinds of carved poles among different Indian groups at contact (Drucker 1955:185). While reports of interior house posts are common in the eighteenth century, the large, freestanding "totem poles" were unusual. Only at Dadans on the Queen Charlottes and at Lituya Bay in Tlingit territory are there early reports of such sculptures. No monumental poles were recorded among the Nootka, Bella Coola, Coast Salish, or Kwakiutl at the time of contact. Poles soon appeared, partly as a result of the greater availability of metal tools, which made carving easier, and partly as a result of the closer relations that the fur trade fostered and that helped promote intertribal cultural exchange.

Trade material was soon adapted into other art forms. The availability of copper allowed its increased use for decorative purposes and crest objects on masks (fig. 13). Bells and thimbles replaced puffin beaks as rattles, and commercial paints made inroads on the use of native pigments. Woolen trade blankets became common as ceremonial garments, often decorated with European buttons. The new materials were used selectively and within traditional designs and methods (Wyatt 1984). The increased wealth and the new tools and materials combined with older techniques and uses to produce what is generally regarded as a golden age in Northwest Coast art.

As with the totem pole, the custom and ceremony of

Fig. 13. Haida bear crest hat. The crouching bear and characteristic funnel-shape hat are carved of cedar, the formline designs executed in red, green, and black. The bear's head is painted yellow; its body is turquoise and red. Strips of copper held by copper nails highlight lips and eyes. Collected by James G. Swan at Ft. Simpson, B.C., 1883; height 44.5 cm.

the potlatch seems to have existed only among north coast groups before contact. There it became more fully developed from the effects of European trade.

The greater wealth brought by the fur trade enabled larger and more frequent potlatches. The size, frequency, and importance of the potlatch increased after contact among the Coast Tsimshian (Grumet 1975:301). Before the establishment of Fort Rupert in 1849, the potlatch was relatively unimportant in Kwakiutl life (Codere 1961: 445). With the presence of a trading post in the area, a dramatic increase occurred in the size and frequency of potlatches, a change that may be attributed to their becoming substitutes for warfare among the Kwakiutl. Until 1849 the Kwakiutl were still using native blankets in gift-giving ceremonies, but these were replaced by the Hudson's Bay Company woolen ones (Codere 1950:95). Substitutions of potlatching for warfare and of woolen blankets for native ones occurred earlier among the Coast Salish (Suttles 1954:46). There seems to have been a complex process in which access to wealth from trade, the availability of blankets, and the decline of warfare—all stemming from the establishment of European trading posts—tended among some groups to stimulate the potlatch.

The increase in intertribal trade fostered the spread of the potlatch to more southern groups. According to native tradition, the Quinault held their first potlatch around 1800 (Olson 1936:124). The lower Columbia people probably did not possess any elaborated gift-giving ceremony even by 1830, acquiring it only later (Hajda 1984:214). Other ceremonials spread too. Concomly seems to have brought a secret society from the north, perhaps from the Quinault (Ray 1938:89).

While some cultural practices and ceremonies expanded and increased, they did not necessarily persist. By 1850 the potlatch had fallen into disuse among Indians in western Washington and Oregon who associated regularly with Whites. Only more remote tribes such as the Lummi and the Clallam continued the practice and then on a considerably reduced scale (Gibbs 1877:205).

Christian Missions

Missionary activity was not a significant factor in Indian-White relations during the early period. The 1830s smallpox epidemic did have the short-term effect of lessening Tlingit faith in traditional medical practices and the consequent conversion of some to Christianity. For the most part, this was a temporary phenomenon in response to a particular crisis. Priestmonk Ivan Veniaminov, who had worked among the Aleut and Eskimo since 1824, lived at Novo-Arkangel'sk (Sitka) from 1834 to 1838. By 1840 there were only 20 baptized Tlingits. The Russian Orthodox missionization was much less successful with Tlingits than with Arctic and Subarctic groups (vol. 4: 508–511, 513).

Evangelical activity was much more pronounced in Puget Sound and the Columbia and Willamette valleys. The Hudson's Bay Company did little to promote evangelization of the Indians, although it did not hinder attempts by religious agencies. Methodist Jason Lee arrived in the Oregon territory in 1834 and established missions along the Willamette River, at Nisqually, Clatsop, and The Dalles. There was little success in either christianizing or acculturating Oregon Indians. Lee found that the Indians were "so exceedingly scattered and migratory . . . as to render it difficult to operate among them" (Loewenberg 1976:91). Attention became focused on children, especially the orphaned and abandoned. Even there, success was meager and often temporary. The young were not easily acculturated, and those who did not run away from school usually died, "so that when I left the country, there were more Indian children in the mission grave yard at Walamet than alive and in the manual labor school" (Lee and Frost 1844:311). The devastation of the epidemics had made the work very difficult, and the mission was dissolved in 1844 (Loewenberg 1976).

Roman Catholic missions were more successful. In 1838 the bishop of Quebec sent two priests, Fathers François N. Blanchet and Modeste Demers, to work in Oregon (Blanchet 1956). They established missions at Cowlitz among the Southwestern Coast Salish and at French Prairie among French-Canadian and half-blood settlers. Joined by secular priests Antoine Langlois and

J.B. Bolduc, they preached in Chinook Jargon to Indians at Fort Vancouver, Nisqually, Whidbey Island, and as far as Fort Langley and Fort Victoria between 1839 and 1843. Using the Catholic Ladder, a pictorial summary of the tenets of the faith invented by Blanchet in 1839 (vol. 6: 149), they baptized many Indians and laid the foundations for permanent Catholic influence among many groups of the area, both Northwest Coast and Plateau (Pilling 1893a:5–6, 20–21; Schoenberg 1987:26–76).

Summary

Contact brought significant change to the Indians of the Northwest Coast. Resources that previously had had only a limited, domestic use suddenly became valuable commodities for export and sale; and new materials and technologies were available. The new resource exploitation, the resulting wealth, and the new goods were incorporated and adapted into existing social and cultural patterns. Change, even enrichment, occurred, but it did not revolutionize Indian society or significantly lessen native autonomy. Indians retained almost unimpaired control over their territory. The fur trade had little interest in placing limitations on Indian land or in more than altering the emphasis of the traditional hunting, fishing, and gathering economy.

Diseases were another matter. Their introduction was both inadvertent and inevitable; their effect, disastrous to the Indians and deplored by the traders. The epidemics of smallpox came in devastating waves; venereal diseases and other introductions were slower in their destruction.

The fur trader sought only to alter native resource exploitation and consumption patterns. Late in the period, missionaries sought to alter Indian life and manners. And, after 1834, settlers began arriving, affecting much more radically the relations between Euro-Americans and the indigenous inhabitants. With them came the beginnings of governmental authority and coercion. Hostility between settlers and Indians bred wars in the Oregon Territory; by 1849 Indian-White relations were characterized by fear and distrust. The murder of some Klamaths visiting the Willamette Valley in 1848 "was such a tawdry affair that even the whites were ashamed of it" (Martin 1969:26). Severe clashes soon followed in the Rogue River area.

Even these portentous occurrences were geographically limited. Indeed, one of the most striking characteristics of the contact relationship on the coast is the unevenness of its effects over the region. There was great variety both in the extent of contact, in the Indians' accommodation to it, and in Indian retention of traditional customs. Groups more remote from contact, like the Chilkat Tlingit, the Oregon Athapaskans, the Makah, the Nishga, and the Quatsino Kwakiutl retained much of their original culture. Their numbers were reduced, but their society remained intact and their power could yet inspire fear in the Europeans. At the other extreme, the societies of the Chinook and their lower Columbia River and Willamette Valley neighbors were radically changed. In 1845 Indians around Astoria were "dwindled in numbers & broken in Spirit by their intercourse with the White Man and by the different diseases consequent upon their intercourse with the so called civilized world" (Warre 1976:90). Though the Chinooks were responsible for most of the settlers' fencing and did most of the boating on the river, this was more a testimony to their dependence than to their successful integration into a settlement economy.

Demographic History, 1774–1874

ROBERT T. BOYD

Aboriginal Population

Before the arrival of Europeans in 1774 as many as 200,000 Native Americans inhabited the Northwest Coast culture area, making it one of the most densely populated nonagricultural regions of the world. Within 100 years, the aboriginal population had declined by over 80 percent.

Figures in the most comprehensive work on aboriginal North American population size (Mooney 1928) are now considered to be too low (Ubelaker 1976:247, 1976a). Although there has been no reassessment of the Northwest Coast area as a whole, Taylor (1960, 1961, 1963) has computed new figures for particular tribal groups based on Hudson's Bay Company censuses not available to Mooney.

New aboriginal Northwest Coast population estimates are presented in table 1. They have been calculated by a variation of the "additive" and disease history methods of ethnohistorical reconstruction described by Dobyns (1966:408, 410–412). The method first establishes a fairly reliable, dated anchor population, selected by ethnohistorical means (reliability of census taker or enumerator, consistency with earlier and later population figures, and internal consistency in the case of censuses). The anchor is then enlarged, by simple addition, to compensate for mortality from preceding disease events. Specific mortalities have been used when available; otherwise average mortalities derived from the epidemiological literature have been applied. Given the succession of disease events in the first century of contact, there is little evidence for significant rebound of any local populations, and it is not assumed here. All aboriginal estimates have been computed on an assumption of a minimum population loss of one-third from the initial Northwest Coast smallpox epidemic, about 1775, and must be considered conservative.

Environment and Demography

Abundant aquatic, and in particular fish, resources, supported dense coastal populations on the Northwest Coast (Kroeber 1939). The productivity of the aboriginal fishery resource in Northwest drainage systems has been correlated with native populations (Hewes 1947, 1973). Close correspondence of native populations and salmon abundance on the lower Fraser has been noted (Sneed 1971; Kew 1976). Donald and Mitchell (1975) likewise demonstrated a close fit between the population of Kwakiutl groups, the salmon resource, and a social correlate, potlatch ranking. The apparent discrepancy in Haida and Tlingit populations on Prince of Wales Island has been tied to a differential adaptation to halibut and sockeye salmon resources (Langdon 1979).

The seasonal and local availability of fish resources had a great impact on Northwest Coast population movements and settlement patterns. The most stable settlement units throughout the coast, in a temporal, social, and ethnic sense, were winter villages (Mitchell 1983). During the warmer part of the year, these populations commonly disbanded and dispersed to locations where resources were seasonally available. Among the Southern Coast Salish, for instance, small units of people normally left their winter villages and migrated to optimal fishing and plant gathering areas, where they resided in temporary lodges (Haeberlin and Gunther 1930:15, 18). On the lower Columbia River, a different pattern obtained. Spring and summer fisheries drew interior peoples to the Columbia River, where they congregated in polyglot concentrations that were much larger than the Chinookan villages that existed in the area during the winter (Boyd and Hajda 1987). These seasonal variations had some effect on early explorers' perceptions of the total population of a given area. Dispersed summer populations tended to give a deflated impression of true aboriginal numerical strength in places such as Puget Sound (Scouler 1905:198). On the other hand, the dense populations observed by Meriwether Lewis and William Clark (Thwaites 1904–1905) on the lower Columbia in spring 1805 were not representative of the true (winter) riverbank populations but included visitors from the entire lower Columbia drainage.

Aboriginal Nondisease Mortality

Aboriginal Northwest Coast nondisease mortality was the product of a multiplicity of causes. Occasional deaths resulted from hunting accidents and interpersonal violence, as well as eating poisoned food, for example shellfish tainted by *Gonyaulax catenella* (Gould 1981: 440–441).

Table 1. Aboriginal Population Estimates

Group	Mooney 1928	1986
Eyak		—
Tlingit	10,000	14,820
Haida	9,800	14,427
Tsimshian Peoples	7,000	14,485
Gitksan	1,500	2,813
Nishga		3,635
Coast Tsimshian	5,500	6,357
Southern Tsimshian		1,680
Haisla	700	1,238
Bella Coola	1,400	2,910
Haihais, Bella Bella, Oowekeeno	2,000	4,540
Kwakiutl	4,500	19,125
Northern Coastal Salish	3,100	4,057
Northern and Central Nootkans		6,000
Squamish	1,800	1,694
Halkomelem	12,600	9,662
Songhees and Saanich	2,700	2,592
Lummi and Samish	1,300	1,975
Nooksack		1,067
Lushootseed Salish	4,800	11,835
Twana	1,000	774
Chemakum	400	150
Clallam	2,000	3,210
Nitinaht and Makah	2,000	4,320
Quileute	500	630
Quinault	1,500	2,250
Lower Chehalis	—	2,340
Chinook and Clatsap	1,100	1,260
Tillamook	1,500	4,320
Alseans	6,000	3,060
Siuslawans		2,100
Coosans	2,000	2,250
Athapaskans—Tututni and Chetco	3,600	4,500
Upper Chehalis	1,000	2,880
Cowlitz		4,320
Kwalioqua and Clatskanie	1,800	1,890
Upper Chinookans—Cathlamet, Multnomah, Clackamas	13,200	9,288
Kalapuyans	3,000	16,200
Takelma and Athapaskans—Upper Umpqua, Upper Coquille, Chasta Costa, Galice, and Applegate	5,700	6,750
Total	114,000	188,344

Starvation

The extent and possible demographic impact of starvation on aboriginal Northwest Coast populations is controversial. Starvation is a frequent theme in coastal folk traditions, referring to occasional sizable vagaries in seasonal and annual food supplies (Suttles 1968:59; Piddocke 1965:247; Cove 1978). However, there is a paucity of historically documented cases of starvation, and it has been claimed that the wide range of potential wild foods available at all times of the year made it highly unlikely (Stewart 1975).

References to food shortages in the oral traditions rarely mention actual cases of mortality. It may be, in some cases, that there was not an absolute lack of food, but only of particular preferred resources (Rivera 1949: 20–21). Seasonal resource shortages may, in fact, have caused nutritional imbalances. Excessive dependence on fish was associated with hypervitaminosis D (Lazenby and McCormack 1985). Winter season lack of sources of vitamin C may have caused symptoms of scurvy (A. Henry 1897, 2:819). Nutritional imbalances such as these, in turn, might have had adverse seasonal effects on fertility, morbidity, and mortality.

Starvation-induced mortality may well have been a rare event, occurring at wide-spaced intervals, and dependent upon long-term cyclical fluctuations in major food resources. Records for six of the seven years of year-round Euro-American occupation at Nootka Sound (1789–1794 and 1804–1805) mention food shortages (Meares 1790: 132; Walker 1982:182; Malaspina 1791:218; Saavedra 1794:290; Vancouver 1798, 3:304; Jewitt 1931:34–35), but only in 1794 were famine-induced deaths (of 80 people) recorded (Saavedra 1794:290; cited in Suttles 1973a:622). Salmon cycles fluctuate greatly; in drainage systems where fewer species were present, or when natural disasters (such as changes in ocean currents or volcanic eruptions) occurred, sudden drops in the runs may have affected the well-being of the populations that depended upon them. Widely spaced but cyclical variations in food supplies may have set an upper limit on aboriginal populations (Hayden 1975).

Warfare and Slavery

Warfare may have been an important cause of mortality in aboriginal times, at least in the northern half of the culture area (Ferguson 1984). Archeological evidence of warfare in the Tsimshian area goes back 3,000 years (MacDonald 1979). Traditional tales (Swanton 1905a:364–447 on Haida; Boas 1916:124–145 on Tsimshian; Sapir and Swadesh 1955:336–457 on Nootka) speak of territorial wars with considerable mortalities. Few of these tales date from the contact period, perhaps because depopulation removed the motivation and means for territorial war. A few groups who received guns early in the contact period were able to carry out wars of extermination and expansion against their less fortunate neighbors. Such a phenomenon is reported for the Lekwiltok Kwakiutl against the Comox Salish (Taylor and Duff 1956) and among the Northern Nootkans (Swadesh 1948). A war of extermination by the Suquamish Salish against the Chemakum has been dated from as late as 1850 (Curtis 1907–1930, 9:141–142; Gibbs 1877:191). Hostilities between Northwest Coast Natives and Euro-Americans were few throughout the contact period and made little contribution to historic population decline. An exception was the Rogue River War of 1854–1855 (Beckham 1971). High mortalities among adult male Indians documented in historical records on this conflict are verified by skewed sex ratios of postconflict Rogue River censuses.

Disease History

Before the arrival of the Euro-Americans the Northwest Coast, like the rest of the Americas, seems to have been relatively free of lethal infectious diseases. One summary lists only a dozen important infectious diseases that are probably native to the western hemisphere (M.T. Newman 1976). None of these belongs to the class of high-mortality density-dependent diseases that regularly caused demographic havoc in the Old World. Once smallpox, malaria, measles, influenza, and the others arrived in the Pacific Northwest in the late eighteenth and early nineteenth centuries, they caused a population decline of unprecedented dimensions.

Possibly Aboriginal Diseases

Forms of at least four chronic Old World diseases are documented in the early contact period and may have been present in the Northwest aboriginally. A "severe purulent ophthalmia" (Townsend 1978:74), often resulting in blindness, may have been a form a conjunctivitis or trachoma. Two historical references from the lower Columbia in the 1840s give clinical descriptions of what appears to be leprosy in Indians (Demers in Landerholm 1956:111–112; J.R. Dunn 1846:28), and a mid-nineteenth-century Comox Indian skull has lesions that have been diagnosed as lepral (Møller-Christensen and Inkster 1965).

Tuberculosis is documented in many precontact American osteological remains (Buikstra 1981), though not yet from the Pacific Northwest. The disease was definitely present among the crew of James Cook's 1778 voyage, which stopped at Nootka Sound (Watt 1979:153); the earliest attested case from a Northwest Coast Indian comes from Nootka in 1793 (Menzies 1793: entry of May 20). The common later ethnohistorical mentions of "scrofula" among Indians most likely refer to the cutaneous manifestation of the disease (for example, Swan 1870:79). The Indians' crowded and unhygienic dwellings have been implicated in creating a favorable environment for maintaining and transmitting the tubercle bacillus. By the late 1900s the disease had become epidemic among semiacculturated Indian populations (Hrdlička 1909).

The geographic distribution of osteological remains showing evidence of treponemal infection (El-Najjar 1979:600–601; C.S. Wood 1979:235–240) suggests that a variety of this disease may have been present in the aboriginal period ("Human Biology," this vol.). Ethnohis-

torical accounts of venereal diseases are very early: both gonorrhea and syphilis were present among Cook's crew (Watt 1979:156). The venereal diseases took hold wherever populations of (mostly male) Euro-American traders came into sustained or continuing contact with sizable Indian settlements: at Nootka Sound by the 1790s (Moziño 1970:43–44; see also Hoskins in Howay 1941: 196), on the lower Columbia by 1800 (Lewis and Clark in Thwaites 1959, 3:232, 4:26, 270), and at Novo-Arkangel'sk in the early decades of the nineteenth century (Khlebnikov 1976:104). Venereal disorders were common complaints at most Hudson's Bay Company forts, judging from frequent references to the "pox" and treatments with mercury.

Introduced Diseases

All the eight major varieties of epidemic diseases documented from the Northwest Coast in the first century of contact (smallpox, malaria, measles, influenza, dysentery, whooping cough, typhus, and typhoid fever) were introduced, ultimately from European sources. Four of these (smallpox, measles, influenza, and whooping cough) are transmitted among humans by "droplet infection" (sneezing) and are dependent on continuous and dense populations for their transmission and maintenance; two (malaria and typhus) are transmitted by insect vectors (mosquitoes and fleas or lice); typhoid and dysentery microbes normally enter the body through polluted water (Benenson 1975). Despite suggestions by Dobyns (1983) of continent-wide epidemic visitations in the 250 years before 1770, there is no evidence—archeological, traditional, or otherwise—from the Northwest Coast that could be used to support a hypothesis of precontact epidemic mortality.

● SMALLPOX, 1775 AND 1801 Of all introduced diseases on the Northwest Coast, smallpox caused the greatest mortality. The disease appeared in epidemic waves, the exact timing and distribution of each visitation being due to the dual factors of introduction from an outside source and the presence on the coast of a pool of susceptibles (nonimmunes) large enough for the disease to take hold and spread. The initial outbreak occurred sometime during the 1770s, seems to have affected the entire coastal region, and was (apparently) not witnessed by Euro-Americans. References in the ethnohistorical literature consist of observations of pockmarked individuals and Indian recollections of the outbreak. It is reported from the Tlingit (Portlock 1789:27; Fleurieu 1801:328; Khlebnikov 1976:29), Haida (Fleurieu 1801:438; Bishop 1967: 83; Green 1915:39), Nitinaht (Hoskins and Boit in Howay 1941:196, 377), Northern and Central Coast Salish (Puget 1793: entry of 3/18/92; Maud 1978, 2:22), Northern Straits Salish (Suttles 1954:42), Southern Coast Salish (Vancouver 1798, 1:217, 241; Menzies 1923:29, 35; Puget

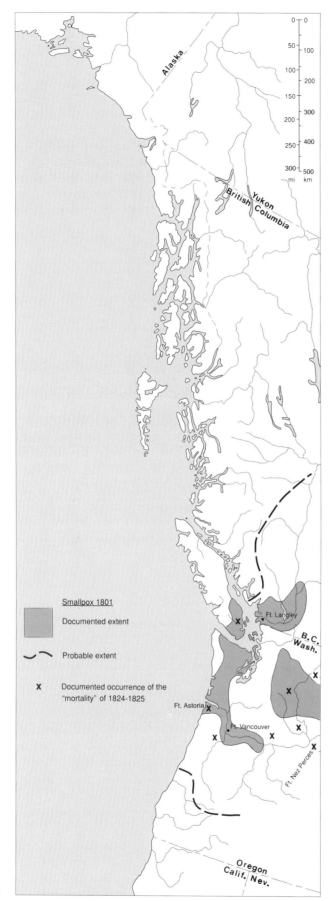

Fig. 1. Documented and probable extent of the smallpox epidemic in 1801 and documented occurrences of the "mortality" of 1824–1825.

Smallpox 1801

Documented extent

~ Probable extent

x Documented occurrence of the "mortality" of 1824-1825

1939:198), Upper Chinookans (Thwaites 1959:4:241), and Tillamook (Haswell in Howay 1941:33). Numerous lines of evidence suggest that smallpox was introduced to the Northwest Coast with the 1775 Bruno de Hezeta–Juan Francisco de la Bodega y Quadra Expedition, though alternative or multiple sources—from the Northern Plains or Kamchatka—cannot be ruled out (Boyd 1985).

Smallpox appeared again on the central coast about 1801, certainly spread from the Plains via the Columbia Plateau (fig. 1) (Teit 1930:212, 315–316). It is recorded from the Chinookan area (in Thwaites 1959, 2:117, 3:50; Stuart 1935:32), the Southwestern Coast Salish and Twana (Elmendorf 1960:272), and the Central Coast Salish (Jenness 1955:34; Elmendorf 1960:272).

Mortality for either of these epidemics is not recorded; however, the conservative figure of 30 percent mortality for initial smallpox outbreaks in the Americas (A.W. Crosby 1972:44; C.W. Dixon 1962:325) has been used. Recorded mortalities from other parts of North America for the epidemic of the 1770s–1780s approximate or exceed this number (for example, Dobyns 1966). These lines of evidence have led to the acceptance of the minimal figure of one-third as the best approximation of the true mortality rate on the Northwest Coast from the smallpox epidemic of the 1770s. Two sources from the Plateau (Work in Chance 1973:120; A.B. Smith 1958:136–137) state that mortality from the second visitation was less than that for the first, and one (Smith) attributes this to a milder strain. A second factor that certainly contributed to the smaller death rate was the fact that a sizable segment of the population, including all those over 25 or 20 years old who had survived an initial infection by the smallpox virus, was immune to subsequent attacks. This epidemiological phenomenon of smallpox and other viral diseases tends to concentrate mortality in the younger segments of populations experiencing sequential epidemics.

● THE "MORTALITY" OF 1824–1825 Scattered evidence, both ethnohistorical and demographic, suggests that there was a third epidemic visitation, of unknown nature, in the central Northwest Coast and the Columbia Plateau, in 1824–1825 (fig. 1). References from Tualatin Kalapuya, Cowichan and Upriver Halkomelem, as well as nearby Plateau tribes, all very ambiguous as to date, name smallpox (Gatschet 1877a:235; *British Colonist* 12/9/ 1862; T.C. Elliott 1912:222; Scouler 1905:203; Teit 1928: 97; Splawn 1944:393, 426). Epidemiologically, sufficient time (one generation) had passed to allow a nonimmune population large enough to support a third outbreak of smallpox. Two sources (ARCIA 1854:499; Barclay in Larsell 1947:90) name measles (among the Tututni and Columbia River peoples, respectively). Again, epidemiologically, the timing is correct: measles is documented from the Subarctic in 1819–1823 (Krech 1981:85) and in 1838 from California (Valle 1973). The Chinook, Cayuse, and Walla Walla are all reported to have suffered from an unnamed "mortality" in 1824–1825 (Scouler 1905: 165–166, 276–277; A. Kennedy 1824–1825; Simpson 1931:127; Ogden 1933:24). Demographic evidence, in the form of low numbers and percentages of children in the 1824–1825 Fort George (Chinookan) and 1829 Colville censuses (Sanpoil-Nespelem, Spokane, and Coeur d'Alene) (Kennedy 1824–1825; Work 1829), also points to an epidemic visitation about 1824–1825. Comparison with possibly similar outbreaks (smallpox 1801 and measles 1848) suggests that mortality from the 1824–1825 epidemic was probably in the 10–20 percent range.

● MALARIA, 1830– A second exotic disease that made a major contribution to the depopulation of the Northwest Coast was called by its contemporaries "fever and ague," "intermittent fever," or some variation on these terms. Although there has been much controversy over the identity of this ailment (typhus, cholera, influenza, and scarlatina have all been suggested), a consensus has formed that it was malaria, sometimes accompanied by secondary diseases (see Scott 1928; M.F. Boyd 1941; Larsell 1947; S. F. Cook 1955; Hodgson 1957; Taylor and Hoaglin 1962; Boyd 1975).

The epidemiology of "fever and ague" supports the malaria hypothesis. Geographically, the extent of the disease corresponded closely to the range of the most likely malarial vector, the mosquito *Anopheles malculipennis*, which is native to the interior valleys of western Oregon, with an especially heavy concentration in the formerly swampy areas of the Portland Basin (Gjullin and Eddy 1972:100). Temporally, the incidence of "fever and ague" matched the pattern of malarial outbreaks in temperate zones. Cases appeared in mid- or late summer, coincident with the breeding season of the mosquito, peaked in number in the fall, and declined with the onset of cold weather.

"Intermittent fever" first appeared on the Northwest Coast in August 1830, in the vicinity of Fort Vancouver (Harriott 1907:260). The common belief of the Indians was that the disease came on one or both of the two American coasters, the *Owyhee* and *Convoy*, that spent the winter of 1829–1830 in the Portland Basin. This is possible, as both ships had stopped at malarial ports on their way to the Northwest Coast, but it is just as likely that the disease came with infected trappers or traders at the fort who had spent time in the malarial Mississippi Valley. By October 11, 1830, according to Chief Factor Dr. John McLoughlin at Fort Vancouver, "three-fourths of the Indian population" in the "vicinity" had died (1948: 139–140). Natives who fled to the fort were driven away because of lack of resources, and at least one depopulated local village was burned to the ground on the orders of McLoughlin (1948:175; Ogden 1933:67–71).

After its initial surge in the autumn of 1830, "fever and ague" remained quiescent for nine months. It reappeared in July 1831, spreading throughout the lower Columbia River from Oak Point to The Dalles and into the Willamette valley (McLoughlin 1941–1944:232–233, 1948:212–213). The epidemic was "raging" at The Dalles by October 18, and had appeared at the mouth of the John Day, its apparent eastern limit, by October 23 (McGillivray 1830–1831). About this time Dr. McLoughlin ordered a shipment of cinchona, in lieu of quinine, the best medicine for malaria and then in short supply, from Oahu (1948:225). The third fever season began in July 1832, and the disease again raged "with great violence" through the fall (1948:289, 296). Numerous infected individuals were among the membership of the annual fur trading expedition to California (Work 1945a), and this expedition probably introduced malaria to the Central Valley of California and the lakes of the Great Basin (S.F. Cook 1955:311–313). Although it appeared annually on the lower Columbia throughout the 1830s, by 1833 the "fever and ague" had passed through its epidemic phase and settled into an endemic status (Bolduc 1979:118). Records of physicians at Fort Vancouver indicate that two varieties of the disease, tertian and quartan, were prevalent (J.R. Dunn 1846:26–27). According to Dr. William Bailey "The ague and fever was not of a dangerous type . . . [and] would not prove so fatal . . . for the natives if they would adopt the European mode of treating it" (Wilkes 1925–1926:47; Colvocoresses 1855:258). Numerous sources state that the Indian practices of steaming in a sweat lodge and jumping into cold water during the period of alternating spells of chills and fever characteristic of malaria hastened death. The exact mechanism of death in such cases remains uncertain; the rapid alternation between hot and cold states while laboring under a febrile disease might lead to shock (J.F. Taylor 1977:58), or these practices may have facilitated the development of pneumonia (Hodgson 1957), in which terminal cases of "fever and ague" included nose bleeds and coughing up blood (Work 1945a:77).

Pre-epidemic numbers in the lower Columbia and Willamette valleys are calculated to have been 13,940, of which around 5,160 were Kiksht-speaking and 8,780 Kalapuyan (Parker 1838:36). In 1841 there were around 575 Chinookans and 600 Kalapuyans (Wilkes 1925–1926: 296). Total losses in the area between 1830 and 1841 are therefore about 92 percent (13,940 to 1,175). Mortality was concentrated in the Kiksht-speaking villages of the Portland Basin, with a probable 98 percent loss (Lewis and Clark 1805–1806). Other loss estimates state "more than 2,000 souls" in the Portland Basin died and 5,000–6,000 on the Willamette (Slacum 1837:15–16). Parker (1844) states seven-eights died, and McLoughlin (in Parker 1844:192–193) estimated nine-tenths died. In 1841, loss figures of around 10,000 for all Chinookan

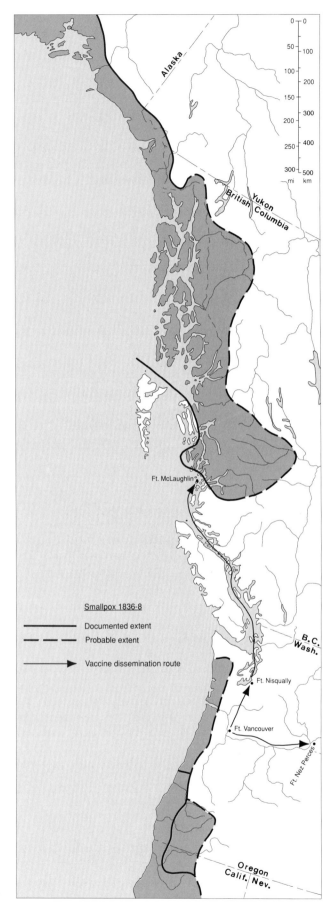

Fig. 2. Probable extent of the smallpox epidemic in 1836–1838 with locations of vaccine dispersion. Presence on northern Oreg. and Wash. coasts is inferred.

Smallpox 1836-8

——————— Documented extent

– – – – – Probable extent

⟶ Vaccine dissemination route

speakers were cited (Duflot de Mofras 1937:174; Hale 1846:215). Dr. Bailey estimated that "one-fourth died off yearly" in the Columbia-Willamette area (Wilkes 1925–1926:57). Outside that zone, but within the malarial region, mortality was less. Total losses in the malarial area of the Northwest are difficult to compute but may have exceeded 25,000, or 85 percent of the total population.

● SMALLPOX, 1836–1838 Smallpox reappeared among the northern peoples of the Northwest Coast in December 1835, at Novo-Arkangel'sk whence it may have been transported by a ship from Asia or Spanish America (fig. 2). Between January and April 1836 smallpox was epidemic at the Russian post; half the Native population of Novo-Arkangel'sk died (Veniaminov 1840). From April through June it spread throughout the Tlingit territory (J.R. Gibson 1982); Russian medical personnel sent out with vaccine encountered great resistance to the treatment from the Indians (Veniaminov 1840:47). In 1837 and 1838 smallpox was epidemic among the Aleuts (Sarafian 1977) and Ingalik Indians (Van Stone 1979).

Smallpox was carried to Fort Simpson, in Tsimshian territory, on board the American coaster *La Grange* from Novo-Arkangel'sk or by a trading party of Stikine Tlingit. The first case was recorded on September 28, 1836; by November 11 "a great number" were dying on the lower Skeena; on December 4 smallpox was on the lower Nass (Finlayson and Work 1834–1838). By the beginning of 1837 smallpox had run its course in Tsimshian territory. A comparison of pre- and post-epidemic (1835 and 1838) population figures from the Fort McLoughlin district (Tolmie 1963:319–320; Douglas 1878) suggests sizable mortality among the Haisla, Haihais, Bella Bella of Dean Channel, Bella Coola, and Bulkley River Carrier (Jenness 1943:475) were also affected. The Kwakiutl were untouched by this outbreak (Simpson 1847:114; cf. Codere 1950:51) as were, by negative evidence, the Haida.

The 1836 epidemic in the north may well have been related to the 1837–1838 smallpox epidemic in California, which was first recorded at the Russian outpost of Fort Ross near Bodega Bay in late 1837 (S.F. Cook 1939:184). The northern California epidemic extended into Oregon, at the mouth of the Rogue River (ARCIA 1854:498), and in the Umpqua River valley (McLoughlin 1941–1944:282; Wilkes 1845:225). The Upper Umpqua Indians blamed the Hudson's Bay Company fur brigade under Michel LaFramboise, which had been on the Sacramento in late 1837, for introducing the disease. Comparison of 1805 and mid-century population statistics from the Oregon and central Washington coasts (Coosan, Siuslawan, Tillamook, Chinook, Lower Chehalis, and Quinault) indicate considerable decline, which may be due to this epidemic.

There is no evidence that the 1836–1838 outbreak

BOYD

spread to the Columbia River drainage or any of the region between Forts Nisqually and McLoughlin. The reasons for this were probably a discontinuity in Indian population distribution and communications as well as extensive dissemination of smallpox vaccine from Fort Vancouver to mid-coast forts and posts (Boyd 1985).

The common wisdom among Hudson's Bay Company officials was that the 1836–1838 epidemic claimed one-third of the population of the north coast (McLoughlin 1941–1944:271; Simpson 1847:123), as shown by table 2. Mortality on the Oregon coast, assuming some acquired immunity from earlier outbreaks, was probably much less than in the north.

● IMMIGRANTS' DISEASES, 1840S The first permanent White settlers in the 1840s brought with them a long list of minor infectious diseases that had previously been present only transiently, if at all, among the populations of the Northwest Coast. The focus of these new diseases was along the main migration route, which comprised the Oregon Trail and the lower Columbia. According to an eyewitness at Cowlitz: "Every fall the Indians were excited as to what new ill was to come . . . .Every year they [the immigrants] brought something new . . . .Whooping cough, measles, Typhoid fever etc . . . .the country was free from all these malidies till then—when first introduced they seemed much more violent than now . . . .All these things we think so lightly of now scourged the poor Indians dreadfully" (G.B. Roberts 1878:16, 48).

Dysentery appeared in 1844 on the lower Columbia (fig. 3); 400 Indians were reported to have died at Vancouver (J.R. Dunn 1846:27), 30 at Cowlitz (Landerholm 1956:238), and "numbers" at the Cascades (Smet 1905, 2:451). The epidemic also spread to the Willamette (Jacobs 1945:6) and The Dalles.

Measles was first reported at Fort Nez Perces at the mouth of the Walla Walla in late July 1847 (Harper 1971:117), prior to the overland immigrations of that year. The disease may have arrived from California with Cayuse and Walla Walla traders (Heizer 1942) or from the Red River (Larsell 1947:90).

From its initial focus on the mid-Columbia, measles spread in all directions. It appeared at Fort Vancouver in December (Douglas 1848a), was epidemic at Cowlitz from mid-December through March 1848 (G.B. Roberts 1962),

and was noted during January and February at Fort Nisqually (Heath 1979) and mid-March through May at Victoria (Finlayson 1848). The disease may have been carried from Fort Nisqually to points north by the Hudson's Bay supply ship *Beaver* (Work 1848). Measles was present at Fort Simpson shortly after the arrival of the *Beaver* in mid-January and eventually appeared at Fort Stikine (Douglas 1848).

Reports of mortality are sparse. On the Columbia Plateau the recorded death rate among the Cayuse and at Colville was about one-third (Craig 1858:27; E. Walker 1976:437); the equivalent figures for the coast south of Fort Nisqually and at Fort Simpson were "a ninth" (Barclay 1848) and 10 percent (Douglas 1848), respectively. One factor that contributed to higher mortalities was the simultaneous presence of secondary diseases: dysentery is reported from nearly all locations; typhus ("camp fever") was present on the lower Columbia; the flu or colds at northern locations. Another factor contributing to mortality was the south coast practice of sweat bathing for febrile diseases. For those groups (on the coast) without adequate statistics, 10 percent is a conservative estimate of mortality from this epidemic.

● SMALLPOX, 1853 AND 1862 In 1853, smallpox was apparently introduced at more than one coastal location by trading vessels from San Francisco. From an initial focus at the mouth of the Columbia (Swan 1857:54–55) the epidemic spread south through Tillamook, Yaquina, and Alsea territory as far as Cape Perpetua (Gibbs 1856:12) and north as far as Quinault territory (Olson 1936:182) and the head of Puget Sound (fig. 4) (Starling 1853). From a second focus at Neah Bay (Hancock 1927:181–182) smallpox was introduced to Nitinaht (Drucker 1951:12) and Clallam lands (W.H. Hills 1853:137). The disease was also reported in Nooksack territory and among the lower Skagit (J.M. Collins 1949a:302). Its entry into Puget Sound itself was apparently stalled by a vigorous program of vaccination (Starling 1853).

Mortality from this outbreak seems to have been greatest at the two points of introduction and along the intermediate portion of the Washington coast, where somewhat more than 40 percent of the Indian population perished. The death rate was considerably less among

Table 2. North Coast Mortality from Smallpox, 1836-1837

	Pre-epidemic population	Post-epidemic population	Percentage loss
Tlingit	9,980	7,255	27
Nishga	2,423	1,615	33
Tsimshian	4,238	2,825	33
Haisla	825	409	50
Kitasoo, Haihais, Bella Bella	875	579	34
Bella Coola	1,940	1,056	46
Total	20,181	13,739	32%

SOURCE: Boyd 1985.

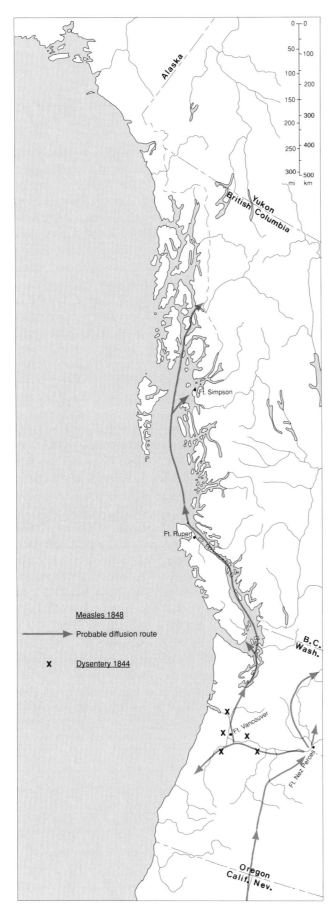

Fig. 3. Documented occurrences of dysentery in 1844 and probable
diffusion routes of measles in 1848.

Measles 1848

→ Probable diffusion route

x   Dysentery 1844

peripheral populations. Total loss in the affected areas of
the coast was about 2,000–3,000 people.

The 1862–1863 smallpox epidemic in British Columbia
(fig. 4) (Duff 1964:42–43; Yarmie 1968; Pethick 1978:
11–23) was introduced by a ship from San Francisco,
which came to port at Victoria on March 13 (*British
Colonist* 3/19/1862,3:1). By late April smallpox was
present at a temporary settlement of Haidas, Tsimshians,
Kwakiutls, Stikine Tlingits, and other Indians assembled
for trading purposes just outside Victoria. Within the
crowded confines of the encampment the disease spread
rapidly (Hills 1863; *British Colonist* 1862). The government's response to the situation was isolation and eviction;
orders were given to restrict Indian entrance into Victoria
and to commence the removal of the Indians to their
homelands (*British Colonist* 4/29/1862,3:1).

Throughout May and June parties of infected Indians
moved toward home, sometimes accompanied by government vessels, leaving numerous dead on islands and
beaches all along the Strait of Georgia (*British Colonist* 6/
13, 6/21, 6/27, 7/11/1862). By this very efficient means
smallpox was transmitted to all the peoples of northern
British Columbia. The Fort Rupert Kwakiutl and the
Bella Bella (McNeill 1862) were decimated. In July a
government surveying party reported 400 Bella Coola
deaths (Palmer 1863:7–8; Wade 1931:149–150). The
Haisla apparently escaped the 1862–1863 epidemic (Olson
1940:197).

"No fewer than 500" Tsimshians at Fort Simpson were
lost (McNeill 1862; Church Missionary Society 1869:88)
in May. At the same time inhabitants of the missionary
settlement of Metlakatla, British Columbia, were spared
infection due to the vaccinating efforts of William Duncan
(1862: entry of 7/11). The Tongass and Stikine Tlingit lost
more than half their numbers (table 3).

The last significant outbreaks of infectious disease on
the Northwest Coast in the first century of contact were in
1868 and 1874. In 1868 measles spread along the
mainland coast north of the Strait of Georgia (J.W. White
1868:7; Teichmann 1963:93, 116, 196). Mortality was
probably minimal and concentrated among those born
since the outbreak 20 years earlier. In 1874 smallpox again
surfaced among the Barkley Sound Nootka and Nitinaht
(Brabant 1972:38–45). At least part of the over 1,200-
person difference in population for these peoples between
1860 and 1881 (Sproat 1868:308; Swan 1870:2–3; Guillod
1882 adjusted; Colson 1953:298) may be attributed to
mortality from this outbreak.

Population History

The demographic disruption that followed Euro-American contact on the Northwest Coast was a product of

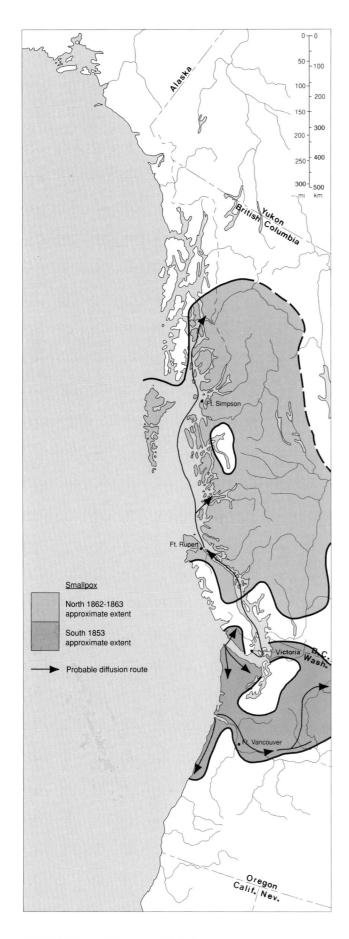

Fig. 4. Approximate extents of smallpox epidemics of 1853 and 1862–1863 along with the probable diffusion routes of the disease.

changes in aboriginal patterns of fertility and mortality. Changes in fertility are difficult to detect because of the lack of detailed statistics, but certain trends are likely on the basis of shared historical experiences with other, more completely recorded, contact-period hunter-gatherer populations. The demographic history of the Northwest Coast in the first century after contact was essentially one of a dramatic increase in mortality rates, leading to decline of some populations and extinction or amalgamation of others. The increase in mortality was due almost exclusively to the introduction of exogenous diseases.

Changes in fertility patterns may have come from a number of sources. Increase in fertility rates might be associated with a shift from seasonal nomadism to a more sedentary existence (cf. Lee 1972). In the early nineteenth century, increased sedentism occurred near many permanent trading posts of the Hudson's Bay Company. Dietary changes, involving more reliable year-round food supplies and an increase in carbohydrate intake, might improve the general health and fat levels of females, extend the childbearing period, and reduce the interval between births, resulting in an increased fertility rate (Frisch 1977). In this instance, the early adoption of potato cultivation by most of the Central and Southern Coast Salish and Haida (Suttles 1951a), who had high ratios of children in contemporary censuses (Douglas 1878), is of interest.

Conversely, fertility rates might decline as a result of changes brought by contact. Secondary sterility among women resulting from infection by venereal disease was a documented cause of depopulation in the missions of California (S.F. Cook 1943:22–30; Aschmann 1959). In 1792 Spanish observers at Nootka Sound, familiar with the situation in Baja California, expressed a fear that the spread of venereal disease among the Nootkans would lead to their eventual extinction (Moziño 1970:43–44).

North Coast Epidemic Area

The North Coast Epidemic Area includes the Eyak, Tlingit, Haida, Tsimshian, Bella Coola, and Haisla. Most of these peoples suffered from the smallpox epidemics of about 1775 and 1836 (Haida and perhaps Gitksan excepted) and 1862–1863 (some Tlingit and the Haisla excepted), as well as measles outbreaks in 1848 and 1868. The population anchor date for most groups is 1842, the year of the most complete surviving Hudson's Bay census (Douglas 1878). For the Haisla and Bella Coola it is Tolmie's (1963:319–320) 1835 house count estimate.

● TLINGIT The population history of the Tlingit is the best known of the northern peoples. Precontact numbers are estimated at a minimum 14,820. In 1835 there were

143

Table 3. Smallpox Fatalities, 1862–1863

	Pre-epidemic population[a]	Post-epidemic population[b]	Percentage loss
Hutsnuwu and Kake Tlingit	1,088	688	37
Stikine and Tongass Tlingit	1,860	803	57
Nishga	1,454	828	43
Gitskan	1,875	1,462	22
Coast Tsimshian	2,543	1,967	23
Southern Tsimshian	936	300	68
Haida	9,618	1,658	83
Bella Coola	950	402	58
Haihais, Oowekeeno, Bella Bella	1,651	508	69
Kwakiutl	7,650	2,370	69
Comox	1,080	506	53
Songhees, Saanich	1,050	486	46
Total	31,755	11,978	62%

[a] Most figures have been decreased by 10% to allow for losses from the 1848 measles epidemic.
[b] Most figures have been increased by 5% to allow for losses from the 1868 measles outbreak.
SOURCE: Boyd 1985.

approximately 9,880 Tlingits (Douglas 1835; Veniaminov 1840:19). By 1842 Tlingit population had dropped to about 7,255 (Douglas 1878, adjusted), certainly due to the 1836 smallpox epidemic. Between 1842 and 1890, while other island Tlingit numbers remained stable, the Hutsnuwu and Kake lost approximately two-thirds of their population, as did the mainland Tongass and Stikine, mainly due to measles in 1848 and smallpox in 1863. Total Tlingit population in 1890 was 4,501 (U.S. Census Office. 11th Census 1893:158).

• HAIDA Haida population statistics from the early contact period are exceedingly rare. The 1842 Hudson's Bay census gives 8,428 individuals (6,693 on the Queen Charlottes and 1,735 Kaigani) (Douglas 1878; Harper 1971; Dawson 1880a). Other early estimates are 10,692 (Parker 1936:124), 9,350 (Veniaminov 1840:19), and 10,000 (W. Duncan 1860). Averaged, these figures yield 9,618, which may be assumed to approximate the early nineteenth-century number. Allowing for mortality from the initial smallpox epidemic, there should have been at least 14,427 Haida aboriginally. There is no evidence that the Haida suffered from any major epidemic between 1775 and 1862. About 1890, total Haida numbers were around 1,200 people, a drop of 88 percent between the 1840s and 1880s. Most of this loss must be assigned to the 1862 smallpox epidemic, the only known event of demographic significance occurring in the Queen Charlottes during this span.

Aboriginal population for the North Coast Epidemic Area is here estimated at 48,952. By the late 1800s there were around 4,500 Tlingits, 4,400 Tsimshians, and 1,200 Haidas (U.S. Census Office. 11th Census 1893:158; Chittenden 1884:23–24).

Wakashan Epidemic Area

The Wakashan Epidemic Area includes the Haihais, Bella Bella, Oowekeeno, Kwakiutl, Northern and Central Nootkans, and Northern Coast Salish. All apparently experienced the epidemic of about 1775 and the "mortality" of 1824–1825. The Haihais suffered from the 1836 smallpox epidemic. The peoples along the inland passage experienced both the 1848 measles outbreak and 1862 smallpox epidemic. Those two diseases seem to have bypassed the Nootka, who suffered from a minor smallpox outbreak of their own in 1874. Population anchor for the Kwakiutl is the 1835 estimate of Tolmie (1963:306, 317–320); for Haisla, Haihais, Bella Bella, and Oowekeeno it is Douglas (1878); for the Nootka the anchor is the 1860 census of Sproat (1868:308). There are no completely reliable figures for the Northern Coast Salish until the 1880s.

• KWAKIUTL The Kwakiutl were not counted until 1882, when there were 2,264 (Blenkinsop 1883:65). Of earlier estimates, Work's (1838) figure of 38,855 is far wrong. Closer to reality is Tolmie's (1963:317–318) 1835 total of 8,500. Douglas (1840:21) and W. Duncan (1860) both cite estimates of 10,000 speakers of Kwakiutl and Heiltsuk languages, which tends to support the 8,500 figure. The precontact Kwakiutl number, using the disease history method of reconstruction, is here set at 19,125. Codere's (1950:52) population figures show a steady decline of Kwakiutl numbers after 1882 to a nadir of 1,088 in 1928.

• NORTHERN AND CENTRAL NOOTKANS Speakers of Nootkan languages made contact with Euro-Americans in 1774, and Spaniards established a settlement at Nootka Sound in 1790. Within a year venereal disease had become established, and by 1793 the first Indian case of tuberculosis was recorded.

144

The earliest and most complete population estimates for any Northwest Coast people are recorded for the Nootka. What is surprising about these figures is their consistent large size. In April 1778 a member of the Capt. James Cook expedition estimated 2,600 as the population of Nootka Sound alone (J. King 1967:1404, 1408). In summer 1788 Meares (1790:229–231) gave 15,900 for the Northern and Central Nootkans. Between 1791 and 1793 Spanish chroniclers estimated 8,500 people at Clayoquot, 8,500 plus at Barkley Sound (Eliza 1933:145–146, 149), and 4,000 in Nootka Sound (Suría 1936:285). Yet in 1792 Menzies (1923:15) estimated the "subjects of" Tatoosh at 500. Jewitt in 1804 (1975:39–41), from his base at Nootka Sound, gave a figure of 2,750 warriors, or (using his own multiplicant of three as applied to Nootka itself) 8,250 people. Mooney (1928) estimates 6,000 Nootkans in 1774; Taylor (1963:163) gives 14,000. The true figure is probably somewhere between (table 1).

Even assuming that the initial estimates of the 1790s are too large, it is apparent that Nootkan population was on the decline from contact. The 4,850 population of the 1840s (Douglas 1878, adjusted) declines to 3,256 in the 1881 British Columbia census. Part of this loss is attributable to the 1848 measles outbreak among the Northern Nootkans and to the 1874 smallpox outbreak among the Barkley Sound people. But it seems likely that there were additional factors at work. After a five-year residence in Barkley Sound, Sproat (1868:278–279) stated that the "principal cause" of the continued decline of the Nootka was the "despondency and discouragement" associated with pronounced cultural change. Sproat perceived an increase in death rate, and there is evidence for an increase in deaths from tuberculosis and respiratory diseases on Vancouver Island arising from a decline in hygiene characteristic of the first stages of the transition to Euro-American clothing and housing. But the birth rate was declining also. Observers commented upon the prevalence of abortion (Grant 1857:304; Sproat 1868:254; Guillod 1882:165). Considering the already low fertility of Nootka women (Walker 1982:88; Sproat 1868:94), abortion, and sterility from venereal infections, it is probable that the population was no longer replacing itself.

The Northern and Central Nootkan population lost a minimum of two-thirds of their numbers between 1775 and 1881. The population nadir was reached in 1939 when the total dipped to 1,605 (Duff 1964:39).

Total aboriginal population for the Wakashan Epidemic Area is here set at at least 38,075. By the 1880s this total had decreased to about 6,876. Kwakiutl depopulation was sudden, with over one-third of the total loss occurring in 1862. Nootkan decline, by contrast, was gradual, attributable in some areas to mortality from chronic diseases accompanied by a perceptible decline in fertility (Sproat 1868:272–286).

Olympic Epidemic Area

The Olympic Epidemic Area includes the Nitinaht, Makah, Quileute, Chemakum, and Clallam. These peoples shared the smallpox epidemics of 1775, 1801, the "mortality" of 1824–1825, and the 1848 measles epidemic. However, it is the mortality from the 1853 smallpox epidemic that sets them off from their neighbors. Hudson's Bay Company censuses of 1839–1842 provide the anchor populations for most groups. The Quileute anchor dates from the 1805 Lewis and Clark estimate (Thwaites 1904–1905).

In 1804–1805 Jewitt (1975:39) allowed 1,000 men, that is, 3,000 total using his proportions, for the Nitinaht plus Makah. In 1805 Lewis and Clark estimated 2,000 for the Makah (Thwaites 1904–1905, 6:118). The Hudson's Bay Company anchor populations of 1839–1842 are 800 Nitinahts and 1,200 Makahs. The aboriginal figure for these two peoples, allowing for disease history prior to 1839, is estimated at 4,320.

The causes of decline after 1839 are clear. Using the more completely documented Makah as a guide, there was a 12 percent decline during the 1840s, undoubtedly due to measles, and the 1853 smallpox epidemic eliminated over one-third. By 1881 there were 869 surviving Nitinahts and Makahs. Estimated total aboriginal population for this epidemic area is 8,310. Total numbers decreased by at least half after 50 years of contact and a minimum of three-quarters after 100 years.

Georgia-Puget Epidemic Area

The Georgia-Puget Epidemic Area comprises the Central Coast Salish, except the Clallam, and the Southern Coast Salish. All suffered from the initial smallpox epidemic in 1775, as 1792 references suggesting depopulation show (Vancouver 1798, 1:229; Menzies 1923:63; Puget 1792:6/28, 1793:9/19). Most of these peoples seem to have experienced the epidemic of 1801. Smallpox or measles may have reappeared in 1824, and measles was definitely present in 1848. The 1853 smallpox epidemic in Washington and the 1862–1863 epidemic in British Columbia marginally affected the Central and Southern Coast Salish (except for the Songhees), due in part to the widespread use of smallpox vaccine around the missions and populated areas.

Continuing White presence in the Georgia-Puget area dates from the establishment of Forts Langley and Nisqually in 1827 and 1833, respectively. The first population estimate is A. McDonald's (1830) list of adult men of the various tribes. Reliable estimates are somewhat later: 1839 for the environs of Nisqually and Langley, and not until the reservation period of the 1850s for the Northern Lushootseed, Nooksack, Songhees, and Saanich.

The Squamish and Halkomelem, due to their proximity to Euro-American settlements, were often counted. The Squamish returned 784 in the 1839 census; the 1884 figure (778) is nearly identical. The precontact number may have been 1,694. There were 2,074 mainland Halkomelem in 1839 (perhaps an undercount—Duff 1952a:129) and 2,649 in 1884 (Vankoughnet 1885:187–188). A Hudson's Bay Company census of around 1839–1845 for the island Halkomelem yields an aggregate of 2,399; the 1883 equivalent is 1,614 (Vankoughnet 1885:189–190). It appears that, despite some shifts in relative numbers, Squamish and Halkomelem populations on the whole remained stable from 1839 through the early reservation period. Mortality from imported diseases among these peoples was probably mitigated by access to Euro-American medicines, in particular smallpox vaccine; in addition the early censuses consistently indicate high fertility. The precontact population of the Halkomelem (mainland and island) may be twice its mid-nineteenth-century mark, or about 9,662.

The Lushootseed speakers were probably the largest and their population history is the best documented of the peoples of the Georgia-Puget Epidemic Area. Hudson's Bay Company censuses of 1839–1842 give a total count of 5,479 for most of the Lushootseed peoples (Douglas 1878; Taylor 1963:163). Given the known disease history of the area, the precontact figure is here set at at least 11,835. In 1856 there were approximately 4,872 Lushootseed speakers (Washington Superintendency of Indian Affairs, various).

Total precontact population for the Georgia-Puget Epidemic Area is estimated at 29,599. By 1820 this precontact estimate had been halved, and after a century it had decreased by over two-thirds.

It should be noted that population decline here is the smallest estimated for any epidemic area on the Northwest Coast. In addition, though there was no perceptible rebound of any member group before the beginning of the reservation period in the late 1850s, censuses taken between 1839 and 1856 suggest that a potential for recovery was present. Central and Southern Coast Salish populations, on the whole, show an unusually high percentage of children. The reasons for this apparent high fertility undoubtedly relate to the nature of their resource base, which included long stretches of coastline, and was broader, and hence more reliable, than most of their neighbors. The adoption of potato cultivation by most Central and Southern Coast Salish by the 1850s was also a factor. When vaccination and effective health care systems were introduced in the mid-nineteenth century the natural tendency to increase seems to have reasserted itself.

However, a few years after moving to reservations, these populations began declining. Only 3,549 Lushootseed Salish were tallied in the 1870 census (Ross in ARCIA 1870:17). Eells (1887:272, 274, 1903) attributed this resumed decline to the prevalence of chronic diseases attendant upon culture change in "clothing and housekeeping" and to venereal diseases.

South Coast Epidemic Area

The South Coast Epidemic Area includes the peoples of the southern Washington and Oregon coasts (Lower Chehalis, Quinault, Chinook and Clatsop, Tillamook, Alseans, Siuslawans, Coosans, and coastal Oregon Athapaskans). Smallpox was the major cause of depopulation; every epidemic—1775, 1801, 1824, 1838, and 1853—spread through this region (but those of 1801 and 1853 did not affect people south of the Alseans). Anchor populations are drawn from the 1805 Lewis and Clark estimate (Thwaites 1904–1905, 6:113–120).

The best-documented group from the South Coast Epidemic Area is the Chinook, whom Lewis and Clark put at 700 for the Chinook, Clatsop, and Shoalwater Bay peoples combined. In the 1824–1825 Fort George estimate there were 750 Chinook and Clatsop plus 290 slaves (A. Kennedy 1824–1825). Allowing for disease mortality 1775–1805, aboriginal numbers may have approached 1,260.

In 1841 there were 429 Chinooks and Clatsops (Wilkes 1925–1926:296), and a total Chinook-speaking population probably slightly over 500. Depopulation during the 1840s was due to mortality from dysentery and measles, depressed fertility from venereal disease and endemic malaria, and losses through outmarriage of women into the White population. By 1851 population was around 279 (Gibbs 1851b; Shortess 1851).

Lewis and Clark give a population of 13,250 for the South Coast Epidemic Area in 1805. Taking into account prior disease mortality, the aboriginal figure would have been 22,080. After a century of contact, the combined populations of the South Coast peoples approximated only 2,885. Only two populations—Oregon Athapaskans and Chehalis-Quinault—survived in sizable numbers, 994 and 563 respectively, in 1853–1854 (ARCIA 1854:495; Stevens 1901:504).

Interior Valleys Epidemic Area

The peoples of what is here termed the Interior Valleys Epidemic Area—(Upper Chehalis and Cowlitz, Kwalhioqua and Clatskanie, Cathlamet, Multnomah, and Clackamas, Kalapuyans, Takelma, and interior Oregon Athapaskans—experienced a precipitous population decline in the first century of contact. Smallpox spread throughout most of the region every generation, in the 1770s, 1801, 1824–1825, 1838 (Takelma and interior Oregon Athapaskans), and 1853 (Washington groups only). Measles was present in 1848. The bulk of the population loss resulted from the introduction and establishment of malaria in an endemic focus after 1830. Population anchors are the Lewis and Clark (1805–1806) manuscript estimate (Chinookans, Kwalhioqua and Clatskanie, and Kalapuyans), Morse's (1822) figures (Cowlitz), and Parker's (1838) journal (Takelma and interior Oregon Athapaskans).

The two largest ethnolinguistic units among the Interior Valleys peoples were the Kiksht-speaking Chinookans of the Columbia River and the Kalapuyans of the Willamette Valley. Aboriginal populations are here estimated at 9,288 and 16,200, respectively. Lewis and Clark (1805–1806) gave 5,160 for the former and 9,000 for the latter.

In 1841 Wilkes (1925–1926:296) estimated 575 in the lower Kiksht-speaking villages and 600 Kalapuyans. The declines of 89 and 93 percent from the 1805–1806 numbers are basically due to malarial mortality. The sudden population drop in the area permitted new peoples to move in, and in the late 1830s Klikitat Sahaptins located permanently in some former Chinookan and Kalapuyan areas. Treaty estimates in 1851 for lower river Kiksht and the Kalapuyans show continued decreases—to 203 and 560—or about one-third of the 1841 totals.

The estimated aboriginal population of the Interior Valleys Epidemic Area is 41,328. By the late 1850s no more than 2,000 of the original number remained.

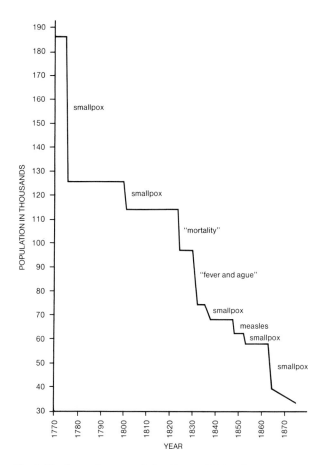

Fig. 5. Northwest Coast population history, 1774–1874.

Summary

Northwest Coast population history in the first century of contact is summarized in figure 5. The aboriginal total of 188,344 is an estimate, based on the assumption of one-third population loss from the first smallpox epidemic. There is a good possibility that the actual figure was considerably higher. Later totals are based on more reliable information. It is clear that Northwest Coast depopulation was an episodic process, with important disease events triggering sudden declines. The most important disease events, rated by demographic impact, were the initial smallpox epidemic of the 1770s, the "fever and ague" epidemics of the early 1830s (about 25,000 mortality), and the 1862–1863 smallpox epidemic (over 19,000 deaths in the Northwest Coast). Decline after 1874 was gradual, with a population nadir for the culture area reached in the early 1900s. Population figures for the twentieth century are given in the tribal chapters in this volume.

The actual process of depopulation varied from group to group, dependent upon their particular disease histories. Abrupt, catastrophic declines occurred among Haida, Kwakiutl, and the peoples of the Interior Valleys Epidemic Area. Although disruption was severe among the first two groups, survivorship was large enough to allow some degree of social and cultural continuity. In those areas where malaria became endemic, there was no recovery. Most Northwest Coast peoples experienced a more gradual decline, punctuated on occasion by sudden losses from epidemic diseases. Population survivorship and cultural continuity was greatest in two areas: among the Halkomelem, Southern Coast Salish, and Northern and Central Nootkans, and among the Tlingit and Tsimshian (excepting the Kitkatla).

Postcontact culture change among the Northwest Coast peoples was certainly influenced by their demographic histories. Two controversial hypotheses about Northwest Coast culture change, in fact, start from an assumption of significant disease-caused depopulation. Codere (1950) attributed the historical increase in the frequency and intensity of Kwakiutl potlatching in part to an increase in and confusion over heritable statuses resulting from a precipitous population decline. Aberle's (1959) "deprivation hypothesis" suggests that the origins of many Plateau and Northwest Coast nativistic cults may lie in part in social disorganization and perceived differences in mortality arising from introduced diseases. And there are other disease and depopulation theories of culture change that may be productive when applied to the Northwest Coast experience.

Sources

The principal sources for contact-period Northwest Coast populations are: Lewis and Clark's 1805–1806 estimates, Hudson's Bay Company censuses and estimates between 1824 and 1856, and censuses on reservations and reserves following 1851.

The 1805–1806 estimates, which cover the Columbia River drainage and Washington-Oregon coasts, have been widely used as indices of precontact population sizes. Lewis and Clark extrapolated from the number of lodges they observed on their route, and they collected informant testimony on numbers for peoples not visited. Their first estimates, compiled in the winter of 1805–1806 from data collected in October and November 1805 (Lewis and Clark 1805–1806), were later considerably enlarged on the basis of information obtained on their return trip (Thwaites 1904–1905, 6:114–120) in March and April 1806. The largest numerical differences between the two versions are for Upper Chinookan (Kiksht-speaking) villages and probably reflect a seasonal difference in population concentrations along the Columbia River (Boyd and Hajda 1987).

Between 1820 and the 1850s, estimates and head counts of Indians were taken by employees at Hudson's Bay Company trading posts. The most complete compilation of fort and district statistics is Douglas's (1878) manuscript census, which includes estimates and censuses taken at various times during the 1830s through the 1850s for Indians between Puget Sound and Fort Stikine. Selected censuses found in Douglas's records were used or printed by Warre and Vavasour (1909:61), Harper (1971:App.)., and Schoolcraft (1851–1857, 5:487–489, with numerous errors). In addition, local censuses from the Northwest Coast and Plateau survive in the Archives of the Hudson's Bay Company, Winnipeg, Manitoba, and in second-hand summary figures from lost censuses of the 1820s and 1830s (Parker 1837, 1838, 1844, 1936).

The Hudson's Bay statistics vary widely in quality. Work's 1838 "census" of the Kwakiutl (cited by Codere 1950:52) is a grossly inaccurate overestimate, and its inflated figures have led to incorrect estimates for the Nootkans (Douglas 1878; Taylor 1963:10). The 1839 Fort Langley census (summary figures in Duff 1952a:28), on the other hand, is a model of careful collection and attention to detail (Douglas 1839). The more comprehensive of the Hudson's Bay censuses offer information of great demographic value: population by categories of age and sex, numbers of slaves, and in some cases details on lodges, canoes, horses, and guns.

In Oregon and Washington reservation-period censuses include counts arising from the treaty-making efforts of Anson Dart, Joel Palmer, and Isaac I. Stevens in the early 1850s, and letters and annual reports from agents at local reservations, preserved in the manuscript records of the Bureau of Indian Affairs and in the annual reports of the secretary of war. In British Columbia initial complete censuses from the early reservation period are found in the annual reports of the Department of Indian Affairs and in the Sessional Papers, commencing in the early 1880s. Inflated nineteenth-century population counts for the Central Coast Salish and Chinooks led to incorrect aboriginal estimates by Mooney (1928). Reservation counts may suffer from incomplete coverage (due to absence of segments of the population) and potential stochastic error in indices because of small numbers. Despite these drawbacks, they preserve important information on demographic decline from disease mortality, changes in fertility patterns, and out-migration.

History of Southeastern Alaska Since 1867

ROSITA WORL

In 1867 Russia, by treaty, sold Alaska to the United States (see D.H. Miller 1981). At the time, the Tlingit objected, maintaining that they were the rightful owners and that the United States should have paid the $7,200,000 to them instead of the Russians (Bancroft 1886:609). The treaty of cession (15 U.S. Stat. 539) did not extinguish the legal aboriginal rights of the Alaska Natives to their land, but Article III was vague about how the United States would settle their possessory rights: "The uncivilized tribes will be subject to such laws and regulations as the United States may, from time to time, adopt in regard to aboriginal tribes of that country" (Gruening 1954:499). The Tlingit, who had maintained their independence through the period of Russian occupation, asserted that they had allowed the Russians to remain in Alaska only because it was mutually advantageous (Bancroft 1886: 609). The land rights of the Tlingit were not to be settled for another 100 years, and their designation as "uncivilized" was also an issue (Gsovski 1950:21–25, 73–86).

U.S. Army Occupation, 1867–1877

The raising of the Stars and Stripes over Alaska began 10 years of administration by the War Department as a military district. The missions of the troops under Gen. Jefferson Columbus Davis were to oversee the fur trade and to end the traffic in alcohol. The army did little to promote law and order: in fact, soldiers sold alcohol to Indians (Andrews 1953) and engaged in armed disputes with them. Because soldiers were often responsible for the conflicts between the Indian and White populations, all Army posts but one were abandoned in 1870 (Utley 1973: 181–183).

One of the first recorded moves toward unification of the politically separate clans of the Tlingit occurred in response to the threat of the loss of their lands. Several councils of clan chiefs met to discuss their objections to the sale of Alaska. In 1869, a special agent of the U.S. Treasury Department recorded their official complaint that Alaska was sold without their consent (Arnold 1978: 62). Some chiefs were in favor of declaring war and driving out the Americans. They abandoned this idea after the Chilkat chiefs convinced the others that their coastal villages were vulnerable to attack by the American war

vessels. This warning was to be realized when in the same year the military initiated a series of bombardments and destroyed the villages of Kake and Wrangell. In 1882 Angoon was destroyed (fig. 1). The military bombarded the villages to punish the Tlingit for acts that the military itself provoked (Bancroft 1886).

The Customs District of Alaska was established in 1868 to regulate customs, commerce, and navigation (Morris 1879). Although the agents lacked legal authority, they began to record squatters' title to land in spite of an order by Secretary of the Interior O.H. Browning in 1867 that forbid White claims as a violation of the Russian treaty and American law (Browning in Morris 1879:119).

The secretary of state advised the secretary of war that "military force may be used to remove intruders" (Seward in Morris 1879:119). In spite of this order the army did not evict any White squatters, and the customs office continued to record their land deeds. These actions initiated a process that began to erode Tlingit and Haida land holdings.

After 10 years, the army was withdrawn from Alaska to fight the Nez Perce Indians in Idaho. The Tlingit immediately moved to reassert their claim over their lands. The Sitka Tlingit tore down the military stockade and occupied the abandoned buildings. Chief Annahootz proclaimed:

> The Russians have stolen this country from us and after they have gotten most of the furs out of the country they have sold it to the Boston Men for a big sum of money, and now the Americans are mad because they have found that the Russians had deceived them, and have abandoned the country, and we are glad to say that after so many years hard fight we got our country back again (Hinckley 1972:129).

The customs agent at Sitka was alarmed that the Tlingit would attack the White citizens since as he said, "Many of these Indians have wrongs to redress and injuries to be made good," which he cited as caused by the military (Morris 1879:31). On the other hand, the customs agent at Wrangell expressed fear for the safety of the Indian population. During this period, Wrangell was the gathering point for the miners and traders who were awaiting transportation to and from the Cassiar mines in British Columbia. The agent felt that the army would be needed to protect the Natives from assaults by the Whites (Morris 1879:23). The cutter *Corwin,* dispatched to Sitka

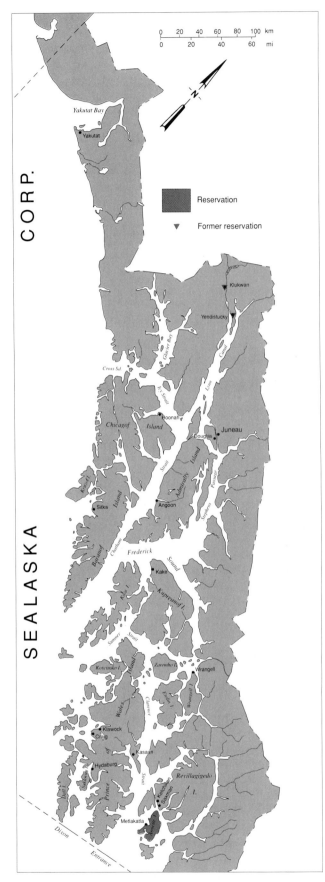

olin-*150* Fig. 1. Selected historical sites in southeastern Alaska.

in 1877 to ease the fears of the Whites, reported no breach of the public peace among the 1,500 Indians, 270 "half-breeds," 15 American citizens, and 5 Russians (White in Morris 1879:127–128). Accounts differ as to the actual danger of the White population, but during the two years in which a military force was absent the feared massacre did not occur.

U.S. Navy Rule, 1879–1884

The Tlingit were soon to realize that the United States had not abandoned its claim to Alaska when the U.S.S. *Jamestown* under the command of Capt. Lester A. Beardslee arrived. By this time, Americans had learned of Alaska's rich mineral and fishery resources and the Navy moved to open Alaska to settlement.

The Chilkat Tlingit had maintained exclusive control over the northern routes to the interior. A major source of their wealth was derived from their monopoly over the trade with the interior Indians. In 1880, Commander Beardslee initiated negotiations with the Chilkat chiefs to open access to the interior for the miners. Beardslee felt that the Chilkat policy of preventing Whites from traveling into the interior deterred the development of Alaska. He assured them that the mining prospectors who wanted to pass through the Chilkat territory to the interior would not engage in fur trade. A warship manned by 20 sailors and a gatling gun escorted five sailboats filled with armed prospectors to the Chilkat country. The officer opened the negotiations by first explaining how the gatling gun worked. He then read them Beardslee's letter. The Chilkat chiefs who had several years earlier warned other Tlingits about the strength of the military reluctantly agreed to open Chilkoot Pass to the gold hunters (Wickersham 1938:7–8).

The Navy also initiated action that began the process to alter Tlingit codes of land ownership and usage. Under their traditional law, each clan had exclusive control over specific geographical areas. In 1881, Commander Henry Glass promoted the signing of a formal treaty of peace between the Stikine Tlingit at Wrangell and the Hutsnuwu Tlingit at Hoonah. Under the terms of the treaty, the clans agreed that other clans "shall be free to travel, hunt, or fish in the territories of either, and shall be under the protection of the head of chiefs of the tribes" (Ct. of Cl. 1962:405).

Although the Secretary of the Navy Richard W. Thompson was reminded that land could not be obtained by immigrants until Congress settled the land issue, the Navy officials in Alaska moved the Tlingit out of the mining town that later became known as Juneau. An officer reported that the Tlingits had been paid by the White men for the damages to their land. To insure that their orders were enforced, a military post was established in the homeland of the Auk Tlingit. The miners praised

WORL

the Navy for removing the Tlingit but complained that the naval officers were using their superior equipment and position to obtain the best claims (Hulley 1953:219). The absence of Tlingit people in this area would be used as evidence in later land claims efforts to show that the Tlingit had abandoned their aboriginal land use and occupancy.

Education

Three Stikine chiefs were the among the first to request that schools and churches be established after the military assumed control of Alaska (P. Miller 1967:180). In addition, they requested churches, based on the relationship they perceived between the progress of the White men and their religion (P. Miller 1967:184–185).

The Organic Act of 1884 ordered the establishment of schools by the secretary of the interior "for the education of children of school age in the Territory of Alaska, without reference to race." Sheldon Jackson, appointed general agent of education in Alaska, used the $25,000 appropriated by Congress to subsidize the mission schools that had been established (fig. 2). Federal subsidies for church schools continued until 1895, when the Bureau of Education assumed control of many of the schools in Alaska (C.K. Ray 1958:23).

The educational policy of the government was to "civilize" the Natives. The official rules stated that "the children are primarily to be taught to speak, read, and write the English language . . . the use of school books printed in any foreign language will not be allowed" (C.K. Ray 1958:25–27). English was to replace the Native languages. Leadership was to be developed by offering to the most intelligent students vocational training in carpentry, boat building, mechanics, fish canning, and domestic sciences. The White population demanded separate schools for White children (C.K. Ray 1958:30).

In 1900 Congress passed legislation that provided for the establishment of independent schools for White children within incorporated towns. In 1905, the Nelson Act called for establishing schools in areas outside incorporated towns for "white children and children of mixed blood who lead a civilized life." The Nelson Act established two separate systems of education with the federal government responsible for Native education. The territorial government was to assume control of White education.

In 1908, when six children of mixed blood were refused admission to a territorial school at Sitka, the issue was brought to court in *Davis* v. *Sitka School Board* (Alaska 481. 1908). Although some of the children came from families that spoke English, dressed and lived as Whites, paid taxes, and were members of the Presbyterian church, the judge ruled them not "civilized" for purposes of attending the territorial school (Worl 1980).

top, Sheldon Jackson College, Stratton Lib., Sitka, Alaska: M-1V-B-2-d.
Fig. 2. Alaska boarding schools. top, Students at Sitka Training School, later called Sheldon Jackson School, established in 1880 by the Presbyterian church. Until 1908 it was the only industrial training school in Alaska. Photograph by Elbridge W. Merrill, 1897–1904. bottom, Marching band from Mt. Edgecumbe High School, a Bureau of Indian Affairs school from 1947 to 1983. Photograph by Bill Hess at Sitka, 1981.

In 1928 the Tlingit again attempted to force the integration of schools through legal suit. Two Indian girls who had been attending the public schools in Ketchikan were advised that they had to transfer to the Indian school in the nearby village of Saxman. William L. Paul, a Tlingit lawyer, initiated a suit against the school board. The Tlingit were successful in this case, but it was not until 1949 that schools were integrated after the Office of Indian Affairs had adopted an educational policy to assimilate Indians into the larger society (Anderson and Eells 1935:215; Drucker 1958:49–51).

Dispossession of Land

The Organic Act of 1884 (23 U.S. Stat. 24) provided for the establishment of a land district and executive and judicial branches of government in Alaska. Laws relating to mining claims were extended to the new territory. The Organic Act also recognized Indian possessory rights: "Indians or other persons in said district shall not be disturbed in the possession of any lands actually in their use or occupation or now claimed by them but the terms under which such persons may acquire title to such lands is reserved for future legislation by Congress" (23 U.S. Stat. 24, section 8; see also Gruening 1954:355–356).

The legislation guaranteed immediate conveyance of title to land held by Whites, but it failed to provide the means for Alaska Natives to acquire title to their land. The first official duty of the land office was to convey legal title to mining claims that had been recorded by the customs office without any legal basis.

Although the Tlingit still legally owned southeast Alaska under aboriginal title, they could not share in the wealth generated by the mineral resources. It was Kaawaa'ee, an Auk Tlingit, who led Joe Juneau and Dick Harris to the gold in Juneau in 1880. The Auk were confined to a small area in Juneau known as the Village. Even their access to the waterfront was cut off. A number of Tlingit attempted to file claims, but they were denied because they were not United States citizens. According to oral tradition, some Tlingits led prospectors to gold under the condition that the prospectors would file the claim and share the wealth with the Tlingit. These accounts do not indicate that the Tlingit shared in the riches from the gold (Worl 1980:163).

Prior to the 1880 gold strike in Juneau, the non-Indian population was less than 400. After the discovery, thousands of miners arrived. The 1890 census reported over 4,200 Whites and 1,800 Creoles in Alaska (Gruening 1954: 75). The Alaska Juneau Gold Mining Company recovered approximately $80.8 million in gold, silver, and lead between 1893 and 1944. The Treadwell properties yielded more than $67.5 million in gold and silver between 1885 and 1922. The Chichagof Mine yielded more than $13.5 million in gold between 1906 and 1938 (Rogers 1960). The Tlingit and Haida landholdings and resources diminished as American economic development expanded.

Realizing that they could not protect their land through military efforts, the Tlingit appealed to the United States government to protect their rights. In 1889 the Tlingit clans organized and retained a lawyer to present their claims to the president of the United States. Chief Shakes of the Stikines was selected to represent the clans. The Tlingit requested the United States to recognize their hereditary rights of ownership to their land and fishing streams and to permit them to govern themselves and regulate their local and domestic affairs (Ct. of Cl. 1962:430–431). These requests were ignored. In 1899 several clan chiefs met in council and selected Chief Johnson of a Taku clan to present their petition to Congress. Chief Johnson emphasized that Indians were the real owners of Alaska and that Russia had no right to sell the land. In spite of this, he indicated that their position was "not . . . to be paid for the lands which were ours by rights. We do not ask that the whites be prevented from coming to Alaska." In the petition they did ask "that the fishing and hunting grounds of their Fathers be reserved for them and their children . . . ." The petition also included additional demands calling for the establishment of reservations and schools. Secretary of the Interior Ethan A. Hitchcock reported to the Senate that in his judgment, "the extension of the reservation system to the Alaskan Indians generally is undesirable and should not be inaugurated" (Ct. of Cl. 1962:433–435).

By 1878 salmon canneries were operating in the Alaska panhandle. Within half a century, Alaska became the world's principal salmon producer, and salmon processing surpassed mining as the major industry (Gruening 1954). The Alaska Packers Association of San Francisco, which had maintained a monopoly over fur trading since the purchase of Alaska, shifted its attention to salmon and became one of the largest salmon packing companies. Several of the companies formed the Alaska Salmon

left, U. of Wash. Lib., Special Coll., Seattle: 905; right, Alaska Histl. Lib., Juneau: PCA 87–66.
Fig. 3. Indians in the money economy. left, Tlingit women selling baskets and jars with beaded and woven covers to Whites near a gold mine. Photograph by Frank LaRoche, Treadwell, Alaska, about 1894. right, Tlingit couple in front of a house with a sign advertising "Washing Woman. Seb. 8, 1896." In towns Indians became domestic and other service workers. Photograph by Lloyd V. Winter and Edwin P. Pond, Juneau, about 1896.

Industry, Inc., to lobby their interests in Washington, D.C. Through this organization, the salmon industries greatly influenced all policies, legislation, and regulations affecting fisheries in Alaska. In 1889 federal legislation was enacted that outlawed aboriginal traps and weirs. A few years later, legislation was adopted that permitted commercial fish traps to be placed at the mouths of salmon streams. Conservation of the salmon resources was ignored by the industry, and warnings about the effects of overfishing went unheeded. These traps, which were owned by the nonresidents, accounted for more than one-half the entire annual salmon harvest. The traps became the symbol of "outside" exploitation to the Tlingit and Haida Indians as well as to the increasing number of resident White settlers.

The Tlingit did not have the financing to open their own salmon canneries or purchase fishing boats until after the mid-1930s. Employment opportunities in the canneries were also limited for the Tlingit. Even if they were able to get work, the canneries paid them less than other workers and they did not receive the benefits extended to the imported workers or fishermen. In this situation, Tlingits entered the larger economy by selling their goods or services as individuals (fig. 3).

By 1889, 14 salmon canneries and several sawmills were operating in Tlingit country. Fishing stations were established at every productive salmon stream. The Tlingit had barely enough salmon to sustain their own needs. Their land holdings were further diminished with the establishment of the Tongass National Forest, which withdrew some 16 million acres in the early 1900s, and the Glacier Bay National Monument, which withdrew over two million acres in 1925.

In 1887 a group of Tsimshian Indians, followers of the Anglican missionary William Duncan, moved from Metlakatla, British Columbia, to Annette Island, Alaska, which became a reservation in 1891 by an act of Congress ("Tsimshian of Metlakatla, Alaska," this vol.).

The Indian Rights Movement

Alaska Native Brotherhood

The Alaska Native Brotherhood, which is the oldest modern Native organization in the United States, was founded in Sitka in 1912 to promote the social and civil welfare of the Indians of Alaska. The founding members included 12 men and one woman from various communities; all except one Tsimshian were Tlingits. The founding members had been greatly influenced by the Presbyterian mission, which had established church-affiliated organizations in nearly every community (vol. 4:456). The affiliate organization, the Alaska Native Sisterhood, was organized in 1923 (vol. 4:311).

The first three chapters, or camps, as they were called,

were established at Sitka (fig. 4), Juneau, and Douglas. Although the persistence of ancient tribal conflicts hindered the formation of new camps (Drucker 1958), by 1925 Brotherhood and Sisterhood camps were organized in many Tlingit and Haida villages.

The Brotherhood's Indian rights effort intensified with the entry of two brothers, Louis and William Paul. William Paul, who was the first Alaska Native to become a lawyer, attacked the political issues identified by his brother through legal processes. William Paul devoted his lifetime to Alaska Native Brotherhood affairs, and is considered the founder of the land claims effort in Alaska.

The 1915 Alaska territorial legislature enacted legislation that allowed Natives to become citizens if they severed tribal relationships, adopted the habits of civilization, passed an examination given by town teachers, obtained an endorsement from five White residents, and satisfied the district judge (Arnold 1976:83). Very few Natives became citizens under these restrictive requirements.

Citizenship for Alaska Natives was one of the highest priorities for the Brotherhood. The opportunity to advance this cause came with the arrest of Chief Shakes and his niece, Tillie Paul Tamaree, in 1922. Chief Shakes was charged with a felony for voting, and Tamaree was cited for aiding in the felony act. William Paul defended Shakes, his great-uncle, and his mother, winning the case in court. Alaska Natives thus secured the right to vote two years before Congress passed the Indian Citizenship Act in 1924.

With the right to vote, the Alaska Native Brotherhood organized to promote their legislative interests and to elect their candidates. Several Tlingits, who had held the office of Brotherhood grand president, were subsequently elected to the legislature, including William L. Paul (fig. 5), Frank Johnson, Andrew Hope, Alfred Widmark, and Frank See.

Tlingit fishermen could not compete against the Whites who used fish traps, and the Brotherhood initiated efforts in 1947 to have fish traps banned (Gruening 1954: 397–399). The fish traps accounted for 70 percent of all salmon taken in southeast Alaska during 1925 to 1934 (Rogers 1960:6). The salmon industry had been successful in promoting legislation in 1947 that prohibited public access to fish trap harvest records. In spite of this, it was quite evident that the salmon stocks were decreasing and that fish traps were responsible for the decline. By 1953, President Dwight Eisenhower declared the fishing communities in southeast Alaska disaster areas. The Alaska Native Service within the Department of the Interior had implemented a program that allowed Indians to establish canneries. The agency held the mortgages on the Indian-owned salmon canneries, but the Alaska Native Service refused the request by the Brotherhood to intercede in the fish trap issue. Even after several Indian-owned canneries

Fig. 4. Alaska Native Brotherhood. Identifications left to right, front row: unknown, Frank Mercer, unknown, Chester Worthington (Wrangell) or John James, Peter Simpson, Paul Liberty, Edward Marsden (Metlakatla, Alaska), James or Haines DeWitt (Juneau), Mark Jacobs, Sr., unknown; middle row: John Willard, unknown, William Kootz, Steven Nicholis (Sitka), Harold Bailey, Ralph Wannamaker one of the next three (others unknown), Charlie Daniels, unknown, Ralph Young, Rudolph Walton, William Jackson, and Frank Price; top row: James Gordon, Andrew Hope, William Stevens, Thomas Williams, John Williams, George Lewis, Sr., and Sergus Williams. Photographed in front of new hall in Sitka, Nov. 1914.

purchased fish traps, the Brotherhood continued to maintain a firm stand against traps until they were abolished in 1959 by regulations of the Department of the Interior (Gruening 1954:533).

Overt economic and social discrimination against the Tlingit was quite common during the first half of the twentieth century. Stores and restaurants often posted signs, "No Dogs or Natives Allowed." Movie theaters sectioned off areas designated for "Natives Only." In 1929, the Brotherhood initiated a series of boycotts against businesses that discriminated. The economic measures were successful, and the offensive signs were removed. The Brotherhood turned its attention to discriminatory legislation that excluded Natives from old-age pensions and aid to women with dependent children. Paul and other Native legislators threatened to stop the payment of all pensions on the grounds of racial discrimination. Legislative action was then taken to include Natives in welfare payments. The Brotherhood successfully lobbied for the enactment by the territorial legislature of the Antidiscrimination Act, in 1946. William L. Paul later lamented, "We were successful in promoting the passage of the Anti-Discrimination Act, but it did not mean the discrimination towards the Natives ended" (Worl 1980: 199).

One of the most successful lobbying efforts initiated by the Brotherhood was the amendment of the Indian Reorganization Act, which had excluded Alaska from its provisions when passed in 1934. In 1936 the Act was extended to include Alaska. After incorporating under the Act, the villages of Kake, Klawock, Hydaburg, and Angoon were eligible for federal loans with which they purchased salmon canneries and fishing boats (Gruening 1954:374).

Hydaburg, a Haida Indian village, petitioned for recognition and confirmation of their land rights under the Indian Reorganization Act. In 1949, the secretary of the interior designated a reserve of 101,000 acres for the village, although the Haida had claimed that they actually owned 900,000 acres. The establishment of the reservation meant a change for the companies doing business on the land—the fisheries and the timber and mining firms. The Hydaburg Reservation was revoked by the U.S. District Court in 1952, in a ruling that the reservation had not been validly created. In contrast to the 1908 court decision in which the Tlingit were found not to be civilized, this opinion held that the Haida Indians were assimilated and that compensation was not due them, but rather to their ancestors who suffered under the impact of civilization. The judge, concluding that "the Haidas have not only

Alaska Histl. Lib., Winter and Pond Coll., Juneau.
Fig. 5. Alaska Territorial legislature, House of Representatives, with the Tlingit William L. Paul third from left. Paul, who represented Ketchikan 1925–1929, was one of 16 house members. Photograph by Lloyd V. Winter and Edwin P. Pond, April 1925.

abandoned their primitive ways of life, but are now fully capable of competing with the whites in every field of endeavor" (Gruening 1954:379), reasoned that compensation in the form of a 101,000-acre reservation would be made at the expense of the Whites who followed and had nothing to do with the exploitation of Indians.

Perhaps the most significant contribution made by the Alaska Native Brotherhood was in the area of land rights. The organization's 1929 convention at Haines prepared the bill that was enacted as the federal Jurisdictional Act of June 15, 1935. The Jurisdictional Act extended the right to the Tlingit and Haida to bring suit for claims against the United States in the U.S. Court of Claims. Passage of the legislation was a significant event, but it was only the beginning of the legal struggles.

The first case initiated by the Tlingit and Haida was dismissed by the courts because the secretary of the interior had not approved of the contract with the attorney who was representing them. The Tlingit and Haida Indians argued that they should have equal rights with the government to supervise their lawyer. Ten years elapsed, and the Tlingit and Haida finally agreed in 1947 to accept the lawyer approved by the Office of Indian Affairs in spite of the fact that many Tlingits did not believe he would represent their best interest. The five chiefs of Yakutat clans organized, and the Stikine and Hoonah chiefs joined in, to protest the move by their lawyer to combine all their tribal claims into a single suit known as *The Tlingit and Haida Indians of Alaska* v. *The United States* (177 F. Supp. 452).

The Tlingit and Haida wanted a settlement based on their aboriginal land ownership by clans. However, they were not successful in changing the language of the suit. One clan initiated action to sue for their own territorial claims. Other clans attempted to do the same, but the time period to introduce their claim in court passed. In 1955 the *ti·ẏ hít-ta·n* clan brought suit in the U.S. Court of Claims alleging that the United States should be required to give an accounting of the monies received from the sale of certain timber in the Tongass National Forest. The clan claimed title to the Tongass National Forest, which had been created by presidential executive order in 1902. William L. Paul argued that aboriginal title could not be extinguished by executive order. The Court of Claims ruled in favor of the United States (*Tee-Hit-Ton Indians* v. *United States*, 348 U.S. Stat. 272).

The Brotherhood initiated the Tlingit and Haida suit against the United States. It contended that over 20 million acres of land in the Tongass National Forest, Glacier Bay National Monument, and the Annette Island Indian Reservation had been appropriated from the Tlingit and Haida. Because the Brotherhood membership included non-Natives, a new organization, the Central Council of Tlingit and Haida, was established to pursue the aboriginal claims. In 1954, the Tlingit and Haida case was transferred to another lawyer, but the outcome of the case was to wait another 12 years.

The Brotherhood remained the single vital political force for Alaska Indians through the 1940s. Through its organizational efforts, the Brotherhood had unified clans, communities, and the Tlingit and Haida people. The Brotherhood reversed its original position against the practice of aboriginal traditions in the late 1960s and became a leading force in the resurgence of traditional culture among the Tlingit and Haida.

Central Council of Tlingit and Haida

The sole function of the Tlingit and Haida Central Council of was to bring suit against the United States for aboriginal claims. In the Tlingit and Haida case, the court rendered the opinion that the federal government had taken lands from the Indians when it created the Tongass National Forest, Glacier Bay National Monument, and the Annette Island Reservation. The court declared that the government was guilty of failing to protect the rights of the Indians from White settlers, miners, and other developers. The court also found that Indian title survived to two and one-half million acres of land in northern Tlingit territory.

The Tlingit and Haida valued the land that had been taken from them by the government at $80 million, but the government valued it at $3 million. The commissioner appointed by the court estimated the land to be worth $16 million, but the actual award was $7.5 million (G. Harrison 1971), which represented 43 cents an acre. William L. Paul noted that the value of the timber alone that had been sold from their forests totaled over $600 million and recommended an appeal, but in 1968 the Central Council of Tlingit and Haida accepted the award (Worl 1980:210). The claims for the remaining two million acres and for fishing claims were carried over to the Alaska Native Claims Settlement Act of 1971.

The Central Council of Tlingit and Haida is composed of elected delegates from the 14 communities in southeast Alaska. In addition, other communities with Tlingit and Haida populations may organize and be represented on the Central Council. Each community is entitled to elect one delegate for every 100 Tlingit and Haida Indians who are registered in their community and approved by the Bureau of Indian Affairs. Communities in Anchorage, Seattle, and San Francisco elect delegates to represent them on the Central Council. In 1985, 86 delegates were elected to the Central Council.

The Central Council developed a plan for the $7.5 million judgment that included $4 million for social and economic programs, which it administers subject to the approval of the secretary of the interior. The Central Council, with headquarters in Juneau, contracts with the Bureau of Indian Affairs and Public Health Service to administer health, education, and social welfare programs.

156

Alaska Native Claims Settlement Act of 1971

In 1966 the Tlingit and Haida Central Council joined with other Alaska Native groups to form the Alaska Federation of Natives to pursue the settlement of their remaining claims against the United States. In December 1971 the Alaska Native Claims Settlement Act (85 U.S. Stat. 688) was passed by Congress (see M.E. Thomas 1986, 1988). Under its terms, 12 regional profit-making corporations and approximately 200 village corporations were created. The Act extinguished aboriginal title to Alaska and conveyed fee simple title to 44 million acres to the corporations. Alaska Natives were compensated by a payment of nearly one billion dollars for the remaining land in Alaska, which they surrendered. The corporations were made responsible for administering the land and money they received. Individual Natives who were alive on the date of passage of the Act and who could establish that they were at least one-quarter-blood Native were enrolled as shareholders in the corporations.

Sealaska Regional Corporation, organized as the regional corporation for southeast Alaska, received 280,000 acres of valuable timber land and $200 million of which $100 million was distributed to the village corporations and at-large shareholders. The majority of the shareholders in Sealaska are Tlingit and Haida.

Nine village corporations were initially incorporated—Angoon, Craig, Hoonah, Hydaburg, Kake, Kasaan, Klawock, Saxman, and Yakutat (table 1). Although historically Juneau, Sitka, Haines, and Wrangell were Tlingit villages, they were not permitted to organize as village corporations because the majorities of their populations were in 1971 non-Tlingit. Juneau and Sitka were designated as urban corporations and were not entitled to receive monies distributed by Sealaska.

The Claims Settlement Act revoked all reservations in Alaska but allowed the villagers to vote on whether they would obtain full title to their former reservations and give up all other Settlement Act benefits. Klukwan elected to maintain its reservation land, while asserting that it was already owned by the tribal government. Under the Act, shareholders who were enrolled to Klukwan but were not living in the village were denied benefits. A later amendment allowed Klukwan to establish a village corporation, thus extinguishing reservation status and permitting receipt of additional lands outside the former reservation. The Tsimshian living on Annette Island Reservation elected to maintain their reservation status.

The first five years after 1971 were devoted to organizational efforts and land selections and conveyances. The second five years were devoted to business development. Sealaska Regional Corporation headquarters was built in Juneau. By 1981, Sealaska was among *Fortune* magazine's top 1,000 United States corporations, with heavy investments in the fisheries and timber

Table 1. Sealaska Village and Urban Corporations in 1974

	Initial Enrollment
Angoon	620
Craig	317
Hoonah	868
Hydaburg	570
Juneau	2,640
Kake	552
Kasaan	121
Klawock	507
Klukwan	251
Saxman	191
Sitka	1,804
Yakutat	334
	8,775
At-large shareholders	7,718
Total sealaska shareholders	16,493
Shareholders residing in region	9,529

SOURCES: Arnold 1976:330–334; Arnold et al. 1978.

industries. Due to setbacks in the salmon canning industry and to falling timber prices, by 1983 Sealaska had lost over $27 million; however, by 1985 the corporation was once again showing a profit.

The Persistence of Indian Culture

The Alaska Native Brotherhood had originally promoted efforts to suppress the traditional language and culture, but it was also the organization that led in the revival of the traditional culture. The Tlingit and Haida readily adopted and mastered parliamentary procedures to run the Brotherhood and Sisterhood meetings. These rules and the protocol governing their organizational behavior were consistent with traditional organizational structure and behavioral norms.

Matrilineal descent continues to be recognized by the Tlingit and Haida through the 1980s. Exogamous marriage rules, which were relaxed somewhat, were still honored. Although marriages between individuals who were both from Raven clans or both from Eagle (Wolf) clans occurred, they were frowned upon.

Potlatching continued (fig. 6) and again flourished beginning in the late 1960s. The čuʼkaneʼdí clan of Hoonah hosted a large potlatch after their chief, Jimmy Marks, died and was succeeded by Willie Marks in 1969. The šankukʷeʼdí clan held a potlatch to commemorate the construction of a new tribal house in Klukwan in 1971. Amounts up to $20,000 are often distributed at these potlatches, and notable Tlingit names are often bestowed. Tlingit dance was brought from the potlatches to the general public in 1968. At that time, the Marks Trail Tlingit Dancers organized and first performed at the Juneau celebration of the settlement of the Tlingit and Haida land claims case. Jenny Marks, a member of the łukʷaʼxʼádí clan, led the group and brought $1,000 in cash to distribute in the event that anyone criticized the performance of Tlingit dances outside the potlatch. The group was renamed the Geisan Dancers. Since 1968 many communities have organized dance groups, often under the sponsorship of Indian education programs.

Tlingit and Haida languages in the late 1980s were spoken only by individuals over the age of 50. Nora Dauenhauer and several other women offered Tlingit language classes and developed curriculum materials. Although it is evident that children are no longer speaking Tlingit or Haida, they continue to sing Tlingit and Haida songs in dance groups.

In the early 1980s Chief Daanaawaak of the łukʷaʼxʼádí clan began teaching traditional Tlingit ways

Alaska Histl. Lib., Case and Draper Coll, Juneau.

Fig. 6. Tlingits from Killisnoo arriving at Sitka to attend a potlatch. Some are dressed in traditional regalia while others wear Euro-American clothes. The canoes display American flags (retouched). Photograph by William H. Case and Herbert Horace Draper, 1904.

157

and clan history to groups of children. In 1985, the cultural survival camp had grown to include nearly 100 children, who arrived from throughout the Northwest Coast.

In the early 1980s the Sealaska Corporation organized and endowed the Sealaska Heritage Foundation, whose primary objectives were to promote and enhance the knowledge of southeastern Alaska Native customs, history, arts, and educational achievements. The Foundation sponsored a number of cultural activities, including two celebrations in which the elders of the region gathered to record their traditional knowledge and dance. During the first celebration, the elders who were most knowledgeable about Tlingit property law met with younger Tlingit lawyers and scholars to discuss and codify the principles governing Tlingit law.

History of Coastal British Columbia Since 1846

J. E. MICHAEL KEW

By 1849 maritime fur trading on the central Northwest coast was in decline and the Hudson's Bay Company had retrenched and stabilized its position by establishing Forts Langley, 1827 (figs. 1–2); Simpson, 1831; McLoughlin, 1833; and Victoria, 1843. These bases, and the steamship *Beaver,* allowed secure access to furs originating on the coast and to any coming from the interior through indigenous trade networks (Rich 1958–1959, 2:621). By the time the British government offered to let the company act as a colonizing agent for the territories, it had already moved a long way from a narrow concern for fur. Commercial farming had been attempted under the banner of the Puget Sound Agriculture Development Company, and cattle and gardens were kept at every suitably situated post. Some coastal tribes had adopted potato cultivation, and a few posts soon recorded substantial trade in the new produce. From the earliest days of the company's activity along the Fraser River, dried and salted salmon, caught and prepared mainly by Indians, were essential items of trade.

Colonization and Settlement

It is inappropriate to speak of the conquest of British Columbia Indians, for contact and settlement were mainly peaceful. This is not to discount occasional acts of violence on both sides. Attacks upon Whites or isolated murders by Indians occurred and evoked alarm in Victoria. Naval vessels were dispatched to bring in the culprits. This usually proved difficult, and officers sometimes resorted to retaliatory shelling and burning of unprotected villages, for example: the Kwakiutl village of Nahwitti in 1850 and 1851, a Halkomelem village on Kuper Island in 1863, a Nootka village in Clayoquot Sound in 1864, and the Bella Coola village of Kimsquit in 1877 (Gough 1984). Naval vessels and land forces were also ordered to Bella Coola in 1864 with an armed contingent of marines and volunteers to assist in quelling the Chilcotins of the interior, who had attacked survey parties and settlers.

These operations were more in the nature of retributive raids meant to impress the Indians than acts of war. Wars were never declared and defeat of villages or tribes was never attempted or achieved. Subordination of Indians did not result from use of military force or even its display,

which was infrequent and isolated. Rather, superiority in technology, the capacity to control valuable trade goods, and political organization gave Whites the upper hand (see Rich 1958–1959, 2:637–638ff.). With the continual immigration of Whites, Indians were outnumbered by others in the province by about 1885. However, Whites were concentrated in the few urban centers while Indians remained proportionately significant in rural districts. In 1901 Indians comprised about 16 percent of the provincial population, but in the Cassiar-Skeena and Alberni census subdivisions of the coast, the proportions were 60 and 80 percent of the population, respectively (Canada 1901).

The Land Question

When James Douglas assumed governorship of Vancouver Island in 1850, he began to negotiate with nearby Indians. By 1854, 14 treaties had been concluded with tribes near Victoria (fig. 3), Fort Rupert, and Nanaimo. Coal had been discovered in the last two localities, while the first was the center for agricultural endeavors and sawmilling. The Indians were paid in goods to relinquish rights to all land except their villages and fields, retaining rights to hunt and fish on unoccupied lands (British Columbia 1875; Duff 1969).

Costs of negotiating these settlements were extremely modest; for example, 50 square miles on the Saanich Peninsula was purchased for slightly over £100 in goods. However, the imperial government and colonial assembly were unwilling to allocate more funds for additional treaties. As settlement proceeded and the mainland was made a colony in 1858 under Douglas's jurisdiction, he continued marking out reserve land for Indians, leaving formal treaty making until such time as funds became available. He repeatedly pressed for such assistance but without success (Cumming and Mickenberg 1972:177–179). Douglas's business sense seems to have been tempered with a genuine concern for Indians and their future welfare, but he had little support. The willingness of the assembly to finance punitive expeditions stands in marked contrast to its attitude toward paying for Indian land.

Upon Douglas's retirement in 1864, Joseph Trutch became chief commissioner of lands and works. His position was a marked contrast: "The Indians have really

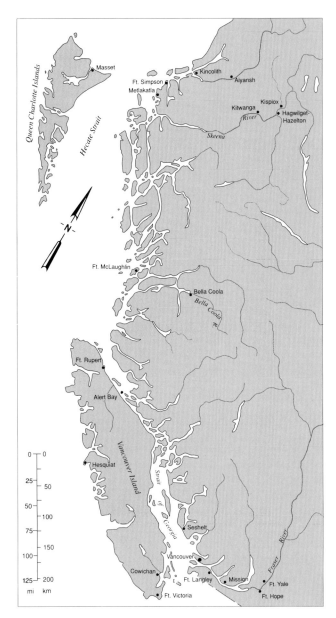

Fig. 1. Selected historical sites in western B.C.

no rights to the lands they claim, nor are they of any actual value or utility to them; and I cannot see why they should either retain these lands to the prejudice of the general interests of the Colony, or be allowed to make a market of them either to Government *or to individuals*" (British Columbia 1875:42; see also Fisher 1971, 1977:164). Trutch proceeded to reduce some reserves that had already been laid out in the Fraser valley.

When British Columbia joined Canada in 1871, Trutch became lieutenant-governor of the new province and continued to defend his policies. The federal government then assumed responsibility for Indians and Indian reserves in British Columbia, but the newly constituted provincial government, by the terms of union, controlled all other land and thus would limit the size and location of future reserves and frustrate the more generous policy

urged by federal representatives.

Both governments agreed in 1876 on the appointment of a Joint Commission for the Settlement of Indian Reserves in the Province of British Columbia. Its task was to try to settle the land question, in particular to allay Indian fears and recurring resentment. The Commission's first efforts were bent toward revision and affirmation of 82 small reserves already laid out, mostly in Coast Salish territory, which had experienced the earliest White settlement. It was almost a decade before the Commission confirmed reserves on the central and northern coasts.

In 1882 Commissioner Peter O'Reilly toured Nootka, Kwakiutl, Bella Coola, Tsimshian, and Haida villages, met with chiefs and leaders, and laid out their main reserves. Representatives of villages or kin groups who were able to meet with the commissioner were asked which sites were for villages and food-getting and which they would like to retain. By this time Indian domestic economies had been modified and diseases had severely reduced most populations. Nevertheless, most of the main village sites, cemeteries, and major fishing stations were reserved—though as specific, separate, small plots of land rather than inclusive territories. The Commission took no note of Indian concepts of ownership even when they were advanced but followed a policy of granting Indians minimal lots leaving most of the land free for settlement by Whites (Duff 1964:68; British Columbia 1888).

In 1913 another joint commission was appointed following agreement between J.A.J. McKenna, on behalf of the federal government, and Richard McBride, premier of the province, to effect "a final adjustment of all matters relating to Indian Affairs in the Province" (Cail 1974: 304). This commission again visited all parts of the province, meeting Indians, interviewing Indian agents, and receiving other evidence. In total more acreage was added than cut off, although that cut off was more valuable at the existing market prices (Canada. Royal Commission on Indian Affairs for the Province of British Columbia 1916). On the coast there were 871 reserves, most of them small parcels of land scattered through the aboriginal territory of each group (table 1).

Neither of the two joint commissions had authority to make treaties or extinguish aboriginal rights. Aside from the early treaties on Vancouver Island, negotiated on behalf of the colony, no treaties or formal surrenders of land were made by Indians on the coast of British Columbia. The Royal Proclamation of 1763, which required that agents of the crown purchase Indian lands by treaty, and the practices of treaty-making pursued in Ontario and elsewhere were simply ignored.

Indian Status: Separate and Unequal

Because the colonial government had never developed an explicit Indian policy or any administrative programs for

Natl. Arch.: Record Group 76: Sketch No. 6.
Fig. 2. Kwantlen village on McMillan I., Fraser River, seen from Hudson's Bay Company's Ft. Langley. Bastion and wall of fort in right foreground. Watercolor by James Madison Alden, 1858.

Table 1. Reserves of B.C. Coastal Tribes

Tribes	Number of Bands	Number of Reserves	Total Acreage	Acres per Capita 1929	1984
Haida	2	37	3,928.2	5.7	2.3
Tsimshian	17	255	89,125.6	24.6	8.5
Kwakiutl, Haisla, Oowekeeno, Haihais, and Bella Bella	17	170	26,356.7	14.2	4.3
Nootka and Nitinaht	15	168	12,251.8	7.5	2.6
Bella Coola	1	7	5,001.0	20.1	6.0
Coast Salish	52	234	61,947.1	14.3	4.8
Totals	104	871	198,610.4	16.1	5.4

SOURCES: Canada 1972, 1984.

benefit of Indians, Israel W. Powell faced a formidable task when appointed superintendent of Indian affairs for the province of British Columbia in 1871. He initiated a system of administration patterned after that prevailing in eastern Canada: the province was divided initially into two "superintendencies," which were later subdivided and renamed "agencies." Each agency contained many separate reserves and bands, as the formally defined and nominally listed local groups of Indians were ultimately termed, within its territory. By 1886 four major agencies had been designated on the coast, each more or less concordant with Indian language groupings: the Fraser River Agency encompassing mainland Coast Salish and a few Lillooet, the Cowichan Agency consisting of all the

Vancouver Island Coast Salish, Kwawkewlth Agency composed of Kwakiutl, and the West Coast Agency for the Nootkan tribes (Dominion of Canada 1887). By 1895 a Northwest Coast Agency had been created and included the Haida, Nishga, Coast Tsimshian, Bella Coola, Oowekeeno, Haihais, Bella Bella, and Haisla. The Gitksan were included with the Carrier in the Babine and Upper Skeena Agency. Over the years a number of changes were made in agency boundaries.

In the early years an agent's contact with the Indians was intermittent and of little influence, as the agents and their supervisors frequently complained in annual reports. Brief mention of British Columbia was made in the report of the Indian Affairs Branch in 1872 (Dominion of *161*

McGill U., McCord Mus., Notman Photographic Arch., Montreal: 69,907-I.
Fig. 3. Victoria, B.C., from Mission Hill with a village of Songhees (Central Coast Salish) in the foreground. This village was allotted as an Indian reserve according to a treaty made with Gov. James Douglas in 1850. In 1910 the Indian village was demolished and the people moved to a new reserve outside the city. Photograph by Benjamin Baltzly, 1871.

Canada 1872:37–38), and in the following year Powell submitted an extensive report (Powell 1873, 23:2–40; Spragge 1873). From then on information about British Columbia Indian administration appears in the annual reports. Much attention was given to reporting efforts to prevent traffic in liquor, provide medical supplies, and issue sundry tools and materials meant to assist in promotion of farming and animal husbandry.

The first schools for Indians were established by missionaries: Methodists at Hope in 1859, Roman Catholics at Mission in 1862 (Begg 1894:482, 486), and Anglicans among the Tsimshian at Metlakatla in 1858 (Arctander 1909:129). Although the earliest schools were church-run day schools, larger "industrial" or residential schools became the favored instruments of Indian education (Dominion of Canada 1894:xviii). Financial responsibility for Indian schooling was eventually assumed by federal government authorities, although management remained for many years with missionaries.

Federal legislation eventually known as the Indian Act applied to British Columbia Indians from the date of confederation in 1871. It created a special status for Indians who were listed on nominal band rolls or general lists and applied special rights and restrictions to them. In 1884 an amendment to the Indian Act prohibited the major Native ceremonies—the potlatch and the winter dance (Fisher 1977:207).

Provincial laws also applied restrictions to Indians as a group. Even prior to confederation, the colony had prohibited Indians from homesteading land, and with other racial minorities in British Columbia, Indians were denied the provincial franchise until 1949. The federal franchise had been available to Indians who were war veterans (and their wives) and to those who chose to waive tax exemptions extended under the Indian Act, but it was not until 1960 that this right was extended without restriction to registered or status Indians.

British Columbia did not extend provincial public services to Indians on reserves. Like other Canadian provinces it treated Indians as noncitizens whose care was solely the responsibility of the federal government, which agreed with this position. The result was the emergence, in effect, of two roughly parallel but separate administrative structures—a provincial one for all persons with non-Indian status (including many of Indian descent but not enrolled on band lists) and a federal one, embodied in the services of the Department of Indian Affairs or Indian Affairs Branch, for legal or status Indians. Thus separate institutional systems emerged for education, welfare, health, and local government.

Indians residing on reserves did not pay school taxes, which are assessed as part of the provincial tax on real property; therefore, their children were excluded from public schools. The inequity lay in the fact that, although some other citizens did not own property or pay taxes, Indians were the only persons excluded from schools for such a reason. Following federal initiative to make funds available to local school boards on a pro-rata basis for Indian students, there was increasing integration of schools and gradual abandonment of segregated residential schools. After 1945 similar trends toward integration of services and extension of provincial grants, such as those to assist home purchases, supplementary old-age assistance payments, and the like, have continued. At the same time, the special administrative powers and services of the Department of Indian and Northern Affairs remained in effect, as did the special legal status of Indians.

Entering the Industrial Economy

The technology of commercial fishing was developed from the expertise of Indians, and it was their equipment that helped start and build the industry. Especially important was their knowledge of fish movement and small boat navigation in the uncharted tidal channels of the coast. Indian women were skilled in fish cleaning and preservation and needed little or no training to work in canneries ("Haihais, Bella Bella, and Oowekeeno," fig. 8, this vol.) and salteries. Additionally, Indians were accustomed to traveling in family groups to fishing stations and to working and living together cooperatively in makeshift camps. These capacities suited perfectly the labor requirements of cannery operators.

Of additional significance was the fact that this new economic activity did relatively little to impede the Indians' capacities to obtain salmon for their own food supply. In fact, sailboats, and later motorboats, factory-made nets (fig. 4), new techniques of preservation by salting and "canning" in jars, as well as a multitude of other innovations, only enabled greater efficiency of subsistence activities and domestic chores. And there remained abundant fish for local use, particularly coho, pink, and chum, which were in little demand by the canneries and often ran abundantly after the seasonal peak of sockeye runs and commercial fishing. However, Indian fishing was also regulated in new ways (fig. 5).

Introduction of gardening and animal husbandry plus continued use of shellfish, waterfowl, deer, wild fruits, and the like, even among Indians living on the fringes of Victoria and Vancouver, enabled Indian families to subsist as seasonal or only casual workers in the fishing and logging industries. In addition, networks of kinship marked by reciprocal obligations of many kinds, including long- and short-term gift exchanges—and reciprocal potlatching—continued to provide a cushion to support individuals, families, and even villages in times of periodic scarcity (Hawthorn, Belshaw, and Jamieson 1958:209ff.; McDonald 1985:80–89; K.A. Mooney 1976, 1978; Suttles 1960; Piddocke 1965).

Of special significance to the White economy was the Indian contribution in the logging, sawmilling, and stevedoring work that developed in Burrard Inlet in the 1860s and gradually extended to other coastal areas. Squamish Indians were key participants, loading sailing vessels in all-Indian work gangs, working in mills and logging camps, and taking an early lead in Indian participation in labor unions (Philpott 1963). Although the Department of Indian Affairs gained little headway making farmers of them, coastal Indians were nevertheless important sources of seasonal labor in hop picking ("History of Western Washington Since 1846," fig. 3, this vol.) and hay growing, which developed on a large scale in the Fraser valley and western Washington.

The importance of Indians to the provincial economy was substantial. This report of the Indian agent for the Fraser District in 1882 gives an account.

> At the fisheries this season there were 1,300 Indian men employed; the average wages are $1.75 per day. The season for summer fishing is about 90 days. Besides, there are at the canneries 400 Indian women engaged cleaning and canning salmon, who receive $1 per day. At the two saw mills, Burrard Inlet, there is paid for Indian labour about $18,000 a year. Mr. Onderdonk [a contractor] pays this year for Indian labor at least $40,000 (Dominion of Canada 1883:61).

The 1,300 Indian men probably included Kwakiutl as well as Salish, so the income was spread among workers who moved in for the season from a wide area. These

right, SSC Photocentre, Ottawa: 66-12124.
Fig. 4. Fishing. left, Fishing boats belonging to the Kwakiutl at Alert Bay, B.C. A great deal of capital is required to compete in the short fishing seasons. Photograph by Vickie Jensen, about 1980. right, Haida fisherman repairing his factory-made nets. Photograph by Chris Lund, Prince Rupert, B.C., 1966.

Fig. 5. Fisheries officers, including Inspector E.G. Taylor, removing a Kwakiutl salmon trap on Marble River, Vancouver I. Imposition of Canadian Dept. of Fisheries regulations aimed at "conservation" of the resource for packing companies resulted in prohibition of some Indian fishing devices. Photograph by Benjamin W. Leeson, 1912.

Indians constituted about half the total labor force in the primary fishing operations in British Columbia for that year (Urquart and Buckley 1965:396). Fishing outside the Fraser District also employed many Indians, and they constituted a substantial portion of the total labor force.

The Depression of the 1930s brought a drastic decrease in the value of production in the fishing industry and a decrease in the number of canneries from 76 to 44 (Jamieson and Gladstone 1950:161). Indian incomes were severely cut. The continuation of subsistence activities may well have reduced the relative impact among coastal Indians of the economic decline (see Sparrow 1976).

With the onset of World War II, the economic picture changed dramatically. Indians benefited from the demand for labor and from the low prices placed on confiscated Japanese-Canadian fishing boats. This period probably marked the peak of Indian participation as owner-operators in the fishing industry. After the war, the fishing industry indebtedness to company financiers grew as required capital investments expanded, and independent participation diminished. In all parts of the province, even in the few economically developed areas, Indians were concentrated in the fishing, logging, and sawmill industries as casual, unskilled, and seasonal workers (Hawthorn, Belshaw, and Jamieson 1958:75–83). They were attached to dispersed and often isolated reserves with an inflexible system of residence created and maintained by the Indian Act. Everywhere Indians had less access to capital than non-Indians, for reserve property could not be mortgaged. In a society that required more formal education and skilled workers in the labor force, Indians were disadvantaged.

Demographic Change

Indian population of the British Columbia coast reached its nadir in 1915 and then began a recovery (table 2).

During this period of growth the population has been, necessarily, one with a high proportion of young people. Reserves have become less viable as economic bases to support this population. As with all segments of the population the amounts of welfare payments, income supplements, and pensions have increased to partially offset the imbalance in earned incomes of reserve populations.

Off-reserve residents in 1984 accounted for 40 percent of total band populations (table 3) whereas the proportion was negligible in 1954 (Hawthorn, Belshaw, and Jamieson 1958). Enrolled Indians who live off-reserve are largely in Victoria, Vancouver, Nanaimo, and Prince Rupert.

There has been a high rate of natural increase among nonstatus Indians (those descended from mixed marriages, or whose ancestors were not included on the lists of status Indians when these were first compiled) and an apparently high rate of immigration to coastal British Columbia of status and nonstatus Indians from central Canada. Information about off-reserve Indian populations is scarce, especially for nonstatus people. In contrast to close and accurate records for registered or status Indians, no records or censuses are routinely compiled for nonstatus Indians. Nonstatus Indians are concentrated in cities and larger towns, they are employed mainly in unskilled or blue-collar occupations, and they suffer high rates of unemployment. Indians in British Columbia's urban centers in the early 1970s differed in levels of income and employment according to educational background, but overall there was a high rate of unemployment and withdrawal from job-seeking (Stanbury and Siegel 1975; Stanbury, Fields, and Stevenson 1972, 1972a).

Band list numbers may grow from an administrative change. The Indian Act was amended in 1985 to abolish the sections that removed Indian women, and in some cases their children, from band lists upon their marriage to non-Indians.

Federal Government Programs

Beginning in the 1960s the federal government attempted to improve education and job placement through upgrading courses, enrollment in colleges, universities, and vocational institutes. Despite government efforts and claims of achievement, school dropout rates and unem-

Table 2. Population of British Columbia Coastal Tribes, 1885–1984

Year	Haida	Tsimshian	Kwakiutl, Haisla, Oowekeeno, Haihais, and Bella Bella	Nootka and Nitinaht	Bella Coola	Coast Salish	Totals
1885	(800)	(4,550)	(3,000)	(3,500)	(450)	(5,525)	(17,825)
1895	(663)	(3,550)	2,401	(2,834)	(340)	4,737	(14,525)
1905	599	3,565	2,052	2,264	288	4,377	13,145
1915	588	3,618	1,917	1,835	253	4,120	12,331
1929	691	3,626	1,854	1,626	249	4,320	12,366
1939	790	3,779	2,148	1,605	259	4,722	13,303
1949	895	4,290	2,817	1,815	334	5,738	15,889
1959	1,062	5,691	3,853	2,501	460	7,686	21,253
1969	1,363	7,545	4,879	3,267	596	10,047	27,697
1979	1,560	9,452	5,768	4,240	745	11,786	33,551
1984	1,701	10,503	6,167	4,720	830	13,044	36,965

NOTE: Figures in parentheses are estimates from Hawthorn, Belshaw, and Jamieson (1958:22).
SOURCES: Figures for 1885 and 1895 are from Duff (1964; H.B. Hawthorn 1968:23). Other data are from Department of Indian Affairs Annual Reports, and Census of Indians of Canada.

ployment remained extremely high and incomes, low. A 1964 survey revealed a range in average annual per capita incomes from gainful employment from $325 to $664 for the Masset band of Haida, Port Simpson band of Tsimshian, Sheshaht band of Nootka, and the Squamish Salish. Skidegate Haida averaged $1,252 of income, the highest in the sample of Indian bands across Canada; however, it was still below the average per capita income from gainful employment of $1,400 for the nation as a whole (H.B. Hawthorn 1968, 1:45–49).

Of growing importance to economies of reserve communities from the 1960s to the 1980s has been the availability of federal funds to band councils for employment of band managers, clerks, secretaries, welfare administrators, and the like. In addition, band councils have had access to modest federal funds for welfare, housing, recreation, and so on. These have been made available as part of a slowly developing federal policy intended to strengthen local government and leadership in Indian communities. Limited success has been achieved, with many bands having, in addition to elected chiefs and councilors, officers who serve as village administrators in a manner analogous to that of municipal clerks. However, there has been relatively little investment of public funds in economic development; moreover, control has remained in the hands of federal administrators. Only a few bands situated adjacent to cities, and leasing land for residential or industrial development and thus deriving substantial revenues of their own, have been able to attain any effective independence from the Department of Indian and Northern Affairs.

Since the first constitutional Conference on Aboriginal Rights in Ottawa in 1983, Indians have pressured governments to build into the Canadian constitution guarantees of Indian rights to self-government. They failed to reach agreement at the third constitutional

Table 3. Registered Indian Population Living On and Off Reserves, 1984

Tribe	On Reserve		Off Reserve	
	Number	Percent	Number	Percent
Haida	867	51.0	834	49.0
Tsimshian	5,822	55.4	4,681	44.6
Kwakiutl, Haisla, Oowekeeno, Haihais, and Bella Bella	3,580	58.1	2,587	41.9
Nootka and Nitinaht	2,380	50.4	2,340	49.6
Bella Coola	606	73.0	224	27.0
Coast Salish	8,850	67.8	4,194	32.2
Totals	22,105	59.8	14,860	40.2

SOURCE: Canada 1984.

HISTORY OF COASTAL BRITISH COLUMBIA SINCE 1846

conference in 1987. The Sechelt band individually reached agreement with the federal government on a specific procedure for granting band control of lands, embodied in a special act of parliament for that band alone. Other coastal bands rejected this model for settlement of the issue. Canadian Indians remained in 1988 heavily dependent upon the federal government and subordinate to its complex administrative services.

Social Conditions and Political Movements

Some Indians have consciously sought assimilation as an avenue to a better way of life; others have turned to their own communities.

The high rate of alcoholism among Indians has had drastic consequences. Accidents have been the leading cause of deaths among British Columbia Indians (Canada 1982:11; British Columbia 1984:39). Suicide and homicide are more common than among the general population, and drinking is an associated factor in these sudden deaths among Indians (Cutler and Morrison 1971).

To some extent all Christian missions sought to change social conditions as well as morals and beliefs, but exceptional and unusually successful were the Metlakatla mission ("Tsimshian of Metlakatla, Alaska," fig. 1, this vol.) begun among the Tsimshian in 1862 by William Duncan, an Anglican (Usher 1974); and the Sechelt (fig. 6), Squamish, and other Salish missions created in the nineteenth century by the Roman Catholic priest and bishop, Pierre-Paul Durieu, O.M.I. (Lemert 1954; Morice 1910). Additional Anglican and Methodist missions with similar reformist approaches were founded among the Haida and Tsimshian (Duff 1964). Personal conversion and reform were promoted, and whole villages under the influence of these missionaries became materially and socially transformed (Rumley 1973).

Renewed growth of Coast Salish spirit dancing (Amoss 1978a) has elements similar to the early utopian Christian communities, although spirit dancing is a complex blending of several indigenous institutions. Reform of individual behavior has become a central theme in the recruitment of new dancers, and dance houses have become winter centers promoting Indian ethics and morality ("Central and Southern Coast Salish Ceremonies Since 1900," this vol.).

Other revivals of Indian culture are evident in dance societies that teach and promote theatrical displays of pan-Indian, as well as modified indigenous coastal styles of dancing. These are more widespread, although perhaps less influential on community life than religious phenomena. There are also many locally organized revivals of sculpture, weaving and basketry arts, myth-telling, and the study of tribal history and culture. Some of these, like the 'Ksan project of the Gitksan, have obtained considerable support from government agencies and have become successful centers for preservation and remolding of elements of Indian culture. These revivals are aimed at rebuilding a sense of ethnic pride among Indians and respect in the wider community. This is evident in the emergence of Northwest Coast art as fine art. While museums played vital parts in assisting this growth, which has seen the emergence of numerous Indian professional artists as well as commercial galleries specializing in the art, the individual contributions of the Kwakiutl, Mungo Martin, and the Haida, Bill Reid ("Art," fig. 23, this vol.) have been outstanding (see Macnair, Hoover, and Neary 1980).

Through political movements Indians have set out to reshape the structural position of Indians in Canadian society. The most common tactic was to petition and lobby governments and their agencies for change of policies and for recognition and formal settlement of land claims. One of the more ambitious of early efforts to organize and present a united front was that of the Coast Salish who sent a delegation of chiefs from several Salish language groups to appeal to King Edward VII in London in 1906 (LaViolette 1961:126–127). Nishga villages also united in protest against the reserve system, and resentment against the section of the Indian Act forbidding potlatches evoked concerted protest from many tribes.

Nishga, Coast Salish, and Interior Salish joined to form the Allied Tribes of British Columbia in order to contest the findings of the McKenna-McBride Commission, 1912–1916. They managed to delay ratification of the decisions of the Commission for several years. Under dedicated leadership from Rev. Peter Kelly (Haida), and Andrew Paull (Squamish), they prepared and presented to the federal government a summary of Indian claims. These were disallowed in 1923 and the Commission's work was ratified by parliament, but the Allied Tribes persisted. Eventually the federal government was pressed into hearing a lengthy submission (Canada 1927a) but again refused to recognize the need for negotiated settlement. With its leadership severely disillusioned, not only by the failure of their appeal but also by introduction in the Indian Act of a section making it an offense to solicit funds for the purpose of pursuing a land claims case (Canada 1927), the Allied Tribes disappeared.

In 1931, following the model of an Alaska organization, the Native Brotherhood of British Columbia was formed at Port Simpson. It soon claimed membership among all tribal groups of the coast and from some Interior Salish and Carrier as well (Drucker 1958). The interests of the Native Brotherhood were broadly conceived and directed to all lawful means by which Indian welfare might be enhanced. After the Native Brotherhood absorbed the Pacific Coast Native Fishermen's Association (primarily Kwakiutl) in 1942, its activities became more firmly centered on the Indians' role in the fishing

left, Vancouver Pub. Lib., B.C.: 19927; right, Royal B.C. Mus., Victoria: PN 8788.
Fig. 6. Intervillage gatherings for Christian ceremonies. left, Six Indian brass bands gathered at the mission in Seshelt, B.C., to play at the dedication of the Roman Catholic church, Our Lady of the Rosary (Mattison 1981:10). Photograph by Charles S. Bailey and Hamilton G. Neelands, June 1890. right, Passion Play enacted by the Central Coast Salish at the Roman Catholic St. Mary's Mission, Mission, B.C. These religious ceremonies were large public occasions that attracted non-Indian as well as Indian spectators. Photograph by Charles S. Bailey, June 1892.

industry, and the Brotherhood became a bargaining agent alongside the militant United Fishermen and Allied Workers union.

Internal dissent and divergence of interest lead to formation in 1945 of a splinter organization among Coast Salish, Nootka, and Interior Salish, the North American Indian Brotherhood. Both organizations continued to strive for support and for changes in legislation and government policies. Their representatives, as well as other citizens, made presentations to a joint committee of the Senate and House of Commons prior to a major revision of the Indian Act in 1951, and this achieved repeal of some glaring discriminatory sections, including those prohibiting potlatching, Indian dancing away from home villages, and collecting money to pursue land claims.

During the 1960s a number of Indian organizations emerged, including a women's group, the Indian Home-makers' Association. Another attempt at forming a united body of British Columbia Indians was made in 1967–1968 when the Confederation of British Columbia Indians was formed in Vancouver (Tennant 1982:39ff.). This was part of a response to advice from the minister of Indian affairs that his government could not attempt to negotiate any land claim unless it could deal with a united and representative Indian organization. Although evoking some interest among Salish bands the new organization failed to receive support from the reactivated Nishga Tribal Council, which had in 1967 gone to court seeking a declaration of the existence of their aboriginal title (vol. 4: 93). The Confederation scarcely got off the ground before it fell from view.

In June 1969 the government of Canada released a paper proposing major changes in Indian policy, including abolition of the Indian Act and the Department of Indian Affairs while disavowing the existence of aboriginal rights. This paper, which evoked strong reaction among Indians across Canada, led to the formation of the Union of British Columbia Indian Chiefs. Joined by a majority of the bands in the province, the organization obtained recognition and financial support from the federal government and established headquarters in Vancouver. Although it assumed some service functions previously provided by the federal administration, its major task was resolution of land claims. To this end a statement of policy was prepared and presented to the government, and a research center for land claims was established in Victoria.

Formed in 1968, the British Columbia Association of Non-Status Indians also obtained government support. The emphasis of this organization has been upon obtaining recognition of the special needs of nonstatus Indians and sponsoring housing. But it too developed concern for recognition of claims to lost land and other rights. The Union of British Columbia Indian Chiefs and the British Columbia Association of Non-Status Indians rejected government funding in 1975, in an attempt to emphasize their independence and expand their activities, but the government simply redirected its funding to the band level (Tennant 1983:116ff.).

Beginning in the mid-1970s regional band organizations were formed ("tribal councils"). In 1987 there were 15 of these among the coastal Indians, with memberships ranging from 2 to 13 bands. Some councils, like the Gitksan-Wet'suwet'en Tribal Council, have focused effort on settlement of land claims. Others, such as The Alliance (Coast Salish of the Mainland) have concentrated upon lobbying for changes in Department of Indian and Northern Affairs administration and assisting member bands to provide services. The tribal councils have also

Vancouver Sun, B.C.
Fig. 7. Protestors from throughout B.C. marching to the home of Minister of Human Resources Grace McCarthy. With the support of the union of B.C. Indian Chiefs they were objecting to the policy of placing Indian children in foster homes outside their own community without consulting bands or tribal councils. Photograph by Ken Oakes, Vancouver, Oct. 1980.

supported wider national organizations such as the Assembly of First Nations in efforts to negotiate settlements of claims and to establish constitutional rights of self-government for native peoples. About a dozen bands, including the Port Simpson and Cowichan, have remained unaffiliated with tribal councils; nevertheless, they participate in wider political activities. For these tribal councils, organization at the local level is of primary importance (Tennant 1983).

A landmark in the long fight for land claims was a supreme court of Canada decision in 1973 on the Nishga request for recognition of aboriginal title (Sanders 1973). Although not providing a definitive ruling it did lead to revision of federal government policy (Canada 1981), and in 1976 negotiations began between representatives of the Nishga and provincial and federal governments. However, the province of British Columbia maintained its refusal to recognize aboriginal title to land. Although other general land claims have been received by the federal Office of Native Claims, the intransigence of the province has prevented any meaningful negotiations. Other groups including the Gitksan-Wet'suwet'en Tribal Council and the Nuu-chah-nulth Tribal Council (Nootka), have entered the courts in efforts to verify existence of aboriginal title.

Political activity among Northwest Coast Indians in British Columbia has been conducted mainly within adopted Euro-Canadian models of organization, and within the constitutional framework and accepted norms of Canadian society (fig. 7). It has been through the courts, by lobbying and petitioning, and by persuasion that Indians have presented their points of view. Rebellion against authorities or separation from the larger society have never been the means of concerted action.

History of Western Washington Since 1846

CESARE MARINO

Before 1846 the area that became Washington State was part of the Oregon Country, a region that by agreement between the United States and Great Britain in 1818, renewed in 1827, was a territory subject to their joint occupation (Scott and De Lorme 1988:19). In 1846, the British and Americans resolved the Oregon question with a treaty that drew the international boundary line at 49° north latitude and midway through the Strait of Juan de Fuca, thus placing all tribes south of that line under the jurisdiction of the United States. Two years later Congress passed the Organic Act, by which the Oregon Territory was created and legal assurance given to the northwestern Indians that their lands would not be taken without their consent (Beckham 1977:117–118). Under pressure from growing numbers of settlers who had laid claims in the Puget Sound area and Willamette Valley under the Oregon Donation Act of 1850, in 1853 Congress organized Washington Territory and appointed Isaac I. Stevens as its governor and ex officio superintendent of Indian affairs (Manypennny in ARCIA 1853:453–457). At the end of an exploration from Saint Paul, Minnesota Territory, to Puget Sound (I.I. Stevens 1855), during which the expedition's ethnologist George Gibbs (1855, 1877) gathered important information on the Indian tribes of Washington Territory, Stevens established himself at Olympia and began to address the Indian question.

The Stevens Treaties

A believer in Manifest Destiny and a strong proponent of westward expansion (see Hazard 1952; Richards 1979), Governor Stevens regarded the tribes under his jurisdiction as an impediment to civilization. White settlement was to be facilitated by extinguishing Indian title to the land, concentrating tribes on reservations and promoting Indian acculturation (ARCIA 1854:455–457). In 1854, Congress allocated some $45,000 for treaty agreements Stevens was to conclude with the tribes in Washington Territory (Coan 1922:12–13). That year, the governor had submitted to the secretary of the interior a detailed census of the tribes west of the Cascades, placing the total Indian population at 7,559 (I.I. Stevens 1855:435–436; ARCIA 1854:457–458). In the winter of 1854–1855 Stevens began his treaty-making mission among the tribes and bands of western Washington. The first of his treaty negotiations (see Trafzer 1986) was concluded in December 1854 on Medicine Creek near lower Puget Sound, with the headmen of the Nisqually, Puyallup, Steilacoom, Squaxin and other bands (Taylor 1974b), who agreed to cede their lands and remove to three selected reservations within one year after ratification of the treaty (Kappler 1904–1941, 2: 661–664). Article 3 of the Treaty of Medicine Creek set a historic legal precedent by securing said Indians "the right of taking fish, at all usual and accustomed grounds and stations . . . .in common with all citizens of the Territory" (Kappler 1904–1941, 2:662; see also Lane 1977). Besides acknowledging their dependence on the United States government, the tribes and bands were also "to free all slaves now held by them, and not to purchase or acquire others hereafter" (Kappler 1904–1941, 2:664), thus altering an important feature of their traditional social organization. The reservations established by the Medicine Creek treaty included the Puyallup, near present-day Tacoma, the Nisqually, near Olympia, and the Squaxin on Squaxin Island in southern Puget Sound. The former two reservations were enlarged in 1857, and the same year the Muckleshoot reservation was created between the White and Green Rivers to accommodate the Salish-speaking bands who had not been explicitly mentioned in the 1854 treaty (fig. 1) (Gosnell in ARCIA 1858:338; see also Lane 1973: [Pt. 7]; Ruby and Brown 1981:131). It was settled mainly by the Stkamish, Skopamish, and Smulkamish.

Amidst growing Indian unrest incited by Nisqually chief Leschi (see Meeker 1905), who refused to subscribe to the Medicine Creek treaty, Governor Stevens, on January 22, 1855, concluded the Treaty of Point Elliott (fig. 2), near present-day Everett, with 82 chiefs and headmen representing the tribes north to the international boundary. Several hundred members of the Duwamish, Suquamish, Snoqualmie, Snohomish, Stillaguamish, Swinomish, Skagit, Lummi, and other tribes gathered for the treaty council, during which, according to popular tradition, the Duwamish-Suquamish leader Seattle is said to have given a famous speech (see Kaiser 1987 for a critical review). In addition to the familiar land cession clause, the fishing rights, antislavery, and annuity provisions, the Treaty of Point Elliott called for the establishment of temporary reservations and the eventual removal

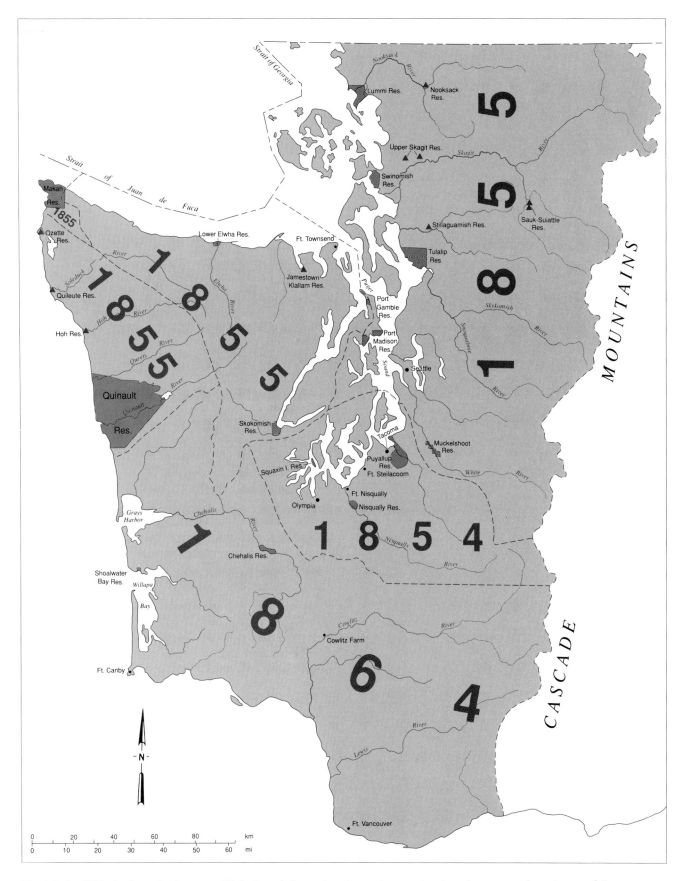

Fig. 1. Indian-White land transfers in western Wash. Dates indicate when the treaties were signed or when an executive order, act of Congress, or order of the secretary of the interior transferred lands. For reference, historic forts and present-day reservations are sited.

MARINO

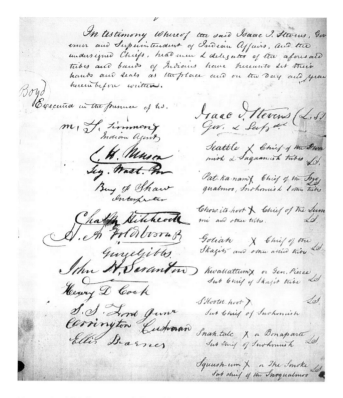

Natl. Arch., Civil Reference Branch: Treaty No. 283.
Fig. 2. Signatures on the Treaty of Point Elliott, 1855, including that of Isaac I. Stevens and the marks of Seattle, Patkanam, and Goliah, leaders of Southern Coast Salish tribes, and Chowitshoot, a Lummi leader (Kappler 1904–1941, 2:672).

and concentration "of all Indians living west of the Cascade Mountains" on the Tulalip (or Snohomish) Reservation (Kappler 1904–1941, 2:670). Besides Tulalip, the smaller Swinomish and Lummi reservations were established farther north, and the Port Madison reservation (also known as the Suquamish, Fort Kitsap, or Seattle reservation) on the Kitsap Peninsula, across the Sound to the south. This reservation was enlarged by executive order in 1864, while new lands were added in 1873 to the Tulalip, Swinomish, and Lummi.

From Point Elliott, Stevens proceeded to the Kitsap Peninsula, where on January 26, 1855, the Treaty of Point No Point was concluded with representatives of the Clallam, Twana, and Chemakum. This treaty reiterated the provisions of the other two agreements and called for the placement of the signatory tribes on what later became the Skokomish reservation at the head of Hood Canal (Kappler 1904–1941, 2:674). The Twana soon concentrated at Skokomish (Elmendorf 1960:273–274), but the Chemakum and most of the Clallam did not relocate there. In time, the Chemakum disappeared as a distinct tribal entity, and three small Clallam settlements became the reservations of Lower Elwha, Jamestown, and Port Gamble.

Having thus dealt with the Puget Sound tribes, Stevens turned to the coastal Indians under his jurisdiction (Seeman 1987:37–67). On January 31, 1855, the governor concluded the Treaty of Neah Bay with the Makah, who

were apparently satisfied with the provisions of the agreement that called for the establishment of what has since been their main reservation (for Ozette see Taylor 1974; Ruby and Brown 1986:161) and recognition of their fishing, whaling, sealing, and hunting rights (Kappler 1904–1941, 2:682; Gibbs 1855a). In the early 1860s an agency was established at Neah Bay; the Makah reservation was enlarged by executive orders in 1872 and 1873 (Gillis 1974). After Neah Bay, Stevens faced the difficult task of proposing a similar treaty to the remaining tribes of the ocean shore, whom he summoned to a treaty council to be held at the end of February 1855, on the Chehalis River near Grays Harbor. The negotiations between Stevens and the headmen of the Queets, Quinault, Satsop, Lower Chehalis, Upper Chehalis, Cowlitz, and Chinook proceeded unsuccessfully for days, with the Quileute and other smaller bands being absent. Opposed to the land cession and indiscriminate removal provisions, and dissatisfied with the federal government's failure to ratify the 1851 treaties of Tansey Point (see Beckham 1977:123–126), the Indians eventually refused to sign the treaty. On March 3, 1855, the Grays Harbor negotiations came to an unresolved end (Swan 1857:327–360). The Quinault, Queets, Hoh, and Quileute agreed to a separate treaty concluded with Special Indian Agent M.T. Simmons on the Quinault River, July 1, 1855. This provided that they were to concentrate on the Quinault reservation (Kappler 1904–1941, 2:719–721), but while the Quinault settled there, together with the Queets, whom they eventually absorbed, the Quileute avoided removal and were granted a small reservation in 1889; in 1893, the Hoh, who had not relocated to Quinault, were given a small reservation. The nontreaty Upper Chehalis and Lower Chehalis, and the Chinook, in addition to other small bands who had been parties to the unratified 1851 treaties of Tansey Point, Oregon, were provided with an inland reservation at the confluence of the Chehalis and Black rivers in 1864 and a coastal one at Shoalwater Bay in 1866. Not all members of these tribes settled on these two reservations, and many chose to relocate among the Quinault and Nisqually; some Cowlitz were even removed east of the Cascades to the Yakima reservation (Ray 1974: 276–277; Fitzpatrick 1986). Still other Indians, both north of the Columbia River and throughout the Puget Sound region, continued to live off-reservation, becoming, in time, the "landless tribes of Western Washington" (Bishop and Hansen 1978).

The disruption brought upon the Puget Sound and Columbia river tribes by dispossession and removal, epidemics, White encroachment, and government delays in the ratification of the treaties had resulted in the short-lived Puget Sound uprising of the winter of 1855–1856. Under Leschi's leadership the Indian coalition, never numbering more than a few hundred warriors—mostly Nisqually, Puyallup, and their Sahaptin allies—attempted in vain to draw all the western Washington tribes into a general war against the Whites. Tribal factionalism and intertribal enmity prevailed over the call for unity (Gosnell 1926; Ruby and Brown 1981:145–154). After two unsuccessful attacks on the town of Seattle in late January and early February 1856 (Blaine, Gansevoort, and Heebner 1956; Nalty and Strobridge 1964), the hostile Puget Sound Indians, joined by a contingent of their Yakima allies, managed to score some victories against the White volunteer troops and their Indian auxiliaries, but by late spring the outbreak was over. Leschi, betrayed by two of his own men, was imprisoned, put on trial, and executed (Bancroft 1890:171–174; D.G. Emmons 1965). The Puget Sound hostilities were connected to the Yakima War (Glassley 1972); both were part of the general Indian unrest in the Northwest caused by increased White settlement in the region and more directly by the Indian policy pursued by Stevens, who was criticized for it by General John E. Wool, commander of the Army of the Pacific (Melina 1986).

Agencies and Reservations

With the failure of armed resistance, the Indians of western Washington entered a period of difficult adjustment to the new order imposed on them by treaties and enforced by the Indian Office. To keep a more direct control over the tribes, in the 1860s separate agencies were established under the Washington Superintendency at Puyallup, Tulalip, Neah Bay, Skokomish, and Quinault (Hill 1974:193–200). Indian agents, many of whom were corrupt, aided by resident farmers, carpenters, and physicians assigned to their respective agencies, embarked on the task of "civilizing" the Indians. Agriculture and schooling were used as the main tools of the government's reservation policy, but neither appeared to have been adopted enthusiastically by most Indians. At Neah Bay, in 1865, the agent reported that "farming operations have thus far been limited" and complained that only a few Indian children had been attending school "with any degree of regularity . . . the great obstacle to their advancement . . . [being] a total indifference of the parents to the benefits of education" (Webster in ARCIA 1865:90). In regard to agriculture, the agent at Skokomish wrote: "I am sorry to have nothing encouraging to report" (Knox in ARCIA 1865:82), while the subagent at Quinault stressed a condition noted elsewhere on the western Washington reservations, that of a "soil . . . almost totally unfit for farming purposes" (J. Hill in ARCIA 1865:96). Better results were reported the same year at Puyallup (Billings in ARCIA 1865:80–81), and to some extent at Tulalip (Howe in ARCIA 1865:72–74; Chirouse in ARCIA 1865:75–77), and on the Lummi reservation where the Indians had "cleared off thirty acres in potatoes and vegetables" (Finkboner in ARCIA 1865:74; see also Suttles 1954). Still, agriculture remained a secondary occupation among the coastal and Puget Sound tribes

who continued to rely on fishing and gathering of shellfish, berries, and roots for subsistence, supplemented by government annuities. Some Indians also found temporary employment as wage laborers in the White-controlled fishing and canning industry or as seasonal workers in off-reservation hop fields (fig. 3). Nevertheless, the economic situation of most western Washington Indians was marginal (fig. 4).

Recurring incidents of smallpox, and other diseases, malnutrition, and the effects of the use of alcohol contributed to population loss. An 1870 census placed the Indian population at 7,657, with 6,223 Indians included under the 1854–1856 Stevens treaties, and 1,434 listed as parties to no (ratified) treaty (S. Ross in ARCIA 1870: 17–18).

During the 1870s, under President Ulysses Grant's Peace Policy (Prucha 1984, 1:479–533), humanitarian organizations and Christian denominations were officially drawn into the formulation and administration of Indian affairs. Local agencies and reservations were placed under the direct control of religious associations and missionary societies to promote acculturation through "the moral and religious advancement of the Indians" (ARCIA 1872:73). In western Washington, the Tulalip agency, administering Tulalip, Port Madison, Swinomish, and Lummi reservations, was assigned to the Roman Catholics, with Eugene Casimir Chirouse, O.M.I., acting both as missionary and Indian agent (Sullivan 1932). Neah Bay agency on the Makah reservation, serving also the Quileute who had not removed to Quinault, was first given to the Christian Union (ARCIA 1872:73) and later placed under the Methodists, who controlled Quinault agency and reservation (ARCIA 1872:73, 1880:279). The Skokomish agency,

U. of Wash. Lib., Special Coll., Seattle: NA 663.
Fig. 3. Hop pickers, White River valley, Wash. Indian families from the western Oreg. and Wash. reservations as well as from B.C. were among those who found seasonal employment in the hop industry, which flourished from the 1880s to 1919. Photograph probably by Ashael Curtis, 1902.

MARINO

Fig. 4. Coast Salish Indian camp on Ballast "Island," Seattle, Wash. This peninsula at the foot of Washington Street was created by deposits of ballast, rocks and rubble, from cargo ships prior to refilling their holds with the marketable goods of coal or lumber. Although an 1865 city ordinance forbade Indians from living alongside streets, they were tolerated on Ballast Island. From there Indians would go into town to sell clams and crafts and to find work. This was also the fall gathering place for Indian hop pickers who were traveling to the White and Snoqualmie river valleys (Dorpat 1984:[44]). Photograph by Arthur Warner, about 1892.

later consolidated with the Puyallup agency (Hill 1974: 195–196), although initially assigned to the Methodists (ARCIA 1872:73), was placed under the Congregational Church; Edwin Eells served as Indian agent there from 1871 until 1895 (E. Eells 1916), while his brother Myron conducted missionary work at Skokomish and among other western Washington Indians from 1874 to 1907. Myron Eells (for example, 1882, 1886, 1985) recorded the history and culture particularly of the Twana and the Clallam, at a time when Indian peoples in western Washington, and throughout the rest of the country, were experiencing considerable stress under the policy of forced assimilation that Eells and many like him advocated. Submission was seen as the only hope of the Indians (ARCIA 1872:9), and the Indians seemed to have adjusted well to the practical elements of White civilization. R.H. Milroy (in ARCIA 1879:149), Indian agent for the Puyallup, Nisqually, Chehalis, and other bands reported that "the condition of the different tribes and bands belonging to [this] agency is much changed from the wild aboriginal state, especially as to dress. All have . . . adopted the style of dress of the whites." Myron Eells (1985:113) noted the adoption of "civilized clothing" among "nearly all the Indians in Puget Sound." Agent Edwin Eells (in ARCIA 1880:163) stated that on the Skokomish reservation the Indians

> have built comfortable houses, barns, wood-sheds and outhouses, have set out small orchards, and have around them the substantial comforts of civilized life. Indoors their

floors are smooth . . . and the rooms are warmed with stoves and fire-places. Their food is cooked on stoves, eaten on tables with knives and forks, in plates and dishes, as white people do. They have . . . bedsteads with feather beds, sheets and pillow cases, as well as clocks and looking-glasses, and they keep their persons as neat as a large majority of the white people living on the frontiers.

In 1879 about a dozen schools, both boarding and day schools, were operating, with a total enrollment of about 300 Indian students out of 1,700 Indian children of school age (ARCIA 1879:242–243). By 1899, the enrollment had risen to about 500 students for the same number of facilities (Office of Indian Affairs 1899: 44–45, 52, 62). Indian students were also sent off-reservation to the Training School for Indian Youth, a boarding school established in 1880 in Forest Grove, Oregon (vol. 4:60), which was moved to near Salem, Oregon, in 1885 and became the Chemawa Indian School (fig. 5). Myron Eells reported that "Puyallup boys took the lead in putting out a small newspaper" at the school, while "on their own reservation Puyallup children had done considerable printing. Snohomish children published a magazine, *The Youth's Companion* from 1881 to 1886" (Ruby and Brown 1976a:86, 104). Other western Washington Indian students were sent as far away as Carlisle Indian School in Pennsylvania and Haskell Institute at Lawrence, Kansas.

Overall, Indian children experienced the same cultural ambivalence that was felt among older generations. Despite the nominal conversion of many Indians, Chris-

Oreg. Histl. Soc., Portland: top 36112; bottom 007202.
Fig. 5. Chemawa Indian Training School near Salem, Oreg. top, Male students who in addition to studying history, geography, English, and arithmetic, learned farming and trades—shoe manufacture, blacksmithing, carpentry, and tinsmithing. The girls took the same academic course as well as learned sewing, cooking, and laundering. The pupils' vocational work provided the support services for the school; the boys cultivated much of the food for the school population, and the girls did all the cooking. In 1886 there were 200 pupils (ARCIA 1886:15–18). Photographed 1886–1890. bottom, Cheerleaders and students, some of whom are from western Wash. In addition to Northwest Coast Indians, pupils enrolled at Chemawa came from Plateau, Plains, northern California, and Great Basin tribes. Photographed March 1949.

tian denominations had not succeeded in eradicating aboriginal beliefs and rituals. At Skokomish and Tulalip, for example, sick Indians still sought out shamans, who administered their traditional cures in defiance of government prohibition (Eells 1985:425–426). A compromise between the old traditions and Christianity spread among the Southern Coast Salish first, and eventually more widely in the form of Indian Shakerism, a religion founded in 1882 by John Slocum, a Squaxin. Syncretic in nature, Shakerism was described as "a curious mixture of the old

Tamahnous religion and Protestantism and Catholicism . . . [and] undoubtedly a decided step in advance of the old religion" (St. John 1914:19). Indian agents were initially suspicious of Shakerism (fig. 6) but eventually grew tolerant toward it, since it called for temperance and restrained behavior: "The Shakers, a peculiar religious sect, are seemingly doing good, as there has been little or no law breaking by their members, and no drunkenness whatever" (C.L. Woods quoted in St. John 1914:20; see also "The Indian Shaker Church," this vol.).

After years of Christian control of Indian affairs, it became clear that throughout western Washington the traditional patterns of subsistence, kinship networks, and intervillage ties persisted, fostering Indian values and the maintenance of Indian identity. For their part, missionaries and agents worked to strengthen the nuclear family, hoping to direct young Indian couples to give up living in multifamily houses and adopt instead single-family houses on separate parcels of land. In an effort to undermine the traditional Indian social structure and speed up the "civilization" process, lands had been allotted as early as 1874 on the Skokomish and Squaxin reservations, and in the mid-1800s at Puyallup, Tulalip, and Nisqually. These

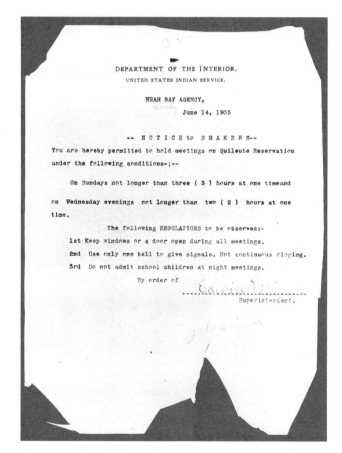

Fig. 6. Letter from Neah Bay Agency Superintendent Edwin Minor, June 14, 1905, ordering Quileute Shaker worshipers to confine their religious meetings to certain hours. Shakers ignored this regulation, and Minor asked reservation police to jail the violators (Powell and Jensen 1976:42).

allotments, which preceded the passage of the Dawes Severalty Act in 1887, were based on provisions in the Stevens treaties. Many western Washington groups, with the possible exception of the Southern Coast Salish (Wayne Suttles, personal communication 1988), recognized individual or family rights to various kinds of real estate such as fishing locations, clam beds, and root beds. The allotment system changed the extent and nature of the ownership of real estate: aboriginally, probably only the heads of important kin groups had property, while with the allotment system every nuclear family was to receive land of its own.

The various tribes reacted differently to the allotment program and some, such as the Lummi, apparently welcomed it (Wayne Suttles, personal communication 1988). Overall, however, the allotment of the already reduced tribal land base allowed White settlers and land speculators to gain legal title to Indian lands that were declared surplus and to buy parcels directly from Indian allottees after the trust period limitations had expired. On Puyallup reservation, the political maneuvering of White officials of nearby Tacoma resulted in the sale of about 7,000 acres, 40 percent of the tribe's alloted lands, "for less than a half million dollars . . . .Some of the land was valuable waterfront property along Commencement Bay in Tacoma and along the Puyallup River" (Ruby and Brown 1981:266; see also Ruby and Brown 1986: 168–169). The agent's complaceny resulted in the loss of tidelands on Squaxin Island, one-third of which came under White ownership. The Nisqually suffered a worse fate at the hands of the U.S. Army, which in 1917 occupied and later expropriated two-thirds of their reservation, forcing the relocation of several Indian families to other western Washington reservations (Kickingbird and Duchencaux 1973:179–195; Ruby and Brown 1986:151–152).

The allotment policy also caused friction among the Indians of different tribes, particularly on the Quinault reservation. Following the issuing of allotments to resident Quinaults in 1892, Congress, on the basis of the 1855 treaty and despite Quinault opposition, in 1907 authorized the Queets and Quileute to acquire allotments among the Quinaults. In 1911 the Hoh and Ozette were included, and in 1932 the Chehalis, Chinook, and Cowlitz Indians were also granted allotments at Quinault, leaving no tribally owned land there (Ruby and Brown 1986:176; Kinney 1937:267–268). Although they acquired Quinault lands, Chehalis, Chinook, and Cowlitz allottees were never given voting rights by the Quinault. The small Ozette, Quileute, Hoh River, and Shoalwater reservations remained unallotted (ARCIA 1912:117).

Fishing Rights

The admission of Washington Territory to statehood in 1889 marked the beginning of a bitter struggle over fishing rights among Indians, non-Indians, and state authorities (Cohen 1986). Under treaty provisions, the Indians had carried on their fishing activities, on both a subsistence and commercial basis, without major interference by non-Indians. By the late 1880s, White-owned commercial fishing and canning operations were well established throughout the Puget Sound region and on the Columbia River, competing among themselves and with the Indians for the seemingly unlimited quantities of salmon. In the Puget Sound area alone, the number of non-Indian commercial salmon canneries rose from 1 in 1890 to 19 in 1900 and to 45 in 1917 (Pacific Fisherman Yearbook 1918:62–65). In practical and political terms the fishing industry left little room for the aboriginal fishermen of Washington State. Even the federal government, whom the Indians had turned to as their trustee, seemed unable or unwilling to stop non-Indians from infringing upon Indian fishing rights. Such was the case for the Lummi who in 1897 sought to protect in court their own off-reservation commercial fishing activities against interference from a non-Indian commercial fishing company. However, Judge C.H. Hanford ruled against the Indians in *United States et al.* v. *Alaska Packers Association* (C.C. Wash., 79F 152): "As a result . . . the Lummi had to abandon their reef-net grounds at Point Roberts and Lummi Island and resort to small-scale subsistence fishing in the Nooksack River adjacent to the reservation" (Boxberger 1988:181). The Lummi filed an appeal that reached the U.S. Supreme Court, which in 1899 dismissed the case (W.A. Jones in ARCIA 1899:140–141).

In 1905 the U.S. Supreme Court handed down its first decision concerning Indian fishing rights in Washington State. In the case of *United States* v. *Winans* (198 U.S. 371), involving the operation of a state-licensed, White-owned, fish wheel at a place traditionally used by the Yakima, a Plateau tribe, the Court upheld the treaty provisions securing to the Indians the rights to fish at "usual and accustomed places." The state could not interfere with tribal rights in granting licenses; furthermore, the Indians "held the right to cross the land, to fish in the river, and to erect temporary houses for curing their catch" (Cohen 1986:55). In essence, the Court put forth what eventually became known as "the reserved rights doctrine" noting that the treaties "documented certain rights the Indians were granting *to* non-Indians, as well as certain other rights the Indians chose to reserve for themselves" (Cohen 1986:56). On the other hand, the Court recognized the State maintained some authority to regulate Indian fishing rights: "the nature and extent of that regulatory authority was left unclear and became the subject of future litigation" (U.S. Commission on Civil Rights 1981:65, passim).

During the early decades of the twentieth century the Indians of western Washington experienced repeated abuses at the hands of state fish and game authorities attempting to extend their control over Indian fishing and hunting both on-reservation and off. Cases were reported whereby two Lummi Indians had been arrested and jailed for fishing without a state license outside their reservation, while a Tulalip Reservation Indian had been jailed for hunting on contested reservation land. This situation led Charles M. Buchanan, Indian agent at Tulalip, to send an address to the 1915 Washington State legislative session urging that "the proper and necessary amendments be made" to state fish and game laws to recognize the Indians' treaty rights, and "make further quarrels, clashes and litigation both unnecessary and undesirable on these said points" (Buchanan 1915:118). Despite the *Winans* decision and the agent's appeal, in 1916 the State Supreme Court ruled against Indian fishing rights in two cases involving, again, a Yakima and a Lummi Indian exercising their treaty rights. The State Court rejected the premise of Indian sovereignty and subjected Indians fishing off-reservation to state regulations (Cohen 1986: 56–57; U.S. Commission on Civil Rights 1981:65–66).

Other aspects of Indian culture underwent change during the early 1900s. The potlatch had disappeared because of legal and social opposition "from religious and secular authorities . . . .[and] the decline . . . of the Native economic system within which the potlatch played its key role as a regulating mechanism" (Suttles 1987a:207). The distribution of goods persisted, although greatly modified, during Indian gatherings such as for winter dances and celebrations held on the Fourth of July (Ruby and Brown 1976a:76–77). Native language proficiency declined among younger generations who were sent to boarding schools, while bilingualism increased among older Indians seeking seasonal employment off the reservation. Intermarriage with Whites was relatively common. Alcoholism plagued many Indian communities despite a law forbidding the selling of liquor to Indians passed by the state of Washington in 1909 (St. John 1914:17–18). By 1921, the Indian population of western Washington had dropped to 5,003, with 3,283 Indians classified as full-blood and 1,720 as mixed-blood (ARCIA 1921:48). Under the Indian Reorganization Act of 1934, most tribes in western Washington replaced the traditional village leadership with a new tribal government based on a constitution and by-laws approved by the secretary of the interior (T.H. Haas 1947:2,-3, 18–19, table 1). Indians saw active duty overseas or joined war industries at home during the two world wars (The Suquamish Museum 1985:46–47).

In 1951, the Makah tribe challenged state regulations that prohibited them from net fishing off-reservation on the Hoko River. In the case of *Makah Indian Tribe* v. *Schoettler* (192 F.2d 224), the Ninth Circuit Court of Appeals "supported the claim of the Makah that [the] State regulation . . . .was not necessary for conservation purposes . . . .[and therefore] the State had no right to

close the river to Indian net fishing" (U.S. Commission on Civil Rights 1981:66). In 1957 the State Supreme Court dismissed the charges of gillnetting in violation of state law brought against two Puyallup Indians. This decision (*State of Washington* v. *Satiacum*, 314 P.2d 400) "encouraged both individuals and families from other western Washington tribes to fish more openly" (Cohen 1986: 68–69). However, in 1963 the State Supreme Court upheld the state's right to periodically close fishing in certain areas for conservation purposes; the state moved quickly to enforce its regulations against Indian fishing off-reservation, and in late 1963 it closed Indian fishing in southern Puget Sound (U.S. Commission on Civil Rights 1981:67). The Indians responded by organizing demonstrations and protests that gained national and international attention; so-called fish-ins were staged by tribal members with the support of militant pan-Indian organizations such as the National Indian Youth Council and the Survival of American Indians Association (La Potin 1987:125–127, 152). After a few years of often violent confrontation between Indian fishermen and their supporters on one side and White fishermen and state authorities on the other, the state of Washington brought suit against the Puyallup and Nisqually tribes in an attempt to assert the legitimacy of its conservation laws over Indian fishing rights based on the 1854 treaty (see American Friends Service Committee 1970). Contradictory opinions were handed down by lower state and federal courts until the United States Supreme Court, in a 1973 review of the case, struck down as discriminatory the state ban on Indian net fishing but allowed for partial state regulation of Indian fishing for preservation purposes (*Department of Game* v. *Puyallup Tribe*, 414 U.S. 44, 46; Cohen 1986:76–82; U.S. Commission on Civil Rights 1981:67–70).

In February 1974 federal district court Judge George H. Boldt gave his landmark decision in *United States* v. *State of Washington* (384 F. Supp. 312). The suit had been filed in 1970 by the U.S. Department of Justice as the trustee for seven, later 14, western Washington tribes seeking to resolve the fishing controversy by asserting the validity of their treaty-based fishing rights vis à vis state laws and regulations. After three and one-half years of in-depth review of the extensive historical, judicial, and scientific record pertaining to fishing in Washington State, Judge Boldt issued a lengthy opinion reaffirming Indian fishing rights. Specifically, the Court ruled that: (1) treaties reserved to Indian tribes fishing rights that are distinct from those of other citizens; (2) off-reservation Indian fishing rights extended to every place each tribe customarily fished; (3) Indians had reserved rights to a fair share—50 percent—of the harvestable fish exclusive of on-reservation catches and of fish taken for subsistence and ceremonial purposes; (4) the state may regulate Indian off-reservation fishing only to the extent necessary

176

Table 1. Federally Recognized Tribes of Western Washington, 1987

Organizational structure approved	
Indian Reorganization Act	*Outside specific federal statutory authority*
Hoh Tribe of Washington	Confederated Tribes of the Chehalis Reservation
Lower Elwha Tribal Community	Jamestown Klallam Tribe
Makah Tribe[a]	Lummi Tribe
Muckleshoot Tribe[a]	Quinault Tribe
Nisqually Indian Community	Shoalwater Bay Tribe
Nooksack Indian Tribe	
Port Gamble Indian Community[a]	
Puyallup Tribe	
Quileute Tribe[a]	
Sauk-Suiattle Indian Tribe	
Skokomish Tribe[a]	
Squaxin Island Tribe	
Stillaguamish Tribe	
Suquamish Tribe	
Swinomish Tribe[a]	
Tulalip Tribes[a]	
Upper Skagit Tribe	

SOURCE: U.S. Bureau of Indian Affairs. Branch of Tribal Relations 1987.

[a] Has federal corporate charter.

for conservation, but not in ways limiting treaty rights to state-preferred times and fishing methods; (5) the state classification of steelhead as a "game" fish restricted Indian fishing rights and violated the treaties; and (6) 14 treaty tribes, plus three more upon federal approval, were entitled to share in the decision (U.S. Commission on Civil Rights 1981:70–71; Cohen 1986:11–15, 83–106). Following the ruling, a Fisheries Advisory Board composed of state and tribal representatives and five intertribal treaty councils, comprising the tribes under the 1854–1855 treaties, were established to coordinate with the Northwest Indian Fisheries Commission the implementation of the court decision and the management of Indian fisheries (Cohen 1986:84–86, 168–169; Northwest Indian Fisheries Commission 1977, 1980, 1986; Vernon and Scott 1977).

Throughout the intense legal and political controversy, the Indians of western Washington continued to pursue fishing as a means of livelihood and a focal point for the preservation of their tribal identity, culture, and traditions. The Lummi, for example, pioneered in the development of an aquaculture facility in the early 1970s (Deloria 1978). Contributing to preservation and repopulation efforts that benefited both Indians and non-Indians, by 1984, 16 federally recognized tribes of western Washington operated 20 tribal hatcheries; total salmon and steelhead releases from so-called treaty hatcheries rose from less than 10 million in 1976 to nearly 33 million in 1983 (Cohen 1986:165, tables 10.4–10.5). The ruling in *United States* v. *State of Washington* also gave the western Washington tribes new legal grounds on which to challenge industrial projects that they perceived as posing threats to the region's rivers and fish. In the late 1970s, the

Upper Skagit, Swinomish, and Sauk-Suiattle invoked the same treaty case law in a battle against Puget Sound Power and Light, a private company planning to build a nuclear plant near Skagit River. Indians and non-Indians alike successfully united against the project, which would have infringed on Indian fishing rights besides having an impact on the environment (Anonymous 1980). A few years later, the Muckleshoot tribe sued for damages caused by the diversion of water from the reservation and its fishery by a hydroelectric plant that had been in operation since 1911 (Arkeketa and Austin 1986).

As the treaty tribes took actions to consolidate their newly recognized fishing rights, the so-called Boldt decision met with strong negative reaction among non-Indian fishermen and state regulators, who appealed the case to the United States Supreme Court. After denying review in 1976, the Court eventually decided to hear the case, which continued to stir controversy and violence in western Washington (fig. 7). In 1979 the Supreme Court upheld much of the 1974 decision but modified the lower court ruling to include in the 50 percent allocation all fish caught by treaty Indians both on and off-reservation, for any purposes (U.S. Commission on Civil Rights 1981: 97–98). Despite the new definition of the equal share clause, the general Indian response was positive, while commercial and sports fishermen expressed their disappointment at the ruling (Cohen 1986:115–117). Ultimately, the decision resulted in better cooperation between the state Department of Fisheries and the treaty tribes, as reflected in joint tribal and state salmon projects on the Nisqually River and at Hood Canal (Cohen 1986:170). It also appears that the 1979 Supreme Court ruling, by

The Seattle Times, Wash.
Fig. 7. Fishing boat blockade by Whites in a demonstration at State Ferry, Wash., on Sept. 11, 1978, against the 1974 ruling in *United States* v. *State of Washington* by Judge George Boldt. Non-Indians who appealed the decision called it racial discrimination and openly violated it (Prucha 1984, 2:1184–1185).

giving the highest judicial sanction to the legitimacy of the Indians' treaty fishing rights, had a positive impact on a number of non-Indians who had previously criticized the Boldt decision (Gassholt and Cohen 1980; for an economic critique of the fishing rights controversy see Barsh 1979; background information is in Swindell 1942; U.S. Bureau of Indian Affairs 1977; J. Ryan 1979; Josephy 1984; cf. also Knutson 1987; Cohen and Bowden 1988).

Landless and Unrecognized Tribes

The partial resolution of the long-standing conflict over fishing rights highlighted another aspect of the Indian history of western Washington—several landless and nonfederally recognized tribes of the region who, besides having to confront non-Indian fishermen and state authorities, also had to face the opposition of federally recognized tribes unwilling to share with them the exercise of historically common, but now judicially separate, treaty fishing rights. The landless status of many Indian groups in western Washington was to a great extent the outcome of the Stevens treaty policy and the partially fulfilled promises made by the government to all the signatory tribes (T.G. Bishop 1915). Following the ratification of the treaties about a dozen tribes and bands, entirely or in part, did not remove to reservations, because

the land reserved was insufficient for the number of Indians, or because of traditional enmity between different tribes assigned to the same reservation or the distance of the established reservation from their traditional homeland. Despite the lack of a land base, these Indian groups maintained their character as distinct Indian communities (McChesney 1906), and their members participated in Bureau of Indian Affairs programs (Lane 1973). They also successfully litigated their land claims before the Indian Claims Commission, which awarded them monetary compensation and between 1958 and 1974 ruled that the landless Samish, Duwamish, Snohomish, Snoqualmie, and Steilacoom each constituted an "identifiable tribe of American Indians [which had] continued to perpetuate [its] identity as a tribal entity into contemporary times" (cited in Barsh and Whittlesey 1988:[4]; see also Indian Claims Commission 1980; Ruby and Brown 1986).

In 1913 these and other landless tribes of Washington, under the leadership of Thomas G. Bishop, a Snohomish, had organized the Northwest Federation of American Indians, an intertribal organization that sought to resolve the landless status of its members and assert their treaty rights (Bishop and Hansen 1978:25–26). The Federation successfully supported the claims of the Port Gamble and Lower Elwha Clallams who, in the 1930s, acquired reservation lands under provisions of the Indian Reorganization Act. In 1942 the United States Supreme Court in *Tulee* v. *Washington* (315 U.S. 681) upheld the right of all Washington treaty tribes to fish without a state license. The Bureau of Indian Affairs implemented this decision by issuing identification cards, "blue cards," to all eligible Indians. "No distinction was drawn in this program between reservation and landless tribes, and the members of the landless tribes fished freely under *Tulee* throughout the 1950s and 1960s" (Barsh and Whittlesey 1988:[3]). During the 1950s, under the threat of termination, both landed and landless tribes joined forces in the Inter-Tribal Council of Western Washington, an organization that opposed termination and tried, unsuccessfully, to prevent the closing of the Cushman Indian Hospital in Tacoma; the closure resulted in the phasing out of health services to landless Indians (Bishop and Hansen 1978:26).

Between 1971 and 1976, at the height of the fishing rights battle, four formerly landless and nonfederally recognized Salish tribes—Nooksack, Upper Skagit, Sauk-Suiattle, and Stillaguamish—were granted federal acknowledgment, thus gaining full participation in the implementation of the Boldt decision. Later, five other nonreservation and unrecognized groups, namely the Duwamish, Samish, Snohomish, Snoqualmie, and Steilacoom, filed a motion to intervene in the treaty fishery established in 1974 by the federal district court. Judge Boldt in 1979 denied the motion by these five tribes and ruled that "only tribes recognized as Indian political bodies by the United States may possess and exercise tribal fishing rights secured and protected by treaties with the United States" (cited in Barsh and Whittlesey 1988a:2). As a result, several other recognized tribes laid claim to the aboriginal fishing areas of those five (Barsh and Whittlesey 1988:[12]).

With the coordination and support of Small Tribes Organization of Western Washington, founded in the late 1960s, these and other landless tribes petitioned the federal government for recognition. Since 1978, when the Federal Acknowledgment Program was established in the Bureau of Indian Affairs, only the Jamestown Klallam Tribe has been granted acknowledgment, in 1981 (table 1). The Samish were denied federal recognition in 1987 (cf. Hajda 1987a; Hajda and Barsh 1988; Roth 1988). In 1988, the petitions of six other landless tribes of western Washington were in the review process at the Bureau of Indian Affairs—the Snohomish Tribe, Snoqualmie Indian Tribe, Cowlitz Indian Tribe, Chinook Indian Tribe, Steilacoom Tribe, and Duwamish Indian Tribe (Barsh and Whittlesey 1988a; U.S. Bureau of Indian Affairs. Branch of Acknowledgment and Research 1987).

Whether landed or landless, recognized or unrecognized, throughout the 1970s and 1980s the tribes of western Washington experienced a resurgence of native culture. Traditional ceremonies and dances as well as arts and crafts were revived, while tribal culture centers and museums and native language and culture programs were established on many reservations. In 1988, the Jamestown Klallam, Quinault, and Lummi were among a group of nine American Indian tribes participating in a self-governance project that allowed them to assume full responsibility and control of programs previously administered and budgeted by the Bureau of Indian Affairs (U.S. Bureau of Indian Affairs 1988:3). The same year, one additional unrecognized group, the Snoqualmoo Tribe of Whidbey Island, submitted a petition for federal acknowledgment to the Bureau of Indian Affairs.

History of Western Oregon Since 1846

STEPHEN DOW BECKHAM

Federal Policies, 1846–1850

Policies of the Bureau of Indian Affairs shaped the course of Indian affairs in the Pacific Northwest and western Oregon in the mid-nineteenth century. By 1850 these policies included: reducing the extent of Indian Country; removal or relocation of Indians to reservations distant from settlement and routes of travel; "civilization" based on agriculture, the English language, Euro-American lifeways, and Christianity; prohibition of the use of alcohol; and peace between Indians and American settlers (Trennert 1975).

Although the Oregon Treaty of June 15, 1846, established American sovereignty between 42 and 49° north latitude, Congress was dilatory in extending federal services to the region. The Cayuse War, which erupted in 1847 on the Columbia Plateau, compelled the federal government to act. On August 14, 1848, Congress passed the Organic Act (9 U.S. Stat. 323) establishing Oregon Territory. This statute prescribed that the governor was to act as superintendent of Indian affairs and appropriated $10,000 to purchase presents for the Indians to secure "the peace and quietude of the country." The Organic Act contained a guarantee: "nothing in this act contained shall be construed to impair the rights of person or property now pertaining to the Indians in said Territory, so long as such rights shall remain unextinguished by treaty between the United States and such Indians" (9 U.S. Stat. 323: para.1). This act extended the Northwest Ordinance of 1787 (1 U.S. Stat. 51: note a) to the Pacific Northwest, which meant that the "utmost good faith" clause of the ordinance, affirming Indian land title, rights, liberty, and protection from undeclared war, was valid throughout the region (9 U.S. Stat. 323: para. 14).

In March 1849 Joseph Lane assumed duties in Oregon as governor and superintendent of Indian affairs. Lane mounted no formal treaty program, though in the summer of 1849 he advocated removal of all bands from the Willamette Valley, and the territorial legislature endorsed this removal (Coan 1921:52–53). Concerned with protecting travelers on the Oregon-California Trail, in June 1850 Lane negotiated a peace treaty with 150 Takelmas in the Rogue River valley, but the agreement was not ratified (J. Lane 1878:88–96).

In 1850 Congress authorized a treaty commission of three members to negotiate with the Kalapuyans for their removal east of the Cascades, created the post of superintendent of Indian affairs separate from the office of governor, and extended the Indian Trade and Intercourse Act of 1834 (4 U.S. Stat. 729) to Oregon Territory. This last provision meant not only that the Oregon Superintendency would attempt to suppress the liquor trade but also that the concept of Indian Country, meaning that until a ratified treaty altered relationships, Indian "law and custom" prevailed in all unceded lands, gained statutory authority throughout the territory.

Although the Organic Act had validated Indian land title, the Oregon Donation Act of 1850 (9 U.S. Stat. 496) provided for grants of up to 320 acres to "every white settler or occupant of the public lands, American half-breed Indians included, above the age of eighteen years, being a citizen of the United States, or having made a declaration according to law, of his intention to become a citizen." Altogether 7,437 claimants in Oregon obtained lands under this act or its amended version by its expiration in 1855 (D.O. Johansen 1957).

The filings on nearly 2,500,000 acres of Indian lands in western Oregon were of singular consequence. Those who came drove the Indians off their claims and away from their villages. Fencing their fields, White settlers attempted to suppress field burning, a practice in the western Oregon valleys whereby the Indians secured crops of tarweed seeds and insured an open forest understory suitable for picking berries. With firearms the settlers decimated the deer, and their livestock usurped vegetal foods. Where food abundance had once characterized the region, the Indians found starvation and widespread dislocation (Beckham 1971:117–126; Riddle 1920:43–46, 54–56; Culver in ARCIA 1854:500–505).

The Treaty Program, 1851–1855

The treaty initiatives of 1851 failed to secure any ratified agreements. The Willamette Valley Treaty Commission could not induce the Kalapuya bands to move east of the Cascades (U.S. Bureau of Indian Affairs 1838–1863, 4,8; Mackey 1974), and the commission was abolished. Territorial Gov. John Gaines negotiated a peace treaty with the Takelma but the Senate ignored it (Gaines 1851).

Anson Dart, the first full-time superintendent for Oregon Territory, launched a treaty program in August 1851 at Tansey Point on the south shore of the mouth of the Columbia. Dart's treaties not only provided for small reservations within the tribes' homelands but also reserved rights of fishing, hunting, freedom of passage, harvest of whales washed ashore, grazing livestock, and cutting timber for fuel and building purposes (U.S. Bureau of Indian Affairs 1838–1863, 8). Dart negotiated additional treaties at the mouth of Rogue River with four bands of Indians, offering 1½¢ per acre for 2,500,000 acres (Dart in ARCIA 1851:221–222). Although signed and forwarded to Washington, D.C., none of these treaties gained ratification (table 1). Samuel Thurston and Joseph Lane, territorial delegates to Congress, were instrumental in blocking Senate action (Spaid 1950:74–85; Coan 1921: 62–63).

Joel Palmer succeeded Dart as superintendent in 1853 and initiated yet another treaty program, negotiating with the Cow Creek Band of Umpqua and the Rogue River Indians in 1853 (table 2) (Kappler 1904–1941, 2:605). Palmer's treaties were primarily agreements of land cession. He made no provision for reserved rights, except for modestly sized reservations of marginal lands in southwestern Oregon. Palmer created three reservations within the homelands of the tribes making cessions: the Table Rock Reservation on the north margin of the Rogue River valley, the Cow Creek Reservation in the South Umpqua valley, and the Umpqua and Calapooia Reservation on Calapooya Creek in the Umpqua Valley. Although Palmer envisioned these tracts as permanent (Kappler 1904–1941, 2:656,659), the persistence of hostilities and aggressions of settlers and miners persuaded Palmer to remove all Indians from southwestern Oregon (Coan 1922:4–5).

Table 1. Unratified Treaties, Western Oregon, 1850–1855

Band or Tribe	Date
Gov. Joseph Lane	
Takelma and probably some Shasta	June 1850
Willamette Valley Treaty Commission	
Santiam band of Kalapuya	April 16, 1851
Tualatin band of Kalapuya	April 19, 1851
Yamhill band of Kalapuya	May 2, 1851
Luckiamute band of Kalapuya	May 2, 1851
Molala	May 6, 1851
Santiam band of Molala	May 7, 1851
Gov. John Gaines	
Takelma	July 14, 1851
Superintendent Anson Dart	
Clatsop	Aug. 5, 1851
Nehalem band of Tillamook	Aug. 6, 1851
Tillamook	Aug. 7, 1851
Nucquecluhwenuck (identity unknown)	Aug. 7, 1851
Cathlamet Chinook	Aug. 9, 1851
Clatskanie	Aug. 9, 1851
Curry and Coos County Indians—Athapaskans and some Miluk Coosans	Sept. 1851
Clackamas	Autumn 1851
Gen. Joseph Lane	
Rogue River Indians	Sept. 8, 1853
Superintendent Joel Palmer	
Tualatin Kalapuya	March 24, 1854
many coastal bands	Aug. 11, 17, 23, 30, Sept. 8, 1855

SOURCES: U.S. Bureau of Indian Affairs (1838–1863, 4, 5, 8); Kappler (1904–1941, 2:1049–1050).

HISTORY OF WESTERN OREGON SINCE 1846

The treaty program did little to curb problems. The entire first round of agreements made promises, reserved rights, and accomplished nothing. The Palmer treaties, which led to a number of ratified agreements, reserved no traditional rights and only limited tracts of land, but they did call for educational and health services. Palmer chose the season for negotiation; when the Indians were hungry, they were more likely to attend the treaty conferences and accede to his offers (Coan 1922:31). Evidence suggests that the treaties were negotiated in Chinook Jargon in hastily called sessions. It is likely that few of the Indian signatories grasped the scope of the treaties terminating their tenure in their homelands or the provisions in the agreements (J. Palmer 1853, 1856).

Warfare, 1851–1856

The discovery of gold on Jackson Creek in the Rogue River drainage in January 1852 and the spread of the rush for resources led to intermittent conflicts with Whites in the years 1853–1856. The gold rush drew an overwhelmingly male population who frequently formed companies of volunteers and in 1853–1854 massacred the Takelma, Shasta, Chetco, and Lower Coquille Indians (Beckham 1971). Although the U.S. Army established Fort Orford in 1851 and Fort Lane in 1853 in the mining district, troop strength was minimal. When Indian agents such as Frederick M. Smith of Port Orford protested about the murders of Indians, he was threatened with death by the volunteer soldiers and fled the region (Minor, Beckham, and Greenspan 1980:40).

The flood of mining debris took a heavy toll on the important Indian fisheries. The miners drove the Indians from the stream terraces where they had established their villages. Reduced to starvation the Takelma (including the Cow Creek people) and the Shasta sometimes broke into cabins or stopped travelers to steal food. Some frontiers-men raped the Indian women, enslaved the children as "pet" Indians, and murdered the men. Driven by hunger, anger, deception, and a sense of desperation, the Indians fought back (Beckham 1977:129–145).

The final Rogue River War erupted in October 1855, when a company of volunteers initiated hostilities by attacking peaceful Indians camped near the Table Rock Reservation. Fearful of more murders, the Takelmas fled the reservation and headed west into the canyons of the Rogue River. Over the next several months volunteer soldiers assailed these refugees. In June 1856 the U.S. Army defeated the various bands at the Big Bend of Rogue River. Several hundred Indians and perhaps 50 settlers and miners had perished. The policy to resolve these difficulties was simple: removal of all Indians to distant reservations (Beckham 1971:169–191).

Removals and Reservations, 1856–1945

Superintendent Joel Palmer proposed removal of the Indians from the Willamette Valley to "a home remote from the settlements" where "they must be guarded from the pestiferous influence of degraded white men, and restrained by proper laws from violence and wrong among themselves." Palmer believed the government should provide houses, agricultural tools and instruction, schools, and missionaries. "If still it fail, the government will have at least the satisfaction of knowing that an honest and determined endeavor was made to save and elevate a fallen race" (Palmer in ARCIA 1853:449).

The Siletz or Coast Reservation, which originally extended nearly 125 miles along the central Oregon coast, was established in 1855. The Grand Ronde Reservation, at the eastern base of the Coast Range, was established in 1857. As executive order reservations, both were vulnerable to reduction (Kappler 1904–1941, 1:891, 886).

The Bureau of Indian Affairs assigned the surviving

Table 2. Ratified Treaties, Western Oregon, 1853–1855

Group	Date of Treaty	Date of Ratification
"Rogue River Tribe," probably Takelma	Sept. 10, 1853	Apr. 12, 1854
Cow Creek Band of Umpqua (Takelma)	Sept. 19, 1853	Apr. 12, 1854
"Rogue River Tribe," Takelma and probably Applegate	Nov. 15, 1854	Mar. 3, 1855
Chasta,[a] Scoton,[b] Grave Creek band of Takelma	Nov. 18, 1854	Mar. 3, 1855
Upper Umpqua and Yoncalla Kalapuya	Nov. 29, 1854	Mar. 3, 1855
Confederated Bands of Kalapuya	Jan. 22, 1854	Mar. 3, 1855
Molala	Dec. 21, 1855	Mar. 8, 1859

SOURCE: Kappler (1904–1941, 2).
[a] Identity unknown; not either Shasta or Chasta Costa.
[b] Identity unknown.

Indians of western Oregon to these two reservations. The refugees from the hostilities in the Rogue and Umpqua valleys began removal in January 1856 to the Grand Ronde Reservation where they joined the surviving Kalapuyans and Molalas as well as some Chinookans. Technically the Tillamook were also under the Grand Ronde agent, but the Oregon Superintendency mounted no removal program for the Tillamook, Clatsop, or other Indians of northwestern Oregon. The Army removed the Indians of the Rogue River canyon and southern Oregon coast to the Siletz Reservation and colonized them about 30 miles up the Siletz River at Siletz Agency. The government held the Coos and Lower Umpqua at the mouth of the Umpqua River from 1856 to 1859 and then moved them to Yachats in the Alsea Subagency on the southern part of the Siletz Reservation (Beckham 1977: 143–145).

The removals were traumatic, commencing in January. Settlers confronted the refugee Indians with threats (Metcalfe in ARCIA 1855:251–253; Ambrose 1856). Over 1,000 refugees departed from Port Orford by steamer for transit to the mouth of the Columbia, ascent to the head of navigation, and a journey by foot via the Willamette Valley and the Coast Range to Siletz. Others were driven north under soldier escort along the coastal trail (Palmer in ARCIA 1857:212–220, 1857a:220–221). Between 1856 and 1859 bounty hunters tracked down, captured, or killed Indians hiding in the mountains of southwestern Oregon (Tichenor 1883). During the summer of 1856 the Army established Fort Umpqua, Fort Hoskins, Fort Yamhill, and the Siletz Blockhouse to surround the two reservations and maintained these stations until the Civil War (Bensell 1959:197–215).

Approximately 4,000 Indians in western Oregon were located on reservations by 1856. Conditions at Grand Ronde and Siletz were poor. The government had made no preparation for housing, medical facilities, or providing for subsistence. None of the streams at Siletz had a spring salmon run. Starvation and disease led to 205 deaths at Siletz in 1857–1858 (Metcalfe in ARCIA 1858:251–253). Population figures from the reservations confirm the consequences of dislocation and warfare in the skewed sex ratio (table 3).

The Bureau of Indian Affairs built day schools at Siletz and Grand Ronde, but the schools operated sporadically. "Though the children exhibit a capacity for learning," wrote the agent at Siletz in 1861, "it is impossible, while under the control of their parents, to get them to attend school. I have, therefore, abandoned it for the present" (Newcomb in ARCIA 1861:161). These problems gradually altered in the 1870s when the Roman Catholic agents at Grand Ronde and Methodist personnel at Siletz established boarding schools. In 1877 the Sisters of the Holy Names began teaching at Grand Ronde (Sinnott in ARCIA 1878:113). In 1880 the U.S. Army opened the

Lane Co. Histl. Mus., Eugene, Oreg.: I3A: L76-233.
Fig. 1. Game of shinny played between Indians of the Grand Ronde and Siletz reservations on Sept. 15, 1884. The event ran for four hours and when each team had won 15 innings, the teams divided the prize money of $50 (*Eugene Guard*, Sept. 20, 1884). Photograph by John A. Winter.

Training School for Indian Youth in Forest Grove. This institution, which became the Chemawa Indian School in 1885, is the oldest Bureau of Indian Affairs boarding school in continuous operation ("History of Western Washington Since 1846," fig. 5, this vol.) (Beckham 1977: 158–159).

Both Methodists and Roman Catholics mounted initial missionary efforts on the reservations in 1856–1857 (Miller in ARCIA 1858:361–368), and both secured control of the agencies under the Peace Policy. Adrian Joseph Croquet, a priest from Belgium, founded the parish of Saint Michael the Archangel at Grand Ronde in 1860 and served until 1898. Annually Croquet visited the Oregon coast and ministered among the Indians from Tillamook to the Siuslaw River (Munnick and Beckham 1987; Bosse 1977).

A number of western Oregon Indians embraced prophetic religious movements in the 1870s and the 1880s. While the Smohalla cult of the Plateau may have influenced these movements (Spier 1935:48), the 1870 Ghost Dance undoubtedly contributed elements to the Earth Lodge cult that emerged in 1871 on the Grand Ronde and Siletz reservations. Depot Charlie, Sixes George, and Coquille Thompson spread the movement's teachings and dances. Some Tillamook embraced the cult and referred to it as the South Wind Dance. The Coos, Lower Umpqua, and Siuslaw followed it enthusiastically and erected a large dance lodge in 1878 near Florence, Oregon. The Earth Lodge cult and its local variations attracted believers through 1880 when it went into decline (Beckham, Toepel, and Minor 1984:90–101).

The Indian Shaker religion first attracted followers on the Siletz Reservation in the 1920s through its ceremonies of healing and the fellowship of the faithful. Unlike at Grand Ronde where the Roman Catholic presence remained strong through the parish church, at Siletz probably a majority of the adults by the 1930s had become Shakers and helped erect a worship building. Ideological differences over the role of the Bible in the religion and the deaths of older members diminished the Shaker influence. By 1945 fewer than 10 members remained, and the community razed the abandoned church in 1976 (Sackett 1973:123–124; Beckham, Toepel, and Minor 1984: 102–106, 123–124).

White trespassers encroached on the reservations in the 1860s to harvest oysters in Yaquina Bay or as settlers in the 1870s on the Alsea and Salmon river estuaries. To the dismay and often vocal opposition of the Indians, the federal government steadily diminished their trust lands. An executive order of December 21, 1865, opened the Yaquina and Alsea estuaries to pioneer settlement (Kap-

pler 1904–1941, 1:891). In 1875 Congress opened for settlement another large section of the reservation (fig. 3) (18 U.S. Stat. 420, 446). In 1888, 1890, and 1894, Congress granted rights-of-way through the Siletz and Grand Ronde reservations for railroads (Kappler 1904–1941, 1:287,381,512). In 1894 (28 U.S. Stat. 286, 323) Congress ratified the Siletz allotment agreement of 1892, wherein the Indians ceded "all their claim, right, title, and interest in and to all unallotted lands" excepting five sections for $142,600 (Kappler 1904–1941, 1: 533–535). President Grover Cleveland opened all the ceded Siletz lands to settlement on July 25, 1895 (Kappler 1904–1941, 1:986–987). In 1904 Congress ratified the

Table 3. Western Oregon Reservation Population, 1856–1857

	Men	Women	Boys	Girls	Total
Siletz Reservation					
Shasta, Takelma, and Rogue River Athapaskans	118	202	109	125	554
Tututni	228	316	141	151	836
Chetco	61	86	40	49	236
Upper Coquille	82	104	59	68	313
Chasta Costa	32	43	19	14	108
Coos	65	87	44	38	234
Lower Umpqua	38	54	14	19	125
Siuslaw	26	42	6	11	85
Alsea (1854)	24	24	8	7	63
Yaquina (1854)	12	14	4	3	33
Total					2,587
Grand Ronde Reservation					
Chinookans					
Clackamas	18	33	10	17	78
Cathlamet					19
Clatsop					41
Tillamook					183
Clatskanie[a]	18	18	6	5	47
Kalapuyans					
Tualatin	33	30	10	8	81
Mary's River	15	18	4	3	40
Chemapo	6	9	1	3	19
Chelamela	5	6	1	2	14
Yamhill	11	12	2	2	27
Luckiamute	8	7	3	2	20
Mohawk River	8	7	1	4	19
Winefelly	7	10	3	5	23
Santiam	29	31	8	17	85
Ahantchuyuk	4	5	4	1	14
Yoncalla	8	13	4	2	27
Molala	35	51	28	21	135
Other small bands of uncertain tribal identification, at Oregon City and on the Umpqua and Rogue rivers	153	254	86	108	601
Total					1,473
Total					4,060

SOURCES: R.B. Metcalfe (1857), Drew (1856), J. Palmer (1854), ARCIA (1858:354–356), J.F. Miller (1857), T.H. Smith (1856).

a Including a group called Nepechuck.

left, Oreg. State U. Arch., Corvallis: P25:614; right, Oreg. Histl. Soc., Portland: 71752.

Fig. 2. Pan-Indian influences on Oreg. Indians. left, John Williams (b. 1865) a long-time resident of Siletz, where he held an allotment, wearing a Plains-style feather headdress and fringed buckskin jacket decorated with what appear to be dentalia. Census records identify him as a Kalapuya and at least one language he spoke was Kiksht Chinookan, but his father was Mexican and his mother Molala. He was a consultant to Du Bois (1938:15) and Boas (Hymes 1984:359–362) (Henry Zenk, personal communication 1987). Photographed about 1900 probably at a July 4 celebration. right, Siletz Indian Feather Dancers. Man seated on the far right with Plains-style feather headdress is John Poncee, Takelma, holding an obsidian knife. At an earlier time the Feather Dance was known as the Dream Dance and was performed in response to an actual dreaming. By this period the Feather Dance had become a secular event (Du Bois 1939:34–35). Photographed at Siletz Indian Fair, Oreg., Aug. 29–31, 1917 (cropped).

Grand Ronde allotment agreement of 1901, wherein the tribe ceded to the United States 25,791 acres, reserved 440 acres, and accepted $28,500 for the cession (Kappler 1904–1941, 3:105–107). In 1910 Congress authorized the platting and sale of town lots in Siletz, "reserving to actual business men and actual residents the rights to buy the land upon which their respective buildings stand" (36 U.S. Stat. 367). This law further prohibited the introduction for 25 years of "intoxicants into the Indian country" (Kappler 1904–1941, 3:454).

The allotment agreements of 1892 at Siletz and 1901 at Grand Ronde and the cessions of remaining tribal properties left later generations of Indians almost landless. Unless they inherited an interest in trust allotments held by older family members, they had no opportunity for securing allotments. At allotment in 1892 the Siletz Reservation contained 225,280 acres; two years later the tribal and allotted land had dropped to 46,000 acres. At Grand Ronde the tribal and allotted land amounted in 1904 to 33,148 acres. The Dawes Severalty Act of 1887 had rapidly accelerated the loss of land by western Oregon Indians (Beckham 1971:168–169); unscrupulous people easily acquired the land (Puter 1908:469–482).

The Siletz allotment agreement of 1892 offered public domain allotments to several hundred off-reservation Indians in western Oregon. The Coos, Lower Umpqua, and Siuslaw, driven from the Alsea Subagency when it was opened to settlement in 1875, had returned to southwestern Oregon. They and other refugee Indians who escaped the reservations came forward between 1892 and 1902 to secure public domain allotments, mostly in Lane, Coos, Curry, and Douglas counties (General Land Office 1892–1901).

Claims Efforts, 1898–1987

The Clatsop and Tillamook were the first western Oregon tribes to mount efforts to settle claims for taking of their lands without ratified treaty or adequate compensation from the United States. The Nehalem Tillamook were granted $10,500 in 1897 (30 U.S. Stat. 78). Led by their attorney Silas Smith, the son of Celiast Smith and grandson of the Clatsop chief Coboway, these tribes joined with the Chinook and Wakaikam and in 1898 obtained a jurisdictional act that permitted suit in the Court of Claims. Tribal members testified in 1902. In 1907

Fig. 3. Indian-White land transfers in western Oreg. Dates indicate when the treaties were signed, or when an executive order, an act of congress, or an order of the secretary of the interior transferred lands; the gradual dissolution of the Siletz and Grand Ronde reservations began after the passage of the Dawes Severalty Act of 1887. Historic forts and present-day reservations are sited. One Indian group within this area maintains federal recognition without a reservation—Confederated Tribes of Coos, Lower Umpqua, and Siuslaw Indians at Coos Bay.

the Court of Claims entered its findings and in 1912
Congress appropriated the judgments: $10,500 to the

Tillamook, $15,000 to the Clatsop, $1,500 to the Nuc-quee-clah-we-nuchs (identity unknown), and $7,000 to the Cathlamet (U.S. Congress. Senate 1912). The government made per capita distributions in 1914 (McChesney 1906; Beckham 1987:75–79).

In 1916 George B. Wasson, a graduate of Carlisle Indian School of Coos and Coquille descent, began a 30-year campaign for claims settlements in western Oregon. Wasson rallied both reservation and off-reservation tribes and pressed the Oregon congressional delegation to introduce bills permitting litigation in the Court of Claims. In 1938, the Court of Claims rejected an unratified treaty and oral testimony as evidence of aboriginal land ownership by the Confederated Coos, Lower Umpqua, and Siuslaw. The court observed that "none of plaintiff tribes has ever possessed any right, title, or interest in or to any designated area of land" except to allotments under the 1892 agreement at Siletz (87 C. Cls. 143).

Twenty-eight bands or groups from the Willamette, Umpqua, and Rogue river valleys, who had ceded lands to the United States in ratified treaties in the 1850s, sued after 1935 in the Court of Claims. In 1950 only the Molala tribe and the Umpqua Band and Calapooia Band of the Umpqua Valley received monetary judgments (U.S. Congress 1954:146–147).

Under the ethnographically erroneous name of *Alcea Band of Tillamooks* v. *United States* 32 bands of western Oregon Indians filed land claims. The Tillamook, Coquille, Tututni, and Chetco were enumerated in this case as "tribes" and gained awards in 1945. The Umpqua, Chinook, Clatsop, Nehalem Tillamook, Confederated Tribes of the Grand Ronde Community, and Siletz Confederated Tribes of Indians were denied awards (103 C. Cls. 494). Congress authorized payment of $2,641,856.73 in 1954 (68 U.S. Stat. 979).

Several western Oregon tribes filed complaints before the Indian Claims Commission between 1946 and 1951. The case of *Tillamook et al.* led to settlements in 1955 of $416,240.85 for approximately 192,000 acres ceded to the United States in 1892 in the Siletz allotment conference. The Commission awarded $72,162.50 to the Nehalem Band and $97,025 to the Tillamook Band for land. The cases of the Kalapuya et al. and the Coos Bay Tribe were both dismissed (Indian Claims Commission 1979; see also Zucker, Hummel, and Høgfoss 1983:116–126).

The Cow Creek Band of Umpqua Tribe of Indians of Douglas County, Oregon, in May 1984 received a settlement of $1,500,000 for lands taken under an 1853 treaty. Unlike all other western Oregon judgments, which were distributed per capita, the Cow Creeks placed their judgment in a permanent endowment, whose interest was to fund programs in education, housing, economic development, and benefits (Beckham 1986:113; Susan Crispen Shaffer, personal communication 1988).

Civil and Economic Status, 1854–1951

In 1854 the territorial legislature prohibited the sale of firearms or ammunition to Indians or half-Indians, ruled that Indians and half-Indians were incompetent to testify against a White person, and prohibited the sale of alcohol to Indians. In 1866, the state legislature prohibited intermarriage between Whites and Indians or half-Indians. Both the ban on alcohol sales and intermarriage remained Oregon laws until May 1951 (Oregon Legislature 1854, 1866, 1951).

Off-reservation Indians such as the Clatsop, Tillamook, Coos, Lower Umpqua, Siuslaw, Yoncalla, Upper Umpqua, and Cow Creek Takelmas endured many problems. In the 1860s and 1870s they were under pressure to remove to the reservations at Siletz and Grand Ronde. Remaining in or returning to their traditional homelands, they were landless and vulnerable to dispossession; they could not obtain title unless they learned of and used the special "trust" provisions of the revisions in 1875 of the Homestead Act. Many eked out an existence as domestics, hop pickers, loggers, and woodchoppers. Some ran traplines, processed hides, and marketed tanned leather goods. After the Siletz allotment agreement of 1892, a number of these Indians obtained public domain allotments (fig. 4). The Coos, Lower Umpqua, and Siuslaw, for example, secured 72 allotments in 1892 and more in succeeding years. In 1910, these public-domain Indians gained modest services from the Bureau of Indian Affairs with the establishment of the Roseburg Superintendency, which until 1918 maintained jurisdiction over the off-reservation allottees in southwestern Oregon. Nominal oversight then passed to the Greenville School at Fresno, California; in 1925, to the clerk of the Chemawa Indian School; and after 1934, to the Grand Ronde–Siletz Agency (Beckham 1984:27–29, 1986:184–185).

Both reservation and public domain allotments served as a vehicle for gaining citizenship for western Oregon Indians in the early twentieth century. The fee patenting of allotments after the Burke Act of 1906, while bringing citizenship, often led to a reversion to landless conditions. The obligations of paying taxes or the allurement of selling the timbered lands to loggers or sawmill owners led over and over again to these Indians' losing their properties (General Land Office 1892–1901; U.S. Bureau of Indian Affairs 1919).

After passage of the Indian Reorganization Act of 1934 (48 U.S. Stat. 984), delegations from the tribes assembled at Chemawa Indian School in March to hear the explanations of the law. The Confederated Tribes of Siletz rejected incorporation under the act; the Confederated Tribes of Coos, Lower Umpqua, and Siuslaw declined to vote on it. Indians at Grand Ronde accepted the legislation and on May 13, 1936, formed a tribal corporation—the Grand Ronde Indian Community. The Grand Rondes were able to secure loans to purchase some lands and to construct a community building. The Bureau of Indian Affairs secured lands for the Confederated Tribes of Coos, Lower Umpqua, and Siuslaw, and erected a tribal hall at Empire, Oregon (Beckham 1977:182–185, 1984).

left, Oreg. Histl. Soc., Portland: 47127; right, U. of Oreg. Lib., Special Coll., Eugene: M-4103.
Fig. 4. Siletz Reservation Indians. left, Jane Simpson (b. about 1838), Coquille; Mary Hill; John Bradford, Rogue River; and Mary Bradford at a camp where they sold baskets. Mary Bradford is wearing a Northern California–type basketry hat and is making a twined basket. She wears shell necklaces and has tattoo marks on her chin. Simpson holds a wallet-style carrying basket characteristic of the Tillamook. The storage rack behind them holds a gathering basket and mats. Tribal identities of Mary Bradford and Mary Hill are unknown, a circumstance that was common after groups were combined on reservations where government records became confused. Photographed at Newport, Oreg., 1905. right, Family of Abram Logan, Tututni, and Louisa Logan, Chetco. The twins, John and Jack, in traditional basketry cradles, were born in 1899. The family resided on allotments on the Salmon River in northern Lincoln County. Photograph by Major Lee Moorhouse, Siletz Reservation, Oreg., 1900.

Fig. 5. Bill Brainard (Coos) and Esther Waters Stutzman (Coos and Siletz) at an annual salmon bake of the Confederated Tribes of Coos, Lower Umpqua, and Siuslaw. Brainard served as chairman of the Confederated Tribes from about 1971 to 1985, through termination to federal recognition. He was also an original member of the Oregon Commission on Indian Services. Stutzman was active in Indian education programs and served on the tribal council of the Confederated Tribes. Photograph by Stephen Dow Beckham, near Coos Bay, Oreg., Aug. 1978.

Termination and Restoration

In 1951 the BIA targeted western Oregon Indians for termination. Gov. Douglas McKay endorsed the program as the means to raise the social and economic status of Oregon Indians. The Termination Act (68 U.S. Stat. 724) of 1954 called for fee patenting of allotments, sale or transfer of tribal lands to special organizations, a transition program of education and training, revocation of the tribal charter of the Confederated Tribes of the Grand Ronde Community, and the end of all federal relationships with 61 tribes and bands. The Confederated Tribes of Siletz and the Business Committee of the Confederated Tribes of the Grand Ronde Community endorsed termination. Several other Indian groups—the Alsea, Tillamook bands, Coquille Tribe, and the Chetco Tribe—passed resolutions in 1950–1951 regarding their wishes for per capita distributions of their pending claims judgments.

The opposition of the Confederated Tribes of Coos, Lower Umpqua, and Siuslaw was omitted from the record (U.S. Congress 1954:153, 159–167).

In 1976 the American Indian Policy Review Commission's Task Force on Terminated and Nonfederally Recognized Tribes heard testimony in Salem, Oregon, on the impact of termination. The western Oregon Indians described their inadequate housing, unemployment and underemployment, and poor health (American Indian Policy Review Commission 1976).

In the 1970s each tribe had to make its own case for restoration. Barred because of termination from using the Federal Acknowledgment Program, the western Oregon tribes each had to convince congressmen to sponsor legislation and to present a record of continued tribal existence. Gradually the tribes mounted the effort and regained a federal relationship (Beckham 1977:191–203).

The Confederated Tribes of Siletz Indians secured restoration in 1977 (91 U.S. Stat. 1415) and obtained a reservation of 3,630 acres in 1980 (94 U.S. Stat. 1072). The Cow Creek Band of Umpqua Tribe secured "recognition" in 1982 (96 U.S. Stat. 1960) and in 1984 purchased 29 acres at Canyonville, Oregon, a tract taken into trust as a reservation in 1986. The Confederated Tribes of Coos, Lower Umpqua, and Siuslaw Indians were restored in 1984 (98 U.S. Stat. 2250) and retained their 6.1 acres at Coos Bay, Oregon, a property they refused to dispose of during termination. Congress passed the Grand Ronde Restoration Act (97 U.S. Stat. 1064) in 1983 and in 1988 created a 9,811-acre reservation for the tribe (102 U.S. Stat. 1594).

Working through the Oregon Commission on Indian Services, participating in the Affiliated Tribes of Northwest Indians, sending delegates to the National Congress of American Indians and responding to the cultural resource laws impinging on the federal land-managing agencies in Oregon were some ways Indians expressed their common concerns. In the 1980s Oregon tribes launched a number of economic development initiatives, participated in housing improvement programs, and secured Indian Health Service benefits for their members.

Eyak

FREDERICA DE LAGUNA

The Eyak ('ē,yak) speak a language that is related to the Athapaskan family as a coordinate branch of a larger grouping called Eyak-Athapaskan.* This grouping may be remotely related to Tlingit.

Territory

In the eighteenth century the Eyak were living on the 300-mile long shore of the Gulf of Alaska between the Tlingit-Athapaskan people of Dry Bay and the Chugach Eskimo of Prince William Sound. Their original homeland extended from Italio River, east of Yakutat, westward to Cape Suckling and probably included the mainland shores of Controller Bay, although the Chugach held the islands (fig. 1). Kayak Island in 1741 was the hunting territory of a Chugach Eskimo band, the čiɬqaɣmiut (Tyitlqarmiut in Birket-Smith 1953:20), named after "Chilkat" village on Bering River at the head of the bay, but they may never have occupied it. An Eyak clan obtained their beaver crest in the vicinity, suggesting early Eyak occupation of the mainland despite Chugach claims, and the name Chilkat itself is of Tlingit origin.

By the late eighteenth century the Yakutat area Eyak were dominated by the expanding Tlingit. In the early nineteenth century Tlingitized Eyak from east of Cape Suckling drove the Chugach from Controller Bay, while more purely Eyak people pushed on to the Copper River delta (fig. 2) and to Cordova, just inside Prince William Sound. By the late nineteenth century the only relatively pure Eyak were those living in this last area, where they

*The phonemes of Eyak are: (plain voiceless stops and affricates) d, λ, ʒ, ž, g, g^w, ġ, ʔ; (aspirated stops and affricates) t, λ̣, c, č, k, q; (glottalized) t̓, λ̓, c̓, č̓, k̓, q̓; (fricatives) ɬ, s, š, x, x^w, x̣, h; (nasals) m, n; (resonants) w, l, y; (short plain vowels) i, e, a, u; (long plain vowels); i·, e·, a·, u·; (short nasalized vowels) į, ą, ų; (long nasalized vowels) į·, ą·, ų·. All short vowels occur before h and before a ʔ that is in the same syllable (not intervocalic); in other positions only i, a, and u are found and a is [ə]. Information on Eyak phonology is from Krauss (1963–1970a:8, 1982:23–24); the transcription of Eyak words into this orthography has been provided or checked by Michael E. Krauss (personal communications and communications to editors 1974, 1984, 1986). The short vowels are written as in Krauss (1982), which writes a for [ə] whether this is the reduced form of a (in prefixes) or the reduced form of e, u, and i (in stems); another solution to this problem of phonemic overlap would recognize a phoneme /ə/ and write the reduced vowels as /ə/ in stems and as /ə/ and /i/ in prefixes.

had a village named Eyak. Evidence for these movements is provided by historical records, traditions of the Tlingit proper, the Yakutat Tlingit, and surviving Eyak of Cordova (Swanton 1909:64–69, 154–165, 326–368; Birket-Smith and De Laguna 1938; De Laguna 1972, 1:210), and by place-names. Many place-names from Cordova to Cape Suckling are Chugach in origin; those from Cape Suckling to Yakutat and farther east are often Eyak (or Tlingit translations).

The Eyak have evidently lived on the Malaspina-Yakutat Forelands for a long time and, prior to Tlingit expansion, may have lived even farther south. Their culture, minus Eskimo borrowings and recent acquisitions, suggests what once may have been characteristic of present Northern Tlingit territory (Birket-Smith and De Laguna 1938; De Laguna et al. 1964).

The Eyak formed four regional groups, none a "tribe" in any political sense. These groups were, first, the Eyak (proper), since 1800–1825 in the Cordova–Copper River area (former Chugach territory). Second were the Eyak on the mainland of Controller Bay, who were becoming Tlingitized by 1850; they were sometimes called Chilkats from their village at the head of the bay. Third were the Eyak of the Gulf of Alaska coast between Capes Suckling and Yakataga, who were also being Tlingitized by 1850 and were sometimes called Yakatags from a village near Cape Yakataga. Emmons (1903) designated them as Guth-le-uk-qwan or Qwolth-yet-kwan from their main village on Kaliakh River and included with them the Tlingitized Eyak of Controller Bay. The fourth group lived around Yakutat Bay and are now completely Tlingitized.

Within this whole area 47 sites have been identified as having been at one time occupied by the Eyak (De Laguna 1972:58–106). Archeological investigations have been made in Controller Bay by Ketz and Johnson (1985) and in Yakutat Bay by De Laguna et al. (1964).

Environment

Eyak groups living on the morainic shore, 15 miles wide at its maximum, between the open Gulf of Alaska and the mountains of the Saint Elias, Robinson, and Chugach ranges (10,000 to 18,000 feet high) tended to be isolated

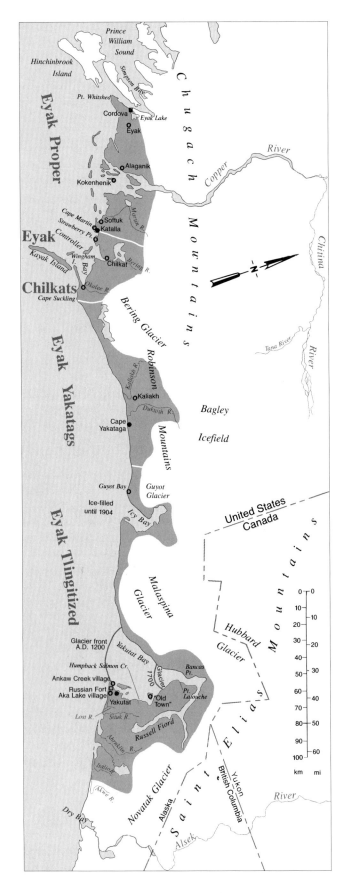

both from each other and from their nearest neighbors. Canoe travel was dangerous except in the shelter of offshore bars; safe landing places could be found only inside the mouths of rivers or behind the islands of Yakutat and Controller bays. Sudden squalls, strong winds, fog, and rain, with heavy winter snows demanded human adaptation to damp and cold, but not to severe freezing.

Yet the surf brought to the outer beaches the precious flotsam of the Pacific: bamboo, spars with drift iron, and stranded whales and sea lions (which the Eyak used but dared not hunt). Advances and retreats of the great piedmont glaciers are said to have overwhelmed ancient villages or opened new bays; where the ice reached tidewater were ideal breeding grounds for seals. The many lakes and lagoons attracted the enormous flocks of the Pacific flyway; berries grew in profusion on the open gravel and sand; the tidal flats provided mollusks and seaweeds.

The only large rivers cutting through the mountain barrier are the Alsek, emptying into Dry Bay east of Eyak country, and the Copper River near its western boundary. The Alsek was used by Athapaskans and Tlingits traveling to and from the interior, and the Copper River was used by Ahtnas bringing native copper and fur to trade. An easier overland route from the Copper River valley across the Bagley Icefields to Eyak settlements on the Duktoth River was taken by Ahtna immigrants and traders, but these routes were seldom if ever attempted by the Eyak.

Culture

Annual Cycle

Beginning in February, eulachon were caught in traps under the ice; later, with dip net or multibarbed spears from lighted canoes. Seals were harpooned on the ice. Edible roots, wild celery, sweet inner bark of the hemlock were gathered, and probably spruce roots for baskets.

In spring and summer, herring were caught and dried, and herring spawn collected. Trout, whitefish, and cod were taken with hook and line. Bird eggs were collected and seaweed picked and dried for winter. During the salmon runs, from early May to the last stragglers in November, chinooks, sockeyes, cohoes, and pinks were taken with traps, harpoons (fig. 3), two-pronged fish spears, or dip nets from river bank or canoe. Most were split and smoked; some were buried to rot.

Summer berries were picked and dried into cakes or preserved in oil. Sea otter were shot with harpoon arrows from encircling canoes. Molting geese and ducks were clubbed. Bears and mountain goats were hunted with dogs and killed with spears and arrows.

In the fall, Kamchatka lily roots and late berries were gathered. Clams, dried on strings, were put in boxes of oil.

Fig. 1. Territory and settlements of the Eyak in the 19th century.

Fig. 2. Copper River delta, covered by spruce, cottonwood, and willow. Mt. Eyak is in the distance. The house, used as a trading post 1898–1900, was built near Alaganik village, abandoned in 1892–1893 following an epidemic (Birket-Smith and De Laguna 1938:21, 360–361) Photograph by Frederica De Laguna near present Alaganik, Alaska, 1930.

Furbearers were trapped in fall and winter, with deadfall and snare; beaver could be taken only in fall and spring, not when protected by thick winter ice. Late fall, when larders were full, was potlatch time.

The poor snowshoes undoubtedly limited winter hunting, though young men attacked hibernating bears, fished for halibut, and snared ptarmigan and grouse. Most people remained home from December to early February, telling stories, making clothing and baskets, or doing other indoor chores.

Structures

The dwelling was a rectangular house of vertical planks, with a gable roof. A movable windscreen was hinged on the single ridgepole that crossed the smokehole. Sleeping rooms across the back and sides were roofed and floored with planks, entered by sliding doors, and illuminated by shell or cobblestone lamps. Bedding consisted of grass mats, pelts, twined goat wool blankets, and a sloping plank as the family pillow. Some Controller Bay houses in

the nineteenth century had shedlike additions. There were also houses for single families, smokehouses for fish and meat in the villages and camps, and boxlike caches on tall posts.

Each village had a fort or palisaded enclosure around some or all of the houses. Every important village also had a potlatch house for each moiety, with carved post (of Eagle or Raven moiety) in front. High benches around the walls served for sitting and sleeping; below were lockers with crest designs on the doors. These houses were equivalent to the Tlingit lineage or chiefs' houses, and like those were named; for example, Raven House, Goose House, and Bark House of the Raven moiety; Eagle House, (Eagle?) Skeleton House, Bed (Platform?) House, Beaver House, Beaver Dam House, Wolf House, Wolf Den House, and Wolf Bath House of the Eagle moiety. One built at Katalla about 1870 had two posts inside, carved with the Eagle, Beaver, and Beaver Dam crests (Barbeau 1950, 2:fig.376 top; Keithan 1963:57).

Graveyards, as well as individual graves or grave houses, were surrounded by fences and also had crest memorials.

Transportation

The Eyak had a variety of wooden and skin boats. These included: a small cleft-prow dugout (fig. 4) for open water hunting, a small heavy-prowed canoe with a ram for sealing in the icy waters of Yakutat and Icy bays, a larger Tlingit-type dugout for 10–16 persons, sometimes with a European mast and sail, a larger war canoe with Raven or Eagle carved on the prow, slender dugouts for racing, Eskimo kayaks and two-hole bidarkas for sea otter hunting, and large canoes like umiaks of goat or sealskin.

Snowshoes webbed only under the feet were aboriginal from Cordova to Yakutat (fig. 6). Sleds were hand-drawn, for dogs were used only for hunting.

Clothing and Adornment

Men wore their hair tied in a bunch, women in a braid,

Fig. 3. Fish harpoon with detachable barbed iron head and cotton cord line. The iron head is 14cm long; the shaft, 356cm long and 3cm in diameter at the middle. The slotted end of the shaft is wrapped with cotton cord to prevent splitting, as the wedge-shaped tang of the barbed head would ram back and twist into the wood at every successive thrust. Abercrombie (1900:397) reported that most of the salmon supply was taken with this implement. Collected by Frederica De Laguna, 1933.

Fig. 4. Yakutat-type canoe, partly finished. Made by Gus Nelson, with an adz, it was thought to be the more traditional shape (Birket-Smith and De Laguna 1938:45). The man beside it is the canoe maker's brother, Galushia Nelson, one of Frederica De Laguna's major informants. Photograph by De Laguna, Old Town, Cordova, Alaska, 1933.

while the shaman's hung long and loose. Both sexes painted the face and wore earrings, nose ornaments, finger rings, and bracelets of native copper. Women, who tattooed their wrists, did not wear labrets except under Tlingit influence at Yakutat. No labrets were found in prehistoric sites.

The Eyak dressed like the Eskimo with trousers, boots, mittens, and a summer shirt with fur inside, over which was worn a hooded shirt in winter. For rain a hooded gutskin parka was donned. In summer men went barefoot and practically naked, for only a breechclout was noted in 1884 (Birket-Smith and De Laguna 1938:70). An apron was worn to war. Men and women wore robes of small furs (preferably ground squirrel) or of twined goat wool. It was taboo for women to dress in fresh sealskins or to sew together land and sea mammal skins in one garment.

U. of Pa., U. Mus., Philadelphia: 33-29-2.

Fig. 5. Broken canoe paddle of characteristic Eyak form, with a crutch handle and an elongate, pointed blade. The handle has been reshaped as an ax handle. According to Birket-Smith and De Laguna (1938:50) it was common for paddles to wear through at the handle from friction with the gunwale of the canoe. Collected by Frederica De Laguna, 1933. Length, 175 cm.

left, Nationalmuseet, Copenhagen: H-2966; right, U. of Pa., U. Mus., Philadelphia: 33-29-3.
Fig. 6. Showshoes of the traditional type, with a 2-piece frame made from spruce; a pointed heel; a rounded, spliced, upturned toe; 2 or 3 crossbars; and webbing of seal thong (Birket-Smith and De Laguna 1938:56, 384). Photograph by Frederica De Laguna, Cordova, Alaska, 1933.

Technology

Tools, utensils, and weapons were like those of the Northern Tlingit or Chugach Eskimo except for the greater use of native copper for knives, ulu blades, scrapers, pins, harpoon heads for arrows, or sharp arrowheads. Eyak boxes, though decorated in Northern Northwest Coast style, were made of four separate pieces for the sides, morticed into the bottom. Abercrombie (1900) reported pipes with crude pottery bowls, the only mention of pottery. Bows were sinew-backed except the automatic bow set in a bear trail. Blunt arrows were used only at Yakutat. Fine spruce root baskets were decorated with false embroidery.

Social and Political Organization

Three classes were distinguished: chiefs and their families, commoners, and slaves. There was no tribal or village government; the moiety (or clan) chief in any village was leader only of his own people, although one chief was likely to be preeminent. Chiefs owned slaves, led war and hunting expeditions, and dressed themselves and their close kin in dentalia and fine clothing. Succession went to a younger brother or maternal nephew. Slaves (war captives and their children) might be killed at the funeral of a chief or his relative.

The Eyak were divided into exogamous matrilineal moieties, Raven (or "Crow") (*či·lehyu·*) and Eagle (*ġu·ǯgalaġyu·*), equated with Tlingit Raven and Wolf-Eagle and with Ahtna Crow and Sea Gull moieties. Birket-Smith and De Laguna (1938:447) believed that the Eyak lacked true clans and that even their moieties were recent, but Yakutat informants named their clans, and De Laguna (1975) has argued that matrilineal clans and moieties were ancient and widespread in northwestern North America. Krauss (1974) doubts their importance among the Eyak and points out that the moiety word for 'eagle' is of recent Chugach Eskimo derivation.

Eyak clans were semi-localized, while local groups tended to be identified as clans. Villages might be said to "belong" to a certain clan, probably because its chief was the most prominent or his clansmen most numerous, although both moieties were represented in each settlement. While Cordova Eyak denied that hunting areas were controlled by clans, this was the case from Controller Bay southward (Goldschmidt and Haas 1946; De Laguna 1972), although any relative of the owners might utilize their resources. The clans were the political and legal units.

According to Yakutat tradition, much Tlingit influence, probably including potlatch ceremonial and crests, was spread westward by *xatga·wé·t*, a wealthy Tlingit chief and shaman of the *te·qʷe·dí* (a Wolf clan), who was born near Dry Bay in the eighteenth century. He is said to have "organized" for trade the backward Eyak speakers of Yakutat, among whom he settled, but he also traveled all over, taking Eyak wives from places as far west as Cordova, bestowing Tlingit clan names on his wives' kinsmen, and introducing Tlingit ceremonial gift exchange (a familiar ploy for acquiring wealth from unsophisticated brothers-in-law). Stories about *xatga·wé·t* belong among the many traditions documenting the northwestward movement of Tlingit into Dry Bay Athapaskan and Eyak territories, through trade, inter-marriage, purchase of lands, or conquest (Swanton 1909: 154–165, 326–346; De Laguna 1972:242–247).

Eyak clans are known chiefly by their Tlingit names (given in the following list unless otherwise indicated). Clans of the Raven moiety were: 1. *ġa·naxte·dí*, 2. *qu·sḱe·dí* (Eyak *qu·sḱe·d*), 3. *łukʷa·xʔádi*, 4. *qahλayahd-daìa·x-dalahġayu·* 'bark house people' (Eyak name), 5. *kʷá·šḱ-qʷá·n* 'pink salmon people', 6. *hiṅy·dí*, 7. *staxʔadí* or *sdaxedi*. Clans of the Eagle moiety were: 8. *ǯi·šqʷe·dí* (Eyak *ǯi·šqe·t-yu·*), 9. *ġu·ǯihyu·* 'wolf people' (Eyak name), 10. *ġałyax-ka·gʷanta·n*, 11. *ła·xa·yík-te·qʷe·dí*, 12. *łux̌ʷe·dí* 'muddy water people', 13. *ẏaṅy·dí*.

Clans 1, 2, and 3 were in the Cordova-Copper River area, while 4 and 9 were "adopted Tlingit" who moved there from Controller Bay. Clan 8 was at Controller Bay, while 9, 10, and 11 were at both Controller Bay and the coast to the east. Clans 5, 6, 7, 11, 12, and 13 were in the Yakutat area, 7 and 13 at Arhnklin River, and 12 at Situk River.

Of clans 3, 6, 7, and 13, nothing more is known. Clans 1 and 5 are said to be branches of an Ahtna Raven clan who emigrated to the coast across the icefields. Those going west were named *ġa·naxte·dí* for the famous Chilkat Tlingit clan by *xatga·wé·t*, who also named clan 2; those who went to Yakutat acquired their name by purchasing Humpback Salmon Creek. Clan 8, considered a branch of 10, is clearly equivalent to the Red Paint People of the Sea Gull moiety of the Ahtna, Upper Tanana, and Tanaina. Clans 11 and 12 were considered eastern branches of 10. Other clans at Yakutat are either Tlingit or of mixed Tlingit-Athapaskan origin.

Ambilateral cross-cousin marriage was preferred, with bride-service, and avunculocal residence. There was polygyny, the sororate, junior levirate (with access to the elder brother's wife during his lifetime), wife exchange, and even wife hospitality. There was avoidance between mother- and son-in-law; father- and daughter-in-law (?), grown brother and sister; but free joking between brother- and sister-in-law.

Killing or even accidental injury to someone in the opposite moiety or in another house (lineage or clan) necessitated payment of damages; grievances were aired in insulting songs.

Life Cycle

Fresh meat or fish were taboo to menstruants or pregnant women, for fear of offending the animals. All men left the house during childbirth; after 10 days of seclusion and taboos, the new parents purified themselves.

A girl's puberty seclusion lasted several months, involving special dishes, sucking tube, and bone scratcher. A boy's first kill was presented with gifts to members of the opposite moiety.

A dead body was laid out in the house for four days, watched by members of the opposite moiety, who tried to cheer the bereaved, then removed the corpse through a hole in the wall to be cremated or interred, according to the relatives' wishes. Slaves, witches, or evil taboo-breakers were always burned. Most of the deceased's property was burned or buried with him; some was saved to be burned or given away at his death potlatch. At this ceremony, the chief of the deceased's moiety acted as host to members of the opposite group, presenting food and gifts in order of rank, with special payments to the undertakers. Guests were addressed by their "potlatch names" (names of the dead in the hosts' moiety who were not yet reincarnated), but they accepted food and gifts on behalf of their own dead. Thus, all the deceased shared what the living enjoyed. Potlatches were also held for building a new "potlatch house," or chief's house.

Religion

All things, animate and inanimate, were believed to have spirit owners, or souls in anthropomorphic form. The human soul left the body temporarily in dreams, trances, or insanity. After death, it was supposed to enter the womb of a woman in the deceased's maternal line to be reincarnated, receiving again the same name and supposedly exhibiting the same personality and appearance.

Hunters cut the eyeballs of game, so that the animals could not see them, and put the heads, entrails, etc., in appropriate places to insure the animals' reincarnation. Bears were treated with respect, and there was a simple first-fish ceremony. Women were tabooed from touching or stepping over a man's weapons. A wife should remain quiet while her husband was hunting or chopping wood.

Cold water baths, use of a rubbing amulet (an incised pebble), sexual abstinence, fasting, bathing, or purging with devil's club infusion could bring good luck in a chancy undertaking or remove the contamination of childbirth or death.

Shamans (fig. 8) could be of either sex. The power was usually inherited though not manifested until after puberty when the spirit helpers appeared in dreams. The novice fasted, observed sexual continence, bathed in cold water, purged with devil's club infusion, and went alone into the woods, where spirits in animal or human form gave him power and taught him songs. Before practicing, the shaman observed the same regimen, put on bone and ivory necklaces, an apron with rattling fringe, a belt, and the special mask or face paint representing the spirit he invoked. Cures were effected by singing, laying on hands, and sucking out disease. Shamans could also prophesy, find lost persons or property, confer good or bad luck, walk on water, handle hot rocks or fire, free themselves from bonds, perform ventriloquist tricks, or make an image move (Birket-Smith and De Laguna 1938: 208–213). (Dolls were, therefore, taboo to girls.)

Witches of both sexes obtained evil power from dead dogs or human bones. They could fly, change shape, and bring misfortune or death. Shamans usually blamed sickness on witches, and those denounced might be fined or suffer death.

Prayers were addressed to the Sun. There was also belief in the Thunderbird, Property-Woman, monster animals, dwarfs, Tree People (giants that steal humans), man-eating Wolf-People, and Land Otter Men that transformed the drowned or lost into creatures like themselves. Northern Lights foretold death. Generosity to the poor or to starving animals was rewarded. Raven cycle myths are said to have been sung; other myths and tales resemble those of the Chugach Eskimo and Tlingit, some

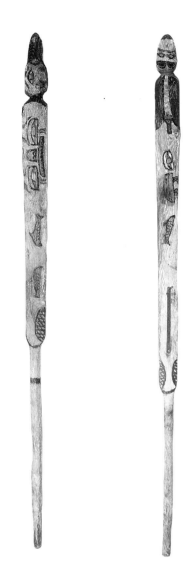

left, Nationalmuseet, Copenhagen: H-2966; right, U. of Pa., U. Mus., Philadelphia: 33-29-3.
Fig. 7. Ceremonial paddles used in potlatches like the dance paddles of the Tlingit, carried by song leaders to direct the singing and motions of their groups. Like Tlingit heirlooms, they could also be thrust between quarreling groups by a peacemaker to end disputes. They are painted with commercial oil-based house paint, in black, red, and white. That on the left belonged to the Raven moiety and was carved at the end to represent the raven. On the sides were paintings probably representing an animal's face, two jumping salmon and a beaver lodge. The other paddle has a bear's head at the end and is painted with figures representing bugs with 6 legs, an anthropomorphic face, a jumping salmon, and beaver lodges. The owner said that the Raven paddle was carried into the potlatch house by the leader of the Raven guests to announce the coming of his group. The Bear paddle followed, and showed that the Ravens were glad to come to the potlatch. Collected in 1933 by Frederica De Laguna; length of left 166 cm, other to same scale.

explaining the origin of crests.

History

In 1783 Nagaiev (Zaikov 1979:1–6) first learned from the Chugach Eskimo of the Eyak living "east of Kayak Island," but the Russians did not encounter any until

Fig. 8. Old Man Dude at his house on Simpson Bay, Alaska. He was a powerful shaman with a reputation among not only the Eyak but also the Chugach Eskimo (Birket-Smith and De Laguna 1938:10, 219–223). Photograph by Frederica De Laguna, 1933.

Fig. 9. Anna Nelson Harry mending a commercial gill net. She was an informant who gave valuable data on kinship terms and tales (Birket-Smith and De Laguna 1938:9–10), and on language (Krauss 1982: 17–18). Photograph by Martha Nelson, Yakutat, Alaska, about 1975.

1792, when Eyak from Cape Suckling and Tlingitized Yakutat Eyak attacked a party under Aleksandr Baranov in Prince William Sound (Baranov 1979:27–37). In 1794 Purtov and Kulikalov (1979:46–52) found no trace of habitation on the lower Copper River but discovered an Eyak village of 50 to 60 persons, at or near Kaliakh River, from which they took the chief and seven others as hostages, including two Yakutat men. In 1796 Baranov himself supervised the establishment of a fort and agricultural colony at Yakutat, securing hostages from the Yakutat (Tlingit?) chief and from the Eyak-speakers of the vicinity. In the late eighteenth century, the Yakutat people were still part Eyak, although the leading families were Tlingit or had adopted their speech and ways (Izmailov and Bocharov 1981; Beresford 1789; Colnett 1788; Malaspina 1885).

Native resentment of Russian tyranny and of poaching by their Aleut and Pacific Eskimo hunters led in 1799 to a massacre of a hunting party returning from Sitka by the Eyak at Cape Suckling; in reprisal an Eyak from Controller Bay was tortured to death by the Russians. The Yakutat people helped to plan the destruction of the Russian fort at Sitka in 1802 (rebuilt in 1804). In August 1805, the Russian post and colony at Yakutat were wiped out, the attack led by an Eyak of the ła·xa·yík-te·qʷe·dí clan; in commemoration the te·qʷe·dí Bear crest was carved on a nearby rock. The Russians never attempted to reestablish a post at Yakutat.

In the early nineteenth century, Tlingits from Dry Bay and southeastern Alaska, in part attracted by loot from the Russian post, completed their conquest of the Yakutat area, absorbing or enslaving the last Eyak people there. Smallpox in 1837–1838 wiped out about half the communities on the Gulf Coast.

From 1806 until about 1825, there were joint Eyak–Yakutat Tlingit attacks on the Chugach Eskimo and Chugach raids on the Eyak and Yakutat. Finally, the Chugach had to surrender Controller Bay, and the Eyak began to settle on the Copper River delta and the edge of Prince William Sound. Some Eyak were later involved in unsuccessful Russian attempts to explore the Copper River, apparently killing their masters. H.T. Allen (1887) used Eyak helpers on his 1885 expedition but could not induce them to venture into Ahtna territory beyond the first village.

Yakutat remained relatively isolated until visited by missionaries, prospectors, traders, and alpinists in the 1880s and 1890s. By 1900, practically all the natives from Dry Bay to Cape Suckling were concentrated at Yakutat, which was becoming a typical Tlingit cannery town, enjoying brief prosperity between 1910 and 1920.

In the Cordova–Controller Bay area the first cannery was built in 1889, but it offered little employment to the Eyak. After 1900 the Eyak found some work in the canneries. The discovery of oil near Katalla and the building of the Copper River and Northwestern Railroad, 1907–1910, forcing the natives from their homes, and the depletion of herring and salmon along the whole coast brought destitution to the remaining Eyak and their neighbors. This was the period in which the Cordova–Controller Bay Eyak were virtually destroyed. Debauched by alcohol, the native population was left to starve in winter or die from epidemics. Many children were shipped off to school at Chemawa, Oregon, from which few returned. By 1920 almost the only Eyak-speakers were those, fewer than 20, who lived at Old Town, Cordova. Population figures are given in table 1.

As a result of the Alaska Native Claims Settlement Act of 1971 (vol. 5:657–661) the Eyak Corporation was established. In 1985, it included 319 Alaska Native shareholders

Table 1. Eyak Population, 1787–1985

Date	Population	Sources
1787	70-80[a] at most at Port Mulgrave	Beresford 1789:87
1788	200[a] at most at Port Mulgrave	Colnett 1788
1791	1,000[a]	Malaspina 1885:345
1818–1819	117 in Controller Bay and Copper River delta	U.S. Census Office 1884:33; Tikhmenev 1978–1979, 1:161
1835	150[b] at Yakatut village	U.S. Census Office 1884:35
1839	150[b] at most "near Mt. St. Elias"	U.S. Census Office 1884:36
	38 families in Controller Bay area	Wrangell 1980:49
1860	148 baptized	Tikhmenev 1978–1979, 1:348
1874	300 in Controller Bay and Copper River delta	Dall 1877:23, 26–27
1880	444	U.S. Census Office 1884:29
1890	236	U.S. Census Office 1893:158
1899	59 Cordova area	Elliott 1900:739
1933	38 Cordova area	Birket-Smith and De Laguna 1938:24
1973	30-40	Krauss 1974
1985	5	Michael E. Krauss, personal communication 1986

[a]Includes Tlingit.
[b]Mostly Tlingit.

of which only two were Eyak. About one-third of the shareholders in the Eyak Corporation lived in the Cordova area (Lucas Borer, communication to editors 1985).

Synonymy

The name Eyak, which is used in English as a self-designation, is taken from the name of the village Eyak near Cordova, where the last concentration of Eyaks lived. The Eyak name of this village is *ʔi·ya·ġ*, a borrowing from Chugach Eskimo *iɣya·q* 'outlet of a lake' (literally 'throat'). The spelling Eyak was first used by Abercrombie (1900:384, 397) in 1884. Other spellings and variants include Ikhiak (Petroff 1884:29), Eeak tella, for the Cordova-Copper River group (Emmons 1903), and perhaps Hyacks, 1869 (cited in Hodge 1907–1910, 1:448).

The Eyak refer to themselves as *ʔi·ya·ġdalahġayu·* (originally used in its literal meaning 'inhabitants of Eyak village') or simply as *daxu̧hyu·* 'human beings'.

The usual name for the Eyak in Tlingit is *gute·x̣qʷá·n*, but the Yakutat Tlingit use this or the variant *ḱuté·x̣ qʷá·n* for 'Chugach Eskimo' (vol. 5:7; Krauss 1970a:280) and call the Eyak *yá·t qʷá·n* 'local inhabitants', because

Eyak was the original language at Yakutat. The Ahtna, though farther up the Copper River, called the Eyak *danġene*, literally 'uplanders' (De Laguna and McClellan 1954–1968; Kari and Buck 1975:59), perhaps because they most often reached them by going up the Chitina and Tana rivers and over the Bagley Icefield to the coast.

The Russians referred to the Eyak as Ugali͡akhmi͡ut- (with Russian inflections), variants having -la- for -li͡a- and -mu- for mi͡u-, and by the Russianized form Ugalent͡sy (Wrangell 1839:51), names which appeared in German as Ugalachmut and Ugalenzen (Teben'kov 1981; Shelekov 1793, 1981; Radloff 1858; Wrangell 1839a, 1980:49). This name is from Chugach Eskimo *uŋala·ɣmiut* 'people of the southeast' according to Krauss (1970a:654). Names that appear to be ultimately variants or corruptions of this include Wallamute (Portlock 1789), Lakhamutes (Petroff 1884), Lakhamit or Lakhamites (Bancroft 1886). Bancroft also applied Agelmute(s) to Eyak from the Copper and Kaliakh rivers. Elliott (1900) named Agaligniute the Indians at Eyak or "Odiak" Village.

The Russians recognized the Eyak as distinct from the Eskimo and as linguistically distinct from the Tlingit, yet they often called them Kolosh (Tlingit) because their culture was like that of the Yakutat Tlingit. Russian I͡Akutatskiĭ 'the Yakutat language' sometimes refers specifically to Eyak (Davydov 1810–1812, 2:appendix).

It was Dall (1870, 1877) who introduced the erroneous notion that Eyak "Ugalakmiut" were really Eskimos transformed into Tlingits. This error was perpetuated by Petroff (1882, 1884), Emmons (1903), Swanton (1908a, 1952), Hodge (1907–1910), and Kroeber (1939). For a time Dall (1877) even confused the Eyak with the Ahtna, supposing that the "Ah-tena" or "Ugalentsi" had a colony on Controller Bay.

Sources

Aside from brief items in Shelekhov (1791, 1793, 1981), Coxe (1803), and in Wrangell (1839, 1970), or references in Tikhmenev (1861–1863, 1978–1979), the earliest ethnographic information on the Eyak is in Jacobsen (1884) and Abercrombie (1900). The major source on Eyak culture, problems of nomenclature, and territorial claims is Birket-Smith and De Laguna (1938), apart from the preliminary sketch of De Laguna (1937). The same problems have been discussed by Johansen (1963), without new data. Additional information obtained at Yakutat, including notes from Harrington and Krauss, is utilized in De Laguna (1972). Archeological data are found in De Laguna et al. (1964). The definitive works on Eyak linguistics are by Krauss (1970, 1970a), which include all information from previous sources.

Stories told in Eyak by Anna Nelson Harry, the last speaker of the language, translations, and a sketch of her life appear in Krauss (1982).

Prehistory of Southeastern Alaska

STANLEY D. DAVIS

The first excavations in southeastern Alaska were conducted in 1934 and 1935 by the U.S. Department of Agriculture Forest Service at the site of the Russian redoubt, "Old Sitka," or Archangel Saint Michael (fig. 1). Some prehistoric materials were recovered, but no analysis was undertaken and no chronological placement can be made, other than that they predated the Russian occupation.

The first systematic archeological investigations by professionals were conducted in the late 1940s and early 1950s (De Laguna and Riddell 1952; De Laguna et al. 1964; De Laguna 1960, 1972) at Angoon and at Yakutat. The assemblage of ground stone and bone artifacts recovered near Angoon, particularly at the sites of Daxatkanada and Whale's Head Fort, indicated a late prehistoric and historic Tlingit occupation (De Laguna 1960). At Yakutat, the excavation of Old Town (De Laguna and Riddell 1952; De Laguna et al. 1964) suggested an occupation 250-400 years ago by an Eyak-speaking group later joined by Ahtnas from the Copper River area.

Archeological investigation in southeastern Alaska was initiated by the National Park Service at Glacier Bay, also including Dundas Bay and Icy Strait eastward to Point Howard on Lynn Canal, from 1963 through 1965, with work in 1971 and 1973. The project resulted in the discovery and excavation of the Ground Hog Bay 2 site and in limited excavation at the Point Couverden site and the historic site of Grouse Fort. Ground Hog Bay 2 yielded the first evidence, supported by controlled excavations, stratigraphic relationships, and radiocarbon dating, that human occupation in southeastern Alaska spanned the entire Holocene (Ackerman 1965, 1968).

Starting in the mid-1970s the Forest Service conducted fieldwork that emphasized both site inventory and testing in areas to be affected by ground-disturbing activities. This work includes excavation or testing of the multicomponent site at Hidden Falls (Davis 1984, 1979, 1980), the Lake Eva site (Swanson and Davis 1983), the Portage Arm site (Stanford 1980), the Starrigavan site (Davis 1985), the Coffman Cove site (Clark 1979a), the Sarkar Entrance site (Rabich-Campbell 1984), Yatuk Creek Rockshelter (Mobley 1984), the Irish Creek site (Roberts 1982), the Young Bay Midden site (Swanson and Davis 1982), the Greens Creek site (Swanson and Davis 1982a), the Traders Island site (Stanford and Thibault 1980), the Russian Cove site (Davis 1985a), the Bear Shell Midden site (Bergey 1983), the Poison Cove site (Swanson and Dolitsky 1985), and the Mud Bay site (Autrey and Davis 1984) (fig. 1).

Chronology

The prehistory of southeastern Alaska has been poorly developed because of the small number of archeological excavations and must be viewed from a regional perspective. The area between Yakutat Bay and Dixon Entrance, including the islands and mainland, comprises southeastern Alaska. This region lies at the northern end of the traditional Northwest Coast culture area. Within this area, a number of prehistoric sites and historic native sites have been investigated and reported upon. Based on this work, the following sequence has been proposed: the Paleomarine tradition, 9000-4500 B.C.; a transitional stage dating 4500-3000 B.C.; the Developmental Northwest Coast stage, divided into an early phase 3000-1000 B.C., middle phase, 1000 B.C.–A.D. 1000, and late phase, A.D. 1000 to European contact; and the Historic period.

The Paleomarine Tradition

The term Paleomarine tradition (Davis 1984, 1980) has been used to define the earliest cultural stage yet identified within the coastal area of southeastern Alaska. The most noteworthy characteristics of the assemblages belonging to this tradition are a well-developed microblade industry with wedge-shaped microblade cores (fig. 2), few if any bifacial artifacts, and an economic pattern based on coastal-marine subsistence. The earliest evidence of human occupation in southeastern Alaska comes from Hidden Falls (Davis 1984, 1979, 1980) and Ground Hog Bay 2 (Ackerman, Hamilton, and Stuckenrath 1979; Ackerman 1968).

Hidden Falls, a stratified multicomponent site situated about eight meters above low tide, contained a buried cultural horizon (Component I) between two glacial deposits. Only one radiocarbon date from charcoal was obtained (7110 B.C. ± 230). The occupation probably

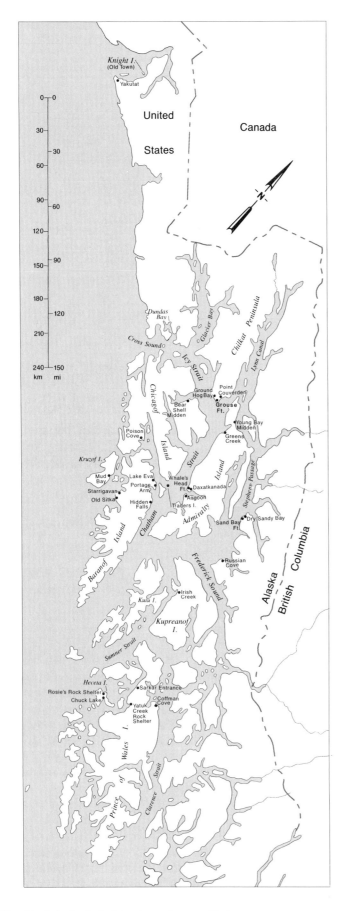

occurred about 7500 B.C. according to both the radiocarbon dates and the geological evidence. The buried paleosol containing the cultural material was deposited between 8300 and 6600 B.C. These radiocarbon dates were based on wood fragments recovered from this horizon. Component I is described as a unifacial tool, microblade, and microcore industry (Davis 1984, 1979, 1980). Other artifacts typical of the assemblage were split cobble and pebble tools, notched scrapers, gravers, and burinized flakes. Bifaces were not present in the assemblage. Fish bone and marine shell suggest a coastal marine subsistence. Two other prehistoric occupations (Components II and III) overlay this early Holocene component.

Ground Hog Bay 2 is situated on a 10–15 meter raised marine terrace. Components II and III were mixed with beach gravels that were deposited as a lag pavement that formed on glacial till above bedrock. Radiocarbon dates of 8230 ± 800, 7270 ± 80 and 7180 ± 130 B.C. were assumed by Ackerman et al. (1979) to date Component III. The only artifacts recovered from Component III were two obsidian bifacial fragments, a water-rolled chert scraper, and five argillite flakes (Ackerman 1968). Component II, also contained within the beach gravels, was defined as a stratum bearing macro and microblade cores. The associated artifact assemblage included examples of side, end, and notched scrapers, choppers, hammerstones, bifaces (2 fragments), a burinized flake, and utilized and non-utilized flakes. The component was dated within a suite of dates from 6850 B.C. ± 125 to 2205 B.C. ± 95 (Ackerman, Hamilton, and Stuckenrath 1979). The site was abandoned 3000–2000 B.C. and reoccupied about A.D. 1000.

Investigations at the Chuck Lake site, Heceta Island, yielded two dates, 6230 B.C. ± 130 and 6270 B.C. ± 125 from a shell midden. The artifact assemblage consists of microblade cores, microblades, pebble cores, flakes, an anvil stone, hammerstone, and a whetstone. Of particular importance is the faunal assemblage: shellfish included horse clam and sea urchin; vertebrate remains included seal, sea lion, waterfowl, beaver, a canid, and possible deer (Robert Ackerman, personal communication 1985).

Transitional Stage

A transitional stage is assumed, because of the technological changes between the Paleomarine tradition and the early phase of the Developmental Northwest Coast stage. At some point in time (presumed to be between 4500 and 3000 B.C.), the technological emphasis changed either by parallel invention or by diffusion to include a ground stone tool industry that became dominant over the microblade and unifacial flaked stone industry by 5,000 years ago. The economic and settlement strategies reflected the adaptation to a changing environment. Three sites have been tested that either have artifact assemblages or radiocarbon dates that could shed light on the probable transitional period. These are the Lake Eva site, the Point Couverden site, and the Irish Creek site.

At the Lake Eva site three occupations were identified; the oldest (Component III) yielded radiocarbon dates of 3830 B.C. ± 90 (SI-5576), 3570 B.C. ± 100 (SI-5578), and 3550 B.C. ± 70 (SI-5580). Component II was dated to 1770 B.C. ± 65 (SI-5577). A date of A.D. 1725 ± 55 (SI-5581) for Component I indicated a protohistoric use of the site. Fire-cracked rock and charcoal were evident in all three cultural horizons. No shellfish or other faunal remains were recovered from any cultural zones. Two significant features were discovered within Component I: a rock-lined depression and a rock pavement consisting of fire-altered rock (Swanson and Davis 1983). The only artifact recovered was an obsidian flake core. Palynological studies conducted on sediment samples (Holloway 1982) revealed high frequencies of pollen of Ericaceae, a family that includes blueberries and huckleberries. This indicated that the plants were probably intentionally brought onto the site for processing (Holloway 1982). The recovery of one artifact adds little to the technological attributes of this period. The importance of this site lies in its chronological placement during the probable transitional stage, its location 2.5 kilometers from the coast, and its probable function as a specialized camp for the gathering and processing of berries.

The Point Couverdon site is located on an 11-meter terrace. A radiocarbon sample dating 240 B.C. ± 70 was taken from above the cultural horizon, suggesting the occupation was of a greater antiquity. The artifact assemblage also suggests that the site belongs to an earlier stage and may be contemporary with the Lake Eva III. The artifact inventory consists of a possible microblade industry, bifacial fragments, core rejuvenation flakes, choppers, and scrapers (Ackerman, Hamilton, and Stuckenrath 1979).

The Irish Creek site, located on a raised terrace, also has a more recent radiocarbon date (290 B.C. ± 70) than the artifact assemblage suggests. The material remains include bi-directional microblade cores, microblades, scrapers, a graver, and unifacial flakes (Roberts 1982). No bone or shellfish remains were recovered. The microblade cores (?) are similar to those from the Queen Charlotte Islands, which could indicate a date more in line with a

a   b   c   d   e

U.S. Forest Service, Sitka, Alaska: a, SIT-119:1554; b, SIT-119:1129; c, SIT-119:3784; d, SIT-119:4126; e, SIT-119:1301.
Fig. 2. Wedge-shaped microblade core and microblades of the Paleomarine tradition, Hidden Falls site, Component 1. Length of a 2.75cm, rest same scale.

transitional stage, 4500 to 3000 B.C.

The Developmental Northwest Coast Stage

The Developmental Northwest Coast stage is distinguished from the Paleomarine tradition and the transitional stage by shell midden deposits, ground stone and bone technology (fig. 3), human burials, and the establishment of larger settlements (winter villages), specialized subsistence camps, and fortifications.

The Early Phase

Component II at Hidden Falls (Davis 1984; Lightfoot 1983) has the earliest evidence in southeastern Alaska of a ground stone and bone industry. This cultural horizon yielded dates between 2670 B.C. ± 110 and 1265 B.C. ± 80 and an artifact inventory including ground stone points, ground single-edge tools, small planing adzes, abraders, unilaterally barbed bone point fragments, labrets, beads, ribbed stone, and utilized flakes. Absent from the inventory were bifaces, burins, flaked stone points, and a microblade industry. A number of post holes and a circular depression about three by four meters in diameter indicated that some type of structure was used by the inhabitants. Faunal remains associated with the occupation include dog, deer, sea mammals, and anadromous and marine fish (Davis 1984). Decomposed shellfish remains were present throughout the horizon but were unidentifiable as to species. Comparisons can be made with the Locarno Beach phase along the British Columbia coast to the south and with the Takli Birch phase on the Alaska Peninsula to the north.

Rosie's Rockshelter, Coffman Cove, and Traders Island also have components that date to the early phase. Coffman Cove is a coastal shell midden where investigations were limited to three test pits, which resulted in the recovery of 170 specimens with diagnostic items numbering less than 10. Artifacts included ground slate points, a bilaterally barbed bone point fragment, bone bipoint, chipped stone, and human osteological specimens. Radiocarbon samples collected from near the surface, 40 centimeters below the surface, and 140 centimeters below the surface yielded dates of A.D. 520 ± 70, 1285 B.C. ± 85, and 1685 B.C. ± 70, respectively (Clark 1979a, 1979). Similarities were found with Component II at Hidden Falls (Davis 1984; Lightfoot 1983).

Traders Island (Stanford and Thibault 1980) is approximately 1.5 kilometers long and .7 kilometers wide. The site consists of three mounds, two of which are separated by a stand of Sitka spruce. The stratigraphy revealed an upper shell concentration containing charcoal and fire-cracked rock and a lower shell, charcoal, and fire-cracked rock matrix separated by a buried forest soil. Charcoal samples taken from 70 to 120 centimeters yielded radiocarbon dates of 1006 B.C. ± 65 (SI-5587) and 1605 B.C. ± 70 (SI-5586), respectively. Identified shellfish remains included heart cockle, butter clam, horse clam, littleneck clam, and bay mussel. The only identified mammalian species recovered were one sea lion phalange and a modified muskrat tooth. A similarity with Hidden Falls is noted. In both sites, the cultural components are separated by sterile buried forest soil at approximately 1000 B.C.

Rosie's Rockshelter contains two cultural levels separated by sterile silts and rockfall (Robert E. Ackerman, personal communication 1985). The upper midden dated 2100 B.C. ± 70 and 2110 B.C. ± 115, while the lower midden deposit dated 1870 B.C. ± 120 and 2200 B.C. ± 80. Both deposits contained mollusk shells and bone. Artifacts from the upper stratum included a unilaterally barbed bone harpoon head with an offset line hole and a pointed long bone.

The Middle Phase

The artifact assemblage of the middle phase exhibits a continuation of the ground stone and bone technology, with more emphasis placed on unilaterally barbed ground bone points, ground stone knives, and heavy hand mauls, with an increased use of nephrite in tool manufacturing. Additions to the artifact inventory include burins, ground burins of bone and nephrite, composite toggling harpoon valves, and possibly small chipped stone points. Assemblages from 10 sites suggest affiliation with this phase.

The uppermost prehistoric component (Component III) at Hidden Falls, dated between 1000 B.C. and A.D. 650, yielded an artifact inventory that included in addition to the preceding, unilaterally barbed bone points without lashing spurs or holes, small planing adzes, gravers, abraders, labrets, bone tubes, incised bone and stone, drilled mammal teeth, and ground stone point fragments. Within this cultural horizon were extensive shell deposits and fire-hearth areas. Post holes, a bark mat, and a pole indicate structures. The most abundant shellfish exploited were bay mussels, littlenecks, and butter clams. Marine fish used included Pacific gray cod, salmon, rockfish, herring, halibut. Mammals were represented by deer, dog, sea otter, and harbor seal; bird remains were also found (Davis 1984). Faunal analysis suggested winter-spring occupation of the site.

The Sarkar Entrance site (Rabich-Campbell 1984) exhibits an artifact assemblage similar to that identified for the middle phase but more limited. The site is three terraces ascending from the beach. The upper terrace contains five housepits; one, which measured about 12 by 10 meters, appeared to have been abandoned by A.D. 1190 ± 90. A date of A.D. 30 ± 120 from the lowest level may reflect earliest site occupation. Present in the collection, but not identified at other sites in southeastern Alaska, is a ground slate projectile point with a fish-tailed base, with

an associated date of A.D. 210 ± 240. Human skeletal remains were recovered within a cultural level dated at A.D. 650 ± 50.

The eight remaining sites that have been tested and radiocarbon dated fit a pattern similar to that of the middle phase—a ground stone technology, extensive shellfish deposits, mammalian (marine and terrestrial), and marine and anadromous fish remains. The evidence suggests these sites are seasonal, limited in size, and used for subsistence procurement. Charcoal samples have yielded dates of 890 B.C. ± 50 (SI-5582) and A.D. 1810 ± 50 (SI-5585) for the Young Bay site; A.D. 5 ± 80 (SI-5569) to A.D. 735 ± 75 (SI-5586) for the Greens Creek site; and A.D. 530 ± 55 (SI-5572) to A.D. 640 ± 60 for the Portage Arm site.

The Late Phase

The late phase is characterized by a move to larger structures, presumably associated with "winter villages," and by sites that were used for defensive purposes. Continuing within this period are sites used while procuring shellfish, sea mammals, fish, deer, and berries. The artifact assemblage reflects a continuing ground stone and bone technology, with labrets, chisels, splitting and planing adzes, and some chipped stone. New elements added to the assemblages include copper tools, stone bowls and lamps, harpoons with lashing holes, the increased use of obsidian for chipped stone tools and in protohistoric times, the introduction of drift iron for tool manufacturing.

Four sites have been investigated that have components yielding radiocarbon dates from this period: A.D. 1290 ± 50 (Beta-10039) and A.D. 1720 ± 50 (Beta-10040) for the Starrigavan site; A.D. 1590 ± 60 (Beta-10037) for Russian Cove; A.D. 1460 ± 75 (SI-5590), A.D. 1205 ± 100 (SI-5589), and A.D. 515 ± 55 (SI-5588) for Bear Shell Midden; and A.D. 1020 ± 70, A.D. 1380 ± 90, and A.D. 1495 ± 85 for Component I at Ground Hog Bay.

Old Town represents three periods of prehistoric occupation. The ages of the parts of the site that was excavated are believed to range from about A.D. 1700 or earlier to 1750.

Faunal remains indicated the most important mammals were the harbor seal, followed by porpoise, mountain goat, and sea otter. Other remains included land otter, black bear, beaver, hoary marmot, muskrat, dog, and whale. The most common shellfish remains were bay mussel, smooth Washington clam, Pacific littleneck, and sea urchin.

There was an abundant use of native copper for arrowheads, knife blades, tiny nails, and ornaments such as bracelets, rings, and beads. Drift iron was used for small knives, scrapers or adz blades, awls, and drills. Small slate woodworking tools, grooved stone axes, beaver-tooth

U.S. Forest Service, Sitka, Alaska: a, SIT-119:4102; b, SIT-119:27; c, SIT-119:3903; d, SIT-119:68; e, SIT:119:550; f, SIT-119:3954; g, SIT-119:28; h, SIT-119:3891; i, SIT-119-50; j, SIT-119:953; k, SIT-119:4029; l, SIT-119:67; m, SIT-119:117; n, SIT-119:1293; o, SIT-119:69; p, SIT-301:26; q, SIT-119:3772; r, SIT-119:60; s, SIT-119:98; t, SIT-119:3981; u, SIT-119:100; v, SIT-119:97; w, SIT-119:3880; x, SIT-119:289; y, SIT-119:48; z, SIT-119:39; aa, SIT-119:79, 3777, 4237; bb, SIT-119:3776; cc, SIT-119:29; dd, SIT-119:29; ee, SIT-119:3; ff, SIT-119:9; gg, SIT-119:53; hh, SIT-119:4; ii, SIT-119:831; jj, SIT-119:1043; kk, SIT-119:383; ll, SUM-041:6; mm, SIT-229:1; nn, SUM-018:128; oo, SUM-018:16; pp, SIT-229:58; qq, SUM-018:7; rr, SUM-042:4; ss, SUM-018:2; tt, SUM-018:128; uu, SIT-229:46; vv, SUM-018:8; ww, SUM-018:13; xx, SUM-018:5; yy, SUM-018:10; zz, SIT-229:26; a′, SUM-018:1.

Fig. 3. Artifacts of the Developmental Northwest Coast Stage. Early Phase: a–d, ground slate points; e–f, unilaterally barbed bone point fragments; g-h, stone labrets; i, stone bead; j, small perforated pebble beads; k, stone adz; l, small stone planing adz; m, whetstone; n, chipped slate blank; o, ribbed stone. Middle Phase: p, lanceolate bone point; q, unilaterally single-barbed bone point; r, unilaterally multiple-barbed bone point; s–t, small unilaterally single and double-barbed bone points; u-v, valves for composite harpoon; w, labret; x, bird bone tube; y–z, drilled seal teeth; aa, perforated shell beads; bb, incised stone; cc–dd, multifaceted burins; ee–ff, small stone adzes; gg, small stone planing adz; hh, nephrite chisel; ii–jj, single edge ground stone knives; kk, ground shell knife. Late Phase: ll, bone point; mm, unilaterally barbed harpoon point with line hole; nn, unilaterally barbed bone harpoon point; oo–pp, bone points; qq, composite harpoon valve; rr, bird bone awl; ss, bone awl; tt, mammal tooth chisel; uu, carved bone; vv, elliptical pulley-shaped labret; ww, small stone planing adz; xx, ground slate chisel; yy, ground single edge knife; zz, ground slate point base; a′, obsidian scraper. Length of a, 5.75 cm, rest same scale.

PREHISTORY OF SOUTHEASTERN ALASKA

chisels, grinding slabs, whetstones, and stone lamps were found. Bone artifacts included detachable unilateral barbed bone harpoon heads with a line hole for spears and arrows, a carved bone socket piece for a dart (representing a duck?), slender unilaterally barbed bone points, and awls. Ornaments included mammal-tooth pendants, beads of bone and coal, and pins for nose or hair. Labrets were not recovered. The abundance of stone lamps and the presence of the harpoon arrow (presumably for sea otters) are Eyak traits as is the absence of the labret.

Daxatkanada and the Russian Cove site were used for defensive purposes. According to tradition, Daxatkanada had been a palisaded fort. The occupants had a well developed woodworking industry. Beads, pendants, and labrets were made of bone, animal teeth, shell, jet, and steatite. Clay or claystone was baked to obtain red pigment. Of particular interest were the pebbles or slabs (amulets?) incised with zigzag lines and faces with weeping eyes. A piece of bottle glass and a brass thimble suggest the site was occupied during the early historic period. One sample produced a radiocarbon date of A.D. 1430 ± 70 (Moss and Erlondson 1985).

The Russian Cove site is located on a high bedrock point. The arrangement and size of the postholes suggests that temporary surface structures were used; no evidence was found for permanent plank houses. A radiocarbon sample of charcoal taken from a hearth in the middle of the cultural zone dated A.D. 1590 ± 60. The initial occupation could have been as early as A.D. 1150 based on comparisons of the artifact assemblage with other sites.

Tlingit

FREDERICA DE LAGUNA

The Tlingit ('tliŋgit, 'tliŋkit; sometimes anglicized as 'kliŋgit, 'kliŋkit) speak a language that is remotely related to Eyak-Athapaskan.*

Territory

They occupy the fjord-indented mainland and islands of the southeastern Alaska panhandle and, before the establishment of the Canada–U.S. boundary in 1906, had some territory in British Columbia (Dundas and Zayas islands; part of the western shore of Portland Canal). In the southeast, about A.D. 1700 according to native tradition, the Kaigani (Haida from Massett) had driven the Tongass Tlingit from Dall Island and the southern part of Prince of Wales Island, although village names in this area (Sukkwan, Howkan, Klinkwan, Kasaan) remained Tlingit. But while the Tlingit were losing lands in the south, they were expanding across the Gulf of Alaska at the expense of the Athapaskans and Eyak, at least to Icy Bay (or even to Controller Bay by 1880), this northwestward movement beginning early in the eighteenth century and culminating in the nineteenth. The Coast Mountains and Saint Elias Range have separated the Coastal Tlingit from their inland neighbors, since the Tlingit abandoned aboriginal rights to certain fishing areas on the upper Taku and Stikine rivers when these places became Canadian.

This article deals with the Coastal Tlingit only. For the Atlin and Teslin Tlingit of Yukon Territory, see "Inland Tlingit," volume 6.

The Tlingit have never formed a political unit but are rather a "nationality" united by recognition of common language and common customs. The Coastal Tlingit comprise three major groups of tribes ($q^w\acute{a}\cdot n$): the people of the Gulf Coast, the Northern Tlingit, and the Southern Tlingit, each group, according to the Tlingit, distinguished by subdialectal differences (fig. 1). Local groups may also possess minor cultural peculiarities, depending upon location, history, and contact with foreigners.

The Gulf Coast Tlingit include descendants of the Hoonah who formerly had camps or settlements at Lituya Bay and vicinity. Farther northwest, at Dry Bay (mouth of the Alsek River) and on the Akwe River, eighteenth-century Tlingit traders from Hoonah and Chilkat country mixed with the Athapaskan residents to form a separate tribe, the Dry Bay (or $\acute{g}una\cdot xu\cdot$ 'among the strangers [Athapaskans]'), also known to the Russians as people of the "Bays of Akoie." Absorption of Eyak speakers from Italio River to Icy Bay in the late eighteenth and beginning nineteenth centuries produced a second Tlingit tribe, the Yakutat, with whom the Dry Bay merged about 1910. Population figures for all these groups are given in table 1. Some writers (Emmons and De Laguna, 1945-1985; U.S. Census Office 1884, 1893) recognize a third tribe farther west, the Kaliakh ("Yakatags" and "Chilkats"), from Cape Yakataga through Controller Bay, but these were more properly Tlingitized Eyak who became virtually extinct in the twentieth century.

The Northern Tlingit include the Hoonah, on the north shore of Cross Sound, who claim the coast as far north as Cape Fairweather; the Chilkat-Chilkoot, Auk, Taku; and Sumdum along the mainland; and Sitka and Hutsnuwu (Angoon) on the outer islands and coasts.

The Southern Tlingit are, on the islands: Kake, Kuiu, Henya, and Klawak; and along the mainland and sheltered waters: Stikine or Wrangell, Tongass, and Sanya or Cape Fox.

Since the fundamental units of Tlingit society were the matrilineal clans of the two exogamous moieties, the tribes listed above were merely local communities, made up of representatives of several clans, united by propinquity, intermarriage, and love for their common homeland. Nor

---

*The phonemes of Tlingit are: (unaspirated stops and affricates) d, λ, $\mathfrak{z}$, $\check{\mathfrak{z}}$, g, $\dot{g}$, g^w, $\dot{g}^w$, $\mathfrak{z}$; (aspirated stops and affricates) t, λ, c, $\check{c}$, k, q, k^w, q^w; (glottalized stops and affricates) $\dot{t}$, $\dot{\lambda}$, $\dot{c}$, $\dot{\check{c}}$, $\dot{k}$, $\dot{q}$, $\dot{k}^w$, $\dot{q}^w$; (voiceless spirants) $\dagger$, s, $\check{s}$, x, $\underline{x}$, x^w, $\underline{x}^w$, h; (glottalized spirants) $\dot{\dagger}$, $\dot{s}$, $\dot{x}$, $\dot{\underline{x}}$, $\dot{x}^w$, $\dot{\underline{x}}^w$; (nasal) n; (resonants) w, y, $\dot{y}$ (unrounded velar); (short vowels) a, e, i, u; (long vowels) $a\cdot$, $e\cdot$, $i\cdot$, $u\cdot$; (tones) high ($\acute{v}$), low (unmarked). Sequences of a velar (or back velar) plus w are distinct from unitary labialized phonemes, and sequences of obstruent plus $\mathfrak{z}$ are distinct from glottalized obstruents. Outside of the Tongass dialect the phoneme $\dot{y}$ is no longer found, being replaced by y; for other dialectal differences see Leer in Williams and Williams (1978:6-17) and the orthographic footnote in "Inland Tlingit" (vol. 6:469). The phonemic transcription of Tlingit words was provided by Jeff Leer (personal communication 1985).

In the practical orthography now in use the Tlingit phonemes are written: d, dl, dz, j, g, g, gw, gw, .; t, tl, ts, ch, k, k, kw, kw; t', tl', ts', ch', k', k', k'w, k'w; l, s, sh, x, x, xw, xw, h; l', s', x', x', x'w, x'w; n; w, y, y; a, e, i, u; aa, ei, ee, oo; high tone ($\acute{v}$), low tone unmarked. Word-initial vowels are written but always correspond to a word-initial $\mathfrak{z}$ followed by a vowel.

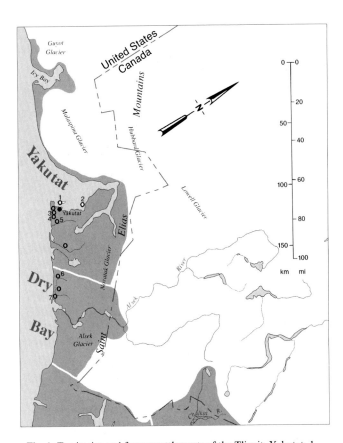

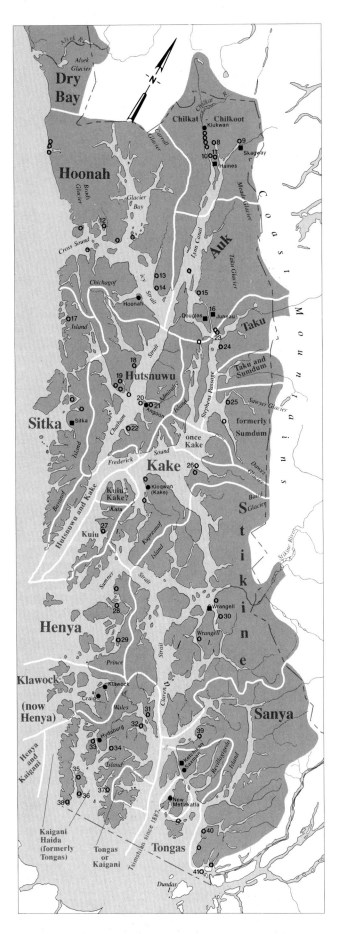

Fig. 1. Territories and former settlements of the Tlingit. Yakutat: 1, Port Mulgrave village, abandoned about 1898; 2, 'Old Town', Knight I., prehistoric, abandoned about 1780?; 3, Lost River Slough village, abandoned about 1880?; 4, Lost River village, prehistoric and historic, abandoned about 1840; 5, Situk, 1860–1916. Dry Bay: 6, Akwe River village, abandoned 1852–1865; 7, Kakanhini Slough village, abandoned about 1930? Chilkat-Chilkoot: 8, Chilkoot, abandoned about 1915; 9, Dyea, Chilkoot camp; 10, Yandestaki, Chilkoot, abandoned 1900; 11, Tanani, Chilkoot camp, abandoned 1898. Hoonah: 12, Tlistee, abandoned; 13, Thluhuggu or Village Point, abandoned 1911; 14, 'Grouse Fort', settled by people from Glacier Bay, abandoned about 1830. Auk: 15, Arnskultsu, part of Auke Bay since about 1900; 16, 'Flounder Water', founded about 1881, now part of Juneau. Sitka: 17, 'Blue Jay Mountain Town', abandoned about 1900. Hutsnuwu: 18, Basket Bay village, abandoned after 1888; 19, Sitkoh, abandoned; 20, Killisnoo, 1878–1929; 21, Daxatkanada Fort, 1820?–1875?; 22, Neltushkin, early 1880s to 1890. Taku: 23, Taku village, founded 1888 by Taku and Auk; 24, 'Ground Stone Bay', site of Ft. Taku, 1840. Sumdum: 25, "Old" Sumdum, abandoned after 1899. Kake: 26, Kake village, abandoned. Kuiu: 27, Kuiu, abandoned after 1892. Henya and Klawak: 28, Shakan, Henya, 1879–1938; 29, Tuxekan, Henya, abandoned about 1900 for Klawock and Shakan. Stikine: 30, "Old" Wrangell, abandoned 1837. Former Tongass villages, occupied by the Haida since the 18th century: 31, "New" Kasaan, founded 1890, now abandoned; 32, "Old" Kasaan, abandoned about 1890; 33, Sukkwan, abandoned before 1920; 34, Hetta, abandoned about 1860; 35, Howkan, abandoned before 1920; 36, Koianglas, abandoned about 1885; 37, Klinkwan, abandoned about 1911; 38, Kaigani, abandoned 1911. Sanya: 39, Loring or Naha, abandoned; 40, Gash, Cape Fox village, abandoned 1896. Tongass village, taken from Sanya in the 18th or 19th centuries: 41, 'On the Cottonwood', Tongass I., abandoned about 1900, Ft. Tongass (1868–1870) nearby. All sites named on the map were occupied in 1987.

Table 1. Tlingit Population, 1740–1930

	1740[a]	1838[b]	1840[c]	1861[d]	1880[e]	1890[f]	1910[g]	1920[h]	1930[h]
Gulf Coast									
Yakutat			150	380	500	354	307		
Lituya Bay			200[i]	590					
Northern									
Hoonah		782	250	742	908	592	625		
Chilkat		498	200	1,616	988	812	694		
Auk		203	400	118	640	279	269		
Sitka			750	1,344	721	815	608		
Hutsnuwu		729	300	600	666	420	536		
Taku		493	150	712	269	223	142		
Sumdum									
Total	2,500								
Southern									
Kake		393	200	445	568	234	325		
Kuiu			150	262	60		29		
Henya		269	300		500	262	214		
Klawak					21				
Stikine		1,410	1,500	697	317	255	189		
Tongass		315	150	333	273	255	184		
Sanya		363	100						
Total	7,500								
Total	10,000	5,455	4,800	7,839	6,431	4,501	4,458	3,895	4,462

NOTE: Figures for 1838 and 1861 include slaves, which may have been non-Tlingit.
[a]Mooney 1928:32.
[b]U.S. Census Office 1884:36–37.
[c]Veniaminov 1840:382.
[d]U.S. Census Office 1884:38.
[e]U.S. Census Office 1884:31–33, 177.
[f]U.S. Census Office 1893:158.
[g]U.S. Bureau of the Census 1915:16.
[h]Swanton 1952:543.
[i]Including Dry Bay people.

were they land-owning groups, for it was the clans that held primary territorial rights, and the tribe lacked a common chief or council.

Environment

Tlingit country is rugged, the mainland from tidewater to lofty mountains nowhere more than 30 miles wide. On the exposed Gulf Coast there are few bays or safe landing places, but the southeastern Alaska coast is cut by deep fjords and protected by an 80-mile wide archipelago. Most of these islands are mountainous and, like the mainland, clothed up to 2,000 or 3,000 feet by dense forests of spruce, hemlock, yellow cedar (red cedar in the south), and by tangles of bushes and abundant berries in certain places. Major rivers, notably the Stikine, Taku, Chilkat, and Alsek, have cut through the mountain barrier, offering access to the interior.

There are few extremes of temperature, except in valleys leading into the mountains. Fogs, rain, and snow are common. Precipitation may occur on 200 to 260 days a year and total 100 to 220 inches. There are gales in fall and winter.

The sea abounds in life: shellfish and seaweeds exposed by the tide, sea mammals (chiefly the harbor seal, but formerly the fur seal and sea otter), and fish (especially the halibut). The important land animals were the blacktail deer (not found north of Cross Sound and Lynn Canal), both black bears and grizzly (Alaska brown) bears, and Dall sheep and mountain goat (on the mainland).

The five species of Pacific salmon furnished the staple food of the Tlingit. Other fish of importance were the eulachon and herring.

Spring and summer bring vast quantities of useful waterfowl, coming up the Pacific flyway to nest in Tlingit waters or pause there on their migrations. From these, and from resident birds, the Tlingit obtained meat, feathers, eggs, and beaks.

Origins

Although there are traditions of now extinct autochthonous groups, usually of the Raven moiety (Swanton 1908a:407), most Tlingit clans believe that they moved northward from the Tsimshian peninsula, while somewhat later, other clans came from the interior down the Skeena, Nass, Stikine, and Taku rivers. Although these traditions are often contradictory and cannot be supported by archeological evidence, it would certainly appear that the center of Tlingit cultural elaboration lay to the south, near the mouths of the Nass and Skeena, and that these cultural influences have moved from south to north, and from coast to the interior (along with small upstream migrations of Tlingit families). Human occupation of the Tlingit coast could have begun 10,000 years ago. While the expansion of the Tlingit along the Gulf Coast in the eighteenth century was probably part of a general northward movement, due to the displacement of Southern Tlingit groups by the Haida, there must have been an earlier occupation of the Gulf and Northern Tlingit areas, between A.D. 1200 and 1700, when the glaciers were smaller than they are now. Tlingit traditions refer to the destruction of villages by advances of the ice in the late seventeenth and eighteenth centuries. Although these areas have been uncovered, no traces of settlements remain. Clan traditions also indicate that those who came from the interior did so when the rivers were all but blocked by glaciers, and people had to pass under ice bridges that have since disappeared.

Culture

Annual Cycle

No one annual cycle of activities was true for all the different local groups, and every community offered a choice of occupations at any given time, so that different families might follow different pursuits during the same period. The detailed summary given by Oberg (1973:65-78) refers specifically to the Chilkat on the mainland and their island neighbors (unspecified); that of De Laguna (1972:360-361), to the Yakutat.

In general, in early spring, there was hunting and trapping of bear, marten, mink, and beaver, on the mainland, or where these animals were available, while halibut were caught in deep waters. Shellfish and seaweed were also gathered. Eulachon were taken at certain streams and their oil rendered. In April, May, and June, many natives hunted sea otter and fur seal. In April herring spawn was gathered. The first runs of Chinook salmon began in April and May.

In summer, June through September, the Tlingit devoted themselves to catching and curing salmon, although there was also berrying, and some groups, especially the Hoonah and Yakutat, caught many harbor seals in early summer, drying the meat and trying out the oil. In the last part of the nineteenth century and up to the failure of the salmon runs in the early twentieth century, salmon fishing was largely for the canneries and was increasingly controlled by government regulations as to localities, seasons, and gear permitted. Trips were made upriver in early spring or late summer, when the water was low. Such trading parties in late summer might catch and hang fish on their way up, winter in the interior, and return by boat in the spring. June and July, months of calm water and most favorable winds, formerly saw fleets of canoes from Hoonah, Sitka, and Chilkat country going to Yakutat to trade, while the Yakutat Tlingit might cross the Gulf to trade with the Ahtna or visit the Russian posts in Prince William Sound (Nuchek) or at Sitka. Summer was also the season for Tlingit wars and slave raids, made on distant Tlingit tribes or on tribes to the south.

In the fall, there was formerly a short season of sea otter hunting. From the late nineteenth century on, salmon were caught and smoked for domestic consumption, and the last berries picked and preserved.

Starting in the mid-nineteenth century, some Tlingit groups harvested their potatoes in the fall; others went directly from the salmon streams to hunt mountain goat, deer, and bear, because the animals are fattest during September through November. By the middle of October, many families were already established at their winter villages.

November and December, when winter supplies were in, were the important months for potlatching. In winter, too, when the rivers were frozen, many mainland clans (of the Dry Bay, Chilkat, Taku, and Stikine) made trading trips into the interior.

Settlement Pattern

In each Tlingit tribal area there was at least one principal village, occupied in winter but usually deserted in summer when families scattered to the fishing and hunting camps. Additional settlements might be founded if an immigrant group were received, or if an old village were being abandoned or divided as a result of disputes, war, or disease. Tradition indicates that such movements were common before recorded history.

Village sites were preferably on a sheltered bay from which there was a view of the approaches. A sandy beach for landing canoes and convenient access to salmon streams, hunting areas, berry patches, clam beds, fresh water, good timber, or special resources (halibut deeps, sealing grounds in ice-filled bays, trails to the interior) were also important.

In the early nineteenth century, such towns consisted of a row of large houses facing the water. The beach in front was crowded with canoes under mats and shelters, with fish racks, and probably with garbage. Behind, or at one end of the row of houses, or on an island opposite, was the graveyard. In southern Tlingit villages tall mortuary totem poles stood beside or in front of the houses (Garfield and Forrest 1948:frontispiece.). In or behind the village were smokehouses for curing fish, caches (small houses on poles or plank-lined pits) for food and belongings, steambath huts, and shelters for women during menstruation and childbirth. Hidden in the woods, where they could do no harm, were boxes containing the paraphernalia of the shamans.

Structures

The aboriginal house (Garfield and Forrest 1948:figs. 32, 33; Emmons 1916; Shotridge and Shotridge 1913:figs. 68-76) was rectangular, with a low-pitched gable roof. It accommodated perhaps six families, plus a few unmarried adults and slaves, totaling 40–50 persons. The house was excavated in the center and planked to form a working and eating place around the central fire. Around this were one or more wide wooden platforms, the uppermost partitioned off with wooden screens, mats, or piles of boxes into family sleeping places. For ceremonies, these temporary partitions could be removed to convert the house and its benches into an amphitheater. The rooms at the back, reserved for the owner and his close kin, were often behind a wooden screen, carved and painted with the lineage (house) or clan crests ("Art," this vol.) (Swanton 1908a: fig. 106; Emmons 1916:1-2). The platform in front of these rooms, "the head of the house," formed the place of honor where the house owner and his family sat, where guests were entertained, or where a corpse might lie in state. Ordinary persons occupied the side benches. Firewood, buckets of fresh water, urinals, fresh game, and other things were placed on the platforms just inside the front door. Here was where the slaves slept, and where the house chief received his guests. In a dark hole under the platforms, an adolescent girl might have to pass her puberty confinement or an accused witch lie in bonds to suffer thirst and hunger until he confessed. A trapdoor near the fire led to a small cellar used for steam baths.

The only openings were the smoke hole in the center of the roof, protected by a screen that could be tilted against the wind, and the oval front doorway, set above the usual level of winter snow and reached by a few steps (fig. 2). It was just big enough to admit a man, bent over and therefore helpless, and could be barred from inside. Wall planks, horizontal or vertical, fitted into slots in the corner or mid-wall posts, or into the heavy plates along the ground and edges of the roof.

The four main house posts were often carved and painted to represent totemic or ancestral figures. Sometimes the facade of the house was painted with a crest design. Totem poles and house screens and posts, like the house itself, all carried personal names, associated with the totemic decorations, the exclusive prerogatives of the owner's lineage or clan.

Single houses or whole villages, especially before European and American cannon rendered such fortifications useless, might be surrounded by palisades.

Some old houses, especially those built in a hurry, might have walls and roof of spruce or cedar bark. Bark houses were usually for temporary shelter, until they were gradually replaced by canvas tents near the end of the nineteenth century (De Laguna 1972, 3:pls. 72–79).

When sawed lumber, nails, and carpentry tools became available in the late nineteenth century, and many Tlingits were becoming wealthy from fishing, they built multifamily frame houses, set on pilings, with commercial windows, doors, and iron stoves (De Laguna 1960:frontispiece, pl. 2). These houses were at first furnished with brass beds and with tables, chairs, suitcases, and boxes in the single room. Later, the interiors were cut up into separate, unheated bedrooms, the walls covered with wallpaper, but people complained that these houses were cold and drafty compared to the old sunken ones. Totemic crests painted on the facades of the houses were obliterated in the 1920s under the influence of the Alaska Native Brotherhood; old screens and house posts were sometimes preserved under sheets, but most were sold to museums.

The old smokehouses (Shotridge and Shotridge 1913: 89–94, figs. 77–82) were built like small dwellings, and

Fig. 2. Yakutat winter village where Chief Yanatchoo lived, Khantaak I., Alaska. A traditional village, it had 5 rectangular lineage houses made of spruce planks with smoke-hole openings in the roof and oval front doorways. Photograph, cropped, possibly by John Q. Lovell, summer 1888.

207

Fig. 3. Children with canoes. While playing in a wooden canoe and with a toy canoe, the boys and girls are learning about watercraft and boat-handling. Photograph by Edward M. Kindle, Taku Harbor, Alaska, May 1905.

usually also served as such, but lacked benches. Above the fire hung a large plank baffle to spread the smoke; rafters above held the cross-sticks on which fish were hung to dry. A movable screen at the smokehole was the early style; but later (under Russian influence?) a fixed wooden roof or "chimney" was set over the smokehole, protecting it from wind and rain, but permitting ventilation (De Laguna 1972, 1:figs. 17–18).

Transport

The most common type of Tlingit canoe, used for hunting, fishing, and travel by small parties, was the 'spruce' (si·t). Extra pieces were morticed on to form the bow and stern, and thwarts set in to hold the stretched sides apart. After European contact, it might carry a square sail of matting (later of cloth) but could sail only before the wind. Normally paddles of yellow cedar were used, the steersman employing a longer one.

The Southern Tlingit were able to make their canoes of local red cedar, but all Tlingit preferred the great Haida canoes, sometimes 60 feet long, with two masts and sails, that could carry six to eight tons of freight. Such "war canoes" were purchased by wealthy Tlingit headmen, who decorated them at bow and stern with carvings or paintings of their crests and gave them personal names. Nootkan "goose canoes" were also traded all the way to Yakutat.

Special types of canoe were made by the Tlingit in certain areas. For example, the heavy-prowed ice-hunting canoe for sealing and the graceful forked-prow canoe, both made at Yakutat, were probably of Eyak derivation. The Chilkat, Dry Bay, and Taku (?) made shallow draft river canoes of cottonwood. The Stikine made a small

"moon canoe," so-called for its upturned ends, for fishing and sea otter hunting. On trading trips to the interior, the Chilkat sometimes made skin canoes. Umiaks, single-holed kayaks, and two-holed bidarkas made at Yakutat in the eighteenth and nineteenth centuries were of Eyak design (presumably derived from the Chugach Eskimo). All were paddled. When going upstream, a canoe might be poled or tracked on a long line. Sometimes it was portaged over a skid road of peeled logs to avoid bad rapids or to cross a narrow isthmus.

The oldest known type of Tlingit canoe had a protruding planklike prow and stern, pierced with holes. These were seen at Lituya Bay in 1786, and at Yakutat Bay in 1788 and 1794 (De Laguna 1972, 1:203-334, fig. 26, 3:pls. 37, 43; Gunther 1972:fig. 32). At this same period smaller dugouts and skin canoes were in use.

The peculiar Eyak snowshoe, netted only under the foot, was used by the Yakutat and Dry Bay only, but they, like others who made trips into the interior, also purchased fine Athapaskan snowshoes. The Chilkat also used large skin packs with tumpline in which they and their male slaves could carry loads of 100 to 200 pounds; their dogs carried 50 pounds in saddlebags. Some mainland groups, like the Hoonah, put spikes on their snowshoes when climbing after mountain goats. The Tlingit of the islands rarely needed snowshoes or packs. They traveled by canoe and needed only a cord to pack game or firewood from the water to the house.

Loads of berries, roots, shellfish, or seaweed were usually carried by women in large pack baskets. Only the Yakutat, Chilkat, and Dry Bay people used hand-drawn sleds of Athapaskan type; otherwise, sleds and toboggans were not part of Tlingit culture.

When traveling or moving camp, personal effects and provisions were packed in boxes with tight-fitting lids, or in waterproof bags of halibut skins or sealskin.

Trade

The Tlingit were involved in extensive intertribal trade with the Eyak, Tsimshian, Haida, and Subarctic Athapaskan tribes, relations that were intensified after the arrival of Europeans.

Among themselves, Tlingits traded largely as gift exchanges between "partners" (ẏaqá·wu, members of different clans in the same moiety), or between "brothers-in-law" (members of opposite moieties), or "fathers- and sons-in-law." These ceremonial but often exploitative arrangements were also imposed on the Athapaskans and Eyak. Leaders of clans that "owned" the "grease trails" into the interior and thereby held monopolies in dealing with the Athapaskans organized trading expeditions to them (Olson 1936a; Legros 1984). But they forbade direct contact between Whites and Athapaskans, denying the latter access to the coast except for a few chiefs under

Tlingit guard. (White prospectors might enter the interior only some years after the purchase of Alaska.) In August 1852, Chartrich or Shotridge, the chief of the Kagwantan clan at Chilkat, led a war party over 300 miles to destroy the Hudson's Bay Company post at Fort Selkirk, and so effectively prevented competition (Davidson 1901).

Native trade brought walrus ivory and hide from the Bering Sea Eskimo, native copper from the interior, and dentalia from the south, as well as fine Haida canoes, Tsimshian carvings, and slaves. Slaves were among the most valuable trade "goods" or war "booty." The interior, Subarctic, tribes furnished furs, especially after the sea otter were all but destroyed in southeastern Alaska by 1825. They also provided the Tlingit with skin garments decorated with porcupine quills and exotic treats like black spruce chewing gum and soapberries, while the Tlingit gave them inferior muskets, ammunition, seaweed, leaf tobacco, and fish or seal oil (Legros 1984).

When the Hudson's Bay Company acquired trading rights in southeastern Alaska from the Russian-American Company in 1839, there was an increased flow of European manufactures to the Tlingit (blankets, china dishes, cloth, dyed feathers, panaches, glassbeads, mother-of-pearl buttons). Also, the Hudson's Bay Company traders served as middlemen in supplying dentalia, sharks' teeth, and abalone shells. From China, traders brought camphor (Canton) chests and fine porcelain. By the middle of the nineteenth century, European manufactures had become essential to Tlingit culture, although breech-loading rifles with cartridges were not available until near the end of the century. In many respects, European-American trade stimulated a flourishing of Tlingit culture up to about 1867. Iron and steel tools, for example, encouraged the carving of large totem poles and house posts, as well as delicate masks and boxes. Although small copper plaques may have been made aboriginally, "coppers," the large shieldlike sheets that represented wealth, seem to have developed only after the natives acquired commercial sheet copper (Keithahn 1964).

Intertribal trade undoubtedly stimulated the development of the crest type of classic Chilkat weaving, for in the eighteenth and the first quarter of the nineteenth century the Tlingit wove blankets with geometric designs only (Osborne 1964; De Laguna et al. 1964:180–181, pl. 18; Shur and Pierce 1976:43; Samuel 1982, 1984).

Subsistence

● HUNTING LAND ANIMALS Hunting and fishing were not simply subsistence activities, but moral and religious occupations, for the Tlingit was killing creatures with souls akin to his own. No animal, especially no little bird, should be slain needlessly, nor mocked, nor should the body be wasted. Rather, the hunter would pray to the dead animal and to his own 'spirit above', explaining his need and asking forgiveness. The dead creature was thanked in song, perhaps honored with eagle down (like a noble guest); certain essential parts (head, bones, or vital organs, depending on the species) were interred, returned to the water, or cremated, to insure reincarnation of the animal.

The hunter had to purify himself in advance by bathing, fasting, and continence, to refrain from announcing what he hoped to kill (bears, in particular, could hear and understand everything that was said), and to start out before dawn. He should fast while hunting but might carry a dried salmon for emergency rations. He would make use of any amulet or magical plant that he might own. His wife, as when her husband was engaged in any dangerous or chancy undertaking, also had to be quiet until his return, and even the behavior of his children might influence that of the game, or the weather, or in some way bring misfortune or death. Bears, the most important land animals, were killed with deadfalls, snares, bow and arrow, but preferably were speared. Although fattest in the fall, bears were usually sought in the early spring, for then the furs were prime and best for men's robes. Many hunters are said to have entered the den to attack the sleeping animal with a spear. A more usual method was to send in three or four dogs to rouse it out, while a group waited with spears or bows and arrows just above the den. Or, the dogs would track a newly emerged bear and hold it at bay until the hunters could kill it.

The spear used for war or bears had a shaft of hemlock or spruce, six to eight feet long, with a double-edged blade of slate, native copper, or later of iron, with a guard at the base to prevent the spear from entering the bear's body so far that the animal could claw the hunter.

Bows and arrows were used for hunting bears, deer, mountain goats and sheep, birds, and other animals. The bow was of yew or hemlock wood, narrowed in the middle, but lacking both the Eskimo sinew backing and the Athapaskan string guard. The arrows, preferably of yellow cedar, were notched for the bowstring, but lacked feathers except at Yakutat. The heads of bone (often barbed), of copper, slate, and later of iron, were intended to remain in the wound, while the hunter retrieved the shaft. Some arrows, for practice or for stunning small animals, had blunt bone heads. Only the Yakutat had the harpoon arrow for sea otter. In shooting, the bow was held horizontally in the left hand, the middle of the arrow gripped between the middle and forefingers, which also served to sight. The butt of the arrow was held between the ball of the thumb and knuckle of the forefinger of the right hand.

The whip sling and dart were also used in the old days. The former was a handle to which a deer thong was fastened; the other end of the cord had a knot to engage the dart. The dart was shaped something like an arrow with a single feather (to enable the hunter to spot it); at the fore end was a detachable socketed bone point.

Female deer could be decoyed by a whistle that imitated the cry of a fawn; young men might hunt deer above the timberline, but old men preferred to have dogs drive them to the shore where they could be shot from a canoe.

Mountain goats and Dall sheep were hunted for their fat, their horns used for spoons, feast dishes, and powder containers, and the goat wool for blankets. Trained dogs would drive the animals down to hunters waiting to spear them in a narrow canyon. Kake people hunted sheep at three places but were careful not to visit the same place for two years, to conserve the game. Goats, sheep, and deer, if killed in the mountain, were usually butchered there and their meat dried, to make it easier to pack it home.

Snares and deadfalls were used for furbearers and many meat animals before the introduction of steel traps. Snares were more often used by the mainland Tlingit, while those on the islands preferred traps. Gulls, ducks, and other waterfowl might be taken by snares weighted with stones in shallow water or caught with baited gorges attached to lines stretched across a stream.

The one land animal that was never purposely killed in aboriginal times was the land otter, since people who drowned or died in the woods were believed to have been captured by otters and transformed into animals like themselves. It was the animal form most often assumed by a shaman's spirit.

● HUNTING SEA MAMMALS The most important sea mammals hunted by the Tlingit were the common harbor seal, fur seal, sea lion, sea otter, and porpoise. Originally sea otter furs were worn, but by the late eighteenth century these were valued primarily for trade, although the flesh was still eaten. By 1825 the animals had been virtually exterminated in southeastern Alaska, so parties of Tlingit and even of Tsimshian used to go to Yakutat and Icy bays on the Gulf of Alaska to hunt sea otter, not always welcomed by the local Tlingits.

Sea mammals were hunted from canoes with the same kind of harpoon as that used for salmon, but often equipped with a toggling rather than barbed head. Only the Yakutat hunted the sea otter with feathered harpoon arrows, equipped with tiny detachable barbed heads and carried in wooden quivers, surrounding the sea otter with a whole fleet of canoes. Even though other Tlingit may have used the surround method, they killed sea otters with harpoons and unfeathered arrows.

The Yakutat and Hoonah were the most expert sealers, exporting skin and oil to other Tlingit, for the best sealing grounds were in Icy Bay, Disenchantment Bay at the head of Yakutat Bay, and Glacier Bay on Cross Sound, where the seals gave birth to their pups on the ice floes.

The hide of the sea lion was valued for heavy cords or ropes, but these animals were probably hunted only by the bravest men. The skins and furs of seals were used for

clothing, the stomachs for floats, and the blubber rendered into oil. Porpoise meat was poor man's food, for it produced a disagreeable body odor. Most Tlingit apparently did not attempt to hunt whales, although Marchand (Fleurieu 1801,1:231) reported that the Sitka killed (small?) whales with a barbed harpoon of bone, cast into the eye. The fat was preserved in gutskin bags, and the "beard" (baleen) was made into combs, spoons, and other household utensils.

● FISHING Because of the importance of salmon in the Tlingit diet, the runs of the five species—chinook, sockeye, pink, coho, chum—virtually dictated the economic cycle. In late spring or early summer, families moved to the fish camps until autumn, except for those whose winter villages were located on salmon streams. Part of the catch was eaten fresh (boiled, baked in an earth oven, or roasted on a spit); most was dried and smoked for winter. The heads were tried out for grease. Cutting, sun drying, smoking, and finally baling the cured salmon involved much more laborious and skillful tasks than catching the fish, tasks performed by the women, aided by male and female slaves. Each woman marked her fish with distinctive cuts and kept her bundles separate in the cache, taking pleasure in sharing them with housemates or visitors. It was probably control over this staple food that gave Tlingit women, and especially the head women in the households, their high status.

Yet fear of offending the fish prohibited menstruants and parturients from approaching the fish streams. Fish had to be treated with respect and the offal returned to streams or burned to insure their reincarnation. But there was no first salmon ceremony.

Most salmon were caught in a rectangular trap of wooden slats, set in a V-shaped weir or fence, the apex pointing upstream. The trap was attached to stakes at the corners so that it could be adjusted to the height of the water. Sometimes an entire stream might be fenced across, with several Vs and as many traps, or a single large trap. Such weirs and traps were controlled by lineage heads, who permitted others to take fish when their own household needs were satisfied.

Only the Chilkat used the funnel-shaped trap for salmon; other groups used smaller models for eulachon.

A wall of stone, topped by branches, might be built across a tidal stream; salmon would enter with the flood, but be caught when the tide fell, and dispatched with spears or clubs.

In August, when streams are so low that fish can barely enter, lines of sharp stakes were set close together across the stream mouths. On these, the jumping salmon would impale themselves, to be collected at low tide.

The same type of harpoon or spear, with detachable barbed and tanged head of bone, antler, native copper (later of iron) was used for fish, seals, sea lions, porpoise, and sea otter. A short line ran from the hole in the tang of

Fig. 4. Northern-style halibut hooks, used in deep water. These hooks were made of 2 pieces of wood lashed together. The attached line was of spruce root or kelp, weighted with a stone, the hook set so as to float 1–2 feet above the bottom. Two men could readily attend 12–15 such lines (La Perouse 1799, 1:406). When set properly, the carved figure faced downward, enticing the halibut to bite, and the fisherman increased its effectiveness with a ritualized speech. left, Hook carved in the shape of a bird standing atop a human head. The lashings are spruce root, and the barb iron. Collected in 1885. right, Hook carved as a pot-bellied man holding an octopus tentacle. The barbed arm is cedar; the carved arm, yew. Lashings and leader are cotton fish cord. Collected in 1936. Height of left 32.3 cm, other to scale.

the head back to the middle of the spear shaft, so that when the fish or animal was struck, the floating shaft would impede its efforts to escape. A second running line, attached to the butt end of the shaft, was often fastened to the canoe, since most salmon were harpooned from canoes. Gaff hooks were more apt to be used to catch salmon from the bank of the stream. Those of the Northern Tlingit were (and are) of hard wood steamed and bent like a hook. Those of the Southern Tlingit had a detachable hook, so that the gaff functioned more like a harpoon. Only the Chilkat used leisters with two barbed sideprongs (sometimes with a third central spike), evidently an Athapaskan rig, especially useful for spearing fish through the ice in winter.

Although hook and line were used for trout, cod, rock cod, and halibut, only the Angoon people took salmon with hooks. They trolled for chinook salmon, using herring for bait (De Laguna 1960).

The most ingenious and efficient hooks were made for halibut (fig. 4). The upper arm, of buoyant yellow cedar, had a sharp barb of bone (later an iron spike); the lower arm, of heavier alder wood, was carved on the bottom with a design to influence the fish. The bait was octopus. One or two pairs of hooks floated up on short leaders from a long bottom line, one end of which was weighted by a boulder, the other leading to a pair of floats (an inflated

seal stomach, and a piece of wood carved like a swimming bird). Since some fish weighed 100 pounds or more, it was a tricky business to haul them up, club them, and slip them over the gunwale into the boat.

Eulachon were prized for their delicious flesh and fine oil, and since the runs in the Alsek, Chilkoot, and other rivers were not enough for their own use and for trade with the Athapaskans, the Tlingit imported oil from the Tsimshian. Eulachon were taken with dip nets (fig. 5) and at Yakutat, Dry Bay, and Chilkoot, with a small cylindrical funnel trap. The first fish of the late February or early March runs were eaten fresh, but those of the larger and later run (end of April to mid-May) were processed for oil.

Herring were also eaten and herring oil rendered, but the roe was the special delicacy, traded particularly from Sitka and Angoon. Here the herring formerly spawned in vast numbers in mid-April and the Tlingit laid down hemlock boughs in shallow water on which the fish would lay their eggs. After spawning and spending the summer in deep water, the herring would return to the bays in schools where they could be caught on a rake, wielded by a man in the bow of a canoe, which his companion paddled. The rake was like a 14-foot slender oar, armed with 30 to 50 sharp bone pins (later nails) to impale the fish.

● FOOD PREPARATION Fresh deer meat, especially the liver, was esteemed. Meat might be cooked or smoked a little, then put up in oil or in a box with liquid fat poured over it.

Salmon and halibut were split open, so thin that the flesh was "unfolded," dried, smoked, and tied in bundles. Salmon heads and eggs when fermented (rotted) were relished like rich cheese. Salmon eggs were often cooked with black seaweed, or with certain kinds of berries.

Fat was rendered from salmon heads, eulachon, herring, seal blubber, and mountain goat fat, to be stored in wooden boxes. Fish and seal fat made better grease if allowed to become rancid before being tried out, so the fish were thrown into a pit and the blubber into a sealskin bag for several days. To render the oil, especially of the

Fig. 5. Dip netting eulachon into a cottonwood dugout canoe. Photograph by Louis Shotridge, Chilkoot River, Alaska, about 1910.

eulachon, a canoe was used as a pot in which water was boiled with hot rocks. After the first oil had been strained into boxes with long-handled dippers, the remaining mass of fish was squeezed in long openwork twined bags, often by women who sat on the fish.

Shellfish and seaweed were eaten fresh only at proper times but were dried or smoked for winter. Clams were not fit to eat from March to August, but cockles and mussels were good all year.

The most commonly preserved berries were blueberries, elderberries, strawberries, and highbush cranberries. These might be slowly cooked until they could be formed into a cake and dried, or might be put up in a wooden box with grease. The sweet inner bark of the hemlock was relished. Roots of the riceroot, ferns, and *Hedysarum* ("Indian sweet potatoes") were dug in spring or fall, when they had the most flavor. Shoots of salmonberries, cow parsnips, and angelica were eaten raw in the spring.

In the nineteenth century, Angoon and Killisnoo were famous for their tiny potatoes, which were apparently introduced by the Russians.

A species of tobacco (*Nicotiana quadrivalvis*) was once cultivated by the Tlingit. The leaves were dried and mixed with ashes of yellow cedar and lime from roasted shells crushed in a mortar, and made into pellets with spruce or cedar gum to be sucked (Beresford 1789:175; Dixon 1933; Heizer 1940a; Turner and Taylor 1972). When Russian leaf tobacco and pipes were introduced in the late eighteenth century, the Tlingit turned readily to smoking, making elaborate carved pipes, often with crest designs, for smoking at funerals, although women continued to use snuff pellets until about 1900.

Fire was kindled with a wooden drill, sometimes a hand drill used by a single person, or a cord drill operated by two. Iron pyrites and quartz were used as strike-a-lights more often by the Northern than the Southern Tlingit, who had red cedar for drills. Wax from the ear was put on the tinder.

Cooking was done by boiling in watertight boxes or baskets containing red hot rocks; spits and earth ovens lined with leaves were also used. Domestic utensils included spoons and dippers of sheep and goat horn and of hardwood, serving dishes and platters, basketry drinking cups, mats, and storage baskets, bags, and boxes. The utensils used for feasts were carved in crest designs and inlaid with abalone shell and red turban opercula. The finest containers were bentwood boxes and bowls (fig. 6) with morticed bottoms and lids or the firmly twined spruce root baskets of the Northern Tlingit, with geometric designs worked in dyed grass and fern stems by false embroidery.

Social Organization

Tlingit social, political, and economic life was based on the fact that every individual (other than a slave of foreign origin) belonged to one of two exogamous moieties: Raven (*yé·ł*) and Wolf (*g̣u·č*) (sometimes called Eagle, *čá·k̲*, in the North). Each of these was, in turn, made up of some 30 clans (*na·*), most of which were subdivided into lineages or house groups (*hít-ta·n*). Membership in moiety, clan, and lineage was matrilineal. Moieties were not social groups, for they never met or cooperated together. Moiety membership simply arranged individuals and matrilines into "opposites" (*g̣une·tkana·ỵí*) that intermarried and performed important social and ceremonial services for each other. The Henya had an Eagle clan that was outside both moieties.

 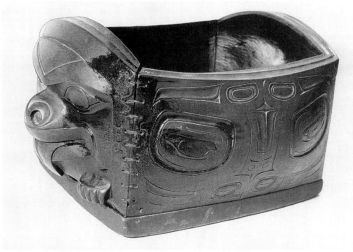

U. of Pa., U. Mus., Philadelphia: NA 4295.
Fig. 6. Bentwood bowl. These were made by kerfing and steaming a single piece of wood at three points, bending these to box form, joining the open edge by passing a cord through drilled holes or pegging with wooden dowels, and anchoring the sides to a bottom plate by means of pegs or nails. This example is symmetrical in design, with a 3-dimensional bear's head carved at each end. Heavily impregnated with grease, this bowl was used to serve oil or pieces of fish in oil at ceremonies. Collected in 1885; length, 33.5 cm.

212

Rank was important, the nobility being the chiefs (headmen of clans or lineages) and their immediate relatives. Commoners of lower rank were in theory their more distant relations in the lineage. Lineages within a clan were sometimes ranked, and certainly among clans there were those of great wealth and status, as well as others of little account. Only slaves were completely outside this social system; but when freed after the purchase of Alaska, they were adopted as the poorest and lowliest members of their former owner's house and clan.

It was the clan, and under it the house, that possessed territories, including rights to all game, fish, berries, timber, drinking water, and trade routes (for Chilkat and Chilkoot); house sites in the winter village; and the prerogatives associated with the totemic crests, represented in the decorations of houses, heirloom objects, and personal names. The chiefs or 'big men' of the clans and 'house owners' of the lineages were trustees and administrators of their group's property. They could assign fishing spots, open or close the hunting season, set a limit on the number of sea otters that a man might take, order the death of a trespasser, and plan and act as hosts in expensive ceremonies in honor of their deceased maternal kin.

The named "house" or lineage was usually so small that its members believed they could trace their genealogical relations to each other or to some founding ancestor. Some lineages seem to have been remnants of once-important clans that had joined stronger clan groups for protection or had been absorbed by them. Others had clearly been formed by subdivision of a clan, just as a house that had grown too big, or in which there was dissention, might found "daughter houses." Some lineages, in fact, became so large that they spread from one Tlingit tribe to another, in effect becoming clans, like the famous Kagwantan (ka·g^{w}a·nta·n), a powerful Wolf clan among the Northern and Gulf Coast Tlingit. Other clans and lineages might be restricted to a single settlement.

The Tlingit are known to have absorbed increments of Haidas and Tsimshians, together with ceremonial prerogatives (like the Henya Eagle clan), just as the Tsimshian and Haida have received some Tlingit groups. The Tlingit have also taken in various Eyak and Athapaskan bands, usually treating these foreign groups as clans, and ascribing them new crests.

● CRESTS The most treasured possessions of clan or lineage were their crests. These represented their totems, that is, certain animals, birds, fish, and invertebrates, heavenly bodies, prominent landmarks, and even ancestral heroes and certain supernatural beings associated with them.

The most important crests of clans in the Raven moiety are: Raven, Owl, Whale, Sea Lion, Salmon, Frog, Sleep Bird, Sun, Big Dipper, Moon, Ocean. Those of the clans of the Wolf moiety are: Eagle, Petrel, Wolf, Bear, Killer-whale, Shark, Halibut, Thunderbird, among others. The Golden Eagle (or Fish Hawk) and Beaver were Wolf crests on the Gulf of Alaska coast but Raven crests from the Hutsnuwu south.

Such crests identify Tlingit clans, subclans, and lineages and serve as guides in aligning Haida or Tsimshian clans with those of the Tlingit for marriage or potlatching. Crests are displayed as paintings or carvings on or inside houses, on totem poles (fig. 7), graves, canoes, feast dishes, ladles, pipes, ceremonial garments (figs. 8–11) (Chilkat blankets or shirts, beaded blankets, hats, masklike headdresses, beaded bibs), armor, helmets, ceremonial equipment (drums, speakers' staffs, dance leaders' poles, rattles, drums), and on the important personal possessions of the group's chief (pipe, powder horn, spoon, feast dishes). Crests may be reflected in personal names, especially titles of house owners, and in the names given to houses, canoes, and other crest objects and heirlooms. Tales of how an ancestor obtained the crest furnish themes for clan songs, sung to mourn the dead at potlatches or by warriors facing death.

The display of any crest or crest object, whether by hosts or guests at a potlatch, requires payment to all members of the opposite moiety who may be present. This is because they serve as witnesses to the right to such display. When the crest illustrates some geographical landmark in the clan's territory, acceptance of the gift affirms the clan's territorial claims (De Laguna 1972, 1: 456, 3: pl. 151).

All clan and lineage property, including territories, songs, crests, or heirlooms, are alienable: by sale, as potlatch or marriage gifts, as indemnity for injuries or as part of a peace settlement, or as booty taken in war. If a crest were seized in a dispute between clans, the original owners would feel under an absolute obligation to redeem it, just as they would if one of their nobles had been captured (Olson 1967:72, 53). At the peace ceremonies used to settle lawsuits, feuds, or wars between clans, special titles, suggestive of their own clan crests, were given by each side to the hostage-ambassadors whom they had taken from the other side, and songs were composed about them. These titles did not, however, become the inheritable property of the hostage's clan.

The totem was clearly more than an emblem or beautiful design. The actual animals, the mountains, glaciers, or bodies of dangerous waters that were associated with clans were addressed by kin terms, according to the relationship of the speaker to the clan in question, and the creature or natural entity would respond. The te·q^{w}e·dí, who had a special claim on the Bear, were therefore great bear hunters; children of te·q^{w}e·dí men could appeal to bears as "father's brothers and sisters." Although totems are thus part of the Tlingit social and moral world, they were not worshiped (Olson 1967:117-118). *213*

top, U. of Oreg. Lib., Eugene: AL-5-1230; bottom left, U.S. Forest Service Photographic Lib., Rosslyn, Va.: 384899; bottom right; Alaska Histl. Lib., Juneau: PCA 87-149.

Fig. 7. Totem poles. top, Dogfish House of Chief Shakes, head of the Wolf *na·nya·ʔa·yí* clan of the Stikine Tlingit, memorial poles, and *Brown Bear Canoe*, Wrangell, Alaska. Poles in front of the house represent: left, a killer whale sitting on a mythological creature, and right, bear paw marks ascending to a grizzly bear sitting on the top, where the ashes of Chief Shakes VI's younger brother were supposedly deposited (Keithahn 1940). The grizzly bear was a crest of the *na·nya·ʔa·yí* clan (Krieger 1928:pl. 11). There were 7 Chief Shakeses in succession (Keithahn 1940; Krause 1956:111; Cole 1985:83). This photograph may have been taken at a funeral of a family member. Photograph by William H. Partridge, 1886. bottom left, Restoration of poles through funds provided by the Civilian Conservation Corps. Photograph by C.M. Archbold, Saxman, Alaska, May 1939. bottom right, Mortuary pole depicting 3 adventures of Raven. Carved in 1902 by Nawiski for a woman of the Raven moiety as a memorial to her 2 sons, the pole was repainted and moved to Saxman Totem Park in 1939 (Garfield and Forrest 1948:13–17). Photograph by Lloyd V. Winter and Edwin P. Pond, Pennock I. cemetery, Alaska, about summer 1903.

DE LAGUNA

Fig. 8. Coudahwot and *yé·ɫ-gu·x̣ú·* (Raven's Slave) in ceremonial clothing. Coudahwot wears a painted hide tunic and wooden hat. *yé·ɫ-gu·x̣ú·* wears a Chilkat woven dance shirt and holds a raven rattle and has his face painted. Both men wear porcupine-quill fringed leggings. Photograph by Lloyd V. Winter and Edwin P. Pond, Klukwan, Alaska, before 1895.

Fig. 9. Carved wooden Bear crest hat worn by Tlingit nobility at potlatches. Basketry cylinders at the top are said to represent the number of times the crest hat was presented and validated through giveaways at the potlatch. At some point, rings may have stopped being added, the hat assuming importance as an heirloom. The grizzly bear crest represents the Wolf moiety. Eyes are abalone, teeth opercula, and the face painted in red, light blue, and black. Whiskers of the northern sea lion outline the crown. Collected 1867–1868; height 41.5 cm.

● ROCK ART While Tlingit rock art (especially petroglyphs) may sometimes have been made to attract the salmon (Keithahn 1940), the figures include clan crests, ancestors, mythological figures, and sailing ships, as well as symbols of wealth or victory (Emmons 1908; Garfield 1947:441; De Laguna 1960:75-78, fig. 8, pl. 11; De Laguna et al. 1964:23, pl. 3b). Tlingit rock art may, like the elaborate totemic figures on poles and house screens, serve as illustrations of important events, mythic or historical, in the clan traditions and so bear witness to the achievements, wealth, or supernatural powers obtained by the clan ancestors.

Law and Warfare

Injury to the property and especially to the person of someone in another clan could be redressed by suitable restitution and peace-making ceremonies. No distinction was made between accident and intent. Even if a man should accidentally injure his beloved wife or child, indemnity would be demanded of him, since they belonged to another clan. However, there was no legal machinery for dealing with intraclan quarrels or killings; one party usually moved away, or a chronic troublemaker might be murdered (Oberg 1934). Local feuds or lawsuits were usually settled by payments of blankets or other wealth, but not necessarily without the sacrifice of a life to even the score. The life of a chief or of a noble woman was worth that of several ordinary persons, and usually necessitated the killing of someone of equal status, without regard to guilt.

Wars were carried on between clans in different tribes, sometimes for plunder, but usually to avenge an injury or insult. Wars were never fought between tribes as such, although wars between clans in distant regions were more savage than local feuds. Enemies might be brutally slain, their heads or scalps saved as trophies; women and children were usually taken as slaves.

To settle a lawsuit or end a war, each side, in a mock battle, "captured" one or more previously selected high-ranking members of the other clan as hostage-ambassa-

Fig. 10. Woman weaving a Chilkat blanket. The pattern, a painted board, was designed by the men and represented clan or lineage crests. The weaving, by the women, was on a single bar loom using 2- and 3-strand twining. The materials used were cedar bark and goat wool, the wool often dyed black, bluish-green, and yellow. It took about one year to weave a single blanket (Emmons 1907; Kaiper and Kaiper 1978:44–45; Samuel 1982; Holm 1982). Photograph by Lloyd V. Winter and Edwin P. Pond, about 1900.

Fig. 11. Ceremonial costumes. The man wears an appliqué and button blanket and tunic representing the Beaver crest, leggings decorated with beads and sea shells, and a wooden hat with 6 potlatch rings; he holds a painted wooden staff. The boy's clothes also reflect the use of contemporary materials in traditional-style clothing. Photograph by Joseph C. Farber, Saxman, Alaska, 1972–1974.

dors. These men or women were treated as if they had died and been reborn as helpless babies, and observed taboos and rituals reminiscent of a girl's puberty. During the eight-day ceremony, they were given names suggestive of the crests of their captors, and finally danced in fine Chilkat blankets to songs composed on the same themes; feasting and dancing ended the ritual.

The Tlingit warrior was armed with a dagger (often with a blade at each end) (fig. 12), a short spear, war club, bow and arrows. When fully equipped, he wore a shirt of untanned moose hide (traded from the interior), over which was armor of wooden slats or rods, which covered his body from neck to the knees (fig. 13). On his head and neck were a wooden visor (or collar) and helmet, with eye slits where the two joined. These were carved like crest animals or ferocious human faces to frighten the enemy. For greater mobility, the warrior might pin his hair on top of his head (like a shaman) and wear only a hide tunic, both face and shirt painted with his clan crests.

Kinship

The Tlingit kinship terms are bifurcate collateral in the first ascending generation, distinguishing 'father', 'father's brother', 'father's sister', 'mother', 'mother's sister' (literally 'little mother'), and 'mother's brother'; the terms for parents' brothers and sisters were extended to father's and mother's clan mates. In the speaker's generation the terms are of the Crow type, merging parallel cousins with siblings, father's sister's children with father's siblings, and mother's brother's children with brother's children.

Cross-cousins are also distinguished by descriptive compounds, such as 'mother's brother's daughter', 'father's sister's son'. Siblings and parallel cousins of the same sex are distinguished as older or younger than the speaker or referent, while those of the opposite sex are not. Grandparents and all relatives of the second and third ascending generation are identified by a single term, and there is a single reciprocal term. There are separate terms for some, but not all, affines. The consanguineal terms have collective forms that may be applied to whole groups of relatives that stand in special relationships to one another.

Life Cycle

● BIRTH Every baby was believed to be a reincarnation of a deceased maternal relative; the time between death and rebirth was when one "was ashes." Many babies are said to have remembered persons and events known in their previous incarnation (De Laguna 1972, 2:776–783; Stevenson 1966:191–240).

Childbirth took place in a bark shelter, where mother and child remained about 10 days, to avoid contaminating

Smithsonian, Dept. of Anthr.: left 9936; right, 60189.
Fig. 12. Fighting knives. left, Classic Northern Northwest Coast–style dagger, bipointed, with unifacially fluted blades, the smaller having an animal head. The eyes are inlaid with abalone, the grip wrapped in elkskin covered with heavy twine. Such knives were hammered out on crude native forges from trade iron. The smaller blade was used to gash the face, distracting the combatant so as to finish him (Caamaño 1938:203; see also Beresford 1789:244; Portlock 1789:260–261). Collected at Sitka before 1870. right, Later version of the Northern dagger. The blade has a midline ridge on one surface; the other is concave. The carved wooden haft is wrapped in heavy twine. The crest is a bear, inlaid with abalone. Collected by J.J. McLean from the Hutsnuwu, Killisnoo, Alaska, 1881. Length of left 10.5 cm; other to scale.

the house and its occupants. She was attended by two or more experienced women, preferably her husband's sisters, who were later well paid.

● CHILDHOOD A small boy's training began in earnest at seven or eight when he went to live with his maternal uncle, who saw to it that the lad toughened and purified himself by taking morning baths in icy water, switching his body, chopping wood, and doing other daily exercises, and who also taught him hunting magic and ritual. The boy had to observe certain food taboos until his first successful hunt, celebrated by a feast, established him as a "master of game." From his uncle, he also learned the traditions and prerogatives of their clan and lineage, especially important if his uncle were a house owner or chief and the nephew his selected heir. Although he could use his uncle's property and even had access to his wife, he was subject to his uncle's orders and had to work for him. A girl also had to learn practical things, and she was subject to food taboos in anticipation of her first menses.

● PUBERTY The most important event in a girl's life was her first menstruation, for her conduct then would determine her own future and that of her relatives. She was confined ideally for two years, but the length depended upon her rank and her father's wealth. During this time she was supervised by her father's sister, although often her mother or maternal grandmother would take charge and teach her the traditions of their clan. She would emerge from the dark cellar or room with the admired transparent complexion, but with legs almost too weak for walking.

Ritual acts were performed to bring wealth. She had to use a special scratcher to avoid self-contamination; she wore a black feather cap and had her hair washed in blueberry juice to preserve its color in old age. For the first eight days she had nothing to eat or drink except for a little water offered on the fourth day and on the eighth. If she reached greedily for the proffered drink, it was thrown away, to teach her self-control. When she broke her fast at the end of eight days, her maternal relatives feasted her "opposites" and gave her dolls to paternal cross-cousins.

During the remaining months of seclusion she was forbidden fresh fish, shellfish, and seaweed and was served from her own dishes. If she looked at the sky, it would bring storms or other disasters; to prevent this she wore a big hood, hung with tassels of dentalia.

At the end of this time, she was bathed, given new clothes, including perhaps a button blanket, gold bracelets, and other ornaments. Her labret hole was pierced or perhaps enlarged for a small stud, and at the potlatch to reward her paternal aunts she was presented as ready for marriage.

● MARRIAGE Marriage was always with a member of the opposite moiety, preferably with a member of the father's clan and house. Marriage of a man with his "father's sister" (or with her daughter or maternal niece, called by the same term), or of a woman with her "father's brother" (or his maternal nephew and heir, also termed alike) were ideal unions, insuring that the spouses were of equal rank. Since an individual's mother's brother was frequently married to his or her father's sister, the cross-cousin sought as a mate was their child, and the two houses or lines were continually linked. The wealth given by the bride's father, in return for the bride price from the groom's relatives, might include crest objects (appropriate since father-in-law and son-in-law were ideally of the same clan), and marriages might be arranged solely to secure such treasures. An established man could take his bride home; a poorer man remained for a time to work for his father-in-law. If a man, as heir, married his uncle's widow or her daughter, there was, of course, no removal; the girl in such a case remained in her father's house.

A man might be married to two or more sisters at the same time. On the death of a wife he was entitled to replace her with her younger sister or other close kinswoman. Similarly, the widow was expected to marry her husband's brother or maternal nephew, although there were said to be a few women of high rank who had several husbands simultaneously. These secondary marriages

Smithsonian, Dept. of Anthr.: top left, 168157; top right, 74343; center left, 9243; bottom left, 74438; bottom right, 130589.

Fig. 13. Armor. top left, Helmet carved as a human head, cut from a solid block of wood. Eyebrows are painted brown, the eyes black, lips reddish brown against a background of light green. On the helmet proper, formlines are painted dark brown against a vermilion background. Remnants of tufts of hair stud the crown. Collected from the Taku, 1893. top right, Wooden collar. It was held in place by a basketry strap passed through the front and clenched in the teeth of the wearer. A strap of leather secured the rear of the collar. Slight indentations at the top permitted limited vision. Collected in Sitka, Alaska, 1888. center left, Wooden body armor, 32 slats of cedar and other woods tightly woven with fine sinew and other cord. Front and back sections are joined at the sides by elkskin cords. The armor is secured to the body with a broad band of elk hide over the right shoulder and a hide tie on the left side of the body. A toggle on the left side of the breastplate was probably for suspension of a quiver. Collected at Sitka, Alaska, before 1859. bottom left, Greave, of 12 tapered hardwood slats and 8 rods woven together with sinew cord. When tied around the leg, the hollowed out sections accommodate the knee and instep. Collected in Alaska, 1884. bottom right, Body armor of walrus and moose hide. The thick walrus hide—2 body pieces and a shoulder guard sewn with sinew—joins 3 pieces of fringed, recycled moose hide armor, front and back, at the open left side. The section of moose hide at back shows a portion of painted bear's crest. Fringes on the right of this recycled armor show that it was used by a right-handed man; the walrus hide armor with the open, fringed side on the left, was evidently used by a left-handed man. Collected in Alaska before 1889. Length of bottom right, 96 cm; center left and bottom left same scale.

218

DE LAGUNA

often united persons of very unequal age, so in compensation a suitably related young person might also be appointed as "future wife," or "future husband," when the older spouse died. It was all but impossible to take a new spouse from another clan, once one was "married into" one, yet instances are not unknown. While marriages of the aristocracy perpetuated alliances between the same two noble lines, those of their junior relatives or commoners might be with various clans in the opposite moiety.

● DEATH Death rites for men, women, and children were similar in fundamentals, although they were most elaborate for a man of rank, those for a lineage head or clan chief ending only with the great memorial potlatch at which his heir was installed. The widow was subjected to more severe mourning restrictions than the widower, repeating some of the observances of her puberty. The death of a shaman involved special rites.

Typically, the death of a man initiated eight days of mourning. The deceased's clanmates assembled to sing four mourning songs (De Laguna 1972, 3:1152–1224, "Sib Potlatch Songs") and contribute wealth to pay for the funeral. Men of the opposite moiety, especially those married to the deceased's sisters, cared for the corpse and later performed all the services connected with the funeral and erection of a memorial. (The corpse of a woman was attended by her husband's sisters; that of a child by the father's.) For four days, the deceased lay in state, the traditional clan design painted on his face, dressed in his ceremonial clothes, propped up at the "head of the house," with the lineage treasures piled beside him. For a chief, one or more slaves might be killed, or set free if he so asked. Cremation usually took place on the fourth day, but the corpse of a great chief might be kept until well decomposed (Krause 1956:163).

During the wake, the widow and the mourners (clanmates of the deceased) dressed in old clothes with ropes around their waists. Their hair was cut off or later burned off in the cremation fire. They were not allowed to work, so although they supplied the food, it was cooked in another house by their "opposites," who fed them and feasted on it themselves. Morning and evening, the bereaved sang four clan songs. The widow fasted for eight days, eating sparingly every other evening, when she put some food into the fire for the deceased. The "opposites," who kept watch by the corpse, enlivened the time with games and songs, admonished the relatives not to weep too much, lest excessive grief cause the death of another relative.

Men of the opposite moiety carried the corpse from the house through an opening made by removing a wall plank. They built the pyre and cremated it (in later times, making the coffin and the grave), while the bereaved clan sang four more clan songs, and the widow's clanswomen, dressed in button blankets, swayed to the music. Valuable possessions of the deceased and even a bound slave were sometimes thrown on the pyre. Finally, the "opposites" gathered the bones and ashes in a blanket and placed them in the lineage grave box or mortuary totem pole.

That evening the mourners feasted their opposites. The hosts did not eat but gave blankets or other wealth to those who had "worked on the grave" or pyre, guests of rank receiving the most, although the ghosts of the bereaved clan were supposed to obtain the spiritual counterpart of the goods. Since the hosts sang their clan mourning songs, Olson (1967:60) calls the occasion a "crying feast," of which there were ideally four, although the wealthy might give eight. After the guests had been fed, the host chief eulogized the deceased and called on all his clan in turn, beginning with those of lowest rank, so that all could introduce a mourning song for their relatives who had died. At the end, the host sang four clan mourning songs, while his clan brothers-in-law handed out wealth for the guests.

With the end of mourning, the widow and mourners were freed from all restrictions. They washed, donned new clothes, and burned all their old garments and the bedding that the widow had shared with her husband.

The funeral of a shaman was somewhat similar, except that the hair of the widow and of the deceased's clanmates could not be cut. The body was not cremated but was put into a little house or cave, with some of his paraphernalia, and an image of a spirit guardian. Other objects were preserved for his successor (Veniaminov 1985:404–405).

Cremation, gradually given up in favor of inhumation under missionary influence, became rare by 1880. Even in the eighteenth century, the scalps and heads of noted warriors and shamans were preserved.

The most ancient graves, particularly in the south, were mortuary columns, carved with clan crests and hollowed out to receive the ashes of the dead (Swanton 1908a:figs. 109–111). At a Yakutat cemetery in 1791, a huge wooden bear held the box of ashes in his paws (De Laguna 1972, 3: pls. 60–61). More characteristic of the north were the boxes for ashes set on high posts. Later Tlingit grave boxes or grave houses were not raised, often had the sides painted with crest designs, or were covered with a Chilkat blanket (Krause 1956:159).

When inhumation was adopted, the little house set on the grave was often complete with doors and glass windows, through which one could see the possessions of the deceased. Finally the grave houses were replaced by cement slabs over the grave; graves were often fenced; and by the late nineteenth century, marble tombstones (often carved in crest symbols from wooden models) were obtained. Those of the late twentieth century bear the conventional inscriptions and Christian emblems.

In former times the bodies of slaves were usually thrown out on the beach, to be washed away or eaten by scavengers (Young 1927:93; Jones 1914:118).

The Potlatch

There were three important feasts or ceremonies: the funeral feast; the memorial potlatch; and a feast for the children, in which the ears of noble children were pierced (Krause 1956:163–165; Veniaminov 1985:419–425). With the new wealth obtained in the late nineteenth and early twentieth centuries, more large potlatches seem to have been given, although the memorial feast and the honoring of children might be combined.

The memorial potlatch consisted of what Olson (1967: 61) has called "four joy feasts" and lasted four, eight, or more days, involving as hosts or guests all members of the community, as well as a guest clan invited from another tribe. Within this series, the potlatch proper was the climax, when the host clan, in honor of their deceased relatives, repaid in full the members of the opposite moiety (their guests) for their services during the funeral feast. While only a wealthy man (or woman) could give a potlatch, the occasion enabled his poorer clanmates to contribute wealth and so pay off their own funeral debts, so that a single ceremony concluded the rites for several deceased persons in the same clan. At this time, the heir and new house master assumed his title, exhibited his crests, bestowed honorable names on the juniors of his clan, or had the ears of his own children pierced. Payments were made to guests not only for their work but also for being witness to the honors and prerogatives claimed by the hosts, which might include territorial rights symbolized by crest objects displayed.

Thus, while the potlatch was primarily to honor the dead, it also served the prestige of the living, and an ambitious man might have his house rebuilt or repaired many times, on each occasion assuming a new title and a new name for his house. Only the great Chief Shakes of the Stikine is said to have achieved the ultimate of eight major potlatches.

The potlatch had to be planned by the house master and fellow hosts well in advance in order to accumulate enough food and property. The wife of the chief host went to all her clan "brothers" to collect property. This was really a loan, for it would be returned to them with additional gifts, but it would help to make a bigger show at the potlatch. In addition, the wife contributed all her own property, while her husband's fellow clanmates pledged their wealth.

The guest clan from another tribe arrived by canoe on the beach, met not only by their hosts in the opposite moiety but also by the local guests, a different clan in their own moiety. Because these two guest clans were rivals who "danced against each other," they met with mutual suspicion, singing peace songs, and the host was careful to treat them alike, to avert trouble.

That evening, the guests were entertained at a smoking feast, in which tobacco was offered via the fire to all the dead of the host clan. Clan mourning songs were sung, the clan history recalled, and perhaps a few gifts distributed.

At the feast the next day, quantities of food were served and some put into the fire for the dead. Often the two guest clans, or their champions, vied with each other in feats of gluttony to honor their hosts. That evening, the guest clans each danced four times to Athapaskan or Tsimshian songs, to thank their hosts.

Sometimes this feasting and dancing might continue for several days, especially if there were several houses of the same or allied clans hosting the guests. The proceedings were enlivened by joking between clan children, between "fathers-in-law" and their "daughters-in-law," by dances performed by members of the hosts' clan imitating their crest animals, or wearing masks like those of their shamans.

On the last day, all the property was brought to the house, and the host dressed in his heirloom regalia, especially his crest hat. All the members of the clan and the clan "grandchildren" to be honored also wore ceremonial garments. The chief recited his clan history; each member of his clan was called on to introduce a mourning song and to indicate to whom his contribution should be given. The wealth in furs, coppers, money, dishes, and blankets went to those who had worked on the house or the funerary memorials, the visiting chiefs receiving the most, perhaps slaves if the host were wealthy.

Then the house owner could take a new name and, though perhaps bankrupt, was honored because he had "finished the body" and could look forward to receiving gifts when his guests potlatched.

Feasts followed on succeeding days, and the guests danced to express their thanks. Because they exhibited their own crest costumes, they paid their hosts to validate this display.

Olson (1967:68–69) reports that a very wealthy chief, who had inherited the right, might give a potlatch to enoble his own children. While given primarily for the oldest child, other children of the same house or lineage were included. For a great potlatch of this kind, guests belonging to the father's moiety, but to a different clan, would be invited from another village or tribe. After several days of feasting and dancing, guest chiefs or noble women pierced the ears of the children or tattooed the hands of the girls. Each guest received gifts, most going to those who decorated the children. The slave who had dressed them was freed. Only people who had been honored in this way as children could properly be called "noble" (ʔaˑnyádi 'child of the town'), and those of highest rank would bear witness to eight potlatches in their honor by the four holes in each ear.

While the Tlingit occasionally gave a potlatch to remove a disgrace, they did not give one to overwhelm a rival. The only rivalry was between the two guest clans.

Harvard U., Peabody Mus.: 69-30-10/1908.
Fig. 14. Charm, worn suspended from the neck or clothing. Charms were made by shamans and given to their clients to ensure good health, good hunting, and the like. This ivory figure represents a shaman as indicated by the crown and long braided hair. The octopus he grasps is his spirit helper. Collected by E.G. Fast, 1867–1868; height 15 cm.

Modern Tlingits refer to the potlatch as an investment, like putting money in the bank, because in the long run such wealth would be returned, and the original gift insured an honored reputation.

Shamanism and Witchcraft

The shaman (*ʔixí*) was the most powerful figure in his own lineage or clan. While most shamans were men, there were some women of reputedly equal power. If consulted in time, and if not opposed by stronger forces, the shaman could cure the sick, control the weather, bring success in war or hunting, send his familiar spirit to communicate with colleagues at a distance or bring back news from far away, foretell the future, rescue and restore those captured by Land Otter Men (humans who after death by drowning or exposure were transformed into land otter form), expose witches, and make awesome public displays of his power. Although he accompanied war parties of his own clansmen, a shaman was not consulted when they were sick, for he could not save them. Rather, when serious or lingering illness suggested witchcraft, the patient called in a shaman of a different clan, preferably from another village, since the witch was likely to be a near kinsman.

The shaman owed his powers to his spirits, whom he controlled and who inspired him, entering his body and speaking through him, some in Tlingit, but many in Tsimshian (for many shamanistic practices evidently came from the south). There is evidence that some (all?) of a shaman's familiar spirits were the souls of those who had died (De Laguna 1972, 2:835–836). Each appeared to the

shaman in both animal and anthropomorphic form, bore a personal name (which the shaman often assumed as his own), was summoned by a special song, and was represented in the shaman's regalia or costume—ivory charms (fig. 14), headdress, mask (fig. 15), face paint, decorated robe or apron, carved rattle (fig. 15), and wand.

At the death of a shaman, his attendant spirits were supposed to remain close to his corpse and his "outfit," while his own spirit or ghost chose his successor, some junior relative who had come into contact with his corpse or grave. The call was signaled by illness, dizziness, fainting, and seizures, or singing the dead shaman's songs. Then the novice would be taken by his assistant into the woods, where he would encounter a spirit in animal form, usually a land otter, and secure its power by killing it and cutting off a slice of its tongue. On subsequent retreats, the shaman would acquire more spirit helpers.

To keep himself fit to receive the spirits, the shaman had to endure frequent and prolonged periods of fasting, thirsting, purging with sea water or devil's club infusions, and sexual abstinence. The shaman and his family could not eat shellfish or seaweed except during the one moon when Property Woman was believed to do so. He could not comb or cut his hair, nor could his wife cut hers. From 1868 to 1893, when the U.S. naval authorities seized shamans accused of torturing witches, they destroyed their powers by forcibly shaving their heads (Scidmore 1893:46–47; Beardslee 1882:58–59; Coontz 1930: 123–124).

While shamans purveyed medicines and amulets, their major function was the detection of a witch (*nu·kʷ śa·tí* 'master of sickness'), who had to be discovered by a shaman in a spirit seance. The witch would be tightly bound, the head strained back by the hair, thorny devil's club pressed into the flesh, and kept until hunger and thirst forced a confession. Sometimes the accused was left on the beach, to be drowned by the rising tide, which would also wash away his evil. The witch was traditionally the unsuccessful jealous kinsman or the slave of the patient and caused his illness or death by putting a doll made from his hair, scraps of clothing, or other "witches' dirt" by the decaying corpse of a dog or human being. If a witch could be forced to remove this and wash it in the sea, the patient would recover (Veniaminov 1985:408–411).

Religion

Aboriginal Tlingit religion was animistic and ethical, although not focused on a high god or gods. While Raven did much in myth time to make the world as it is now, he was not a creator; as a trickster-transformer, he was often actuated by base motives.

All living things and even natural features and the celestial bodies were believed to have indwelling spirits or souls. These could and should be respectfully addressed by

221

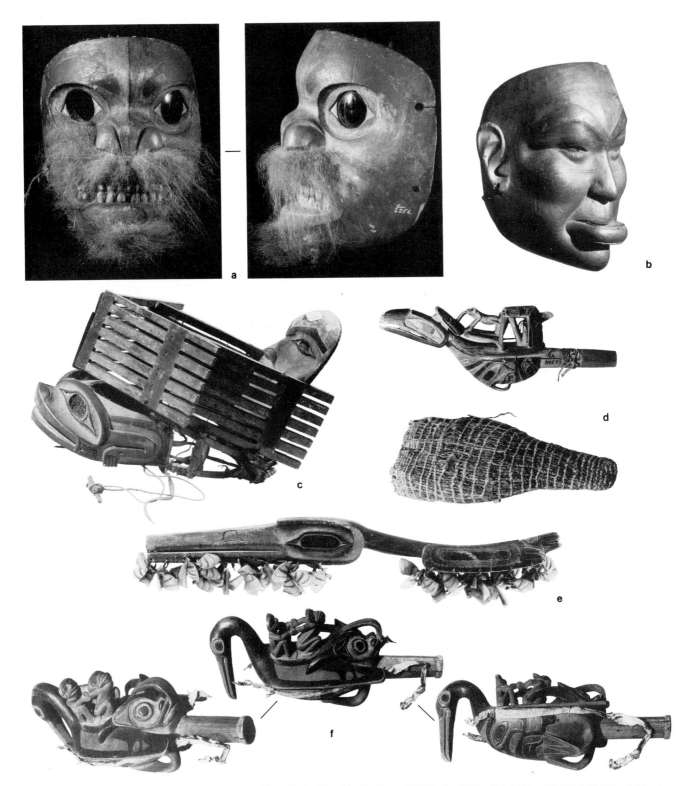

Amer. Mus. of Nat. Hist., New York: a, E/2356; c, 16.1/1047; b, R.I. School of Design, Mus. of Art, Providence: 45.089; U. of Pa., U. Mus., Philadelphia: d, NA 9467; f, NA 1674; e, Smithsonian, Dept. of Anthr.: 20828.

Fig. 15. Masks and rattles. a, Doctor's mask taken from a cave on the Porpoise Is., Alaska. Teeth are opercula, eyes are green bottle glass, and the beard is Alaska brown bear fur. It is painted in black, red, and green. Collected by G.T. Emmons, before 1894. b, Mask of a woman with labret, nose ring, and face painting. Portrait masks were used by shamans to represent spirits, and others were made for dancing at potlatches and for sale to whites. Collected about 1830. c, Wooden ceremonial headdress of a fish trap, used in public performances to act out myths and stories. Collected by E.H. Harriman in 1899. d, Raven rattle and cover woven of woolen twine and bark. A raven is carved on the tail, and a hawk depicted on the belly. The human figure on the bird's back is connected by a tongue to a frog, likely symbolizing the transfer of power from a spirit helper. Collected by Louis B. Shotridge before 1923. e, Rattle carved in abstract form to represent a bird (a crane?) and bedecked with puffin beaks. Collected by James G. Swan on Prince of Wales Is., Alaska, 1875. f, Oyster-catcher rattle, exclusive property of a shaman. A goat's head is carved near the handle; on the bird's back is a witch torture scene. Collected 1908–1914. Height of a, 23.5 cm; b to same scale. Length of c 39 cm; d–f to same scale.

DE LAGUNA

human beings who needed to win their active help or friendly acquiescence; disaster might follow neglect, disrespect, or incorrect invocation. Some manufactured articles (such as halibut hooks and canoes) were at time exhorted as if they were alive.

The world was believed full of mysterious beings, able to help or harm man. Thus, there was Property Woman who roams the woods and the mysterious underwater monster, both of which could bring good fortune and wealth to the person who saw them and knew what to do.

While death ended life in this world, it was only an introduction to existence on another plane, which in turn would end with reincarnation. Those who died a natural death journeyed through a thorny forest and crossed a river to the Town of the Dead (the cemetery with grave houses), where they warmed themselves by the cremation fires, subsisting on the food and drink put into the fire by their relatives, or consumed in their memory at potlatches. Those who died by violence went to a "heaven," or land above the sky. The very wicked (liars, thieves, witches) went instead to "Raven's home" or "Dog Heaven" (Swanton 1908a:461; De Laguna 1972, 2:771-772).

History†

The first recorded contact between Tlingits and Europeans occurred in 1741, when the Russian explorer Alexei Chirikov lost two boats in what seems to have been a brief hostile encounter. Contact may not have occurred again until 1775, when the Spanish explorer Bruno de Hezeta explored in Klawak, Sitka, and Hoonah territory and accidentally infected the Sitka Tlingit with smallpox. During the next 20 years the Tlingit were visited by several European exploring expeditions, including Jean Francois Galaup, comte de LaPérouse in 1786, Alejandro Malaspina in 1791 (fig. 16), and George Vancouver in 1793-1794, as well as by a number of fur traders, mainly British at first but increasingly American. During this period the Russians were occupied farther west, in the Aleutians and on Kodiak, and were gradually expanding their quest for furs eastward along the Gulf of Alaska. In 1788 they reached Yakutat Bay. During the 1790s they explored farther into Tlingit territory, and in 1799, Aleksandr Baranov established a fort at Sitka. In 1802 a group of Tlingits captured this fort, but in 1804 the Russians defeated the Indians and built a new fort Novo-Arkangel'sk (New Archangel). In 1808 this became the headquarters of the Russian-American Company and the administrative center of Russian America until Alaska was purchased by the United States in 1867.

During the Russian period, the Tlingit maintained their independence away from Sitka and a second Russian fort at Wrangell. But at the posts they acquired tools,

Museo de América, Madrid: 191.
Fig. 16. Yakutat woman and child. The woman wears an unadorned hide cloak and skirt and displays a lower lip labret. The infant, with nose decorations possibly of dentalia, is in a basketry cradle with hide cover (De Laguna 1972:503–504). Pencil sketch by Tomás de Suría, Port Mulgrave, Khantaak I., Alaska, on Malaspina Expedition, 1791.

cloth, and other goods, and a number were converted to Russian Orthodox Christianity, especially after the severe smallpox epidemic of 1835-1839. In 1839 the Russians leased a part of Tlingit territory to the Hudson's Bay Company, but the Tlingit resisted British attempts to break their own monopoly of trade with the interior. Meanwhile, they continued to trade with American ships, which, contrary to Russian and British regulations, freely supplied them with liquor and firearms. By the late 1850s Tlingit canoes were also going south as far as Victoria and Puget Sound for trading, seasonal work, and occasional raiding. In spite of conflict and disease, the period from 1840 to 1867 was one of great Tlingit prosperity.

During the early years after the purchase, the posting of U.S. troops at Sitka, Fort Tongass, and Fort Wrangell and the influx of prospectors and adventurers brought prosperity followed by a depression. Drunken and lawless soldiers and miners debauched the natives, especially after a soldier taught the Hutsnuwu to distill moonshine liquor. Conflict was frequently exacerbated by the Americans' failure to understand and respect Tlingit legal principles, especially liability and compensation for deaths and injuries. Such conflict resulted in 1869 in the destruction of Kake villages and the bombardment of the Stikine

† The section on History was written with the help of Wallace Olsen.

223

village at Wrangell and in 1882 in the destruction of Angoon.

The 1870s and 1880s saw the development of commercial fishing which provided employment for Natives, and of tourism, which provided a market for Indian curios. The gold rush of 1898-1899 brought thousands of miners through Chilkat-Chilkoot territory, where the natives earned good wages as packers, though very few struck it rich themselves.

Meanwhile, Christianity was becoming more influential. American Presbyterians began mission work with the Tlingit in 1877 (Jackson 1880:140) and by 1882 they were operating six schools in the region, three of them boarding schools (Jones 1914:245). They made many converts, especially among younger people, and took a strong stand against much of traditional Tlingit culture. During the late 1890s and early 1900s, there was a great increase in Tlingit membership in the Russian Orthodox Church (fig. 18), which was more accommodating to native culture and more attractive to conservative clan leaders, some of whom came to occupy important positions in church-sponsored temperance and mutual aid societies. The Orthodox clergy also opposed the removal of children from their families to go to boarding schools (B.S. Smith 1980:26). Particularly attractive to some Tlingit were the elaborate Orthodox mortuary and memorial rites, some of which became syncretized with the indigenous ones (Kan 1985). At Sitka, by the early 1900s, Protestant or Orthodox Christmas as well as Orthodox Easter (with its elaborate processions, blessings of the native houses and

fishing boats, and exchanges of ritual food) became an integral part of the Sitka Tlingit annual cycle. The Salvation Army and the Episcopal Church also gained some converts during this period, and the Church of God after 1950.

By 1900, acculturation of the Tlingit was well advanced, through work for the canneries, contact with miners, merchants, and missionaries. The Tlingit increasingly shifted from a subsistence economy to one based on wage work and commercial fishing. Small settlements were abandoned, their people moving to major towns and in summer to the canneries. Many worked in British Columbia canneries also or continued to pick hops in Washington. Slavery was obsolete, and slaves were adopted as poor relatives of their former masters.

Potlatches became smaller and less elaborate as ceremonial objects were sold to museums and lineage houses were replaced by small dwellings. Some younger and more Americanized Tlingits turned away from potlatching altogether, but a greater number were committed to hiring members of the opposite moiety to perform funerary services and then compensating them at a memorial

Fig. 18. Tlingit leaders with Russian Orthodox Archimandrite Anatolii Kamenskii, and Kharlampii Sokolov, an interpreter and psalm reader. Front row, far left (wearing a top hat) is Ioann L'aanteech, a chief of the ka·gwa·nta·n clan of Sitka; third from left is Chief Jack; far right is Aanyaalahaash, a chief of the ġa·naxʔádi clan of the Taku. Photograph, cropped, by William H. Case, Sitka, Alaska, 1898.

Fig. 17. Wooden pipe said to represent a young eagle, presumably the owner's crest. Aboriginally, tobacco was chewed or sucked as snuff. Pipe smoking was acquired from sailors during the earliest periods of White contact, and pipes became popular items of embellishment, often elaborately carved in naturalistic or fanciful forms and decorated with crests or figures representing myths or mythic events. Collected by G.T. Emmons from the Stikine, Alaska, before 1894; length 12 cm.

224

Alaska Histl. Lib., Juneau: PCA 87-223.
Fig. 19. qa·-ẋa·qtí 'man's slain body', chief of the Raven ʔa·nẋa·k hít-ta·n clan of the Hutsnuwu, an Indian policeman, in the door of his house at Killisnoo, Alaska. Over the door is a shield probably depicting the Indian village over the Stars and Stripes and a poem ridiculing his claim to a position of high status. His rival was Killisnoo (or Saginaw) Jake, chief of the Raven de·ši·ta·n clan of the Hutsnuwu. Photograph by Lloyd V. Winter and Edwin P. Pond, Killisnoo, Alaska, about 1900.

potlatch.

Rapid acculturation was the express goal of the Alaska Native Brotherhood, founded at Sitka in 1912 to work for the advancement of the Native people and to combat discrimination. This organization arose out of a background of experience in Protestant church-sponsored societies but differed in that it was not confined to a single village and it was free of non-Indian guidance. It was probably also to some extent inspired by White organizations struggling for home rule in Alaska. The Alaska Native Sisterhood was soon organized, and by the mid-1920s there were branches of these organizations in all Tlingit villages (Drucker 1958).

Table 2. From Tlingit Tribes to Corporations

Historic Identity	Location in 1980	Village Corporation
Yakutat	Yakutat	Yak-tak Corporation
Hoonah	Hoonah	Huna Totem Corporation
Chilkat	Klukwan and Haines	Klukwan Corporation
Auk } Taku }	Juneau[a]	Goldbelt Corporation
Sitka	Sitka	Shee-Atika Corporation
Hutsnuwu	Angoon	Hootznoowoo, Inc.
Sumdum	Juneau[a]	
Kake	Kake	Kake Tribal Corporation
Kuiu	Kake[a]	
Klawak	Klawock	Klawock Heenya
Henya	Craig	Shaan-Seet, Inc.
Stikine	Wrangell[a]	
Tongass } Sanya }	Ketchikan[a]	Cape Fox Corporation

[a]Under the Alaska Native Claims Settlement Act of 1971, villages located in historic sites as Native villages were allowed to form village corporations. By this time, however, some historic villages had been abandoned and the descendants of these people were living in other southeastern towns or had moved elsewhere. The towns given in the list are those in which many members of historic villages resided in 1980.

In 1915 the territorial legislature enfranchised those Alaska Natives who could show they followed a "civilized way of life" (Arnold 1976:83). In 1924 all Alaska Natives were enfranchised by federal law. Tlingits became active in public affairs, several being elected to the territorial legislature. The Alaska Native Brotherhood's campaign against racial segregation resulted in the Antidiscrimination Act of 1946.

Acculturation and participation in the economic and political life of Alaska did not obliterate tribal identity. Most of the mid-nineteenth century Tlingit tribes continued to exist as separate villages, though some moved and a few became assimilated into others (see table 2).

The Organic Act of 1884 guaranteed that the Natives would "not be disturbed in the possession of any lands actually in their use or occupation or now claimed by them" (Gruening 1954:355) and then put off giving them any way of getting legal title. The Tlingit had little protection against encroaching Whites. Then in 1907 any possibility of expanding what lands they had managed to keep seemed blocked by a presidential proclamation creating the Tongass National Forest of all lands not in private hands.

Tribal economies were helped in the late 1930s, when some villages incorporated under the Indian Reorganization Act and acquired canneries, sawmills, fishing boats, and other capital. But settling the land question was an on-going concern, which led to the formation, during World War II, of the Central Council of Tlingit and

Fig. 20. Fishing cooperative, Yakutat, Alaska. Fish and crabs are brought in by native-owned boats to be processed and sent to Anchorage, Alaska. The decline in salmon runs since about 1900 has resulted in the state's policy of severely limiting the number of commercial fishing licenses, which have become valuable private property. The cost of a license and boat therefore limit the number of Tlingits who can fish commercially. Fishing for home consumption is still possible without a license but is not nearly so productive as in the past. Photograph, cropped, by Judy Ramos, 1980.

Haida. This organization worked for a land claims settlement of $80 million but in the end received $7.5 million. Under the Alaska Native Claims Settlement Act of 1971, the Tlingit and Alaska Haida formed the Sealaska Regional Corporation and village corporations in the 10 historic villages still occupied (table 2). The regional corporation retained title to 194,000 acres, later adjusted to about 200,000 acres; each of the 10 village corporations received title to surface rights to about 23,000 acres, while the regional corporation held subsurface rights to this additional area of about 230,000 acres. Both the Sealaska and the village corporations became active in logging and fishing.

In numbers the Tlingit dropped from a possible 10,000 in the eighteenth century to a low of less than 4,000 in 1920 (table 1), to increase again to nearly 10,000 in 1985 (U.S. Bureau of Indian Affairs. Financial Management Office 1985:10) largely because of greatly improved health services. In the mid-1980s many Tlingits were continuing to live in their traditional villages, though some members of every tribe had chosen to live in urban centers in Alaska or to go south to Seattle or elsewhere. In 1985, it was estimated that over 40 percent of the Sealaska shareholders (which included Alaska Haida) lived outside southeastern Alaska (Wallace Olsen, personal communication 1985).

Village life held amenities such as telephones, television (perhaps by satellite), and freezers, though electricity was often generated by diesel power and expensive. Every village had a grade school and some had high schools. Often the Alaska Native Brotherhood–Alaska Native Sisterhood hall served as a community center. Every village had at least one church—Russian Orthodox, Presbyterian, or Salvation Army.

The traditional clan system had declined in importance, some of its functions being performed by the newer

social groups, but extended family ties were still strong. Some use of Native foods and practice of Native crafts survived, and the Tlingit language was still spoken by some people over 40, especially at Klukwan, Hoonah, Angoon, and Kake. Memorial potlatches for the dead were still held in 1985 (Kan 1985). Since 1970 there has been a revival of many aspects of Tlingit culture, including potlatching, the associated singing and dancing, and crest arts.

Synonymy

The name Tlingit comes from the Tlingit name for themselves, łi·ngít 'human being(s)'; historical spellings include Clingats, Klinket, Thlinket, Tlinkit, and others. An earlier name appearing as Kaloshes, Kolloshians, (German) Kaljuschen and Koljuschen, (French) Koloches, etc., is from the Russian designation, variously written Koloshi, Kaloshi, Koliushi, Koliuzhi, Kaliuzhi (plurals, pronounced with the accent on the first syllable); according to Veniaminov (1985:380-381) this was derived from Aleut kalu·kax̣ 'wooden dish' (Russianized diminutive kalushka), referring to the wooden labrets of the Tlingit women (Krause 1956:64; Hodge 1907-1910, 1:723, 2:764-765; Grinev 1986). While this designation is carefully restricted to the Tlingit by some writers, others applied it loosely to all Northwest Coast peoples. The Tanaina borrowed this name as gulušutna, gulušuhîana (Kari 1977:44).

The Haida call the Tlingit łi̓nagît (Swanton 1905:105, 107) and łaŋgas (Lawrence 1977:225); the Coast Tsimshian referred to them as gʸid-ġbane̓dz 'people of the north (?)' (Boas 1916:44). The Nishga knew them as kiti-kan 'people among the trees' (Emmons and De Laguna 1945-1985), while the Tahltan called them to-tee-heen 'people of the stinking [salt] water'. According to Jewitt (1815:161), the Nootka referred to the Tlingit as "wooden lips." The Eyak were acquainted only with the Tlingit from Yakutat, whom they called λaʔxaʔlahġ, reflecting the Eyak-Tlingit name ła·xa·yík 'Yakutat Bay' or a related form (Krauss 1970:92; De Laguna 1972, 1:58), but the Chugach Eskimo even knew of the Stikine and called the Tlingit axłut 'killerwhales' (Birket-Smith 1953:100), perhaps referring to the totemic crest of the most aggressive raiders from Yakutat. The Ahtna, associating the Tlingit with Canadian trade routes or with Hudson's Bay Company goods, called them genʒu·y, as if 'King George (men)' (De Laguna and McClellan 1954-1960; Kari and Buck 1975:59); a similar name was used by a number of other Subarctic tribes.

Tribes and Clans

The Tlingit tribes are listed here with the clans represented in each, referred to by the numbers on table 3.

Table 3. Raven and Wolf Clans

Raven Clans	Wolf Clans
1. ġa·naxʔádi	1. ka·gwa·nta·n
2. tá·kʷʔa·ne·dí.	2. kadakʷʔadí (?)
3. ġa·naxte·dí	3. qu·kʷ hít-ta·n
4. ʔí·x̣ʔádi	4. ǯi·šqʷe·dí
5. ʔiški·ta·n or ʔiška hít-ta·n	5. ču·kane·dí
6. łukʷnaxʔádi	6. ġaẏé·šhít-ta·n
7. x̣atka̓ʔa·ẏí	7. daġisdina·
8. qu·sḱe·dí or xa·s hít-ta·n	8. šankukʷe·dí or ša-ngukʷe·dí
9. x̣ałčane·dí	9. qa·x̣us hít-ta·n
10. kiksʔádi	10. ša·ʔa·qʷa·n (?)
11. ti·ẏ hít-ta·n	11. na·ste·dí
12. ti·ẏine·dí	12. na·saxʔádi (?)
13. de·ši·ta·n	13. kú·n hít-ta·n
14. ʔa·nx̣a·kíta·n or ʔa·nx̣a·k hít-ta·n	14. kagʷax hít-ta·n (?)
15. ṫi·ne·dí	15. nika·x̣ʔádi
16. ṫaqde·nta·n	16. ẏanẏe·dí
17. łukʷa·x̣ʔádi	17. wu·ški·ta·n
18. nu·wšaka̓ʔa·ẏí	18. na·nẏa·ʔa·ẏí
19. kʷá·šḱiqʷá·n or kʷá·šḱ-qʷá·n	19. šiknaxʔádi
20. wéx̣hine·dí	20. λenta·n
21. ẏí·sqane·dí (?)	21. ca·ti·ne·dí or ca·ṫine·dí
22. łu·kʷhine·dí	22. waṡi·ne·dí or waṡ-hí·n-ʔádi
23. kuye·dí	23. ne·sʔádi
24. tí·łhít-ta·n	24. ṡi·łqʷe·dí
25. saqʷti·ne·dí or suqʷti·ne·dí	25. kaẏá·ška hít-ta·n
26. kiǯu·kʷ hít-ta·n or giǯu·kʷita·n	26. xu·x̣ʷe·dí (?)
27. tane·dí	27. daqławe·dí
28. qa·čʔádi	28. ca·gʷe·dí
29. ku·qʷ hít-ta·n	29. ga·w hít-ta·n
30. kaẏa·ʔádi	30. łux̣ʷe·dí
31. tuqʷẏe·dí or tuqʷwe·dí	31. xe·ł-qʷá·n
32. ka·sx̣agʷe·dí	32. te·qʷe·dí
33. ta·łqʷe·dí	33. ġałyax-ka·gʷa·nta·n
34. quẏé·q̓ʔádi	34. q̓aq̓a·hít-ta·n (?)
35. hinẏe·dí	35. ʔa·nšukʷahít-ta-·n
36. staxʔádi	36. ḱu·xine·dí
37. tax̣hít ta·n	
38. qagʷe·dí or qakʷʔe·dí	

NOTE: For the tribes in which each clan is represented see the list in the synonymy. The list of clans principally follows De Laguna (1972) and Emmons and De Laguna (1945–1985), with phonemic transcriptions (conjectural where queried) supplied by Jeff Leer and Nora Dauenhauer (personal communications 1985). Some of the listed clans are extinct and some are considered house groups rather than clans by some Tlingits.

Yakutat (ya·kʷdá·t qʷá·n, ła·x̣a·yík qʷá·n). Raven clans: 6, 8, 19, 35, 36. Wolf clans: 16, 29, 30, 32, 33.

Kaliakh (ġałyax̣ qʷá·n). Raven clans: 3, 8, 19. Wolf clan: 4.

Dry Bay (ġuna·xu·). Raven clans: 6, 7, 8, 17. Wolf clans: 1, 3, 7, 8.

Chilkat (ǯiłqá·t qʷá·n). Raven clan: 3. Wolf clans: 1, 7, 27.

Hoonah (xuna· qʷá·n). Raven clans: 6, 7, 8, 16, 37. Wolf clans: 1, 5, 6, 17.

Chilkoot (ǯiłqut qʷá·n). Raven clans: 17, 18. Wolf clans: 7, 8.

Auk (ʔá·ḱʷ qʷá·n). Raven clans: 4 or 30, 15. Wolf clans: 17 or 20.

Sitka (ši·ṫká qʷá·n). Raven clans: 6, 7, 8, 10. Wolf clans: 1, 3, 5, 6, 34 (part of 1?).

Hutsnuwu (xucnu·wú); Angoon. Raven clans: 13, 14, 31, 38. Wolf clans: 17, 27, 28, 32.

Taku (ṫa·qú qʷá·n). Raven clans: 1, 5, 29, 30, 31. Wolf clans: 16, 19, 21, 24.

Sumdum (ṡawdá·n qʷá·n). Raven clan: 1. Wolf clans: 16, 24, 31.

Kake (qé·x̣ qʷá·n, qí·x̣ qʷá·n). Raven clans: 9, 25, 26, 27. Wolf clans: 10, 11, 22, 23, 28.

Kuiu (kuyú qʷá·n), Kuyu. Raven clans: 22, 23. Wolf clans: 10, 11, 12, 13.

Henya (he·nẏa qʷá·n, hinẏa·qʷá·n). Raven clans: 2, 12, 20, 21, 24. Wolf clans: 8, 11, 14, 15, 35.

Klawak (ławá·k qʷa·n), Klawock. Raven clans: 1, 30, 31. Wolf clans: 9, 14.

Stikine (štax̣hí·n qʷá·n); Wrangell. Raven clans: 10, 11, 28, 32, 33. Wolf clans: 18, 19, 26, 31.

Tongass (ta·nṫa qʷá·n; ṫanga·s qʷá·n, ṫanga·š qʷá·n). Raven clan: 1. Wolf clans: 8, 27, 32.

Sanya (sa·nẏa· qʷá·n). Raven clan: 10. Wolf clan: 32. Eagle clan: ne·x̣ʔádi.

Sources

Ethnographic sketches of the Tlingit appear in some works of more general character, such as Veniaminov (1840), Wrangell (1839, 1839a, 1970), Holmberg (1855-1863, 1), Dall (1870, 1877), U.S. Census Office (1884, 1893) volumes on Alaska, and a number of other reports in *Compilations of Narratives of Explorations in Alaska* esp. Abercrombie (1900) and Schwatka (1900). There are also sketches by Bancroft (1886), Grinnell (1901), Shotridge (1917), as well as the more scholarly overall study of the Northwest Coast Indians by Drucker (1955). Guidebooks to Alaska with useful information on the Tlingit and their homeland are those by Scidmore (1885, 1893) and Colby (1939).

Historical works that either include the Tlingit or provide a useful background are: Andreev (1952), Coxe (1803), Gunther (1972), Bancroft (1886, 1886a), Tikhmenev (1978-1979), Holmberg (1855-1863, 2), Okun (1951), Swineford (1898), Gormly (1977), and Drucker (1958).

Of the earlier explorers and traders who met the Tlingit, the most interesting accounts are, with the dates of their observations: Chirikov with Bering, 1741 (in Golder 1922-1925); LaPérouse, 1786 (1799; and in Chinard 1937); Beresford with Dixon, 1787 (Beresford 1789); Suría with Malaspina, 1791 (Malaspina 1885; Suría 1936); Marchand, 1791 (in Fleurieu 1801); Vancouver, 1793, 1794 (1801); Lisianskiĭ, 1804-1805 (1814); Langsdorff, 1805-1806 (1813-1814, 2); Kotzebue, 1825 (1830, 2); Litke, 1826-1829 (1835-1836, 1); and Simpson, 1842 (1847).

Personal accounts from after the purchase of Alaska in 1867 are those of U.S. government agent Colyer (1870), Beardslee (1882), Willard (1884), Muir (1915), Young (1927), and Salisbury (1962).

General ethnographies of the Tlingit are: Krause (1885, 1956, 1981), Knapp and Childe (1896), Swanton (1908a), Jones (1914), Keithahn (1963), De Laguna (1972), Oberg (1973, largely Chilkat), and Emmons and De Laguna (1945-1985).

Works on Tlingit archeology, including petroglyphs, are by: Ackerman (1964, 1965, 1968, 1974), Drucker (1943), Emmons (1908a), Keithahn (1940, 1962), De Laguna (1953, 1960), De Laguna et al. (1964), and Harlan I. Smith (1909).

Tlingit material culture is discussed by Drucker (1950), Emmons (1903, 1907, 1908a), Weber (1986), Holm (1982), Keithahn (1954, 1964), Kissell (1928), Niblack (1890), Osborne (1964), Paul (1944), Samuel (1982), and Shotridge (1919a, 1921, 1928). Many of these focus on basketry and blanket weaving, whereas Shur and Pierce (1976) are especially useful for clothing in 1818.

Villages, houses, and totem poles are treated by Barbeau (1950), Drucker (1948), Emmons (1916), Garfield and Forrest (1948), and Shotridge and Shotridge (1913). Krieger (1928) contains some inaccuracies. Goldschmidt and Haas (1946) survey Tlingit and Alaska Haida land use.

Art is well covered in Boas (1897a), R.T. Davis (1949), Emmons (1930), Collins et al. (1973), Gunther (1962, 1966), Henry (1984), Holm (1965, 1983b), Holm and Reid (1975), Jonaitis (1978, 1981, 1986), Inverarity (1950), MacCallum (1969), and Wardwell (1964, 1978), to mention only a few of the many excellent titles.

Social and intellectual life are stressed in Baugh (1978), Durlach (1928), Garfield (1947), De Laguna (1952, 1954, 1965, 1975), Kan (1983), McClellan (1954), Oberg (1934), Olson (1936a, 1956, 1967), F. Shotridge (1913), Shotridge (1929), Stevenson (1966), and Swanton (1909). Sociopolitical organization and government are discussed in De Laguna (1983).

Averkieva (1971) sketches social history from a Marxist viewpoint. Aspects of acculturation are discussed by Drucker (1976), Klein (1975, 1976), W.M. Olson (1983), Kan (1985), and Tollefson (1977, 1978, 1982, 1984).

Prehistory of the Northern Coast of British Columbia

KNUT R. FLADMARK, KENNETH M. AMES, AND PATRICIA D. SUTHERLAND

Though speaking languages with no proven genetic relationship, the Tsimshian and Haida shared a similar cultural pattern that, with the Tlingit, forms Drucker's (1955) "Northern Province" of the Northwest Coast. In historic times North Coast cultural homogeneity was fostered by institutionalized trade networks, kinship bonds, shared ranking systems, and warfare, which maintained a constant interchange of concepts, goods, and people between the tribes. While late prehistoric cultures in the Haida and Tsimshian areas appear to be similar, those of earlier periods do not; and the nature of the origin and development of the north coast interaction sphere or area cotradition is a major archeological question (Mac-Donald 1969).

Environment

North Coast cultural homogeneity is in contrast to varied environmental conditions between Haida and Tsim-shian territories. In prehistory these differences are often amplified by differential paleo-environmental changes on the inner and outer coasts. Fluctuations in the abundance and dependability of major food resources have been critical in shaping the overall course of Northwest Coast prehistory (Fladmark 1975), and an understanding of northern coast culture change can only come with knowledge of local paleoecology.

Environmental inequalities between Haida and Tsimshian areas primarily derive from the marked isolation and endemic features of the Queen Charlotte Islands. The 4,000-square-mile island group is one of the most disjunct large landmasses associated with North America, and its environmental history exhibits considerable independence from the continental stream of events (Foster 1965).

Tsimshian territory is dominated by the Skeena and Nass rivers, major drainage systems with no equivalent on the Queen Charlotte Islands. The inland distribution of Tsimshian speakers reflects both the suitability of these low-gradient rivers for coast-interior communication and the importance of anadromous fish resources. Massive spawning runs of salmon and eulachon provided a natural cycle of abundance around which the Tsimshian regulated their yearly activities. In addition, communication with the interior and control of a large land area gave the Tsimshian access to a wide variety of terrestrial resources.

In comparison, the historical environment of the Queen Charlotte Islands seems somewhat impoverished. While salmon do spawn in the small island streams, short drainages and a lack of major lakes reduce the productivity of the sockeye and coho runs. Local pink salmon have a two-year periodicity making this species less frequently available than on the mainland, and the islands entirely lack eulachon. The Charlottes' terrestrial fauna are limited. Only two forms of large land mammals are native to the islands: an insular variety of black bear and a now extinct species of dwarf caribou (Foster 1965). Partially compensating for these lacks are intertidal resources at least equivalent to those of the mainland, and a greater access to halibut and other pelagic species, such as northern fur seal. It is crucial to understand that the environment of the region has changed in important if poorly understood ways over the past 10,000 years. Two of the critical factors in these changes are sea levels and climate.

Geological evidence from the northern mainland coast indicates sea levels up to 40 meters above the modern position as late as 5500 B.C. (Armstrong 1966; Heusser 1960). However, work on the upper Skeena River estuary shows that the highest marine transgression into the Skeena occurred at approximately 8500 B.C., at a level 200 meters above present-day sea levels. The sea may have achieved its present position in the Skeena River valley by 6000 B.C. (Clague 1984, 1984a). The modern mainland shoreline has been continuously occupied for 5,000 years, the minimum period for sea-level stability on this coast.

On the Queen Charlottes, sea levels before 8000 B.C. were 30 meters below their modern level (Nasmith 1970; Fladmark 1975), and Hecate Strait would have been quite narrow though it is unlikely the Charlottes were ever connected to the mainland. Sea levels rose to a maximum of 15 meters above modern sea level by about 7000 B.C. This highstand continued until about 2500 B.C., producing a raised strandline around the islands. After 2500 B.C. sea level gradually and continuously declined to its present position.

Postglacial temperatures rose from a nadir of perhaps as low as nine degrees C below the modern yearly average around 8500 B.C. to two to three degrees C above the modern average at 6000 B.C. After that date, annual temperatures continued to fluctuate but with declining amplitude to their modern averages by 4000 to 3000 B.C. It is also likely that the period from 8500 to 6000 B.C. was marked by decreasing rainfall. After 6000 B.C., when annual precipitation was lower than now, rainfall increased to its modern high levels by 4000 B.C. These long-term trends mask shorter cycles in temperature and rainfall that no doubt were also significant to the people of the time.

The composition of local biotic communities changed as coastlines, temperature, and rainfall changed. Organisms do not respond instantaneously to environmental changes, so while the modern mainland coast is probably at least 5,000 years old, the modern climax forest of the region may not have become fully mature until 3,000 years ago (Hebda and Mathewes 1984, 1984a). Fladmark (1975) has argued that stabilization of the mainland coastline at about 3000 B.C. was the critical factor in the development of the rich salmon runs. On the Queen Charlottes, the gradual decline of sea levels starting about 2500 B.C., after several thousand years' stability, implies that the Island's ecosystem may have begun to degrade slightly from former climax levels about 1,000 years after the mainland environment had begun to stabilize.

History of Research

Early work on the North Coast emphasized Prince Rupert Harbour sites (fig. 1). Harlan I. Smith (1909, 1929), Drucker (1943), and Borden (Calvert 1968) indicated some prehistoric time-depth and pointed out certain archeological traits distinctive of the northern coast but did not establish a reliable cultural chronology. Smith (1930) recorded 18 sites on the Skeena River. Very limited tests were conducted on the Queen Charlottes (Duff and Kew 1958:50–54).

In Prince Rupert Harbor 11 sites were excavated between 1966 and 1978, over 200 sites recorded, and some 18,000 artifacts recovered (MacDonald 1969, 1971; MacDonald and Inglis 1981; Ames 1976; Inglis 1973, 1973a; May 1979; Sutherland 1978). A significant element of this project has been the analysis of a very large sample of prehistoric human skeletons (Cybulski 1972, 1975, 1978).

On the Queen Charlottes, several sites were excavated by MacDonald (1969) and Fladmark (1970a, 1970, 1971, 1973, 1975, 1979). Excavations at Blue Jackets Creek and Tow Hill represent the only extensive prehistoric site excavations on the Islands (Severs 1974, 1974a).

Prehistoric research on the Skeena has focused on Kitselas Canyon, where two sites, Gitaus and Paul Mason,

Fig. 1. Archeological sites in the Queen Charlotte Islands and Skeena River areas.

have been excavated (Allaire 1978, 1979). Some survey (Ames 1973) and testing (Ames 1979; MacDonald 1969) has been done elsewhere along the river and its tributaries. The bulk of the research on the Skeena has been oriented toward the historic period.

Early Period Cultures

The prehistory of the Northwest Coast can be conveniently split into two major periods at 3000 B.C., when shell middens appear on the coast.

These two periods are termed here the Early period (8000–3000 B.C.) and the Recent period (3000 B.C. –A.D. 1800). Early period components come almost exclusively from the Queen Charlottes, although materials dating to the end of the period from Kitselas Canyon have been described. The Recent period is represented primarily by components from Prince Rupert Harbour, but significant data have been recovered on the Charlottes and at Kitselas (table 1).

Prince Rupert Harbour

There are no recorded archeological materials on the mainland coast that predate 3000 B.C., although such assemblages have been recovered to the north, in southeastern Alaska (Ackerman 1968; Ackerman, Hamilton, and Stuckenrath 1979; vol.5:136–148; Davis 1979; Lightfoot 1983) and to the south on the British Columbia Coast (Hester and Nelson 1978; Carlson 1979). This absence is not easy to explain. It may be due to sea level changes, and the early sites are located on abandoned beaches back in the forests above the modern coast, or they are drowned. It may be due to the nature of the archeological sample itself. Shell middens are the only sites that have been recorded along this portion of the coast. Early non–shell midden sites would be extremely difficult to locate below the luxuriant vegetation of the coast. It is possible, though unlikely, that the area was unoccupied.

Queen Charlotte Islands

Research on the Queen Charlottes, particularly along the raised 7000–2500 B.C. beach line, has produced most of the Early period data. The bulk of this material is assigned to the Moresby tradition (6000–3000 B.C.). There is some scattered evidence of yet earlier materials. Hobler (1978) recovered water-rolled pebble cores and flakes from a series of sites in the modern intertidal zone on the southern portions of Moresby Island. If the sea level curves sketched above are applicable, these materials must predate 8000 B.C.

A very small set of early artifacts was recovered throughout an eight-meter thick stratified gravel beach deposit at the Skoglund's Landing site on Graham Island. The collection consists of pebble choppers and a flake core. These materials are seen here as the result of a site eroded out by the rising waters of the sea level highstand, and the lowest artifacts may be 9,000 years old. Weathered pebble tools and cores have been found on old surfaces and, with the south Moresby beach assemblages and the Skoglund's Landing assemblage, may be part of an early, simple flaked stone industry. These materials differ technologically from those of the Moresby tradition.

Fourteen excavated components of the Moresby tradi-

Table 1. Concordance of North Coast Cultural Sequences

		Prince Rupert Harbour	Queen Charlotte Islands	Kitselas Canyon
Recent Period	1000	I		Historic ?
	500			
	B.C. A.D	II	Graham Tradition	Kleanza
	1000			Paul Mason
		III		Skeena
	2000			Gitaus
	3000		Transitional Complex	Bornite
Early Period	4000		Moresby Tradition	
	5000	?		?
	6000			
			Intertidal Assemblages ?	
	7000			

tion occur in the deeply stratified sites of Lawn Point and Kasta with related surface collections from five other locales, associated with the 10–15-meter high strandline (Fladmark 1971). Radiocarbon dates range between 5400 B.C. on the second oldest component at Lawn Point and 3400 B.C. on an upper level at Kasta. Occupations consist of limited scatters of lithic detritus and artifacts around small unlined hearths on old beach surfaces, entirely lacking fire-cracked rocks (ubiquitous in most later sites), or structural features. Soil acidity at these nonshell sites precludes any organic preservation. The Moresby tradition is characterized by unifacially flaked stone tools and microblades made on locally available tool stone. Of approximately 6,000 lithic specimens from all components there are no bifaces or ground stone tools of any type. Sandstone abraders do appear by 4000 B.C., indicating the presence of a bone and antler industry that has not been preserved. Some technological changes are observable in the lithic technology. Microblade technology changes from a prepared core and blade technology in the early components to a bipolar percussion method by the end of the tradition.

The data indicate that Moresby tradition people practiced a mobile hunting-fishing-gathering way of life, and that they used watercraft (needed to get to the Queen Charlottes). However, these data are scanty and few conclusions can be drawn from them.

231

Skeena River

The Bornite phase (3000–2300 B.C.) is represented by a single component at the Paul Mason site in Kitselas Canyon. The most common artifacts are obsidian microblades and cobble tools. Ground stone tools are a minor element in the assemblage. There are no flaked tools such as bifaces. The microblade industry is represented by over 100 microblades and two microblade core rejuvenation flakes. There is no evidence of habitations, and there are no faunal remains. Coupland (1985) speculates that this material represents a temporary, seasonal camp. This assemblage is very similar to the earlier Moresby tradition assemblages on the Queen Charlottes on several points: microblades, emphasis on cobble tools, and the absence of bifaces. For these reasons it is placed in the Early period, despite its relatively late age.

Recent Period Cultures

Prince Rupert Harbour

The following summary is based upon MacDonald and Inglis (1981), MacDonald (1983a), and Ames (1984a).

Citations are limited to information from other sources.

Only four of the Prince Rupert sites have significant Prince Rupert III (3000–1500 B.C.) components. The middens associated with these components are relatively small, and artifact densities are low. Analysis of faunal remains and material culture indicates a broad-based hunting-gathering-fishing economy focusing more heavily on land mammals, including deer and wapiti (elk), than the economy of later periods, though marine mammals, mainly seals, were taken.

The basic tool kits of historic Tsimshian technology are present, though not so complex as in later periods (fig. 2). Tools of bone and antler dominate the assemblages, but ground stone tools as well as cobble tools occur. Flaked bifaces are exceedingly rare. No microblades have been found.

Hunting and fishing equipment includes the bifaces, fixed bone points, rare ground slate points, two styles of harpoon, and fishhook barbs. Cobble spalls may have functioned as fish knives. The middens themselves are evidence of the collection of intertidal shellfish. Manufacturing and processing tools include the general purpose cobble tools, abraders, awls, and needles. Bone and antler wedges, shell adzes, and beaver and porcupine incisor

Natl. Mus. of Canada, Ottawa: a, GbTo-18:741; b, GbTo-18:675; c, GbTo-18:356; d, GbTo-18:711; e, GbTo-18:731; f, GbTo-18:642; g, GbTo-18:401; h, GbTo-18:730; i, GbTo-18:652; j, GbTo-18:187; k, GbTo-18:678; l, GbTo-18:537; m, GbTo-18:358.

Fig. 2. Period III artifacts from Dodge Island, Prince Rupert Harbour, B.C. a, bilaterally barbed antler harpoon point; b, unilaterally barbed bone point fragment; c, rodent incisor tool; d, perforated canine pendant; e, chisel made from a section of mammal long bone; f, awl made from mammal long bone; g, ground nephrite chisel or adz blade; h, perforated and incised ground stone tablet; i, cortical spall tool; j, ground slate pencil; k–m, cortical spall tools. Length of a 5.3 cm; rest to same scale.

adzes represent the woodworking technology. The specialized, heavy duty woodworking tools of later periods such as ground adzes and hammers are not yet present, though cobble tools may have performed some of those functions.

There is no evidence of structures. Small postholes, postmolds, and hearths indicate that domestic structures were probably small. Bird bone tubes and beads, canine pendants, and pigments are the only items of personal adornment. The pigments and obsidian are the only exotic materials. Period I populations were probably relatively small and mobile, but nothing is known of their settlement patterns.

Prince Rupert II (500 B.C.–A.D. 500) is marked by major social changes, rapid population growth, and an expansion and intensification of the subsistence base. Most of the evidence for the social changes comes from the major burial complex, which disappears by its end.

This period is represented by 12 components, with thick midden deposits and relatively high artifact densities. Midden accumulation during Prince Rupert II is rapid.

Fishing and sea mammal hunting appear to have become increasingly important, while land mammal hunting declined in importance. Net weights appear, a third style of harpoon is added, and ground slate points increase in frequency. Sea mammal remains may become more frequent in the deposits (Calvert 1968). There is, however, a tremendous variety in the food resources exploited during the entire Recent period in Prince Rupert Harbour (Stewart 1977; May 1979), including many species of birds, fish, marine invertebrates, and sea and land mammals, which indicates an intensive exploitation of most of the major microenvironments in Prince Rupert Harbour. The presence of eulachon in at least one site (May 1979) suggests that the spring movement from Prince Rupert Harbour to the mouth of the Nass River by nineteenth-century Tsimshian may have begun during or by this period. The presence of salmon implies movements to either the Nass or, more likely, the Skeena. The sites vary among themselves in the kinds and frequencies of subsistence-oriented artifacts and their faunal remains, pointing to intensive use of very local environments. Seasonality studies (Stewart 1977) indicate year-round occupation of the harbor, but with winter and spring the major occupation periods.

Stone adzes, chisels, bark shredders, and bark peelers are added to the bone and antler woodworking technology of the previous period. These more durable tools indicate an expansion in the role of wood in the material culture of the period. An anthropomorphic handle for an incisor adz dates to the beginning of this period. The design is very similar to an adz handle found near Vancouver dating to about 2290–1500 B.C. (Matson 1976). Wooden artifacts from waterlogged deposits dating to this period include kerfed boxes, basketry, and carved objects similar in style to those of the historic period.

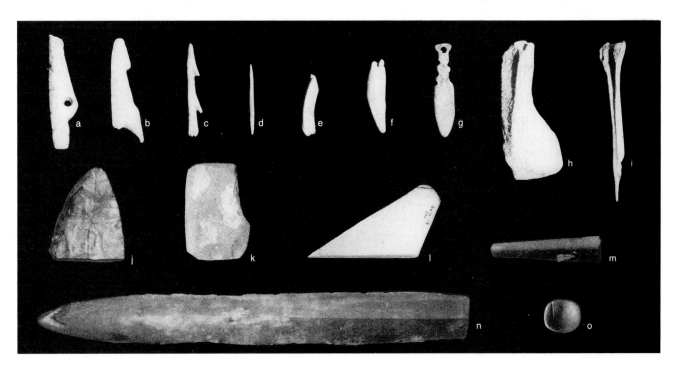

Natl., Mus. of Canada, Ottawa: a, GbTo-18:481; b, GbTo-18:470; c, GbTo-18:407; d, GbTo-18:116; e, GbTo-18:338; f, GbTo-18:389; g, GbTo-18:236; h, GbTo-18:689; i, GbTo-18:59; j, GbTo-18:438; k, GbTo-18:565; l, GbTo-18:570; m, GbTo-18:191; n, GbTo-18:631; o, GbTo-18:544.
Fig. 3. Period II artifacts from Dodge Island, Prince Rupert Harbour, B.C. a, Bone harpoon point fragment with hole for line attachment; b–c, unilaterally barbed bone point fragments; d, bone barb; e, rodent incisor tool; f, perforated canine pendant; g, bone pendant shaped like a tiny dagger; h, bone wedge fragment; i, splinter awl made from a mammal long bone; j, chipped biface fragment; k, ground stone chisel or adz blade; l, shaped abrasive stone; m, ground slate pencil fragment; n, ground slate dagger; o, frontal labret of jet. Length of a 6.2 cm; rest to same scale.

The number and variety of decorated tools and decorative motifs increases relative to the previous period. The styles of decoration fall within the canons of the historic art.

There is only indirect evidence of domestic structures, including the woodworking tools that indicate the capacity to build the large, cedar plank lineage houses of the early nineteenth century, and extensive, superimposed hearth and floor features. The presence of small square houses in Kitselas Canyon at this time is also indirect evidence that such structures were being built in Prince Rupert Harbour during this period.

The burial complex, marked by interment in the middens, provides intriguing evidence of some aspects of social organization, of warfare and of ritual. However, the more than 200 graves span the full 2,000-year period of Prince Rupert II and do not represent a single mortuary population. Despite that caveat, the burial complex does suggest that there were differences in social rank or status among individuals and perhaps occupation sites, that warfare was endemic, and that there probably was an extensive trade network.

Differences in rank among individuals and sites is suggested by a variety of evidence. The graves vary among themselves in the style of the grave, in whether grave goods are present or not, and whether the grave goods are utilitarian or nonutilitarian. Nonutilitarian items include copper objects, amber and shell beads, shell gorgets, stone and bone clubs, ground and flaked stone daggers (fig. 4), labrets, pendants, and sea otter teeth. These items are concentrated in only three sites in the Prince Rupert area: Boardwalk; Dodge Island, immediately adjacent to Boardwalk; and Garden Island, which is a short distance by boat away. Some of these artifacts, such as the labrets, were status markers during the historic period. Finally, Boardwalk is unusual in that it has a higher frequency and greater diversity than any other site of decorated items, nonutilitarian objects, and manufacturing tools in addition to holding the major concentration of graves.

The high frequency of warfare is inferred from three lines of evidence (Jerome Cybulski, personal communication 1985). First, the skeletal population has a disproportionally high ratio of men to women. Second, these males show unusually high levels of trauma including parry fractures of the forearm and depressed skull fractures. Third, the bone and stone clubs, bipointed ground stone objects, and ground slate daggers are clearly weapons.

Dentalia, copper, pigments, amber, and obsidian are evidence of trade. Other exotic goods may include the whale bone used for clubs. The exploitation of salmon and eulachon suggests seasonal movement to the Nass and Skeena Rivers and contact with other peoples there, while the anthromorphic adz handle is evidence of at least shared art styles with peoples as far south as the Fraser delta.

Natl. Mus. of Canada, Ottawa: GbTo-31:521.
Fig. 4. Bifacially flaked and ground stone blade found in association with middle period burials at the Boardwalk site, B.C., dated about 2500 B.C. Length, 19 cm.

The evidence indicates growing populations, living in partially to fully sedentary villages, intensively exploiting most if not all the habitats available within the harbor and the region. Subsistence was broad based but may have emphasized sea mammal hunting, fishing, and shellfish collecting. It is likely that individual social statuses and perhaps villages as well were ranked in relative prestige. Contacts within and beyond the region appear to have been extensive. Warfare was frequent.

The Prince Rupert I period (A.D. 500–1830) differs in some ways from the preceding one, but there are many continuities between the two. The burial complex ceased, and there were no further midden burials. The causes of this change are unknown. While it seems likely that the historic burial practices began at this time, these included cremation, and no cremations have been recovered. Other historic burial practices, excluding certain specialized burials, are very unlikely to leave archeological traces.

Rates of midden accumulation slowed, suggesting a stabilization in population levels. Subsistence practices as described above continued, but shifts in sea mammal hunting tackle may suggest a decline in its importance, which in turn may have been due to greater emphasis on fishing. Settlement patterns remained the same.

Period I artifacts associated with historic high status positions and with period II burials include labrets, clubs, shell gorgets, shell bracelets, amber and shell beads, and copper. Cedar plank houses of the historic type are present in the middens. While there is no skeletal evidence for

234

Natl. Mus. of Canada, Ottawa: a, GbTo-31:X-1046; b, GbTo-31:1200; c, GbTo-33:2786; d, GbTo-31:X-166; e, GbTo-31:2245.
Fig. 5. Late Period ground slate and nephrite artifacts from the Boardwalk and Lachane archeological sites. a, Slate point or dagger; b, slate projectile point; c, notched slate palette; d, slate labret; e, small nephrite adz bit. Length of a, 15 cm; others to same scale.

warfare, the weapons are present.

Large, grooved splitting adzes and hafted mauls are added to the woodworking technology. These tools are frequently decorated with zoomorphic designs. These tools, with shell knives, carving and cutting tools, indicate the full development of woodworking and carpentry. The number and variety of decorated artifacts is greater than previous periods (fig. 6). MacDonald and Inglis (1981) interpret these data to show that the prehistoric version of historic Coast Tsimshian culture, including ranked social statuses and matrilineal house groups, existed during period I. The changes in burial practices and population dynamics point to important changes at the beginning of this period.

Queen Charlotte Islands

The majority of data on the Recent period comes from the Blue Jackets Creek site (Severs 1974, 1974a). This and other material has been organized by Fladmark (1975, 1984) into two contemporary archeological manifestations: the Transitional complex (3000 B.C.–at least 2,000 years ago) and the Graham tradition (2200 B.C.–A.D. 1800). The most notable differences between the Early and the Recent periods are the disappearance of the microblade industry and, as elsewhere, the appearance of shell middens.

Originally defined as the Transitional period (Fladmark 1972, 1975) and conceived as a short phase of intermixture between the Moresby tradition and new elements from the mainland about 2000–3000 B.C., the Transitional complex is now seen as a recurring cluster of distinctive technological traits possessing considerable temporal continuity.

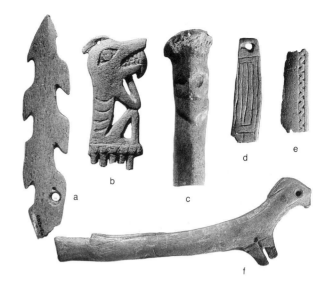

Natl. Mus. of Canada, Ottawa: a, GbTo-36:149; b, GbTo-23:850; c, GbTo-33:2853; d, GbTn-1:117; e, GbTo-33:840; f, GbTo-31:211.
Fig. 6. Periods I and II bone and antler artifacts from the Baldwin, Boardwalk, Garden Island, Lachane, and Grassy Bay archeological sites. a, Bilaterally barbed harpoon point with line hole; b, bone comb carved in a wolf motif and dated about A.D. 800; c, anthropomorphic design carved on the proximal end of an antler tine; d–e, decorated bone pendant and bone fragment; f, zoomorphic antler club or pendant. Length of a 10 cm; b–e to same scale. Length of f 18.7 cm.

The Transitional complex includes a variety of unifacially retouched convex-edged basalt flakes and a system of bipolar reduction of pebble cores, the end-product of which was elongated microbladelike flakes. The method of stone tool production is reminiscent of the Moresby tradition, and the retouched flakes that functioned as scrapers are similar to those found in Moresby tradition assemblages. Fladmark has recognized the Transitional complex in Graham tradition sites as well as in non–shell midden contexts (Zone II at Skoglund's Landing and Component 1 at Lawn Point).

There is controversy over whether the Transitional complex represents a cultural entity contemporary with but separate from the Graham tradition (Fladmark 1984) or a distinctive element of Graham tradition technology and settlement patterns (Sutherland 1980).

The Graham tradition begins about 3000 B.C. and lasts until European contact, A.D. 1774 for the Queen Charlotte Islands, but after about A.D. 1 it is poorly represented in the archeological record. Excavated components include the deposits at Blue Jackets Creek (Severs 1974, 1974a), the 3000-year-old Honna River site (MacDonald 1969), the 3000 to 2000 year old deposits at Tow Hill (Severs 1975), and the 1,400-year-old-Council site (Severs 1974b).

While microblade industries are absent in Graham tradition sites, some of the artifact types seen earlier in the Moresby tradition, such as basalt unifacial tools, pièces-esquillée, and abrasives, are present (fig. 7). This evidence suggests some degree of continuity between the two cultural periods. In addition, bifacial chipped stone technology, which was absent in the Moresby tradition, is lacking until relatively late in the Graham tradition; and at Blue Jackets Creek, the bifacial tools that do occur are manufactured from mainland obsidian (Carlson 1983). Cobble tools and cortical spall tools are ubiquitous.

In Graham tradition sites, particularly after 2000 B.C., chipped stone tools are associated with a wide range of pecked and ground stone and organic artifacts. Battered fragments of small flaked adzes or chisels that were finished by pecking and grinding are common throughout the deposits at Blue Jackets Creek. These artifacts are distinctive to the Graham tradition. Ground slate points and knives occur but are very rare. The large splitting adzes commonly associated with heavy woodworking on the northern coast at a later date have not been recovered from Graham tradition sites, and there are only a few examples of complex ground stone artifacts, such as

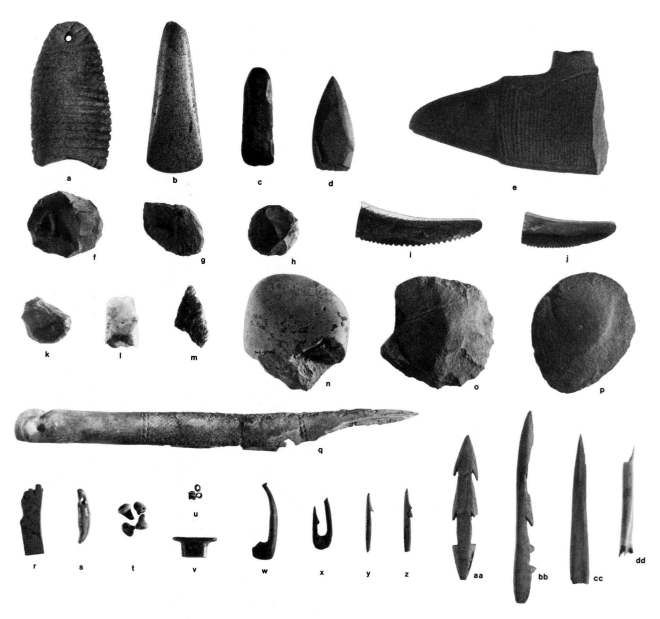

Natl. Mus. of Canada, Ottawa: a, FlUa-4:219; b, FlUa-4:160; c, FlUa-4:146; d, FlUa-4:215; e, FlUa-4:185; f, FlUa-4:979; g, FlUa-4:581; h, FlUa-4:181; i, FhUa-1:10; j, FlUa-4:2000; k, FlUa-4:2036; l, FlUa-4:1179; m, FlUa-4:555; n, FlUa-4:884; o, FlUa-4:414; p, FlUa-4:287; q, FlUa-4:1611; r, FlUa-4:72; s, FlUa-4:660; t, FlUa-4:2333; u, FlUa-4:431; v, FlUa-4:2169; w, FlUa-4:1393; x, FlUa-4:419; y, FlUa-4:1293; z, FlUa-4:1425; aa, FlUa-4:1481; bb, FhUa-1:12; cc, FlUa-4:224; dd, FlUa-4:63.

Fig. 7. Graham Tradition artifacts from the Queen Charlotte Is., B.C. a, perforated and ribbed stone; b–c, ground stone chisel or adz blades; d, ground slate point; e, zoomorphic stone club fragment; f, retouched, convex, asymmetrical basalt flake; g, "nosed" basalt scraper; h, discoidal basalt scraper; i–j, shaped abrasive stones; k, chalcedony end scraper; l, chalcedony pièce-esquillée; m, broken obsidian biface; n, cobble tool; o, retouched cortical spall tool; p, unretouched cortical spall tool; q, caribou metapodial tool with incised line decoration; r, decorated antler comb fragment; s, perforated canine pendant; t, sea otter tooth beads; u, shell disk beads; v, ground jet frontal labret; w, bone fishhook shank; x, single-piece bone fishhook; y–z, single and multiple barbed bone points; aa, bilaterally barbed antler harpoon point; bb, unilaterally barbed bone harpoon point; cc, splinter awl of mammal long bone; dd, bird bone awl. Length of a 6.5 cm; rest to same scale.

FLADMARK, AMES, AND SUTHERLAND

zoomorphic clubs, fragments, a ribbed stone, and a labret.

Bone and antler tools at Blue Jackets Creek include barbed harpoons, the most common of which is a bilateral type associated with early contexts throughout the Northern Northwest Coast. There are fishhook shanks, absent in Prince Rupert Harbour sites but occurring farther south on the west coast of Vancouver Island (Dewhirst 1980). There are also a variety of awls and punches, needles, barbed points, and rare single-piece fishhooks. Bone combs, some with geometric surface decoration, and pendants and beads of bone, tooth, ivory, and shell were recovered at Blue Jackets Creek. Some items of personal adornment came from burial contexts, as did two matching caribou metapodial tools decorated with a geometric design of cross-hatching, zigzagging, and enclosed circles.

Fourteen human burials representing 25 individuals were excavated at Blue Jackets Creek (J.S. Murray 1981). Three individuals were interred, in an upright sitting posture, and one burial consisted of the remains of two subadults. Red ocher was found in association with these four burials. The remainder were flexed burials, and some individuals were interred with grave goods. Three of the skeletons displayed "buccal abrasion" on the upper and lower premolars and molars, which is interpreted as labret wear (Severs 1974b). Four radiocarbon dates on bone collagen from the human remains range between 2900 and 2000 B.C., but most of the burials probably date around 2000 B.C. These dates place midden burials at least 500 years earlier on the Queen Charlotte Islands than in Prince Rupert Harbour, and they also suggest that the use of labrets and elaborate grave goods may have occurred earlier on the Charlottes than elsewhere on the northern coast of British Columbia.

Other features at Blue Jackets Creek include hearths with fire-cracked rocks, pits, living floors, and small postholes. None of the features indicates the presence of large dwellings similar to those of the historic period, nor do the deposits point to full-scale village life. However, there is the suggestion of a more sedentary pattern of settlement than that inferred for the Moresby tradition. Faunal evidence from Blue Jackets Creek indicates that the site was utilized at different times of the year. In contrast, the site of Tow Hill seems to represent a short-term, seasonally specific occupation. The beginnings of semipermanent settlement pattern involving a seasonal round are suggested by Graham tradition data.

There are certain aspects of the Graham tradition that distinguish it from developments on the mainland. There is a higher frequency of stone tools relative to bone and antler. The woodworking industries of the two areas are quite distinctive. With the exception of a few imports, there is no bifacial chipped stone technology on the Charlottes. Several lines of evidence point to a heavier emphasis upon sea mammal hunting on the Charlottes, and the massive shell midden sites that occur throughout

Prince Rupert Harbour in the Recent period do not seem to be present on the Islands until relatively late.

The distinctive character of the Islands' prehistory is maintained until approximately 1000 B.C. After this time, one begins to see parallels with developments in Prince Rupert Harbour (Sutherland 1980) and more evidence of trade, of which obsidian is the best indicator (Carlson 1983). The increase in ground stone specimens, in particular complex artifacts, is noteworthy; perhaps more significant is the presence of zoomorphic club fragments like those found in Prince Rupert deposits of the same age. One of the conditions for these changes might have been the expansion of the Western red cedar in coastal forests, which occurred slightly later on the Charlottes than elsewhere on the northern coast (Hebda and Mathewes 1984, 1984a). Mature stands of cedar would have facilitated the building of large canoes suitable for traveling the treacherous waters that separated the Queen Charlotte Islands from other areas of the coast.

Skeena River–Kitselas Canyon

Components from Gitaus and Paul Mason are assigned to the Gitaus phase (2300–1600 B.C.), which is markedly different from the preceding Bornite phase. Microblades virtually disappear, though cobble tools continue to be very common, particularly cobble spall tools, which may have been used for preparing fish. Ground stone increased in frequency and diversity, with an increase in abraders and the addition of ground stone points and slate saws. These tools suggest that working bone and antler and perhaps wood was becoming more important. Leaf-shaped projectile points are present, though rare. Coupland, following Allaire (1978), interprets this material as representing a seasonal occupation, perhaps a fishing camp. Both authors stress the similarities of this material with Early Period components in Prince Rupert Harbour. Coupland suggests this phase may represent the use of Kitselas Canyon for salmon fishing by people who wintered in Prince Rupert Harbour. There are no structural remains.

The Skeena phase (1600–1200 B.C.) is represented by assemblages from Gitaus and Hagwilget (Allaire 1978, 1979; Ames 1979). Bifaces, particularly leaf-shaped projectile points, increase significantly in frequency, as do shaped abraders. Other ground stone, including points, continue to be present. Cobble tools remain the dominant element in these assemblages, indicating the continuing importance of general utility processing activities. Allaire (1978, 1979) and Coupland (1985) view the increased importance of projectile points as suggesting a greater emphasis on hunting in the economy. However, Allaire sees the Skeena complex as representing the movement of interior peoples into Kitselas Canyon, displacing the coastal peoples of the previous period, while Coupland   *237* argues that the differences between the Gitaus and Skeena phases may reflect subsistence adjustments by the coastal people utilizing the canyon. He regards this occupation as a seasonal one. These issues cannot be resolved with the available data. There is no evidence for structures.

The Paul Mason phase (1200–700 B.C.), documented only at the Paul Mason site, is extremely important to the understanding of social changes on the Northern Coast during the last 5,000 years. The Paul Mason phase component is a small village of 10 rectangular houses (there are 12 houses at the site, but the temporal assignment of two is not clear) in two house rows. The houses were partially excavated into a steep slope above the river, producing distinct house depressions. The houses are rather small, the largest one being 6.6 by 11 meters, a size that falls well within the average size of houses in western North America during this period (Ames 1984). Changes among the artifacts include a reduction in the relative frequencies of chipped stone tools, including projectile points and a relative increase in the importance of ground stone forms. Cobble tools continue to be important. Coupland (1985) interprets the reduction in chipped stone tools as indicating a reduction in the importance of land mammal hunting.

The significant change of this phase is the appearance of a sedentary village that displays the general pattern of village spatial organization in the historic period, but without the differences in house size that indicated differences in the status and prestige of the lineage occupying the house. The village also very probably means year-round occupation of the canyon, the formation of multi-generational extended kin groups, and the intensive exploitation of salmon (Coupland 1985).

The Kleanza phase (700 B.C.–A.D. 500) is represented only at Gitaus. The general outlines of the material culture repeat earlier phases. Shaped abraders, probably reflecting bone and antler tool manufacturing, increased in frequency. Additions to the artifact inventory include net sinkers, indicating an intensification of fishing; labrets; ground slate daggers and ground slate mirrors (high status or ritual markers); and ground stone adzes. There is no direct evidence of structures, though Coupland (1985) suggests a large pit outline at Gitaus may be a postmold, implying that the houses of the Paul Mason phase continued to be built, as is likely. These changes are quite similar to the changes occurring at roughly the same time in Prince Rupert Harbour at the end of period II.

Conclusions

The Moresby tradition represents the earliest well documented cultural manifestation on the Northern Coast. The intertidal assemblages on Moresby Island and the Skoglund's Landing materials hint of an earlier, technologically different occupation. The Moresby tradition technology is based upon microblades and cobble tools. Microblade technology is a method of producing many cutting tools from limited lithic resources; they are usually mounted in handles, shafts, and points and replaced as they dull. Cobble tools are multi-purpose, easily made tools. This technology is also present in the Bornite phase in Kitselas Canyon, the earliest, well documented cultural manifestation on the mainland.

These microblade industries have their ultimate technological connections with early microblade traditions in Alaska and to the earliest component at Namu (Carlson 1979; Hester and Nelson 1978). The users of these tools appear to have been mobile hunter-fisher-gatherers few in number, equipped with boats. The exact nature of their economy and society is unknown, although their technology seems geared to maximum flexibility. Lack of organic preservation makes estimation of early subsistence difficult, but the location of Moresby tradition sites on tidal beaches and an absence of any stone projectile points (though microblades could have armed wooden or bone projectile points) suggests an orientation toward littoral resources.

On the Queen Charlotte Islands the Transitional complex contains some traits of the Moresby tradition as well as the succeeding Graham tradition. It is not clear how the Transitional complex articulates with these and whether it represents a distinct social or cultural group, or a distinctive technological aspect of the Graham tradition.

Just after 3000 B.C. there is an important change in the archeological record of the region with the appearance of shell middens, indicating, among other things, exploitation of the intertidal zone. Artifact assemblages recovered in the middens show a generalized adaptation that included hunting of terrestrial and marine mammals, fishing, and collecting of intertidal shellfish and probably plant foods. These people appear to have been mobile, moving seasonally in small groups. The basic subsistence technology of the next 5,000 years was in use by this time.

Two points need to be raised here. First, this new technology, heavily reliant upon organic raw material for tools—bone, antler, and wood—appears in the sites already well developed. This makes it likely that it already existed in the region before 3000 B.C. The presence of abraders in Moresby tradition contexts by 4000 B.C. may mark the actual initiation of the changes leading up to the beginnings of shell middens. Similar technology was present elsewhere on the coast by 7800 B.C., and it seems unlikely it was absent here before 3000 B.C.

Second, there are significant differences between Graham tradition and Prince Rupert material cultures until rather late in the prehistoric period, despite broadly similar subsistence patterns in both areas. In Prince Rupert Harbour, less dramatic but still important differences exist among the sites. The areal variations probably reflect both the environmental differences and some kind of cultural distinctions, while the differences in Prince Rupert minimally indicate differential utilization of local micro-environments and perhaps some social differences between village sites. There is evidence that the intensive exploitation of local habitats was coupled with seasonal movements to other areas to exploit critical resources such as eulachon and salmon.

By 700 B.C. at least one sedentary village existed in Kitselas Canyon, and it is very likely that similar villages will be found in Prince Rupert Harbour and on the Queen Charlottes. Faunal remains in Prince Rupert Harbour point to year-round occupation. There is evidence for a more sedentary way of life on the Queen Charlottes. Sedentism was probably the single most important change of the last 5,000 years.

The establishment of sedentism was accompanied by a series of other, important changes. In Prince Rupert Harbour populations appear to have grown rapidly. The subsistence base was diversified in Prince Rupert; sea mammals became more important and fishing was intensified by increasing the catch and by exploiting a greater array of fish habitats. On the Islands, there is evidence for a broadening, maritime subsistence. In Kitselas Canyon, subsistence may have focused primarily on salmon.

The burial complex in Prince Rupert Harbour is a significant change. It seems clear that some form of social ranking of individuals was present by 500 B.C. and that warfare was endemic. Woodworking became increasingly important, and the Northwest Coast art style had been developed by this period, coincident with and no doubt related to the maturation of the western red cedar forest.

The evidence of trade, seasonal subsistence movements, similarities in artifact styles between this area and other coastal regions, particularly the southern British Columbia coast where similar developments were also occurring at roughly the same time (Burley 1980) means that the Recent period can be understood only from the perspective of the entire Northwest Coast. MacDonald's (1969) area co-tradition or interaction sphere very likely developed between about 1500 and 500 B.C.

These trends are clear until about A.D. 1 to 500. The archeological record for both the Queen Charlottes and Kitselas Canyon is poorly documented after this time until the historic period. In Prince Rupert Harbour burial practices may have shifted to their historic form. For whatever reason, midden burials cease. However, the art and woodworking technology continued to develop after this date, large plank houses were present, and status markers and weapons continued to occur, indicating basic cultural continuity between the period before A.D. 500 and the historic period. Population size may have stabilized or declined. There is equivocal evidence for a contraction in the diversity of the resource base, perhaps reflecting a continued intensification of salmon fishing. The lack of evidence on the Charlottes and in Kitselas is most likely the result of the archeological sample of excavated sites, and not any significant population shifts.

All areas of the Northern Coast of British Columbia participated in these developments. It is clear that the people of Kitselas Canyon and Prince Rupert Harbour were part of the same regional cultural tradition during the last 4,000 years. The people of the Queen Charlotte Islands retained their distinctive cast, the result of their insular location.

Causal explanations for these developments vary somewhat in their emphasis (Ames 1981, 1985; Burley 1980; Coupland 1985; Fladmark 1975; Matson 1983, 1985) but share a focus upon the development of sedentism, the intensification of fishing, particularly of salmon, and the development of social complexity. Of major concern is explaining the sudden importance in collecting intertidal shellfish at 3000 B.C., the changes in family organization indicated by the appearance of plank houses, the formation of sedentary villages, the causes and effects of population growth and warfare, the development of social ranking, the changes in burial practices, shifts and variation in subsistence, and the effects of environmental changes.

239

Haida: Traditional Culture

MARGARET B. BLACKMAN

Language

The Haida ('hīdu) speak a language that has no demonstrable genetic relationship with any other (see "Languages," this vol.).

There is little direct information on the dialectal differences that must have existed among the stable towns of the nineteenth century, but the dialects fell into Northern and Southern groups. Northern Haida was spoken on northern Graham Island, where it survived in the twentieth century at Masset, and in Alaska, where it survived as a distinct Alaskan variety at Hydaburg. Southern Haida was spoken at Skidegate Inlet and to the south, its most divergent variety being the Kunghit (or Ninstints) dialect, spoken in the southernmost villages. Southern Haida survived at Skidegate, but the Kunghit dialect is extinct.* Northern and Southern Haida differ greatly, "allowing only partial mutual intelligibility without practice" (Krauss 1979:838). In the 1970s and 1980s the number of Haida speakers was rapidly diminishing.

---

*The phonemes of the Masset dialect of Haida are: (unaspirated stops and affricates) b, d, ȝ̌, λ, g, ġ, ʕ, ʔ; (aspirated stops and affricates) t, č, λ, k, q; (glottalized stops and affricates) t̓, c̓, λ̓, k̓, q̓; (fricatives) s, ł, x, x̣, ḥ, h; (nasals) m, n, ŋ; (liquid) l; (glottalized liquid) l̓; (semivowels) w, y; (short vowels) i, a, u; (long vowels) i·, e·, a·, u·; high and low tones. Corresponding to Masset ʕ (a pharyngeal stop) the Skidegate dialect usually has ġ and the Alaskan dialect ʔʰ (a glottal stop released with aspiration); corresponding to Masset ḥ Alaskan has ḥ and Skidegate usually has x̣. (Skidegate lacks ʕ and ḥ, and Masset and Alaskan have ġ and x in only a few words.) Skidegate has a glottalized nasal (ṅ) and an additional vowel (ə) not found in the other dialects. A period (.) is used within words as a syllable separator in Masset and Alaskan.

The accentual systems differ in the three dialects; Masset and Skidegate have a tone system, with level high and low tones, and Alaskan has a pitch-accent system. In Masset "heavy" syllables (those with a long vowel or ending in a resonant—a nasal, liquid, or semivowel) have a contrast between high tone (unmarked) and low tone, marked with a grave accent on the long-vowel syllables (v̀·) and by doubling the final resonant otherwise (corresponding to the phonetic realization); other ("light") syllables have only low tone (unmarked). Skidegate has the same system and notation, except that there are no low-tone heavy syllables ending in a resonant. Alaskan has high pitch (v́) on the first syllable of each word that has a high tone in the other dialects, and a low pitch (unmarked) elsewhere.

Information on Haida phonology and the transcription and glossing of Haida words and names was furnished by John Enrico (communication to editors 1986). The cited Haida words are in the Masset dialect unless otherwise stated.

Territory

Haida territory encompasses the Queen Charlotte Islands in British Columbia and a portion of the Alexander Archipelago in southeastern Alaska. The Queen Charlotte Islands comprise two large islands and nearly 150 smaller ones situated 30-80 miles off the coast of northern British Columbia. From Langara (or North) Island in the Queen Charlotte chain, some Haidas migrated across Dixon Entrance (probably in the eighteenth century) to settle on Long, Sukkwan, Dall, and Prince of Wales islands.

At the time of the first recorded contact with Europeans, in the late eighteenth century, the Haida lived in a number of "towns," each composed of houses of one or more matrilineal lineages. These settlements did not form any larger political units, but six groups of them can be distinguished on the basis of geography, tradition, and speech, following Swanton (1905:105). From north to south these were: the Kaigani people, traditionally from Dadens on Langara Island, at Sukkwan, Howkwan, Koianglas, Klinkwan, and Kasaan; the people of the north coast of Graham Island, traditionally from Rose Point, with their principal villages at Yaku, Kiusta, Kung, Yan, Kayung, Masset (Old Masset), and Hiellen; the Skidegate Inlet people at Skidegate; the people of the west coast of Moresby Island at Chaatl and Kaisun, and later at Haina; the people of the East coast of Moresby Island at Cumshewa, Skedans, and Kloo (Tanu); and the southern (or Kunghit) people, whose principal village was Ninstints on Anthony Island. Standing outside this classification were the Pitch-Town-People, an anomalous group on the west coast said to have lacked the crest system (Swanton 1905:90). In the 1970s the Masset Haida still distinguished four groups of Haidas, corresponding to the major dialectal differences (see Synonymy); the east and west Moresby peoples were not recognized as distinct from the Skidegate Inlet people, a reflection of the late nineteenth-century resettlement at Skidegate of all the Haida to the south.

Environment

The aboriginal homeland of the Haida, the Queen Charlotte Islands, comprises a biotic province distinct

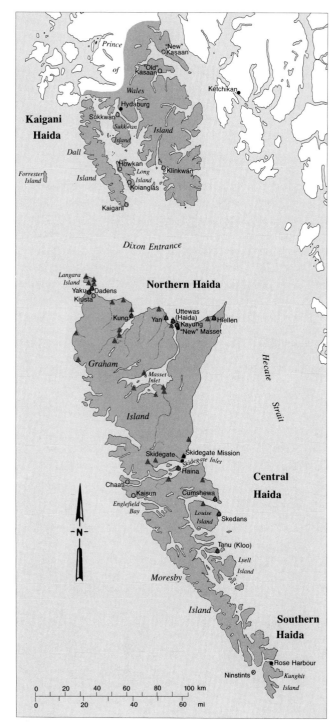

Fig. 1. Territory and principal towns of the Haida in the early to mid-19th century.

each area. Only along the coastal plain are sizable expanses of sandy beach found. Shingle beaches are found in the plateau region, and along the west coast of the southern islands the rocky cliffs slope precipitously to the sea. Rainfall patterns also vary. The eastern portions of the islands receive an average of 47-63 inches per year (Calder and Taylor 1968:29), while the mountainous west coast often receives more than triple that amount. Probably of greater significance than the contrasts within the Queen Charlotte habitat are the differences between that archipelago and the Alexander Archipelago inhabited by the Kaigani Haida. The Alaska islands, in general, are more storm protected; their climate is slightly more extreme (colder winters, warmer summers), and rainfall everywhere is higher than along the eastern shores of the Queen Charlotte Islands. The most important differences for the Haida, however, undoubtedly lay in available flora and fauna. The Kaigani had a larger inventory of economically useful plant and animal species (berries, deer, wolf, beaver, mink, and many waterfowl species that nested on Forrester Island). At the same time, some species were reputed to be more abundant (halibut, chum), or of better quality (red cedar) in Queen Charlotte Haida territory.

Settlement Pattern

Swanton and Newcombe recorded 126 habitation sites remembered from about 1850-1860. But Swanton (1905: 268) cautioned, "it is questionable whether so-called 'towns' were really anything more than camps, and it must not be supposed that a large number of the others were ever occupied at the same time." Twenty were winter village sites; their locations are shown in figure 1.

A number of factors appeared to enter into the selection of winter village sites: natural protection from storms and enemies, proximity to halibut banks and shellfish resources, availability of drinking water, and adequate beachfront for landing canoes. Houses, built close together, nestled against the treeline and faced the beach in a long, even row. Several villages contained two rows of houses (Ninstints, Kloo, Cumshewa, Chaatl, Kasaan). Houses of the most important individual ("town" chief) tended to be located either in the center of the village (Masset, Kiusta, Kayung, Cumshewa) or at one end of the village (Kloo, Skedans, Chaatl, Kung, Klinkwan, Kasaan). Above the storm tide mark along the beachfront were erected the "forest" of totem poles so frequently remarked upon by nineteenth-century visitors to Haida villages (fig. 2). Among the carved posts were those (sometimes plain, sometimes carved) containing the remains of the dead. Small gravehouses architecturally similar to the dwellings stood behind the habitations or at one end of the village.

from the mainland Coast Forest to the north and south (Cowan and Guiguet 1965:19). Within the archipelago itself there exists considerable environmental variation. The northeastern portion of the islands is coastal lowlands, which rise in elevation to form a plateau in the west. In the southern portions of the Charlottes this plateau gives way to a mountain range. These physiographic differences are most apparent in the different shorelines in

241

Culture

Structures

Haida houses were constructed of red cedar timbers and planks. Though similar in finished form, two basic types of Haida house can be distinguished. House type A has seven roof beams, six running full length and projecting several feet beyond the front and rear facades, and one, the central or ridge beam, broken in the middle for the smoke hole. These beams are supported by the front and rear plates, which are borne by pairs of posts near the center, front and rear, and by being mortised into four corner posts. Upper and lower plates in the front and rear of the house are grooved for reception of the wall planks and the outermost roof timber on each side of the house is likewise grooved. House type A was most common in the villages of the central Queen Charlottes where, at Skedans for

example, it was the exclusive type of house in the mid-nineteenth century. It was not found in Kaigani villages.

House type B has only four beams, which do not project, the two central ones supported by four internal posts. Front and rear plates are similarly mortised into corner posts and grooved for wall planks. House type B occurred throughout the Queen Charlotte Islands and in the Kaigani villages. A variation of this type of house, B′, is distinguished by the long horizontal beam running the width of the front and rear facades. House type B′ was infrequently found, in the late nineteenth century in Yan, Kasaan, and Howkwan villages. Archeological features also reveal its presence at Koianglas. Both types of Haida house were roofed with sheets of heavy cedar bark, and all houses had a centrally located square hole framed by a plank shield, for the emission of smoke from the house fire. The house of the Masset town chief, built around 1840, was reputed to be one of the largest Haida houses

Public Arch. of Canada, Ottawa: PA-37756.

Fig. 2. Skidegate, Queen Charlotte Is., B.C. Each house has associated with it totem poles of different kinds, carved with figures representing crests (Swanton 1905:122–135; MacDonald 1983:22–30). The houses and poles have been identified by MacDonald (1983:50–52). At the left is a mortuary column raised for Chief Skedans. It has a burial chamber on top covered by a plaque bearing a moon with a thunderbird (or hawk) face, and it represents a mountain goat (above) and a grizzly. The painted designs that would have been on the plaques of the other mortuary columns that are visible have weathered away. Behind the column is House Chiefs Peep at from a Distance, built about 1875 by Though Younger Brother Must Be Obeyed, who later became Chief Skidegate. The housefront pole has, from the top, a dogfish with a killerwhale in its mouth, a raven with a sculpin in its beak, and a killerwhale eating a harbor seal; human watchmen in potlatch hats are on either side of the dogfish tail and atop the corner posts. The second house, Raven's House, was owned by Skidegate VI, chief about 1860–1870. The principal figures on the frontal pole are a raven, dogfish, and killerwhale eating a harbor seal. The frontal pole of the next house is topped by 7 potlatch cylinders, originally painted alternately black and white. In the distance are two memorial poles, with their smooth tops visible against the sky, one bearing a separately carved raven. Photograph by George M. Dawson, July 1878.

Fig. 3. Houses and wealth display. left, Chief 'Highest Peak' with 2 coppers in front of his house, known as House Where People Always Want to Go, Haina, Queen Charlotte Is., B.C. It is a Northern 6-beam house and has a frontal pole with cutout entryway at base, which was the original doorway into the house. The figures on the pole are 3 watchmen, Raven (a crest of the owner), sea grizzly and smaller creatures associated with Raven, and Thunderbird (a crest of the owner's wife) (MacDonald 1983:64). right, Interior of Chief Wiah's house, *na ʔiwʔaˑns*, 'big house' (sometimes called Monster House), Masset, Queen Charlotte Is. The central housepit, with open fireplace, has 2 levels and is exceptionally deep (approximately 8 feet). Above the fireplace are 2 drying racks. On the upper level, with open doors, is a gabled sleeping compartment, probably of Chief Wiah (Blackman 1972; MacDonald 1983:18, 142–143). Euro-Canadian furnishings include tables, chairs, and stairways. Haida traditional wealth artifacts, such as boxes, are also visible. Photographs by Richard Maynard; left, 1888; right, 1884.

(fig. 3, bottom right) measuring 54 by 55 feet (Blackman 1972). Chief Gitkun's house at Kloo and Chief Skowal's house at Kasaan were similarly large.

The more opulent Haida houses boasted a centrally excavated pit, often terraced with several tiers leading to the base of the excavation. In the center of the housepit burned the house fire, which served for cooking, drying clothing (and fish, in inclement weather) and heating. Meals were prepared in the housepit, and there the household slaves slept. Living and sleeping places within the house were apportioned according to rank, those of highest position occupying the perimeter of the ground level tier, those of lower rank occupying intermediate tiers. The highest ranking member of the household, the house chief, had reserved as his sleeping quarters the rear central portion of the upper tier.

A carved totem pole, up to 50 feet in height, normally stood against the house facade. The bottom figure of this centrally positioned pole occasionally provided the entryway to the house through a hole placed in its stomach or mouth. Swanton (1905:292) believed that this frontal pole evolved from a short, carved block of wood that in earlier times graced Haida house fronts.

Houses without entryways through the frontal pole were entered through elliptical doorways cut into the front

Fig. 4. Halibut hooks. left, Two-piece hook lashed with cedar bark and nettle fiber twine. The barb is iron lashed to a snood of spruce root. Bait was tied to the arm just below the barb. right, One-piece hook made from the fork of a tree. The barb is iron. Niblack (1888:290) says this type of hook was "very strong and serviceable, often bringing up halibut weighing from 50 to 120 pounds." Both specimens were collected by J.G. Swan at Massett, Queen Charlotte Is., B.C., 1883. Length of left 25.5 cm; other to same scale.

facade of the house. These doorways were often covered with painted plank doors. Rarely entire house fronts were painted with zoomorphic designs. Other possibilities for house adornment were realized in carved corner posts, roof timbers, and interior house posts.

Haida houses were named and a house might bear more than one name. Names derived from a number of sources: the crests of the house owner (for example, Moon House, Dogfish House), the largesse of the house owner or the abundance of his economic resources (House Where One May Always Expect Food), events related to the actual construction of the house (Weasel House derived from a weasel that ran from under a house timber as it was lifted into place), and physical features of the house (Big House). House names were considered personal property and were often transferred to a new house in a new village when the house owner moved. Haida houses from the late nineteenth century and their attendant totem poles are described, village by village, in MacDonald (1983).

Subsistence

Fish and shellfish comprised the bulk of the aboriginal diet, probably followed in order by sea mammals, vegetal products, and land mammals. Most important were resources that were preservable; seasonal variability of food resources required that large quantities of food be stored for the lean winter period.

Halibut were probably quantitatively the most important fish (Dawson 1880:44B). They were caught offshore by hook and line, using the V-shaped hook (fig. 4) and octopus bait. They were sliced in thin strips and sun-dried on racks or, less often, smoked; however, salmon, particularly chums, were identified by Masset people in the 1970s (Blackman 1979) as the most important winter food. The Haida caught sockeye, coho, pink, and chum salmon in traps in tidewater, in traps set in weirs in streams, or with the harpoon (Drucker 1950:166–167). The Alaska Haida also trolled for chinook salmon (Langdon 1977:186). Chums, especially in the Queen Charlottes, were important for their low fat content, large size, and late fall runs. Many other fishes were used, the most important perhaps being the sable-fish ("black cod") and the herring. The eggs of pink and chum salmon and of herring were eaten. Dawson (1880:110B) reported that the people of the west shore of Moresby Island extracted oil from the "pollock" (perhaps actually the sable-fish) to use as a substitute for eulachon oil, which other Haida had to get in trade from the Tsimshian.

The Haida hunted seals (fig. 5), porpoises, sea lions, fur seals, and sea otters, and they used stranded whales. Land animals used included deer and beaver (in Alaska only), caribou (on the Queen Charlottes only), and bear. Seal, deer, and bear meat were preserved by smoking and drying. Some 25 species of birds also contributed to the

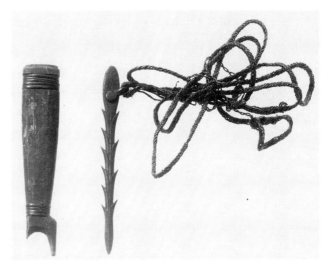

Smithsonian, Dept. of Anthr.: 88890.
Fig. 5. Iron harpoonhead for sealing and its sheath. Iron quickly replaced harpoon points made from bone, antler, and shell. Any metal object was likely to be used to manufacture implements modeled on traditional aboriginal designs. This specimen was cut with a chisel from cast iron and ground smooth (Dawson 1880:144). In use, the butt of the iron head was fixed in a socket at the end of a long, light, cedar shaft. It was designed to detach easily upon striking the seal. When not in use, the iron point was kept in a wooden sheath as shown here. Collected by J.G. Swan at Masset, B.C., 1883; length of barbed head, 20 cm.

diet of the people of northern Graham Island (Blackman 1979).

Fifty species of edible plants (Turner 1972) and 27 species of edible marine invertebrates (Ellis 1976) have been recorded for the Skidegate Haida. Plant foods that were preserved included seaweed, several species of berries, clover and cinquefoil roots, and the cambium of hemlock and spruce. Some berries were preserved best by boiling slightly and storing in water. Others were mixed with water and boiled till nearly dry. Crabapples were often preserved in eulachon grease. Other vegetal foods were sun-dried. Many foods, though collected only occasionally or sporadically, were nonetheless important to the diet. Shoots of several plants (cow parsnip, fireweed, salmonberry) picked early in the spring, incidentally to other food-getting, provided welcome fresh greens after a winter of eating dried provisions. Other plants, such as bracken and swordfern rhizomes, were relied upon primarily in times of real scarcity. Shellfish, though used through the year, were probably critical during severe winters following poor autumn salmon harvests. Some shellfish, such as chitons and barnacles, were readily available year round and used when other foods were in short supply or gone. In addition, following storms, there were clams, cockles, scallops, and abalones churned up on the beaches and available to stormbound villagers for the picking.

The cycle of subsistence activities varied regionally because of local variations in available species and seasonality, but everywhere periods of intense economic

Fig. 6. Northern canoe. The bow is on the left. The largest canoes, those intended for long voyages, were over 40 feet in length and had a strong, upward sloping spur at both bow and stern. These could carry 40 men and baggage (Dawson 1880:145). The upsweeping bow and stern sections were separate pieces, lashed to the main body of the canoe. Typically, the outer hull was blackened, the inner decorated with fine patterns of regular chisel marks, and the bow and stern sections painted in formline designs representing mythic creatures. Collected by George Gibbs in 1862. Scaled at one inch to one foot, this model represents a canoe measuring about 36 feet in length with a hull depth of 2 feet, one inch. Actual length, 91.5 cm.

activity alternated with inactivity. In April canoeloads of families from northern Graham Island headed for Langara Island and the nesting sites of the ancient murrelet and Cassin's auklet to hunt these birds and collect their eggs. Halibut fishing and seal hunting also began in spring and continued until September, the favored month for halibut. People left for their sockeye streams in late May and early June. From then until late fall they were busy with food-getting activities, which reached a peak in late July and early August as women collected and processed berries and again in October as the last berries ripened and people dispersed to their chum salmon streams. October was also the time for hunting ducks and geese and

trapping bears and martens. Before the end of November the smoked chums had been boxed and transported to the winter villages, where people were gathered from December to some time in March. If resources had been plentiful, the smoked salmon would last until April. The yearly rounds of the Alaska Haida and Skidegate people differed importantly in having a spring herring season.

Foods were valued differently. Those held in highest esteem were the scarce, seasonal, and socially or geographically restricted (including exotic) foods. Shellfish, occurring in the public domain and available to all, although eaten daily and relished, were not prestigious. In contrast, salmon and other valued resources (cranberries, crabapples, cinquefoil roots) coming from lineage-controlled lands, were prestigious enough to be offered to guests at feasts or as gifts to certain kin.

Division of Labor

The division of labor in Haida society was along sex and, to some extent, class lines. The different spheres of women's and men's labor were summarized in the 1970s by a Masset man who said, "Every woman's got to have her digging stick and every man his fishing line and devilfish [octopus] stick" (Blackman 1979:52). Women gathered roots, berries, and seaweed for food and cedar bark and spruce root for weaving. They processed and preserved all food items, prepared animal skins, and made all clothing and basketry.

Fig. 7. Clothing. left, Painted and fringed buckskin mantle, adorned with humanlike figures with animal claws and columns of complex formline design, all done in red and black pigment. Collected by J.G. Swan on Prince of Wales I., Alaska, 1875; width, 160 cm. right, Man's dance shirt of dark blue stroud decorated on the front with a dogfish appliqué done in scarlet broadcloth outlined in white seed beads. On the back is a wolflike creature in scarlet broadcloth alone. Collected by J.G. Swan at Skidegate, B.C., 1883; width, 75 cm.

Smithsonian, Dept. of Anthr.: left to right, 89022, 88905, 20548, 20548, 88905.

Fig. 8. Incised stone paint dish and brushes. Pigment was pulverized and mixed with oils or grease in the dish and then applied with a carved wooden brush tipped with bristles. Often, paint pots were undecorated. This one is unusual, incised with a complex split formline design surrounding a human head. Collected by J.G. Swan at Skidegate and Masset, Queen Charlotte Is., B.C., 1883. Length of paint dish, 23.8 cm, brushes to same scale.

Men fished, hunted sea and land mammals, constructed houses and canoes, and undertook carving and painting. They gathered the heavier spruce roots for making fish traps and snares and the bulky outer sheets of cedar bark for roofing. Both sexes collected shellfish. Men normally "hunted" octopus and speared sea urchins and crabs, but both sexes collected chitons and dug clams. Both men and women also hunted birds. Men hunted waterfowl using snares and bows and arrows. Women and children brandished clubs and joined the men in hunting auklets and murrelets.

Certain economic activities were considered more prestigious than others. Canoe makers and carvers were highly esteemed for their skills, and proficient sea otter hunters were held in high regard. Fishing, which contributed so heavily to the Haida diet, was not an especially prestigious form of labor. In fact, high-ranking Haida who owned slaves entrusted the task of fishing to their male slaves. That several halibut banks off northern Graham Island in the Queen Charlottes were named for certain slaves who regularly fished them points to the economic importance of slaves (Mitchell and Donald 1980). Formerly numerous among the Haida, slaves were "hewers of wood and drawers of water" (Dawson 1880:132B).

Although slaves were exploited for their labor, high-ranking individuals were by no means idle. Concerned parents worked hard to garner the resources to potlatch for their children, and ambitiousness combined with success in hunting and fishing were qualities sought by the high-ranking in a man. Swanton's (1905:50) statement that "A young, unmarried woman was not allowed to do much work, and lay in bed a great deal of the time . . . . so

that she might marry a chief, and always have little work to do" is more reflective of a ritual act to assure wealth than of the actual industry of high-ranking women. Overall, individuals, regardless of rank, who were lazy were disdained.

Trade and Warfare

Many necessary items were acquired by the Haida through trade with neighboring groups, particularly the Coast Tsimshian and the Tlingit. To the Tlingit the Haida traded canoes, slaves, and shell (opercula?) for copper, Chilkat blankets, and moose and caribou hides (Oberg 1973:108). With the Coast Tsimshian, the Haida exchanged canoes, seaweed, and dried halibut for eulachon grease, dried eulachons, and soapberries (Curtis 1907–1930, 11:134). The Haida acquired slaves in trade from the Kwakiutl (Oberg 1973:108). Occasionally some items were traded internally, between Haida village groups. The Skidegate people, for example, traded "winter seaweed" and herring spawn to those at Masset who lacked these resources in their own territory.

Trade with non-Haida was conducted sometimes under the protective auspices of a formal relationship established between two chiefs of equivalent moieties (Tlingit) or phratries (Tsimshian), which established a bond of brotherhood between the two individuals, their lineages or clans and heirs, and prohibited warfare between them (Murdock 1934:377).

The Haida were renowned for their bellicosity and warred against the Coast Tsimshian, Nishga, Bella Bella, and Southern Tlingit. Occasional raids were also made against some Kwakiutl tribes, Coast Salish, and Nootkans. Internal conflicts also occurred; the Northern Haida in the 1980s regarded the Ninstints people as having been the most feared of Haida warriors. Swanton (1905a: 364–448) recounts external and internal wars among the Haida reported by Skidegate informants. Plunder, revenge, and the capture of slaves were the primary motivations for warfare.

Transportation

Several forms of canoes provided efficient transport to scattered resource stations, villages, and trading centers (fig. 6). The occupation of canoe maker was recognized as an economic specialty. The main body of a canoe was cut from red cedar timbers during February and March. The canoe form was roughed out and hollowed in the woods before being towed to the village where the shaping was finished and the hull steamed and spread with thwarts. Murdock (1934a:229) records seven basic types of Haida craft; most or all of these fall into Drucker's (1955:64–65) "Northern" canoe type. The Haida were outstanding canoemakers, and their craft were traded north and south

top, Smithsonian, Dept. of Anthr.: 20856; center, British Mus., Mus. of Mankind, London: NWC 25; bottom, McGill U., McCord Mus., Montreal: 1180.

Fig. 9. Bowls. top, Mountain sheep horn bowl inlaid with green abalone shell (*Haliotis cracherodii*). Horn bowls like this one were used to serve at feasts, were highly acclaimed gifts, and liable to become family heirlooms. Their graceful form was achieved by steaming the tough horn until malleable enough to be held in a mold to the desired shape. Walls were then given a final thinning and the outer surfaces carved. The horn was obtained through barter with the Tsimshian and other mainland groups (Dawson 1880:142). This species of abalone was brought by the earliest fur traders from Monterey Bay, Calif. (Heizer 1940:400). Collected by J.G. Swan in 1876. center, Wooden grease dish carved as humanoid figure lying on its stomach. The sides of the bowl bear abstract designs representing flippers or wings. Collected on Capt. James Cook's voyage, Queen Charlotte Is., B.C., July 1787. bottom, Wooden grease dish showing a raven with a human figure clasped in its beak and a hawk face carved on the tail. These bowls were favorites among the Haida and non-Indian visitors and collectors in the late 19th century. Collected on the Queen Charlotte Is., B.C., 1876–1878. Length of top 19 cm, others to scale.

on the coast.

Art

Haida art shared so many similarities with that of the Tlingit, Tsimshian, and Bella Bella that Holm (1965: 20–21) states that it is impossible to differentiate two-dimensional designs of these four northern groups. Haida art was largely an applied two-dimensional surface-decorated art, though the Haida are perhaps best known and renowned for their monumental sculpture. The majority of these totem poles (*gya·.a·ŋ* 'housefront pole'; *q̇a·l* 'memorial pole'; *sa·ɬaŋŋ ḥa·d* 'mortuary column'), although three-dimensional in appearance, were primarily two-dimensional in concept—flat designs wrapped around a semi-cylindrical surface (figs. 2–3) (Holm 1965: 25). Wood was the major medium for art work, and decorated items included (in addition to totem poles) canoes, house fronts, house posts, housepit retaining walls, screens, settees, weaponry, tools, spoons, dishes (fig. 9), trays, storage boxes, masks, rattles, and frontlets.

The human body was also artistically embellished. High-class individuals of both sexes were tattooed, and both men and women wore face paintings (fig. 10) on ceremonial occasions.

Deerskins and basketry were sometimes painted with designs; horn and stone were other media for carved designs. Argillite, a soft carbonaceous slate, may have been decoratively carved in prehistoric times, but was intensively quarried only after it was produced by Haida to meet White demands for curios in the nineteenth century. After contact, traditional art motifs were also appliquéd to cloth (ceremonial "button" blankets) and carved in silver and gold (bracelets, earrings, brooches).

Principal colors used in Haida art were black, red, and blue-green. Even on naturalistic carvings the elements of design were highly stylized (Holm 1965). The most commonly represented forms in Haida art were the zoomorphic crest figures of the matrilineages. Events and beings from Haida myth were also amply represented (MacDonald 1983).

Technology

Basketry, made by women from spruce root and the inner bark of red cedar, was used for the gathering, processing, and storage of foods as well as for ceremonial purposes. Openwork twined baskets were made for holding clams, seaweed, and potatoes, and later, for trade to Whites (fig. 11). Close twined baskets of various sizes and shapes were used for berries and treasures ranging from shamans' charms to the eagle down used in dance performances. Close twined baskets were occasionally decorated with bands of false embroidery.

The finest basketry was exemplified in spruce root hats with twined brims; these were frequently also embellished with painted crest designs. Utilitarian mats and bags were plaited from the inner bark of the red cedar.

Cosmology

The Haida universe was divided into three main zones. Above the flat, circular earth was a solid firmament *247*

left, Prov. Arch. of B.C., Victoria: PDP 1333; right, Royal B.C. Mus., Victoria: PN 1053A.

Fig. 10. Body decoration. left, Detail showing the wife of a Queen Charlotte Is. chief with red face paint and labret, holding a child whose face is also painted. The vermilion was "usually . . . rubbed on with little regard to symmetry or pattern" (Dawson 1880:107). Wooden labrets were inserted in the lower lips of girls when they reached maturity. The size of the labret was a measure of the social importance, wealth, and age of the wearer. Each succeeding year, the size of the labret would be increased, a point of beauty to the Haida (Niblack 1890:256–257). Sketch by Sigismund Bacstrom, Rose Inlet, Queen Charlotte Is., B.C., March 1793. right, Woman with large labret. Photograph by Richard Maynard, Haina, Queen Charlotte Is., B.C., 1884.

supported by a pillar, and below it an expanse of sea on whose surface rested 'Inland Country' (the Queen Charlottes) and the 'Seaward Country' (the mainland). The first was supported by a supernatual being, Sacred One Standing and Moving, who in turn rested upon a copper box (Swanton 1905:12).

As their world of social relations was hierarchically organized, so the Haida conceptualized relations within the nonhuman world. Animals were especially important to the Haida, and consequently hierarchy in the animal kingdom was highly elaborated.

Possessing souls like those of humans, animals were classified as special types of people with abilities and intelligence surpassing those of ordinary humans. They lived in villages in their respective sky, land, and sea worlds following a social order like that of their human counterparts. Unlike humans, however, animals could change their form at will, transforming animal into human visage. The Haida prayed and made offerings of grease, tobacco, and flicker feathers to the masters of the game animals and beings who gave wealth (Swanton 1905: 13–32).

Social Organization

● DESCENT GROUPS   The Haida recognized a division of their society into moieties (called clans by Swanton 1905), Raven and Eagle, each composed of a number of lineages (called families by Swanton, clans by Murdock 1934, and lineages by Drucker 1955:110). In 1900–1901, elderly Haidas recalled 22 Raven and 23 Eagle lineages, numbers that had surely fluctuated through time as lineages grew in size, split apart in conflict, and formed new groups. (Haida lineages differ from Tlingit lineages in that fission is complete; there is no larger group, at the level of the Tlingit clan, composed of related lineages.)

Haida lineages trace their origins to several supernatural women of the Raven and Eagle moieties, and their autochthonous beginnings go back to a series of mythical "story towns" (Swanton 1905:72–106) on the Queen Charlotte Islands. Swanton (1905:maps opp.103, 104) plotted the mythical migrations of the lineages and, noting that the most important supernaturals were Ravens and that some Eagle names and lineages were of foreign origin, suggested that the Eagle moiety might have been of foreign, perhaps Tsimshian, extraction.

248

Haida lineages were named, and their names most often have reference to the group's place of origin. In other instances the lineage name refers to a special property or quality that the group possessed. Several lineages, particularly those whose members had migrated to Alaska to form the Kaigani Haida, were further divided into sublineages. These sublineages, conceptualized in Haida as "houses," may well reflect the Tlingit influence on the Kaigani Haida, which early ethnographers acknowledge was pronounced.

Lineages controlled both real and incorporeal property. Vested in the lineage were rights to certain salmon spawning streams, lakes, trapping sites, patches of edible plants (cinquefoil, fireweed, high-bush and bog cranberry, and crabapple), stands of cedar trees, bird rookeries, and stretches of coastline. Swanton (1905a:31) and Niblack (1890:335) wrote that lineages owned halibut banks, but in the 1970s Masset Haida stated that while halibut banks were named, neither they nor the sea were aboriginal lineage properties.

Lineages also owned house sites in the winter villages. Swanton (1905:66) noted that "it would seem that in olden times each town was inhabited by one family [lineage] only. The women in such a town would all have belonged to outside towns." By 1840–1850, however, virtually all winter villages were comprised of house owners of several lineages, and in most villages house owners belonged to

both moieties (Swanton 1905:282-295; see also Stearns 1984:203–205). House sites as well as economic properties could be transferred from one lineage to another. Occasionally a man would give his son a house site from his lineage properties, thus passing it to an individual of the opposite moiety. Dawson (1880:165B) cites an instance in which Chief Skidegate received the area of land known as Tlell (on the east coast of the Queen Charlottes) in marriage and later divested himself of it by presenting the land to Chief Skedans as blood payment.

Incorporeal properties included a repository of names (personal, canoe, fish-trap, house, spoon names), dances, songs, and stories. The most important incorporeal lineage properties were the crest figures. Swanton (1905:113–115) listed 70 distinct crests used by the Haida, while Newcombe (1906) claims to have recorded more than twice that number. These were mostly zoomorphic, though rainbow, rockslide, evening sky, cirrus, stratus, and cumulus clouds occur. A few crests, such as eagle and killerwhale, were common to all lineages in a moiety; other crests were unique to particular lineages. Crests were the identifying symbols of the lineages and, in cases where an individual claimed exclusive right to a crest, it was indicative of individual rank within the lineage. Crests were carved on totem poles, tattooed on the body (fig. 12), painted on the face, carved or painted on household utensils, boxes, and feast dishes. Crests were also dis-

left, Field Mus., Chicago: 854; right, Smithsonian, Dept. of Anthr.: 88965.

Fig. 11. Basketry. left, Woman from Masset, B.C., weaving a close-twined spruce root basket. Spruce roots were roasted over a fire to loosen the bark, which was then stripped by pulling the roots through a split stake. The roots were soaked to soften them, split, bundled, and stored in a dry dark place. Photograph by Edward Allen, 1897. right, Plain close-twined basket with brown-dyed bands on the natural buff background, a characteristic of Haida basketry decoration. Collected by J.G. Swan at Massett, B.C., July 1883; height, 41 cm.

249

a

b

c

e

d

f

g

Amer. Mus. of Nat. Hist., New York: bottom left, 32960; e, 16/397; Smithsonian, Dept. of Anthr.: a, 89038; b, 20875; c, 89052; f, 74750; d, Royal B.C. Mus., Victoria: CPN 10630; g, McGill U., McCord Mus., Montreal: ME892.30.

Fig. 12. Ceremonial garb. bottom left, Men in ceremonial clothing, including 2 masked shamans. The man second from left is ǩude·, nicknamed Dr. Kude, a famous chief and shaman. On the far right Chief xana· of Grizzly Bear House has arm and chest tattooing in charcoal of a hereditary crest (Dawson 1880:108B; Niblack 1890:257; Swanton 1905:107). Bird down, used in ceremonial decoration, is in the hair and around the shoulders of the participants. All wear skirts and leggings with puffin beaks and quillwork decorations. Photograph by Edward Dossetter, Masset, Queen Charlotte Is., B.C., 1881. a, Ulala carved wooden dancing figure, red and white, part of a headdress that represents the cannibal spirit (Caamaño 1938:292). Collected by J.G. Swan at Laskeek, B.C., in 1884; height 122 cm. b–c, Rattles, used by the shaman as a tangible link to the spirit world or by performers to dramatize social rank. b, Bear's head rattle used in secret society performances (Boas 1897:654). Collected by J.G. Swan at Kootznahoo Inlet, Admiralty Is., Alaska, in 1875; length 33 cm. c, Dance rattle ornamented with carved figures. This style is usually considered Tsimshian, but J.G. Swan collected this piece from Tsilwak, a shaman at Gold Harbor, Queen Charlotte Is., B.C., in the 1880s; length 30 cm. d, Shaman's hand drum, which, together with a rattle and a "soul-catcher," was an essential element in the exorcism of sickness from a patient's body. Purchased in Vancouver, B.C., 1930; diameter 62.4 cm. e, Carved wooden shaman figure, attributed to Charles Gwaytihl (Holm 1981:176). It shows the long hair of the shaman bound in a knot, a Chilkat blanket apron with deer hooves on buckskin fringes, and a rattle. The shaman's pierced nose once held a bone ornament. Power transformation of the shaman is shown in the bird figure done as an integral part of his chest and back. Collected in 1869; height 51 cm. f, Raven mask painted in black and red, with movable beak and eyes. Collected by J.G. Swan at Laskeek, B.C., 1884; height 26 cm. g, Ulala society mask, one of 4 that were worn sequentially in performing a transformation of mythical creatures. Collected by George Mercer Dawson in 1878; height 25.3 cm.

played on ceremonial garments, headdresses, helmets, basketry hats (fig. 13), drums, weapons, and canoes. Crests were acquired occasionally in ceremonial exchange with the Tsimshian, and, according to Swanton (1905: 107), a man might allow his children to use his crests. This practice may have existed only among the Southern Haida.

• KINSHIP Haida kinship terminology is of the Crow type, in which terms are cross-generationally skewed. In particular, the term for father's sister (sqa·nn) is extended to all women of the father's lineage of his generation or below. (In Crow systems the term for father is normally extended to include the male offspring of women of father's lineage, but in the Haida system this was not the case.) In parents' generation the terms are bifurcate merging, mother and mother's sister being equated and distinguished from father's sister, father and father's brother being equated (at least in Southern Haida) and distinguished from mother's brother. In one's own generation, parallel cousins are equated with siblings and distinguished from cross-cousins; father's sister's daughter (sqa·nn) and mother's brother's daughter are distinct in both surviving dialects, while father's sister's son and mother's brother's son are distinct in Southern Haida only. Second ascending generation terminology (with the exception of sqa·nn) is generational; grandparents, their siblings, and cousins are called by grandparent terms. Second descending generation terms (again with the exception of females of father's lineage) are similarly generational with kin being called by grandchild terms. In the first descending generation, own children and children of same sex siblings are classed together and distinguished from children of opposite sex siblings. A number of kin terms in the Haida system vary according to sex of the speaker, males using one term, females another.

Affinal terms are distinct from those for consanguine kin; however, both categories of kin terms, appear to have been widely extended, some encompassing all same-sex members of the speaker's or the opposite moiety. In addition, primary relationships were generated from a secondary consanguine kin relationship referred to by the verbal expression gud-ʔał qi·.uwa· 'have fathers that belong to the same lineage'. People in this relationship called each other by sibling terms and their offspring called each other by the appropriate cousin terminology.

In traditional Haida society there were patterns of kin avoidance and familiarity. Brothers and sisters, while strongly supporting one another, as adults had to treat each other with reserve; a man and his sister's daughter were especially formal; and a woman and her son-in-law avoided speaking directly to one another. On the other hand, men whose fathers belonged to the same lineage could ask for each other's property and play practical jokes on each other, while cross-cousins of the opposite sex and in-laws of the opposite sex could joke and flirt and have semisanctioned affairs (Murdock 1934).

• RANKING There was no overall ranking among Haida lineages, though one informant listed three Raven lineages and three Eagle lineages that ranked above all the others (Swanton 1905:70). Some Masset Haida, commenting in the 1970s on the existence of lineage rank, asserted that one lineage was inferior to all the rest because that group owned very little land.

Each lineage was headed by a hereditary chief who was the trustee of the lineage properties. His permission had to be secured before others of different lineages could have access to those properties and their resources. He was consulted on lineage matters and could call together the lineage for counsel or to declare war. If a lineage were divided into sublineages, chiefs of these divisions were also recognized. The owner of a cedar plank dwelling was a house chief whose authority extended over all those resident in his household. He decided when the household members left the winter village for the fish camps, and he could call together his sisters' sons for warfare. In single lineage towns, the lineage chief was the highest authority in the village. In multilineage settlements the highest authority was called the "town master" or "town mother" (Swanton 1905:68). This title was held by the highest-ranking, wealthiest house chief of the lineage that owned the village site. In actuality, the position was occasionally held by a lineage chief whose ancestral properties lay *251* elsewhere.

Swanton (1905:69) noted that most questions regarding the interests of the townspeople as a whole were decided by the town chief. Curtis (1907–1930, 11:119) concurs, while Murdock (1934a:238) states that no chief wielded any authority outside his own lineage. In the 1970s Masset people indicated that while the town chief needed the support of the house chiefs and lineage chiefs of his village, he did wield a considerable amount of authority in respect to matters affecting the village as a whole. Boelscher (1985) explores the relationship between rank and respect as well as its dependence on reciprocity and public scrutiny.

Chieftainships were handed down within a lineage in accordance with matrilineal principles of inheritance. Normally a title would be passed on to the next oldest brother, any younger brother, and the oldest sister's oldest son (Stearns 1984:195). Success in the acquisition of wealth was an important chiefly criterion, and an unproductive sister's son might be passed over for a more remote but successful "nephew." Occasionally a chieftainship was transferred to an individual of another sublineage or lineage of the moiety, though public pressure militated against this practice. Rarely, it would appear, a chieftainship might be given to an individual of the opposite moiety, the title passing from father to son. The Masset town chieftainship, held by the *sgida·qaw* Raven lineage and passed to the *sʕaʒu·gà·ł la·na·s* Eagle lineage about 1840 from a father to his son, is an example (Blackman 1972, 1981:115)

The internal ranking of Haida society was evident at feasts and potlatches when guests were seated in accordance with their rank.

In addition to a rank order the Haida recognized a class system. High-ranking people (*yahʕi·d*) were those who, as children, had had potlatches given in their honor by their parents and thus bore one or more potlatch names. Both sexes wore the markers of their status in the form of tattoos. These "nobles" were the house owners and heirs to lineage and sublineage chieftainships and high names. People who were not high-ranking had not had potlatches given for their benefit. They did not own houses, were not heirs to high-ranking names, and, through either improvidence or "unluckiness" were not so successful in their economic endeavors as the high-ranking. They did not display the visible symbols of rank and did not host potlatches or feasts (Murdock 1936:18–19). Slaves (*ḥalda·ŋ*) were war captives and the offspring of war captives. They were regarded as chattels and their position was hereditary.

Ceremonies

Haida ceremonies were directly related to the rank structure of Haida society. The major ceremonial events, feasts, potlatches, and dance performances were given by high-ranking people; in fact, the hosting of such affairs was one of their responsibilities. In order to maintain prestige in the eyes of the people, a chief was expected to give frequent feasts; to succeed to a chiefly title, to guarantee the noble standing of his children, or to build a house, he was constrained to give a potlatch.

Property was ceremonially distributed from host group to guest group for a variety of reasons. The largest and most elaborate wealth distribution was the *ʔwa·ła·l*, a potlatch given upon completion of a cedar-plank dwelling and its frontal pole. The several wealth distributions of the lengthy *ʔwa·ła·l* acknowledged the new house owner's accession to the position of house chief and served to reimburse those who had performed important functions in the actual construction of the house. Equally important, the *ʔwa·ła·l* was hosted for the benefit of the house owner's children. They received potlatch names (often newly invented) and tattoos and were subsequently accorded high-ranking status. A less elaborate version of the *ʔwa·ła·l* was given solely to assure the standing of a couple's children. No house was constructed, but a freestanding totem pole bearing the childrens' crests was carved and erected.

The mortuary potlatch (referred to with the verb *saḱa* 'to host a ceremonial payment for interment') marked the death of a high-ranking individual and the succession of his heir to the deceased's position. The carving and erecting of a mortuary column or a memorial pole preceded the wealth distribution.

Minor property distributions were given to mark female puberty; to respond to a high-ranking member of the opposite moiety who had impugned one's status (referred to as *ga da·ŋ* 'to throw things away' to him); and to erase the memory of a mishap causing loss of composure (usually falling or slipping), in which a member of the opposite moiety came to one's assistance (referred to as *ʔagaŋ saŋa·da* 'to fix one's high rank'). With the exception of the *ʔwa·ła·l* distribution of property was to members of the moiety opposite the host. In the case of the puberty potlatch, the mortuary potlatch, and the *ʔwa·ła·l* the primary recipients of wealth were members of the father's lineage (of the girl, the deceased, and the children receiving names, respectively).

While potlatches generally included feasting, feasts were also hosted separately. Occasions for feasts included the first naming of a child, marriage, death, the honoring of high-ranking visitors, and the enhancement of one's own prestige. Like potlatching, feasting was governed by a precise etiquette. Guests were seated relative to their rank, certain foods were eaten, and special carved and sometimes painted feast dishes and spoons were used.

The performance of the shamans (*sʕa·ga·* 'be a shaman, be possessed') or members of the dancing "societies" was another accompaniment to the potlatch

Fig. 13. Painted basketry hat. Designs painted in red, black, and shades of blue show a crest belonging to the wearer. The hat was worn in conjunction with decorated clothing and other costume on ceremonial occasions where the family's privileges and honors were displayed. The crown is supported by an inner wooden framework. Leather chin straps anchored the large hat to the head. Collected by J.G. Swan at Masset, Queen Charlotte Is., B.C., 1883; diameter 60 cm.

(fig. 12). The dances were acknowledged copies of Northern Wakashan winter ceremonial dances but were neither so significant nor so elaborate as the originals. Curtis (1907–1930, 11:139), in fact, contends that the dances were taught to the Haida by uninitiated Bella Bella war captives, as the more esoteric aspects and the underlying mythology of the dances were unknown to the Haida. Boas (1897:651) also attributes a Heiltsuk origin to the Haida dances, but Haida oral tradition (Swanton 1905:156–160) places their actual acquisition in the vicinity of Kitkatla (Coast Tsimshian).

Dance performances (Curtis 1907–1930, 11:143ff.; Dawson 1880:127B; Swanton 1905:156; Drucker 1940: 223–224) were given at major potlatches, both the ʔwa·ɬa·l and the mortuary potlatch (Swanton 1905:162, 176). As in the Wakashan performances from which they were copied, the sequence began with the supposed capture of initiates by spirits and was followed by the return of the initiates to the village, the exorcism of the possessing spirits through dance, and the distribution of property by the initiates to guests for witnessing the performance. A man high enough in rank could be initiated by a new spirit at each successive potlatch. Possessing spirits were moiety specific, and one could not be possessed by a spirit that came to members of the opposite moiety. In addition, two dances were regarded as the specific property of two different lineages (Curtis 1907–1930, 11:146, 148). Among the Southern Haida, the initiates collectively formed an exclusive sodality, but they may not have done so among the Northern Haida, for whom these performances were less important (Drucker 1940:223–224).

Life Cycle

According to Murdock (1934a:248), the Haida preferred female to male children because the former insured the perpetuation of the lineage. Pregnant women (as well as

Fig. 14. Ceremonial staffs. left, Wand of office held by a chief when giving out gifts at the potlatch. When a recipient was named, the staff was thumped on the floor boards. At top is a beaver crest; at bottom, an eagle. Collected by J.G. Swan at Skidegate, B.C., 1883; length 122.6 cm. right, Staff carved in 2 jointed sections. When pulled apart at the socket, the chief retaining one section in each hand, the distribution of presents began (Niblack 1890:272). Collected by J.G. Swan at Masset, B.C., 1883; length 82.2 cm.

their husbands) were subject to a number of taboos (Swanton 1905:47–48), the observance of which was for the benefit of the unborn child. In addition, a woman performed several rituals to assure an easy delivery.

A Haida infant was welcomed into the world by a woman of its father's lineage who assisted the mother in childbirth. The infant received a name, given usually by its parents and drawn from among the personal names of the child's father's father's lineage. This name is usually conferred at a small feast. When the infant is quite young (some modern Haida say four days old), he may have his ears pierced. Further ear piecing and tattooing (of the arms, legs, chest and back in males and the arms and legs in females) by women of the child's father's lineage takes place at ʔwa·ɬa·l or mortuary potlatches hosted by the child's father. The child also receives additional names at its father's potlatches. During childhood high-ranking females had the lower lip pierced for the wearing of a labret (fig. 10). According to one observer, the size of a woman's labret was related not only to her rank but also to the number of children she had borne (Harrison 1911–1913).

Nearly every Haida child was regarded as the reincarnation of a deceased ancestor. The identity of the ancestor is indicated either in birthmarks or other physical characteristics, features of personality or behavior, or statements made by the child that point to past memories (Stevenson 1975). Swanton (1905:117) noted that individuals are reincarnated into their own moiety and usually own lineage while in the 1970s Haida stated that reincarnation was not lineage or moiety specific.

Haida children were instructed formally as well as informally. Young boys learned from their fathers, but at an early age they went to reside with their mother's brothers, whom they were expected to assist and from whom they received instruction in lineage matters and proper behavior. Boys were toughened by their uncles, who periodically made them swim in the cold winter sea. Other, more ritual training served to instill appropriate qualities. For example, a boy would eat dragonfly wings to be a rapid swimmer, suck on diving duck tongues to be longwinded in the water and on bluejay tongues in order to be a fast climber. There was no ceremonial attention given boys at puberty.

A girl was under the tutelage of her mother and might at a young age assist her in collecting spruce root, cedar bark, seaweed, and berries. A girl's first menstruation (referred to by the verb *taguna*) was ritually acknowledged. The girl was secluded behind a screen or partition in a rear corner of her parents' house where she remained for a month or longer. The higher her rank, the longer the seclusion. A number of taboos were enjoined upon her at this time. She could not venture near the central house fire lest her face turn permanently red. In order to strengthen herself, she slept on a stone pillow, ate little, and drank no water. She avoided looking at the sea, and so that her future children would not be bedwetters, she ate no shellfish. She was forbidden to talk or laugh during her seclusion, and when she left the house she could not use the regular exit. Hunting, fishing, and gambling equipment were kept as far as possible from the menstruating girl to avoid their pollution. During her seclusion the girl was attended and instructed by her father's sisters. At the end of the isolation period, the girl was ritually cleansed, a feast was given to mark her entry into womanhood, and her father's sisters were given property by her mother. Swanton (1905:49–50) reports a number of additional taboos observed by the girl for the next two to five years. Additionally, at each menstrual period a woman went into brief seclusion.

Marriages among the Haida were arranged, frequently during the childhood (even infancy, in Skidegate) of the couple. The arrangements were made by the parents of the couple if the betrothed were very young; if the marriage was proposed when the couple were older, the man's lineage met with the girl's parents and, frequently, her maternal uncle to offer the marriage proposal. For both

Fig. 15. Burial of Chief Sonihat. Rev. Edward Marsden, a Tsimshian Presbyterian minister, is second from right, and the chief's 2 sons hold the blanket epitaph. Photograph at Kasaan, Prince of Wales Is., Alaska, Jan. 1912.

sexes the preferred partner was someone of the father's lineage (Vaughan 1976; Boelscher 1985:222). The regular practice of bilateral cross-cousin marriage is suggested in the fact that several lineages had long histories of intermarriage (Swanton 1905:67). Marriage called for the exchange of property between the parents of the couple, gifts of property from the groom to the girl's mother's brothers, and a several-fold reciprocation of property from the girl's uncles and father to her husband. Feasting accompanied marriage, but the property exchanges were not regarded as potlatches.

Polygyny, restricted to chiefs, was evidently infrequent in practice. Upon the death of a spouse, an individual usually remarried. A woman was expected to marry a man of her husband's lineage, often a younger brother or a nephew of her husband. Similarly, a man might remarry into his wife's lineage, preferably her younger sister or sister's daughter.

Of all Haida life cycle events, death was accorded the most ceremony, and the elaborateness of the ritual was correlated with the deceased's rank (fig. 15). At death the body was cleansed, costumed, and the face painted by women of the deceased's father's lineage. The body, surrounded by personal property, lay in state in the rear of the house for several days so that friends and relatives might file past the body and sing crying songs. Men of father's lineage constructed the bent-corner coffin. Once in the coffin, the body was removed from the house through a hole in a side wall and placed in a lineage grave house behind the main dwelling. There the body remained until it was transferred to a niche in a newly carved mortuary column; if a memorial pole was erected instead, the body would remain permanently in the grave house. The mortuary potlatch was given when the grave or memorial pole was put in place. The mortuary potlatch for a man was given by his heir; that of a woman was given by her husband. Commoners were not normally placed in grave houses with the high ranking, and carved poles were not erected in their honor. Slaves were cast into the sea at death.

At death a man's property would be taken by his younger brothers and nephews. Often the deceased's house would be literally cleaned out by his heirs, leaving the widow with only her cooking utensils and personal property. A woman's property devolved upon her daughter at death. As a sign of mourning a widow fasted for several days and "treated herself like a slave" (Swanton 1905:52). This custom was still practiced in the early 1980s by older conservative Haidas. He deceased's near relatives and close friends mourned by cutting their hair and blackening their faces with pitch. The widower underwent mourning rituals like those of a widow (Murdock 1934:373).

Often an individual near death would express a reincarnation promise, occasionally specifying the parents to whom he would be reborn. At death, the deceased individual was transported by canoe to the Land of Souls.

History

The first recorded contacts with the Haida were made in 1774 by the Spanish explorer Juan Perez and his crew at Langara Island in the Queen Charlottes and again at Dall Island in Alaska. Numerous trading ships plied Queen Charlotte and southeastern Alaska waters in the late eighteenth century and early nineteenth. Conducting their trade from shipboard, European and American mariners exchanged manufactured goods with the Haida for sea otter pelts. These traders introduced a great variety of goods to the Haida, some in substantial quantities. Among the most significant items were iron pieces (called "toes" in mariners' records) that were worked into adz blades by the natives, chisels and knives, sheet copper, muskets, tin wash basins, kettles, liquor, cloth, and items of clothing.

Potato cultivation was introduced by traders, and by 1825 the Haida were growing large quantities of potatoes that they exchanged with the Coast Tsimshian and, later, with the Hudson's Bay Company.

Several early traders remarked upon the Haida skill in trade and the exacting and changing native tastes in foreign goods. The Haida often refused to trade pelts with one ship either because they were not interested in the goods offered or because they knew another ship whose captain offered better bargains would soon arrive.

It is difficult to ascertain the effects of this early trade on the Haida, as contacts with traders were cursory and seasonal. The eighteenth century sea trade was, for the most part, peaceful, though hostilities broke out in 1791 and the Haida wreaked revenge for this incident in succeeding years. There are no data on population decline resulting from the introduction of disease by traders,

U. of B.C., Vancouver: A1584.
Fig. 16. Northwest trade gun, lockplate stamped "Parker, Field, and Co., 1861," and typical of smoothbore muskets traded well into the late 19th century. On the side opposite the lockplate is a dragon sideplate characteristic of these guns, regardless of maker. The barrel has been shortened, and the stock carved. Collected on the Queen Charlotte Is., B.C., 1893–1930; length 83 cm.

though the Haida had contracted smallpox as early as 1791 (Fleurieu 1801:438; Bishop 1796). Doubtless the native economic system was affected by the channeling of increasing amounts of energy into the pursuit of sea otter.

The sea otter trade began to decline after 1810, and by 1830 it was defunct. Four years later, the sea trade was superseded by the Hudson's Bay Company, which established Fort Simpson in Coast Tsimshian territory. This post became a meeting ground for Tsimshian, Southern Tlingit, and Haida who went there to trade for the next 40 or so years, not only with the White traders but also with one another. The Hudson's Bay Company disbursed its famed blankets, rice, flour, and other staples, cloth, and clothing to the Haida in exchange for furs (mostly land furbearers), dried halibut, potatoes, and dried herring spawn. After the Fraser gold rush in 1858 the Haida also regularly journeyed to the burgeoning town of Victoria to trade, and they traveled at least as far north as Sitka on trading expeditions. A small Hudson's Bay Company post founded at Masset on the Queen Charlottes in 1869 attracted Haida from outlying villages, but it does not appear to have curtailed Haida trading ventures to the mainland.

Trading trips to Victoria were detrimental to the Haida. Warfare broke out between them and the Kwakiutl groups whose villages lay along the route, and in Victoria they fell prey to drinking and prostitution, vices introduced during the maritime fur trade period. Travelers to Victoria in 1862 brought a devastating smallpox epidemic back to the Queen Charlotte Islands. Within two years the population had been so severely reduced that entire villages were gradually abandoned, and their remnant populations resettled within the next 15 years at Masset and Skidegate. The population continued to decline, reaching a low of 588 on the Queen Charlottes in 1915 (Duff 1964:39; cf. Fisher 1977:116).

The first Christian missionary to visit the Haida was a Methodist, Jonathan Green; in 1829, in response to an expression of interest from Chief Skidegate, he visited Skidegate Village and went on to meet two Kaigani chiefs on Dall Island (Green 1915). Somewhat later the Haida received, through the Tsimshian, something of the message of the Carrier prophet Bini and perhaps other native   *255* reinterpretations of Christianity (Swanton 1905a: 311–315; Spier 1935:39).

William H. Collison, an Anglican and former assistant to William Duncan at his successful Metlakatla mission among the Coast Tsimshian, established the first mission at Masset in 1876. Within 10 years a church had been constructed, the erection of grave posts and memorial totem poles had ceased, and the Haida consented to bury their dead in a cemetery the missionary had surveyed. Dancing performances were apparently abandoned under missionary pressure, and the missionaries reported that the power of the shamans was on the decline; however, potlatching and feasting remained integral to Haida culture.

Invited to the village of Skidegate in 1877 by a Christianized Haida, Missionary Collison heard the following request: "We cannot give up all our customs. We want to give away property as formerly and to make feasts and burn food when our friends die. Our people must continue to paint their faces. We would also like to have a sawmill that we might build good houses and a store where we might purchase cheap goods as at Metlakatla" (Collison 1878). Although the Skidegate Haida requested a missionary and lay teacher, the Anglicans, due to a lack of funds, were unable to meet the request. A request sent by Skidegate villagers to the Methodist mission at Fort Simpson led to the appointment of George Robinson in 1883 and informal agreement between the denominations that the Methodists would control Christianization of the central and southern Haida villages and the Anglicans, the northern villages (Henderson 1974:304).

In Alaska the Presbyterians organized a mission to the Kaigani at Howkwan in 1880 and established a branch mission at Klinkwan under a native lay minister after 1900. Populations from Sukkwan and Koianglas gradually resettled at Howkwan and Klinkwan, leaving Kasaan as the only unmissionized Kaigani village.

The Indian Reserve Commission, appointed by the Canadian federal government, arrived on the Queen Charlotte Islands in 1882 to survey reserves for native use. As a result the Haida were granted rights to 3,484.5 acres; the reinvestigation of the reserve lands question in 1913 resulted in the allotment of an additional 360.1 acres to the Haida (Canada. Royal Commission on Indian Affairs for the Province of British Columbia 1916). A resident Indian agent appointed for the Queen Charlottes in 1909 established his agency at Masset. Agents served the Queen Charlotte branch until 1966, when it was removed to Prince Rupert on the mainland.

Kasaan was abandoned in 1902 when its members were persuaded by officials of the Kasaan Bay Mining Company to move to the vicinity of the mining operations. They were offered permanent winter and summer employment in the mining industry, schooling, and assistance in laying out a new village (Jackson 1908). White-style cottages

top left, Peabody Mus. of Salem, Mass.: E3494; top right, Harvard U., Peabody Mus.: 94-57-10/R163; bottom, Smithsonian, Dept. of Anthr.: 89001.

Fig. 17. Carvings of argillite, quarried historically in the Queen Charlotte Is. Soft enough to carve with steel-bladed woodworking tools, it also has the attribute of taking on a fine lustre from the blades of the tools, needing no further polishing. Although argillite was worked in the precontact period, it was an insignificant craft until the introduction of steel-bladed tools and a thriving curio market. There are well-documented examples of strictly aboriginal motifs on carvings dating as early as 1820. top left, Pipe carved as a cluster of mythological figures. Collected before 1830; 9.5 cm wide. top right, Platter characteristic of the late 19th century, ovate and carved only on the upper surface. Earlier platters tended to be round, carved inside and out, and displayed flowers, simple geometric forms, designs from U.S. coins and insignia, as well as names and letters. Later carvers incorporated sculptural figures representing characters in Haida mythology. Here 2 human figures struggle with an octopus, based on a Kaigani story (Swanton 1905:259–260). Collected in the Queen Charlotte Is. before 1894; length 52 cm. bottom, Miniature chest, probably modeled after the wooden chests designed to hold ceremonial objects in chief's homes. The argillite chests are far more fanciful in design and formline layout. They were done for sale, the artists catering to foreign tastes. Lids, bottoms, and sides are all separate sheets of argillite, glued and pegged with wooden dowels. This box probably portrays one of the many legends concerning human hunters and their struggles with the grizzly bear. The heads at the side of the box are probably the sea lion, holding a salmon (Niblack 1890: pl.XLIV; cf. Barbeau 1957:64). Collected by J.G. Swan at Skidegate, B.C., 1883; 34.5 cm long.

were built in the new village, also named Kasaan. The Haida remained here until the mine closed its operations, after which they migrated in the late 1940s and 1950s to Ketchikan.

By 1910 Howkwan and Klinkwan Haida were experiencing economic difficulties. As seasonal cannery workers they migrated from these villages to the crowded quarters of cannery housing during fishing season, and as commercial fishermen they faced unfavorable competition from cannery-owned fishtraps and consequent reduction in wages. Out of these conditions emerged a group of Howkwan and Klinkwan Haida favoring relocation to a single village where they could earn a livelihood and reside year-round. The U.S. federal government supported such a move because, among other things, it meant centralization of school facilities. Under the auspices of a representative of the Bureau of Education, the Haida selected a village site with an ample supply of water (a problem at Howkwan and Klinkwan), and Hydaburg was established in 1911. Its founding was accompanied by the signing of an unusual document. This statement, drawn up by the village founders, asserted that old tribal customs had been abandoned and requested full U.S. citizenship (Blackman 1981:34), granted with the Indian Citizenship Act of 1924. In 1933 Hydaburg was incorporated as a town, with local government functions residing in an elected mayor and town council. The people of Hydaburg petitioned the government for a reservation, and in 1949 the 101,000-acre Hydaburg Reservation was created. It was invalidated by a U.S. District Court decision in 1952 (Gruening 1954:364–381).

The most dramatic changes in Haida culture were effected during 1875–1910. The Haida were increasingly acculturated, as White-style housing appeared among the cedar plank dwellings. The last traditional house building and frontal totem-pole raising occurred in the winter of 1881. By 1905 the last traditional house had disappeared from Masset.

The population decline, which reached its nadir in 1915, led to rearrangements in settlement pattern, the extinction of some lineages, and severe constraints upon ceremonial organization. Missionaries wrought specific changes in mortuary practices, traditional ceremonies, and marriage patterns. When the potlatch was outlawed in Canada in 1884, missionaries to the Haida assisted in enforcing the ban. Wage labor, available in the burgeoning fishing and canning industries, enhanced the economic resources of the people, while the Canadian government's allotment of reserves without regard to lineage landholdings undercut the economic base of the lineages. Lineage organization was further diminished by the adoption of nuclear family dwellings and the subsequent disappearance of the house-building potlatch (Blackman 1977). However, the mortuary potlatch, temporally truncated and altered in content but not form, continued to be a feature of twentieth-century Haida culture (Blackman 1973). Feasting, a traditional custom given missionary approval, continued unabated and may even have gained momentum as nontraditional events become occasions for celebration by feasting. Matrilineal organization contin-

Table 1. Size of Haida Towns

	1836–1841 (Work in Dawson 1880:173B)		about 1850–1860 (Swanton 1905: 282–295)	
	houses	population		houses
Alaska				
Sukkwan	14	229	Sukkwan	7
Howkwan	27	458	Howkwan[a]	
Koianglas	8	148	Koianglas[a]	
Klinkwan	26	417	Klinkwan	13
Kasaan	18	249	Kasaan[a]	
"You-ah-noe"	18	234	Kaigani[b]	
Total	111	1,735		
Queen Charlotte Islands				
"Lu-lan-na"[c]	20	296	Yaku	8
			Kiusta	9
"Nigh-tasis"[d]	15	280	Kung	12
Masset[e]	160	2,473	Yan	20
			Kayung	14
			Masset	33
			Hiellen	3
"Ne-coon"	5	122		
"A-se-guang"	9	120		
Skidegate	48	738	Skidegate	22
			Haina	13
Chaatl	35	561	Chaatl	30
Kaisun	18	329	Kaisun	20
Cumshewa	20	286	Cumshewa	21
Skedans	30	439	Skedans	27
Kloo	40	545	Kloo	26
Ninstints	20	308	Ninstints	20
"Too"	10	196		
Total	430	6,693		277
All Haida	541	8,428		

[a]Town listed, but number of houses not collected.
[b]A summer site, for trading.
[c]Assumed to correspond to Yaku and Kiusta.
[d]Assumed to correspond to Kung.
[e]Encompasses Yan, Kayung, and Masset on the Swanton list.

ued to function in a restricted ceremonial context. The ceremonial context, though, is significant, for the ceremonial links with the past are what give modern Haida culture its distinctive identity.

Population

The only population figures for Haida villages prior to the dramatic decline of the population in the late nineteenth century were compiled by John Work, a Hudson's Bay Company factor commissioned to enumerate the Northwest Coast native population, 1836–1841. Table 1 compares the villages inventoried by Work with Swanton's (1905) informants' listing of Haida houses by village. While there are a number of correspondences (Cumshewa, Kaisun, Hiellen, Ninstints), there are significant discrepancies (Masset, Skidegate, Kloo). According to Murdock (1934a:237) a Haida household might number as many as 30 or more individuals, but mean household size as calculated from Work's data ranges from a low of 13 to a high of 24.

Swanton (1905:106) estimated 900 in 1901, "largely mixed-bloods." Haida population continued to decline, reaching the nadir of 588 in 1915 (Duff 1964:39). However, the 1920s and 1930s were marked by a steady recovery. In 1963 the Queen Charlotte Agency, British Columbia, reported 903 Masset and 321 Skidegate for a total Canadian Haida population of 1,224 (Duff 1964:18, 39). In 1970 Alaska Haida (Kaigani) population was estimated at around 240 concentrated mostly in Hydaburg (Van den Brink 1974:232; contemporary figures for Canadian and U.S. Haida are discussed in "Haida Since 1960," this vol.).

Synonymy†

The name Haida has been in general use in English since Dawson (1880); earlier spellings were Haidah, Hai-dai, Hydah, and Hyder (Hodge 1907–1910, 1:523). This name is an adaptation of the Northern Haida self-designation, (Masset) ḥàˑieˑ, ḥàˑdeˑ, (Alaskan) haˑdéˑ, haˑdáˑy, also meaning 'the people', a nominalization of the verb (Masset) ḥàˑtaˑ, ḥàˑdaˑ 'to be human, to be a Haida'. In the Skidegate dialect the noun is xàˑydǝgaˑy and the verb xàˑydǝgaˑ; the Skidegate name is the source of the English form Hidery used by Deans (1899).

The Tlingit call the Haida deˑkiˑnaˑ (Naish and Story 1976:86).

Subdivisions

Kaigani Haida. The Kaigani, or Alaska, Haida are called in Masset q̣iˑs ḥàˑdeˑ 'people of Langara Island', after the island from which they traditionally came. Dawson (1880: 172B–173B) sometimes refers to them as the Kai-ga-ni Haidas and sometimes as the Kai-ga-ni Indians as distinct from the Haida, who in this usage were only those on the Queen Charlotte Islands. The name Kaigani was that of a traditional town or summer camp (Swanton 1905:281), in Alaskan Haida k̓áyk̓aˑníˑ, a loan blend of Tlingit xáˑx ʔaˑní 'Crabapple Town' and Haida k̓áy 'crabapple' (Jeff Leer, communication to editors 1986). Early variant spellings include Kaiaganies, Kegarnie, Kiganis, Kigarnee, and Kyganies (Hodge 1907–1910, 1:642).

Masset Haida. The names for the Masset Haida refer to their residence on Masset Inlet: (Masset) ʕaww ḥàˑdeˑ 'inlet people', (Skidegate) ǯaxuˑsdǝ xàˑydǝgaˑy 'mouth-

of-the-inlet people'. Another Skidegate name, equivalent to the Masset one, is given by Swanton (1905:105). They were traditionally from Rose Point (Rose Spit), Masset nàˑy kun.

Skidegate Haida. The Skidegate Haida call themselves łga gilda xàˑydǝgaˑy, after the name of the town of Skidegate, and the Masset Haida call them qa·łgwaˑ ḥàˑdeˑ 'up-inlet people', a geographically inappropriate label that apparently plays on the name the Skidegate people give those at Masset.

Kunghit Haida. The Haida name for the Kunghit people, Masset ʕaŋ.iˑd ʕud ḥàˑdeˑ 'people of the end of Anthony Island' and Skidegate ġǝŋxiˑd xàˑydǝgaˑy 'people of Anthony Island', refers to the island on which the major village of Ninstints was located, not to the larger Kunghit Island. These are the Ninstints people of Swanton (1905:105, 277).

No names are recorded for the historical divisions on the opposite coasts of Moresby Island (Swanton 1905: 105). The traditional group that Swanton (1905:90, 105) calls the Pitch-Town-People were the q̣aˑs laˑnaˑs 'the pitch ones'.

Villages

Swanton (1905:277–282) gives the names of 126 Haida towns. The following list treats 20 of these, the 17 "principal towns" for which Swanton (1905:282–294) lists the house names and three additional Alaska towns (fig. 1). The name of the town chief is given if it is the source of the English name. The names of the Kaigani towns, whose people eventually moved to Hydaburg, are given in the Alaskan dialect; the names of the northern Graham Island towns, whose people ended up at Masset, are in the Masset dialect; and the names of the remaining towns, whose people moved to Skidegate, are in the Skidegate dialect. These dialectal distinctions probably correspond roughly to the major dialects of the period when the towns were inhabited (about 1850–1860), but each town presumably had its own characteristic speech, and Swanton (1905:105) reports that there was a noticeable difference between the Kunghit dialect and that of Skidegate.

Sukkwan. This name and the Haida sahq̣wa.aˑn are from Tlingit suqʷkaʔaˑn 'town on the fine underwater grass'. Variants are Shaw-a-gan (John Work in Dawson 1880:173B) and Shakan, Shākwan, and others listed by Hodge (1907–1910, 2:648).

Howkwan. The Haida name is ʔʰáwk̓yaˑn. A Tlingit derivation cannot be confirmed, and Swanton's (1905:282; Hodge 1907–1910, 1:573) Tlingit explanations are apparently just folk-etymologies. Other spellings are How-a-guan (Work in Dawson 1880:173B) and Houkan, Howakan, Howkan, and others in Hodge.

Koianglas. This is Haida q̣wíˑ ʔʰánλaˑs 'wet earth', given by Swanton (1905:282) as q!wēᶜAnḷas lᵑagaˑ-i and

† This synonymy was written by Ives Goddard; the Haida forms written in italics were furnished by John Enrico, and the Tlingit forms were furnished by Jeff Leer (communications to editors, 1986).

also appearing as Qui-a-hanless (Work in Dawson 1880: 173B), Gu-ai-hendlas, Koiandlas, Kwaihāntlas, and Kweundlas (Hodge 1907-1910, 1:747).

Klinkwan. The English name and the Haida *łanqwá·n* are from Tlingit *łenquʔa·n* 'tideflats-place-town'. Variants include Chlen-kŏ-ān, Klinquan, and other forms in Hodge (1907-1910, 1:714). Work (in Dawson 1880:173B) referred to Klinkwan as Click-ass, after the name of Klakas Inlet, the estuary to the north of the village.

Kasaan. The English and the Haida *gasá·n* are from Tlingit *kasaʔa·n* 'pretty town'. This name also appears as Kassan (Hodge 1907-1910, 1:660). According to Swanton (1905:295) Kasaan is the town referred to by Work as Chat-chee-nie (in Dawson 1880:173B), the name of a camping place nearby; this is also rendered tcatchi'nî (Swanton 1905:282).

Yaku. The Haida name *ya·k̓u* has been rendered iā'k'ō (Boas 1898:22) and by the misprinted Kāk-oh (Dawson 1880:162B) and Yukh (Deans 1899:94). Swanton (1905:295; Hodge 1907-1910, 2:984) conjectured that this, or this and Kiusta, might have been the Lu-lan-na of Work (in Dawson 1880:173B).

Kiusta. Haida *k̓yu·s̓ta·* appears as Kioo-sta (Dawson 1880:162B) and Kūstā (Hodge 1907-1910, 1:710).

Kung. The Haida name is *qaŋ*, appearing as Kung already in Dawson (1880:163B). Swanton (in Hodge 1907-1910, 1:735, 2:70) conjectured that this town was the one called Nigh-tasis by Work (in Dawson 1880:173B), a variant of which is Nigh-tan.

Yan. The Haida name *ya·n* is given as Yān in Dawson (1880:163B) and rendered as ia'an and Yēn (Hodge 1907-1910, 2:987).

Kayung. The Haida name *q̓à·ya·ŋ* was rendered Kayung by Dawson (1880:163B), becoming Kayung in Hodge (1907-1910, 1:670) and Kayang in MacDonald (1983).

Masset. Masset is named for Masset Inlet, and early sources apply the name (and variants such as Massette) to all the towns on the inlet, including Yan and Kayung (Dawson 1880:163B-164B; Work in Dawson 1880:173B). The English name of the inlet is generalized from that of a small island called *mà·sad gwa·ye·*. The village of Masset is called *ʕad ʕayuwa·s* 'the flat white hanging expanse' (Skidegate *ġadə ġaxiʔwa·s*), an allusion to the front of the hill called *ʔi·ċa·w*. The Masset dialect name appears in Dawson (1880:163B) as Ut-te-was; other variants are in Hodge (1907-1910, 1:818). Masset, together with Kayung, came to be referred to as Old Masset after the Euro-Canadian town of Masset was constructed to the south; locally it is also called Haida (Dalzell 1968:52).

Hiellen. The Haida name *ł̓ʔya·laŋ* was rendered Hiellen by Dawson (1880:164B); Swanton coined the spelling Hlielung appearing in Hodge (1907-1910, 1:553), and MacDonald (1983) uses Hiellan. The synonymy in Hodge identifies Hiellen with the village Boas (1899:650) calls

ia'gen, but this is rather Swanton's (1905:281) Yā'gAn. Swanton (1905:295; in Hodge 1907-1910, 1:553) first accepted but later rejected Dawson's (1880:165B) identification of Hiellen as the town referred to by Work as Necoon (in Dawson 1880:173B), which is rather Naikun (Hodge 1907-1910, 2:12).

Skidegate. The English name is from that of the town chief, *sgi·dəgi·ds*, earlier rendered Skid-de-gates (Work in Dawson 1880:173B) and Skit-e-gates, Skittagets, and others in Hodge (1907-1910, 2:589); Deans (1899:14) calls the town and its chief Skidegat, and his use of the expression Skidegat's town suggests that the loss of the final -s in the English name may have been due to metanalysis as the possessive suffix. The Haida name of the town is *łga gilda*. Swanton (1905:279) was apparently informed that *łga yu·*, the name of a town nearby to the north, was shifted to Skidegate.

Haina. The Haida name *xəyna·* was given the English spelling Haena by Swanton (in Hodge 1907-1910, 1:519). This village is also referred to as New Gold Harbour Village (Dawson 1880:168B), New Gold Harbor (Swanton 1905:289).

Chaatl. The Haida name *ċa·ʔał* has been rendered Chaahl (Swanton in Hodge 1970-1910, 1:230), Cha-atl (Dawson 1880:168B), and, apparently equivalent, Kowwelth (Work in Dawson 1880:173B).

Kaisun. The Haida name *qəysʔun* appears as Kaisun (Swanton in Hodge 1907-1910, 1:643), Kai-shun (Dawson 1880:168B), and Kish-a-win (Work in Dawson 1880: 173B). This is the village Dawson locates at "Gold Harbour, or Port Kuper," for which he also gives the name Skai-to; although Kaisun was sometimes referred to as Gold Harbour or, to distinguish it from Haina, Old Gold Harbour, Gold Harbour itself, on which was the briefly occupied Haida camp Skaito, was some distance up-inlet to the east (Swanton in Hodge 1907-1910, 1:643, 2:586). Swanton's (1905:280, 288) earlier application of (Old) Gold Harbor to Chaatl is erroneous, as is Boas's (1899:651) equation of Dawson's Skai-to with Tlg·ā'it, a village near Skidegate (Swanton 1905:279, no. 57) from which several families at Chaatl traced their origin; Boas's list thus has three towns corresponding to Chaatl and Kaisun.

Cumshewa. The English name is from that of the town chief, *ga·msiwa·*; spellings listed by Hodge (1907-1910, 1: 371) include Casswer, Comshewars, Gumshewa, Koumchaouas, and Kumshiwa, and Work has Cum-sha-was (in Dawson 1880:173B). The Haida name is *łqinʔul*, rendered Tlkinool by Dawson (1880:168B), who gives the Tsimshian name as Kit-ta-wās.

Skedans. The English name is an alteration, perhaps by contamination with the name Skidegate, of the name of the town chief, *gida·nsda*; variants include Skee-dans (Work in Dawson 1880:173B), and Kiddan, Skidans, and Skiddan (Hodge 1907-1910, 2:588). The Haida name is *259* q̇u·na·, appearing as Koona (Swan in Dawson 1880: 169B).

Kloo. This name, from the town chief's name χyu·, has appeared as Clew, Klue, and Tlu (Hodge 1907-1910, 1: 715), in addition to Cloo (Work in Dawson 1880:173B) and Tlō (Boas 1899:652). The Haida name is ʻtanu·, appearing as Tanoo (Dawson 1880:169B) and Tanu (MacDonald 1983). This village is sometimes called Old Kloo, to distinguish it from a later temporary settlement also called Kloo. The Tsimshian name Laχ-skīk (Dawson 1880:169B) appears as Laskeek.

Ninstints. The English name is that of the town chief, nǝn sdins, also rendered Ninstance (Dawson 1880:169B). The Haida name is sġǝn gwa·y lǝnǝga·y 'Red Snapper Island Town', referring to the small island in front of it. Dawson gives the Haida name as Kun-χit, which is actually ġǝnχi·d 'Anthony Island'. Swanton (1905:295; in Hodge 1907-1910, 2:73) concluded that Ninstints was the village referred to by Work (in Dawson 1880:173B) as Quee-ah, and Duff and Kew (1958) confirmed this identification with documentation that this name was based on that of an earlier town chief.

Sources

The earliest mention of the Haida occurs in the accounts of late eighteenth-century maritime traders (Bartlett 1925; Caamaño 1938; Dixon 1789; Hoskins 1941; Fleurieu 1801). Later historical accounts are those of Green (1915), based on an 1829 visit, Poole (1872), and Chittenden (1884).

Major ethnographic works on the Haida are Swanton (1905), Dawson (1880), and Curtis (1907–1930, 11). Swan (1876), Niblack (1890), Boas (1890), Collison (1915), and Harrison (1925) provide some additional ethnographic information. Murdock (1934a) gives a summary of Haida culture. Swanton (1905), the single most important ethnographic source for the Haida, leans heavily toward mental and social culture with little information on material culture and economy.

Other aspects of aboriginal and historical Haida culture are treated in papers, books, and dissertations: Allen (1954, 1955), Murdock (1934), and Anker (1975) on kinship; Murdock (1936) and Blackman (1973, 1977) on the potlatch; Stearns (1984) on chiefship; Boelscher (1985) on social and symbolic systems; Barbeau (1950, 1957), Gessler (1971), Holm (1981), Kaufmann (1969), and MacDonald (1983) on art; Turner (1974) on ethnobotany; Duff and Kew (1958), Fladmark (1973), and MacDonald (1973) on archeology; Cybulski (1973) on physical anthropology; Swanton (1905a, 1908) and Barbeau (1953) on myth; and Blackman (1981) and Stearns (1981, 1984) on ethnohistory. Van den Brink (1974) should be used with caution. Krauss (1973) summarizes the state of Haida linguistics to 1971. Levine (1977) and Enrico (1980) have written on language.

Unpublished archival materials pertaining to the Haida abound. Swan's (1883) and Dawson's (1878) accounts of their travels on the Queen Charlottes are available on microfilm. C.F. Newcombe's extensive ethnographic notes on the Haida are housed in the Provincial Archives in Victoria, British Columbia, and Swanton's unpublished notes are located at the Smithsonian's National Anthropological Archives. Records from Haida missions can be found at the Church Missionary Society in London; the United Church Archives in Toronto, Ontario; and the Presbyterian Historical Society in Philadelphia.

Major North American ethnographic collections of Haida material are located in the National Museums of Canada, Ottawa, Ontario; the British Columbia Provincial Museum, Victoria; the University of British Columbia, Museum of Anthropology, Victoria; the American Museum of Natural History, New York; the Museum of the American Indian, Heye Foundation, New York; the Field Museum of Natural History, Chicago; and the Smithsonian Institution. Historical photographs of Haida culture can be found in most of these museums.

Haida Since 1960

MARY LEE STEARNS

The centers of Haida culture in the 1980s were Masset and Skidegate on the Queen Charlotte Islands of British Columbia and Hydaburg on Prince of Wales Island, Alaska. While sharing a common culture and similar habitats, the Canadian and Alaskan communities were shaped by different historical experiences and national policies; however, underlying their differing relations with their respective governments are several common features.

Significant differences between the communities may be traced to the frontier period when Alaska natives campaigned for self-government and full citizenship while Canadian natives were segregated on reserves. Drucker (1958:17–19, 103–104) stresses the importance of missionary influence in both countries, citing the founding of local church societies, which served as models for elected village councils. Instructive was the example of White Alaskans who waged a long campaign for civil rights and self-government (Drucker 1958:14–15). Haidas participated with Tlingits in founding the Alaska Native Brotherhood at Sitka in 1912, "avowedly to further their own acculturation" (Drucker 1976). This regional association, which eventually had local "camps" in 20 villages, aimed at opposing racial prejudice, increasing educational opportunities, and establishing the civil rights of natives.

The political history of the Alaska Haidas is one of incorporation in wider, overlapping frameworks: in municipalities under the laws of the territory and then of the state of Alaska; as clients of the Bureau of Indian Affairs and other federal agencies; and, finally, as participants and shareholders in regional organizations, including the Tlingit-Haida Central Council and Sealaska, formed to manage awards obtained in land claims settlements.

Canadian Haidas, in contrast, were placed under the jurisdiction of the Indian Act, administered by a Department of Indian Affairs that centralized control over all agencies dealing with Indians. Native villages were designated as bands and grouped in regional Indian agencies under the personal supervision of an agent. Isolated on reserves, the Indians were deprived of control of their internal affairs while their relations with the outside world were mediated by department officials. In the early decades of federal administration, the agent was expected to oversee the whole of community life, supervising the home, education, economic activities, moral behavior, health care, and governance (Stearns 1981:49). Under this "compulsory system of relations," native people could make little progress in overcoming the disabilities of their status (Stearns 1981:17). The British Columbia Native Brotherhood, inspired by the Alaska model, was more effective as a trade union for fishermen than as a voice for native rights. After World War II, the government's custodial orientation toward native peoples began to shift to integrative goals. With reorganization of the Indian department the agent was gradually removed from personal association with the people, and his duties were reassigned to a host of civil servants in various agencies.

In preparation for the natives' integration into mainstream society, emphasis was placed on improving educational and economic opportunities. Political participation was encouraged by the granting of Canadian federal voting rights in 1960. During the following decade, Indian agencies were consolidated, local department officials were transferred, and the management of band affairs was turned over to native administrators, subject to the continuing authority of the Indian Act. Even this minimal experience of self-determination inspired a cultural renewal on the Northwest Coast. The 1970s saw the recreation of the arts of singing, dancing, carving, and the pageantry of "potlatching." In the 1980s groups of natives across the country joined in the battle to entrench aboriginal rights in the new Canadian constitution, thus paving the way for the settlement of outstanding land claims. In Canada it is the provinces that control the disposition of Crown lands. In late 1985 the government of British Columbia still refused to recognize aboriginal rights, thus blocking negotiations of the extinguishment of native title.

As a consequence of historical and political factors, then, there are major differences in the structure of Alaska and Canadian Haida communities and in their relations with their respective national societies.

Alaska

The community of Hydaburg operates within two frames of reference: as the seat of Haida culture in Alaska and as a node in a network of state, federal, and regional organizations. These include the City of Hydaburg, the Alaska

Smithsonian, NAA.

Fig. 1. Building a wood frame house in a one-family Euro-American style, Hydaburg, Alaska. The village was founded in 1911 when the people of Howkan, Klinkwan, and Sukkwan abandoned their old villages to take up common residence. This resettlement, undertaken to qualify for programs offered by the territorial Bureau of Education, reflected the Haidas' determination to adopt the customs of their White neighbors and to become full citizens of the United States. Photograph by Joseph C. Farber, 1968.

Native Brotherhood and Sisterhood, the Indian Reorganization Act Council, the Hydaburg Cooperative Association, the Tlingit-Haida Central Council, the Haida Corporation, and Sealaska (CASA 1983:26–27). Hydaburg's dual orientation is displayed physically in the interspersal of modern public buildings among the weathered houses and the monuments in the totem pole park. It is expressed socially in the churchgoing elders and clan heads who assume the roles of city official and corporate director.

In 1983 the village population of about 400 persons comprised one-third of the total U.S. population of Haidas. Most of the absent members resided in urban centers, especially Ketchikan and Seattle. The town occupies 189 acres extending along the waterfront in a strip a mile long and 600 feet wide. Of the surrounding land, Sealaska has 60,000 acres of high quality timber north of Hydaburg, and south of town is the 23,040-acre tract of less choice timber held by the village-owned Haida Corporation (CASA 1983:15, 16).

For most of its history, the village was accessible only by float-plane, private boat, or monthly barge. In 1983 a road was opened connecting Hydaburg with the Prince of Wales Island highway system. The immediate effect of this road link was to increase the volume of travel and to reduce the high cost of transporting goods to the village.

In addition to state revenue sharing, municipal assistance, and capital funding totaling $15 million in one decade, the city received federal funding for housing and education, economic development, training programs and social services that was channeled through the Tlingit-Haida Central Council (CASA 1983:31). The Council was established in 1965 to develop programs for the management of the $7.5 million settlement awarded by the U.S. Court of Claims in 1967–1968. As participants in the Alaska Native Claims Settlement Act, the Tlingits and Haidas were included in the more than 16,000 shareholders of Sealaska Corporation (Drucker 1976). The holdings of Haida Corporation, with 560 shareholders, included Haida Oil, Haida Seafoods, and Haida Corporation–Timber Division (CASA 1983:21–23, 31).

Few Hydaburg residents appeared to benefit from their corporate holdings. The local economy was based upon traditional subsistence activities (CASA 1983:49, 19–21) and limited commercial development of land and sea resources. Fishing (for salmon, halibut, crab, and shrimp), hunting deer, digging clams, and gathering wild berries and dulce were seen not only as economic but also as cultural activities that reaffirmed Haida identity. Commercial fishing produced about 60 percent of the villagers' cash earnings. Skilled jobs, such as teachers and clerical workers, were generally held by outsiders. Activities associated with timber harvesting by the Haida Corporation and its subcontractors employed 50 Haidas out of a total payroll of 90 in 1983.

The social life of the native community revolved around the extended bilateral family and matrilateral networks. To a lesser extent, voluntary associations such as the church and the Alaska Native Brotherhood and Sisterhood fostered interaction between the various kin factions. The people have been members of the Presbyterian Church since about 1900. The establishment of the Assembly of God Church in 1975 was controversial at first, but most Haidas, observing an ethic of hospitality and respect, began to attend services of both churches. In Hydaburg, as in other southeastern Alaska communities, the role of the Brotherhood and Sisterhood has become more fraternal than political.

Responsibility for instruction in traditional arts has been assigned to the school. The language program and classes in drawing and carving have been incorporated in the curriculum with elders helping to teach the children. Examples of traditional carving are preserved in the park where old totem poles were restored and erected in the 1930s. The dancing and singing revived for the dedication ceremony inspired many of the younger generation to learn the old forms (Daniel Vaughan, personal communication 1985).

British Columbia

In Canada the native community is the domain of a discrete cultural group, but, unlike the Alaska municipality, it is no longer the property-holding corporation. Its political and economic functions have been usurped by the band, an administrative unit whose members and boundaries are defined by the Indian Act. The people themselves distinguish "the village," whose members are related by matrilineal descent and bound by coresidence and tradition, from the band structure, which they recognize as an instrument of external authority. Although the bands are not self-governing units, the elected councils have assumed much of the responsibility for managing their lands and moneys. The councilors, who represent the interests of all band members, are elected every two years from among those ordinarily resident on the reserve. The band council channels relations with federal agencies, administering grants and supervising employees and projects. The estate of the Masset band includes 26 ancient village and fishing sites on northern Graham Island as reserves, totaling 2,214 acres. The Skidegate band holds 11 reserves on Graham Island and the southern Charlottes with an area of 1,677 acres.

The Haida town of Masset on Masset reserve is three miles north of the town of New Masset. Skidegate reserve is eight miles east of Queen Charlotte City. These pairs of adjacent villages have become interdependent. For wage work and a market for their fish, as well as for education, medical care, and other services, the natives were drawn into daily interaction with Whites in the towns, participating in the mainstream culture and subject to its distinctive norms, values, and expectations (Stearns 1981:17–18, 45–48).

Life in the native community, in contrast, focused on the obligations of kinship and rank, religious and ceremonial activities, the subsistence economy, and recreation (Stearns 1981:193–282). Since the late nineteenth century each village has had a church and school, and later a community hall. Native-owned businesses, such as a store, sawmill, boatyard, poolroom or coffee shop, have been few and usually short-lived. Rarely has a non-native business, such as a cannery, been permitted to operate on a reserve.

The aboriginal pattern of seasonal migration continued as the people sought wage work in mainland canneries. While some activities, such as trapping, seal hunting, gardening, basket making, and carving had waned by 1950, the skills of carpentry and boatbuilding flourished. By 1950 Masset had become "the home of one of the largest and finest seine-boat fleets of any community on the coast" (Gladstone 1953:34). For a brief period during and after the Second World War, when non-natives were otherwise occupied, the Haidas participated in the specialized salmon seine fishery. But in the 1950s conditions in the fishing industry deteriorated with the depletion of fish, intensified competition, technological change, and market fluctuations. For native people those conditions meant low returns, long-term indebtedness to the fishing companies, and displacement (Friedlaender 1975; James 1984).

By the 1960s Masset fishermen had reverted to the small boat pattern of the early decades—a pattern defined by the composition of the fleet, reliance on a mixed economy, and constriction of the social world. The long fishing voyages along the coast came to an end as the men returned to the inshore fishery centered on the Queen Charlotte Canners, a small, locally owned crab, clam, and salmon processor in New Masset (fig. 2). The villagers were still overwhelmingly dependent on the fishing and processing industry, which in 1965 engaged 89 percent of employed persons. Since the fishing season lasts for six months at most, 80 percent of the male work force was unemployed for half the year. Of 59 employed women, all but one worked in the cannery (Stearns 1981:88). When Queen Charlotte Canners was taken over by a Vancouver company in 1966, the canning of crab and salmon ceased, at the cost of 75 jobs.

Skidegate was much less dependent on the fishing industry. The timber resources of its reserves and wage work in nearby logging camps provided a major source of income. In 1966 this village of 278 persons enjoyed full employment. In many cases fishermen sought part-time work in logging in order to maintain their vessels.

During the 1960s native people were as concerned as

Public Arch. of Canada, Ottawa: PA 123909.
Fig. 2. Employees at crab canning factory at New Masset, Queen Charlotte Is., B.C. Cannery jobs were one of the main sources of employment for Indian women, who were paid about 13 cents per pound of picked crab meat in the 1960s (Stearns 1981:107). At the height of production the factory employed about 80 people (Van den Brink 1974:212–213). Photograph by Gar Lunney, July 1956.

government officials with opening up opportunities for Indians in employment and education. Strenuous efforts by the Indian affairs department to create alternate employment resulted for the most part in short-term jobs, mainly in slashing bush and construction work. Those few industries that accepted inducements to locate in the Queen Charlottes and practice preferential hiring of Indians shut down as world economic conditions worsened in the late 1960s. For many Masset people, the only realistic opportunities for employment required leaving the islands. Even work in the logging industry entailed relocation, for the nearest logging camp was at Juskatla, 48 miles away. About one-third of the band members had established residence off the reserve in 1966; by 1984 half of all band members had moved away.

An Indian day school operated on the Masset reserve in 1966, enrolling 74 children in grades one to three, and 129 native children were in grades 4 to 10 at the New Masset schools, where they constituted 48 percent of the student body (Stearns 1981:78–84). Skidegate children went directly to the provincial school at Queen Charlotte City, with 58 enrolled in grades 1 to 10. A few students attended boarding schools and training programs. No Haidas attended university at that time.

The organization of Haida social life during the 1960s was similar in the three villages—Masset, Skidegate, and Hydaburg—with respect to family, subsistence, religious, and recreational activities. However, only in Masset was the old potlatch model of kinship obligation and ceremonial exchange observed in rituals of death and nametaking (Stearns 1975, 1977, 1981:246–282). In each community the coresidential family group, based on the conjugal bond and paternal authority and comprising one, two, or three generations, was the basic social and economic unit. Of Masset's 99 households in 1966, for example, 37 percent consisted of parents and children while 40 percent were three generations in depth (Stearns 1981:124–125). The labor force provided by adult dependents allowed heads of three-generation households to undertake more extensive economic, social, and ceremonial activities than could be carried out by nuclear families (Stearns 1981:121). The linked households of senior couples and their married children formed a narrow circle of continuously interacting, bilaterally related kinsmen who performed many of the functions formerly carried out by matrilineages.

Although the matrilineal model continued to govern community relations, the lineage had become a shadow structure in which only the principal, name-holding members were visible. Aside from names and titles, other symbolic properties associated with the rituals of rank—crests, songs, and dances—were no longer publicly displayed (Stearns 1981:217, 221–227). Traditional ideas about the meaning of wealth and the prestige of rank persisted, but their overt expression was inconsistent with the people's need for pensions and welfare assistance and with the reality of the Haidas' subordinate political status (Stearns 1981:216, 234–236, 292).

Even in the neotraditional life cycle feasts at Masset, only a narrow range of matrilateral kin could be mobilized on any ceremonial occasion.

The reorganization of ceremonial relations permitted the continuing observance of traditional obligations such as gift exchange, life cycle rituals, and the honoring of matrilateral kinsmen in spite of extensive changes in social structure. The participation of a significant proportion of community members in these ceremonies expressed and

left, SSC Photocentre, Ottawa: 66–12492. right, Royal B.C. Mus., Victoria: 13866-1.
Fig. 3. Skidegate, Queen Charlotte Is., B.C. left, Indian boys going fishing on the beach. Photograph by Chris Lund, 1966. right, Herring spawn on kelp drying in a back yard. Photograph by Marilyn Chechik, May 1978.

reinforced old Haida norms and values (Stearns 1981: 290–292). In the more acculturated communities of Skidegate and Hydaburg, voluntary associations played an important role in ritual activities. The Sons of Skidegate conducted burials as a public service, accepting "gifts" in return (Hawthorn, Belshaw, and Jamieson 1958: 183). The Alaska Native Sisterhood chapter sponsored memorial feasts at Hydaburg.

In all three villages, the most important social service groups were associated with the churches (Blackman 1982:45, 116–117; Stearns 1981:247, 257, 258; Hawthorn, Belshaw, and Jamieson 1958:426–427).

The established church at Masset was Saint John's Anglican Church, founded by the first missionary, William Henry Collison, in 1876. Its evangelical arm, the Church Army, has also been important in the life of the community. The Pentecostal Church was introduced at Masset in 1962 when a minister who had married a band member moved into the village and began holding prayer services. Members of this group joined the congregation at New Masset in building a church in that community. There has been no interdenominational conflict in Masset, where many individuals attend all religious services. In 1980 there were three native Anglican ministers in Masset, along with two Pentecostal lay readers (Boelscher 1985: 172). Skidegate people are identified with the United Church of Canada, which has also operated a medical mission hospital at Queen Charlotte City since 1955.

When the Queen Charlotte Agency closed in 1966, responsibility for the management of local affairs was turned over to the band councils. Up to that time the Masset villagers, perceiving that little power or prestige was attached to the office of councilor, took their problems directly to the agent. Officials spoke of a "leadership vacuum," concluding that more than five decades of government supervision had rendered the people incapable of making their own decisions (Stearns 1981:239). Even in the late 1960s, native officeholders enjoyed little autonomy in grappling with the social and economic problems of the reserve. The Indian Act was still in force, and the bands depended upon federal financial support. Nevertheless, the councilors, with little training or experience, grew into their jobs. The new roles of band manager, bookkeeper, home school coordinator, community health worker, alcohol counselor, legal aid counselor, and welfare administrator allowed the natives to participate in the provision of support and social services.

The 1970s were a time of cultural rediscovery on the Northwest Coast, sparked by the emergence of several major artists. In Masset Robert Davidson, grandson of the noted Haida artist, Charles Edenshaw, carved the first totem pole to be raised in his village in more than eight decades. This pole raising in 1969 was the first of the public events that large numbers of outsiders were invited to attend. By the late 1970s the work of Davidson and Bill Reid had received wide acclaim. These artists set up training programs for apprentices in their respective villages of Masset and Skidegate. For a time more than 30 artists were at work in Masset alone. Looking back to the traditional culture for inspiration intensified their interest in other aspects of old Haida culture—the food, the beliefs, the medicines. The making of red-bordered dance blankets, with crests outlined in pearl buttons, became a cottage industry. Dance groups appeared, and soon every public event featured native dancing, drumming, and singing (Stearns 1981:294–296; Boelscher 1985:132–133, 172). Carving replaced fishing as the most prestigious

Royal B.C. Mus., Victoria: left, PN 13974-31A; right, PN 13974-13A.
Fig. 4. Charles Edenshaw memorial house, Masset, Queen Charlotte Is., B.C. left, Exterior of house. The architecture demonstrates the adherence to traditional forms achieved by Haida artists in the 1970s. right, Interior at house dedication, Nov. 4, 1978. The inside post visible was one of two. A B.C. flag is on the right. Florence Davidson, daughter of Charles Edenshaw, is seen center left full face. Photographs by Alan Hoover.

occupation. Interest in genealogical relationships was revived as kin links were manipulated in the competition for symbolic capital (Boelscher 1985). At Skidegate, a traditional house and totem pole were raised. The ancient art of canoe making was revived under the supervision of Bill Reid.

In the 1980s "issues such as the ongoing land-claims, and resurgent native militancy against the exploitation of the Islands' resources by multi-national companies have created interest in patterns of aboriginal land use and ownership among young and middle-aged as well as Elder Haida" (Boelscher 1985:39). For the first time the two Haida villages banded together to pursue their common goals, forming the Council of the Haida Nation (see Pinkerton 1984). In addition to organizing public demonstrations, such as the blockade of Lyell Island in 1985, the Council drew up proposals for the co-management of fisheries and other resources.

Reflecting the trend to participation in regional associations, Haida representatives were appointed to the Queen Charlotte Health and Human Resources Board, which was responsible for medical and welfare services to the entire population of the Charlottes. Haidas served on the board of the Queen Charlotte Museum Society and other intervillage organizations.

The membership of the Skidegate band totaled 464 persons in 1984, 249 of whom lived on the reserve. Of Masset's band population of 1,237 persons, 618 lived on the reserve in 1984. The high proportion of nonresident members reflects both the problems of unemployment and housing shortages on the reserves and the increasing mobility of native people. A crucial factor in that mobility is education. Enrollment figures show that in 1984–1985, Skidegate sent 67 children to public schools and 6 to postsecondary institutions. In Masset 175 children were enrolled in schools and 15 in postsecondary training. The local provincial schools offered studies in Haida culture and language, drawing upon the resources of the elders. In the reserve nursery schools, instruction was provided in Indian dancing.

Unemployment continued to be a major problem as participation in commercial fishing declined and the logging industry as a whole suffered a loss of markets. Salmon enhancement programs sponsored by the Department of Fisheries and Oceans offered training and employment to a small number of persons and the hope of a long-term commitment to aquaculture programs. Herring fishing provided a lucrative income for a few license holders. Fishing for salmon for subsistence became more important during a period of low cash incomes (Stearns 1981:193–216, 293–298).

Tsimshian Peoples: Southern Tsimshian, Coast Tsimshian, Nishga, and Gitksan

MARJORIE M. HALPIN AND MARGARET SEGUIN

The Tsimshian ('tsĭmshē͵ăn, locally also 'sĭmshēən, 'chĭmpshēən) are a group of linguistically and culturally related peoples whose languages constitute the Tsimshian family, which is not closely related to any other.* The Tsimshian live in northwestern British Columbia along the Nass and Skeena rivers and on the inlets and islands between their estuaries, extending south to Milbanke Sound. They comprise four major divisions: the Nishga ('nĭshgə), on the Nass River; the Gitksan (gĭtk'săn), on the Upper Skeena above the canyon at Kitselas; the Coast Tsimshian, on the lower reaches of the Skeena and the adjacent coast; and the Southern Tsimshian, on the coast and islands to the south (fig. 1).

Languages

Linguistically, the major division is between the Coast and Southern Tsimshian on the one hand and the Nishga and Gitksan on the other. These are clearly two separate languages, though many Nishga and Gitksan people once spoke Coast Tsimshian, which was more prestigious, especially for ceremonial purposes. Southern Tsimshian, nearly extinct by the 1970s, is close to Coast Tsimshian but the two may not have been mutually intelligible. Nishga and Gitksan are mutually intelligible.

*The phonemes of Coast Tsimshian, as here transcribed, are: (plain stops and affricate) p, t, c, k, kʷ, q, ʔ; (glottalized stops and affricate) ṗ, ṫ, ċ, k̇, k̇ʷ, q̇; (continuants) s, ł, x, h; (plain sonorants) m, n, l, w, y, ÿ, (an unrounded velar glide); (glottalized sonorants) ṁ, ṅ, l̇, ẇ, ẏ, ÿ̇; (short vowels) i, e, a, o, u; (long vowels) i·, e· ([ɛ·]), a·, o·, u·, i·; (stress) v́. The plain nonglottal stops and affricates are contextually voiced to [b], [d], [ʒ], [g], [gʷ], [g̈], the velars are palatalized to [kʸ, gʸ] and [k̇ʸ] before o(·) or u(·) and optionally before other vowels. It may be possible to analyze the vowel system as having only three phonemic short vowels, with what are here written as i and e as allophones of i, and u and o as allophones of u.

Nishga-Gitksan may be transcribed with the same inventory of phonemic symbols plus ƛ, x, xʷ; there is no ÿ, ÿ̇, or j·.

Considerable dialectal variation in the shape of Coast Tsimshian words is documented by J.A. Dunn (1978); the transcriptions used here follow John A. Dunn (communications to editors 1974, 1985, 1986). Information on Tsimshian phonology was also obtained from Bruce Rigsby (communications to editors 1973, 1986); Hindle and Rigsby (1973), and J.A. Dunn (1978, 1979). The editors are responsible for the particular selection from and interpretation of these materials used in the *Handbook*.

Territory

In traditional Tsimshian thought, each village "was held to be a world apart, distinct in history, custom and law; to enter the territory of another village (or even of another lineage segment) was to enter a foreign land, whether a nearby one which shared the same language or a more distant Haida or Tlingit one" (Seguin 1985:1). Each local group customarily occupied a single winter village, moving in the spring to fishing villages on the lower Nass and in the summers to fishing camps on other rivers. The 26 groups known for the nineteenth century (Duff 1964: 18–20) are shown on figure 1.

The historic Southern Tsimshian villages are: Kitasoo, Kitkiata, and Kitkatla. The Kitasoo live in the 1980s in Klemtu with the Haihais. The original village of the Kitkiata was abandoned between the 1860s and 1880s when the people joined the mission village of Metlakatla established by William Duncan (W. Duncan 1853–1916; Wellcome 1887). The present village was founded at a new site in 1887 by 27 people who returned to their own territories rather than follow Duncan to New Metlakatla, Alaska (for a history of the Kitkiata, see Campbell 1984). The Kitkatla have been regarded by Indians and anthropologists as being the most conservative of the Tsimshian villages.

Ten groups of Coast Tsimshian had winter villages on the lower Skeena River below its canyon: Gitwilgyots, Gitzaklalth, Gitsees, Ginakangeek, Ginadoiks, Gitandau, Gispakloats, Gilutsau, Gitlan, and Gitwilkseba (Duff 1964:18). In late prehistoric times, they extended their territories coastward and built new villages on the islands of Venn (Metlakatla) Pass, where the weather was milder. There is evidence of some 5,000 years of occupation in the Prince Rupert Harbour area ("Prehistory of the Northern Coast of British Columbia," this vol.). They continued to return to their territories on the Skeena in the summers for salmon fishing. After the Hudson's Bay Company moved Fort (later Port) Simpson to its present location in 1834, nine groups moved to the area surrounding the fort (the Gitwilkseba were extinct by this time). William Duncan reported that there were some 2,300 Indians living in 140

267

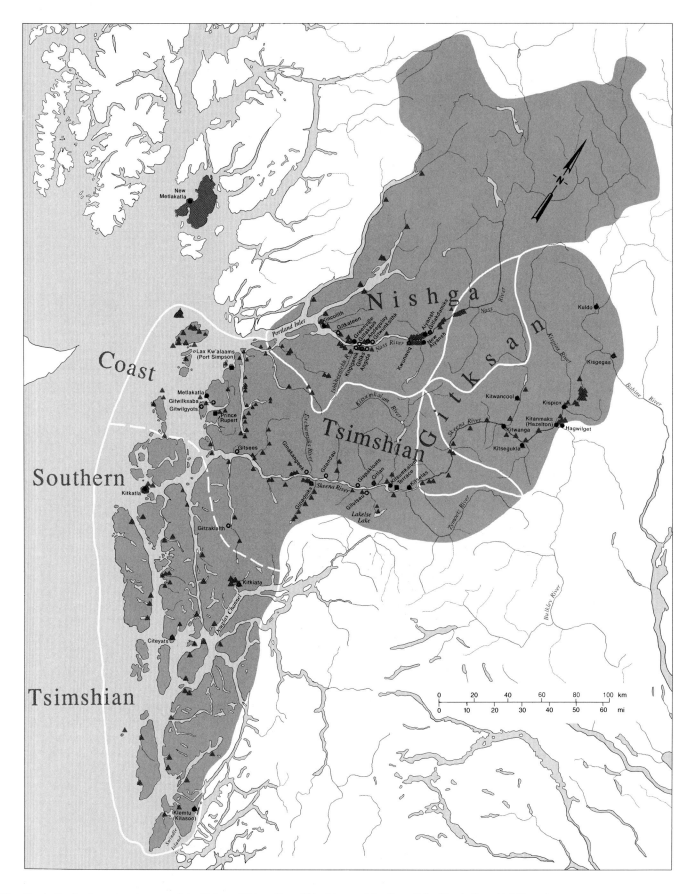

Fig. 1. Territories and settlements of the Gitksan, Nishga, Coast Tsimshian, and Southern Tsimshian in the mid-19th century.

houses around Fort Simpson in 1857.

In the 1980s these people comprised the Port Simpson and Metlakatla bands in British Columbia, and there is a population of the descendants of Duncan's followers at New Metlakatla on Annette Island in Alaska ("Tsimshian of Metlakatla, Alaska," this vol.). The bulk of the published literature on the Tsimshian refers to the Port Simpson people (Boas 1896, 1916; Barbeau 1917; Garfield 1939, 1966; Barnett 1941, 1942; Beynon 1941).

Also classified as Coast Tsimshian are the Kitselas, who lived in two winter villages on either side of Kitselas Canyon on the Skeena River, and the Kitsumkalum, who lived below them near the mouth of the Kitsumkalem River.

The Nishga of the lower Nass were divided into two groups: the Gitkateen and the Gitgigenik, a small group that moved a short distance upriver to the village of Andegulay. The four villages shown on figure 1 for the Gitkateen (16a–16d) were nineteenth-century ('totem pole') villages.

The Nishga of the upper Nass were the *kitanwili´·ks* ('people staying temporarily', referring to their movement downriver at eulachon fishing time). They were divided into the Gitwunksithk, who lived at the canyon, and the dominant Gitlakdamiks, who lived a few miles above them.

The Nishga were relatively inaccessible and little studied until well into the twentieth century. The documentation of their land claims has added much to the literature.

The seven Gitksan groups each occupied a single winter village, six of them on or near the Skeena and one, Kitwancool, to the north on a "grease trail" (eulachon oil trade route) to the Nass. About 1880 another small group, the Anlagasamdak, joined the Kisgegas. The traditional villages in their order upriver are: Kitwanga, Kitwancool, Kitsegukla, Kitanmaks (Hazelton), Kispiox, Kisgegas, and Kuldo.

Environment

The villages and hunting territories of the Coast Tsimshian and Nishga were within the Coast Forest biotic area, a heavily forested region of high precipitation. The winters are relatively mild and summers cool. Along the coastal fiords the land rises precipitously from the shore except for a few favored locations (frequently near small streams) that have a more gentle slope. The winter villages were generally the choicest of these locations, that is, those with available fresh water, a variety of plant and animal food resources nearby, shelter from strong winter winds, and preferably some defense against attack. Transportation between sites for most activities was by canoe, and only in a few areas were there networks of trails. Elsewhere it was, and is, time-consuming and difficult to walk more than a short distance into the bush due to the heavy cover of undergrowth lying over layers of deadfall.

The climax forest along the coast is dominated by western hemlock, red cedar, Sitka spruce, mountain hemlock, yellow cedar, and grand fir. Preclimax areas are dominated by red alder and broadleaf maple.

The Gitksan winter villages were also in the Coast Forest biotic area, but some of them (notably the Kitwancool, Kispiox, Kuldo, and Kisgegas) had hunting territories in the Upper Nass and Skeena drainages, which were in the Subalpine Forest biotic zone. This is a higher and dryer region, containing a larger proportion of valley land than along the coast, which was penetrated by a number of well-used trails.

Culture

Annual Round

Boas (1916:399) discusses Coast Tsimshian seasonal activities, from which J.A. McDonald (1985:98) has extracted a reconstruction of the aboriginal cycle. His account of that cycle is supplemented here with information on the Southern Tsimshian area (Mitchell 1981; Seguin 1984a).

At the end of winter before the river ice breaks up (roughly February to April), the main activity was eulachon fishing on the Nass. The man who caught the first eulachon gave it to the oldest child of his eldest brother, who gave gifts in return. The fish were either dried or processed into a nutritious (iodine-rich) oil or "grease" that was highly prized (fig. 2). The Tsimshian monopoly on the grease trade brought them wealth. Although some people remained at the winter village site (Mitchell 1981:84), a very large proportion made the journey to the Nass, after which they returned to their winter villages and stored the grease and eulachon in their permanent houses.

May was the time for the Coast and Southern Tsimshian to gather and dry seaweed from rocks along the coast, generally residing for a month or more at special seaweed camps. While there men fished for halibut, which women sliced into thin filets for drying on racks in the sun. Large quantities of herring spawn were also gathered at this time, either from thick deposits on grass and kelp or on branches suspended in the water for the purpose. Supplies of the inner bark of the red cedar were collected for winter weaving, and the cambium of several species of trees (hemlock, spruce, and lodgepole pine) was collected for eating.

The eggs of sea gulls and oyster catchers were gathered in early June, and abalone was taken at the lowest tides during the summer months. The first salmon of the year began to enter the tidal waters during the seaweed season, at which time they were caught by trolling. In myths, 269

Fig. 2. Eulachon preparation, Nass River, B.C. People from all divisions of the Tsimshian and even Tlingit and Haida came here. For the Gitksan who came overland the trip to eulachon sites in late winter was physically rigorous but was enjoyed for the social opportunities as well as the economic rewards (People of 'Ksan 1980:89). top left, Fishing camp with dozens of racks of drying eulachon. Photograph by Benjamin A. Haldane, 1903 or before. top right, Loads of the fish left to ripen (decompose) in large pits for from 10 days to 3 weeks depending on the weather. bottom left, Boiling the decomposed fish in large wooden boxes with fire-heated rocks. After boiling several hours the mixture was allowed to stand and cool, so that the oil could be skimmed off the top. bottom right, Extracting more oil from the fish residue, placed in a stiff, open-meshed container made of heavy cedar splints (Laforet 1984:236). The basket was placed over a grid on a box and squeezed with a lever on a flat stone. top right, bottom left, and bottom right, Photographs by Richard Maynard, 1884.

shamans are described as performing a ceremony over the first salmon of the year (Boas 1916:449–450).

As the salmon began to enter the rivers in early summer, people moved to traditional fishing sites where seasonal camps were maintained. The sites for fishing were under the control of the "houses" (corporate matrilineages) managed by the chiefs. Also during the summer, women were active in harvesting berries from house territories, beginning with the early-ripening salmonberries and continuing through the summer until the wild crabapples and high bush cranberries could be gathered and stored in the autumn. The woman who picked the first salmonberry of the year gave it to her husband's or father's sister, who would return gifts of high value. Some berries were dried while others were preserved in grease. Various roots and shoots were collected for fresh consumption, particularly early in the season.

Early autumn (September and October) was a period of intense activity, including the preservation of the major supplies of salmon. The chum salmon that had begun moving up the rivers were ideal for preservation, because the fat content was lower and the product was less likely to go rancid; they were smoke-dried in great quantities. The failure of a salmon run could presage a winter of privation, and many myths refer to actual starvation (Cove 1978). However, since each house controlled several different fishing stations, access to all five salmon species provided some insurance against famine. The habits of each species were extremely well known, and weather specialists monitored and predicted the annual runs.

After the supply of preserved salmon had been safely stored, the territories for hunting game were used. Hunting was undertaken by groups smaller than those for the spring and summer activities; permission to use hunting territories was granted by the house chief. Men purified themselves before hunting or fishing. They fasted, bathed, drank the juice of the root of the devil's club, and practiced sexual continence. Animals were said to be offended by unclean persons and to refuse to allow themselves to be caught by them. In myths, gamblers were said to purify themselves for luck. Other sources of luck were to cohabit with a "lucky woman," who was paid for her services, or to meet the Crying Woman in the woods (see Halpin 1981). There was also a bird similar to a robin (called *haċanás* 'good luck') that conferred luck to those who saw it. Bear taboos and killing ceremonies are described in myths (Boas 1916:449).

J.A. McDonald (1985:105) lists the following game regularly hunted by the Kitsumkalum: deer, elk, seal, sea lions, sea otter, mountain goat, mountain sheep, bear, porcupine, raccoons, eagles, marmots ("groundhogs"), caribou, moose, mountain lion, hares, lynx, swans, geese, ducks and other waterfowl.

Sporadic hunting was an option through the winter, but most people spent the season in the permanent villages. Shellfish abounded in the coastal waters, and huge shell middens attest to their importance as food; among the shellfish used were cockles, several varieties of clam, and mussels. All except abalone were gathered primarily during the winter months on nearby beaches exposed by very low tides. Many individuals were occupied with weaving (women) and carving (men) during the winter months, and the midwinter was the period when most ritual and ceremonial events were held, with the exception, of course, of those dictated by life cycle events. Potlatches and secret society dances were held only during the winter. The long period of relative inactivity was also a favored time for gambling and storytelling.

The annual round of activities for Gitksan and upper Nass River Nishga groups was similar to that of Coast and Southern Tsimshian villages, with accommodations to their riverine environment (fig. 3). Shellfish and seaweed, which were not available, were obtained by trade with coastal groups. Certain plant foods, including soapberries, were available in greater abundance and were harvested and processed for trade as well as use. There was a greater emphasis on land hunting (figs. 4–5), and a somewhat

greater variety of game available: beaver, marmot, and moose were more abundant, and the hunting of bear and mountain goats was a significant activity.

Chiefs managed the diverse resources available from house territories to provide food throughout the year, surplus for trade, and the liberal quantities of special delicacies served at feasts. The foods that were most valued were those that were scarce, available only seasonally, required intensive labor (and entailed organization by a person of rank), "imported items" (including European foods as they became available), grease, and anything preserved in grease. In general, prestige foods were foods that required some evidence of supernatural efficacy, such as luck in hunting or propitious weather, to obtain.

Structures

Tsimshian winter houses were constructed of massive timbers hewn from red cedar. In 1792 the chief's house at Ksidiy'ats was about 50–55 feet long and 30–35 feet wide "and at some time must have been much larger, as around and above it stood heavy forked posts with cross timbers" (Caamaño 1938:293). The largest house at Fort Simpson was about 60 by 40 feet (Church Missionary Society 1869: 26); the average house was 50 by 55 feet (Drucker 1965: 119). According to Boas (1916:46–48), the walls were independent of the post, beam, and roof structure. Thick upright base planks at the front, rear, and sides were set just outside the corner posts and grooved to receive thinner horizontal planks. Vertical wall planks are also reported (Drucker 1950:178–179). Garfield (1939) reports that some people carried their house planks to their spring and summer camps.

An excavated pit, five feet deep and 30 feet square, usually lined with cedar plank retaining walls, formed the main living space and contained the central fireplace, which was lined with sand and the beach cobbles that were used for stone-boiling. Cedar-bark mats were used as insulation in the winter. Some houses had narrow platforms around the main pit; narratives tell of famous chiefs' houses with multiple platforms. The ground level platform served as a storage area. The door (apparently either rectangular or oval) was at the gable end facing the beach. Some houses had entrance doors cut through totem poles placed at the front of the house. House names were inherited as crests.

The only published plans of Tsimshian houses are in Boas (1896:580–583). Tsimshian houses with vertical wall planks are shown in Boas (1916:pl. II).

The chief and his immediate family occupied one or more cubicles at the rear of the house; people of lesser rank had family quarters along the side walls. Sacred red cedar bark was used to transform chiefs' dwellings into dance 271 houses during the winter ceremonial season.

Housefronts were painted with crest designs (fig. 6) (see MacDonald 1984). One of Barbeau's (1929:15) informants said that "the housefront paintings . . . were the most important; they were the real crest boards. The poles . . . were merely commemorative." Housefront paintings sometimes had projecting beaks (fig. 7). Painted "false fronts" were added to the houses at ceremonial times. Wooden screens painted with sacred designs were erected at the inside rear of the house.

Other structures included menstrual huts (MacDonald 1984a:71), summer houses, sweat lodges, and underground caches (Drucker 1950:252–253, 180–181).

Tsimshian totem poles are well known through several surveys (Barbeau 1929, 1950; Duff 1952). Although some scholars (for example, Barbeau 1950) have suggested that

U. of Pa., U. Mus., Philadelphia: top, 14953; bottom left, 14954; bottom right, Royal B.C. Mus., Victoria: PN 11987.

Fig. 3. Fishing. The basic item of subsistence was fish, which was served at every meal (People of 'Ksan 1980:30). top, Weir (a wooden lattice fence that guided migratory salmon into traps) across a shallow river. A salmon trap is on the shore at right. bottom left, Gitksan youth with salmon trap made by lashing sticks together. The fish would swim through a small opening made with split sticks and could not get out (H. Stewart 1977: 112–113). top and bottom left, Photographs by Louis Shotridge, Kitwancool, B.C., 1918. bottom right, Fishing platform and salmon trap being set by a Gitksan on the west side of Hagwelget canyon, Bulkley River, B.C. (Barbeau 1930:144). The trap consists of a vertical barrier set between posts, a long chute, and fish basket. Photographed about 1920.

272

Fig. 4. Daniel Wiqaix or Wigaix, a Kisgegas chief with furs, including bear, fox, wolverine, beaver, ermine, fisher, mink, otter, and marten. Some land game was used for food, but animals such as marten, fox, otter, and mink were taken only for their furs, which were then traded (People of 'Ksan 1980:45) for Euro-Canadian goods. The appliqúed, fringed skin shirt and snowshoes show Subarctic influence. Photograph by C. Marius Barbeau, Hazelton, B.C., 1923.

Fig. 5. Arthur Derrick and family ready to go hunting. An infirm individual, probably an old woman, is wrapped in blanket and tied onto the sled. Such winter transportation is evidence of Subarctic influence. The wooden cradle has a rod with beads on it in front of the baby's face. Photographed probably at Kitwanga, B.C., about 1920s.

Technology

they were a postcontact phenomenon on the Northwest Coast, Duff (1964a) clearly demonstrated that they existed before contact in some areas. Whether or not this was true for the Tsimshian remains to be established.

Totem poles were carved from large red cedar logs by people standing in the relationship of "fathers" to the pole's owners, that is, affinal relatives of the house commissioning and erecting the pole. If no good carver stood in the proper relationship, one was appointed by a "father" who "stood over him" (Barbeau 1929:7; see also Shane 1984). The most elaborate totem poles were erected in honor of deceased chiefs by their successors. Poles featured the crests of the house erecting them, although a crest of the carver's house was sometimes included as a "signature."

Basketry was made by women. Coast women mainly used the bark of the western red cedar for mats and containers, while upriver women also used maple and birch bark and spruce roots for containers. Throughout the region, the techniques of greatest importance were plaiting (checker weaving) and twining, with a greater emphasis on plaiting on the coast (see Laforet 1984 for an illustrated survey of Tsimshian basketry). Functional classes of Tsimshian basketry include plaited bark containers used for berries and the transport of goods, plaited mats, eulachon baskets, and twined-root cooking baskets. There are stylistic differences between the coast and upriver peoples, with the Nishga sharing in both traditions.

Utilitarian wooden objects made by men, of the same types as those of the Haida and Tlingit, included a wide

Fig. 6. Painted Tsimshian housefront, presumably the only complete example in a museum collection. It was acquired by J.G. Swan at Fort Simpson, B.C., probably in 1875, for exhibition at the 1876 Centennial in Philadelphia. It measures 11.6 m in length and 3.6 m in height.

TSIMSHIAN PEOPLES: SOUTHERN TSIMSHIAN, COAST TSIMSHIAN, NISHGA, AND GITKSAN

Fig. 7. Minesqu House, Gitlakdamiks, B.C. The elaborately painted housefront has a projecting beak. Commemorative poles are in the front. Photograph, cropped, taken in 1903.

variety of storage boxes (fig. 10) and chests, the northern type of canoe, woodworking tools, and fishing and hunting gear. Many are described in Drucker (1950) and illustrated in Boas (1916).

Social Organization

● DESCENT GROUPS The customary anthropological picture of Tsimshian society has been that it had a four-fold structure, being divided into four exogamous matrilineal clans (Garfield 1939:173), also called "exogamic groups" (Boas 1916:488), "phratries" (Barbeau 1917), and "crests" (Adams 1973:23) by anthropologists and "tribes" or *pte·x* by the Tsimshian themselves. The four clans are listed in table 1.

Fig. 8. Carved wooden bark shredder of the type commonly used to shred the inner bark of the cedar. However, this specimen was used to shred young alder bark, which was put into a bath with shredded cedar bark to dye the cedar a reddish brown—the color required for shamans' headdresses. Collected at Angida, B.C., by G.T. Emmons, before 1921. Length 45.5 m.

This four-clan structure appears to have been the case only in the postcontact villages of Port Simpson and Metlakatla, where most of the early fieldwork was done. Fieldwork done since the 1960s (Adams 1973; Dunn and Dunn 1972; J.A. Dunn 1984, 1984a; Kasakoff 1984) suggests that, *at the village level*, Tsimshian society traditionally had a dual or moiety structure.

The basic social unit in Tsimshian society was a corporate matrilineage called a "house" (*wa·lp*), the members of which, together with affines, children belonging to other lineages, and slaves, occupied one or more dwellings. Barnett (1938:349–350) identified the *wa·lp* as the functioning unit in the potlatch, in which case the term refers only to members of the same kinship group (see also Garfield 1939:174). Houses fluctuated widely in size, and hence in productivity, at times resorting to adoption to prevent extinction, at other times growing so large that they fissioned into two or more separate houses. Garfield (1939: 278–282) analyzes the membership of the house of Grizzly Bear at Port Simpson, and Adams (1973) has published a study of house composition and dynamics for the Gitksan.

Each house owned fishing, hunting, and gathering territories and localities, which it exploited under the direction of the house chief (the man, and in exceptional circumstances, the woman, who bore its highest-ranking name). The house owned crests, songs, names, and other privileges, also under control or stewardship of the chief. The transfer of the right to use natural resources to another house by gift or through seizure in payment of a debt was fairly common. Matters of mutual interest, such as defense, were discussed with the chiefs of other houses in the village. Each interacting group of chiefs had an established rank order, which determined their rights to precedence in both political and ceremonial events.

● KINSHIP The kinship system was of the Iroquois type, with separate terms for affines. Gitksan and Kitkatla kin terms are listed in Kasakoff (1984); Nishga terms in Sapir (1920); Coast Tsimshian in Boas (1916:489–495) and Durlach (1928). Dunn and Dunn (1972) list Kitlatka terms, J.A. Dunn (1984) compares Coast and Southern

Fig. 9. Poling a spoon canoe on the Skeena River, B.C. Photographed about 1910–1920.

274

Royal B.C. Mus., Victoria: PN 4330.

Fig. 10. Nishga chiefs of Gitlakdamiks, B.C., with ceremonial equipment. left to right: 3 children; Andrew Nass, wearing shirt with coppers and ermine-decorated headdress; John Nass in light-colored skin robe, holding a rattle, his dance headdress showing a carved frontlet; James Skean wearing Chilkat blanket and decorated leggings and dance apron; Philip Nass, wearing Chilkat blanket, neck ring, 3-ringed headdress, and dance apron decorated with puffin beaks; 2 children; Charlie Brown, in shirt with inverted face holding a painted drum; Eliza Brown, in button blanket with neck ring; Matilda Peal in button blanket; child. Both women have down in their hair. Displayed are masks, frontlets, dance headdresses, and carved wooden boxes. Photograph possibly by C.H. Orme, about 1903.

Tsimshian and Nishga kinship terms, and J.A. Dunn (1984a) compares them to Haida and Tlingit lists. While most analysts have worked on the referential meaning of the kin terms, Kasakoff (1984) considers the nonliteral or extended use of kinship terms where these intersect with and accommodate the demands of the potlatch system.

The relationship with father's side was extremely important throughout an individual's life. Pole-carving and canoe-carving were also purchased from the father's side.

Affinal relationships between clans were expressed in a relational naming system unique to the Tsimshian on the Northwest Coast. Children's names, which were owned by the matrilineage, referred to physical and behavioral characteristics of the two major crest animals of the father's clan (Sapir 1915a). Some examples of such cross-

clan names are "mocking raven," "the eagle never flies crooked," and "the eagle has nothing to eat" (Duff 1964). Several authors (C. Ackerman 1975; Cove 1976; Rosman and Rubel 1971) have developed analyses that assume that names reflect perpetual affinal relationships between clans. This assumption has been disputed by Kasakoff (1984:83).

● CLASS The Tsimshian recognize four named social distinctions, often called classes (Seguin 1984:110–136; Garfield 1939:178ff.). Women were of the same levels as men, although their names and status did not ordinarily entail the same sort of political power. All marriages were supposed to be between social equals; the children of parents of unequal rank inherited rank no higher than that of the lower-ranked parent. The social distinction between the *smkikét* 'real people' (singular *sm?ó·ket* 'chief'), that

Table 1. Tsimshian Clans with Haida and Tlingit "Friends"

Coast Tsimshian	Killer Whale	Wolf	Eagle	Raven
	(*kispuwutwáta*)	(*laxkipú·*)	(*laxskí·k*)	(*qanháta*)
Southern Tsimshian	Killer Whale	Wolf	Eagle	Raven
Gitksan	Fireweed	Wolf	Eagle	Frog/Raven
	(*kisǧaha·st*)	(*lax kipu·*)	(*lax xski·k*)	(*lax se·l̦/ qanata*)
Nishga	Killer Whale	Wolf	Eagle	Raven
Haida	Raven	Raven	Eagle	Eagle
Tlingit	Wolf	Wolf	Raven	Raven

275

is, the chiefly families, and the *liq̓akikét* 'other people', that is, those who had names of lesser rank, was maintained through intermarriage with other chiefly families, including those from Tsimshian-speaking as well as other language groups (Tlingit, Haida, Haisla, and Heiltsuk). Free people who had not taken ancestral names in the potlatch system were termed *wahʔáʔayin* 'unhealed people' (explained as "without origin" or "having no relatives"). Slaves (*xa·* or *ɬú·nkit* were captives taken in war or purchased from slavers, especially from the south, and their children; their status was hereditary, and it was unthinkable for free persons to marry them (Garfield 1939:177–178, 1966:28–31; Seguin 1985).

● CRESTS   Crests are images and privileges (acquired by one's ancestors during encounters with supernatural beings) that are owned as property by a house and ceremonially displayed by its members. When listing crests and their owners (Duff 1964a; Halpin 1978, 1984), Tsimshian informants often mentioned the kinds of artifacts on which the crests could, and more rarely could not, be represented. Categories of artifacts most often specified for crest representations were: architectural features—totem poles, including house entrance poles, house posts, housefront paintings, beams, rafters, and ceremonial entrances; costume features—robes and head-dresses (fig. 11); and feast dishes and ladles. In other words, crest images were worn in the potlatch, used in the feast, and represented on the houses where potlatching occurred. Sapir (1915a:6) notes that "one cannot even pay a neighbour a visit and wear a garment decorated with a minor crest without justifying the use of such regalia by the expenditure of property at the house visited."

Fig. 11. Wooden ceremonial crest hat displaying a bear's head surrounded by 5 human hands (one not visible) and bearing 3 basketry potlatch rings. The hat proper is painted green, the bear's head painted red and black with abalone inlays for eyes. The hands are painted red with eye designs in green on the back of each one. Collected at Port Simpson, B.C., about 1900. Height 28 cm.

Each Tsimshian clan was associated with and identified by two primary crest animals: for the Blackfish or Fireweed clan, the grizzly and killer whale (in local English, "blackfish"); for the Wolf clan, wolf and bear; for the Eagle clan, eagle and beaver; for the Raven clan, raven and frog. These animals were the building blocks of the crest system and, with rare exceptions, could be displayed by all members of the clan. Halpin (1984) identifies secondary animals for each clan, some of which served to identify subclans (groups of related houses).

Additionally, there were other animals, mythological beings, celestial phenomena, some items of costume (armor, ladles, feast dishes), plants, water phenomena (whirlpools, riptides), and varieties of fires that were claimed as crests. One factor that accounts for the abundant use of human faces in Tsimshian art is that many of the crests identified as celestial phenomena and mythological creatures were represented by stylized human faces (Halpin 1984; see also MacDonald 1984). Special crests that could be made of real animal heads and skins, and included ermine and abalone decoration, were restricted to the chief (Halpin 1984). This introduction of the dimension of rank into the crest system sets the Tsimshian apart from the Haida and Tlingit.

Political Organization

Since descent among the Tsimshian was reckoned matrilineally, succession to a man's names and position went in theory to a younger brother or sister's son (see Garfield 1939:179 for a ranked succession order). Actual succession, which involved a number of situational factors, was often a source of controversy.

The role of village chief was present only among the Coast and Southern Tsimshian (Mitchell 1981; Boas 1916: 429–434; Garfield 1939:182–191, 1966:32–37). The village chief was the chief of the highest-ranking house in the village, and the other houses, in all clans, were ranked under him in descending order. Gitksan chiefs, on the other hand, were not organized above the clan level, and the chief of the highest-ranking house in a clan did not have authority over the other clans. Nishga chiefs seemed to be vying for hegemonies of the Coast Tsimshian type.

Garfield (1939:182) reports that a chief had other (non-ritual) economic support from and obligations to his group: "While a chief can expect constant and liberal economic support from his tribesmen, he does not contribute to potlatches given by them. He is responsible for their economic welfare, must feed them when necessary and has to lay aside supplies for this purpose."

Traditional narratives report that the Southern Tsimshian chiefs received tribute in the form of the first sea otter and seal caught by each canoe of sea hunters and other fur animals captured by land hunters. It is also reported that chiefs hunted sea lions and mountain goats, activities that required courage and endurance, but that they seldom participated in other hunting, except to perform a supervisory role (Garfield 1966:17). As chiefs, they could expect slaves and other hunters to provide for them (Boas 1916:429). In Kitsumkalum the people were said to give a chief everything he needed so that he did not have to produce for himself at all (Boas 1916:278; J.A. McDonald 1985:97). Duff (1964), Mitchell (1981), MacDonald (1984a), and M.P. Robinson (1978) suggest that some chiefs, including Legaik of the Gispakloats, at Port Simpton, Sebassa of Kitkatla, Neqt of the Gitksan, and Chief Mountain of the Nishga, achieved unusual influence through fortunate placement in the fur trade. Mitchell (1981:85) traced the recorded mentions of Sebassa in the journals of fur traders for the year 1835, finding that the "glimpses we have of his year find him playing host to a visiting chief, in turn visiting and trading with the Bella Bella, trading with Europeans and seeking revenge for wrong done him or his group by a trader."

Life Cycle

Important events in an individual's life activated a series of duties and wealth exchanges between the houses of the father and mother (Garfield 1939:329ff.; Seguin 1984: 123).

The birth of a child was attended by its father's sister and other women of his lineage, who brought gifts for the infant. If the family were of high rank, the chief announced the birth, for which he was compensated; otherwise, it was announced by the father's relatives. The birth announcement was accompanied by the distribution of marmot skins provided by the mother's house. A first naming ceremony was held at which the chief or the father's relatives announced the name, for which they were again compensated. Such a ceremony was often included as a minor element in a potlatch.

When children of both sexes were about seven, they were given their first initiation ritual, in which a chief "threw" power into them. A father's sister or other female relative pierced her ear as a sign of rank; high-ranking girls also had their lips pierced for labrets (fig. 12).

Both boys and girls were given their first names at puberty ceremonies, at which time their lineage relatives made gift distributions. Girls were secluded in menstrual huts at their first menstruation.

Marriages were arranged. The boy's mother and her brother made the initial call upon the girl's relatives, bringing gifts. Several further gift exchanges between the relatives of the bride and groom were made, including at a potlatch when the marriage was announced to others. The Tsimshian are said to have a rule of preference for marriage with a man's mother's brother's daughter (Boas 1916; Garfield 1939:321, 1966:23), although late twentieth-century research has been unable to verify it. It seems

Mus. of the Amer. Ind., Heye Foundation, N.Y.: 9/8044.
Fig. 12. Mask representing an old woman, with long stringy strands of hair, and a labret inlaid with abalone. The size and treatment of the labret indicates an old woman of high status. Collected from the Nishga, B.C., probably 1825–1850. Height 24 cm.

likely that the Tsimshian favored marriage with either cross-cousin (Cove 1976). What is clear is that the primary goal of marriages was the consolidation of wealth and position. The ideal postmarital pattern, at least for the high-ranking men who inherited noble names, was one of avunculocal residence. In fact, a boy went to live with his mother's brother as a child, later succeeding to his name and position. Polygyny was permitted for chiefs, although it was apparently rare, and a widow was expected to marry her husband's successor or brother. Divorce was probably frequent (Garfield 1939:235).

Death was announced by the distribution of marmot skins by the deceased's own lineage, which contributed to a funeral fund. Other clan relatives were also expected to contribute. The preparation of the body and the coffin and related tasks were the responsibility of the deceased father's lineage, for which it was compensated from the *277* funeral fund. Traditionally cremation was practiced. Secret society regalia were burned with the body. The bodies of shamans were placed in caves or special grave houses.

Ceremonialism

● FEASTS AND POTLATCHES Though the secret society dances were the most flamboyant expression of Tsimshian ceremonialism, the feast complex was apparently the core around which the social system revolved. Through various types of feasts the social order was maintained and expressed, inheritance and succession were validated, and conflict was expressed and managed. Since sacred and secular were not distinct domains for the Tsimshian, the feasts were organized by premises that can properly be seen as religious. Seguin (1985) has suggested that the feast complex was a discourse with supernatural powers who were represented at the event by the chiefs from other houses invited as guests. This allowed a house to purify itself by distributing property, in an act reminiscent of the ritual fasting and cleansing required by a man who wished to attract fish or game. The ability to manage the territories of the house and gather the support of contributors made it self-evident that the house was ritually clean and the event proper.

The most obvious constant features of a $ya \cdot k^w$ 'potlatch' were the division of the people into two groups—hosts and guests—and the public distribution of wealth by the hosts to the guests. The specific action of the feast varied according to the purpose of the event the guests were called to witness; there were house-building, marriage, naming, funeral, and cleansing feasts. This last event "washed off" a mistake or indignity from an individual or group and "shut the mouths" of the guests.

Tsimshian potlatches were ritual statements of the social relationships of the participants. Members of the host clan sat together near the entrance while members of the several guest clans were seated together in prescribed ranked arrangements around the house (see Adams 1973: 54). A chief's successor sat in front of him, the next in line behind him. Contributions to the potlatch fund were made publicly by those affirming solidarity with the potlatch giver and his local lineage segment. In a Coast Tsimshian chief's potlatch to chiefs from other villages these were all the houses in the village. In other potlatches donors were lineage, clan, and affinal relatives. The amount of the contribution was a signifier of the relationship and of past obligations owed to the potlatch giver or his deceased predecessor. Disbursements or gifts to the guests were made in accordance with their rank, those of highest rank receiving the largest gifts. Food was served at all potlatches, sufficient in quantity for chiefly guests to redistribute on their return to their own houses.

According to information Beynon (1916) received at

Fig. 13. Copper, "the ultimate symbol of wealth" (MacDonald 1984: 133). It was beaten out of a sheet of metal into this standard form, the central T-shaped ridge separating the flared upper panel and the two rectangular lower panels. The engraved designs varied, but in any case were not crests; coppers changed ownership and so could not symbolize kin groups. They were displayed at namings and were essential to potlatches honoring the dead. The followers of a Tsimshian chief bought a copper for him, preferably a very valuable one and broke it up after his death, identifying the pieces as his "bones" and distributing them to other chiefs (Garfield 1939:264). The design on the upper panel of this copper may be a hawk. Collected about 1800; height 110.7 cm.

Kitkatla, the most important potlatch was the last of three mourning potlatches at which a successor assumed his deceased predecessor's name and position. It was known as *wilxmás*, the "feast of red," referring to the fact that, at this feast, the black facial markings that had been worn by the successor since the "feast of black" (*wilxtúʔuck*) were replaced with red stripes on each cheek. Second in rank was an *ʔoix* potlatch (*ʔoix* 'to proclaim or make known'). These were the feasts of assuming a name, validating a crest, or erecting a totem pole. Rivalries and challenges were also typically expressed through crest displays within the *ʔoix* potlatch framework. Other kinds of potlatches were said to rank behind these two. The prestige accorded the potlatch-giver, of course, depended upon the amount of wealth he displayed and gave away (fig. 13). Boas

Fig. 14. Chief's dance headdress worn in his role of *smhaláit* or 'real dancer'. The carved frontlet represents a crest. The double rows of small faces around the periphery are distinctively Tsimshian, and common on the flattened globular rattles. Abalone sections are inlaid around the face and used for eyes and teeth. Sea lion whiskers form the standing crown atop assorted feathers over a canvas headdress and printed cloth trailer, which are both lined with strips of ermine. Collected by C.M. Barbeau on the Nass River, B.C., in 1927 or before. Height 48 cm with whiskers.

(1916:538–541) and Garfield (1939:192–219) are second-hand descriptions of Tsimshian potlatches. In eyewitness accounts of a 1965 Gitksan potlatch (Adams 1973:51–78) and a 1980 feast (Seguin 1985:76–87) many traditional forms and idioms were no longer present, but the events were recognizably continuous with a 1792 account (Caamaño 1938; Gunther 1972; Seguin 1985).

● RELIGIOUS ORGANIZATION Establishing and maintaining supernatural power and well-being was not relegated to religious specialists but was the responsibility of the political leaders, *smkikét* p.18 (Halpin 1973; Guédon 1984a). Their religious responsibilities included demonstrating respect for animals and spirits in all activities (such as hunting, fishing, and the consumption of animal foods), and also during the particularly volatile periods around rituals, birth, and death.

The spiritual leadership of the *smkikét* can be separated into four types of activity. In their role as house chiefs they were active in ritual occasions such as the feasts and naming ceremonies; at these occasions they wore their crests and ceremonial robes and headdresses (fig. 10). In their role as *naxnóx* 'power' dancers they dramatized and validated the powers of their ancestors and their house by masked dances and dramas. As *smhaláit* 'real dancers', garbed in their *k*ʷ*ushaláit* (Chilkat dance robes) and *ʔamhaláit* (frontlet headdresses not covering the face), with the raven rattle as a symbol of power, they initiated young people into ritual roles. The final formal named

role for a leader was the *wihaláit* or 'great dancer', the leader of the four secret societies, into which many of the people were initiated (fig. 14). For this role the *wihaláit* wore red cedar-bark neck rings and danced to the music of whistles and drums. The secret society dances were apparently borrowed from the Haisla and Heiltsuk-speaking people just before contact with Europeans; they were most fully expressed among the Southern Tsimshian, who obtained them directly from the Heiltsuk speakers, and had only partially been received by the other divisions. Most of the names for the dancers are Northern Wakashan in origin. (Accounts of the dance societies appear in Garfield 1939; Boas 1916; Drucker 1940.)

The chiefs' roles in ordering sacred relations were complemented by the activities of specialists called *swánsk haláit* 'blowing shamans', who were particularly active during serious illness or times of "bad luck" such as failure in a salmon run (Barbeau 1958; Guédon 1984). Such events were understood to be due to events in the domain of power. Illness, for example, was believed to be at least partly due to spiritual weakness or impurity, and the practices of the shaman marshaled the spiritual resources of the community to strengthen and purify the spirits of the patients, who were symbolically cleansed by the shaman sucking "dirty" objects from them and rubbing them with clean substances. The *swánsk haláit* were not a separate social stratum like the *smkikét* and in fact some *smkikét* were shamans as well.

● WITCHCRAFT Not classified as sacred were the *haltá·ukit* or witches, men or women who worked in secret to harm others. They did not have spirit-helpers but employed physical objects such as dolls or nail parings to create a state of "dirtiness" that was the opposite of the purity required for a supernatural encounter. Witches were depicted in a "horrid manner" (Guédon 1984a:148). Their favorite ingredients were bits of corpse; Boas (1916: 564) gives a detailed example of the witch's "recipes."

Beliefs

Tsimshian beliefs in reincarnation were not well reported by early ethnographers, although they were still widespread in late twentieth-century villages (Seguin 1984; Halpin 1984a; Adams 1973; B. Campbell 1975). The traditional belief seems to be that people were reincarnated in their lineage grandchildren, although other connections are also reported. Seguin (1984:123) goes so far as to suggest that the potlatch was structured so as to *"make it possible for lineage members to be reincarnated properly."* That the same terms are used to refer both to a cradle and a gravebox (*ẇo*) and that a person's baby song and mourning dirge (*li·mḱói*) are the same song is evidence in point.

279

Natl. Mus. of Canada, Ottawa: VII-C-215 (67).
Fig. 15. Wooden shaman's rattle. This characteristic flattened, globular rattle is made in halves, joined with lashes, and pegged at the handle. Both front and back shown. It is carved in bas relief and left unpainted. Arrangement of design elements is typically Tsimshian, although other northern groups also had these rattles ("Haida: Traditional Culture," fig. 12, this vol.). Collected at Gitlakdamiks, B.C., 1905; height 30 cm.

Mythology

There are two types of Tsimshian myths: those that were known generally and could be told by anyone, such as the Raven cycle (Boas 1916), and those, called *ʔatáuҳ* that were owned by a particular house and could be told only by a trained and authorized house member.

The Raven cycle tells of the exploits of *tҳá·msm*, who was known to the Nishga and Gitksan as *wi·két* ('great person' or 'giant'), a trickster and shape-changer. One of his accomplishments was the liberation of light from a box in the Sky Chief's house. He also brought fire to humans and taught them the use of the eulachon rake. While *tҳá·msm* cannot be called a creator, since the elements and creatures with which he worked were already in existence, he put the world in its present order.

The *ʔatáuҳ* are historical in character. Many tell of the original home of the lineage ancestors, their migration to and possession of their present territories, and their acquisition of power and crests from supernatural ancestors. The most famous of the Tsimshian homelands was Temlaham (Barbeau 1928; Boas 1902:221–225), said to have been a large town stretched along the west bank of the Skeena just below present Hazelton. Episodes in *ʔatáuҳ* were widely known, such as the story of a girl who married a bear, and were interpreted by each house to its own ends. Portions of a great many Tsimshian *ʔatáuҳ* have been published (Barbeau 1929, 1953, 1961; Boas

Nat. Mus. of Canada, Ottawa: 69616.
Fig. 16. Frank Bolton, a lower Nass River chief of a leading Eagle clan, portraying a medicine man helping the "patient" Robert Pearl of Gitlakdamiks. The singers are, left to right: Albert Allen, of Kincolith; Henry Smart, chief of a Wolf clan on upper Nass River, with a skin drum; and William Foster, chief of an Eagle clan at Gitwunksithk (Barbeau 1951:105–106). In shamanistic performances techniques used by the healer to get himself and patient ready for treatment are drumming, tapping rhythm sticks, singing specific songs, and manipulation of objects given to the shaman by supernatural helpers. The noise and physical activity help pull the concentration of the shaman and patient together (Guédon 1984:187–188). A shaman's rattle, an essential part of the equipment, is lying on the "patient." Photograph by C. Marius Barbeau, near Hazelton, B.C., 1927.

1902, 1916; see also Harris 1974). Lévi-Strauss (1967) and his commentators have analyzed the myth of Asdiwal.

External Relations

Garfield (1939:230ff.), Boas (1916:519–523), and Swanton (1905:66) reported that the four Tsimshian clans paralleled the moieties of their Haida and Tlingit neighbors. Marriages were forbidden with foreign "friends," that is, clans sharing the same crests (table 1). J.A. Dunn's (1984a) comparison of Haida, Tlingit, and Tsimshian kinship terms reveals a number of borrowings that bring all three societies into symbolic relations with one another. He argues that from the Tsimshian point of view, the Haidas were seen as supernatural animal "fathers" and the Tlingit as "little sisters."

Toward the interior the Tsimshian had as neighbors the Tsetsaut, whose last members affiliated with the Nishga, and the Carrier, matrilineal Athapaskan-speaking peoples. Some items of the Subarctic groups' material culture, such as snowshoes and work with porcupine quills, were borrowed by the Nishga and Gitksan, but most cultural borrowings flowed in the other direction. The Carrier, for example, took over the coastal complex of the potlatch and crests from the Gitksan. This "Gitksanization" of the Carrier (Jenness 1943) continued in the late twentieth century, and in fact some of the Carriers politically affiliated with the Gitksan villages in the Gitksan-Wet'suwet'en Tribal Council.

According to Tsimshian oral histories, dancing societies were received from the Haisla and Heiltsuk; Swanton (1905:156–160) reports that the Haida, in turn, received them from the Tsimshian of Kitkatla.

The greatest aboriginal trading center on the northern Northwest Coast was at the mouth of the Nass River during the eulachon fishing season in the early spring. Tlingit, Haida, Gitksan, and Nishga from the upper Nass converged each February on the lower Nass River from Red Bluff to Fishery Bay to fish and trade with the coastal Nishga and Coast and Southern Tsimshian who owned fishing stations there.

Formal trade relationships have been reported for a number of groups, both within and between the Tsimshian-speaking divisions and with Haida and Tlingit groups (MacDonald 1984a). Trade goods included foods (eulachon and grease, halibut, seaweed, soapberries), carved horn spoons, and slaves. Boas (1916:398) inferred village specialization in commodity and craft production, but Allaire (1984) analyzed the myth upon which that conclusion was based and suggests that the text was a "mental map" or code of Coast and Southern Tsimshian groups based upon a metaphorical relationship between containers (coastal), food (interior), and ceremonial paraphernalia (southern).

About 1750–1835 forts were built at Kispiox, Kisgegas, Gitlakdamiks, Kitwanga, and Kitselas, probably in response to trading networks that brought European goods into the area in advance of settlement. They were connected by "grease trails," 22 of which have been plotted for the Skeena-Nass-Stikine river systems (MacDonald 1984a).

History

The Southern Tsimshian were the earliest contacted by Europeans. The joint fur trading expedition of Capt. Charles Duncan in the vessel *Princess Royal* and James Colnett in the *Prince of Wales* visited what was probably the village of Kitkatla in 1787 (Moeller 1966). Colnett believed that he and his men were the first Europeans seen by the villagers, although they already had trade goods and were eager for more. In 1792 the Spanish explorer and captain of the *Aranzazu*, Jacinto Caamaño, visited a village on Pitt Island. This village has been identified as Ksidiya'ats, known as an archeological site (Seguin 1985: 28); Caamaño (1938:287) called it Citeyats.

The Gitksan were in contact with Europeans at Fort McLeod and Fort Saint James during the first decade of the nineteenth century, although they were not intruded upon by White settlement until the late 1860s, when Kitanmaks became the site of the Skeena River trading town of Skeena Forks or Hazelton.

Capt. George Vancouver explored Coast Tsimshian waters and sailed up Portland Canal into Nishga territory in 1793, but he left only scanty information about the few

Indians he saw. The documentary history of these two groups begins with the establishment of the Hudson's Bay Company at Fort Simpson on the Nass River in 1831.

Fisher (1977) has claimed that the native cultures were little disrupted by the traders, although Grumet (1975) analyzed changes in the potlatching patterns of the Coast Tsimshian who relocated around Fort Simpson.

It was the coming of the missionaries that inaugurated a much greater change in the cultures of the Tsimshian. The story of William Duncan and the establishment of the Christian village of Metlakatla has been told several times (Wellcome 1887; Arctander 1909; Usher 1969; Duff 1964: 93–94). An Anglican lay preacher, Duncan arrived at Fort Simpson in 1857 and learned enough of the language to preach his first sermon in Tsimshian in June 1858. In May 1862, he led a group of about 50 converts to found a village at the site of the old winter villages on Venn Passage. Soon after they departed, smallpox struck Fort Simpson, and others followed them. Barnett (1941, 1942) records instances in which people moved to Metlakatla because of political difficulties at Fort Simpson and concludes that Duncan offered an alternative life to people who had little chance of advancement in traditional Tsimshian society or who were otherwise in difficult or shameful positions.

The community prospered. By 1879 the population of the village was about 1,100 (Duff 1964:93). In 1887, after several years of conflict with officials of the Anglican Church, Duncan and his followers left British Columbia and founded New Metlakatla on Annette Island in Alaska (Usher 1974; Beynon 1941; Murray 1985).

The people remaining at Fort Simpson after the founding of Metlakatla, British Columbia, continued to follow traditional practices, but only for a few years more. In 1874 Rev. Thomas Crosby, a Methodist, went to Port Simpson at the invitation of Alfred and Kate Dudoward, high-ranking people who had been converted the previous year in Victoria. When Crosby arrived, there was only "one shingled 'European'" house outside the fort, but within a few years, Port Simpson resembled Metlakatla as a model Christian community. By 1878 "most of the original carved posts" at Port Simpson had been "cut down as missionary influence spread among the people" (Dawson 1880a:115B). An 1873 visitor to Metlakatla exclaimed: "I say these men are not Indians, they are White men" (Fisher 1977:134). However, the succeeding century has shown that the cultures of the Tsimshian were more resilient than that evaluation implies. Several authors have argued that the Tsimshian were active participants in their own missionization and that they developed a uniquely Tsimshian Christianity, suited to their new context dealing with a colonial society (Patterson 1982; Seguin 1985).

Missions in the Nishga and Gitksan areas quickly followed on the success at Metlakatla. In 1864 Rev. Robert Doolan founded a mission village at Kincolith; in 281

1880 Rev. William H. Collison, who had assisted Duncan at Metlakatla since 1873, was sent to Hazelton; another mission in the Gitksan area was founded north of Kispiox in 1879 by Robert Tomlinson, who had moved a mission founded at Greenville to Aiyansh in 1878. Patterson (1982) discusses Nass River missions.

The years during which the missions were growing were active in other ways as well. Trapping for trade led to shifts in annual cycles among most groups, though the traders' journals imply that most Indians continued subsistence production. After a minor gold rush along the Skeena in the early 1870s, there were prospectors in the area for many years. Most significant, the first salmon cannery was established on the Skeena in 1876, to be followed by a number of others. The labor of the local Indians was sought by the new industry, and a pattern of summers spent residing in company houses at the salmon canneries was quickly established. J.A. McDonald (1985) traces the development of the modern economy of the north coast area, pointing out that many Tsimshian people developed businesses and worked for wages during the nineteenth century.

Population

Duff (1964:39) estimated the 1835 total population of Tsimshian-speaking peoples at 8,500, of which 1,200 were Southern Tsimshian, 3,000 were Coast Tsimshian, 1,700 were Nishga, and 2,600 were Gitksan. In 1885 the total Tsimshian population in British Columbia had been reduced to 4,500; in 1887, 817 Tsimshians moved to Alaska. By 1895, the lowest year on record, the British Columbia population had shrunk to 3,550; there were 465 Tsimshians at New Metlakatla, Alaska, in 1900. The population began to grow in the twentieth century, and by 1963 there were 6,475 Tsimshian people in British Columbia. In 1980 there were 9,494 of which 3,149 were Gitksan, 2,893 were Nishga, and 3,452 Coast and Southern Tsimshian (Canada. Department of Indian Affairs and Northern Development, Indian and Inuit Affairs Program 1980:50).

Synonymy

The name Tsimshian is derived from *ċmsyan*, literally 'inside the Skeena River', the designation the Coast Tsimshian and Southern Tsimshian use for themselves. It appears in English as early as 1836, when Duncan Finlayson referred to "The Pearl Harbour, and Skeenah Indians called the Chimmesyan tribe" (E.E. Rich 1941: 323). Boas (1890:804) and Hodge (1907–1910, 2:827) used the spelling Tsimshian, though Hodge (1907–1910, 1: 270–271) continued to use the same name in the older spelling Chimmesyan for the linguistic family as a whole, following Powell (1891:63–65). Other spelling variants given by Hodge (1907–1910, 2:827) include: Chimseyans, Chymshean, Chimpsain, Shimshyans, Simseans, Simpsian, Tsimsean, Tsimseyans, Tsimsheeans, Tsimpsean, T'simpshean, and (German) Zimshīan.

Gitksan is from the Gitksan people's name for themselves in their own language, *kitxsan*, literally 'people of the Skeena River' (Hindle and Rigsby 1973:2). In Coast Tsimshian they are referred to as *kitksyán*. Spelling variants given by Hodge (1907–1910, 1:707) include Kitksan, used as the heading of the entry, and Gyitksa´n, Gyitkshan, Kiksàn, Kit-ih-shian, and Kit-ksun. Locally the spelling 'Ksan has some currency.

Nishga is also a self-designation, *nisqá?a*; the etymology of this word is uncertain. Spelling variants given by Hodge (1907–1910, 2:75–76) in the entry Niska include: Náss, Naas River Indians, Nascah, Nascar, Nishgar, Nishka, and Nis-kah. The spelling Nisgha is used by the Nisgha Tribal Council.

The Tsimshian-speaking peoples do not have a common name for themselves. The coastal people refer to the upriver people as *ċmsyán kilháuli* 'upriver Tsimshian'; the interior people call the coastal people *alukikét* 'standing-out people'. The Coast Tsimshian speakers differentiate their own language, which they call *sm?álkax* 'the real language', from Southern Tsimshian (*ski·xs*) and Nishga-Gitksan (*qe·lmx*) (John A. Dunn, communication to editors 1974).

Names for the Tsimshian in other Indian languages include: Tlingit *ċu·cxán* (Davis 1976:86), Tongass dialect *ċù·cxan* (Williams and Williams 1978:32–33); Haida *kílda·, kílada·* (Lawrence and Leer 1977:250); Squamish *ċamšián* (Kuipers 1969:39); Heiltsuk *kwē´təla* and Bella Coola *elxī´mix* (Boas 1890:805, normalized).

Variant forms of the names of the principal Tsimshian-speaking villages are given with the sources abbreviated as follows: B (Boas 1916:482–485, 959–966), H (Hodge 1907–1910), MB (Barbeau 1950).

Nishga

Gitiks (*kit?áiks* 'people of *?áiks!*'), G·it-aiks (B), Gitiks (MB), Kitaix (H).

Kwunwoq (*kʷinwo?a* 'where people sleep over'), Gwunahaw (MB), Gwinwork (H).

Angida (*nkitẏáh* 'where they rake eulachon'), Angyadæ (MB), Ankeegar (H).

Gitlakaus (*kitlax?áus* 'people on the sand bar'), G·it-lax-a´us (B).

Andegulay (*?antekʷile·*), Andegualē´ (B).

Gitwunksithk (Canyon City) (*kitwinksí·łk* 'people of the place of lizards'), G·it-wunksē´łk (B), Gitwinksihlk (MB), Kitwinshilk (H).

Gitlakdamiks (*kitlaxtá·miks* 'people on the place of springs'), G·it-lax-dā´mîks (B), Gitlarhdamiks (MB), Kitlakdamix (H).

Gitksan

Kitwanga (*kitwingáx* 'people of the place of rabbits'), Kitwanga (MB), Kitwingach (H).

Kitwancool (*kitwanɫkúʔul* 'people of the little place *or* narrow valley'), G·it-wunlkṓɫ (B), Gitwinlkul (MB), Kitwinskole (H).

Kitsegukla (*kicikúkʷɫa* 'people of Sagukhla Mountain'), G·idzig·úkɫa (B), Gitsegyukla (MB), Kitzegukla (H).

Kitanmaks (Hazelton) (*kitʔanmá·xs* 'people where they fish by torchlight'), G·it-an-mā́k·s (B), Kitanmaiksh (H).

Kispiox (*kispayákʷs* 'people of the hiding place'), G·ispa-yô̄ks (B), Kispayaks (MB), Kishpiyeoux (H).

Kisgegas (*kisqaqáʔas* 'people of the seagulls [?]') G·isgagas (B), Kiskagas (MB), Kishgagass (H).

Kuldo (*qaltóʔo*), Qaldo (B), Kauldaw (H).

Coast Tsimshian

Gitwilgyots (*kitwilkó·c* 'people of the kelp'), G·id-wul-g·ấdz (B), Gitwilgyawts (MB), Kitwilgyoks (H).

Gitzaklalth (*kitsaxɫá·ɫ* [c?] 'people of [?] berries'), Kitsalthlal (H).

Gitsees (*kitcí·s* 'people of the salmon trap'), G·it-dzī⁻ᵒs (B), Kitzeesh (H).

Ginakangeek (*kinaxʔankí·k* 'people of the mosquitoes'), G·inax'ang·ī⁻ᵒk (B), Ginarhangyeek (MB), Kinagingeek (H).

Ginadoiks (*kinató·iks* 'people of the swift water'), G·inadấᵒxs (B), Ginaihdoiks (MB), Kinuhtoiah (H).

Gitandau (*kitʔantó·* [?] 'people of the weirs'), G·it!andấ (B), Gitandaw (MB), Kitunto (H).

Gispakloats (*kispaxluʔuc* 'people of the elderberries'), G·i-spa-x-lấᵒts (B), Gisparhlawts (MB), Kishpachlaots (H).

Gitwilkseba (*kitwilksipá·*), G·id-wul-ksE-bā́ᵒ (B), Kitwilksheba (H).

Gilutsau (*kilucá·ÿ* 'people of the way inside'), G·i-lu-dzā́r (B), Gillodzar (MB), Kilutsai (H).

Gitlan (*kitlí·n* 'people of two passing canoes'), G·it-lā́n (B), Gitlæn (MB), Kitlani (H).

Kitsumkalum (*kitsmqé·lm* 'people of the plateau'), G·its!Emgā́lôn (B), Kitsumkælem (MB), Kitzimgaylum (H).

Kitselas (*kitsalá·sÿ* 'people of the canyon'), G·its!alā́sEr (B), Gitsalas (MB), Kitzilas (H).

Southern Tsimshian

Kitkatla (*kitqxá·ɫa* 'people of the channel'), G·it-qxā́ɫa (B), Gitrhahla (MB), Kitkatla (H).

Kitkiata (*kitqaʔáta* 'people of the ceremonial cane'), G·it-q!ā́ᵒda (B), Kitkahta (H).

Kitasoo (*kitiscú·*), G·idEsdzū́ (B), Kittizoo (H).

Sources

The first written record of Tsimshian people is in the 1787 journal of Colnett (1798; Howay 1940; Moeller 1966). The most complete explorer's account is the journal based on Jacinto Caamaño's extended sojourn among Southern Tsimshians in 1792 (Caamaño 1938). There are a few other reports of Coast and Southern Tsimshian people during the next three decades. The establishment of Fort Simpson by the Hudson's Bay Company in 1834 began a period of more regular records (Hudson's Bay Company 1834–1838). Mitchell (1981, 1983a) used records from the fort and trading vessels from 1835 as the basis for a discussion of the annual round of a Kitkatla chief in 1835. Patterson (1982) summarizes most of the early accounts of the Nishga. Large's (1957) history of the Skeena River includes information on the Coast Tsimshian and Gitksan peoples. William Duncan's papers (1853–1916) are preserved in Metlakatla, Alaska, and his reports to the Church Missionary Society are preserved in the Society's archives in London (both sets of papers are available on microfilm from the University of British Columbia Library, Special Collections Division, Vancouver).

There are no ethnographies of the Tsimshian in the sense that a traditional ethnography is an attempt to describe a whole culture on the basis of information gathered from informants and from the observation of behavior. Boas worked with Tsimshian people in Victoria in 1886 and on the Nass in 1894, and between 1903 and 1914 he corresponded with Henry Tate, a Port Simpson Tsimshian, who sent him a large body of texts. Boas's primary interest was in mythology, and the result was two volumes (Boas 1902, 1912) of texts with translations and one collection (Boas 1916:58–392) in English only. His ethnographic publications consist of a piece on the Nishga (Boas 1895:569–583) and a general description of the Tsimshian peoples incorporated into his work on their mythology (Boas 1916). This consists of a short account of material culture (1916:43–57), a description of Tsimshian culture as reflected in their myths (1916:398–477), and an analysis of social organization using other sources and comparative data (1916:478–564). While much of this work is convincing in the light of later work, insofar as it depends on myths it must be used with caution. Myths are not a reliable source on actual behavior.

During the 1930s Boas received extensive collections of notes from William Beynon, of Port Simpson, but never published from these materials, some of which are in the Columbia University Library, New York, and are available on microfilm, and some of which are in the Library of the American Philosophical Society, Philadelphia. Beynon also sent material to Philip Drucker in the 1950s, which is preserved in the National Anthropological Archives, Smithsonian Institution, Washington.

Sapir (1915a, 1920) published information on Nishga social organization gathered from chiefs who visited the National Museum of Man in Ottawa. Berger (1981) summarizes the important Nishga land claim case.

Viola Garfield, a student of Boas, did fieldwork among the Coast Tsimshian at Port Simpson during the 1930s; she also worked extensively with William Beynon. Her monograph (1939) is a detailed investigation of their social organization, with considerable information on potlatches and *haláit*. She also wrote a useful popular summary (1966), which is the best general introduction to Tsimshian culture available. Garfield's field notes and papers are preserved in the University of Washington, Seattle.

Marius Barbeau was an active Tsimshian scholar for a number of years from his first fieldwork during 1915. William Beynon worked with him throughout the period, and the collection of unpublished Tsimshian notes and texts in the Barbeau room at the Centre for Folk Culture Studies at the National Museum of Man, Ottawa, is the most significant resource for Tsimshian scholars (Duff 1964a; Halpin 1978). It is available on microfilm. Beynon collected an enormous volume of material from the Coast and Southern Tsimshian and the Gitksan, most of it myths and narratives, between 1915 and 1957. Much of it remains unpublished, and what was published by Barbeau (notably 1929, 1950, 1953, and 1958) was poorly edited and organized in support of outdated theoretical assumptions (see Duff 1964a).

Grumet (1979) published a thorough bibliographic essay on the Tsimshian. Significant contributions include Seguin (1985) on feasts, Patterson (1982) on Nishga missionization, McNeary (1976) on Nishga social and economic life, J.A. McDonald (1985) on the Kitsumkalum economy, and two edited collections. Seguin (1984b) includes chapters on feasts, archeology, basketry, cosmology, secret society carvers, and shamanism. Miller and Eastman (1984) include discussions of mythology, totemism, inheritance, potlatch, kinship, house fronts, and religion.

Important museum collections from the Tsimshian groups are in the Royal British Columbia Museum, Victoria; the National Museum of Man, Ottawa; the Royal Ontario Museum, Toronto; and the Museum of the American Indian, Heye Foundation, New York. These repositories include both artifacts and photographs.

Tsimshian of British Columbia Since 1900

GORDON B. INGLIS, DOUGLAS R. HUDSON, BARBARA R. RIGSBY, AND BRUCE RIGSBY*

During the nineteenth century missionaries, in the process of converting the Tsimshian (Coast and Southern Tsimshian, Nishga, and Gitksan) to Christianity, fostered the formation of elected village councils and the adoption of Euro-Canadian dress, personal names, and house styles. With the entry of British Columbia into the Canadian Confederation in 1871, Indians became the administrative responsibility of the federal government, and during the next two decades the Tsimshian villages became "bands" under the Indian Act. Reserves were established for each band at traditional village, burial, and subsistence sites, and the bands came under the administration of Indian agents. The reserve allocations were unilaterally imposed by the provincial and federal governments. All the Tsimshian groups protested the attempt at usurpation and have continued to assert title to their entire aboriginal territories. The major comprehensive land claims rising from this history were not settled in 1986; settlements were reached in 1982 for the specific claims rising from the unilateral "cutting off" of some allocated reserves from Port Simpson, Metlakatla, and Kitwanga by the acts implementing the recommendations of the McKenna-McBride Commission (Canada. Royal Commission on Indian Affairs for the Province of British Columbia 1916).

Political Structures

The culture and society of the Tsimshian groups have been pressured by external forces. The early maritime fur trade, wage labor, and other economic enterprises created new forms of wealth that were integrated into the Tsimshian systems. Depopulation, missionization, and government controls also had to be incorporated. What has remained is a core of land and titles; the relationships between particular titles and particular tracts of land or resource areas are recalled in traditions and recounted at feasts in which titles are transferred along matrilineal lines.

Following missionization, English names were added

to, but did not replace, native names. A few names were anglicized, and in the 1980s there was a dual naming system in operation: English names, which were used on an everyday basis as family names, and traditional name-titles, which are used to denote house membership and social standing along traditional lines. High-ranking names have remained, while some lesser ranking names have either fallen from use or have not been transferred.

By the beginning of the twentieth century a basic pattern was established, many features of which persisted in the 1980s. Although there was no lack of conflict, the villages were organized units in which the aboriginal kinship and political systems and White-influenced institutions and organizations fit together in a community structure. Native social structure underwent some changes, but it continued to fulfill social control functions and to regulate marriage and personal relationships to some degree, and remained the context in which inheritance and territorial ownership were asserted. Traditional chiefs and leading men were elected to the village councils, or, if they were not, exerted much influence over elected councilors. Delegations of chiefs were sent to Ottawa and London to press for recognition of land claims. Much of the native ceremonial and esthetic expression was suppressed by the missionaries and replaced by clubs, organizations, musical bands and choirs modeled after those of English or eastern Canadian towns and villages.

This complex village structure was in some places in the 1980s still most evident at funerals and weddings, when the aboriginal kinship system provided an organizational pivot, and church organizations, clubs, bands, and choirs each played a part in the ceremonial. Road access in the Nishga and Gitksan areas, rapid travel by aircraft to coastal communities (since 1956), and the coming of television in the early 1960s had powerful effects. All the villages, at varying rates in different institutional sectors, have undergone similar processes of secularization and urbanization. The influence of the aboriginal sociopolitical structure in daily life has waned, and "commoners" may take the lead in band councils. In some cases hereditary chiefs and principal men have lived away from their villages (sometimes by necessity due to the government policy of forced enfranchisement of women who

*This chapter was edited by Margaret Seguin, using material submitted separately by Inglis on the Coast and Southern Tsimshian, Hudson on the Nishga, and Rigsby and Rigsby on the Gitksan.

285

married out); some have died without their names being formally transferred to heirs. Wedding receptions were sometimes held in private homes rather than in village halls, with only immediate kin and close friends invited; funerals sometimes took place in Prince Rupert or Terrace, with the traditional "business" of transferring title and privilege being postponed and sometimes never held. These processes were most evident in the coastal villages closest to urban centers and seemed to be an indication of acculturation, but the direction of change reversed in the last half of the twentieth century as the influence of the feast and naming systems was reasserted in those villages. While these processes were interpreted as evidence of culture loss and assimilation by many outside observers, it has become apparent that in general they are most appropriately viewed as manifestations of vitality and cultural growth as each of the groups has incorporated useful elements into what remain essentially Tsimshian cultures.

Name-titles are still transferred through feasts with chiefs acting as witnesses; the extent to which other community members participated varied among the groups. The transfer of names was a serious matter, as the holdings of the corporate house group are embodied in particular titles.

The most important ceremony in the 1980s was the memorial or settlement feast, when a title is publicly transferred. Such a ceremony follows the death of a chief, after the leading men and women of a house and clan have decided on the successor and have amassed enough money and goods to repay those from other clans who performed services for the deceased. Members of the deceased's father's clan play an important part in providing these services. Though different in detail in each of the communities, the memorial feast allows the heir and his house group to "settle" the debts incurred with members of other clans and publicly have the transfer of title witnessed and validated.

In one domain change has been consistently in the direction of strengthening and formalizing traditionally oriented institutions. The transmission and ratification of ranked names tied to territories provided the structural skeleton for the modern institution of tribal councils, which continued to assert territorial sovereignty vis-a-vis the provincial and federal governments. The Nishga tribal council was the first of the three present tribal councils incorporated, in 1955; it is effectively a council of chiefs, backed by the moral authority of the aboriginal name-title system, continuing the assertion of sovereignty over territory. The Gitksan incorporated a similar organization in 1968; several Carrier villages were included in this organization, called the Gitksan-Wet'suwet'en Tribal Council. In some respects the better road connections among the Gitksan villages enabled their council more easily to maintain the integration of the villages. The

North Coast Tribal Council for Coast and Southern Tsimshian villages was incorporated in 1980; headquartered in Prince Rupert, it was less actively engaged in managing traditional activities, such as the feast system and associated land claims, which remained village-organized in this area, but it was successful in channeling program funding formerly administered by the Department of Indian Affairs.

With increasing emphasis by Indian Affairs authorities on self-government for the bands, village structure was becoming more centralized as band councils involved themselves in the areas of recreation and community development. Church-sponsored village organizations seemed to be declining in importance.

Until the middle of the twentieth century missionaries provided education in the villages, but for many children the school year was interrupted to accommodate seasonal moves by the family, and few children progressed beyond primary grades. A few children were sent to residential schools in Port Alberni, Alert Bay, Coqualeetza, and Edmonton. In the second half of the twentieth century the federal government replaced the missionary teachers by a federal school system. The village schools of the Coast Tsimshian were integrated into the provincial school system (Prince Rupert District) by a master tuition agreement; the Gitksan village schools were part of the Terrace School District; the Nishga formed a separate school district. In all three areas bilingual-bicultural programs were introduced. Levels of educational attainment remained below provincial averages.

Economic Activities

Most activities of the Natives in the modern economy of the region were of a kind that could be integrated into the aboriginal subsistence cycle, and for the last of the nineteenth and the first third of the twentieth century the Tsimshian villages enjoyed comparative affluence fed by income from fishing, trapping, freighting, and commerce. However, technological changes such as the introduction of gasoline-powered fishboats and the growth of large non-Indian populations at Prince Rupert, Terrace, and Hazelton after the First World War brought about a centralization in the economy of the area, drawing employment and capital away from the villages.

The economic base of the Tsimshian groups in the 1980s was a combination of commercial fishing, logging, professional positions (especially in education and the clergy), band office jobs, and a small amount of trapping. Band-owned logging companies operated at Canyon City on the Nass and at Moricetown (a Carrier village) on the Skeena. The use of traditional marine, river, and land resources is a significant component of household consumption; in many village households the locally harvested foods (fish, shellfish, herring eggs, game, eulachon and

Table 1. Registered Indian Population, 1983

	On Reserve	Off Reserve	Total
Coast and Southern			
Tsimshian Bands			
Port Simpson			
(Lax Kw'alaams)	882	692	1,574
Metlakatla	117	147	264
Kitkatla	493	511(+1)[a]	1,005
Hartley Bay	230	218	448
Kitselas	44	68	112
Kitsumkalum	74	65	139
Kitasoo	269	52	231
Total	2,109	1,754	3,773
Nishga Bands			
Kincolith	402	680(+2)[a]	1,084
Greenville			
(Lachkaltsap)	378	547	925
Canyon City	116	82	198
New Aiyansh			
(Gitlakdamiks)	654	409(+3)[a]	1,066
Total	1,550	1,723	3,273
Gitksan Bands			
Kitwancool	292	77	369
Kitwanga	323	174	497
Kitsegukla	326	137	463
Hazelton			
(Kitanmaks)	524	375	899
Glen Vowell	143	74	217
Kispiox	456	267	723
Total	2,064	1,104	3,168

SOURCE: Canada. Department of Indian Affairs and Northern Development (1984).

[a]Indians residing on Crown land.

seal grease, berries, and seaweed) comprised well over half the diet. Participation in this economic sector with modern harvesting and storage technology entailed an expenditure of cash income for boats, nets, fuel, canning equipment, and freezers.

Fishing continued in the 1980s to be the biggest source of earned income in the villages, but public sector employment increased to a substantial level; jobs in this sector included band management, teaching and other standard positions, permanent and temporary employment in sponsored economic development projects such as hatcheries and sawmills, and a plethora of temporary make-work projects. Transfer payments grew after 1950 to a substantial portion of the economy; these included off-season unemployment insurance payments to salmon fishermen, pensions, and social assistance. Tsimshian fishermen have since the 1930s faced stiff competition from better-financed and hence better-equipped non-Indians and suffered from a lack of interest among the cannery companies in the small company-owned gill netters that provided a major part of Indian participation

in the fishery. Several federally commissioned studies (Pearse 1982; Hawthorn, Belshaw, and Jamieson 1958) have noted the dramatic decrease in Indian participation in the fishing industry; one recommendation that has been implemented is the use of special Indian-only licenses for vessels, at reduced annual cost. A native-owned cooperative operated in Port Simpson 1975–1985. The 1970s saw a short-lived boom in the industry as a new fishery for roe herring for export to Japan yielded huge returns during the early years; a combination of overfishing, overcapitalization and an erratic market rapidly made this fishery a risky investment. Two villages had special licenses to pen herring in ponds and produce roe-on-kelp. The largest fishing company, B.C. Packers, in the 1980s sold its rental gill-net fleet of over 225 vessels to a government-sponsored Northern Native Fishing Corporation, organized by the three tribal councils. The 1980s have also seen a rapid growth in support for hatchery projects to enhance the salmon stocks, and the development of "fish-farming"; the downriver and coastal villages have reaped some employment benefits from these programs.

Seasonal cycles of key resources continued to influence the movements of people. One of the most important aboriginal fisheries, for eulachon, continued to draw a considerable number of Nishga people in the spring to the mouth of the Nass River; a few individuals from the village of Hartley Bay made grease together with people from Kitamaat at Kemano each spring. Thus the making of grease continued to begin the economic year, followed by the collection of seaweed by coastal people, salmon fishing for food, commercial fishing, and other harvesting activities. The extent of exploitation of local food sources by households varied considerably, depending on access to boats and equipment and flexibility in cash-income employment; networks of sharing distributed the locally obtained land foods throughout the Tsimshian communities.

Population

Population figures (table 1) refer only to people of legal Indian status as of the census date and thus include a small number of non-Tsimshian women who have become band members by marriage; these figures also do not reflect the revision of the Indian Act in the 1980s restoring status to women who lost official status by reason of marriage to non-status men, and to the children of those marriages. Most band members listed as "off-reserve" lived in and around Prince Rupert and Terrace, but some lived elsewhere in British Columbia and a few in other parts of Canada. There is some movement back and forth between reserve and town as employment opportunities fluctuate.

U. of Ill., Dept. of Anthr., Urbana.

Fig. 1. Spreading out commercial fish nets to dry and mend in the cannery town of Sunnyside, near Prince Rupert, B.C. Residences built by the cannery for its workers are in the background. Photograph by Julian Steward, 1940.

Coast and Southern Tsimshian Communities

Port Simpson, the largest concentration of Tsimshian people, is relatively close to Prince Rupert, having daily scheduled flights by light aircraft and a regular ferry service. Ceremonial expressions of traditional culture, as at funerals and weddings, seemed to be declining rapidly in frequency and importance until the 1970s when renewed interest by many younger people became apparent; this has had the most obvious impact on the feasts associated with funerals and on the architecture and decoration of public buildings. Most adults at Port Simpson in the 1970s could point out the sections of the village that were once tribal territories, although the tendency to patrilineal inheritance of houses eroded the spatially distinct character of the tribal units by the 1930s (Garfield 1939:175, 177). Tribal, as well as clan, membership is recognized as passing in the maternal line, so that the tribes have become weakly defined matrilineal groups, but there has been much "adoption" by fathers, and many people claim membership in two tribes. Renewed interest in land claims has led to local research, including an effort to sort out the tribes and reassert their role in political processes.

The relative size of Port Simpson compared to the other coastal communities has led to some difficulties in building an effective organizational structure for the North Coast Tribal Council; there was pressure for Port Simpson to split off from the other villages.

Metlakatla had a high proportion (56%) of off-reserve members in 1983 (table 1) and perhaps the highest rate of enfranchisements. The population of Metlakatla was drawn from the same nine aboriginal groups that formed Port Simpson; it became a distinct community when William Duncan built his original village in 1862. The population of Metlakatla was drastically reduced when many people went with Duncan to Alaska in 1887, and many others returned to Port Simpson or other aboriginal villages. Band members, some of whom live in Prince Rupert, have attempted to develop the village as a tourist attraction, helped by archeologists from the National Museum of Man, Ottawa.

Kitsumkalum and Kitselas were in the 1980s practically residential suburbs of Terrace. Rates of employment were high for both bands, and both have reasonable incomes from land leases and band enterprises. Kitsumkalum has a band-sponsored museum and craft outlet. Both bands belong to the North Coast Tribal Council, and Kitsumkalum has been especially active in researching its aboriginal land claim.

At Port Simpson and Metlakatla, Kitkatla has the reputation of being the "most Indian" of the Tsimshian villages, which concurs with the assessment given by Dorsey (1897:280). While relatively isolated it had regular flights in the 1980s and received television from Prince Rupert. Older villagers deplored what they perceived as a rapid decline of village organization.

Hartley Bay was, by some measures, more isolated than Kitkatla but has a history of greater outside interaction. All the people from this village joined the Metlakatla missionary community. The village was re-established by people who planned their own new village on the mission model (Campell 1984). Hartley Bay seems to most closely represent the early twentieth-century pattern of village organization. Seguin (1985:15) suggested that from its re-establishment after the return from Metlakatla "the community defined itself as a progressive, Christian Tsimshian village, with equal emphasis on each aspect of their definition."

The village of the Kitasoo band (popularly called Klemtu) was "almost deserted" in 1897, part of the population having gone to Alaska, and part to Bella Bella (Dorsey 1897:280). It is farther from commercial centers than the other villages and, in the 1980s, had a much smaller proportion of members living off the reserve. Indian Affairs officials estimated that the band was about evenly divided between Tsimshian and Haihais. Klemtu has been economically rather successful, having its own hydroelectric power project, a village-owned sawmill, salmon hatchery, and herring roe-on-kelp license. It was a stop on the route for coastal ferries and had regular seaplane service.

Nishga Communities

The Nishga live in four villages on the Nass—New Aiyansh, Canyon City, Greenville, and Kincolith (table 1)—and in urban centers in British Columbia. People of Nishga ancestry also live in Alaska.

Fig. 2. Nishga children with flags of the British Commonwealth and a banner saying "Canadians All," on steps of McCullaghs Community Hall. They are dressed for a pageant during a Dominion Day celebration. Photograph by Wilson Duff, Old Aiyansh, B.C., 1949.

These villages are the consolidations of a number of other villages. The other village groups are often referred to as "tribes," especially in the earlier anthropological literature. Thus, the Nishga can be seen as four "tribes," although a traditional distinction between "upriver" and "downriver" Nishga is maintained.

The village of New Aiyansh was created in the early 1960s and connected by road to Terrace. The previous village, across the river, had been flooded out, and the move was made to facilitate access to services. Prior to this, there had been five other villages in the immediate area identified with this group of people. The most recent were Gitlakdamiks (Horetsky 1874:128; Shotridge 1919: 128) and Aiyansh, a Christian village established in 1875 or 1883 (Fisher 1977:137).

The village of Canyon City is the last of a number of villages in the vicinity. It was accessible only by boat or across ice bridges in the winter until the construction of a foot bridge in 1969.

The two downriver villages, Greenville and Kincolith, are closely linked. A Church Missionary Society missionary, Rev. Robert Doolan, founded a mission in the vicinity of present-day Greenville in 1864; Greenville itself was founded in 1872 by Rev. W.S. Green, with inhabitants of a Nishga village, Gitiks. Kincolith was established in 1867 with people from the Greenville area, and close social ties have been maintained. Until 1984, when a vehicular bridge was built across the Nass River upstream from the village, Greenville was accessible only by boat in the summer or across the river ice in the winter.

In the 1980s all villages were associated with the Anglican Church, except for Canyon City, which affiliated with the Salvation Army in the 1920s (Patterson 1982, 1982a).

Non-Nishga populations have been incorporated into Nishga society over time. In the early 1900s, Gitksan from the Skeena River watershed moved to Aiyansh and its mission (Barbeau 1929:151), and the Athapaskan Tsetsaut of Portland Canal were integrated into the Nishga population at Kincolith in the late 1800s (see vol. 6: 454–457). The impact of World War I substantially reduced non-Nishga settlement of the middle and upper river regions. The major movement in the lower region came with the canneries, with the first cannery opening on the Nass in 1881, with much of the labor force drawn from Nishga villages (Knight 1978:78, 91). In the late 1940s, logging commenced in the Nass region, accelerated by the construction of a road from Terrace in 1958, and the creation of logging camps.

The Nishga social world continued in the 1980s to be one of kinship obligations, and rights and responsibilities that have their base in matrilineal descent groups called pte·q 'clan' and wilp 'house'. Through this social system, resources are controlled and harvested. At the core of the resource-harvesting system are corporate groups, that is, groups that own property, land, titles, and traditions. These corporate groups (houses) own fishing and hunting places and show and exercise control through leaders with titles or high-ranking names. The basic elments of the resource ownership and harvesting system—land, titles, traditions, houses—work together to ensure the continuity of the Nishga form of sovereignty.

High-ranking chiefs in particular houses are identified as village chiefs (sim'o·kit, sg.). Having a sim'o·kit name means assuming certain responsibilities. A sim'o·kit manages the resources and territories of his house and is expected to live in the village located in the vicinity of the house's lands in order to do this.

While titles are tied to particular pieces of land, the land is owned by matrilineal descent groups, in this case, a house. People describe and define their rights to use land in the Nass River area in accordance with membership in particular house groups. The physical landscape is thus a social one; the Nishga own the Nass River valley and adjacent coast through their matrilineal social system.

There are about 65 houses in the four major Nishga villages, each with territories in the vicinity of their villages.

The clans do not control resources and territory in the same way as the houses. They primarily function to regulate marriage and to serve as a way of integrating village house groups in an exchange system that joins the Nishga with other groups. The clans are exogamous; thus house groups in the same clan cannot intermarry, even though they may belong to different villages.

In addition to the clan structure, a number of voluntary and Church organizations serve to integrate the Nishga. Each village has athletic clubs and a church musical band. Both of these organizations carry out services associated with funerals and ceremonies. Nishga fishermen belong to

289

the Native Brotherhood of B.C., an organization representing Indian fishermen.

In 1890 the Nishga bands formed a land committee and protested White settlement of the Nass Valley. In 1913, Nishga sovereignty was reaffirmed in what has become known as the "Nishga Petition." In 1975 the Nishga tribal council adopted a contemporary version, the "Nishga Declaration."

A number of issues in the 1960s–1980s brought the position of the Nishga to public attention (Raunet 1984). In 1967 the Nishga sued the British Columbia provincial government for recognition of aboriginal title to the Nass Valley. The Nishga lost in the provincial courts in 1969 but took their case to the Supreme Court of Canada in 1971. They lost again, but this court's decision in 1973 had far-reaching implications for government policies; the judges were evenly split on the issue of aboriginal title (Canada. Department of Indian and Northern Affairs 1981:43).

Negotiations among the Nishga, the British Columbia government, and the federal government over Nishga assertions of ownership of the Nass River watershed and adjacent coast began in 1976. Meetings ceased in 1978 but were reinstated in 1981. In order to document the extent of its territory, the Nishga tribal council directed a study in the early 1980s of land ownership and use in its land claims area. The land claims area covers about 15,000 square kilometers, from Portland Canal to Meziadin Lake, and including the Nass River watershed, none of it allocated in any treaties. As a statement of their cultural and political unity, the Nishga raised what has been called the "Unity Pole" in New Aiyansh in 1977, with crests of the major clans carved on the pole.

In 1976 the Nishga School District was created, with several schools in the villages, including a high school and student residences in New Aiyansh. An important part of the curriculum is a bilingual and bicultural program.

In addition to land claims, the 1980s brought the Nishga into conflict with a multinational corporation, AMAX, over its disposal of mining effluent from a molybdenum mine in Alice Arm, an inlet falling within the Nishga land claims area, and used for food gathering. Poor market conditions for the metal resulted in a closing of the mine, but the issue remained unresolved from the Nishga point of view.

Gitksan Communities

Traditional Gitksan cultural and social forms have been supplemented with new forms to give content to and to maintain a distinctive Gitksan identity that differs from that of the Anglo-Canadians who live alongside the Gitksans in the Middle Skeena valley. Although the Gitksans wore the same clothes, drove the same cars, lived in similar houses, and shared common public facilities and amenities with their Anglo-Canadian neighbors, they remained Gitksans and the public and private worlds had features different from those of the Whites.

The Gitksans lived principally in six village communities: Kitwancool, Kitwanga, Gitsegukla, Hazelton, Glen Vowell, and Kispiox (fig. 3) (table 1). A number of non-Indians lived in Hazelton, too, and controlled the town and its businesses. Glen Vowell was established before 1900 as a Salvation Army village by people from Kispiox. Kisgegas and Kuldo, other traditional Gitksan villages farther up the Skeena River, have been deserted since at least 1949 and 1939 respectively. The Kisgegas people and their descendents lived in Hazelton and Kispiox, while those of Kuldo were in Kispiox. The mission villages of Andimaul and Carnaby were gone, but some people remained at Cedarvale.

Villages, which remain important social units for the Gitksans, have their own community halls, churches, and athletic fields. Formal village government rests with the band councils, whose members are elected and tend to be the younger chiefs and chiefly heirs. Villages have their own sports teams, they sponsor sporting events and celebrations, and there is keen intervillage rivalry. The Christian churches in the villages—Anglican, Pentecostal, Salvation Army, and United Church—are loci of social activity and sometimes of factions. The houses in the villages range from modern ranch-style homes to old unpainted dwellings. Households generally consist of a single nuclear family of husband, wife, and their children, augmented sometimes by an elderly widowed kinsperson.

The villages were integrated through the Gitksan-Wet'suwet'en Tribal Council, which continued and formalized the role taken since the nineteenth century by councils of chiefs in asserting Gitksan sovereignty over their territories vis-a-vis external governments. These

Royal B.C. Mus., Victoria: PN 7037.
Fig. 3. The Gitksan town of Kispiox. Each of the 6 totem poles is owned by a different family (Barbeau 1929:40, 86–88, 110–112, 220, 240, 250). Photograph by Wilson Duff, 1952.

INGLIS, HUDSON, RIGSBY, AND RIGSBY

councils of chiefs were in turn externally oriented manifestations of the political functions of the chiefs of Gitksan houses in ratifying inheritance and succession.

Memberhip in one of the four clans (*pte·q*; called 'tribes' or 'crests' in local English) is inherited in the maternal line. Thus, a Gitskan is from birth an Eagle (found only in Kitwanga), a Fireweed (or Killer whale), a Frog (or Raven), or a Wolf, unless adopted into another clan, and he or she will marry a person from another clan. Attachments between young people of the same clan were discouraged in the 1980s, and intra-clan marriages drew strong community disapproval.

Particularly in the winter season, when most villagers are in residence, the Gitksans hold ceremonies that see the operation of more traditional social structure and organization (fig. 4). The ceremonies are in fact potlatches at which a host group distributes money and goods to its guests and a proper public witnesses some change in social status. Potlatches are most commonly held following death and burial.

The major social groups at a potlatch are the houses, although several sorts of social categories play parts too. Gitksan houses are resource-holding corporations, and they include a number of named, ranked chiefly statuses. In former times, many members of a house indeed dwelt together in a large winter house, utilizing resources and territories in common under the direction of its chiefs. In the 1980s Gitksan people lived in single-family houses, but the house groups continued to claim and transmit ownership of territories and symbolic property such as legends (*?ata·wq*), totemic crests (*?ayuk^w s*), and names. Houses were not unitary matrilineal descent groups. Rather they included unrelated matrilineages (a matrilineage being the

descendants of the same mother's mother) who belonged to the two 'sides of the house' (*stu?wilp*) and were competitors for the controlling head chiefship of the house.

Gitksan villages tended toward dual organization in that the houses that owned the associated village territories belonged to only two phratries. Houses of a third pharatry may be resident, but they did not own land. Thus, the major Kitwancool houses belonged to the Wolf and Frog phratries. The resident Fireweed houses did not own land but used that of their Wolf and Frog fathers' houses.

Upon a death, the house of the father of the deceased person—the "fathers" (*wilksiẁitx^w*)—has the responsibility of making and carrying out the funeral arrangements and duties. Ideally, burial takes place on the third day, and that evening the house of the deceased—the "hosts"—holds a feast and a potlatch at which they repay the "fathers" for their funeral expenses and labors. The first part of the ceremony is a feast (*liĺikit*) at which the "hosts" and the house of the father of the main heir feed the "fathers" and the invited public. The potlatch proper follows (*yuk^w* is the Gitksan word; *pa·ɬac* from Chinook Jargon *potlatch* is also used).

Most marriages take place between fellow villagers, and potlatches generally involve houses of the same village, but not necessarily. Kitwancool has many links with the Nishga houses of Aiyansh on the Nass, and Kitwancool, Kitwanga, and Gitsegukla often potlatch together, while Hazelton and Kispiox also go together. Houses that decline in numbers due to demographic vicissitudes are usually not permitted to die out; rather they adopt new members. The overall ethos of the potlatch system is one of balanced reciprocity, not competitiveness, and the Gitksans sometimes describe it as their own "social insurance" scheme. Adams (1973) gives a detailed account and interpretation of the Gitksan potlatch in the 1960s.

Subsistence fishing for salmon was an important food source for Gitksan households in the 1980s. Salmon were taken at traditional locations along the streams; moose, deer, and the occasional black bear provided welcome game contributions to the larder. Sharing networks, based mainly upon kinship and friendship, ensured that fish and game were distributed among the households in the villages. Many families had smokehouses for preserving fish, and home-canning outfits and freezers were common. People also picked quantities of the many berry species when ripe for immediate consumption and preserving.

The largest surviving numbers of totem poles on the Northwest Coast were found in the Gitksan villages. In the late 1960s there was a revival of art and craft work in wood (fig. 5), gold, and silver that centered mainly in the buildings of the 'Ksan Association at Hazelton (Canada. National Museum of Man 1972). Several artists there turned out excellent poles, masks, and jewelry for sale to the public. A reconstructed winter village there—'Ksan—displayed items of traditional material culture, some old

Natl. Mus. of Canada, Ottawa: 97539.
Fig. 4. Gitksans raising a pole. A pole was often a memorial to a deceased chief, raised by his successor in a potlatch ending the mourning period. On the pole are carved figures that illustrate the lineage and personal history and possessions. The raising of a pole was not done by the owner or his lineage; it had to be done by invited guests. Once the pole was raised it could not be repaired or moved without the ritual of a potlatch (Garfield 1939:209–210). Photograph by William Beynon, Kitsegukla, B.C., 1945.

291

top, 'Ksan Assoc., New Hazelton, B.C.; bottom left, SSC Photocentre, Ottawa: 73-3299.
Fig. 5. Contemporary art. top, "Carving House of All Times," at 'Ksan Indian Village near Hazelton, B.C., a workshop for local carvers and for the Kitanmax School of Northwest Coast Indian Art. This is one of 7 museum and exhibition buildings opened to the public for the purpose of preserving and teaching the cultural history of the Tsimshian. Vernon Stephens, a member of the Wolf clan, designed the house front painting (People of 'Ksan 1972:19). Photograph by Ron Burleigh, 1986. bottom left, Sam Wesley, Gitksan, carving a ceremonial wooden hat. The piece is first painted then carved. Photograph by Crombie McNeill, Kshwan, B.C., 1973. bottom right, Norman Tait, Nishga from Kincolith, B.C., carving a wooden bowl. Photograph by Mary Randlett, Vancouver, B.C., 1979.

and some newly made, for tourists. A group at 'Ksan collected and wrote down traditional legends, myths, and lore, and published several books (People of 'Ksan 1980; 'Ksan Book Builders 1977).

All Gitksans in the 1980s spoke English as their main language, although older people preferred to speak Gitksan at home. Gitksan was used on all public occasions, such as at potlatches, but English was the language of most children's play groups, and many young people used it almost exclusively. Some Gitksans were concerned by the prospect of the loss of their native language and attendant cultural knowledge and so worked for the development and introduction of bilingual-bicultural curriculum materials into the local schools.

Tsimshian of Metlakatla, Alaska

JOHN A. DUNN AND ARNOLD BOOTH

Metlakatla (or "New Metlakatla") maintained in the 1980s much of its character as a successful utopian community, the dream child of its missionary founder, William Duncan. It is a Native American community literally saved by this excommunicate Anglican adventurer from White oppression and reservation degradation (Barnett 1942; Beynon 1941). Metlakatlans placed strong emphasis on the common good and communal effort as opposed to individual profit motive. The Metlakatla city council discouraged economic enterprises that served individual interest to the detriment of the common village good. A service or institution was considered valid only if the whole community cooperated to effect it and made specific material contributions to its development. These attitudes were part of the Duncan society model, one of three cultural systems that organized social interaction in Metlakatla. The other two cultural systems were the aboriginal native Tsimshian (the spelling Tsimpshean was preferred by Metlakatlans in 1986) and the Anglo-Alaskan. The Duncan society manifested itself primarily in a set of utopian communal ideals and in much of the managerial activity of the city council. The Anglo-Alaskan system manifested itself in profit-motivated market-economy enterprises and in the organization of the public school complex. The aboriginal native system was a disarticulated collection of survivals and syncretized survivals of a dimly remembered past; it was most evident in factionalism and vague matrilineal structures.

History

The story of the founding of Metlakatla has been told in the literature (Barnett 1941, 1942; Beynon 1941; Matthews 1939; Usher 1974; P. Murray 1985). William Duncan (fig. 1, bottom right) went to Port Simpson, British Columbia, in 1857 to work among the Tsimshian Indians. He first learned their language and then began making converts to the Anglican Church. In 1862 he led a group of his converts away from Port Simpson to found a religious colony (now Old Metlakatla—fig. 1 top left) about 15 miles to the south on the Tsimpsean Peninsula. It was composed primarily of Kitlan, Kispakloats, and Kitkatla people. In 1887, beset by religious factionalism and charges of heresy (leveled at him by his bishop),

Duncan moved his colony of about 830 Tsimshian people to Alaska (Wellcome 1887). About 70 miles north of Old Metlakatla, on Annette Island, which had been given to him by President Grover Cleveland, he founded a community at first called Port Chester, later, Metlakatla (fig. 1 top right). The pioneers of this colony included (in addition to the Old Metlakatlans) Nishga and Gitksan as well as Kitselas and more Kitkatlas. Duncan designed a complete political and social order for the colony; it was democratic, utopian, and communalistic. A Native American government incorporating this sociopolitical order was established on August 7, 1887, under a constitution entitled the "Declaration of Residents." Admission to this community had as prerequisites a renunciation of the Tsimshian way of life and a commitment to the Duncan model society. In 1891 all of Annette Island, including Metlakatla, was created an Indian reservation by an act of Congress. This act explicitly contained a resolution recognizing and praising the form of government set up by the "Declaration of Residents."

In 1898, Edward Marsden, a Tsimshian from New Metlakatla and an ordained Presbyterian minister ("Haida: Traditional Culture," fig. 15, this vol.), founded a mission at Saxman, Alaska, 12 miles from Metlakatla. In the following years an anti-Duncan faction slowly emerged with Marsden at its center. His faction manifested itself originally in his support of an heir to a chiefly line among the Kitlan people in an aborted attempt to replace the "Declaration of Residents" government with a native chiefdom. Beginning in 1914 the Marsden faction seized and destroyed much of Duncan's property and much of the common property of the "Declaration" government. In 1915, Secretary of the Interior Franklin K. Lane at the insistence of the Marsden faction approved the dissolution of the "Declaration" government and established the city council form of government. In 1916 Marsden was appointed "secretary" of the reservation, an extraordinary, non-elected office, which he held until his death in 1932. Marsden had already established a Presbyterian church in Metlakatla; he forbade Duncan to practice his ministry and, according to some, even had him arrested for baptizing children. Duncan survived this harassment and kept the loyalty and respect of the major part of the community until his death in 1918. With his

294

death the Episcopal faction lost control of the community. From about 1920 until the mid 1930s, under the ravages of the ensuing and often violent factional struggle, Metlakatla declined. In 1936 the population had dwindled to 532 persons (U.S. Congress. Senate. Subcommittee of the Committee on Indian Affairs 1939:18401). Since that time the community has been making a slow and arduous recovery (P. Murray 1985).

The Duncan Society Model

The political structure of Metlakatla centered around a powerful city council composed of a mayor and 12 council members, all elected for limited terms in office. The city council exercised practically absolute economic control over the community. This economic control was the major Duncan legacy surviving from the "Declaration of Residents" government. Metlakatla corporately owned a cannery and cold-packing plant, which processed and froze seafood products, including some, such as salmon roe, that had no market in the United States, and also contracted for a sawmill and logging operation. The products of both these industries were for the most part sold directly to Japanese businessmen whose freighters took on their purchases in the Metlakatla harbor. Profits maintained all the community services, which were also managed directly by the city council. These included a clinic staffed by medical personnel from the Coast Guard station on Annette Island, a police force with a fleet of patrol cars, a fire department, an electric power system, a water and sewage system, a street system, and a marina. The two community-managed industries and the city services employed most of the Metlakatla labor force. Public buildings maintained by the city council included the city hall, the clinic, a fire station, the power plant, and a community hall.

Because the power structure of Metlakatla was neither Tsimshian nor White, but Native American–Duncanian, the community was able successfully to incorporate a sizable minority of non-Tsimshians as full-fledged members. These included Tlingits, Haidas, and mixed bloods.

Tsimshian Culture

Despite Duncan's abolition of the Tsimshian way of life, there remained a few survivals of the native culture. These included vestiges of matrilineality and the ranking system, a viable traditional factionalism, and the Tsimshian language.

In addition to having English surnames Metlakatlans maintained and recognized totemic matrifamily affiliations. These were no longer phratric; there were quite a few, many more than the four mentioned for the British Columbia Tsimshian (Boas 1916; Garfield 1966). They were perhaps survivals of a coalescence of the clan or phratry (*pte·x*) and house (*naia·ł*) designations. A fairly rigid and complex status system was expressed in many aspects of village life, especially in the preference for electing high-ranking persons to city government office.

There were in the 1980s two institutionalized factions in Metlakatla: the Duncan (Episcopal) faction and the Marsden (Presbyterian) faction. The Duncan-Marsden conflict provided an opportunity for the incarnation of traditional factionalism into modern institutions (Beynon 1941:84; Matthews 1939). The interfactional power structure was covert and strong. Its strength probably lay in the inscrutability of its checks-and-balances functions. It appeared to be effective in influencing city council and school board decisions in a manner that completely baffled outsiders who do business with the Metlakatlans. If an idea or proposal originated in one faction, the other faction tended to oppose it and to marshal logic, rhetoric, and a variety of social pressures against it. A decision could generally be made in favor of a course of action only if the antagonist faction could not organize a competent opposition to impress the city council or school board.

Less than 100 members of the Metlakatla community spoke Tsimshian in 1986. This linguistically conservative minority spoke a dialect of Coast Tsimshian (Dunn 1978) that displays a relatively minimized phonological elaboration, that is, more simplified phonological processes, than the conservative, peripheral dialects spoken at Hartley Bay, Kitkatla, and Klemtu, British Columbia.

Efforts to maintain or reinstate Tsimshian cultural elements were manifested in two ways—a cultural enrichment program in the public school and the formation of a nativistic Tsimpshean Committee. Elementary and high school courses in the Coast Tsimshian language, as well as courses in traditional history, local geography, and Tsimshian folk art, have been taught since the early 1970s. Thus, the Metlakatla school system complies with Alaska state law, passed in 1972, that requires the maintenance and enrichment of native cultural systems. The Tsimpshean Committee, consisting of three chapters, one each in Seattle, Ketchikan, and Metlakatla, has come to be recognized as the authority in matters of traditional history and geography.

The Tsimshian in British Columbia have become a reference group for the Metlakatlan nativists; Metlakatlans felt that the British Columbia groups maintained more of the traditional culture than did the Alaska community.

Perspective

The Metlakatla people are unique among the Indians of southeastern Alaska in being immigrants—refugees from religious turmoil and unsettled land questions—and in having been granted a reservation. They have not generally participated as a group in the activities of the Tlingit

296

Smithsonian, NAA: top left: 42977-C; center left: 38583-C; bottom left, Amer. Mus. of Nat. Hist., New York: 42307; top right: Natl. Geographic Soc., Washington: FS-N1; U. of Wash. Lib., Special Coll., Seattle: center right, 2750; bottom right, 2779.

Fig. 1. Old and New Metlakatla. top left, Old Metlakatla, B.C., which had standardized frame houses (uniform to foster the ideal of equality), a fish cannery plant, sawmill, brickyard, sash factory, blacksmith shop, bakery and weaving house, carpenter shop, trading post, hospital, school, and church (Usher 1974:68–75). Photograph possibly by Edward Dossetter, about 1880. center left, Interior of Rev. William Duncan's Mission Sunday School, Old Metlakatla, showing carved poles with crest representations. Duncan permitted some of the traditional use of Tsimshian crest organization, which he felt was beneficial in keeping social order (Usher 1974:93, 153). To live in "Old" Metlakatla "people had to conform to 15 laws of conduct, which required them to give up many features of the old life, such as native dances, potlatching, shamanism, gambling, face-painting, and alcohol, and also to attend religious instruction, observe the Sabbath, send their children to school, build neat houses, pay the village tax, and be cleanly, industrious, peaceful and honest in trade" (Duff 1964:93). Photographed before 1883. bottom left, Women taught the Euro-American manner of spinning. Weaving of wool, part of the industrial education, was intended to develop into a profitable business. Photograph by Edward Dossetter, Old Metlakatla, 1881. top right, New Metlakatla, Annette I., Alaska. Photograph by Amos Burg, 1929. center right, Interior of Indian Church, New Metlakatla. Photograph by John N. Cobb, 1908. bottom right, Rev. William Duncan, who established the Christian mission. Photograph by John N. Cobb, probably New Metlakatla, 1909.

and Alaska Haida. They did not organize a camp of the Alaska Native Brotherhood (Drucker 1958:20–21, 74–75), join in the fight for a land settlement, or become a party to the Alaska Native Claims Settlement Act of 1971. Nevertheless, individual Tsimshians from Metlakatla played important roles in these movements and events. Peter Simpson was one of the founders of the Alaska Native Brotherhood, and William Paul, the Tlingit leader in the fight for land settlement, gave Simpson credit for having inspired him to begin the fight (Tlingit and Haida Indian Tribes of Alaska 1985:15, 17). The Rev. Edward Marsden was also an early supporter of the Alaska Native Brotherhood (Drucker 1958:17).

In 1985 the resident Indian population at Metlakatla was estimated to be 1,300 (U.S. Bureau of Indian Affairs. Financial Management Office 1985).

Prehistory of the Central Coast of British Columbia

PHILIP M. HOBLER

The Central Coast of British Columbia extends from Douglas Channel on the north to Rivers Inlet on the south, a distance of some 240 kilometers. In age, Central Coast archeological sites (fig. 1) range from nearly 10,000 years to the historic period. Components from the early period are represented at several sites. Throughout most of this long span, human population appears to have remained small. Even taking into consideration factors of natural site destruction and the low visibility of the earlier archeological sites, the first 5,000 years or so on the Central Coast of British Columbia must have seen a relatively low human population. The number of archeological sites began to increase about 2,000 years ago. This growth had its roots as early as 4,500–5,000 years ago when a complex of factors began to contribute to increasing settlement stability. It is manifest archeologically in the accumulation of shellfish remains at sites.

By late prehistoric times, if not before, the region was presumably inhabited by the ancestors of the historic peoples, the southernmost Tsimshian at Kitkaata and Kitasoo, the Northern Wakashan–speaking Haisla, Haihais, Bella Bella, and Oowekeeno, and the Salishan-speaking Bella Coola.

Systematic archeology has been conducted in the Bella Bella area (Drucker 1943; Pomeroy 1980), the Bella Coola area (Hobler 1970), Milbanke Sound (Simonsen 1973), Rivers and Fish Egg inlets (Donald Mitchell, personal communication 1985), and the Douglas Channel area (Mishra 1975). Hobler (1982) reviewed the history of Central Coast field work.

For the archeologist, the lists of old settlement names and locations (Boas 1898; McIlwraith 1948; Olson 1955) have been particularly useful. These provide an understanding of the nature of aboriginal settlement distributions. Specifically they have made it possible to narrow the search for archeological sites in the difficult terrain and heavy vegetation of the Central Coast.

The method of ethnographic analogy remains the soundest framework for the interpretation of the prehistory of the Central Coast over the last 4,000–5,000 years. Adaptive strategies and techniques, once developed, have tended to persist over long periods of time. This gives an archeological picture of cultural stability. Archeological classifications have tended to magnify the importance of small changes in technology over time, but it should be emphasized that the principal pattern is really one of continuity.

Culture

Cultural activities varied with the environment. Salmon were, of course, of paramount importance throughout the area. On the inner coast, with its large steep rivers, salmon were concentrated in a small area. Summer and fall saw impressive numbers of salmon entering the rivers to spawn, although a few were available almost year round. The inner coast rivers were also favored with a major run of eulachon in the early spring. There the hunting of land mammals, particularly deer and mountain goat, provided a major supplemental food source. In contrast, on the outer portions of the coast salmon are distributed over a large number of smaller spawning streams, and land mammal hunting was not so productive. The intertidal resources and bottomfish were of much greater importance in Native diet. In the ethnographic pattern the aspects of Native technology that most stand out are the working of wood and plant fibers; large houses, massive carvings, canoes, bark clothing, basketry, and matting dominated Native technology. Because of factors of preservation such items are all represented poorly if at all in most archeological inventories. Another complex that is characteristic of the ethnographic pattern is ceremonialism with its related emphasis upon wealth and social rank. Understandably, this too is seldom seen in the archeological record.

Despite the primacy of artifacts made of wood and plant fibers in ethnographic collections, virtually all artifacts recovered from most archeological sites are of nonperishable materials such as stone, bone, antler, shell, and tooth. Excavations at the late prehistoric site of Axeti at Kwatna have provided a measure of the magnitude of this bias (Hobler 1976). The matrix at part of Axeti was a black anerobic mud deposited in the intertidal zone where the Kwatna River mixes with the sea. Midden deposits extended from the land down into the mud of the intertidal zone. Normal absence of organic artifacts was found in the midden of the shore, but once in the waterlogged zone the anerobic mud resulted in the preservation of a large and remarkable sample of artifacts of wood or plant fiber. Since Axeti had both a waterlogged and a nonwaterlogged side it was possible to estimate what information is lost through normal decay processes. The comparison indicated that a significant proportion of artifact types, probably more than half, are lost.

Structures

Posts and beams from historic plank houses of traditional construction are not uncommon (fig. 2). Also observed were several isolated sites with the remains of scaled-down versions of traditional post-and-beam Native houses associated with historic refuse. These are known to have been used as seasonal camps by trappers and others and may be a hint as to the nature of shelter types that were used at prehistoric seasonal camps.

Architectural pit and depressions observed on the Central Coast are of two kinds: subterranean storage pits and rectangular house depressions. House depressions are not common, and only a few examples are known from clearly prehistoric contexts, such as the site of Anutcix at Kwanta. Two unique sites at Kimsquit are true villages with numbers of large contiguous rectangular house depressions. The largest of these has more than 20 such structures arranged in rows (Hobler 1972). Associated refuse indicates a brief occupation in the mid-eighteenth century (Hobler 1984). Some historic Native sites have depressions from root cellars, a probable European introduction used to store garden products.

The remains of planks, probably from a house, were encountered at Grant Anchorage in a shell midden deposit about 2,000 years old (Simonsen 1973). At a site on top of Mackenzie's Rock in Dean Channel, excavation in a shell midden revealed the preserved remains of a floor joist with planks running at right angles to it at a depth of 1.5 meters (Hobler 1983). Radiocarbon dates suggest an age of A.D. 1200–1500 for the Mackenzie's Rock structure. At Kwatna, deposits of about the same age and depth at the site of Nutlitliqotlenk revealed a thin uniform compacted surface in a subrectangular outline, 6 by 10 meters (Carlson 1972). Shallow depressions are suggestive of post or hearth areas, but a definitive pattern of house posts could not be identified.

Shell Middens

Shell middens are the most significant archeological remains and represent the locus of concentrated cultural activities. In other areas of the coast tiny shell middens (less than 2.5 cubic meters) greatly outnumber larger

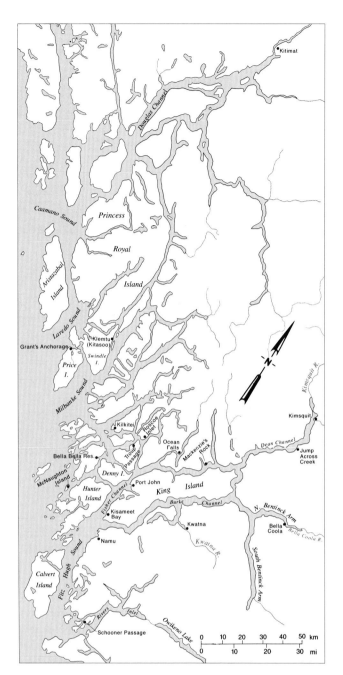

Fig. 1. Archeological sites in the central B.C. coastal area.

middens, but on the Central Coast this pattern is not present. Almost half the shell middens in the Central Coast sample are classed as large (greater than 25 cubic meters), and several are estimated to be greater than 2,000 cubic meters. The amount of shell present in middens decreases as one enters the relatively fresh waters of the inner coast's fiord zone. The outer coast middens are rich in shell, many containing large areas of nearly pure unfragmented shell. Most midden sites contain evidence of occupations extending over long periods of time, but usually survey collections do not permit the identification of the range of phases or time periods present below the surface.

299

Fig. 2. Remnants of a mid-19th century house, with 4 carved posts still standing. On Troup Pass 20 km north of Bella Bella, B.C., this house was excavated (Carlson 1984). Photograph by Philip M. Hobler, 1983.

Fig. 3. Pictograph at Port John, B.C., the largest rock art site (FaSx 4) recorded on the central coast. The style suggests a late prehistoric date. The largest figure measures about 1.2 m. Photograph by Philip M. Hobler, 1968.

In the 1970s an aged Bella Bella informant provided names for his recorded shell midden sites and identified the major winter villages (Pomeroy 1980). Surprisingly, the largest, deepest shell middens often had no names or were referred to as insignificant. In contrast, the important winter villages often showed little shell midden. This contradicts the predisposition among coastal archeologists to equate massive midden accumulation with winter village occupation (Fladmark 1975).

Pictographs and Petroglyphs

On the Central Coast, rock art sites represent the third most common site type. Pictographs significantly outnumber petroglyphs (figs. 3–4). Despite the considerable difference in the method of execution (painting as opposed to pecking), there is definite overlap in subject matter and even style, which suggests that it may not be correct to consider them to be of different ages. Historic subjects are uncommon, little traditional knowledge about the sites has been recorded, and so most of the work may be prehistoric. A common element in Bella Bella area rock art is a pattern of repeated dots with anywhere from two to several dozen arranged in rows (Hobler 1975). Two pictographs show ships with high aft cabins and rigging suggestive of Asian junks (Hobler 1983). Two rock art studies taking a coast-wide perspective deal in part with Central Coast sites (Lundy 1974; Hill and Hill 1974).

Burials

From Kwatna eastward burials in shell middens are practically nonexistent. The rocky fiord environment provided numerous small rockshelters that were used extensively for burial. Typical is a small rockshelter with from one to four cedar boxes, each with the remains of one or more individuals. Mummification has been observed in the driest shelters. Bella Coola ethnographic accounts relate the once extensive use of box burials in trees, but only one such site has been recorded. Some inner coast villages with historic components are associated with cemeteries with flexed burials in cedar boxes.

In contrast, in the Bella Bella area rockshelter and tree burials are far less common than on the inner coast. Historic burial sites are usually near villages. They consist of from one to three grave houses, each containing from three or four to as many as a dozen burials each in a wooden box. The grave houses are semi- or fully underground rectangular log and plank structures measuring three to four meters on a side. Roofs are low and flat, often almost level with the ground surface. Prehistoric outer coast burials are commonly found in shell middens, a marked contrast to the inner coast. The burials recovered from Namu included two distinct types: single inhumations and group burials. The group burials may be of people who died together through warfare or disease (Curtin 1984). An alternate explanation is that they are simply all that is left after a structure like the historic Bella Bella burial house decomposed.

In the Namu skeletal population Curtin (1984) found exaggerated sexual dimorphism in comparison with other coastal sites. A few Namu burials have elaborate grave goods. In the late prehistoric levels of Namu there is a decline in total number of burials and status-related grave goods are found with children and adolescents as well as with adults. Some of the Namu and other Central Coast survey skeletal samples have been described by Finnegan (1972).

Fig. 4. Petroglyph site at Jump Across Creek on upper Dean Channel, B.C. This is one of several human figures on the bedrock in the upper intertidal zone. The size of the figure is about 90 cm. Figure has been chalked. Photograph by Philip M. Hobler, 1972.

Fig. 5. Fish trap enclosing wall of stone at half tide, Troup Passage, B.C. Photograph by Philip M. Hobler, 1972.

Fish Traps

In riverine settlements weirs have been poorly preserved because of flooding and channel change, and thus they are probably significantly underrepresented in the archeological site sample. In contrast, from Kwatna westward to the outer coast, stone wall intertidal fish traps (fig. 5) are typical (Hobler 1970; Pomeroy 1976). They are designed so that fish swim over the walls on a high tide and are trapped as the tide runs out. They appear to have fallen into disuse early in the historic period, as little information concerning their function is available. Some of the walls, more than 100 meters long, show complex histories of renovations and additions. While weirs in the big inner coast rivers were used exclusively for salmon, stone wall intertidal traps may have functioned for both salmon and a variety of small bottomfish that feed near the shore.

Intertidal Lithic Artifacts

In the middle and outer portions of the Central Coast are sites that consist of flaked stone, sometimes in considerable quantity, distributed within the intertidal zone. Generally sites are without contiguous deposits on the shore. Because they are surface sites they are difficult to place in time. They include a lot of diversity from site to site and thus may represent an extended period (Apland 1982). The original interpretation of these unique site situations was that they represented camps occupied during a time when sea levels were one to three meters lower than at present. Rising sea levels subsequent to abandonment would result in their present locus in the intertidal zone. An alternative interpretation, that the cultural material was simply washed out from the land, was rejected in a study (Hobler 1979) that tested for sorting of the intertidal artifacts through downslope

movement on the beach by wave action.

Most archeologists working on the outer parts of the Central Coast have recognized that the lowermost levels of the older shell middens are presently being undercut by the sea. Hydrographic observations record a submergence rate for the outer part of the coast around Bella Bella of two millimeters a year (F.E. Stephenson, personal communication 1982). Assuming the current subsidence rate for the outer coast has been consistent through time, intertidal lithic sites could be on the order of 2,000–3,000 years old. Artifact typology suggests they may be older, although the near absence of microblades and microblade cores may set lower limits at not much greater than 5,000 years. An independent argument for mid to late Holocene lower sea levels on the outer Central Coast comes from a series of wave eroded dunes. These seem to have begun to develop prior to 4,000 years ago when lowered relative sea levels subjected large freshly exposed areas of beach sand to reworking by wind action (Andrews and Retherford 1976).

Site Distribution

Most of the largest shell middens are on the outer portions of the coast. Sites older than about 500 B.C. tend to be found mostly in the outer and middle areas, although this pattern may be due to factors of preservation. Pomeroy (1980) undertook a reconstruction of the traditional territories of each of the bands that came together as the Bella Bella. Within these territories he specifically considered the stream-by-stream salmon escapement data compiled by government agencies as a way of assessing the resource potential for each territory. These he related to archeological site distributions.

Two quantitative studies dealing somewhat more generally with Central Coast site distributions have been undertaken in the Bella Coola and Bella Bella territories. *301*

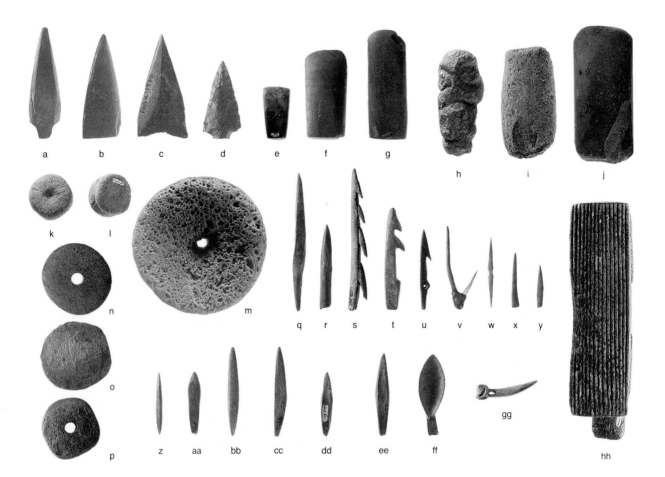

Simon Fraser U., Mus. of Achaeol. and Ethnology, Burnaby, B.C.: a, FaSu 2–1335; b, FaSu 2–2157; c, FaSu 2–1946; d, FaSu 2–1965; e, FaSu 2–2980; f, FaSu 1–962; g, FaSu 2–1419; h, FaSu 1–1905; i, FaSu 2–459; j, FaSu 2–1557; k, FaSu 2–1366; l, FaSu 2–281; m, FaSu 1–1320; n, FaSu 2–2521; o, FaSu 2–61; p, FaSu 2–1321; q, FaSu 2–2659; r, FaSu 2–1734; s, FaSu 10–605; t, FaSu 2–2156; u, FaSu 2–2393; v, FaSu 1–107; w, FaSu 2–245; x, FaSu 2–351; y, FaSu 2–2546; z, FaSu 2-2235; aa, FaSu 10–1042; bb, FaSu 2–1673; cc, FaSu 2–1918; dd, FaSu 2–617; ee, FaSu 2–1893; ff, FaSu 10–358; gg, FaSu 10–978; hh, FaSu 2–500.

Fig. 6. Artifacts from late prehistoric sites: a-c, ground slate projectile points; d, small flaked stone projectile point; e-g, ground nephrite and greenstone adz blades; h-i, hammerstone-grinders; j, stone hand maul with oval cross-section; k-l, circular stones; m, perforated stone disk; n-p, discoidal objects ground from sea mammal bone; q-r, awl-like pointed bone tools; s-u, unilaterally barbed harpoon points, with u perforated for a line to the harpoon shaft; v, small composite fishhook found in waterlogged deposits at the Axeti site; w, simple bone fish gorge; x-z, bone points from composite fishing implements; aa-cc, bipointed arming tips from composite toggling harpoons; dd-ee, valves from composite toggling harpoons; ff, carved bone spoon with broken handle; gg, carved zoomorphic bone blanket pin; hh, whale bone cedar bark beater, viewed from the grooved lower surface. Length of a, 5.2 cm; b-d to same scale. Length of e, 4.1 cm; e-g, q-r, w-z, aa-ee to same scale. Length of h, 9.8 cm; i-p, s-u, ff-hh to same scale. Length of v, 4.4 cm.

The first deals with site grouping (Hobler 1981). In the more open terrain west of Fisher Channel archeological sites are relatively uniformly distributed. In contrast, east of Fisher Channel, distributions are discontinuous and sites occur in definite clusters. The analysis of these clusters began with a calculation of distances between each site and its closest neighbor. The results showed that some 58 percent of the sites in the sample have their nearest neighboring archeological site within less than one kilometer. Pictographs and intertidal lithic sites are the most widely dispersed archeological features with the least tendency to occur in clusters. House pits, burials, and shell middens are the most likely to be found in groups.

Another study of Central Coast archeological site distributions examined the correlation between site concentrations and the salmon productivity of the region's streams (Hobler 1983a). Using spawning records of the 1940s–1980s, this analysis correlated the tonnage of spawning fish in each stream with the number and kinds of archeological features within a five-kilometer radius. This produced a rough measure of the extent to which productive spawning areas attracted human settlement. On the outer portion of the coast where factors of terrain and other river spawning species could be held constant, the results were clear: the amount of salmon in a stream showed no correlation with the amount of archeological evidence in the vicinity of that stream. Looking at these results without the ethnographic record to guide interpretations one might be tempted to speculate that salmon were not an important food resource. The best explanation is that, although the salmon were paramount in providing a rich and stable existence, on the outer coast during most of the year salmon were not available for harvest. Smoking and drying the harvested salmon allowed for year-long

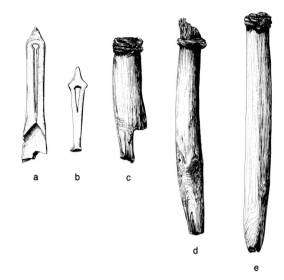

Simon Fraser U., Mus. of Archaeol. and Ethnol., Burnaby, B.C.: left, FaSu 1–1929; right, FaSu 10–710.
Fig. 7. Carved figurines. left, 2 individuals standing back to back, separated by a perforation running from top to base; antler, length 75 mm. right, Human figure of unusual form; bone, length 183 mm.

Simon Fraser U., Mus. of Archaeol. and Ethnol., Burnaby, B.C.: a, FaSu 1–1257; b, FaSu 1–437; c, FaSu 1–416; d, FaSu 1–1309; e, FaSu 1–1273.
Fig. 8. Wooden spoons and wedges recovered from the water-logged deposits of the Axeti site. These splitting wedges exhibit the usual twisted withe collets. Drawings by Barbara Hodgson. Length of e, 32 cm, others to same scale.

preservation, thus making it possible for winter villages and other kinds of seasonal settlements to be distributed in response to a broader range of locational considerations. These probably included accessibility for trade and the seasonal availability of other resources.

Comparison of Excavated Sites

For purposes of systematic comparison, collections from a number of excavated sites or portions of sites have been selected. Most site collections included have more than 200 artifacts. Historic components, where present, were excluded from the analysis. The artifact types were organized under the categories flaked stone, ground stone, bone and antler, shell, and tooth. At EeSu 5 (Chapman 1982) the huge sample of obsidian debitage was omitted from the tally as it would have obscured all other variation.

Collections from sites or subsections of sites included in the comparison were: both the nonwaterlogged portion and the waterlogged portion of Axeti excluding artifacts of perishable materials; Nutlitliqotlenk at the mouth of the Kwatna River; the site of Nutl at Kimsquit near the mouth of the Dean River; Anutcix on the Kwatna River; shell midden at Grant Anchorage; the O'Connor site near Port Hardy, just south of the Central Coast as defined here (Chapman 1982); Namu; ElTb 10 on McNaughten Island; and Joashila in Kwatna Inlet.

The quantitative analyses of these assemblages are based upon the Central Coast pattern of relative stability of material cultural inventories over the time these sites were occupied. Thus, even though not all collections may represent exactly the same time there is some justification for making the comparisons.

An average linkage cluster analysis compared the assemblages on the basis of the simple presence or absence of individual artifact types. The results reflect clusters that are understandable in the light of both regional ethnic divisions and site chronologies. For example, sites at Kwatna and Kimsquit fall into the first recognizable cluster. All are of Bella Coola or of mixed Bella Coola–Bella Bella origin. The terms Kwatna phase and Anutcix phase have been used to refer to components present at these sites (Carlson 1983a). Artifact types that seem to set this group apart are circular stones (both perforated and unperforated), greenstone adz blades and fragments, and a tool type called hammerstone-grinders. Another cluster encompasses sites located in the outer coast. The cluster analysis places the O'Connor site at Port Hardy within this group, though it is located within the area of the Kwakiutl. Artifact assemblages within this category share with the first grouping a well-represented small bone tool industry but have somewhat more diversification of sea mammal hunting technology and lack the other diagnostics of the first category. A third cluster consists of relatively early sites or ones where some earlier materials are present.

Change Through Time

Over the last 10,000 years there has been measurable cultural change on the Central Coast. The first 5,000 years (Carlson 1979; "Cultural Antecedents" this vol.) saw the establishment of an initial population probably as part of general southward coastal population movements. Archeological evidence for this period, at least at its beginning, is only thinly represented. But trade contacts, as evidenced

303

by obsidian source studies, indicate even at this early time, intimate knowledge of area resources extending into the mountains of the Coast Range beyond the heads of the fiords. Certainly by 3000 B.C. there was a widely distributed, small population throughout the Central Coast. This must have included the valleys of the inner coast rivers with their rich salmon resources. The apparent absence of earlier archeological sites in these river valleys is probably a result of their frequent flooding and channel change. For example, only half the known mid-nineteenth century village sites in the Bella Coola Valley remained visible in the 1980s. At the same site loss rate, half per century, over the last 5,000 years it is understandable why older sites are not commonly found in these valleys.

A major shift in the nature of the archeological evidence occurs after roughly 2500 B.C. At about this time the rate of accumulation of refuse deposits increases markedly and mollusk shells begin to show up in quantity, forming middens. These changes appear to be coast-wide (Borden 1975; Fladmark 1975). A similar phenomenon has been observed at coastal sites in some areas of the world other than the Northwest Coast (Nash 1983). It has been suggested that the changes may relate to as yet poorly understood climatic shifts that resulted in western red cedar rapidly becoming codominant with western hemlock in coastal forests (Hebda and Mathewes 1984).

After about 2500 B.C. microblade and core technology are gone, and the relative importance of stone flaking begins a slow decline. In some sites it maintains its importance as late as A.D. 1–400. Although never totally absent in later excavated collections, flaked stone after about A.D. 200 nowhere constitutes a significant item of technology. In some sites, perhaps, mostly on the outer portions of the coast, the near disappearance of flaked stone seems to have taken place 1,000 years or so earlier. Circumstances of preservation before 3000 B.C. may obscure potential continuities in bone tool technology although nonartifactual bone is represented. Certainly, between about 2500 B.C. and A.D. 1, bone tools, most of which are related to fishing, begin to characterize the material cultural inventories. Pecked, ground, and polished stone steadily gained in frequency and appeared to be replacing flaked stone for wood working and other functions.

The cultural pattern of the later prehistoric is typified by several excavated sites at Kwatna and Kimsquit. Collections show the virtual absence of flaked stone although small quantities of obsidian micro-debitage are found in the Kimsquit sites, and a few small triangular notched points of basalt (fig. 6d) are found in both areas. Common pecked stone artifacts in these late sites are the loaf-shaped hammerstone-grinders. Showing battering on the ends and smoothing on the nether surface, many are made of soft granite and would have been of limited utility

as tools. Native informants recall stories of their use in a game in which they were thrown at targets. Of comparable frequency are greenstone adz blades and fragments (fig. 6 e-g). These were probably used in wooden hafts. When broken, they were reduced by bipolar percussion to produce quantities of small flakes that appear to have been used without further modification. Less common but still highly characteristic of late prehistoric assemblages are circular stones (fig. 6k-l). In surface treatment they range from smooth through dimpled to fully perforated. They are of uncertain function although one elderly informant suggested their use as rolling targets used in bow practice. Other ground and polished tools include a few triangular slate points (fig. 6a-c) possibly used as arming tips in composite toggling harpoons.

In later prehistoric collections many types of tools of bone and antler are found. Most frequent are small bone objects, some pointed and others not. A few are clearly fish gorges (fig. 6w). Others may be parts of various kinds of composite fishing and sea mammal hunting tools such as composite fishhooks (fig. 6x-z), composite toggling harpoons (fig. 6aa-ee), and possibly other types. Less common objects of art are shown in figure 7.

The waterlogged cultural deposits at Axeti at Kwatna yielded more than 1,000 artifacts of normally perishable materials such as wood and plant fiber (figs. 6v, 8). These include a broad variety of objects such as wooden stakes, splitting wedges, hafts, bent fishhooks, small two-piece fishhooks, and spoons. Plant fiber artifacts in the Axeti collection consist largely of hundreds of rope, cordage, and string fragments, many with knots. There are bark mats, openwork and plaited bags and baskets, and complex basketry hats.

How far back the archeological evidence can be identified with historic peoples is a difficult question. A distinction can be made between sites in historic Wakashan (Haihais, Bella Bella, and Oowekeeno) and Salishan (Bella Coola) territory, reflecting both cultural differences and environmental preferences. This distinction goes back to the first century A.D., but earlier it becomes blurred. The increased number of sites after about A.D. 1200 is probably the result of in-place population growth rather than migration, since a number of sites show considerable cultural continuity from about A.D. 1200 onward. Thus it seems reasonable to infer some 1,800 years of Wakashan and Salishan presence in the region.

Going back earlier is more speculative. Archeology suggests that the inhabitants of the region of some 10,000 years ago came as bearers of a maritime culture from the north. But linguistic relations and distributions seem to argue against a model of continuous southward movement. The Wakashan and Salishan languages of the region are the northernmost members of their respective families, and they may have reached their historic territories from the south. One interpretation (Suttles and Elmendorf

1963; Kinkade and Powell 1976:91–92) suggests that Bella Coola is the northern end of a once continuous distribution of Salishan extending northward from Georgia Strait, perhaps in inner coast and river environments, and that this continuum was broken by an expansion of Northern Wakashan, perhaps from the northern end of Vancouver Island. The discontinuity in the archeological record around 2500 B.C. and the changes that occurred between then and A.D. 1 may reflect the movements of speakers of Salishan and Wakashan.

Haisla

CHARLES HAMORI-TOROK

The Haisla ('hīslä) are the native people of the upper reaches of Douglas Channel and of Gardner Canal on the northern, inner coast of British Columbia. Their language belongs to the Northern branch of the Wakashan family and is the northernmost member of the family.* In the nineteenth century there were two divisions of Haisla, the Kitamaat of Douglas Channel and the Kitlope of Gardner Canal (fig. 1). Population loss among the Kitlope was especially great, and the survivors gradually moved to Kitamaat. Haisla culture began to change radically with the arrival of missionaries in the late 1870s. Information on traditional culture comes mainly from work in the 1930s with the Kitamaat people and refers to conditions in the late nineteenth and early twentieth centuries, though historical narratives reach back to an earlier time.

External Relations

The Haisla were somewhat isolated from other Wakashans. Their nearest neighbors were the Southern Tsimshian at Kitkiata at the lower end of Douglas Channel and at Kitkatla and Klemtu on the outer coast. The Coast Tsimshian of the Lower Skeena were on the coast to the north, and from Kitamaat it was also easy to reach the Coast Tsimshian of the Skeena Canyon by way of the Kitimat River and Lakelse Lake. The Haisla also had contact with the Gitksan and the Bulkley River Carrier by this route and with the Carrier while hunting in the Coast Mountains (Jenness 1934:232–233, 1943:480–481). From the Kitlope village there was an overland route to the Bella Coola village of Kimsquit, and these two villages intermarried (McIlwraith 1948, 1:17, 2:505). The nearest Wakashans and closest linguistic relatives of the Haisla were the Haihais, Bella Bella, and Oowekeeno.

* The phonemes of Haisla are (unaspirated stops and affricates) b, d, ꝫ, λ, ġ, gʷ, g̣, g̣ʷ, ʔ; (aspirated stops and affricates) p, t, c, ƛ, k, kʷ, q, qʷ; (glottalized) p̓, t̓, c̓, ƛ̓, k̓, k̓ʷ, q̓, q̓ʷ; (voiceless continuants) s, ł, x, xʷ, x̣, x̣ʷ, h; (plain resonants) m, n, l, y, w; (glottalized resonants) m̓, n̓, l̓, y̓, w̓. Phonetic vowels are i, u, ə, and a. However, Lincoln and Rath interpret i and u as allophones of y and w respectively and ə as conditioned by a syllabic resonant, leaving a as the only vowel with phonemic status (Lincoln and Rath 1980:25–30). Phonetic vowels appear in transcriptions of Haisla words given here. The stress accent (v̀) is realized as stress or low tone, for some speakers accompanied by pharyngealization.

Origins

Haisla traditions suggest that they are in origin an amalgam of Northern Wakashans and Tsimshians. One tells that the village of Kitamaat was founded by people from Rivers Inlet, who were joined by people from the Tsimshian village of Kitselas (Olson 1940:187; Lopatin 1945:21; Drucker 1950:159). Another tradition (Olson 1940:192) ascribes a Haida origin to the Eagle clan.

Culturally the Haisla were close to the Tsimshian, especially in technology and social organization. They were the only Wakashan-speaking people with a fully developed matrilineal clan system. On the other hand, like other Northern Wakashans, they had a well developed set of secret societies.

Their clan system was almost certainly Tsimshian in origin, just as the Tsimshian secret societies were probably largely Haisla in origin. Tsimshian traditions (Boas 1890: 831, 1916:509–510) say that the Gispakloats people got the secret societies along with the famous name Legaik through a marriage with the Kitamaat, while the Kitkatla people got their secret societies through marriages with the Kitlope and the Bella Bella.

Environment

Haisla territory falls within the Northern Inner Coast climatic region (J.M. Powell 1965:fig. 1). It experiences greater extremes in temperature than the outer coast, with hot, dry summers and colder winters with heavy snow. During the period 1931–1960, Kitamaat received an annual mean snowfall of 118 inches (Canada. Department of Transportation 1968:18). It also experiences strong winds. Over several generations the Kitamaat people moved their village a number of times in search of a more sheltered location (Drucker 1950:159).

Culture

Subsistence

All five species of Pacific salmon run in Haisla waters, but cohoes, chums, and pinks were the most important. The Haisla took salmon in the salt water in stone tidal pounds

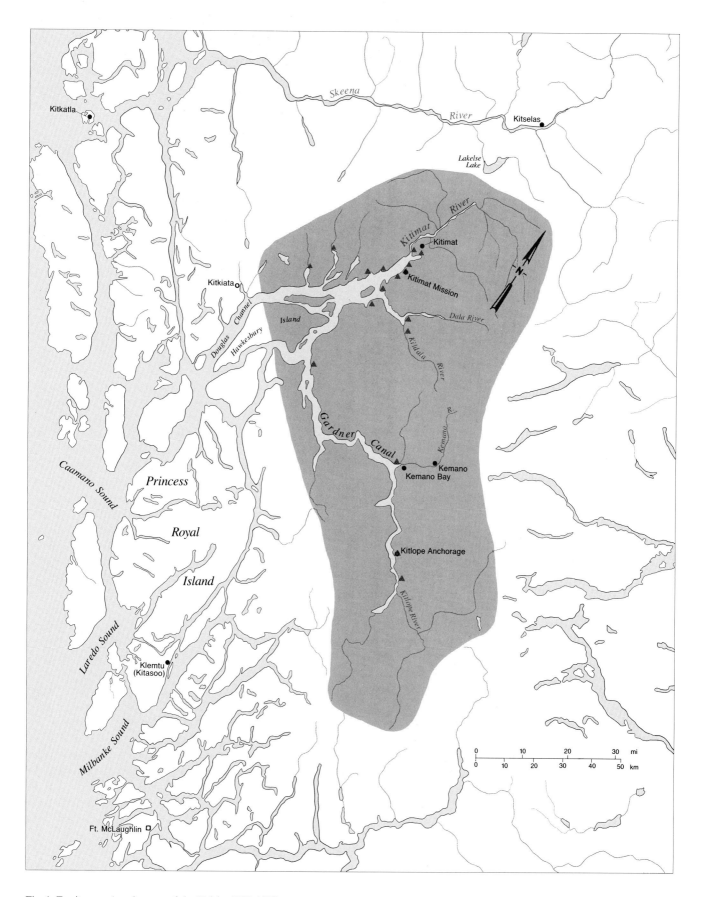

Fig. 1. Territory and settlements of the Haisla, 1860–1890.

HAISLA

and in rivers in traps and weirs, as well as with harpoons, leisters, dip nets, and trawl nets. Eulachon were especially important, with runs in the Kitimat, Kildala, Kemano, and Kitlope rivers. These fish were caught in such numbers that they were an important export. They were caught in a long funnel-shaped net that is widely used on the northern Northwest Coast and that tradition says was invented by a Haisla girl who was inspired by watching a bullhead (sculpin) swallow young trout (Drucker 1950: 240). For halibut the Haisla used the northern-style two-piece, V-shaped hook.

Land mammals were much more important than sea mammals. Hunters took mountain goats by driving them with dogs and spearing them, deer by driving them with dogs into the water, and black bears, grizzlies, and marmots in deadfalls. Haisla women gathered shellfish and a variety of vegetable foods. Berries were especially important, and the Haisla burned areas to encourage their growth (Lopatin 1945:14). Kitlope was famous for crab apples, and, according to the Bella Coola, people from as far away as Kitkatla had rights to harvest them there (McIlwraith 1948, 1:133, 2:505).

Technology

Haisla technology shared many features of other northern Northwest Coast peoples. Woodworkers used the chopping adz, hafted stone ledge, and elbow adz. The usual house had a gable roof, double ridgepole, vertical wall planks inserted into slotted roof plates and sills, a painted facade, a central fireplace and smokehole, and walls of sleeping areas lined with cedarbark mats. Canoes were of the northern type, those for river use made without the usual vertical cutwater, and some of cottonwood rather than cedar. Containers included wooden dishes, kerfed-corner boxes and chests, burden baskets made by wrapped twining, and storage baskets by plain twining.

Woodworking was a man's occupation. Women made shredded cedar bark, wove mats and fabric for robes and packstraps, and made baskets. Both sexes dressed hides.

Clothing and Adornment

Clothing included spruce-root rain hats and fur caps and robes of sewn skins or woven yellow cedarbark or mountain-goat wool. Women wore aprons of shredded cedarbark or buckskin. Men went naked in good weather. Traveling overland, people wore leggings of woven cedarbark for protection against brush. They usually went barefoot, but for traveling in snow, "rich men and good hunters" had moccasins of sealskin or bearhide, while others "wrapped pieces of cedarbark matting around their feet" (Drucker 1950:260). The Haisla also used snowshoes that were oval in form and had withe fillers.

308   Both sexes wore the hair long, men loose or in a knot,

women in a single braid. Both sexes were tattooed with clan crests and wore ear and nose ornaments. Women wore labrets.

Social Organization

The basic social unit was the matrilineal clan, which had territorial rights, crests, and a set of ranked men's and women's names. The clans functioned independently for ordinary purposes but formed alliances for ceremonial ones. Marriage within the clan was forbidden; between members of allied clans it was not forbidden but it was rare (Olson 1940:169, 185). It appears that during the nineteenth century and perhaps into the twentieth the number of clans changed, as some became nearly extinct and merged with others, and that there were shifts in alliances. Researchers in the 1930s identified five functioning clans—Eagle, Beaver, Raven, Blackfish (Orca), and Salmon (also called Wolf), as well as a nearly extinct Crow (Lopatin 1945:21; Olson 1940:161; Drucker 1950: 281; cf. Boas 1891:604, 1897:328).

Clans were allied, producing a set of three ceremonial groups: Eagle, Beaver-Raven-Crow, and Blackfish-Salmon. In feast and potlatches, the hosts always sat near the door, while the other two groups sat on opposite sides of the house; for example, when the Blackfish or Salmon were hosts, members of these clans sat near the door, while the Eagles sat on the right and the Beavers, Ravens, and Crows sat on the left. Clan chiefs and upper-class members had regular seats. The hosts presented gifts in a fixed order, first to the highest ranking person on one side, next to the highest on the other, then to the second ranking person on the first side, and so on, giving alternately to right and left sides (Olson 1940:172–173).

Haisla society was divided into nobles, commoners, and slaves. There were also two chiefs at Kitimaat, the heads of the Beaver and Eagle clans, and one at Kitlope, the head of the Beaver clan, who had a special title. Within each clan there were both nobles and commoners. Nobles were persons who had received inherited names, validated through potlatching. They occupied ranked seats at potlatches, were eligible for initiation into the higher grades of the secret societies, and could succeed to chiefly positions. Commoners were untitled people, some the younger siblings of nobles.

A clan chief was usually succeeded by the eldest of his sisters' sons. If he had no nephew, his successor might be a younger brother, a sister's daughter, or a sister. Succession to any title required a potlatch.

Marriages were arranged between young people who were members of different clans but were of the same social status and, preferably, were cross-cousins. A young man of the upper class would most likely marry his mother's brother's daughter but possibly his father's sister's daughter (Olson 1940:185). Drucker (1963) notes a third preference, for father's brother's daughter, while Olson gives another (possibly best for commoners), for mother's father's sister's son's daughter. (Presumably these last two were possible only if the parties belonged to different clans; they could belong to the same clan.) For a proper marriage, the prospective groom's clansmen had to give wealth to the prospective bride's clan to mark the engagement. The wedding came as much as a year later, when the groom and his clan brought more wealth to the bride's house. The couple then lived in the bride's house until her people "redeemed" her, that is, reciprocated with gifts to the groom's family of greater value than what they had received. After this the couple lived in the groom's house, until the death of his mother's brother.

The Haisla kinship terms are bifurcate merging in the parents' generation, merging mother's sister with mother and father's brother with father, while distinguishing mother's brother and father's sister. They are of the Iroquois type in ego's generation, merging parallel cousins with siblings while distinguishing cross-cousins with a separate term (Olson 1940:184). The Haisla terms are structured like those of Tsimshian rather than like those of other Wakashan languages. Comparison of Haisla and Kwakiutl terms for parents, aunts, and uncles suggests that in Haisla an earlier lineal terminology was restructured to fit a unilineal social system (Lowie 1960: 128–129). However, the Haisla did not adopt all of the behavior patterns associated with unilineal descent; unlike their matrilineal neighbors and like their fellow Wakashans, they did not have classes of kin whom they had to avoid and classes with whom they enjoyed privileged familiarity (Olson 1940:185; Drucker 1950:222). Nor did a boy go live with his mother's brother (Olson 1940:187). His father had authority over him and subjected him to the hardships required for membership in the secret societies (Lopatin 1945:81).

Ceremonies and Beliefs

A number of life crises and changes in status were publicly marked by feasts and potlatches. These occasions included birth, naming, a girl's puberty, initiation into a secret society, and graduation into shamanhood. At less important occasions the family of the person being honored invited no more than members of his or her clan. But higher-ranking names and titles to property had to be validated by one or more potlatches to which the host clan invited the other clans and even guests from other tribes. The most important potlatches were to prepare a young man to take the position of clan chief, to mark the completion of his new house, and to legitimize his succession after the death of his predecessor, usually his uncle. On such occasions the new chief usually gave away "hundreds of gallons of eulachon oil" (Olson 1940:179).

Once a year the Kitamaat people put on a parody of the potlatch at which men dressed as women and women as men, speakers pretended to be great chiefs from distant tribes, and the guests were given "great names"—in fact names of animals, obscenities, and titles of real chiefs in other tribes. Olson (1940:199), reporting this as practiced in the 1930s, says "the whole party is carried out in an hilarious spirit."

The Haisla had three sets of ritual performances restricted to initiates said to form "secret societies" (Boas 1897) or "dancing societies" (Drucker 1940): a shamans' series called hìlikəla, a m̓iƛa series, and a nùɬəm dance. The shamans' series consisted of six ranked performances. In most the novice, who had inherited the right to perform, became possessed at the sound of whistles, ran into the woods, was kept there for a time, and then reappeared with miraculous powers. The highest ranked was the Cannibal Dance (tànis), in which the novice ate (or appeared to eat) human flesh. This was restricted to the highest ranking chiefs. The second was the Fire-Throwing Dance, in which the novice swallowed or walked on hot coals. Another was a performance restricted to real shamans. Several involved the use of masks, rattles, and rings of red cedarbark. The m̓iƛa series differed in the use of horns rather than whistles and the novice's reappearance from the sea rather than the woods. In the nùɬəm dance the novice ate a live dog. (This identification follows Drucker 1940:216–219; cf. Olson 1940:175–177 and Lopatin 1945:80–89.)

Interpretations of shamanism differ. Drucker (1950: 223) recorded that Haisla shamans got their powers solely from the "spirits" of the secret societies, that is, the entities that possess the initiates. On the other hand, Lopatin (1945:63) reported that there were two kinds of shamans, one kind essentially a division of the secret societies, the other consisting of persons (usually men) who had individually sought power or had it come unsolicited because of some unusual physical feature. Olson (1940:147) said that a boy showing signs of special powers might be chosen by the chiefs, sometimes for the fees they could extract from his father.

Being publicly acknowledged a shaman required potlatching and demonstration of power. In public performances, shamans treated illnesses believed caused by soul loss, intrusive object, or intrusive spirit, and they were especially important in detecting contagious magic. In such cases, the shaman could effect a cure only by discovering the magician and forcing him or her to undo the harm (Olson 1940:197)

There were several other, less structured ceremonial activities. Lopatin (1945:60–61) reported prayers used by hunters and fishermen. A hunter killing a mountain goat cut four pieces from its tongue and offered them to the masters of the sky, the mountains, the sea, and his luck (see also Drucker 1950:266). Olson (1940:199) reported ritual treatment of the first chinook and coho salmon and the first eulachon.

Little is known, however, about the beliefs that seem to be implied by these practices or, in fact, those of the secret societies and the shamans. An origin myth, in which Raven creates the world and the first people (Lopatin 1945:61), seems unrelated to any ritual activities.

The souls of the dead, it was thought, lingered for a time near their former homes, where they were a danger to the living; they then went to a land of the dead, which was like this world but without hardship; and finally they were reincarnated in their descendants (Lopatin 1945:61–63; Olson 1940:181–182, 198–199).

History

The first contact with Europeans may have occurred in July 1792, when Juan Zayas, one of Jacinto Caamaño's officers, took a boat up Douglas Channel (Caamaño 1938: 280). In June 1793, Joseph Whidbey of the George Vancouver expedition explored both Douglas Channel and Gardner Canal (Vancouver 1798). The maritime fur trade probably involved the Haisla at least indirectly; the traders generally worked the outer coast, people of the inner coast going out to meet them or dealing through middlemen. The Hudson's Bay Company established Fort McLoughlin near Dean Channel in 1833. In 1831–1832 the Kitkatla chief Sebassa was selling Kitamaat furs to the company (Æmilius Simpson in Mitchell 1981:86), but in February 1834 the Kitamaat were trading at Fort McLoughlin (Tolmie 1963:269). This trade probably did not greatly alter the native economy or social organization.

Christianity first appeared among the Haisla through the conversion of a Kitamaat native, Charlie Amos. While visiting Victoria in 1876 he was converted to Christianity by listening to a sermon by the Rev. W. Pollard (Crosby 1914:250). Amos upon his return to Kitamaat told his fellow villagers about his new religious beliefs. His activities eventually resulted in the conversion of a small number of people. In spite of resistance by the traditionalists, Charlie Amos continued his proselytizing. At this time the dancing societies and the shamans were still active in the village (Crosby 1914:249–258).

The coming of a White missionary teacher in 1883 and the settling at Kitimaat Mission by the Rev. George H. Raley of the Methodist Church in 1893 resulted in the breakdown of Kitamaat religious and sociopolitical structures (Methodist Church 1895:xvii).

The Kitlope people were influenced by Christianity somewhat later, through a Roman Catholic mission established at Kemano. The breakdown of Native structures was hastened by the government's banning of the potlatch and associated practices.

The Kitamaat Band was allotted four reserves in 1889, four more in 1910, and six more in 1916, totaling 1,432

Royal B.C. Mus., Victoria: PN 11366.
Fig. 2. Grave marker at Kitimaat. Wooden monuments on graves were traditional; the adoption of marble memorial stones, often with figures representing crest animals, show the integration of traditional elements with Euro-American technology (Lopatin 1945:56-57). Photograph by George Henry Raley, 1902–1906.

acres. The Kitlope Band was allotted three reserves in 1889, and one more in 1913, totaling 370.4 acres (Barbara Lane, communication to editors 1985).

From the 1890s to the mid-1950s commercial fishing and work at canneries were the mainstay of Haisla economy. Haisla fishermen were active in the Native Brotherhood of British Columbia, and one, Guy Williams, served in various executive posts from the 1950s to the 1970s. Other sources of income in the early part of the twentieth century were provided by handlogging and trapping. In the early 1950s a major change occurred with the building of the Aluminum Company of Canada's smelter complex and the growth of the new town of Kitimat. By the 1970s, work at the smelter complex and in the new town were the most important sources of cash income (Band Council of Kitamaat, personal communication 1978).

In the 1930s the Kitlope people began moving to the Kitamaat area, and the two bands amalgamated.

The earliest official census of the Haisla is for 1889; it

gives a total of 367 (261 Kitamaat and 106 Kitlope) Some movement of people or inaccuracy in counting is indicated by the next year's total of 392 (Canada. Dominion of 1890: 272, 1891:244). Population seems to have remained under 500 until the 1950s. By 1983 it had risen to 1,041 (Canada. Department of Indian and Northern Development. Indian and Inuit Affairs Program 1984:00065).

Synonymy

The name Haisla has been used since the 1840s. It appears as Hyshalla (Scouler 1848:233), Haishilla (Tolmie and Dawson 1884:117), Qāisla' (Boas 1890:805, 1891:604), and Ha-isla' (Boas 1897:328). The native source is *xà?isəla* '(those) living at the rivermouth, (those) living downriver'.

The Kitamaat people have perhaps been more commonly identified under this name. W.F. Tolmie (1963: 269) mentions them as Kitimats in his journal for 3 February 1834. The name also appears as Gyit'amā́t (Boas 1890:805), G·it!ama't (Boas 1916:356), both apparently for [gʸitamá·t], Kitamat (Hodge 1907–1910, 1:705), and Gitamat (Barbeau 1950,2:473). Hodge (1907–1910, 1: 705) lists other variants. The source is Coast Tsimshian *kitama·t*, literally 'people of the falling snow', the name of the principal village. The name is written Kitimat for the river and town, but the native people prefer the spelling Kitamaat, used by the Methodist missionaries.

The Kitlope people are identified by their Tsimshian name as Gyitlṓp (Boas 1890:805), G·it-lâ˚p (Boas 1916: 356), gᵻtk-lɔ́·p (Garfield 1939:176), and Kitlawp (Barbeau 1950,2:473). Hodge (1907–1910, 1:707–708) gives other variants. The source is Coast Tsimshian *kitlo·p*, literally 'people of the rock'. They have also been identified as Keimanoeitoh (Tolmie and Dawson 1884: 117), Gyimanoitq (Boas 1890:805), and Gīmanoîtx (Boas 1897:328), renderings of Haisla *kìmanu?idxʷ*, which refers strictly to the people of the village of Kemano.

Because the name Kwakiutl has been extended to refer to the whole of Northern Wakashan (Boas 1897:328), the Haisla, along with the Haihais, Bella Bella, and Oowekeeno, have commonly been identified as Northern Kwakiutl (Duff 1964:20; Hawthorn 1979:2). This extention of the name Kwakiutl has tended to obscure linguistic and cultural differences among the Northern Wakashans and the close social ties between the Haisla and the Tsimshian. Probably because of these ties, the Haisla have also been identified, incorrectly, as Southern Tsimshian (Barbeau 1950, 2:473).

Sources

The principal published sources on the Haisla are Drucker (1940, 1950), Lopatin (1945), and Olson (1940). These studies are based on information from only a few informants and, possibly due to the authors' neglect of specifying time referents, they tend to contradict one another on certain aspects of sociopolitical structure.

Hamori-Torok's (1951, 1956) information was primarily supplied by Gordon Robinson, then chief councillor at Kitamaat, as well as by Charles Shaw and Charles Walker. Robinson's description of Haisla sociopolitical structures reflects the situation of the 1880s and 1890s. Robinson (1962) provides a valuable addition to Olson's and Lopatin's works.

Various Methodist publications cited in the text describe the early contact-period Native culture and the conversion to Christianity in some detail.

Pritchard (1977) describes how the traditional social system was abandoned as the Haisla participated in the new economy, accepted Christianity, and declined in numbers.

Haihais, Bella Bella, and Oowekeeno

SUSANNE F. HILTON

The Haihais ('hī͵hīs), Bella Bella (͵bĕlə'bĕlə), and Oowekeeno (ōō'wēkē͵nō, ə'wēkə͵nō) are speakers of Heiltsuk-Oowekyala, the central member of the northern branch of Wakashan.* Heiltsuk ('hāltsək) is the language of the Haihais and Bella Bella, and Oowekyla (ōō'wēkyələ) that of the Oowekeeno. The two approach mutual intelligibility. Their aboriginal territories cover a portion of the central coast of British Columbia, extending along the shores of Queen Charlotte Sound from Price Island at Milbanke Sound to the southern shore of Rivers Inlet and into the channels and inlets northward and eastward (fig. 1).

The Haihais, Bella Bella, and Oowekeeno each consisted of a number of local groups that owned and used village and resource sites on both the mainland and coastal islands. Although the majority of the Oowekeeno winter villages were situated at the head of Rivers Inlet, on Wannock River, and around Owikeno Lake, the Oowekeeno owned resource sites down the inlet, on Calvert Island, and northward on the mainland to the vicinity of Koeye River and Koeye Lake where a separate group, the Koeye, lived in a number of villages. This group was considered half–Bella Bella, half-Oowekeeno with individuals moving either to Bella Bella or to Rivers Inlet Village

in historic times (Drucker 1943:99, 1950:158–159; Hilton, Rath, and Windsor 1982:2; Olson 1954:213–215, map facing p. 213, 1955:320–323, 344; D. Stevenson 1980: 9–10, 1985:6–7).

Environment

The territories of the Haihais, Bella Bella, and Oowekeeno included numerous inlets, islands, peninsulas, mountains and valleys. Rivers and streams cascade into the sea through heavy forests and dense undergrowth, although few are navigable much beyond tidal influence. On the windward side of Pacific storm systems, the region is characterized by high winds, dense fogs, heavy rainfall, and rapid and severe weather changes. Thus while transportation by water was the rule, heavy swells on the outer coast, and strong tides and currents on inland waters made travel treacherous at times.

Except for a few scattered alpine zones found above the timberline, this region falls within the Coast Forest Biotic zone, which is noted for its mild winters, moderate summers, and high precipitation. The mean annual temperature ranges 5–9° C (41–49°F). Annual rainfall measures above 100 inches and approximates close to 200 inches in some locations. The climax forest consists mainly of western hemlock, western red cedar, Sitka spruce, amabalis fir, and, at the higher altitudes, mountain hemlock and yellow cedar. Succession growth includes western yew, red alder, bigleaf maple, and crabapple. Other flora include a wide variety of shrubs. Those providing edible fruits include salal, soapberry, thimbleberry, salmonberry, several huckleberries, and high bush cranberry (Cowan and Guiguet 1965:19, 25, 26; Krajina 1970:35; C. Lyons 1952).

Blacktail deer and wolf are found on both the mainland and islands while the mountain goat, black bear, and grizzly bear (particularly at the heads of inlets and in river valleys) are present on the mainland. Many small fur-bearing mammals are also available, such as the mink and beaver on the mainland and islands, and the hoary marmot, fisher, marten, short-tailed weasel, and river otter on the mainland. Other small mammals inhabiting both the mainland and islands are mice, voles, and lemmings, and rarely, porcupine on the mainland.

---

*The phonemes of Heiltsuk-Oowekyala are (unaspirated stops and affricates) b, d, ɜ, λ, g, gʷ, g̣, g̣ʷ; (aspirated stops and affricates) p, t, c, λ̓, k, kʷ, q, qʷ; (glottalized stops and affricates) ṗ, t̓, c̓, λ̓, k̓, k̓ʷ, q̓, q̓ʷ; (voiceless continuants) s, ł, x, xʷ, x̣, x̣ʷ; (plain resonants) m, n, l, y, w, h; (glottalized resonants) m̓, n̓, l̓, y̓, w̓, ʔ. Vowels are i, u, a, and ə. Heiltsuk has a high tone and a low tone (unmarked); Oowekyala has a stress accent (v́). The resonants are phonetically syllabic or vocalized in certain environments, with the vocalic segment showing various conditioned vowel qualities; the *Handbook* orthography writes these vocalized segments as i before y and y̓, u before w and w̓, a before ʔ (abstractly h̓), and ə elsewhere. Information on Heiltsuk-Oowekyala phonology is from Lincoln and Rath (1980:6–16, 30–36) and Rath (1981:4–63). For words common to both dialects, only the Heiltsuk forms are cited in the *Handbook* if Oowekyala differs only in the position of the accent. Village names are given in the dialect of the village.

In the practical orthography used by the Heiltsuk Cultural Centre in Bella Bella the phonemes are written: b, d, z, dh, g, gv, ǧ, ǧv; p, t, c, th̲, k, kv, q, qv; ṗ, t̓, c̓, t̲h̲, k̓, k̓v, q̓, q̓v; s, lh, x, xv, x̲, x̲v; m, n, l, y, w, h; m̓, n̓, l̓, y̓, w̓, ˀ; i, u, a, and ə.

Information on the transcription of Heiltsuk-Oowekyala words has been provided by Neville J. Lincoln (communication to editors 1986) and John C. Rath and D. Stevenson (personal communications 1986). The editors are responsible for synthesizing and interpreting the available data and for the aspects of the *Handbook* orthography that differ from the sources used.

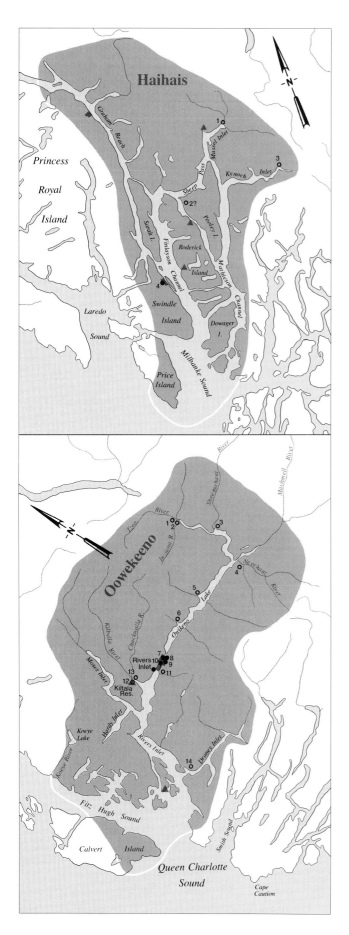

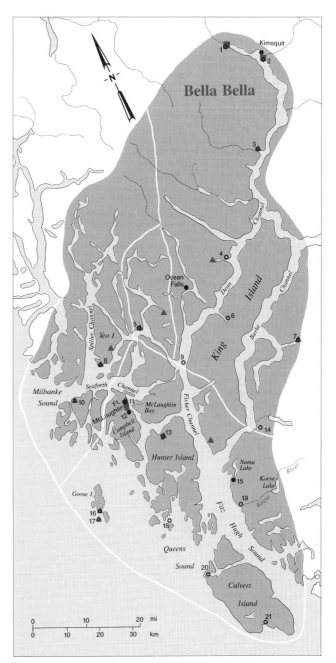

Fig. 1. 19th-century territories and settlements of the Haihais, Bella Bella, and Oowekeeno, with 20th-century reserves. Haihais: 1, *láiq* (Mussel River); 2, *sxiẏálákʷ*; 3, *qínát*; 4, *ɬⁿdu* (Kitasoo Res. [Klemtu]). Bella Bella: 1, *cáckʷ* (Chatscah Res. [Bella Coola]); 2, *k̓m̓x̣k̓ʷitx̣ʷ* (Kemsquit Res. [Bella Coola]); 3, *sxʷáxʷiylkʷ* (Skowquiltz River Res. [Bella Coola]); 4, *ʔáɬkʷu* (Elcho Res.); 5, *xʷənís* (Hoonees Res.); 6, *yaʔís* (Jenny Inlet); 7, *k̓ʷáɬħa* (Kwatlena Res. [Bella Coola]); 8, *q̓ábá* (Kokyet Res.); 9, *k̓ʷátus* (Stokes Is.); 10, *q̓ʷúq̓ʷai* (Koqui Res.); 11, *wágəlísəla* (Bella Bella Res.); 12, *q̓ə́lc* (Bella Bella Res.); 13, *húẏat* (Howeet Res.); 14, *nútm* (Nootum River); 15, *n̓əxʷám̓u* (Namu); 16, *yáláx̌i* (Yellertlee Res.); 17, *wák̓ənálakʷ* (Werkinellek Res.); 18, *n̓úlú*; 19, *k̓ʷiẏái* (Koeye River); 20, *lúx̣ʷbál̓ís* (Pruth Bay); 21, *ʔuwíga* (Chic Chic Bay). Oowekeeno: 1, *čiyú* (Tzeo River); 2, *k̓siyán̓uwa* (Inziana River); 3, *suwə́mx̣uɬ*; 4, *núxʷənc* (Neechanz River); 5, *ʔásxʷələm* (Ashlulm Creek); 6, *q̓ʷápx̣*; 7, *ləx̣ʷləg̓ʷís* (Katit Res.); 8, *k̓ítit* (Katit Res.); 9, Oowekeeno (Katit Res.); 10, *q̓ʷáxsawa* (Katit Res.); 11, *x̣ʷísiq̓ʷa* (Nicknaqueet River); 12, *gə́ldala* (Kiltala Res.); 13, *čág̓ʷala* (Chuckwalla River); 14, *g̓áləmbalis*. Bella Bella village nos. 1–3, and 7 were jointly occupied with Bella Coola.

313

This part of the coast is on the migratory routes for waterfowl such as ducks, geese, loons, and cormorants. Many other birds of economic or mythological importance including the sandhill crane (Bella Bella area only), grouse, seagulls, eagles, crow, and raven are also present with the last four in great numbers throughout the year. Most birds and bird eggs were eaten but crows and ravens were not.

All five species of Pacific salmon migrate to freshwater rivers to spawn throughout the area but are not evenly distributed. Chinook salmon, for example, require specialized habitats and are therefore not found in Bella Bella rivers. Similarly, the eulachon spawn only in certain rivers, such as the Wannock at the head of Rivers Inlet. Drucker (1950:239) reports the presence of small eulachon runs in Haihais territory but an absence in the Bella Bella region. Steelhead trout, cutthroat trout, and Dolly Varden were also available. Saltwater species were numerous, including halibut, herring, rockfish, lingcod, Pacific cod, flounder, dogfish, and hake. Invertebrates such as octopus, squid, clams, mussels, scallops, barnacles, sea urchins, abalone, cockles, periwinkles, and crab were also gathered and eaten.

Sea mammals located in the vicinity either occupying offshore rocky islets or migrating along the coast include: sea otter, northern sea lion, hair seal, northern fur seal, porpoise, and a variety of whales (Cowan and Guiguet 1965; Drucker 1950:166–177, 239, 247; Hilton 1968–1969).

External Relations

Culturally, the Haihais, Bella Bella, and Oowekeeno were located between two major traditions. The Southern Tsimshian and Haisla, like other peoples to the north, had a matrilineal system, while the Bella Coola and Kwakiutl, like other Wakashans and Salishans to the south, reckoned kinship bilaterally. The Haihais, Bella Bella, and Oowekeeno had, in varying degrees, a social organization that featured aspects of both the northern matrilineal organization and the bilateral organization of the central Northwest Coast. In material culture too, they stood between the northern and the central Northwest Coast. For some features the dividing line fell between the Bella Bella and the Oowekeeno or between the Oowekeeno and the Kwakiutl. For others the traditions overlapped, with one or more of the three peoples having features of both traditions. In ceremonialism, and perhaps in art, the Haihais, Bella Bella, and Oowekeeno were at the center of developments that were, in historic times, influencing peoples both north and south.

Compatible social organization and shared ceremonialism, as well as geography, promoted social and economic ties among neighbors. The Oowekeeno, who were relatively isolated from the more coastal Bella Bella, had close ties with the Bella Coola and Kwakiutl, made possible by mountain passes. One such pass connects the upper Owikeno basin with South Bentinck Arm where relations with the Bella Coola on this inland route included events described as "like Olympic Games" (Hilton 1968–1969), festive and a great attraction for the young, with cliff climbing and other activities. Intermarriage between the Bella Bella and Bella Coola occurred to such an extent that some villages were bilingual.

The Bella Bella traded saltwater resources such as clams, seaweed, and herring spawn with the Bella Coola, Oowekeeno, and Kitamaat for eulachons and eulachon oil. The Oowekeeno, who were well supplied with salmon, traded sockeye for vegetal foods with the Talio tribe of the Bella Coola. Similarly, the Haihais gained access to resources through intermarriage and trade with the Kitasoo Tsimshian and Haisla (Drucker 1950:159; Hilton 1968–1969; Olson 1954:217; McIlwraith 1948, 1:17, 19, 21, 40; Simonsen 1973:21).

Hostilities occurred mainly with more distant tribes. The Bella Bella traveled far into Haida, Tsimshian, and Kwakiutl territories and, as a result, were themselves constantly on guard for marauding warriors especially during the spring when calm water prevailed and ceremonial and economic activities were at a minimum. Unlike the Haihais and Oowekeeno, the Bella Bella were so well organized in leadership and military strategies that the Bella Coola frequently sought a Bella Bella to lead their war parties. The Oowekeeno were out of the main path of the war canoes, being well protected by the easily defendable Wannock River. On the other hand, the Haihais, who were few in number, had no chance to be peaceable as they were forever embroiled in and afflicted by attack from both the northern tribes and the Bella Bellas, having to defend against predatory expeditions directed toward their resource base and to protect themselves from these warring tribes who wanted to practice on them in preparation for more major expeditions. Revenge, territorial possession, violation of dancing society rituals, and seasonal shortages of food supplies were motivations for warfare (McIlwraith 1948, 2:20, 342, 349, 352, 376; Drucker 1950:159, 1965:82; Olson 1954: 218, 1955:344).

Culture

Subsistence

Central to the subsistence economy was the seasonal migration of families to a series of resource sites, many of which were owned by families, local groups, or crest groups. The seasonal round began in late winter and lasted until October or November when families returned to their winter villages to observe the ceremonial season and to manufacture or repair equipment. All three divisions responded to seasonal harvesting determined by tidal cycles and by the spawning cycles of several anadromous fish species.

Largely as a result of their location at the head of Rivers Inlet, the Oowekeeno were more inland in their orientation than the other two divisions, a natural result of their resource base in the Owikeno basin. Owikeno Lake provided an ideal habitat for sockeye salmon and the rivers for eulachon (fig. 2). Nonetheless, the Oowekeeno, like the more coastal Bella Bella and Haihais, had access to most resources found on the coast as their seasonal migrations extended down to the mouth of the inlet and farther to harvest seaweed, herring eggs, and other seafoods. They did hunt sea mammals incidentally on these expeditions but placed greater emphasis upon land mammals such as the mountain goat (Drucker 1950:241; Hilton 1968–1969; McKervill 1964:93; Olson 1954: 213–214).

Subsistence methods were numerous and varied. Salmon was caught by stone and wooden stake weirs, fish traps, two-headed harpoons typical of the south, dipnets, and clubs. The Oowekeeno residing in upper Owikeno Lake employed a collapsable weir in the narrows designed to survive flash-flooding tendencies of the upper watersheds. For halibut the Haihais used the V-shaped hook of the northern Northwest Coast, the Oowekeeno the U-shaped hook of the central coast, and the Bella Bella both. Herring spawn was collected by immersing hemlock branches, against which the fish spawned, and by a herring rake.

Sea mammals were hunted with harpoons, clubs, and bow and arrows. The sealing harpoon used for hair seals, porpoises (with the exception of the Oowekeeno), and sea otter was northern in type consisting of a single point with a detachable foreshaft. Seals and sea lions were also clubbed on rocks, and the Oowekeeno and Haihais sometimes hunted sea otters with a bow and arrow. None

of the divisions hunted whales, but the Bella Bella and Haihais took stranded ones mainly for their blubber.

Land animals such as mountain goat and deer were hunted with dogs and either snared or speared. The Oowekeeno manufactured snares for mountain goats, which were not found in the territory of the other two divisions. Bears and small game were caught with deadfalls; hibernating bears were killed with lances. Waterfowl were shot with a bow and arrow, clubbed, or snared. Digging sticks were used for gathering roots, primarily the activity of women, although men frequently helped in gathering of vegetal foods while on land expeditions and of sea foods such as clams, abalone, and seaweed (Drucker 1950:166–176, 246).

Structures

At their semipermanent winter villages all divisions had rectangular cedar plank houses that were northern in style with vertical wall planks, gabled roof, double ridgepole, carved interior posts (fig. 3), adjustable central smokehole, and mat-lined walls in the sleeping compartments to keep out drifting snow. With the exception of some Bella Bella dwellings that had removable sheathing, wall planks were permanently attached to the house frame (Tolmie 1963:270, 274), and as such were not removed for use at summer camps. Instead plank houses similar in design to the winter houses, with the exception of little or no decorative features, were built at major resource sites. Bark houses were used at hunting stations and minor camps. The Oowekeeno diverged from this pattern by not having bark houses and by replacing the central fireplace with ones built in the corners in the Kwakiutl style (Drucker 1950:178–180, 249, 251).

Clothing and Adornment

In clothing these peoples differed little from their neighbors. But what was truly distinctive was the combination, among the Haihais and the Bella Bella, of the northern Northwest Coast practice of wearing labrets (by high-status women) and the central coast practice of head deformation (for both sexes). The Oowekeeno practiced head deformation only (Drucker 1950:188–189; Hilton 1968–1969).

Technology

Northern and central styles in woodworking tools were also noticeable in this region. The Haihais and Bella Bella used the northern style hafted stone maul or hammer as well as a pear-shaped hand maul typical of the Oowekeeno and more southern tribes. All three divisions had the northern-style elbow adz but only the Oowekeeno combined it with the D adz from the south while using both

U. of B.C., Mus of Anthr., Vancouver: A253.

Fig. 2. Oowekeeno woman stringing eulachon in order to dry them. Photograph by C. McKay, Rivers Inlet, B.C., 1952.

Fig. 3. House frame with interior post carved to represent a grizzly bear, Bella Bella, B.C. Photograph possibly by Harlan I. Smith, about 1920s.

implements for different functions. The elbow adz was used for heavier rough work followed by the D adz for finer, more precise lines (Drucker 1950:182–183, 256).

Transport

All three divisions used the northern style cedar dugout canoe and, in the case of the Bella Bella and Haihais, cedar bark canoes suitable for traveling on lakes. But distinctive designs also emerged that were neither part of the northern nor the southern traditions. For example, the Oowekeeno, Bella Bella, and Haihais had a specialized shallow-bottom canoe balanced and rounded to suit rocky, sweeping rivers. The blade of the common crutch-handled paddle did not follow the typical leaf-shape pattern; instead all three divisions used a round-tipped blade (Drucker 1950:181–182, 252–253; J. Carpenter, personal communication 1986).

Art

A significant feature of Bella Bella society was the development of a cadre of highly skilled artisans noted for their construction and decoration of bentwood boxes (fig. 4), chests, canoes, and horn spoons and ladles. After

316

Fig. 4. Bella Bella water bucket and dipper. The bucket (left) is a bent-corner box (the 4 sides made of a single board, kerfed, steamed, and folded into a box shape, the ends joined and a bottom attached with wooden pegs) with a wooden handle across the top. The dipper (right) is a smaller bent-corner box with a long handle carved from the piece that forms the bottom. Designs are done in red and black, and borders and handles in red. The bottom of the ladle carries the eye-within-the-hand motif. Collected as a set by J.G. Swan at Bella Bella, B.C., 1876; height of bucket 26 cm; other to same scale.

White contact the skills of these artisans were turned to the market demand for canoes and boxes. A clearly identified school of artistic creation flourished in Bella Bella. Light, narrow formlines, extensive open backgrounds, bilaterally symetrical design with fully parallel hatching, and particular green and possibly red pigments are characteristic. All are within the context of northern rules of form but with unique presentation. Distinctive designs in portrait masks show "a flattened orb with a narrow and sometimes sharply cut rim in the eye socket . . ." (Holm 1983a:41; see also Crosby 1914:187; Holm and Reid 1975:132–133; McIlwraith 1948, 1:39, 529; Macnair, Hoover, and Neary 1980:37–38).

Political Organization

The basic social and political unit was the local group whose members descended from a common male or female ancestor. This unit was politically autonomous with its own chiefs, resource sites, traditions, names, and ceremonial prerogatives. Among the Bella Bella, some local groups in close proximity to each other formed tribes by congregating at one or more winter villages. The Bella Bella recognized six or more tribes that were not politically integrated; each local group maintained its autonomy. In historic times, these tribes merged at a village near a trading store and mission and formed a loose confederation that did not co-opt local group autonomy (Boas 1924:325; Drucker 1943:80, 1950:220, 1965:47, 72; Olson 1955:320, 324; Hilton 1968–1969).

The extent to which the Haihais and Oowekeeno had a tribal organization is unclear. For the Haihais, Olson (1955:344) reports at least two "tribe-villages," a term indicating that a tribe and village did not necessarily correspond. On the other hand, Drucker (1950:159, 1955:122) believed that the Haihais consisted of a few small local groups and doubts that they ever developed a more complex organization. Boas (1897:328), Drucker (1955:14, 122), and Curtis (1907–1930, 10:305) list three to six tribes on Owikeno Lake, Wannock River, and at the head of Rivers Inlet; but Olson (1954:215) found that the Oowekeeno only recognized a number of villages while granting the possibility that the villages on upper Owikeno Lake may have formed a tribe. Unlike the individual Bella Bella who identifies himself as a member of a tribe as well as a village, an Oowekeeno refers only to the village that he came from (Hilton 1968–1969; Olson 1954:215).

Kinship Terminology

Bella Bella and Oowekeeno kinship terms imply bilateral descent. They are lineal in parents' generation, making no distinction between father's and mother's side, and Hawaiian in ego's generation, making no distinction among cross-cousins, parallel cousins, and siblings. In address, the actual relationship between the speaker and the person addressed was superseded by the relationship between the previous bearer of the speaker's name and the person addressed (Olson 1954:253, 1955:335). There is no information on Haihais terms or usage.

Social Organization

● CREST GROUPS In addition to the social groups based on residence, there were groups based on descent, the crest groups. These are the "clans" of Boas (1924) and the "septs" of Olson (1954:214–215, 1955:324–325).

For the Haihais and Bella Bella, the crest groups were the counterpart of the exogamous matrilineal clans of the tribes to the north. Their names were similar, and their existence no doubt made intermarriage more acceptable to the northerners. But they were neither rigidly exogamous nor consistently matrilineal. People were aware of the northern marriage rules but did not agree on whether they should be followed. Parents tended to place their children in the mother's crest group, but membership was not necessarily permanent.

Both the Haihais and Bella Bella had a Raven, Eagle, and Orca crest group. The Uyalit tribe of Bella Bella had a fourth, a Wolf crest group. The first three were represented in all Bella Bella tribes. The crest groups owned crests and a series of ranked names or titles. Each Bella Bella crest group had its own style of face painting displayed at feasts. Information on this and other practices is lacking for the Haihais.

The Bella Bella crest groups were ranked, Raven being highest, followed by Eagle, Orca, and Wolf. Members of a crest group sat together at feasts and potlatches, the arrangement depending on the rank of the group. Crest group membership provided a basis of identification with members of other tribes, Bella Bella and foreign. After a death, there were memorial duties performed by the crest group of the father of the deceased. A council of crest group chiefs decided on questions of succession. Generally a title passed along a line of surviving brothers and then to the eldest sister's son. But chiefs often circumvented this matrilineal pattern by adopting their eldest sons, who ordinarily belonged to their mothers' crest groups, into their own. A woman's titles went from sister to sister and then to the eldest sister's eldest daughter (Boas 1924; Olson 1955:324–329, 336, 344–345).

The Oowekeeno had four crest groups that were named not for their crests but with names designating groups of people, such as "those who receive first." Unlike the Bella Bella crest groups, they were not evenly distributed among villages, they were not an important basis of identity, and beyond determining who sat where at feasts they seem to have had few ceremonial functions. An individual could choose which parent's crest group to affiliate with and even claim membership in several at one time. A title passed from a man to his eldest son, though some prerogatives were reserved for the youngest (Olson 1954:214–215, 220–221, 1955:324). In all, the social practices of the Oowekeeno crest groups resembled those of the numayms of the Kwakiutl and lacked many features of the Bella Bella and Haihais crest groups, which shared a northern orientation.

● STATUS DIFFERENCES Society was divided into a number of named categories distinguishing degrees in social rank. The main divisions were chiefs (both men and women), commoners, and slaves. The Belia Bella and Oowekeeno made further distinctions by identifying people of low class. Further, Bella Bella recognized three levels of chiefs: two top-ranking chiefs of equal status, who are the only ones with rights to become *tánis* dancers; chiefs; and nobility or chiefs of lower rank. Symbols of prestige and privilege for members of high rank included tattoos, elaborations of ornamentation, possession of coppers, and the possession of chiefly titles, which were limited in number and denoted high social value. Commoners had names of minor social value without honorific titles, held smaller feasts, and did not have inherited rights to upper level dances. Low class commoners were the unambitious, orphans, or those who did not have kinsmen to sponsor them at potlatches and feasts. Slaves could be bartered for wealth items and were usually war captives or their progeny. If freed their status was elevated to low-rank freemen (Boas 1924:330–331; Drucker 1940:208, 1950:190–191, 221, 260–261; Olson 1954:220, 1955:326, 337, 344; Rath 1981, 1:302, 2:704).

● MARRIAGE AND RESIDENCE The marriage of cousins (first cousins among the Bella Bella, second cousins among the Oowekeeno) was permitted and even encouraged if it meant a consolidation of claims to hereditary

a, Amer. Mus. of Nat. Hist., New York: E/962; b, Royal Ont. Mus., Toronto: 902.2.6; U. of Aberdeen, Mus. of Anthr., Scotland: 93; right, Royal B.C. Mus., Victoria: PN 2523.

Fig. 5. Masks and ceremonial costume. a, Mask representing the ʒúnúqʷa, an ogress of great strength whose mouth is rounded in creation of her fearsome cry. Compare this mask and its definite apelike quality with that in "Kwakiutl: Traditional Culture," fig. 11c, this vol., which is bearded and male in appearance. The ogress, bukwus, wild woman, wild man, and wild beast of the woods became androgynous, indistinct beings in the masks. Collected by G. T. Emmons in 1894. b, Bukwus 'man of the woods', a malevolent being who collects and transforms travelers by enticing them to eat bukwus food and also gathers the souls of drowned people into his retinue. Bukwus masks are characterized by a strongly arched and hooked nose, lips either drawn back over exposed teeth or pushed forward, and ears, if present, small and pointed. This mask was made by Daniel Houstie, a Bella Bella artist, before 1902. c, Wolf mask with human faces carved on the ears, and moveable jaw and anterior appendages. Human hair trails from the carved heads on the ears. Glass beads serve as the wolf's eyes. Collected at Port Simpson, B.C., 1850. Height of a, 32.8 cm; others to scale. right, Oowekeeno man wearing a bukwus mask and costume. Photographed at Rivers Inlet, B.C., about 1920.

names. Postmarital residence was usually with the husband's family, but occasionally Haihais and Oowekeeno men lived with their wives' families.

If divorce occurred, the Oowekeeno children stayed with the father, while the mother kept the children among the Haihais and Bella Bella. The levirate and sororate were usual.

Bride price was paid to the bride's family with an expected repayment of at least double at a later date. Repayment by the bride's family to the groom's kin bought back their daughter, and she was then free to leave her husband if she desired. Associated with this custom was what Olson (1954:223) called an "investment" type of marriage, a marriage arranged for the express purpose of enhancing one's status. The husband, his wife, their children, and the wife's father all benefited in rank and prestige from such a union. Normally, only those men of high rank engaged in this type of marriage as it required

318 wealth at the outset to maximize the return (Drucker

1950:214–216, 278–279; Olson 1955:334).

Ceremonies

The year was divided into a summer secular season, the time for subsistence activities, and a winter sacred season, the time for ceremonies. The major ceremonies were performed by groups identified as "dancing societies" (Drucker 1940) or "secret societies" (Boas 1897). Members of a dancing society were persons who had, by hereditary right, been initiated into it. There were two or perhaps three societies, each with a series of dances, varying somewhat among the Haihais, Bella Bella, and Oowekeeno. In each series the dances were ranked. All three peoples had a číčáiqa 'shamans' series, in which the highest ranking performance was the tánís or hámaċa, the Cannibal Dance. All had a second series, performed after the season for the first was over, called λuẇəláxa 'coming down again' or ṁíλa, which included a wáwínalał 'war dancer' performance. The Bella Bella and perhaps the Haihais had a *núɫəm*, known as the dog-eating dance, separate from the other two series. The Oowekeeno did not have this last but had another, about which little is known.

Each performance was inspired by some powerful being who had been, in the tradition of the society, encountered by an ancestor. The performance itself was a dramatization of the encounter; the initiate was supposedly possessed by the being as the ancestor had been, and in the course of the performance he or she was captured and tamed by members of the society. Performances involved masks and other paraphernalia as well as extraordinary feats demonstrating the possession of power (Drucker 1940:202–216; Olson 1954:239–249, 1955:337). Traditions suggest that the Haihais, Bella Bella, and Oowekeeno were the source of much of this ceremonialism among their neighbors both north and south. (For a discussion of this and a description of the related Kwakiutl forms, see "Kwakiutl: Winter Ceremonies," this vol.)

High-ranking chiefs owned the highest-ranking dances, while commoners had rights to dances of less importance that represented minor spirits. Those of low rank who were few in number were excluded from participation in the dances. Women were not allowed to perform in the higher order dances of Oowekeeno Shamans' society but could perform in all but the *tánís* dance of the Bella Bella. There were no dances exclusively for women (Drucker 1940:202, 225; Olson 1954:239, 1955:337).

The correlation between ceremonial rank and social status was directly related to wealth as well as heredity. The acquisition of ceremonial prerogatives required the ability to call on the resources of others to accumulate wealth to sponsor a dance, with its attendant feasts, payment of services, and a potlatch held to validate an individual's right to the dance and to receive his or her new title. Ideally an individual danced in the lower order of dances of a society before assuming his hereditary right to a higher ranking dance, with some lower order dances seen as preparatory to specific higher level ones (Olson 1954:239–249; Drucker 1940:202–216).

The winter ceremonials were managed by a council of chiefs who gave permission for a dance to take place, adjudicated a claimant's right to a dance, and ensured that the rules were followed. Central to their concern was whether a sponsor had the means to provide wealth essential to proper conduct of procedures. The Oowekeeno council comprised chiefs who all had rights to the Fool's Dance, the second highest ranking dance in the Shamans' series. For the Bella Bella, management was in the hands of the nobility or chiefs or lower rank. It would appear that the head chiefs of both the Oowekeeno and Bella Bella, while having secular authority, did not have control over the ritual season, suggesting a possible division between secular and ritual authority. The council in each case had no formal powers yet their decisions were not questioned and were enforced with religious sanctions (Boas 1924:331; Olson 1954:217, 240).

History

The first recorded contact with Europeans occurred in 1793, seven years after the beginning of the maritime fur trade, when two explorers on separate expeditions penetrated Bella Bella territory. Capt. George Vancouver surveyed channels and inlets while heading north into Haihais country and beyond; Alexander Mackenzie traveled overland down the Bella Coola River into Dean Channel. Their encounters with the Bella Bellas were brief and what trade in furs did occur was limited. Soon afterward maritime fur traders seeking the valuable sea otter pelts entered Bella Bella territory stopping frequently at Milbanke Sound to trade. Rich for fur collection, Milbanke Sound continually attracted both British and American ships even though some contact with the Bella Bellas had been marked by violence. A second major trading center was established in Bella Bella territory in 1833 when the Hudson's Bay Company built Fort McLoughlin on Campbell Island. From 1833 to 1843, when it was abandoned, Fort McLoughlin was the only fort serving the central Northwest Coast. About 1850 a small Hudson's Bay Company store was opened on the same site, and it continued to operate for many years.

With two trading centers within their territory, the Bella Bella were able to establish themselves as middlemen

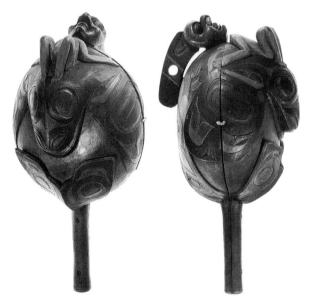

Smithsonian, Dept. of Anthr.: 20584.

Fig. 6. Bella Bella carved wooden rattle (front and side views). A human figure at the top lies with his back to the killerwhale that encircles the rattle. The whale's dorsal fin rises from the back of the figure's head. Carved features are painted in red, green, and black. This specimen, said to have been the property of a "medicine man," was used in the secret societies according to Boas (1897:654). Collected by J.G. Swan at Fort Simpson, B.C., 1875; length 32.5 cm.

Amer. Mus. of Nat. Hist., New York: 42310.

Fig. 7. Bella Bella, B.C. No totem poles are evident because their manufacture was discouraged by the Methodist missionaries (Olson 1955:336). Photograph by Edward Dossetter, about 1881.

and to manipulate the competition between the British-owned fort and American ships (Duff 1964:56; Dunn 1844:261; Fisher 1977:29, 31; Work 1945:15, 79; Large 1968:3–4; Tolmie 1963:403).

Following the height of the fur trade was a period of rapid social and economic change, which began with the devastating smallpox epidemic of 1862. The years that followed saw the process of missionization, growth of the commercial salmon canning industry (dating from 1882 in Rivers Inlet) and logging, shifting settlement patterns as groups amalgamated into central villages, and drastic population decline from disease and warfare. Accompanying these forces was the severance of ownership of land with the establishment of reserves without treaty, a process that began about 1880. Each of the three communities, one per division, was formed in this colonial context. The Bella Bellas, who numbered 1,598 (including 159 slaves) in 1835 (Tolmie 1963:304, 306–307), counted only 204 in 1890 (Canada, Dominion of 1891:243). From about 1862 to 1900 the Bella Bella tribes moved into McLoughlin Bay to be near the store and a mission built in 1880. The settlement of Bella Bella was considered to be a model Christian village by the Methodist missionaries, with European-style housing, church, and educational facilities (fig. 7). In 1898, the resident medical missionary precipitated a move to the present site of Bella Bella two

miles north in search of better space, beach, and water supply. By 1902, a hospital was completed at the site (Hilton 1971; Lyons 1969:169; Large 1968:7, 10, 13; McKervill 1964:39, 49; Olson 1955:320, 321; Tolmie 1963:306–307; Crosby 1914).

While the centralizing forces for the Bella Bella were the fur traders and missionaries, for the Oowekeeno it was the burgeoning salmon and logging industries. Around 1900 two Oowekeeno villages were established at the foot of Wannock River close to a cannery and sawmill. From 1900 to 1935, Oowekeeno villages were vacated as groups moved to join those at Kitit on the Wannock River. Destruction of that village by fire in 1935 led to the eventual location of the village at its present site at the lower end of the Wannock River close to the commercial activities at the head of the inlet.

The Oowekeeno, in their attempt to retain their traditional culture, accepted neither the ideas nor assistance of the Methodist misssionaries. In contrast to the Bella Bella population, which began to increase by 1916, the Oowekeeno population trend did not reverse itself until about 1940 (Olson 1954:214 ff.; D. Stevenson 1980: 63–66, 85, 90–91).

The Haihais vacated their former villages about 1870 to move to Klemtu on Swindle Island, a camping site that became a fuel depot for steamships. Haihais families

Fig. 8. Bella Bella women and men packing salmon at cannery at Namu, B.C. Photograph by John Mailer, 1945.

traded cordwood, furs, fresh meat, and fish in exchange for European goods. No known records exist to add details to this era for the Haihais (Drucker 1950:159; Olson 1955:344; Storie and Gould 1973a:54).

The intervening decades led to expanding populations coupled with displacement from the fishing and logging industries through competition with non-native populations, technological advances, license limitations restricting native access to the commercial resources and associated technologies, and loss of rights to the land. The result is high unemployment and out-migration but with continuing strong ties between migrants in the Vancouver area and the home communities (Hilton 1973–1975; D. Stevenson 1980:70–79). These communities are determined to preserve their cultural knowledge and to control economic and social development.

Synonymy

The Haihais, Bella Bella, and Oowekeeno have sometimes been grouped together under the name Heiltsuk (Boas 1897:320; Hawthorn 1979:xix, 2), and these peoples together with the Haisla have been identified as Bella Bella (Murdock and O'Leary 1975, 3:22) or Northern Kwakiutl (Duff 1964:20). However, none of these usages has any counterpart among the native peoples. They have had no collective term for themselves. They have used Heiltsuk and Bella Bella simply for the tribes that joined together at Bella Bella in historic times.

The name Bella Bella (Heiltsuk *pə́lbálá*) has been in use since 1834, when it appears, as Bilbilla, in Tolmie's (1963: 204, 278) journal at Fort McLoughlin. The name referred to the site of the fort and the native village that grew around it (Walbran 1909:45). It is said (Hodge 1907-1910, 1:140) to be based on the native pronunciation of Milbanke borrowed back into English. The resemblance to Bella Coola represents convergence within English.

Heiltsuk, from *híɬʒaqʷ* (meaning unclear), dates from the same period. Tolmie (1963:278) uses Haeeltzuk (misread Haceltzuk by his editor, read correctly by Walbran [1909:45–46]) seemingly as a synonym for Bilbilla. John Scouler (1848:233) used Haeeltsuk as a general term for the Northern Wakashan speakers while also identifying the term with one of two tribes on Milbanke Sound, the other being the Esleytok, presumably the *ʔísdaítxʷ*. Boas identified (1891:604) Hḗʼiltsuk· as both the language of the North Wakashan speakers north of the Kwakiutl and the people of Bella Bella, but he later (1897:328) separated the Haisla and identified Hḗʼiltsuq as the language of the Haihais, Bella Bella, and Rivers Inlet people.

The tribes that gathered at Bella Bella were reportedly (Olson 1955:320) once also collectively called by the name of the tribe that owned the site, *ʔúyalitxʷ* (Uyalit).

The four principal Bella Bella tribes were the *qʷúqʷaẏaítxʷ* 'qʷúqʷai people', *ʔuwíƛitxʷ* 'landward people', *ʔúyalitxʷ* 'seaward people', and *ʔísdaítxʷ* 'ʔísda people' (Rath 1981:2). These are identified by Olson (1955:320) as the K!oʼkwaeʼdox, Uwiʼtlidox, Oʼyalidox, and Eʼstedox, respectively.

The name Oowekeeno is from *ʔuwíḱinuxʷ*, at one time the name for the people living on the Wannock River just below the outlet of Owikeno Lake. The name has appeared as Weekenoch (Scouler 1848:233), Oweckano (Sproat 1880:145), Wikeinoh (Tolmie and Dawson 1884:117), Awíkyʼēnoq (Boas 1891:604), Awīkˑʼēnôx (Boas 1897: 328), and Wikeno (Hodge 1907–1910, 2:952). The language name Oowekyala is from *ʔuwíḱala*.

The name Haihais, from *xíxís*, the tribal name, has appeared as Hyhysh (Scouler 1848:233), Haihaish (Tolmie and Dawson 1884:117), Qēʼqaes (Boas 1891:604), and Xāesxaes (Boas 1897:328). The Haihais have also been identified as the China Hat or Chinaman Hat people, a name that probably refers to Cone Island opposite Klemtu and one the Haihais do not care for (Olson 1955:344).

Sources

Few published ethnographic accounts exist for the Haihais, Bella Bella, and Oowekeeno. Olson (1954, 1955) deals mainly with social and ceremonial organization and tribal histories. When Olson conducted his fieldwork in 1935 and 1949, he concluded that the traditional culture had not been practiced as part of daily life for several decades with few people even remembering the old customs. Consequently, his reports are incomplete. Drucker, who carried out research about the same time, published a comparative account of dancing societies (1940) and a cultural element distribution list that provides the only broad coverage of these three cultures (1950). Drucker's (1943) archeological survey gives eth-

321

nographic notes on village sites and material culture. Boas (1928, 1932), published Bella Bella texts that included Oowekeeno traditions as well and a short article on Bella Bella social organization (1924). His trips to Bella Bella in the early 1900s were brief and accompanied by a Kwakiutl interpreter from Fort Rupert. His reliance on this man may have affected the authenticity of his myth collections, translations, and transcriptions (John C. Rath, personal communication 1985). Traditions were collected from the Bella Bella, Haihais, and Oowekeeno (Storie and Gould 1973, 1973a; Storie 1973a). A fourth volume from this collection was published by Hilton, Rath, and Windsor (1982).

Pomeroy (1980) concerns an ethno-archeological analysis of Bella Bella settlement patterns and subsistence. Hilton (1971) wrote a preliminary analysis of Bella Bella tribes and village sites based on ethnohistorical and ethnographic accounts. D. Stevenson has produced a manuscript on Oowekeeno social history (1980), and one on Oowekeeno ceremonial names and their distribution (1985).

Historical sources, such as explorers' journals and fur trader's accounts and diaries, provide some details about traditional Bella Bella culture and their reactions to European contact. Vancouver (1798, 1–2), Tolmie (1963), Work (1945), and Dunn (1844) describe settlement patterns, tribal chiefs, trading practices, and ceremonial activities from 1793 to about 1840. Missionary accounts (Crosby 1914; Pierce 1933), reports, and letters published by the Methodist Church describe Bella Bella from the beginning of missionary activity in the 1870s. These sources give only a superficial treatment of Bella Bella culture because most contact was brief and oriented to the concerns of the outsiders. Two popular books on missionary activities describe Bella Bella life and history (McKervill 1964; Large 1968).

The Royal Ontario Museum in Toronto, Ontario; the National Museum of Man in Ottawa, Ontario; and the University of British Columbia Museum of Anthropology in Vancouver have collections containing Bella Bella and Oowekeeno art and ceremonial objects.

A program of archival and ethnographic data collection was begun in Bella Bella in 1973 under the auspices of the Heiltsuk Cultural-Educational Center. Integral to this program is the revival of Heiltsuk language and culture, as exemplified by a resurgence of potlatching, which began in 1977 with the first potlatch given in over 50 years. The resident linguist, John Rath, and native colleagues have collaborated on an extensive study of Heiltsuk language resulting in a number of papers and publications (Rath 1981; Lincoln and Rath 1980, 1986).

Bella Coola

DOROTHY I.D. KENNEDY AND RANDALL T. BOUCHARD

Language

The Bella Coola (ˌbeləˈkōōlə) speak a Coast Salish language* that is geographically isolated from the rest of the Salishan family and forms a separate division within it. Bella Coola is surrounded on the south, west, and north by Wakashan languages, and on the east by Athapaskan languages.

Territory

At the time of European contact in the late eighteenth century, the Bella Coola occupied a number of permanent villages (fig. 1) situated alongside and at the mouths of major rivers and creeks in the Bella Coola valley, North and South Bentinck Arms, Dean Channel, and Kwatna Inlet. The last two areas were also occupied by groups of the Bella Bella. In earlier times the Bella Coola may have occupied the habitable lands along the east front of the Coast Range south of Anahim Lake (vol. 6:402).

Beginning probably around the time of contact and accelerating rapidly thereafter, the Bella Coola abandoned village sites in the inlets and up the Bella Coola Valley, in favor of sites at the mouth of the Bella Coola River. By the early 1900s, most of the Bella Coola were living at the village of ʔatqlax̣ł situated on the north shore of the Bella Coola River mouth. But in 1936, by which time all the other village sites had been abandoned, a severe flood forced the people to move from ʔatqlax̣ł across the river to q̓ʷumk̓ʷuts̓ where they have lived since.

Environment

The present village of Bella Coola is situated approximately 120 kilometers from the Pacific Ocean. This entire area is particularly rugged, with high mountains rising steeply from the shores of the inlets and along both sides of the

narrow Bella Coola valley. Extensive estuaries are found at the mouths of the larger rivers emptying into these inlets and there are lowland areas along the river valleys.

The area used by the Bella Coola falls within the Coastal Western Hemlock Biogeoclimatic Zone, but other vegetation zones are also encountered, including the Mountain Hemlock Zone, the Englemann Spruce–Subalpine Fir Zone, and the Cariboo Aspen–Lodgepole Pine–Douglas Fir Zone. The community types contributing most to the Bella Coola were the well-vegetated estuarine flats and the various types of forest communities. Common tree species in Bella Coola territory are western hemlock, mountain hemlock, Sitka spruce, western red cedar, Douglas fir, amabilis fir, yellow cedar, lodgepole pine, red alder, Sitka alder, black cottonwood, Rocky Mountain maple, and wild crabapple (Turner 1974:9). The climate within this Coastal Western Hemlock Zone is characterized by a mean annual temperature of 41-49°F, total annual precipitation of 65-262 inches, and annual snowfall of 5-295 inches (Krajina 1969:35, 40).

Culture

This description of Bella Coola culture is summarized primarily from McIlwraith (1925, 1948, 1964), who conducted anthropological fieldwork among the Bella Coola between 1922 and 1924; fieldnotes of the archeologist Harlan I. Smith (1920-1924); and the ethnographic fieldnotes compiled by Kennedy (1971-1977) and Bouchard (1971-1977). The data of McIlwraith and Smith reflect culture as the Bella Coola believed it to have been around the time of contact with Europeans, whereas data compiled in the 1970s reflect the Bella Coola culture of the late nineteenth century.

Culturally the Bella Coola are similar to their western neighbors, the Bella Bella, whom they respect for their dramatic ceremonials and credit as the source of many of their customs. Although the Bella Coola are very much aware that their eastern neighbors, the Carrier and the Chilcotin, lack in this rich ceremonialism, still there is one characteristic of these Athapaskans that they especially admire—their tracking and hunting skills.

The Bella Coola did intermarry and trade with the

---

*The phonemes of Bella Coola are: (plain stops and affricate) p, t, c, k, kʷ, q, qʷ, ʔ; (glottalized stops and affricates) p̓, t̓, ƛ̓, c̓, k̓, k̓ʷ, q̓, q̓ʷ; (voiceless fricatives) s, ł, x, xʷ, x̣, x̣ʷ, h; (nasals and lateral) m, n, l; (semivowels) w, y; (short vowels) i, a, u; (long vowels) i·, a·, u·.

The transcriptions of Bella Coola words appearing in the *Handbook* in italics were supplied by Randall T. Bouchard. This analysis differs in some details from that in Davis and Saunders (1980).

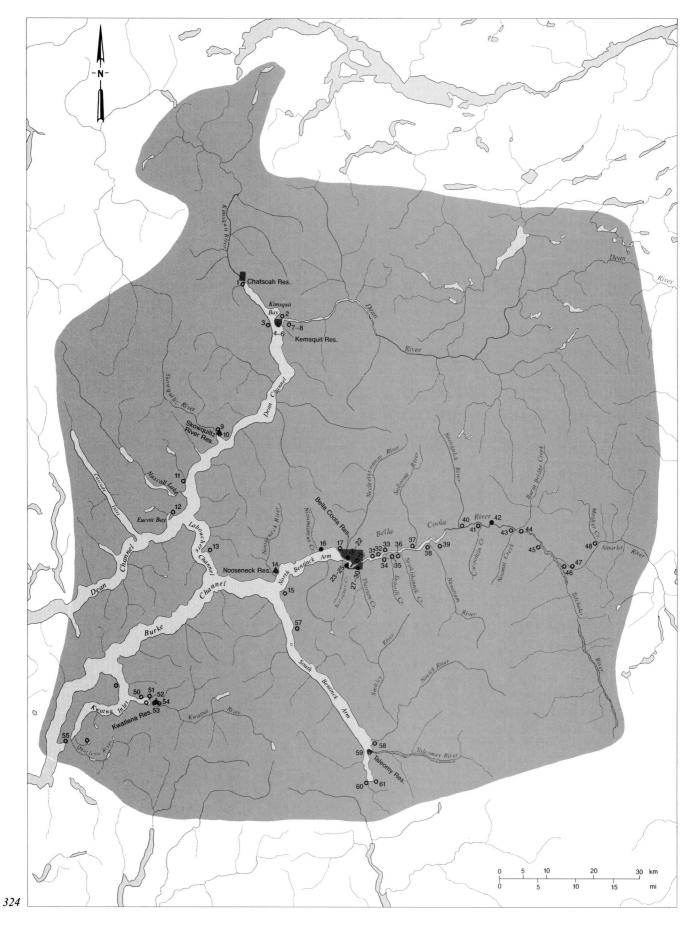

Fig. 1. Territory and settlements of the Bella Coola about 1850. Villages: 1, *sack*ʷ, 2, *txaλsik* 'behind the village', 3, *nuxʷlst*, 4, *snuwapata·x* 'closed at the mouth of river', 5, *nuλl* 'canyon', 6, *usʔusq̓ʷp* 'bare place', 7, *axati* 'mound', 8, *nucqʷalst*, 9, *sxʷaxʷilk*, 10, unknown, 11, *umλum* 'sound of small waves splashing on shore', 12, *aɬλλiqʷ* 'crevasse pattern criss-crossed in rock', 13, *siɬimtimut* 'appears suddenly', 14, *nusxiq̓*, 15, *saɬya*, 16, *numamis* 'fly place', 17, *isaɬ* 'salty feet', 18, *aɬq̓laxɬ* 'stockaded place', 19, *asa·qta*, 20, *anucqʷuc* 'labret', 21, *numu·kʷ*, 22, *nusmaɬayx*, 23, *scki·ɬ*, 24, *q̓ʷumkʷuis*, 25, *cwankʷus* 'cold spring of water', 26, *usʔusq̓ʷp* 'bare place', 27, *snxɬ*, 28, *cumu·ɬ* 'obstructions in the water', 29, *sq̓ʷumaɬ*, 30, *snuʔunikʷlxs* 'point of land intruding into river', 31, *nuʔi·xmaq̓ʷs* 'place of mud smelling of rotted fish', 32, *clkt* 'bald eagle', 33, *nuqa·xmac* 'place of many ferns', 34, *snuɬli* 'place of chum salmon', 35, *uq̓ʷmik* 'hunched over', 36, *nukic* 'water going in all directions', 37, *salmt*, 38, *asasani*, 39, *nunutwinm* 'visible intermittently', 40, *nusq̓lst*, 41, *ascani*, 42, *nuxʷnu·xʷskani* 'place of many soapberries', 43, *numc* 'sound of berries being crushed', 44, *nuλɬi·xʷ* 'place without a waterfall', 45, *λaya·ɬ* 'black bear footprint' or *twina·ɬ* 'visible footprint', 46, *stwix*, 47, *q̓ʷliyuɬ* 'low vegetation only', 48, *snuλlaɬ* 'apparently blocked area', 49, *cu·sila*, 50, *ɬixlikʷuɬank*, 51, *pakʷana* 'big' (in Heiltsuk), 52, *k̓nc* 'any whale', 53, *anuɬxʷumxʷmi* 'underground sound caused by a river', 54, *waxwas*, 55, *ciq̓ʷi*, 56, *q̓ʷusalq*, 57, unknown, 58, *axati* 'mound', 59, *talyu*, 60, *asi·xʷ* 'end of inlet', 61, *q̓ʷapx*. Nos.47–48 were verified as village sites by McIlwraith (1948, 1:8) and Smith (1920–1924) but were known only as place-names to informants in the 1970s (Bouchard 1971-1977).

Carrier and the Chilcotin, as well as with the Bella Bella, yet they have had "wars" with all these groups.

Subsistence

Bella Coola territory provided its inhabitants with a plentiful supply of food and other resources. Because of the area's abundance, its residents were able to remain relatively sedentary throughout the year, apart from small excursions to seasonal camps to exploit specific resources.

Fish was the main Bella Coola food. Five types of salmon were caught, as well as steelhead trout. These fish were procured mainly by traps set in weirs across rivers and creeks. Apparently the fish weirs were once owned by descent groups, but during the nineteenth century, as these weirs began to be abandoned, ownership of them began to be claimed by individuals rather than groups.

By the late nineteenth century gill nets had become the usual gear for taking salmon in rivers, although traps continued to be used in creeks until around the 1920s. Villages along the inlets depended upon tidal traps to obtain the majority of their salmon. In the rivers and creeks, salmon were also taken with a dip net or by means of a harpoon having either one or two foreshafts.

Leisters, hook and line, and gaffs (which were used occasionally to procure salmon) were the most common implements used to catch rainbow and cutthroat trout. These species, eulachons, and Pacific herring, provided boiled, barbecued, or smoke-dried staple food.

Because of their abundance and their value as a trade item, eulachons (particularly when rendered into highly valued grease) were second only to salmon in importance to the Bella Coola. A cylindrical basketry trap and a conical net were formerly used to trap them. In the 1980s most eulachons were caught with seine nets (fig. 2).

Pacific herring were raked from the water in April or scooped up with the same small dip net that was used to empty the eulachon trap. Herring eggs, usually found on blades of boa kelp or giant kelp, were received through trade with the Bella Bella. Pacific halibut, starry flounder, various species of perch and sole, and rockfish were also common food items.

There were complex rites governing the handling, butchering, and cooking of the first chinook salmon as well as the first eulachon run.

Certain intertidal species, including various clams and mussels, could only be found in the outer channels and were dug with the aid of a yew wood digging stick.

Hair seals and northern sea lions, both killed with harpoons, provided a source of meat and oil as well as skins that were used for moccasins and blankets. Beached whales were eaten occasionally.

The hunting of animals was permitted in any territory claimed by an individual's descent groups. Because it was believed that animals had the ability to know a hunter's thoughts, a man had to cleanse himself not only physically by bathing and scrubbing himself with boughs but also spiritually by praying and practicing ceremonial chastity. Only certain men had the ancestral prerogatives to be professional hunters.

The mountain goat was economically the most important animal for the Bella Coola. It was hunted not only for its flesh, which was smoke-dried for winter, but also for its wool, which was woven into blankets, and for its fat, which was used externally as an ointment, internally as the base for a number of medicines, and as a condiment for food.

A variety of deadfall traps, snares, spears, and bows and arrows were used traditionally by the Bella Coola to kill game. The black bear, grizzly bear, Canada lynx, snowshoe hare, American beaver, and hoary marmot were hunted for their skin as well as for their meat. Mule deer were killed in the Bella Coola Valley, South Bentinck, and Kwatna areas.

Fowl, including ducks, geese, and seagulls, as well as the common loon, ruffed grouse, and blue grouse were killed with a bow and specially designed bird arrow (fig. 3). However, fowl did not form a staple part of the Bella Coola diet.

Over 135 plant species were traditionally used for food, materials, and medicines (Turner 1973; Smith 1929a). Plant foods were numerous and varied. In the spring, the young sprouts of plants such as fireweed, thimbleberry, salmonberry, and stinging nettle formed an important food source. Another major plant food was the cambium layer of the western hemlock tree, which was scraped off in the summer and steamed overnight in large pits lined with skunk cabbage leaves. The cooked cambium was then pounded and air-dried in baskets laid out on drying racks; *325*

Natl. Mus. of Canada, Ottawa: 56884.
Fig. 3. Jim Pollard, a Kimsquit resident, showing the usual Northwest Coast way of holding the bow. The arrow release (tertiary) is probably not usual. The multi-pronged arrow was used in bird hunting. Photograph by Harlan I. Smith, 1922.

top, Royal B.C. Mus., Victoria: PN 4579.
Fig. 2. Fishing for eulachon. top, Spoon canoe filled with its catch. Made of a cedar log, the canoe was hollowed out with an adz. It was then widened and hardened by steaming the inside with heated rocks dropped into the canoe and covered with matting, at the same time forcing the sides apart. The canoe was 20–30 feet long and 4 feet wide and was propelled by the use of 10-foot poles (McIlwraith 1948, 2: 538–539). These long canoes were stable and easily navigated the rapids and swift currents of the local rivers. Photographed about 1930. bottom, A load of fish being dragged onto the riverbank. To seine the fish, one end of the net was held by a man standing on the shore while the other was attached to a punt (in background). The punt circled downstream corralling the eulachons in the net and then landed on the river bank at the place where the other end of the net was held. The fish were chased into the net by rocks thrown by men in another punt downstream from the school of fish. Photograph by Dorothy Kennedy, Bella Coola Indian Reserve, B.C., 1977.

Numerous varieties of berries were eaten either fresh or cooked into a thick sauce and poured into rectangular molds to be air-dried for winter use. Either in the spring or in the fall, the roots of wild clover, cinquefoil, and fritillary could be steamed in a pit and eaten with eulachon grease (Turner 1973).

Clothing and Adornment

Both men and women wore fur robes, capes, and sometimes moccasins. Women also wore aprons. Robes were of whole skins and were worn belted in cold weather. Capes were commonly of woven yellow-cedar bark, strips of rabbit skin or mountain goat wool, and trimmed with otter or sea otter. For long distances, caribou skin moccasins were used, although Bella Coola people mostly walked barefoot.

Both sexes wore their hair long and occasionally

the resulting dried cambium was soaked in warm water
326   and mixed with eulachon grease before being eaten.

braided. Personal adornment included necklaces, bracelets, and nose and ear ornaments of shell and bone. Copper and dentalium shells were highly prized (Smith 1920-1924). Tattooing was common for both sexes but not universal (McIlwraith 1948, 1:80, 371, 436).

Structures

Houses were large and constructed from red cedar planks; often they were built on stilts, not only to accommodate the riverbank slopes and periodic flooding but also to provide defense from attacks by raiding parties. House fronts were frequently decorated with the houseowner's "crest," the animal form in which his first ancestor descended to earth (figs. 4-5) (Boas 1892a:410-411).

For winter use, red cedar plank rectangular houses were sometimes constructed in excavated pits. Only the roofs of these winter houses were visible above the ground's surface. The roof was covered with a thick layer of earth; several steps led from the entrance at one end of the winter house up to the surface of the ground.

Technology

Common household items included dishes and vessels made from wood, bark, and stone. Mats and bags were woven of red cedar bark, and boxes were shaped from red cedar wood or made of bark. Spoons of maple wood and mountain sheep horn, and beaver-tooth knives were used until they were replaced by iron implements (Smith 1920-1924).

Transportation

Most travel was by canoe. A long, narrow spoon canoe, made from a single red cedar tree, was used in rivers. This was the most common canoe type used among the Bella Coola. Four types of large sea-going canoes were also used, some of which were obtained from the Bella Bella and the Fort Rupert Kwakiutl and were painted and carved according to the owner's family history. Others of these sea-going canoes were painted all black. Sails of skins or red cedar mats were occasionally used on sea-going canoes. Paddles were carved from red alder.

Two types of snowshoes were used: a temporary snowshoe made from a single red cedar limb, and a sturdier snowshoe made of caribou or deer lacing stretched on a maple-wood frame. The babiche lacing was often obtained from the Chilcotin or Ulkatcho Carrier (Smith 1920-1924).

Royal B.C. Mus., Victoria: PN 7195-B.

Fig. 4. q̓ʷumk̓ʷuʔs village, Bella Coola, B.C. The village was made up of a single row of houses built on pilings. The front doors opened onto wooden platforms that extended the length of the village and acted as a sidewalk. These were all gable-roofed houses, but this fact is obscured in some by a painted false facade of a type unique to the Bella Coola. It consisted of a high central panel of vertical planks and 2 lower lateral panels of horizontal planks (Drucker 1950:251). Conical fish traps and a notched log stairway leading up from the beach are evident. Israel W. Powell, the commissioner of Indian affairs in B.C., and his inspection expedition are in the foreground (Duff 1964:63). Photograph by Richard Maynard, 1873.

Fig. 5. Structural art in the village. left, Old Bella Coola village, B.C. The house at far left has a figure of a man on the roof peak. The house with 5 peaks, representing Mt. *nusq́lst*, has a memorial sign on it to Chief Clelamen who died in 1893, and who, according to the sign, gave away goods valued at $4,000 at his eighth potlatch. A carved figure of a man breaking a stone and mountain goats protruding out of a gable window also embellish this dwelling. The house on the right has a carved pole. At the top of such a pole was carved the crest animal, then a representation of the owner's mother's, wife's, or other groups; lower designs represent beings who helped more recent ancestors (McIlwraith 1948, 1:249–252). The group in front display a copper, an object of great value (McIlwraith 1948, 1:252–264). Photograph by Iver Fougner, about 1897. right, House of Noomts used as a classroom for cultural activities. Entry pole carved by Dave Moody. A Canadian flag flies from pole, right foreground, and the United Church is on the left. Photograph by Wayne Suttles, Bella Coola Indian Reserve, B.C., 1971.

Kinship Terminology

Bella Coola kinship terminology is lineal in the first ascending generation, distinguishing father and mother and merging father's sister and mother's sister as aunt, and father's brother and mother's brother as uncle. Grandparents, especially those living with their grandchildren, are often addressed by the grandchildren using the terms properly applied to parents. In ego's generation the terms are Hawaiian in type, merging siblings and cousins and distinguished only by the relative ages. Blood relatives are distinguished from affines.

McIlwraith (1948,1:404-405) reported the practice of polyandry among the Bella Coola and glossed the term *maxsays* as 'co-husband in a polyandrous household'. However, kinship data obtained from Bella Coola people in the 1970s did not support McIlwraith's claim. They stated that *maxsays* actually refers to 'husband's brother's wife' and can also be used to address a 'co-wife in a polygynous household'; they also felt that the term McIlwraith glossed as 'husband's brother's wife', *k̓ʷuks*, actually has a collective meaning of 'all the wives in a polygynous household'.

Social Organization

The Bella Coola shared a common language, culture, and territory, but the villages did not form a political unit. They were, however, grouped by proximity into four subgroups: the villages of the Bella Coola Valley, whose inhabitants were referred to collectively as *nuxalkmx*; South Bentinck Arm villages, the Talio or *talyumx*; Dean Channel villages, the Kimsquit or *sucɬmx*; and Kwatna Inlet, the *k̓ʷaɬnamx*.

Within Bella Coola territory there may have been as many as 60 occupied sites, although it is unlikely that all were ever used at the same time. Boas (1898:48-50) was given the names of 31 village sites, Smith (1920-1924) 43, McIlwraith (1948,1:5-16) 45, and Bouchard (1971-1977) 61 (fig. 1). A village consisted of from two to 30 houses arranged in a row along the bank of a river or creek. Apparently there was no ranking of houses within the village.

The household acted as the unit of social structure most

operative in providing for the daily economic needs of its members and for assisting in potlatches (Rosman and Rubel 1971:110). The composition of the Bella Coola family probably varied "according to the importance of its head" (McIlwraith 1948,1:150). A wealthy and powerful man's household was sometimes occupied by the husbands of his daughters, his wives, his married sons, and the aged relatives of both his wives and himself (McIlwraith 1948,1:144-145). Around 1900 in the village of q͟ʷumk͟ʷuîs, households are said to have consisted of from two to six brothers and their wives, plus their children and their elderly relatives.

Between the household and the village was the *mnmnts* 'descent group', which McIlwraith (1948,1:119) calls the "ancestral family." Members of this unit are "those whose ancestral names, embodying definite prerogatives, are embodied in a single origin myth" (McIlwraith 1948,1:127). Such a myth is a *smayusta* 'family history', which describes the descent to earth of one of the "first ancestors." It relates how groups of two, three, or four (occasionally more) brothers and sisters were created under the direction of *aɬk͟ʷntam*, the supreme deity, and dropped down to earth to populate the world. Each of these first ancestors wore a cloak representing an animal or bird and possessed one or more names and ancestral prerogatives. Each had some food that was used to supply the world's future inhabitants. Equipped with tools and ceremonial knowledge acquired from the deities, each group descended to a mountain top, established a village at its base, and took territory for subsistence activities. The first marriages were necessarily exogamic; however, realizing that a continuation of this practice would diffuse valuable prerogatives to outsiders, the descent group is said to have adopted the endogamic marriage principle (McIlwraith 1948, 1:120). Thus, as presented in the myths, each descent group occupied its own village where its members intermarried. In reality, society was much more fluid. Marriages occurred both within the descent group and between descent groups. When a woman married outside her descent group, her child, at birth, would become a member of two distinct descent groups, thus giving him or her the right to use the territory belonging to both groups, and providing him or her with the opportunity to validate numerous ancestral names. An individual could thus claim membership in as many as eight different descent groups. Although descent was traced ambilaterally, residence in the father's village tended to reinforce bonds with the dominant descent group; and in time relationships to other descent groups, through the mother, became lost (McIlwraith 1948,1:119-120).

The fluidity of Bella Coola social structure is substantiated by the following: (1) two individuals may claim different ancestors for the same village, indicating that several family histories could be associated with one

Mus. für Völkerkunde, Berlin: IV A 7692.

Fig. 6. Raven mask, probably a Sisaok, representing the form in which an ancestor first appeared, the cloak he wore, and hence a crest of the descent group he founded. Raven is also an important figure in mythology, an inventor and teacher but also a trickster, who stole the sun and brought light into the world (McIlwraith 1948,1:36, 81–91; Stott 1975:78–79). Collected by Fillip Jacobsen; length 61 cm.

village; (2) the "hero" of a *sma* ('myth, legend, story') could be adopted as a first ancestor, thus creating a *smayusta*; and (3) family histories were never told in full except to members of the descent group whose names were embodied in them. Bella Coola people in the 1970s suggested that as the villages became amalgamated, any acknowledged identity between descent group and village became lost, thus accounting for the considerable difference in the accounts of the family histories that have been recorded for each of the villages. The *smayusta* recorded by Boas (1898:50-73) were quite different from those recorded 30 years later by McIlwraith (1948,1:292-360), and the *smayusta* known to the eldest generation of Bella Coola Indians in the 1970s were only fragments of what had been recorded earlier.

Boas (1892a:409) stated that villages were comprised of social units he identified as "gentes," which were known by the name of their first ancestor. Although this unit clearly corresponds with McIlwraith's "ancestral family" there is no consistency between the names of the first ancestors and their founding villages as recorded by Boas and McIlwraith. Furthermore, Boas (1898:48-50) later did not use the term "gentes" and instead listed the "mythical ancestors" of the "village communities." Again this list of ancestors differed both from the list Boas himself compiled in 1892 and from the list provided many years later by McIlwraith.

● STRATIFICATION The status of a Bella Coola man depended, to a great extent, upon his ability to distribute gifts on ceremonial occasions. Therefore, chieftainship was contingent not only upon possession of a high-ranking ancestral name carrying with it a number of prerogatives but also upon lavish generosity. The term *numiɬ* was used to designate a chief who had hosted four potlatches. A woman who had been "rebought" a number of times, thus helping her husband attain greater status, was called *yacalt* and was recognized as a chief herself.

Social mobility was possible among the Bella Coola. Thus a commoner could increase his or her status by the distribution of goods. A slave was on the lowest level. McIlwraith (1948,1:159) stated that "a slave's greatest misfortune lay in the fact that he had no ancestral home, and hence no rights." Nevertheless, some owners gave their slaves Kusiut dance prerogatives, thus allowing them to become influential members of the village (McIlwraith 1948,1:160).

Cosmology

The Bella Coola believed that there were four (some say five) "worlds," one above the other. The center world was where the Bella Coola lived in human form. Above this there were two upper worlds; below it was an underworld, inhabited by ghosts. Boas (1898:27) recorded an account of a second underworld where ghosts, after they had died a second death, sank and never returned. This concept was known only to the older people in the 1920s (McIlwraith 1948,1:25); by the 1970s, none of the oldest Bella Coola Indians was familiar with this belief.

The center world was thought of as a flat, circular island, kept from capsizing by a supernatural being who maintained tension on ropes that were fastened to this island. It was believed that earthquakes occurred when this being became tired and adjusted its grip on the ropes.

The sky was thought of as an inverted dome whose bottom edges rested on those of the world, yet whose upper edge was a flat land. Many deities were believed to live in this flat land, in a large house called *nusmata* 'place of myths, legends, stories'. Among them was the supreme deity, *aɫkʷntam*. According to Boas (1892a:420, 1898:29-30), the Bella Coola believed the sun was the master of this upper world, although Bella Coola people in the 1970s said that the term glossed as 'sun' (*snx*) was used in this context to mean the supreme deity. The list of synonyms for the supreme deity (McIlwraith 1948,1:32) demonstrates how the many names by which this deity was known were a reflection of the many functions it served.

According to Bella Coola belief, the supreme deity did not create itself; it has always existed. *aɫkʷntam* decided to modify the world and created four supernatural carpenters whose task it was to create land features, flora and fauna, and, under the supreme deity's direction, to carve human figures and give life to them (Boas 1892a:420, 1895:241-243, 1898:32-33; Jacobsen 1890; F.B. Jacobsen 1895a; McIlwraith 1948,1:35).

An uppermost world was described by Boas (1898:28) as being the final repository for spirits who had died in the first upper world, but as McIlwraith (1948, 1:25) explained, belief in this uppermost world was not a concept held by all Bella Coola people; it was shared only by two families who learned of its existence through their family history. Boas described this uppermost world, *nuqʷliyals* 'place of green', as being like a prairie without any trees, where a wind was blowing continually. In the far east stood the house of the female deity, *qamayc* 'dear one', who in the beginning of time made war on the mountains, causing them to remain in one place and reducing them to their present size. Occasionally *qamayc* visited the earth, causing sickness and death (Boas 1898:28). One elderly person in the 1920s said that long ago the dead used to dwell in the house of *qamayc*, and another declared that "prayers" were addressed to her, suggesting that *qamayc* may once have been more important to the Bella Coola (McIlwraith 1948, 1:42).

According to Bella Coolas in the 1970s, the traditional belief was that immediately below the world of the living was a world inhabited by ghosts, in which everything was opposite to normal. Food was scarce in this lower world, so ghosts frequently visited the world of the living, making themselves known by whistling or by singing. They could be heard near the burial area on the fourth day after a death. It was at this time that the curtain separating the living from the dead was pulled aside to allow the newly deceased to join his or her relatives. Boas (1898:38) noted that the souls of the dead were at liberty to return to the upper world where they were reborn and sent back to earth by the deities.

In addition to these worlds, there was a cosmos situated below the ocean that was described as being similar to the normal world, but where fish and marine mammals existed in human form (Boas 1895a:39, 1895:258; McIlwraith 1948, 1:26).

The Bella Coola calculated time by observing the summer and winter solstices and counting the lunar months after each, and they believed that the months marked the comings and goings of spirits governing the ceremonial cycle (Boas 1898:41; McIlwraith 1948, 1:27). They believed that animals had powers and were able to assume at will the form of any other object or being. The entire world was populated by spirits, and a peculiar event, a task well accomplished, or a sudden thought all were attributed to supernatural intervention (McIlwraith 1948, 1:513). Individuals could gain favor with the supernatural through prayer, offerings, and ceremonial chastity followed by ritual sexual intercourse (McIlwraith 1948, 1:104–116).

Life Cycle

Pregnancy was believed to occur when the supreme deity asked the four supernatural carpenters to carve a new child (McIlwraith 1948, 1:361). During and after pregnancy, both parents observed restrictions concerning diet and behavior.

When the labor pains began, the woman, accompanied by two hired midwives, went to a birth hut in the woods.

The newborn child was wrapped in furs and the afterbirth was buried immediately.

During the time a child was in its cradleboard, the child's head was wrapped in weasel skin, a head-presser was set in place on its brow, and its body was massaged daily to make it strong and straight. If the parents were wealthy, the infant's name-giving ceremony was accompanied by the distribution of food and gifts to gain public recognition (Drucker 1950:205–208). In former times, infanticide and abortion were sometimes practiced (McIlwraith 1948, 1:36).

According to Bella Coolas in the 1970s, twins were attributed to a salmon's entering the body, and parents of twins had to observe rituals to avoid "offending" salmon. Both the twins and their parents in later life could induce the annual salmon runs by throwing gifts, carved in red cedar wood as miniature salmon, into the river.

Responsibility for a child's upbringing rested primarily with the parents, although other members of the household (particularly the grandparents) and the descent groups also assisted. Much of the care of children was magical in nature: young boys were taught by their fathers to bathe daily in the river and to pray for spiritual aid. They were also whipped with boughs to make them strong. Young girls were taught household chores by female housemates (McIlwraith 1948, 1:702–712).

The nose septum and both ears of boys and girls were pierced with porcupine quills during childhood. The nose was furnished with a nose ring and the ears were decorated with copper, abalone shells, or dentalium shells. Drucker (1950:208) noted that the first ear piercing was done at a potlatch and additional piercings were made at subsequent potlatches.

For adolescent girls, the menarche was marked by a four-day seclusion. These girls' activities and diet were restricted for one year after this. Such girls, when menstruating, were confined in an enclosed area where they lay with their knees bent together tightly against their chests and consumed little food or water. At the end of the year, if the girl's father was a person of high status, he would put up a feast to announce her "return to the people" (Boas 1892a:418; McIlwraith 1948, 1:370–372; Drucker 1950:209–221).

Apparently there were no initiation procedures or restrictions associated with a boy's pubescence, although Bella Coola Indians in the 1970s noted the belief that a boy would have good luck in his life if he noticed blood in his urine during the time of puberty. The first game killed by a boy or the first berries picked by a girl were distributed to the villagers at a small feast hosted by their parents (Drucker 1950:209).

Marriage was an extremely important rite for the Bella Coola, not only because a carefully selected wife ensured that the future children would be firmly established in a descent group but also because the union of two families provided economic assistance in potlatching and opportunities to gain new ancestral prerogatives or regain old ones lost through a previous marriage. It was believed that these matters were too important to be entrusted to young people easily swayed by affection, thus the choice of a mate was the responsibility of the parents and elderly relatives.

Marriage with a close relative, including a first cousin, was prohibited, but marriage with a more distant cousin was possible or even preferred, if it kept prerogatives from leaving the descent group. On the other hand, arranging a marriage with another tribe could bring in new prerogatives. Both strategies were followed (McIlwraith 1948, 1: 375–378; Rosman and Rubel 1971:117).

Preparation for marriage began a few years after the birth of a daughter with her fictitious marriage to an influential man. The emphasis was on the exchange of goods and rise in status, so much so that a man lacking a daughter could ally himself with a chief by performing a fictitious marriage rite with a part of his own body (such as a finger, leg, or hand) representing the bride. Unlike a real marriage, the fictitious marriage was terminated when the bride was first rebought, that is, when the family of the bride assisted the groom in potlatching (McIlwraith 1948, 1:424–425). Fictitious marriages raised the status of the bride's future children.

A normal Bella Coola engagement was initiated when an intermediary acting on behalf of the groom's parents went to the house of the prospective bride to present the proposal. If the parents accepted, they were given various goods to bind the engagement. Wishing to increase their position even more, relatives of sufficiently high status helped to provide these goods.

During the engagement, the relatives of the groom gave prerogatives to the bride in the form of ancestral names from their family history. These names were to be held in trust for the children resulting from the union. They also gave goods to the bride's relatives. The groom was bound to a period of servitude to the bride's father and was required to perform menial tasks such as chopping firewood (McIlwraith 1948, 1:383).

It was the bride's parents who decided when the wedding ceremony would occur. At this ceremony, the guests witnessed the transfer of additional goods from the groom's family to the bride's family. These goods were referred to as "weapons of war" (McIlwraith 1948, 1:392). The bride's father often presented the groom with ancestral names, ceremonial prerogatives, or the special use of a hunting territory, all of which were meant for the forthcoming children and did not become the property of the groom's descent group. Goods given by the bride's family to the groom's relatives were termed "bed coverings" or "rope fastenings" because they were the binding mechanism of the wedding. As McIlwraith (1948, 1:396) noted concerning these goods, "the greater their value, the greater her prestige." After the marriage, both the bride's family and the groom's family assisted each other by providing the goods to be distributed whenever either family was involved in a ceremonial affair (McIlwraith 1948, 1:403).

After the marriage, the relatives of the bride who were involved with the initial ceremony were expected to rebuy her at every potlatch hosted by the groom. Without their aid, the groom could not amass the necessary goods for distribution. The goods also served to validate ancestral names, to increase the status of the groom's children and of the donor's children, and to govern the bride's status in the community (Boas 1892a:418; McIlwraith 1948, 1: 408–409).

If the bride died before she was rebought, her relatives were expected to return the goods received during the marriage transactions. If the groom died before his wife was rebought, the bride's parents were not required to return the marriage goods, but if they did so it raised their status. Levirate and sororate practices were common (McIlwraith 1948, 1:417).

Marriages could be dissolved because of cruelty and neglect. An elaborate ceremony was held to shame a husband or wife who deserted his or her mate for a lover (McIlwraith 1948, 1:418–422).

The Bella Coola, believing in the omnipresence of the supernatural, attributed death to the intervention of supernatural forces. Soon after death, the body was washed and dressed by a relative. The nose ring had to be placed in the septum, for if this was not done, the body would not decay, it was believed; rather, it would roam the earth as a phantom, causing injury to anyone who saw it (Boas 1892a:419; McIlwraith 1948, 1:436).

Funeral rites varied according to the status of the deceased. Most often the corpse was bound into a squatting position and placed in a wooden burial box. A stone was placed on the back of the head to prevent the deceased's ghost from returning and bothering people. Most corpses were buried, but twins were placed in burial boxes in trees. Formerly, coffins were placed in caves, on top of memorial poles displaying the deceased's crest erected in the graveyard, or on scaffolds behind the village houses. Bella Coola people in the 1970s stated that in precontact times, corpses were wrapped in bearskins and left on tree stumps in the forest. Boas (1892a:419) also recorded this but indicated that the corpse was buried. Apparently the use of individual grave houses was a more recent practice that was adopted from the Bella Bella.

Ceremonials occurring after burial included payment of all those who assisted with the funeral and the actual purification both of the relatives of the deceased and of those who handled the corpse.

Much of the deceased's valuable personal property was burned at the funeral, a practice that persisted into early 1980s. Ancestral prerogatives could be inherited by members of the deceased's descent group, but whoever received these prerogatives had to validate them through distribution of goods (McIlwraith 1948, 1:127).

Ceremonialism

Probably the most prominent characteristic of Bella Coola life was its extremely rich and complex ceremonialism, dominated by two secret societies, the Sisaok (*sisawk*) and the Kusiut (*kʷusiyut*), and by the potlatch (McIlwraith 1948; Boas 1892a; F.B. Jacobsen 1891, 1895a; Jacobsen 1891, 1892).

Membership in the Sisaok society was limited strictly to the children and relatives of certain chiefs. Sisaok names, carrying with them the prerogatives of performing a Sisaok dance, were the potential property of those descent group members in whose family history these names were embodied. Many Sisaok prerogatives were acquired by marriage from the Bella Bella. Members of the Sisaok society performed at potlatches, funerals, and occasionally at gatherings of less importance.

Initiation into the Sisaok society included a two-week to four-month seclusion in the back room of the house belonging to the host of the potlatch. Also part of this initiation was the composition of two songs (based on a few of the more prominent points in the initiate's family history), and a public display of a masked figure representing the initiate's crest. This embodiment of the crest provided the initiate with a mask that was used on rare ceremonial occasions (fig. 7) (McIlwraith 1948, 1: 198–203).

The members of the host's family who provided the goods used to validate Sisaok names received public recognition. These goods, which were distributed to all the guests, were said to have "flowed away" and did not have to be returned on any future occasion. Presents made to a few individuals after this general distribution would be returned with interest. After the distribution, singers, who were also Sisaok members, beat the time of one of the initiate's songs. The Sisaok initiate emerged from the back room wearing a blanket, a collar of dyed and pounded inner red cedar bark decorated with pendant weasel skins, and a headdress consisting of a frontlet (a small mask worn on the forehead) affixed to a headband of swan skin, underneath which was a red cedar bark framework with sea lion whiskers extending upwards from it. The whiskers formed a cage from which eagle down feathers would fly as the wearer danced. White weasel pelts hung down from the back of the headdress (Bill Holm, personal communication 1977). A hollow rattle, carved in the shape of a bird and held with the belly up, was clasped in the right hand (McIlwraith 1948, 1:204–206).

The Bella Coola potlatch was said to have originated at the beginning of time when the first ancestors who descended from the upper world prospered in the Bella

Vancouver Mus., B.C.: AA 117.

Fig. 7. Sisaok mask showing a frog draped atop the head of a bear. It was a crest displayed at the Sisaok dance, wherein an ancestral or Sisaok name was validated by transferal of goods. The bulbous face form and solidly painted U-forms on this mask are characteristic of Bella Coola work. It was carved in alder. Painting is in light blue with red, black, and white accents. Brown and gray horsehair forms the crown. Height 32 cm.

Coola country until they were able to invite guests to their homes and show what they had achieved. The supreme deity had told these first ancestors to give away their surplus. The Bella Coola word *ɬlm*, most often glossed as 'potlatch', originates from the root *ɬl* 'throw away something that is no good', referring to the food that would otherwise rot if not distributed.

The most important reason for hosting a potlatch was to invite guests to witness rites in connection with an ancestral myth, especially to "wash away the grief." It was necessary for the host not only to possess an account of his family history but also to have enough wealth to validate whatever was going to take place. The host sought supernatural assistance through supplication and ceremonial chastity, in order to ensure success in the proceedings (McIlwraith 1948, 1:182–243).

Potlatches were held most often in October, before the start of the Kusiut ceremonials, when there was an abundance of food to distribute. Guests, especially those from outside the area, were a very important component of a potlatch for they carried back home with them the news of the host's elevated status.

Those participating in the potlatch occupied certain "seats"; these were not seats in the literal sense, although people did sit in generally specified areas of the house. Rather, potlatch seats were defined by the goods that were expended and the ancestral names that were validated. Apparently a fixed order of ranking these seats did not exist, other than for chiefs who as a rule sat in a row near the fire at the back of the house (McIlwraith 1948, 1:

167–169).

Potlatches were held for the following reasons: the return of a dead ancestor, the strengthening of the host's name and his seat in the house, the repurchase of a wife, the strengthening or establishment of seats for young relatives of the host, the initiation of young people into the Sisaok society, and the giving of an ancestral name to a child. An additional component of the potlatch was the destruction and rebuilding, or remodeling, of a house and the erection of a totem pole (fig. 5) recording the glories of the host's ancestors (McIlwraith 1948, 1:184–185, 195, 249–252).

The *skʷanat* 'memorial potlatch' contained most of the components of the *ɬlm* and was hosted to honor the memory of deceased relatives. Most prominent at the memorial potlatch was the appearance of one of the deceased's crests (McIlwraith 1948; 1:458–459). This not only increased the status of the host but also validated the transfer of the deceased's ancestral names to the close relative who was to occupy his or her former position (Rosman and Rubel 1971:125). Carpenters were hired to carve a figure commemorating the dead relative. This was placed in the graveyard and apparently (in former times) remained there only for one year, after which time it was cut down (McIlwraith 1948, 1:463).

To teach his child the principles of potlatching, a chief would arrange for a 'play potlatch' (*nusʔa·xqamx*) to be held, usually in February. The child was given a name drawn from a myth, and a number of boys, who were chosen to act as singers, were taught the song associated with this name. The play potlatch was characterized by feasting, singing, dancing, and the distribution of goods (in the form of miniature canoes, baskets, bows and arrows, etc.); all these activities were modeled on those of the real potlatch. When it was over, the children paraded in front of the village, singing (McIlwraith 1948, 1: 289–291).

Bella Coola ceremonials, held from November through March, were dominated by the proceedings of the Kusiut society. Preparations began on the fourth day after the September moon was full, at which time, it was believed, a special canoe called *anuwakʼxnm*, commanded by a supernatural being with the same name, left the land of the salmon-people and went up the Bella Coola River. Other supernatural beings joined *anuwakʼxnm* and performed Kusiut dances while waiting for the arrival of *aɬkʷntam*, who was considered the leader of the Kusiut society (McIlwraith 1948, 2:41–51; Jacobsen 1892:437).

The effectiveness of this secret society depended not only upon the profound belief of the uninitiated in the supernatural powers of the Kusiut members but also upon the ability of these members to act as a unit to deceive and impress the uninitiated. Kusiut marshals, those society members who were the earthly representatives of *anuʔulikʷucayx*, the female spirit guarding repositories of *333*

Natl. Mus. of Canada, Ottawa: 56907.

Fig. 8. Willie Mack and one of his sons wearing Kusiut society ceremonial costumes. Willie Mack is impersonating the spirit of a murdered slave woman buried in a great chief's house, to give strength to it (McIlwraith 1948,2:226–229). He wears rags and carries a bundle on his back that represents an infant. The mask, with plug of abalone shell in lower lip, depicts a woman from a northern tribe, probably Haida. The boy, as the initiate, is dressed to be the dancer in the ceremony. Photograph by Harlan I. Smith, Old Bella Coola, B.C., 1922.

power, forcibly recruited young men and instructed them in the methods of deception used by the society. They also urged them to spy on any nonmember who appeared skeptical or too inquisitive. Apparently any nonmember who managed to learn Kusiut secrets was either killed, or, if a prerogative was available to him, was inititated into the society (McIlwraith 1948, 2:14–18). Kusiut members who divulged the secrets of the society were punished by death (Jacobsen 1892:438).

Initiation could take place at any time during the winter ceremonial season. The face of the novice was blackened and he wore a blanket, as well as anklets, wristlets, collar, and headdress all of dyed inner cedar bark (fig. 8). Each novice was required to visit the repository where his Kusiut name was held and then to return to the village on a dancing platform set between two lashed-together canoes. Around him on this same

platform danced several Kusiut members. The novice's spirit had to be adjusted by a *siki* 'professional healer'. In addition, it was necessary for the novice's relatives to distribute gifts to validate his Kusiut name. A song was composed for him. The novice was generally not permitted to hold a dance until the following Kusiut season, and his attendance at all dances during the first year was compulsory (McIlwraith 1948, 2:31–41).

A person who wished to hold a dance notified the marshals of his intention, and the senior Kusiut members would determine whether or not this would be permitted. The summer months were spent in training the initiates (Jacobsen 1892:438). Occasionally permission to perform the more complicated dances such as Cannibal, Scratcher, Breaker, and Fungus was refused if the marshals felt that the dancer was not competent and would possibly expose secrets of the society to the eyes of the uninitiated (McIlwraith 1948, 2:24).

The regular Kusiut ceremony lasted four days, during which time the novices and those dancers who had already performed slept in the house where the dance was being held. During the first three days, songs were composed for the dancers, masks were carved, and a platform with raised sides was constructed where the dancer could conceal himself during the remainder of the ceremony. On the fourth day, after the marshals had decided who would wear the masks, the singers took their place behind the fire. Certain dancers hid behind a mat enclosure in one of the back corners of the house, ready to dash out to distract the nonmembers' attention if the dancer erred. Near the door huddled the fearful uninitiated, witnessing the dramatic representations of supernatural beings (McIlwraith 1948, 2:58).

Immediately after the dancing and singing were finished, nonmembers were told to leave and the masks were usually burned. The Kusiut members gathered outside the house and sang the host dancer's song once more to send his "call," the supernatural power that allowed him to dance, back to the upper world (McIlwraith 1948, 2:27).

The masks used by the Kusiut dancers were carved of red alder wood (fig. 9). Some of the names of masks most easily recognized were: *anuʔulikʷucayx*, Thunder, Echo, Laughter, and Hawhaw (a long-beaked supernatural bird) (McIlwraith 1948, 2:27; Stott 1975:97). Carvers were praised more for producing new mask designs than for duplicating standard ones (McIlwraith 1948, 2:54). Sketches of mask types can be found in Boas (1898), and photographs are in Stott (1975).

Other Kusiut dance paraphernalia included small wooden whistles, bellows (used to imitate the voices of the supernatural), bull-roarers, and occasionally small carved wooden figures representing humans, animals, or birds.

McIlwraith (1948, 1:273–285) assumed that another secret society, called *alkʷ*, existed among the Bella Coola

Ethnografiska Museet, Stockholm, Sweden: 1904.19.16.
Fig. 9. Kusiut mask of a man with a bruised face and swelling eye. This mask was probably used in a series of dances where the dancers undergo feigned mutilation and death and then rise whole back into the realm of the living because of their supernatural power. The right side of the face is mostly unpainted, exceptions being small spots of light blue, a light red ear, a red line over the eye, and a black eyebrow. The left side of the face has black lines with red spots, an unpainted ear, and a red forehead with black spots. The lips are red. This mask was bought from a dealer in Victoria, B.C., in 1893. Height 26 cm.

and stated that as it became less important, the *alkʷ* society apparently became amalgamated with the Sisaok society. However, Drucker (1940:220) stated that the term *alkʷ* referred to the 'master of ceremonies' of the Kusiut dances. Furthermore, a description of both Kusiut and Sisaok dances compiled by F. Jacobsen (1895) suggested that the *alkʷ*, in addition to functioning in the role that Drucker described, also acted as a messenger who invited people to feasts. The *alkʷ* was appointed by the village chiefs and although he received large gifts during potlatches, the *alkʷ* was never required to return them. Elderly Bella Coola people in the 1970s recognized the term *alkʷ* only as 'any messenger'.

Shamanism and Medicine

The Bella Coola believed that their first ancestors were so close to the supernatural that virtually all of them were shamans. Later, human beings had much less power, although each, regardless of status, had the potential to receive supernatural power, allowing him or her to become an *ałukʷala* 'shaman', an *asqnkʷuc* 'shaman with power from ghosts', or a *sxak* 'sorcerer' (McIlwraith 1948, 1:539, 740).

An *ałukʷala* obtained his or her powers through being visited by *ẋica·pliłana*, a supernatural woman who gave him or her a name, four songs, and sometimes the ability to cure sickness. This supernatural visit occurred either while the person was ill or while he or she was seeking shamanistic powers through magical means. An *asqnkʷuc* received power from ghosts and had the ability to see dead

people; such a person, who was not considered evil, transmitted the needs of the dead to the living relatives and cured diseases said to be caused by ghosts. However, a *sxak*, who obtained power from corpses, was considered evil and was very much feared (Smith 1925).

Although shamans were not necessarily members of any secret society, they felt akin to the Kusiut because of their shared contact with the supernatural. Thus, at the conclusion of Kusiut ceremonials, any shaman who had received supernatural authorization performed a dance and conjuring feat to impress the uninitiated (McIlwraith 1948, 1:565).

Herbal remedies were known to many people, although some of them were owned by descent groups and passed on through inheritance. Detailed information concerning the medicinal use of plants is found in Boas (1892a: 423–424), Smith (1929a), McIlwraith (1948, 1:693–763), and Turner (1973:193–220).

Warfare

McIlwraith (1948, 2:338) noted that for the Bella Coola people, "war was secondary in importance to ceremonial rites." He added that peace reigned during the winter, and members of groups who were hostile to the Bella Coola were even received as guests at some dances. Although such enemies might be subjected to insult at potlatches, seldom was there actual violence offered either to envoys or guests.

The lack of centralized authority among the Bella Coola often made retaliation difficult, and raiding parties

335

frequently deserted their task when the fighting was not going in their favor. Sometimes a war party leader was chosen by popular opinion, but not even a chief could compel anyone, other than his own slaves, to fight (McIlwraith 1948, 2:339–342).

Bella Coola raiding parties traveled in canoes. Apparently there was formerly a fixed order in which the canoes traveled. Each man provided his own weapons and carried shields of moosehide or wore armor made from slats of maple or birch (Boas 1892a:421–423; McIlwraith 1948, 2: 341–342).

Attacks were made at dawn; women and children were taken as slaves, but all the men were killed. Before leaving, the raiding party looted and burned the village. When the successful raiding party got within sight of its home village, the captain of each canoe sang a victory song (McIlwraith 1948, 2:344).

Probably the last "war" in which the Bella Coola participated was with the Kwakiutl in the late 1850s (Boas 1897:426–430, 1892a:422–423).

Art

Bella Coola carving style, expressed mainly in masks and monumental sculpture, is most similar to that of the Kwakiutl and other Northern Wakashans. But it is distinctive and generally easily recognized for the hemispherical or "bulbous" form of the face, with surface painting consisting of solid U-forms both following and crossing the strongly defined intersections of carved planes (Holm 1972:80; Macnair, Hoover, and Neary 1980: 49–50). Boxes, spoons, and combs were also carved and occasionally painted.

Both pictographs and petroglyphs are found throughout Bella Coola territory. Smith (1920–1924) recorded a story associating one particularly large petroglyph site with an account of how a first ancestor who was a Cannibal dancer received a special power while at this place. He kept this power hidden there under a stone. Several times each year he invited his friends to this site to sing and dance.

Music

A significant amount of Bella Coola music has been recorded since 1885–1886 when nine Bella Coola singers visited Germany (Stumpf 1886). McIlwraith (1948, 2: 267–337) published a thorough description of the sociocultural content and performance practice norms of Bella Coola songs, with accompanying wax cylinder recordings (now held by the National Museum of Man, Ottawa) and song texts. In 1946 Thornton (1966:300) made several records of Bella Coola songs; in the 1960s the Bella Coola people themselves began to record their songs on magnetic tape; and in the 1970s several non-Indian researchers

taped Bella Coola songs.

Bella Coola songs can be grouped into two major categories: ceremonial and nonceremonial. Ceremonial songs include the following types: Headdress or Sisaok, Hamatsa or *lxʷuɬla*, Mourning, Dance of the Kusiut, and Entrance songs. Nonceremonial songs include: love, lahal (bone game), animal, and story and game songs. Shamans' songs were used both in ceremonial and nonceremonial contexts (Kolstee 1982:8).

Ceremonial songs were composed by specialists who met secretly to discuss which newly composed melodies would be employed for an upcoming ceremony. Texts and wordless choruses were then added. Singing of these songs was an indispensable feature of the validation of ancestral prerogatives. Although considered private property, these songs were sung by a choir (who used sticks and drums to outline the rhythmic design) led by three principal performers: a main singer, an announcer, and a prompter. Various wind instruments, employed to symbolize supernatural beings, were sounded outside the singing area (Kolstee 1982:19).

History

The first non-Indian contact made with the Bella Coola was by Capt. George Vancouver and his crew in June 1793. After anchoring his ship in Restoration Bay, Vancouver used a small boat to survey Dean Channel and Cascade Inlet, while a crew member surveyed Burke Channel and North and South Bentinck Arms in another small craft. Both men encountered the Bella Coola and exchanged iron, copper, knives, and trinkets for much-needed fresh fish and a variety of animal skins (Vancouver 1967, 2:260–276).

On July 17, 1793, Alexander Mackenzie entered the Bella Coola valley from the east, stopping first at the village of *nuɬ̓ti·xʷ*, Burnt Bridge (which Mackenzie called Friendly Village), and proceeded downriver to the sea. Mackenzie's journal (Lamb 1970:358–394) provides valuable comprehensive data concerning Bella Coola village sites, technology, and Native use of European trade goods.

From their encounter only one month earlier with Vancouver, the Bella Coola had acquired a preference for certain items, especially iron, copper, and brass. Mackenzie stated: "When I offered them what they did not choose to accept for the otter-skin, they shook their heads, and very distinctly answered 'No, no'. And to mark their refusal of anything we asked from them, they emphatically employed the same British monosyllable" (Lamb 1970:377).

Bella Coola people in the 1970s have given their own accounts of the arrival of Mackenzie: "The chief put a feather on Mackenzie's head to guide him. They spread the contents of his chamber-pot on the trail, before and after him. They thought that he had returned from the dead, so this would prevent him from disappearing" (Kennedy 1971–1977).

In 1833 the Hudson's Bay Company established Fort McLoughlin near the present village of Bella Bella. Apparently the Bella Coola went there to trade furs for non-Indian commodities, but there exists very little documentation concerning this period; the fort was abandoned in 1843 (Kopas 1970:139).

The Carrier traded their furs with the Bella Coola, who prohibited their passage to the coast and maintained a monopoly on trade with Whites (Palmer 1863:19). Palmer (1863:7) also reported that smallpox broke out in 1863, decimating the population of the numerous villages along the Bella Coola River.

A Hudson's Bay Company post was established in Bella Coola in 1869 and was abandoned in 1882 (Kopas 1970:139–140). Company correspondence from this period indicates that iron and trinkets were no longer as much in demand as they had been (F. Kennedy 1877).

In 1883 the Bella Coola Chief Tom invited a Methodist minister, Reverend William Pierce (a mixed-blood Coast Tsimshian Indian) to establish a mission in Bella Coola (Pierce 1933:44). Other religious denominations established missions, and in the 1970s Protestant faiths were dominant (Goodfellow 1950).

In 1885 nine Bella Coola Indians accompanied Norwegian brothers, Capt. J. Adrian Jacobsen and Fillip B. Jacobsen, to Germany (fig. 10). For 13 months they performed dances and sang songs for European audiences, including the ethnologist Franz Boas, who was inspired by these Bella Coolas to begin his life-long studies of Northwest Coast Indians (Rohner 1969:17).

In 1894 the first major non-Indian settlement, a Norwegian colony, was established at Hagensborg in the Bella Coola valley (Kopas 1970:241).

By the early 1900s few of the traditional Bella Coola villages remained; introduced diseases had depleted their population drastically. In the early 1920s, the Kimsquit, Talio, and Kwatna people requested permission from those living in the villages at the mouth of the Bella Coola River to come and live with them (McIlwraith 1948, 1:16).

As the Bella Coola economy changed from that of a hunting, fishing, and gathering society to one engaged in commercial fishing and logging, the physical structure of the community also changed. By the 1930s, the traditional, extended-family houses had been abandoned in favor of modern, nuclear-family dwellings.

Cultural Persistence

In the early 1920s the descent groups were no longer so operative in village affairs, several of the Sisaok and Kusiut ceremonials had merged, and many of the songs had been forgotten. And although McIlwraith (1922) stated that the Bella Coola were very proud of their own

Glenbow-Alberta Inst., Calgary, Atla.: NA-250-8.

Fig. 10. One of the troupe brought to Germany by the Jacobsens. He wears a cedar bark neck ring and headdress of fur and feathers. The troupe had a contract that agreed "to pay each Indian $20 per month plus food, lodging, clothing, and medical expenses, and personally to supervise and care for 'the welfare and reasonable comfort of the parties,'" who were not to be separated. In return the Indians contracted to perform for 7½ hours each day, "Indian games and recreations in the use of bows and arrows, in singing and dancing and speaking and otherwise in showing the habits, manners and customs of the Indians." As surety for the Bella Coolas' return to B.C. by Aug. 1, 1886, the Jacobsens deposited a $1,000 performance bond with Indian Commissioner Israel Powell (Cole 1985:68). Photograph by E. Hattorff, Hamburg, Germany, 1885.

customs, it was with his assistance that the dances were performed "in better style than they [had] been for several years" (McIlwraith 1923). Elderly Bella Coola people in the 1970s recalled McIlwraith's role as song prompter during the ceremonials and remember him by his Bella Coola nickname, *wina* 'warrior', which was derived from a Bella Coola myth that he found particularly amusing. In the 1970s, several Bella Coola families owned copies of "*wina*'s books" and consulted them regularly concerning Bella Coola traditional culture.

© Natl. Geographic Soc., Washington.
Fig. 11. Celebration of the Allied victory over Germany in World War II. The women wear left to right: black robe originally woven from bear hair and decorated with skulls carved of wood, a costume used in the cannibal ceremony (McIlwraith 1948, 2:7); a button blanket representing Man from the Bottom of the Sea and a spruce root hat with potlatch rings (representation of the number of potlatches given by the owner of the hat). Photograph by Clifford R. Kopas, Bella Coola Reserve, B.C., 1945.

The music records produced by Thornton (1966) also became an important reference for the Bella Coola people. Using these records, along with tape recordings of Bella Coola music made by the people themselves, members of the Bella Coola United Church Women's Guild initiated a program in the early 1960s to relearn the old songs.

In the 1970s, new masks were carved, dancing blankets were made, and Bella Coola dancers and singers began performing for fundraising events. Throughout the 1970s, the Bella Coola singers and dancers traveled to many areas of British Columbia, participating in Indian dancing competitions and providing entertainment at Indian gatherings.

This renaissance of Indian dancing (fig. 12) corresponded with a renewed interest in Indian rights and reawakened a strong sense of Bella Coola identity in the community. As an expression of this, the Bella Coola Band Council began, around 1980, to refer to their people as the Nuxalk Nation (Kennedy and Bouchard 1985).

The contributions of Bella Coola people to anthropological and linguistic scholarship have been significant. In recognition of her invaluable role in assisting non-Indian researchers from the mid-1960s through the mid-1980s, Margaret Siwallace was awarded an honorary doctorate by the University of British Columbia, Vancouver, in May 1985.

Synonymy

Bella Coola is an anglicization of the Heiltsuk (Bella
338 Bella) name *bə́lxʷəlá*, which is applied to all of the

Fig. 12. Performance at Bella Coola, B.C., in celebration of a new hospital. The male dancer wears a recently made Thunder mask, which is painted black and has twigs and down feathers protruding upward, and red cedar bark fastened on either side of the mask. He wears a button blanket with a copper decoration and wooden wings, a dance apron, and wool anklets. The female dancer has on a button blanket, what appears to be a bag decorated with a sun, buttons, and deer hoofs, and a button-decorated hat. Thunder was the most powerful being portrayed in the Kusiut ceremony. His performance at special ceremonies gathered all the spirits together. The dance of Thunder was also sometimes performed as a nonsacred dance (Stott 1975:83–85). Photograph by Dorothy Kennedy, 1977.

speakers of the Bella Coola language (Rath 1981, 1:188). The name is rendered *plxʷla* in Bella Coola (Boas 1898:26; Bouchard 1971–1977). It appears as Billichoola in W. F. Tolmie's journal for November 1834 (1863:292), possibly its earliest recording. It also appeared as Bellaghchoola (Dunn 1844:271), Bellichoola (Scouler 1848:234), Belhoola (Gibbs 1877:267), Bī́lxula (Boas 1897:320), and in other forms (Hodge 1907–1910, 1:141).

There seems to have been no native term for all the speakers of Bella Coola. The Bella Coola themselves used the name *nuxalkmx* for the people of the Bella Coola Valley (from *nuxalk* 'Bella Coola Valley', *-mx* 'people') (Boas 1892a: 409, 1898:49; McIlwraith 1948, 1:11; Bouchard 1971–1977). Since the consolidation of the Bella Coola people at Bella Coola in the 1920s, this term has designated them all; the spelling Nuxalk was adopted about 1980.

Kimsquit is from the Heiltsuk *k̓imxk̓ʷitxʷ*, which refers to the Bella Coola–speaking people at the mouth of the Dean River. The name appears in Tolmie's journal (1963: 292) as Kummuchquetoch and in a few other forms

(Hodge 1907–1910, 1:688). The Bella Coola name for the people of Dean Channel is *suc̓lmx* or, less commonly, *nux̓lmx*.

Tallio is from the Bella Coola *talyu*, the name of one of the villages on South Bentinck Arm. The term *talyumx* can be used for the people of this village but can also refer to all of the people of South Bentinck Arm (McIlwraith 1948, 1:3). The name has also appeared as Tālio′mH (Boas 1892a:409) and in other forms (Hodge 1907–1910, 2: 678–679). At one time the Department of Indian Affairs (Canada, Dominion of 1901, 2:162) listed the Tallio people as Tallion and the Bella Coola as a whole as the Tallion Nation.

Kwatna is from the Bella Coola *k̓ʷatna*, the name for Kwatna Bay and the surrounding area (Bouchard 1971–1977), and *k̓ʷatnamx* designates the Bella Coola–speaking people of the area. At one time a Heiltsuk-speaking group also occupied the Kwatna area (Boas 1892a:409, 1898:48; Smith 1920–1924; McIlwraith 1948, 1:19; Bouchard 1971–1977).

Sources

Beginning with Alexander Mackenzie in 1793, several explorers and travelers recorded summary accounts of various aspects of Bella Coola culture, but the first systematic investigation of Bella Coola began with the work of Boas (1886, 1886a, 1887a, 1892a). Boas described masks (1890b), social structure (1892a), and mythology (1895, 1895a, 1898).

Jacobsen published on mythology (1890) and ceremonialism (1891, 1892), and F.B. Jacobsen published on ceremonialism (1891, 1895) and mythology (1895a).

As a result of the Bella Coola Indians' 1885–1886 visit to Germany, Goeken (1885) described ceremonialism; Stumpf (1886) described music; and Virchow (1886) described the physical anthropology of the Bella Coola.

During the summers, 1920–1924, Harlan I. Smith, an archeologist with the Geological Survey of Canada, Ottawa, traveled throughout Bella Coola territory gathering both archeological and ethnographic data. The originals of Smith's very extensive ethnographic field notes are held by the National Museum of Man, Ottawa. Smith's publications (1924, 1924a, 1925, 1925a, 1929a) as well as his field notes (1920–1924) show that his interests were specifically in those topics that McIlwraith did not describe, that is, technology and subsistence activities. Thus Smith's work is complementary to McIlwraith's.

The principal source of information on the kinship, ceremonialism, and songs of the Bella Coola area is the excellent and voluminous work of McIlwraith (1925, 1948, 1964). McIlwraith's (1922–1924) original Bella Coola field notes are held by the University of Toronto, Ontario.

An outline of Bella Coola culture is provided in the survey conducted by Drucker (1940, 1950). As part of a linguistic study begun in the mid-1960s and continuing through the mid-1980s, Davis and Saunders (1980) taped, translated, and transcribed a number of traditional Bella Coola texts. Stott (1975) studied the relationship between ceremonialism and art. Storie (1973) taped and transcribed a substantial collection of Bella Coola stories in English. Turner (1973, 1974) conducted ethnobotanical fieldwork in Bella Coola. Kennedy (1971–1977) and Bouchard (1971–1977) gathered a considerable body of ethnographic and linguistic data. Edwards conducted extensive interviews regarding Bella Coola Indian health care and traditional medical practices and published on various aspects of Bella Coola culture (Edwards 1978, 1979, 1980).

In the early 1980s, a research team studied the nutritional content of traditional Bella Coola foods (Nuxalk Food and Nutrition Program 1984; Kuhnlein 1984; Kuhnlein, Turner, and Kluckner 1982; Kuhnlein et al. 1982; Lepofsky, Turner, and Kuhnlein 1985; Turner and Kuhnlein 1982; Kennelly 1985; Lepofsky 1985).

Prehistory of the Coasts of Southern British Columbia and Northern Washington

DONALD MITCHELL

The prehistoric cultures under review in this chapter existed in a part of the Pacific Coast lying entirely west of the Coast and Cascade Mountains south from the northern entrance of Queen Charlotte Strait to the Strait of Juan de Fuca and the entrance to Puget Sound. At the time of contact, the area was mainly the home of Northern and Central Coast Salish, Kwakiutl, and Nootkan tribes (fig. 1).

The organizing concept adopted is that of the culture type, basically "a group of components distinguishable by the common possession of a group of traits" (Spaulding 1955:12). The taxonomic units are broadly defined because regional phases characterized by extrapolation from single assemblages or even from a geographically concentrated cluster of assemblages are particularly suspect in an area known, ethnographically, to have been occupied by people whose annual round of activity required seasonal moves of substantial populations over very considerable distances (Abbott 1972). The culture types should be viewed as tentative, largely intuitive archeological units whose strength and probable endurance lie in the generality of their definition. The summaries include lists of "distinctive archeological characteristics"—component attributes that cluster to define the unit.

All discussions of chronology involving radioactive carbon estimates use dates that have been recalibrated with the aid of the conversion table published by Damon et al. (1974).

Strait of Georgia Area—Northern and Southern Strait

Environmentally one of the most distinctive segments of the north Pacific coast of North America, the Strait of Georgia area (locally called the Gulf) was occupied at the time of contact by speakers of eight Salish languages comprising the Northern and Central Coast Salish. The cultures appear to have been based on river and marine resources supplemented by diversified hunting and gathering, and it seems likely that in their most general forms, ethnographic models will be applicable to at least the last 5,000 years.

Boundaries of the Strait of Georgia Salish area encompass several more or less distinct regional cultural variants (Barnett 1939, 1955; Jorgensen 1969). Comparable studies of the distribution of archeological traits have not been done, although partly empirical, partly intuitive analyses were attempted for stone sculpture (Duff 1956a) and for several other classes of material (Mitchell 1971).

The Northern and Southern Strait subareas are reviewed as one unit, the Fraser Canyon as another. In part, this separation reflects differences in the nature of the data: because of very poor organic preservation, Canyon assemblages are almost entirely confined to lithic materials. In addition, parts of the Canyon sequence are so inadequately reported that there are real difficulties in incorporating the proposed phases in an area-wide scheme of cultural units.

Excavations at Locarno Beach, Marpole, Whalen Farm, Beach Grove, and Musqueam, all situated at or near the Fraser River mouth, formed the basis for an outline of phases for the Southern Strait (Borden 1950, 1968, 1970) that has strongly influenced assemblage taxonomy for the whole Northern and Southern Strait of Georgia Salish area. A.R. King's (1950) San Juan Island scheme was reinterpreted by Carlson (1960) and fitted to the Fraser Delta sequence. Matson's (1974) analysis of the resemblances among several components of Locarno Beach, Marpole, and Strait of Georgia forms supports these groupings.

Many carbon-14 date estimates are available for Northern and Southern Strait of Georgia components, suggesting an arrangement of culture types in the following sequence: Charles, 4500–1200 B.C.; Locarno Beach, 1200–400 B.C.; Marpole, 400 B.C.–A. D. 400; and Strait of Georgia, A.D. 400–1800.

Even after dates based on marine shell are corrected, (after Robinson and Thompson 1981), some estimates for each unit in the sequence overlap estimates for succeeding or preceding culture types. It is likely that some or all of the apparent overlap is a product of the inherent inaccuracies of the radioactive carbon-dating process or, simply, ambiguity in component classification. In an evolutionary sequence, assemblages from "transitional" periods may be difficult to classify.

For relative age estimates, the picture is clear and consistent. All known examples of culturally stratified sites confirm this chronology.

Characteristics of the Charles culture type are surveyed in "Cultural Antecedents," this volume. The detailed review here is confined to the post-1500 B.C. era.

Locarno Beach Culture Type

Components of Locarno Beach form (Borden 1950) have been identified at 29 excavated sites whose distribution, extending even beyond the Strait of Georgia area, is shown in figure 1. When Borden (1951) described an occupation by people with a culture of "Eskimoid" stamp, lacking many characteristics of the later, distinctive Northwest Coast culture, the phase became the focus of considerable speculation about "Eskimo" underpinnings of Northwest Coast culture (for example, Drucker 1955a). Although the type is obviously possessed of some uncommon traits, the reconstruction plays down the apparent difference between Locarno Beach and other Strait of Georgia ways of life. Distinctive archeological characteristics (after Borden 1970:96-99; Charlton 1980; Mitchell 1971:57; Peacock 1981; Trace 1981) (fig. 2) include: medium-sized flaked basalt points, many with contracting stems; microblades and microcores, many based on quartz crystals; flaked slate or sandstone tools of generally ovoid shape; crude pebble and boulder spall implements; microflakes of cryptocrystalline and fine-grained rock, produced mainly by bipolar flaking techniques; large, faceted ground slate points and similar points of bone; thick ground slate knives, often only partially ground; small, well-made ground stone celts, generally rectangular in plan and cross-section; Gulf Islands complex items; ground stone and coal labrets, of T and oval disk shape; grooved or notched sinkers; handstones and grinding slabs; sandstone abraders, sometimes carefully shaped; heavy bone wedges; unilaterally and bilaterally barbed antler points, generally with enclosed barbs; antler toggling harpoon heads of one-piece or composite form; antler harpoon foreshafts; antler wedges; sea mussel shell celts; and clay-lined depressions and rock slab features. These items are often associated with deposits containing little shell or shell that is much decomposed. When shells are present, bay mussel is prominent. These characteristics are derived from reports of conventional, "dry" site excavations.

Attributes provided by excavation at the Musqueam Northeast wet site (about 1250 B.C.) consist of twine and cordage of various sizes and styles (single, two, three, and four strand); large gauge netting; basketry; and other products of wood and bark. The most common basketry technique, used for construction of many openwork vessels, has been described as plaited (that is, checker-woven) wrapped twining (Archer and Bernick 1985). The rigid split cedar-withe warps and a rigid member of the paired weft elements are plaited and then wrapped by the second, more flexible, weft strand. Other techniques included checker and twilled weaving, plain twining, and diagonal twining. Several baskets have structural decoration consisting of bands of these different weave types. A common form was the burden basket, produced with a rectangular twilled base.

Among other basketwork forms and objects produced were finely twined knob-top hats. Wood and bark items include yew wedges with twisted withe grommets around the poll, bentwood fishhooks, and a distinctive series of cedar bark slabs reinforced by a few thin splints driven into their edges (Archer and Bernick 1985; Borden 1976).

● SUBSISTENCE Borden (1950, 1951) argued that Locarno Beach was set apart from other Fraser Delta phases by a relatively greater dependence on sea mammal hunting, but after including all components now known and recognizing that some may be seasonal variants, the subsistence base seems comparable in variety and emphasis to that of later times. Deposits include remains of land mammals, especially wapiti and coast deer; sea mammals such as sea lion, harbor seal, and porpoise; birds; fish; and a wide variety of shellfish.

The place of plant resources in the diet is less easily established. At two seasonal sites on or near the Pitt River in the Lower Fraser Valley, occupants were primarily using fish, waterfowl, and large mammals as food (Patenaude 1985; Peacock 1981). On the grounds they were available during the seasons of occupation, Patenaude has also suggested gathering of berries, roots, and other plant foods from the Pitt River camps.

At the Tsable River and Buckley Bay sites of the Northern Strait, year-round collection of shellfish, with the greatest period of collecting activity in the spring and summer, is likely (Keen 1975). Analysis of mammal, bird, and fish remains from the same sites indicates a similar pattern, although the main collecting activity covers a somewhat greater part of the year (Wigen 1980). Patenaude (1985) infers late summer and fall use of the Pitt River site for the collection and processing of salmon, wapato, and berries.

● TECHNOLOGY Hunting and fishing devices seem to have been of sorts that are fairly common throughout the past 5,000 years except the throwing board, which was present in Locarno Beach times but possibly not later (Borden 1970:98). There are toggling harpoons; lance, spear, or knife blades; points for arrows or darts; line or net sinkers; and bone points suitable for a variety of fishing devices.

Small, unretouched flakes of fine-grained or cryptocrystalline materials (crystal and vein quartz, obsidian, chert) are viewed as possible cutting blades for small, easily made fish-cutting knives (Flenniken 1981). On such flakes from the Telep site there are examples of adhering   *341*

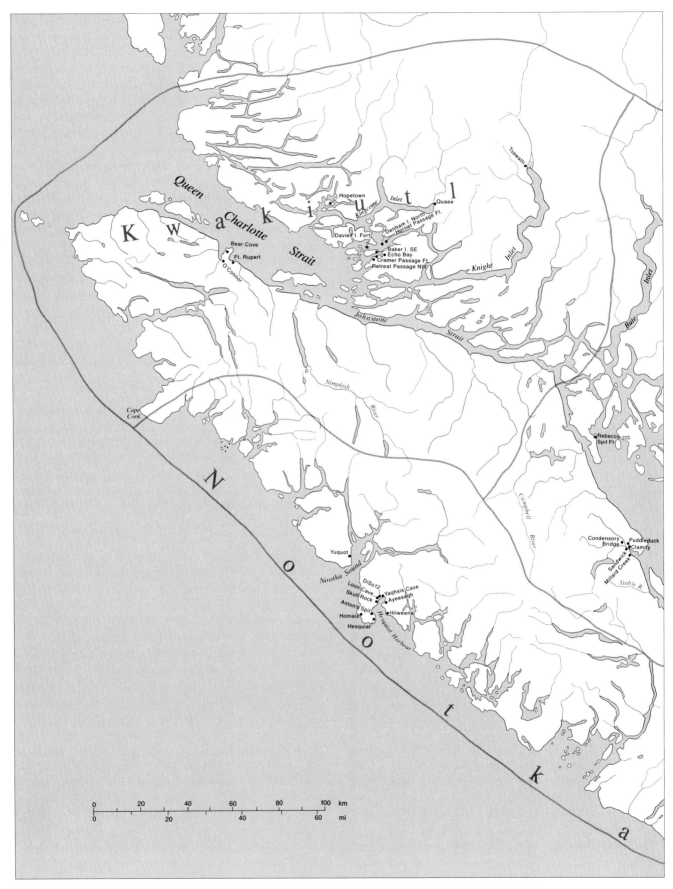

Fig. 1. Archeological sites and divisions of the coasts of southern B.C. and northwest Wash.

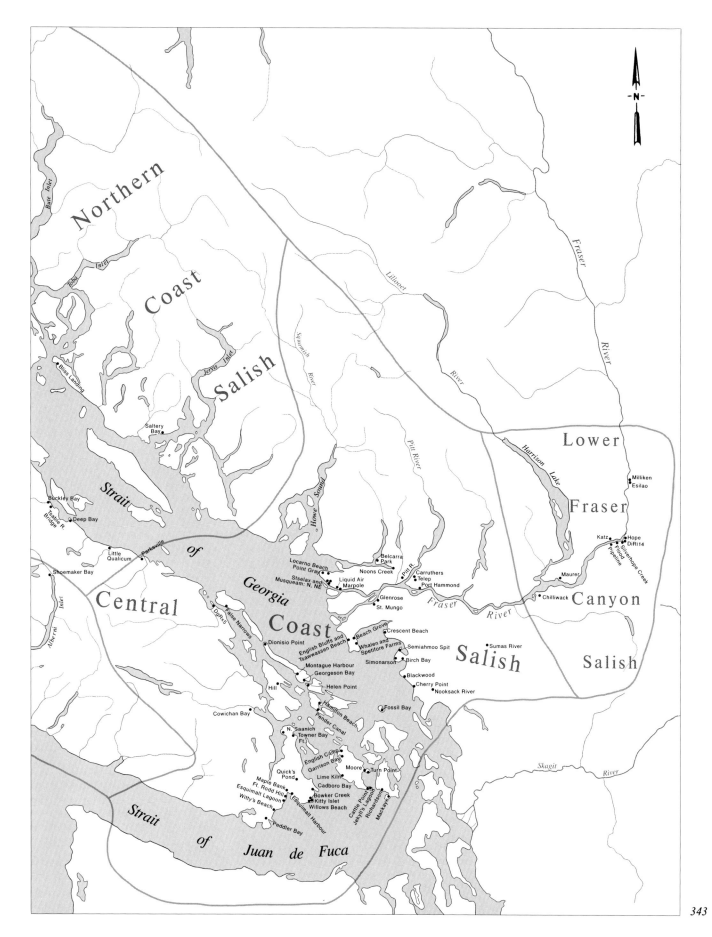

Northern

Coast

Salish

Strait

of

Georgia

Central

Coast

Salish

Lower

Fraser

Canyon

Salish

Strait of Juan de Fuca

Bute Inlet

Toba Inlet

Jervis Inlet

Howe Sound

Squamish River

Lillooet River

Pitt River

Harrison Lake

Fraser River

Fraser River

Skagit River

• Bliss Landing

Saltery Bay •

Buckley Bay •
Tsable R. •
Bridge •
• Deep Bay

Little • Qualicum
Parksville •

Shoemaker Bay •

Alberni Inlet

False Narrows
DgRx5

Dionisio Point •

English Bluffs and •
Tsawwassen Beach

Montague Harbour •
Georgeson Bay •

Hill •

Helen Point •

Cowichan Bay •

Hamilton Beach •
Pender Canal •

N. Saanich •
Towner Bay •
Ft. •

English Camp •
Garrison Bay •

Quick's • Pond
Lime Kiln •

Maple Bank •
Ft. Rodd Hill •
Esquimalt Lagoon •
Witty's Beach •

Cadboro Bay •
Bowker Creek •
Kitty Islet •
Willows Beach •

Esquimalt Harbour

Peddler Bay •

Locarno Beach •
Point Grey •
Stselax and •
Musqueam: N, NE
Liquid Air •
Marpole •

Noons Creek •

Belcarra •
Park •

Pitt R. •
Carruthers •
Telep •
Port Hammond •

Glenrose •
St. Mungo •

Beach Grove •
Crescent Beach •

Whalen and •
Spetifore Farms
Simonarson •

Semiahmoo Spit •
Birch Bay •

Blackwood •
Cherry Point •
Nooksack River •

Sumas River •

Fossil Bay •

Moore • Turn Point •

Castle Point •
Jekyll's Lagoon •
Richardson •
Mackaye •

Milliken •
Esilao •

Katz •
• Hope
DlRi14 •
Flood •
Pipeline •
Silverhope Creek

Maurer •

Chilliwack •

PREHISTORY OF THE COASTS OF SOUTHERN BRITISH COLUMBIA AND NORTHERN WASHINGTON

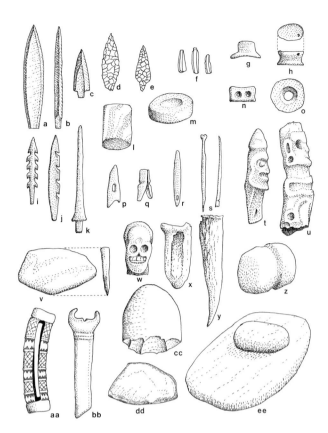

Fig. 2. Artifacts characteristic of the Locarno Beach culture type (1200–400 B.C.), Northern and Southern Strait of Georgia archeological area cultural sequence: a-c, ground and faceted slate points; d-e, simple lanceolate and shouldered flaked stone points; f, microblades; g-h, labrets; i-k, bilaterally barbed antler point, unilaterally barbed bone point, and antler composite harpoon shaft; l, stone celt; m and o, perforated stone disks; n, polished stone pendant; p-q, one-piece toggling harpoon head and paired composite toggling valves; r, bird bone awl; s, eyed and notched needles of bone; t, carved anthropomorphic antler tine hook for throwing board; u, carved antler figurine; v, ground slate knife; w, human skull effigy carved in the split distal end of a deer metapodial; x, bone wedge or chisel; y, antler wedge; z, grooved cobble sinker; aa, slotted antler section decorated with geometric motifs, incised, and carved in bas-relief; bb, bone knife with whale tail motif; cc, cobble chopper; dd, flaked slate or shale knife; ee, handstone and grinding slab. Artifacts not drawn to scale.

residues of animal origin (Peacock 1981:207). Quantities of cracked and shattered oval pebbles are interpreted as byproducts of cooking by stone boiling and possibly by pit steaming methods.

For Locarno Beach culture as a whole there are signs of at least a modest woodworking industry (including the use of heavy splitting wedges and chisels or adzes, and quantities of wood chips from the Musqueam Northeast wet site). Although information on the form of dwellings is lacking, it might be argued that the heavy wedges were employed to produce split planks to cover dwellings. Location of sites suggests that watercraft were important. Woodworking technology seems adequate to the task of dugout production, and it appears logical that this sort of vessel would be used rather than ones of hide or other material (cf. Borden 1951:47).

The highly distinctive Gulf Islands complex (Duff 1956) of carefully shaped small soapstone, coal, and bone artifacts seems to be associated with this culture type although such items are not found in all components.

There are several decorated objects associated with Locarno Beach components (Borden 1983:140-143). Among those reported are bone carvings of a human skull, of a head with conical headdress and prominent chin, and "whale flukes" from the Locarno Beach site; carved antler-tine spoons from Musqueam Northeast; and small antler-tine carving (possibly spoon handles) from the Helen Point site (J.L. Hall 1968), Pender Canal, and the Tsable River Bridge site (Mitchell 1985). Several specimens resemble figures of the Marpole culture sculpture complex, and in their posture, proportions, and style details such as prominent eyebrows, some seem to foreshadow historic Northern Northwest Coast art. However, there is little similarity to carvings of the Coast Salish people of historic times. On stylistic grounds, Borden (1968a) attributed to this culture an ornate throwing board recovered from the mouth of the Skagit River.

● SOCIAL ORGANIZATION There are no specific estimates of community size, although compared to subsequent culture types, settlements appear to be smaller. The very few burials reported show no major differences in the mode of disposal of individuals, nor are there signs of wealth accumulation. Head deformation is rare (Beattie 1980:190-206); of the number known, four are male and one female, and in all cases the deformation is lambdoidal. Six males showed tooth abrasion indicative of labret use. In Locarno Beach society, it seems these decorative practices may have been principally reserved for males. What significance may have been attached to the disfigurement is not clear. It may have represented a class distinction, as many interpret the practice for later occupants of the coast, or it may have been a group identifier, with no implications of social stratification. On the whole, the few clues available on Locarno Beach society suggest more egalitarian arrangements than appear to have characterized the subsequent culture types.

Marpole Culture Type

Components attributable to the Marpole culture form have been reported for 33 sites spread over an area similar to that of its predecessor. The type was named and briefly described by Borden (1950), although there are descriptions by Hill-Tout (1895, 1948) who referred to it as "Pre-Salishan," and by Harlan Smith (1903, 1907). The most thorough examination of the type and its variants was produced by Burley (1980).

Distinctive archeological characteristics (after Borden 1970:99-107; Burley 1980:19-30; Carlson 1970:119; and Mitchell 1971:52) (fig. 3) are: flaked stone points in a number of forms, both stemmed and unstemmed, most medium size, some large well-made leaf-shapes, both contracting and expanding stem forms; microblades and microcores; large leaf-shaped and smaller triangular ground slate points, some faceted, others of lenticular cross-section; thin ground slate knives; ground stone celts of various sizes, many large and of flattened oval cross-section, many with angled bit; disk beads of shale or clamshell; ground stone labrets, generally T-shaped; stone hand mauls, with nipple or decorated top; perforated stones of various sizes; handstones and grinding slabs; sandstone abraders, occasionally decorated by incising; stone sculpture, including decorated bowls, large heads with depressions in the top, seated human figures, decorated straight pipe bowls, incised siltstone; sectioned and split bone awls; barbed, nontoggling antler harpoon points with a tang for attachment to shaft and line guards and/or line hole, most unilaterally barbed; antler sleeve hafts; antler wedges; antler sculpture; native copper ornaments; burials with plentiful inclusions of dentalia, disk beads, rock cairn burials; skull deformation; and large post molds and house outlines.

● SUBSISTENCE Considering the distribution of the majority of Marpole sites, it seems likely that Fraser River salmon, whether approaching or in the river, were an important food source. At the same time, there is evidence other resources—including small sea mammals, land mammals, birds, shellfish—supplied a substantial portion of the diet. Seasonal use and perhaps seasonal occupation are indicated for at least the Glenrose site (Matson 1981).

● TECHNOLOGY The subsistence technology of the Marpole type is recognizably like those of its predecessors and successor, differences being primarily in form rather than function. One obvious but as yet unexplained difference lies in the harpoon forms. Marpole culture is principally associated with a barbed, nontoggling variety, while the earlier Locarno Beach and later Strait of Georgia had toggling forms. Thin ground slate knives are common at some of the prime fishing locales and it seems reasonable to assume that such knives were then, as they were in historic times, mainly used for butchering fish for the drying racks. The smaller perforated stones may be net or line sinkers, and the pointed bone artifacts are suitable for various fishing and hunting devices. Many of the medium-sized and smaller ground slate and flaked stone points were probably used for arming arrows.

Components of the Marpole culture type provide ample evidence of a woodworking industry. Hand mauls (fig. 3q), adz and chisel blades (fig. 3i-j), and antler splitting wedges (fig. 3v) are well represented at some, although not all, sites.

Heat-cracked rocks, present in great numbers at Marpole sites, indicate that cooking techniques included the use of boiling stones. Layers of heated stones may also have been used in roasting or steaming pits.

Marpole settlements seem to have been large, with a

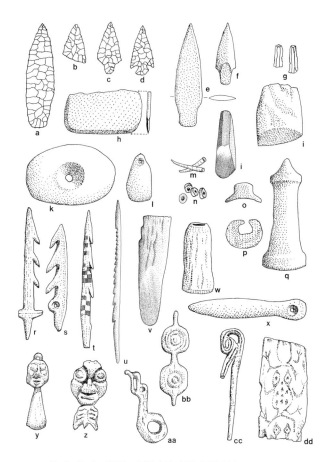

y-z, aa, cc-dd, after Borden 1983:figs. 8:19b, 8:19c, 8:17b, 8:17d, 8:16a.

Fig. 3. Artifacts characteristic of the Marpole culture type (400 B.C.-A.D. 400), Northern and Southern Strait of Georgia area cultural sequence: a-d, chipped stone points; e-f, ground slate points; g, microblades; h, ground slate knife; i, ground stone chisel; j, ground stone celt; k-l, perforated stones; m, dentalia; n, disk beads; o, labret; p, crescentic copper object; q, nipple-topped stone hand maul; r-u, unilaterally barbed antler harpoon head, unilaterally barbed antler harpoon head with proximal hole for line attachment, and unilaterally barbed antler points; v, antler wedge; w, antler adz haft; x, stone club; y, z, and bb, carved antler sculptures; aa, antler buckle or cord adjuster carved in the stylized form of a raptor; cc, long-shafted antler pin with the head of a long-beaked bird carved at the proximal end; dd, incised stone object. Artifacts not drawn to scale.

village layout that saw the big, rectangular, heavy-timbered structures arranged along the shore, backed and separated from one another by mounds of midden refuse. Dwellings may have been of row-house style, as was later the case for the region, or may have been single, very large units.

Water transport was surely important, and considering that suitable woodworking implements were available and that they were so employed by historic peoples, it is likely that dugouts were produced.

At least some of the distinctive stone sculpture of the region (fig. 4) is attributable to the Marpole culture (Borden 1968:19, 1983:147–155; Duff 1956a:95). In addition, there are a number of decorated antler and bone items recovered from Marpole sites (fig. 3y–cc). Common motifs include turtlelike animals with prominent eyes, 345

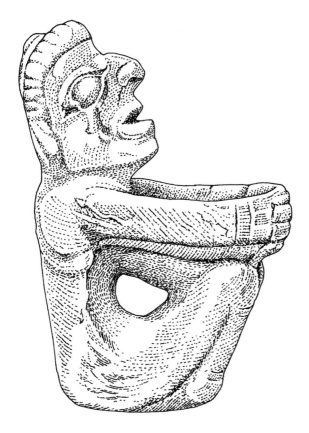

The British Mus., Mus. of Mankind, London: 96-1-25-1.
Fig. 4. Seated human figure bowl carved in steatite, from Cowichan Bay, B.C. This sculptural representation is characteristic of the Marpole culture type stone sculpture complex. Height, 42 cm.

snake or sea monster representations, herons and other birds, and seated emaciated humans. Most design was representational.

• SOCIAL ORGANIZATION Some settlements appear to have been larger than those of the earlier types, but they seem of approximately the same size as those of the later occupants. There are indications that persons of quite different status were to be found in the villages. Some burials are rich in dentalia and shale and shell beads, while others are without enduring inclusions, a finding that suggests distinctions based on the relative wealth of individuals. Similarly, there are persons with deformed skulls and others lacking this feature, possibly indicating a difference in ascribed status from infancy. Beattie's (1980) study of cranial deformation indicates that lambdoidal flattening was usual, but that there was also a high frequency of the frontolambdoidal variety. Deformation was applied equally commonly to males and females.

• COMPONENT VARIATION Burley's (1980) analysis of interassemblage variability, expanding earlier work (Matson 1974; Monks 1973, 1976; G. Thompson 1978), provides the best data for a discussion of regional and temporal variants. His comparisons suggest that some time segregation can be seen, with a group of early

components sharing, among other attributes, a higher proportion of contracting stem points, leaf-shaped points, and microblades. There is also an obvious eastern strait–western strait division. Of the 18 components considered, the Marpole site itself stands as the sole exception to this pattern. Mainland components have relatively large numbers of flake tools; island components are characterized by shaped abraders, saws, and handstones. Finally, there is some support for isolation of a "Beach Grove" variant of the Marpole culture type (Mitchell 1971:56), which would include at least the False Narrows assemblages as well.

Strait of Georgia Culture Type

Most investigators have considered the cultures at and immediately preceding contact as constituting a single culture type variously referred to as the Developed Coast Salish, Late, Recent, or Strait of Georgia form. As figure 1 shows, the type is widespread in the area.

Distinctive archeological characteristics (after Borden 1970:100–112; Carlson 1970:120; Mitchell 1971:48) (fig. 5) of the type are: small triangular flaked basalt points; thin triangular ground slate points, many with thinned base; thin ground slate knives; large ground stone celts, generally well made; flat-topped stone hand mauls; sandstone abraders, generally of irregular outline; unilaterally barbed bone points, usually with many enclosed barbs; bone single-points and bipoints; split and sectioned bone awls; antler composite toggling harpoon valves; decorated bone blanket or hair pins; decorated antler combs; antler wedges; triangular ground sea mussel shell points; skull deformation; large post molds and house outlines; and sites with protective ditches and wall or palisade features.

Investigations of two wet-site components, English Camp on San Juan Island (Sprague 1976) and Little Qualicum River (Bernick 1983), add to this list twisted withe cordage of various sizes; checker weave, open plain twining, open wrapped twining (fig. 6), and plain twined basketry and matting; wooden wedges, bentwood fishhooks, and wooden stakes; and folded cedar bark canoe bailers.

• SUBSISTENCE Site locations, artifacts, and faunal material all point to the conclusion that the culture was built on fishing, hunting, and gathering, with a heavy reliance placed on fishing for salmon.

The relative dietary contributions of the different subsistence pursuits are difficult to assess. Although good faunal data are available for a number of Strait of Georgia components (Bernick 1983; Boehm 1973; Boucher 1976; Mitchell 1980, 1981a; Monks 1977, 1980; Patenaude 1985), these are all, evidently, seasonal assemblages. Moreover, most analyses are of spring occupations, a very few of summer and fall, and there are none for winter

346

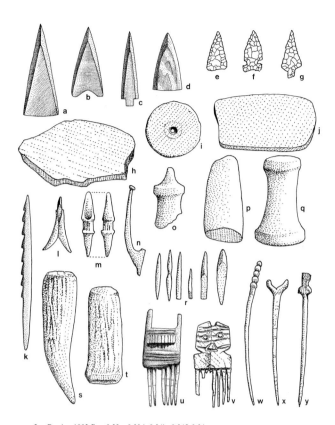

u-y after Borden 1983:figs. 8:32c, 8:32d, 8:34b, 8:34f, 8:34g.
Fig. 5. Artifacts characteristic of the Strait of Georgia culture type (A.D. 400–1800), Northern and Southern Strait of Georgia area cultural sequence: a-d, ground slate points; e-g, chipped stone points; h, abrasive stone; i, spindle whorl; j, ground slate knife; k, unilaterally barbed bone point; l, composite toggling harpoon head with wedge-based arming point; m, dorsal and ventral views of composite toggling harpoon valve with lashing groove and stepped point bed; n, fishhook shank; o, bone points and bipoints; p, head of nipple-topped stone hand maul; q, ground stone celt; r, complete flat-topped stone hand maul; s, antler wedge; t, antler haft for an adz; u-v, carved combs; w and y, hair or blanket pins; x, blanket pin. Artifacts not drawn to scale.

settlements.

Spring data show the considerable importance of shellfish and herring fisheries, and summer and fall, of the various salmon runs. Flatfish (sole, flounder), dogfish, and rock fishes are seasonally and locally important. In all sites, remains of coast deer, wapiti, and dog are particularly common although their relative significance varies from site to site. Dog bones, in contrast to those of other mammals, are often articulated and seldom shattered, suggesting that in the past, as at contact, they were not considered a food source. The most common bird remains, especially prominent in spring assemblages, are species of waterfowl and gulls.

● TECHNOLOGY The many fish-catching, mammal-hunting, and plant- and shellfish-gathering devices known to have been characteristic of the area at the time of contact have undoubtedly been a part of Strait of Georgia culture for some considerable time. Assemblages include artifacts that are likely the remains of herring rakes, fish

B.C. Prov. Mus., Victoria: DiSc-1:165.
Fig. 6. Wrapped twined openwork basket fragment from the Little Qualicum River site, Vancouver I., Strait of Georgia culture type. Width, 36 cm.

gorges, leisters, toggling harpoons, composite fishhooks, trolling hooks, barbed arrow and spear points, net or line weights, and net gauges.

River and saltwater traps of several kinds were important to occupants of the Strait of Georgia area at contact and they were obviously present in earlier times. The remains of large stone tide traps and river weirs are known, particularly from the Northern Strait. Tide traps were probably primarily for taking flatfish and sculpins, although Monks (1977) argues use of the huge Deep Bay trap for herring. Segments of sturdy, open-twined basket-ry of cedar bark and split fir have been interpreted as the latticework from a fish weir on the Little Qualicum River (Bernick 1983:286). Concentrations of anchor stones and net weights attributable to reef net gear have been located at traditional fishing sites in Straits Salish territories of the Southern Strait. One set of these clusters, the location of from three to five rigs, is at least 300 years old (Easton 1985). The differing waterfowl assemblages reported for the Crescent Beach (Lawhead 1980) and Deep Bay sites could be explained by use of a pole net at the former and submerged nets at the latter (Ham 1982:355).

Evidence for food preparation techniques is contained in abundant heat-cracked rocks. Cooking techniques probably included boiling with heated stones and steaming or roasting in pits containing hot stones.

Woodworking implements are comparable to those of the Marpole culture type, from which they differ mainly in minor, specific detail rather than in general form. Hand mauls, for instance, are commonly flat-topped rather than nipple-topped or decorated. From wet-site components there is evidence of weirs and perhaps other traps, fishhooks, and wedges. Bark and plant fiber products known from these water-saturated deposits include baskets of various sizes, forms, and weaves; mats; cordage; hats; and bark canoe bailers.

Settlements consist of one or more rows of dwellings along a shore and sometimes include both row-house and single dwelling structures. Located nearby may be a refuge formed by walls and ditches enclosing temporary shelters. Houses had heavy timber framing and were probably clad in split cedar planks.

Artistic products of the Strait of Georgia culture type are infrequently reported (but see Borden 1983:161–163), perhaps in large measure because the major Northwest Coast decorated objects were of very perishable materials—grass, wood, bark, split root, or wool. Among the ornamented pieces recovered archeologically are spindle whorls, combs, and blanket or hair pins (fig. 5i, u-x). Designs are frequently geometric or curvilinear, and there are proportionately fewer that are representational than was the case for the Marpole culture type.

• SOCIAL ORGANIZATION Variations in the sizes of sites, association of those sites with different faunal assemblages, and data on months when fauna were collected suggest, for at least some parts of the Strait, a seasonal pattern of settlement much like that of the Northern and Central Coast Salish, with large winter and sometimes large summer village groups and smaller spring, summer, and fall encampments at gathering and fishing locales.

In differential burial practices there are indications of status differences. It is uncertain whether head deformation signifies class differences or group affiliation.

The widespread distribution of sites with trench embankment features argues for intergroup conflict of sufficient frequency and severity to justify the considerable labor entailed in construction and maintenance. Because they are generally lacking an obvious source of fresh water and because midden remains associated with them are usually shallow, they are better viewed as refuges than fortified villages. Such an interpretation is consistent with the historic pattern of fighting, which involved opportunistic raids rather than seige.

• COMPONENT VARIATION There are noticeable differences among the assemblages attributed to this culture type. It seems likely that many are the result of seasonal differences in site use, but there seem also to be some broad regional distinctions that may eventually be tied to the historically recorded "ethnic divisions" (Barnett 1955) or, perhaps, to culture clusters such as those identified by Jorgensen (1969) or Mitchell (1971:29–30).

Carlson (1970) associates his San Juan phase components with the forerunners of the several historic Straits

Salish groups, but even within this cultural division variability arises from seasonal pursuits and seasonal movement of the population. Within the Halkomelem speakers' territory at least some of the east-west regional variation (canyon, delta, island) must be explainable by seasonal activities and seasonal moves (Abbott 1972). Some of the same groups were regularly occupying sites in all three regions. Two of the more obvious of these perhaps seasonally related geographical distinctions are the relatively higher proportion of flaked stone artifacts from Vancouver Island and Gulf Island portions of Halkomelem territory than from the delta area and the significantly greater abundance of ground slate knives along the Fraser River than on the islands.

Strait of Georgia Area—Lower Fraser Canyon

The Lower Fraser Canyon region consists of a portion of the Fraser River valley extending from within the Coast-Cascade Mountain system downstream to about the vicinity of Chilliwack. Its archeological distinctiveness is attained largely by the presence of remains of semi-subterranean winter dwellings, by the absence of shell midden, and by the resulting near absence of bone and antler artifacts and faunal remains from the assemblages. There is, in addition, a prominent soft stone carving industry that is poorly represented in coastal assemblages.

Major excavations in the area (fig. 1) include work at the adjoining Milliken and Esilao Village sites (Borden 1961, 1968; Mitchell 1963), at the Katz site (Hanson 1973; Von Krogh 1976), several sites on the left bank of the Fraser River a short distance downstream from Hope (Archer 1980; Eldridge 1982), and the Flood and Pipeline sites (Von Krogh 1980). On the basis of material collected at the first two sites, Borden (1968), proposed a long series of "phases," to which subsequent workers have attempted, with varying success, to fit their results. The last five of Borden's cultural units were the Eayem, Baldwin, Skamel, Emery, and Esilao phases. Baldwin was distinguished from the others by the presence of microblade technology and labrets, rings, earspools, numbers of beads, and other small products of a soft stone carving industry. Skamel was distinct for the absence of those artifact categories that characterized the preceding phase and for the presence of many items made of cryptocrystalline rock. The Emery phase saw the return of the softstone carvings with the addition of straight pipes to the list of products, while the Esilao phase was characterized by small triangular point forms.

These Milliken and Esilao components are combined here with assemblages from several downstream sites to form three distinct culture types. The third one, an amalgamation of the Emery and Esilao "phases," has been named the Canyon culture type both to parallel the terminology for the coastal Strait of Georgia sequence and to indicate a belief the type will eventually be identified for the late period in all parts of the central and lower Fraser canyon.

Radioactive carbon estimates indicate a progression from Baldwin through Skamel to Canyon culture types but the boundary between the first two is unclear as there is a 200-year period of overlap within which fall two Baldwin and four Skamel estimates. There is also a substantial 700-year gap between the earliest Baldwin estimate and the last date for a component of the preceding Charles culture type. Half of the overlap and half of the gap have been assigned to the span of each adjoining culture type in the following estimate of time values for the Canyon sequence: Charles, 4500–1700 B.C.; Baldwin, 1700–500 B.C.; Skamel, 500 B.C.–A.D. 500; Canyon, A.D. 500–1800.

The Charles culture type characteristics are reviewed in "Cultural Antecedents," this volume. Only the post-1700 B.C. portion of the sequence is considered here.

Baldwin Culture Type

The least securely defined and yet probably the most distinctive of the lower Fraser Canyon culture types is known from but three components: one each at the Milliken, Esilao Village (Borden 1968:15–16), and Component 2 at DiRi 14 (Eldridge 1982).

Distinctive archeological characteristics (fig. 7) of the type consist of: flaked stone points of various sizes and forms, both stemmed and unstemmed, medium to small; cortex spall tools; numerous retouched and utilized flakes; pebble core tools; microblades and microcores; ground slate knives; ground stone celts; a soft stone industry with products including pendants, disk beads, labrets, earspools, "rings," and small anthropomorphic and zoomorphic carvings; hammerstones; and quartz microflakes.

● TECHNOLOGY A major distinguishing characteristic of the culture type is the plentiful evidence for the working of talc, steatite, schist, and shale by carving, drilling, abrading, and polishing. The objects manufactured are all of a nonutilitarian, occasionally ornamental nature. Borden (1968:15) suggested that small stemmed points characteristic of the components at Milliken and Esilao Village were likely arrow rather than dart, spear, or knife points, but few other inferences have been made about the use of Baldwin artifacts.

At the Skamel culture type Katz site, cortex spall implements would be suitable for preparing fish for drying and storage (Hanson 1973); perhaps the numerous utilized flakes, large and small, and the small pieces of apparently unused quartz debitage were so used here. Many of these microflakes may have been used in the manner reconstructed by Flenniken (1981). But because of the poor bone preservation at Canyon sites, evidence of subsistence is lacking.

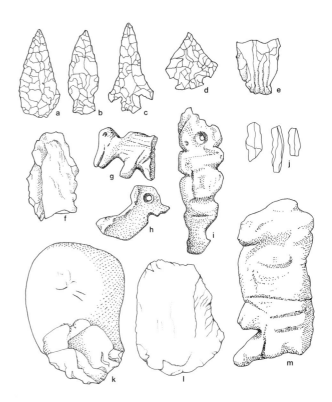

a-f, j, after Eldridge 1981:figs. 5, 18g, 18h, 18d, 18f; g-i, m, after Borden 1983:figs. 18j, 18k, 18o, 18l.

Fig. 7. Artifacts characteristic of the Baldwin culture type (1700–500 B.C.), Lower Fraser Canyon–Strait of Georgia archeological area cultural sequence: a-d, flaked stone points; e, microblade core; f, bifacially flaked stone knife; g-h, zoomorphic stone figures; i, stone figure of a fantastic segmented creature; j, microblades; k, cobble chopper; l, spall tool; m, probable miniature death mask carved in stone. Length of l, 4.7 cm; b-h and j to same scale. i and k-m not drawn to scale.

At three sites excavated, there is no sign that pit houses were in use; However, they have been attributed to the earlier Charles culture type at the Maurer site (LeClair 1976), and they occur in later components.

With only three components (and two of these inadequately reported) it is not wise to make much of the apparent differences between the Milliken and Esilao assemblages and the one from DiRi 14. The principal divergence lies in the prevalence of carved stone items. There is not anything like the same wide range of ornaments at DiRi 14.

Skamel Culture Type

Excavated Skamel components are found at Esilao Village (Borden 1968:16); the Katz site where the Zone A and B assemblages identified by Hanson (1973) and the Zone C by Von Krogh (1976) seem to fit the Skamel pattern; the Flood site Component 1 (Von Krogh 1980); the Pipeline site (Von Krogh 1980); and Silverhope Creek Zone A (Archer 1980).

Distinctive archeological characteristics (fig. 8) of the   *349*

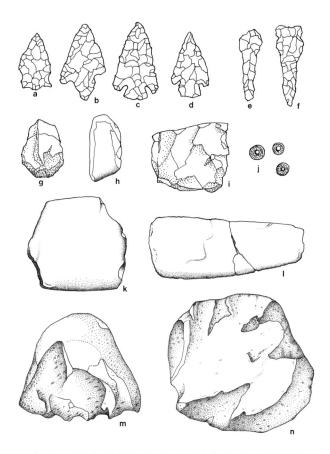

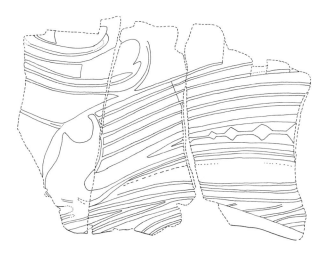

after Borden 1983:fig. 8:28.
Fig. 9. Fragment of a charred wooden board, engraved with an elaborate curvilinear design. From the Skamel component of the Esilao site, B.C. Length, 21.3 cm.

a-k, after Archer 1980:figs. 17, 19, 19g, 19i, 22k, 31, 19k; l after Von Krogh 1980:fig. 43f; m-n after Von Krogh 1976:figs. 35, 19.
Fig. 8. Artifacts characteristic of the Skamel culture type (500 B.C.-A.D. 500), Lower Fraser Canyon–Strait of Georgia archeological area cultural sequence: a-d, flaked stone points; e-f, key-shaped flaked stone drills; g, flaked stone end scraper; h, ground stone celt; i, large retouched stone flake; j, disk beads; k, tabular stone saw; l, ground slate knife; m, pebble chopper; n, spall tool. Length of a, 2.6 cm; b-j to same scale. k-n not drawn to scale.

culture type include: flaked stone points, including leaf-shaped, contracting stemmed, corner notched, and basal notched varieties, many made of cryptocrystalline rock; flaked stone drills; formed flaked end scrapers; cortex spall tools; numerous retouched and utilized flakes; pebble core tools; ground slate knives; ground stone celts; shale and slate disk beads; schist and sandstone saws; abrasive stones; and circular pit houses and cache pits.

Excavations at Esilao revealed burned timbers from a forerunner of that village's semisubterranean winter dwellings. Preserved in the collapsed structure were charred remnants of checker weave matting, coils of fine two-strand line with small perforated stone sinkers, wooden objects looking very much like modern net shuttles or small handline reels, and a carved wooden box or tray (fig. 9).

What most obviously sets this culture type apart are the absence of any evidence of microblade technology and the near absence of the stone carving complex. Additionally, a shift from basalts and cherts to glassy textured materials

for flaking distinguishes Skamel from its predecessor, Baldwin.

● TECHNOLOGY Without significant quantities of faunal remains, it is difficult to reconstruct the subsistence patterns or to arrive at conclusions about tool function. Those who have reported on Skamel assemblages have uniformly suggested that salmon were being processed and have identified ground slate knives and cortex spall tools as probable butchering implements. From the presence of celts and pebble core tools some (Archer 1980) have inferred a woodworking industry. The profusion of unifacial "scrapers" is taken as evidence of hide processing.

As there are sites with and sites without the remains of semisubterranean dwellings, there is likely seasonal occupation of at least some settlements. Excavations of house pits have so far disclosed little about the superstructure. All are circular, oval, or subrectangular in plan; and most possess a raised earth bench around the nearly flat interior floor. One or several hearths may be present.

The presence of multiple hearths in a single large dwelling suggests use by more than one family unit. Certain kinds of activities were spatially separated within settlements (Archer 1980; Eldridge 1982; Hanson 1973; Von Krogh 1976). At DiRi 14 and the Silverhope Creek sites (both without house pits) the distribution generally conformed to a "ring" model, with a central area for cooking, food processing, and light manufacturing, and a peripheral zone for "messy" space-consuming tasks (Archer 1980:137; Eldridge 1982:81).

● COMPONENT VARIATION Between the earliest of the Skamel components (Silverhope Creek) and the latest (Pipeline) there is very little difference that cannot be accounted for by the fact that one is and one is not a pit house settlement. For a span of about 1,000 years, the

MITCHELL

Canyon saw a comparatively unchanging lifeway.

Intersite variation is also most easily explained as resulting from differences in the nature of the settlement. Given the historic pattern of a marked winter-summer distinction in dwellings, it is likely that pit house sites are at least winter occupied and that "non–pit house" sites are spring, summer, or fall settlements.

Canyon Culture Type

Borden's (1968:22–24) Emery and Esilao phase components from the Milliken and Esilao Village sites join Component 3 at DiRi 14 (Eldridge 1982) and Components 2–5 at the Flood site (Von Krogh 1980) to form the Canyon culture type, representing the late occupancy of the Lower Fraser Canyon.

Distinctive archeological characteristics (fig. 10) comprise the following: flaked stone points, including basal-, corner-, and side-notched forms, generally small; flaked stone drills; cortex spall tools; retouched and utilized flakes; ground slate knives; ground stone celts; soft stone industry, including disk beads, small figurines, and trumpet-shaped straight pipes; sandstone and schist saws; sawn nephrite pebbles; abrasive stones; stone hand mauls; circular pit houses and cache pits.

Reappearance of stone carving and, in particular, the production of finely made, occasionally elaborately decorated, pipes and other soft stone objects set the Canyon culture type off from the earlier Skamel.

The large quantities of ground slate knives—traditional implements for preparing salmon for drying and storage—suggest that the salmon fishery was important throughout at least A.D. 500–1800. A very few faunal remains were preserved in the upper deposits of the Esilao Village site. These include some goat horn cores (Borden 1968:23), possible evidence of hunting excursions into the mountains.

Numerous small flaked stone points, especially the late triangular side-notched variety, are almost certainly for arming arrows. Even more numerous are the ground slate knives. Bark rolls, charred at one end and plentiful in the Esilao Village deposits, may be the remains of torches to assist in night-time fishing.

Stages in the manufacture of disk beads and stone pipes have been reconstructed from partly and completely finished objects and waste material as it was evident these objects were being produced in the one house excavated at Esilao Village (Mitchell 1963).

The semisubterranean dwellings were much like those of the Thompson people (Teit 1900:192–195). For one house at Esilao Village (Mitchell 1963) there was evidence of four uprights within the dwelling, four main rafters, and subsidiary hip rafters. A rock slab near the central hearth may have served as protection for the base of the notched log entry ladder.

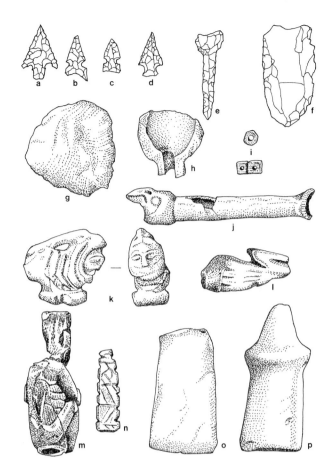

a-e, h-j, l after Mitchell 1963:pls. l, lv, lx; f-g, k, o-p, after Von Krogh 1980:figs. 25b, 28a, 53k, 38h; m after Borden 1983:fig. 8:29a.
Fig. 10. Artifacts characteristic of the Canyon culture type (A.D. 500–1800), Lower Fraser Canyon–Strait of Georgia archeological area cultural sequence: a-d, flaked stone points; e, flaked stone drill; f, burinated flake; g, cortex spall tool; h, flared stone pipe bowl fragment; i, stone disk bead and bead blanks; j, stone bird effigy mouthpiece for a tubular or straight pipe; k, anthropomorphic stone pipe; l, problematic carved steatite object; m, seated human effigy pipe of stone; n, decorated steatite pendant; o, ground stone celt; p, nipple-topped stone hand maul fragment. Length of a, 5.9 cm; b-j, l-n, to same scale. Length of k, 4.5 cm, o-p to same scale.

There are sites with house pits and sites without, which may be interpreted as evidence of seasonal use of some sites.

It is likely that characteristics of Upper Stalo society at the time of contact (Duff 1952a) will also apply to the Canyon culture type in prehistory. However, there is very little evidence on which to base a reconstruction. Winter dwelling units within a settlement vary considerably in size, suggesting the composition of households was also variable, and there is a wide range in the number of house pits found in the settlements themselves.

Seasonal site differences probably account for most of the interassemblage variability. In particular, it seems that stone carving was mainly a winter site activity; it is poorly represented at the spring, summer, or fall DiRi 14 but very visible in the nearby Flood site winter village and at Esilao Village.

351

The major division in the time sequence comes with the late appearance of small triangular side-notched flaked stone points. Their arrival at about A.D. 1200 coincides with a change in pipe form; an earlier "effigy" style does not continue (Borden 1968:22–23).

Culture History of the Strait of Georgia Area

Speculations about the beginning of the Locarno Beach culture type have focused on similarities with coastal Alaska assemblages and interpreted these as grounds for derivation of Locarno from the more northern culture form or for descent from an older, shared basal culture on the west coast (Borden 1951; Drucker 1955a). However, as details of the early portions of the area sequence fill in, it becomes increasingly clear that there are suitable antecedents in what has come to be known as the Charles phase or culture type (Borden 1975).

Charles culture type components at the St. Mungo Cannery (Calvert 1970), Glenrose Cannery (Matson 1976), Crescent Beach (Percy 1974), Pitt River (Patenaude 1985), Maurer (LeClair 1976), Helen Point (Carlson 1970), and Tsable River Bridge (Mitchell 1985) are characterized, to varying extents, by assemblages bearing considerable resemblance to those of the Locarno Beach culture type. In particular, there are similar contracting stem points, mircoblades, celts, antler wedges, and, at some sites, a comparable high incidence of bipolar flake production of cryptocrystalline mircoflakes. In the Northern Gulf especially, late Charles components incorporate items of the distinctive Gulf Islands complex.

Without abrupt change in the character of the assemblages the transition from Charles to Locarno Beach is seen as an evolutionary one. Ground slate implements improved in quality and their production increased; the Gulf Islands complex items, whatever may have been their use, became more popular; a wider range of artifacts was made of bone, antler, and shell (and probably of wood) as abrading became an increasingly important manufacturing technique.

In its basics, the Locarno Beach way of life closely resembles that of its predecessors. A wide variety of land mammals and marine mammals, anadromous and marine fish, birds and shellfish were taken for food and materials. A woodworking industry was prominent. There is evidence that the pattern of seasonal occupation of sites for exploitation of the resources available from those sites was also continued.

In Locarno Beach there is evidence some males were distinguished from other males (and from most females) by head deformation and the wearing of labrets, but it is not clear that this is an indication of rank or stratification of society.

It seems reasonable to assume that Locarno Beach culture evolved into Marpole form. Some of the apparent overlap of the culture types may simply result from forcing transitional Locarno Beach and Marpole components into one or the other category.

In the archeological sequence for the Strait of Georgia area, the Marpole culture type stands out as a sort of "florescent" stage. However, as Ham (1983:88) and Mitchell (1971:72) have argued, Marpole may more properly be seen as the attainment of a plateau than a peak. There is little reason to view the later culture type as a decline in any significant way from its forerunner.

Evidence for the Marpole–Strait of Georgia cultural plateau in the archeological record is most conveniently explained as the full development of the southern Northwest Coast culture. With Marpole it seems certain that all the material aspects were in place: large settlements; substantial, heavy-timbered houses; a technologically superior woodworking industry; efficient tools for the butchering of fish; and quantities of "wealth" items. Marked differences in treatment of the dead suggest some degree of social distinction, probably of stratification, and this appears in part to be associated with the wealth objects: disk beads, dentalia, and copper.

What circumstances caused the full development of this pattern in the centuries around 500–400 B.C.? It is most likely that the explanation lies in some relationship between the evolving salmon stocks and developments in harvesting and preservation technology, but the role of conflict should also be considered.

The change from Marpole to Strait of Georgia culture types can best be interpreted as indigenous and evolutionary. An alternate explanation is a migration from the interior plateau region, but there seem to be enough continuities in assemblage composition to suggest the one simply grew out of the other. Between Marpole and the Strait of Georgia there is evidence of a transitional period and form that has led to difficulties in classifying those components falling in the A.D. 300–800 period. However, cultures of essentially Strait of Georgia form were present by about A.D. 400–500.

It is difficult to fit the lower Fraser Canyon sequence into this review of culture history. There are significant differences among the component assemblages, but it is not clear what processes have produced those differences. Borden (1968:16) favored population replacement as an explanation for the Baldwin-Skamel break and a fusion of "Skamel phase culture with traditions characteristic of the Baldwin and Marpole phases" to account for the distinctive Emery component. Von Krogh (1980) makes a similar interpretation, partly on the grounds that he sees Baldwin and Skamel as having coexisted for several centuries.

But it is also possible to emphasize the continuities in Canyon assemblages, and, as with the coastal sequence, to reconstruct a picture of indigenous evolution. In this case, although many technological traditions continue, there is a puzzling 1,000-year interruption represented by the great reduction in stone carving during the Skamel.

These several centuries of seeming "impoverishment" become all the more perplexing when comparing Canyon with nearby coastal developments. Baldwin and Locarno Beach are contemporaneous and probably similar enough to suggest they should be considered variants of but a single culture type.

However, the Skamel/Marpole correlation that chronological estimates suggest presents an apparent anomaly, as the rich Marpole and spare Skamel assemblages are superficially very unlike. The difference becomes more understandable by recognizing that much of the Marpole appearance of richness lies in products of bone, antler, and shell—materials not preserved in Canyon soils. Certainly, the flaked stone points are similar in form, variety, and quality; and ground slate implements, especially thin knives, are prominent in both kinds of assemblages. The major demonstrable differences are in the soft stone industry and winter house form. These remain distinctive regional traits.

The contemporaneous Canyon and Strait of Georgia culture types have much in common. It is possible to see them, too, as variants of a single general Strait of Georgia Salish area culture type.

Kwakiutl Area

The Kwakiutl archeological area was occupied at the time of contact by the various Kwakiutl tribes, all speakers of a common language. Resource exploitation followed a pattern comparable to that outlined for the Strait of Georgia Salish although many of the specific resources were different. Each tribe spent the winter months at its village engaged in ceremonial activity and feasting. Seasonal moves were made to camp or village locations for gathering shellfish, berries, and rootcrops and fishing for halibut, salmon, or eulachon. The largest annual aggregations (Mitchell 1983) were at the eulachon fisheries of Tsawatti (at the head of Knight Inlet) and Quaee (at the head of Kingcome Inlet).

Site location surveys have been completed for most of the marine shoreline portions of the area (Carlson and Hobler 1976; Mitchell 1969, 1972) and for the Nimpkish River system on Vancouver Island (Ham 1980). Excavated assemblages from sites of the last 5,000 years (fig. 1) are available only from Fort Rupert (Capes 1964), the O'Connor site (Chapman 1982), and Bear Cove (C. Carlson 1979, 1979a, 1980), all on Vancouver Island near Hardy Bay; from Hopetown Village on Watson Island (Mitchell 1979); and from eight sites at Fife Sound (Mitchell 1981b). Components from the area fall in two, possibly three, distinct groups of assemblages: the Obsidian culture type (2800–500 B.C.), with a relatively high proportion of flaked stone categories, and the Queen

Charlotte Strait culture type (500 B.C.–A.D. 1800) with very little flaked stone but much ground bone.

Obsidian Culture Type

Components of the obsidian culture type include the early portion of O'Connor II (Chapman 1982), a part of the Bear Cove III assemblage (C. Carlson 1979a, 1980), Hopetown I (Mitchell 1979), and the early levels of the Echo Bay site (Mitchell 1981b). For the O'Connor site, the upper levels may be separated from the lower levels of the O'Connor II component by differentiating between an assemblage with a high density of obsidian microflakes, low occurrence of ground stone, and small number of bone tool categories, and one with ground slate points, ground stone celts, unilateral barbed bone harpoons and points, bird bone awls, needles, and comparatively few obsidian flakes. Three radioactive-carbon estimates date from the obsidian-bearing component.

The upper, shell-bearing, levels of Area 2 at the Bear Cove site (C. Carlson 1979, 1979a, 1980) also form a horizon rich in obsidian flakes. This zone is dated at approximately 2800 B.C. and had been placed in the Bear Cove III component, for which there are radioactive-carbon estimates ranging to A.D. 900. The Area 2 shell zone assemblage is isolated because it apparently contains the bulk of the site's obsidian flakes, and because associated with it is an age estimate some 1,750 years older than the earliest estimate for shell zones in Areas 1 and 3.

Distinctive archeological characteristics (after Chapman 1982; Mitchell 1985a) (fig. 11) include: rare, leaf-shaped flaked stone points; very few formed flaked stone tools but numerous obsidian microflakes, mainly produced by bipolar techniques; hammerstones; irregular abrasive stones; bone composite toggling harpoon valves; bone bipoints; bone singlepoints; ulna tools; mussel shell celts; and mussel shell knives.

The principal defining characteristic is the great quantity of flaked obsidian. Pieces range considerably in size but are typically small. Many of the flakes display crushed and step-flaked edges—distinctive signs of the bipolar flake production technique. In general, the flaked stone fraction of the assemblage is large and bone is infrequent when compared with the later Queen Charlotte Strait culture type. In Hopetown I, for example, bone comprises 12 percent and flaked stone 74 percent of the assemblage. This is to be compared with 56 percent and 1 percent for the same materials in Hopetown III.

Faunal remains from the few sites for which data are available indicate exploitation of a wide range of resources, and, in contrast to the later culture type, emphasis on harvesting several rather than a few species. The principal shellfish collected were: clams, especially butter clam, littleneck, and horse clam; whelks; and barnacle, with the last being locally, perhaps seasonally,   *353*

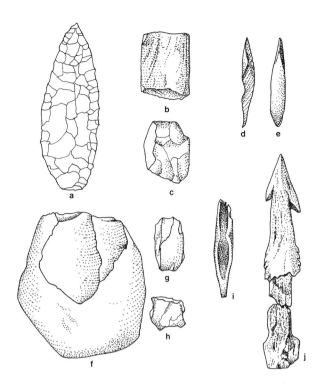

a, e-f, after Mitchell 1980b:figs. 32g, 32d, 32e; B.C. Prov. Mus., Victoria: b, EfSq2:228; c, EfSq2:1147; d, EfSq2:1649; g, EfSq2:1171; h, EfSq2:1359; i, EfSq2:717. j after Chapman 1982: fig. 3.18.

Fig. 11. Artifacts characteristic of the Obsidian culture type (2800–500 B.C.), Kwakiutl archeological area cultural sequence: a, flaked leaf-shaped stone point; b, celt of sea mussel shell; c, bone splinter bipoint; d, bone point; e, bipolar obsidian core; f, obsidian pebble core; g-h, obsidian flakes produced by bipolar technique; i, bone valve with chanelled point bed for composite toggling harpoon; j, bilaterally barbed non-toggling harpoon head. Length of a, 7.9 cm; b-i to same scale. j not drawn to scale.

very significant. Among fish, salmon and herring are clearly the most important, followed by ratfish, rock fishes, and greenlings. For the mammals, there is reasonably strong dependence on coast deer, with harbor seal placing a distant second. Bird remains indicate ducks, large gulls, crows, loons, and grebes were all taken in significant numbers.

The working of obsidian is an important industry although the products seem mainly to be small, simple flakes. The main means of primary flake detachment is bipolar percussion, probably with the aid of a hammerstone and stone anvil. Some tools are produced by abrasion of stone, bone, and shell.

Fish were likely taken with a variety of devices that made use of the bone bipoints and singlepoints, and sea mammals and fish would have been caught with toggling harpoons, the heads of which appear to have been armed with sturdy bone singlepoints. It is not clear what artifacts were used for the obviously important land mammal hunting.

As with microflake assemblages from the Coast Salish area, the small artifacts were probably mounted and used for butchering fish and other foods. Large amounts of fire-

broken rock throughout Obsidian deposits indicate stone boiling or steaming as means of cooking.

Woodworking is indicated by the presence of both ground stone and sea mussel shell celts. If splitting wedges were used, they were not made of material that has lasted under ordinary site conditions.

At Hopetown Village there are signs of a buried, substantial, level house platform in the beachfront portion of the midden. Hearth ash deposits are found.

The O'Connor site was occupied in late spring and/or early fall. It may be significant that assemblages do not include items readily interpreted as wealth.

Queen Charlotte Strait Culture Type

Distinctive archeological characteristics (after Chapman 1982; Mitchell 1981b, 1985a) (fig. 12) include: flat-topped hand mauls; stone disks; hammerstones; irregular and shaped abrasive stones; ground stone celts; unilaterally barbed bone points; unilaterally barbed, nontoggling bone harpoon points; bone composite toggling harpoon valves; bone bipoints; bone singlepoints; bone splinter awls; ulna tools; whalebone bark beaters; bone spindle whorls; bone blanket or hair pins; sea mussel shell celts; and sea mussel shell knives.

Bone items, particularly bipoints, singlepoints, and fragments of points, and sea mussel shell implements form major parts of the assemblages. Bone ranges upward from 45 percent of the artifact total. In Hoptown III, bone and shell together account for 96 percent of the assemblage; bone 56 percent (Mitchell 1979).

Although the range of resources used is as wide as the earlier culture type, there is a pronounced dependence on a few species. Harbor seal and salmon are overwhelmingly prominent in the mammal and fish categories, and their numbers are also such as to indicate importance in relation to all resources. Shellfish gathered in quantity included butter clam, littleneck, cockle, horse clam, barnacle, and whelk. After salmon, herring rank a distant second among the fish (although methods of archeological recovery mean they are underrepresented), and for the mammals, coast deer and porpoise rank well below the seal. The pattern of bird exploitation is very similar to that for the Obsidian culture type except that crow remains are insignificant.

The dominant means of tool production are carving and abrading, with the principal durable raw material being bone. Coupled with the great reduction in importance of stone flaking, this technological emphasis is very much in line with what is known of Kwakiutl culture in the early historic period. In Queen Charlotte Strait culture type assemblages there are so many items recognizably like what were being produced and employed by the historic Kwakiutl that there is little need for a lengthy reconstruction of the technology.

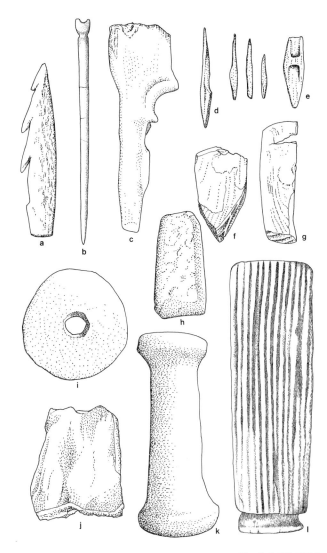

a, h, j after Chapman 1982:figs. 3.18; 3.13b; 3.16e. B.C. Prov. Mus., Victoria: b, EfSq2:727; l, EfSq2:412. c-g; i after Mitchell 1980b: figs. 37a; 33; 38k; 35e; 35f. k after Boas, 1909: fig. 36b.
Fig. 12. Artifacts characteristic of the Queen Charlotte Strait culture type (500 B.C.-A.D. 1800), Kwakiutl archeological area cultural sequence: a, unilaterally barbed non-toggling harpoon head; b, bone blanket or hair pin; c, ulna tool; d, bone points and bipoints; e, valve for composite toggling harpoon; f, fragment of sea mussel shell knife; g, fragment of sea mussel shell celt; h, ground stone celt; i, bone spindle whorl; j, abrasive stone; k, flat-topped stone hand maul; l, ribbed whalebone bark beater. Length of a, 8.1 cm; b-c, e-i to same scale. Length of d-left, 6.6 cm; j-l to same scale.

It is evident from variation in site size and faunal assemblages that a pattern of seasonal concentration and dispersal of population was in effect.

The few burials reported, most dating from the early part of the cultural type's existence, display marked differences between individuals in the elaborateness with which they were interred. As these differences extend even to children, the distinction would seem to be ascribed rather than achieved.

Conflict is suggested by the presence of fortified sites, although examination of the artifact and faunal assemblages (Mitchell 1981b) does not indicate the sites were anything more than very defendable locations at which otherwise ordinary activities were carried on. From their prevalence, fighting and raiding were probably commonplace.

So few assemblages have been recovered and reported that the contributions of seasonal specialization and change over time cannot now be separated from what may later prove to be a more general pattern of regional variation. It is likely that many of the apparent spatial differences stem from seasonal activity at periodically occupied sites.

There is a possibility that an early variant of the Queen Charlotte Strait culture type should be distinguished. Hopetown II (a distinctive burial complex with an age estimate of about A.D. 350) (Mitchell 1979) and the later part of O'Connor II (Chapman 1982) both resemble Marpole culture type assemblages from the adjacent Strait of Georgia Salish area at about the same time. The burials are rich in inclusions, particularly disk clamshell beads, and O'Connor II contains unilaterally barbed points and nontoggling harpoons very like those found in Marpole components.

Culture History of the Kwakiutl Area

During the last 5,000 years, the Kwakiutl archeological area was home to populations of at least two successive ways of life, distinguished from one another in the record by their relative emphasis on flaked stone and ground bone and shell technologies and by their degree of dependence on particular food sources. The Obsidian culture type is especially characterized by a simple, flaked obsidian technology and a fairly broad-based subsistence economy. The succeeding Queen Charlotte Strait culture type emphasized particularly the grinding of bone and shell and placed relatively heavy reliance on salmon and seal as food resources. In most important respects, this late (post-500 B.C.) culture type is recognizably like the way of life described for the Kwakiutl people.

Nootkan Area

Extending along the west coast of Vancouver Island from Cape Cook to the Strait of Juan de Fuca, the Nootkan area was occupied at the time of contact entirely by speakers of Nooktkan languages.

The pattern differed somewhat from that described for other areas of the southern British Columbia and northern Washington coasts in that besides the periods of spring and fall dispersal and winter aggregation of each local group, there was for many a period of summer concentration of the groups of a "confederation" in summer villages. These summer assemblies seem mainly to have been at the prime whale hunting locales (often on or with immediate access to the open coast) while the other villages and camps were chosen for their particular advantages of winter shelter or resources access.

Substantial excavations have been undertaken at Yuquot Village in Nootka Sound (Dewhirst 1980), the Shoemaker Bay site at the head of Alberni Inlet (McMillan and St. Claire 1982), and the vicinity of Hesquiat Harbor (Calvert 1980; Haggarty 1982) (fig. 1).

Only at the Shoemaker Bay site is there evidence for more than one major culture type during the past 5,000 years. Components at all other sites fall into what are here referred to as the West Coast culture type, which is present by at least 2800 B.C. at Yuquot and A.D. 140 at Hesquiat Harbor. It lasts until contact. The Shoemaker Bay sequence starts before 1100 B.C. and ends sometime after A.D. 850.

West Coast Culture Type

Distinctive archeological characteristics (fig. 13) (after Dewhirst 1980; Haggarty 1982) consist of: ground stone celts; ground stone fishhook shanks; hand mauls; abrasive stones; unilaterally barbed bone points; single barb points; bone fishhook shanks; unilaterally and bilaterally barbed bone nontoggling harpoon heads; bone single points; bone bipoints; large and small composite toggling harpoon valves of bone or antler, small ones with two-piece "self-armed" variety with ancillary valve; sea mammal bone foreshafts; bone needles; bone splinter awls; ulna tools; whalebone bark beaters; whalebone bark shredders; perforated tooth and deer phalanx pendants; mussel shell celts; and mussel shell knives.

One of the obvious distinguishing characteristics is the near absence of any flaked stone artifacts or flaking detritus. Even ground stone items are comparatively infrequent. The only common stone artifacts are abraders, presumably used to produce the numerous categories of ground bone tools and objects.

Items recovered from a large historic burial cave at the head of Hesquiat Harbor (Bernick 1985) include yellow cedar bark robes, some with fur collars; both twined and sewed tule mats; checker weave and twilled cedar bark mats; small checker weave cedar bark pouches and larger rectangular storage baskets; and cordage. The cordage, of cedar bark, cedar withe, and kelp, is of two- and three-strand construction.

Thorough study of the Hesquiat Harbor faunal remains (Calvert 1980; Haggarty 1982) and partial analysis of Yuquot materials (Clarke and Clarke 1980; Fournier and Dewhirst 1980; McAllister 1980) disclose use of a wide range of food sources but some obvious emphasis on certain species, but Hesquiat Harbor is an atypical segment of the west coast. Hesquiat territories include few salmon streams, and those few are well below average productivity.

356   In Hesquiat Harbor, by element count or minimum

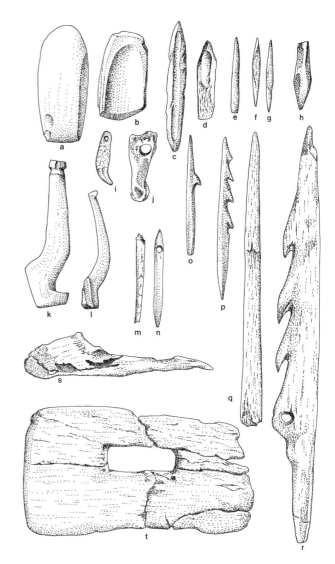

after Dewhirst 1980:figs. 46, 68, 167, 177, 106, 108, 187, 232a, 235f, 127, 119, 97s, 97r, 109, 203f, 152a, 215, 93d, 99b.

Fig. 13. Artifacts characteristic of the West Coast culture type: a, round-polled narrow celt; b, sea mussel shell celt; c, self-armed valve; d, ancillary valve, probably used paired for composite harpoon heads, but lacking the distinctive foreshaft channel; e, thin wedge-based point of bone for double-pointed fishhooks; f-g, spindle-shaped bone points for composite fishhooks; h, ventral face of channeled antler valve for composite toggling harpoon head; i, perforated hair seal canine; j, perforated deer phalange; k, rectangular-based stone fishhook shank; l, curved-stem bone fishhook shank; m-n, eyed needles or shuttles; o, unilaterally single-barbed point for sharp-angled composite fishhook; p, unilaterally barbed arrowpoint; q, tapered whalebone harpoon foreshaft; r, large whalebone unilaterally barbed harpoon head with line hole; s, deer ulna awl; t, whalebone bark shredder. Length of a, 7.6 cm; rest to same scale.

number of individuals, fish evidently ranked first among the nonshellfish resources; and of these, rock fishes were dominant. Of lesser importance were salmon, herring, and dogfish; however, in some site assemblages herring dominated, followed by salmon and midshipmen. Among the mammals, whales, seals, and porpoises were all important with coast deer placing after these. Birds commonly taken included albatross, loons, gulls, geese, ducks, and murres—a pattern that is substantially repeated at Yuquot. Butter clams, littleneck clams, and horse clams collectively comprised the bulk of the shellfish remains in the sites, with sea snails and mussels ranking next.

The archeological assemblages are so like described Nootkan material culture that a lengthy reconstruction of the technology is not necessary. There are artifacts interpretable as whale, small sea mammal, and salmon harpoons; parts of composite fishhooks; knives suitable for butchering salmon or herring or for preparing other fish and foods; woodworking tools; and tools for shaping the numerous bone implements. It is significant that although the artifact sample is very small, these tools and techniques are represented even in the 2800–1200 B.C. levels at Yuquot Village.

Data concerning site size, location, faunal remains, and availability of resources combine to suggest winter season population concentration and spring, summer, and fall dispersal.

The Shoemaker Bay Sequence

Excavations at the Shoemaker Bay site (McMillan and St. Claire 1982) indicate occupation at the head of Alberni Inlet of different character from that seen farther west. The inlet cuts so deeply into Vancouver Island that its head lies very close to the eastern shore. Artifacts from excavated and surface assemblages bear their closest resemblance to artifacts from the Strait of Georgia sites, and it is possible to see the sequence for the head of Alberni Inlet as but an extension of that for the area to the east.

Within the site, Zones C and D (grouped by McMillan and St. Claire 1982 with B and the very small collection from E to form Shoemaker Bay I) together seem most like the northern Locarno Beach culture type. They share with this type flaked slate or schist knives, microblades, quantities of quartz crystal and obsidian microflakes, faceted ground slate points, small rectangular ground stone celts, toggling harpoon valves, and a generally low ratio of bone and antler to stone. Zone C has a radioactive-carbon estimate placing it about 1100 B.C.

Zone B, while exhibiting many resemblances to C and D, differs in a great increase in bone and antler artifacts (only in part attributable to preservation factors) and a marked decrease in the microblade and microflake industries. Although no radiocarbon age estimates are available the stratigraphic position (between Locarno Beach and Strait of Georgia culture type assemblages) is in accord with the general Marpole "flavor" of the assemblage.

Shoemaker Bay II (in Zone A) is quite distinctly an assemblage of Strait of Georgia form, yet it differs and does so in the direction of the contemporaneous West Coast culture type. There are, for example, fishhook shanks and some ground stone celts whose forms closely

approximate such artifacts from Yuquot Village and Hesquiat Harbor.

Culture History of the Nootkan Area

From the modest amount of information available the post-3000 B.C. period can be characterized as one of relatively little change in subsistence and other aspects of technology. One apparent change was the Nootkan replacement or absorption of what was probably a Salish population at the head of Alberni Inlet in late prehistoric or early historic times. Boas (1891:584), Sapir (1914:77), and Drucker (1951:93) have all referred to an earlier Salish presence that archeological data indicate was of long duration.

Summary

The three subareas present very dissimilar prehistories, when the Strait of Georgia and Nootkan areas are compared but more alike when either of these is compared to the Kwakiutl area. Specifically, the Obsidian culture type of the Kwakiutl area most closely resembles the Charles and Locarno Beach culture types of the Strait of Georgia, while it is obviously very unlike the contemporaneous West Coast culture type of the Nootkan area. In contrast, the later Queen Charlotte Strait culture type bears very pronounced resemblances to the West Coast culture type, but, apart from an early possible Marpole style similarity, its assemblages are unlike those to the south.

The following model of events is possible. Prior to about 500 B.C., two distinct populations and ways of life inhabited the southern coast. The ancestors of Wakashan–speaking peoples (including the Nootka and Kwakiutl) occupied the west coast of Vancouver Island, while those of the Salish speakers lived along the protected waterways of Puget Sound, the Strait of Georgia, and Queen Charlotte Strait. As well, populations ancestral to the Salish may have held the coast north at least to the Bella Coola River valley.

Around 500 B.C., speakers of the Northern (Kwakiutlan) branch of the Wakashan languages expanded—probably from the northern part of Vancouver Island's west coast—into the Queen Charlotte Strait area and then, perhaps much later, northward along the mainland shore. In this spread, Salishan and likely some Tsimshian groups were all absorbed or replaced excepting the Salishan-speaking Bella Coola. Inroads against the Salishans to the south continued into the historic period.

What would motivate this postulated expansion? Initially, the goal could have been the rich salmon runs of the Nimpkish River on Vancouver Island or the eulachon fisheries of Knight and Kingcome inlets. And it is possible that the development of warrior sodalities (remnants of which could perhaps be seen at contact in the organization

357

and presentation of the winter ceremonies) may have given the aggressors a decisive superiority.

It is even possible to view the post-500 B.C. Marpole culture type, with its suggestion of improved use of resources, increased population, and greater attention to individual and group status as characteristics of a coincidental or induced development that effectively countered the Northern Wakashan advantage. The Kwakiutl move south was thus blocked until differential access to firearms tipped the scale in their favor in the early historic period and the Salishan speakers again lost part of their territory.

Kwakiutl: Traditional Culture

HELEN CODERE

Language and Territory

The Kwakiutl ('kwäkē,ootəl) speak a language that is the southernmost member of the northern branch of the Wakashan family.* The center of Kwakiutl territory is Queen Charlotte Strait on the central coast of British Columbia. They formerly lived along the outer coast from Smith Sound to Cape Cook, on the shores of Queen Charlotte Strait and the inlets leading into it, eastward along Johnstone Strait, and, by the middle of the nineteenth century, as far as the northern end of Georgia Strait. There are two groups of Kwakiutl dialects, one spoken on the outer coast, the other within Queen Charlotte Strait and eastward (Boas 1966:37).

The Kwakiutl once consisted of around 30 autonomous groups usually identified as "tribes"; the name applied to the Kwakiutl people as a whole is generalized from that of one tribe, who are the Kwakiutl in the narrow sense. Each tribe had its territory, winter village, and several sites occupied seasonally. Each consisted of several corporate kin groups. The kin group, called ńəmíma 'one kind', anglicized numaym (Boas 1921:1) or numayma (Boas 1966:37), had its own resource sites, myths, and crests.

Although the tribes may have all been in origin simply people sharing the same winter village, it would be confusing to call them "villages." During historic times, tribes have moved from their individual winter village sites to form joint winter villages without losing their separate identities. In a few instances such coresident tribes have later moved apart. There are also instances of small tribes merging with others, of one tribe becoming a numaym within another, and of a numaym splitting off to form a separate tribe (Duff 1960). Figure 1 shows the winter villages and territories of the tribes in the early nineteenth century. Figure 2 shows the merging of the tribes in historic times.

Intertribal Relations

Relations among the Kwakiutl tribes were not stabilized on any Kwakiutl-wide basis until about 1900 when potlatching with its attendant social alliances, relations, and social ranking of tribes became a system in which all participated. In the earlier days of the historical period, which is well reported upon from about the mid-1800s, the picture is one of fairly close and dependable alliances between neighboring tribes, but more infrequent and even strained relations beyond such clusters of neighbors. However, even relatives in neighboring tribes were not safe from the type of head-hunting that took place on the occasion of the death of some close relative and was designed to both honor the deceased and to "let someone else wail" (Boas 1921:1375), and acts of blood revenge in which the aim was to kill either a person of social rank equal to that of the deceased or several persons of lower rank in the offending kin group (Boas 1966:109). By about 1850 (Curtis 1907–1930, 10:120–123) such practices had ceased.

External Relations

Kwakiutl external relations were even less free of the possibility of violence than their internal relations until 1865, which is the final date of any intertribal hostilities (Codere 1950:112). The kind and degree of violence ranged from the sort of mourning or revenge raid that could take place among the various Kwakiutl tribes themselves to the outright predatory warfare the south-ernmost Kwakiutl, the Lekwiltok, waged against the Comox (Northern Coast Salish), driving them out of their lands and villages between the Salmon River and Cape Mudge (Taylor and Duff 1956). The Lekwiltok also raided Central and Southern Coast Salish groups, taking heads and captives (Hill-Tout 1907:43–44; Codere 1950:104). The scale and territorial aims of Lekwiltok set them apart from other Kwakiutl.

In one view (Codere 1950:99–117, 1961:483–440; Hawthorn, Belshaw, and Jamieson 1958:37), the term "warfare" is inappropriate for the kind of raiding,

---

· *The phonemes of the Kwakiutl language are (unaspirated stops and affricates) b, d, ʒ,λ, g [gʸ], gʷ, ġ, ġʷ, ʔ; (aspirated stops and affricates) p, t, c, λ, k [kʸ], kʷ, q, qʷ; (glottalized stops and affricates) ṗ, ṫ, c̓, λ̓, k̓ [k̓ʸ], k̓ʷ, q̓, q̓ʷ; (voiceless continuants) s, ł, x̣, xʷ, x, xʷ, h; (plain resonants) m, n, l, y, w; (glottalized resonants) m̓, n̓, l̓, y̓, w̓; (vowels) i, ϵ, a, ɔ, u, ə; (stress) v́. A more abstract transcription is possible in which ə and the stress accent are eliminated, their occurrences being predicted by rules.

Information on Kwakiutl phonology is from Lincoln and Rath (1980: 17–25); the transcription of words into the orthography used here has been supplied by Neville J. Lincoln (communications to editors 1986).

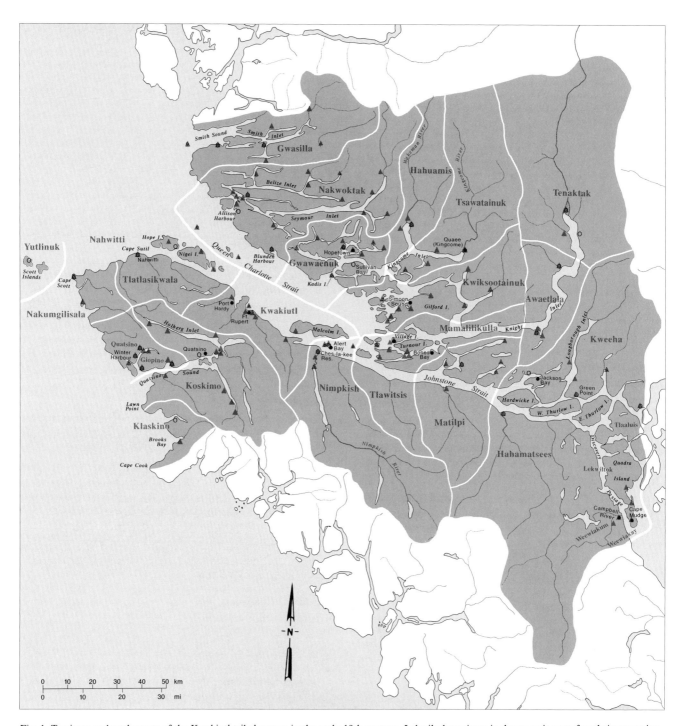

Fig. 1. Territory and settlements of the Kwakiutl tribal groups in the early 19th century. Lekwiltok territory is shown as it was after their expansion into Comox territory.

headhunting, and opportunistic acts of violence the Kwakiutl, apart from the truly warlike Lekwiltok, practiced and suffered. In another view (Ferguson 1984: 301–307), the Kwakiutl, like other Northwest Coast peoples, fought for loot, slaves, and territory as well as for vengeance.

Regardless of the motives of raiders, fear of them was well-founded and resulted in a pervasive feeling of insecurity. Therefore the friendly relations the Kwakiutl had with several neighboring peoples cannot have been maintained without tension or interruption. The most dependable of such relations existed with the Haisla, Haihais, Bella Bella, Oowekeeno, and Nootkans. Communication with the Haisla and Bella Bella was mostly of a social and ceremonial character and included intermarriage. The Nimpkish commanded a regular overland trade with the Nootkans, whom they supplied with eulachon oil. By 1792 the Nimpkish had obtained European goods,

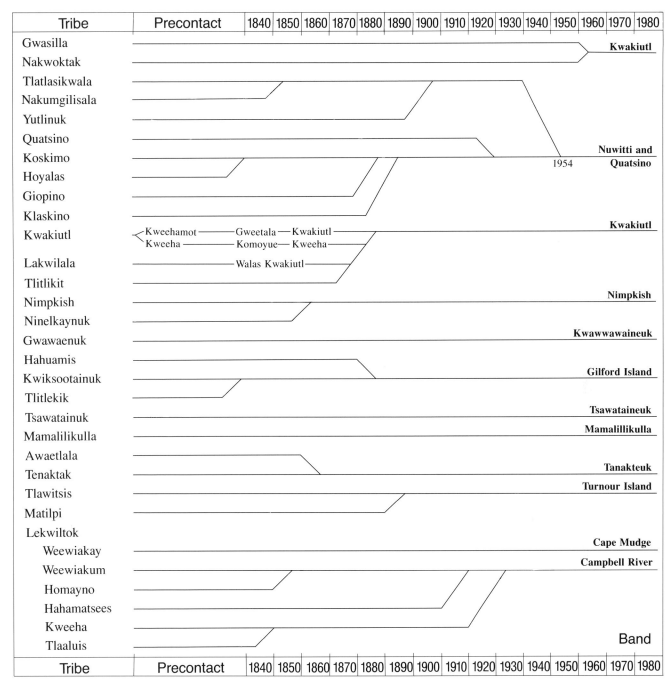

Tribe	Precontact	1840	1850	1860	1870	1880	1890	1900	1910	1920	1930	1940	1950	1960	1970	1980

Gwasilla
Nakwoktak — **Kwakiutl**

Tlatlasikwala
Nakumgilisala
Yutlinuk
Quatsino
Koskimo — 1954 — **Nuwitti and Quatsino**
Hoyalas
Giopino
Klaskino

Kwakiutl — <Kweehamot — Gweetala — Kwakiutl — **Kwakiutl**
Kweeha — Komoyue — Kweeha

Lakwilala — Walas Kwakiutl
Tlitlikit

Nimpkish — **Nimpkish**
Ninelkaynuk

Gwawaenuk — **Kwawwawaineuk**
Hahuamis

Kwiksootainuk — **Gilford Island**
Tlitlekik

Tsawatainuk — **Tsawataineuk**
Mamalilikulla — **Mamalillikulla**

Awaetlala
Tenaktak — **Tanakteuk**

Tlawitsis — **Turnour Island**
Matilpi

Lekwiltok
  Weewiakay — **Cape Mudge**
  Weewiakum — **Campbell River**
  Homayno
  Hahamatsees
  Kweeha
  Tlaaluis

Band

Tribe	Precontact	1840	1850	1860	1870	1880	1890	1900	1910	1920	1930	1940	1950	1960	1970	1980

Fig. 2. Historical merging of Kwakiutl tribes into modern bands. The Comox band does not appear because it was originally a Northern Coast Salish group.

including muskets, over this "grease trail" (Vancouver 1798,1:348; Menzies 1923:86–88), and the success of Lekwiltok expansion in their war against the Comox has been explained by the fact that they obtained guns from their former Nimpkish neighbors before the Comox got them (Taylor and Duff 1956:64).

The lack of dependability of friendly relations and the possibility of violence both among the Kwakiutl themselves and externally are features important to recognize to understand the society and culture of the people at the end of the nineteenth century when it was fully reported upon. By then both internal and external violence had ceased, and under this condition Kwakiutl culture flourished, developing and elaborating its most distinctive features, particularly those connected with the potlatch.

History

Spanish and British exploration and activity around Nootka Sound in the 1770s may have had consequences felt

362

CODERE

top left, Hydrographer of the Navy, Taunton, England; top right, Smithsonian, NAA: 26789; B.C. Prov. Mus., Victoria: center left, PN 235; center right, PN 2709; bottom right, PN 2051; bottom left, Amer. Mus. of Nat. Hist., New York: 329173.

Fig. 3. Structures. top left, Cropped view of "Cheslakee's village" (probably xʷəlkʷ), on the Nimpkish River, B.C. The village, arranged in regular streets, had 34 houses. The larger houses decorated with paintings and other ornaments belonged to the more important personages in the village (Vancouver 1798, 1:346). Engraving, after compilation drawing by W. Alexander based on sketch by John Sykes, July 1792. top right, Indians, probably of the Gwasilla tribe, on beach in front of houses of both shed-roofed and gable-roofed types, with horizontal plank walls. Photograph, cropped, by Richard Maynard, Smith Inlet, B.C., 1873. center left, John Scow's house (painted front), called Sea Monster House. The house to the left has a carved beam at roofline in a sisiutl (double-headed serpent) form (Hawthorn 1967:124–126). Photograph, cropped, by Charles F. Newcombe, Gilford I., B.C., 1900. center right and bottom left, Thunderbird-lifting-a-whale design on house of gigəġam, a Nimpkish numaym, Alert Bay, B.C. center right, A carved figure of a man with harpoon (?) stands on the roof and the thunderbird's large beak is clearly visible. Photograph by Richard Maynard, 1874. bottom left, The same house repainted and refurbished. A copper and flag hang from pole on the roof and over the door is the identifying sign "Tlah.Go.Glass,Nimkessh Chief." Photograph probably by Richard Maynard, 1884. bottom right, Graves at Alert Bay,B.C. The sign which appeared over the house is now identifying the chief's grave. Photographed about 1912–1915.

by the Kwakiutl, especially those of the outer coast of Vancouver Island. The first recorded contact occurred in 1786, when the British trader James Strange discovered Queen Charlotte Strait (Strange 1929:29–32; Fisher and Bumsted 1982:130–131). The next recorded contact was in 1792, when the Queen Charlotte Strait people were visited successively by Americans under Robert Gray (Howay 1941:402–404), British under George Vancouver (1798,1: 343–351; Menzies 1923:86–86), and Spanish under Dionosio Alcalá Galiano and Cayetano Valdés (Wagner 1933). The Vancouver expedition visited the Nimpkish village of xʷəlkʷ at the mouth of the Nimpkish River (fig. 3, top left) and saw muskets and other evidence of trade, either with Europeans directly or with the Nootkans. By the early nineteenth century contact was frequent. The village of Nahwitti at Cape Sutil was a favorite port of call, especially for Americans (Reynolds 1938:22).

From the 1830s on, the Hudson's Bay Company was active in the region, having established Fort Langley on the Fraser River in 1827 and Fort McLoughlin on Milbanke Sound in 1833, while maintaining ships to compete with the Americans. The Kwakiutl themselves soon took an active part in the trade. In 1838 "Native Coquilt [Kwakiutl in the narrow sense] Pedlers" had established friendly relations with the Musqueam at the mouth of the Fraser and were siphoning off furs that would otherwise have gone to Fort Langley and selling them at Fort McLoughlin for a higher price (Douglas 1941:245, 281). In 1843 the company established Fort Victoria, which became a major trading post and an attraction for Native people from far north of the Kwakiutl, who had to pass through Kwakiutl territory to get there. The Kwakiutl too were frequent visitors.

In 1849, because of the presence of coal, the Hudson's Bay Company established Fort Rupert on Beaver Harbour. The coal was mined for a brief period only, but the company maintained a post there until 1873 or 1878, when it was sold to the last factor Robert Hunt (Healey 1958:19). When the fort was established, four tribes (who were the Kwakiutl in the narrow sense) settled at the site, forming what became the largest Kwakiutl settlement and, in time, the center of regional ceremonial activity. Because of this prominence and the vast amount of information recorded by Robert Hunt's son George, Kwakiutl culture and history have been seen largely from the viewpoint of Fort Rupert.

During the 1850s and 1860s disasters struck the Kwakiutl. Disputes with the colonial authorities resulted in the destruction of Nahwitti in 1850 and of the village at Fort Rupert in 1865 by the British Navy, which also stopped the expansion of the Lekwiltok. In 1857 or 1858 the village of Gwayasdums was destroyed by Bella Coola raiders. And in 1862 the region was swept by smallpox brought north from Victoria. Another loss occurred in the late 1880s, when Indian Reserve Commissioner P. O'Reilly established reserves for some bands of Kwakiutl and in effect formalized the crown's claim to the rest of their aboriginal territory.

Fort Rupert maintained its central position until about 1900, when it was superseded by Alert Bay as the center for the people of Queen Charlotte Strait. Alert Bay had its start in 1870, when two White men established a salmon cannery there and sought Indian labor. In 1877 the Anglican missionary Rev. A.J. Hall began work at Fort Rupert but soon moved to Alert Bay. By 1881 he had a school there and a home large enough to accommodate several young girls taught "domestic duties" by his wife, and by 1888 he had built a sawmill to provide employment and lumber for single-family houses. In 1881 the federal government established a Kwawkewlth Agency at Fort Rupert, but this too moved to Alert Bay. In 1894 the Department of Indian Affairs opened an industrial school for boys at Alert Bay. The same year a day school opened at Cape Mudge. Meanwhile, Mrs. Hall's program had grown into a residential school for girls (Healey 1958: 24–31; Halliday 1935:229–232; Canada, Dominion of 1882:171, 1883:161, 1895:158, 160).

Kwakiutl material and economic life changed rapidly under the circumstances of contact. During the period of maritime fur trade, iron and steel replaced native materials in tools. After Fort Rupert was established, the older style robes were replaced by Hudson's Bay blankets, acquired in vast numbers for potlatching. By the 1880s, White-style clothing was in general use. The Kwakiutl were also becoming assimilated into the Canadian economy and dependent on money income. This development led to a period of great prosperity between 1900 and the mid-1920s. Wealth became widespread, primarily because the old organization of production, knowledge of local resources, and industrious habits fit the new opportunities   *363*

Fig. 4. Ma-Ma Yockland, a Quatsino woman, picking salmonberries. Her elongated head was the result of purposeful deformation as an infant. The berries are held in a wrapped-twine, openwork carrying basket. Photograph by Benjamin W. Leeson, Vancouver I., B.C., about 1912.

offered, particularly those of the commercial fishing industry, which needed seasonal labor (Hawthorn, Belshaw, and Jamieson 1958:109–110). Just as the Kwakiutl had moved seasonally in the old days, they entered into commercial fishing and canning and other seasonal occupations that yielded a cash income, while continuing to produce their own food. The high incomes that resulted (Codere 1950:43–49) were used to purchase Euro-Canadian goods, particularly the quantities that were used in potlatching. Kwakiutl prosperity suffered a setback in the 1920s with the difficulty of financing power boats (introduced in 1911). Difficulties lasted through the Depression but prosperity was restored by the boom in the fishing industry during World War II.

Culture

In the exploitation of a shore environment that was especially rich in all forms of marine life Kwakiutl artisanship, technology, work habits, and organization of production resulted in a secure abundance of food and a wealth of material objects of every sort. Their permanent villages, material wealth, and capacity to support an extensive ceremonial, potlatching, and artistic life makes them much less comparable to the hunters and gatherers with which they are often classified than to settled agriculturalists, although in their case they "farmed" the woods, the shores, the salmon streams, and the sea.

Subsistence

364 Each Kwakiutl tribe had some easily accessible food

resources. Fort Rupert was famous for its large and numerous clams; the Nimpkish had a fine salmon stream in the Nimpkish River; all had some berry patches (fig. 4) and marine shore life such as mussels, sea urchins, and barnacles. However, the members of each tribe exploited the food resources of a wide area traveling in canoes to herring spawning places, berry patches, clover-root fields, halibut fishing grounds, and salmon streams. Claims to many of these resource areas were hereditary and based upon numaym membership, which meant that a man and wife could each have claims to different sites of the same resource and the members of a tribe would have multiple claims. Other resource sites were common property. One of the largest food-getting expeditions was the trip to the head of Knight Inlet for the spring eulachon run. Twenty-one numayms of nine different tribes had claims to dip-net sites, viburnum patches, mountain-goat hunting grounds, and other resource sites at Knight Inlet (Boas 1934: map 22). The Kwakiutl of Fort Rupert traveled by canoe about 250 miles there and back to get this supply of eulachon oil. This expedition forms a model of Kwakiutl food production—travel to the site of the resource; application of an effective technology (dip nets, herring rakes, fish weirs); and preparation for storage by processing (oil-trying by stone-boiling, drying, smoking) and placing in containers (kelp-tubes, baskets, wooden boxes and chests). In food production the Kwakiutl were geared to cropping and storing as large and various a harvest as possible. The mobility afforded them by their canoes gave them range and flexibility in their food quest, and their large wooden houses gave them space for storage in boxes and on racks under the roof.

People who did not have direct access to a resource they needed could trade for it. For eulachon oil, the Gwasilla and Koskimo traded dried herring roe and the Nahwitti tribes dried halibut (Duff 1960:6).

Technology

Kwakiutl production of material goods was characterized by the same high productivity and special skill and technology in the handling of wood. Men's techniques in woodwork and women's in fiberwork were similar to those of the tribes to the north (Boas 1966:28). Some 130 Kwakiutl manufactures and technological processes have been described in detail with illustrations and diagrams by Boas (1909:310–516, 1921:57–172). Except for clothing, which was scanty, the Kwakiutl inventory of objects of every sort seems very large.

In craft production as in food production they placed an explicit value upon industriousness, and they aimed at a level far above mere subsistence and utilitarian needs. Much that they made was embellished by carving and painting, and their manufacturing replicated various items many times over, so that each household had many boxes, mats, dishes, spoons, and canoes (Codere 1950:19). Kwakiutl wealth in material goods was produced by all the people. There were no full-time specialists in craft production, although there were some men whose special knowledge and skills were required and called upon for some difficult process such as steaming open a dugout canoe, and there were artists whose skill in painting and carving set them apart and earned them special commissions.

The Kwakiutl economic year was seasonally organized. The prime food harvesting season began in spring with the first run of chinook salmon and lasted well into the fall with the final run of chums. The winter months were free of the necessity of any important food getting activities and, except for ceremonial visits to other villages, the people were in permanent residence in their winter villages and craft production was at its peak.

Structures

At the time of first contact, in the 1790s, the Kwakiutl were evidently living in shed-roofed houses like those of some Nootkans and Coast Salish. By the middle of the nineteenth century, the Kwakiutl had early versions of the type known from the late nineteenth century, houses with low two-pitched roofs and walls of huge planks held horizontally between pairs of upright poles. There were no painted facades or external carvings visible. By the 1870s, there were Kwakiutl houses with vertical wall planks, perhaps of milled lumber, painted facades, and external carvings (fig. 3).

The late nineteenth-century Kwakiutl house was 40 to 60 feet square, built with a gabled side facing the water, the door in the center of that side. Some earlier houses may have been built on pilings; houses of this period often had platforms in front of them, if they were built right at the shore.

Late nineteenth-century houses were built with three types of framework. Type A had four central posts, a pair near the front and a pair near the rear, each supporting a crossbeam. Two longitudinal beams, making a double ridgepole, rested on the crossbeams. At each side, three smaller posts supported an eaves beam. Type B had three central posts, a large one at the rear and a pair of smaller ones at the front, only the doorway width apart, holding up a short crossbeam. A single ridgepole rested on the top of the rear pole and on the crossbeam. As in Type A, there were six side posts and two eaves beams. In Type C there were only two central posts with the ridgepole directly on them. With all three types there were rafters and stringers holding the roof planks, which ran from ridgepole to eaves, interlocking like tiles. In the front and rear there were vertical poles fastened to the rafters and serving to hold the wall planks. The front and rear wall planks were set into a sill, where the side wall planks were set directly

Royal B.C. Mus., Victoria: PN 29.

Fig. 5. House interior of Harry Mountain, Mamalilikulla. The posts, which support a crossbeam, are carved with crest figures—the cannibal bird sitting on a grizzly bear. Five wooden feast bowls are displayed, 2 carved in the shape of killer whales, 2 as wolves, and a square bowl, the food in which was said to cause loose bowels (Newcombe 1912:notebook 24-a). Photograph by Charles F. Newcombe, Village I., B.C., 1912.

into the ground, their top ends fitted into the eaves beams.

In late nineteenth- and early twentieth-century houses, the central posts were nearly always carved with crest figures, and the side posts might also be carved (fig. 5). But Curtis (1907–1930,10:7–8) was told that before 1865 carved posts were not common, most houses were of type B, and there were a few of Type C in which the door was an opening between the legs of a carved figure.

In most houses there was a single platform extending around the walls; a few reportedly had more than one level. Most houses were occupied by four families, each in a corner, partly partitioned off, with its own fireplace on the earth floor and a large settee before the fire. In some houses the occupants had small houselike structures on the platform. Smokeholes were made by raising a roof plank (Boas 1889:198–202; Curtis 1907–1930,10:6–9).

Canoes

Late nineteenth-century canoes were mainly of the Northern type, having a high bow with a vertical cutwater and a high stern. These varied in length from about 10 to over 50 feet. The Kwakiutl also had canoes of the west coast type, having a long tapered bow and low vertical stern; this may have been the usual type on the outer coast of Vancouver Island.

In earlier times the Kwakiutl also had a type called mánga, identified as a war canoe, which had a long, narrow, heavy hull, a high flaring bow with two perforations, and a nearly vertical stern, like that of a west coast canoe but with a more flaring, flat upper surface. According to tradition, they also once had a type called *gáɔ*, in which both bow and stern projected as long thin fins, the bow high and nearly vertical, the stern high and slanted (Boas 1909:444–445; Curtis 1907–1930,10:12–13; Drucker 1950:253).

Clothing and Adornment

In warm weather women wore only aprons of strands of cedar bark while men went nude. For more cover both wore a blanket of woven yellow cedar bark or of sewn skins, tied with a belt. When needed, they wore conical rain hats and rain coats made of cedar-bark matting. All generally went barefoot. Both sexes wore their hair long, men's loose or knotted, women's parted and braided. Some men let their facial hair grow. Both sexes who could afford it wore nose and ear pendants of abalone shell. Women also wore necklaces, bracelets, and anklets of dentalia. Tight anklets were believed to keep the feet small.

Painting the face and body (for protection against sunburn) were common. Tattooing was uncommon.

All the Kwakiutl tribes reshaped the heads of infants in their cradles. Among the tribes of the outer coast of Vancouver Island, high-ranking women had elongated "sugar-loaf" heads (fig. 4), while among the tribes of the upper end of Queen Charlotte Strait both sexes had flattened, broadened heads (Boas 1909:451–457; Curtis 1907–1930, 10:4–6, 52–53; Drucker 1950:188–192).

Social Organization

● THE NUMAYM Each Kwakiutl tribe was made up of from one to seven numayms, usually three or more. The numaym was a social division that traced its crests back to a supernatural ancestor. Each numaym had claims to real property in a section of house sites in the village, at least one of the large houses there, and a number of other sites that were principally food resource sites. Just as important as this real property were the numaym claims to crests and titles in a multitude of forms ranging from designs on house fronts, poles, posts, and feast dishes to privileges such as the use of a certain kind of betrothal ceremony, and certain songs, house names, and titles, even to the fixed and particular numaym name for the dog and the canoe that belonged to its head. The most important titles owned by the numaym were named potlatching positions, called standing places or seats in the numaym.

The numaym should be considered first of all as the holder of certain inalienable titles, crests, and property, and this feature of the numaym remained stable. However, in the important matter of its social character, there seems to have been an early (1835–1850) high population numaym and a later (1875 on) low population numaym. Many social features concerning corporativity, membership, position holding, ranking, marriage, and residence

Royal B.C. Mus., Victoria: PN 2209-b.
Fig. 6. Aboard the H.M.S. *Boxer*, a Kwakiutl wearing a basketry hat and button blanket. Indians were frequent visitors on European ships as official delegates, as traders, or as curious onlookers. Photograph by Richard Maynard, Cape Caution, B.C., 1873.

are understandable when assigned to the early or the later numaym whereas they are confusing and contradictory when lumped together without regard for demographic and other historical development.

The drastic population reduction of the Kwakiutl (table 1) caused a reduction in size of the major Kwakiutl social units, the village and its constituent numayms. The number of numayms among the Kwakiutl (about 100) and the number of individual positions within each numaym seem reasonable and quite workable for the early days of far higher population when the numaym seems to have been an important corporate group organizing and controlling the economic activities and the social relations of its members in their daily and ceremonial lives within the village and with other villages. The earliest dependable population estimates, for the year 1835, yield an average numaym membership of 75, assuming the number of numayms to have been the same as that recorded later by Boas (1966:38–41), 100 numayms or some 90 if the Lekwiltok are excluded, which it is necessary to do for some computations. The figure of 75 is not far from that of 100, which Boas (1966:47) thought to have been the early size of the numaym. However, in 1887 the average number of numaym members was only 15 and by 1895 it dropped to 10 and remained at that low figure through the 1920s. These averages are for the total population, so that the

CODERE

Table 1. Kwakiutl Population, 1835–1954

Date	Population	Source
1835	7,500–8,000	Codere 1961:439
1853	about 7,000	Hall 1889
1872	3,500	Codere 1950:52
1877	3,000	Codere 1950:52
1880	2,500	Codere 1950:52
1885	2,160	
1890	1,754	
1895	1,597	
1900	1,527	Hawthorn,
1905	1,278	Belshaw, and
1910	1,227	Jamieson 1958:24
1915	1,161	
1929	1,088	
1939	1,220	
1954	1,891	

NOTE: Some estimates before 1835 are over 8,000, but they seem unreasonably high (Curtis 1907–1930,10:303; Kroeber 1939:142).

average adult membership would be only about half the total, and would have dropped from about 37 in 1835 to from seven to eight in 1887 and to only five from 1895 on. It is important, also, to consider that not all numaym members were co-residents in the numaym house or houses in the village where the numaym was located. The largest number of nonresident members would be women who married men of other numayms or of other villages. Some male numaym members might also reside in their wives' villages, although virilocal residence was far more usual.

In addition it is known for the later period that individuals generally held positions in more than one numaym and could not possibly remain active and fully contributing members of each numaym with its concerns as a social group. The post-1895 numaym with its very small size and dispersed membership could not have been anything like the earlier numaym as an important functioning corporate social group. Rather it was primarily an organized scheme of positions with their titles, crests, ceremonial privileges, and property claims all going back to mythic times as the source of their value and sanction. These positions were used and maintained, enhanced and lowered in their relative social rank by potlatching.

The total number of individual positions within the various numayms was 794, based on position titles listed by George Hunt (Rosman and Rubel 1971:137). For a mid-century Kwakiutl population the 794 figure would mean that many adults including many adult men could not have had a numaym position at any one time, and, perhaps, could never have one. Numaym positions with the value of scarcity could reasonably be expected to be remembered and continued as the population decreased (Boas 1920:115), as it did, to the point where there were more positions than adults to fill them.

If the Kwakiutl saw their 794 numaym positions as seats that had to be filled even as their population was markedly decreasing, this may account for practices of the later period, notably a flexible and opportunistic use of every possible means of filling the positions and using them in potlatching. Ambilaterality, primogeniture, the use of any kind of claim based on descent, however thin, and of gifts and bequests to nonrelatives, and the frequent holding of multiple positions are all means that would keep the positions filled and in use. These devices may have existed in the earlier period as recourses to be used when a man had no son. But given the patrilineal bias that Boas (1966:52) saw, it seems likely that earlier, when there were many more adults than positions, there would have been a much greater favoring of the male line of succession to position and inheritance.

Flexibility, early and later, is implied by the view of Lévi-Strauss (1982:163–187) that the Kwakiutl numaym was a "house" in the medieval European or Japanese sense, an institution that can, when it needs to, use descent through females or even affinity as a basis for succession.

● MARRIAGE In addition to the inalienable titles, crests, and property rights that were connected with the numaym and with any numaym position, individuals acquired and transmitted other crests and privileges and, in particular, the highly valued rights to present various dances of the winter ceremonial. The line of transmission of this individual property in crests and rights was through marriage from father-in-law to son-in-law, or to members of the son-in-law's family. This was, in effect, a transmission through a succession of daughters with their husbands most frequently the bearers and users of the privileges (Boas 1920:118). The most important and valued of these crests and rights came into the hands of those who were highest in rank in the numaym organization, since marriages were arranged between those of equal or comparable social rank. An important consequence was that the social organization of the winter ceremonial, in which an entirely new series of titles, offices, and positions replaced those of the rest of the year, nevertheless paralleled that of the numaym order with the same individuals holding the highest positions in both systems.

There was no definite marriage rule among the Kwakiutl (Rosman and Rubel 1971:147), and there was an unusual variety of permissible forms of marriage. The two least frequent forms were: the marriage of unusually close relatives—children of the same father, a man and his younger brother's daughter, children of two full sisters (Boas 1920:117, 1921:781, 1966:50); and the serial marriage of the highest ranking chiefs and numaym heads. In this second form a woman was married four times, with each marriage dissolved, whether or not there were children, after the marriage exchanges were duly made between father-in-law and son-in-law (Boas 1966:54–55). *367*

Two opposite tendencies seem to have been at work here. One was to retain privileges, the effect of the highly "endogamous" marriages, which made affines of close kin and allowed them to receive privileges. The other was to speed up the transfer and dissemination of privileges, the effect of the sequential marriages of brief duration. Both tendencies are understandable for the early period when these crests and privileges were first being obtained by the Kwakiutl, through marriages with women of northern tribes, and through warfare against the northerners, and were very rare.

Numaym endogamy was also among the most infrequent types of marriage (Boas 1966:50). Village endogamy and village exogamy seem about equally frequent (Rosman and Rubel 1971:148), but the family histories indicate that for those of highest social rank it was usual for marriages to take place with women of comparable rank in other villages.

The crests and privileges that were transferred by marriage were regarded as so important that they were not allowed to lapse in the event that a man had no daughter through whom to transfer them. In such a case, a man declared his son's foot or half of his body to be a woman, and a fictitious marriage was arranged and performed with a man to whom the privileges were then transferred (Boas 1966:55).

● KINSHIP TERMINOLOGY The Kwakiutl kinship system is bilateral. Consanguines were distinguished from affines. In ego's own generation the terminology does not distinguish between siblings and cousins but does use an age distinction for siblings and cousins of the same sex.

● CHANGES The complexities of Kwakiutl social structure are best understood when it is seen that acquiring, transferring, and above all preserving the existence of all available crests and privileges justified the use of a large variety of available social devices, so that no rule was without exceptions, and customary procedures were flexible and never without strategic recourse. The reasons for this seem clear. What had once had great social scarcity among the people became widely available. A condition in which only the most important individuals in the highest numaym positions could mobilize the wealth necessary to assert them by use, that is, validate the crests and privileges involved by giving potlatches, was replaced by a situation in which industry, good planning, and successful adjustment to new opportunities for earning wealth in the Canadian economy could support the necessary potlatching activities.

Between about 1835 and 1895 Kwakiutl social structure underwent significant change in the direction of much greater social equality. The earlier structure consisted of what amounted to a noble minority and a commoner majority. Women seem rarely to have been holders of noble positions, and there was even a small slave group of war captives. Slavery ceased to exist soon after 1849.

Although an overall system of social ranking of tribes and numayms developed through the potlatch, the system was far more egalitarian. As potlatching decreased in importance and frequency, the inequalities of the ranking system also began to erode. By the 1950s the social greatness of the Kwakiutl of Fort Rupert, once the highest-ranking tribe of all, had been extinguished for all except a few oldsters. Fort Rupert was an out-of-the-way village, and social status was connected with the wealth and modernities associated locally with the town of Alert Bay.

The Potlatch

The word potlatch, as it applies to the Kwakiutl potlatch of the late nineteenth and early twentieth centuries, was a public ceremonial and social event, often of impressive size in the amount of property distributed and the numbers of people gathered for the occasion. It was also a complex process in which all those who gave potlatches had to accumulate the necessary property through work and preparatory loans and plan for its distribution in response to the potlatch gifts they had received in the past. The potlatch was an institution that contributed to the integration and dynamic drive of Kwakiutl society by validating social status and giving material manifestation to an expanding and changing network of social exchanges and reciprocities.

The occasions for potlatches were numerous and varied greatly in importance according to the amount of property distributed, the social prominence of the potlatcher, and the number and social standing of the guests invited. The least important were those given for children and youths at various life cycle points: naming according to the place of birth, bestowing a child's name at 10 months, removing the arm and leg straps put on the child four days earlier at the naming ceremony, and assigning a youth's name. The potlatch required to wipe away the shame of some accident, such as falling out of a canoe in front of the village, was also usually a modest and local matter. Potlatches of moderate size were given when a youth first was assigned a potlatch position in his numaym and when he danced in a winter ceremonial and was given a winter dance name, usually by his father. There were similar occasions for young women. The most important potlatches, those to which the Kwakiutl gave the name *ṁáxʷa* meaning 'doing a great thing' were those to which guests from other tribes were invited. These occasions included: the assumption of an important or chiefly name and position within the numaym, a grease feast, the buying and selling of coppers, the erection of crest or memorial poles and houses, and marriage, when potlatches were given alternately by the father-in-law and son-in-law with property each received from the other for the purchase of the bride and the return gift for her repurchase.

Along with all these serious potlatches there was a half-serious kind, in which property was given away in the course of a theatrical skit intended to be amusing, and a quite unserious kind, the play potlatch, in which all the dignified pretentions of real potlatching were lampooned, sometimes the women mocking the men among themselves, sometimes with the two sexes taking sides as rival potlatchers (Codere 1956).

For whatever reason the guests were assembled by the main potlatcher, others gave potlatches as well. The main guests and recipients often came prepared to do so, and others merely seized the occasion of the gathering. All potlatches, even the simplest, were ceremonious, and all, even the greatest ones, included feasting, informal socializing, and fun (Boas 1897). Ceremony and drama were embodied in the display of goods to be distributed, the strictest precedence in the distributions made according to the social rank of the recipients, and in the formal speeches, special songs, and displays of crest heirlooms, such as feast dishes, and of dances and theatrical performances the potlatcher had the hereditary right to put on.

The accumulation of property was accomplished by financial means as well as by direct earnings in the European market. Shortly after 1849 the Kwakiutl used a cheap Hudson's Bay woolen blanket in great quantities for potlatching and treated the blanket as a standard of value for measuring all other goods and the overall size of any potlatch. They also loaned out blankets at high rates of interest—100 percent for a year's loan, proportionally less for shorter terms. These interest rates were in line with the fact that goods distributed in a potlatch were later returned with an increment, not always the 100 percent increment that Boas (1897:343) claimed.

"Coppers," a unique Northwest Coast invention, were shield-shaped plates of European copper (Drucker and Heizer 1967:14-15) usually decorated with a design in the form of a face (fig. 7). Each copper had a name such as "Beaver Face" or "All other coppers are ashamed to look at it" (Boas 1897:344). A copper's value was that of the property distributed at the potlatch in which it had last changed hands, and it could be bought only at double that amount, a fact that so inflated the cost of coppers by the 1920s that, even when options were taken on them and downpayments made, transfers were rarely completed (Codere 1961:468). They played a special role in rival potlatches when one chief either broke off a piece or pieces, "burned" the copper by placing it in the fire, or completely destroyed it by throwing it into the sea, and the rival chief was obliged to treat a copper of equivalent value in the same fashion or acknowledge his inferiority.

● DEVELOPMENT Before 1849 the Kwakiutl potlatch seems to have had none of the features that were later to make it famous. Potlatches were modest in the amounts of property distributed and in the number of tribes invited as guests and recipients. Potlatch goods, all of native manufacture, consisted of canoes, dressed skins, mats, occasionally slaves, and fur blankets, the blankets being the major item (Codere 1950:90–94).

In 1849 four Kwakiutl tribes moved to found a super-tribe or confederacy at Fort Rupert. It is from the point of view of the Fort Rupert Kwakiutl that the expansion of the system is most clearly seen, since the expansion occurred as the Fort Ruperts enlarged the number of tribes that were invited to their potlatches and so were brought into potlatching relationship with one another. In the early historical period there seem to have been six clusters of tribes who potlatched with one another. Potlatch invitations were to one tribe at a time within the cluster. The Fort Ruperts next invited all the other tribes of their potlatch area simultaneously, and thereafter all four Fort Rupert tribes were invited as a body when potlatches were reciprocated. The Kwakiutl of Fort Rupert next included a northern cluster of tribes, then three central clusters, and the Lekwiltok last (Drucker and Heizer 1967:35–45). Lekwiltok potlatching up to that time had a quite isolated and distinct character, revolving around shares in large canoes of traditional manfacture that had become not merely obsolescent but useless beached hulks (Drucker and Heizer 1967:62).

Severe population decrease was occurring during the same period. There is no doubt about expansion of potlatch ties with more and more tribes brought together as festival or guest groups at any one time. The absolute size of the gatherings after the population decline may not have been larger in numbers than the earlier ones where a single tribe invited one other tribe, but their social character is the issue. Social position was in a Kwakiutl-wide rather than in a tribal-cluster context, and all the people could participate in the upper levels of the system, for there were more than enough numaym potlatch positions for everyone.

A potlatch ranking of the Kwakiutl tribes developed with the Kwakiutl of Fort Rupert in the first position and the ranking of the remaining tribes varing over time. The tribal ranking, along with the ranking of positions within the numaym and the creation of a special group of "Eagles" who received property first at potlatches but who had none of the other prerogatives of rank, all depended upon acquiring wealth and using it in potlatching. No hereditary position, however high, and no rank in the system could be maintained without being affirmed in the potlatch. Increasing wealth from European sources, particularly commercial fishing, inflated the size of potlatches; and very large quantities of European goods, up to several thousand dollars' worth, were distributed (fig 8). A 1921 potlatch included gas boats, gas boat engines, pool tables, sewing machines, gramophones, furniture, and musical instruments (Codere 1961:464).

The European sources of wealth that had fed the

Royal B.C. Mus., Victoria: CPN 9251.

Fig. 7. Mungo Martin's "Killer Whale" copper, one of the few coppers preserved in ethnological collections that retains its history (Duff 1981). It was bought by Chief Mungo Martin from Peter Scow about 1942 for $2,010. Willie Seaweed painted the killer whale design on the blackened surface. The top corner was broken off by chiefs invited to do so at the initiation of Martin's son David into the hamatsa secret society. The bottom section was broken off by Martin to shame a rival chief who had publicly questioned the status of his son as a hamatsa. The piece was never given to that chief, since Martin decided the man did not have the power to respond; instead, he threw it into the sea at the death of his brother. It was also used in Dec. 1953 at the opening ceremonies of Mungo Martin's house in Thunderbird Park, B.C., as part of a cradle ceremony for his son's daughter, wherein the copper was placed in an elaborately decorated cradle as the child's symbolic "comforter." Just as the original display had "filled his son's belly" as a hamatsa, showing that he would never be hungry, this later display showed that the baby would never be cold, that it would always be wrapped in the softest of blankets. The copper was last used in public display as the "coffin" for his dead son. It was given by Mungo Martin to the B.C. Provincial Museum in 1960, because with the death of his son, it could go no further. The value of this copper had increased with its sale and display. Its being broken in no way diminished its value; rather, it added to its prestige and worth. When broken sections of coppers were riveted together, the refurbished copper would carry an even greater value. People in a village or along a long section of coast would know all the valuable coppers, who owned them, what displays they had been used in, and what titles or names they had been used to validate. Coppers were greatly coveted by those wanting to increase their prestige. Height 63 cm.

potlatch system began to dry up and fall short of its needs in the 1920s, and the Depression made for a prolonged

period of poor money incomes (Codere 1961:483–484). Past potlatches went unreciprocated, and there was bitterness both on the part of those who considered they were owed return gifts and those unable to make them. Many "left the potlatch" as they phrased it, and conversion to the Pentecostal church, which was strongly opposed to the potlatch and other Indian ways, was frequently the occasion for doing so (Drucker and Heizer 1967:23).

The Kwakiutl potlatch had survived and even flourished to its greatest point of development in spite of legislation forbidding it (the Indian Acts of 1885 and 1915) and the disapproval of many non-Indians who held that it was a profligate custom that reduced the people to want in their daily living. It also survived a later period of strong enforcement of the anti-potlatching law by going underground, using Canadian money, which was not visible as a potlatch good, in order to make private distributions to one or a few recipients at a time. As a Kwakiutl-wide institution the potlatch did not continue during bad times from the 1920s to the 1960s. A revival of potlatching took place in the 1970s under the stimulus of the proud assertion of Indian rights, identity, and ties with tradition.

● INTERPRETATION   There is wide agreement that the Kwakiutl potlatch shared the general characteristics of the Northwest Coast potlatch (Barnett 1938b:349–358, 1968). These are the ceremonial distribution of property to guests specially invited to witness and recognize assertions and demonstrations of social prerogative and status. The special features that set the Kwakiutl potlatch apart, particularly those of its dramatic scale and overwhelming importance in Kwakiutl social and cultural life, require explanation in terms other than those that would apply to Northwest Coast potlatching in general. The development of the special features of the Kwakiutl potlatch took place during the last quarter of the nineteenth century (Codere 1950, 1961), and an explanation of the Kwakiutl potlatch must center on the changes in Kwakiutl social structure that accompanied severe population decline and greatly increased wealth. A static structural or functional interpretation will not account for the increasing importance of the potlatch to the point of becoming the dominant institution in Kwakiutl social and cultural life.

The old social structure of the period of high population can be viewed as one in which the comparatively large tribes had both a high degree of isolation from a number of other Kwakiutl tribes and the demographic possibility of a rich and highly organized and differentiated social life of their own. Evidence indicates their political and economic cohesion as well as social unity and independence.

The social structure of the period from the mid-1880s when the population had been reduced to a fourth its former size to the 1920s when it was halved again was significantly changed. Once-important tribes became so

CODERE

Fig. 8. Potlatching. top, Gathering goods for a potlatch given by Bob Harris, a Tenaktak. Some of the goods shown are traditional dance aprons and frontlets hanging on line to right, native-made silver bracelets on poles, hundreds of enameled basins at left, coffee pots, kettles, sewing machines and pails. Photographed at Alert Bay, B.C., about 1900. bottom left, Women's potlatch goods. The men in center rear are probably the host and tally keeper who carefully record the goods. Some of the gifts have been distributed and their grouping in units of 10 is similar to the distribution of the blankets (Blackman 1976:55). Photograph by Harlan I. Smith, Fort Rupert, B.C., 1898. bottom right, Ceremonial distribution of Hudson's Bay Company blankets at a feast sponsored by Franz Boas for the Kwaikutl, Nakwoktak, and Koskimo tribes. Boas supplied the food (apples) for the feast; and while he initiated the ceremony and recorded it, it was conducted by Indians, according to Kwakiutl custom (Jacknis 1984:21). The man giving the speech is Lagius, a Kwakiutl from Fort Rupert (not Olsīwit, chief of the Mamalilikulla, as implied by Boas 1897:348). The Nakwoktak are seated in the background listening to the speech. Photograph by Oregon C. Hastings, Fort Rupert, B.C., Nov. 28, 1894.

reduced that their remnant populations abandoned their villages and moved to still existing ones. Except for Fort Rupert, which was the seat of a confederacy of four tribes from its beginning, and Alert Bay, the site of a new Nimpkish village and a new Canadian town that had attracted members of other tribes as well, villages lacked the population to sustain their former internal social life and its stratified organization. What survived were the ranked social and potlatch positions with all their prerogatives and perquisites, and there were more than enough of them to go around. Every adult had the opportunity to potlatch and to gain status, public recognition, and glory. The Kwakiutl had always spoken of especially important potlatches as ones to which "all the tribes" were invited. Formerly this was a grandiloquent rhetorical usage and referred only to a gathering of two to four tribes. It became literal as more and more tribes were simultaneosly invited to a potlatch, finally including even the remote Lekwiltok. Travel throughout the area had only to contend with natural hazards and was otherwise safe. The gatherings may have been no longer than those of the earlier days when only one other tribe was invited, but its new composition of all participants being position holders and its pan-Kwakiutl character certainly enhanced the social significance and glory of the occasion for all its participants, who had the individual wealth to make the most of it until the mid-1920s.

Religion

All nature and all things had a wonderful or supernatural aspect, *náwalak^w*, which individual men and women addressed with prayer and thanks in the course of their daily lives. The sun could be asked and thanked for a good day, the beaver for his skill and industry in felling trees, a woodworking tool for help in carving, a plant collected as a medicine for a successful cure. Such prayers were simple and unformulaic statements made for a host of everyday desires as they might occur and on a host of occasions that ranged from killing an animal to picking berries or seeing an otter slide. There were some occasions, for example, that of calling up a shift in the wind, on which an individual performed a ritual along with his prayer. The rituals usually derived from some mythic episode (Boas 1966:155–165).

Witchcraft too was a private practice. It required only the knowledge of how to harm or control intended victims through the use of their hair or body wastes and such powerful ingredients as bits of corpses, snakes, and toads. Knowledge of how to guard against it or to cancel the effectiveness of attempted witchcraft was equally available. The practice does not seem to have been so frequent or serious that it added much fear or menace to life.

Shamanism was limited to those who had formed a relation with a supernatural helper and who had been initiated by shamans. Usually sickness signaled the calling and some animal spirit appeared to the prospective shaman; among the Kwakiutl of Fort Rupert it was the killer whale or loon (Boas 1966:135). The initiation by shamans followed a period of solitary seclusion in the woods after which the new shaman was publicly presented in a ceremonial at which he danced and sang the sacred songs he had received from his supernatural helper. There were varying degrees of shamanistic power, the highest including the ability both to cure and cause disease, and those with such powers were attached to chiefs to protect them and kill their enemies. Lower degrees conferred the

Fig. 9. A shaman's curing ceremony. The patient lies on a new mat surrounded by Sitka spruce branches hung with strips of cloth. Another new mat, against the wall, might be used to cover the doctored patient. An openwork basket hanging above the mat has sharpened sticks in it called "Quills to hurt the Woman-Doing-Evil." The shaman wears a neck ring over one shoulder through which the patient was passed in order to purify him. With down in his hair, the shaman is actively blowing or sucking out the place of the sickness (Codere 1966:127, 133, 136). Photograph probably by George Hunt, Ft. Rupert, B.C., 1901–1905.

ability to cure or to merely diagnose disease. The lowest of all had no special powers, but were those who had been cured by a supernatural. Shamanism does not seem to have brought high material rewards (Boas 1966:120).

Shamanistic cures were called for when the sickness fell into some unusual and poorly understood category or when the cures available in a large body of folk medical lore had been applied without success. They were public ceremonials and quasi-theatrical events involving sacred songs, rattles, and other paraphernalia, the most important item of which was the purification ring of hemlock or cedar (fig. 9). Intervals of rapid time-beating and violent trembling on the part of the shaman occurred at climaxes in the performance, and the shaman often resorted to tricks in which objects that had been hidden in his costume or mouth were produced as if by magic.

The Winter ceremony of the Kwakiutl was a many-sided public event in which the entire tribe, and often visiting tribes as well, were involved in both the ceremonials themselves and in the associated feasting, potlatching, entertainment, and theatrical activities. The event could last many days. A Winter ceremonial at Fort Rupert in 1895, which lasted more than 20 days, has been described in detail (Boas 1966:179–298).

The sacred aspect of the ceremonials derived from the belief that a number of supernatural beings came to visit the village in wintertime. During this sacred season, which was distinct from the ordinary secular life of the rest of the year, all quarrels were supposed to give way to general good will. Secular names and offices were put aside and sacred ones assumed. The ceremonials themselves (see "Kwakiutl: Winter Ceremonies," this vol.) were based on the dramatic theme that the supernaturals captured and spirited away the various men and women who were to be the actual dancers and performers, initiated them, and imbued them with their awesome and often horrendous qualities. It was then necessary that they be recaptured and tamed back to their human condition. The public ceremonial was the performance and taming of the possessed dancer, who had disappeared from the village some time before, often under dramatic circumstances, and had been in seclusion in the woods or in a special room.

In the mid-nineteenth century, as warfare ceased, social relations intensified over a much wider area, and potlatching became far more important, the various winter dances, which were largely privileges a man received from his father-in-law or had hereditary right to display, were used to maintain or enhance a man's social standing when they were presented with potlatches. Wike (1952:103) identified the process that occurred as secularization, seen especially in "the increasing emphasis upon the economic aspect of the potlatch."

Mythology

The mythology of the Kwakiutl reflects the overriding preoccupation with crests and privileges that exists in Kwakiutl social relations, potlatching, ceremonialism, and art. Although Kwakiutl myths share many elements of other Northwest Coast tribes, and although two groups of tales, the anecdotal animal tales and those in which Raven, Mink, and the Transformer figure are typical of the culture area, the great body of recorded Kwakiutl tales is either wholly concerned with obtaining and transferring crests and privileges or gives the subject extraordinary attention and space (Boas 1910:297–309, 1966:305).

The most distinctive Kwakiutl tales are those of the origins of the numayms. They tell of a supernatural ancestor who came from the sky, sea, or underground, in the form of a Thunderbird or other fabulous being, assumed human form, often by removing his mask or costume, and created the human members of his group. Representations of the supernatural ancestor and of other beings who figure in his adventures are numaym crests. In quasi-historical tales further crests and privileges are obtained and transferred as chiefly human ancestors travel to foreign tribes to marry the daughters of their chiefs, often several in succession. Identifying the rights to dances of the Winter ceremony and the dance masks and paraphernalia that are transferred to a man from his father-in-law makes up an important part of these tales.

Denver Art. Mus., Colo.: 1969.406.

Fig. 10. Dance apron. Ornately beaded surfaces with elaborate designs, unusual in Northwest Coast art, probably were borrowed from Subarctic Athapaskans. Seed beads in many colors are sewed on commercial cloth. Beaded figures are eagles, bears, and a sisiutl, all traditional forms. The beaded triangle motif along the bottom of the apron is done in larger white beads than used elsewhere, and these may be considerably older. Brass thimbles are suspended from the base of the sisiutl and the triangle motifs as tinklers. Both the triangle motif and floral borders are adoptions from the Subarctic tribes. Purchased from Mary Waddums, a Kwakiutl of Alert Bay, B.C., in 1969, the apron is estimated to date from about 1880. Dimensions, 74 cm square.

An associated and typical group of tales are those of a man who confronts some supernatural being and receives powers and ceremonies.

This large body of crest tales does not form a systematic tribal mythology, since each tale is either particular to the numaym concerned or related at most to those of only a few other numayms and tribes (Boas 1930:177–178).

Art

Kwakiutl art in its style, forms, and cultural functions was a distinctive variant of Northwest Coast art. During its golden age, 1890–1921 (Duff 1967), it developed its greatest elaboration, exuberance, and distinctiveness.

In carving its style, like that of the Bella Coola, was basically sculptural, in contrast to the more graphic and flatter styles of the north, particularly of Haida and Tsimshian (Hawthorn 1967:11). Unlike the northerners who worked within the constraints of the cylindrical field of the tree trunk in the carving of monumental poles and house posts, the Kwakiutl added protuberances in the form of beaks, fins, wings and so on. A similar development was the Kwakiutl attachments to masks. Some masks were provided with hinges and strings so that beaks

a

b

c

d

e

374

a, Field Mus., Chicago: 19174; b, Mus. of the Amer. Ind., Heye Foundation, New York: 6/9153; c, The British Mus., Mus. of Mankind, London: 1949 AM 22.63; d, Natl. Mus. of Canada, Ottawa: V11-E-49; e, Glenbow-Alberta Inst., Calgary, Alta.: R.180.219.
Fig. 11. Masks, portraying creatures in Kwakiutl mythology and worn to recreate the accounts of ancestral encounters. a, Wolf who carries the novice of the Cannibal of the Ground to the house of the cannibal spirit, who initiates them. Twists of cedar bark portray scraggly hair and mane. Collected by George Hunt, Vancouver I., 1893. b, xʷíxʷi, who is said to shake the earth when he performs. His dance is held to be a certain means of bringing back the hamatsa initiate (Boas 1897:497). Collected by D.F. Tozier, 1894-1907 (Cole 1985:186, 219-220). c, ʒúnuq̓ʷa, a wild woman who lives in the woods, who steals children, places them in her basket, and eats them. She is said to sleep most of the time. When she is awake, as in this mask, her mouth is pushed forward to make her cry of "ū, hū, ū, ū" (Boas 1897:372). Collected before 1949. d, Iakim (ỹágəm 'badness'; Boas 1897:480), a water monster that obstructs rivers, endangers lakes and the sea, and swallows and upsets canoes. The sea is said to boil when he rises, and all the tribes fear him. Masks portraying Iakim take many forms, as all versions of sea monsters are called by this term. The wooden head is painted in black and white, with fragments of mica on the black. The lower lip is movable. Collected by Franz Boas at Nimpkish Reserve, B.C., 1889. e, Transformation mask representing a large fish, probably a salmon. Red cloth encircles an opening in the belly of the fish, into which the dancer inserts his head. When opened by the dancer (bottom), the head of the fish fell back to reveal a sisiutl with a humanoid face at the center and the water monster's snakelike face on the inner surfaces of the flanking boards. The jointed tail also moved, imitating the salmon's motion in swimming upstream. Made by Mungo Martin. Collected from the Scow family at Simoom Sound, B.C., before 1968. Length of e 1.58 m; others to scale.

could be opened and closed, fins raised and lowered, and various attachments revolved. Double (transformation) masks opened to reveal an inner face (fig. 11).

In painting the Kwakiutl used the stylized design units characteristic of other Northwest Coast art, for example, the eye forms for body joints and sockets; and they used many of the symbols and conventions in portraying particular animals or beings. Yet, Kwakiutl painting style cannot be described as can Northern Northwest Coast painting in terms of the "form line" or "continuous flowing grid over the whole decorative area" (Holm 1965: ix, 29). There is not only less form line continuity but also a freer use of color, the use of design units not found elsewhere in Northwest Coast art, and other peculiarities (Holm 1965:36, 38). Boas (1927:288) has described the distortions in Kwakiutl painting as, if anything, more daring than those of Haida; but, as in the case of carving, there seems less tendency to interlock figures and to fill the entire design field as the northerners do.

While most Kwakiutl art was in the general Northwest Coast style, it was unusual in maintaining both a geometric and a realistic style. Many everyday objects were decorated with geometric design, particularly boxes and trays (Boas 1927:281), and realistic carvings of human beings were produced (fig. 12). Some were portrait carvings for use in ceremonial performances in which a beheading or immolation was theatrically simulated (Boas 1927:185, 289). There were also caricature portraits used to lampoon rival potlatch chiefs by showing them in foolish or defeated postures, often with prominently visible ribs signifying poverty and, therefore, incapacity to potlatch (Boas 1909: pl. 46, 1966:342–346).

Kwakiutl art was everywhere: embellishing housewares, furnishings, and tools; in the monumental and commemorative housefront paintings, house posts, and so-called totem poles; and on the secular or sacred occasions of potlatching and ceremonial life in which masks, statuary, feast dishes, and many other ceremonial objects were used. This visual art was embedded in a total aesthetic field that also included rhetoric, song, dance, theater, and special ritualistic ways of acting. The meaning of all the arts was primarily heraldic. It was a crest art manifesting the hereditary distinction, history, and glory of the numayms.

Kwakiutl art history is closely connected with Kwakiutl social and cultural history. An early Kwakiutl style in which both geometric and realistic design figured, as they did among their Salishan neighbors, was overlaid by the Northern Northwest Coast style, probably in the first decades of the nineteenth century. Family histories tell of the transfer of crests from the early 1800s (Boas 1921: 836–1277). The Cannibal Dance ceremony with its rich artistic panoply of masks and paraphernalia was obtained through marriages with the Bella Bella and Oowekeeno and also, in an incident during the war with the Bella Coola about 1856, through killing a group of Bella Bella chiefs (Boas 1966:258). From mid-century on, the battery

U. of Pa., U. Mus., Philadelphia: 29-175-452.
Fig. 12. Feast dish carved as a human figure. The body consists of a single hollowed out piece of wood; the head is detachable. The figure is completely painted: hands and face, white; hair, red; mouth, tongue, nostrils, and ears, orange-red; mustache, eyes, and eyebrows, black; body, brown. The head, carved on a half-cylinder form, with rounded, sloping forehead, round eyes with sharply contracting lids, and forward projecting chin, is distinctively Kwakiutl. Collected on Vancouver I., B.C., before 1917. Height 76 cm.

375

of crests, particularly ones of animal forms, seems to have been present among the Kwakiutl, and there was a continuing history of crests being acquired through marriages with women of northern tribes. Once crests with their titles, accompanying myths, ritual privileges, and artistic representations were acquired, they were passed on in the transfer of numaym positions and in succeeding marriages.

Synonymy†

The English designation Kwakiutl was used by Boas in a long series of influential publications beginning in 1887 (Boas 1887:227) and has become standard in anthropological usage.

Boas used the term Kwakiutl on four levels of classification, in order of diminishing inclusiveness: the Kwakiutl group, those speaking what he referred to as the Kwakiutl language (Boas 1897:320, 328, 1966:12); the grouping of the speakers of the Kwakiutl dialect, corresponding to what is called Kwakiutl in the *Handbook*; the grouping of the speakers of the Kwakiutl subdialect, which excluded those on the north and northwest of Vancouver Island; and the Kwakiutl tribe (Boas 1897: 329–330). The Kwakiutl of the *Handbook* are the equivalent of the Southern Kwakiutl of Duff (1964:15), his Northern Kwakiutl being the Haisla, the Heiltsuk-speaking Haihais and Bella Bella, and the Oowekeeno. The Kwakiutl of Boas's highest level of classification, embracing the Northern and Southern Kwakiutl of Duff, are the Northern Wakashans of the *Handbook*. Idiosyncratically, Kwakiutl has been used to include the Kwakiutl and the Haisla but not the geographically intervening "Bella Bella" and "Heiltsuk"—though the inconsistent map implies some confusion (Murdock and O'Leary 1975: 2–3), and to include Kwakiutl and Oowekeeno but not the rest of Northern Wakashan (Canada. Department of Energy, Mines and Resources. National Geographical Mapping Division 1980). The spelling Kwawkewlth is used in Canada as the name of the agency that administers all the Kwakiutl tribes. Among other spellings of Kwakiutl, in various applications, in early sources (from Hodge 1907–1910, 1:744–745, except where noted) are: Coquilt (Douglas in Rich 1941:244), Coquilths, Kwagiutl (Hall 1889), Kwagutl, Kwahkewlth, Kwakiool, Qā-gūtl, Quackewlth, Quackolls, Quackuli (Canada. Indian Affairs 1873:7), Qua-colth, Quacós, Quagheuil, Quahkeulth, Quakeolth (Lamb in Rich 1941), Quakult, Quaquiolts, Qualquilths, Quoquoulth, Quawguults, Qwaquill (Finlayson in Rich 1941:327, 334).

The broader senses of the name Kwakiutl have been generalized from the name of the Kwakiutl tribe. In Kwakiutl this is $k^{w}águ\sevenh$, (phonetically [$k^{w}ág^{y}u\sevenh$]), the analysis of which is uncertain (Boas 1897:330). This generalization of the name presumably reflects the fact that it was the Kwakiutl tribe with whom the Europeans became familiar earliest, when they established the Hudson's Bay Company post at Fort Rupert, where the Kwakiutl tribe settled in 1849.

To avoid using the name of one tribe for the whole people, the Kwakiutl terms $k^{w}ák^{w}ak\partial\dot{w}ak^{w}$ 'Kwakiutl-speaking people' and $k^{w}ák^{w}ala$ 'Kwakiutl language' have been adopted in local English and by some scholars; the common spellings of these in English are Kwakwa-ka'wakw and Kwakwala.

Tribes

In nearly every case, the tribal name used as standard here comes from Duff (1964:20–22).

Gwasilla ($g^{w}a\sevenh s\partial lá$), Goasi'la (Boas 1897), Gwaᶜsᴇla´ (Boas 1966:38), Quawshelah (Canada. Royal Commission on Indian Affairs 1916, 2:434).

Nakwoktak ($\dot{n}ák^{w}axda\cdot\dot{x}^{w}$), Nā´q'oaqtôq (Boas 1897: 329), ᶜna´k!wax·daᶜxᵘ (Boas 1966:38), Nahkwockto (Canada. Royal Commission on Indian Affairs 1916, 2:430).

Tlatlasikwala ($\dot{\lambda}á\lambda asiq^{w}\partial la$), La´lasiqoala (Boas 1897), L!a´Lasiqwäla (Boas 1966:38).

Nakumgilisala ($n\partial q\partial mg\partial lis\partial la$), Naqô´mg·ilisala (Boas 1897), NaqE´mg·Elisäla (Boas 1966:38).

Yutlinuk ($yú\dot{\lambda}inu\dot{x}^{w}$), Yu´L!enoxᵘ (Boas 1966:38).

Quatsino ($g^{w}a\sevenh cínu\dot{x}^{w}$), Gua´ts'ēnôx (Boas 1897), Gwa´ts!enoxᵘ (Boas 1966:38).

Koskimo ($\dot{g}úsgim\partial\dot{x}^{w}$), Qō´sqēmox (Boas 1897), Ǧo´s g·imᴇẋ̣ᵘ (Boas 1966:38).

Giopino ($\dot{g}ópinu\dot{x}^{w}$), G·ôp'ēnôx (Boas 1897), G·â´p!enoxᵘ (Boas 1966:38).

Hoyalas ($\dot{x}uyalas$).

Klaskino ($\dot{\lambda}ásqinu\dot{x}^{w}$), Tlaskeno (Boas 1887), L'ā´sq'ēnôx (Boas 1897:329), L!a´sq!enoxᵘ (Boas 1966:38).

Kwakiutl ($k^{w}águ\sevenl, k^{w}águ\sevenh$), Kwa´g·uł (Boas 1966:39), Kwawkewlth (Canada. Royal Commission on Indian Affairs 1916, 2:422). Subtribes: Kweehamot (?), or Gweetala ($g^{w}ít\partial la$), Gwe´tEla (Boas 1966:39); Kweeha ($k^{w}íxa$), Kwishkah (Canada. Royal Commission on Indian Affairs 1916, 2:385), or Komoyue ($\dot{q}úmuyo\sevenh i$), Q'ōmoyue (Boas 1897:330), Q!o´moyâᶜe (Boas 1966:39); Lakwilala ($láq^{w}i\sevenh l\varepsilon la$) Lâ´kuilila (Boas 1897:330), La´qwi-ᶜläla (Boas 1966:39), or Walas Kwakiutl ($\dot{w}álas k^{w}ág^{y}u\sevenh$), ᶜwálas Kwag·uł (Boas 1966:39), Walaskwawkewlth (Canada. Royal Commission on Indian Affairs 1916, 2:385); Tlitlikit ($\dot{\lambda}í\lambda\partial\dot{g}it$) or Komkiutis ($\dot{q}úm\dot{k}u\sevenh\partial s$), Q'ōmk·ūtis (Boas 1897), Q!o´mk·!ᴇs (Boas 1966:39); and Matilpi ($madi\dot{l}bi\sevenh$), Ma´diłbeᶜ (Boas 1966:39).

Nimpkish ($\dot{n}\partial m\dot{g}is$), NE´mqic (Boas 1897), ᶜnE´mgis (Boas 1966:40), Nimkeesh (Canada. Royal Commission on Indian Affairs 1916, 2:385).

† This synonymy was written by Ives Goddard, Helen Codere, and Wayne Suttles.

Ninelkaynuk (n̓in̓əl̓k̓inux̣ʷ).

Gwawaenuk (gʷáwaʔinux̣ʷ), Guau´aēnôx (Boas 1897), Gwa´wǎenoxᵘ (Boas 1966:41), Kwawwawineuch (Canada. Royal Commission on Indian Affairs 1916, 2:386).

Hahuamis (həx̣ʷáʔmis), Haxuā´mîs (Boas 1897), Hǎ-x̣wa´ᶜmis (Boas 1966:41), Ahkwawahmish (Canada. Royal Commission on Indian Affairs 1916, 2:386).

Kwiksootainuk (qʷíqʷəsut'inux̣ʷ), Qoēxsot'ēnôx (Boas 1897), Qwe´x̣ᵘsot!enoxᵘ (Boas 1966:40), Kwicksitaneau (Canada. Royal Commission on Indian Affairs 1916, 2: 438).

Tlitlekit (λíλəg̓it).

Tsawatainuk (ȝáwadəʔinux̣ᵘ), Ts'āwatEēnôx (Boas 1897), Dza´wadEenoxᵘ (Boas 1966:40), Tsahwawtineuch (Canada. Royal Commission on Indian Affairs 1916, 2: 386).

Mamalilikulla (mámaliliqəla), Mǎ´maleleqǎla (Boas 1966:39), Mahmahlillikullah (Canada. Royal Commission on Indian Affairs 1916, 2:385).

Awaetlala (ʔəẃaʔíλəla), A´wa-iLEla (Boas 1897), AᶜwǎiLEla (Boas 1966:40), Ahwaheettlala (Canada. Royal Commission on Indian Affairs 1916, 2:386).

Tenaktak (dən̓áxdaʔx̣ʷ), T'Ena´xtax (Boas 1897), DE-ᶜna´x·daᶜxʷ (Boas 1966:40), Tanockteuch (Canada. Royal Commission on Indian Affairs 1916, 2:420).

Tlawitsis (łáwiċis), Lau´itsis (Boas 1897), Ła´wits!es (Boas 1966:40).

Lekwiltok (líǵʷiⱡdaʔx̣ʷ), Lē´kwîltôq (Boas 1897), Le´g-wiⱡdaᶜxᵘ (Boas 1966:41), Laichkwiltach (Canada. Royal Commission on Indian Affairs 1916, 2:416); Euclataw (Duff 1964). Subtribes: Weewiakay, Wī´wēqaē (Boas 1897), Wi´weqeᶜ (Boas 1966:41); Weewiakum (listed as a clan by Boas 1897, 1966:41); Homayno, Q'ōm´ēnôx (Boas 1897), Q!omᶜenoxᵘ (Boas 1966); Hahamatsees, Kahkah-matsis (Canada, Royal Commission on Indian Affairs 1916, 2:410), Xā´xamatsEs (Boas 1897), Xa´xamats!Es (Boas 1966:41); Kweeha (kʷixa?), Kweahkah (Canada. Royal Commission on Indian Affairs 1916, 2:416), Kuē´xa (Boas 1897), Kwe´xa (Boas 1966:41; Tlaaluis (?) La´luîs (Boas 1897), Łāa´lEwis (Boas 1966:41).

Sources

The basis of Kwakiutl studies has to be the ethnographic reporting of Boas, with the help of George Hunt (especially Boas 1897, 1909, 1920, 1921, 1925, 1930, 1935–1943, 1966), and the many texts of myths, tales, and family traditions recorded by Boas and by Hunt under Boas's direction and editorship (especially Boas 1910,

1935–1943; Boas and Hunt 1902–1905, 1906). A complete bibliography of Boas, including all his publications on the Kwakiutl, appears in Andrews et al. (1943). Most of Hunt's manuscripts (14 volumes) are in Special Collections at Columbia University, New York; other Boas and Hunt materials are in the Library of the American Philosophical Society, Philadelphia, and in the National Anthropological Archives, Smithsonian Institution.

Other reporting based on fieldwork includes general accounts by Dawson (1888), Jacobsen (1884, 1977), and Curtis (1907–1930, 10) a culture element list (Drucker 1950), and works on ceremonialism and the potlatch (Drucker 1940; Codere 1956), art (Hawthorn 1967, 1979; Holm 1983), life history (Ford 1941; Spradley 1969), community life (Rohner 1967; Rohner and Rohner 1970; Wolcott 1967; T. Inglis 1964), and culture history (Codere 1961; Mauzé 1984).

A number of anthropological works deal with the interpretation of Kwakiutl ethnographic and historical materials. On the potlatch are Barnett (1938b, 1968), Codere (1950), Piddocke (1965), Weinberg (1973), Drucker and Heizer (1967), Rosman and Rubel (1971), Kobrinsky (1975), and Dundes (1979); many other works deal with the Kwakiutl potlatch in the context of the potlatch as a regional phenomenon. On social stratification are Codere (1957) and Donald and Mitchell (1975). Benedict (1934) offers an interpretation of the relationship between Kwakiutl culture and personality. Interpretations of Kwakiutl beliefs, ceremonies, and myths as an integrated symbolic or religious system include those of Locher (1932; cf. Boas 1933), Müller (1955), Goldman (1975; cf. Holm 1976; Suttles 1979), Reid (1973, 1976, 1979), Walens (1981), and M.J. Reid (1981, 1984).

Because of the interest in Northwest Coast art, examples of Kwakiutl carving and painting are found in museums throughout the world. The American Museum of Natural History, New York; the University of British Columbia Museum of Anthropology, Vancouver; and the Provincial Museum of British Columbia, Victoria, are notable for collections and exhibits that recreate the traditional life of the people.

The historical sources date to 1792 with George Vancouver's visit to the area (Vancouver 1798; Menzies 1923). Sources between that date and the 1860s are meager with the major firsthand reports those of Hudson's Bay personnel (Rich 1941, 1943). After 1860, sources are numerous, for example, Mayne (1862), Lord (1866), and, of special value, the annual reports of the Canadian Department of Indian Affairs, which began in 1872.

Kwakiutl: Winter Ceremonies

BILL HOLM

Ceremonial complexes that featured dramatic representations of supernatural beings, dramatizations of the contact of ancestors with those beings, and the demonstration of supernatural power were pan-coastal features of culture at the time of European contact. The specific form taken by these performances varied from place to place on the coast in accordance with the differing cultural emphases and traditions. At the same time, within any one group, there were great variations in the character of these dramatic acts, depending upon the specific purpose of the ritual and its place in the cultural whole.

The traumatic cultural upheavals of the late nineteenth and early twentieth centuries resulted in the eradication of many of these traditions and the drastic curtailment or modification of others. However, even before European contact, the dramatic complexes were not fixed or static. There is ample evidence to show that both specific ritual acts and whole concepts were moving from group to group during the early historic period and, according to native tradition, for generations before that. Changes in form and function are inevitable in any such transfer, and the relationships are often clear enough to allow some reconstruction of the direction of diffusion, sometimes corroborated by oral traditions of the receiving group.

Among the most complex, and at the same time most consciously theatrical, of Northwest Coast ritual performances were those of the Kwakiutl peoples of northern Vancouver Island and the British Columbia mainland along Queen Charlotte and Johnstone straits. Not only have these rituals been recorded and described in more detail than others, but also they have survived in more complete form. It is surprising that the Kwakiutl people have managed to retain many of their ceremonial traditions when their active and persistent participation in those traditions brought them, in the late nineteenth and early twentieth centuries, overt Canadian government opposition (La Violette 1961:59–97; Sewid-Smith 1979). Canadian federal legislation, the Indian Acts of 1885 and 1915, prohibited winter ceremonies and potlatches. In spite of the efforts of missionaries, Indian agents, and police to abolish the institution of the potlatch and the accompanying dance dramas, the Kwakiutl continued them almost without interruption. For a period after the most zealous attempts at suppression in the early 1920s

these ceremonial activities were rather furtive, but they continued, somewhat modified by the need for secrecy and the difficulty of assembling large groups of people without attracting the attention of the authorities (Drucker and Heizer 1976:47–52; Ford 1941:224).

Considerable modification took place during the 1940s with advances in communications and increased outside contacts associated with World War II (Holm 1977:5–24). Even so, the basic structure of the ceremonies and many of the individual dances survived, and on the basis of their form in the 1980s, it is possible to interpret the earlier descriptions of those dances and ceremonial acts no longer a part of the ritual.

Cedar Bark Dance (c̓éqa)

There were in the 1980s two major ceremonial complexes in Kwakiutl life. Formerly there were a number of others of lesser importance and of more limited distribution. Of the two major ceremonial festivals, by far the more important is that called c̓éqa (pl. c̓íc̓eqa) and in English Cedar Bark Dance by the Kwakiutl and designated the Winter ceremony by anthropologists. The native term has never been entirely satisfactorily translated, but it seems to imply 'acting', or perhaps 'making manifest the powers of the spirits'. Curtis (1907–1930, 10:170) wrote that the term was not used in the presence of the uninitiated, but neither the Boas-Hunt texts (Boas 1897) nor twentieth-century usage support that statement (Holm 1956–1976). Typically the festival was held in the winter and was analogous to ritual complexes of other Northwest Coast people involving demonstrations of supernatural power or contact with supernatural beings also held in winter. There is nothing in the native term that refers to the winter season, and, although formerly very unusual, it was possible to hold c̓éqa performances at any time, given the proper circumstances (Boas 1921:1073).

It seems certain that the c̓éqa as known historically was descended from guardian-spirit power dances, probably not unlike those of the historic Coast Salish. Family traditions that describe the first contact of an ancestor with a supernatural being and his acquisition of power and privilege from that being are similar to Salish tales. Aggressive Kwakiutl dancers like the Cannibal Dancer (hámaċa) and Cannibal of the Ground (hə́mshəmċəs) ran wildly in the early stages of their initiation and were restrained by their attendants in much the same way as were certain newly initiated Salish Spirit Dancers. The cedar-bark harness worn by the Salish initiate was similar to the crossed rings worn by novices in the Kwakiutl Winter ceremony. Possession, or the appearance of it, could be triggered in both by startling acts or the sound of a taboo word (Barnett 1955:280–281; Jilek 1982:78; Curtis 1907–1930, 10:193–194). Other similarities are numerous.

Many features of the late twentieth-century ċéqa such as the use of rattles to soothe the dancers, the constant references to the motivating spirits, the use of emblems that were spoken of as sacred such as red-dyed cedar bark and eagle down, and the dramatized possession of many dancers recall a time when the religious aspect of the ceremony predominated. Historically, the main motivation has been social. The dances and their accompanying songs and ritual were seen as valuable inherited privileges, graded in rank, that had as their principal function the manifestation of the prestige of noble families. A marriage of persons of high rank was a usual motivation for the ceremony, since the dances were typically transferred as part of a dowry to a man's son-in-law. They were ultimately for the children of the marriage, and so they were again performed by their proper owners when they come of age, on the occasion of the return of the bride price. The memorial potlatch for a deceased chief was another frequent occasion for Winter dancing.

Kwakiutl dramatic arts cannot be separated from the potlatch. The dances and dramatic presentations that characterize ċéqa and the other ceremonial festivals of the Kwakiutl must be validated by public showing and the payment of witnesses. They were, like names, ranks, and other prerogatives, part of the body of inherited privilege around which the potlatch institution was built. Their performance then was more to be considered a display of privilege than art or entertainment. Yet the dramatic and esthetic motivations were very strong, as evidenced by the continuing elaboration of masks and ceremonial paraphernalia (Holm 1983:86–120), the strikingly imaginative use of illusions and sleight-of-hand in certain performances, and the theatrical staging of events.

The recipients of the various dance privileges were said to be motivated by the supernatural beings whose original contact with the dancers' ancestors began the tradition. The dances were dramatic reenactments of the ancestors' adventures or demonstrations of the power or characteristic actions given them by supernatural beings. The principal spirits motivating ċéqa dances were báxʷbakʷalanuxʷsiwɛʔ, the man-eating spirit, and wínalagəlis, the warrior spirit, although a number of other supernatural beings, animals, and monsters were emulated by the dancers. Certain dance recipients, especially those motivated by báxʷbakʷalanuxʷsiwɛʔ, disappeared from

the sight of man for extended periods prior to their appearance in the ċéqa They were supposed to be in the hands of the spirits, learning their new roles.

Preparations

The Cannibal Dancer, whose dance is the most prestigious of those motivated by báxʷbakʷalanuxʷsiwɛʔ, was gone typically for four months, and the others for lesser periods. In historic times the stay was shortened until by the 1960s it was not unusual for an initiate to forego this disappearance entirely. The dramatic possibilities of the new dancer's disappearance and absence were not lost on the Kwakiutl, and the incidents were elaboredly staged to make it appear that the initiate was magically taken by the spirits (Curtis 1907–1930, 10:161–163). Whether or not all those not party to the ruse were deceived cannot be known with certainty, but there is a good chance that many were not. Kwakiutl tales about persons who were completely taken in by tricks of the Winter ceremony suggest that the general appearance of belief was a traditional simulation that was part of the drama.

The disappearance of a novice dancer was an early public sign that a ċéqa festival was in the offing. The host and those others who planned to participate actively were already deep in preparation, and this continued and intensified. Quantities of food had to be amassed for feasting. The objects that manifested the privileges to be shown—masks, rattles, blankets—had to be made or arranged for. Masses of inner bark of the red cedar had to be shredded and dyed, to be used as headrings by the participants, hung from masks and ceremonial objects, tied in the hemlock boughs that festooned the dance house, and worn as dress by many of the dancers. The red cedar bark was the principal symbolic material of the ċéqa In the late twentieth century it was still spoken of as sacred. Its use advertised the fact that the ċéqa was in effect and that the taboos and customs of the ceremony must be observed.

When the preparations were complete and the time for the festival had come the guests were invited. The invitation itself was developed dramatically. In earlier times, if the guests to be called were from other villages, the inviting party made their call from a canoe. The chief inviter was a high-ranking man from the host's tribe, and even his crewmen were often of chiefly rank. The well known incident by which the Fort Rupert people acquired the Cannibal Dance privilege by killing the owners involved a Bella Bella inviting party made up entirely of high-ranking chiefs (Boas 1897:427–443).

The inviters paddled to some quiet cove just out of sight of the village where they donned their ceremonial dress. Then, singing a paddling song traditionally used by inviters, they slowly paddled into the village bay, coming to a halt somewhat offshore. The villagers, having heard the song of the approaching inviters, assembled on the beach in festive dress. As the canoe drifted offshore the chief of the inviters stood and called the people to come to his village to witness the initiation of the children of the host chief. This richly metaphorical speech, delivered in dramatic style from the great canoe, was answered in kind by the village chief, who then called the inviters ashore and into his house where a feast was prepared for them. They were formally thanked and paid for their efforts. After a short rest, the members of the inviting party left for the next village, finally returning to their starting point, where a dramatic report of their travels was delivered to the host chief. Frequently, as the canoe approached the beach, one of the party stood on a platform of planks laid across the gunwales in the bow and danced to the singing of the crew members, who accompanied their song by beating the grips of their paddles on the gunwales. The dance was one appropriate to the ceremony for which the people were being called. On the beach dances were performed in reciprocation. The inviters' chief then reported, in dramatic fashion, on his travels and announced that the tribes were coming.

Preparations for housing the coming guests then proceeded in earnest, and before long their canoes appeared. The dramatically staged approach of the inviters was repeated, with songs, dancing, and speeches of welcome and thanks. Then the guests went ashore and were dispersed through the village in the homes of relatives and friends.

Much of the drama of the canoe invitation and the arrival of the invited tribes has been lost with the demise of canoe transportation. Until the late 1950s invitations were still occasionally made from boats, although powered fishing boats had been substituted for the traditional cedar canoes. In the 1960s chiefs began sending printed invitations, often bearing crest designs, to guests of rank, supplementing word-of-mouth invitations and the custom of making a general invitation at a previous gathering.

A great deal of functional preparation (amassing goods for payments, food and necessary materials, composing and practicing songs) had been going on for up to several years before the event. Various activities associated with the ceremony, but functionally part of the potlatch business, such as the repayment of the marriage debt, cannot be separated from the dramatic whole. Symbolic actions, metaphoric speech, dancing, and singing characterize both. The theatrics of the repayment were equal to those of the ćéqa itself (Boas 1897:421–424). Rows of goods, paid the husband by the wife's father to be distributed in turn by the husband, were laid out in a great square bounded by a line of ancient box lids inlayed with sea otter teeth. The display is called háwanaqa, the term for a catamaran made of canoes tied together and decked with house planks on which household goods were transported in earlier times. At a certain point in the ritual

of transfer, a man of the husband's numaym split one of the box lids with an ax or harpoon, symbolically sinking the catamaran. This dramatic display has persisted in modified form.

Beginning

Every event of the ensuing ceremony was developed dramatically. George Hunt described in detail the mythical background and the complex ritual attending the preparation and presentation of the ceremony (Boas 1930: 57–174). Each act was performed by the hereditary privilege owner in stylized form. The principal host of the Winter ceremony and those others who intended to coordinate their displays with him, along with the owners of the privileges of conducting the various activities of the ceremony, met and planned the ceremony. The participants were divisible into three groups—those without privilege (bíbaxʷəs 'ordinary men'), the active dancers and initiates (mí²əmgʷat 'seals'), and those who had dance privileges but were currently inactive (ġʷí²ġʷəӡa 'sparrows'). This last group included the managers of the ceremony, those who held the hereditary posts of cedar bark distributor, master of ceremonies, and song leader among others.

In order to clear the air of sorrows, mourning songs were sung. These were either traditional family dirges, or, if the gathering was on the occasion of a memorial to a deceased chief, stylized recitations of his accomplishments. Sometimes a masked figure representing one of the chief's prerogatives was brought into the house by an escort of high-ranking men (Curtis 1907–1930, 10:57; Ford 1941:221–223). The dance following was spoken of as the last appearance on earth of the departed chief. After the departure of the masked dancer, the escorting chiefs returned with the mask and regalia, symbolizing the privileges retained by the heirs. The mourning ceremonies were always completed before sunset. As of the 1980s they were still performed at the beginning of ćéqa.

At the appointed time, traditionally four days after the planning meeting, four sparrow messengers went from house to house and called the people to a meeting. The last to enter the house were the seals. There those privileged by inheritance to do so brought out the emblems and paraphernalia of the ceremony—tallow and charcoal for the participants' faces, shredded red-dyed cedar bark for their headrings, eagle down to be placed on their heads, the drum, and the singers' batons. Several traditional versions of this ceremony have been described in great detail (Boas 1930:59–72, 92–98, 121–132). The only part of this dramatic sequence to survive into the second half of the twentieth century was the distribution of red cedar bark, and even this action had almost ceased by the 1960s. Since then certain of the ceremonial procedures have been revived, including the bringing in of the ring of red cedar bark around a woman. Even in its much abbreviated late form it was always performed by the privilege owner in a solemn and impressive manner. Each ritual movement was made four times and each circuit of the house, accompanied by rattle and song, was made in a counterclockwise direction with a pivot to the left at front and rear of the house, customs that prevailed throughout the entire ritual.

Cannibal Dance

Throughout the following four days, while preparations were being made for bringing out the privilege dances, the sparrows followed a round of feasts, and during the nights the people danced. During this time people who were scheduled to inherit minor dances were abducted from the dance house by masked or hemlock-shrouded figures. On the fourth night of dancing whistles representing the supernatural power of the Cannibal Dancer were heard during the presentation of a dance, usually the Ghost Dance, which was considered to have a special attraction for the man-eating spirit. The Cannibal Dancer's return from his sojourn with *báxʷbakʷalanuxʷsiwεʔ* was announced by a loud thump on the roof. Immediately the singers began to beat rapid time with their batons. Pushing aside a board, the dancer thrust his torso through the roof of the firelit house, shouting his hungry cry, "*hap!*" He ran around the roof, repeating his appearance in each of the four corners, and finally he dropped into a blanket held by his attendants. His dress consisted of hemlock branches tied in his hair, in wreathes crossing over his shoulders, and around his wrists and ankles (fig. 1 top left). Closely surrounded by his attendants, his secret whistles sounding, he dashed around the floor in an apparent frenzy and finally disappeared as suddenly as he had arrived. The most intense excitement prevailed in the house. The dancer's whistles were heard receding in the distance along with his ever fainter cry.

In his wild state the dancer displayed his cannibalistic hunger by biting the arms of spectators, or even devouring human flesh. So much of the *ćéqa* was illusionary that it is not at all certain that cannibalism actually ever took place. The Kwakiutl avoided contact with the dead, and the thought of eating human flesh was abhorrent and consequently awe-inspiring. However, biting living persons by Cannibal Dancers is well documented, at least for the Bella Bella (Tolmie 1963:259, 292–293). Since about 1900 even this has been simulated.

At dawn the next morning the people reassembled. Those who had recently disappeared were brought back. The dancer and his female attendant were ceremonially captured on the beach and brought into the house. Then followed several (traditionally four) nights of dancing, during which the newly inherited dances were publicly shown and the names associated with them bestowed on

their new owners. Many of the customs just described survived, in gradually diminishing detail, into the 1940s. Since then much of the preliminary ritual has ceased. In the mid-twentieth century only the mourning ceremony was certain, and sometimes a distribution of red cedar bark. Only the Cannibal Dancer disappeared, usually overnight, and even this symbolic absence was often omitted. He usually appeared briefly, in a wild state, following the mourning or the cedar bark distribution, to return later that night to complete his dances.

In general each dance privilege can be seen to have four phases—the abduction of the initiate by the motivating spirit, the return and capture of the initiate, the demonstration by the initiate of the appearance or power of the motivating spirit, and the taming or purification of the initiate. Although historically the most important of the *ćéqa* dances, and more elaborate than the others, the Cannibal Dance followed the same sequence. In his first appearance after his recapture the dancer acted the part of a man-eater, in fact impersonating *báxʷbakʷalanuxʷsiwεʔ*. As he became progressively tamer his hemlock branch dress was changed for that of red cedar bark (fig. 1, top right), and he danced in an upright position. In one of his songs a word or phrase was used that excited him to possession, and he dashed around the house and disappeared behind the curtain stretched across the rear of the room. Immediately a man wearing the great mask representing one of the birdlike associates of *báxʷbakʷalanuxʷsiwεʔ* danced into the firelit room. Up to three other masked dancers followed him, each accompanied by an attendant, as were all dancers in the Kwakiutl ceremonial performances. This dance, called *hámsəmala* 'wearing the cannibal mask', was one of the most dramatic in the *ćéqa* and, as of the 1980s, one of the least altered by the passage of time.

The sight and sound of these dancers was said to be exciting to former Cannibal Dancers, and at the close of the *hámsəmala* one or more may run wildly about the house and out behind the curtain. Later he returned and performed to one of his songs, following which he promised to pay the people for the temporary renewal of his Cannibal Dance, and at the same time he bestowed names on some of the younger members of his family.

Finally, accompanied by his female associate and his many attendants, each shaking a large, round rattle, the newly initiated dancer performed his final, tame dance, dressed in a blanket, apron, and cedar bark rings. Later all his female relatives danced, honoring him and signifying his return to the human condition.

Other *ćéqa* Dances

Among the many other *ćéqa* dances, that of the *túxʷʔid* gave the Kwakiutl dramatic flair its greatest opportunity. The *túxʷʔid* dancer acquired magical powers from the

top left, Amer. Mus. of Nat. Hist., New York: 22866; top right, U. of Pa., U. Mus., Philadelphia: 12588; bottom left, Smithsonian, NAA: S.I. 3946.

Fig. 1. Cannibal Dance. top left, Untamed cannibal dancer clothed in hemlock branches. Photograph probably by George Hunt, Ft. Rupert, B.C., 1901–1902. top right, Partially tamed dancer, wearing cedar bark. Photograph by Benjamin W. Leeson, Vancouver I., 1912. bottom left, Fully tamed cannibal dancers with cedar bark rings and blackened faces at Franz Boas's apple feast. Photograph, cropped, by Oregon C. Hastings, Ft. Rupert, B.C., Nov. 25, 1894. bottom right, Simon Dick, dressed as a fully tamed cannibal but dancing as an untamed one at the opening of the U'mista Cultural Centre, Alert Bay, B.C. Photograph by Vickie Jensen, Nov. 1, 1980.

Fig. 2. Representation of a severed human head carved in solid wood that was used in the *túxʷʔid* performance to make the audience believe the dancer has been decapitated. Human hair is pegged into the crown. Collected by J. Adrian Jacobsen in 1881. Height 32 cm.

Fig. 3. War Dancer with hoisting frame attached to his body. Charles Nowell, who posed for this picture at the Field Museum, Chicago, was one of the last Kwakiutls to be suspended by his pierced skin (Ford 1941:115–117). The paraphernalia is at the Field Museum (Weber 1985:75). Photograph by Charles H. Carpenter, 1904.

warrior spirit. After enduring the ridicule of the audience, the *túxʷʔid* dancer, often a woman, brought out her *λúgʷɛʔ*, or supernatural treasure, to the amazement of the people. Examples of her power were to give birth to a giant frog, cause birds to fly about, or the moon to rise, wax, wane, and set in the house. The opportunities for dramatic spectacles were limitless. The most impressive *túxʷʔid* performances demonstrated the power of invulnerability. The dancer asked to have her head cut off or pierced with a splitting wedge, be stuffed into a box and burned to ashes on the fire, be disemboweled or thrown, weighted, overboard of a canoe. Finally someone agreed to do the deed, and it was accomplished with gruesome realism (fig. 2). Always she returned, again whole, to dance, but often with the telltale marks of her ordeal.

Among the other performances that dramatically demonstrated acquired power was the War Dance (*həwínaɬ*), in which the dancer allowed himself to be suspended by his pierced skin, to demonstrate his insensibility to pain (fig. 3). Actual suspension of the War Dancer ceased around 1900, while the graphic simulation of violence in the *túxʷʔid* dance continued at least into the 1930s. Another dancer who demonstrated acquired supernatural power was the *ṁaṁaq́a* 'thrower' who caught and

threw a debilitating power into the audience.

After all the initiates had demonstrated their inherited privileges, the people stood and sang the closing song of the *ćéqa*, while removing their cedar bark headrings. These were collected by a man who by this act signified his intention to sponsor a *ćéqa* the following season.

The next day the people assembled and the business of paying them for their services as witnesses was concluded. The goods that may have been displayed before the *ćéqa* were again brought out and distributed to the people. The order and the amount payed each recipient was determined by rank. By the 1960s the closing ritual of the *ćéqa* and the distribution of the payments had been very much simplified and shortened. Immediately following the last dance the goods to be given were brought out and displayed on the floor of the house and distributed, along with payments in money. The distribution was made in the order in which the people were seated in the house, rather than that of rank as in former times, but the amount of each payment is related to the rank of the recipient.

The *ćéqa* clearly had religious antecedents. All the active participants were referred to as *pípəxəla* 'shamans'; and the hemlock branches, cedar bark rings, and round rattles used in the ceremony were very similar to shamanistic paraphernalia. The many ritual prayers and songs and the constant references to supernatural beings demonstrate this relationship. Nevertheless, the emphasis in the twentieth century, as it had been historically, was on the demonstration of inherited privilege.

For the duration of the ceremony the secular power of the chiefs and the organization of the numayms were suspended and superseded by the hierarchy of dancers. The Kwakiutl expressed this by saying that during the *ćéqa* the chiefs are like ordinary men, and the high-ranking dancers are chiefs. For all practical purposes there was little change, since those of high secular rank were also the owners of the important dances. These dancers have been described as making up secret societies. However, they had no actual function as societies and perhaps should be seen as groups of individuals with similar dance traditions, who may sit together and act together somewhat informally during the time of the ceremony. The clearest indication of change in the social order during the ceremony is the fact that the names associated with secular rank were put aside by the participants in favor of the names belonging to their current *ćéqa* positions.

λa²səlá Ceremony

The other important Kwakiutl ceremonial complex, the *λəẃəlaxa* or *λa²səlá* has been erroneously referred to as the Summer Dance, perhaps because of its seeming opposition to the *ćéqa*, which has been called the Winter ceremonial. Kwakiutls sometimes call it Weasel Dance, referring to the headdress. In the twentieth century the Kwakiutl term *λa²səlá* supplanted the word *λəẃəláxa* 'come down from above', the term used to designate the ceremony by the Bella Bella and Oowekeeno, from whom it is said the dance was derived.

Although ownership of a *λa²səlá* dance was considered a valuable privilege, the whole ceremony was recognized as being foreign in origin and was held in somewhat lower esteem than the *ćéqa*. The dances represented the appearance of figures that had the status of numaym crests, rather than being demonstrations of the power of supernatural beings.

Traditionally the *λa²səlá* was never held at the same time as the *ćéqa* and never in the same house. Some accounts describe it as being held on the four days preceding the *ćéqa*. Active *ćéqa* participants were not allowed to be present at a *λa²səlá* performance. By the mid-twentieth century the two ceremonies had modified to the point that they followed one another in the same

Fig. 4. Joe Seaweed performing the Headdress Dance of the *λa²səlá* ceremony. Photograph by Bill Holm, at opening of Sea Monster House, Pacific Science Center, Seattle, Wash., 1971.

house on the same evening, with the same participants. The *ćéqa* usually preceded the *λa²səlá*.

The initiate in the *λa²səlá*, the *hílikəlat*, appeared from behind a curtain wearing a dancing blanket, apron, and complex crownlike headdress adorned on the forehead with a carved and shell-inlaid representation of a crest figure, an upstanding circlet of sea lion whiskers, and a long trailer of ermine skins down the back (fig. 4). He carried a rattle, which was traditionally the classic Northern Northwest Coast raven rattle rather than the globular rattle used by *ćéqa* performers. He danced with short, quick jumps with his elbows spread to display the blanket and ermine trailer and bobbed his head rhythmically to distribute the down that was placed in the top of the headdress. His attendants teased him by mocking his movements until he lost his self-control and dashed out of the house. The attendants followed and came back carrying his blanket and headdress, which they announced is all that there was to be found. The assumption was that he had been taken away by the being from which his *λa²səlá* privilege was derived. Presently the sound of horns or whistles was heard from outside the house and the attendants went cautiously to investigate. They announced that some creature was approaching the house, and on its arrival they escorted it in, identifying it to the people as the lost dancer returned in the form of his crest figure. The singers started the appropriate song, and the

Fig. 5. Echo Dance of the λaʔsəlá series. The mask has many mouths, which are changed to correspond to the different creatures mentioned in the song. This one, worn by the dancer Steve Brown, represents the grizzly bear. The attendant dancer, in background, is Jack Hudson. Photograph by Bill Holm at the Sea Monster House, Pacific Science Center, Seattle, Wash., 1972.

Fig. 6. Woodman emerging from the forest. The mask is in "Art," fig. 13, this vol. Photograph by Edward S. Curtis, before 1914.

masked dancer moved into the firelight, surrounded by the attendants who blew eagle down over him.

The masks and costumes worn by the dancers were often extremely elaborate. The transformation masks for which the Kwakiutl are renowned were used in this dance (fig. 5). The complex mask sometimes represented two different creatures in a dancer's tradition or else graphically illustrated a mythical transformation.

When the dance was finished the attendants chased the dancer behind the curtain with cries of "wə̀ wə̀ wə̀!" The dancer was not the initiate himself but a hired performer chosen for his dancing ability and for his skill in operating the mask. In former times the initiate danced three nights before his disappearance and return as the crest figure (Boas 1921:873–875). Goods were distributed following each performance. Since the 1940s the first three nights of dancing have been eliminated and a single distribution was held at the close of the λaʔsəlá. A great many different creatures were represented. Some of them, like q̓úmugʷɛʔ, the chief of the undersea world, and bə́k̓ʷəs, the woodman (fig. 6), were manlike, while others represented various creatures of the land, sea, and air. The northwesternmost

Kwakiutl groups celebrated a ritual called by them núnɬəm, which in many ways was analogous to the λaʔsəlá, and by the early twentieth century it had been largely superseded by that ceremony.

Sources and Influences

Since the legalization of Kwakiutl Winter dancing by the revision of the Indian Act in 1951 there has been a continual increase in public ceremonial activity, and attempts have been made to revive some of the details that had been eliminated. Since the 1940s the entire ćɛ́qa and λaʔsəlá together, from opening ritual to final distribution of payments, may be concluded in one day.

Kwakiutl dramatic arts were not limited to these ceremonial complexes. The transfer and bestowal of names and secular privileges; the buying, selling, and breaking of coppers; feasts; and speeches were all elaborated dramatically. The other Northern Wakashan peoples, especially the Bella Bella and Oowekeeno, seem to have been the sources for many ceremonial concepts. The Kwakiutl themselves recognize these groups as the source of many of their privileges and in fact customarily insert words and phrases from the northern languages into their dance songs.

The influence of the Kwakiutl and the other Northern Wakashans has been far-reaching in the ceremonial life of the coast. The Winter ceremony performances of the Haida, Tlingit, and Tsimshian have been strongly influenced if not derived from the dances of the Haisla and Bella Bella, a diffusion most clearly demonstrated by the northern use of Wakashan terms for figures that resemble those in Bella Bella and Kwakiutl ceremonial systems. To the south a similar influence can be seen, one clear example being the Nootkan term for their Winter ceremony, *λuꞏkʷaꞏna* or *λuꞏkʷaꞏli*, apparently derived from the Kwakiutl term *λúgʷala*, meaning 'having supernatural power'. Even the Kwakiutl *xʷíxʷi* dance, which they acquired from the Comox (Northern Salish) by marriage and war (Boas and Hunt 1902–1905, 1:237–239; Boas 1921:892–894), may have been influenced in earlier times by Kwakiutl concepts of inheritance, of bestowing prestige, and of masking itself. On the other hand, similarities in the actions of the newly captured Cannibal Dancer and the novice Spirit Dancer of the Salish may be due to a common derivation from an earlier coast-wide tradition of spirit power dancing.

Kwakiutl Since 1980

GLORIA CRANMER WEBSTER

Each of the 15 bands of the Kwakiutl* is an independent political unit governed by a band council made up of one elected member for each 100 band members; for example, in 1985 the Nimpkish had 10 councilors and the Kwiakah Band, with 5 members, had one (see table 1). The bands were subsumed within the Campbell River District (until 1969 the Kwawkewlth Indian Agency headquartered at Alert Bay) of the British Columbia Region of the Department of Indian and Northern Affairs. A tribal political organization, the Kwakiutl District Council, was set up in 1974 for the purpose of lobbying for greater control of reserves and to take over various functions previously administered by the Department of Indian Affairs. In 1982, the four Kingcome Inlet bands departed from the Kwakiutl District Council, later joined by the Nimpkish, to set up the Musga'makw Tribal Council. Band councils operate much like municipal councils, in charge of housing, water, sewer, sanitation, and road maintenance. In some areas bands incorporate responsibilities handled at the provincial level in the rest of Canadian society. These areas include supervision of health care (including drug and alcohol-abuse counseling and treatment), welfare services, and in some cases education. Many bands manage economic enterprises of various kinds, such as marinas, salmon enhancement projects, an oyster hatchery, tourist related businesses, cafeterias, laundromats, and a shipyard. Funds for general band operation and economic development derive from federal and other grant monies. Law enforcement is handled by the Royal Canadian Mounted Police, but band councils may pass by-laws binding upon band members and visitors on reserve lands.

Band membership was available to all hereditary Kwakiutls until 1951 (with the provision that any band member could apply for enfranchisement, that is, removal from the band list with payment for their share of band funds). In that year, changes to the Indian Act irrevocably deprived Native women of their Indian status upon marrying non-Indians. In 1986 federal legislation revised the Indian Act so that marriage to a non-Indian no longer

*The term Kwakiutl and the synonyms for it that are preferred by many are discussed in the synonymy in "Kwakiutl: Traditional Culture," this vol.

Table 1. Kwakiutl Band Population, 1983

	On Reserve	On Crown Land	Off Reserve	Total
Tanakteuk	7	7	102	116
Tlowitsis-Mumtagila	11	29	121	161
Tsawataineuk	110	0	198	308
Tsulquate	325	0	19	344
Campbell River	109	0	124	233
Cape Mudge	300	0	115	415
Comox	62	1	28	91
Kwa-wa-aineuk	14	5	0	19
Kwakiutl (Fort Rupert)	144	1	152	297
Kwiakah	6	0	8	14
Kwicksutaineuk	68	0	126	194
Mamalillikulla	28	25	145	198
Nimpkish	620	2	319	941
Nuwitti	3	5	13	21
Quatsino	136	0	44	180
Totals	1,943	75	1,514	3,532

SOURCE: Canada. Department of Indian Affairs and Northern Development. Indian and Inuit Affairs Program 1984:54–55.

revoked Indian status. Some bands decided to re-admit previously excluded women and their children. Many of those deprived of Indian status have continued to maintain their hereditary ceremonial responsibilities; the entire issue of status is for many Kwakiutls irrelevant—an issue of "White law."

Whereas in the past many Kwakiutls worked off-reserve in logging, construction, canneries, and mining, the onset of comprehensive welfare and unemployment benefits in the 1960s allowed Natives to pursue traditional seasonal economic patterns. Most band members are seasonally engaged in commercial fishing of various types. In some communities, native ownership of commercial fishing boats was quite common. Alert Bay boasted the second largest Indian-owned fishing fleet on the British Columbia coast for many years). But increasing restriction and waning fish stocks have made fishing a less predictable livelihood and resulted in less native ownership of boats and fewer opportunities for younger band members to engage in fishing. Other employment is offered by band administration and enterprises, for example, clerical, janitorial, teacher aide, and homemaker assistant jobs.

Education has changed over the years. Since the first school in the area was set up at Alert Bay by the Anglican Church around 1880 Native children have been taught in residential schools or day schools operated by the Department of Indian Affairs, whose last residential school in the area closed in 1974, and later in the provincial public schools. Education of Native children in Canada continues to be a federal responsibility, although most Kwakiutls are educated in provincial schools situated near reserves. However, the Nimpkish, Tsawataineuk, and Tsulquate operate band-administered schools, set up because of perceived failures in the public school system to confront special needs of native children (for example, statistics for 1978 showed a 99% dropout rate among the Nimpkish). Band members have increasingly recognized the need for and taken advantage of opportunities for academic and vocational training. Community college and band-initiated programs in carpentry, office skills, fisheries technology, forestry management, and traditional art have resulted in trained local personnel for band operations and self-employment. Since 1960, some young people have graduated from college and entered the professions.

Band politics reflect traditional family alliances and allegiances. Even ordinary aspects of community interaction often become politicized and competitive, rather than allowing community cooperation for achievement of long-term goals.

Traditional practices in life cycle activities were observed in the 1980s. Most children were born in hospitals and cared for by physicians. A pattern of grandmaternal child-rearing, prevalent until the 1970s, was replaced by childcare facilities and pre-school programs, since the elderly almost always maintained their own households, rather than living in an extended family arrangement. Children were commonly baptized, even in families where parents did not regularly attend church. Newborns and toddlers may also be given names at potlatches (sometimes before they are born, a practice that requires names appropriate to either sex).

Few in the 1980s learned the Kwakiutl language at home; English replaced the Kwakiutl language in the usage of most people under 50. However, children were taught the Kwakiutl language, ceremonial dancing (fig. 1), and associated mythology, and the conventions of traditional art in primary school programs, which have become common since the late 1970s. The success of these programs has been in increasing cultural awareness and providing a positive Indian identity in the young, rather than in revitalizing native speech and ceremonial habits.

As young as 10, boys and (less frequently) girls may be initiated as Cannibal Dancers or members of other secret ceremonial societies, depending upon their family's rights

Fig. 1. Traditional dance instruction at Alert Bay School, B.C. Vera Cranmer on left teaches a girl how to hold a paddle model while dancing. Programs to teach the language and traditional skills are well established in the local schools. Photograph by Vickie Jensen, 1983.

to these prerogatives. Girls are sometimes recognized at potlatches as having reached puberty, at which time they will be given another name. Toys will be distributed to symbolize the end of childhood, and soap and combs are given out to portray purification after the onset of menses.

Marriage is no longer generally recognized as requisite to child-bearing, but it is common. Although aboriginally incest restrictions in choosing marriage partners may have been less of a consideration than projected inheritance benefits, the old people still sometimes remark that present-day marriage partners are "too closely related (according to traditional kinship reckoning)"; but in general European customs of first-cousin incest avoidance are the rule. Most marriages are performed in churches according to Christian rites but are on occasion followed by an "Indian wedding"—a potlatch involving a mock competition for the bride, gifts of wealth and prerogatives from the bride's family to the groom's, and feeding of the new bride by elderly women of virtue. The couple will usually assume residence in single-family housing in the groom's village, although employment opportunities regularly take precedence in making these decisions.

Young adults expect to inherit their parents' assets and also may fall heir to names and other ceremonial prerogatives from more distant relatives in the course of their lives. Funeral ceremonies take place in churches (after embalming procedures), and burials are in reserve cemeteries. Those attending the funeral are then provided a light meal by the family of the deceased in an informal ceremony at which eulogies and moralizing instruction will be offered by the guests. The family may give notice of their intent to hold a memorial potlatch (often about a year following the funeral). This period of a year may be one of mourning behavior, and relatives will participate in the mourning songs with which subsequent potlatches

Kwagiulth Mus., Cape Mudge, B.C.
Fig.2. The Kwagiulth Museum at Cape Mudge, Quadra I., B.C. The museum opened in June 1979 to house the returned potlatch paraphernalia. Photograph by Brian Kyle, about 1983.

begin. The old people may still avoid mentioning the name of the dead; for instance, a widow might refer to her husband as "the deceased father of my children" rather than using his name. Memorial potlatches may begin with the appearance of an *imas* mask, worn by a relative to indicate the desire of the deceased to have his/her prerogatives remain with the family (some rights and privileges are allowed to die with the deceased according to their wishes).

After potlatches were permitted to be conducted openly in the 1950s, most were held in Alert Bay. Because other activities such as soccer tournaments and the annual weekend of sports festivities in June brought out-of-town groups together there, a tradition developed to hold potlatches in June (they still occurred infrequently

throughout the year in other villages). Ceremonial big-houses already existed at Gilford Island and Kingcome Inlet, and new ones were built in Comox in 1962 and Alert Bay in 1963. On smaller reserves such as Cape Mudge, Campbell River, and Quatsino, potlatches are held in community halls. Besides memorial and wedding pot-latches, families may give potlatches for pole raisings (since about 1937 done only rarely as an obligation of an heir), to wash away shame, to transfer titles, and for events of public note such as the opening of community buildings. Traditional reasons for potlatches, such as initiation of Cannibal Dancers, name givings, transfer of titles, and wiping off shame, may be held together with potlatches given for other reasons. Since 1981 fewer potlatches were scheduled at Alert Bay in June; this may be evidence of change from June as potlatch time. The bighouses may also be used for nontraditional activities such as community functions, reception of dignitaries, and fundraising dance performances for tourists. Spradley and McCurdy (1975:579–597) discuss the commencement of performing private dances for tourists as an example of culture change.

In 1978, the National Museum of Man, Ottawa, returned the ceremonial masks, regalia, and coppers that had been surrendered in 1922 in order to obtain reduced sentences for some of the 45 people arrested in 1921 for holding a potlatch at Village Island (Codere 1950; Sewid-Smith 1979). The collection was divided, and museums were built to house the artifacts, the Kwagiulth Museum at Cape Mudge (fig. 2) and the U'Mista Cultural Centre at Alert Bay (fig. 3). These institutions provided a locus for systematic community attempts to document and revital-ize cultural life by recording oral histories, producing language and culture curricula, preparing exhibits, orga-nizing and administering classes on cultural topics (such

Fig. 3. Opening of U'Mista Cultural Centre, Alert Bay, B.C., Nov. 1, 1980. left, Building front design based on a house front of a Nimpkish chief at Alert Bay, depicting a thunderbird carrying a whale ("Kwakiutl: Traditional Culture," fig. 3, this vol.). Guests from other Kwakiutl villages arrived costumed and dancing aboard seine boats. They are being welcomed with eagle down and the Peace Dance. right, Preparing the feast for the potlatch. About 300 salmon were barbecued and goods distributed. Photographs by Vickie Jensen.

as traditional songs, button blankets), and assisting with the planning of potlatches. The U'Mista Cultural Centre produced movies presenting the Native view of potlatch prohibition and a statement about cultural survival (U'Mista Cultural Society 1975, 1983). Carving programs such as those carried out by Tony Hunt and Doug Cranmer have helped train a new generation of carvers, although carving had continued as an art among individuals in almost all Kwakiutl communities. Native-designed jewelry, plaques, and other nonfunctional carvings, introduced during the nineteenth century, continue to be produced, but serigraph prints represent a new departure in native art. A few old people have continued to make basketry; although the young have been introduced to these crafts, restrictions on the gathering of cedarbark and other materials have resulted in the continuing decline of basketry crafts.

Discussions of contemporary life among the Kwakiutl include Rohner (1967), Rohner and Rohner (1970), Wolcott (1967), Spradley (1969), and Haegert (1983: 21–24). The place of art in everyday life is treated by Arima and Hunt (1975), Holm (1983), and Macnair, Hoover, and Neary (1980). Studies of language produced for Native use and for teaching include Powell et al. (1981), Grubb (1977), Wilson and Henderson (1980–1981), and Hemphill and Hemphill (1984). Mythic narratives have been presented in Wallas (1981).

Nootkans of Vancouver Island

EUGENE ARIMA AND JOHN DEWHIRST

The Nootkans of Vancouver Island are the speakers of Nootka ('nōōtkə) and Nitinaht ('nĭtĭ,năt), two members of the Wakashan language family.* These two, together with Makah, constitute the southern branch of this family.

The aboriginal territory of the speakers of Nootka and Nitinaht extends along most of the Pacific side of Vancouver Island for some 250 miles, from Cape Cook to Point No Point (fig. 1). Nootka is spoken north of Pachena Point and Nitinaht to the south. Culturally a distinction has been made (Drucker 1951:4–6, map 1) among the Northern Nootkans, north of Estevan Point, the Central Nootkans, between Estevan Point and Pachena Point, and the Southern Nootkans, south of Pachena Point and including both the Nitinaht and the Makah, who live around Cape Flattery on the Olympic Peninsula.

Component Groups

Large inlets and sounds along the Nootkan coast were natural units of sheltered sea fostering sociopolitical groupings (Sproat 1868:10–12; Drucker 1951:6–7). Local kin groups linked by ambilateral descent held defined territories (P.L. Newman 1957:4–8). A myth usually derived the group from a legendary ancestor at a particular locality (Sapir and Swadesh 1955:52–53). The senior, chiefly line of descent owned territory and resources material and immaterial and was the nucleus of the local group. Such local groups often united through alliance or conquest to form a distinct "tribe" with their ranked chiefs, common winter village, and ceremonials (Drucker 1951:220). Northern Nootkan tribes joined to form confederacies with their chiefs ranked in a single series and a common summer village (Drucker 1951:220, 246). Within the larger associations the local groups

retained their identities and territorial rights, and they acted as ceremonial units (Sapir and Swadesh 1955:45). A tribe was named after one of its component units, and a confederacy after one of its tribe or local groups. There were no native terms for these levels of organization. Major groups in the late nineteenth century are listed below, (after Drucker 1951:222–241); their native names are given in Nootka for the Northern and Central Nootkans and in Nitinaht for the Southern Nootkans. More existed earlier, but after White contact many vanished, were exterminated, or were absorbed by other groups. These were reduced again by governmental merging to just 15 officially recognized "bands."

Northern Nootkans

1. Chickliset (čiˑqλisˀatḥ), a tribe occupying Ououkinsh inlet, having five salmon streams, an "outside" site for halibut fishing and sealing, a winter village at ˀiquˑs, a summer site at ˀapsuˑwiˑs, and territory extending from Cape Cook to the beach opposite Whiteface Island. In the mid-twentieth century they moved to reside with the Kyuquot, and were governmentally subsumed under that band (Kenyon 1973:28).

2. Kyuquot (qaˑẏuˑk̓ʷatḥ), an old confederacy of four tribes (qanupittaqamɬ, šawispˀatḥ, qʷixquˀatḥ, ƛaˀaˑˀatḥ) uniting 14 local groups of Kyuquot Sound, each named after its salmon stream. The confederacy summer village at ʕaqtiˑs had 27 houses, duplicating those in the four tribal winter villages. Their chiefs claimed territory from Whiteface Island to Rugged Point.

3. Ehattesaht (ˀiˑḥatisˀatḥ), a confederacy of three tribes: ˀiˑḥatisˀatḥ of Zeballos and Espinosa inlets, hawiɬtaqimɬˀatḥ of the outside coast, and činixnitˀatḥ of Queen's Cove, where all concentrated in the twentieth century. The traditional confederacy summer village was at Tatchu Point.

4. Nutchatlaht (nučaˑɬˀatḥ), a confederacy of several groups seemingly left over from the Ehattesaht and Mowachaht, with its summer village at the north of the mouth of Nuchatlitz Inlet. Winter tribal villages were inside the inlet and, cut off by the Ehattesaht, in Port Eliza and Espinosa inlets.

5. Mowachaht (muwačatḥ), formerly the Nootka Band,

*The phonemes of Nootka are (plain stops and affricates) p, t, c, č, λ, k, kʷ, q, qʷ, ˀ, ˁ (a pharyngealized [ˀ]); (glottalized stops and affricates) p̓, t̓, c̓, č̓, ƛ̓, k̓, k̓ʷ, q̓, q̓ʷ; (voiceless continuants) s, š, ɬ, x, xʷ, x̣, x̣ʷ, h, ḥ (a pharyngealized [h]); (plain resonants) m, n, w, y; (glottalized resonants) m̓, n̓, w̓, y̓; (short vowels) i, e, a, u; (long vowels) iˑ, eˑ, aˑ, uˑ. The phoneme inventory of Nitinaht is similar except that Nitinaht has two voiced stops, b and d, and the plain and glottalized resonants l and l̓ (Sapir and Swadesh 1939:12; Turner et al. 1983:144).

The editors are responsible for synthesizing and selecting information on the transcription of Nootka from the available sources, including Barbara Efrat and John Thomas (communication to editors 1987).

391

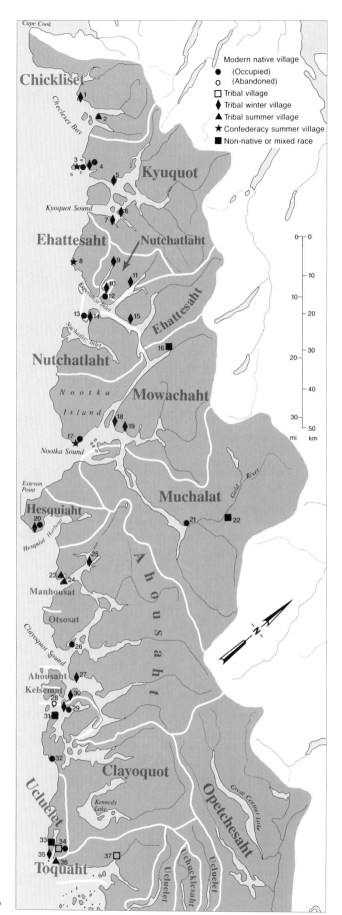

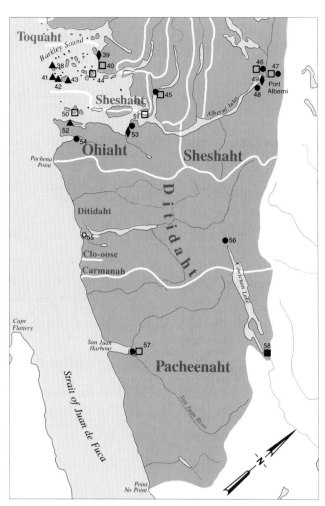

Fig. 1. Territories and major settlements of the Nootkan tribal groups in the late 19th century. 1, *ʔiqu·s* (Acous Res.); 2, *ʔapsu·wi·s* (Upsowis Res.); 3, *ʕaqti·s* (Village I. Res.); 4, *hu·psitas* (Houpsitas Res.); 5, *šaẁispa* (Guillod Pt.); 6, *maḥqit* (Markale Res.); 7, *qʷixqu*; 8, *ṭaču·* (Tatchu Res.); 9, *ʔuqa·c* (Occosh Res.); 10, *činix̣nit*; 11, *čačačink* (Savey Res.); 12, *maḥti·ʕas* (Chenahkint Res.); 13, *nuča·ł* (Nuchatl Res.); 14, *ʔapaqtu* (Ahpukto Res.); 15, *hu·kʷḥ* (Oke Res.); 16, Tahsis; 17, *yukʷa·t* (Yuquot Res.); 18, *ƙu·pti·* (Coopte Res.); 19, *ʔu·wis* (Hoiss Res.); 20, *ḥišk*ʷ*i·* (Hesquiat Res.); 21, *ʔa·ʔaminqis* (Ahaminaquus Res.); 22, Gold River; 23, *sumaxqʷu·ʔis*; 24, *ma·n̓uʔis* (Openit Res.); 25, *ʕałmaʔa*; 26, *ma·qtusis* (Marktosis Res.); 27, *ċati·kʷis* (Sutaquis Res.); 28, Clayoquot; 29, *ʔupicatḥ* (Opitsat Res.); 30, *λułpič* (Cloolthpich Res.); 31, Tofino; 32, *hisa·wista* (Esowista Res.); 33, Ucluelet; 34, *ƙʷa·yimṭa* and *hitaču* (Ittatsoo Res.); 35, *hi·napi·ʔis*; 36, *ṭukʷa·* (Dookqua Res.); 37, *ṭi·kyakis* (Deekyakus Res.); 38, *čiša·* (Benson I.); 39, *hi·kʷis* (Equis Res.); 40, *λučpitis*; 41, *ma·kλʕi·* (Wouwer I.); 42, *hucacwił* (Dicebox I.); 43, *hu·m̓u·wa* (Omoah Res.); 44, *λiḥu·wa* (Cleho Res.); 45, *hu·čuqλis* (Elhlateese Res.); 46, *ču·maʕas* (Tsahaheh Res.); 47, *ʕaswin̓is* (Ahahswinis Res.); 48, *ṭi·pis* and *ḥu·mapt* (Alberni Res.); 49, *nu·pčiqapis*; 50, *ʔa·ʔatsuẁis* (Hamilton Pt. Res.); 51, *qawašu̓ł* (Cowishil Res.); 52, *ki·xʔin* (Keeshan Res.); 53, *numaqami·s* (Numukamis Res.); 54, *ʕanaqƛa* (Anacla Res.); 55, *λu·ʔu·ws* (Clo-oose); 56, Nitinat; 57, *ṗa·či·daʔ* (Gordon R. Res.); 58, Lake Cowichan. Many other minor villages and sites also existed throughout the Nootkan territory.

ARIMA AND DEWHIRST

a confederacy of Nootka Sound of two tribal groupings (*muwačath̦*, uniting six local groups of Tlupana Inlet, and *k̓u·pti·ʔath̦*, composed of eight local groups, the product of earlier fissions, in Tahsis Inlet) (Drucker 1951: 228–231). Curtis (1907–1930, 11:181) listed 18 groups. The confederacy summer village at Yuquot had 13 houses traditionally. Most Mowachaht have lived at Gold River since the late 1960s.

6. Muchalat (*mačɬa·th̦*), a tribe formed in historic times from the war-decimated remnants of perhaps seven local groups on Muchalat Inlet and along Gold River. In the early twentieth century they moved to Yuquot and in 1935 joined the Nootka Band.

Central Nootkans

7. Hesquiaht (*h̦išk̓ʷi·ʔath̦*), a tribal merging in historic times of several local groups of Hesquiat Harbour. After their village *h̦išk̓ʷi·* was destroyed by a tidal wave in 1964 they dispersed, mainly to Port Alberni and Victoria.

8. Manhousat (*ma·n̓uʔisʔath̦*), a local group in Sidney Inlet that may have been part of the Otsosat but amalgamated with the Ahousaht.

9. Otsosat (*ʕuču·sʔath̦*), a tribe of Flores Island, Millar Channel, and Shelter and Herbert inlets who were practically annihilated by the Ahousaht in the late eighteenth and early nineteenth centuries and later amalgamated with them.

10. Ahousaht (*ʕa·h̦u·sʔath̦*), a large tribe, originally a local group of Vargas Island and the mainland to the north who conquered the more numerous Otsosat and occupied Flores Island.

11. Kelsemat (*qiɬčmaʔath̦*), a tribe of Vargas Island whose loss in 1886 of many men sealing in the Bering Sea fostered amalgamation with the Ahousaht.

12. Clayoquot (*ƛaʔu·k̓ʷiʔath̦*), a Kennedy Lake tribe that dominated Clayoquot Sound, exterminating or subordinating at least eight groups from about contact to mid-nineteenth century. Curtis (1907–1930, 11:181–182) listed 16 local groups. The tribal village is Opitsat on Meares Island.

13. Ucluelet (*yu·ɬuʔiɬʔath̦*), a tribe of west Barkley Sound. They took Effingham Inlet from a Sheshaht group and Nabmint Bay on Alberni Inlet from another group in the early nineteenth century.

14. Toquaht (*ɬuk̓ʷa·ʔath̦*), a tribe of Toquart Bay, Mayne Bay, and west Barkeley Sound, reduced by warfare by mid-nineteenth century (Sproat 1868:104). Boas (1891: 584) listed 11 local groups.

15. Uchucklesaht (*h̦u·čuqλisʔath̦*), a tribe of Uchucklesit Inlet who once claimed east Barkley Sound and the open coast eastward to Tsusiat Creek.

16. Sheshaht (*čiša·ʔath̦*), an amalgamation of four local groups in central Barkley Sound plus five less independent groups under them (Sapir 1910–1914: xxiv, 4–5). In the

late eighteenth century some of these groups expanded up Alberni Inlet, exterminating a group in Effingham Inlet.

17. Opetchesaht (*hu·pačasʔath̦*), amalgamated three originally Salish groups, *λiku·tʔath̦*, *m̓u·h̦u·ɬʔath̦*, and *ču·maʕasʔath̦*, on Sproat and Great Central lakes, Somass River, and Alberni Inlet down to Hell's Gate. They were partially displaced by three other groups and Nootkanized.

18. Ohiaht (*hu·ʕi·ʔath̦*), a tribe occupying east Barkley Sound, joined before White contact by groups from Cape Beale and Pachena Bay. They took San Mateo Bay from the *h̦u·čuqλisʔath̦* who had it after an earlier group died out (Sapir 1910–1914:xxiv, 7, 7a).

Southern Nootkans

19. Ditidaht (*di·ti·d̓a·ʔtχ*), until 1984 the Nitinaht Band, a tribe around Nitinat Lake including four local groups. In the mid-twentieth century Clo-oose and Carmanah were incorporated into Ditidaht.

20. Clo-oose (*λu·ʔu·wsaʔtχ*), a group just east of Nitinat Lake on the Cheewat River with territory from Clo-oose to Carmanah Point.

21. Carmanah (*qʷa·ba·duwʔa·ʔtχ*), a group on a bight of outside coast between Carmanah and Bonilla points.

22. Pacheenaht (*p̓a·či·d̓a·ʔtχ*), the southeasternmost Nootkan tribe on Vancouver Island, centered on San Juan Harbour and claiming the coast from Bonilla to Point No Point.

Environment

The West Coast of Vancouver Island has an open outer coastline broken by a series of sounds on which groups of inlets converge. To the Nootkans their country presents two equally important environments, "outside" and "inside." "Outside" refers to rocky coast, relatively unbroken and exposed. Sheltering islands lie mainly within sounds and inlet mouths. Offshore reefs, rocks, and islands support rich pelagic and intertidal food resources. Along the outer coastline and inlet mouths is a low plain under 500 feet elevation and up to about three miles wide except at Hesquiat Peninsula and Long Beach where it is nearly seven miles wide. This plain has few lakes and relatively few streams with significant salmon runs. "Inside" consists of inlets penetrating inland from a few miles to as much as 40 miles in Alberni Inlet. Inlets range from a few hundred yards to nearly two miles across with nearby hills and mountains rising 2,000–4,000 feet. There are fewer marine resources than "outside," but the streams have rich salmon runs. Nitinaht country has few inlets, but both environments are present in compressed form.

The Nootkans live in the Coastal Western Hemlock biogeoclimatic zone (Krajina 1969:35–41). Humid and rainy, it has 165–665 centimeters annual precipitation, which increases closer to the Vancouver Island Mountains. Winters are mild (January mean –4 to 5°C) and wet with 30–40 percent of the annual precipitation. Summers are cool (July mean 13–18°C) and relatively dry with 7–15 percent precipitation. There are 120–250 frost-free days. Two subzones exist, primarily resulting from differing precipitation. The wetter subzone typical of most of the region supports a predominantly coniferous forest characterized by Douglas fir, western hemlock, western red cedar, Pacific silver fir, Sitka spruce, lodgepole pine, western white pine, and yellow cedar. The drier subzone has the above conifers except for Pacific silver fir and yellow cedar. Also the grand fir is common. Conifers dominate but deciduous trees are frequent: western alder, black cottonwood, bigleaf maple, vine maple, and bitter cherry, with madrona only on the driest sites. This subzone occurs mostly at the upper Alberni Inlet and on the leeward slopes of the mountains beyond.

External Relations

Trade, warfare, and intermarriage occurred with neighbors. For the Northern Nootkans the trail to the Nimpkish Kwakiutl, overland via Woss Lake and the Nimpkish River, was a major trade route (Drucker 1951: 151, 298, 354; Curtis 1907–1930, 11:3). For the Central Nootkans, the main route overland led from the head of Alberni Inlet to the Qualicum River. By the mid-nineteenth century, the (originally Coast Salish) Opetchesaht and others were in conflict with the Pentlatch and Qualicum (Northern Coast Salish) and Nanoose (Central Coast Salish) (Boas 1891:584; Sapir 1915:19; McMillan and St. Claire 1982:13–14; Brown 1873–1876, 1:42–43; Walbran 1909:350).

The Central Nootkans and the Nitinaht had contact, both friendly and hostile, with the Makah and their neighbors across the Strait of Juan de Fuca (Jewitt 1976; Irvine 1921; Touchie 1977:77). In the late eighteenth century the Nitinaht had friendly relations with the Sooke and Songhees Coast Salish (Wagner 1933:96–97, 108), but conflict occurred in the nineteenth century (Walbran 1909:465).

Culture

Subsistence

All resource sites were owned by local groups, who sought to maximize access to seasonal resources both "outside" and "inside" through warfare and intermarriage (Dewhirst 1978:7). The two-phase economic cycle was typical of about the mid-nineteenth century (Moziño 1970; Jewitt 1807, 1815; Sproat 1868; Sapir 1910–1914; Sprot 1928; Koppert 1930a; Drucker 1951; Arima 1976, 1983a;

McMillan and St. Claire 1982; Calvert 1980; Clarke and Clarke 1975, 1980; McAllister 1980; Fournier and Dewhirst 1980; Ellis and Swan 1981; Turner 1975, 1978; Turner and Efrat 1982; Turner et al. 1983).

The "outside" phase began in late February when the local groups that gathered in winter tribal villages up the sheltering inlets were exhausting their dried salmon stores. As herring reappeared, people dispersed down inlet to take them with rakes and dip nets. Chinook salmon were taken by trolling with a sharp-angled hook. In March and early April the herring spawn was collected on floating fences of hemlock boughs and dried. Also dried were egg-covered kelp and eelgrass.

Migratory waterfowl were hunted on dark nights from canoes. A mat held before a fire on board cast a shadow where the birds gathered only to have a net cast over them (Sprot 1928:141; Drucker 1951:24, 42–43). On the sea, hunters hidden behind branches on their canoes drifted close to shoot arrows (Drucker 1951:43). Baited gorges, trolling hooks, and snares were also used. Nets were stretched across duck flyways such as Nitinat Narrows (Turner et al. 1983:129–131). At Yuquot over 60 bird species appear archeologically with 23 in significant numbers, mainly diving sea birds such as the common murre, the marbled murrelet, cormorants, loons, grebes, scoters, and the American merganser (McAllister 1980). The short-tailed albatross was the most abundant bird species. Large gulls, mew gull, black-legged kittiwake, and bald eagle were eaten.

Marine invertebrates, always abundant outside, were significant in spring when relatively few foods were available and heavy seas curtailed hunting and fishing. Low spring tides during daylight increased access. Women, sometimes helped by men, did the gathering wearing a tightly woven cedarbark back protector and packing an openwork basket with tumpline. Men carried a woven cedarbark sack. Digging and prying sticks of yew were used (Ellis and Swan 1981:75–80). Over 20 species of marine mollusk were utilized (Clarke and Clarke 1975, 1980; Calvert 1980). Archeology suggests that primarily rock-dwelling species, particularly the sea mussel and fringed dogwinkle, were collected prehistorically; but historically, more sand and mud dwellers were taken, notably butter and littleneck clams. Also eaten were horse clams, razor clams, cockles, weathervane and rock scallops, bay mussels, turban snails, limpets, and goose and acorn barnacles. Chitons were favorites, as were sea urchins collected with a special spear and dip net (Drucker 1951:35; Ellis and Swan 1981). Sea cucumbers, anemones, crabs, and octopus were enjoyed.

As weather improved local groups moved to outside villages whence they dispersed to halibut and sea mammal grounds. Offshore halibut banks were located by lining up landmarks such as mountain peaks. Various rigs with U-shaped hooks of dense wood were used (Arima 1976).

Fig. 2. Chief's shrine, a house filled with carved images of dead whalers, whale carvings, and human skulls, where the Yuquot chief performed rituals to bring in herrings and dead whales (Drucker 1951: 171–172; Boas 1930, 2:257–269). The skulls were formed into a pallet for the whaler's wife to lie on during the whale ritual. The Kwakiutl George Hunt purchased the house and contents from the first and second chiefs of the Mowachaht for Franz Boas and the American Museum of Natural History, much to the consternation of their people (Cole 1985:160–161). Photograph by George Hunt, Jewitt's Lake near Yuquot, B.C., 1904.

Harbor seals, always about, were sought especially in late spring. When hauled up they could be clubbed, harpooned, or impaled on stakes hidden in seaweed (Curtis 1907–1930, 11:178). Net traps were set (Arima 1983). On water, seals, porpoises, and sea lions were harpooned. The northern fur seal migrating far offshore were not hunted aboriginally (Drucker 1951:46) except perhaps for the injured or stragglers inshore (Dewhirst 1980:307–309; Rick 1980:28). Sea otter were hunted with harpoon or bow in kelp beds where they might be found asleep. In historic times, the animal became rare and valuable, and mass hunts developed, with aligned canoes systematically sweeping large areas (Drucker 1951:46–48).

Whaling began in March and lasted through the summer. The most important species were the California gray whale, which migrates northward along the shore in the spring and south in the fall, and the humpback whale, which was abundant through the summer, often entered sounds and inlets, and may have been the one most commonly taken (Kool 1982; see also Sapir 1924:79–81; Arima 1983). The right whale may also have been occasionally taken.

Whaling was the noblest calling, and the whaler was always a chief. To ensure success he prepared for months, bathing and scouring his body, praying, and swimming in imitation of actions desired in the whale, his wife holding him on a line. His equipment consisted of a harpoon with a heavy yew wood shaft 14 to 16 feet long and a single toggling harpoon head armed with a musselshell blade, two lines of 40 to 60 fathoms, sealskin floats, and lances. His crew consisted of six paddlers and a steersman, all

ritually prepared. A whaling expedition usually consisted of the whaler and his crew accompanied by other canoes with junior relatives and their crews.

When they sighted a whale, the whaler had to approach it from the rear on the left side and thrust his harpoon into it behind the left flipper just as it was submerging. Any other spot or moment could be disastrous. It took great patience and skill to meet these conditions, and expeditions were often unsuccessful. The instant the harpoon struck, the canoe had to veer to the left as the line payed out and the floats went overboard, each man performing his task precisely. After a successful hit and the whale resurfaced, other canoes could move in to attach more harpoons and floats. A weakened whale was finally dispatched with a lance. When dead, its mouth had to be tied shut to keep it afloat, and it had to be towed home. There it was cut up, the whaler first receiving a part of the back that was treated ritually, others receiving according to participation and rank, blubber going to the whole tribe (Drucker 1951:48–56; Koppert 1930a:56–60).

Some whalers used effigies of whales in secret rituals (fig. 2) that were believed to cast whales onto the shore dead. These drift whales were often ones that had been struck and lost; they furnished good oil if not always good meat (Hunt in Boas 1930, 2:261–269; Sayachapis et al. 1985).

Whales were important in Nootkan subsistence; even a few taken annually provided a significant dietary amount of oil (Cavanagh 1983; Arima 1983; Inglis and Haggarty 1983). Sea mammals supplied a lot of preferred food.

Spring plants were welcome additions to the diet. Women dug silverweed roots, sword-fern rhizomes, and tiger lily and rice-root bulbs for roasting or steaming. Bracken fern fiddleheads were boiled. Several sprouts or stalks were eaten raw: salmonberry, thimbleberry, cow parsnip, horsetail. In early summer, roots of eelgrass and surfgrasses were eaten raw. Common camas, great camas, and tiger lily bulbs were dug from blooming season through the summer. A series of berries ripened into late summer: salmonberry, thimbleberry, Alaska blueberry, oval-leafed blueberry, red huckleberry, strawberry, blackberry, black cap, red elderberry, saskatoon, stink currant, white-flowered currant, gooseberry, high-bush cranberry, bunch berry, kinnikinnick. Crabapples were picked green and stored to ripen. Also in late summer Nootkans dug and steamed perennial clover rhizomes, their most important root.

The rugged outer coast supports numerous fishes. Offshore, Nootkans caught halibut, cod, and red snapper on U-shaped hooks. Unusual deep sea species like bluefin and albacore tuna were likely brought by tongues of warm water close enough in to be caught by trolling (McMillan 1979). Sandy and muddy bottoms provided flounder, ratfish, and skate. Around reefs, rocks, and headlands, rockfishes, greenlings, tomcod, Pacific cod, lingcod,

395

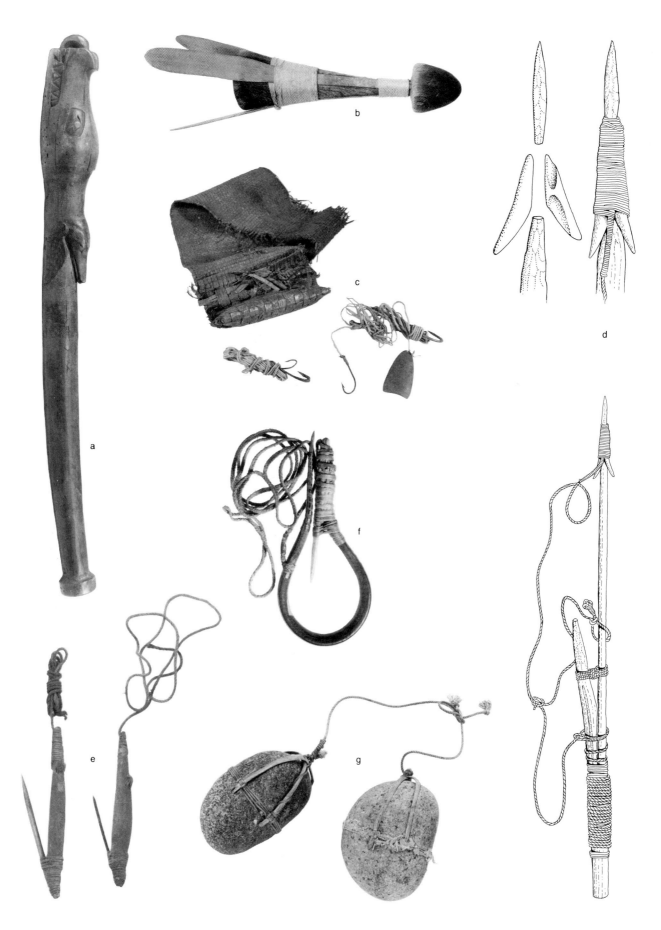

a

b

c

d

e

f

g

a, Denver Mus. of Nat. Hist., Colo.: 2737; b, Glenbow-Alberta Inst., Calgary, Alta.: AA-1375; Amer. Mus. of Nat. Hist., New York: c, 16/9412; e, 16/1702; g, 16/2103; d, Smithsonian, Dept. of Anthr.:289693; f, British Mus., Mus. of Mankind, London: NWC 78.

Fig. 3. Fishing equipment. a, Carved wooden salmon club. Figures depicted may represent the "feathered serpents" and "dogs of the thunderbird" of Nootkan mythology. Collected before 1954; length 60 cm. b, Lingcod lure. Three fins of cedar are lashed to the carved wooden body with string. Collected at Ucluelet, Vancouver I., B.C., 1966; length 35.5 cm. c, Plaited cedar bark wallet with commercial fishhooks, twine leaders, and metal spoon. Collected as a set by George Hunt in 1904; length of wallet 85 cm. d, Salmon harpoon, of the 2-foreshaft type, equipped with toggling heads of 3 pieces of bone wrapped in nettle fiber cord and covered with pitch. Close-up views show construction of the heads. Collected at Nootka Sound, Vancouver I., B.C., before 1916; length 46.3 cm. e, Trolling hooks, of the kind used for trolling for spring salmon and fishing for cod or dogfish. Shanks of spruce root were armed with a wood, bone, or iron point, lashed on with nettle fiber string. Nettle fiber also attached the hooks to the lines of kelp stem (Drucker 1951:21–22; Niblack 1890: fig. 143). F. Jacobsen, who collected these specimens at Vancouver I., B.C., in 1897, states they were used to catch ducks; length of left 11cm. f, Bentwood hook for cod. The bone point is lashed to a steam-bent shank. Leaders are nettle fiber. Collected on Capt. James Cook's third voyage, at Nootka Sound, 1778; length 24 cm. g, Sinkers, unmodified stones wrapped in a support cage of split roots and commercial twine. Collected by F. Jacobsen at Clayoquot, Vancouver I., B.C., 1897; length of left 12.5 cm.

sculpins, midshipman, and wolf eel were caught with straight-shanked angled hooks and gorges (fig. 3e–f). A shuttlecock-like lure (fig. 3b), pushed down on interconnected poles spun upward when released, attracting lingcod and sablefish for harpoon or dip net. These fish also followed a live herring, shiny stone, or kelpfish on a line. Kelpfish and perch, mainly for bait, were caught in globular baskets baited with cracked mussels. Small fish such as shiners were caught in low stone weirs on shallows exposed at low tide. In late summer when shiners and perch school in coves, they were driven to shore with a line of weighted fir boughs held down from canoes and taken with herring rakes and dip nets.

Sockeye, chinook, and coho salmon begin to spawn in late summer in advance of the main season, so the chiefs sent groups to the streams. As the season advanced, more joined those fishing so that by September all local groups were at their fall fishing stations, beginning the "inside" phase of the subsistence cycle. A succession of salmon species ascended the spawning streams: sockeye, chinook, coho, chum, and pink, as well as steelheads. The main part of each run was taken with rodwork weirs and traps set progressively upstream. Harpoons (fig. 3d) and harpoon-leisters were used as the runs thinned. Gulls and diving ducks were taken with gorges or nooses (Drucker 1951: 33–34). The salmon were smoked and dried.

By mid-November much salmon was put up for provisions, and the local groups were assembled in the winter villages. Salal berries had been dried in cakes. Evergreen huckleberry was picked October to December. Also available were roots and rhizomes of bracken fern, silverweed, skunk cabbage, and spiny wood fern. Potatoes became important in historic times. Fishing for cod, rockfish, kelpfish, and perch continued. A few whalers went out on the winter ocean.

Coast deer, the most important land mammal, were taken with deadfall or bow throughout the year. The Muchalat and Opetchesaht, oriented to inland river systems, used simple snowshoes to run down deer and elk in deep snow and kill them with yew lances. Deadfalls were used for furbearers: bear, mink, marten, raccoon, and beaver (Sproat 1868:237–238; Drucker 1951:32–33). Dried salmon, berries, clams, sea mammal blubber and oil, and reduced subsistence activities supported the

Nootka into late February when once again they watched for signs of the returning herring.

Structures

Villages and principal fishing stations had large multifamily houses lined along the beach. Houses were rectangular, consisting of a permanent cedar log frame covered with removable planks. Northern and Central Nootkan houses were low-gabled; Southern Nootkan houses had shed roofs. Usually there was one door at an end of the house. Along the walls were low platforms and storage boxes with low partitions between family areas, a hearth in each. Dried fish and bladders of oil hung from rafters above. House posts and ridge beam were often carved (fig. 4) and painted with hereditary designs. Only chiefs had the right to erect freestanding figures. House size varied by group size and wealth, ranging 40–150 feet long, 30–40 feet wide, and 8–10 feet high (Cook in Beaglehole 1967,3:317–318; Jewitt 1815:61–64). Houses beside a beachward bank often had verandas. Temporary camp dwellings were small versions of the big house, some with single-pitch shed roofs (Drucker 1951:75).

In the late nineteenth century people began living year-round in the summer villages. Houses changed to face the water and have permanent vertical siding sometimes painted with privileges and incorporating doors, windows, and other features of European houses. In the early twentieth century these barnlike houses were superseded by smaller White-style family dwellings.

Clothing and Adornment

On warm days men wore no clothing. Both sexes wore yellow cedarbark robes and, for added warmth, short conical capes. Underneath women wore a skirtlike apron of shredded cedarbark. For rain a cape of double matting and a hat of tightly woven red cedarbark and spruce root were used. The commoner's hat was a plain truncated cone. Chiefs wore whaler's hats with a top knob and whaling scenes (fig. 5). They also wore a bearskin when whaling. On ceremonial occasions they wore robes of sea-otter or mink and marten pelts (Drucker 1951:100–101). War chiefs wore elkhide armor with painted designs (Drucker 1951:335; Jewitt 1815:66–68).

398

top, British Lib., Dept. of Manuscripts, London; center, Royal B.C. Mus., Victoria: PN 4648; bottom left, Harvard U., Peabody Mus.: N26744; bottom right, Smithsonian, NAA: 43220.
Fig. 4. Yuquot, B.C. top, Members of the James Cook expedition meeting Nootkans on the beach. Behind them is a large midden on which sit 2 rows of houses. A log and plank platform projects over the midden bank. The racks of poles are for drying fish. bottom left, Interior of a house. Along the walls are platforms for sitting and sleeping, bent-corner storage boxes for ceremonial paraphernalia, and baskets. The 2 large carved posts and whaler's dorsal fin trophy beside the left post ("Prehistory of the Ocean Coast of Washington," fig. 11, this vol.) are prerogatives of the chief. On the right, plank partitions separate family units within the house. In the center a woman boils water by using tongs to place hot stones into a box filled with water. Small fish are being roasted over the open fire, and other fish are being dried on the rafters. The people wear capes and blankets of cedar bark, ear ornaments, and facial decorations. top and bottom left, Watercolors by John Webber, 1778. center, Late 19th-century houses with permanent vertical plank siding (not the traditional removable planks), glass windows, and doors that face the water. Chief Maquinna's house has a painted crest. Photograph by Edgar Fleming, 1896. bottom right, House frame with carved ridge pole in the form of a sea lion with teeth of bone. Such a beam, which projects from the house, was the hereditary prerogative of a chief (Drucker 1951:69). The rear support of the ridge pole is carved in human form. The double supporting posts form the entranceway. Photograph by Richard Maynard, 1874.

Faces were painted for adornment and protection with black, red, white, and glittering mica. Nasal septums and earlobes were pierced for ornaments of dentalia, abalone shell, trade beads, copper, and brass (Beaglehole 1967,3: 314; Drucker 1951:100–101; Jewitt 1815:77–79). Other ornaments included bracelets of copper, horn, and dentalia, sea otter fur, and painted elkhide; anklets of sea otter or elkhide; dentalium necklaces; and false braids.

In the mid-nineteenth century trade blankets replaced the cedarbark robes and capes. Men adopted flannel shirts and head bandannas; women, cloth dresses. Missionization brought complete non-Indian dress.

Canoes

Transportation was by red cedar dugouts ranging from large freighters and war canoes to small fishing and hunting canoes (Arima 1975:15–17; Drucker 1951: 83–84). Paired canoes bridged with house planks moved large loads of goods and people. Sails were adopted early (Meares 1790:264).

Social Organization

Kinship and hereditary rank were fundamental in the organization of Nootkan society (Drucker 1951:219).

Kinship terminology is lineal in parents' generation and Hawaiian in ego's generation, consistent with ambilineal descent and the option to shift residence (Rosman and Rubel 1971:72). The generations are consistently distinguished, and within ego's generation, senior and junior lines are distinguished. Parents' older and younger siblings' children are called by the terms used for own older and younger siblings, and the distinction continues in subsequent generations, so that an old man might call a boy 'older brother', if the boy's grandparent was the older sibling of his own grandparent (Sapir 1916:364). This usage is consistent with the importance of primogeniture.

Brother and sister treated one another with reserve, especially while unmarried. Those called brother and sister could not marry, even if remote cousins, but if kinship was so remote that links could not be traced it was possible "to marry one's own," usually to get back hereditary rights that had left a descent line (Sapir 1910–1914:xvii, 43 n.). Parent-child relations were close,

and grandparent-grandchild especially close, as children often stayed with grandparents. Aunts and uncles were like parents, and one helped oneself to their things without asking. With parents-in-law there was great familiarity. Step-father and step-daughter kept their distance. Descent was ambilateral and kinship traced in any line allowed an individual to claim membership in more than one local group (Drucker 1951:278–280; Rosman and Rubel 1971: 71–75). Residence with a given group activated membership in it as a kinsman, and while there the individual gave it his loyalty and participated in its activities. Although residence was mainly patrilocal, in the long run there was no set rule. People were constantly moving between groups.

Rank was closely linked with kinship, positions, such as chief, being inherited by primogeniture (Drucker 1951: 245; Jewitt 1815:170; Moziño 1970:31; Sproat 1868:116). A chief (the native term, ḥawił, also means 'wealthy, upper class') was simply the highest ranking member of a kin group of whatever level. Rank was founded on inherited rights called tupa·ti, thought of as property, which governed the ownership and use of practically everything of value. tupa·ti, depending on their nature, could be inherited by an eldest son, shared by several children, held by an eldest daughter until her marriage and then transferred to her brother, or given to a son-in-law as common alternatives (Drucker 1951:267). There was a sense of a patrimony of rights in a local group to be kept as intact as possible as it passed down through successive chiefs (Sapir 1916:363–364). The inheritance of tupa·ti tended to be through males.

Over generations a number of descent lines developed in a group in a ranked relationship made explicit at feasts and potlatches in the order of seating, serving, and gift receiving. Rank was also constantly embodied in the place occupied in the big house (Drucker 1951:71,221; Jewitt 1815:63; Koppert 1930a:19; Sapir 1921:242; Sproat 1868: 42–43). The top chief and house owner occupied the right rear (right for one facing the entrance), the next in rank, a brother or other close kinsman, the left rear. In between might be the head's married sons. Left and right front corners belonged to the third and fourth ranked. Middle sides could be for fifth and sixth ranked. Such interior locations were hereditarily owned.

By the entrance were the slaves (qu·ł), mostly war

399

Fig. 5. Clothing. left, Man at Nootka Sound, B.C., wearing a hat, with a whaling scene, made of cedar bark and grass and a fur cloak. His ornaments consist of facial painting, ear pendants, a nose ring, a bracelet, and fur anklets. He carries a bow and fur quiver containing arrows with barbed bone points. This type of bow was used for hunting sea otter, land game, and warfare (Drucker 1951:31). Watercolor by John Webber, on James Cook's third voyage, 1778. a, Conical basketry hat showing whaling scenes. These hats were made by plain twining, using split spruce root with strands of red cedar bark for wefts. Designs were introduced with surf grass overlay. Whaler's hats were not made after the early 1800s, but other conical hats done in wrapped twining with grass overlay were made until the late 1800s (Gunther 1972:30; J.C.H. King 1981:82). Collected by Capt. James Magee at Nootka Sound, Vancouver I., B.C., 1794. b, Wooden rattle painted red and black. Beaglehole (1967, 3:299, 1090) records descriptions of similar rattles used to accompany the welcoming speeches of chiefs to Capt. James Cook's ships each day at Nootka Sound. Collected by Captain Cook at Nootka Sound, Vancouver I., B.C., 1778. c, Cloak woven of yellow cedar bark and nettle fiber. Cedar bark forms the warp, and twined nettle bark fiber, in places mixed with mountain goat wool, the weft. The painted design may depict a raven flanked by 2 abstract flat fish, both enclosing human faces (J.C.H. King 1981:86). Painting is done in red and black. Bands of geometric decoration are yellow-dyed goat wool on a dark brown cedar background. Collected by Capt. James Cook at Nootka Sound, Vancouver I., B.C., 1778. Height of a 23 cm, b to same scale; c, 154 cm wide.

captives, who were significant as trade objects, protective attendants, and even sacrificial victims (Donald 1983: 110–115). Commoners (*masčim*) were either those living with a chief, often quite close relatives, or less definitely associated transients along the sides (Drucker 1951:279). They always belonged to some chief who addressed them as kin. Even secondary chiefs were *masčim* to a head chief (Sapir 1910–1914:xxii, 17n., xv, 50n.). Although rank was graded continuously, an upper stratum could be distinguished consisting of indisputable chiefs with potlatch seats and titles to resource sites plus closely associated supporters, generally immediate relatives. Chiefs were the nuclei of Nootkan society; they owned practically everything and ideally did not work but directed followers (Drucker 1951:244, 247–248). A chief and his family wore

richer dress, abalone and dentalium ornaments, sea otter or fur-trimmed robes, and decorated rain hats and owned powerful symbols (fig. 6). For the use of resource sites the chief collected a tribute in kind, of no fixed amount, with which he would give a feast (Drucker 1951:251–252). However, big sea or land mammals belonged to the hunter who gave a feast with his catch.

A chief's sons and younger brothers were subsidiary chiefs, war chiefs, and speakers, but the eldest son nominally took the top position while still a youth to ensure succession, the father continuing to actually run affairs. Some younger brothers of chiefs became independent chiefs through conquest of other groups. Other avenues to chiefship were potlatching or marriage to a woman of high rank. A chief and his more distantly

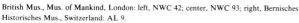

British Mus., Mus. of Mankind, London: left, NWC 42; center, NWC 93; right, Bernisches Historisches Mus., Switzerland: AL 9.

Fig. 6. War clubs, symbols of the status of war chief as well as functional weapons. left, Whalebone club, sharpened along both edges, decoration carved down the blade, and a carved bird's head at the finial. Similar clubs have abalone inlays and handles wrapped in cherry bark, cedar bark, or human hair. center, Daggerlike crusher of fine-grained stone. Traces of ocher suggest a ritual function (King 1981:64). right, "Slave-killer," a ground stone blade set into the mouth of a human head as a tongue. These may have been used for ceremonial killing (Gunther 1972:39–41, 60), but they seem principally to have been badges of office and weapons for fighting (Beaglehole 1967, 3:1101–1102). Most war chiefs had ritual names for their clubs and consistently referred to them by these names or some euphemism. All collected at Nootka Sound, Vancouver I., B.C., 1778. Length of left, 51.5 cm; others to same scale.

British Mus., Mus. of Mankind, London: NWC 38.

Fig. 7. Staff or baton of yew wood with the finial (detail at left) carved in the form of an owl-like bird. This type of implement may have been a baton used in dancing or beating time (Gunther 1972:209) or as a speaker's staff (Boas 1897:382; Dockstader 1978:169). Collected on Capt. James Cook's third voyage, at Nootka Sound, 1778; length, 56 cm.

related commoners were interdependent, the maintenance of his high standing resting on the support of the commoners, who in return had their children named ceremonially, were assisted in marriages, often lent privileges for social use and even granted minor rights. The chief of a group was regarded as a father looking after his children, authoritarian but beneficent (Wike 1958:219-220). Drucker (1983:95) holds that only the local group was a true political unit since larger aggregations lacked a control authority. Within his group a chief could coerce commoner relatives with his slaves as potential enforcers of his will (Donald 1983:113). On the other hand, when he failed to provide feasts and security, allegiance diminished, commoners left for better chiefs, and the chief could even be killed and replaced by a rival relative. When in such jeopardy a chief might have his slaves protect him or employ his supernatural powers malevolently (Jewitt 1815:144–146).

Feast and Potlatch

Feasts and potlatch distributions often occurred together and were given principally by chiefs. When food and goods were accumulated they were given away with public ceremony, thereby gaining for the givers acceptance of

claims to status, bringing them prestige, forestalling envy and hostilities, and fostering alliances (Ferguson 1983: 135–137). Frequent feasts helped keep a following (Jewitt 1815:171). Potlatches were less common earlier, when native-produced goods accumulated slowly, but became frequent after the advent of trade goods and money.

The chief held a feast when he received first fruits or tribute from the use of a resource, a gift of food from in-laws, or substantial "leftovers" at a feast elsewhere. Other occasions were individual life crises and public events. Certain individuals to whole tribes were invited. Seating order was important, embodying ranked status. Chiefs usually sat at the rear of the house, beginning in the middle and alternating to the sides or in single order from right to left. The rest, including retired chiefs, sat along the sides, men right and women left, facing the entrance. Down the middle in a double row sat the war chiefs.

Potlatches were given primarily to transfer chiefly privileges and status to successors on occasions such as life crises or the Wolf ritual in the witnessing and validating presence of guests. Nootkan potlatches rarely featured competition, shaming of rivals, property destruction, or hostile behavior. If a potlatcher sought to outdo anyone, it was not a living rival but an illustrious ancestor (Drucker 1951:383–384).

To give a potlatch, a chief first feasted his group to announce intentions and plan procedure. Supporters volunteered contributions. For a major potlatch, as at a chief's daughter's puberty, a new house might be built (Sapir and Swadesh 1939:139–145). The inviting of another tribe by a special canoe party involved considerable ceremony in itself. Guests arrived in canoes, dressed up, dancing and singing, as the hosts did before their houses. After preliminary feasting and gifts, each guest was called loudly in order of rank to the potlatch donor's house. Usually there was a feast first. When the goods were brought out by the young men, the speaker announced the reason for the potlatch, amounts, and sources of wealth. Ceremonial privileges were also announced, their dances displayed, and the guests thanked for viewing them. Finally the chief sang his wealth song, and the goods were given away with each recipient's name and gift called out. Gift value was according to rank at no fixed proportional rate. Potlatches were returned, but not necessarily with matching wealth, and even chiefs who rarely potlatched continued receiving according to rank (Drucker 1951:381). Greater return was expected in a secondary potlatch form (ńušmiꞏs), an elaboration of the invitation visit. Giving and receiving generally evened out with wealth circulating and being consumed (Drucker 1951:382–383, 385), while privileges were validated in exercise or transfer, and the associated ambilateral lines of descent were spelled out (Rosman and Rubel 1971:104).

Music and Art

Music and dance were the predominant esthetic forms. Nootkans loved music, singing enhanced with drumming, rattling, and devices such as solo and group parts, contrasting song patterns, varying beat, rising or falling cries (Roberts and Swadesh 1955:203–229; Halpern and Duke 1978:63–69). Ceremonial occasions featured impressive songs and dances, commonly imitative of secular activities. Masked dance and drama represented assorted supernatural or otherwise special beings. Lively oratory and storytelling were arts, too.

Songs were of a dozen types for activities such as informal socializing, gambling, doctoring, potlatching, and marriage. Many were restricted hereditary rights. New songs were composed, learned from elsewhere, or obtained from spirits, typically at striking or beautiful spots. The major instrument was a raised plank beaten with hardwood billets or, less common, a long narrow box pounded with padded fists. In the late nineteenth century the single-headed "tambourine" drum was acquired from the Coast Salish along with the bone game. Wooden floors when adopted were pounded with sticks or feet. Rattles were of wood (often bird-shaped), baleen or split mountain-sheep horn folded over, or scallop shells on a hoop. Dance aprons hung with deer or elk hooves or bird beaks added rhythmic noise. More for dramatic effects were whistles, some with reeds or multiple notes, featured in the Wolf ritual; bull-roarers for earthquakes; and a long box with rolling rocks for thunder.

Nootkan sculpture and painting changed after the mid-nineteenth century. Earlier carving is simple and naturalistic, freely and strongly shaped in the "Old Wakashan"

402

British Mus., Mus. of Mankind, London: top left, NWC 63; bottom, NWC 51; top right, Amer. Mus. of Nat. Hist., New York: 16/2005.

Fig. 8. Carved wood figures, very common among the Nootkans. (Beaglehole 1967, 3:319–320, 1329; W. Ellis 1783, 1:219). top left, Woman kneeling, holding a baby in a cradle across her thighs. The upright board at the head of the cradle had been broken off and mended aboriginally with sinew. The child is a male, his penis protruding through a hole in the cedar bark blanket, the traditional practice that let urine escape (Drucker 1951:124). The head of the child is covered with a head flattener of cedar bark, which was left tightly bound to the head until the malleable bones of the forehead assumed their distinctive slope. The whole carving was once painted with red pigment (J.C.H. King 1981:76). Collected on Capt. James Cook's third voyage, at Nootka Sound, Vancouver I., B.C., in 1778. top right, Pregnant woman with her unborn child visible through diamond-shaped holes in her belly and back. The body and facial carving are more realistic than in the earlier carvings. Collected by F. Jacobsen at Clayoquot, Vancouver I., B.C., 1897. bottom, Bowl with 2 human figures as handles. The globular form with side fluting was characteristic of cups used by chiefs for drinking oil or water. The wood is alder (J.C.H. King 1981:74), used in preference to cedar for eating utensils because it did not taint the food (Drucker 1951:90). Collected on Capt. James Cook's third voyage, at Nootka Sound, 1778. Height of top 16 cm; others to same scale.

style (Holm 1972:77); later, clean lines, smoothly finished forms, and painted designs seem characteristic (fig. 8) (Arima 1983a:160). Large red cedar sculpture occurred as carved house posts and roof beams, simply ornamented grave posts, and ritual figures like those used in drift whaling. Elaborate grave monuments and interior displays stem from dramatic ceremonial devices. Much later carving was in a "prismatic" style (Holm 1972:79–80) with two flattened sides angled to meet down the front midline of masks and Kwakiutl-derived "totem poles." This style may derive from the light headdress masks of two cut-out and painted cedar boards joined by a small crosspiece at the nose of the represented creature. Earlier painting on masks, face, body, architecture, screens, and so forth was quite free and simple, whether naturalistic or geometric. In the late nineteenth century, the Northern Northwest Coast style influenced the Nootkans by way of the Kwakiutl. Nootkan painters did not fully apply its formline principle of composition but emphasized some of its elements, such as the "feather" (split-U) form. As commercial pigments came into use, Nootkan art became brightly colored. Basket makers also switched from natural to synthetic dyes and increasingly produced small trinket baskets, shopping bags, and other forms for the commercial market.

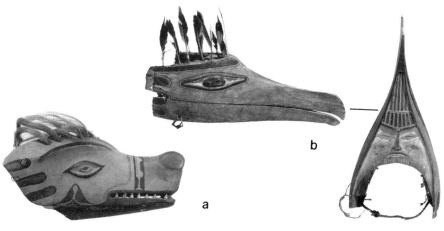

a, Smithsonian, Dept. of Anthr.: 56464; b, British Mus., Mus. of Mankind, London: NWC 55; bottom left, Alberni Valley Mus., Port Alberni, B.C.: PN 1873; right, Smithsonian, NAA: 43225.
Fig. 9. Masks and totem pole. a, Wolf mask or headdress, probably part of the paraphernalia of the Wolf ritual, worn not by the wolves who abduct the novices but by chiefs who own that privilege. Collected at Clayoquot, Vancouver I., B.C., before 1882. b, Bird mask or headdress with hinged beak, one of the many types of masks used in the winter ceremonial. The eye treatment—large, with open and pointed eyelids showing little or no orb—is typically Nootkan. Details are done in black and white paint. The irises were coated with mica set in spruce gum. A small rattle of limpet shells, tied to the inside of the upper beak with sinew twine, would sound as the dancer moved (J.C.H. King 1981:80). Collected by Capt. James Cook at Nootka Sound, Vancouver I., B.C., 1778. Length of a 32.5 cm, other same scale. bottom left, Ceremonial costumes worn during a Dominion Day parade. Chief Dan Watts carries a sign on back of the truck that reads "We Are The Real Native Sons of Canada" in response to another float of non-Indians that proclaimed "The Native Sons of Canada." left to right: James Rush (on roof of cab) wearing bird headdress; Rochester Peter wearing a transformation mask; Porter Ned wearing wolf headdress; Mrs. Seymour Callick wearing wolf headdress; Mrs. Doctor Ned, wearing wolf headdress and skin bib (?); unidentified; Mrs. James Rush holding cradle. Others are not identified. Photograph by Joseph Clegg, Port Alberni, B.C., about 1929. right, Napoleon Moquwinna, head of the Mowachaht (on right); and Captain Jack, another chief of the Mowachaht; and his son Benedict. The adults wear headdresses patterned after the Kwakiutl x^wix^wi mask. The totem pole, which belonged to Captain Jack, was erected about 1877 when he married a Muchalat woman. Figures include the Thunderbird and Whale, Callicum holding tail of lightning snake (a Nimpkish Kwakiutl–derived perogative), Bear, Owl, King of Sea (Nimpkish perogative), Snake, Sea Otter, Wolf, and wealth figure. The pole crests are a combination of his wife's and his crests. Photograph at Clayoquot, Vancouver I., B.C., about 1928.

NOOTKANS OF VANCOUVER ISLAND

In traditional Nootkan culture, art was not a separate category. Great whaling canoes inlaid with snail opercula, carved whalebone clubs, fine harpoons, painted screens, and chief's hats with whaling scenes were made with great care and may qualify as art in European eyes, but they were prized by the Nootkans as manifestations of inherited privilege.

Cosmology

The Nootkans saw evidence of spirits everywhere. They often prayed for power to the Four Chiefs of Above, Horizon, Land, and Undersea (Curtis 1907–1930, 11:45; Drucker 1951:152). In a pleasant sky country was *ka·ʔu·c*, the supreme controller of primary resources, communicated with by chiefs only (Boas 1891:595; Curtis 1907–1930, 11; Jewitt 1815: 120, 171; Moziño 1970:26; cf. Drucker 1951:152). Moon and Sun, husband and wife, were the highest powers for most, prayed to for food and luck, especially Moon (Arima 1983a:8). Swallowing of either by a great Sky Codfish caused eclipses (Drucker 1951:155; Jewitt 1815:165). The Thunderbird's flapping wings made thunder, and lightning flashes were feathered serpents, his dogs.

Spirit beings were not systematized but particularistic (Drucker 1951:151). Beneath the sea the Salmon and Herring peoples lived in two halves of a great house, dangerous if angered as by ritual neglect. In other houses were the Whales and Harbor Seals. Killer Whales and Wolves, neither dangerous, were related, transforming into each other. Giant canoe-gulping sharks lived in deep holes under cliffs; elsewhere were huge but harmless squids. Seeing the giantess *kapča·* slowly surface was death, but one of her long hairs was a powerful charm. In the mysterious forest were humanoid *yaʕi·* who bestowed powers but killed the ritually unclean. Tall and shaggy red-skinned *či·ni·ʔatḥ* chased people with spears. The bristly giant *maλu·ḥ* knocked people over with shouts alone (Moziño 1970:27–28). *pukmis*, the nearly drowned, were malevolent swift white beings with claws and protruding eyes. Shaman-Squirrels, Minks, and Ravens singing and shaking tiny rattles over writhing rotten logs gave medicine power, as did a Right Hand with a rattle sticking out of the ground. A Left Hand was fatal. Other fantastic creatures included brilliant headless ducks, birds with human faces, a backward-walking cougar with a lancelike tail, shadowy tree souls who could kill, small snakes that leaped into body openings, and dwarfs who enticed people inside mountains to dance and get the "earthquake foot." In an encounter with such a being, one obtained power by seizing some part of or token from it rather than by establishing an enduring relationship with the being as one's "guardian spirit" (Sapir 1928, 12:592).

Spirits could be controlled by ritual acts (Drucker 1951:164–181). One sort was compulsive magic with automatic effect like formulaic prayers, medicines, figures imitating sought results, harmful spells and victim-linked substances; details, originally revealed by spirits, were family secrets. A powerful ritual act used corpses to draw dead whales ashore (fig. 2). Ritual cleanliness was another main set of procedures. Human odor repelled spirits, including animals, so it was erased by prolonged bathing in cold water and vigorous scrubbing with fragrant or magically potent plants, often to torturous degree. This *ʔu·simč* ritual (a variety of self-mortifying vision quest, though many never sought or met spirits) was done with the waxing moon, while practicing continence and partial fasting, the details adapted to specific goals. There was also routine bathing for general luck and well-being; bathing toughened if not overdone. Other rituals honored and pleased animals—whale, salmon, herring, bear—so that their spirits, reincarnated, allowed themselves to be recaptured.

Myths were full of action and humor, commonly ribald. Stock animal characters had idiosyncratic speech and caricatured qualities such as Deer's simple-mindedness and Raven's gluttony. Mink (*kʷatya·t*) was the culture hero and transformer from Barkley Sound to the southeast, and Snot Boy north of Barkley Sound.

Winter Ceremonies

There were two winter ceremonies, the *λu·kʷa·na* (Nitinaht *λu·kʷa·la*) 'Wolf ritual', which was held throughout the Nootkan area, and the *ċa·yiq* 'Doctoring ritual', which was held among the Central and Southern Nootkans only. Both were performed by groups of initiated persons and involved the seizing and initiating of others.

The Wolf ritual was sponsored by a wealthy chief in order to initiate a son or other younger relative. It could last 10 days or more and was accompanied by potlatching. Nearly the whole village participated, many roles being hereditary privileges. The ritual consisted of the capture of the principal novice and others by members impersonating wolves, isolation of the novices, their recapture by other, high-ranking members, and their performance of dances taught by the "wolves." Other performances included the eating of a dog and dancing with skewers through the flesh. The whole ritual involved masks (fig. 9), theatrical illusions, and comic entertainment. Several Wolf Rituals might be held in a village during a winter, all but small children might be initiated, and a person could play the role of novice repeatedly. There were many local variations (Sapir 1911:20–28; Curtis 1907–1930, 11: 68–91; Drucker 1940:225, 1951:386–443; Ernst 1952: 63–81). Possible historic connections between this ritual and the Kwakiutl winter ceremonies have been discussed by Boas (1897:632–644), Curtis (1907–1930, 11:91–92), and Drucker (1940).

404

The Doctoring ritual was generally performed on behalf of a sick person by a group of people with songs of a special class, often obtained through dreams. They wore undyed yellow cedar bark, sang individually and wept, and used the occasion to initiate new members. This performance seems to have resembled and had some historic connection with the winter dancing of the Central Coast Salish (Drucker 1951:215–218).

Life Cycle

Individual life crises elicited protective rituals and public ceremonies elaborated according to rank (Boas 1891: 591–594; Curtis 1907–1930, 11:41–3; Sapir 1914, 1921; Drucker 1951:118–150). Birth was in a temporary hut, the mother's mother assisting. The newborn was manipulated toward physical ideals and properly positioned in a matting cradle, head pressed with pads on brow and sides for shaping, flexed legs bandaged for calf bulging. The afterbirth was buried with treatments to improve the child's development. Ears were pierced, and the first name given. After 10 days a wooden cradleboard was used and seclusion ended. The mother observed dietary taboos for a year. Twins, associated with the Salmon Spirits, entailed severe prohibitions including remote isolation of infants and parents for one to four years.

Children were raised with much instruction, stressing correct behavior and ritual knowledge (Sayachapis in Sapir and Swadesh 1939:184–209). Industry, peacefulness, and social responsibility were encouraged. Misbehavior brought a private lecture instilling fear of family shame. Lengthy family traditions taught where rights originated; current anecdotes illuminated social relations. Maturing, boys accompanied their fathers on various expeditions while girls stayed indoors learning womanly tasks. A boy's first game or girl's first berries or clams occasioned a feast. But the main childhood pursuit was play, often imitating adults, with play feasts and potlatching and shamans' dances and shamanizing. Activities included spear and stone throwing contests, archery, slinging, hoop and dart, tops, shuttlecock, ring and pin with a seal humerus, cat's cradle, dice, the bone game, hide and seek, tag, tug-of-war, mock battles, and dolls (Drucker 1951:444–452). Much time was passed in canoes (Sapir 1921:243).

A girl's first menses occasioned major ceremonials and her family's greatest potlatch (Boas 1891:592–594; Curtis 1907–1930, 11:42–43; Sapir 1914; Drucker 1951:137–144; Sapir and Swadesh 1955:243–253). Observances varied, but typically a well-born girl stood outside between two masked dancers representing thunderbirds or whales, great torches flaming on either side. Four times, four men poured water at her feet. She then fasted four days behind a screen inside. Family songs, dances and games, some dramatizing legendary suitor tests, were performed.

Ha-Shilth-Sa, Port Alberni, B.C.
Fig. 10. Members of the Frank family performing a canoe dance at a memorial potlatch for David Frank, Sr. The canoe is the last of over 100 canoes he made. Photograph by Bob Soderlund, Thunderbird Hall, Marktosis, B.C., 1986.

Guests improvised songs satirizing sexual relations and requested gifts. Feasting, announcement of the girl's new name and potlatch distribution followed. Seclusion ended with purificatory bathing outdoors. A Wolf ritual might follow. Lighter seclusion and restrictions continued for 4 to 10 months, the girl wearing special hair ornaments of rows of dentalia (fig. 12). After this period ended with a feast and perhaps a potlatch, she remained largely indoors, chaperoned, until marriage. Boys had no special puberty rites but as they began adult pursuits became subject to rigorous training rituals including abstinence from food, water, sleep, and sex. Youths tended to be assistants overshadowed by elders.

Names changed repeatedly through life, especially before adulthood, as new ones were bestowed at feasts and potlatches. They were inherited through lines of ancestors and had detailed histories, which came out when they were assumed.

Marriage was primarily an alliance between families (Sproat 1868:97; Drucker 1951:286). Unsanctioned relationships were degrading. Marriage age was about 16 years in the late nineteenth century (Brabant 1926:84). Parents or guardians arranged first marriage, preferably with distant kin, beyond second cousins. Child betrothal, practiced by high-ranking families, involved pledges of valuable blankets but at times was terminated by mutual agreement or when a greater chief sought the girl. Chiefs often paid bride price for girls only 8 or 10 to keep them from rivals (Koppert 1930:49–53). Polygyny was practiced by chiefs who could afford repeated bride prices (Moziño 1970:32; Drucker 1951:301). When a spouse died, sororate or levirate was common.

Among several ways of marrying (Drucker 1951: 287–303), for a first one without betrothal the suitor's father sent a proposal party repeatedly, between the

Alberni Valley Mus., Port Alberni, B.C.: PN 1681.

Fig. 11. Potlatch. The large painted screens are the type used in a girls' puberty ceremony and represent privileges the girl's children would inherit (Drucker 1951:141). In front of the screen is a fire where the feast food might have been prepared. Photograph by Fred Brand, Port Alberni, B.C., about 1910.

chiefly families before it was accepted. Rank mattered most for consent, though a chief with an only daughter might prefer a lower ranking son-in-law who would join his household. If the suit was accepted, the suitor's father feasted his group to plan the marriage. The marriage party typically arrived at the bride's on two big canoes planked across for a floating stage (Boas 1891:594), singing its chief's marriage songs and displaying ceremonial privileges such as masked dances. With each performance a speaker praised the groom's ancestry and traced the relationships between the families. Finally the bride price was presented to the bride's group, only to be refused at first. The party could wait outside up to four days, singing, orating, and offering the bride price. After acceptance came suitor's tests such as climbing a greased rope, walking a shaky horizontal pole, running a gauntlet of torches, sitting by a hot fire, carrying a heavy stone, or breaching a line of strong men. Feasting and a potlatch distribution from the bride's side followed. The bride danced formally for the groom's party and was handed over then or delivered later if puberty observances were incomplete or her dowry was not ready. When the bride

arrived at her new home, the in-laws danced, feasted, and bestowed gifts, including, if she was chiefly, rights to territory and resources, ceremonial seats, names, dances, and so forth. A chief's daughter also brought various privileges for eventual inheritance by her children. Periodic gift exchange, principally of food, continued between the families. For an elopement or marriage of elderly, a few relatives of the man went to the woman's family to give a small amount of blankets or money, usually without performance of ceremonial privileges. No dowry was given.

Divorce was by simple separation, the wife being sent back or leaving by herself (Curtis 1907–1930,11:67). Marriage gifts were not repaid, but transferred privileges reverted to their original owners. Paternal claim was usually the stronger for any children. Commonest grounds for divorce were childlessness and incompatibility. Adultery, unless persistent, was usually smoothed over, but with a chief's wife it meant banishment for a man of rank or death for a commoner and a whipping for the woman (Moziño 1970:43).

At death chiefs, war dead, and good men always

406

Fig. 12. Ehattesaht girl with puberty hair ornaments. Her hair is worn in 2 rolled-up braids, each covered with a hair ornament. The elaboration of the ornament was dependent on the rank and wealth of the family (Drucker 1951:138–140). It consists of a wide wool band with strings of beads tipped with thimble jinglers. This dual braid style of ornament indicated that the girl was a younger daughter. An eldest daughter wore a single ornament. The comb pinned to her cloak enables her to scratch her head without violating menstrual restrictions (Drucker 1951:144). Photographed about 1910.

praying to Sun and Moon went to the fine land above; the rest, to a poor netherworld (Mozino 1970:28; Sproat 1868: 209-214; Boas 1891:597; Curtis 1907–1930,11:44). Death was attributed to physical reasons or illnesses like disease objects inside, soul loss, spirit possession, or malevolent magic (Drucker 1951:205–206). Sometimes autopsies were performed. The corpse was flexed and placed in a box, or sometimes a canoe, placed in a tree, cave, or on a point (Drucker 1951:147–149). The poor were buried in mats or worn blankets in shallow graves (Mozino 1970:29; Sproat 1868:259). Mourning was elaborate for chiefs, simple for commoners. Women wailed for hours. Relatives blackened faces, cut their hair short, dressed poorly, ate little, and walked with a staff as if very weak (Curtis 1907–1930,11:44). A chief near death might have his achievements publicly recounted and his personal effects distributed (Sproat 1868:261–262). If the dying wanted them along, belongings, often including the house, were burned (Sapir 1921:366; Drucker 1951:150). Valuables

were also deposited with the dead. A memorial post with a painted crest or a carved figure depicting a notable quality was erected for the high ranking (Sproat 1868:260–261). For a hunter a carving of his favorite game was put on a pole in a canoe by his grave (Curtis 1907–1930,11:43). Large painted sculptures could form a leading chief's memorial. After a chief's burial his successor was announced at a feast. Later a potlatch announced procedures such as destroying the old chief's big canoe, shelving certain privileges, and tabooing his name for a year or two. For lesser chiefs and well-to-do commoners a feast was held with gifts given to chiefs, and the name was avoided for a time before close associates. A chief upon losing a close relative such as an eldest son would make death companions for the lost one by killing slaves or sending warriors against another tribe (Curtis 1907–1930,11:43; Drucker 1951:333–334).

History

For an unknown period before contact with Europeans, the Nootka acquired iron and other metals through native trade networks and shipwrecks.

First direct contact with Europeans occurred in 1774, when Juan Pérez, captain of the Spanish frigate *Santiago*, briefly exchanged gifts with men in canoes off the west coast of the Hesquiat Peninsula. Native accounts identify the location as near the village of Padsista (Brabant 1900a).

First prolonged contact with Europeans took place in 1778, when Capt. James Cook anchored at Nootka Sound for nearly one month to repair his ships and take on provisions. He was welcomed by the people of Yuquot, who eagerly traded sea otter pelts for iron and other metals. The Yuquot people quickly took control of the trade, becoming middlemen to other Nootkan groups seeking to trade with Cook's ships (Cook in Beaglehole 1967,3:299, 302). Cook's crews later found that the sea otter pelts could be sold in China for great profits, thereby establishing the basis for the maritime fur trade on the Northwest Coast.

The first trading ship arrived at Nootka Sound in 1785. Yuquot, or "Nootka" as it was called by Europeans, soon became a major trading port. Clayoquot Sound and Barkley Sound also became important trading areas. The growing involvement on the Northwest Coast of Great Britain, Russia, and the United States led Spain to establish a military post at Yuquot from 1789 to 1795.

The maritime fur trade was largely controlled by the natives (Fisher 1977, 1977a). Chiefs of groups in the trading centers operated as middlemen between the traders and other native groups. Access of relatively few groups to the trade made their chiefs, such as Maquinna of Yuquot and Wickaninnish of Clayoquot, enormously wealthy and powerful. Middlemen groups acquired firearms early and used this advantage to seize resource territories from weaker neighbors. The balance of power among many local groups was disturbed, resulting in intensified warfare. The population was declining through venereal disease from prostitution of native women to sailors (Moziño 1970:43) and probably from other diseases.

The fur trade on the west coast of Vancouver Island declined rapidly in the 1790s. By 1792 the sea otter population there had become severely reduced, and the trade was shifting to more distant areas on the Northwest Coast (Moziño 1970:91). Some traders desperate for pelts resorted to theft and extortion. The greatly diminished flow of trade goods weakened once powerful middlemen. These circumstances may have motivated some groups to capture trading ships. In 1803 the Yuquot people seized the *Boston* (Jewitt 1807, 1815; Brathwaite and Folan 1972), and in 1811 the Clayoquot captured the *Tonquin* (Howay 1922). These attacks in effect brought an end to the maritime fur trade in Nootkan territory and the beginning of an era of sporadic contact with Europeans that lasted until the mid-nineteenth century.

Confederacy and tribal levels of organization were present among some groups prehistorically but developed mainly from population decline and extended warfare for resources in the late eighteenth and early nineteenth centuries (Drucker 1951:220–243, 332–365; Swadesh 1948; Sapir and Swadesh 1955:412–439). Warfare, together with disease, dislocation, and stress, destroyed many groups. Weak or decimated groups joined more powerful neighbors, resulting in the formation of confederacies among the Northern Nootkans and tribes among the Central and Southern Nootkans. The number of native groups remaining in the late nineteenth century was but a fraction of those present at the time of European contact. The local groups that joined others were (if twentieth century salmon runs reflect earlier conditions) those with less productive streams (Morgan 1981).

The total population at contact is not known. Estimates of 25,900 (Meares 1790:229–231) for most Nootkan groups in 1788, when disease and warfare were beginning to take their toll, are accepted by some scholars but considered too high by others. In the early 1840s a Hudson's Bay Company estimate of 7,093 Nootka (Taylor 1963:160) is much too high ("Demographic History, 1774–1874," this vol.). As Nootkans became increasingly integrated into the commercial economy their population continued to decline (table 1).

In the mid-nineteenth century several Nootkan attacks on traders and vessels in distress resulted in government warnings and attempts by naval authorities to arrest the persons responsible (Gough 1984:108–128, 172–175). The most serious incident was the Ahousaht capture in 1864 of the trading sloop *Kingfisher* and killing of her crew. Investigating naval forces found the Ahousahts armed as a

Table 1. Nootkan Population, 1835–1984

Date	Population	Source
1835	7,500	Duff 1964:39
1860	5,514	Sproat 1868:308
1881	3,613	Canada, Dominion of 1882:164
1888	3,160	Canada, Dominion of 1889:312
1898	2,636	Canada, Dominion of 1899:239
1908	2,093	Canada, Dominion of 1908:255
1915	1,835	Canada, Dominion of 1915:14
1924	1,459	Canada, Dominion of 1924:35
1929	1,626	Canada, Dominion of 1930:51
1934	1,622	Canada, Dominion of 1934:35
1939	1,605	Duff 1964:39
1944	1,680	Canada. Department of Mines and Resources. Indian Affairs Branch 1945:11
1949	1,815	Canada. Department of Citizenship and Immigration. Indian Affairs Branch 1950:14–15
1954	2,100	Canada. Department of Citizenship and Immigration. Indian Affairs Branch 1955:14–15
1959	2,501	Canada. Department of Citizenship and Immigration. Indian Affairs Branch 1961:38–41
1963	2,680	Canada. Department of Citizenship and Immigration. Indian Affairs Branch 1963:34
1967	3,135	Canada. Department of Indian Affairs and Northern Development, Indian Affairs Branch 1967:26
1970	3,409	Canada. Department of Indian Affairs and Northern Development, Indian Affairs Branch 1970:42
1974	3,810	Canada. Department of Indian Affairs and Northern Development 1975:86–87, 92–93
1977	4,071	Canada. Department of Indian Affairs and Northern Development 1978:66–67, 74–76
1980	4,331	Canada. Department of Indian Affairs and Northern Development 1982:57–58, 65–67
1984	4,720	Canada. Department of Indian Affairs and Northern Development 1985:54, 62–64

NOTE: Figures after 1924 were compiled from official band lists. After 1951 figures reflect only status Indians, a reliable indication of the population, as there has been relatively little intermarriage with Whites.

tribe and unwilling to surrender those responsible. In retaliation, gunboats destroyed nine Ahousaht villages and killed at least 15 Indians. In 1869 the Hesquiahts plundered the shipwrecked bark *John Bright* and shot some crew members who had reached shore. The British Navy, after burning houses and shelling canoes, forced the surrender of two suspects; they were tried, found guilty of murder, and hanged before the assembled tribe at Hesquiat.

The Nootkans became integrated into the commercial economy by taking up occupations based on their

Fig. 13. Basket making. Emma David weaving a shopping basket on a wooden form. The basket, either split spruce root or red cedar bark wrap, is twined with rafia and sharp grass or bear grass. The decorative designs were created with dyed grasses. The oval wooden tool in the box is a grass splitter with a pair of cutting blades for trimming the grass to an even width. The basin contains water for soaking the trimmed grass to make it pliable for weaving. Weaving shopping baskets for sale to tourists was a household industry. Photographed at Polly's Point, Alberni Indian Reserve, 1951.

Fig. 14. Twined basketry pouch, typical of basketry knicknacks done for the late 19th-century tourist trade, although the envelope form is a traditional design. Other nontraditional products included twined basketry covers for bottles and vials, White-style straw hats, and serving trays decorated with whaling scenes (Swan 1870:45–66; Drucker 1951:93). Collected about 1900; length 23 cm.

traditional subsistence patterns and skills. Since the land-based fur trade reached the Pacific coast in the early nineteenth century, the Nootkans supplied trading posts and visiting schooners with furs and provisions. The sea otter was taken only rarely, and the continuing fur trade was based on elk, deer, mink, marten, and northern fur seal.

From the 1850s until the end of the century, the Nootkans were major producers of dogfish oil used as skid grease in the logging industry. Nootkans caught dogfish and basking sharks for their livers, which they rendered into oil and sold to White traders (Swan 1870:29).

In the early 1870s commercial pelagic sealing became the preferred occupation of the Nootkans. Their traditional expertise in sea mammal hunting played a key role in the fur seal industry. Sealing schooners took on board Nootkan hunters with their canoes and gear to intercept the fur seal herds off California in the spring and in the Bering Sea during the summer and fall. The Nootkans also hunted offshore in canoes when the northward migrating herds sometimes passed within 20 or 30 miles of Vancouver Island. Sealing was highly lucrative. Several successful Nootkans bought their own schooners, and the crews of many schooners were largely Nootkan. In 1911 the North Pacific fur seal fishery was closed by international treaty, but sealing by natives was still permitted and continued for some time.

Nootkans also became involved in the expanding commercial fishery, particularly after 1880. In mid-summer many families left their villages for the salmon canneries on the Fraser River and on Rivers Inlet. The men fished for the canneries, and the women prepared the fish for canning. When the commercial fishing season was poor, many families went hop picking on Puget Sound, returning to their villages for the winter.

Traditionally crafted curios for sale or trade to Whites became an important cottage industry among the Nootka as early as the 1860s. Women wove fine sedge baskets and basketry-covered bottles decorated with brightly colored motifs. Men carved small totem poles, masks, and model canoes.

In 1871 British Columbia joined Canada, and the Nootkans became part of the Indian reserve system of the federal Department of Indian Affairs. In the 1880s the Department, without native surrender of any land, allocated for the Nootkan tribes small reserves based largely on village sites and fishing stations then in use. Tribal territories and many land resources used in the recent past were not given reserve status. The total area of all the Nootkan reserves was 12,200.25 acres (Canada. Royal Commission on Indian Affairs for the Province of British Columbia 1916, 4:851). The Department, responsible for native education and health, financed missionaries to carry out programs in those areas.

Missionization of the Nootkans began in 1875, when Reverend A.J. Brabant established a mission at Hesquiat (Brabant 1900). After 15 years, Brabant had largely converted the Hesquiaht to Roman Catholicism (Moser 1926:121). During this period Roman Catholic missions or churches were also established among the Chickliset, Kyuquot, Ehettesaht, Nutchatlaht, Mowachaht, Ahousaht, Clayoquot, and Ohiaht (Moser 1926:151–153, 158–159; Canada, Dominion of 1891:122). The Presbyterian Church began missionary work among the Nootkans 409 in 1892, establishing a mission school near the Sheshaht in Alberni (Canada, Dominion of 1893:235). Protestant mission schools were set up among the Ahousaht, Kelsemaht, Ucluelet, Ohiaht, and Ditidaht (Canada, Dominion of 1899:240–241). By 1900 about 60 percent of the Nootkans were at least nominally converted to Christianity (Canada, Dominion of 1901:149). In the late 1890s the Presbyterians set up the Alberni Residential school, and in 1900 the Roman Catholics built Bishop Christie Indian Residential School at Clayoquot Sound. The boarding schools separated children from their families, deliberately suppressed native language and culture, and taught Euro-Canadian values and beliefs. Within a few generations the Nootkan language and traditional culture declined severely.

In the early twentieth century the fishing industry expanded and became the major employer of Nootkans. Many worked as fishermen and inside workers for several saltries, canneries, and reduction plants. The logging industry also employed many Nootkans. Men continued to trap mink and marten. Many families still went hop picking in Puget Sound and in the Fraser Valley. Women continued to make tourist curios. The Depression of the 1930s caused most fish processing plants and logging operations to shut down.

World War II gave brief respite to Nootkan fishermen, but after the war the fishing industry consolidated and centralized, making native participation increasingly difficult (Shoop 1972). In the 1950s and 1960s outlying reserves became depopulated as numerous families in search of employment, housing, and education moved into regional centers such as Victoria, Port Alberni, and Gold River. Children were integrated into the British Columbia public school system and families into provincial government social programs. Off-reserve families generally maintained strong ties with their home reserves.

Potlatching continued in spite of government opposition. Among the Northern Nootkans in the 1970s the occasions for potlatching included weddings, girls' puberty, and occasionally funerals and the "washing" (purification) of someone who had suffered an accident (Kenyon 1977). A Central Nootkan potlatch given in 1977 by a widow and her children, to honor their deceased husband and father, began with a dinner of fish, ham, and turkey, included performances of hereditary dances and the assumption of hereditary names by the children and several grandchildren, and ended with the giving away of a large quantity of blankets, dishes, and other household goods, jewelry and beaded headbands, several thousand dollars in cash, and silkscreen prints produced by one of the sons (Efrat and Langlois 1978:40).

During the 1960s and 1970s, as Nootkans became more involved in mainstream Canadian society, a pan-Nootkan or "independence" movement developed. Its basic goals were the establishment of a positive Nootkan identity, socioeconomic improvement, and complete control by the Nootkans of their own affairs.

The Nootkans attempted to achieve these goals through their own political organization. From the 1930s on they expressed economic and political concerns through the Native Brotherhood of British Columbia. In 1958 they formed their own organization, the West Coast Allied Tribes, later called the West Coast District Council, that was modeled after the Nishga Tribal Council (Tennant 1982:37–38). In 1978 the West Coast District Council devised the name Nuu-chah-nulth for all the Nootkan peoples and renamed their organization the Nuu-chah-nulth Tribal Council. In 1985 the council was elected by all Nootkans and funded by most bands, except the Pacheenaht. A primary goal was to achieve recognition of aboriginal title and a land claims settlement.

Synonymy

While Nootkan tribes and groups had specific names, the Nootka had no overall name for themselves as a people (Drucker 1951:3). The ethnic name Nootka was transferred from the name bestowed by Cook on Nootka Sound in the mistaken belief that this was the native name (James Cook and William Griffin in Beaglehole 1967, 3:30). Conceivably Cook misunderstood a use of the verb *nu·tka·* 'circling about' (Walbran 1909:359–360; Sapir and Swadesh 1939:276). Nootka has also been the name used for the village of Yuquot (Jewitt 1974:24), the Mowachaht tribe and band, speakers of the language, and even the speakers of all the Southern Wakashan languages. Variant spellings include Nutka (Moziño 1970; Kroeber 1939), Nutca, Noutka, Nuca, Noca (Wagner 1968:400; Gormly 1977: 59, 73), and Nootkah.

Cook proposed the name Wak'ashians, based on the Nootkans' cheers of *wa·ka·š* 'bravo!' (Beaglehole 1967, 3: 323). Gallatin (1836:15) used Wakash, which was later extended to include the entire Wakashan family. The name Aht (Sproat 1868:312), based on the Nootka suffix -ʔatḥ 'residing at' that forms all names for groups of people, was used for many years by the Department of Indian Affairs. The Nootka referred to themselves for many years as West Coast, a designation they officially adopted in 1958 for their political organization, the West Coast Allied Tribes. In 1978 they devised the name Nuu-chah-nulth (*nuča·ńuɬ* 'all along the mountains'), a reference to the mountains of Vancouver Island that are common to all the Nootkan tribes.

Sources

The literature on the Northern and Central Nootkans is comparatively full. The most complete ethnography is Drucker's (1951) work, based on fieldwork in 1935–1936, but other observations span two centuries. Beginning in

410

the late eighteenth century, there are the observations of James Cook and other members of his expedition edited by Beaglehole (1967), Spanish observations ordered into a relatively full account by Moziño (1970), and accounts by Meares (1790), Strange (1929), Walker (1982), Haswell and Boit (Howay 1941), and Menzies (1923). In 1803–1805 John R. Jewitt was held captive at Nootka Sound, and his experiences are told in his journal (1807) and reworked narrative (1815). Heizer (1975:ix–x) lists the editions of these works. Sproat (1868) describes the people of the Alberni area in the 1860s, and Robert Brown (1873–1876, 1:20–152) includes material from the same place and time. Boas (1891:582–604) gives a brief ethnographic report. Curtis (1907–1930, 11) emphasizes ritual and mythology but summarizes other aspects of culture.

Work begun by Sapir in 1910 and 1913–1914 in the Alberni area produced a collection of texts in the Sheshaht dialect. Myths and some aspects of culture (Sapir and Swadesh 1939, 1955) as well as a biography of a primary informant (Sapir 1921) were published.

Sources on specific topics include Densmore (1939) on music, Koppert (1928) on mythology, Koppert (1930a) on technology and subsistence, J.C.H. King (1981) on eighteenth-century artifacts, and Swadesh (1948) on warfare. After about 1950 Nootkan ethnology tended to emphasize problems in the analysis of social organization (Newman 1957; Wike 1958; Kenyon 1973, 1975, 1976; Langdon 1976; Mitchell 1983). Other studies include Mowachaht ethnohistory (Folan 1972), Barkley Sound ethnohistory (St.Claire 1984a), ethnohistorical summaries of Barkley Sound and Southern Nootkan groups (Inglis and Haggarty 1986), Ahousaht ethnography (Webster 1983), Ahousaht geography (St.Claire 1984), Manhousaht ethnobiology (Ellis and Swan 1981), Pachenaht technology (Arima 1976), Hesquiat ethnobotany (Turner and Efrat 1982), and Nitinaht ethnobotany (Turner et al. 1983). There are popularly written collections of stories (Clutesi 1967, 1969) and an ethnographic interpretation (Clutesi 1969) by a Nootkan artist and writer.

Roman Catholic missionary activity from 1874 to 1925 is recorded in Moser (1926), which includes reminiscences of Brabant and his ethnographic observations (1900). The Annual Reports of the Canadian Department of Indian Affairs in their West Coast Agency sections are another major historical source form 1872 on.

Sendey (1977) gives a collection of early drawings and photographs. Arima (1983a) presents a concise general ethnography of all of the Nootkans, including the Makah.

Prehistory of the Ocean Coast of Washington

GARY WESSEN

The ocean coast of Washington consists of the coastal watershed of the westernmost portion of the state. The region extends from the rocky entrance of the Strait of Juan de Fuca on the north to the broad expanse of Willapa Bay on the south. To the interior, this includes all the major north- and west-flowing drainages of the Olympic Peninsula and much of the Chehalis River system. In early historic times the coast was populated by numerous groups of native peoples with considerable social and economic interaction. They spoke: Makah (Wakashan family); Quileute (Chimakuan family); Clallam, Quinault, and Lower Chehalis (Salishan family); and Chinook (Chinookan family). Although this diversity of languages implies a variety of heritages, Washington coast peoples displayed a remarkable degree of similarity in their material cultures. These peoples used a similar range of natural resources and applied technologies.

Environment

The ocean coast of Washington enjoys a maritime climate characterized by moderate temperature and heavy precipitation. Flora and fauna, though variable in concentration, are largely continuous throughout the region. Before the historic period, the coast was cloaked in a forest of cedar, hemlock, spruce, and alder. Substantial populations of deer, elk, bear, cougar, beaver, otter, and raccoon inhabited the coastal forest, and the coastal waters contained large numbers of sea otter, seal, sea lion, porpoise, and whale. Beaches and the nearshore environments contained many species of birds and shellfish; and marine and anadromous fishes such as salmon, herring, smelt, sculpin, rockfish, and cod were well represented.

The ocean coast of Washington, despite its overall similarity, is easily divisible into two major environmental subzones: the Olympic coast to the north and the bay coast to the south. Point Grenville marks the boundary between these two regions. The Olympic coastline is largely composed of harsh narrow beaches with numerous offshore rocks and islets. Here the interior rises steeply into the Olympic Mountains, and with the exception of several river valley floodplains, little flat ground occurs. South of Point Grenville, the coast opens into a wider, more gentle expanse of coastal plain with broad sandy beaches and two large and well protected saltwater bays. The southern interior too, is generally of gentler relief and lower elevation.

The heavy precipitation, dense vegetation, acidic soil, and frequently rugged relief, combined with the erosive effects of swift rivers and exposed beaches result in an environment that favors neither the preservation nor recognition of archeological resources. The ethnographic record clearly indicates that the material culture of Washington coast peoples was dominated by organic materials, yet few archeological sites in this region offer depositional conditions that are likely to preserve such items. This situation has lead to the recognition of two very different types of archeological localities: "dry" sites and "wet" sites (Croes 1977). Most of the archeological sites of the region occur in sediments that are normally dry. These deposits are subject to alternate wetting and drying (with weather conditions), have moderate exposure to oxygen, and typically offer poor preservation of organic materials. Wet sites, situated in sediments that are permanently wet, and exposed to only limited oxygen, thus provide outstanding organic preservation. Wet sites have provided most of the knowledge of the prehistoric cultures of the ocean coast of Washington.

The Archeological Record

The archeological record for the ocean coast of Washington, like that for the Northwest Coast as a whole, cannot be regarded as extensive. The first archeological work undertaken in this area was by Reagan (1917, 1928), who reported on the distribution and contents of shell middens at locations along the Olympic coast. Controlled archeological fieldwork began with Daugherty's (1948) systematic site survey of the coast.

The inventory of sites is largely the product of archeological site survey efforts, but the substantial environmental problems for such surveys have produced significant biases in this database. The overwhelming majority of sites occur in the relatively accessible modern beach environment (Daugherty 1948; Stallard and Denman 1956; Friedman 1976). A few sites associated with relict beach features are known (Wessen 1984), but these were chance finds, and there has been no systematic effort to investigate the occurrence of cultural deposits with earlier sea-level stands. Despite ethnographic accounts of settlements along rivers throughout most of this area (Olson 1936; Pettit 1950; Singh 1956), the survey of streamways has had mixed results. While cultural materials have been reported along various portions of the Chehalis River (Jones, Campbell, and Studenmund 1978), investigation of the steeper gradient rivers of the Olympic Peninsula has rarely produced sites (Rice 1966; Wessen 1978; Daugherty 1983). Further, although fortuitous discoveries have demonstrated that prehistoric sites are present in the dense forest areas, archeological site survey programs have consistently failed to locate any (Righter 1980; Dalan et al. 1981; Wessen, Gallison, and Virden 1985). In sharp contrast, a single survey of alpine parkland areas in the Olympic Mountains (Bergland 1984) has indicated that sites are widespread in this relatively open upland setting.

While more than 110 archeological sites have been recorded in this region, only 15 have been excavated to any extent (fig. 1, table 1). All but one of the excavated sites are shell middens situated on or near a modern saltwater beach, and most of them are in the northernmost portion of the coast.

The recovered collections from these 15 archeological sites are relatively well dated. All but one of the sites have been dated by radiocarbon measurements, and more than 40 dated samples are available (see table 1). Most of the sites contain evidence of occupation within the last 1,500 years, and at least 10 of them also contain early historic deposits. The single undated site, Toleak Point, is probably also a member of this group. Only three sites are wholly prehistoric—Martin, Sand Point, and the Hoko River wet site—and these sites all date between 1000 B.C. and A.D. 500. Despite evidence from the eastern Olympic Peninsula of human activity in a late glacial context (Gustafson, Gilbow, and Daugherty 1979), no known ocean coast site has been demonstrated to contain deposits older than 1000 B.C. However, this apparent lack of early coastal occupation is probably an artifact of the survey biases, and it is likely that humans were present on the Washington Ocean coast for as long as is reported for the eastern Olympic Peninsula.

Ozette and the Hoko River wet site contain both wet and dry components. While both of the wet sites have been extensively investigated, 8 of the 13 dry sites have been examined only to a very limited extent. Between them, the Ozette and Hoko River wet sites account for approximately 60 percent of the excavated volume and 90 percent of the prehistoric artifacts for the entire ocean coast region.

The sites and their contents may be conveniently reviewed not only as wet and dry sites, but also with reference to the northern and southern coast subareas. From this perspective, regional distinctions are also apparent.

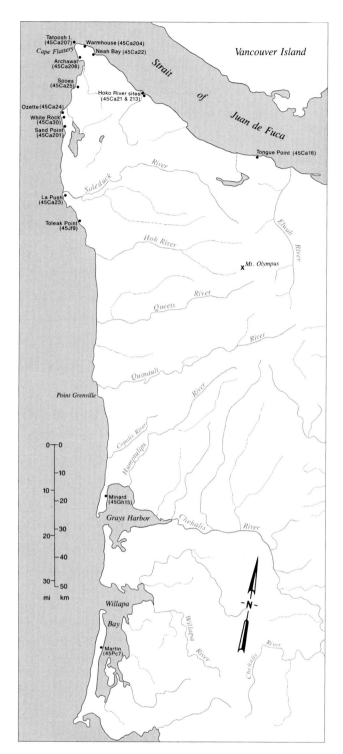

Fig. 1. Archeological sites along the ocean coast of Wash.

Northern Area

Dry sites in the northern coastal area include a small number of inland lithic-scatter sites and a large number of shell middens. While none of the lithic-scatter sites has been a subject of detailed study, they all appear to occur on reasonably level ground surfaces, often near water sources. Most of the alpine parkland sites are members of   *413* this group. Cultural materials in such sites include chipped stone detritus and an occasional flaked cobble or leaf-shaped point. All artifacts appear to be produced with a simple percussion technique, and there is little evidence of pressure flaking. The vast majority of all these objects are made of basalt; cryptocrystalline stones are virtually unrepresented. Faunal materials of any kind, either as tool forms or as debris, are absent. These sites and their contents appear to be much like the Olcott complex (Kidd 1964) to the east of Puget Sound. While suggested to be of early postglacial age, much about the character and dating of the Olcott complex remains unclear, and therefore its relationship to these northern coast inland sites is problematic.

Most sites of the northern coastal region are late prehistoric shell midden deposits; overall they are quite similar, and much like late prehistoric shell middens from elsewhere on the Northwest Coast. These sites consist of masses of food refuse, ash, and cultural materials in complex linear bands parallel to the present saltwater shoreline. Nearly all such sites are situated on first terraces adjacent to the beach, although the Hoko River Rockshelter occurs in a wave-cut rock face adjacent to the beach.

While these shell middens invariably offer abundant faunal materials for economic and environmental study, artifacts are usually sparse, and stratigraphic features are complex and often difficult to discern. Typically, such sites contain only small numbers of stone, bone, and shell artifacts. Chipped stone objects are virtually absent from these sites. Common stone tools include: ground slate knives and ground or pecked stone mauls, net and line weights, and whetstones or abrading stones probably used in the fashioning of bone and shell. In most of these sites worked stone items comprise 10–15 percent of the recovered artifact sample.

Bone objects constitute the vast majority of the artifacts recovered from the late prehistoric northern coast shell midden sites. Small modified bone splinters fashioned into single- or double-ended points are by far the most common bone artifacts, comprising 30–60 percent of the collection from such sites. The historic peoples used such bone points as awls, comb teeth, herring-rake teeth, fishhook barbs, fish gorges, and arming elements for a variety of harpoon, spear, leister, and arrow forms. Yet despite various typological approaches (Drucker 1943; Roll 1974; Friedman 1976) and detailed morphological analysis of this class of objects (Ames 1976), remarkably little is known about this type of artifact, and convincing criteria for inferring the purposes for most specimens are lacking. In addition to bone points, these shell middens contain bone composite toggling-harpoon valves, unilaterally barbed points, and wood-working wedges.

Ground shell artifacts produced from the valves of California mussel comprise a third group of artifacts commonly occurring on the Washington coast. Mussel shell was worked into a variety of cutting and piercing tools such as knives, harpoon blades, and adz blades. While nowhere numerous, these artifacts appear to have been used in functional roles that were filled by ground or chipped stone objects on other portions of the Northwest Coast.

The artifact assemblage from the Sand Point site, the only older relict shoreline associated shell midden yet studied, departs from this pattern in only one respect: in addition to all the above materials, it contains significant quantities of chipped stone. The recovered sample is composed mostly of debitage, providing little insight into the styles of finished forms. A relatively wide range of stone is present, and both simple and bipolar percussion as well as pressure flaking techniques were employed.

In addition to the materials normally encountered in the shell middens, the Ozette and Hoko River wet sites contain a broad range of wooden, woven, and twisted fiber artifacts. Ethnographic sources describe the Washington coast peoples' material culture as dominated by plant fiber objects, but these are the only archeological sites that offer collections approximating those records. Such artifacts comprise better than 80 percent of the recovered sample from each site. Ozette represents the late prehistoric period while Hoko River provides insights into the oldest securely dated materials currently available.

The Ozette site is an extensive shell midden deposit

Table 1. Excavated Sites on the Ocean Coast of Washington

Sites	Radiocarbon Dates	Sources
Tongue Point	650 B.C.– A.D. 955	Wessen 1981
Hoko River Rockshelter	A.D. 1030–1800	Croes 1985
Hoko River wet site	820–260 B.C.	Croes and Blinman 1980; Blinman 1980
Neah Bay	modern	Friedman 1976
Warmhouse	A.D. 1750	Friedman 1976
Tatoosh Island	A.D. 990	Friedman 1976
Achawat	A.D. 1800	Friedman 1976
Sooes	A.D. 840–970	Friedman 1976
Ozette	60 B.C.–A.D. 1510	K.H. McKenzie 1974; Gleeson 1980a; Friedman 1976; Mauger 1979
White Rock	A.D. 1563	Guinn 1963
Sand Point	320 B.C.–A.D. 350	Wessen 1984
La Push	A.D. 1185–1480	Duncan 1977; Wessen 1977
Toleak Point		Newman 1959
Minard	A.D. 870–1085	Roll 1974
Martin	A.D. 90–510	Kidd 1967; Shaw 1977

[a]Site has one or more historic components.

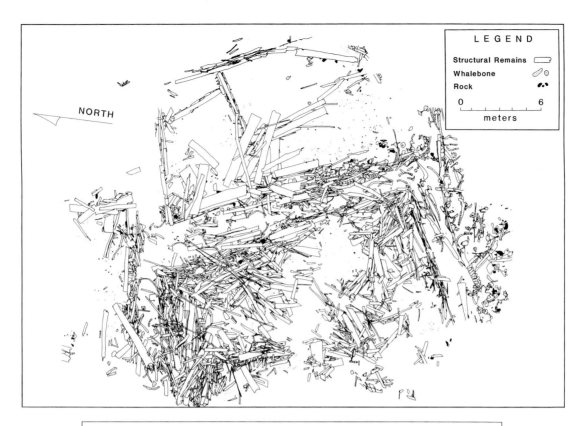

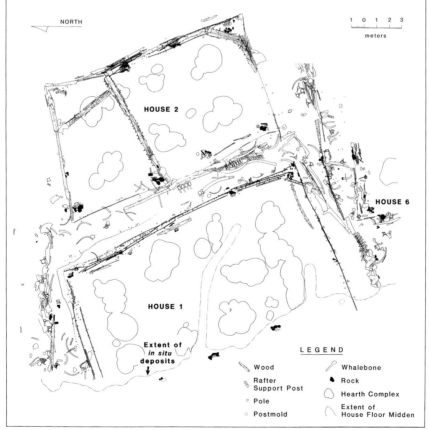

Samuels 1983.

Fig. 2. Ozette houses. top, Plan drawing of exposed remains of at least 3 structures. bottom, Floorplans of the 3 structures. Plank drains on the House 2 floor directed rain water into a series of plank and whalebone gutters to the east and south of House 1. Drawings by Stephan Samuels.

representing more than 2,000 years of occupation in the vicinity of Cape Alava. Although most of the site is dry and much like most other shell middens in the region, a portion of Ozette is waterlogged and contains a cultural record unparalleled on the Northwest Coast. Approximately A.D. 1500 a clay slide buried at least four cedar plank houses and the exterior surfaces immediately adjacent to them. The clay sealed house remains and associated materials into a deposit permanently saturated by subsurface water flow. The result is an area marked not only by outstanding organic preservation but also by unprecedented clarity in the recognition of cultural features. Excavations at Ozette between 1970 and 1981 produced a sample of more than 50,000 prehistoric artifacts and more than 1,000,000 pieces of associated faunal material.

The Ozette houses are large, split cedar plank, shed roof structures. Nearly 20,000 structural members including roof, wall, bench, and drain planks, rafter support posts, and support poles for walls, benches, and drains (Mauger 1978) littered the excavation area (fig. 2). At least three of the houses contain drainage-control trenches or drains to divert ground runoff from rainfall from house floor surfaces. Outside the houses, these drains combined into an elaborate drain system of cedar planks and whale bones that controlled the water as it passed through the community. These drains were essentially storm sewers, and the system amounts to a rudimentary example of community planning.

Ozette contains a very broad range of other types of artifacts. Approximately 6,000 woven or twisted plant fiber objects were recovered (figs. 3–4), including many varieties of cordage, basketry, garments, hats, sleeping mats, and cradles (Croes 1977). Wooden artifacts such as wedges, fishhooks, clubs, bows and arrows, small points, and kerfed-corner boxes (Mauger 1982) are also well represented. All the usual shell midden artifacts are present, but in reduced roles; the normally ubiquitous bone points comprise less than 5 percent of this collection.

Significant inorganic artifacts also occur at Ozette. Chipped stone artifacts, though present in older portions of the site, are virtually absent in the wet deposits; however, the houses do contain moderate amounts of ground slate knives, mauls, line and net weights, and abrading and grinding stones. These late prehistoric strata at Ozette also contain a limited quantity of iron and copper. The iron generally occurs in small pieces as cutting elements in woodworking tools and knives (fig. 5). The copper occurs in a more decorative context, usually in the form of pendants. Little is known of the origins of either metal; while copper may be indigenous on the Northwest Coast, the iron's ultimate origin is probably in the Old World.

The functional context of the Ozette materials offers yet another dimension to the interpretive value of this site.

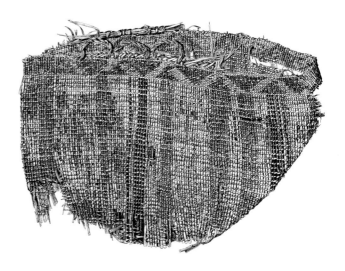

Fig. 3. Ornamented, open-twined weave basket with bear grass overlay, recovered from Ozette. Similar baskets were also found at the Hoko River site. Width 72 cm. Drawing by Chris Walsh.

The houses contain many associations of artifacts that represent kits of whaler's gear (fig. 6), seal hunter's gear, fisherman's gear, woodworker's gear, and the complete range of equipment used in weaving, slate grinding, and many other technological pursuits. Analysis of the house-floor deposits has determined individual nuclear family areas and activity zones representing food preparation, artifact fabrication, and storage (Samuels 1983). Therefore, in addition to a wealth of economic and technological information, the site also offers outstanding conditions for the detailed study of social interactions at both the household and community level. As such, Ozette is not only a unique opportunity to examine prehistoric culture but also an invaluable standard for assessing the poorly preserved dry shell middens much more typical of this region.

The Hoko River wet site consists of cultural materials discarded in or near the river, which became incorporated within the river channel and were subsequently uplifted and exposed by the river. Most of the wet site is situated within the range of tidal fluctuations, and much of it can only be examined during low tides. The dry deposits are above the tidal zone immediately adjacent to the river, and a more recent shell midden site, the Hoko River Rockshelter, is located nearby.

The Hoko River wet site has produced a collection consisting largely of plant fiber artifacts. No structural remains have been recovered, and the site lacks clear evidence of structures. Cordage represents nearly 70 percent of the artifact sample. The site also contains significant amounts of basketry and various forms of fishhooks. In addition to the ground slate knives and the ground stone mauls, net weights, and abraders common to all the coastal sites in this area, the Hoko River wet site contains abundant evidence of chipped stone. It has

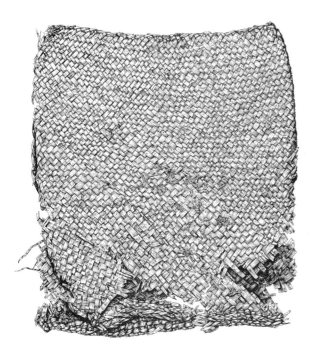

Makah Cultural and Research Center, Neah Bay, Wash.: 111/evc/92.
Fig 4. Infant's face cover from Ozette, twill on bias weave. Height 27 cm. Drawing by Chris Walsh.

Makah Cultural and Research Center, Neah Bay, Wash.: 71/iv/32.
Fig. 6. Plaited, checker weave storage basket for whaling gear from Ozette. Height 90 cm. Drawing by Chris Walsh.

produced extensive indications of a bipolar microlithic industry (fig. 7) (Flenniken 1980) as well as examples of microblades and bifacially flaked stemmed projectile points. From its waterlogged deposits, the site has yielded complete knives consisting of bipolar microliths hafted in simple wooden handles. While similar tools may have been widespread on the coast, Hoko River offers the only direct evidence of them.

Southern Area

The southern portion of the ocean coast of Washington contains an apparently similar range of sites, but it has been the subject of substantially less study. Interior areas are known to contain lithic-scatter sites, some of which may be similar to those described to the north. Other lithic sites here appear to be characterized by various stemmed projectile points made of cryptocrystalline stone, and in this respect differ from those to the north. Most sites on the southern coast are dry shell middens, and this group includes the only excavated sites: the late prehistoric

Makah Cultural and Research Center, Neah Bay, Wash.: 29/iv/109.
Fig. 5. Deteriorated base metal knife blade set in simply carved wooden haft. Recovered from Ozette. Length 47 cm.

Minard site and the somewhat older Martin site. Much like on the northern coast, these sites consist of masses of food refuse, ash, and small quantities of artifacts in complex and often unclearly structured deposits. While their recovered samples are similar to those from northern Washington sites, Minard and Martin nevertheless share traits that are uncharacteristic of that area.

Most of the artifacts recovered from the Minard site are objects of either bone or stone. Consistent with most coastal sites, more than half the bone tools are bone splinters modified into simple unipointed and bipointed forms. Other important bone tools at Minard include: composite toggling-harpoon valves, unilaterally barbed points, and wedges. Unlike the late prehistoric northern coast shell middens, Minard also contains moderate amounts of chipped stone. These consist of triangular and contracting stem projectile points, bifacial knives, scrapers, and modified flakes.

The sample from the Martin site also represents a dry shell midden with chipped stone, but this collection stands in some contrast to the rest of the ocean coast of Washington. At Martin, chipped stone objects comprise more than half the total artifact collection. As at Minard, triangular and contracting stem projectile points, bifaces, and scrapers of various forms are the most common stone artifacts. Bone tools, while still important, are less abundant; and bone splinter points constitute no more than 8 percent of the sample. Bone and antler wedges are well represented at the Martin site, but unilaterally barbed points are scarce, and composite toggling-harpoon valves have not been reported. In total, while clearly occupied by coastal people, the abundant chipped stone and relatively reduced importance of bone artifacts—particularly forms such as the splinter points and harpoon valves—suggest relatively greater contact with the more interior lower Columbia River or southwest Washington areas.

Most sites in this area contain large quantities of faunal remains. Every shell midden site that has been studied has produced evidence of broad economic activity including the exploitation of fish, shellfish, birds, and mammals. Like the artifacts, recovered faunal collections show great overall similarity, although some important subareal patterns are also apparent. The clearest distinctions between northern and southern coast faunal materials may be seen in the relative importance of mammals. In northern coast sites, marine mammals such as whale, porpoise, and seal are prominently represented. Northern fur seal is especially significant in this regard, and it frequently accounts for 50–80 percent of all mammal bones recovered from a site. Marine mammals constitute only a very small percentage of the recovered samples on the southern coast and were clearly not a principal focus of hunting activities. Land mammals such as deer, elk, and rabbit are dominant in southern coast samples and decidedly secondary in the north.

Culture Patterns

Review of the archeological record of the ocean coast of Washington reveals it to be of limited time-depth, and frequently, of limited detail. Given both the many obvious biases in this record and the complex social and economic behaviors of the ethnographic peoples, no regional phases or other explicit geographically oriented integrative units have been proposed for the Washington coast. Indeed, Abbott (1972) has raised important questions about the application of such terminology for the entire southern Northwest Coast area. In addition to the specific attributes of artifacts, faunal remains, and cultural features, ethnographic analogy has provided a basis for most of the interpretations of the archeological record of this region. Considering the limited nature of their contents, and their "obvious" continuity with the early historic cultures, many sites have been interpreted almost exclusively by this means.

Not surprisingly, interpretations of most of the archeo-

logical record of the Washington coast closely reflect ethnographic perceptions of its early historic cultures. However, the early historic cultures are not well documented; like the region's archeology, some portions of the coast have seen repeated study while others have been virtually ignored. Further, while often containing useful information, ethnographic and early historic accounts generally tend to stress social and ceremonial behavior and sometimes contain little specific information about the basic economic and technological conditions most immediately reflected by the archeological record.

The historic peoples of the ocean coast of Washington were remarkably knowledgeable about the coastal forests, beaches, intertidal areas, and coastal waters, and few, if any, resources were ignored in this area. They were hunters, fishermen, and plant material collectors. The coastal people were skilled technicians and artisans, and they produced a wide variety of both utilitarian and decorative goods. They were highly mobile people and followed a yearly cycle of movements between small, seasonal, economically oriented camps and larger, multi-season villages of broader economic and social focus. Coastal hunting and fishing camps were occupied mostly during the spring and summer months. In the autumn much activity probably shifted to fish-trap camps on nearby rivers in order to exploit the salmon runs. Following the salmon season, many people returned to the coastal villages for the winter. People of the Washington coast participated in most of the social elements of Northwest Coast societies. They were organized in local kin-based groups associated with particular named localities. These groups controlled camp and village house sites and resource-collection areas, and they owned dances, songs, and other ceremonial properties. Intermarriage and trade were important mechanisms of regional interaction, and exchange networks linked these peoples with each other and with the residents of other portions of the Northwest Coast.

The archeological record of the Washington coast is compatible, for late prehistoric cultures, with the ethnographic accounts of early historic people in the same region. The upland sites in the Olympic Mountains are the only currently known sites that appear to lack a close relationship to the ethnographic pattern, but these materials are undated, and there is no reason to conclude that

Makah Cultural and Research Center, Neah Bay, Wash.: 113/ax/22, after photograph.
Fig. 7. Drawing of a bipolar microlith knife, showing method of hafting. The handle is simply a folded strip of cedar. The blade is held by bark wraps. Oil covers the entire knife. Found at the Hoko River site. Length 12 cm.

418

Fig. 8. Unilaterally barbed wood points, probably arrowpoints, found at Ozette. Similar points were found at the Hoko River site. Length of each about 13 cm.

they are late prehistoric in age. Little about the contents of the dated sites contradicts knowledge of ethnographic patterns, but only the Ozette and Hoko River wet sites offer the data necessary to test specifically most implications of this interpretive framework. The record from these two sites has greatly enhanced the detail of prehistoric reconstructions while generally corroborating traditional interpretations. The Ozette and Hoko River wet sites reflect occupations very much like ethnographically derived notions of large multiseason villages and small seasonal camps, and both sites document patterns that probably were representative of much of the northern Washington coast.

The Ozette site was a large multiseason community. The major economic activities at Ozette—seal and whale hunting (Gustafson 1968) and marine fishing for salmon, halibut, and lingcod (Huelsbeck 1983)—were principally in the spring and summer months. However, seasonal determinations from shellfish remains (Wessen 1982) indicate that the site also had a significant autumn and winter occupation. Thus, while population levels probably fluctuated seasonally, it seems likely that Ozette may have been occupied for much of the year. Archeological sites at La Push, Sooes, and Neah Bay probably represent similar types of settlements.

Although relatively few strictly ceremonial objects have been recovered at Ozette, the site contains considerable evidence of social and ceremonial relationships both within and beyond the community. The distribution of household decorations within houses clearly indicates variation in the social standing of individual nuclear families. Similarly, the occurrence of whale hunting trophies (fig. 11) and other symbolic items indicates

differences in economic orientation and social standing among the represented houses. Exotic materials at the site record the community's contacts with many other portions of the Northwest Coast: dentalium and abalone shell from western Vancouver Island, coiled basketry from the Puget Sound–Georgia Strait region, and carved wooden bowls from the Columbia River mouth.

The Hoko River wet site was a camp for marine and riverine fishing. Located near the river mouth, the site offered access to different fish species in different seasons and may have been occupied from spring to late summer or early autumn. Although mammal, bird, and shellfish remains do occur there, halibut, Pacific cod, and rockfish appear to have been the chief focus of interest (Huelsbeck 1980); and the artifacts from this site indicate that hook-and-line and net fisheries were the most important activities. Warmhouse, Achawat, White Rock, and Toleak Point sites probably represent similar types of settlements.

The dry shell midden sites of the southern Washington coast offer somewhat less potential to expand ethnographic perceptions of cultural patterns. In many respects the southern coast people were much like their neighbors to the north. A major difference that is reflected in both archeological and ethnographic records concerns their orientation within the environments available to them. The pelagic marine mammal hunting and fishing widely pursued by the northern groups has no analog on the southern coast. While marine fish and marine mammals, such as harbor seal, were important on the southern coast, they were probably obtained from the large saltwater bays more frequently than from the coastal waters. This bay rather than ocean orientation is also reflected in the shellfish fauna from the southern coast sites and, in combination with a relatively greater emphasis on terrestrial mammals, the southern coast people followed economic pursuits similar to Puget Sound people.

Fig. 9. Unilaterally barbed, double-pointed, wooden arrowheads held to the wood shaft by bark wraps. Recovered from Ozette; similar ones were found at the Hoko River site. Length of top 18 cm, bottom to scale.

Fig. 10. Fishhooks from Ozette. left, Bent wood Southern Northwest Coast-type halibut hook with bone point; height, 16 cm. center, Single-barbed "bottom" fishhook with bone point; height, 12 cm. right, Double-barbed "bottom" fishhook, with bone points; height, 5 cm.

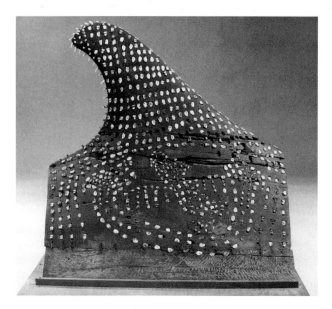

Makah Cultural and Research Center, Neah Bay, Wash.: 28/v/5.
Fig. 11. Whale dorsal fin effigy, from Ozette. Presumably a whaling trophy, it is carved wood, inlaid with sea otter teeth. Inlaid on the side are thunderbird and double-headed serpent motifs. "Nootkans of Vancouver Island," fig. 4, this vol., shows an identical specimen on display within a house. Length 90 cm.

Origins

Although nearly all the excavation in the region has taken a direct historical approach, this approach has been restricted by an inability to recognize specific historic peoples in every site. While all the late prehistoric and early historic sites may be assumed to reflect the local historic cultures, none of the wholly prehistoric deposits can be demonstrated to represent any particular group. Further, while the large number of late prehistoric coastal sites and the much smaller number of older sites may appear to suggest a substantial increase in population during the last 1,500 years, consideration of the biases in site survey coverage indicates that this perception may well be a product of sample error.

Before considering culture history as reflected by the archeological materials, it is worthwhile to consider what other data have suggested about it. Elements of language, material culture, and social life have traditionally provided the basis for anthropological assessments of cultural relationships among Northwest Coast peoples, and some such observations of relationship, or suggested relationship, are relevant to any reconstruction of the culture history of the ocean coast of Washington. The linguistic diversity of the coast has suggested cultural-historical relationships to many researchers. Similarly, aspects of economy and technology have also been cited as evidence of such relationships.

Suggestions of economic or technological evidence of cultural-historical relationship are limited to the northern coast peoples and tend to focus on that most remarkable

Makah Cultural and Research Center, Neah Bay, Wash.: 164/v/23.
Fig. 12. Wood-working chisel made of beaver incisor wedged into a carved wood haft. The proximal end sports a human face with characteristic West Coast hat. Recovered from Ozette. Length 17 cm.

activity, whaling. Whaling techniques and other material culture similarities have been cited as examples of historical relationship between Wakashans from western Vancouver Island and Bering Strait Eskimos (Collins 1937; Lantis 1938; Heizer 1943; Borden 1951). Makah people were thus considered to have carried whaling to the Washington coast where Chimakuan and Salishan peoples subsequently adopted it.

Against this background, the archeological record of the ocean coast of Washington presents a picture of remarkable stability and continuity. With the exception of the upland sites, all the known sites of this region reflect cultures much like those of the early historic period, and the regional patterns of northern coast offshore hunters and fishermen and southern coast bay fisherman and coastal woodland hunters appear to have persisted throughout the time represented. At Ozette, where wet and dry portions of the site combine to offer approximately 2,000 years of occupation, relatively little change in either artifacts or faunal remains is evident. Similarly, a comparison of woven fiber artifacts from the Ozette and Hoko River wet sites reveals many elements of continuity

Fig. 13. Carved front panel from a kerfed-corner wooden box. Sea otter and pile perch teeth were used as inlays. Found at Ozette. Length 82 cm.

Fig. 14. Zoomorphic, double-headed wooden mat creaser, from Ozette. Length 16 cm.

over the last 2,500 years (Croes 1977).

The apparent absence of chipped stone in late prehistoric sites of the northern coast appears to be a consistent temporal pattern, but its technological implications are uncertain. Chipped stone objects are common in the oldest Ozette dry site deposits, at Sand Point, and at the Hoko River wet site; they are virtually absent from all later collections. This disappearance may indicate a greater reliance on ground shell tools, or it may be related to the as yet unexplained presence of iron on the coast. In any event, the decline in stone chipping does not appear to have had major consequences; functionally equivalent objects produced from other materials were common and neither artifacts nor faunal assemblages show associated changes.

Archeological perceptions of culture history are generally consistent with what is known of historic peoples. Impressions of long-term continuity in the Salishan and Chimakuan portions of the coast are in agreement with linguistic speculation, but these areas are poorly represented archeologically. The Martin site, with both coastal and possible lower Columbia River elements, may be a prehistoric Chinookan site. The many similarities between collections from the northernmost Washington coast sites and those from western Vancouver Island (Dewhirst 1978; Haggarty 1982; McMillan and St. Claire 1982) support the suggestion of a northern origin for the Makah.

The northern coast, with its better documented archeology, offers insights not totally consistent with ethnographic thought. If Wakashan-speaking peoples arrived in Washington as recently as A.D. 1000 (Kinkade and Powell 1976) their arrival is not reflected in the archeological record. This condition is similarly unclear with respect to whaling. While both Sand Point and the Hoko River wet site contain whale bone, neither site offers clear evidence of the actual hunting of these animals. However, whaling is closely associated with fur seal hunting in both ethnography and in late prehistoric archeology, and fur seal hunting is well documented at Ozette and Sand Point for at least the last 2,000 years. Thus if Wakashans are as recent as suggested, they did not introduce fur seal hunting to Washington, and perhaps not whaling either. This circumstance may be taken to indicate that northern coast Chimakuan speakers were marine mammal hunters prior to the arrival of the Wakashans or that the Wakashans have been present in northern Washington for more than 2,000 years.

While anthropologists have traditionally associated marine mammal hunting with the western Vancouver Island Wakashans from whom Washington Wakashans are probably derived, equally important is the question of whether other Washington coast peoples lacked the capability or inclination for such pursuits prior to the Wakashan arrival. Indeed, whaling and fur seal hunting are as well documented on the northern Washington coast as on Vancouver Island. It may be that marine mammal hunting developed at the western entrance of the Strait of Juan de Fuca as part of a maritime tradition in which people of both the northern and southern shores participated. The water was an avenue of communication and transportation for seafaring peoples; the skill required to cross the strait was probably only one prerequisite to successful marine hunting.

The archeological data indicate that the historic cultures were the products of cultural traditions that persisted longer than the known physical evidence of them. All the historic peoples exhibited sophisticated adaptations to the coastal environment; and this condition, perhaps more than any other, argues for a relatively long coastal residence for these cultures. Thus, while not necessarily in their historic positions, all the peoples of the region probably have been coastal people for thousands of years.

421

Makah

ANN M. RENKER AND ERNA GUNTHER

Language and Territory

The Makah (məˈkä) language is the southernmost member of the Wakashan family.* It belongs to the Southern or Nootkan branch and is closest to Nitinaht, from which it separated about 1,000 years ago (Jacobsen 1979:776). Three varieties of the language are discernible, probably reflecting earlier differences among villages (Renker 1980–1985).

The Makah are the people of the area around Cape Flattery at the northwestern tip of the Olympic Peninsula (fig. 1). Early in the nineteenth century, Makah territory extended eastward along the Strait of Juan de Fuca as far as the Hoko River (which they reportedly shared with the Clallam) and southward along the ocean shore beyond Cape Alava, perhaps as far as Cape Johnson, and it included the drainages of the streams flowing into the sea between these places, the offshore islands and reefs, and the ocean out to Swiftsure Bank.

Villages

Five Makah villages existed in precontact times: Neah Bay (diˑyaˑ), Biheda (biʔidʔa), Wayatch (waʔač̓), Tsoo-yess (čuˑyas), and Ozette (ʔuseˑʔiɬ). The first four were located on sites within the 1986 contiguous reservation; Ozette's location was 22 kilometers south of Cape Flattery. Some authors use the geographical distance from Ozette to the other Makah villages as evidence supporting a tribal distinction between Ozette dwellers and Makah people (Riley 1968). The majority opinion regards Ozette as one of five semiautonomous villages linked by language, kinship, and common traditions (Swan 1870; Densmore 1939; Taylor 1974).

These villages were inhabited all year long. In the

spring and summer when the weather cleared and the winds abated, some people moved to summer residences at Achawat, Kydikabbit, and Tatoosh Island. All the people of one village did not necessarily go to the same fishing sites. If a headman owned rights to multiple sites, he could divide the labor in his household to accommodate the need for groups at different sites.

Environment

Makah territory experiences fierce storms and incessant rain during the winter months, contrasted with calm, sunny summers. The average minimum and maximum temperatures do not vary greatly on a seasonal basis, with a temperate range of 53°F maximum and 46°F minimum, while wind and rainfall increase dramatically with the onset of winter. Annual precipitation ranges from 90 to 110 inches and falls approximately 199 days annually. These rainy days occur predominantly in winter and spring, while winds greater than 40 miles per hour are restricted to the period of November through March. Snow is not plentiful, and figures indicate an average snowfall of eight inches for the winter months (Phillips and Donaldson 1972).

The lands and waters comprising Makah territory provide habitats for abundant land and sea mammals, birds, and freshwater, saltwater, and anadromous fishes. Several smaller streams in Makah territory have runs of coho and chum salmon and steelhead, the Sooes and Ozette rivers have runs of chinook salmon, and the Ozette River and Lake Ozette have a run of sockeye. Particularly important to the Makah were the halibut banks off Cape Flattery and the fur sealing grounds off Cape Alava.

The environment supported a variety of flora as well, abounding in plants with technological, medicinal, and nutritional value. Large, straight-grained red cedar trees were reportedly (Swan 1870:4) less abundant in Makah territory than to the north or south, but cedar was present, though perhaps less accessible (Gill 1983).

All the resource areas in Makah territory, in addition to technological innovations directed at subsistence, could be owned by a Makah headman. This economic, as opposed to ceremonial, privilege (Drucker 1951:247–248) allowed a headman and his family privileged access to

---

*The phonemes of Makah are: (voiceless stops and affricates): p, t, λ, c, č, k, kʷ, q, qʷ, ʔ; (glottalized stops and affricates) p̓, t̓, λ̓,c̓, č̓, k̓, k̓ʷ, q̓, q̓ʷ; (voiced stops) b, d; (voiceless fricatives) ɬ, s,š, x, xʷ, x̣, x̣ʷ; (nasals) m, n; (voiced resonants) w, l, y; (short vowels) a ([ə]), e ([ɛ]), i ([ɪ]), o ([ɔ]), u ([u]); (long vowels) aˑ ([a]), eˑ [æ]), iˑ ([i]), oˑ ([o]), uˑ ([u]). Other vocalic nuclei represented are: ay ([ay]), oy ([ɔy]), ey ([e]), iy ([iː]), aw ([aw]), uy ([uˑy]).

This orthography, based on one developed by William H. Jacobsen, Jr., has been the one used by the Makah Language Program; x is written x̌ and xʷ is x̌ʷ.

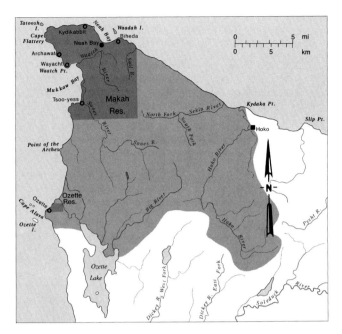

Fig. 1. Territory and settlements of the Makah in the mid-19th century.

certain resources, in addition to providing a mechanism for coping with more than one plentiful migration.

External Relations

Culturally the Makah were closest to their fellow Nootkans, especially the Nitinaht, and they generally followed Nootkan patterns of subsistence activities, social organization, and ceremonialism. But they shared some features of material culture, most conspicuously the shed-roof house and the two-bar loom, with their Salishan and Chimakuan neighbors. Socially, the Makah had ties with neighbors on all sides. During the nineteenth century, Makah families had fishing rights on the Lyre River in Clallam country, where they caught chum salmon (Waterman 1920:55), while Clallam and Quileute families went to the Cape Flattery area for halibut, and Quileute went to Lake Ozette for salmon (Riley 1968:78, 80–81; Singh 1966:38). The Makah served as middlemen in trade between the Lower Columbia and Vancouver Island (Swan 1870: 30–31), and they carried on trade with the Clallam and others up the Strait of Juan de Fuca. But there are also traditions of conflict with the Quileute (Curtis 1907–1930, 11:56–59), the Clallam (Swan 1870:50–51), and even their close relatives, the Nitinaht (Irvine 1921).

Culture

Social Organization

Makah social organization adhered to the Nootkan pattern, which emphasized the integrated concepts of hereditary ranking and kinship recognition as a means of

forming alliances (Drucker 1951:219). An ambilateral descent system allowed kinship reckoning via a number of avenues and allowed an individual or a family group to choose the most advantageous social situation possible.

By far, the most restrictive places in Makah society were the opposite ends of the Nootkan social continuum: headmen and their immediate families (ča·baɫ) and slaves (quɫu·). Like Nootkans to the north, headmen tested and affirmed their positions during potlatches, and Makahs in the middle social group could advance or fall back slightly in prestige through marriage and acquisition of privileges.

Within a house, occupants were ranked by the headman relative to himself. As was usually the case with Nootkan people, the headman might be a whaler, who relied on a series of specialized activities within his household to maintain his prestige. In the case of Makahs, this might have included a fur seal hunter.

Ceremonies

Additional Makah practices that indicate their Nootkan affiliation include the ƛu·kʷa·li· or Wolf ritual (Swan 1870; Ernst 1952; Drucker 1951) and the ča·yiq or healing ceremony (Swan 1870; Densmore 1939). Other spiritual matters, especially regarding whale rituals performed to hunt live whales and bring dead whales to shore (Drucker 1951:170–174, 180), follow the Nootkan patterns.

The Makah life cycle also is Nootkan in intent and nature (Swan 1870; Densmore 1939; Taylor 1974, Goodman 1978), as are Makah tastes in aesthetics (Daugherty and Friedman 1983).

Subsistence

The Nootkan pattern of social organization, the harvestable quality of resources, and occupational specialization allowed the Makah to be selective in exploiting their food resources. While a predominantly marine diet may appear monotonous, Makahs perceived a great variety and abundance of sustenance in the environment (Swan 1870; Renker and Gill 1985; Gill and Renker 1985).

Sea mammals may have contributed the most to the Makah diet, followed by halibut, other marine fishes, and salmon.

In addition to the prestigious occupation of whaling (fig. 2) ("Nootkans of Vancouver Island," this vol.) (Waterman 1920), fur seal hunting evolved as a major factor in precontact economics. Both occupations involved knowledge of complex systems of navigation on the open ocean, the ability to interpret the activities of the prey prior to the kill, and a reliance on ritualized activity to secure the success of the hunt. While the ritualized nature of whaling was intense (Drucker 1951; Gunther 1942) and the occupation strictly an inherited privilege, seal hunting involved less ritual to perform, and there

a

c

b

Wash. State Histl. Soc., Tacoma: top left, 56519; center left, 19220; lower left, 31002; Smithsonian, NAA: top right, 86–3621; center right, 77–10045; bottom right, Smithsonian, Dept. of Anthr.: a, 74208; b, 23338; c, 72637.

Fig. 2. Whaling. top left, Harpooner ready to thrust the harpoon into the whale. The skill of the steersman and crew to come up on the left side of the whale at the critical moment were all necessary for a successful strike. The harpoon was too heavy to be thrown, and once implanted in the whale, extreme care had to be taken to keep the crew clear of the fast-running tow lines. The final kill was accomplished with a lance. The whaling canoe carried a crew of 8--6 paddlers, a steersman, and the harpooner (McCurdy 1961:104). Ceremonial preparations preceded a whaling trip, and one who had not been ritually purified would not be allowed in a whaling canoe. Photograph probably by Shobid Hunter, a Makah whaler, Neah Bay, Wash., about 1910. top right, 6 canoes towing a whale ashore, Tatoosh I., Wash. The ropes used for towing were made from cedar limbs and spruce roots (Swan 1870:39–40). Drawing by James G. Swan, 1861. center left, The whale towed onto the beach. To insure that the catch would not sink, its mouth was tied shut by a diver and sealskin floats were attached. center right, Butchering the whale, an activity participated in by the whole village. The whaler retained possession of the prized piece surrounding the dorsal fin. Other people might have claims to particular pieces by hereditary right or by previous agreement with the whaler. lower left, Lighthouse Jack, with whaling canoe, harpoon shaft, and sealskin floats (McCurdy 1961:103–108). The 13–18 foot shaft was made of yew wood. center left, bottom left, and center right, Photographs by Asahel Curtis, Neah Bay, 1905–1910. a–b, Harpoon heads fitted with mussel shell (a) and metal (b) blades. The 3-piece toggle heads consist of 2 antler valves lashed to the blade with cherry bark and spruce gum. Harpoon heads were uniquely marked so that carcasses would be properly credited to the harpooner. Lanyards, whale sinew wound with nettle fiber string, were attached to heavy cedar rope that was run out once the whale was struck. c, Wooden reel carved in the form of whale tails for nettle fiber string. Collected by J.G. Swan: a, 1883; b, 1876; c, 1883. Length of c, 42 cm; others to scale.

were few or no restrictions on the occupation itself. Any able-bodied man could become a sealer, and success was linked with the diligence of someone who ritually prepared himself correctly (Gunther 1936; Renker 1980–1985).

The northern fur seal was hunted by a few other tribes in the region (the Nitinaht, Quileute, and Quinault), but the Makah were in the most favorable location to hunt this species, because in its spring migration northward it generally comes closest to the coast in large numbers at a feeding ground off Umatilla Reef, three miles from Ozette. The Makah hunted fur seals in canoes holding three or four men, the sealer using a double foreshaft harpoon and a pair of inflated floats, which served to wear out a struck seal or to buoy up the canoe in bad weather (Scammon 1874:154–155, 159). Makahs preferred the taste of fur seal and its oil (fig. 3), and so other seal species were not fully exploited. Archeological evidence, especially at Ozette, shows long, heavy use of the fur seal (E. I. Friedman 1976; Huelsbeck 1983).

Halibut were caught mainly during the spring and summer from offshore banks with U-shaped hooks and kelp lines. Chinook and coho salmon were caught by trolling in the ocean and strait through the summer; these two species and chums were taken in weirs and traps or with harpoons and gaffs in smaller streams during fall and winter; and sockeye were taken with trawl nets in Lake Ozette. Archeological evidence (Huelsbeck 1983: 114–117) suggests that, for some households, lingcod, rockfish, and other marine species available throughout the year may have been more important than halibut or salmon.

Land mammals and birds provided a limited food source and an additional source of raw materials such as bone and antler. Despite the fact that land animals were accessible to Makah people, the poor representation of land animal remains in the archeological record and ethnographic accounts strongly indicates Makah preference in sea foods (Swan 1870; Densmore 1939; Gunther 1936; Taylor 1974; Wessen 1982; Huelsbeck 1983).

One of the most dependable food sources for Makah people was the intertidal zone (Wessen 1982). The availability and variety of the foods in this environment offset the possibility that winter storms could preclude other subsistence activities, especially in the event of unexpected company. Intertidal food consisted of many varieties of clams, octopus, mussels, and other shelled animals such as chitons, barnacles, and limpets (Wessen 1982). These foods also provided raw material in the way of shell for cutting tools, eating implements, and adornment.

Hunting and fishing activities were restrcited to men in precontact times; women's activities centered around gathering shellfish and plant resources and processing the animals killed by men, with the exception of the ritualized activities that surrounded butchering whales (fig. 2) and, to a lesser extent, seals (Swan 1870; Waterman 1920). Women cleaned, then smoked or dried halibut, salmon, clams, and whale products for winter use and for trade.

Plant gathering fell almost exclusively to women, with the exception of certain plants a man needed to complete a ritualized behavior or fulfill a *tupa·t*, or inherited privilege (Gunther 1945; Gill 1983). Plant foods gathered by women included salmonberries, red and blue huckleberries, blueberries, cranberries, and wild strawberries. Roots of the sand verbena, surf grass, and buttercup were steamed or baked in a pit oven. Camas, a favorite food, was not found in Makah territory but received in trade from the north (Gunther 1945; Gill 1983; Singh 1966:25).

Additional uses of plants included medicines (Densmore 1939; Gunther 1945; Gill 1983), raw material, and entertainment.

Structures

The Makah house was of the flexible shed-roof type (Mauger 1978), built on a permanent framework that could reach 60 feet in length by 30 feet in width by 15 feet in height. The roof was nearly flat and consisted of planks that could be easily shifted for ventilation or removed for use at another site. The wall planks were held horizontally between pairs of poles, the outer member of each pair   *425*

Southwest Mus., Los Angeles: 2294-G-1.
Fig. 3. Oil container made from the stomach of an animal, probably a seal. Oil was a staple of the Makah diet, used to flavor dried meat, fish, and plant foods. Whale oil and fur seal oil were the most highly prized. Collected about 1900; length 44 cm.

rising above the roof to support a fish drying rack. The flat roof also served as a platform for laying out fish to dry. The house was usually occupied by several families. Occupants secured privacy by means of partitions that were easily removed to accommodate dancing, feasting, and gambling. At such times the family fires too could be moved to the center of the house and a new smokehole opened in the roof. Houseposts bore carved or painted designs, but more often the house contained a wide plank with carved designs (Swan 1870:5).

Transport

Makah canoes were nearly all of the Westcoast type, which was made in six standard sizes and styles adapted to carrying freight, war, whaling, sealing, and other activities (fig. 5). These graceful, seaworthy craft were essential to whaling, pelagic sealing, and trading voyages. They were also an important trade item. The Makah made some of their own canoes and acquired others from the Nootkans of Vancouver Island. They were suppliers of the Westcoast type of canoe to the people of the south and east.

Smithsonian, Dept. of Anthr.: 1137.
Fig. 4. Carved alder trencher. Wooden bowls and feast dishes saw general use as containers for oil, soups, fish, or plant food. Carved in many forms, elaborate pieces were used by the wealthy on special occasions. Collected by J.G. Swan at Neah Bay, Wash., 1866. Length, 76 cm.

Waterman (1920:9–29) gives a detailed account of the Makah canoe and its equipment.

Technology

Makah material culture was based on the use of western red cedar and other woods like yew, spruce, alder, and hemlock (J. Friedman 1975; Gleeson 1980). The cellular structure of cedar allowed the wood to split straight enough to form house planks, and the inner bark could be beaten soft enough to make diapers and clothing. The majority of the Ozette artifacts were made of western red cedar (Friedman 1975), though craftsmen used yew wood when the task required heavier, denser wood. Clubs, whaling harpoon shafts, bark beaters, and bows (fig. 6) all were made of yew (J. Friedman 1975).

Carved wood was the result of a complex wood technology that exhibited specific techniques and tools for a particular type of wood. Makah craftsmen did not select wood randomly for a task, for the needs of a project dictated the choice of wood and the techniques for preparation of the article (Gleeson 1980). Bent-corner boxes provided a means for cooking, storing belongings, and, in the case of whalers and wealthy Makahs, a means

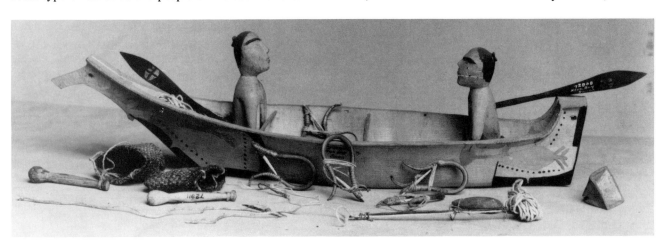

Smithsonian, Dept. of Anthr.: 72907–72914.
Fig. 5. Model of a Westcoast canoe and fishing equipment, including woven fish bags and wooden clubs, halibut hooks and set line rig with stone sinker, and carved wooden bailers. The making of models does not seem to have been solely for the White tourist trade, since miniature tools, figures, and other objects have been recovered from the Ozette archeological site. Collected by J.G. Swan at Neah Bay, Wash., 1883.

Mus. of Hist. and Industry, Seattle, Wash.: 1173.
Fig. 6. Man using a steel knife to make the shaft of an arrow. Makah self-bows were typically of yew with a lock of hair wrapped in nettle twine at the grip. Arrows had bouyant cedar shafts, were tangentially fletched, and armed with barbed bone points or copper points fashioned from heavy gauge wire. Feathers and points were secured with wraps of sinew or thin strips of bark. Cylindrical wooden quivers were embellished with carved crest figures. Photograph by James G. McCurdy, Neah Bay, 1912–1913.

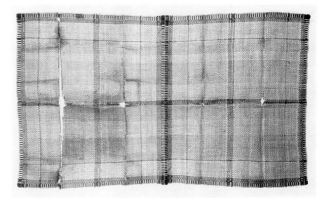

Smithsonian, Dept. of Anthr.: 74794.
Fig. 7. Mat of checkerwoven cedar bark, incorporating strips dyed in different colors to create geometric designs. Cedar bark mats were said to have been used for canoe sails, though they found most common use as blankets to wrap cargo (Swan 1870:45). Collected by J.G. Swan at Neah Bay, Wash., 1883; length 150 cm.

for proclaiming wealth or *tupa·t*.

The versatility of cedar allowed Makah women to develop a highly prized skill of basket weaving. Makah women produced numerous types of baskets, from those with large open weaves to facilitate intertidal gathering to those that held water and could be used for cooking and storage. Makah basketry was predominantly an exercise in cedar (fig. 7), but women used other materials such as cherry bark, cedar root, cattail, tule from Ozette, and spruce root with the same discretion as male carvers showed in their choice of materials (Gill 1983). Makah women also wove textiles on the two-bar loom, using spun dog wool or a cordage made of stips of birdskin, the down left on, twisted around a fiber twine (Swan 1870:43–44; Drucker 1955:83, fig. 53).

History

Makah contact with the Europeans was first recorded when John Meares anchored off the coast of Tatoosh Island in the spring of 1788 (Gunther 1972:56–57). Spaniards sailed into Neah Bay in 1790, beginning two years of contact (fig. 8) that culminated in the establishment of a fort in the village there in 1792. The fort lasted four months before the Spaniards abandoned the venture (Gunther 1972:67–72; Pethick 1980).

In 1809–1810 several ship-wrecked Russians and "Aleuts" (probably Pacific Eskimos) were temporary captives of the Makah (Owens 1985). In 1833 three ship-wrecked Japanese were held (Rich 1941:122, 128–129; see also H. Davis 1872:71–73).

Early contact intensified Makah trade and the tribe's use of non-Indian goods. It also introduced a series of epidemics that decimated the population. By 1852 Biheda was abandoned because of smallpox, and residents moved into nearby Neah Bay (Taylor 1974:6). Representatives from the four remaining villages negotiated with Gov. Isaac Stevens of Washington Territory (with the help of an interpreter speaking Chinook Jargon) before signing the Treaty of Neah Bay in 1855 (Gibbs 1855a). Makahs ceded land in return for education, health care, and the right to fish in "usual and accustomed grounds and stations" (Kappler 1904–1941, 2:682).

Subsequent Indian policy revolved around the assimilation of Makah people through an educational system that ignored Makah priorities and prohibited the use of the language (Whitner 1977; Gillis 1974). Instead of capitalizing on the Makah's knowledge and expertise regarding marine hunting and navigation, as well as fishing, the Indian Service emphasized agriculture in an area unsuited to cultivation (Whitner 1977).

Other policies revolving around the school system served to suppress and eradicate Makah culture. The school placed in Neah Bay changed from a day school in 1863 to a boarding school in 1874, and back to a day school in 1896; the last date also marked the beginning of a compulsory attendance policy for Indian children. Agents effected these changes to accommodate the belief that each type of school was the best means, in its time, to protect Makah children from Indian barbarism and "superstitious" practices (Colson 1953; Gillis 1974; Whitner 1977).

The school had an additional effect on intervillage 427

relations. Neah Bay increased in importance because the Indian agency and the school were maintained there. With the closing of the boarding school in 1896, the population from other villages had the choice of sending their children away or moving with their families to Neah Bay. While isolated families continued to live at Ozette, Tsooyess, and Wayatch after 1914, Neah Bay became the primary village of residence and the center of the cash economy on the reservation (Colson 1953; Taylor 1974).

Special prosperity for Makahs accompanied the tribe's commercial sealing ventures. Makah involvement with pelagic sealing went through several phases. Prehistorically, fur seals were very important, but for a good part of the nineteenth century the migration route missed the region and they were virtually unknown (Colson 1979:21). The animals reappeared in great numbers in 1866, and, partly because there was a market for the skins, the Makah began hunting them again (Swan 1884–1887, 2:394). During this phase the Makah hunted with harpoons in three-or four-man canoes (Scammon 1874:154–155, 159). By the 1880s, White-owned sealing schooners had appeared, and Makahs were hiring on as hunters. This work was so profitable that the Makah temporarily abandoned whaling (Swan 1884–1887, 2:396; Waterman 1920:48). It was also broadening, taking Makahs and other Indians as far away as the Bering Sea and Japan. (On the experiences of British Columbia Indians in pelagic sealing, see Knight 1978:107–112.) By the 1890s several Makah sealers had their own schooners and were hiring White navigators (Colson 1953:159). But by this time the number of sealers and the use of firearms had greatly diminished the seal population, and so in 1894 international treaties began to restrict it. Reportedly the Makah became skilled poachers, but their schooners were confiscated, and commercial sealing came to an end. Some returned to traditional whaling. However, a treaty signed in 1911 gave certain groups of Indians, including the Makah, the right to continue pelagic sealing by aboriginal methods only, in canoes with harpoons (Broderson and Hopkins 1939). This practice continued for several decades.

The introduction of cash and the availability of non-Indian goods were not the only factors that affected the reservation in the early twentieth century (Densmore 1939; Colson 1953), but they played a dramatic role in Makahs' acceptance of measures that linked the reservation to non-Indian territory. Before State Road 112 was completed in the 1930s, the reservation was accessible only to water travelers. With the road, Makahs had the opportunity to travel to other towns on the Olympic Peninsula, and tourists gained the means to visit the reservation. Tourist access increased in the following decade when the Army Corps of Engineers completed the breakwater linking Waadah Island to the mainland. The breakwater created a sheltered harbor attracting tourist boats and fishing vessels.

Fishing, logging, and the tourist trade became the major occupations (Colson 1953; Taylor 1974; C. Hall 1983) on the reservation, and as government Indian policy gradually allowed the tribe more power in decision-making processes, cultural life began to reemerge from decades of secrecy. While the Neah Bay Agency's policy was designed to eliminate potlatches and other cultural

Museo de América, Madrid: left, 240; center, 239; right, 241.
Fig. 8. Tatoosh and his wives. left, Tatoosh wearing a whaler's hat, made of spruce root with a whaling scene, and a bearskin robe. The onion-shoped top on the hat indicated his higher status; the tops of commoners' hats were flat. center, First wife with infant with a bound head-deformation device (Gunther 1972:70). right, Second wife. Both women wear robes of shredded cedar bark edged with fur. The women wear nose, neck, ear and hair ornaments made of dentalium and olivella shells and what are probably trade beads. Watercolors by José Cardero, an artist with the Alejandro Malaspina expedition, 1791.

428

Fig. 9. Makah Day, an annual celebration. Helen Peterson (left), shaking a scallop shell rattle, and her sister Mable Robertson (right) drumming, wear headbands made of olivella shells. The girl at left wearing a basketry hat is a Nootkan from Vancouver I., B.C. On other occasions, such as birthdays, Makah Museum and Makah tribal council functions, and potlatches, families also bring out their particular songs and dances. Photograph by Ruth Kirk, Neah Bay, Wash., 1975.

practices (Colson 1953; Gillis 1974), Makahs had discovered means to disguise and preserve outlawed Indian traditions. The shift of reservation power to the tribe allowed Makah language and culture an opportunity to regain a public place in Makah territory.

Some elders were concerned that Indian agency policies had disrupted the traditional transmission of information about Makah language and culture. By the 1960s, speakers held informal language and culture classes in the public elementary and high school on the reservation. This early effort grew into a Makah cultural renaissance in 1970, when excavation at the Ozette archeological site began to reveal the precontact life of Makah people (Renker and Arnold 1988).

Ozette, where a catastrophic mudslide buried five houses about A.D. 1500, has been extensively excavated (Kirk 1974; Huelsbeck 1983). Young Makahs in the earliest public school culture classes in the 1960s later worked with the investigative teams and received formal training and degrees in anthropology as college students (Renker and Arnold 1986). The interest generated in Makah language and culture, in addition to the sheer number of Ozette artifacts—50,000 artifacts, as well as countless structural remains and faunal samples—caused the tribe to commit its resources to the development of a tribal museum that would maintain and display the Ozette archeological collection. Plans evolved into a cultural center housing archival, linguistic, educational, and ethnographic research and outreach programs (Renker 1985). The Makah Cultural and Research Center (MCRC), opened in 1979, administered one of the most

active and successful language preservation programs in the United States. In operation for eight years in 1986, the Makah Language Program raised Makah language proficiency from 50 percent in adults and 33 percent in children in 1980 (Renker 1980) to 57 percent in adults and 78 percent in children in 1985 (Renker 1985). By 1986, elders and Makah instructors were conducting Makah language and culture classes for 297 children in the reservation's Headstart program and in grades kindergarten-12 in the public school system (Renker 1985a).

In 1986 the Makah Reservation encompassed approximately 44 square miles of land on the Olympic Peninsula. In addition, the tribe was granted in 1970 a one-square-mile reservation around the Ozette archeological site, and in 1984 Tatoosh and Waadah Islands were given back to Makah jurisdiction. In 1983, 811 of the 1,049 enrolled Makahs lived on the reservation (C. Hall 1983).

Synonymy

The name Makah is based on the Clallam *màq̓áʔa* (the tribal name, no other meaning known), which has been rendered Macau (ARCIA 1850:162), Ma-caw (ARCIA 1852:170), Mak-kah (Swan 1870:1), Mi-caw (D.F. Jones 1857:7), Maccaw (ARCIA 1858:337) and in other similar ways. This name has been in official use since the 1850s.

The Makah call themselves *qʷidičča̓ʔatx̱* 'residents of *qʷidičča*', a name said to refer to the Cape Flattery region (Swan 1870:1), to a place near Ozette (Waterman 1920a: 4), or, according to one older Makah in the 1960s, to the north end of Vancouver Island (William H. Jacobsen, communication to editors 1973). Swan (1870:1) recorded the name as Kwe-nēt-che-chat, with a nasal (n) for the voiced stop (d), perhaps the usual pronunciation in the mid-nineteenth century. Versions of this name were used by peoples to the south and are seen in the Chinook name recorded Quinechart, Quinnachart by Lewis and Clark (Thwaites 1904–1905,6:70, 4:169) and Que-nait′sath by Swan (1857:211) on Willapa Bay.

Eighteenth-century visitors knew the Makah as the people of *tutu·tš* 'thundering, one of three thunderbird brothers', a powerful chief (Tatoosh) identified with the island off Cape Flattery (fig. 8). The name was rendered Tatootche (Meares 1790:231), Tootooch (Hoskins 1941: 196), Tutusi (Moziño 1970:65), and in other spellings, and the island officially became Tatoosh. Moziño (1970:91) also used the name Tutusi for the Makah themselves, and this usage occurs later, as in Nicolay's (1846:143) Tatouche for the Makah.

The Makah have also been identified by versions of their Nootka name, *x̱a·ʔasʔatḥ* 'people outside, toward the sea' (Sapir and Swadesh 1939:148, 310), rendered Klaiz-zarts (Jewitt 1815:75), Classet (Farnham 1843, 2:310; Scouler 1848:235), Clatset (Dunn 1844:231), Clossets (ARCIA 1852:171), and Tlā′asath (Boas 1891:30). In *429*

Makah the term *λa·ʔasatx* 'southerly people' refers to tribes from Quileute southward (William H. Jacobsen, communication to editors 1973).

Sources

Precontact Makah life is documented by the reports from the Ozette archeological excavation (J. Friedman 1975; Mauger 1978, 1979; Gleeson 1980; Wessen 1982; Huelsbeck 1983; Gill 1983), which explore the complex links between procurement, processing, and utilization (Gleeson 1981) of resources and Makah social structure.

These sources are especially important in light of the scanty literature generated during the early contact and early historic periods. Gunther (1972) and Pethick (1980) present comprehensive accounts of the earliest Makah-European encounters. Other sources (Gibbs 1855a, 1877; Hancock 1927; Swan 1870; Densmore 1939; Colson 1953; Taylor 1974) offer discussions of Makah life in the early years of the reservation. Swan's (1859–1866) observations are invaluable as firsthand description of Makah life at a time when major aspects of the aboriginal culture were still highly visible. The descriptions of material culture and technology are more complete than his accounts of social and political organization or his explanations of ceremonies and inherited rights.

Makah sources include Wike (1958), Riley (1968), and Gunther (1962a) on social patterns; Lane (1973) on economy and the Makah treaty of 1855; Densmore (1939) and Goodman (1978) on songs and potlatches; Gunther (1936, 1945), Gill (1983), Renker and Gill (1985), and Gill and Renker (1985) on ethnobiology; and Colson (1953), Gillis (1974), Whitner (1977, 1984), and Miller (1952) on acculturation.

A large body of sources emerged from the research programs at the Makah Cultural and Research Center (Renker 1980–1985, 1980), the Makah Language Program, and from Jacobsen (1979b). Of special interest are the massive amounts of ethnographic information contained in the Makah Language Program curriculum (1981–1986) and in studies designed to update and correct previous work (Renker and Ward 1984; Gill 1983).

Quileute

JAMES V. POWELL

The Quileute ('kwĭlē,ōōt) speak a language* of the Chimakuan family, which consists of Quileute and the extinct Chemakum (J.W. Powell 1891:62–63). Linguistically homogeneous subdivisions of the Quileute live at the Quileute (La Push) and Lower Hoh River reservations on the Pacific coast of the Olympic Peninsula, Washington. In 1986 approximately 10 Quileute speakers remained.

Aboriginal Quileute territory extended from south of Cape Alava to Destruction Island (Powell and Jensen 1976:4; Powell and Woodruff 1976:488; Powell et al. 1972:105; Curtis 1907–1930, 9:175–176). Inland, it encompassed the drainages of the Quillayute River and its tributaries, along Jackson Creek and the Hoh River, and the south shore of Ozette Lake (fig. 1). Linguistic and toponymic evidence corroborate mythic references that suggest that the Cape Flattery area was controlled by Chimakuan peoples before the arrival of the Nootkans (Kinkade and Powell 1976:94–99). Some evidence supports statements made to Curtis (1907–1930, 9:176) and Frachtenberg (1916, notebook 3:115–121) that the people at Lower Hoh River originally spoke Quinault. The Quileute name for the Hoh River people (čalá·i) was sometimes used for the Quinaults as well, and the Quinault language is called čalá·l. However, place-names along the Hoh River are unquestionably of Chimakuan etymology and suggest a considerable period of Quileute usage there.

The entire region receives in excess of 110 inches of rainfall annually. Tangled rainforest vegetation extends from the seashore to the less dense fir, spruce, and red cedar forests at the river headwaters in the 5,000–8,000 feet heights of the Olympic Mountains. The natural beauty of the Quileute shorelands is so striking that, aside from the reservations at La Push and Lower Hoh River, the entire littoral is preserved as the Pacific Coast Area of Olympic National Park.

*The phonemes of Quileute are: (voiceless stops and affricates) p, t, c, ƛ, č, k, kʷ, q, qʷ, ʔ; (glottalized stops and affricates) p̓, t̓, c̓, ƛ̓, č̓, k̓, k̓ʷ, q̓, q̓ʷ; (voiced stops) b, d, g; (voiceless fricatives) s, ł, š, x, xʷ, x̣, x̣ʷ, h; (voiced continuants) w, l, y; (short vowels) i ([e], [ɛ], [ɪ], [i]), a ([a], [ə]), o ([o], [u]); (long vowels) i·, æ·, a·, o·; (stress) v́ (primary), v̀ (secondary). A description of Quileute sounds, using a practical orthography, is in Powell and Woodruff (1976:vii–xiv); a more complete technical treatment is in J.V. Powell (1975:20–32).

External Relations

Relations of trade and intermarriage existed, primarily with the Makah and Quinault. Occasional hostilities broke out due to trespassing or insult. Quileute raids were made as far north as Vancouver Island and south to Gray's Harbor. A fortress was maintained atop James Island, to which the Quileute retreated when attacked.

Culture

Subsistence

Although some Quileute families maintained settlements on the upriver prairies, most Quileutes wintered in permanent shed-roofed plank houses at the stream mouths. During warmer months (April–November) house groups would fragment into smaller nuclear family units, some of which moved upriver or along the coast to areas in which the family had hereditary hunting, fishing, and gathering rights. Some traveled as far as the halibut grounds at Tatoosh Island. Family groups often lived in cattail mat huts or brush lean-tos as they followed the annual subsistence cycle in gathering foods (including 16 types of fruits and berries, tuberous roots, edible sprouts and seaweed; see Reagan 1934, 1934b) and in collecting the raw materials of Quileute handicraft (spruce roots, hemlock, cedar, and willow bark, kelp, and a variety of reeds and grasses; see Gunther 1973).

Fishing was the primary subsistence activity, the adjacent waters providing five species of salmon, steelhead, halibut, smelt, trout, flounder, dog-fish, skate, octopus, and others. Remains of more than 50 species of shellfish have been discovered in the middens at La Push (Reagan 1917). Hunting land mammals, especially deer and elk, with the bow and arrow, deadfalls, and snares provided part of the Quileute diet. However, the hunting of marine mammals was considered the most characteristic occupation for Quileutes in late prehistoric times: whaling and hunting of hair seals, fur seals, sea lions, and porpoises (Reagan 1922; 1907–1930, 9:145–147; Frachtenberg 1916, notebook 3:88–126). The diet was supplemented by snared small game and birds, a variety of eggs

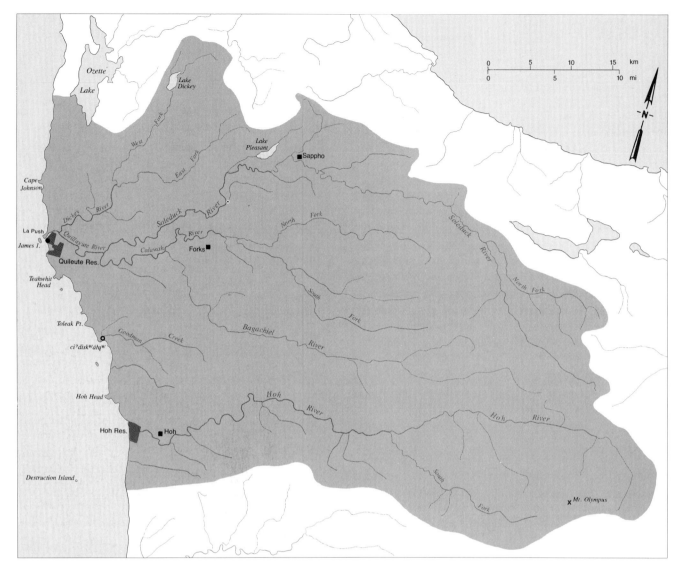

Fig. 1. Territory of the Quileute in the mid-19th century.

(primarily seagull), camas, and other edibles. The Quileute traded camas and sea mammal blubber for oysters (from Puget Sound), sockeye salmon (from Quinault), and eulachon grease (from the north via the Makah and other Nootkans). Bearberry (kinnickinnick) was gathered for smoking.

Political and Social Organization

The social stratification distinguished a hereditary class of chiefs and those in line for family headship (*pił̓áqłi*), commoners (*cíx pó · ʔoqʷ*), and slaves (*ʔá · woqʷoł̓*) procured in raids or trading. Village politics revolved around the pursuit and maintenance of individual and family status. Two hereditary village chiefs with equal powers were recognized. The nature of village leadership is reflected in the word for 'chief', *ʔá · čit*, which also connotes 'rich' and 'head of family'. Besides wealth and the generosity that it allowed, the criteria of rank and prestige included the rights to names, dances, songs, and designs, the proven assistance of guardian spirit powers, and membership in secret societies.

Extended families had their territorial rights and their heads, but they seem not to have had separate myths or symbols. Although Farrand (1910:340) believed there was evidence for an earlier "clan system," Frachtenberg (1916, notebook 4:39) found no basis for such a claim.

Kinship was reckoned bilaterally with lineal terminology (that is, mothers and aunts, both mother's and father's sisters, are called by different terms) and Hawaiian or generation type terminology (sister and all cousins called by same term) with distinctions between elder and younger siblings. Ten different types of marriage were recognized, including levirate and sororate. Residence was usually patrilocal. Polygamy and divorce were common, and premarital intercourse was strongly discouraged.

432

Life Cycle

Pregnancy and childbirth were attended by taboos affecting the diet and demeanor of both parents. Mothers gave birth sitting up, with the help of midwives. The umbilical cord was not tied, and afterbirth was ceremoniously hidden with gifts. Eight months of taboos followed the birth of twins in a family. Cradleboards were used and noble families attached a padded headpiece to flatten and slope the forehead. Traits of cleanliness, moderation, and generosity were taught the young through stories and tasks. Games of skill and competition developed endurance, dexterity, and a taste for adult games of chance or prepared boys for spirit questing, which they would begin in their late teens. At puberty, girls were confined in a screened corner of the house for five days.

The dead were buried in canoes or hollow logs above ground. Mourners cut hair and painted their faces with ocher. Widows observed taboos such as being forbidden to sleep lying down. Name taboo was practiced, the family asking others with the same or similar names as the deceased to adopt another name. Representations of the guardian spirits of the deceased were destroyed, and personal effects of the dead were either burned or disbursed with the assumption that they would be taken away from the village.

Ceremonies

The Quileute had five ceremonial societies that were identified with occupational groups and served as ritual dance fraternities, and leadership of a society was a source of prestige. Membership could be bought by holding a status-validating potlatch (ʔixʷá·q̇ol) or by showing evidence of a guardian spirit power appropriate to the particular group. The societies in order of prestige (Frachtenberg 1921) were: λokʷá·li, Wolf ritual or Black Face Society for warriors (fig. 2); ćá·yiq, fishermens' ritual; qiλáʔkʷał, hunters' society; sibàxʷolá·yoʔ, whale hunters' society, literally 'oily voiced'; and čalá·layoʔ, weathermen's society, literally 'southern song or voice'. The first two societies are identical in name and similar in their performances to the Wolf ritual and the Doctoring ritual of the Nootkans of Vancouver Island and the Makah, and they are probably of Makah origin. The fourth is believed to be a late prehistoric adoption from the Makah, and the last is a Quinault tradition, the songs of this group being sung in the Quinault language. Thought to antedate the introduction of the other groups, the hunters' society is of Quileute origin. Initiations to these ceremonial societies took place primarily during the winter months (hence, the term winter ceremonials) and were generally accompanied by potlatches.

The potlatch-like feast (haʔwókʷsil) also accompanied naming ceremonies, births, and marriages, a child's coming of age or assuming inherited honors, memorials for the dead, or periodic maintenance of claims to property rights. These ceremonies lasted four to six days. Invited guests were reimbursed according to their status for witnessing the event, and individuals or families sponsoring the potlatch achieved status according to the amount of distributed wealth.

Technology and Art

The most extensive museum collections of Quileute artifacts are of basketry and weaving: twined watertight boiling baskets, openwork pack baskets with tumpline, and rainhats (of spruce root), twilled and twined storage baskets (vine maple limbs, cedar bark, and bear grass), mats (cattail and swamp grasses), skirts and capes (cedar bark), and a variety of dolls and figurines. A waterproofing treatment of boiled hemlock bark was often applied. Blankets were woven of fiber and occasionally of mountain goat wool, apparently obtained in trade from the Cascades area. Frachtenberg (1916, notebook 1:65) mentions memory of wool-bearing dogs at La Push in precontact times. Skins often substituted for blankets and also provided capes, drumheads, sealskin floats, and trim on clothing. Ropes and strings were made from spruce root, cedar withes, nettle fiber, whale sinew, and kelp.

Quileute carvers made and often decorated bent-corner boxes, platters, dishes, bailers, fishhooks, rattles, masks, and headdresses. Hunting equipment included harpoons (one a three-pointed sealing harpoon), lances, bows and arrows, and clubs, most of which did dual purpose as weaponry. Canoes of red cedar in six sizes were recognized, primarily of the Nootka (Chinook) type, and they made a variety of paddles. Both the straight and D-adz were used in carving and hollowing out trees (fig. 3) felled by controlled burning and split with yew wedges.

The Quileute decorated houseposts with representations of guardian spirits, which also appear on shamans' spirit figures and wands. Earlier they did not erect carvings outside the houses or at graveyards, although a few crude welcoming figures and thunderbird-whale carvings were done early in the twentieth century. Motifs common to Nootkan art were used in decoration, but features of the Northern Northwest Coast style were known only through trade items and apparently copied roughly. Geometric and representational designs were carved into tools and utensils, woven into basketry, and applied to wooden pieces by patterned hammering of teeth (usually sea otter) into the surface. Tattoos were not uncommon, and body painting was practiced during ceremonials. Rock art has not been found in Quileute territory.

Stone was used in hammers, mortars, scrapers, and in fashioning dolls for children. Mussel shell provided harpoon points and knives. Antler served as awls and

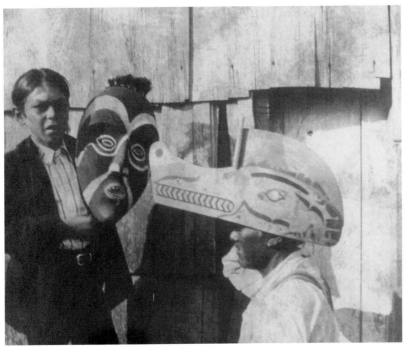

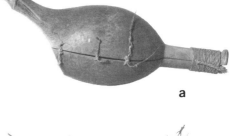

a

b

c

d

434

Smithsonian, NAA: top left, 86–11558; top right, 86–11557; center left, 86–4118; U. of Pa., U. Mus: a, NA 2329; c, NA 2314; b, Smithsonian, Dept. of Anthr.: 299067; d, Mus. of the Amer. Ind., Heye Foundation, New York: 10/8080.

Fig. 2. Ceremonies and ceremonial equipment. top left, Dance of the Black Face Society. Some of the dancers are dressed as wolves, while others are outfitted with salal branches and blow bark whistles (Reagan 1907:sec. 9:61–65). Drawing by Jimmie C. Hobucket, Quileute Day School, Mora, Wash., 1906–1907. top right, Contest of two medicine men to show which has more power. They might grapple with invisible objects, make objects disappear, pick up and carry scorching hot stones, handle fire, dance on burning objects, or drink buckets of water or oil (Reagan 1907:sec. 10:8). Drawing by Ernest Y. Obi, Quileute Day School, Mora, Wash., 1907. center left, Men displaying masks, probably of the Black Face Society (Powell and Jensen 1976:46). Photograph by Albert B. Reagan, La Push, Wash., 1903–1907. a, Rattle carved in stylized bird form, of the type used to accompany singing. Pebbles fill the two hollowed out wooden sections. Collected before 1914; length 57 cm. b, Head ring of the Black Face Society, worn by a man who owned a guardian spirit. Ring and tresses are cedar bark, from which are suspended clam shell rattles. Collected before 1917; length 52 cm. c, Dance skirt with a sea otter skin waist band and dyed porcupine quill-wrapped thongs ending in deer hoof tinklers. Collected before 1914; length 57 cm. d, Large mask that may have been used in secret society initiations, since leaders of the Wolf ritual of the Black Face Society originally wore only "round face masks" (Pettitt 1950:15). Collected before 1921: height 30 cm.

scrapers. Bone was used in adz handles, borers, and the bones of the bone game (slahal). Other gaming equipment included beaver-tooth dice and wooden disks. Hemlock bark slabs were fashioned into buckets and troughs for stone boiling.

Weirs and drag, dip, and gill nets were made. Engineering was involved in building the horizontally planked, shed-roofed, excavated houses and in constructing fish traps and deadfalls.

Cosmology and Shamanism

The world was conceptualized as including a nature-universe essence (*čiq̓á·ti*) and a creator-transformer (*q̓ʷá·ti*), a variety of monsters and myth creatures (Frachtenberg 1916, notebook 5:18–43), ghosts of the dead (*yalá·*), and spirit-powers (*t̓axí·lit*) that instructed, empowered, and variously affected the lives of the Quileute. Individuals often claimed numerous guardian spirits, acquired either by spirit questing or being adopted by a spirit-power (such as that of an ancestor). Also, everyone had a soul (*titipá?d*) that left at death to journey to the underworld and inner (*ƚibìtitipá?d*) and outer (*t̓áxƚis titipá?d*) personal spirit shadows, replicas of the body that dwelt in the person.

Either or both of these spirit shadows could be kidnapped or lured away by sinister spirit-powers directed by shamans, or they might simply wander away from their owner's body. Shamanistic medicine was then necessary to recover the spirits and replace them. Bodily injuries and sores were also sometimes treated by shamans (although herbal remedies, charms, and amulets were also common), who drew their powers from spirits living along a river to the southeast protected by five mighty rapids.

Mythology and Music

The Quileute are the most southerly group on the coast to have a myth cycle in which Raven (*bá·yaq*) serves as culture hero; Blue Jay (*k̓ʷášk̓ʷaš*) appears as trickster in the mythology of all groups south of the Quileute. However, Raven is by no means so strong a protagonist in Quileute myth as he is in the mythologies of the northern groups. For instance, the theft of light and creation are attributed in Quileute myth to *q̓ʷá·ti*, who created

Quileutes from wolves. Thunder and lightning and certain rains were caused by Thunderbird (*t̓ístilal*), whose lair was the Blue Glacier on Mount Olympus. High tide was caused by *dásk̓iya*, the kelp-haired child snatcher, and eclipses were caused by one of a host of other monsters biting away chunks of the sun or moon. The stars were people and formed a tribe of their own. A legendary flood had separated the Quileute from the Chemakum, and various legendary ancestors were revered and thought to linger as spirits in the region.

Quileute songs were inheritable personal property. Singing was accompanied with whistles; deer hoof, shell, and carved rattles; drums; and drumming planks. In addition to spirit songs there were gaming songs, love ditties, and lullabies. In myth narration, mythic characters often sang personal songs, and various formalized narrational styles were used to distinguish characters (Frachtenberg 1920a).

History

Early contacts with Europeans earned the Quileutes a reputation for ferocity. The Spanish schooner *Sonora* in 1775 and the British *Imperial Eagle* in 1787 both lost landing parties in the Hoh River area. In 1808 a Russian-American Company ship, *Sviatoi Nikolai*, was wrecked off the mouth of the Quillayute River, and the survivors spent some months in Hoh country, mainly as slaves. Most were ransomed by American traders (Owens 1985).

In 1855 Quileute met with representatives of Gov. Isaac I. Stevens of Washington Territory and subsequently signed a treaty with the United States, according to which they were to move to the Quinault reservation (Kappler 1904–1941, 2:719–721). Apparently misunderstanding the provisions of the treaties, Quileutes were still "unremoved" in 1889, and in that year President Grover Cleveland signed an executive order setting up a one-mile square reservation for the 252 inhabitants at La Push. Four years later, the 71 inhabitants at Hoh River were provided with a reservation.

Some Quileute children went to Neah Bay to attend the school established by James G. Swan in 1864, but this arrangement was not satisfactory, and in 1882 a school was set up at La Push. A.W. Smith, first schoolmaster, was responsible for providing Quileutes with names from

Fig. 3. Ted Hudson making a canoe from a cedar log. This type of canoe is sometimes equipped with an outboard motor and used for river travel, fishing, and racing. The hull was first roughed out with a power saw. top left, Making a series of cuts through the center with the saw, so that the wood can be split out with an ax. top right, Using the ax to hollow out the center. The chips were left in to keep the bottom from drying out and cracking. bottom left, D-adz, with a traditional carved whalebone handle and a modern single-bitted ax blade, bound with commercial line, used for finishing the bottom of the canoe. bottom right, Using a drawknife to finish off the bow, which is a separate piece added to the hull. The patch of sheet metal where the bow is secured to the hull is nontraditional, as is the use of hardwood from a lumber yard for the rubrail on the gunwale. Canoe making, which Ted Hudson learned from his father, was a craft followed by only the best carvers (Pettitt 1950:52). Photographs by Ruth Kirk, mouth of Hoh River, Wash., about 1964.

the Bible and American history. All 26 houses at La Push were destroyed in a fire in 1889, causing the loss of nearly all precontact artifacts.

The Indian Shaker religion, introduced in Quileute territory around 1895, was embraced with such fervor that in 1905 Indian agents advised local authorities to limit meetings to three two-hour sessions a week. The constitution and by-laws of the Quileute Tribe, adopted in 1936, and the corporate charter of 1937 recognize the Quileute people as an independent, self-governing political unit within the United States. On the Quileute Reservation the tribal council consists of five members elected to three-year terms, and a similar governing body acts at Lower Hoh River. A number of tribally owned economic ventures were undertaken at La Push beginning in the mid-1970s, including a fish-buying company, cooperative store, trailer park, and fishing gear store to supply salmon trollers that harbor at La Push during the commercial fishing season. Visited during warmer months by thousands of tourists, the Quileute shorelands revert to quiet

436

Indian villages in the rainy winter months. Most Quileutes have remained fishermen, although a few have regularly worked in the lumbering industries of the area.

In 1985 there were 383 Quileutes at La Push and about 91 residents at Lower Hoh River (U.S. Bureau of Indian Affairs. Financial Management Office 1985).

Synonymy

The name Quileute is from *kʷoʔlí·yot*, the name for the village at the site of La Push; its literal meaning is unclear. An alternate spelling Quillayute has also been used locally, and early recordings include Kwilleʹhiūt and Kwe-dée-tut (Gibbs 1877:173), and Quilahutes and (misprinted) Kuille-pates (Farrand 1910:340).

The name Hoh is apparently derived from *hóx*, the Quinault name for these people; the meaning is unknown. Variant spellings include Hūch and Hooch, and they have also been called Kwāāksat (Gibbs 1877:173; Farrand 1907a:556).

Sources

The earliest information on the Quileute is found in Timofei Tarakanov's account of his shipwreck, flight, and captivity of 1808–1809 (Owens 1985). James G. Swan (1861, 1881) reported on fishing activities (see also L. McDonald 1972).

Frachtenberg visited La Push in 1915–1916, making extensive ethnographic notes and collecting museum specimens. His manuscripts are extant (1916), and he wrote on Quileute beliefs (1920), narrational voice techniques (1920a), and secret societies (1921). The schoolmaster at La Push from 1905 to 1909, Albert B. Reagan, described Quileute ethnobotany (1934b, 1934), fishing (1922), whaling (1925), and other aspects of Indian life (1911, 1934a). His manuscripts are in the archives of Brigham Young University, Provo, Utah. Reagan also provided a corpus of Quileute (1929, 1934c, 1935; Reagan and Walters 1933) myths, but not so carefully edited nor so extensive as that compiled by Andrade (1931), a work which includes many stories collected by Frachtenberg. Other legends were published by a Quileute, Harry Hobucket (1934), and by Farrand (1919).

Ernst (1952), includes a discussion of Quileute ritual in her study of the Wolf ceremonial, and Densmore (1939) collected Quileute songs at Neah Bay. Botanical lore was published in Gunther's (1973) ethnobotany, supplemented by Powell and Woodruff (1973). Pettitt (1950) gives an account of Quileute history and life at La Push in the early 1940s. The aboriginal economic system is described by Singh (1966). Ray (1973) identified Quileute and Hoh village sites and resource gathering areas. Daugherty (1949) recorded Hoh ethnographic data. Data on fishing are summarized by Lane (1973). At the request of the La Push tribal council, Powell and Jensen (1976) prepared an introduction to the Quileutes for outsiders.

Curtis (1907–1930, 9), who describes Quileute life in general, took a word list and list of Quileute village sites. Other place-names were made available by Powell et al. (1972). First serious linguistic research was undertaken by Frachtenberg (1916), but Andrade's (1933) grammar was the first published account of the Quileute language.

The Quileute Culture Committee has produced grammatical workbooks (J.V. Powell 1975a, 1976), a dictionary (Powell and Woodruff 1976), and children's bilingual books (Jensen and McLaren 1976) as part of the program to provide teaching materials on language and culture.

Historical material is found in the papers of A.W. Smith at the Washington State Library, Olympia. Important museum collections are in the Smithsonian Institution; Museum of the American Indian, Heye Foundation, New York; Burke Memorial Washington State Museum, Seattle; and the Field Museum of Natural History, Chicago.

Chemakum

WILLIAM W. ELMENDORF

The Chemakum ('chĕməkəm, less frequently 'chĭməkəm) were a small tribe or village community at the northeastern corner of the Olympic Peninsula, Washington. By the early twentieth century the Chemakum had disappeared as a separate people; their language was no longer spoken, and their descendants had become absorbed by the Clallam, the Twana, and the larger non-Indian society.

Language

The Chemakum language* has been grouped with Quileute in a Chimakuan family (Swan 1861; Eells 1889:646; Powell 1891:62–63). In the middle of the nineteenth century all neighboring native groups were speakers of Coast Salish languages: Clallam to the west, along the Strait of Juan de Fuca, Lushootseed to the east and southeast, and Twana to the south, in the Hood Canal area. Salish influence on Chemakum, in vocabulary and possibly other features, is apparent (Eells 1880:52, 1886-1888:5–6; Swadesh 1955). However, the Chemakum language is not a member of the Salishan family, and its clear relation to the territorially separated Quileute carries implications for the prehistory of native populations in the Olympic Peninsula region.

Territory and Environment

Aboriginally the territory of the Chemakum comprised the immediate area around Port Townsend and Hadlock Bay, and probably a section of shore south to Port Ludlow. How much more extensive it may have been at one time is uncertain. Spier (1936:33, 42–43 map) shows their area as extending from the mouth of Hood Canal, north of Port Gamble, north to the present town of Port Townsend and west to Discovery Bay (fig. 1). This is probably too large an area to represent Chemakum occupation in mid-nineteenth century. Spier's mapping

*The phonemes of Chemakum are assumed to have been as follows: (voiceless stops and affricates) p, t, c, č, kʷ, q, qʷ, ʔ; (glottalized stops and affricates) p̓, t̓, c̓, ƛ̓, č̓, k̓ʷ, q̓, q̓ʷ; (voiceless fricatives) s, ł, š, xʷ, x, x̣ʷ, h; (nasals) m, n; (voiced resonants) w, l, y; (short vowels) i, a, o; (long vowels) i·, a·, o·; (stress) v́. The inventory of Chemakum phonemes is based on the analysis by J.V. Powell (1975:32–36) of the recordings by Boas and Andrade.

appears to be based on varying statements of Gibbs (1855: 430–431, 1877:167, 177) and Eells (1881:301–302, 1886-1888:5–6, 1889:606–607).

It would appear from other evidence (for example, Gunther 1927:177–178) that Discovery Bay was an area of Clallam occupation well before 1850, and it is safest to regard Chemakum territory in the 1840s as according with Gibbs's (1855:431) statement of "the shore from Port Townsend to Port Ludlow." Curtis (1907–1930,9:3) is in error in describing the Chemakum as "on the Strait of Juan de Fuca in the neighborhood of Port Angeles." J.M. Collins (1949:150–151) sought to extend Chemakum territory northeastward through the San Juan Islands on the basis of what may have been a misrecorded or misinterpreted place-name; her hypothesis was criticized by Suttles (1957a:166–167).

Within the Chemakum area there was a single village, čičabus, near the head of Hadlock Bay, surrounded by a stockade (Elmendorf 1940: item 36; Eells 1886-1888:5–6, 1889:606–607, as Tse´ts-i-bus). A Twana name for the isthmus between Hadlock Bay and Oak Bay was recorded as łaławəltəbáxʷ, possibly interpretable as 'portage country' (Elmendorf 1940: item 5.13).

The Port Townsend region is within the rain shadow extending northeast from the Olympic Mountains and is one of the driest portions of western Washington. It contains one small stream, Chimacum Creek. A folktale, from a Twana source, describes the Chemakum as undergoing a drought, their creek running dry, and saved from hunger by an underwater being who marries one of their girls (Elmendorf 1961:128–130). Compared with surrounding regions, Chemakum country seems to have been relatively restricted, not only in size but also in resources.

Culture History and Population

There is virtually no specific ethnographic information on the Chemakum. Gibbs (1877:178) says, simply, "In their modes of subsistence, habits, etc., they do not differ noticeably from their neighbors." Most of the meager available data deal with implications of their linguistic position or with factors in their catastrophic decline as a people in the second half of the nineteenth century. Early observers remarking on the population phenomenon stress

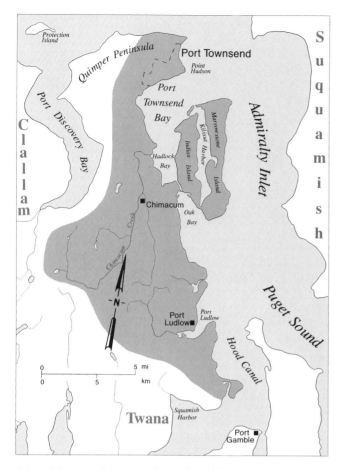

Fig. 1. Territory of the Chemakum before 1840.

belligerence, intertribal warfare, and disease as major causes. The Chemakum, who had warred at one time or another with Makah, Clallam, Twana, Snohomish, and Duwamish are described as "very troublesome neighbors, and on bad terms with all" (Gibbs 1877:191).

By the time they came to the attention of White observers, the Chemakum seemed to be losing social cohesion and declining in numbers. It is possible that their disintegration as a community dates from the late 1840s, after a devastating raid on their stockaded village by the Suquamish, from Puget Sound. Gibbs (1855:431) calls them "formerly one of the most powerful tribes of the Sound, but which, a few years since [about 1847–1848] is said to have been very nearly destroyed at a blow by an attack of the Snoqualmoos [Snoqualmies]. Their numbers have been probably much diminished by the wars in which they were constantly engaged." Elsewhere Gibbs (1877: 191) identifies the attackers as Suquamish. Curtis (1907–1930, 9:141–143) and Elmendorf (1940: item 36) obtained traditional accounts of this affair, from a Suquamish and a Twana informant, respectively. Both accounts indicate that the Chemakum survivors, including the chief, joined the Skokomish, on Hood Canal. However, Chemakum were present in their original area some years later, although apparently in diminished

numbers. The chief, General Gaines, reported 73 in 1860 (table 1).

Gibbs reported on March 4, 1854 (1855:431) that the Chemakum "now occupy some fifteen small lodges on Port Townsend Bay, and number perhaps seventy in all. Lately, the Clallams have taken possession of their country, and they are, in a measure, subject to them." In 1860 they were living in 18 lodges in a camp at Point Hudson, where they were intermixed with Clallam. During this period the Chemakum signed the Treaty of Point No Point (1855) with the Clallam and the Twana-Skokomish; however, few if any of them seem to have taken up residence on the Skokomish Reservation, Washington Territory, as provided in the treaty.

It is fairly clear that, after 1850, one factor in the decline and ultimate disappearance of the Chemakum was their assimilation by other ethnic groups. Despite earlier hostilities, the Chemakum remnant seems, during the second half of the nineteenth century, to have largely married into other Indian communities. Eells (1884:35, 37) mentions 16 Chemakums married to Clallams (fig. 2), and 9 to Twanas. These intermarriages were apparently accompanied by loss of language and of ethnic identity.

Linguistic Relationships

Chemakum and Quileute traditions agree in asserting an original connection of the two peoples, which accords with their special linguistic relationship. A legend shared by both tribes derived the Chemakum from the Quileute as a section of the Quileute whose canoes broke away and drifted eastward to Port Townsend during a tidal inundation (Swan 1857:344; Eells 1880:52, 1886-1888:5–6; 1889: 606–607). Curtis (1907–1930, 9:149–150) and Andrade (1931:200–203) present Quileute accounts of the Chemakum separation following a deluge. The folktale motif of separation in a flood is widespread in the region and by no means confined to the two Chimakuan groups; it cannot be taken as historical evidence that the Chemakum wandered or drifted east from the Quileute homeland. However, its occurrence does indicate recognition of a

Table 1. Population

Date	Numbers	Source
1841	70[a]	Gibbs 1855:435
1854	70	Gibbs 1855:435
1855	90	Gibbs 1877:177
1857	95–100	ARCIA 1858:337, 335
1860	73	Swan 1859–1866: item for Oct. 25, 1860
1870	27	Eells 1889:612
1878	13	Eells 1889:612
1881	15–20	Eells 1881:301–302
1887	7+	Eells 1886-1888:5–6
1890	3 speakers	Boas 1892:37

[a]Port Townsend area.

Smithsonian, NAA: 3040-b.

Fig. 2. Studio portrait probably from a daguerreotype. Ketsap on left (Clallam), his wife Souscitsa, and her sister or daughter, Wiltoh, in center. Both women were identified as Chemakum. Their Euro-American style clothing at this early date emphasizes their early acculturation. Photographed in Port Townsend, Washington Terr., 1860.

special relationship between the two groups separated in the nineteenth century by approximately 90 miles of mountainous Olympic Peninsula.

Between the Chemakum and the Quileute were the Salishan Clallam, along the south shore of the Strait of Juan de Fuca, from Discovery Bay west to Hoko River. West of these, the Nootkan Makah occupied the Neah Bay area, at the tip of the Olympic Peninsula. Both peoples may have been intrusive in the region, from the north; the Makah from the west coast and the Clallam from the southern end of Vancouver Island, areas where in both cases their closest linguistic relatives are found. If so, it is then plausible to assume an earlier continuous distribution of Chimakuan-speaking peoples through at least the northern part of the Olympic Peninsula. This hypothesis (Farrand 1907:269) would see the two Chimakuan groups as the western and eastern end remnants of a once more widespread speech family.

The degree of relationship between the Chemakum and Quileute languages was characterized by Andrade (1953:212) as comparable to that between English and German, and as less close than that between Spanish and Italian.

Swadesh (1955:60) found 41 percent agreement between the two in a basic-vocabulary test list and inferred a date of about 21 elapsed centuries since they began to diverge from one another. This glottochronological date, approximate at best, need not refer to the putative Clallam intrusion; Quileute and Chemakum may already have been linguistically separate when they became territorially separated. But, drifted-canoe traditions aside, it does appear that Chimakuan may once, some centuries ago, have been the linguistic family of northwestern Washington.

Synonymy

The name Chemakum is an anglicization of the term for this people in several Salish languages; Twana čə́bqəb (Elmendorf 1940:item 36, 1960:296, cf. Chŭbakŭb in Curtis 1907–1930, 9:171), Lushootseed čə́bəqəb (Hess 1976:90), which also appears in Quileute as číbeqib for the place, and číbeqibiʔ for the people (Andrade 1931: 200–203). Eells (1889:606–607) was unable to learn any etymology for this ethnic name. The Chemakums' own term for themselves was given by Eells (1887:5–6, 1889: 606) as aʹ-hwa-ki-lu; by Boas (1892:37) as axoqúlo (in modern transcription); by Swadesh (1955:63, from Boas's material) as ʔaxu·qulu·.

Chemakum (Swan 1857:344; ARCIA 1860:335; Eells 1879:250, 1881:301, 1889:607; Boas 1892:37; Andrade 1931:200; Spier 1936:33) has been rendered Chimakum (Gibbs 1855:431; Powell 1891:62–63; Farrand 1907:269; Curtis 1907–1930, 9:11–13), Chimicum (ARCIA 1860: 395, 398), and Tsemakum (Gibbs 1877:177, 191). (For other variations and presumable misprints see Farrand 1907:269.) The Chemakum have also been identified as the Port Townsend (Gibbs 1855:435).

Sources

There are at least two sets of manuscript materials. One of these includes a vocabulary by George Gibbs (1853) and linguistic material recorded by Franz Boas (1890a). A second valuable set of data was recorded by Manuel Andrade (1928, 1930–1953), in the course of rechecking some of Boas's notes with his informant of 40 years before. The Gibbs, Boas, and Andrade materials are in the American Philosophical Society Library, Philadelphia; J.V. Powell (1972) has used them for linguistic analysis.

Notes on Chemakum appear in the notebooks of Eells (1985).

Northern Coast Salish

DOROTHY I.D. KENNEDY AND RANDALL T. BOUCHARD

The Northern Coast Salish are the speakers of the Comox ('kō,mäks), Pentlatch ('pĕnt,lăch), and Sechelt ('sē,shĕlt) languages, three closely related members of the Central division of the Salishan family.* In 1792 Northern Coast Salish territory included roughly the northern half of the Strait of Georgia, from Bute Inlet and Johnstone Strait southward to Parksville on Vancouver Island and Roberts Creek on the mainland (fig. 1). Comox was spoken by groups identifiable as the Island Comox, at that time on Vancouver Island from Kelsey Bay to Cape Lazo and the islands at the northern end of the Strait of Georgia, and the Mainland Comox, comprising the Homalco (hō'mălkō), Klahoose (klu'hōōs), and Sliammon (slī'ămən) people on the mainland shores and inlets as far south as Lang Bay.

Component Groups

Island Comox

Formerly the Island Comox consisted of at least five named groups. Those whose locations are known are: the Sasitla, said to have spent the summer at Salmon River and the winter at Cape Mudge; the Tatpoos, on the northern part of Quadra Island; the Kaake, on the southern part of Quadra Island; the Eeksen, on Oyster Bay south of Campbell River; and the Kakekt, in the vicinity of Kye Bay and Cape Lazo. But beginning in the mid-1700s, apparently, the territory of the northernmost groups was gradually usurped by the Lekwiltok, a Kwakiutl tribe. Warfare, combined with epidemics, further depopulated the Island Comox in the early 1800s. By this time the remaining Island Comox were wintering mostly in two villages, one in the vicinity of Cape Mudge and the other at Campbell River. In summer they dispersed to at least 10 sites throughout their former territory. Among these sites were Salmon River, a village that seems to have been occupied in the early 1800s by both Lekwiltok and Island Comox people, and Comox Harbour, a village then occupied by both the Island Comox and Pentlatch. By the mid-1800s, all Island Comox territory was under the control of the Lekwiltok (Barnett 1955:25; Boas 1887a:131-132, 1888:201; Taylor and Duff 1956). By the late 1800s the Island Comox had been acculturated into the Kwakiutl. The Comox band is considered a Kwakiutl band.

By the 1980s, there was only one speaker of the Island Comox dialect.

Mainland Comox

The Homalco had winter villages in Bute Inlet near the mouths of the Homathko and Southgate rivers and on Orford Bay; the Klahoose had winter villages in Toba Inlet on Brem Bay and along the Toba River; and the Sliammon had two main winter villages, at Grace Harbour and at Sliammon Creek.

By the 1920s, Church House on Sonora Island and Orford Bay were the only Homalco villages, apart from a very small settlement on Maurelle Island (Kennedy and Bouchard 1983:89). The Klahoose by the 1920s had abandoned all their Toba Inlet villages, except for one at the mouth of the Toba River, and resided instead either at Squirrel Cove or at Sliammon Creek.

All the inlet villages were abandoned by the mid-1950s. By the 1980s, the population of Church House was reduced to one family, and only a handful of people lived at Squirrel Cove. Most of the Mainland Comox population was living on the Sliammon Indian Reserve (table 1). *441*

*The phonemes of Comox are: (plain stops and affricates) p, t, θ, č, ƛ, k, kʷ, q, qʷ, ʔ; (glottalized stops and affricates) ṗ, ƚ̇, θ̇, ċ, ƛ̇, ḱ, ḱʷ, q̇, q̇ʷ; (voiced affricate and stop) ǯ, g; (voiceless continuants) s, θ, š, ɫ, xʷ, x, x̣ʷ, h; (resonants) m, n, l, w, y; (glottalized resonants) ṁ, ṅ, l̇, ẇ, ẏ; (short vowels) i ([i] to [ɛ]), a, u ([u] to [ç]), ə; (long vowels) i· ([ɛ·]), a·, u·; (stress) v́. This inventory follows the listing in Kennedy and Bouchard (1983:147-148).

The phonemes of Sechelt are: (plain stops and affricates) p, t, c, č, k, kʷ, q, qʷ, ʔ; (glottalized stops and affricates) ṗ, ƚ̇, ċ, c̣, ƛ̇, ḱ, ḱʷ, q̇, q̇ʷ; (voiceless continuants) s, š, ɫ, x, xʷ, x̣, x̣ʷ, h; (resonants) m, n, l, w, y; (glottalized resonants) ṁ, ṅ, l̇, ẇ, ẏ; (vowels) i ([i] to [e]), a, u ([u] to [o]), ə· (stress) v́. In the practical orthography used by the Sechelt Band Language Committee and in local language programs these phonemes are spelt: p, t, ts, ch, k, kw, k̲, k̲w, ʔ (or 7); p', t', ts', ch', tl', k', kw', k̲', k̲w'; s, sh, lh, x, xw, x̲, x̲w, h; m, n, l, w, y; i, a, u, e; v́. The glottalized resonants are not represented in this orthography, as they were distinct phonemes only in the speech of the oldest speakers in the 1980s when it was established. Information on Sechelt phonemes and orthography is from Beaumont (1985:3-13).

Pentlach, which had a similar phoneme inventory, was extinct in the 1980s. All italicized Comox and Sechelt words are transcribed by Randy Bouchard.

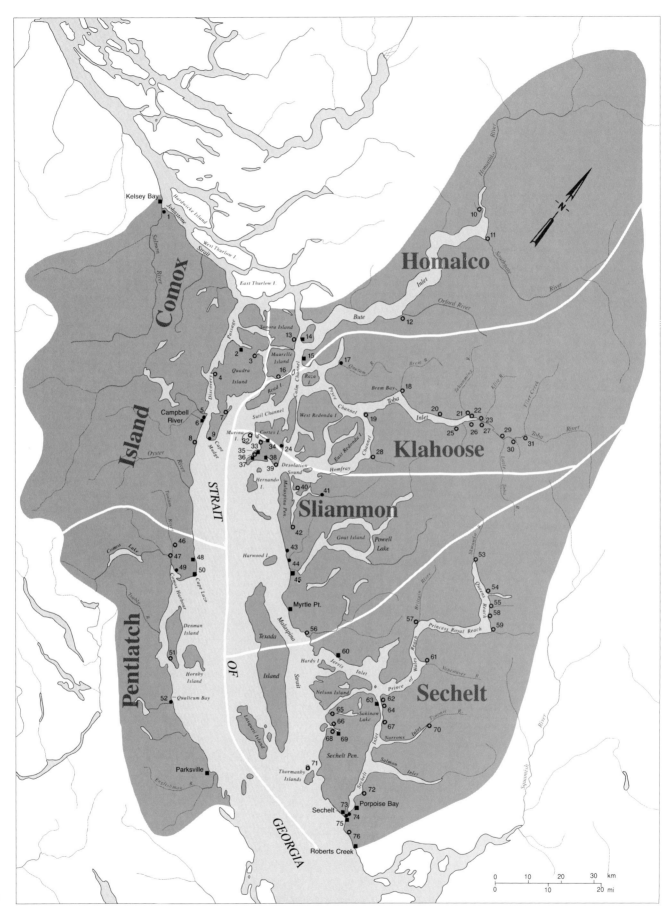

Fig. 1. Late 18th-century territory and primary villages of the Northern Coast Salish. Island Comox villages: 1, xʷə́sam 'having fat or oil', Salmon River Res.; 2, qáṅis, Granite Bay; 3, gáẏat, Waiatt Bay; 4, qáʔgičn 'bent over back'; 5, ƛáṁhatəxʷ, Campbell River Res.; 6, kʷútxʷiqʷ 'hollow point', Campbell River; 7, žíˑičn 'cross over back', Drew Harbour Res.; 8, Willow Point; 9, čqʷúwutn 'Indian-game place', Cape Mudge Res.   Homalco villages: 10, xʷə́maɫkʷu 'swift water', Homalco Res.; 11, míˑmáẏa; 12, píʔpqnəč 'white a little bit on the back end', Orford Bay Res.; 13, múˑšqin, Old Church House, Mushkin Res.; 14, číčxʷiẏaqaɫ 'clear passage in between', Stuart Is.; 15, ɫɫuqʷəm 'basin shaped', ʔuʔp, Church House, Aupe Res.; 16, ɫáɫpuʔus 'goes dry a little bit on the face side', Tatpo-ose Res.   Klahoose villages: 17, páɫxen 'flat open area', Deep Valley Res.; 18, qʷiqʷtičanam 'having lots of humpback salmon', Salmon Bay Res.; 19, sáyip 'water passage between two points', Brettell Pt.; 20, ʔiẏqsn 'point of land'; 21, qíxʔə́min 'slide place'; 22, ƛə́mƛəms 'many houses', Klahoose Res.; 23, híháymin 'canoe-making place', Klahoose Res.; 24, tuʔqʷ, Tork Res.; 25, híwʔə́min 'place to throw things into fire'; 26, sísʔúˑmin 'shake splitting place', Klahoose Res.; 27, xáʔẑəys 'rock', Klahoose Res.; 28, ʔáˑpúkʷm 'having maggots', Ahpokum Res.; 29, xʷə́θə́yin 'long cross over'; 30, náˑθúwəm; 31, nɪ́šʔuˑθin 'in middle at mouth'. Sliammon villages (as named by Klahoose speakers): 32, šítqáʔẑi 'tie rope around tree'; 33, yípiˑkʷu, 'break ice', Gorge Harbour entrance; 34, sáẏɫ 'two waters in one', inside Gorge Harbour; 35, ɫáytuˑθin 'facing inward at mouth', Mansons Landing; 36, ṕáqíʔaẑim 'place where maple leaves turn brown', Paukeanum Res.; 37, kʷúˑmáxən 'shelter inside arm', Smelt Bay; 38, žíˑmuθin 'blocking the mouth', Cortes Bay; 39, gíɫəxʷ, Mary Pt.; 40, qáqiqi, Kahkaykay Res.; 41, túˑqʷánən, Toquana Res.; 42, túxʷneč 'stretched-out rear end', Tokenatch Res.; 43, ƛíkʷanem, Sliammon Res.; 44, ɫášusm, Sliammon Res.; 45, tískʷət 'wide riverbed', Powell River.   Pentlatch villages (as named by Island and Mainland Comox speakers): 46, ċúwəm; 47, kʷiƛt 'upriver', Pentledge Res.; 48, táwusəman 'river parallel to beach', Little River; 49, qʷúmuʔxʷs, Comox Res.; 50, qiʔ, Cape Lazo; 51, Repulse Pt.; 52, kʷúʔuxʷm 'having smoke-dried salmon', Qualicum Res.   Sechelt villages: 53, xə́ničən, Hunaechin Res.; 54, swíwlát 'facing the rising sun's rays', Swaywelat Res.; 55, (s)čílúcin, Chelohsin Res.; 56, qʷə́qʷnis 'whale', (originally Sliammon, now Sechelt), Cokqueneets Res.; 57, sɫɫəm, Slayathlum Res.; 58, (s)píqiɫxan 'wide shoulders', Paykulkum Res.; 59, ċúnay 'sheltered', Tsooahdie Res.; 60, sqəɫp, Saltery Bay; 61, (s)kʷákʷiyám, Skwawkweehm Res.; 62, čətxʷánač 'black bear's posterior' or ċəċxʷənáčəm 'wash posterior end', Egmont Res.; 63, sqʷəláwt(xʷ) 'sword fern', Egmont; 64, kʷatámus 'high bluff'; 65, (s)cə́xʷna, Saughanaught Res.; 66, səxʷʔámin 'herring-spawn place', Sawquamain Res.; 67, čačlíɫtənam 'having lots of fish', Tchahchelailthtenum Res.; 68, ċə́lqʷám 'water trapped inside'; 69, smíšalin, Kleindale; 70, (s)ƛíxʷim, Klayekwim Res.; 71, sxʷə́lap 'deep furrow'; 72, píqílak 'wide beach'; 73, čátlíč 'outside', Seshelt Res.; 74, ʔáɫtúlíč 'inside', Seshelt Res.; 75, qə́laxan 'stockade', Selma Park; 76, ċúqʷum, Tsawcome Res.

Some were living off-reserve in the town of Campbell River (Kennedy and Bouchard 1983:149-151).

Formerly there were subdialects among the Mainland Comox groups, but the only dialect differences that were recognized by linguists in the 1970s were between Island Comox and Mainland Comox (J.H. Davis 1970; H. Harris 1977; Hagège 1981:10; Bouchard 1971-1981). In the 1980s, Mainland Comox continued being spoken fluently by about one-third of the population and was the most viable of all Salishan languages.

Pentlatch

Pentlatch territory included the eastern shore of Vancouver Island from Cape Lazo south to Parksville and the islands offshore, including Denman and Hornby islands.

Each of the four named Pentlatch subgroups comprised one or more winter villages from which the people traveled each summer to specific resource sites.

Disease, battles with Nootkans, and the southward movement of the Lekwiltok and Island Comox all contributed to the demise of the Pentlatch. Pentlatch territory was encroached upon by Cowichan people who began using the Qualicum fishery in the 1860s (Barnston 1864) and by some Nanaimo people who began residing permanently at Qualicum around 1875 (Sproat 1876).

In 1886 only one family of Pentlatch remained at Comox Harbour (Rohner 1969:59). The Pentlatch language became extinct in 1940 (Barnett 1955:6; Bouchard 1971-1981).

Sechelt

There were four Sechelt subgroups, each associated with a particular geographical area. These were: the Hunechen, whose principal village was situated at the head of Jervis

Table 1. Northern Coast Salish Population Registered in 1987

Group	Band	Population
Mainland Comox	Homalco	245
	Klahoose	127
	Sliammon	560
Pentlatch	Qualicum	55
Sechelt	Sechelt	708
Total		1,695

SOURCE: Canada. Department of Indian Affairs and Northern Development 1987.

Inlet; the Tsonai, with their main village at Deserted Bay; the Tuwanek, with their main village at the head of Narrows Inlet; and the Skaiakos, with their main winter village at Garden Bay and possibly another settlement on the Thormanby Islands. Sometime in the nineteenth century, the Tuwanek people resettled at Porpoise Bay (Beaumont 1985:xvii; Barnett 1955:30-31; Hill-Tout 1904:21).

Although Sechelt people were residing at approximately 12 sites when Indian reserves were established for them in 1876, most of the Sechelt population was living at a large village established at Trail Bay in the late 1860s under the direction of Roman Catholic missionaries. By the 1980s the only permanently occupied Sechelt villages were Trail Bay and Porpoise Bay.

External Relations

There are traditions of prolonged hostile relations with the Lekwiltok, and the Pentlatch are believed to have been the victims of Nootkan raids (Douglas 1840, 1853; Curtis 1907-1930, 10:108).

According to traditions, in the 1840s some of the Island Comox began to join with the Lekwiltok in their attacks against other Coast Salish groups to the south. In response, the Coast Salish allied together to avenge the decades of injury inflicted on them by the Lekwiltok and mounted a decisive retaliatory expedition aimed at incapacitating their enemy. But despite heavy losses, the Lekwiltok domination continued. In the 1860s, by which time Lekwiltok villages had been established on Quadra Island and Arran Rapids, the Lekwiltok annually visited fisheries at Comox Harbour or Qualicum on Vancouver Island, and at the mouth of the Homathko River.

Trade goods among the Northern Coast Salish consisted of surplus seasonal foods that were exchanged among themselves and with the Squamish, Halkomelem, Nootkans, and Lillooet. The Lillooet brought baskets, berries, animal furs, and snowshoes in return for smoked salmon, dentalia, fish oil, and deer hides (Teit 1906:232). The Chilcotin occasionally visited the Northern Salish for the smoke-dried fish.

Environment

The Northern Coast Salish occupy an area of the coast that is classified into the Coastal Western Hemlock zone and the Coastal Douglas Fir biogeoclimatic zones (Krajina 1969). Both zones are characterized by mild climates moderated by the ocean, with relatively high numbers of frost-free days and low annual ranges of temperatures.

The Coastal Douglas Fir zone, extending along the east coast of Vancouver Island, north to beyond Campbell River, along the Sechelt peninsula on the mainland, and encompassing the islands in between, is drier, due to the rain-shadow effect of the Vancouver Island mountains. Precipitation averages 65–175 centimeters per year, with only 25–160 centimeters of snowfall. The forested areas are often fairly open, with a shrub cover of ocean spray, wild rose, salal, thimbleberry, red huckleberry, and snowberry.

At higher elevations in the southern part of Northern Coast Salish territory, and throughout the northern part on the mainland from Powell River northward, is the Coastal Western Hemlock zone. The climate is wetter, with an average annual precipitation of 74–665 centimeters, of which 18–80 centimeters is snowfall. This zone is generally more heavily forested, sometimes also impenetrably, with a dense undergrowth of salal, salmonberry, thimbleberry, several blueberry and huckleberry species, and many other shrubs.

A third biogeoclimatic zone, the Mountain Hemlock Zone, is found at subalpine elevations above 800–1,000 meters. Besides mountain hemlock, other common trees of this zone are yellow cedar, amabilis fir, and western hemlock.

Culture

The cultural summary that follows is based primarily on ethnographic accounts compiled between 1885 and 1935, supplemented by additional data elicited in the 1970s. These data describe native life as it was in the mid-nineteenth century.

Subsistence

The Northern Coast Salish were primarily fish-eaters, although sea mammals and ungulates also formed a significant part of their diet. Of particular importance were the five species of Pacific salmon available seasonally in varying quantities throughout the Strait of Georgia.

All the Northern Coast Salish smoke-dried large numbers of the chum salmon that entered the spawning rivers during October and November. This fish's lean flesh dried hard, making it well-suited for long storage. Pink salmon, caught in late summer, could also be smoke-dried. Although chinook, sockeye, and coho salmon were occasionally dried in this manner, it was done mostly for the flavor that was imparted rather than as a means of preserving the oil-rich flesh. Summer runs of these species, where available, were normally eaten fresh.

The arrival of the first salmon was marked by the ritual handling, butchering, and cooking of the fish. The Island Comox honored the year's first catch of sockeye salmon, whereas in the Mainland Comox area, where sockeye were scarce, the ritual was performed with the first chinook salmon.

In open water, the Northern Coast Salish trolled for chinook and coho salmon or caught them in gill nets; however, most salmon were taken either at the entrances to spawning streams and rivers or in these waters themselves. Basketry traps and weirs were used, and as the salmon swimming upstream were congested on the downstream side of these devices, they could also be caught individually by fishermen using both gaff hooks and single- and double-shafted harpoons. The Northern Coast Salish also constructed tidal pounds using stakes or rocks near the mouths of spawning streams and trapped the salmon within them once the tide ebbed.

Another device that took advantage of the rising and falling tide was used across the narrow neck of a bay or river mouth both by the Sechelt and by the Mainland Comox. This consisted of a latticework fence fastened only along the bottom to a weir framework. At low water it lay flat and exposed. Then, once the tide had come in, the fence was pulled to an upright position by means of lines fastened to its top. The outward flow of the water kept the latticework in place against the framework. When the tide went out, fish would be impounded in the trap and left on the dry sand where they were gathered (Barnett 1955:83; Kennedy 1971–1981).

Herring were scooped from the water with dip nets or impaled on comblike herring rakes. Gill nets and seine nets largely replaced these traditional devices by the early 1900s. Herring eggs were collected on boughs or small trees of red cedar or western hemlock that had been submerged in the water for several days during the spawn. These eggs were eaten fresh or sun-dried.

Other species of some importance to the Northern Coast Salish included lingcod and greenling, taken with a shuttlecock lure and spear; steelhead, which along with chinook and coho salmon could be caught trolling; and flounder and sole, taken in shallow water using a spear or simply stepped on and tossed into a canoe. Among the Mainland Comox rockfish comprised a significant part of the diet. The best fishermen owned special songs that they sang to the rockfish as they jigged for them.

Sea mammals hunted by the Northern Coast Salish included northern sea lions, harbor seal, and harbor porpoise. Professional hunters trained specifically for this task. Hunting was usually accomplished by two men in a canoe; the bowsman was armed with a heavy harpoon fixed with a trident-butt and detachable head. Fastened to the head was a long line on the end of which was a cedar float specially carved to identify the owner. Once the harpoon head was imbedded deep into the animal's flesh, the float was thrown overboard and the wounded animal allowed to struggle until it expired.

Seals were occasionally approached near their rookeries by a hunter disguised in a seal skin and imitating the sound of a seal. The kill was made once the hunter was close enough to use a club or harpoon.

Deer was the most important land animal hunted. Until the early 1900s, deer hunters used trained dogs to herd the deer toward the shore where other hunters would be waiting, armed with bows and arrows, clubs, or knives. Deer were also caught in pitfalls, snares, and nets that were constructed on deer trails. Some hunters used deer calls.

Only a few Northern Coast Salish men obtained the skills necessary to hunt mountain goats. Evidently certain families had their own mountain goat hunting territories. Family expeditions would sometimes camp in the mountains, the women drying the meat while the men hunted. Once an animal was killed, it was butchered and the meat partially roasted so that it would be lighter to pack.

Hunters went after bears with bows and arrows; sometimes they prepared camouflaged pits in which sharpened stakes were set, or heavy deadfall traps baited with fish or deer meat.

Elk were found only in the territory of the Island Comox and Pentlatch. But smaller animals like beaver, otter, mink, marten, raccoon and porcupine were available to all the Northern Coast Salish.

Birds were clubbed with long poles, entangled in nets laid across the water's surface, blinded by torchlights so

Fig. 2. Preparing clams for barbecuing. Rose Mitchell is pounding the end of the stick to prevent the threaded clams from slipping off. Photograph by Dorothy Kennedy, Sliammon Indian Reserve, B.C., Nov. 1974.

that they could be grabbed and their necks could be wrung, or shot with bird arrows. The Sechelt are said to have used aerial duck nets (L.R. Peterson 1968). Numerous types of waterfowl and two species of grouse were eaten, as were the eggs of the pigeon guillemot and several species of gull. As well as eating great blue heron and Canada goose flesh, the Mainland Comox also used the heron's fat and the geese's dung for their medicinal value.

Shellfish such as butter clams, littleneck clams, horse clams, and cockles were available on beaches in the Strait of Georgia for most of the year. During the winter, when the tides were low at night, the people dug clams by the light of pitchwood torches. Particularly good shellfish beds were cultivated by moving the rocks to one side. Clams were prepared boiled, steamed, or barbecued (fig. 2). For storage, the clams were first barbecued, and then either smoke-dried or sun-dried. Chitons, sea urchins, and sea cucumber were gathered.

Food from plants included fruits (berries and seeds), green vegetables (shoots and leaves), underground parts (roots, bulbs, tubers and rhizomes), and cambium. Women and children picked large quantities of ripe berries and dried them into cakes to be eaten during the winter, but most plant foods were eaten fresh.

445

Structures

Four types of dwellings were constructed: the shed or single pitched-roof plank house; the gabled-roof plank house (fig. 3); the semisubterranean plank house; and temporary shelters. House planks could be removed and transported by canoe to summer villages where the planks were then fastened onto another permanent framework. Some houses remained wholly constructed year-round; only the residents moved from site to site.

Shed houses were the preferred type of house in summer villages for both Comox and Sechelt, but Comox people of status preferred gabled-roof houses for winter dwellings. The Pentlatch used both types of dwellings (Barnett 1955:43, 47–49).

Some shed houses were 60–70 feet in length, and half as wide. Each house had several fires, built down the center in the narrow houses and along the sides in the larger ones. The floor of a shed house was sometimes excavated among the Sliammon. The Homalco and Klahoose sometimes dug storage pits in the dirt floor of their houses (Hill-Tout 1904:29; Barnett 1955:43–52).

Among the Pentlatch and Island Comox the gabled-roof house contained features not commonly found elsewhere, including excavated earth floors, enclosed sleeping partitions, and separate smoke-drying sheds.

Some of the houses that were built on hillsides had special platforms jutting from their fronts. Besides guarding from attack, these platforms provided a comfortable sitting area.

Semisubterranean plank houses were used by the Klahoose. These dwellings were rectangular in shape, constructed in pits excavated to a depth of about 10 feet, roofed with a series of poles, brush, and bark, and covered with a layer of dirt. A gangway sloped down to the floor level for entry at one end. A concealed tunnel led out the back way. The Homalco, Sliammon, and Sechelt used semisubterranean plank houses during periods of frequent enemy attacks.

Throughout the northern Strait of Georgia, houses were sometimes fortified with stockades of logs on top of which they stored large rocks to hurl down on raiding parties. Others were protected by deep trenches dug around the perimeter.

Temporary shelters consisted of simple, bough-covered lean-tos and crude pole frameworks draped with mats.

House fronts, beams, and ridgepoles of gabled-roof houses were frequently decorated with anthropomorphic figures. These designs were inherited prerogatives among the Pentlatch and Island Comox, but apparently among the Mainland Comox and Sechelt they could be bought or obtained through dreams (Hill-Tout 1904:27; Barnett 1938a:128, 1955:56). House posts might be carved to represent sea lions, seals, porpoises, and killer whales (Barnett 1935–1936, 1955:47–52).

Prov. Arch. of B.C., Victoria: C9265.
Fig. 3. Gabled-roof plank house with wooden figure in front. The wall planks were tied horizontally between pairs of upright poles, overlapping in a clapboard manner. Most of the carvings in this village were painted with red and blue features (Dally 1866:14). Photograph by Frederick Dally, Comox, B.C., Aug. 1866.

Technology

Household items included a variety of containers for carrying and storing food. Possibly the most characteristic of the area were the openwork, wrapped lattice pack baskets made from cedar limb splints or roots woven in different-size mesh for carrying fish, clams, berries, or firewood. Women also wove inner-red-cedarbark baskets using a checkerwork technique. Over the years different styles of baskets have been developed (fig. 4).

Flat bags, and large mats used to line the walls of houses, were sewed from inner red cedarbark or cattail leaves. Sechelt and Mainland Comox women manufactured imbricated, coiled basketry of banded cedar slats; it appears that this craft was learned from Interior Salish women (Hill-Tout 1904:30–31; Barnett 1955:122–124; Kennedy and Bouchard 1983:76–79).

Wooden dishes and spoons were hollowed out of red cedar, red alder, and big-leaf maple wood. Western yew, because of its hardness, was ideal for wedges and digging sticks, while barbecue sticks, canoe poles, and harpoon poles were made from red cedar wood, and bows and arrows were made from the wood of young yellow cedar.

Twilled mountain goat wool blankets, woven on roller looms, were restricted to the Sechelt. Other Northern Coast Salish used a 3-piece suspended-warp loom for weaving blankets of twined inner red cedarbark and mountain goat wool (Hill-Tout 1904:28–29; Barnett 1938a:125, 1955:119–121).

Stone and bone were also vitally important to technology, and archeological sites of the area are filled with numerous examples of their uses as scrapers, knives, choppers, abraders, sinkers, palettes, chisels, awls, toys, and tools.

Canoes

Travel was primarily by water, using a number of canoe

Fig. 4. Jeannie Dominick making an imbricated coiled basket of cedar slats and roots for the tourist trade. Photograph by Dorothy Kennedy, Squirrel Cove Indian Res., Cortes I., B.C., July 1977.

types, ranging from narrow, one- or two-man trolling canoes to war canoes designed to carry 20 men. Most canoes were carved from red cedar, although the Mainland Comox also used yellow cedar, cottonwood, and cedar bark, the last for a small canoe used in lake travel and in beaver hunting. Separate paddles for men and women, and also different styles for use in rough weather, for night hunting, and for sealing were carved from big-leaf maple and red alder. Other canoe gear included cedar bark bailers and small mats for sitting on (Barnett 1955: 111–118; Kennedy and Bouchard 1983:79–81).

Kinship Terminology

Among the Northern Coast Salish, kinship was reckoned bilaterally, creating kin groups that were nondiscrete units consisting of both parent's relatives.

The system is lineal in that separate kinship terms are used for 'mother', 'father', and 'child.' Both male and female siblings and cousins are called by the same term, depending upon their relative age to the speaker. The kinship terms are therefore of the Hawaiian system. A single term is also used for 'aunt-uncle' regardless of the

reference to a parent's sibling or cousin, though a different term is used after the parent's death. Similarly, the children of these relations are referred to by a single 'niece-nephew' term.

Among the Mainland Comox, the next-older generation is distinguished by sex. The father and male siblings of one's own parents are referred to by the term 'grandfather.' Both the mother and female siblings of one's own parents are called by the one term, 'grandmother'. Kinship terms recorded by Boas (1886b) among the Pentlatch indicate they also distinguished 'grandfather' and 'grandmother' terms. The Sechelt refer to a grandparent and all the grandparent's siblings, regardless of sex, by the one term 'grandparent'.

Terms applied to relatives a generation older or younger do not distinguish on the basis of sex and the lineal and collaterals are merged.

Both males and females refer to their 'siblings-in-law' by common terms, though a different term is used after the death of the linking spouse. The term used to refer to a deceased child's spouse is distinguished only by a suffix indicating he has died or separated.

Social Organization

The Northern Coast Salish family consisted of a husband, wife, their children, dependent young adults, old people, and slaves. A number of related families formed a household, each occupying its own section of the house and each cooking its own meals, but cooperating in various economic and social activities. Couples were free to live in the household of either parents and could therefore take advantage of fluctuating prosperity. Families or larger groups of kin scattered for their summer activities to resource sites. Ownership of some of these summer sites was an inherited prerogative.

Among the Sechelt, Pentlatch, Island Comox, and possibly also the Mainland Comox, the "local group" was the social unit whose members all acknowledged descent from a mythical first ancestor who descended from the sky to a particular village or harvesting site.

Local groups were present among the Mainland Comox, yet their unifying feature does not appear to have been a first ancestor. Even though each local group tended to be identified with a certain area, several local groups would often be represented in a winter village. Each local group likely owned fishing sites as well (Boas 1892c: 62–63, 1892b:65; Sapir 1939; Barnett 1955:25; Kennedy and Bouchard 1983:64).

Life Cycle

Pregnancy and childbirth were surrounded by taboos restricting the diet and behavior of both parents, particularly the mother. Women gave birth in a squatting

447

position assisted by female relatives and, when available, by a paid midwife. The afterbirth was covered with oil and ceremoniously hidden in a dry place, in the belief that this would protect both the child and the mother from injury. Head deformation was practiced throughout the northern Strait of Georgia, resulting in a wedge-shaped head with a flat, broad forehead (Barnett 1955:75; Kennedy and Bouchard 1983:43–44).

A baby was called by a nickname during the first year, after which an ancestral name was bestowed upon the child at a public name-giving ceremony.

Girls at the onset of menses were secluded in a cubicle above the family's sleeping platform where they remained for up to 16 days while their behavior and diet were severely restricted.

Boys at puberty underwent training to develop their physical and mental character, part of which focused upon the acquisition of guardian spirit power. Quests for such spiritual helpers were conducted alone and lasted for up to a year, during which time the seeker bathed in cold water, took sweatbaths frequently, and ate little. The guardian spirit power was received in a dream or trance from a bird, an animal, or even from an inanimate object. Some of these powers provided the seeker with special skills such as those to be used for hunting, fishing, or canoe-making. Those young men who continued their training over many years became shamans (Hill-Tout 1904:32; Barnett 1955:141–152; Kennedy and Bouchard 1983:47–52).

Marriage occurred any time after puberty. Proposals were initiated by the young man, accompanied by his father and influential male relatives traveling by canoe to the village of the chosen woman. Even if both parties lived in the same village, the approach was always made by canoe. Betrothals were occasionally made during the couple's infancy and later formalized by the exchange of gifts and feasting, once the betrothed were past puberty. Polygyny was common; co-wives resided in the same household, but in different compartments. Divorce was accompanied by the return of the marriage gift by the bride's family. A widow or widower could remarry once he or she had undergone the prescribed rituals. Levirate and sororate marriages were not the custom, although people of high-class families followed this practice to ensure that the children would be well provided for (Barnett 1955:204; Kennedy and Bouchard 1983:53).

At death a person's soul, which was believed to be located in the head, left the body. The body was washed, placed in a flexed position, wrapped in a blanket, and stowed in a wooden mortuary box that was then set in a cave or rock crevasse on a nearby island, or at a site away from the village. Among the Sechelt, Island Comox, and Pentlatch, mortuary boxes were also placed high in trees (Barnett 1955:217).

The Comox and Pentlatch erected carved and painted poles commemorating the dead either at the gravesite or in front of the deceased's family dwelling. Possessions of the deceased were burned so that they might be used by them after death. In the spring families gathered to burn food for their dead ancestors.

Potlatches

Men of high status maintained their prestige by the frequent and generous distribution of goods at ceremonies that marked a change in their social position or that of a family member. Gatherings for such purposes were known as potlatches.

The simplest potlatch was held for all the members of the host's own village, and only food was distributed. Another intravillage affair, where both food and goods were distributed, was held to "wipe away shame" that had been cast upon the family by a clumsy action of one of its members.

Guests from both within the host's village and beyond were called to receive food and gifts at a potlatch held to witness events such as a name-giving, a marriage, or the erection of a memorial pole. The last was sometimes accompanied by a public display of the host's dancing prerogatives.

Among the Comox, such a display could include the prestigious sxwayxwey ($x^w\acute{a}yx^way$) dancers. This dancing privilege was owned by certain high-class men and used exclusively by their families. Such dancers wore masks distinguished by protruding eyes, a gaping mouth from which projected a large tongue, a bird's head for a nose, horns of either bird or beastlike heads, and a crest of feathers (fig. 5). The rest of the costume included a scallop-shell or wooden rattle, stiff neck shield, rows of overlapping swan feathers extending from chest to knees, leggings, anklets, and a skirt of swan feathers or white grass (Barnett 1955:158, 170).

Winter Ceremonials

Comox and Pentlatch winter dancing seems to have consisted of two forms: spirit dancing, participated in by the majority of the people, and a more exclusive masked dancing order performed only by certain high-status families.

Genuine spirit possession and initiation were not necessarily prerequisites for joining the winter spirit dancing, although a willingness to participate was manifested by a supposedly uncontrollable moaning or singing. When this occurred, previously initiated dancers gathered round and softly beat a drum to help "bring the song out." Having learned how to sing and dance in a possessed state, the dancer was then permitted to participate in any winter dance.

Transmissible dance prerogatives were most developed among the Island Comox, where members formed danc-

448

Amer. Mus. of Nat. Hist., New York: 16-4724A.

Fig. 5. Sxwayxwey mask, Island or Mainland Comox. Kennedy and Bouchard (1983:63–64) describe use of these masks among the Island Comox. Collected at Comox, B.C., before 1898.

Mus. of the Amer. Ind., Heye Foundation, New York: 19/9039.

Fig. 6. Tal mask with deep-set eyes, bent nose, protruding cheeks, and open mouth. Holes lining the crown probably once held tufts of hair. Tal was a legendary giantess who kidnapped and ate children. She could only be thwarted by singing, which would always compel her to dance. The privilege of owning a Tal mask was inherited or purchased. The masks were used at life cycle rites and at winter dances. Collected at Church House, B.C., before 1938; height 25 cm.

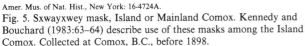

ing orders, each having its own patron spirit, song, regalia, and myth recounting how the original member had acquired the dance. Some of these dances appear to have been of Kwakiutl origin (Sapir 1939:49). In fact, direct Kwakiutl influence is shown in the occasional use of the Kwakiutl name ȝúnuq̓ʷa for Tal masks (fig. 6). The hamatsa dancing orders included the grizzly bear, warrior, wolf, and ghost dancers.

Klahoose and Sliammon people sometimes underwent a four-day seclusion in the woods where they were subjected to a ritual initiation similar to that of the Central Coast Salish. Later, the initiate publicly announced the successful acquisition of his spirit power by singing and dancing.

Sechelt winter dances conformed more to the dances of their southern neighbors than to those of either the Comox or Pentlatch, although initiation was not a requirement for dancers other than those classed as "bleeding mouth" dancers. No masks and only a mini-mum of costumes were worn by Sechelt winter dancers while they were in a possessed state. The inherited, privileged performances owned by certain Sechelt families were not given at winter dances, only at intervillage potlatches.

History

In summer 1792 two fleets of foreign ships entered the northern Strait of Georgia, becoming the first non-Indian explorers to have contact with the native people of this region. The British fleet was commanded by George Vancouver; the Spanish fleet by Cayento Valdés and Dionisio Alcalá Galiano. The reception they received was amicable, and they traded beads, medals, iron, and copper for supplies of fresh and dried foods.

A few years later the maritime fur trade was active on the outer coast of Vancouver Island, but the absence of the sea otter in the northern Strait of Georgia excluded these people's direct participation in this trade. Only the Sechelt were recorded as visitors to Fort Langley on the Fraser River during the late 1820s.

None of the Northern Coast Salish tribes escaped the epidemics of diseases introduced with White contact. The Pentlatch, already nearly exterminated by Nootkan raids, were hit hard by disease. Their territory was taken up by the Island Comox who in turn had been driven south by the Lekwiltok. Locations of Sechelt villages may have shifted, but the boundaries of their territory remained substantially the same.

A second period during which the Northern Coast Salish underwent profound changes likely began in the

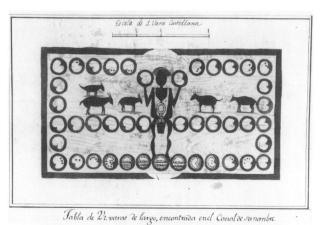

Museo de America, Madrid: 219.
Fig. 7. Representation of a wooden plaque found in Toba Inlet by explorers of the expedition of Dionisio Alcalá Galiano and Cayento Valdés. It was both carved and painted with geometric and realistic figures, among which were 5 mountain goats (Jane 1930:131). Drawn by José Cardero, 1792.

1860s when they came under the influence of Roman Catholic missionaries who were members of the Oblates of Mary Immaculate. The Oblates' conversion of these native people to Christianity included the renunciation of winter dancing and potlatching and the establishment of Indian "theocratic states" consisting of self-sufficient Christian villages (Lemert 1954). In such settlements a strict moral and economic order was maintained by a missionary-selected village hierarchy comprised of men given the titles of "Captain," "Watchman," and "Bell-man."

In the realm of social life, polygyny and slavery were no longer tolerated. Dissidents were punished and native traditions were discouraged. By the 1890s the Easter Passion Play was as much a part of Indian life as intravillage feasts had been only a few decades earlier. In addition to the church on Seshelt Reserve (fig. 8), there was a Catholic boarding school for native children where indigenous languages were discouraged.

Also beginning in the late 1800s were new economic conditions. Northern Coast Salish men were employed longshoring on the Burrard Inlet waterfront, or found themselves competing with non-Indians for timber cutting permits to hand-log their traditional lands. Entire families were hired as farm laborers in the Fraser Valley hop fields and as fishmen and inside workers in the Fraser River canneries.

Many traditional lands and resources had already been alienated by the time Indian reserves were officially established in 1876 and later confirmed by the Royal Commission on Indian Affairs in 1913–1916.

Several Indian organizations were formed beginning in the early 1900s to pursue government recognition of aboriginal title. The Northern Coast Salish communities were represented in organizations such as the Allied Tribes, the Native Brotherhood of British Columbia and, beginning in the 1970s, the Alliance of Tribal Councils. These Native organizations served to foster a political unity among the Indian people. Perhaps one of the most tangible results of this long political struggle occurred in the 1980s when the Sechelt Indian Band developed its own self-government legislation, which was enacted in 1986 as the Sechelt Indian Band Self-Government Act by the federal government and by the province of British Columbia in 1987. This resulted in the Sechelt Band being the first in Canada to be granted self-government, with constitutional and legislative powers similar to those of municipal governments.

Synonymy

Comox is from Kwakiutl $\acute{q}^w úmux^w s$ (derived from $\acute{q}wm$-'rich'), which was applied to the Comox Harbour area and later used to refer to the people who settled there in the mid-1800s. Originally this term may have referred to one division of the Island Comox. Variants include kowmoo-chsheah (Tolmie 1963:317–318), comaux (Yale 1838–1839), commagsheak (Scouler 1848:234), ko-mookhs or s'ko-mook (Gibbs 1877:269), qōmoks (Boas 1887a:132), k·ṓmoks (Boas 1890:806), comox (Canada. Royal Commission on Indian Affairs for the Province of British Columbia 1916, 1:278), and q'ó·mo·xᵘs (Sapir 1939:49). Nootka has $\acute{q}o·mo·ʔoxšʔatḥ$ (Sapir and Swadesh 1939:150, 295).

Island Comox

The Island Comox have called themselves $sá\text!tu\text!ltx^w$ in the twentieth century, but apparently earlier pronounced the name $θá\text!tu\text!ltx^w$ (as it is pronounced in the Mainland Comox dialect), and possibly used it to designate the northernmost division only. The name appears to contain $-tx^w$ 'house' but is otherwise unanalyzable. This term has appeared as tisilholts (Douglas 1853), sath-luths (Brown 1864:25), s'tlaht-tohtlt-hu (Gibbs 1877:269), çatlṓltch (Boas 1887a:131), çatlṓltq (Boas 1890:806), sŭhlúhl̄ (Curtis 1907–1930,9:34), saLaLt (Barnett 1955:25), and $θa\textł óltx^w$ (Vool 1961–1962).

The subgroup name Eeksen (Island Comox $ʔíʔiqsn$) is a normalization by Hodge (1907–1910, 1:418) of éeqsen (Boas 1887a:131); variants are eiksan (Barnett 1955:25), íʔiqsin (Sapir 1939:54), and eyəqsən (Vool 1961–1962).

The name of the Kaake subgroup was coined in this form by Hodge (1907–1910, 1:637) as an anglicization of the phonetic transcription chāaché (Boas 1887a:132); other renderings are xá·ʼᵃxe· (Sapir 1939:50), xaxe (Barnett 1955:167), and xáᵃxey (Vool 1961-1962).

The subgroup name Kakekt (Hodge 1907–1910, 1:644) was based on the recording by Boas (1887a:132) of qāq'ēcht; this was transcribed by Vool (1961–1962) as

KENNEDY AND BOUCHARD

Fig. 8. left, Catholic Church Our Lady of the Rosary, Seshelt Reserve, B.C. Outdoor worship was necessary because the church could not hold the number of Indians who came for its opening. Tin can bells decorate the altar. The flags, which bear the words "Religion," "Civilization," and "Temperance," identify the bearers as members of the Temperance Society. Photograph by Charles S. Bailey or Hamilton G. Neelands, June 1890. right, Our Lady of the Lourdes, built in 1907 to replace Our Lady of the Rosary, destroyed by fire. Photograph by Leonard Frank, 1924.

q̇aqɛxt.

The name of the Sasitla subgroup (sásiƛa) appears in Barnett (1955:25) as säsitla. The name of the Tatpoos subgroup (ťáťpuʔus) was coined by Hodge (1907–1910, 2: 698) on the basis of Boas's (1887a:132) transcription t'ātpoós; Vool (1961–1962) recorded t'áᵃtpoᵒs.

Barnett (1955:25) has transcribed names for four additional Island Comox groups: yayaqwiLtah, katka-duL, komokwe, and papusenitc.

Mainland Comox

Homalco (Canada. Royal Commision on Indian Affairs for the Province of British Columbia 1916, 3:633) is from Comox xʷámɬkʷu 'swift water', which has appeared as humáhīkyu (Curtis 1907–1930, 9:32) and homaLko (Barnett 1955:26). Another form, xʷíxʷmaɬkʷu, has appeared as chuéchomātlqō (Boas 1887a:132). Hodge (1907–1910, 1:334, 557) used Homalko and Homaltko.

Klahoose (Canada. Royal Commission on Indian Affairs for the Province of British Columbia 1916, 3:631), is Comox ƛúhus, the name of a species of sculpin. It has been recorded as tlohoose or cle-house (Yale 1838–1839), tlahū̃s (Boas 1887a:132), tlăkyús (Curtis 1907–1930, 9: 32), and kLahus (Barnett 1955:26). Hodge (1907–1910, 1: 302) used Clahoose.

Sliammon (Canada. Royal Commission on Indian Affairs for the Province of British Columbia 1916, 3:637; Hodge 1907–1910, 2:602) is Comox ɬáʔamin, which has appeared as tlamay (Douglas 1840), tlaāmen (Boas 1887a: 132), hlaamı̆n (Curtis 1907–1930, 9:32), slaiäman (Barnett 1955:29), and ɬaʔamən (Hagège 1981:5).

Pentlatch

Pentlatch is from Sechlet and Comox pə́nƛəč; it is not known if the Pentlatch had a name for themselves. This name may formerly have referred exclusively to the Pentlatch people in the vicinity of Comox Harbour. The term has appeared as puntlatch (Douglas 1853), pɛntlatsch (Boas 1887a:132), pentledge (Canada. Royal Commission on Indian Affairs for the Province of British Columbia 1916, 1:278), and pɛnLätc (Barnett 1955:23).

The Pentlatch subgroup residing in the vicinity of Qualicum was called sáʔaɬəm, also recorded as saathlam (Douglas 1853) and sāámen (Boas 1887a:132). Brown

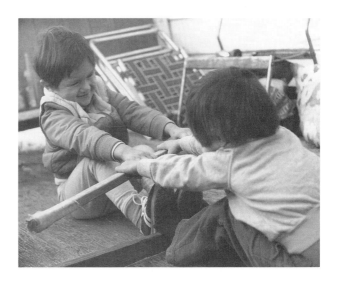

Fig. 9. Homalco children Aaron Wilson (left) and Ian Wilson playing a traditional game known as "pull the lazy stick." The object of the game is to pull your opponent over the plank. In this game, it's the winner who ends up on his back. Photograph by Dorothy Kennedy, Sliammon Indian Reserve, B.C., 1983.

NORTHERN COAST SALISH

451

(1864:25) transcribed this term as saa-tlaam or saat-lelp 'place of green leaves'.

A division of the Pentlatch residing formerly around Union Bay and Deep Bay was identified as s:uckcan by Barnett (1955:24) and s'óksŭn by Curtis (1907–1930, 9: 21).

Boas (1887a:132) recognized a southernmost division of the Pentlatch whose name he recorded as chuãchuatl. This term has also appeared as wahatl (Barnston 1864), swakulth (Brown 1864), wor-cal-tlas (Buttle 1865), and wachellall (T.H. Lewis 1864).

Sechelt

Sechelt (Canada. Royal Commission on Indian Affairs for the Province of British Columbia 1916,3:633) is from Comox šíšáɬ, the name applied to that area of Seshelt Indian Reserve No. 2 that faces Trail Bay on the southeastern extreme of the Sechelt peninsula. This name has been recorded as tseashall (Yale 1838–1839), sĩschiatl (Boas 1887a:132), nĩ́ciatl (Boas 1890:806), sĩciatl (Hill-Tout 1904:20), sicɛLt (Barnett 1955:30), and se-shalt´ (L.R. Peterson 1958–1963).

The subgroup name Hunechen (Sechelt x̣ə́ničən) is used here in preference to Kunechin, an anglicization by Hodge (1907–1910, 1:735) of qúnētcin (Hill-Tout 1904: 21); variants are hane:tcan (Barnett 1955:30), x̣ənečən (Grekoff 1965), and hunaé-chin (L.R. Peterson 1958–1963). The name of the Tsonai subgroup (Sechelt čúnay) is from the recording tsónai (Hill-Tout 1904:21), normalized by Hodge (1907–1910, 2:829); another spelling is tsoh´-nye (L.R. Peterson 1958–1963). The subgroup name Tuwanek (Hodge 1907–1910, 2:858), from Sechelt təwánkʷ, has appeared as tūwãnekq (Hill-Tout 1904:21), tuwankw (Barnett 1955:30), and tuh-wahn-kwuh (L.R. Peterson 1968). The name of the Skaiakos subgroup (Sechelt sx̣íx̣ʔus) is the normalization by Hodge (1907–1910, 2:585) of sqaiaqos (Hill-Tout 1904:21); other renderings are xexoats (Barnett 1955:30), sx̣ex̣ʔós (Grekoff 1965), and klaý-ah-kwohss (L.R. Peterson 1968).

Sources

Early historical sources providing ethnographic accounts of the Northern Coast Salish include the journals kept by members of the 1792 British and Spanish expeditions (Vancouver 1801; Menzies 1923; Jane 1930; Meany 1942; Wagner 1933) and the diary of Hudson's Bay Company Factor James Douglas (1840). Roman Catholic missionary activity beginning in the 1860s is described in Fouquet (1870) and Lemert (1954). An important source beginning in the late 1870s is the voluminous documentation published in the Annual Reports of the Department of Indian Affairs and in the unpublished records of the Department at the Public Archives of Canada, Ottawa.

The first ethnographic work among the Northern Coast Salish was undertaken in 1886 by Boas. Boas collected Comox and Pentlatch myths in English translation, texts in the Pentlatch and Comox languages with translation, and extensive Sechelt, Comox, and Pentlatch word lists (Boas 1885, 1886d, 1886b, 1886c, 1888, 1891a, 1892c:62–63; 1895).

Hill-Tout (1904) reported on Sechelt ethnography and language, with particular emphasis on spiritual aspects of this culture. Curtis (1907–1930, 9 and 10) published brief notes on the Sechelt and Comox. Sapir (1915, 1939) recorded Comox linguistic data and information about songs and traditions relating to a Comox dancing mask.

It was not until the mid-1930s that ethnographic research was conducted among the Mainland Comox, by Barnett (1938a, 1939, 1944, 1955). Unpublished field notes are held by the University of British Columbia Library, Vancouver.

Duff compiled data concerning the Island Comox and Pentlatch from manuscript and published sources; they are found among his field notes at the Royal British Columbia Museum, Victoria. Suttles (1961, 1973) recorded Island Comox place-names.

In the 1950s–1960s, local historians collected data among the Sechelt and Mainland Comox (L.R. Peterson 1968, 1958–1963; Stanley 1954, 1968; Orchard 1965), and Sismey (1961) and Meade (1980) collected Island Comox data from Lekwiltok informants. Beyond these sources the major collections of ethnographic data for Sechelt and Comox are those of Kennedy (1971–1981), Bouchard (1971–1981), and Kennedy and Bouchard (1983).

Linguistic research among the Northern Coast Salish includes studies among the Mainland Comox and Island Comox (J. Adams 1961; J.H. Davis 1970; Hagège 1981; H. Harris 1977; Vool 1961–1962). Comparative Mainland Comox and Island Comox word lists were compiled by Thompson and Thompson (1964a) and by Bouchard (1971–1981), who also developed a practical orthography for Comox.

The earliest linguistic work on Sechelt is a collection of prayers (Durieu 1874). Similar materials were written in the Duployan shorthand (LeJeune 1896). Sechelt linguistic research has been undertaken by Willmott (1961), Thompson and Thompson (1964), Grekoff (1965), Timmers (1977), who published a classified word list, and Bouchard (1971–1981), who also developed a practical orthography for Sechelt. The major source of Sechelt linguistic materials is the work of Beaumont (1973, 1985).

Central Coast Salish

WAYNE SUTTLES

Central Coast Salish refers to the speakers of five languages: Squamish ('skwamish), Halkomelem (ˌhălkəˈmāləm), Nooksack ('no͞okˌsăk), Northern Straits ('strāts), and Clallam ('klăləm).* Before the European invasion they possessed the southern end of the Strait of Georgia, most of the Strait of Juan de Fuca, the Lower Fraser Valley, and some adjacent areas. Their territory thus includes parts of both British Columbia and Washington (fig. 1).

*Unless otherwise identified, the forms cited in this chapter are from the Musqueam (Downriver) dialect of Halkomelem, whose phonemes are: (voiceless stops and affricates) p, t, c, č, k, kʷ, q, qʷ, ʔ; (glottalized stops and affricates) ṗ, t̕, θ̓, c̓, ƛ̓, k̓, k̓ʷ, q̓, q̓ʷ; (voiceless continuants) θ, s, ɬ, š, x, xʷ, x̣, x̣ʷ, h; (resonants) m, n, l, w, y; (glottalized resonants) m̓, n̓, l̓, w̓, y̓; (short vowels) i, e, a, u, ə; (long vowels) iˑ, eˑ, aˑ, uˑ. Island dialects differ from Musqueam in having a voiceless affricate θ̓ and lacking the voiceless continuant x and possibly the glottalized stop k̓; they have š corresponding to Musqueam x. Upriver dialects differ from Musqueam in having a c̓ and the vowel o, in having high- and mid-pitched stress (marked ´ for high and ` for mid), in having extra-long vowels (marked iˑ, etc.), and in lacking the resonant n and the glottalized resonant series; they have l for Musqueam n (Elmendorf and Suttles 1960; Suttles 1984; Leslie 1979; Galloway 1977).

In the practical orthography used by the Coqualeetza Education Training Centre the phonemes of Upriver Halkomelem are written: p, t, ts, ch, k, kw, q, qw,'; p', t', th', ts', tl', ch', k', kw', q', qw'; th, s, lh, sh, x, xw, x̠, x̠w, h; m, n, l, w, y; i, a, o, u, e. The vowel o is written ō, and stress is as in the technical orthography; vowel length is marked : (Galloway 1980).

The phonemes of Squamish are: (voiceless stops and affricates) p, t, c, č, k, kʷ, q, qʷ, ʔ; (glottalized stops and affricates) ṗ, t̕, c̓, ƛ̓, č̓, k̓, k̓ʷ, q̓, q̓ʷ; (voiceless continuants) s, ɬ, š, xʷ, x̣, x̣ʷ, h; (resonants) m, n, l, w, y; (vowels) i, æ a, u, ə (Kuipers 1967–1969:21–23).

The phonemes of Nooksack are: (voiceless stops and affricates) p, t, c, č, k, kʷ, q, qʷ, ʔ; (glottalized stops and affricates) ṗ, t̕, c̓, ƛ̓, č̓, k̓ʷ, q̓, q̓ʷ; (voiceless continuants) s, ɬ, š, xʷ, x̣, x̣ʷ, h; (resonants) m, n, l, w, y; (vowels) i, æ, a, u, ə. Some speakers have θ, θ̓, and x as a result of Upriver Halkomelem influence; a may occur only in loanwords (Galloway 1983).

The phonemes of the Songhees dialect of Northern Straits are: (voiceless stops and affricates) p, t, c, č, k, kʷ, q, qʷ, ʔ; (glottalized stops and affricates) ṗ, t̕, c̓, ƛ̓, č̓, k̓ʷ, q̓, q̓ʷ; (voiceless fricatives) s, ɬ, š, xʷ, x̣, x̣ʷ, h; (resonants) m, n, ŋ, l, w, y; (short vowels) i, e, a, o, ə; (long vowels) iˑ, eˑ, aˑ (M.R. Mitchell 1968 [with a correction]). The Saanich dialect has θ and θ̓, probably under the influence of Halkomelem; the Sooke dialect has y where other dialects have l (a feature in which it resembles Clallam).

The phonemes of Clallam are: (voiceless stops and affricates) p, t, c, č, k, kʷ, q, qʷ, ʔ; (glottalized stops and affricates) ṗ, t̕, c̓, ƛ̓, č̓, k̓ʷ, q̓, q̓ʷ; (voiceless continuants) s, ɬ, š, xʷ, x̣, x̣ʷ, h; (resonants) m, n, ŋ, l, w, y; (vowels) i, e, a, u, ə. The phonemes k and l occur mainly in loanwords (Thompson and Thompson 1971).

Component Groups

The names Squamish, Nooksack, and Clallam each designate the people who spoke these languages and are thus names of "tribes" in a nonpolitical sense. Halkomelem and Northern Straits refer simply to languages, each of which is spoken by a number of named groups varying in size from one to more than 20 villages; these named groups are identifiable as the Halkomelem and Northern Straits "tribes." Some of these may be historically late groupings.

Squamish

The Squamish language seems to have been homogeneous, with no dialect differences. Squamish territory included the shores of Howe Sound, the drainage of the Squamish River (possibly excepting the Upper Cheakamus, which may have been Lillooet hunting territory), and, at least since the middle of the nineteenth century, most of Burrard Inlet. It appears that early in the nineteenth century there were 16 or more Squamish villages on the Squamish River, all within about 25 miles of its mouth. Most of these had summer sites on Howe Sound or Burrard Inlet. Parties of Squamish were also making trips up the Fraser in the late 1820s (Duff 1952a:25–26).

Halkomelem

The Halkomelem language is spoken along the eastern shore of Vancouver Island from Northwest Bay to Saanich Inlet and on the mainland from the mouth of the Fraser eastward to Harrison Lake and the lower end of the Fraser canyon. Three main dialect groups are distinguishable: an Island group, spoken by the people whose winter villages were on Vancouver Island; a Downriver group, spoken by those whose winter villages were on the mainland around the mouth of the Fraser River and upstream about as far as the Stave River; and an Upriver group, spoken by those who lived above the Stave River. Between Island and Upriver dialects the differences are fairly great (Elmendorf and Suttles 1960; Gerdts 1977). Seasonal movements gave the Halkomelem people a greater unity than these facts suggest. For the summer

453

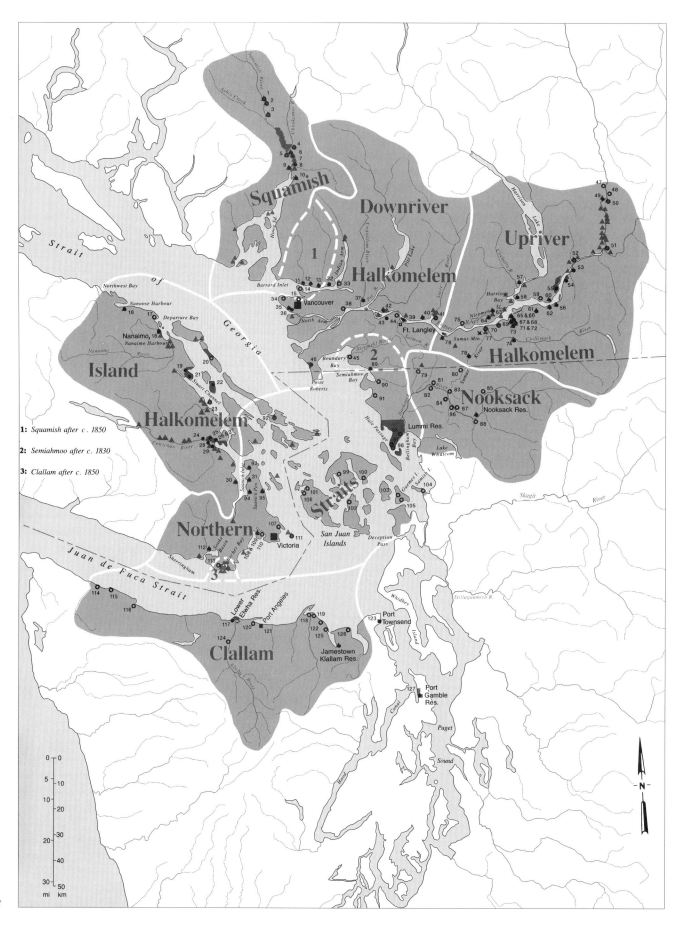

Strait of Georgia

Squamish

Downriver

Halkomelem

Upriver

Northwest Bay

Nanoose Harbour

Departure Bay

Nanaimo

Nanaimo Harbour

Island

Halkomelem

Cowichan River

Boundary Bay

Point Roberts

Semiahmoo Bay

Nicomekl River

Ft. Langley

Sumas Mtn.

Chilliwack

Halkomelem

Nooksack

Nooksack Res.

Lummi Res.

Lake Whatcom

Skagit River

1: *Squamish after c. 1850*

2: *Semiahmoo after c. 1830*

3: *Clallam after c. 1850*

Straits

San Juan Islands

Deception Pass

Northern

Victoria

Juan de Fuca Strait

Sooke Basin

Becher Bay

Sherringham

3

Whidbey

Stilluguamish R.

Port Townsend

Lower Elwha Res.

Port Angeles

Clallam

Jamestown Klallam Res.

Port Gamble Res.

Hood Canal

Puget Sound

N

0   0
5   10
10   20
20   40
30   50
mi   km

Fig. 1. Territories and principal villages of the Central Coast Salish in the early 19th century.

Squamish. 1, p̓uy̓ám̓, Poyam Res.; 2, čə́q̓cəqc 'dirty mouth or edge', Chuckchuck Res.; 3, skáwšən 'foot going down', Skowshin Res.; 4, čiáqməs 'salmon-weir place', Cheakamus Res.; 5, yə́k̓ʷc 'upstream mouth', Yookwitz Res.; 6, wíwəq̓əm 'opening', Waiwakum Res.; 7, syíc̓am 'full', Seaichem Res.; 8, kawtín, Kowtain Res.; 9, yək̓ʷápsəm 'upstream neck', Yekwaupsum Res.; 10, stá̓məs, Stawamus Res.; 11, x̌ʷməlčctən, Capilano Res.; 12, sɬə̓án̓ 'head of bay', Mission Res.; 13, číčlx̌ʷi̓q̓ʷ, Seymour Creek Res.; 14, x̌ʷáyx̌ʷay 'sxwayxwey masks', Lumberman's Arch; 15, sn̓áq̓ʷ, False Creek. Numbers 11–15 may have been Musqueam before 1850.

Island Halkomelem. Nanoose: 16, snəw̓náwəs 'facing inside', Nanoose Res. Nanaimo: 17, sɬ̓íləp; 18, x̌ʷsáx̌ʷəl 'grassy place', Ksalokul. Chemainus: 19, šcəmínəs, Chemainus Res.; 20, léyəqsən 'fir-bark point', Lyacksun Res.; 21, səq̓əmín, Siccameen, Chemainus Res.; 22, pənéləxəθ 'buried edge', Penelekuts, Kuper I. Res.; 23, x̌əléltxʷ 'painted house', Halalt I. Res. Cowichan: 24, s̓ámənə̓, Somenos; 25, k̓ʷáməcən 'hunchback', Quamichan; 26, q̓əməyéqən, Comiaken; 27, xínəpsəm, Kanipsim; 28, x̌ʷəlq̓ʷséla, Koksilah; 29, ɬəmɬəmələc, Clemclemalitz. Malahat: 30, méləxəɬ, Malahat Res.; 31, x̌ʷpáq̓ʷčən, Paquachin, Cole Bay Res.

Downriver Halkomelem. Saleelwat (səlílwətə̓ɬ 'belonging to Indian River'): 32, ̓ácnac 'bay', Burrard Inlet Res.; 33, təmtəmíx̌ʷtən. Musqueam (x̌ʷmə́θk̓ʷəy̓əm 'place of the plant mə́θk̓ʷəy̓'): 34, ̓əy̓álməx̌ (possibly shared with the Squamish); 35, máləy, Musqueam Res.; 36, scəléx̌ʷ, Stselax, Musqueam Res. Coquitlam: 37, k̓ʷík̓ʷiƛ̓əm, Coquitlam Res. Kwantlen: 38, Chitsulus (cíčləs 'steep slope'); 39, McMillan Island Res.; 40, x̌ʷhú·naq̓ʷ 'pink salmon head', Whonnock Res.; 41, sx̌áyəqs, Langley Res. Katzie: 42, q̓íc̓əy 'moss', Katzie Res. No. 1; 43, x̌ʷθə́x̌θəxəm 'nettle place', Katzie Res. No. 2. Nikomekl (snák̓ʷəməɬ): 44, snák̓ʷəye; 45, q̓ʷəmáyəs 'dog face'. Tsawwassen: 46, scəwáθən 'seaward edge', Tsawwassen Res.

Upriver Halkomelem. Tait: 47, c̓ak̓ʷé·m 'skunk-cabbage place', Tsakuam; 48, ̓esəléw̓, Asilao; 49, syəlk̓ʷéɬ, Yale Res.; 50, x̌əɬéɬ, Kuthlalth Res. (Kelatl); 51, ̓iwáwəs, Aywawwis Res.; 52, sq̓əwé·lx̌ʷ, Skawahlook Res.; 53, šx̌ʷ̓əwhéməl, Ohamil Res.; 54, sk̓ʷétəc, Peters Res.; 55, Seabird Island Res.; 56, pápk̓ʷəm 'puffballs', Popkum Res. Chehalis: 57, scə̓íləs 'set on the beach', Chehalis Res. Scowlitz: 58, sq̓əwləc 'turn at bottom', Scowlitz Res. Pilalt: 59, pəláltxʷ 'buried house', Pilalt; 60, siy̓ə́lə, Tseatah Res.; 61, sx̌əléwtxʷ 'painted house', Schelowat Res.; 62, x̌ʷcí·yà·m 'strawberry place', Cheam Res. Nicomen: 63, ləqéməl, Lakahahmen Res.; 64, sk̓ʷiyá·m, Skweahm Res. Chilliwack (scə́lx̌ʷíq̓ʷ): 65, šx̌ʷhéy 'canoe-making place', Skway Res.; 66, sq̓ʷé 'hole', Skwah Res.; 67, q̓ʷəq̓ʷə̓ápəɬp 'crabapple trees', Kwawkwawapilt Res.; 68, sx̌ʷayhéla 'container of many who died', Squiala Res.; 69, ̓éθələc 'edge at bottom', Aitchelitch Res.; 70, léxəwey, Lackaway Res.; 71, sq̓əwqíl 'turn at the head', Skulkayn Res.; 72, yəq̓ʷyəq̓ʷíws 'burnt out', Yakwqeakwioose Res.; 73, čiéqtəl 'weir', Tzeachten Res.; 74, θəwéli, Soowahlie Res. Hatzic: 75, xéθeq 'measure penis'. Matsqui: 76, méθx̌ʷi, Matsqui Main Res. Sumas: 77, səméθ, Sumas Cemetery Res.; 78, k̓ʷək̓ʷə̓íq̓ʷ 'head facing up', Upper Sumas Res.

Nooksack. 79, máməq̓ʷəm 'marshes'; 80, təmíx̌ʷtən; 81, íčélus; 82, sq̓ʷəhélič; 83, k̓ʷénəč; 84, x̌əlxeleltxʷ 'painted houses'; 85, x̌ʷk̓ʷuləx̌ʷiy 'chum salmon place'; 86, spélxən 'prairie'; 87, yəxséy; 88, nəx̌ʷ̓iyəm 'clear water'.

Northern Straits. Semiahmoo (səmyámə): 89, tá̓tələw̓ 'creek', Semiahmoo Res.; 90, s̓íləč; 91, šcé·wəx̌. Saanich (x̌ʷsé·nəč): 92, ̓eleləŋ 'houses', Mayne I. Res.; 93, x̌ʷsə́y̓qəm 'clay place', Tsaykum, Union Bay Res.; 94, x̌ʷčaɬəɬp 'big-leaf maple place', Tsartlip, South Saanich Res.; 95, šcé·wətx̌ʷ, Tsawout, East Saanich Res. Lummi: 96, x̌ʷə́ɬqəy̓əm 'snake place', Old Lummi Village; 97, íemx̌ʷiqsən 'gooseberry point'; 98, sx̌ʷəlísən; 99, ̓eleləŋ 'houses'; 100, x̌ʷtáčɬ; 101, səméyə; 102, sɬəlx̌ə́lnəp 'homesite'. Samish (s̓éməš): 103, gʷəŋq̓ʷəŋéla; 104, ̓e·cílqən; 105, sx̌ʷáyməɬ. Songhees: 106, pq̓ʷi̓élwəɬ 'rotten-wood side'; 107, sŋe̓qə 'snowy'; 108, sx̌ʷiméɬəɬ, Esquimalt Res.; 109, New Songhees Res.; 110, k̓ʷčəŋíləɬč 'bitter cherry trees', Old Songhees village; 111, sqəŋínəs, Discovery I. Res. Sooke: 112, su̓ukʷ 'stickleback', Sooke Res.

Clallam. 113, čiyánəx̌, Cheerno; 114, ƛeƛewáis, Klatlawas; 115, xəŋínət, Hunnint; 116, pəšct, Pysht (Pistchin); 117, ̓iɬx̌ʷa, Elwha; 118, čə́q̓ʷ, Tsako; 119, statíɬəm, Stehtlum; 120, čix̌ʷícən, Tsewhitzen; 121, ̓i̓ínəs 'good beach'; 122, nəx̌ʷŋiə̓áwəɬč 'grand firs', Jamestown; 123, qá̓tay, Kahtai; 124, ti̓éɬ, Indian Creek; 125, sx̌ʷčk̓ʷiə̓ŋ, Sequim; 126, k̓ʷak̓ʷíəɬ, Kaquaith; 127, nəx̌ʷq́íyət, Little Boston.

SOURCES: Kuipers 1967–1969, 2:33–38; Richardson and Galloway 1986; Galloway 1986; Suttles 1946–1952, 1952–1971.

runs of salmon, many of the Island people crossed Georgia Strait and camped along the Fraser, mainly in the Downriver area, and many Downriver and Island people went to the Upriver area (Duff 1952a:25–26).

The Island Halkomelem were: the Nanoose (ˌnă'nōōs), in a single village on Nanoose Harbour; the Nanaimo (nə'nīmō), consisting of five named groups, one with its winter village on Nanaimo Harbour and the other four in a joint winter village on Departure Bay; the Chemainus (chə'mānəs), with at least 10 villages on Stuart Channel, the best known being Penelekuts (pə'nĕləkəts) on Kuper Island; the Cowichan ('käwĭchən), with at least six villages on the lower course of the Cowichan River; and the Malahat, in a single village on Saanich Inlet. Most of the Stuart Channel people also had sites on the banks of the Cowichan River, where tradition (Boas 1887a:132) says they fled during the war with the Lekwiltok.

The Downriver Halkomelem were: the Musqueam ('mŭskwēəm), on the North Arm of the Fraser and on Burrard Inlet; the Tsawwassen (chə'wäsən, tsə'wäsən, tə'wäsən), on the delta south of the main mouth of the Fraser; the Saleelwat (sə'lēlwət), on Indian Arm; the Kwantlen ('kwäntlən), on the Fraser from the upper end of the delta upstream perhaps as far as the Pitt River; the Coquitlam ('kōkwĭtləm), on the Coquitlam River; the Nicomekl ('nĭkō,mĕkəl), in a territory extending from the Fraser south to Boundary Bay via the Salmon and Nicomekl rivers; and the Katzie ('kätsē), on Pitt River, Pitt Lake, and a short stretch of the Fraser above Pitt River. This was, according to traditions, the situation before European contact. Smallpox, probably the epidemic of the 1770s, wiped out the Nicomekl and possibly several other groups above them on the Fraser. After 1827, the Kwantlen abandoned their villages at what was to be the site of New Westminster and established themselves near Fort Langley and in the area depopulated by the epidemic. Later the Musqueam were replaced by the Squamish on Burrard Inlet.

The Upriver Halkomelem were: the Matsqui ('mătskwē), on the south side of the Fraser below Sumas Mountain; the Sumas ('sōō,măs), on Sumas Lake (which covered the lowland southeast of Sumas Mountain until it was drained in the 1920s) and Sumas River; the Nicomen (nĭ'kōmən), along Nicomen Slough; the Scowlitz ('skäwlĭts), around the mouth of the Harrison Bay; the Chehalis (chə'hāləs), on the Harrison River from below the mouth of the Chehalis up into Harrison Lake; the Chilliwack ('chĭlə,wăk), on the Chilliwack River; the Pilalt (pə'ält), on the Fraser at the upper end of the broader part of the valley; and the Tait ('tāt), in more than 20 villages on up the Fraser. According to traditions, until early in the nineteenth century the Chilliwack River flowed into Sumas Lake, and the Chilliwack people, who then spoke a dialect of Nooksack, all lived up the

455

Chilliwack River in the mountains. When logjams caused the Chilliwack River to change its course and flow north into the Fraser, the Chilliwack people moved into the valley, where, by the middle of the nineteenth century they had some 12 villages and were abandoning their original language for Halkomelem (Duff 1952a:43–44; Boas 1894a:455–456; Hill-Tout 1903:355–357). The Chilliwack, Pilalt, and Tait have been grouped together (Duff 1952a) as the Upper Stalo.

Nooksack

Nooksack territory included the drainage of the Nooksack River above the mouth of Bertrand Creek, the upper Sumas River, the south end of Cultus Lake, most of Lake Whatcom, and possibly the shores of Bellingham Bay between the mouths of Whatcom and Chuckanut creeks. Most of the 20 or more Nooksack villages were in the level valley below the confluence of the north and south branches of the Nooksack River (Fetzer 1951; Richardson 1974).

Northern Straits

Northern Straits was spoken on Vancouver Island from Saanich Inlet to Sherringham Point, through the San Juan and southern Gulf islands, and along the mainland shore from Point Roberts and Boundary Bay to Deception Pass. There were dialect differences among the six Northern Straits tribes identifiable in the mid-nineteenth century. These were: the Sooke ('sōōk), around Sooke Harbour; the Songhees ('sôŋ₁hēz), with several winter villages in the Victoria area; the Saanich ('sănĭch), with winter villages at Brentwood, Patricia, and Saanichton bays on the Saanich Peninsula; the Semiahmoo (sĕmē'yämōō), on the mainland around Semiahmoo Bay; the Lummi ('lŭmē), with their two principal winter villages on Hale Passage; and the Samish ('sămĭsh), in villages on Samish and Guemes islands (Suttles 1951). According to traditions, in the late eighteenth century the Songhees, Saanich, Lummi, and Samish all had winter villages in the southern Gulf and San Juan islands. The survivors of two other groups, the Klalakamish on the north end of San Juan Island, and the Swallah, on East Sound on Orcas Island, are said to have joined the Lummi, who moved to the mainland only after taking the mouth of the Nooksack River away from a non-Straits group, possibly Nooksack speakers, the Skelakhan (Curtis 1907–1930, 9:25–30; B.J. Stern 1934:107–108, 115–120).

Clallam

The Clallam occupied the northern slope of the Olympic Peninsula from the Hoko River to Port Discovery Bay (Gunther 1927:177). There were about a dozen Clallam villages on the Strait of Juan de Fuca and one inland on the Elwha River. The people from the Elwha westward are said (Eells 1889:608) to have differed a little in speech from those to the east. The Clallam hunted inland as far as the higher Olympic Mountains and had fishing camps outside their home territory, in Twana country, Skagit country, and with relatives among the Northern Straits people in the San Juan Islands and on the southernmost shores of Vancouver Island. By the middle of the nineteenth century they had expanded northward and eastward, settling on Becher and Parry bays on Vancouver Island in what had been Sooke territory and on Port Townsend at the eastern end of the Olympic Peninsula in what had been Chemakum territory.

Environment

The territory of the Central Coast Salish is varied in topography, climate, flora, and fauna (Suttles 1962: 526–530). Around the eastern end of the Strait of Juan de Fuca, in the rain shadow of the Olympic Mountains, annual rainfall is less than 30 inches; in the Fraser and Nooksack valleys it is 40–60 inches, while to the north of the Fraser on the lower slopes of the Coast Mountains and westward along the Strait of Juan de Fuca, it rises to 80–100 inches (Kendrew and Kerr 1955:79; Phillips 1960: 17). Differences are similarly great in the ranges of temperature and amount of sunlight experienced by different parts of the area.

In the dryer part of the area vegetation is of the Gulf Islands Biotic type (Munro and Cowan 1947), characterized by Garry oak and madrona as well as Douglas fir and by a good deal of open land. In the wetter parts, vegetation falls into two other types, the Coast Forest type in the Squamish Valley and the Puget Lowland type in the Fraser Valley and on the mainland southward. Characteristic trees are Douglas fir, Western hemlock, Western red cedar, big-leaf maple, and red alder, with black cottonwood along river banks and a greater variety of smaller deciduous trees in the Puget Lowland type. Extensive bogs and sloughs in the Fraser Delta distinguish it from other parts of the region.

External Relations

The Central Coast Salish tribes intermarried with adjacent peoples both within their own region and beyond, regardless of differences in speech and customs. Nanaimo negotiated marriages with Alberni Nootka; Sooke with Nitinaht; Clallam with Makah and Twana; Samish, Lummi, and Nooksack with Northern Lushootseed; Upper Stalo with the Thompson and Lillooet; and Squamish with Sechelt. All these marriage ties involved ritual exchange and promoted trade.

There were also hostile relations both within the region and with people of adjacent regions, but usually these involved groups that were not close neighbors. Occasional conflict between the Clallam and Makah may have been exceptional. The Clallam and Lummi were traditionally friends, and both had unfriendly relations with the Cowichan. The Samish, according to traditions, once fought with the Skagit and perhaps other Northern Lushootseed people. The Nooksack occasionally fought with Thompson hunting parties. The Tait were on fairly good terms with the Thompson, and the Chehalis were on good terms with the Lower Lillooet, but the Tait and Lower Lillooet were reportedly enemies. The Squamish fought with Lillooet and Chilcotin raiding parties.

Throughout the region, during the first half of the nineteenth century, the principal enemy was the Lekwiltok Kwakiutl, who raided as far south as Puget Sound. Traditions of battles with them have been recorded among the Cowichan (Curtis 1907–1930, 9:32–35), Lummi (B.J. Stern 1934:100–101), and Musqueam (Suttles 1962–1963).

Culture

The sketch that follows is based in part on what can be gleaned from the accounts of the late eighteenth-century explorers and the early nineteenth-century fur traders and others, but it relies more heavily on ethnographic work dating from the end of the nineteenth century and from the 1930s and 1940s. Unless otherwise specified, it describes culture as of the mid-nineteenth century.

Subsistence

● FISHING Fishing, especially for salmon, must have contributed the greatest amount of food, especially as stored food during the winter. All five species of salmon were present, but at different places and times. People on the salt water could catch chinooks and cohoes by trolling from late winter through spring, but these species were not available to people upriver until late spring or summer. Sockeye and pink salmon generally arrive in the Strait of Juan de Fuca about mid-July and take the same routes around the southern shore of Vancouver Island, through the San Juan and Southern Gulf islands, around Point Roberts and into the Fraser. Along saltwater salmon routes the Northern Straits and Vancouver Island Clallam people used a reef net, which consisted of a rectangular net suspended between two canoes in the path of the migrating salmon (Suttles 1951:152–222; H. Stewart 1977: 93). Anchor lines were arranged in such a way as to resemble a rising reef; this guided in the fish, which were promptly hauled up. The reef net owner or his "captain" engaged a crew of 6–12 men who helped construct the net, set the anchors, and operate the gear. At the height of a good run, a reef net might take several thousand fish a day. The fish were preserved by drying outside on high racks that stood permanently at the reef-net camp.

Sockeye are fatter than other species and were highly valued for flavor, but they do not keep as well as the leaner species caught later in the year.

As the sockeyes and pinks entered the Fraser, nearly all of the Halkomelem, the Squamish, and some of the Northern Straits came for them. In July they fished in the lower course with trawl nets and dip nets operated from canoes. As the season progressed, many went upriver as far as the lower end of the canyon, where they and the local people fished with dip nets from platforms built out over eddies (fig. 2) and dried the fish in the open air or extracted the oil (Duff 1952a:62–67).

Some of the smaller rivers of the area had spring runs of chinooks and summer runs of chinooks and cohoes; many rivers and creeks had fall runs of chums; some had winter runs of steelhead. These fish were caught by fishermen individually with harpoons, leisters, gaffhooks, four-pronged spears, dip nets, and basket traps, or cooperatively with weirs and trawl nets, all depending on the size of the stream and clearness of the water.

The Central Coast Salish weir consisted of a row of posts, braced on the downstream side, holding two horizontal logs, this framework supporting sections of woven withes. Openings in the weir led into traps installed on the upstream side. Building a weir required the cooperation of a number of people for several days and was directed by a man with the necessary technical and ritual knowledge. Once the weir was built anyone could freely gaff fish stopped by the barrier. Disposal of the contents of the traps may have been shared by the kin group only or by a whole village. Fall runs of fish had to be preserved by smoking inside a house.

In channels near the mouth of the Fraser the Musqueam and Tsawwassen had tidal pounds, made of long rows of stakes driven into the bottom, in which they took larger salmon and sturgeon. These were owned by kin groups, the descendants of the men who had built them.

Halibut were caught by fishermen in nearly every village on the saltwater. They were taken from late spring through summer in water from 15 to 40 fathoms with the U-shaped hook and octopus bait. Other saltwater fishes of some importance were herring, taken with the herring rake, lingcod, taken with a shuttlecock lure and spear, and flounders, taken with a multiprong spear.

Sturgeon were harpooned in bays around the mouth of the Fraser with a sealing harpoon. In the Fraser itself, harpooners used harpoons with shafts up to 50 feet long, holding the shaft vertically and "feeling" along the bottom for the fish (MacMillan and McDonald 1827–1830:9; Lord 1866, 1:181; Idiens 1987:50). The trawl net was also used for sturgeon and for the few strictly freshwater fishes of the region, such as whitefish and suckers. Eulachon in the Squamish River (Barnett 1955:31) and in the Fraser (Duff 1952a:70–71) were important as fresh food but not as a source of oil.

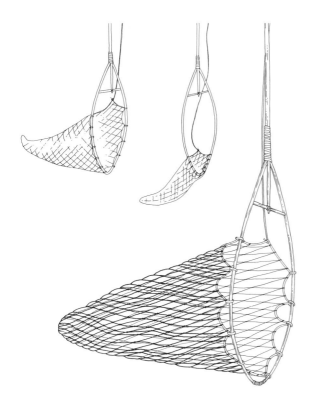

left, after H. Stewart 1977:91; right, Royal B.C. Prov. Mus., Victoria: PN 6262.
Fig. 2. Dip net fishing on the Fraser River. left, Dip net, attached to rings that slipped around the hoop at the end of the shaft. The net was kept open by means of a line that was pulled taut. When a fish swam into the net, the line was released, allowing the rings to slide down the hoop, trapping the fish. right, Dip netting from a platform over the Fraser River, probably in the Fraser Canyon. Photograph by John Pease Babcock, 1901–1910.

• HUNTING The professional sea hunter used a double-foreshaft harpoon with a trident butt for the hair seal and the porpoise. Hunters also caught seals in nets set around their hauling-out rocks and, at a few places where the tide left them high enough, clubbed them before they could reach the water. Seals and porpoises were probably most important as a source of oil, which was commonly used with dried fish.

When sea lions were sighted, Chemainus hunters went out in two-man canoes, each harpooner with his paddler. If one struck a sea lion too large for him to handle alone, a second struck it, possibly a third, and a fourth. The carcass was divided by order of striking, following fixed rules. Some Squamish also hunted sea lions, but no other Central Coast Salish did (Suttles 1952).

The Clallam were, with the Quinault, the only Coast Salish who practiced whaling. The species taken was probably the humpback whale, which came into the Strait of Juan de Fuca. Clallam whalers, unlike those of the outer coast, did not undergo elaborate ritual preparation and go out in search of whales; they were simply ready whenever a whale was sighted (Gunther 1927:202, 210). There were lookout points where a watch was kept, such as on Dungeness Bay (Waterman 1920a:60). Because one harpoon was usually not enough, several canoes went out together. After a harpooner struck a whale, he offered the

blubber of one half of the lower jaw to the second to strike it. If a third was needed, the first man offered the other half of the jaw, and if a fourth, the underpart of one of the flukes. The great whalers had vision power to help them and sang their songs when they struck a whale (Suttles 1946–1952).

Land hunters caught deer by trapping them in a pitfall, with a snare, or simply with sharpened stakes set behind a barrier in a trail; by stalking them with a bow and arrow, some using a deerhead disguise or a whistle sounding like a fawn and some aided by dogs; by driving them into a narrow pass where they could be netted (Lamb 1960:98) or shot; or, on dark nights, by using a flare in a canoe to make shadows that drove them into the water, where they could be easily dispatched. Elk and black bear were hunted with bow and arrow. Bears were also caught in deadfalls and smoked out of their winter dens. Mountain goats were found only in rugged terrain on the mainland, where hunters killed them with the bow and arrow. Beaver were shot, speared, or clubbed. Hunters occasionally shot raccoons but usually ignored the smaller mammals and avoided grizzlies, cougars, and wolves.

Hunters sought hides, antler, horn, mountain-goat wool, and beaver teeth, as well as meat. Some land hunters, like sea hunters, achieved a kind of professional status and were designated by a special term. They spent whole summers in the mountains, with their families, drying meat and preparing hides, or went into the hills in winter when most people stayed close to their villages on the shore.

The bow was of yew, two and one-half to three feet long, with a flat grip. It was held horizontally. Vancouver (1798,1:109) describes recurved sinew-backed bows acquired at Port Discovery.

Several species of waterfowl were present the year round, and over 30 species pass through seasonally or spend the winter. All were used to some extent. Hunters shot large waterfowl, such as swans and geese, with bow and arrow from behind blinds in canoes. Various ducks were taken at night by a two-man team with a flare in their canoe and a net on a pole (for marsh ducks) or a multiprong spear (for saltwater diving ducks). During herring runs, nets were anchored horizontally underwater over beds of eel-grass to catch diving ducks feeding on the roe. Probably the most productive device was a net hung between poles across a spit or channel where flocks were known to pass. The poles, 30 feet or more high and as much as 100 feet apart, were permanent structures, the property of the families who erected them and claimed the sites (Wagner 1933:99; Vancouver 1798,1:61; Meany 1942:85–86). The net was raised by blocks and lines at dawn or dusk or in foggy weather when visibility was poor; as soon as a flock hit it, the persons stationed at the poles released the lines and let the net drop, while others rushed out to wring the birds' necks. Two species of grouse were taken with snares, but other land birds were not commonly eaten.

● GATHERING At least 40 plants provided edible sprouts and stems, bulbs and roots, berries and fruits, or nuts. Most of these were quite limited in availability. However, four starchy bulbs or roots were important enough that the best beds were held as family or individual property—camas among the Northern Straits tribes, brake ferns at Musqueam, wapato at Katzie and perhaps elsewhere on the Fraser, and wild carrots at Nooksack. Women kept their camas beds productive by reseeding and burning (Turner and Kuhnlein 1983:211). Camas and wapato were preserved. Blackberries, salal berries, service berries, crabapples, and possibly a few other fruits were also preserved. A great many plants were used for medicinal purposes (Turner and Bell 1971).

Women gathered sea urchins, crabs and barnacles, and a variety of mollusks, including Washington butter clams, horse clams, littleneck clams, cockles, and bay mussels. The most famous butter-clam and horse-clam beds were owned by kin groups. These two species were preserved by steaming and drying.

Technology

Men worked stone by grinding, chipping, and pecking; antler by sawing, graving, drilling, carving, and abrading; and shell by abrading and graving (Mitchell 1971:220). These techniques produced the tools of woodworking, which provided much that was basic to native life. Products included house posts, beams and planks, canoes, bent-corner boxes, pegged corner boxes (that is, boxes with the four sides dovetailed and held together with a single long peg inserted through each corner), dugout dishes (fig. 3), tools, weapons, and ceremonial paraphernalia.

Men made heavy cordage, of twisted cedar withes, kelp, gut, sinew, and hide. Women made finer cordage, of nettle fibers, willow bark, cedar bark, and Indian hemp (imported from the Plateau). Men made most nets. Women shredded red cedar bark by beating it on a sharp-edged wooden anvil with a sharp-edged bark beater, and they used the shredded cedar bark for towels, cradle mattresses, and skirts. Men used whole cedar bark for canoe bailers as well as makeshift huts and canoes.

Women sewed mats of cattail leaves and tules in three sizes: large house mats used for lining the walls of winter

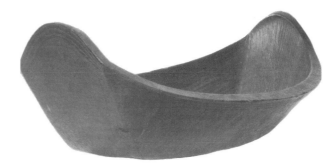

Fig. 3. Cowichan carved wooden bowl for everyday use. This is the characteristic form of food receptacle, carved of a single block of wood, slim, with flared ends. More elaborate dishes had human or animal heads carved at the ends and the rim inlaid with haliotis (Barnett 1955:65). Collected by G.T. Emmons before 1907; length 59 cm.

Fig. 4. Lummi Bill James and his mother Fran James making cedar bark baskets. Photograph by Mary Randlett, Lummi Indian Reservation, Wash., 1986.

a

b

c

d

e

460

top left, Natl. Mus. of Canada, Ottawa: 71525; Stark Mus. of Art, Orange, Tex.: center left, 31.78/96, WWC 97; bottom left, 31.27/73, WWC 73; a-e, Smithsonian, Dept. of Anthr.: 221179-A-E.
Fig. 5. Weaving. top left, Mrs. George Johnnie, Squamish, fulling mountain-goat wool on a cattail mat and beating diatomaceous earth into the wool. On her loom is a partly finished blanket. Photograph by Harlan I. Smith, Musqueam Reserve, B.C., 1928. center left, Songhees woman spinning roving into yarn on her spindle. bottom left, Saanich woman weaving a dog-hair blanket on a 2-bar loom, set up in what appears to be a summer house made of poles and mats. These and other sketches are the basis for an oil painting, which is better known but less reliable than the sketches (P. Gustafson 1980:82-83). center left and bottom left, Watercolor sketches by Paul Kane, 1847. a-e, Spindle whorls embellished with stylized zoomorphic and hominoid designs carved by men. The designs may have been indicative of purification, signifying the importance of the spindle whorl in transforming wool into wealth (Suttles 1983:86). The carved convex surface faced the spinner. a-e, Collected by G.T. Emmons from Cowichan, Vancouver I., B.C., in 1903. Diameter of a, 19.3 cm; rest to same scale.

Public Arch. of Canada: PA-123916.
Fig. 6. Cowichan sweaters. Ed Underwood and his wife, joint managers of the Goldstream Indian Cooperative on the East Saanich Reserve, B.C. He holds a traditional spindle, while she sits at a spinning machine. Photographed about 1960s. The home knitting industry, widespread among the Coast Salish, is a melding of traditional elements and European technology. The knitting technique is European but some of the early designs were from aboriginal basketry. The machine for making the spun wool is based upon the aboriginal spindle, but the machine itself is a local improvisation derived from a sewing machine. The industry began about 1920, and by the late 1940s the sweaters had become popular with non-Indians in B.C. and Wash. and were being exported to other regions including Europe. It had a substantial impact on the Native economy and the status of women knitters in the community, who acquired an independent income while the men were still dependent on seasonal labor (Lane 1951).

houses and covering pole frames for summer shelters, medium-sized bed mats used for mattresses and temporary rain covers, and small canoe mats used for sitting or kneeling on when traveling. Less commonly they wove mats of strips of cedar bark; these were also imported from the outer coast.

Women made several types of containers, including openwork wrapped lattice burden baskets for gathering roots and shellfish, tightly made coiled or twined burden baskets for picking berries, and flexible cattail bags with drawstrings for storing dried fish. Of more limited use were baskets made of woven strips of cedarbark (fig. 4) with reinforced rims, trunks and lidded boxes made of cedar slats, and birchbark vessels (perhaps limited to the Upper Stalo and received in trade from the Plateau).

The Central Coast Salish were at the center of an area where a distinctive form of weaving was practiced. Its features included the use of wool from a special breed of dog, as well as mountain-goat wool, waterfowl down, and fireweed cotton; spinning with an unusually large spindle, by a method not reported from elsewhere; and weaving on a two-bar loom with a continuous warp (Kissel 1916; W.C. Orchard 1926; P. Gustafson 1980).

The wool dog (Howay 1918) seems to have become extinct as a separate breed by the middle of the nineteenth century. It was described as a small to medium-sized, Pomeranian-like, nonbarking animal, generally white, with a thick, compact coat that was shorn with a knife in the spring.

The weaver fulled a mixture of wool and down by beating diatomaceous earth into it (fig. 5 top left). She then twisted it into a loose roving, which she spun on a spindle into a thick yarn. The spindle consisted of a shaft up to four feet long and a wooden whorl up to eight inches in diameter. The spindle was held in the two hands below the whorl (Barnett 1955:118–121); the roving was attached above the whorl after passing through a ring or simply over a beam to maintain tension (Kissel 1916; Lane 1951:19–20). The warping was done on a two-bar loom (fig. 5 bottom left) by passing a continuous strand around the two rollers and around a cord or rod that could be withdrawn after the weaving, so that the finished product opened out with four selvedges. The width of the piece was determined by the distance between the posts, while the length was twice the distance between the rollers. The weaver used thin boards to make sheds or simply worked the weft in with her fingers. The most common technique was twilling, but more elaborate fabrics were made by twining or combining twilling and twining.

Weavers made blankets in several sizes. Smaller ones were large enough to serve as robes or bed covers; larger ones, measuring 12 feet or more, were primarily items of wealth. Most made in the late nineteenth century were twilled, of undyed wool, or with some dyed strands forming stripes. But Fraser (Lamb 1960:101) saw plaid dog-wool blankets. Others were twilled of undyed wool in the center but given borders decorated with geometric 461 forms created by twining. A rarer type was made entirely by twining with an organized pattern of geometric forms (Kissel 1929; Drucker 1965; Feder 1971:pl. 32; P. Gustafson 1980).

Weavers also made a fabric of yarn produced by mixing waterfowl down with nettle fibers, and they made pack straps by twining on suspended warps, incorporating some of the design elements seen in the blankets.

Structures

Winter villages were always on water, usually where canoes could be easily beached. A village could consist of a single house, a row of houses, or two or more rows of houses. In the early nineteenth century the most common winter dwelling was a shed-roof house consisting of a permanent framework of posts and beams and a removable cover of roof and wall planks ("Introduction," fig. 2, this vol.). It was generally built parallel to the shore with the roof sloping to the rear, 20–60 feet in width and twice or more in length. If the terrain permitted, a structure

Fig. 7. House post representing the famous warrior Capilano (*qiyəplénəx*ʷ), who fought the Lekwiltok. It is said to have been carved at the Capilano River and towed around to Musqueam to support a beam in a house built by Capilano II, the nephew of Capilano. Standing beside it is Charlie, Capilano III, the nephew of Capilano II. The face on the post is carved in Central Coast Salish style, a flat oval with small eyes and mouth. The post was acquired by the U. of B.C., Vancouver. Photograph by Harlan I. Smith, Musqueam Village, B.C. 1898.

might be extended indefinitely, possibly with plank partitions separating households (Barnett 1955:43). Fraser (Lamb 1960:103–104) saw a structure 640 feet long, 60 feet wide, and 18 feet high on the front side.

House posts were often decorated with carving or painting, perhaps everywhere in the region (fig. 7). Decorated house fronts were seen on the Lower Fraser, in 1808 by Fraser (Lamb 1960:103–104) and in the 1850s by Wilson (1866:287–288; Stanley 1970:37), Gibbs (journal quoted in Beckham 1969:209), and Alden (Stenzel 1975), and in the Squamish Valley by Mayne (1860), but they are not mentioned for other places.

The Upper Stalo and the Nooksack (M.W. Smith 1947; Duff 1952a:46–47) built Plateau-style semisubterranean houses, for use during the coldest time of year. The Squamish and Downriver Halkomelem also had a few excavated refuges for times of war as well as extreme cold (Barnett 1944, 1955:53, 55).

Fortified war refuges were built in precontact times, evidently with ditches and walls of horizontal planks (Mitchell 1968:44). During the early nineteenth century, fortifications may have become more elaborate; Northern Straits traditions tell of trenches with sharpened stakes, walls around whole villages, escape tunnels, poles for hoisting flares, and doors with protective devices (Suttles 1946–1952).

Other structures include summer mat houses, huts of slabs of cedar bark, wooden grave houses (fig. 8), sweat lodges of poles and mats, and, perhaps in the Upper Stalo area only, raised caches of planks.

Transport

Most travel was by canoe. There were five distinct types of cedar dugout: the Coast Salish canoe, the westcoast canoe, the shovelnose canoe ("Introduction," fig. 3, this vol.), the reef-net canoe, and the war canoe.

The Coast Salish canoe type was used for saltwater fishing and hunting and was the style most commonly used by the Island Halkomelem, Musqueam, Northern Straits, and Clallam. A version of this type with less sheer and a vertical cutwater was used by the Squamish and Upper Stalo. It was said to be less easily handled on the salt water but better on rivers.

The West Coast canoe was the most seaworthy type and was used especially by the Island Halkomelem, Northern Straits, and Clallam. Up to nearly 40 feet in length, these could hold 20 to 30 people. This type was made in small numbers, even by the Upper Stalo (Duff 1952a:51–52) but was probably more often obtained from the Nootkans.

The other three canoe types were adapted for specific uses. The shovelnose canoe was mainly used by the Upper Stalo and Nooksack for poling in rivers. The reef-net canoe was used by the Northern Straits. The war canoe

left, Stark Mus. of Art, Orange, Tex.: 31.78/88, WWC 89; right, Natl. Mus. of Canada, Ottawa: 71406.

Fig. 8. Graves. left, Clallam graves and carved human figure, perhaps representing a deceased person, near the village of ʔiʔínəs at the east end of Port Angeles, Wash. The inscription on the face of the painting "Idol and Graves, Vancouver Island" is not by the artist, and, in fact, gives the incorrect locality. This has occurred on a number of Kane's works (Harper 1971:xi). Watercolor sketch by Paul Kane, 1847. right, Musqueam tomb near Vancouver, B.C., consisting of a box resting on a board support. On the front of the box are four fishers (carved from the same slab of wood as the box front itself) that represent the "cleansing device" of the deceased (Jenness 1955:72–73). The front of the support is carved in low relief, and the front edge of the lid is incised. Photograph by Harlan I. Smith, 1928.

was similar to the West Coast canoe type but with a high, vertical flaring bow blade (Boas 1891:566; Barnett 1955: 115, fig. 45; Gunther 1972:71, fig. 28; Kane sketches in Harper 1971:254–255, figs. 185–187). Some of these war canoes were obtained in trade from the Lekwiltok (MacMillan and McDonald 1827–1830:17).

Where nearby villages could not be easily reached by water, there were well-used trails, as between the Nooksack and the Matsqui on the Fraser (Reid 1987:78). There were also trails used in emergencies; a famous Semiahmoo runner used one to warn the Lummi of enemy attacks.

Clothing and Adornment

A flattened head was the sign of a free (nonslave) status everywhere except among the Upper Stalo, who did not regularly flatten infants' heads (Duff 1952a:90–91). Permanent frontal and occipital flattening was produced by the pressure of cedarbark pads on the head of the infant in its cradle. Ears were pierced and often the septum of the nose. Some women had lines tattooed on their cheeks or chins, and a few persons of both sexes had tattooing on their arms and legs (Harper 1971: pl. 45; Boas 1891:574, fig. 11).

Both sexes ordinarily let their hair grow long, exceptions being mourners and male slaves. Men wore their hair loose, held with a cedarbark headband or gathered in a knot behind. Women parted their hair in the middle, marking the part with red paint, and tied or braided the two ends. Some men plucked all facial hair, but many left moustaches and a few, beards (fig. 9).

In warm weather, men wore no clothing at all or simply a robe thrown over the shoulders, or over the left shoulder and under the right arm, and held with a pin or two. Women wore a short apron or skirt, and usually a robe around the shoulders. Some men and women wore conical (Lamb 1960:100) or mushroom-shaped basketry hats.

Some men wore fur caps. Ordinarily all went barefoot. Robes were mainly woolen blankets, but some were made of skins or shredded cedarbark (Vancouver 1798, 1:106–108).

In colder weather both sexes wore a shirtlike garment made of down-and-nettle fabric, covered with a robe or, in wet weather, a poncho of cattail matting or woven cedarbark. Men who went hunting inland wore a hide outfit consisting of a pointed hood, shirt, leggings, mittens, and moccasins, and they used snowshoes. Warriors wore a knee-length shirt of several thicknesses of elk hide.

European visitors commented on the variety and quantity of paint the Natives put on their bodies. Fraser (Lamb 1960:101, 103) saw the people of one Tait village who seemed to have reddish skin and hair and those of another who looked "fair," the result of red and white paint. Clallam, Lummi, and others in 1825 made "regular lines on their faces" with red ocher, charcoal, and powdered mica (Scouler 1905:201). Paints mixed with tallow were applied not only for decoration but also for protection against insects (Stanley 1970:63).

Europeans also commented on the variety of ornaments, which at first contact already included European items (Lamb 1960:100; Wilson 1866:285,297). In 1790, Clallam were wearing earrings made of copper and beads as well as English, Portuguese, and Chinese coins (Wagner 1933:109). At Point Roberts in 1792 the Spanish saw engraved brass bracelets (Wagner 1933:187).

Social Organization

Kinship was reckoned bilaterally; kin terms made no distinction between father's and mother's relatives, and the incest rule applied equally to both sides. In theory, marriage was forbidden between persons related as

463

distantly as fourth cousins, but in practice distant cousins did marry.

Residential groups were the family, household, local group, and winter village. The family occupied one section of the winter house, where it had its own fire. It consisted of husband, wife, and minor children, possibly expanded to include plural wives (though co-wives might have separate fires), spouses of young adult children (though younger couples would eventually have their own section and fire), dependent older relatives, and slaves. It kept its own stores, generally cooked and ate apart from other families within the household, and might go its own way in summer.

The household was composed of several families related through either males or females, who cooperated economically and socially.

In stronger houses the core of blood relatives constituted the functioning members of the $x^w n\partial\check{c}\acute{a}l\partial w\partial m$ 'one family', a cognatic descent group identified by Jenness

Museo de America, Madrid: 232.
Fig. 9. Nanaimo chief from Descanso Bay, B.C. He wears a woven cloak possibly of cedar bark with fur trim and an elaborate headdress, probably also of woven material decorated with feathers and shells. Black and white sketch by José Cardero on the Alejandro Malaspina Expedition, 1792.

464

(1934–1935:52) as the "house" in the sense used by European nobility. Members of the kin group were the descendants of some notable ancestor, and they shared inherited rights to resources, names, and ceremonial activities and paraphernalia. In theory all descendants, those in the ancestor's village and those elsewhere, were members. In practice, the management of resources remained in one house and tended to become concentrated in the hands of an elite, through a preference for primogeniture modified by a policy of restricting technical, ritual, and other information to children who showed special aptitude.

The named local group was identified in the Fort Victoria treaties (Duff 1969) as a "family," by Boas (1889c:321) as a "clan" or (1889c:322) "gens" or (1891: 563) "sept," and by Hill-Tout (1904a:312, 1907a:308) as a "sept" or "local community." Hill-Tout (1907a:308) describes it as a group having a sense of identity and a myth of descent from a "first man," even though its members did not all regard themselves as kinsmen and were divided into distinct classes. Most local groups consisted of the household of an established kin group and several dependent households. Men identified as chiefs of local groups were probably heads of leading households or kin groups.

Some local groups may have had their own winter villages, while others had adjacent houses in the same winter village; probably all had their own seasonal fishing sites. The Nanaimo, for example, consisted of five local groups; four wintered in one village on Departure Bay, while the fifth had its own on Nanaimo Harbour, and all five had houses where they fished on the Nanaimo River (Barnett 1955:22–23).

The larger winter villages consisted of several houses representing several kin and local groups. Members of different households within the village cooperated in some subsistence activities, as in a deer drive or building a salmon weir, and the houses within the village, like the families within the house, shared temporary abundances of perishable foods. Houses also cooperated in some ceremonial activities and in mutual defense. But such cooperation was not forced upon them by any village organization; houses also acted independently in such matters. Larger winter villages, being composed of kin groups with different inherited rights and different external ties, were not culturally homogeneous. Segments of a village might even differ in speech (Elmendorf and Suttles 1960). Neighboring villages cooperated in mutual defense, perhaps under the leadership of some noted warrior, but there is little evidence for any formal intervillage organization.

In 1790 Quimper found "no superior chief" among the Sooke and the New Dungeness Clallam (Wagner 1933:99, 130–132), and nothing in the reports of the Spanish and British expeditions of 1791–1792 contradicts this judgment. "Chiefs" encountered by Fraser (Lamb 1960: 102–105) in 1808 and Scouler (1905:196–205) in 1824 seem to have been wealthy men who provided their visitors with food and guidance; there is nothing to indicate that they had authority beyond their villages. In 1852 Douglas (1854:246) reported that villages on the Cowichan River had headmen with great influence but no power to govern.

In the Native view society was divided into worthy people, worthless people, and slaves. A worthy person was called siʔém, a term that implies unblemished ancestry, good manners, extrahuman support, and wealth. This term was used in reference for the head of a house, kin group, or local group (and so is sometimes translated "chief") and in address for any respected person, male or female.

Some villages had separate segments occupied by siéxəm 'worthless people', and few villages have been identified as altogether 'worthless people' (Suttles 1958).

A slave (sk̓ʷə́yəθ) was the personal property of his master. Slaves lived in their masters' houses and often worked with them, but they were socially nonpersons and mainly lived lives of drudgery.

Conflict

Conflict both within and between villages seems to have been common. An injury or death caused by another, whether accidental or intentional, was grounds for a demand for compensation, but if payment was not immediate, conflict might follow (Barnett 1955:270). The Clallam (Gunther 1927:266–267), and probably others, saw payment as dishonorable, and refusal to pay was a common cause of conflict. Within a village, on-going conflict was resolved by the stronger party's paying the weaker to end it (B.J. Stern 1934:99–100) or by the weaker party's moving somewhere else. Between people in different villages, conflict could lead to raiding, generally led by professional warriors, men with special vision power for the role.

The raid, whether organized for vengeance, gain, or a show of power, was typically a surprise attack, at night or at dawn, the warrior taking the lead in clubbing and beheading men, capturing women and children, and carrying off loot. The heads were set up on poles as trophies and the captives held for ransom or sold as slaves. Intervillage conflicts did not necessarily involve everyone; relatives might be exempt from attack. But there were instances of successful campaigns against adjacent groups that allowed the victors to expand their territory.

Life Cycle

Babies were not formally named but were called by pet names, some of which lasted into adult life. They were cradled in wooden or basketry cradles and, unless born of slave mothers, had their heads flattened. The cradle was usually carried in the arms rather than on the back, and it was often hung from a bent pole that bounced at the tug of a string.

From an early age, children were toughened by being roused out of bed to bathe in icy water and sent out on stormy nights to run in the rain. This "training" culminated at adolescence in questing for the vision believed to be the source of many kinds of success in later life.

Families with proper traditions gave their children, often individually and secretly, sniw 'advice' consisting of their genealogy and family history, gossip about other families, and rules of proper behavior (Suttles 1958).

A boy's first kill and his change of voice were given minor ceremonial recognition. When a girl reached puberty her family publicly announced it, if possible, with a feast, display of hereditary privileges, and gifts to witnesses. During her menstrual periods a woman had to eat and sleep apart.

A family might give hereditary names to children at any time after late childhood, but when they did so depended on their means, since it required gifts to witnesses (fig. 10).

Families of substance sheltered their daughters and sent their sons, accompanied by uncles, to sue for the hands of daughters of equal status in other villages. The young woman was able to reject a suitor whom she strongly disliked, but parents urged a daughter to marry a husband of means. The ideal wedding involved the exchanges of roughly equal bride price and dowry (the dowry perhaps including rights to hereditary names and performances) and was celebrated with cleansing ceremonies and gifts to witnesses. However, some couples eloped and patched things up later.

The ideal marriage initiated a series of exchanges of food and wealth between the co-parents-in-law, and these continued over the years. If a spouse died, an ideal second marriage was with a sibling or other close relative of the deceased. This remarriage was not required, but it was encouraged if the families wanted to continue the alliance.

At childbirth the parturient was isolated in a separate structure with a woman attendant for several days. After the birth, both parents were restricted in their activities. Parents of twins were isolated for as much as a year.

After death the body was wrapped in blankets by someone with ritual knowledge and placed in a raised canoe or gravebox, and the family and house were ritually cleansed with burning boughs. Several years later the bones of the deceased were rewrapped with new blankets with a display of hereditary privileges and the payment of witnesses. Graves were marked by carvings. Names of the dead were not publicly spoken until they were bestowed again.

Fig. 10. Potlatch. The boy and girl standing in the canoe are to be given hereditary names. They are wearing strands of mountain goat wool, which are typical attire of the adolescent during this ceremony. They will be ceremonially "washed" by sxwayxwey dancers (Barnett 1955:159), an important part of the public rite. The boy is holding a ritualist's rattle. Traditional canoes, native woven mats and blankets, a portrait (probably of a deceased relative), and the mat screen for dancers are visible. Piles of commercial blankets and cloth on the scaffold are to be given away. Photographed at Quamichan, B.C., about 1913; cropped.

Beliefs

● MYTHOLOGY In myths there was an age when the world was different, its people were like both humans and animals of the present age, and it was full of dangerous monsters. The myth age ended when xéˑls the Transformer came through the world, transforming monsters and other myth-age beings into rocks and animals, and setting things in order for the people of the present age. In the myths, Mink and Raven play minor roles as tricksters, but the Transformer is serious and concerned for human welfare.

Traditions of local groups usually told how the group's founder dropped from the sky at or near its winter village or summer camp, where the Transformer gave him technical and ritual knowledge, and where he established special relationships with local resources. Marriage with a non-human establishes an affinal relationship with its obligations of reciprocity, as in the Katzie myth of the ancestor who married a sockeye salmon woman and was taught how to perform the rite that ensures the return of her people, the summer run of sockeye salmon (Jenness 1955:17–21). Or a human being simply becomes a valuable non-human being, as in the Katzie myth of the ancestor whose daughter becomes a sturgeon (Jenness 1955:12).

● BASIC CONCEPTS It was believed that the living human being has components visible only to persons with special powers. These are the šxʷhəlí 'life', the sməstáyəxʷ 'person', and perhaps others identified as the 'mind' and the 'shadow'. One of these, usually identified as the 'person', could spontaneously leave the body, as in dreams and vision, or could be lured away by dangerous beings or the dead. One of the principal tasks of the shaman was to restore such lost entities. After death, one of these entities became the *spəlqʷíɬaʔ* 'ghost' (also 'corpse'), which lingered about the grave or on the edge of living society, sometimes requiring gifts of food and clothing and perhaps eventually being reborn as a descendant. A separate land of the dead was part of Clallam eschatology (Gunther 1927:296) but seems absent elsewhere.

A distinction was made between the ordinary and the *xéʔxeʔ* 'sacred, forbidden, powerful', a term applied to anything that might be a source of danger or power, as an abnormal baby, pubescent girl, recently bereaved person, abnormal animal, or unusual phenomenon. The term was also applied to what some believed to be the most powerful force of all, the *swéyəl* 'daylight, day, sky'.

● VISION POWER The vision experience was described as an encounter with an animal or with a being in human form who revealed himself to be an animal, tree, or "natural" phenomenon, such as the sun. In the encounter the seeker loses consciousness and is given some desirable knowledge or skill. There was often a logical relationship between the being encountered and the gift received; a famous woodworker received power from a pileated woodpecker, a weaver from a snake. The most powerful beings gave those they favored the ability to become gamblers, warriors, and shamans, or simply rich men. The being encountered in the vision experience was thought to act as a "helper," guiding its human protégé in dreams and even bringing material benefits directly, as when a hunter's wolf helper drove deer to his door. What was seen in the vision was also the source of, or was realized in, a song that possessed the human protégé and gave him or her the most direct access to its powers. Shamans, seers, diviners, warriors, and a few others sang their songs before or while exercising their powers, but most people sang them only as participants in the "spirit" dance.

A distinction was made between the ordinary person's *sʔə́lyə* 'vision' and the *snéʔem* 'shaman's helper' of the *šxʷnéʔem* 'shaman'. Shaman's helpers were not different in species from other helpers; they simply gave special abilities. Both men and women became shamans. Public recognition required no special ceremony, simply success in healing. Treatment included singing to bring a helper, diagnosis by looking into the patient or scrying in a vessel of water, dramatizing the recovery of a lost 'person', and using the hands and mouth to extract a harmful intrusive entity.

There were other shamanlike uses of vision power. The seer, usually a woman, could see into the distance and learn of the health of relatives or the approach of enemy raiders. The possessors of two types of songs ordinarily used in the spirit dance could also use them to discover lost persons and objects.

● SPELL POWER Contrasting with vision power and rivaling it in importance was *siẃíṅ* (or *syəẃíṅ*, Clallam *skʷís*), the power of spells, verbal formulas using secret names for things addressed and believed capable of influencing or controlling them. Spells were addressed to cedar wood to keep it from splitting, to the feet of a hunter to make him swift and silent, to a wounded animal to subdue it, to the daylight, to the dead to hold back a rival canoe in a race, to human feelings to turn indifference into love or love into contempt. They were used by many persons who knew enough of them to help in their own occupations, perhaps especially in hunting and wood-working. But the *wəɬθíʔθə* 'ritualist' knew spells for special occasions or emergencies and could be hired to use them. Ritualists combined the inaudible recitation of the spells with ritual acts involving red ocher, white bird down, and hogfennel seeds. Some had cryptic designs they painted on persons' bodies to strengthen them (Jenness 1955:38) and used the rattles identified as 'cleansing devices'. Incantations with spell words were sung by hunters to quell wounded bears or sea lions and by ritualists in the first salmon ceremony and in cleansing ceremonies.

Ceremonies

● THE SPIRIT DANCE During the coldest months of every year, in every village, many nights were devoted to *smíɬə*, called "spirit dancing." For smaller dances one house in a village invited people from other houses; for larger dances one village invited the people of neighboring villages. The hosts provided food for the guests and usually every dancer present performed, individually, and so the dance might last many hours. A dancer was any man or woman who had a *syə́wən* (Clallam *skʷnúcən*), "spirit song" that he or she had learned to dance with. A *syə́wən* was acquired through the return of the vision power acquired when young, through mourning, and through initiation after kidnapping by a group of dancers hired by the family and isolation (usually four days) (Barnett 1955:278–282). The new dancer wore a special costume and was subject to special taboos during his or her first season.

These songs belonged to several distinct categories distinguishable by musical form, dancing style, red or black face paint, and elements of costume and paraphernalia. Dancers with songs classed as *sqə́yəp* used red paint, wore cedar bark, and (according to tradition) danced with knives piercing their flesh. Dancers with *skʷənílɔc* songs could cause cedar boards or hoops to become animated and reveal past events and things not visible to ordinary people. Dancers with *wəẏqéʔen* songs wore black paint, headdresses of hair with twirling feathers and shirts patterned after those of warriors ("Central and Southern Coast Salish Ceremonies Since 1900," this vol.). The

Fig. 11. Sxwayxwey dance. left, Dance practice at Musqueam, B.C. left to right, Andrew Charles, Ed Sparrow, Sr., and Henry Louis (the fourth dancer is not fully visible). They are at the point in the cleansing ceremony when the subject (who is absent at the practice) would be brushed off by red cedar boughs. Photograph by Wilson Duff, 1949. top right, Sxwayxwey mask collected from Nanaimo performers in Victoria, B.C., 1864. Height 43 cm. bottom right, Scallop shell rattle. Strips of red and blue stroud, wrapped with 3 bands of red stroud, secure hawk feathers at the grip. The spruce root hoop holds 16 shells. Among the tribes who practiced the sxwayxwey, rattles of this type were carried by the sxwayxwey dancers; among the Clallam they were used by spirit dancers (Eells 1985:53, 380) or shamans. Collected by J.G. Swan from Clallam at Port Townsend, Wash. Terr., 1873. Diameter of hoop, 18 cm.

words of the songs and movements of the dance hinted at the identity of the vision power but usually did not reveal it clearly.

● FIRST SALMON CEREMONY Throughout the region, people treated one catch of salmon with special reverence. The species and the details of the ceremony varied, but the basis was the same. The salmon, it was believed, were beings who lived like people in their own world but came yearly as fish to give their flesh to humans, who were obliged to treat them properly. The salmon were carefully carried in by children, cooked in a special way, eaten by all, and their bones were ritually returned to the water. The group participating varied in size from the people at a single reef-netters' camp to a whole village at a weir site.

● CLEANSING CEREMONIES The most important ritual property a kin group could have was a $\theta\mathring{x}^w tén$ 'cleansing device', meaning a performance involving ritual paraphernalia, spells, and an incantation. Such a ceremony was used to wipe away a disgrace, as of a captured girl to make her marriageable, and, more commonly, to enhance occasions such as the bestowal of an inherited name, a girl's puberty, the initiation of a new dancer, a wedding, or the display of a memento of a deceased relative. The subject (the person or memento) was presented with speeches, the performance itself was presented, and some or all of the guests were given gifts to thank them for

witnessing the event.

Among the Halkomelem, Squamish, and some of the Northern Straits people, the two most important cleansing ceremonies involved the ritualist's rattle and the sxwayxwey. The rattle, usually made of big-horn sheep horn and trimmed with mountain goat wool, was used by a female ritualist while escorting the subject of the ceremony into the house. The sxwayxwey ($sx^w\acute{a}yx^w\partial y$) was a performance by two or more young men wearing distinctive costumes and masks (fig. 11), who danced around the subject. Other cleansing ceremonies included performances in which stuffed skins of fishers, minks, bears, wolves, and flickers appeared to come to life, stones to float on water, baskets to fly through the air, young men to play catch with red-hot stones, or thunder sound and lightning flash in a darkened house. These were used more widely than the rattle and the mask, perhaps by all but the Nooksack and Clallam, and were taken less seriously, being used primarily as entertainment during potlatches (Jenness 1955:72–74; Suttles 1951:413–420).

● THE SECRET SOCIETY The ceremonial group called by the Clallam $x\partial nx\partial n\acute{t}ti$ 'growling at one another' or $s\mathring{t}\acute{u}k^wali$ (from the Makah for 'wolf dance') was active among the Clallam, Sooke, and Songhees, as among their neighbors the Nitinaht, Makah, Twana, and Suquamish. By the late nineteenth century there were a few members among the

468

SUTTLES

Saanich, Samish, and Lummi. The right to become initiated was hereditary. The principal ceremony seems to have been the initiation of new members, which was attended by members from several tribes and was the occasion for large potlatches. Prospective members, often children, were seized, apparently killed, and then brought back to life by the ceremony. Ceremonial paraphernalia included wolf masks and masks with moving parts (fig. 12). Ceremonial acts are said to have included the eating of a live dog (Gunther 1927:287). Parts of the ceremony were witnessed by members only, and details are not available. An interpretation of the secret society as a counterbalance to the power of shamans (B.J. Stern 1934: 86) is questionable.

Feasts and Potlatches

For families with social position to maintain, major life crises of important members required a *sx̣ánəq* 'potlatch'. In contrast with a feast (*sx̣éxən*), which might be held any time of year and was usually indoors, a potlatch was usually held in good weather and outside. A few famous wealthy men potlatched independently, but typically several or all the houses of a village prepared long for the event, invited guests from other villages over a wide area, and potlatched one by one. Each marked its own

members' change of status with its own cleansing ceremony and gave its own wealth. The hosts piled their wealth on their roofs, and a speaker called out the names of the invited guests and passed the gifts down to them. Remaining goods were thrown to the crowd (figs. 10, 13).

Wealth was a category distinct from food; it included capital such as canoes, bows and arrows, and slaves, and also ornaments of dentalia and other materials, fine hide shirts, and especially woolen blankets. Native blankets, and in time Hudson's Bay Company blankets, were to some degree used as a measure of value. (Dentalia were evidently not used this way.) It appears that potlatchers did not expect that potlatch gifts would be returned with interest, nor even that they would all be returned. Potlatchers invested for fame, which might have its material rewards in secure relations with neighboring villages and tribes and in good marriages for their children.

Games and Music

Three games were played for stakes of wealth items: *sləhél*, the hand game or bone game, played by opposing teams with much drumming, singing, and dramatics (fig. 14); *sləhéləm*, the disk game, played with wooden disks hidden in shredded cedarbark, by men with special vision power;

Field Mus., Chicago: left, 19921; right, 19924; Mus. of the Amer. Ind., Heye Foundation, New York: top center, 18/6941; bottom center, 19/8992.
Fig. 12. Secret society masks and rattle. Masks were used in the initiation rites of the secret society (Barnett 1955:285–287). left, Mask of a hominoid face surmounted by a carved wooden bird. Strings at either side of the face, when pulled, caused the feathers of the wings to flap. Collected by C.F. Newcombe, 1905. top center, Saanich mask of a man's face, painted in green and white. Holes above the upper lip once held tufts of hair for a moustache. Collected by George Heye on the South Saanich Reserve, Vancouver I., B.C., before 1934. right, Cowichan mask of a hook-billed bird with a corona of movable carved feathers. Collected by C.F. Newcombe, 1905. bottom center, Saanich wooden rattle carved in the shape of a ducklike bird, the tail elongated to form the handle. Collected by George Heye on the South Saanich Reserve, Vancouver I., B.C., before 1938. Height of left, 44 cm; others to same scale.

469

CENTRAL COAST SALISH

and *məɬáli*, played with dice made of beaver teeth, by women only (Maranda 1984).

Sports included a form of shinny, sometimes played by teams from different villages for a trophy, foot races, canoe races, and wrestling matches. Boys played a game of shooting arrows at a hoop. They also played with bull-roarers, though perhaps only when sent out to do so, because the action was believed to bring a heavy rain. Girls played a game of battledore and shuttlecock.

Singing for pleasure was common. Songs composed for pleasure, called *stíləm* (often translated 'love song'), expressed nostalgia, grief at parting, the effects of alcohol, and other secular experiences. Other classes of songs included gambling songs used in the bone game (W.B. Stuart 1972), shaman's songs, songs used in spirit dancing, incantations, and war songs. Each of these classes is stylistically distinct.

Art

House posts, grave monuments, tools, and utensils were decorated in a variant of a Coast Salish regional style ("Art," this vol.). Not all house posts were decorated, but many had figures carved in high relief, and some were carved in the round. Three-dimensional carvings were mainly likenesses of humans, animals, and birds, or humans with nonhuman creatures. Those of humans probably most commonly portrayed ancestors. Some of the nonhuman creatures may have, especially in the Northern Straits area, represented vision powers, but others, perhaps most in the Halkomelem area, represented cleansing devices. Similar carvings appear on grave monuments and some tools and utensils.

A more distinctive style existed mainly in the Halkomelem area, where it appears on spindle whorls, ritualists' horn rattles, the smaller figures on sxwayxwey masks, combs, and horn bracelets (Suttles 1983; Kew 1980; Feder 1983). This style is primarily two-dimensional, with some variation depending on the material used; on wooden spindle whorls the figures appear in low relief, while on horn rattles they are produced by incising. Subjects include human faces, whole human figures, birds, beasts, and fishes. When human and nonhuman figures appear together, the human dominates the design. Recurring designs on rattles include a human face with radiating rays or fish, a bird with concentric circles on its body, and a facing pair of birds enclosing a space that becomes a human face. Nothing is known of the meaning of these designs.

History

The Strait of Juan de Fuca was discovered by the fur trader Charles Barkley in 1787. During the next several years other traders may have sailed as far as Coast Salish territory, but believing sea otters were scarce there, they generally kept to the outer coast (Wagner 1933:3). Exploration began in 1790 when Manuel Quimper explored both shores of the Strait of Juan de Fuca. In 1791 Francisco de Eliza explored the southern end of the Strait of Georgia. In 1792 Spanish exploration continued, and the British expedition under George Vancouver charted most of the region but missed the Fraser River. Its existence was not established until 1808, when the North West Company fur trader Simon Fraser made the difficult descent through the canyon of what he had hoped was the Columbia. The Spanish and British explorers of the 1790s and Fraser too saw that the Natives had some European goods, probably obtained through Native middlemen from the maritime fur traders on the outer coast.

The land-based fur traders, seeking beaver pelts, established themselves at the mouth of the Columbia in 1811, and it is likely that the Central Coast Salish soon felt their influence too, as neighbors to the south began trading there. In the early 1820s the Hudson's Bay Company began exploring the region, and in 1827 it founded Fort Langley on the Fraser River. The Kwantlen people welcomed the traders, and they and others

Royal B.C. Mus., Victoria: PN 6810.

Fig. 13. Potlatch. The hosts sit on the roof of the house with the gifts to be distributed. The guests sit on the ground. A mat screen at the base of the house is for use of ceremonial participants. Photograph by Richard Maynard, Old Songhees, B.C. 1872.

provided materials, labor, and wives for the traders (Maclachlan 1983). This post, with its farm, smithy, and other facilities, became a center of European influence as well as the center of Indian trade over a wide region. In 1843 the company founded Fort Victoria in Songhees territory, again employing local Indian labor, and this post became an even greater magnet for Indian trade, at first drawing people throughout the Strait of Juan de Fuca, Puget Sound, and the Strait of Georgia but by the 1850s drawing people from as far north as Alaska.

In 1846 the Treaty of Washington split Central Coast Salish country into British and American portions, which thereafter experienced different political histories and administrative systems—a Canadian system, which made every large Indian village into a band with one or more tiny reserves, and an American system, which combined villages into tribes and gave some larger reservations but left others landless ("History of Coastal British Columbia Since 1846" and "History of Western Washington Since 1846," this vol.).

On the British side, in 1850 and 1854, James Douglas purchased the lands of Sooke, Vancouver Island Clallam, Songhees, Saanich, and Nanaimo bands (Duff 1969), but otherwise no Native titles were extinguished. Douglas began designating some land as reserves, but the process was not completed until the 1880s.

On the American side, in 1855, Washington Clallam headmen signed the Treaty of Point No Point, and Lummi headmen the Treaty of Point Elliott. According to these treaties, the Clallam ceded all their lands and were to go to the Skokomish Reservation, while the Lummi got a reservation that included their principal village and weir sites but were expected to share it with the Samish and the Nooksack. In fact, most of the Clallam, Nooksack, and Samish chose to live at or near their old villages.

Settlers were arriving in the 1850s, especially on the American side of the boundary, but the non-Indian population was still relatively small until 1858, when gold was discovered on the Fraser, whereupon thousands of miners streamed into the region. The Songhees, Lummi, Nooksack, and Stalo people were in the path of this migration, but the whole region was affected. From this time on the Native people were greatly outnumbered in the region.

From the late eighteenth century the Native population had been declining. The first smallpox epidemic may have come in the 1770s, with other epidemics in the early nineteenth century. Lekwiltok raiders, who appeared frequently through the second quarter of the nineteenth century, also accounted for some losses.

The first Christian missionary to reach the region was the Catholic priest Modeste Demers, who was warmly welcomed by the Lummi and by the Kwantlen and others at Fort Langley in 1841 (Landerholm 1956:102–107). The chiefs whom Demers appointed catechists (Whitehead

1981) may have already had some experience as religious leaders. These men seem to have maintained some practices through a period of only occasional instruction by priests until 1858, when the Oblate order moved its headquarters from Puget Sound to Vancouver Island. Two Oblate schools became influential, one founded in 1859 by Father Eugene Casimir Chirouse at Tulalip, on the Snohomish Reservation, attended by a number of Lummies, the other founded in 1863 by Father Leon Fouquet at Saint Mary's Mission on the Fraser, for children north of the boundary. During the 1860s and 1870s a number of bands adopted Bishop Paul Durieu's system, which converted reserves into "theocratic states" (Lemert 1954). The school at Mission became the scene of an annual Passion play. South of the boundary the Lummi were known as "strict" Catholics. In 1890 a Roman Catholic residential school was established on Kuper Island.

Meanwhile Protestant churches made converts. A Methodist school for Indians was established at Hope in 1859. In the 1860s Methodist missionaries Thomas Crosby and James M. Tate were active among the Songhees, Nanaimo, Chilliwack, Tait, and Nooksack (J.W. Grant 1984:132–133). Anglicans were active at Nanaimo and among the Tait about the same time. The Coquileetza Institute was founded by the Methodists as a residential school near Chilliwack in 1886. The Congregational minister Myron Eells established a mission on the Skokomish Reservation in 1874 and began preaching to the Clallam.

From the founding of Fort Langley on, some local people had been employed by the Hudson's Bay Company, not only at tasks they were already skilled at, such as fishing and hunting, to supply the post, but at new tasks such as working as loggers, farm hands, stevedores, and sailors. Some became expert trappers, and a few were powerful middlemen in the fur trade, but the fur trade was not of first or lasting importance. By the 1860s, many Central Coast Salish worked as loggers, mill-hands, and stevedores. Some continued to sell fish, shellfish, cranberries, and other native foods to Whites. By the 1870s canneries employed men as fishermen and women and some children in the canning process. By the 1880s, on the Lummi Reservation and on reserves in the Cowichan and Fraser valleys, there were some successful Indian farmers (Knight 1978:67–71; Suttles 1954). Others worked seasonally picking berries and hops for non-Indian farmers in the Fraser Valley and on Puget Sound.

By this time much of Native material culture had changed. Yet much of the old social relations and ceremonies survived, with potlatching perhaps grander than ever. At a Saanich potlatch held in August 1876, some 3,000 Indians were present and goods valued at about $15,000 were distributed (I.W. Powell 1876:36). After the prohibition of the potlatch in British Columbia

©Natl. Geographic Soc., Washington.

Fig. 14. The hand game. Played by 2 teams lined up facing each other, each with a drumming board to beat with sticks and one or more hide drums. The game is generally played with 2 pairs of bone cylinders, one of each pair marked and the other unmarked, and a set of tally sticks. The leader of the team with the bones gives them to 2 players to hold, and while they shuffle and juggle them (left), he leads his team in drumming and singing (right), challenging the other team to guess which hands hold the unmarked (or marked) bones. Guessing is by gestures. A wrong guess loses a tally stick; a correct guess gains a tally stick and the bones. The team that gets all the sticks wins the stakes. The game is played at summer gatherings throughout the Coast Salish and adjacent regions (Maranda 1984; W.B. Stuart 1972). Photographs by O. MacWhite, Lummi Indian Reservation, Wash., June 1964.

in 1884, the Cowichan in particular resisted the law (LaViolette 1961:46–50), and big summer potlatches were held on Vancouver Island until around 1912.

The first half of the twentieth century saw a decline in economic opportunities for Indians made worse by the Depression (Knight 1978:8), a decline in use of Native languages, due especially to their suppression in residential schools (Levine and Cooper 1976), and a decline in influence of mission-founded churches, coinciding with the spread of the Shaker Indian Church, and the revival of spirit dancing with incorporated features of the potlatch.

In 1910 the Songhees reserve in the heart of Victoria was ceded for a cash payment, and the group moved to Esquimalt (Duff 1969:43–44). By the 1980s greater autonomy allowed the Squamish and Musqueam to lease valuable urban land, generating band incomes spent mainly on housing, community buildings, and education.

In the 1980s there were 47 Central Coast Salish bands in British Columbia, with a total enrollment in 1987 of about 13,000 persons (Canada. Department of Indian Affairs and Northern Development 1987). They ranged in size of enrollment from two to over 2,000. The two largest bands, the Cowichan and Squamish, were the product of early amalgamation of closely related bands, and in the Cowichan case, with contiguous reserves. But the equally closely related Chilliwack still consisted of nine small bands.

The Central Coast Salish of Washington have had even more varied histories. During the 1870s and 1880s a number of Nooksacks were able to take homesteads (held in trust by the federal government) in the Nooksack Valley, where they continued to live among White settlers (Richardson 1979). Because of their status as homestead-

ers, for nearly a century the Nooksack lost their status as a tribe, but the Bureau of Indian Affairs restored it in 1971 (Amoss 1978a:26).

About 1875 the Samish were forced to abandon their village on Samish Island, and rather than move onto a reservation, they established a new village on land purchased on Guemes Island. Until it had to be abandoned early in the twentieth century, this village was a center for winter dancing and potlatching, then forbidden on the reservations. In 1987 the Samish were still seeking federal acknowledgement.

The Clallam continued to live at several of their old village sites and at Little Boston on Port Gamble, where some worked at the sawmill built there in 1853. Around 1875 the Dungeness people were forced off their traditional site and bought land nearby to establish the settlement of Jamestown. In 1936 Little Boston became the Port Gamble Indian Reservation. Under the Indian Reorganization Act, land was purchased for the Lower Elwha Reservation. Jamestown received federal acknowledgement in 1980.

Having a reservation and tribal status did not ensure the Lummi protection against non-Indian encroachment. During the 1890s they lost their principal reef-netting locations when canneries built salmon traps in front of them, and they lost direct access to Bellingham and then their village because of a log jam and flooding (Suttles 1954:77–79; Boxberger 1980). During the next few years they also lost land through the sale of individual parcels. However, by the 1930s the Lummi were able to complete a dike and bring delta land under cultivation and to acquire land along the new course of the Nooksack River. An aquaculture project begun in the late 1960s did not

472

SUTTLES

achieve all the goals hoped for, but it left the tribe with a fish hatchery and a salmon-rearing facility (Deloria 1978; Boxberger 1986:255–256).

The restoration of Indian fishing rights in the 1970s encouraged individual enterprise, and the Lummi fishing fleet increased greatly in the late 1970s and early 1980s (Boxberger 1986:285–289).

By the 1980s the Lummi seine boats were ranging from California to Alaska and bringing in over a quarter of the fish harvested in Washington. The Lummi Tribe had reacquired over 10 percent of the Lummi Reservation in its own name. In the 1980s the tribe purchased a restaurant-boating complex, built a fish processing plant, and opened its own school for kindergarten to grade eight. It also operated the Lummi Community College, one of the few tribally chartered and operated institutions of higher learning in the United States.

In spite of the differences between Canadian and American systems, and among bands and tribes, the Central Coast Salish continued to form a social network (Suttles 1963), linked together and increasingly with other Coast Salish, by summer festivals with canoe racing (fig. 15) and "Indian" pageantry (Dewhirst 1976), intergroup *sləhél* games (Maranda 1984), winter dancing, the Indian Shaker Church, and self-awareness stimulated by cultural programs (for example, Galloway 1988) developing in nearly every group.

Population

Before the great epidemics of the late eighteenth century, the total Central Coast Salish population may have exceeded 20,000 (roughly 9,700 Halkomelem, 4,100 Northern Straits, 3,200 Clallam, 1,700 Squamish, and 1,100 Nooksack), but by the late nineteenth century the total had dropped to less than 7,000 (see "Demographic History, 1774–1874," this vol.). By the early 1980s the total had climbed to over 16,000.

Synonymy

The eighteenth-century explorers recorded few Native names and none that can be identified with tribal names used later. The earliest tribal name recorded is Misquiame, for Musqueam, noted by Fraser in 1808 (Lamb 1960:106). Others date from the 1820s.

Squamish, from *sqxʷúʔmiš*, composed of an unidentifiable root and the suffix *-miš* 'people', has been rendered Chomes, Whoomis (MacMillan and McDonald 1827–1830:24, 61), Squohámish (Wilson 1866:278), Sqchómisch (Boas 1887a:132), Sk·q̄ō′mic (Boas 1890: 806), and Squawmish (Hodge 1907–1910, 2:631).

Halkomelem is from Halkōmē′lEm, Hill-Tout's (1903) transcription of *həlq̓əmíyləm*, the Upriver form of the name of the language. The Downriver form, *həńq̓əmíńəm*,

Royal B.C. Mus., Victoria: top, PN 11782; bottom, PN 8950.

Fig. 15. Canoe racing. top, Crew of the *West Saanich No. 5*, left to right, Johnny Sam, Issac Bartleman, Joe Bartleman, Leslie Tom, Fred Miller, Howard Olson, Fred Huston, Paul or Peter Henry, Chris Tom, Joe Seymour, Baptiste, and Marshal Harry. All hold painted paddles. Eleven-man racing canoes of this style have been made only since around 1900. Photograph by Ernest W. Crocker, South Saanich Reserve, B.C., about 1920s. bottom, Canoes taking their positions at the start of a race at the Gorge, Victoria, B.C. Photographed about 1940s.

is the source of Crosby's (1907) An-ko-me-num. The name is derived from *ləq̓émal* (Upriver) or *nəq̓émən* (Downriver) 'Nicomen'. The present spelling, introduced by Duff (1952a), was in general use among linguists by the 1960s. The language was earlier identified as Cowichan (Boas 1890:806; Hodge 1907–1910,1:355). The Halkomelem term *xʷəlməxʷ* (Island and Downriver) or *xʷəmləxʷ* (in some Upriver dialects) 'Indian' (probably earlier 'village, tribe') is the source of Whull-e-mooch (Deans 1886:42, 1888:109) and Hue-la-mu and Hum-a-luh (cited in Hodge 1907–1910,1:355). Deans identifies the Whull-e-mooch as "dwellers on Whull, Puget Sound," but a connection between *xʷəlməxʷ* and the Lushootseed *xʷəlč* 'sea' is not supportable.

Nanaimo, from *snənáyməxʷ*, composed of the nominalizing prefix *s-*, an unidentifiable root, and the suffix *-məxʷ* 'bunch, people', has been rendered Nanaimooch (MacMillan and McDonald 1827–1830:27), Snanaimooh (Tolmie and Dawson 1884:120B) and Snanaimuq (Boas 1889c). The translation 'the whole' or 'big, strong tribe' (Walbran

1909:348) is not linguistically supportable.

Cowichan is from *qáẃəcən* 'warm the back', the name for Mount Tzouhalem, a bare face of rock north of the mouth of the Cowichan River, and in local usage "Cowichan people" refers to those of the valley overlooked by this mountain. The term has been extended to include: the Chemainus (Douglas 1854:246), who speak the Cowichan dialect and have a historical connection with the Cowichan Valley; all speakers of Halkomelem (Boas 1890:806); all the Central Coast Salish in British Columbia (Wilson 1866:278); and all Coast Salish in British Columbia (Goddard 1934, map). The name was perhaps first recorded in 1824 by Work (in T.C. Elliott 1912:212, 219) as Coweechin, from the Downriver form *qəẃícən*. His identification of the Fraser as the "Coweechin River" reflects the prominence of the Cowichans among the tribes fishing there. Other recordings include Cowitchan (Wilson 1866:275), K·au̓itcin (Boas 1890: 806), and others given by Hodge (1907–1910,1:355).

Kwantlen is from *q̓ʷaʔəṅƛəṅ, q̓ʷa·ṅƛəṅ, q̓ʷáʔəṅƛə̓l*, or *q̓ʷá·ṅƛə̓l* in Downriver and Island dialects, *q̓ʷa·lƛə̓l* in Upriver dialects. Its etymology is unknown. The difficulty of the name for non-Indians and the variety of pronunciations may be responsible for the variety of spellings and the ultimate replacement of the name. The name was perhaps first recorded by Work (in T.C. Elliott 1912:218, 221, 222) in 1824 as Cahoutetts, Cahantitt, and Cahotitt. Other versions are Quoitland, Quitline, and Quatline (MacMillan and McDonald 1827–1830:56, 89, 98), Quaitlin (Scouler 1848:234), Quãltl (Wilson 1866:278), K·oã́antEl (Boas 1894a:454), and KwántlEn (Hill-Tout 1903). Since the beginning of the twentieth century the Kwantlen have been more commonly called the Langley Indians.

Chilliwack, from *sc̓əlxʷíqʷ* 'upstream head (?)', has been recorded Chilcocooks, Chiliquiyouks, Chil.whoo.yook (MacMillan and McDonald 1827–1830: 28, 50, 94), Chilukweyuk (Wilson 1866:278, Tc'ilEQué̄uk (Boas 1894a:454), and Tcil'Qé̄uk (Hill-Tout 1903:355). Wilson (1866:278) gives Squahalitch as a synonym for Chilliwack, but this name appears to be *skʷhélič*, an important Nooksack village.

Tait, from *tíyt* or *tə̓yt* 'upstream', appears as Tituns, Titens (MacMillan and McDonald 1827–1830:121, 158), Teates (Mayne 1862:295), and Té̄it (Boas 1894a:454). Boas says this was a collective term for all the tribes above the Nicomen, but MacMillan and McDonald distinguish the Titens from the Chilliwack and Pilalt, corroborating Duff's (1952a:19) identification of the term with those above Pilalt. The Thompson name for the Halkomelem, *sʔécnkʷu* (phonetically [š?ǽčıngʷu]) 'outside water', is probably the source of Fraser's achinrow or Ackinroe, identified as the people from Spuzzum downstream (Lamb 1960:97), and Mayne's (1862:295) Sa-chin-ko.

474   Stalo, from *stá·ləw* (Upriver) or *stáˏləẃ* (Downriver and

Island) 'river', was adopted by Duff (1952a:11) for the people of the Fraser Valley. The name appears as Sto:lō in the orthography used in the Chilliwack area beginning in the 1970s.

Nooksack, from *nəxʷséʔeq* or *xʷséʔeq* 'place of bracken roots', a village and prairie at the mouth of Anderson Creek where families from most villages had root beds, has been recorded Ossaak (MacMillan and McDonald 1827–1830:167), Neuksacks (Fitzhugh in ARCIA 1858: 328), and Nootsak (Hill-Tout 1903:357). The gloss 'mountain men' (Hodge 1907–1910, 2:81) is fanciful. The Nooksack name for the Nooksack language is *ɬə́čələsəm*.

Straits refers to a group of dialects sometimes identified as a single language (Boas 1891:563; Suttles 1954:29-30; Elmendorf 1960:277), but perhaps better identified as two, Northern Straits and Clallam (L.C. Thompson 1973: 1010). Grant (1857:295) identified this group of dialects as "the Tsclallum or Clellum language," and Kane (in Harper 1971:103) used Clallam for Northern Straits as well as Clallam people. Straits was first used by Suttles (1951, 1954). Northern Straits is identified by some speakers as *ləkʷəŋínəŋ*, from *ləkʷə́ŋən* 'Songhees'.

Songhees is from *sćáŋəs*, the name of the local group at Esquimalt Lagoon and Albert Head. This name or its Halkomelem equivalent *sə̊ɂáməs* have been used, perhaps mainly by others, for all the people of the Victoria area or simply Victoria. It has been written Sandish, Sonese (MacMillan and McDonald 1827-1830:154), Sangas, Sangeys (Kane cited in Harper 1971:306), Songhees (Douglas in Duff 1969:23), Tsaumas (Wilson 1866:278), Thongeith (Sproat 1868:311), and Songish (Hodge 1907–1910, 2:615; Curtis 1907-1930, 9:25). Songhees is the usual local English form. Most Songhees call themselves *ləkʷə́ŋən* (etymology unknown), recorded Lku'ñgEn (Boas 1891: 563) and LEkúñEn (Hill-Tout 1905).

Lummi is from *xʷlə́məỷ* or *xʷlə́miʔ* (in an older style *nəxʷlə́məỷ*), said to be adapted from *xʷlálæməs* 'facing each other', the name of a great L-shaped house at Gooseberry Point (B.J. Stern 1934:107–108). The name was perhaps first recorded, as Lummie, in 1824 by Scouler (1905:199). Other spellings include Holumma, Whullumy (MacMillan and McDonald 1827-1830:46, 159), Wholerneils, 1841 (Demers in Landerholm 1956:102), Whellamay (Harper 1971:307), and Nooh-lum-mi, 1844 (Tolmie in Gibbs 1855:434).

Clallam is probably from the Northern Straits or Halkomelem form *xʷsƛéləm*, rather from the Clallam name for themselves, *nəxʷsƛáyəm*, which has *y* for the *l* of neighboring languages. The name was recorded, perhaps for the first time, in 1824 by Scouler (1905:196) as Klallum. Other spellings include Tlallum, 1853 (Douglas in Duff 1969:23), Noosdalum (Scouler 1848:234, no doubt a misprint for Noosclalum), S'Klallam (Treaty of Point No Point, 1855, in Kappler 1904–1941, 2:674–677), and Klallam (Gunther 1927). The gloss 'strong people'

(Hodge 1907–1910, 1:302) is unsupportable.

Sources

The eighteenth-century Spanish accounts are found in Wagner (1933) and Jane (1930), British accounts in Vancouver (1798, 2:52–200) and Menzies (1923:58–61). They give brief but valuable observations of the Native people apparently untouched by previous contact. Gunther (1960, 1972:76–78) discusses the objects collected by the Vancouver expedition at Discovery Bay in Clallam country. Fraser's account of his 1808 journey gives the earliest view of the Mainland Halkomelem; Lamb's (1960: 97-107) edition is more reliable than Masson's (1889–1890). There is information on the Native peoples from the 1820s on in the journals, letters, and records of employees of the Hudson's Bay Company such as Work (T.C. Elliott 1912; Work 1945:82–92), Scouler (1905), MacMillan and McDonald (1827–1830), and Ermatinger (1907). Kane's sketches (in Harper 1971), done in and around Victoria in 1847, are especially valuable. Dating from the mid-nineteenth century are accounts by Wilson (1866:278–292) and Brown (1873–1876, 1:20–152), relating mainly to the Halkomelem, and by Eells (1985), with material on the Clallam.

Boas (1887a, 1889c, 1891, 1894a) published a short piece on tribal distribution with an excellent map and short accounts of the Nanaimo, the Songhees, and the Mainland Halkomelem. The Squamish, Mainland Halkomelem, Cowichan, and Songhees were discussed by Hill-Tout (1900, 1903, 1904a, 1905, 1907a; mostly reprinted in 1978). Curtis (1907–1930, 9) includes material on the Central Coast Salish, especially the Lummi and the Cowichan.

Fuller ethnographic works, attempting to describe Native cultures before greatly modified by contact, are those by Gunther (1927) on the Clallam, B.J. Stern (1934) on the Lummi, Jenness (1934–1935) on the Saanich and the Katzie (1955), Barnett (1939, 1938a, 1955) on the peoples around the Strait of Georgia, Suttles (1951) on the Northern Straits, Duff (1952a) on the Upper Stalo, and Bouchard, Miranda, and Kennedy (1975) on the Squamish.

Topical works include Gunther (1945), Turner and Bell (1971), Kennedy and Bouchard (1976), and Galloway (1982) on ethnobotany; Kennedy and Bouchard (1976a) and Rozen (1978) on ethnozoology; Suttles (1951a, 1958, 1960, 1962, 1963, 1987a) and K. Mooney (1976) on social organization and economy; Lane (1953) on religion. A number of Central Coast Salish myths are included in Boas (1895); other collections of myths are Gunther (1925) and Lerman (1976).

Ethnohistorical works include Suttles (1954) and Boxberger (1986) on the Lummi. Studies relating to the 1960s to 1980s include Kew (1970) and Weightman (1976) on the Musqueam, C.L. Lewis (1970) on the Cowichan, K. Mooney (1976) and M.R. Mitchell (1976) on the Songhees, and Amoss (1978a) on the Nooksack.

Manuscript materials on the Squamish are in the archives of the British Columbia Indian Language Project, Victoria; and on the Upper Stalo in the Coqualeetza Resource Centre, Sardis, British Columbia.

Central and Southern Coast Salish Ceremonies Since 1900

J.E. MICHAEL KEW

By the 1950s a complex of ceremonies rooted in traditional culture began playing an increasingly important part in the community life of the Central and Southern Coast Salish, providing social links among reserves, reservations, and settlements scattered over much of the region. Beliefs and practices centered in spirit dancing and care of the dead provided the ideological focus of these modern ceremonies, but they are combined, as they always have been, with values and actions derived from systems of social rank and exchange, the so-called potlatch complex.

By 1900, conversion to Christianity, mainly Roman Catholicism, was nearly universal among the Central Coast Salish. The Indian Shaker Church had also spread by that time to Central Coast Salish villages of British Columbia. Pressured by missionaries generally opposed to shamanism and spirit dancing and by Indian agents opposed to potlatch activities, indigenous religious ritual had declined in frequency and participation. Potlatches anywhere and Indian dances outside a home reserve were unlawful in Canada between 1884 and 1951 and severely restricted by Bureau of Indian Affairs regulations in the United States. In many villages they almost disappeared. But even in those villages where houses for extended family, called smokehouses, had ceased to be maintained and spirit dancers were no longer being initiated, dancers sang in the privacy of modern homes or re-occupied the old smokehouses in winter. Spirit dancing continued despite opposition from missionaries, Indian agents, and Indian Christian converts. In some places too, personal names continued to be conferred on younger family members, puberty ceremonies were held for some women, memorials for deceased. The old pattern of gift giving and feasting continued, albeit in modified form and probably in reduced frequency. Funerals had always been potlatch occasions, that is, times when ritual services were required of nonkin and reciprocated with gifts, and although these gradually incorporated elements of Christian services, they preserved Indian belief about the dead and dependence on ritualists to attend the dead and their possessions (Kew 1970:210 ff.). In this way Indian ceremonial life persisted as people fitted into niches in the surrounding society and their villages became engulfed by urban centers.

The Spirit Dance

The spirit dancing of the 1980s is a variant of the widespread guardian-spirit complex. Spirit powers manifested in personal songs, dances, face paintings, headdresses, and other items of costume are celebrated during winter at invited gatherings held in family dwellings. Early observers usually referred to these by the Chinook Jargon term *tamahnous*, as in "*tamahnous* dancing" or "*tamahnous* spirit" (see Eells 1985:361, 395, 408; Elmendorf 1985:452). Guardian-spirit and spirit dancing are the terms used in later accounts. The same terms have found some degree of usage among Indians, although some in Washington have used "powwow" for spirit dance. Increasingly the term used to refer to spirit dancing is *syə́wən*, the Halkomelem and Northern Straits word for what is conferred upon the individual by spirit power, that is, a song and dance.

A spirit power may come to an individual unsought or unannounced and lie dormant, perhaps giving strength or aid in unknown ways. It may also be purposefully sought in a quest, and it may be conferred upon a person or inspired by actions of another spirit dancer. Presence of a power, if it is not latent, is often made apparent by illness, uneasiness, or restlessness. When spirit power or sickness is diagnosed as the cause, the individual is initiated at the onset of winter, or during the winter season, as a spirit dancer. Some observers have suggested that these initiations are rights of passage in which subjects experience symbolic death, rebirth, and reincorporation into society (Amoss 1972:56; Jilek 1982:64; Kew 1970:24, 172). While the original Indian terminology does not indicate the notion of death and rebirth to have been explicitly developed, there is such a suggestion in the English terminology, such as "baby" for initiate and "babysitter" for attendant. Furthermore, dancers sometimes speak of one another's anniversaries of initiation as "birthdays," and count their ages in years since initiation. In any case, the initiate undergoes a transformation in social status signified by ritual participation, everyday behavior, and by Indian and English terms for nondancer, initiate, and fully initiated dancer.

Initiation from the 1950s to the 1980s most frequently followed upon a diagnosis of "syə́wən sickness" or upon decision by an individual or an individual's family to effect initiation. Such a decision might be taken as an overt, conscious act of therapy in a holistic sense—an effort to redirect an individual considered to be using alcohol or drugs excessively, or acting in other ways threatening to self and others. Spirit dancing was frequently said by participants in the 1970s and 1980s to be an avenue to a better way of life, an Indian way that provides strength and protection.

Initiation begins with a dramatic ritual act termed "grabbing." The candidate is seized by painted dancers usually of the same sex as the candidate and then laid down, blindfolded, in a partitioned enclosure or tent, inside a dwelling or a smokehouse. Under supervision of ritualists, that is, persons possessing power and recognized as proficient in its use for others, attendants carry candidates around the house in morning and evening exercises for four days. During this time an initiate is allowed no food and only a little tepid water, is kept lying down and wrapped in blankets, and is confined to a cubicle or tent in the house. During this seclusion the initiate usually begins to sing a song received in a dream. On the fourth morning, following receipt of a song, the initiate is bathed, dressed in new clothing, and in the evening, dons a costume including a headdress of wool, cedar bark, or human hair (figs. 1–2). His face is painted red or black, the color depending on the class of song received. Attendants feed a ritual meal of dried salmon to the initiate and then, in an entranced state, singing the song, the initiate dances according to directions also given in the dream. For the remainder of the winter dance season the initiate, now a "new dancer," wears the special costume and remains secluded under the care of an attendant. Each morning at daybreak both initiate and attendant bathe in freshwater pools or streams.

Dwellings in which initiates reside are the sites of social gatherings and spirit dancing each evening for the remainder of the winter season. On the fourth day, at the conclusion of the first stage of initiation, invitations are extended throughout the village and often to neighboring villages. Guests fill the house, are given a meal, and are invited to dance. Initiates are also expected to attend dances in other homes and villages. Their winter evenings become an unbroken sequence of spirit dances, intervillage gatherings on weekends, and local assemblages on other days.

A requirement of spirit dancing is access to wilderness. Spirit dancers use such places for ritual bathing when they

Royal B.C. Mus., Victoria: left, PN 8745; right, PN 11787.

Fig. 1. Spirit Dance costumes. Photography of costumed dancers was occasionally permitted in the early 1900s, but display of dances and costume outside of dance settings was never common. left, Three costumed initiates: Ernie Jack, Arthur Joe, and Dominic Joe, of Somenos, B.C., Cowichan Band. The Joes' mother is between them, and their father is on the far right. The initiates have painted faces and wear wool headdresses with feathered tops. Costumes include knitted sweater and stockings, embroidered shirt and leggings, and a shirt decorated with wooden pendants. Drinking tubes and head scratchers are suspended on strings around their necks, and they hold fir-sapling staffs decorated with wool and feathers. At the end of initiation the staffs and costumes are deposited in trees or caves apart from ordinary human activities and left, like cradles and baby rockers, to decay (Barnett 1955:281). Photograph by F.A. Monk, Duncan, B.C., 1918-1929. right, Cris Paul, Saanich, displaying one type of costume worn by a fully initiated spirit dancer. He wears a human hair headdress, embroidered shirt and leggings, and deer hoof rattles around his ankles. Wooden pendants on the shirt also rattle when the wearer moves. Photograph by Ernest Crocker, about 1920s.

477

CENTRAL AND SOUTHERN COAST SALISH CEREMONIES SINCE 1900

feel a need for strengthening and renewing their powers. For initiates such places are essential for their prescribed daily bathing and as depositories for items of their costume at the conclusion of initiation. All villages actively participating in the complex use certain favored locations of this kind. After passage of the American Indian Religious Freedom Act of 1978, United States agencies were directed to protect such areas. Accordingly officials of the Mount Baker–Snoqualmie National Forest and representatives of Washington State tribes made an inventory of spiritually significant places within the Forest (Blukis-Onat and Hollenbeck 1981). The Alliance of Tribal Councils, which includes the Upper Stalo bands of the Fraser Valley, surveyed spiritual sites (Mohs 1987) and pursued protection of such sites and validation of aboriginal title to them.

Late Twentieth-Century Potlatches

In earlier times, potlatches were held for any occasion involving a status change of family members, but during the early twentieth century such events were held more and more frequently in the winter at spirit dances (Suttles 1963:518). Families wishing to confer names on younger members, or to bestow other family prerogatives such as the use of sxwayxwey masks and ritualist's rattles, or to hold memorials for deceased members, commonly do so in winter, traveling to other villages and visiting smoke-houses to issue invitations. Large gatherings for these combined potlatch and spirit dance events are usually held on Fridays or Saturdays, and invitations in the 1980s were issued up to a year in advance.

Older, well established persons, both male and female, were usually the sponsors of these gatherings. They took the initiative in planning and organizing them and acted as the host or hosts. They were supported by a circle of close kin, who pooled money, gifts, and labor to prepare for the event. Often at the start or conclusion of the dance season the most active participants in spirit dancing organized a cooperative or "company" dance with community sponsorship. Major potlatch ceremonies are not usually a feature of these gatherings.

The large gatherings often assembled 1,000 guests and required use of a modern smokehouse, since the 1970s generally called a longhouse. These are rectangular, dirt-floored buildings, warmed by two or three open fires. They have apertures in the roof for smoke to escape, two to four tiers of benches around the perimeter, and an attached kitchen and dining hall. The host family engages men to direct parking as visitors arrive in later afternoon. Other appointed men stoke the fires, direct guests to seats (usually grouped according to village), and invite guests to the dining area for a meal. The arrival and feeding of guests is accompanied by continuous singing and drumming as visiting spirit dancers and initiates become

Stark Mus. of Art, Orange, Tex.: 31.78/108, WWC 102H.

Fig. 2. Culchillum, a Cowichan, wearing a "medicine cap" believed by the artist to be made of the hair of people killed in battle and worn only on special occasions (Harper 1971:103). A similar headdress, made of human hair and with twirling feathers, but without the woven part over the forehead, is often worn by 20th-century spirit dancers who have songs of the type once sung by warriors. Watercolor sketch by Paul Kane, Ft. Victoria, B.C., 1847.

entranced and sing and dance, surrounded and accompanied by their own village mates. During this "warm-up," dancers' movements are restricted to the immediate vicinity of their seats and two or more dancers may be singing in different parts of the house.

After this initial period of singing, the hosts address their guests through professional speakers. Witnesses are called by the host's speaker and given small gifts of cash, and then the principal events begin. These (called "the work") may vary considerably in their elaboration. All services, including the mere presence of guests, are acknowledged, and gifts of blankets, towels, household wares, and money are made. Visitors indebted to the hosts or wishing to assist them use speakers to announce formal repayments or gifts of cash to hosts. Members of the host's family appointed for the purpose record all such repayments or gifts, noting donors' names, amounts, and any specific directions.

When the principal event is completed, and all accumulated gifts have been distributed, a procedure that may take several hours, the remainder of the night is given over to spirit dancing. Beginning with guests seated adjacent to the host's village and proceeding in a counterclockwise direction, spirit dancers moved to dance do so singly and in turn. First women, then men of each village group dance, and this is repeated by those in the next village section. In an altered state of consciousness, an individual dancer rises and dances around the house in a counterclockwise direction, between the fires and seats. Songs are led by singers with drums and are joined by the whole assembly. The host's village and members of the host's family sing last. Coffee and sandwiches are usually served to guests as village groups complete their singing by seven or eight o'clock in the morning.

In the 1980s most potlatch gatherings were combined with spirit dances and therefore occurred during the winter season, from mid-November until early April. Occasionally potlatches for namings or marriages, celebrated with traditional cleansing rites, are held outside the spirit dance season. These are usually smaller in scale and, although attended with formalized payments to the sponsors and giving of gifts as well as feasting, are of shorter duration.

Ceremonies Honoring the Dead

Funerals are well attended and usually convoke visitors from several villages. They are always occasions for repayment of obligations to the deceased and bereaved, or for making gifts of money to assist those in mourning. These are made during visits to bereaved households, especially the evening of the wake, and during funeral dinners that follow church services and interment. The bereaved family as host provides food for visitors and after the funeral luncheon makes gifts of money to nonfamily members who have provided requested services such as sitting up with the deceased during the wake, digging the grave, serving as pallbearer, or cooking food for visitors.

A continuing practice that requires ritual service from outside the circle of close kin is burning the possessions of the deceased. By the afternoon of the funeral all the clothing and small personal possessions of the deceased will have been removed from the residence. Under direction of a ritualist these will be taken to a site away from dwellings where a wood fire is lighted. The mourning family provides freshly cooked foods, usually things preferred by the deceased. Separate plates of these are presented to the deceased and to other remembered dead members of the family whom the ritualist calls by name. The food is placed in the fire and thus conveyed to the dead. The clothes of the deceased are similarly disposed.

Often a cherished ritual possession, such as a spirit dancer's costume, staff, or drum, will be saved by the family to be ritually burned at a future memorial ceremony. Such occasions, and also the placing of a tombstone on the grave, are times when a family may be moved to employ a ritualist to feed the dead members of the family. But feeding one's deceased kinfolk may also be done at any time of the year.

It became the practice in the 1980s to make village collections of money for bereaved families. These are modest sums ranging up to a few hundred dollars per village. Most monetary assistance continues to be given to the bereaved in the conventional potlatch manner by a speaker publicly identifying the giver by name and the exact sum being given. These exchanges of money at funerals, spirit dance activities, and potlatches comprise a single system of exchange. Debts or obligations are carried over from one event to another, and payments or gifts are made to discharge or create obligations on different occasions. The gifts and repayments are part of a continuing system of ceremonial exchanges between individual persons, usually not closely related, and often living in different villages. It is an exchange network that links people from separate villages within the wider Indian community and also sets them apart from non-Indians.

Resurgence of the Spirit Dance

From the early decades of the 1900s, when the number of dancers was probably at its lowest point, spirit dancing has shown a marked resurgence. Since 1950 the absolute number of dancers has grown rapidly. In 1961 the total number of dancers on the mainland was estimated to be less than 100 (Wayne Suttles, personal communication 1986). For several years in the 1980s the annual number of initiates alone, on the mainland, approximated that figure. On Vancouver Island, where a larger core of dancers existed, the increase was just as great.

The growth and spread of spirit dancing is also attested in the increase in numbers of new structures built expressly to host intervillage gatherings. These doubled in number between 1970 and 1986. In 1987 there were ceremonial houses on Vancouver Island at Nanaimo, Chemainus Bay, Ladysmith, Kuper Island, Cowichan (three), Malahat, Cole Bay, Brentwood Bay, and Esquimalt; on the British Columbia mainland at Capilano Creek, Seymour Creek, Musqueam, Sumas, Tcheachton and Skulkayn, and Chehalis; and in Washington on the Lummi (four), Nooksack, Swinomish, Upper Skagit, Tulalip, and Skokomish reservations. The greatest expansion has been in the Puget Sound and Fraser Valley areas.

This resurgence coincided with removal of the prohibition on potlatching in the Canadian Indian Act of 1951. However, the change of law itself was probably less significant than gradual relaxation of opposition to dancing among those in authority. While some Protestant clergy active among Indians opposed spirit dancing (Amoss 1972:46–47), the Roman Catholic church showed

479

accommodation. In the 1960s individual clergy began to attend dances occasionally, and in the 1970s one non-Indian member of a religious order was initiated as a spirit dancer and later ordained as a priest. Roman Catholic clergy on Vancouver Island and among the Squamish in the 1980s have also sponsored memorial services for Christ as the focal event of invitational gatherings in smokehouses at Easter, which usually coincides with the end of the winter dance season. A painting of Christ has been carried round the house for viewing by assembled guests, and small mementos have been distributed. This approximates the manner in which photographs of deceased relatives are displayed in memorial potlatches.

Recognition by the Roman Catholic Church of the worth of Indian tradition was also conveyed at a service in St. Paul's Church, North Vancouver, British Columbia, in August 1987. Louis Miranda, a Squamish scholar and exponent of Indian tradition, and Jessica Miranda, who had once been refused the sacrament for participation in spirit dancing, were made honorary members of the Oblates of Mary Immaculate.

Indian opposition to spirit dancing has also diminished with the change in the position of the Catholic church, and although some Indian Shakers in Washington voiced opposition to spirit dancing, those in British Columbia did not. Their members often participated fully in the winter dancing. More serious challenges followed on a few cases of injury or death, which have been experienced by initiates and investigated by coroners or police. Some of the practices of initiation such as fasting, bathing in cold water, and physical lifting are carried out more rigorously than others and have proven injurious to initiates in frail health or with unsuspected disabilities. In some villages, at the request of court officials, medical examinations are required of prospective initiates. Criminal charges against dancers participating in initiation rites have also been brought in cases of injury or reluctance of initiates to submit.

A notable feature of the resurgence of spirit dancing and accompanying potlatch activities among these Salish groups is the fact that the ceremonies are not presented for display to the public. The gatherings, up to the 1980s, have remained invitational affairs within the Indian community. Recordings of spirit dance music and photographs of dance performances are strictly forbidden. They would be considered to be dangerous and potentially harmful to the dancer. In contrast, when a First Salmon ceremony was revived on the Tulalip Reservation in 1979, non-Indians were invited to participate in recognition of the interdependence of humans and salmon (Amoss 1987).

Sources

The brief accounts of spirit dancing and other ceremonies in the early ethnographic literature, except for those of Eells (1985:395–426), do not seem to be based on observation. In British Columbia in the 1930s, Jenness (1934a, 1955) and Barnett (1938a, 1955) got valuable information on Native beliefs and practices from informants and yet seem not to have witnessed any of the ceremonies then taking place. These events were in winter, at night, indoors, and, because of official opposition and missionary condemnation (Crosby 1907:102–104), generally closed to outsiders.

In Washington circumstances were more favorable. A revival of spirit dancing about 1912 (J.M. Collins 1949a: 323–324; Suttles 1954:80–83) led to an annual Treaty Day dance on the Swinomish Reservation (on the anniversary of the signing of the Treaty of Point Elliott on January 22, 1855) at which non-Indians were welcome. Beginning in the 1920s, Professor Erna Gunther of the University of Washington attended (Garfield and Amoss 1984:399), and by the mid-1930s she was taking students and colleagues and encouraging research. B.J. Stern's (1934: 61–69) account of spirit dancing may be based in part on observations there, but the first full and best account of the ceremonies of that period is that of Wike (1945). Brief accounts by Underhill (1944:185–188) and Altman (1947) are also based on observations at a Treaty Day dance. Ethnographic work by J.M. Collins (1974), Suttles (1951), and Duff (1952a), Lane's (1953) analysis of religion, and Snyder's (1964) analysis of mythology, while attempting to reconstruct the earlier culture, incorporate understandings gained from observation of contemporary ceremonies. Works concerned with the role of the ceremonies in contemporary Central and Southern Coast Salish society include S.A. Robinson (1963), Suttles (1963, 1987), Kew (1970), Amoss (1972, 1978a), and Ryan (1973). Jilek (1974, 1982) explores the psychotherapeutic consequences of spirit dancing and other ceremonies. Jilek and Todd (1974) and Kew and Kew (1981) describe the work of contemporary shamans. Todd (1975) reports on a medical case resulting from initiation practices of a sort rejected by many initiators. Photographs of spirit dancers in costume appear in Curtis (1907–1930, 9:facing pp. 74, 76), B.J. Stern (1934), and Underhill (1944:185).

Prehistory of the Puget Sound Region

CHARLES M. NELSON

Puget Sound, the interconnected series of fiords and channels from Deception Pass and Admiralty Inlet in the north to Budd Inlet in the south (fig. 1), contains a heterogeneous series of microenvironments rich in seasonal and perennial resources. Islands, deltas, tide-flats and marshes, estuaries, the tidal portions of rivers, shallow bays, open water, and beaches of many varieties are interwoven along hundreds of miles of waterways and over 1,000 miles of shore (Kroeber 1939:170). Yet Puget Sound and its attendant waterways and contained in an area less than 170 miles long and 40 miles wide. The food resources concentrated in this small area were prodigious (Bryan 1963:App. B; M.W. Smith 1940:228–252; Haeberlin and Gunther 1930:20–29; Elmendorf 1960; Kidd 1964) and included shellfish; saltwater fish; seasonally spawning fish such as salmon, smelt and herring; porpoise; seal; sea lion; waterfowl; and substantial populations of deer, elk, mountain goat, beaver, bear, otter, raccoon, and other small animals.

Puget Sound is set in a broad, hilly, lake-studded trough between the Olympic and Cascade mountains. At contact, this trough was covered with mixed forests of Douglas fir, red alder, red cedar, grand fir, big-leaf maple, and cottonwood, as well as scattered parklands dotted with oak and Douglas fir (Piper 1906; McLaughlin 1971). The forests were relatively open with dense undergrowths of shrubs and herbs. Game was plentiful; and edible plants, including camas, fern, wapato, cow parsnip, clover, and many kinds of berries were abundant for about eight months of the year (M.W. Smith 1940:247–252).

Archeological Remains

In littoral areas, most excavated sites are complexes of shell middens that contain abundant, well-preserved faunal remains but very low concentrations of tools, made mainly of bone and shell, which are functionally and stylistically quite variable. Bryan's (1963:App. A) data from the Whidbey Island area provide a good illustration of this situation. Not counting classes of fragments or contact trade goods, Bryan recognized 170 different categories in the analysis of only 656 tools. Moreover, these 656 implements came from 14 sites, some of which contained numerous stratigraphic components. Assemblage complexity persists even at sites that are relatively simple stratigraphically and have yielded relatively large assemblages. For example, Mattson (1971) classified 528 implements from four phases at the Pedersen 2 site into 118 categories. The Duwamish 1 site (S.K. Campbell 1981), which contains only four main depositional units, yielded 482 artifacts that were divided into 122 analytical classes. In this case, the functional and stylistic elements of the technological assemblages were separated, allowing depositional units laid down over a 700-year period at the site to be compared with one another. The result showed functional stability and modest stylistic change through time in two specific tool categories, flaked stone projectile points and beads. The quantitative analysis of faunal remains coupled with the functional analysis of technology holds out real promise for understanding the function of individual sites and the evolution of littoral adaptations in the Puget Sound basin (G. Thompson 1978; Dunnell and Fuller 1975; S.K. Campbell 1981).

Sites from the riverine sector of the Puget Sound basin present a very different series of problems. Highly acid sediments destroy almost all faunal remains together with bone and shell implements. However, flaked stone artifacts are abundant and frequently standardized (Nelson 1962). Unfortunately, too few sites have been excavated to construct a general riverine sequence or to describe adequately the geographic variation in technologies known to exist along the eastern side of the basin.

Waterlogged sites preserving perishables are known from both riverine (Nordquist 1960a, 1961) and littoral contexts (Munsell 1970, 1976; Blukis Onat 1976; Blukis Onat et al. 1979), but too few have been excavated to establish a sequence for perishable technology in either setting.

The Littoral Sequence

Knowledge of the littoral sequence comes chiefly from the Skagit River delta and adjacent islands. When modified by later research (Kidd 1964, 1966; Mattson 1971; G. Thompson 1978; Blukis Onat et al. 1979; Carlson 1983), Bryan's (1957, 1963) interpretation of the littoral sequence remains the most useful. Influenced to some extent by others (A.R. King 1950; Carlson 1954, 1960; and

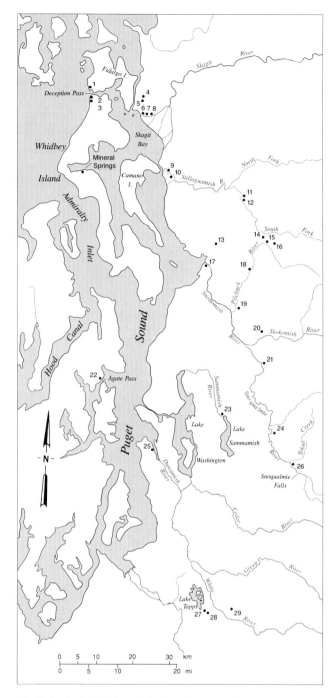

Fig. 1. Archeological sites of the Puget Sound region: 1, Rosario Beach (45SK07); 2, Cornet Bay (45IS90); 3, West Beach (45IS91); 4, Pedersen 2 (45SK51) and (45SK53); 5, Pedersen 1 (45SK54) and (45SK52); 6, Fish Town (45SK33); 7, (45SK34); 8, Dunlap (45SK35); 9, Kwatsakwibxw (45SN01); 10, Drawbridge (45SN64); 11, Jim Creek (45SN33); 12, Olcott (45SN14); 13, Mattson (45SN201); 14, Tusagou (45SN32); 15, James (45SN28) and Ray Gray (45SN73); 16, Scherrer (45SN58); 17, Hebolb (45SN17) and Legion Park (45SN61); 18, Burke (45SN24); 19, Myrick (45SN48); 20, Schuler (45SN62); 21, Biederbost (45SN100); 22, Old Man House (45KP2); 23, Marymoor Farm (45K19 and 45KI10); 24, McDevitt (45KI55); 25, Duwamish 1 (45KI23); 26, Tokul Creek (45KI19); 27, Imhof (45PI44); 28, Schodde/Anderson (45PI45); 29, Jokumsen (45KI5).

Nelson 1962), this formulation was modeled on Borden's (1951) outline of culture history in the Fraser River delta,

50 miles to the north.

The earliest known cultural remains, at Cornet Bay (Bryan 1963; Nelson 1962a), Rosario Beach (Bryan 1963) and, possibly, Old Man House (M.W. Smith 1950:6; Gaston and Jermann 1975) are thought to represent an adaptation to coastal land hunting and intertidal, littoral gathering. The early history of this development is known from excavations in the Fraser River delta (Borden 1975, 1979), but only indirectly on Puget Sound probably due to inundation of most littoral sites dating prior to 2000 B.C. Thus, knowledge of this adaptive phase is limited to a few components believed to date between 500 and 2000 B.C.

While there is little evidence for marked adaptive change over the last 2,000 years, there is evidence for stylistic change in local technologies (Mattson 1971; Kidd 1964; Bryan 1963; S.K. Campbell 1981). Intermediate, Late, and Protohistoric components are often found associated at the same site and consistently occur at ethnographically documented sites. The Protohistoric is defined by the occurrence of European (Bryan 1963:App. A; Nesbitt 1969; W.A. Snyder 1956a; Rice 1965a) and exotic aboriginal trade goods such as flaked stone knives from the Plateau (Bryan 1963:fig. 17/4; M.W. Smith 1950a: fig. 2/17; Garner 1960).

Interpretations of the littoral sequence have been based on inferred changes in subsistence patterns rather than artifact seriation demonstrating periodic shifts of cultural style (Bryan 1963; V.L. Butler 1983; cf. Carlson 1983). This reflects the general paucity of tools and abundance of faunal remains. In developing local sequences, most authorities (Carlson 1954; Bryan 1957; Kidd 1964) have relied on gross midden composition, continuity of occupation, inferred subsistence activities, inferred artifact function, and similarities between flaked stone tools from their site and surrounding areas such as the Fraser River delta, interior British Columbia, and the Columbia Plateau. Reliance on such criteria can lead to errors in the absence of long stratified sequences, radiocarbon dates, and large artifact assemblages. For example, it was shown that relative frequencies of certain species of shellfish and artifact types were related to the exploitation of delta and nondelta environments rather than to cultural succession at a number of sites in the Skagit River delta (G. Thompson 1978; Stilson 1972). Complex geomorphic changes effecting the distribution of food resources and subsistence activities were common throughout the Puget Sound basin (Schwartz and Grabert 1973) and might easily account for many of the differences thought to have been temporal and cultural by Bryan (1963) and Kidd (1964).

The Riverine Sequence

Data pertinent to constructing a sequence for the riverine sector of the Puget Sound basin are limited to (1) Olcott assemblages from the surface and shallowly stratified sites best known from terraces overlooking rivers in the Snohomish River basin (J. Thomson 1961; Miles 1972; Chatters and Thompson 1979), (2) a complex assemblage from Marymoor Farm near the mouth of the Sammamish River (Greengo 1966; Greengo and Houston 1970), (3) material from the partly waterlogged Biederbost site on the Snoqualmie River (Nelson 1962, 1976), and (4) assemblages from late prehistoric or protohistoric contexts (Onat and Bennett 1968; Stilson and Chatters 1981; Lewarch 1979; Lewarch and Larson 1977). Many have speculated about the significance of these sites (Butler 1961; Kidd 1964, 1966; Greengo 1966; Nelson 1976).

The Olcott complex (J. Thomson 1961; Stilson and Chatters 1981; cf. Dancey 1969), consisting of cobble implements and leaf-shaped points, is similar to material dating from 8000 to 4000 B.C. in the Fraser River valley (Borden 1960, 1961) and is probably of comparable age in the Puget Sound basin. Olcott material is known from surface collections throughout the basin and to the south (Welch 1983), typically in riverine settings well away from littoral environments. The absence of other assemblages that date to later periods suggests that the Olcott complex may have persisted until 2000 B.C.

Following the Olcott complex is the regional representative of the Cascade phase first excavated from the Marymoor site, which contains the classic association of Cascade and Cold Springs Side-Notched points, types that spread in association through the Columbia Plateau between 4500 and 2000 B.C. (Nelson 1969). It is likely their spread west of the Cascades occurred no later than 1800 B.C. Radiocarbon dates from the upper and lower levels at Marymoor indicate occupation at the site in 550 B.C. and A.D. 90; but it is difficult to know which, if any, of these dates is associated with the Marymoor phase (Nelson 1976), since the assemblage from Marymoor, itself, contains later materials, probably as a result of mechanical mixture (Greengo 1966:7–10). Related assemblages have been recovered in the southern and western sectors of the basin (Welch 1983).

Surface (Nelson 1976; Lewarch and Larson 1977) collections from the eastern and southern (Welch 1983) portions of the Puget Sound Basin contain numerous points that are similar to the Frenchman Springs phase in the adjoining Columbia Plateau (Nelson 1969). This suggests the presence of a poorly documented phase in the Northwest Coast dating between about 1000 and 200 B.C.

The subsequent phase is best represented by the Biederbost site, which contains a single, well-defined component associated with a date of A.D. 10 ± 80. It contains a rich lithic industry dominated by large corner-notched points, end and side scrapers, gravers, and cobble tools. The smaller tools are made on blades and micro-blades in exotic raw materials. Twined basketry, fish-hooks, and bound net weights have been preserved in a waterlogged part of the site (Nordquist 1960a, 1961a). The projectile points from this component are like those from the Quilomene Bar phase in the western Columbia Plateau (Nelson 1969), which dates to the first millennium B.C.

The most recent phase in the riverine succession, best represented at Tokul Creek (Onat and Bennett 1968), contains an association of cobble tools representing a continuity in local tradition and small flaked stone tools identical to those of the Cayuse phase in the western Columbia Plateau (Nelson 1969; Lewarch and Larson 1977).

The riverine sequence is still poorly understood. It is based on changes in artifact form and manufacture (Nelson 1976), and there are few data pertinent to subsistence activities (Onat and Bennett 1968; Nordquist 1960, 1960a, 1961b, 1961; Stilson and Chatters 1981:62–65). The riverine and littoral sequences cannot be correlated in detail.

External Relationships

External relations are difficult to discern in the littoral sequence. Early point types have isolated analogs in the riverine sector of the Puget Sound basin and in the San Juan Islands and Strait of Georgia, but it is impossible to trace the spread of complexes or individual types. Late assemblages have general analogs in southern British Columbia and on the ocean coast of Washington (Borden 1950a, 1951; Guinn 1962, 1963; Carlson 1983). Scallop, dentalium, and olivella shells, graphite, and jade adzes were traded throughout this area and are commonly found in Late-period components (Weld 1963; C.G. Nelson 1959; Rice 1965a; Bryan 1963; Kidd 1964). Interior trade items are known mainly from Protohistoric contexts.

Throughout the riverine sequence, stylistic features of stone tools are tied to the Plateau and Fraser Valley. The Olcott assemblages have close counterparts to the north and east (Borden 1960, 1961; Nelson 1969), the Marymoor assemblage to the east and south (Nelson 1969), the Biederbost material to the western Plateau (Nelson 1962, 1969, 1976), and the Tokul Creek assemblage to material in the Mount Rainier area and western Plateau (Onat and Bennett 1968; Rice 1964a, 1964, 1965, 1969; Warren 1959; Fugro Northwest 1980). Material from the upper Skagit River appears closely linked with the lower Nooksack River and Fraser River valleys (Lee 1963; R.V. Emmons 1952; Borden 1950a, 1951). These relationships may reflect diffusion of stylistic elements and technological processes, such as blade production, through adjacent riverine technologies.

Data, especially from the Biederbost site (Nelson 1962, 1976), suggest that people in the eastern riverine sector of the basin participated in a highly active, stable trading network, which funneled silica, obsidian (Fugro Northwest 1980), and lignite northward along the Cascade foothills; realgar (for pigment), dentalia, and finished tools from northern Puget Sound into the interior; and jade adzes southward from the Fraser and Skagit drainages. Silica also may have been traded from the Plateau via numerous mountain passes (Rice 1964a).

Developmental Models

Borden (1975, 1979) offered a model for the development and spread of major components of the economic adaptation characteristic of Northwest Coast culture. In this model, an adaptation focusing on intertidal gathering and fishing, with attendant riverine and upland components, spread northward from the Fraser River delta, while a very different kind of adaptation focusing on deepwater sea mammal hunting and fishing spread southward from the Aleutian Islands. The two adaptations met and fused in the area of the Queen Charlotte Islands. The synthesis, which forms the adaptive basis for classic Northwest Coast culture, spread from this central area, reaching the straits to the north of Puget Sound by about 500 B.C. Many of the subsistence and economic patterns characteristic of northern Northwest Coast culture never spread southward into the Puget Sound basin because there was no environmental basis for deepwater sea mammal hunting and fishing. This perspective helps to explain the minimal elaboration of art in the Puget Sound basin (cf. Suttles 1983) and why there are substantial differences in archeological assemblages as the basin is traversed from north to south. It also suggests that significant differences between these areas in subsistence, economy, and interdependent components of the social organization are deeply rooted.

Matson's (1983) model of resource utilization intensification centered around salmon fishing, and Whitlam (1983) is a model of extensification. Intensification is made possible by technological improvements in the taking, processing, and storage of salmon, and by the ownership of resources. Although intensification in the utilization of salmon was almost certainly necessary to the development of Northwest Coast culture, it is equally likely that it was not sufficient, of itself, for such a development. Indeed, if intensive salmon utilization were the only ingredient necessary for the development of classic Northwest Coast culture, then the Puget Sound basin should contain a far more complex manifestation of this cultural pattern. Based on site distributions in the Puget Sound region and the Strait of Georgia, Whitlam's (1983) model of extensification is used to describe the process in which more and more microenvironments come to be exploited over time, reflecting greater complexity in economic activity. This approach certainly warrants development, but Whitlam's particular model is too simple structurally, and the data he cites from the Puget Sound littoral insufficient, to measure extensification reliably.

Southern Coast Salish

WAYNE SUTTLES AND BARBARA LANE

Southern Coast Salish refers to the speakers of two Coast Salish languages, Lushootseed (lə'shōōtsēd) and Twana ('twänə).* Lushootseed is the language of a number of tribes whose territory extended from Samish Bay southward to the head of Puget Sound and included the drainages of the rivers flowing into this sheltered salt water. Lushootseed consists of two groups of dialects, Northern and Southern. Twana is the language of the people of Hood Canal and its drainage. Dialect differences within Twana were slight (fig. 1).

Component Groups

Before the treaties of 1854–1855 and the reservation system, there were over 50 named groups or "tribes," each having one or more winter villages, several summer camps, and resource sites. Neighboring groups were linked by ties of marriage, joint feasting and ceremonial activities, and use of common territory. These ties were especially strong within the same waterway or drainage system, but there were no breaks in the social network, which extended throughout the Southern Coast Salish region and beyond.

Within a waterway or drainage there were sometimes differences among groups in numbers, wealth of resources, defenses (professional warriors and fortifications), and status; and there were instances of groups standing in patron-client or even master-servant relationships. It also appears that the name of the most important group within a waterway or drainage was often used by outsiders as a collective name for all the groups there. Nevertheless, there were no formal political institutions uniting these local groups into multiband tribes.

One of the goals of the treaty-makers was precisely to create such units (Lane 1973:17–18), combining hitherto politically autonomous groups into tribes and appointing head chiefs and subchiefs to create an authority structure. Further complicating matters, anthropologists (for example, M.W. Smith 1941) have attempted to classify the aboriginal groups according to geographical or cultural criteria, in some instances reassigning tribal names to new groupings.

Table 1 lists the tribes whose names appeared in the treaties and early official reports or whose memory survived into the twentieth century. Because of the accidents of history, it is not a complete list of precontact tribes. Probably, as Waterman (1920a) concluded, a complete list of tribes "would be nothing more than a list of villages." In the following paragraphs the more important or best-known of these tribes are identified.

Speakers of Northern Lushootseed included the Swinomish ('swĭnōmĭsh), on Swinomish Slough; the Skagit ('skăjĭt) on Penn Cove, Whidbey Island; the various tribes that have come to be known as Upper Skagit, on the Skagit River; the Stillaguamish (stĭlə'gwämĭsh), on the Stillaguamish River; the Snohomish (snō'hōmĭsh), around the mouth of the Snohomish River; and the Skykomish (skĭ'kōmĭsh) on the Skykomish River.

Speakers of Southern Lushootseed included the Snoqualmie (snō'kwälmē), on the Snoqualmie River; the Suquamish (sōō'kwämĭsh), on Agate Pass; the Duwamish (dōō'wämĭsh), on the Black River; the Puyallup (pyōō'äləp), at the mouth of the Puyallup River; the Nisqually (nĭs'kwälē), at the mouth of the Nisqually River, and the Squaxin ('skwäksĭn) on Case Inlet.

Speakers of Twana included the Quilcene ('kwĭl,sēn), on Quilcene Bay; the Skokomish (skō'kōmĭsh), at the elbow of Hood Canal and on the Skokomish River; and the Duhlelap (də'lälĭp) at the head of Hood Canal.

Environment

The territory of the Southern Coast Salish lies entirely within the Puget Sound Basin, a region of sheltered salt water with numerous bays, inlets, and channels.

The rain shadow of the Olympic Mountains makes the northern saltwater part of the region drier than the rest; at Coupeville on Whidbey Island annual precipitation is

*The phonemes of Lushootseed are: (plain stops and affricates) p, t, c, č, k, kʷ, q, qʷ, ʔ; (glottalized stops and affricates) ṗ t, ċ, č̓, ƛ̓, k̓, k̓ʷ, q̓, q̓ʷ; (voiced stops and affricates) b, d, ȝ, ž̧, g, gʷ; (voiceless continuants) s, š, ł, xʷ, x, x̌ʷ, h; (resonants) w, y, l; (glottalized resonants) w̓, y̓, l̓; (vowels) i, a, u, ə. The voiced stops b and d developed within historic times from nasals m and n, and these nasals are still used in some proper names and ritual terms and in some styles of speech (Hess 1976:15).

Twana has an inventory of phonemes like Lushootseed with the addition of the vowels e [ɛ] and o [ɔ] and the restriction of the voiced stops and affricates ȝ, ž̧, g, and gʷ to loans from Lushootseed (Drachman 1969:1).

485

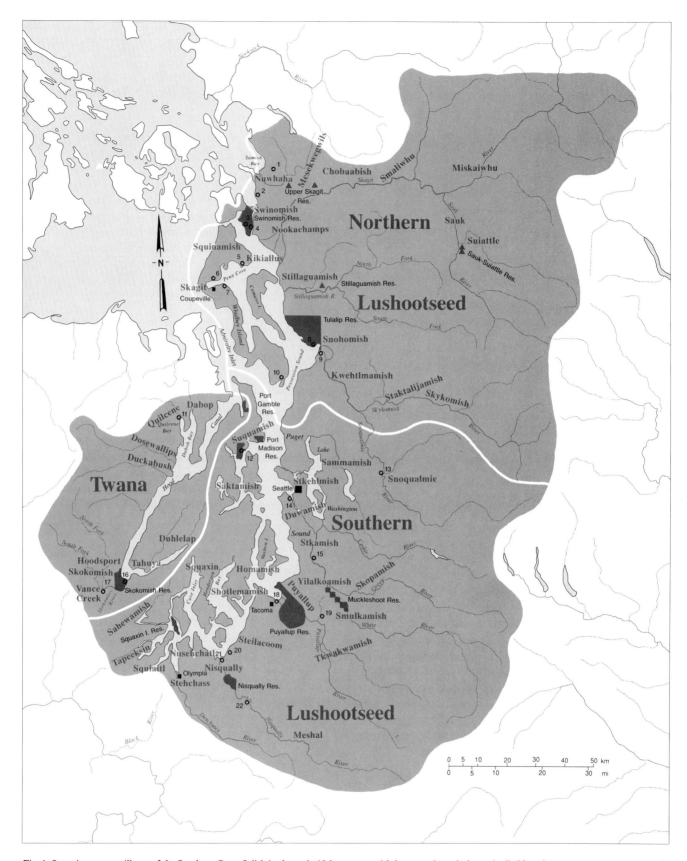

Fig. 1. Some important villages of the Southern Coast Salish in the early 19th century, with language boundaries and tribal locations.
1, sə́gʷsəgʷq̓ʷ; 2, łáłaʔus; 3, sdíʔus; 4, dxʷiúʔuӡ; 5, c̓ə́ɬúsəb; 6, húbqs; 7, čubəʔálšid; 8, čə́ƛ̓aqs 'rocky point';
9, hibúləb; 10, dəgʷáӡx; 11, qʷə́lsíd; 12, xʷsə́q̓ʷəb; 13, xaláltxʷ 'painted house'; 14, t̓uláltxʷ 'herring house'; 15, stə́q 'log jam'; 16, təbádas;

486   17, yəlálqo 'forks of river'; 18, šáčqəd; 19, stəx 'gouged through'; 20, Sequalitchew; 21, dxʷsqʷə́li; 22, Muck Creek.

Table 1. Southern Coast Salish Tribes

English		Treaty Spelling	Hodge 1907–1910
		Lushootseed	
1.	Nuwhaha[a] *dx^wʔáha*	Noo-wha-ha	Towhaha 2:796
			Nuchwugh 2:90
2.	Swinomish *swə́dəbš*	Swin-a-mish	Swinomish 2:662
3.	Squinamish *sqʷədábš*	Squin-ah-mish	——
4.	Skagit *sqáǯət*	Skagit	Skagit 2:585
5.	Kikiallus *kíkiyàlus*	Kik-i-allus	Kikiallu 1:687
6.	Nookachamps[b] *dúqʷəčàbš*	Nook-wa-chah-mish	Nukwatsamish 2:97
7.	Mesekwegwils[b] *bshík^whig^wìlc*	Mee-see-qua-guilch	Miseekwigweelis 1:870
8.	Chobaabish[b] *čúbəʔàbš*	Cho-bah-ah-bish	Chobaabish 1:287
9.	Smaliwhu[b] *sbáliʔx^w*	——	Smalihu 2:610
10.	Miskaiwhu[b] *bəsqíx^wix^w*	——	——
11.	Sauk *sáʔk^wbix^w*	Sah-ku-mehu	Sakumehu 2:414
12.	Suiattle *suyáx̌bix^w*	——	——
13.	Stillaguamish *stùləg^wábš*	Stoluck-wha-mish	Stillaguamish 2:637
14.	Snohomish[c] *sduhúbš*	Sno-ho-mish	Snohomish 2:606
15.	Kwehtlmamish *dx^wk^wíx̌əbabš*	N'Quentl-ma-mish	Kwehtlmamish 1:747
16.	Staktalijamish *sʔəq̓táliǯabš*	Sk-tah-le-jum	Staktalijums 2:596
17.	Skykomish *sq̓íx^wəbš*	Skai-wha-mish	Skihwamish 2:591
18.	Snoqualmie *sduk^wálbix^w*	Snoqualmoo	Snoqualmu 2:606–607
19.	Suquamish *suq̓^wábš*	Suquamish	Suquamish 2:652
	also called *ʔítak^wbix^w*		Etakmahu 1:439,
			Skahakmehu 2:588,
			Stuckre 2:645 (?)
20.	Saktamish *sx̌áq̓tabš* (?)	——	Shaktabsh 2:521
21.	Duwamish *dx^wdəwʔábš*	Dwamish	Dwamish 1:407
22.	Stkehlmish *sacakaɫəbš* (?)	Sk-tahl-mish?	Stkehlmish 2:596
23.	Sammamish *scabábš*	Sam-ahmish	Samamish 2:421,
			Stsababsh 2:645
24.	Stkamish[d] *stqábš* (?)	St-kah-mish	Sekamish 2:498
25.	Yilalkoamish[d] *yilálq^wuʔabš*	——	Syilalkoabsh 2:662
26.	Skopamish[d] *sq^wəpábš*	Skope-ahmish	Skopamish 2:595
27.	Smulkamish[d] *sbalxq^wuʔábš*	Smalh-kamish	Smulkamish 2:604
28.	Homamish *sx̣^wubábš* (?)	——	Shomamish 2:553
29.	Puyallup *puyáləpabš*	Puyallup	Puyallup 2:331
30.	Tkwakwamish[d] *dx^wx^wáq̓^wəbš* (?)	——	Tkwakwamish 2:761
31.	Steilacoom *čtílq^wəbš*	Steilacoom	Steilacoomamish 2:636
32.	Nisqually *dx^wsq^wəliabš*	Nisqualli	Nisqualli 2:76
33.	Meshal *bəšáləbš*	——	——
34.	Shotlemamish *sx̣^wux̌bábš*	——	Shotlemamish 2:558
35.	Squaxin *sq^wáksədabš*	Squawksin	Squaxon 2:631
36.	Sahewamish *səhíʔwəbš*	Sa-heh-wamish	Sahewamish 2:409
37.	Tapeeksin *təpíqsədabš*	T'Peeksin	Tapeeksin 2:691,
			Sawamish 2:481 (?)
38.	Squiaitl *sq̓^wayáɫ* (?)	Squi-aitl	Squiatl 2:632
39.	Stehchass *sʔəčásəbš*	Stehchass	Stehtsasamish 2:636
40.	Nusehchatl *dx^wčičaʔáɫ*	——	Nusehtsatl 2:99
		Twana[e]	
41.	Dabop *čttáʔbux^w*		
42.	Quilcene *sq^wəlsídbəš*		Colcene 1:322
43.	Dosewallips *čtduswáylupš*		
44.	Duckabush *čtdux^wyabús*		

487

Table 1.   Southern Coast Salish Tribes   (*Continued*)

	English	Treaty Spelling		Hodge 1907–1910
45.	Hoodsport	čtslaḷaⱡlaⱡtəbəxʷ		
46.	Skokomish	sqʷuqʷóʔbəš	Sko-ko-mish	Skokomish 2:595
47.	Vance Creek	čtq̓ʷəlqʷéli		
48.	Tahuya	čtta·xúya		
49.	Duhlelap	čxʷlílap		Tulalip 2:835

^aAlso called Upper Samish and Stick Samish.

^bNumbers 6–10 are collectively called Upper Skagit.

^cThe reservation established in Snohomish territory was called Tulalip from *dxʷlilap* 'Tulalip Bay', 'distant bottom'.

^dThe reservation established for numbers 24–27 and 30 was called Muckleshoot from *bə́qəlšuⱡ*, the name of a prairie between the Green and White rivers.

^eFrom Elmendorf 1960:264–265.

about 17 inches, while at Seattle it is 34 inches, and at Olympia 45 inches. The foothills of the Cascades receive considerably more; at Snoqualmie Falls it is about 60 inches (Phillips 1960).

Most of the land was heavily timbered, but there were also a good many prairies, ranging in size from a few acres in the more northern river valleys to more extensive ones on Whidbey Island and from the Puyallup Valley southward. These were probably maintained by native burning practices (Norton 1979; R. White 1980:20–26). Red cedar, spruce, and hemlock were common, but the dominant tree was Douglas fir. Deciduous trees included big-leaf maple, alder, vine maple, and others that grew nearly everywhere at lower elevations, cottonwood and Oregon ash in river valleys in the southern part of the region, and madrona and garry oak in the drier parts of the region. In areas of greater precipitation, the vegetation approached rain-forest density, and these conditions resulted in huge log jams that blocked some rivers and covered large areas.

External Relations

The marital, economic, and ceremonial ties that linked groups within the Southern Coast Salish region extended into adjacent regions. The Suquamish and Twana intermarried with the Clallam, the Swinomish and Skagit with the Northern Straits, the Upper Skagit with the Nooksack, the Twana with the Upper and Lower Chehalis, and the tribes of Southern Puget Sound with the Upper Chehalis. The Squiaitl of Eld Inlet may have been as much Upper Chehalis as Lushootseed in speech (see "Southwestern Coast Salish," this vol.).

Contact between inland groups was by well-known trails. Even the Cascade Range was not a barrier; the Upper Skagit had some contact with Interior Salish such as the Chelan, while the Snoqualmie and upriver people in the Puyallup and Nisqually drainages had considerable contact with the Sahaptin-speaking Kittitas and Yakima.

In the middle of the nineteenth century there were perhaps as many speakers of Sahaptin as of Lushootseed in some villages in the upper Puyallup and Nisqually valleys (M.W. Smith 1940:13, 21–22). The people of one of these have been identified as both Sahaptin and Salish. Jacobs (1931:95) was told by Sahaptin speakers that a small band of Sahaptins called Meshal lived on the upper Nisqually River, but M.W. Smith (1940:13) identified this group as the *bəšáləbš*, a Nisqually group on the Mashel River.

With more distant tribes or ones seldom encountered there was conflict or at least the expectation of conflict. Most of the Southern Coast Salish probably viewed the Cowichan with suspicion or hostility. But the real enemies of all, for much of the first half of the nineteenth century, were the Lekwiltok Kwakiutl, who raided the area for slaves and loot. According to traditions, on one or two occasions leaders of several of the Southern Coast Salish tribes organized retaliatory expeditions (Brown 1873–1876,1:70–72; Curtis 1907–1930, 9:14–16).

Culture

Except for casual observations by members of the George Vancouver expedition of 1791, there is no information on this region prior to the entry of the Hudson's Bay Company in the 1820s and no very systematically gathered data before the 1850s. The sketch that follows describes native culture as of the second quarter of the nineteenth century.

Subsistence

The Southern Coast Salish may have depended to a greater extent on vegetable foods and land game than peoples to the north and on the outer coast; nevertheless, fish and especially salmon were the staple. All five species of salmon, and steelhead, ran somewhere in the region, though pinks were less common and sockeye were limited to small runs in the Skagit and Duwamish river systems. There was also a population of kokanee in Lake Washington and the Sammamish drainage. In the salt water, fishermen took salmon by trolling and with seines and gill nets. In rivers they built weirs and traps, used trawl nets, dip nets, gaff hooks, harpoons, and leisters.

The Southern Coast Salish weir (Ballard 1957; Elmendorf 1960:64–73) consisted of a row of tripods, two legs of each on the upstream side supporting three sets of horizontal poles, which in turn supported a row of removable lattice sections that stopped the fish. On the downstream side there were several platforms, from which the fishermen operated lift nets (fig. 2). The lift net was a bowl-shaped net attached to a hoop held by crossed poles; The net was generally used at night. The weir was generally built by a number of men and belonged to a village, but the Twana lift-net platforms were individually owned.

On Swinomish Channel the Swinomish had a trap consisting of a V-shaped weir with an opening at the apex, a pair of canoes moored there, and a net lowered between them across the opening. The sites and gear were individually owned (Suttles 1947–1952).

In the saltwater, herring and smelt were taken with herring rakes used from canoes; flounders were taken with seines by groups of people wading at low tide; flounders and other flatfishes, lingcod, and rockfish were taken with leisters or two pronged spears used from canoes; and sculpins were caught with baited gorges. Halibut were available only at the north end of Hood Canal and in Admiralty Inlet.

Sturgeon were harpooned in the Skokomish and Snohomish rivers and perhaps other larger streams. Freshwater fishes available to upriver people included cutthroat, Dolly Varden, rainbow trout, mountain whitefish, and suckers.

Among the Twana (Elmendorf 1960:84–113) and probably elsewhere, hunting was a specialization, with sea hunters, land hunters, and fowlers distinct professions. The sea hunter used a harpoon from the bow of a two-man canoe, his partner paddling in the stern. In places where seals habitually hauled out, hunters took them by surprise and clubbed them or drove them onto sharpened stakes or nets. Beached whales were used, but whales were not hunted.

The most important land mammals were blacktail deer and elk. Deer hunters used bow and arrows, usually hunting individually, with a dog or dogs to help locate the game and to track a wounded animal. Deer were also taken in pitfalls, with snares, in drives with nets or with several hunters surrounding them or chasing them into the water so that they could be clubbed, and at night from canoes with flares that frightened them into the water. Elk were also taken with bow and arrow and in drives. Twana villages held community elk drives in the fall and dried the

flesh for the winter (Elmendorf 1960:93). The Stillaguamish used a mountain pass where they could drive elk over a cliff (Suttles 1947–1952). Hunters also used deadfalls and snares to trap black bear, beavers, raccoons, marmots, and other smaller animals.

Around 20 species of waterfowl were caught. Hunters went out on dark nights with fires in their canoes and caught ducks with a multiprong spear or a net on a shaft. They caught ducks in long nets raised between pairs of high poles, in nets anchored underwater over places where herring were spawning, and in snares. Seagulls were caught with gorges.

Shellfish were abundant (Belcher 1985). Important mollusk species included the littleneck clam, butter clam, horse clam, cockle, geoduck, bay mussel, and native oyster. Cockles, mussels, and oysters are surface dwellers and were simply gathered. The other species required digging with a digging stick. Butter clams, horse clams, and cockles were dried for later use or trade. Crabs (probably both Dungeness and red) and sea urchins were also eaten.

Vegetable foods included sprouts, roots and bulbs, berries, and nuts (Gunther 1945). The most important roots and bulbs were probably bracken, camas, and, especially in the Duwamish area, wapato. Important berries included the salmonberry, thimbleberry, trailing blackberry, blackcap, serviceberry, salal berry, red huckleberry, blueberry, and red and blue elderberry. Some berries were harvested with comblike devices not reported from elsewhere (Waterman 1973:54). Acorns were relished but not widely available; people from around Puget Sound went in the fall to the Nisqually plains to harvest them (Curtis 1907–1930, 9:58). They were evidently not leached but roasted fresh (Gunther 1945:27–28).

Technology

The principal men's craft was woodworking, and the principal tools were spool-shaped stone mauls, wedges of elk antler and yew wood, and adzes of a distinctive regional type having a handle with a flared end (fig. 3). Skill at woodworking was responsible for the plank houses and canoes of the region and for several kinds of household utensils. The Southern Coast Salish made bent-corner boxes and enclosed water containers, dishes, and spoons, though not with the variety or form and decoration found farther north.

Women worked with cedarbark and made most cordage, mats, baskets, and blankets. The inner bark of the red cedar was shredded by laying it over the edge of a paddle and beating it with a bark shredder. Women made twine of nettle fiber, cattail fiber, and Indian hemp traded from east of the Cascades. Men made heavier cordage of bear gut and rope of twisted cedar withes.

Women made sewed cattail and tule mats in three sizes,

top left, Wash. State Arch., Olympia; Smithsonian, NAA: top right, 864145; bottom left, 55389; bottom right, U. of Wash. Lib., Special Coll., Seattle: NA 709.

Fig. 2. Fishing. top left, Yelm Jim's weir on the Puyallup Reservation, Wash. A fisherman is lifting a net containing a salmon. Photograph by John E. Mitchell, 1885. top right, A long cylindrical trap made of willow withes used to catch steelhead trout. Photographed before 1957. bottom left, Swinomish men operating a scoop net to transfer the fish from the community-operated trap to the hold of the scow. Photograph by Andrew T. Kelley, Swinomish Reservation, Wash., Aug. 1938. bottom right, William Weahlup of the Tulalip Reservation smoking salmon and roe on the beach. Photograph by Norman Edson, 1906.

used as house mats, sleeping mats, and canoe mats (fig. 4). The house mats were reportedly about five feet wide and 12 to 20 feet long (Eells 1985:76; M.W. Smith 1940:296 gives the dimensions as 6–8 feet by 20–30 feet). They were used to line the walls of plank houses in winter and to cover frames of poles for summer houses. Bed mats were about three feet wide and 8 to 15 feet long; denser and double-layered, they were springy and comfortable. Canoe mats were about two feet wide and two to four feet long. These mats were made from the flat leaves of the cattail or the round stems of the tule, selected by length according to the desired width of the mat.

The Southern Coast Salish also made twined mats of cattails and tules and checkerwork mats of strips of cedarbark. Most of the cedarbark mats used were obtained in trade through the Clallam from the Makah and other Nootkans, who in turn received cattail and tule mats (Eells 1985:78).

Baskets were made by coiling, plain twining, wrapped twining (fig. 5), and checker weaving; coiled baskets were decorated by imbrication and beading and twined baskets by overlay (Waterman 1973:1–29; Thompson and Marr 1983). Coiled baskets were made watertight and could be used for stone boiling.

Using the two-bar "loom" (see "Central Coast Salish," fig. 5, this vol.), women wove blankets of mountain-goat wool, dog wool, and a mixture of bird down, fireweed down, and perhaps other substances. Mountain goats could be hunted only in the Cascade Range, and so the saltwater Puget Sound tribes and the Twana obtained the wool from upriver peoples such as the Skykomish. The saltwater peoples kept a breed of wool-bearing dog. On Whidbey Island in May, 1782, an explorer saw "about forty dogs in a drove, shorn close to the skin like sheep" (Meany 1942:162). Puget Sound weavers used a spindle with an undecorated whorl. Twana weavers reportedly spun yarn on their thighs, without a spindle (Elmendorf 1960:198). Woven blankets were used for bedding and as robes and were important as wealth. Fabrics were also

Fig. 3. William Shelton, Snohomish, carving a totem pole with a crooked knife. An elbow adz rests on the animal's back. Traditionally the Coast Salish carved house posts and grave monuments but did not erect free-standing monuments, "totem poles" in the narrow sense, like those used to commemorate the assumption of titles on the northern Northwest Coast. Shelton's poles, which he began carving in 1911, illustrated Lushootseed myths and legends and symbolized the relationship between the Indians and their environment. Shelton lectured on Indian traditions and worked to promote good will toward Indians among Whites in the Puget Sound region. Photograph by Ferdinand Brady, Tulalip Reservation, Wash., before 1938.

made by twining, the most common being of heavy warps of shredded cedarbark, used for clothing.

Skin dressing was practiced by both sexes but perhaps mainly by women. Deer hides, and less commonly elk hides, were dehaired and cured with brains and oil to make buckskin. Bear skins with the fur intact were made into robes. Skins of beavers, raccoons, mountain beavers, sea otters (obtained in trade or as potlatch gifts), and even of birds were sewed together to make robes. Mountain-beaver robes were common among the Twana and were traded to the Lower Chehalis. Skins of a species of duck were dried and twisted to make cord from which blankets were woven (M.W. Smith 1940:301). The horse-using Nisqually made parfleches of elk hide, using them to carry food and to store smoked meat (Haeberlin and Gunther 1930:33).

Structures

Three types of plank house were built in this region: shed-roof houses, gambrel-roof houses, and gable-roof houses ("Introduction," fig. 2, this vol.) (Waterman and Greiner 1921). Most were built as dwellings, but wealthy men sometimes built extraordinarily large potlatch houses, simply for use during these events and putting up guests.

The shed-roof house was probably the most common and perhaps once the only type. It was similar to or identical with that of the Central Coast Salish. The largest known was Old Man House, at the Suquamish village on Agate Pass. Built as a potlatch house early in the nineteenth century, it was at least 500 feet long and varied from 40 to 60 feet in width (Gibbs 1877:215; W.A. Snyder

Fig. 4. A woman, probably Stillaguamish or married to a Stillaguamish, demonstrating cattail mat making. The wide, spongy leaf of the cattail, identified as the "female" part of the plant, is used. Properly dried, these provide all the materials—the leaves themselves, a coil of cord made from their tough edges to sew them with, and lengths of braided leaves for selvedges. She uses wood needles, long and slightly bowed, and a creaser with a grooved edge that fits over the top of the needle. The process begins by laying the required number of leaves side by side between two selvedges and securing them by one course of twining. The needle is then laid on the ground flat-side down and the selvedges and leaves are threaded onto it. Pressing the creaser down on the perforated leaves, the worker bends them around the needle, forming an opening through which the cord can be pulled as the needle is withdrawn. The leaves are sewn at an interval of about 3 inches and the mat is finished off by braiding the ends of the leaves (Waterman 1973:24–26; Underhill 1944:107; Johnson and Bernick 1986:25). The mat was probably intended for use in a canoe. Photograph by Harlan I. Smith, Stanwood, Wash., 1900.

1956:20; Mauger 1978:230–234).

The gambrel-roof house, a type unique to Puget Sound (fig. 6), had a roof form somewhat like a truncated pyramid.

Gable-roofed houses may have been most common at the southern end of the region. Wealthier Twana built them as the more prestigious type. The wall planks were either set vertically into the ground, in the manner of Southwestern Coast Salish houses, or were held horizontally between pairs of poles, as the shed-roof house. Inside, the bed platform occupied the space between the walls and the posts. In a larger house there were two rows of fireplaces in the earth floor (Elmendorf 1960:154–165; M.W. Smith 1940:282–286).

In all these houses, the center was open, without partitions between the sections. The house posts were sometimes carved or painted. Gibbs (1877:215) reports that those of Old Man House were "carved with grotesque figures of men, naked and about half size."

The temporary house set up at a summer campsite was usually a gable-roof structure made of a frame of poles covered with housemats (fig. 7).

Stockades were built in some villages, as in a Skagit village (Wilkes 1845, 4:511), perhaps only after the 491

Fig. 5. Skokomish wrapped-twined basket with simple geometric designs done in grass overlay. Collected before 1924; height 25.3 cm.

increased danger of Lekwiltok raids in the early nineteenth century. A Snohomish "fort" was defended with ditches concealing sharpened stakes (Gibbs 1877:223).

Transport

The Southern Coast Salish used canoes of several types ("Introduction," fig. 3, this vol.), essentially the same ones used by the Central Coast Salish. The largest were built in the Westcoast style, with the rising tapered bow and the vertical stern (fig. 6). These were used for movements of groups of people and for warfare. Probably most were obtained in trade from the outer coast. For most subsistence activities people used canoes made in the Salish style. The largest of these, designated the "freight canoe" (Waterman and Coffin 1920) or women's canoe (M.W. Smith 1940:289), was used to move household goods. A smaller and slenderer variety with a forward slanting cutwater, capable of holding two or three men, was used for trolling and hunting. A still smaller version of this was used as a one-man canoe. Upriver people used a third major type, the shovelnose, which had a broad bow and stern and was generally propelled with a pole rather than a paddle (fig. 8). Finally, for children and casual use by adults, there was a "knockabout" type with identical blunt bow and stern. Waterman and Coffin (1920) and Elmendorf (1960:170–192) give the fullest accounts.

Fig. 6. Duwamish Westcoast canoe. The mats draped over it may be house mats and were probably there to protect it from the sun. A gambrel-roof house is in the background. Photograph by Clarence L. Andrews, near Renton, Wash., on Cedar River, 1893.

Men and women used different paddles; men's were longer and more tapered, women's broader with a more rounded tip. For travel in rivers the Twana also used a paddle with a notched end, a type common on the Lower Columbia. The paddler knelt on a cattail canoe mat, which rested on a coarse cedar-limb mat that kept it out of any bilge-water. The Puget Sound peoples used the cedarbark canoe bailer also used by the Central Coast Salish; the Twana used the wooden scoop type also used by the Quinault. Sails of mats or planks were used in the nineteenth century but perhaps not before European models arrived. Upriver people made rafts of logs for crossing streams or travel downstream (M.W. Smith 1940: 287). On the salt water, people traveling to and from major summer locations laid house planks across a pair of canoes to make a temporary catamaran.

For carrying goods on land, packers used a tumpline passed around the forehead or across the chest. Hunters who went into the mountains in winter used snowshoes. The Twana snowshoe was a short oval or ellipse in form (Elmendorf 1960:193–194).

Horses reached the southern end of the Puget Sound Basin perhaps in the late eighteenth century. The only peoples who made serious use of them were those of the inland villages of the Puyallup and Nisqually (M.W. Smith 1940:292–294). Horses and gear were probably obtained from the Sahaptins.

Clothing and Adornment

In good weather men wore only a cedarbark or hide breechclout or else went naked. Women wore at least an apron of cedarbark and usually a cedarbark skirt (fig. 9). Both sexes also wore blankets woven of mountain goat wool or made of skins sewed together. In colder weather men wore hide shirts and leggings or trousers. Some southern Puget Sound women had long shirts and leggings of buckskin. Both sexes wore hide moccasins (Haeberlin and Gunther 1930:37–38).

Among the Twana both sexes wore brimless basketry hats, and men also wore fur caps. Among the Puget Sound

Fig. 7. Summer mat house of migrant pickers. The baskets were used in the collection of hops. Photograph by Asahel Curtis, White River, Wash., 1902.

Fig. 8. Phillip Starr poling a shovelnose canoe. Photograph by Arthur Ballard, Green River, Wash., 1919.

tribes some people also had broad-brimmed basketry hats.

Nearly all of both sexes wore earrings of dentalia and abalone shell, and some wealthier people also wore abalone nose ornaments, suspended from their perforated septa. Women wore necklaces of shells, teeth, and claws, and were tattooed on their legs and chins. Twana men wore their hair long and done up in a knot. Nisqually men parted their hair in the middle and braided it or let it hang loose, sometimes wearing a skin headband or tying hawk or eagle feathers into the braids (Haeberlin and Gunther 1930:39), seemingly in Sahaptin fashion. Women parted theirs and wore it in two braids. Slaves wore their hair short. Young men plucked their beards, but older men might let them grow. Except for slaves and the very poor, all had their heads flattened in infancy. The earliest European visitors reported that the Natives smeared themselves with oil and paint, especially red ocher and a black mica-bearing substance, that some men had bushy beards and others chin tufts and moustaches, and that they had ornaments of copper (Meany 1942:131; B. Anderson 1939:201).

Forms of Wealth

Wealth was a category distinct from food. Wealth consisted of dentalia and clamshell disk beads, blankets of dog and mountain goat wool, fur robes, pelts, bone war clubs, canoes, and slaves. Dentalia (presumably received in trade from the Nootkans of Vancouver Island) were commonly used in one-fathom length double strings; the clamshell beads (produced locally?) in single strings. Haeberlin and Gunther (1930:29) report that the strings of dentalia were a unit of value and give some equivalences, probably reflecting early or mid-nineteenth century values. Elmendorf (1960:331) reports that when the Twana gave wealth items, the gifts were graded according to the rank of the recipient, but when they gave packages of food at feasts the gifts were of equal quantity for all.

Social Organization

The basic residential groupings were the village, the household, and the family. The village consisted of one or more big plank houses and perhaps one or more smaller structures; the household consisted of the families that shared a plank house during the winter; and the family consisted of the occupants of one section of the plank house. The family was usually a man and his wife or wives and their children, but it might include another unmarried relative or two and, for the wealthy, one or more slaves. The family usually had its own fireplace. Sometimes co-wives in a polygynous marriage occupied adjacent sections of the house and had their own fires.

Among the Twana a couple usually resided with the husband's parents, and so the male family heads were usually related patrilineally (Elmendorf 1960:311). Among the Puget Sound people the composition of the household was more varied. In the Duwamish area a couple often lived with the wife's parents until the birth of the first child, if not longer (Waterman 1920a). Among the Upper Skagit, a woman's parents sometimes persuaded a useful son-in-law to stay with them (J.M. Collins 1974:83). Generally one family head was acknowledged head of the household.

The village seems to have been a more closed and permanent unit in the southern part of the region. Among the Twana (Elmendorf 1960:255, 306–307) and southern Puget Sound tribes (M.W. Smith 1940:36, 40) village membership was permanent. Among the Duwamish (Waterman 1920a:90) and Upper Skagit (J.M. Collins 1974:85–86) people moved rather freely from one village to another.

Society was divided into upper class freemen, lower   *493*

left, Smithsonian, NAA: 79-4346; right, U. of Wash., Thomas Burke Memorial, Wash. State Mus., Seattle: L4233.

Fig. 9. Women's clothing. left, Muckleshoot girl, granddaughter of Anne Jack, wearing skirt and cape of cedar bark, which were effective in shedding rain. The tumpline is made of maple bark imbricated with bear grass. She is carrying imbricated coiled baskets. Photographed about 1910. right, Studio portrait of a Nisqually woman and her charge, Master McElroy. She wears an elaborate dentalium headdress and a breastplate, which indicate traditional wealth. Photographed in 1868.

class freemen, and slaves. Upper class people (Twana *swǝlwálas*, sing. *swǝlús*; Lushootseed *siiʔáb*, sing. *siʔáb*) were those of good birth and wealth, who participated in the appropriate ceremonial activities. Among the Twana there may have been some sort of ranking of the upper crust of a village (Elmendorf 1960:323, 1971), but there seems to be no evidence of this elsewhere. Lower class people were those without the wealth required for participation in the more prestigious ceremonies, without close kinship with the wealthy, and perhaps with the taint of slave ancestry. Slaves were war captives and their descendants, held as property by their masters.

Each village was linked to several others through the marriages of its leading families and consequent ties of kinship and through common participation in a number of

ceremonial activities (Elmendorf 1960:302–303). High status within the village, Elmendorf argues (1960:403–405, 1971), was dependent on recognition within the intervillage network.

Political Organization

Usually the wealthiest house head was the acknowledged leader of the village, whose role was to sponsor feasts and potlatches. However, there was no formal office of village headman. (Only Twana had terms for 'house head' and 'village head'). At the death of a village headman, the role was often assumed by a younger brother or son, but because of its requirements it was not strictly hereditary. There was also no formal village council. In a Twana

494

SUTTLES AND LANE

village there were two other functionaries, a chief's speaker and a village crier, the latter a man who took on the task of waking people in the morning and calling out advice and opinion (Elmendorf 1960:314–315).

Kinship

Kinship was reckoned bilaterally, and there were no lineage-like kin groups. Lushootseed and Twana kinship terms are like those of other Coast Salish languages in making no distinctions between relatives on father's and mother's side, in separating lineal and collateral relatives in parents' and children's generations but merging them in others, and in having substitute terms for uncle/aunt and nephew/niece after the death of the linking relative. There is some variation in the sibling/cousin terms; in Northern Lushootseed (Hess 1976:366; cf. J.M. Collins 1974: 86–90), as in Straits and Halkomelem, the terms for older and younger siblings are used for cousins of senior and junior lines of descent (the child of a parent's older sibling being called 'older sibling' even if younger than the speaker), while in Southern Lushootseed (Ballard 1935; M.W. Smith 1940:174) and Twana (Elmendorf 1946) these terms are used according to the relative age of the cousins. The affinal terms have a structure quite different from that of Straits and Halkomelem; parents-in-law and children-in-law are merged, man's brother-in-law is distinct, man's sister-in-law and woman's sibling-in-law are merged. Kinship was acknowledged by persons who shared known ancestors, and marriage with known kin was incestuous.

Conflict

There were professional warriors, but warfare was, at least in the nineteenth century, largely defensive. People were generally on good terms with their closer neighbors, with whom they intermarried and had kinship ties. Visitors from outside this circle, regardless of language or cultural similarities, were seen as possibly hostile. What warfare there was can be attributed to the ambition of professional warriors and the desire for revenge. Occasionally a warrior led a small party into territory where they had no relatives, hoping to waylay unarmed women and children and to be able to take a few as slaves, perhaps by intimidation rather than violence. If the victims' village was sufficiently provoked, could identify the aggressors, and had a warrior, he might lead another small party in a surprise dawn attack on the aggressors' village, attempting to kill the men, burn the houses, smash the canoes, and make off with captives and loot. But there was no institution through which warriors could be mobilized, and so fighting of this sort did not develop into more organized warfare, except in response to persistent raiding by the Lekwiltok.

A warrior's weapons included a war club (of bone, stone, or wood, flat and double-edged), a dagger, short spear, and bow and arrow (possibly with arrow poison). He wore a hide shift, but no armor (Elmendorf 1960: 465–473; M.W. Smith 1940:150–161).

As a substitute for physical aggression, a Twana village could hire a shaman for a public use of his power to harm another group (Elmendorf 1960:474–475, 1970). The practice has not been reported for Puget Sound.

Conflict between individuals or families within the circle of normal friendly relations could lead to a killing, in which case close relatives of the murdered person demanded blood money in compensation. This was usually negotiated and paid, but if not the result was likely to be an extended feud. Any person who had killed another had to undergo a long purification.

Games and Pastimes

Three games were played for stakes—dice, the disk game, and the hand game. The dice, made of beaver incisors, were used by women only. The disk and hand games were played by men. They played the disk game (Lushootseed *sləháləb*, Twana *slahál*) with a set of wooden disks, one marked distinctively. One man shuffled the disks within a wad of shredded cedar bark, divided the wad in two, and challenged his opponent to guess which held the marked disk. This game was played within villages and in intervillage gatherings (Culin 1907:250–252). Once the most popular game in the region, in the late nineteenth century it was replaced in popularity by the hand game. The hand game (Lushootseed *sləhál*), usually called "bone game" in English, was played with one or two pairs of bone cylinders, one of each pair marked. In an early version two played, one passed a pair of bones back and forth between hands and challenged his opponent to guess which hand held the unmarked bone. In a later version two teams faced each other, two men on one side each holding a pair of bones while their teammates drummed and sang, and a man from the other side guessed the positions of both unmarked bones.

Contests involving physical abilities included shinny, wrestling, foot racing, weight lifting, and one in which two groups of guests at a potlatch pushed at a pole separating them. Canoe racing, important in twentieth-century intertribal gatherings, may have developed only in the nineteenth century. After Southern Puget Sound people got horses, horse racing became popular.

Boys played a hoop and pole game, had archery contests, and made noises (believed to cause rain) with bull-roarers and buzzers. Young women and girls played on swings; girls played with dolls.

People in the southern part of this region obtained tobacco and elbow-type stone pipes from east of the Cascades reportedly before the first European contact. *495*

Older persons and especially shamans smoked more than younger people, mixing tobacco with kinnikinnick (bearberry). They smoked for pleasure rather than for any ritual reason (Elmendorf 1960:245–246). Smoking may not have been practiced in the northern part of the region.

Life Cycle

There were no ceremonies associated with birth, but both parents observed taboos for the safety of the infant. The usual cradle was a flat board with bindings to hold the swaddled baby. For an upper-class baby, a short flattening board was bound against its forehead to produce the desired head shape. The mother suspended the cradle from a springy bent limb or carried it on her back. Children were kept on the cradleboard until able to walk. Among upper-class families, as children approached adolescence, girls were more strictly trained and limited in their activities than were boys. Both sexes were expected to seek visions, both before and after puberty.

At her first menses a girl was isolated in a mat hut, restricted by taboos, and encouraged to perform tasks believed to make her industrious in later life. After her isolation during her first menstruation, an upper-class girl's family gave a feast that announced her marriageability. Because menstrual blood was thought to be powerful, during every menstrual period a woman retired to a menstrual hut away from the houses.

There was no formal recognition of a boy's puberty. It was expected that adolescent boys would seek sexual experience, but opportunities were probably limited. Masturbation was discouraged because semen was believed polluting and so inimical to success in the vision quest. Boys were married young, in part to keep them from masturbating or getting into trouble with married women (Elmendorf 1960:434).

Marriages, especially among the upper class, were arranged by presumably unrelated families in different villages. A proper marriage involved a formal suit on the part of the young man's family, a wedding in which the bride was ceremoniously brought to the groom's village, the payment of a bride price to her family from the groom's and a dowry from her family to the couple, and subsequent exchanges between the two families. Among wealthy families divorce was difficult, though not impossible, and a widow or widower was expected to marry a close relative of the deceased in order to maintain the family alliance and keep the children in their natal house and village. Among poorer people marriage was less formal and more brittle.

Death was given greater ritual attention than other life crises. The family of the deceased held a wake. Relatives and friends brought gifts to the dead. Professional undertakers prepared the body, which was removed from the house through a side wall, taken to the cemetery, and put into a canoe supported on a frame or put into a box that stood on the ground. After the disposal of the body there was a feast, at which personal property of the deceased was given away. A widow's hair was cut for mourning.

Beliefs

The Twana believed that a living and well human being contained a life soul (shəlé) and a heart soul (yədwás). The first could leave the body, in the form of a tiny replica of its owner, causing illness. After death, the life souls of all but infants went to the first land of the dead, while heart souls died with the body. At the same time some quality of a person could appear near human habitation as a ghost. To reach the first land of the dead the life soul took a trail that went underground and across a river. There the dead lived as in this world but with day and night, summer and winter, and other things the reverse of what they are in this world. Each village in this world had a corresponding village there. After a time the life soul died a second death and went on to the second land of the dead, from which it was reborn as an infant in this world. An infant dying in this world could leave this cycle of rebirth and become a parent's guardian spirit (Elmendorf 1960:512–521). The Puget Sound peoples believed in a land of the dead where conditions are reversed and in the possibility of reincarnation, but nothing like the Twana two-tier hereafter with automatic recycling of souls has been reported.

Southern Coast Salish myths tell of a myth age when there were beings with both human and animal qualities. This age ended with the coming of the Transformer (Lushootseed dúkʷibəł, Twana dúkʷibəł), who changed many of the myth age beings into animals, changed some dangerous creatures into stone, and gave human beings the rudiments of culture (Elmendorf 1961:11–12, 20–27; Eells 1985:362–366). In Twana belief the myth age beings may also emerge in the vision experience as the guardian spirits of the present world (Elmendorf 1984). For the Upper Skagit there were other transformers as well, one being sgʷədílič, who became an important guardian spirit himself (J.M. Collins 1974:158, 211).

For the Twana the sun and the earth were deitylike entities concerned with ethics. Prayers were addressed to the sun, who rewarded good behavior, while the earth punished bad. But these beliefs were not integrated into any larger system (Elmendorf 1960:530–531).

Salmon were believed to be people in their own country. For the Twana each species had a "chief" for which a first salmon ceremony was performed. Other species also had their prototypical "fathers," and after the communal elk drive the elk "father" was given ritual treatment. In the wilderness away from human habitation there were several races of humanlike beings—earth dwarfs, who could steal souls; forest giants, who stole food; and underwater people, known to have taken human wives.

There were a few practices that imply belief in impersonal forces. These included the use of love charms, of harmful contagious magic, and of verbal formulas believed to control the behavior of those for whom they were recited or sung. However, these practices were of minor importance, there being nothing comparable to the development of spells and the role of the ritualist among the Central Coast Salish.

The Guardian-Spirit Complex

Every skill and success was attributed to help from a guardian spirit. There were two classes of guardian spirits, layman's spirit and shaman's spirit. Lay spirits were classified according to the kind of power they conferred, major classes being those bringing success in gaining wealth, war, soul-recovery, gambling, land hunting, sea hunting, and animating ceremonial objects. In addition there were many unclassified spirits conferring minor powers, such as freedom from fleabites. Most lay spirits were described as having the appearance of animals or humanlike beings, but a few plants, artifacts, and natural phenomena were also identified as sources of power, and perhaps in theory anything might be.

Shamans obtained power from some of the same animal sources as laymen, but two very powerful spirits gave power to shamans only. These were the ʔáyahus, described by the Twana as a two-headed serpentlike being and by some Lushootseed speakers as a giant elklike creature, and the stáduk^{w}a (Twana), an alligatorlike being that appeared sliding down talus slopes in the mountains.

Guardian spirits were usually acquired through the vision quest. The training that began in early childhood had the purpose of preparing for this, so that from the age of about eight on children could be sent out away from other human beings to seek visions. The child was instructed to get rid of human pollution by fasting, bathing, and purging. Adolescent boys removed beard and body hairs. Girls quested before their first menstrual periods and again directly after. The seeker often first heard some manifestation of the spirit and then saw it, perhaps in animal form. The seeker approached the spirit, made physical contact, and fell into a trance. The spirit, perhaps now in human form, transported the seeker to its house, where it gave the seeker power and, especially, a song to be used later in life. After regaining consciousness, the seeker receiving a layman's power returned home and said nothing about the experience except perhaps to indicate that something had occurred. A young person might go on seeking encounters with other spirits and collect several, but he was expected not to talk or even think about them.

After a period that could extend to 20 years a spirit returned. Its presence was first manifested through an illness in early winter. Typically a shaman diagnosed the illness for what it was, and the patient sponsored a winter dance, at which he began to sing the song given him by the spirit, dance, and perhaps show other evidence of the spirit's power. This performance made the patient well and established his partnership with the spirit. In subsequent winters his spirit or spirits returned and he sang and danced.

Laymen's spirits were also occasionally acquired through inheritance rather than questing. The spirit simply came unsought to cause the sickness that led to becoming a winter dance.

Shamans' spirits conferred on the seeker the power to diagnose and cure certain illnesses and also to cause illness and even death. Curing by a shaman was a public event with an audience of the patient's relatives and neighbors. The shaman made his diagnosis by singing a power song while covering his eyes with a crooked arm, the audience singing along with him. Types of illness included intrusion of a foreign object or entity (requiring extraction), return of the guardian spirit (requiring the patient to become a singer), and loss or theft of life soul or theft of guardian spirit (requiring search and recovery). Because a shaman could do harm as well as good, he might come to be regarded with suspicion and even killed.

Ceremonies

Feasting and gift-giving were required to validate and publicize events in the lives of members of upper-class families, such as taking or giving a name and announcing a daughter's puberty. The family invited others in the village to a feast followed by distribution of gifts of food and wealth. These were ceremonies performed primarily for the benefit of one person, with his or her family gaining indirectly in recognition. A larger number of people were more directly the beneficiaries of four other ceremonies—the winter dance, the soul-recovery ceremony, the potlatch, and the secret society.

The winter dance was sponsored by an individual diagnosed by a shaman as suffering from the illness caused by the return of a guardian spirit, lodged in his chest as a song. In charge was a song leader responsible for knowing the songs of the guests and for any ritual paraphernalia required. During the evening, the song leader, the shaman who diagnosed the case, and perhaps other experienced persons worked on the sponsor, trying out drumbeats and phrases appropriate to the kind of song he was believed to have, and gradually brought the song out. His face was painted. The sponsor then got up and danced, possessed by his power and singing his song. After this performance others whose power required it could, one at a time, do the same. When all had satisfied the requirements of their powers, there was a feast and the sponsor or his family

497

distributed gifts.

Performances varied according to the kind of *sqǝlálitut* 'vision power, vision power song'. The dancer with *sqáyǝp* (or *sqíp*) used red paint, carried a cluster of deer-hoof rattles, and (according to tradition) danced with a knife piercing his body. The dancer with *q̓ʷǝ́xqǝd* was able to animate a *tǝ́stǝd* 'striker', a pole used to beat time against the roof planks, so that it moved by itself. The dancer with *sgʷǝdílič* had a pair of boards or hoops, each of which was held by two young men (fig. 10). When the owner sang the boards became animated and pulled the young men around the house. The *sgʷǝdílič* ("guarding power" in Collins 1949) was especially important in the Northern Lushootseed area, where it was used for purifying a house for ceremonies and for finding lost articles.

The soul-recovery ceremony (fig. 11) was practiced by all but the northernmost Lushootseed tribes. It was performed by several men, often shamans but not necessarily so, who had guardian spirit power to recover lost souls. It was believed that souls were often stolen by the dead, who wanted the living to join them, and so the task of the men hired for the purpose was to travel to the land of the dead (the first of the two for the Twana) and

Fig. 10. *sgʷǝdílič* board. The red dots are said to represent songs taught by the spirit to the owner. Collected by T.T. Waterman at Tolt (Carnation), Wash., before 1920; height 73 cm.

498

get back any stolen souls. The performance was held at night before as large an audience as possible. The performers each had a thick plank painted with a representation of a guardian spirit, a carved and painted post representing one of the earth dwarfs, and a painted staff. They set the planks and post up to outline a rectangle that represented a canoe (for which the performance has been called the "spirit canoe ceremony"). Standing within it, singing their power songs, and paddling with their staffs, the performers set out on the long trail deep into the underworld, dramatizing getting through tight places and overcoming obstacles along the way. The performance lasted at least two nights. The climax of the performance consisted of rescuing the missing souls by outwitting and outmaneuvering the dead and meeting them in pitched battle (Haeberlin 1918; Waterman 1930).

The youth who managed in his vision quest to encounter a wealth power, *tiyúɫbax̌* or *dxʷhíidǝ*, was destined to become wealthy and also obligated to serve this guardian spirit by hosting an intervillage giveaway. This ceremony (Lushootseed *sgʷíhgʷih*; Twana *s?íwad*) was the Southern Coast Salish potlatch. It was usually held in early fall or summer, when food was plentiful. It was sponsored by either a single owner of a wealth power or several who decided to use the same occasion. Messengers were sent out to other villages to invite the leading men of each, calling out their names and presenting them with little sticks as tokens. Elmendorf (1960:339) reports that the Twana potlatcher had to make sure that in any village the messenger had to invite men in the order of their rank; this concern is not reported for the Lushootseed tribes. The recipients of invitations were expected to bring their people with them. Each group of guests made a ceremonial approach to the host village, with dancers performing on a stage made of planks laid across two canoes. Guests brought food and wealth for the potlatcher. The event was held in the dwelling of the potlatcher or in a potlatch house. Each group of guests was put up in its own section of the house, but there was no ranking of villages or tribes. The event lasted several days, during which there were games and contests, secular songs and dances (that is, those not inspired by visions), and (according to Elmendorf 1960:342) guardian-spirit songs sung for entertainment. People present could use the occasion to distribute wealth to others to validate changes in status, as at intravillage feasts. As the main event, the sponsor's speaker called out the names of the invited guests and each came forward to receive his gift. Finally, the sponsor sang his wealth power song, with all present joining as at a winter dance.

Among the Twana, the Suquamish, and perhaps some other Lushootseed tribes there were members of the secret society, called 'growling' or "black tamanawis" (from the Chinook Jargon word for 'power', 'guardian spirit'). This

left, U. of Wash., Thomas Burke Memorial, Wash. State Mus., Seattle: L3911/3; right, Smithsonian, NAA: 80–4536.

Fig. 11. Soul-recovery ceremony. left, Snoqualmie men reenacting a portion of the ceremony called "paddling upstream." left to right, Jerry Kanim, Tommy Josh, Ed Davis, and Gus James or Gus Shelton. They were using a set of boards of two-thirds size purchased by T.T. Waterman for the Museum of the American Indian, Heye Foundation, New York. The men were devout Shakers and opposed to the work of shamans, but they posed for the photograph because the money from the sale of the boards would be used in legal work for the tribe (J. Miller 1988). Photograph by Douglas Leechman, Tolt, Washington, July 1920. right, Ceremonial planks on exhibit at the Northwestern Federation of American Indians convention, Everett, Wash. Photograph by Arthur Ballard, July 1932.

ceremony had undoubtedly spread through intermarriage from the Nitinaht and Makah via the Clallam. Although much of the ceremony was secret, it may be misleading to refer to the members as a "society," as they seem not to have acted together other than to initiate new members. These were adolescents of both sexes whose parents were upper class and able to afford the expense of the initiation.

The clearest description of the initiation has been given by Elmendorf (1948) for the Twana. The ceremony could be held at any time of year but was most often held in winter. The initiators had to be invited from other villages. Each group of initiators had a leader who could throw the power into the initiates. The ceremony began with the members dancing as a group, some using bird-shaped rattles (fig. 12) and some becoming possessed and vomiting blood. The initiates were then led out, and the head initiators shot the power into them, causing them to fall down in a trance. There followed one or more nights of performances featuring the levitation of objects and the singing of ordinary spirit songs strengthened by the power of the society. (Unlike Central Coast Salish participants, Twana members did not use masks.) Next the initiates were revived with blood spat on them, and they ran off and had to be captured. They were taught dances imitating those of desired guardian spirits. After this they became possessed by the secret society spirit, bled from their mouths, and had to be restrained with ropes. On the final night, the hosts paid the initiators and presented gifts to guests.

History

The earliest known contact with Europeans occurred in 1792 when the British expedition under George Vancou-

ver explored Puget Sound and Hood Canal (Vancouver 1798; Menzies 1923; B. Anderson 1939). At this time the Southern Coast Salish showed evidence of having experienced a smallpox epidemic and they possessed some metal, but they appeared not to have encountered Europeans before. Upriver people in the Puyallup drainage may have already possessed horses, but the Europeans did not see them. During the next three decades there was probably little contact; sea otters were scarce inside the Strait of Juan de Fuca, and the maritime fur traders had no other reason for coming into the region.

In 1824 John Work led a Hudson's Bay Company party through the region (T.C. Elliott 1912), and in 1827 the company founded Fort Langley on the Fraser. Possibly some Puget Sound people were trading on the Columbia earlier, but after 1827 there were certainly Snohomish, Skagit, and others trading on the Fraser. In 1833 the company established Fort Nisqually as a trading post and farm, beginning continuous contact within the region, not only with Whites but also with Hawaiians, Iroquois, and others working with them (Tolmie 1963). Changes in material culture occurred as the company moved in. Firearms became common, elements of European and frontier clothing were adopted, and women began growing potatoes (Suttles 1951a). New ideas also arrived and not all from the company, as when forms of the Plateau Prophet Dance were brought from east of the mountains (Suttles 1957).

This provided a basis for interest in the first Roman Catholic missionaries. In 1839 and 1840 Fathers Francis Norbert Blanchet and Modeste Demers traveled through Puget Sound teaching Christian doctrine, prayers, and canticles, by means of Chinook Jargon and the Catholic Ladder, a representation of human history and the role of   *499*

U. of Wash., Thomas Burke Memorial, Wash. State Mus., Seattle: L4363.
Fig. 12. Annie Rogers (right), Suquamish, with an unidentified woman. Rogers has secret society paraphernalia including a black tamanawis rattle in the shape of a duck, staff, and feathered headdress possibly made of beaten cedarbark with eagle feathers. Her face is painted in black streaks for the black tamanawis ceremonies. Photographed about 1910.

the church (Whitehead 1981). Several Indians were soon leading their tribes in worship and enforcing the new rules (L.M. Lyons 1940:110–116). Demers visited the region again in 1841 and Father J.B.Z. Bolduc passed through it in 1843, but by then the Indians' enthusiasm seems to have diminished. From 1840 to 1842 a Methodist missionary, Dr. J.P. Richards, was at Fort Nisqually, but he seems to have had no success at all (Meany 1927:111–112). It appears that the interest that Blanchet and Demers encountered was in part the result of the political use Salish leaders were finding in the new rituals and rules (J.M. Collins 1974).

While the region was under joint British and American jurisdiction, the Hudson's Bay Company made an unsuccessful attempt to establish Canadian settlers, and in 1845 the first American settlers arrived and established themselves at the head of Puget Sound. In 1846 the Treaty of

500

Washington gave the region to the United States, and more Americans arrived. In 1850 the Donation Land Act of Oregon allowed settlers to take land. Between 1850 and 1852 settlements were established on lands belonging to the Nisqually, Puyallup, and Duwamish and their neighbors.

Washington Territory came into being in 1853, and Territorial Governor Isaac I. Stevens was given the task of making treaties with the Indians. In 1854 and 1855 the Southern Coast Salish became parties to the Treaties of Medicine Creek, Point Elliott, and Point No Point, which reserved for them seven tracts of land, which in time became the Squaxin, Nisqually, Puyallup, Port Madison, Tulalip, Swinomish, and Skokomish reservations. The dissatisfaction of many Indians, especially in inland southern Puget Sound, led to their participation in the Indian War of 1855–1856, and in 1857 the Muckleshoot Reservation was established by executive order. Many, however, did not move onto any reservation.

By the 1850s most Southern Coast Salish were involved in the non-Indian economy, selling furs, other natural resources, and their labor to non-Indians. Some had learned farming from the Hudson's Bay Company. During the 1850s and 1860s sawmills were established throughout the region, and many Indians became loggers. Commercial fishing provided employment for more. In the early 1870s hopyards were established in the Puyallup valley, and both local and British Columbia Indians found seasonal work picking hops.

Missionary work began again in 1848 when the Oblate priest Father Pascal Ricard founded the first permanent mission on Puget Sound at what became Olympia. In 1858 the Oblates moved their headquarters to British Columbia, but Father E.C. Chirouse was left behind to found a mission and school on the Tulalip Reservation (Cronin 1960). As a result of the federal government's Peace Policy of 1869, the Roman Catholics were assigned the Swinomish, Tulalip, Suquamish, and Muckleshoot reservations, and the Congregationalists got the Squaxin and Skokomish reservations. In 1874 the Rev. Myron Eells arrived on the Skokomish Reservation, where his brother Edwin was already the agent. In the early 1880s Eells (1886) saw the rise of the Indian Shaker Church, which was inspired by the apparent death and resurrection of a Squaxin logger, John Slocum, and signs of divine grace shown by his wife Mary. That religion spread far beyond the Southern Coast Salish region (see "The Indian Shaker Church," this vol.).

The 1980s

The Southern Coast Salish tribes in the 1980s experienced economic, political, and cultural revitalization, partly an outcome of national policies and legislation initiated since 1965 that enabled federally recognized tribes to exercise greater control over tribal affairs. In part the enhanced economic situation of the tribes and individual tribal members was directly attributable to the fishing rights litigation of the 1960s and 1970s and in particular to the landmark case *United States* v. *Washington*, decided by Judge George Boldt in 1974. All the Southern Coast Salish tribes, and some other tribes in western Washington, were parties to this litigation. The Boldt decision held that the traditional fisheries of these tribes are protected by the treaties negotiated with them in 1854 and 1855. The decision was upheld almost in its entirety by the Supreme Court of the United States in 1979. The courts have held that the Indians holding treaty-protected fishing rights are entitled to an equal opportunity with others to take fish at their usual and accustomed fisheries outside the reservations.

As a result of the court decision tribal members received training in all aspects of business management and fisheries biology. Tribal fish patrols and tribal courts were responsible for enforcing tribal fishing regulations. Taxes collected by tribal governments from the individual fishermen funded enhancement of fisheries, and, in some tribes, social services such as child care or funerals, which continued to be a major ceremonial occasion.

Almost all the tribes undertook fishery enhancement projects such as saltwater aquaculture with floating rearing pens for various species of salmon, or freshwater hatcheries for stocking of local streams and for sale of eggs and fry.

Some tribes developed fishing fleets, including some large seine boats, but most craft were small gill netters. Trolling and beach seining were the other main saltwater techniques. In the rivers weirs were no longer used, and the bulk of the salmon and steelhead were taken in set nets.

One of the voluntary intertribal organizations that developed since 1974 is the Skagit System Cooperative, whose members are the three treaty tribes who fish the Skagit River and its tributaries—Swinomish, Upper Skagit, and Sauk-Suiattle. They pool their resources to provide saltwater and freshwater enhancement of the salmon stocks using the river system.

The Upper Skagit and Sauk-Suiattle became federally recognized tribes in 1972, and the Upper Skagit reservation was proclaimed in 1981. In 1983 the Upper Skagit tribe completed construction of 50 wooden frame houses, which permitted development of a tribal community with a community center and a new smokehouse where winter dances were held in the winter of 1986–1987.

Winter spirit dancing, bone games, and other traditional cultural features drew Southern Coast Salish people together for intertribal or intercommunity gatherings. The improved economic status of the tribes, and of some individual tribal members, helped to foster marketing of traditional crafts such as Salish weaving, cedar boxes, and basketry. The Suquamish developed a museum in Suqua-

mish, Washington, to display their history (The Suquamish Museum 1985). Other tribes have established their own schools and care facilities for children and the elderly. The Muckleshoot also ran their own school on the reservation.

All the Southern Coast Salish tribes had tribal governments with planning departments and business enterprises such as retail stores, cigarette and liquor outlets, marinas, and restaurants.

Population

Preepidemic population is estimated at about 12,600, Lushootseed speakers numbering about 11,800 and Twana about 800 (see "Demographic History, 1774–1874," this vol.). Mooney (1928:15) gave the Southern Coast Salish an estimated 5,800 for 1780, but this is probably too low, being only slightly more than the Hudson's Bay Company counts in the 1820s and 1830s, which suggest a population of about 5,000 after major epidemics. Counts taken in the 1850s also total about 5,000. By 1885 numbers appear to have dropped to less than 2,000 (Eells 1985:31), but the counts probably did not include all Indians off reservations. Numbers began to rise early in the twentieth century. In 1984 the population of tribes in the Lushootseed area with reservations totaled 15,963, and that of the Twana reservation at Skokomish was 1,029. With the addition of the several unrecognized tribes, the grand total of persons of Southern Coast Salish descent who identified themselves as Indians may have been over 18,000.

Synonymy

The language name Lushootseed is an anglicization of *dxʷləšúcid*, composed of a root *ləš* 'Puget Sound region' and the affixes *dxʷ-*, *-úcid* 'language' (Hess 1976:xiv). The language has also been called Niskwalli (Tolmie and Dawson 1884), Puget Sound Salish (W.A. Snyder 1968), and Puget Salish (Hess 1976). There is no collective name for the Lushootseed-speaking people. The majority of tribal names in Lushootseed are composed of a root, sometimes preceded by a prefix, and the suffix *-abš ~ -əbš ~ -bš* 'people'. When the native names were assimilated into English, the native *b* and *d* were generally interpreted as m and n, and so the suffix usually appears as -amish or -mish. Thus *stùləgʷábš* 'river people', from *stúləkʷ* 'river', became Stillaguamish, and *sqíxʷəbš* 'upstream people', from *sqíxʷ* 'upstream', became Skykomish. A few tribal names are formed with the suffix *-bixʷ* 'people' (a doublet of *-bš*) or with the prefix *bəs-* 'possessing', and a few have no such affixes (see table 1).

Twana is from *tuwáduxq*, their self-designation (Elmendorf 1960:1). It first appears as Too a nook, 1838 (Douglas in Rich 1941:262); other spellings are in Hodge

501

(1907–1910, 2:859). The name Skokomish has sometimes been used for all of the Twana, because the Skokomish were the most important Twana tribe and their home territory became the site of the reservation. In Twana some tribal names are formed with the suffix -bəš 'people', as is sqʷuqʷóʔbəš 'Skokomish', from sqʷuqʷóʔ 'river'. Variant spellings of tribal names can be found in Hodge (1907–1910) as cited in table 1.

Sources

Brief glimpses of the Southern Coast Salish appear in the journals of members of the British expedition of 1792 (Vancouver 1798; Menzies 1923; B. Anderson 1939; Meany 1914–1915), who saw the Natives at their summer camps but probably not at any winter village. No native groups were identified by name. Gunther (1960, 1972: 80–84) discusses the artifacts collected. The earliest identification of the tribes of the region appears in Work's 1824 journal (T.C. Elliott 1912) and in Tolmie's 1833 journal (1963), which documents the social network of the time.

Gibbs (1877) gives the first sketch of native culture, based on observations made in the 1850s. Gibbs covered a much larger area than that of the Southern Coast Salish, but he probably knew southern Puget Sound best. His dictionary of Nisqually (Gibbs 1877:243–361) contains cultural data. He also wrote on mythology (Clark 1955–1956).

The most prolific nineteenth-century observer was Eells, who answered in detail an ethnographic question-naire (Eells 1877). Portions of an expansion of this work were published as journal articles (Eells 1886–1888) and as a monograph (Eells 1889) before an unabridged version appeared (Eells 1985). Ruby and Brown (1976a) repro-duce many of his drawings. Eells's attempts to interpret aboriginal culture are not reliable, but the picture he gives of contemporary Indian life is unparalleled, and his account of his missionary work (Eells 1886) is the most important published source on the origins of the Indian Shaker Church. His unpublished journal accounts of this have been used by Castile (1982).

Curtis included a few pages on the Southern Coast Salish in a volume (1907–1930, 9) that covers all the Coast Salish.

Haeberlin, who worked principally with the Snohom-ish, wrote an article on the soul-recovery ceremony (Haeberlin 1918) and one on songs (Roberts and Haeber-lin 1918). After his death Gunther used his material to compose an ethnography (Haeberlin and Gunther 1930). She also edited his collection of myths (Haeberlin and Gunther 1924).

T.T. Waterman published on canoes (Waterman and Coffin 1920), house types (Waterman and Greiner 1921), ritual paraphernalia (Waterman 1930), and technology in general (Waterman 1973). An unpublished manuscript on place-names (Waterman 1920a) contains material on social organization.

Ballard published on mythology (1927, 1929), kinship (1935), the calendar (1950), and the building of a salmon weir (1957).

From the mid-1930s to the mid-1940s work was done that resulted in the most complete ethnographies of the region, M.W. Smith (1940) on the Puyallup-Nisqually, Elmendorf (1960) on the Twana, and J.M. Collins (1974) on the Upper Skagit. Of these, Elmendorf's is by far the fullest, though based on work mainly with two infor-mants. M.W. Smith also published an article on Puyallup acculturation (1940a) and one on tribal and cultural divisions in the Puget Sound region (1941). Elmendorf has also published a collection of tales (1961) and articles on kinship (1946), the secret society (1948), sorcery (1970), social ranking (1971), and power concepts (1984). A collection of ethnological narratives (1940) remains in manuscript. J.M. Collins has published a biography of a shaman (1949a), an account of the growth of class distinctions during the early contact period (1974a), and an article on kinship (1979).

Other mid-twentieth century ethnographic work in-cludes Wike (1941) on spirit dancing, Snyder (1964) on Skagit values reflected in mythology and (1975) on Skagit values and the potlatch, and Tweddell (1974) on Snohom-ish social organization. Bruseth (1949) presents a sympa-thetic settler's view of the Stillaguamish. Sampson (1972) gives a Native view of Salish culture and history. Folktales, myths, and ethnographic narratives as well as analyses of native categories can be found in linguistic work by W.A. Snyder (1968, 1968a), Hess (1976), and Hilbert (1985). N.A. Roberts (1975) gives an account of the history of the Swinomish Reservation. Lane (1973) describes economic and political change in several parts of the region.

Southwestern Coast Salish

YVONNE HAJDA

Southwestern Coast Salish refers to the speakers of four closely related Salishan languages: Quinault (kwĭ'nôlt; locally 'kwĭnôlt), Lower Chehalis (chə'hālĭs, locally shə'hālĭs), Upper Chehalis, and Cowlitz ('käwlĭts).* This Tsamosan division (formerly called Olympic) of the family constituted a dialect continuum, with the coastal Lower Chehalis and Quinault and the inland Upper Chehalis and Cowlitz forming two subgroups (Elmendorf 1969:225; Kinkade 1963–1964:181).

During the first half of the nineteenth century, Southwestern Coast Salish territory stretched along the coast from north of the Queets River south to perhaps the center of Willapa Bay and included the drainages of the Queets, Quinault, Chehalis, and other rivers flowing into the ocean between these points, as well as the lower drainage of the Cowlitz, a tributary of the Columbia River (fig. 1).

The following discussion pertains to the people of the area before the mid-nineteenth century. Information from the early contact period is primarily about the people living nearest the Columbia River, and ethnographic information was collected mainly from more northerly groups.

Component Groups

In the early nineteenth century, the people of the region's politically independent villages referred to themselves by village names but grouped distant villages together, on the basis of common speech and contiguity, under generic terms. In the 1850s, White treaty makers used these generic terms as names for tribes or bands, creating "fictive political units that had no basis in native society" (Lane 1973,2:8). Following are the early nineteenth-century, nonpolitical groups identified by language.

Quinault was spoken by the Queets (kwēts), the Quinault, and the Copalis (kō'pālĭs). The Queets lived in several villages in the Queets drainage (the principal ones on the south bank at the mouth of the Queets and on the north bank near the mouth of the Clearwater). The Quinault lived in a number of villages in the Quinault drainage (the principal ones on the south bank at the mouth and on the south bank above Mounts Creek, a few as far inland as Lake Quinault and the upper river). The Copalis were on the Copalis River and southward to North Bay (their principal village at Oyhut). The Quinault also had seasonal fishing sites on the north shore of Grays Harbor at the Humptulips River, Chenois Creek, and the Hoquiam River, on the northern end of Willapa Bay, and probably at the mouth of the Columbia River. Seasonal presence of Quinault on the north shore of Grays Harbor may have led Curtis (1907–1930, 9:9) to identify the Humptulips as Quinault speaking.

Lower Chehalis was spoken by: the Humptulips (hŭmp'tōōlĭps), on the north shore of Grays Harbor and the Humptulips, Hoquiam, and Wishkah rivers (with the Hoquiam and Wishkah people possibly considered separate groups); the Wynoochee (wī'nōōchē), on the Wynoochee River; the Chehalis proper, on the south shore of Grays Harbor (with their principal village at Westport) and the Chehalis River perhaps as far upstream as Cloquallam Creek; and the Shoalwater Bay people on the north end of Willapa (Shoalwater) Bay and the lower Willapa River (Gibbs 1877:171; Curtis 1907–1930, 9:6–9, 173; Olson 1936:16–17; cf. Ray 1938:36).

Upper Chehalis was spoken by the Satsop ('sătsəp), on the Satsop River, and the Upper Chehalis proper, who comprised five groups: the sɫačáẃamš, on the Chehalis River from Cloquallum Creek to the mouth of the Black River; the sq̓ʷayáyɫq̓, called Squiaitl or Kwaiailk (Hodge 1907–1910, 2:632, 1:744), on the Black River and northward to the head of Eld Inlet; the ɫmášluws, near the site of Tenino; the ʔílawiqs, near the site of Chehalis; and the c̓axʷásnʔ, on the Upper Chehalis River around the site of Pe Ell (Kinkade 1963–1964:181; M. Dale Kinkade,

*The phonemes of Upper Chehalis are: (voiceless stops and affricates) p, t, c, č, k, kʷ, q, qʷ, ʔ; (glottalized stops and affricates) p̓, t̓, c̓, č̓, ƛ̓, k̓, k̓ʷ, q̓, q̓ʷ; (voiceless continuants) s, š, ɫ, xʷ, x, xʷ, h; (resonants) m, n, l, w, y; (glottalized resonants) m̓, n̓, l̓, w̓, y̓; (short vowels) i, e, a, o, u, ə; (long vowels) e·, a·, o·; (stress) v (low), v́ (high), v̀ (secondary). Information of Upper Chehalis phonology is from Kinkade (1963–1964) and M. Dale Kinkade (communication to editors 1988).

Quinault has the same consonant phonemes as Upper Chehalis, with the addition of x and g; its vowels are (short) i, a, u, ə, and (long) i·, a·, u·. Quinault phonemes are described by Gibson (1964).

Lower Chehalis has the same consonant inventory as Upper Chehalis; its vowels are the same as those of Quinault. Cowlitz has the same phonemes as Upper Chehalis, with the addition of x. Information on Lower Chehalis and Cowlitz phonemes is from M. Dale Kinkade (communication to editors 1988).

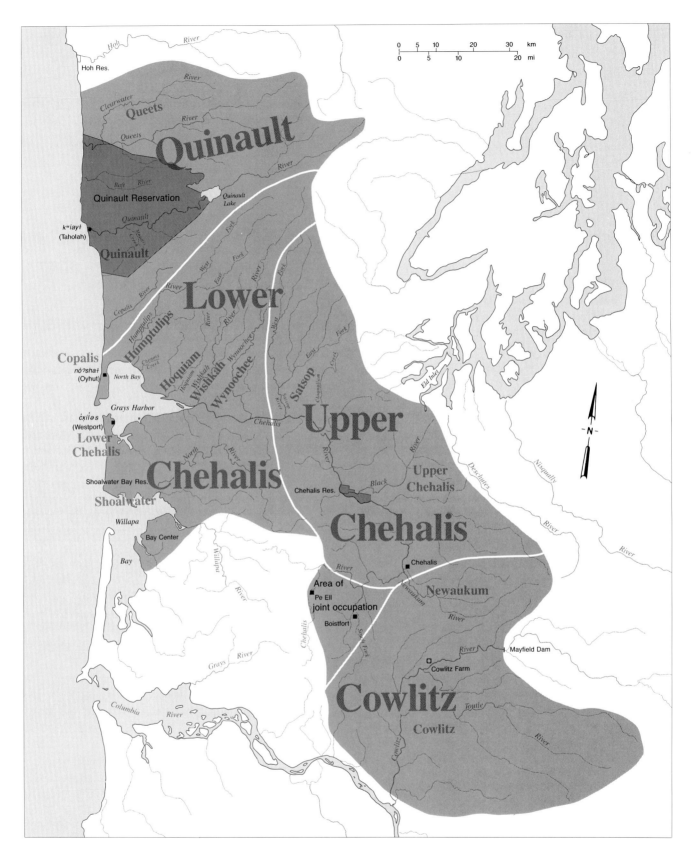

Fig. 1. Selected villages and early 19th-century territory of the Southwestern Coast Salish with language boundaries and tribal locations. Linguistic and social boundaries did not coincide. The Pe Ell–Boistfort area was jointly occupied by the Cowlitz, Upper Chehalis, and Kwalhioqua. Although names or locations of about 150 villages are known (Olson 1936:15–19; Curtis 1907–1930, 9:172–173; Gibbs 1853a), their status is not clear, and so they do not appear on the map. Not all were inhabited at the same time (Lane 1973:20); seasonal settlements cannot be certainly distinguished from winter villages; size is often uncertain; and many villages had become extinct at the time of recording.

HAJDA

personal communication 1987). A group speaking a dialect transitional between Upper Chehalis and Cowlitz lived on the South Fork of the Chehalis around the site of Boistfort.

Cowlitz was spoken by the Cowlitz proper, in the drainage of the Cowlitz River from just above its mouth to just below the site of Mayfield Dam; a group along the Toutle River; a group in the drainage of the Newaukum River; and the transitional group on the South Fork of the Chehalis (Adamson 1934:x–xi). The villages near the mouth of the Cowlitz were jointly inhabited by Cowlitz and Chinookans, while those farthest upstream were shared with the Taitnapam (Curtis 1907–1930, 9:5, 172–173).

Environment

The Southwestern Coast Salish peoples were alike in that the territory of each centered on a major salmon stream, but their aboriginal territories are in some other respects very different. Those of the Quinault and Lower Chehalis face the ocean and are largely within the Sitka spruce forest type. But Quinault territory includes open ocean shore, rain forest with an annual precipitation well over 100 inches a year, and the western slopes of the Olympic Mountains, while Lower Chehalis territory includes the sheltered salt water of Grays Harbor and Willapa Bay, generally lower elevation, and more moderate precipitation of 70–90 inches. The territories of the Upper Chehalis and Cowlitz were entirely inland, in the Douglas fir forest type, where precipitation may be as low as 45 inches a year, and prairies could be maintained by annual burning.

External Relations

Early reports of area Indians outside their winter territories include accounts of a proposed Quinault-Chinook marriage (Bishop 1967:119–120), Cowlitz Indians trading for sturgeon at Oak Point on the Columbia in 1825 (Work 1824–1825:56), and Cowlitz on their way to the Willamette Valley in the 1830s and 1840s to trade camas for salmon (Tolmie 1963:186; Wilkes 1845, 4:318–319). There were frequent reports of Lower Chehalis on Baker's Bay in the Columbia River (for example, Howay 1941; Franchère 1969:88–89). In the earliest records the Lower Chehalis and Chinook proper were already highly intermarried (D. Douglas 1904:253, 333).

Accounts of Indian exchanges in the early records indicate that food and raw materials on the one hand and durable goods on the other were rarely exchanged for each other, and that dentalium shells served as a medium of exchange for durable goods. Trading with Whites blurred earlier distinctions, and beads and blankets as well as dentalia served as currency in transactions between Whites and Indians (Hajda 1984:205–262).

Travels and contacts among groups were sometimes disrupted by conflicts among neighbors. The dispute between Upper and Lower Chehalis over territory is one example (Donovan 1960:13), but this conflict, like others, was undoubtedly only among the villages immediately affected; whole "tribes" did not make war on each other. Such conflicts were eventually settled by the payment of valuables (Olson 1936:116–117) and perhaps by a marriage between the disputants, after which social contacts would be resumed. To the south, slaves were not taken in conflicts among related groups, and the fights appear to have been regulated to some degree; these restrictions seem to have been observed less often in the north (Adamson 1926–1927:85; Olson 1936:97; A. Henry 1897: 878–900; Franchère 1969:80–81; Ross 1855; Hajda 1984: 212–222).

Culture

Subsistence

Fish were the dietary staple everywhere. Though the type of fish varied with location, salmon were of major symbolic as well as nutritional importance. Statements about aboriginal fisheries are somewhat hypothetical, since twentieth-century dam-building, fish-stocking, and ocean fishing have warmed and slowed rivers and altered numbers and types of fish available. On the Queets and Quinault rivers, five species of salmon ran, though the pink run was insignificant. Sockeye (locally called blueback), the most important, was not available in quantity elsewhere in the region. The major run in April provided a surplus for trade. On the Chehalis and its tributaries, chinook, chum, and coho ran; pink and sockeye were rare and probably not indigenous. Coho, chum, and fall but not spring chinook ran in the Willapa Basin. On the Columbia, in addition to chum and coho, the late spring–early summer run of chinook was especially important and drew Lower Chehalis, Quinault, and others from the north (Swan 1857:242–243). The Cowlitz salmon runs of coho, chum, and fall chinook were of great importance. Spring chinook was available (Hugh Fiscus, personal communication 1987), but early reports suggest it was not or that it was not taken (A. Henry 1897:839; Simpson 1847:176; Wilkes 1925–1926:208). (Western Washington salmon fisheries are reviewed by Phinney and Bucknell 1975.)

The first appearance of salmon was marked with a First Salmon ceremony. Among the Quinault, the first salmon—usually a sockeye, caught sometime between December and March—was laid on the bank with the head upstream, then was cut up, using only a musselshell knife and cutting only lengthwise. The head was left attached to the backbone and the entrails were removed, while the heart was burned in the fire. Fish caught later might be cut crosswise, but the

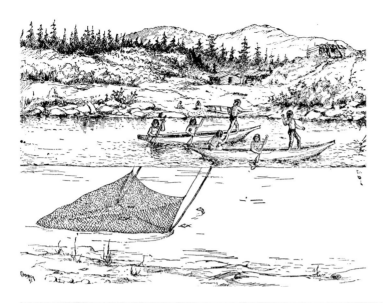

Smithsonian Lib.: top left, Willoughby 1889:fig 3; bottom, Wilkes 1845:313; top right, Smithsonian, NAA: 86-4150.

Fig. 2. Fishing. top left, Quinault using a trawl net. The net is lowered between 2 canoes, held down with poles, and held open with lines. The canoes move downstream faster than the current so that the net will billow out behind. A man in the stern of each canoe holds a pole and a line, while one in the center paddles and one in the bow throws rocks ahead to scare the fish into the net. The net is closed by releasing the lines and is raised with the poles. top right, Quinault removing fish from gill net. Photograph by Edward S. Curtis, 1912. bottom, Salmon weir on Chehalis River. Engraving after sketch by Charles Wilkes, 1841.

hearts were always burned, and the bones were thrown on the river bank. Everyone in the village received a portion of this first fish (Olson 1936:34). At the Upper Chehalis first salmon ceremony, the village head or shaman would eat first (Adamson 1926–1927:52).

Other fisheries included the summer sturgeon (probably white sturgeon) fishery in Willapa Bay and on the Columbia River, which drew people from the north (Franchère 1969:88–89). Trout were trapped on many smaller streams. The runs of eulachon (locally called "smelt"), especially on the lower Cowlitz River in late winter and early spring, came at a time when other food

supplies were running low. In dried form, these fish were a desirable trade item (Boyd and Hajda 1987). Shellfish, collected along the ocean beaches and especially in the bays and estuaries, were also dried and traded; strings of dried clams from Willapa Bay went far to the east (Swan 1857:86). Ocean fish, such as halibut and cod, were taken by the Quinault especially. Other fish included surf smelt and herring on the coast (Olson 1936:40–41) and lampreys inland (Wilkes 1845, 4:313). Eggs and milt of chinook salmon were eaten, sometimes roasted in ashes (Jacobs 1934,1:226; Olson 1936:40–41). Barnacles were popular with the Quinault but not on Willapa Bay (Swan 1857:

86–87). The Lower Chehalis, but not the Quinault, ate herring eggs (Van Syckle 1982:75; Willoughby 1889:269).

Techniques for catching fish varied according to type and location. On the Quinault, upper Chehalis, and smaller streams, at least, each village had one or more fish weirs (fig. 2), from which fish were taken with a dip net; salmon were then killed with a club (fig. 3). On lesser streams, fish traps were used to catch trout and other smaller fish (Tolmie 1963:190; Wilkes 1845, 4:313; Jacobs 1934, 1:225; Olson 1936:26–29, 36; Swan 1857:27). At the mouth of the Quinault, dip nets, drift nets, and harpoons were employed, while herring were caught with a herring rake, and hook and line were used for ocean fish (Olson 1936:29–34, 38). On streams entering Willapa Bay, and probably elsewhere, salmon were speared or gaffed, and sturgeon were taken with gaffhooks (Swan 1857:38–41, 137, 245–246, 264; Olson 1936:34).

Fish and shellfish not cooked and eaten at once were preserved by drying over a fire. Dried fish were eaten as is, or boiled or roasted. To extract eulachon oil, used especially with dried fish, the Quinault boiled the eulachon and skimmed off the oil, then pressed the eulachon to extract the remaining oil (Olson 1936:40–41).

In the Quinault highlands, hunters took elk, deer, bear, and many small mammals such as beaver, land otter, and rabbit. Most of these were eaten, and the skins of all were used. Beaver teeth served as dice in the women's gambling game. The larger mammals were generally taken with bow and arrow, but a deadfall was sometimes used for bears and a pit and noose for deer and elk. Many small animals were caught by snare or deadfall. Besides taking birds with bow and arrow, snare, or noose, nets were employed to

catch ducks. Bird feathers and skins were used and the flesh eaten (Olson 1936:41–44, 49–51). Swans, geese, and other waterfowl were especially plentiful on Willapa Bay, where pelicans and gulls were also hunted (Swan 1857:29).

All coast dwellers used beached whales, finding them important enough that territories along the coast were demarcated so as to determine who was entitled to them; families inherited the right to use particular parts of a whale. The Quinault were the southernmost people on the coast to hunt whales, and very few men followed this dangerous pursuit with its many taboos. The Quinault and Lower Chehalis also hunted other available sea mammals—fur and hair seals, porpoises, sea lions, and sea otters (Olson 1936:44–49; Swan 1857:83–85, 91).

Plants, while utilized as food everywhere, seem to have been especially important in inland areas. Camas—a major product of inland prairies especially—was less important for the Quinault and Lower Chehalis, though the latter traded it from Quinault or inland people (Olson 1936:52–53; Van Syckle 1982:76; Gibbs 1877:167). The Upper Chehalis and Cowlitz, on the other hand, harvested great quantities of camas, enough for exchanging with others (Wilkes 1845, 4:318–319; Tolmie 1963:186). Camas might be pit roasted, then mashed and formed into cakes for drying and storage or trade (Swan 1857:90–91; Olson 1936:52–53). Berries of all kinds were also extensively gathered. They were eaten fresh, or for storage were dried, sometimes after mashing (Jacobs 1934, 1:225). Other foods included crabapples, fern roots, clover roots, cattail roots, salmonberry shoots, cow parsnip, and wild celery roots (Swan 1857:87–89; Van Syckle 1982:76; Olson 1936: 53–55). Hazelnuts were collected in inland areas (Jacobs 1934, 1:225).

Travel and Transport

Dense vegetation, particularly in coastal areas, made water travel a necessity. The Southwestern Coast Salish were expert in handling canoes and were excellent swimmers. The importance of canoes is reflected in their use for burials and in the shaping of cradleboards to resemble canoes (Swan 1857:167–168).

All canoes except the shovelnose were based on the Westcoast design, varying in form and size according to function. Quinault canoes ranged from the ocean canoe, with high sides and bow, 35–40 feet long and some five feet wide, to a duck-hunting canoe under 18 feet in length. All types were locally made, but most of the larger ocean canoes and many others were made by more northerly people and traded to the Quinault, who in turn traded them to people to the south. The shovelnose canoe was the only kind used by inland groups (Adamson 1926–1927: 147; Gibbs 1877:215), and it was adopted by the Quinault in the mid-nineteenth century (Olson 1936:66–67). Paddle blades were notched or double-tipped, rounded or dia-

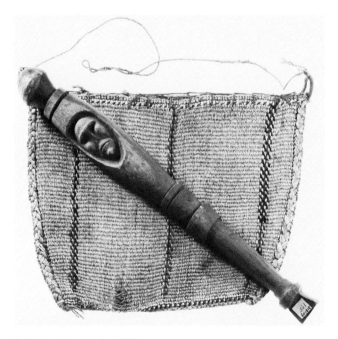

Smithsonian, Dept. of Anthr.: 313109.
Fig. 3. Quinault fish club and plain twined fish bag. Collected on the Quinault Reservation before 1920; width of bag 30 cm.

mond-shaped, with relatively short handles in relation to the blade. The diamond-shaped paddle was used with ocean canoes, and the double-tipped with the shovelnose. A double-ended paddle may also have been used (Olson 1927, 1936:66–67; Swan 1857:79–82).

One trail followed the coast from the village of Chinook on the Columbia River to Neah Bay, with canoes used to cross Willapa Bay and Gray's Harbor; rafts were kept at rivers where no villages existed to ferry travelers across. Other trails ran from villages to prairies or hunting areas (Olson 1936:88). These were more important in inland areas such as the stretch between the Chehalis and Cowlitz rivers, where streams were too infrequent or difficult for canoes and land was more open.

Whites saw Indians on horseback in inland western Washington in the early nineteenth century (A. Henry 1897:839). In the mid-nineteenth century, Gibbs (1877: 178) described the Upper Chehalis as "equestrian in their habits."

Clothing and Adornment

As was typical for the region, men generally went naked in summer, while women wore a knee-length skirt of shredded cedar bark. In winter both sexes might add a fur or skin garment, varying from a single skin around the shoulders to an ankle-length robe. These were sometimes woven of dog wool—perhaps only by the Quinault—or of strips of rabbit or bird skins (Olson 1936:56; Adamson 1926–1927:8). Sea otter skins were limited to the wealthy. Winter wear for Quinault men sometimes included sleeveless buck or elkskin shirts and breeches, with leggings and moccasins for mountain hunting. By the early nineteenth century the Quinault were getting buffalo skins and robes from the lower Columbia (Olson 1936:57). For rain, both sexes might wear waterproof capes of cattail and other fibers (fig. 4), and women had cattail skirts (Jacobs 1934, 1:225; Olson 1936:57–58; Landerholm 1956:40). Quinault rain hats were of twined split spruce roots, often with designs. These were of the kind familiar to neighboring people, in the form of a flattened cone or inverted bowl. One kind, with a distinctive knob on top, was traded from the north (Olson 1936:55; Swan 1857:163). European clothing and items such as blankets were popular very early. By 1857, young people on Willapa Bay dressed mainly in European clothes (Swan 1857:154–155).

Both sexes painted the face and the part in the hair, especially for dancing. Black, red, and white paint were used for simple designs, with black favored by warriors and red by others. Both men and women tattooed rows of dots or lines on forearms and lower legs with charcoal, but only men tattooed the face. Men plucked out their beards, but hair was cut only during mourning. Men and women wore dentalia and other shells as necklaces, and men wore

Harvard U., Peabody Mus.: 5-7-10/65511.
Fig. 4. Quinault woven fiber raincape. This is the cone-shaped type, one of three defined by Olson (1936:58). Near the smaller end a hole is left for the head. These were woven of cedar bark, spruce root, cattail, or tule. Collected by Lewis H. Farlow before 1905; length folded, 58 cm.

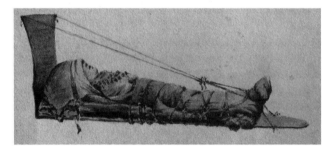

Stark Mus. of Art, Orange, Tex.: 31.78/10, WWC 10.
Fig. 5. Head deformation. Child of Caw-wacham, Cowlitz, with its head being flattened in a cradleboard. The process starts at birth and lasts from 8 to 12 months (Harper 1971:93, 99, 302). Watercolor by Paul Kane, 1847.

them in the nasal septum. Dentalia were traded from Vancouver Island. Beads and metal objects of European origin were later additions (Olson 1936:69, 61).

Heads were flattened in the Chinook style. The infant, who was carried in a cradleboard, had a pad of shredded cedar bark tied over the forehead by thongs attached to the sides of the cradle, with the thongs periodically tightened until the desired shape was obtained (fig. 5) (Olson 1936:102; Swan 1857:167–168; Adamson 1926–1927:112, 125). Groups closest to the lower Columbia were probably most rigorous in carrying out flattening (Gibbs 1877:211–212).

Structures

The usual winter dwelling was the cedar-wood, gable-roof house. The Quinault were the northernmost people on the coast to build houses with gable roofs (Olson 1936:61). Houses were oriented east-west, in a row along the river, with a doorway at one or both ends. Houses held, on average, two to four nuclear families (Olson 1936:61, 63), but some might be much larger: the Cowlitz house was said to hold 10 families (Jacobs 1934, 1:225), and an Upper Chehalis said that 8–12 were usual (Adamson 1926–1927:99, 70, 116). The Quinault house was described as about one-and-a-half to two times as long as it was wide—20–30 feet by 40–60 (Olson 1936:61, 1927)—but houses with 10 or 12 families must have been bigger than that. Wall planks were placed vertically, the ends set into the ground. A plank supported by elk thongs covered the oval doorway (fig. 6). Outside the house was a platform for seating (a feature not noted for houses south of the Quinault).

Inside, a sleeping platform about four feet high and four feet wide ran around all four walls. In front of this was a second bench about two feet high for sitting. A small section of the platform might be walled off for pubescent or menstruating girls. The space under the platforms, and a shelf over the eaves, served for storage. The sand-covered floor of a Quinault house may have been unexcavated or excavated to the depth of about a foot; Lower Chehalis and inland houses might have been excavated deeper than that. The walls might be lined with mats.

Temporary summer dwellings were built of cedar-bark slabs or of pole frames covered with mats or boughs. Planks from the winter house might also be moved to other sites in summer (Adamson 1926–1927:116; Donovan 1963:11; Olson 1936:65).

Technology

In all groups there were woodworkers who made houses and canoes. Quinault woodworkers made bent-corner boxes (the sides of one piece and the bottom pegged on)

and also bent-bottom boxes (all of one piece, the sides folded up and sewed or pegged together), as well as bowls, dishes (fig. 7), spoons, and canoe bailers (Olson 1936: 79–81). A principal carving tool was the adz (fig. 8). Information is lacking for other groups.

Probably women of all groups shredded cedar bark and sewed or twined mats (Swan 1857:161–163). The Quinault, but perhaps none of the other Southwestern Coast Salish, kept a breed of dog for its hair and used a spindle and frame (a two-bar loom?) to weave blankets of dog-hair yarn and elk sinew. Other blankets were woven from strips of rabbit fur or bird skin (Olson 1936:66–86; Adamson 1926–1927:8).

All groups made a variety of baskets for storage and carrying, as well as mats, mainly by twining or weaving. Coast people generally used spruce roots as the basic material (Olson 1936:82–84; Thompson, Marr, and Volkmer 1980). Coiling was rare on the coast, but the Cowlitz produced outstanding coiled baskets (fig. 9) (Haeberlin, Teit, and Roberts 1928:136–137; Gogol 1985).

Upper Chehalis weapons included mussel-shell knives and whalebone daggers, while elkhide shirts and helmets, double-thick deerskin shirts, slatted wood breastplates, and cedar shields provided protection (Donovan 1960:13, 1963:11). The Quinault weapons inventory included war spears of yew with whalebone or mussel-shell points, whale-rib and stone clubs, and bows and arrows. Protective equipment included the elkhide shirt and slat armor of wood or whalebone, but helmets and shields were reportedly unknown. Knives were made of iron as soon as the metal became available (Olson 1936:117–118). Guns were rapidly adopted for hunting as well as warfare.

Division of Labor

The type of occupation depended on sex, status, talent,

left, Lib. of Congress: Swan 1857:339, right, U. of Wash. Lib., Special Coll., Seattle: NA 1113.
Fig. 6. Habitations. left, House and canoes on river bank, Shoalwater Bay. A top board in the roof next to the ridgepole would be moved to allow smoke from the interior fire to escape. The oval doorway, to the left of the standing figure, was just large enough to crawl through. It was covered with a single board, hung by a thong. Engraving based on an original sketch by James G. Swan, 1852–1855. right, The home of Old Shale, a Queets, at the mouth of Raft River, Wash. (Marr 1983:107, personal communication 1987). The buildings are late 19th century, covered with cedar shakes and milled lumber. Photograph by Albert Henry Barnes, 1907.

SOUTHWESTERN COAST SALISH

Fig. 8. Quinault D-shaped effigy adz with ax-head blade and carved whalebone handle. This one was used exclusively for making canoes. Collected at Quinault before 1905; length 22.5 cm.

Fig. 7. Quinault dishes carved from solid chunks of yew. Willoughby (1889:269) says that all ancient dishes were made of yew, but Olson (1936:80) asserts that eating utensils were usually made of alder or maple, because these woods imparted no taste or odor to the food. Collected by Charles Willoughby at the Quinault Reservation, Wash., before 1887; length of bottom, 17 cm.

and possession of an appropriate spirit power. In general, men hunted and fished, and made objects of wood or stone; women gathered plant foods and shellfish, and created fabrics and baskets. However, some men specialized in hunting elk or whales, some were noted for canoe-making or woodworking; some women were especially skilled basket makers; and only some people told stories. The guardian spirit revealed to its possessor what occupation the person should follow. Shamans were ordinary people who happened to have exceptionally powerful spirits (Adamson 1926–1927:115, 121, 345, 348, 290; Jacobs 1934, 1:227; Olson 1936:94–95; Swan 1857:161–164).

Social and Political Organization

The basic social distinction was between slave and free. Slaves were captured in raids or traded in. Some Quinault slaves came from nearby groups (Olson 1936:97), but elsewhere most came from distant people among whom relatives could not be found. The prohibition on slaves' flattening the heads of their children seems to have been stronger in the southern part of the area than in the north, perhaps because the Quinault were more likely to have flatheaded slaves from neighboring groups. Even if a slave should escape or be rescued, he or she retained the slave stigma. Occasional marriages between slave and free were strongly disapproved. The slave ancestry of descendants of such marriages was remembered in spite of potlatches given to remove the taint (Adamson 1926–1927:14–15, 125, 147, 256, 360; Olson 1936:102; Swan 1857:166–168; Gibbs 1877:188–189).

The exact nature of distinctions within the free population is not known, though at any one time the Southwestern Coast Salish, like their neighbors, certainly also had "nobles," or people of inherited status and wealth, "commoners," and the poor, who might include those of part-slave ancestry, ne'er-do-wells, runaways, and other unfortunates. Since all could trace some kind of kinship to noble families, absolute class distinctions would be difficult to maintain. The abilities to acquire wealth and to pursue outside contacts were probably essential in achieving or losing status.

Village leaders tended to come from certain families, with eldest son following father if possible, other male relatives succeeding if not. If several candidates were available, the people of the village might decide which one was best. These leaders had to be wealthy enough to distribute wealth to others; without this, a "chief" might lose status to the point of being considered a commoner. He probably owned several slaves, so that he did not have to work as hard as other men did. He gave advice and settled disputes, but he had no power to punish offenders (Adamson 1926–1927:50–51, 70, 85, 112, 146, 194, 350–361; Elmendorf 1960:302, 1971; Olson 1936:92–93, 95–96).

Leaders of larger Quinault villages (and probably others) had "speakers," men who announced the chief's intentions to his villagers and conducted negotiations with other villages. A speaker was chosen by the chief on the basis of qualifications such as a loud voice, ability to speak

Smithsonian, Dept. of Anthr.: 2614.

Fig. 9. Cowlitz type basket, coiled foundation and imbricated design surface. Fiber bundles serve as coils. Dyed strands are carried along the outside of the wall, folded over, and the edges caught by stitches securing the foundation coils. Originally this basket had a lid. While all coiled and imbricated baskets from western Wash. are called the Cowlitz type, those made on the Cowlitz and Lewis rivers are considered the finest (Mason 1904:428). The 4-field design is characteristic of the precontact style (Marr 1984:47–48). Collected during the United States Exploring Expedition, 1841; length, 20 cm.

several languages, and negotiating skills. The office was not hereditary. Some larger villages might also have individuals who acted as jokers or buffoons, also a nonhereditary position (Swan 1857:265; Olson 1936: 96–97).

Typically for the central Northwest Coast, the winter village was the largest organized sociopolitical unit. The "tribe," consisting of people who shared at least one language and lived in a certain winter territory, had no distinguishable social cohesion. If each house in a village held, on average, four nuclear families, and a village consisted of one to perhaps 10 houses, a winter village might well be as small as 25 people or perhaps as large as 300. Reports of larger settlements may indicate sites for fishing or other activities for which large numbers of people gathered during warmer weather or may date from post-treaty times (Curtis 1907–1930, 9:5–6, 172–173; T.C. Elliott 1912:206–207; Olson 1936:89, 93).

The village was conceived of as a group of relatives, being in theory if not always in fact a patrilocal extended family. The household might consist of a man with his wife or wives, their unmarried children, adult sons and sons' wives and their children, slaves, poor relatives, orphans, visitors, and hangers-on. A son-in-law too poor to exchange goods for his wife might live with her and her parents. A group of brothers or male cousins could also constitute a household core. When the household head died, the remaining householders might tear the house down and rebuild it nearby, or the component families might take their individually owned house planks and build separate houses nearby or elsewhere.

The "owner" of the house was the man who contribut-

ed materials and labor to its building, though he actually owned only his own section. On the death of the owner, the eldest remaining male might assume authority, while "ownership" of the house passed to the eldest son of the previous owner or other next of kin. The household and family heads also directed activities such as weir-building, with each controlling the use of a section of the weir where his father had fished before him (Adamson 1926–1927:50, 85, 112–113, 150, 263, 361; Olson 1936:92–94).

Because of the practice of village exogamy, children growing up in one village had relatives living in others. A child was considered as much a part of his mother's place as of his father's, and he traveled back and forth a great deal. The resulting familiarity with other places and people was useful in adult life, since much of the year was spent not in the winter village but fishing or gathering resources elsewhere, and participation in events in other places required frequent travel. If an individual or family needed to move away from its village, there were always other places to make new homes. Participation in regional networks based on activities such as marriage, ceremonies, fighting, and resource-gathering was especially characteristic of higher-status individuals (Adamson 1926–1927: 26–27, 32, 113, 263, 372; Elmendorf 1960:302; Hajda 1984:124–132; Olson 1936:40, 90).

Kinship Terminology

Kinship terms reflected the equal importance of maternal and paternal relatives. Quinault terms, the best documented, are approximately Spier's (1925:74) "Salish" type: sex of relatives was obligatorily expressed in the terms for all relatives older than the speaker but in none for those younger except son and daughter; parents but not grandparents were distinguished from their siblings; one's own cousins were referred to by the same terms used for one's siblings. Children were distinct from nephews and nieces, but grandchildren and grand-nephews and grand-nieces were called by a single term. Two terms, applying to either parent's siblings, distinguished them by sex. Older and younger sibling-cousins were terminologically distinct. This set of terms, plus one meaning "by marriage," was used for in-laws. A different set applied to certain relatives when they, or those connecting them to the speaker, had died (Elmendorf 1961a; Olson 1936:90–92).

Life Cycle

A first marriage, especially for those of high status, required an exchange of goods between the two families, with the groom's family giving somewhat more than the bride's. Subsequent marriages might be arranged by the groom himself and required less in the way of goods. Exchanges of food continued between the two families thereafter. On the death of a spouse, the family of the *511* deceased was expected to provide a replacement, and the surviving spouse was expected to accept the replacement. In general, people tried to marry into families of their own or higher status (Adamson 1926–1927:2, 82, 263; Olson 1936:108–109; Jacobs 1934, 1:227).

After a death, persons hired for the purpose placed the body in a canoe or box; among the Quinault, at least, the head of the body was usually to the east (Olson 1936:111); among the Cowlitz, it was in a downriver direction (Demers in Landerholm 1956:52). In canoe burial the canoe was "killed" by drilling holes in the bottom, and a second canoe was often inverted over it to cover the body. The canoe or box was usually placed on four posts or in the branches of a tree. Slaves were not given formal burial; their bodies were taken away from the village (Donovan 1966:13; Landerholm 1956:52, 147; Olson 1936:111–113; Swan 1857:185–186, 267; Willoughby 1889:276–277).

Several variants have been mentioned for the Quinault (Willoughby 1889:276–277; Olson 1936:111–113), including placing the body, with or without the canoe or box, in a grave house. These burials were sometimes covered or surrounded with cloths, a practice noted from the mid-nineteenth century. Earth burial was probably the result of contact with Whites (Harrington 1942–1943a).

If the dying person had enough time, he might indicate some items to be buried with him and some to be given to particular people. Other objects, some or all rendered useless, were placed on or around the grave. Some remaining property might be distributed at a minor ceremony soon after the death. The house was purified or, in some cases, abandoned, destroyed, or burned (Olson 1936:112; Gibbs 1877:203; Adamson 1926–1927:150, 295). The dead person's name was tabooed for about a year. Survivors might change their names, particularly if the names resembled that of the deceased. After a year or two, those with means might clean and rewrap the remains and place them in the same or another spot; for the Quinault and coastal Lower Chehalis, the remains were placed in the ground. For the well-to-do, a ceremony marked the reburial (Olson 1936:112–113; Swan 1857:185–189; Adamson 1926–1927:70, 83, 118; Gibbs 1877:204).

Mythology

Beliefs about the origin of the present world and the nature of its former inhabitants are present in the mythology but seem to have had little direct relationship with religious practices. In the mythology, the world did not yet have its present form. Actors merge nonhuman (usually animal) and human characteristics. *mə́sp*, Moon, Coyote, and *x^wə́n* (the form of the name varies by language) appear in the myths as transformers, changing dangerous or inappropriate persons and conditions into ones suitable for the present generation. Coyote and *x^wə́n* are tricksters as well (Coyote's appearance in Cowlitz mythology may be due to Plateau influence). Bluejay appears as a buffoon everywhere. Like the myths of the Chinookans and others to the south and east, Southwestern Coast Salish myths are characterized by the pattern number five: five brothers, five actions, five objects (Farrand 1902; Jacobs 1934, 1; Adamson 1934; Gibbs 1955–1956).

Religion and Shamanism

Religious interest centered primarily on individual relationships to guardian spirits. Success in life depended on acquiring such a spirit. Many spirits came from the land of the dead, but others took the form of animals or plants, monsters, and natural phenomena. Certain spirits gave wealth or gambling power, enabled the possessor to find souls, and cured illness. Women often had fewer spirits than men, but like men they might become shamans, people with especially powerful spirits. Even slaves might acquire guardian spirits (Adamson 1926–1927:45, 121, 139, 141, 356; Olson 1936:141–144).

Training to acquire a spirit began at the age of seven or eight; the quest for a spirit was undertaken in adolescence or at least before marriage. When the spirit appeared, it instructed the person as to what occupation to follow, what paraphernalia to use or wear, and the appropriate song and dance to perform. Failure to follow the spirit's instructions could result in serious illness. Later on, spirits could be acquired with little effort or even involuntarily. A spirit left homeless by its owner's death might seek out a relative (Adamson 1926–1927:40, 46, 139, 141, 356; Jacobs 1934,1:227; Olson 1936:141–144; Swan 1857:171, 175–176).

Shamans diagnosed and cured illnesses caused by soul loss or the presence of a disease object in the body. Most diseases were of this kind, though others, for which natural cures were used, were also recognized. A sudden fright, or the attempts of a ghost to seize the soul, might cause the soul to leave the body, causing disease or death. The shaman and his helper cured this condition by recapturing the soul. If an intrusive object caused the disease, the cure was usually by sucking to remove the object (Olson 1936:158–159, 179–181; Swan 1857: 180–184). During the curing, a Quinault shaman set small wooden representations of his spirit powers around the sick person (Willoughby 1889:275, 278–279). These "image boards," seen also on the Satsop (Colvocorresses 1855: 247; Wilkes 1845, 4:313) and Cowlitz rivers (Demers in Landerholm 1956:52), may have been made and kept by anyone with a spirit power, not just by shamans (fig. 10) (Gibbs 1956–1957:127).

The shaman was paid for his efforts whether or not he effected a cure, possibly from fear of his power. Shamans could cause illness or death as well as cure, and a rich person might hire a shaman to kill someone. Magic, which

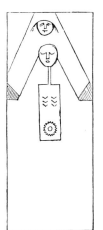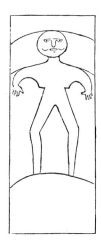

Fig. 10. Carved planks, probably representing the guardian spirits of their owners. left, Drawing of 5 that had been painted red. Engraving after an original sketch by Henry Eld, United States Exploring Expedition, 1841. right, Lower Chehalis or Chinook plank, Bay Center, Wash. Photograph by Harlan I. Smith, 1898.

could be used by anyone, was often used for evil (Adamson 1926–1927:131; Landerholm 1956:51; Olson 1936:158–159, 164, 141–143; Swan 1857:176–177).

Ceremonialism

Quinault and Upper Chehalis data indicate two kinds of gatherings involving gift-giving, the great intertribal potlatch and the feast or "small potlatch" involving local people only. Because the Lower Chehalis and Cowlitz are mentioned as guests in the great potlatches, it is likely that they also hosted them. The Quinault great potlatch was sponsored by a village headman, who had or built a big house for the event. His purpose was to give a name to a child, to honor a deceased relative, or to obey the command of his wealth guardian spirit. Most potlatches were in winter. The host sent a speaker to other villages inviting the leading men of each in order of rank. On the day set the guests arrived singing, there were games, and guests and hosts danced. On the third day a mat was spread in the house, the gifts were piled on it, and the host and his speaker presented them to the guests, beginning with the tribe farthest north and giving in order of rank within each tribe. According to Quinault tradition, their first great potlatch was given about 1800, when people from Vancouver Island to the Oregon coast were guests (Olson 1936:123–129).

Upper Chehalis potlatches were held to name the young, to honor the dead, to celebrate a daughter's puberty, the piercing of children's ears, or a wedding, to mark the end of conflict and the payment of damages, or to oblige the guests to forget some cause for embarrassment. Potlatching could raise a commoner's status and failure to potlatch could lower that of a headman. Small

gatherings held in winter for singing guardian spirit songs were also occasions for gift-giving (Adamson 1926–1927).

Winter "spirit singing" is also reported for the Cowlitz (Jacobs 1934,1:226), but there is no indication of any associated gift-giving. The Quinault do not seem to have had a spirit dance, but their potlatches included shaman's singing (Olson 1936:129). The Quinault also had two secret societies, acquired through intermarriage with the Makah and Quileute. "Klokwalle" members used black paint, red cedar bark, masks, and rattles, and cut themselves; "tsadjak" members used red paint and cured the sick (Olson 1936:120–123). These practices may have spread to the Lower Chehalis but evidently not to the inland groups.

History

The earliest recorded encounter between Europeans and any of the Southwestern Coast Salish occurred at the mouth of the Quinault River in 1775 when seven members of the expedition of Bruno de Hezeta and Juan Francisco de la Bodega y Quadra, attempting to get water and firewood, were killed and their longboat torn apart for the iron fittings (Wagner and Baker 1930:227–229, 240–242; Campa y Cos 1964:70–71; Majors 1980:212–221). Friendlier contact must have followed. In 1788, off Willapa Bay, Meares (1790:164–165) met Indians who seemed used to trading with Europeans. In 1792, Boit (Howay 1969: 395–397) saw some of the same people at the mouth of the Columbia that he had seen at Grays Harbor, the first mention of Lower Chehalis visits to the Columbia. When Meriwether Lewis and William Clark were on the lower Columbia in 1805–1806, local Indians could name 13 traders who visited the river mouth regularly in spring and

513

fall. Lewis and Clark's population estimates for the Lower Chehalis and Quinault are the earliest for Southwestern Coast Salish (table 1).

After the founding of Astoria on the Columbia estuary in 1811, Indians came from an increasingly wide area to trade and visit there (Franchère 1969:88–89). Fur traders based there traveled up the Cowlitz River in 1812, the first Whites to penetrate Cowlitz territory (Stuart 1935:46). In 1824 John Work (T.C. Elliott 1912) traveled to Puget Sound by way of the Chehalis and Black rivers and may have been the first to meet the Upper Chehalis. The opening of Fort Vancouver by the Hudson's Bay Company in 1825 led to greatly increased traffic inland. In 1833 the Company established Fort Nisqually on Puget Sound, reached by way of the Cowlitz Trail, which ran through Cowlitz and Upper Chehalis territory. In 1839 the company established Cowlitz Farm on Cowlitz Prairie at the southern end of the trail.

This development gave the inland people more direct access to trade for foreign goods, eliminating Chinookan middlemen (Bagley 1915–1916). It also enabled these groups to influence the flow of trade between Whites and Indians; the Cowlitz chief Schannanay competed with the Chinook chief Concomly and his son-in-law Casino at Fort Vancouver for control of trade (Simpson 1931:86). The Upper Chehalis formed a connecting link among the Cowlitz, Lower Chehalis, and Southern Coast Salish tribes (Gibbs 1877:172).

In the early 1830s an epidemic of malaria (Boyd 1985) devastated the Lower Columbia Valley and adjacent regions, resulting in changes in the composition of some groups. On Willapa Bay the surviving Chinook and Lower Chehalis became a bilingual population (Swan 1857:211) known as Shoalwater Bay Indians with Lower Chinook eventually replaced entirely by Lower Chehalis (Ray 1938:30). At the mouth of the Cowlitz, villages that had been Cathlamet became Cowlitz (Gibbs 1855:428). The Willapa division of Kwalhioqua became absorbed by the

Shoalwater Bay group, the Suwal division by the Upper Chehalis and Cowlitz. Sahaptin groups in the Cascade Mountains, generally identified as Klikitats (Jacobs 1931: 94–96), began filling the vacated territory (Gibbs 1877: 170–171). One, the Taitnapam, already intermarried with neighboring Cowlitz villages, moved into Cowlitz Prairie and by 1841 were being called Cowlitz (Wilkes 1845,4: 316). Another group of Klikitat moved into former Chinookan territory on the Lewis River, and they too may have eventually joined the Cowlitz (Ray 1974).

The Treaty of Washington in 1846 and the Oregon Donation Act of 1850 allowed American settlers to enter the region and take land. The inland groups suffered earlier and worse than the coast groups. They were increasingly fenced out or driven away from their hunting, fishing, and gathering grounds and out of their very homes. In 1855, as part of a wider program to extinguish Indian title to lands already being settled, Gov. Isaac I. Stevens called together the Chinook, Lower Chehalis, Quinault, Queets, Satsop, Upper Chehalis, and Cowlitz, all of whom were represented, for a meeting on the Chehalis River (Swan 1857:337). Government policy was to concentrate the Indians in as few reservations as possible (Stevens 1901, 1:454), and for this region only one reservation was proposed, to be located between the Makah and Grays Harbor. Although others had urged that two reservations be established, Stevens ignored them (Ford in ARCIA 1858:345; Swan 1857:345–346). The Lower Chehalis and the inland groups objected to leaving their homes and living with the Quinault, and Stevens broke off negotiations. Later in 1855, the Quinault and Quileute signed a treaty, later called the Treaty of Olympia, by which they kept a large reservation on the mouth of the Quinault River, but the others were never given a second chance.

Many Upper Chehalis, some Cowlitz, and other Indians continued to live on an unofficial reservation on the Chehalis River, which became official in 1864

Table 1. Population

Year	Quinault	Lower Chehalis	Upper Chehalis	Cowlitz	Source
1805	1,250	1,300			Thwaites 1904–1905
1812		936[a]		1,000[a]	Stuart 1935
1822		1,400		2,400	Morse 1822
1840				240[a]	Douglas 1931
1841		200[b]	40[c]	300–350	Colvocorresses 1855; Wilkes 1925–1926;
1844			207		Tolmie 1963
1857	158	217	216	140	Swan 1857
1910	288	282[d]		105	U.S. Bureau of the Census. 13th Census. 1915

[a]These figures are estimates of total population, calculated by multiplying numbers of "men" by four.
[b]Grays Harbor only.
[c]Satsop only.
[d]Includes both Lower and Upper Chehalis.

(Kappler 1904–1941, 1:903). The Chehalis Reservation was intended for the Upper Chehalis and the Cowlitz and for the coastal people south of the Quinault, but most of these never moved there, preferring to remain near their old homes. The Humptulips, Cowlitz, and Shoalwater Bay Indians, in fact, refused to accept distributions of goods by reservation officials, fearing that by accepting these goods they would be thought to have given up title to their lands (Milroy in ARCIA 1872:335). Another small reservation on Willapa Bay was similarly established in 1866 for Lower Chehalis, Chinooks, and others living in that area (Kappler 1904–1941, 1:924).

Indians on the reservations were subject to the usual attempts of Whites to "civilize" them: they were expected to become diligent farmers, abandon native religions and adopt Christianity, send their children to school, adopt English and forget their own languages, and in general pattern their lives after the Whites. Reservation agents were given food and goods to distribute annually, but these were not always sufficient or appropriate, and hardships often resulted (G. Ford 1862). Some reservation officials sold or otherwise misused the goods (Paige 1863). Of necessity, nontraditional ways of making a living had to be learned, though whenever possible fishing, hunting, and gathering continued.

The Quinault land was not suited for agriculture, though along the river almost every family had a small patch of land for potatoes, carrots, and turnips. Fishing continued to be a major occupation, but logging became increasingly important (ARCIA 1890:226–228, 1885: 189–192). On Willapa Bay, both local Indians and those from Quinault and elsewhere had long worked for White oystermen and continued to occupy themselves in fishing and related activities on the bay and on the Columbia River (Swan 1857:78, 250; ARCIA 1865:81–82, 1880: 162–163). Many people on the Chehalis reservation worked for neighboring White farmers or were otherwise dispersed among the general population, but they preferred hunting and fishing and following "the old ways" (ARCIA 1870:150–151). The reservation in 1890 was a collection of homesteads, and railroads offered new employment. In 1879, about 275 Cowlitz were still in their own territory, though White settlers had gradually pushed them out of lands on Cowlitz Prairie to areas farther up the Cowlitz. The nonreservation Cowlitz made a living by working for Whites and running canoe and ferry services on the Cowlitz River. Whites bought fish the men caught and berries picked by the women. Logging and railroading provided jobs in the 1870s and 1880s, and logging continued to be important in the early twentieth century (Irwin 1987).

In the late nineteenth century, hop harvests, especially on the Puyallup and Cowlitz rivers, became major gathering places for large numbers of Indians, on and off reservations, from a wide region. One hopyard near Olequa drew 1,000–2,000 Indians in the fall, about half of whom came from eastern Washington. These gatherings were as important socially as they were in providing income. With Prohibition, the hop industry collapsed (Irwin 1987).

Because the reservations never provided adequate employment, people moved into towns and cities looking for work. According to one estimate (Dietrich 1985:3–5), in 1985 unemployment on the Quinault reservation was 30 percent, at Shoalwater Bay 33 percent, and at Chehalis 39 percent.

In the 1980s, the Quinault Indian Nation was composed of seven affiliated tribes: Quinault, Quileute, Chinook, Hoh, Chehalis, Queets, and Cowlitz, with the first four comprising most of the enrollment. Most people at Quinault, and elsewhere, traced descent from more than one "tribal" group. Of the 2,036 enrolled members, 1,556 lived on the reservation. Thirty-five percent of the population was under 18. Most of the Quinault economy was based on fishing. Government-related jobs employed 88 permanently and 33 part-time or seasonally. This is a total of 690 jobs of all kinds (Quinault Historical Foundation, personal communication 1987). The reservation, 190,000 acres, was 32 percent owned by non-Indians.

The Shoalwater Bay Reservation consisted of 640 acres. In 1985, non-Indians owned 48 percent of the reservation. Of the 123 tribal members, 30 to 40 lived on the reservation, and most of the rest lived nearby (Shoalwater Bay Tribe, personal communication 1987).

The Chehalis Reservation's 4,215 acres were over 50 percent non-Indian-owned; 1,952 acres were held in trust. The Chehalis Tribe had 425 enrolled members who, with their families, comprised a service population of 742, who were of Chehalis, Quinault, Muckleshoot, Nisqually, Clallam, and other descent (Richard Bellon, personal communication 1987).

A sizable body of people of Cowlitz–Upper Cowlitz descent were not affiliated with the reservations and maintained an independent organization, not federally recognized. The Cowlitz Indian Nation had 1,424 members (Jean Y. Neal, personal communication 1987). A number of Cowlitz descendents of a group who migrated around 1900 lived on the Yakima Reservation (Fitzpatrick 1986:161–164).

Lower and Upper Chehalis and Cowlitz Indians were not compensated for lands taken from them until the Indian Claims Commission decided their claims in 1960 and 1969, respectively. The Cowlitz award was held in trust in 1988, pending settlement of a dispute among the claimants. The non-treaty Indians were not covered by the 1974 decision on fisheries, *United States* v. *State of Washington*.

515

Synonymy

The name Quinault is from *kʷínayɬ*, their name for their largest village, which stood near the present site of Tahola. The name was first recorded by Meares (1790:232), at Clayoquot Sound in 1788, as Queenhithe, said to be the southern limit of the "district" of the Makah chief Tatoosh. The name appears as Quinielts and Quiniilts (Lewis and Clark in Thwaites 1904–1905,6:70; in Biddle 1814, 2:474), Kwenaiwitl (Hale 1846:212), Kwinaiutl (Gibbs 1877:172), and in other spellings found in Hodge (1907–1910, 2:343).

Chehalis is from *ċxíləs*, the Lower Chehalis name for their principal village, at the site of Westport on Grays Harbor. The name was first recorded by Lewis and Clark (in Biddle 1814,1:map) as Chilts. It has also appeared as Tsihailish or Chikailish (Hale 1846:211), Tsihalis (Gibbs 1877:171), Tsheheilis (Tolmie and Dawson 1884:121B), and other forms found in Hodge (1907–1910,1:241). Hale (1846:map between pp. 196 and 197, 212) included the Quinault and Upper Chehalis under this name, and he invented a combining form seen in Tsihaili-Selish, his term for the language family now called Salish or Salishan. (Chehalis is also the name of a group in British Columbia; see "Central Coast Salish," this vol.)

The Upper Chehalis are the Holloweena or Halloweena of Work (T.C. Elliott 1912:207–212, 226), who met them on the Black River and at the head of Eld Inlet in 1824; this name is a rendering of the Chinook Jargon for 'others'. They were identified as Upper Chihalis and Upper Tsihalis by Gibbs (1855:435, 1877:172). Their self-designation is *sqʷayáyɬq̓*, taken from the name for Mud Bay (the southern end of Eld Inlet), which was used for the Black River–Eld Inlet group (Kinkade 1963–1964: 181), possibly a mixed group including speakers of both Upper Chehalis and Lushootseed. The Quinault and Lower Chehalis name for the Upper Chehalis is *tʔáwən*, from the name of a small prairie near the Chehalis Reservation. The Puget Sound tribes knew the Upper Chehalis as *stə́q̓tábš* 'inland people', recorded Stak-tamish by Gibbs (1877:172).

Cowlitz is from *káwlic* 'Cowlitz River' and *káwlicq* 'language, people of the Cowlitz River' (M. Dale Kinkade, personal communication 1988). The name has appeared as Kowilitzk (Franchère 1969:80), Kawelitsk or Cowelits (Hale 1846:211), Cawalitz (Lee and Frost 1844:99), and other forms found in Hodge (1907–1910,1:355). The Cowlitz have also been called Lower Cowlitz to distinguish them from the Sahaptin-speaking Taitnapam or Upper Cowlitz, who assimilated with them by the mid-nineteenth century.

Subgroups

The Salishan names of the local groups of the Southwest-ern Coast Salish are listed here (M. Dale Kinkade, communication to editors 1987).

Queets: Quinault *q̓ʷícxʷ*, Lower Chehalis *(s)q̓ʷícxʷ*; Quaitso (Hodge 1907–1910, 2:332).

Quinault: Quinault and Oakville Upper Chehalis *kʷínayɬ*, Lower Chehalis *kʷí·ńiɬ*; Quinaielt (Hodge 1907–1910, 2:342).

Copalis: Quinault and Lower Chehalis *kʷupíls*.

Humptulips: Quinault *xʷəmtúlapč*, Lower Chehalis *xʷəmtúlapš*, Oakville Upper Chehalis *xʷəntúlapš*.

Wynoochee: Quinault *xʷənút̓ču*, Lower Chehalis *xʷənút̓č*, Upper Chehalis *xʷənút̓či*.

Chehalis proper: Quinault *ċəxíls*, Lower Chehalis *ċxləs*, literally 'sand', Oakville Upper Chehalis *ɬáčuq*, literally 'downstream language'.

Satsop: Quinault *sácapč*, Oakville Upper Chehalis *sácapš*, literally 'made stream'.

Cowlitz proper: Cowlitz *sɫpúlmx*, literally 'downstream people', Upper Chehalis *sɫpúmš*.

Newaukum: Cowlitz *náwaqʷm*, literally 'big prairie'.

The names of the Upper Chehalis subgroups, for which English terms are generally not in use, are given in the text.

Sources

Accounts of the contact between the Hezeta-Bodega y Quadra expedition of 1775 and the Quinaults are found in Wagner and Baker (1930) and Campa y Cos (1964). Later eighteenth-century explorers and traders who encountered Southwestern Coast Salish included Meares (1790), Boit (Howay 1941), and Whidby (Vancouver 1801). The journals of the fur traders at Astoria included information on the Lower Chehalis and Cowlitz (Cox 1957; Franchère 1969; A. Henry 1897; Ross 1849, 1855; Stuart 1935). Morse (1822) compiled population figures from information provided by Astorian traders. John Work (Work 1824–1825; T.C. Elliott 1912; Annance 1824–1825), Tolmie (1963), and Douglas (1931) described their journeys through Southwestern Coast Salish territory.

A farmer at Cowlitz Farm (G.B. Roberts 1962), priests from the Cowlitz mission (Landerholm 1956), and travelers through the area (Slacum 1837) provide a picture of early life among the Cowlitz. The Wilkes expedition of the early 1840s (Wilkes 1845, 1925–1926; Colvocoresses 1855) and the Belcher Expedition (Hinds 1839) left descriptions of Lower Chehalis country.

Swan (1857) provided the first direct account of Willapa Bay and its people in the early 1850s. Gibbs (especially 1877, 1855) produced descriptions of the region's Indians in connection with the treaty-making efforts. Stevens (1901) includes some information on the context of the treaties.

The annual reports and correspondence from agents, farmers, and teachers at the Quinault and Chehalis reservations provide invaluable accounts of conditions in the late nineteenth century (ARCIA 1857, 1868, 1885, 1890). Willoughby (1889) gave a brief account of the Indians at Quinault Reservation.

Most ethnographic data on the Southwestern Coast Salish come from the Quinault (Olson 1936) and the Upper Chehalis (Adamson 1926–1927). Curtis (1907–1930, 9) has village lists for Cowlitz and Willapa Bay, as well as sketches of most groups and additional information on locations. Donovan (1960, 1963, 1964, 1966) interviewed people at the Chehalis Reservation and elsewhere, collecting myths as well as cultural information. Jacobs (1934, 1) wrote a brief note on Cowlitz ethnography. Irwin (1979, 1987) has interviewed many Cowlitz people and collected valuable ethnographic and historical information. Farrand's (1902) collection of Quinault myths is complemented by Adamson's (1934) extensive compilation of Upper Chehalis, Cowlitz, and other interior mythology. Gibbs (1955–1956) collected myths from the area. Kinkade (1963–1964) described Upper Chehalis phonology and morphology, and Elmendorf (1969) considered aspects of the linguistic relationships among Southwestern Coast Salish languages.

The *Seattle Times* (Dietrich 1985) published a summary of the conditions of Washington Indians as of 1985. Irwin (1987) discussed the Cowlitz struggles for federal recognition.

Prehistory of the Lower Columbia and Willamette Valley

RICHARD M. PETTIGREW

The drainage area of the Lower Columbia River contains two regions that were culturally distinct at the time of Euro-American contact in the eighteenth century—the Lower Columbia valley with its primarily Chinookan population, and the Willamette Basin, the home of the Kalapuya and the Molala. The two areas were neatly divided at Willamette Falls, with the Willamette below the falls and its tributary the Clackamas River belonging in the Lower Columbia region.

It appears that only one major category of the effective environment, aquatic wildlife, sets the two valleys apart in any way similar to the cultural separation. The Columbia River has a much broader variety of fishes, and a larger fish population. At least 13 species of fishes found in the Columbia River did not inhabit the Willamette River system to a significant extent. Among these are sturgeon, salmon, and eulachon (Loy et al. 1976:160-161). Also worthy of mention in this context is the harbor seal, a sea mammal at home in freshwater in the Columbia River but not the Willamette below the falls. This brief comparison of the two valleys strongly suggests that the relative abundance of aquatic food resources in the Lower Columbia Valley and their corresponding lack in the Willamette Basin was the major factor influencing the divergence of the two cultures.

Early sites appear to reflect the hunting emphasis that presumably characterized the ancestral culture that first populated the southern Northwest Coast. Some suggestions of an early distinctiveness for Lower Columbia culture are found in the stylized ground stone tools (stone weights called bola stones, cobble celts, loaf stones) found regularly in undated early sites there but not in the Willamette area. Diverging developmental trends were probably well under way by 6000 B.C., if not earlier, and much of the divergence appears to have taken place by the time represented by dated bottomland sites in both valleys.

Lower Columbia Valley

For the Lower Columbia area chronologies have been devised for the Portland Basin (Pettigrew 1977, 1981) and for the Columbia Estuary (fig. 1) (Minor 1983). The Portland Basin chronology is a culture sequence originally defined to apply to the area between the Sandy River on the east and Rainier, Oregon, on the west, though it has been extended to include the area around Bonneville Dam (Pettigrew 1981:iii). The Portland Basin sequence covers only the time since about 600 B.C., because of the rarity of firmly dated assemblages older than that time.

The Portland Basin sequence includes two cultural phases, Merrybell and Multnomah, with the latter divided into three subphases. Various temporal markers are used to distinguish these phases and subphases. Most useful, because they are most common, are the projectile points, which shift from high proportions of large, broad-necked, stemmed points in the Merrybell phase to the predominance of smaller, narrow-necked, corner-notched, and then small side-notched points as the Multnomah phase unfolds (fig. 2). Other Merrybell diagnostics include flaked cylindrical bipoints and crescents, graphite, perforated ground stone pendants, peripherally flaked pebbles, and atlatl weights. Multnomah yields notched or perforated netsinkers, mule-ear knives, clay figurines, and incised clay tablets. After 1750, in Multnomah 3, historic trade goods and copper tubes are found.

The culture sequence for the Columbia Estuary (Minor 1983) covers the period of time from 6000 B.C. to A.D. 1851, though it is documented by radiocarbon dates only from about 1200 B.C. Human occupation at the mouth of the Columbia River is grouped into four temporally separate units: the Youngs River complex (6000-4000 B.C.), the Seal Island phase (4000 B.C.-A.D. 1), the Ilwaco phase (A.D. 1-1775), and the Historic phase (A.D. 1775-1851). The Ilwaco phase is divided into Ilwaco 1 (A.D. 1-1050) and Ilwaco 2 (A.D. 1050-1775). Projectile points, grouped by means of the Portland Basin typology (Pettigrew 1981), are very important diagnostic elements, but other artifact classes such as stone weights, atlatl weights, composite toggling harpoons, and dentalium shell beads are essential discriminating elements in the scheme as well (fig. 3). Sites from each of the phases have been excavated, but the Youngs River complex is represented only by surface collections from some of the sites

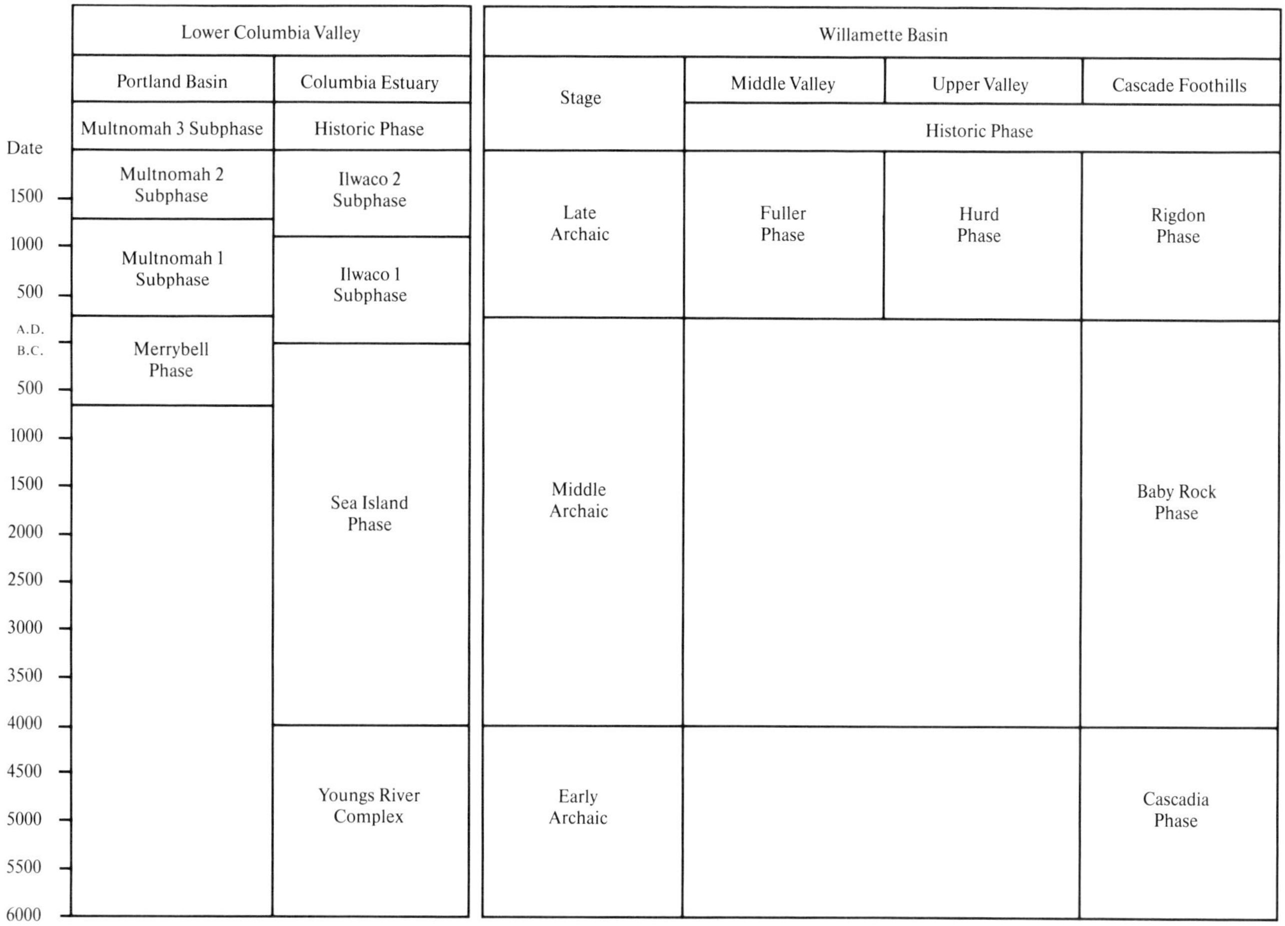

Date	Lower Columbia Valley		Willamette Basin			
	Portland Basin	Columbia Estuary	Stage	Middle Valley	Upper Valley	Cascade Foothills
	Multnomah 3 Subphase	Historic Phase		Historic Phase		
1500	Multnomah 2 Subphase	Ilwaco 2 Subphase	Late Archaic	Fuller Phase	Hurd Phase	Rigdon Phase
1000	Multnomah 1 Subphase	Ilwaco 1 Subphase				
500						
A.D. B.C.	Merrybell Phase					
500			Middle Archaic			Baby Rock Phase
1000						
1500		Sea Island Phase				
2000						
2500						
3000						
3500						
4000						
4500		Youngs River Complex	Early Archaic			Cascadia Phase
5000						
5500						
6000						

Fig. 1. Chronologies for the Lower Columbia Valley and the Willamette Basin.

presumed to be the oldest yet discovered in the area. A curious exception to the Columbia Estuary sequence is the Martin site (45PC7) (Kidd 1967; Shaw 1975) on North Beach Peninsula, where nearly all points are stemless, though the radiocarbon dates (A.D. 90 and 510) fit within the Ilwaco 1 subphase, in which small stemmed points predominate.

Youngs River complex diagnostics are shouldered lanceolate and willow-leaf-shaped points, stemmed scrapers, and stone weights. In Seal Island phase, broad-necked, stemmed points predominate. In Ilwaco 1, there are occasional atlatl weights and a low proportion of broad-necked points. By Ilwaco 2, broad-necked points are absent, and small side-notched points are evident.

Although earlier sites on the floodplain may exist, the earliest firmly dated cultural deposit in the Lower Columbia area is site 45CL31, on the southeastern shore of Vancouver Lake. A hearth feature there produced dates of 1560 and 1410 B.C. (Wessen and Daugherty 1983: B–110). Unfortunately, no tools were directly associated with the hearth. The next earliest firm date on the Lower Columbia area is at the Eddy Point site near the mouth of the Columbia River (Minor 1983:112–129). The lower-

most stratum there produced a date of 1180 B.C., making it the earliest known component of the Seal Island phase (Minor 1983:184–188). Nearly as old is the lowest stratum of the Merrybell site (Pettigrew 1981:67–79) in the Portland Basin with one date of 930 B.C. and two of 900 B.C. These three sites mark the beginning of the period for which there is well dated evidence for human exploitation of the area.

Types of Sites

Signs of prehistoric human occupation on the Lower Columbia are found mostly in the narrow lowland belt (fig. 4). The Columbia River is at sea level (and has been so for much if not all of the past 10,000 years) for nearly all the distance up to the Cascades. Sea level began to rise shortly before 8000 B.C. and did not stabilize at its present elevation until perhaps 3000 B.C. (Fladmark 1975). Consequently, all sites located on the floodplain prior to about 3000 B.C. have probably been drowned and covered with alluvium.

It is not surprising, then, that the earliest known sites in the Lower Columbia region downstream from The Dalles

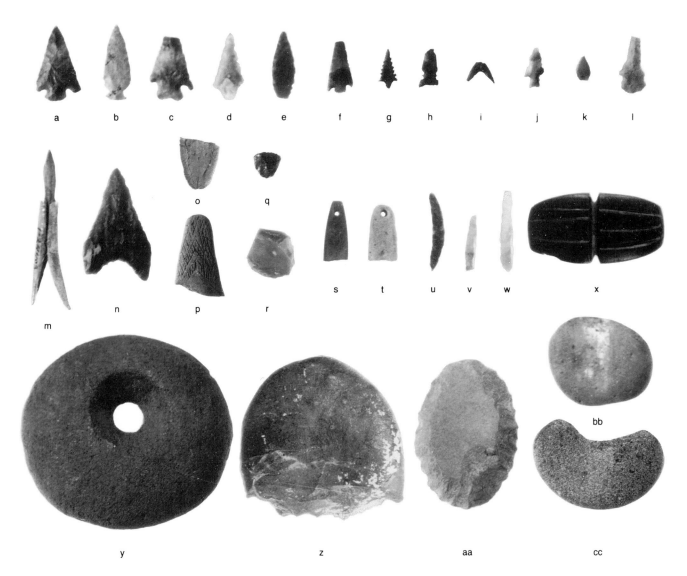

Fig. 2. Artifacts from the Merrybell and Multnomah phases, Portland Basin: a, Type 1 projectile point, Merrybell; b, Type 2 projectile point, Merrybell; c, Type 3 projectile point, Merrybell; d, Type 5 projectile point, Merrybell; e, Type 6a projectile point, Merrybell; f, Type 7 projectile point, Multnomah; g, Type 9 projectile point, Multnomah; h, Type 12 projectile point, Multnomah subphases 2–3; i, Type 13 projectile point, Multnomah subphases 2–3; j, Type 15 projectile point, Multnomah subphases 2–3; k, Type 16 projectile point, Multnomah subphase 1; l, stemmed drill, Merrybell; m, composite toggling harpoon head, Multnomah; n, mule-ear knife, Multnomah; o, clay figurine, Multnomah; p, clay tablet, Multnomah; q, small end scraper, Multnomah; r, large end scraper, Merrybell; s-t, perforated pendants, Merrybell; u, flaked crescent, Merrybell; v-w, flaked bipoints, Merrybell; x, atlatl weight, Merrybell; y, perforated sinker, Multnomah subphases 2–3; z, unifacially flaked cobble, Merrybell; aa, peripherally flaked cobble, Merrybell; bb, "wrap-marked" sinker, Multnomah subphase 1; cc, notched sinker, Multnomah subphase 1. Length of x 7.5 cm; rest to same scale.

are above the floodplain on surfaces that have been free of the depositional and erosive effects of the river since the end of the Pleistocene. These sites in the Portland Basin and Cascades zones can be divided into two categories: the upland sites, which are more than one kilometer from the river, and the peripheral sites, which are within one kilometer. Representative artifacts from these sites are shown in figure 5.

The best known of the upland sites is the Geertz site (Woodward 1972), just west of the Cascade Mountains. This site appears to be a seasonal hunting camp. The projectile points were all large willow-leaf-shaped forms, known to have been most common in adjacent regions from 6000 to 4000 B.C. The Geertz site may have been used by hunting parties whose homes were located on the Clackamas or Columbia rivers.

Another upland site (45CL54) (Tuohy and Bryan 1958–1959:29–32) appears to belong roughly to the same period as the Geertz site but has a much more heterogeneous assemblage, including all the artifact classes that the Geertz site produced, but also manos and metates, mortars and pestles, a sculpted cobble, a perforated cobble

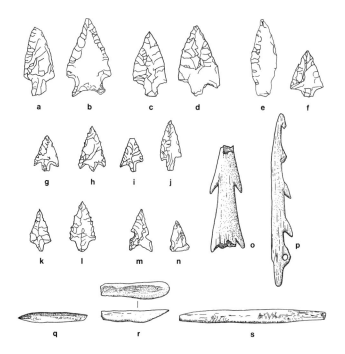

after Minor 1983:105, 122, 124, 137, 140, 156, 167, 177.
Fig. 3. Projectile points from the Columbia Estuary: a, Type 2, Seal Island phase; b, Type 3, Seal Island phase; c–d, Type 4, Seal Island phase; e–f, Type 5, Seal Island phase; g–j, Type 9, Ilwaco phase; k–l, Type 10, Ilwaco phase; m–n, Type 12, Ilwaco subphase 2; o–p, single-piece harpoon heads, Seal Island phase, absent in Ilwaco subphase 2; q–s, composite toggling harpoon, with point (q), barbs (r), and foreshaft (s), Ilwaco phase. Length of s, 8 cm; rest to same scale.

with an edge-ground facet, a ground stone pipe, pitted cobbles, and hearths. Furthermore, the site produced a large sample of stone weights ("bola stones") known from components of the Windust phase on the Lower Snake River, dated 8500 to 6000 B.C. (Rice 1972), and from the Roadcut site at The Dalles, dated about 9000 to 6000 B.C. (Cressman et al. 1960). The projectile points are nearly all willow-leaf-shaped, and these and the ovate bifaces found at both sites are similar to those belonging to the Cascade phase on the Lower Snake River, dated 6000 to 2500 B.C. (Leonhardy and Rice 1970; Brauner 1976), and found in deposits of similar antiquity at the Roadcut site. Certainly hunting was a major activity at 45CL54, but the milling stones and the mortars and pestles represent the processing of vegetable foods as well. The ground stone pipe and the sculpted cobble suggest that this site was more than simply utilitarian.

The peripheral sites are all on forested or formerly forested surfaces that have not been subject to flooding by the river since about 9000 B.C., so that human use of these areas at any time since then could have left exposed traces. Because the cultural deposits at these sites are purely surficial, and there is no charcoal preserved for radiocarbon dating, the only possible means to date them is to compare their assemblages with other nearby and objectively dated assemblages.

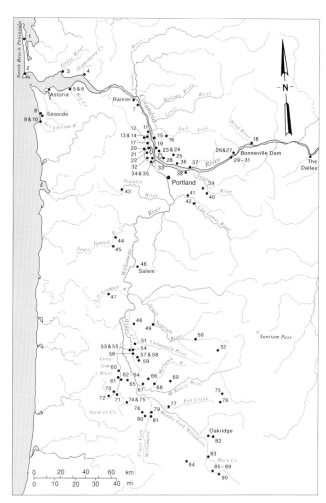

U. of Oreg., Oreg. State Mus. of Anthr., Eugene.
Fig. 4. Archeological sites in the Lower Columbia and Willamette valleys: 1, Martin; 2, Fishing Rocks; 3, Burkhalter; 4, Skamokawa; 5, Ivy Station; 6, Eddy Point; 7, Trojan; 8, Ave. Q; 9, Par-Tee; 10, Palmrose; 11, Powell; 12, Decker; 13, Malarkey; 14, 35C03; 15, Bachelor Island; 16, 45CL54; 17, Meier; 18, Home Valley Park; 19, Herzog; 20, McClarin; 21, Pump House; 22, Cholick; 23, Kersting; 24, Duck Lake; 25, Schultz Marsh; 26, Caples; 27, 45SA11; 28, 45CL31; 29, 45SA12; 30, 45SA19; 31, 45SA13; 32, Coplin; 33, Lyons; 34, Merrybell; 35, Douglas; 36, Bishopbrick; 37, Lady Island; 38, Blue Lake; 39, Geertz; 40, Sandy; 41, Mostul Village; 42, Feldheimer; 43, Scoggins Creek; 44, Fuller Mound; 45, Fanning Mound; 46, Hager's Grove; 47, Luckiamute Hearth; 48, Templeton (Tangent); 49, Lebanon; 50, Cascadia Cave; 51, Halsey Mound; 52, Tidbits; 53, Kropf; 54, Miller Farm; 55, Simrock; 56, Barnes; 57, Davidson; 58, Lynch; 59, Spurland Mound; 60, Lingo; 61, Virgin Ranch Mound; 62, Benjamin; 63, Smithfield Mound; 64, Kirk Park; 65, Flanagan; 66, Beebe; 67, Hurd; 68, Mohawk River Clovis find; 69, Halverson; 70, Hannavan Creek; 71, Perkins Peninsula; 72, Long Tom; 73, Indian Ridge; 74, Bradley-Moen; 75, Ralston; 76, Sardine Confluence; 77, Fall Creek; 78, 35LA70; 79, Simons; 80, 35LA92; 81, 35LA118; 82, Baby Rock Shelter; 83, Buck Creek; 84, Bohemia Mining District Clovis find; 85, 35LA528; 86, 35LA529; 87, 35LA573; 88, 35LA574; 89, 35LA599; 90, Rigdon's Horse Pasture Cave.

Types of Artifacts

The most common artifacts found at the peripheral sites are unifacially flaked cobbles and projectile points. Other kinds of tools found include cobble celts, loaf stones, stone   *521*

U. of Oreg., Oreg. State Mus. of Anthr., Eugene.
Fig. 5. Artifacts from upland and peripheral sites, Portland Basin: a-b, Type 6a projectile points; c-d, Type 5 projectile points; e, ovate biface; f, unifacially flaked cobble; g, loaf-shaped stone; h, bola stone; i, cobble celt. Length of i, 21.6 cm; rest to scale.

weights, and foliate bifaces. Most of these tool classes are useful in estimating the temporal depth of the sites (Pettigrew 1981). Unifacially flaked cobbles at excavated sites on the floodplain are infrequent after 100 B.C. and practically absent after A.D. 200, and these generalizations should probably be applied also to the peripheral sites. The projectile points found are nearly all of early styles (large corner-notched, willow-leaf-shaped, broad-stemmed lanceolate) that suggest an antiquity of perhaps 8000 B.C. to as recent as 500 B.C. Cobble celts have a geographic distribution that centers in the Portland Basin, with specimens reported from as far away as Astoria to the west, the mouth of the Snake River to the east, and the Eugene area to the south. The only specimen found in a buried context is from the Flanagan site in the southern Willamette Valley, recovered below a level dated to 1350 B.C. (Toepel and Minor 1980). Bola stones suggest a date from 8500 to 6000 B.C., and foliate bifaces such as have been found in the peripheral sites are similar to others dated 6000 to 2600 B.C. Overall, then, it would appear that the peripheral sites were used mostly within the period 8000 to 1000 B.C.

The uses to which these sites were put are unclear. The frequency of flaked cobbles and the forested vegetation suggest that wood products were being collected and processed. The presence of projectile points may indicate that hunting was a major activity. The cobble celts, loaf stones, stone weights, and foliate bifaces might have been originally deposited there as mortuary furniture; these areas may have been used for platform or tree interment, a practice known for the region in the historic period. Supporting this conjecture is the fact that nearly all the cobble celts and loaf stones reported from these sites are broken in half, a possible result of the ritual "killing" of the possessions of the deceased.

The only peripheral site that has been intensively studied is the Home Valley Park site (45SA17) (Dunnell and Lewarch 1974). Located in the Columbia Gorge on the northern margin of Lake Bonneville about 50 feet above the original floodplain of the Columbia River, the site contains a basically surficial cultural deposit. The horizontal patterning of the site showed many discrete clusters of debris, suggesting repeated use by small groups. The only chronologically diagnostic tool found was a fragmentary willow-leaf-shaped point. Small unifacially flaked tools were numerous. Also relatively numerous was the flaked cobble, which has become a hallmark of this type of site. Fire-cracked rock was also common, indicating frequent cooking activities; this kind of artifact is not usually reported in peripheral sites. The prehistoric function of this site seems to have been as a temporary seasonal camp used by small groups for hunting and gathering activities, a function that appears to distinguish it from the other known peripheral sites.

Apparently early but undated sites have also been noted at the mouth of the Columbia River by Minor (1983, 1984), who refers to this group of sites as the Youngs River complex. These sites, on terraces above Youngs River and Lewis and Clark River, have produced shouldered lanceolate and willow-leaf-shaped projectile points as well as stone weights and a kind of stemmed scraper (fig. 6).

A most unusual find that may also represent a period earlier than the earliest dated floodplain sites is the Kadow Collection, which was dredged from the bottom of Vancouver Lake (Wessen and Daugherty 1983:79–96). A majority of the projectile points were willow-leaf-shaped or broad-necked shouldered points. Among the other tools found were edge-ground cobbles, unifacially flaked cobbles, and a cobble celt.

Although the cultural chronologies for the Lower Columbia area clearly show stylistic change in artifact styles, as well as some probably functional additions or replacements of artifact classes, no fundamental change in the lifeway seems indicated for the last 3,000 years (a list of reported sites from this best documented period is given in table 1). For this reason, Minor (1983) was able to use sites from this entire period to illustrate the settlement and subsistence system used by the fully developed culture at the mouth of the Columbia River. The Eddy Point site contains a wide variety of faunal remains, including salmon, as well as many kinds of bone and antler tools, including specialized fishing tools such as barbed bone points and composite toggling harpoon valves. During the Merrybell phase rectangular house structures were built

522

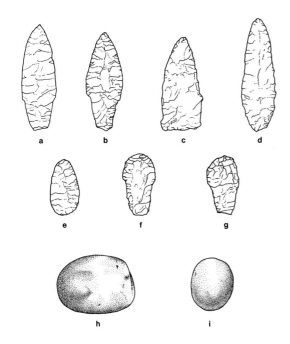

after Minor 1984:6, 9, 14.

Fig. 6. Artifacts from the Youngs River complex, Columbia Estuary: a-b, shouldered lanceolate projectile points; c, straight-based lanceolate projectile point; d-e, foliate projectile points; f-g, stemmed scrapers; h-i, bola stones. Length of a, 6.5 cm; rest to same scale.

(Jermann, Lewarch, and Campbell 1975; Pettigrew 1981: 115). Large riverside settlements appear already to have been established by Seal Island phase and Merrybell phase times. A strong riverine orientation throughout this period seems indicated.

Development of the Historic Pattern

Woodworking seems to be a very ancient attribute of Lower Columbia culture, if the interpretation of flaked cobbles and cobble celts in the peripheral sites as woodworking tools is correct. Small ground-stone adz blades are present in the Merrybell phase, so they may have been introduced prior to that time. Woodworking as a major industry on the Lower Columbia was very likely already developed shortly after the end of the Pleistocene, when the coniferous forests of the Coast Range and the Cascade Mountains evolved to their present form. Cedar was already a major forest component in the Lower Columbia area by 7000 B.C., considerably earlier than in areas to the north (Hebda and Mathewes 1984a).

When the culture became heavily dependent on the salmon runs is difficult to determine. Notched netsinkers are very commonly found in sites affiliated with the Multnomah 1 subphase but are rare in sites of the Merrybell phase. Perhaps this indicates that seine nets were not used in the Merrybell phase. Surely salmon was an important resource in the Early period at The Dalles, where hundred of thousands of salmon vertebrae at the Roadcut site were found. It may be that the "bola stones"

at the Roadcut site, as well as those in peripheral sites in the Portland Basin and in the Columbia Estuary, are netsinkers. Salmon have probably been taken on the Lower Columbia, at least at rapids and falls, since shortly after the end of the Pleistocene.

One of the most elusive aspects of prehistoric Lower Columbia culture is the development of the rich artistic tradition. The archeological problem apparently is that most artistic representations on the Lower Columbia were rendered on woods. The remaining examples of aboriginal art are petroglyphs and portable sculptures of stone, bone, and clay (Peterson 1978; Wingert 1952). Artistic representations occur in the Multnomah 1 subphase (A.D. 200–1250), but examples of art earlier than that are very rare.

Just when Lower Columbia culture evolved to a pattern similar to that recorded at contact is not possible to say. Surely the woodworking technology was a very early development; beyond this all that can be said with confidence is that the other hallmarks of the protohistoric culture were present at least as early as the beginning of the Multnomah phase. It seems that the most basic nonstylistic patterns were already in place by 1000 B.C., if not earlier.

Change did take place, as the Columbia Estuary and Portland Basin culture sequences show. Documented change was mostly stylistic, though many traits probably have functional and technological correlates. A major innovation between about 500 and 100 B.C. was the bow and arrow, which eventually replaced the atlatl. The introduction of the bow is evidenced by the appearance of small, narrow-necked projectile points thought to have tipped arrows and distinct from the more massive, broad-necked points that armed the atlatl dart. The degree of advantage offered by the bow is uncertain, but the two weapons systems were used side by side on the Lower Columbia for at least several hundred years, as indicated by the persistence of broad-necked points and atlatl weights in the Multnomah 1 and Ilwaco 1 subphases and by the discovery of whalebone atlatls at two sites (Phebus and Drucker 1975). These sites, on the coast near Seaside, probably affiliate with the Ilwaco 1 subphase. The atlatl disappears from the record by about A.D. 700 throughout the Lower Columbia area.

The Cascade Landslide

The changes wrought by a catastrophic event, the Cascade Landslide, may have been much more profound. At approximately A.D. 1250 a mountainside collapsed into the Columbia River near the present site of Bonneville Dam (Lawrence and Lawrence 1958), apparently creating a temporary earthen dam that impounded the waters of the river, which eventually broke through the dam and spilled out destructively into the valley downstream. The

Table 1. Documented Prehistoric Sites of the Lower Columbia Dated After 1000 B.C.

Phase	Site	Source
Merrybell	Merrybell (35MU9)	Pettigrew 1981
	Lady Island (45CL48)	Woodward 1977
	Kersting (45CL21)	Jermann, Lewarch and Campbell 1975
	Schultz Marsh (45CL29)	Chatters 1974
	Bachelor Island (45CL43)	Pettigrew 1981; Steele 1980
Seal Island	Eddy Point I (35CLT33)	Minor 1983
	Burkhalter (45WK51)	Minor 1983
	Skamokawa (45WK5)	Minor 1978, 1980, 1983
	Palmrose (35 CLT47)	Phebus and Drucker 1975
Multnomah 1	Cholick (35MU1)	Pettigrew 1981
	35CO3	Pettigrew 1981
	Malarkey (35CO4)	Pettigrew 1981
	Trojan (35CO1)	Warner and Warner 1975
	Sandy	Woodward 1974
Ilwaco 1	Ivy Station I (35CLT34)	Minor 1983
	Fishing Rocks I (45PC35)	Minor 1983
	Eddy Point II (35CLT33)	Minor 1983
	Skamokawa (45WK5)	Minor 1978, 1980, 1983
	Ave. Q (35CLT13)	Phebus and Drucker 1975
	Par-Tee (35CLT20)	Phebus and Drucker 1975
Multnomah 2	Meier (35CO5)	Pettigrew 1981
	Lyons (35MU6)	Pettigrew 1981
	Pump House (35CO7)	Pettigrew 1981
	45CL31	Wessen and Daugherty 1983
	Blue Lake (35MU24)	Archibald 1984
	Duck Lake (45CL6a)	Slocum and Matsen 1968
	Sandy	Woodward 1974
	Feldheimer	Woodward 1974
	45SA11	Skinner 1981
	Caples (45SA5)	Dunnell and Beck 1979
	45SA12	Dunnell and Campbell 1977
	45SA13	Dunnell and Campbell 1977
	45SA19	Dunnell and Campbell 1977
Ilwaco 2	Fishing Rocks II (45PC35)	Minor 1983
	Ivy Station II (35CLT34)	Minor 1983
Multnomah 3	Meier (35CO5)	Pettigrew 1981
	Lyons (35MU6)	Pettigrew 1981
	Pump House (35CO7)	Pettigrew 1981
	Herzog (45CL4)	Slocum and Matsen 1968; R. Jones 1972; Foreman and Foreman 1977
	Decker (35CO2)	R. Jones 1972
	Powell	R. Jones 1972
	Mostul Village	Woodward 1974
	45SA11	Skinner 1981

flood appears to have changed the floodplain topography and may have destroyed many, if not most, settlements in the Portland Basin and downstream. None of the prehistoric sites dated in the vicinity of the Bonneville Dam–Cascades area of the Columbia Gorge predates the landslide, which created the Cascades of the Columbia River, the series of rapids that made navigation so hazardous and the fishing so good for the aboriginal people of that locality. Furthermore, in the Portland Basin, sites that were occupied both just before and after the landslide are extremely rare or nonexistent (Pettigrew 1981:36). It would appear that settlement destruction and landform changes were so severe that virtually all subsequent floodplain sites were relocated. Though Minor

524

PETTIGREW

(1983:192) sees no evidence that the flood had any effect in the Columbia Estuary, with the possible exception of the abandonment of the Skamokawa site (Minor 1980:37), the evidence from his excavated sites on the river fits well with the Portland Basin data. The only excavated site on the river in that area that has components assigned to both the Ilwaco 1 and Ilwaco 2 subphase is the Ivy Station site. This site was assigned in part to the Ilwaco 1 subphase on the basis of a single radiocarbon date (A.D. 580), yet the assemblage found there is typical of Ilwaco 2 and Historic phase components (including small, side-notched points and historic debris) and contains no objects uniquely diagnostic of Ilwaco 1 or earlier phases (such as broad-necked, stemmed points, single-piece nontoggling harpoon points, girdled netsinkers, or atlatl weights). On this basis, it seems probable that Ivy Station is an Ilwaco 2–Historic phase site and that the riverine area of the Columbia Estuary may have suffered also from the Cascade Landslide flood.

The population loss caused by the catastrophe may have presented an opportunity for neighboring peoples to encroach upon this territory. The Caples site, situated on Cascade Landslide debris (Dunnell and Beck 1979), contains 41 circular housepits occupied within two or three centuries after the landslide. These circular depressions are clearly anomalous in the Lower Columbia area and may represent a short-lived intrusion by a group from the Plateau area.

In the centuries following the Cascade Landslide, it is clear that the population of the Lower Columbia rebounded and settlements were reestablished throughout the valley. The economic basis of the society was probably quite similar to its status before the landslide, but some suggestion of change comes in the form of an apparent replacement of the notched netsinker by the larger perforated sinker in the Portland Basin (Pettigrew 1981: 121). Perforated sinkers may have weighted heavy lines used in sturgeon fishing (Dunnell and Campbell 1977).

Willamette Basin

The culture sequence for the Willamette Basin includes the Cascade upland as well as the bottomland zone (Beckham, Minor, and Toepel 1981:157–175). As shown in figure 1, this chronology characterizes each of three areas (Middle Willamette Valley, Upper Willamette Valley, Cascade Foothills) in terms of both evolutionary stages and cultural phases. The Archaic stage is divided into Early (6000–4000 B.C.), Middle (4000 B.C.–A.D. 200), and Late (A.D. 200–1750). Early Archaic is the Cascadia phase (6000–4000 B.C.) in the Cascade Foothills, characterized by willow-leaf-shaped projectile points. No contemporaneous phase is defined for the Willamette Valley for lack of evidence. For the Middle Archaic broad-necked stemmed point types are diagnostic, and there is

abundant evidence of plant processing. In the Late Archaic, narrow-necked point types are evident. In the Fuller phase, antler and bone tools are diagnostic, and there is evidence of fishing. Grave goods, especially marine shells, are found with burials. A list of some reported Willamette Valley sites is given in table 2, and sites from the Cascades Foothills in table 3. Characteristic Willamette Basin artifacts are shown in figure 7.

Sites and Artifacts

Early sites in the Willamette area are even rarer than on the Lower Columbia. Besides the two fluted points discussed above, two sites suggest evidence associating artifacts with remains of mammoth, thought to have become extinct in the Willamette Valley by about 8000 B.C. At the Lebanon site (Cressman and Laughlin 1941) a possible (but disputed) cobble tool was found directly associated with mammoth bones.

The earliest dated site in either the Willamette or Lower Columbia areas is Cascadia Cave (Newman 1966), in the Cascades foothills alongside the South Santiam River. Charcoal from a hearth near the bottom of the cultural deposit in this rockshelter was radiocarbon-dated to 5960 B.C. Evidence found in the excavation indicates that the cave was used not only for hunting mammals and birds but also for collecting and processing hazelnuts. Hunting tools (projectile points, large ovate bifaces) were found, as well as tools possibly used for milling vegetable foods (manos and metates, edge-ground cobbles). It is also important to note that Cascadia Cave is located on the best trail route linking the Willamette Valley and central Oregon (via Santiam Pass), so the site may have been a way station for travelers. The lower portion of the deposit contained only willow-leaf-shaped projectile points (thus the earliest dated style for the region), to which in the upper levels are added large side-notched and corner-notched specimens. No clearly recent styles were found, though it must be kept in mind that in places more than half of the culture deposit had been sifted by artifact collectors before the reported excavation was carried out, leaving only the lower portions of the deposit intact. Consequently, a terminal date for the occupation of the site is not possible to fix, and the rockshelter may have been used by aboriginal groups up to the time of contact.

The only other reported site in the Cascades foothills area that is firmly dated to before 5000 B.C. is Baby Rock Shelter (Olsen 1975), just east of the city of Oakridge. Though no radiocarbon dates were obtained from the site, the lowermost of four culture-bearing strata lies just below a layer of volcanic ash identified with the eruption of Mount Mazama (Crater Lake), dated to approximately 4200 B.C. Excavation of the site was limited in scale, and only a very small sample of artifacts was recovered from beneath the ash, so that nothing can be said about it except *525*

Table 2. Selected Prehistoric Sites of the Willamette Valley

Site	Date or Stage	Sources
Halverson (35LA261)	A.D. 1790	Minor and Toepel 1982; Minor and Pickett 1982; Toepel and Sappington 1982
35LA568 (Kirk Park 2)	A.D. 1555, 1800+	Cheatham 1984
Lynch (35LIN36)	A.D. 670, 1150, 1950	Sanford 1975
Halsey Mound	Late Archaic, Historic	Laughlin 1941
Fanning Mound	Late Archaic, Historic	Murdy and Wentz 1975
Fuller Mound	Late Archaic, Historic	Woodward, Murdy, and Young 1975
Hurd (35LA44)	850, 830 B.C., A.D. 830 900, 900, 970, 1010, 1100, 1280, 1440, 1490, 1620, 1800, 1850, 1950	White 1975
Davidson (35LIN34)	Middle, Late Archaic, Historic	Davis, Aikens, and Henrickson 1973
35LA565 (Kirk Park 1)	A.D. 430, 780, 1410	Cheatham 1984
35LA118	A.D. 970	White 1975a
Perkins Peninsula (35LA282)	A.D. 730, 865	Cheatham 1984; L.R. Collins 1951
Simons (35LA116)	Late Archaic	Pettigrew 1975
Spurland Mound	Late Archaic (?)	Laughlin 1941; L.R. Collins 1951
Beebe (35LA216)	Late Archaic	Follansbee 1975
Simrock (35LIN21)	Late Archaic	W.A. Davis 1970
Kropf (35LIN22)	Late Archaic	W.A. Davis 1970
Miller Farm I (35LIN23)	Late Archaic (?)	Oman and Reagan 1971
Miller Farm II (35LIN24)	Late Archaic	Oman and Reagan 1971
Barnes (35LIN25)	Late Archaic	Oman and Reagan 1971
35LA70	Late Archaic	White 1975a
35LA92	Late Archaic	White 1975a
Virgin Ranch Mound	Late Archaic	White 1975a; L.R. Collins 1951
Smithfield Mound	Late Archaic	White 1975a; L.R. Collins 1951
35 MA9 (Hager's Grove)	1790 B.C., A.D. 730, 810, 1550	Pettigrew 1980
35MA7 (Hager's Grove)	1850, 920, 900, 730 B.C. A.D. 760	Pettigrew 1980
35LA567 (Kirk Park 3)	960, 810 B.C., A.D. 770	Cheatham 1984
35LA566 (Kirk Park 4)	1360, 530 B.C., A.D. 110	Cheatham 1984
35LA41 (Benjamin)	370 B.C., A.D. 310	F.E. Miller 1975
35LA42 (Benjamin)	Middle, Late Archaic	F.E. Miller 1975
Flanagan (35LA218)	3800, 3620, 1350, 1280 B.C., A.D. 110, 150, 170, 190 230, 270, 990, 1110, 1490	Toepel and Minor 1980; Beckham, Minor, and Toepel 1981
Scoggins Creek (35WN4)	Middle, Late Archaic (?)	W.A. Davis 1970a
Lingo (35LA29)	2180, 95 B.C.	Cordell 1975; White 1975a
Long Tom (35LA439)	2160, 1930 B.C.	O'Neill 1987
Bradley-Moen (35LA624)	2340 B.C.	R.D. Cheatham, personal communication 1984
Luckiamute Hearth	3300 B.C.	Reckendorf and Parsons 1966
Ralston (35LA625)	4575 B.C.	R.D. Cheatham, personal communication 1984
Hannavan Creek (35LA647)	5800, 4880 B.C.	Cheatham 1984; R.D. Cheatham, personal communication, 1984
Lebanon	Paleo-Indian (?)	Cressman and Laughlin 1941
Templeton	Paleo-Indian (?)	Cressman 1947

that it indicates use of the site at that early time. The levels above the ash produced a larger, though still small, sample of cultural debris that included willow-leaf-shaped, large side-notched, large corner-notched, small corner-notched, and small side-notched projectile points. These styles seem to represent a continuous, though perhaps not intensive, use of the site from 5000 B.C. to the contact period. That the terminal occupation of the site is so recent is indicated by art on the rockshelter wall that includes representation of a horse and rider. Other cultural debris produced by the site includes a variety of unifacially and bifacially flaked stone tools, manos, a pestle, a mortar, an olivella shell bead, and an assemblage of faunal remains dominated by the bones of deer. Artifacts from the site and its location indicate use as a hunting and gathering camp.

The dated cultural record from the Willamette River drainage area is considerably older than that of the Lower Columbia area, with some of the oldest documented sites in the Cascades foothills. The oldest bottomland site is the Hannavan Creek site west of Eugene with dates of 5800 and 4880 B.C. on charred camas bulbs from an oven feature. These early dates on a camas oven are a surprising development in the context of previous reconstructions of Willamette Valley prehistory. The next oldest site from a bottomland setting is the Ralston site, not from the Willamette Valley proper but from a tributary valley on Spencer Creek southwest of Eugene, with a radiocarbon date of 4575 B.C. from a fire hearth and rock cluster buried in the creek bank. No food remains were recovered (Richard D. Cheatham, personal communication 1984). The Flanagan site, with dates of 3800 and 3620 B.C. from the lowest levels (Beckham, Minor, and Toepel 1981:136), contained low densities of flaked stone tools, suggesting that the location was used as a task-specific hunting camp (Toepel and Minor 1980:40).

The next earliest dated site in the lowland portions of the Willamette Valley is the Luckiamute Hearth site (Reckendorf and Parsons 1966). The hearth, in a pit 80 centimeters wide and 41 centimeters deep, included five charred acorns and was radiocarbon-dated at 3300 B.C. It seems clear that by 3300 B.C. the collection and processing of acorns was a part of the aboriginal economy.

The Long Tom site has yielded radiocarbon dates of 1930 and 2160 B.C. from a thick oven feature buried in alluvium. Though the site was almost devoid of flaked stone tools, it produced a charred acorn and two unidentified fruits, suggesting that the site represents the procurement and processing of plant foods.

Nearly as old but apparently different in function are the cultural deposits investigated at Hager's Grove in the city of Salem (Pettigrew 1980), where the earliest dates from the two excavated sites are 1850 and 1790 B.C. The earliest deposits at Hager's Grove give no evidence of the use of camas, while oven features dated about 900 B.C. suggest that it was in use by that time. Projectile points of about 1800 B.C. appear to have been almost exclusively willow-leaf-shaped in the northern Willamette Valley. After that time, perhaps by 900 B.C., broad-necked corner-notched points became established, though leaf-shaped points continued in lesser proportions.

At the Flanagan site an earth oven with charred camas bulbs was radiocarbon-dated to 1280 B.C. Aside from the much earlier dates from the Hannavan Creek site, this is the earliest date for the use of camas in the Willamette Valley.

The Flanagan site is typical of those excavated in that it is a mounded bottomland site of limited areal extent, occupied mostly within the last 3,000 years. A bottomland site that differs, in its greater areal extent and lack of a mound, is the Hurd site (White 1975), which has produced the only possible house feature—a circular pit house—found in the Willamette Basin. The only reported professional excavations of substantial size on the bottomland of the northern Willamette Valley are those from Hager's Grove (Pettigrew 1980). Other Willamette Valley sites are listed by White (1975a), Minor et al. (1980), and Beckham, Minor, and Toepel (1981).

Development of the Historic Pattern

Archeological evidence from the Willamette Valley sug-

Table 3. Selected Sites in the Cascades Foothills

Site	Date or Stage	Source
Rigdon's Horse Pasture Cave (35LA39)	500 B.C., A.D. 1800	Baxter et al. 1983
Baby Rock Shelter (35LA53)	Early, Middle, Late Archaic, Historic	Olsen 1975
35LA574	Late Archaic	Baxter 1983
35LA573	Late Archaic (?)	Baxter 1983
Indian Ridge	Middle, Late Archaic (?)	Henn 1975
35LA33 (Fall Creek)	Middle, Late Archaic (?)	D.L. Cole 1968
Buck Creek (35LA297)	Middle, Late Archaic	Baxter 1984
35LA529	Middle, Late Archaic	Baxter 1983
35LA528	Middle, Late Archaic	Baxter 1983
Tidbits (35LIN100)	Middle Archaic	Minor and Toepel 1982a
35LA599	Middle Archaic	Baxter 1983
Sardine Confluence (35LA539)	Middle Archaic	Connolly and Baxter 1983
Cascadia Cave (35LIN11)	Early, Middle, Late (?) Archaic	Newman 1966

gests that the basic economic pattern of life documented for the historic Kalapuya, including the use of camas, was in place at least as early as 1280 B.C., though collection and cooking of camas is apparently documented 4,000 years before that. At least in the southern valley, sites dating since 1000 B.C. are frequent and scattered throughout the bottomland, evidencing a dispersed settlement pattern in which small family groups used one or more base camps throughout the growing season to take advantage of food resources that were available in particular zones at particular times of the year. The excavated bottomland sites of this period show a diversity of tools and features to indicate a great variety of economic activities, the most important of which were the collection and processing of vegetable foods, mostly camas (camas bulbs, earth ovens, mortars and pestles), and the hunting of birds and mammals (projectile points, faunal remains).

The cooking activities, and perhaps other kinds of activities as well, at these sites included the frequent digging of pits. This pit-digging, combined with the very diverse nature of the aboriginal activities, has made these sites difficult to interpret because of the churned nature of the cultural deposits and the consequent loss of the original context of the cultural items. Most valley bottom sites display a single dark culture-bearing stratum with no natural internal subdivisions, the only record of an average of about 2,000 years of intensive human activity. Therefore, the prehistory of the Willamette Valley over the past 3,000 years is very imperfectly understood, despite the significant number of sites excavated and reported for the period.

Changes in projectile point styles in the Willamette Valley followed the basic pattern described for the Lower Columbia Valley (Pettigrew 1981), with some differences. Broad-necked corner-notched points were common by 900 B.C., though willow-leaf-shaped points persisted. The bow and arrow apparently was introduced between about 500 and 100 B.C., signaled by the appearance of small, narrow-necked points. Small, side-notched points arrived some time after A.D. 1250, becoming more frequent shortly before contact. A form not known on the Lower Columbia, the "Christmas tree" style (small, triangular, unstemmed, with deep serrations), appears only in the southern Willamette Valley perhaps around 500 B.C., persisting about 1,000 years.

While the subsistence basis of Willamette Valley culture apparently remained fairly constant over the last 3,000 years, there is evidence that in protohistoric time some groups were heavily oriented to accumulation of wealth, a trait presumably derived from the cultures of the Lower Columbia and Lower Klamath rivers. Grave goods from burials found in the Fanning (Murdy and Wentz 1975) and Fuller (Woodward, Murdy, and Young 1975) mounds in the Yamhill River valley include: waisted

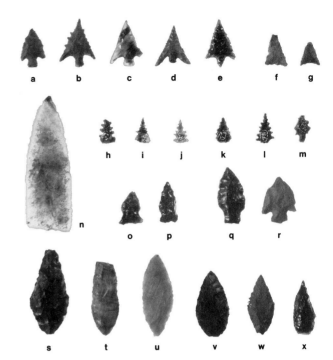

U. of Oreg., Oreg. State Mus. of Anthr., Eugene.
Fig. 7. Willamette Basin projectile points: a-e, narrow-necked, corner-notched projectile points (Late Archaic); f-g, triangular, concave-base projectile points (Late Archaic); h-m, "Christmas tree" projectile points (Middle and Late Archaic); n, lanceolate biface (possibly Early or Middle Archaic); o-p, small side-notched projectile points (Late Archaic); q-r, broad-necked projectile points (Middle Archaic); s-x, foliate projectile points (Early and Middle Archaic). Length of n, 7.2 cm; rest to same scale.

obsidian ceremonial knives, whalebone clubs, ear spools, olivella and glycymeris shell beads, and brass, copper, and glass trinkets. The extent of the accumulation of such wealth in the Willamette Valley is unknown; the only occurrences of something similar in the southern portion of the valley are a copper bead and dentalium shells from a burial at the Shedd Mounds on the Calapooia River (White 1975a:79–83).

The presence of early historic trade items in Willamette Valley sites is almost exclusively limited to the northern half of the area, suggesting that the southern half was somewhat insulated from Euro-American influences. The cultural distinction between the northern and southern halves of the valley is suggested by Beckham, Minor, and Toepel (1981:170) to have a time-depth of about 2,000 years.

Cascade Foothills

Cultural adaptation in the western Cascades Mountains seems not to have changed basically since about 8000 B.C. A primary dependence on hunting apparently persisted. The few sites there (table 3) have all yielded assemblages and have been located in places suggesting a hunting emphasis. Though no sites that may be winter encampments or villages in low-elevation valleys have been

528

investigated, the nature of the lithic debris at known sites is different enough from Willamette Valley bottomland sites to support the notion of a separate Cascades cultural province (D.L. Cole 1968; Grayson 1975; Baxter et al. 1983).

Cultural change in the Cascades Mountains area appears to have been only stylistic, with projectile point styles changing in much the same way as in adjacent areas. Early willow-leaf and large side-notched forms occur at Cascadia Cave in the period around and just after 6000 B.C. (Newman 1966), followed by broad-necked, corner-notched styles that were in vogue by 500 B.C. at Rigdon's Horse Pasture Cave (Baxter et al. 1983). As elsewhere in the region, the bow and arrow was introduced about 2,000 years ago, when corner-notched points became narrow-necked. The most popular style at contact appears to have been the small side-notched point (often called Desert Side-notched though it is found outside the Great Basin), as documented by its predominance at Rigdon's Horse Pasture Cave in the upper levels.

Conclusion

Cultural adaptation and development followed different courses in the Lower Columbia and Willamette regions. Presumably descended from a common cultural ancestor, cultures diverged most likely as a result of differing economic opportunities. Efficient utilization of the natural environment for human ends meant riverside nucleation and intensification of fishing activities to take advantage of the immense salmon runs in the Lower Columbia area, while the abundant but more dispersed resources of the Willamette Basin discouraged nucleation and encouraged a dispersed pattern of base camps or small villages and a more diverse array of primary economic activities. The cultural and economic distinctiveness of the two areas had already developed by the time periods represented by the earliest well-dated sites, possibly 5800 B.C. for the Willamette Valley and 1560 B.C. for the Lower Columbia Valley.

Kwalhioqua and Clatskanie

MICHAEL E. KRAUSS

The Kwalhioqua (‚kwäl(h)ē‘ōkwə) of southwestern Washington and the Clatskanie ('klătskə‚nī) of northwestern Oregon spoke a language, Kwalhioqua-Clatskanie, belonging to the Athapaskan family.*

The vocabulary attested for Kwalhioqua and Clatskanie is sufficient to show that they were a single language and shows no consistent differences between the two. Curtis (1907–1930, 9:153) and Teit (in Boas and Goddard 1924:40) mention dialect differences between Willapa and Suwal speech. According to a tradition recorded by Gibbs (1877:171), Curtis (1907–1930, 9:154), and Teit (in Boas and Goddard 1924:40), the Clatskanie once lived on the Skookumchuck River but migrated across the Columbia where the hunting was better. If this tradition is correct, Suwal speech may have been as close or closer to Clatskanie than it was to Willapa.

Territory and Environment

Early in the nineteenth century the Kwalhioqua occupied an area northeast of the Columbia estuary centered in the Willapa Hills (fig. 1). They consisted of two groups, the Willapa ('wĭləpə) and the Suwal (sə'wäl). Willapa included the Willapa River drainage above the site of Raymond; below this the Willapa went seasonally, and some may have lived there with the Lower Chehalis and Chinook (Curtis 1907–1930, 9:173; Teit in Boas and Goddard 1924). The Suwal group are said (Curtis 1907–1930, 9: 173) to have occupied the drainage of the Chehalis River above the site of Centralia, but Upper Chehalis and even groups of mixed Upper Chehalis and Cowlitz have also been reported for the sites of the towns of Chehalis, Boistfort, and Pe Ell (fig. 1).

The Clatskanie lived south of the Columbia. Their territory included the extensive Upper Nehalem drainage and also the headwaters of the Klaskanine and Clatskanie rivers. At least at times they also occupied the shore of the Columbia around the mouth of the Clatskanie River, perhaps sharing it with Chinookans, and they may have seasonally visited the Portland Basin at Scappoose Creek.

Except for the foothold the Clatskanie may have had

on the Columbia, both they and the Kwalhioqua lived up away from this main salmon stream of the region in upland valleys where there were fewer salmon runs. Their territories were largely dense forest, but there were also many small prairies (Suckley and Cooper 1860:21 describe those in the upper Willapa valley), where there were abundant deer and elk as well as edible roots and berries.

External Relations

Both groups occasionally intermarried with their Chinookan neighbors and probably with Salishans. Some Clatskanies accused of killing three White men at Fort George (Astoria) in 1811 had relatives among the Indians there, presumably Clatsop or Chinook (Ross 1956:32, 133). Charles Cultee, the principal source for knowledge of the Chinook and Cathlamet languages, had a Kwalhioqua grandfather and Clatsop grandmother (Boas 1901:5). This Kwalhioqua-Clatsop marriage must have been made early in the nineteenth century. The existence of mixed Athapaskan and Salishan villages in the Willapa and Chehalis drainages also implies intermarriage.

Differences in resources between upland and riverine environments promoted trade. In 1814 Alexander Henry (Coues 1897,2:794) saw a village of "shoshones" (that is, inlanders, and so probably Clatskanie) at the mouth of what was probably the Clatskanie River and reported that they "subsist upon flesh and roots, which they barter with the natives at Oak Point [Skilloots] for salmon, etc." But trade did not preclude conflict. The Clatskanie who killed the Whites at Fort George also killed some people at Oak Point (Ross 1956:133).

Hale (1846:204) and Wickersham (1899:372) reported contact and even intermarriage between the Clatskanie and the Upper Umpqua. Hale's map (1846: between pp. 196 and 197) shows Clatskanie and Upper Umpqua territories in contact through the Coast Range, but no later work supports this contiguity, which may have been simply conjectured upon the discovery that both peoples spoke Athapaskan languages.

Culture

From the linguistic and historical sources only a few

*Kwalhioqua-Clatskanie became extinct before a phonemic analysis could be made.

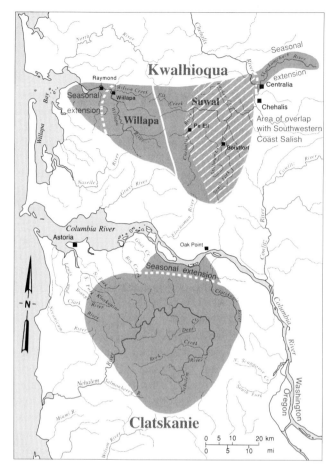

Fig. 1. Early 19th-century territory of the Kwalhioqua and Clatskanie. Cowlitz shared some of the territory of the Suwal.

specific observations can be made about Kwalhioqua-Clatskanie culture. It was a hunting and gathering way of life, centering in the uplands, but seasonally perhaps included salmon fishing at the lower reaches of the Willapa and Clatskanie rivers. The Kwalhioqua and Clatskanie "subsisted on game, berries, and roots" (Hale 1846:204). According to Teit (1910; Boas and Goddard 1924:40), these Indians constructed lodges of split cedar poles, covered with bark, furnished with rush mats; their canoes were the short-nose kind only; they fished with spears, weirs, and traps with drop; they made only soft baskets, not the coiled type, which was recently learned from the Cowlitz.

The system of kinship terms is typically Athapaskan as far as can be determined; the cousin terms are not attested. As so little is specifically documented about their culture, the rest can only be inferred from the nature of their physical and cultural environment and from the general Athapaskan way of life they brought with them from the north.

In a Kwalhioqua myth told by Cultee (Boas 1901: 187–195), the hero trains for power, is rewarded with dentalia, which he distributes to his people; he has his Thunderbird helper bring a whale (not recognized by some of his prairie people), which he uses for a potlatch; and he becomes a great chief. This myth suggests that to some extent the Kwalhioqua may have shared Northwest Coast values.

History

Throughout what little is recorded of Kwalhioqua-Clatskanie history, relations with their Indian neighbors and with Europeans were beset with conflict. Kwalhioqua are estimated at a population of 200 for 1780 (Mooney 1928:15, 17) or 400 (Taylor 1963:162–163). Accounts of bloody conflict with Europeans began immediately with the establishment of Astoria in 1811 (Ross 1956:133). Simpson (1931:170) in 1825 estimated Clatskanie at 175, already perhaps not low, as the Clatskanie seem to have undergone somewhat earlier and more intense European contact than the Kwalhioqua, and swifter decline. Both were no doubt severely weakened also by the epidemics that devastated the area in the 1830s (Taylor and Hoaglin 1962; Taylor 1963). Hale (1846:204), noting in 1841 that the Clatskanie and Kwalhioqua "neither of them comprising more than a hundred individuals ... are somewhat more bold and hardy than the tribes on the river and coast, and, at the same time, more wild and savage," is the last to mention them as viable entities.

Lee and Frost (1844:99) already called the Clatskanie "very nearly extinct." On August 9, 1851, at Tansy Point, Oregon, Anson Dart (ARCIA 1851:214) reported that "two small remnants of bands, called the Wheelappers and Quillequaquas, have ceded to the United States a considerable tract of country ... They number thirteen." On that day there the Clatskanie also signed such a treaty, according them a few hundred dollars annually in goods and cash (Dart 1851, 1851a; Coan 1921:58–86). This group consisted of eight adults (Coan 1921:73). That none of the Indian signatories' names appears to be Athapaskan may reflect either on naming customs by then or on the nature of the treaties, which were never ratified. Gibbs (1855:428) wrote that the Kwalhioqua "may be considered as extinct, a few women only remaining, and those intermarried with the Chinooks and Chihalis," but in 1856, while obtaining a vocabulary (190 items), Gibbs (1877:171) found that "there are yet, it appears, three or four families living on the heads of the Tsihalis River above the forks." As for the Clatskanie, Alexander Caulfield Anderson (1854–1855, 1876) collected a vocabulary in 1854 or 1855 from a part-Clatskanie whom he believed to be the last speaker of the language. The Indian agent W.W. Raymond reported for 1857 that the Clatskanie population was eight (ARCIA 1858:354).

After that these people seem virtually to disappear from recorded history, except as individuals found by ethnographer-linguists searching for surviving speakers of the language from 1890 on (Rohner 1969:120; Boas

1895b:588–592). In 1898 James Wickersham found at Boistfort, Washington, two speakers of Kwalhioqua and also met Maria Harris, the last of the Clatskanie (Wickersham 1898, 1899:371–374). In 1910 Curtis (1907–1930, 9:153–154, 173, 199–200) recorded a Kwalhioqua vocabulary and information on place-names, Teit (1910, 1910a) recorded a Kwalhioqua vocabulary and some ethnographic information (Boas and Goddard 1924), and Frachtenberg (1910a) got a Kwalhioqua vocabulary. Harrington's Kwalhioqua material is largely spurious (Stirling 1943:50–51; Mills 1981, 1:47–54) and can be used only with great caution. Krauss (1963–1988) has collated and analyzed the linguistic material.

Synonymy

The Kwalhioqua and Clatskanie are both known by borrowings of their Chinookan names; there is no record of what they called themselves. Kwalhioqua, also Qualiogua (Hale 1846:198; Hodge 1907–1910, 1:746), Quillequaqua (ARCIA 1851:214), and Qualioqua (Gibbs 1855:428), is from Chinook *tkᵂlxiugᵂáikš* (Michael Silverstein, communication to editors 1987). A Salishan name for the Kwalhioqua, or perhaps only the Suwal, is (Upper Chehalis, Cowlitz) *q̓ᵂaláwc* (M. Dale Kinkade, communication to editors 1987); this corresponds to *nq̓uláwas*, the Chinook name of a Kwalhioqua village (Boas in Hodge 1907–1910, 2:745–746, phonemicized).

Clatskanie, also Tlatskanai (Hale 1846:204; Hodge 1907–1910, 2:763; vol. 6:67–68), is from Chinookan *ɬáck̓ani* 'those of the region of small oaks' (Michael Silverstein, communication to editors 1987). Silas Smith (Lyman 1900:322) identified the name with a place in the Nehalem Valley; it could be reached by ascending either the Klaskanine River or the Clatskanie, and so the early Whites came to call both rivers by versions of the name. Borrowings of this name in other Indian languages include Upper Chehalis *ɬácqənəyu* (Harrington 1942a, phonemicized; M. Dale Kinkade, communication to editors 1987), Tillamook *tɬécqnáyu* (Jacobs 1933a), and Tualatin Kalapuya *aɬatsx̣nei* (Jacobs 1945:188). The Lower Chehalis name for the language of the Clatskanie was *scə́ləhə́t* (Harrington 1942a:17,836, phonemicized; M. Dale Kinkade, communication to editors 1987).

The name of the Willapa, also Willopah (Gibbs 1855:428) and Wheelappers (ARCIA 1851:214), was based on that of their principal village, on the site of the town of Willapa; they called themselves *wəlá·pəx̣yú* (Curtis 1907–1930, 9:153; Harrington 1942a, normalized). The same name was used for a Chinookan (Hodge 1907–1910, 2:955–956) or more likely Salishan group on the lower course of the Willapa River. A similar name is used in Salishan and other neighboring Indian languages, but the direction of the diffusion is uncertain: Satsop and Oakville Upper Chehalis *ʔuxᵂílapš*, Cowlitz and Tenino Upper Chehalis *ʔuxᵂílapx* (M. Dale Kinkade, communication to editors 1987), Chinook *xᵂilápax̣* (Boas 1901:5, phonemicized), Kalapuya *ówilapsh* (Gatschet in Hodge 1907–1910, 2:955–956).

The name of the Suwal is from Cowlitz and Upper Chehalis *swál* (Harrington 1942a; Curtis 1907–1930, 9:153, both phonemicized; M. Dale Kinkade, communication to editors 1987); these people were also called (Oakville Upper Chehalis, Lower Chehalis, Quinault) *swaláwmš*, (Cowlitz) *swəláwmx* (M. Dale Kinkade, communication to editors 1987).

Coues (1893, 3:915, 931) identified with Clatskanie the name Clackstar, given by Lewis and Clark for a village on Scappoose Creek (in the Portland Basin), whose inhabitants traded with the Tillamook. The name is Chinookan *ɬáʔaqštaq* 'roundheads' (Michael Silverstein, communication to editors 1987). The identity of the Clackstar is not proved, and they might have been Kalapuyans.

Sources

There is no good primary ethnographic description of the Kwalhioqua and Clatskanie. The available data have been presented in the sources cited in the text and in Spier (1936), Berreman (1937), J. Hazeltine (1956), and Ruby and Brown (1986). More is known about their language, thanks to the vocabularies compiled by Hale (1846), Anderson (1854–1855), and Gibbs (1877), discussed by Krauss (1973:917–919, 1979:869–870) and Krauss and Leer (1981:55–58); less substantive are Wickersham (1898, 1899), Teit (1910, 1910a; in Boas and Goddard 1924), Frachtenberg (1910a), and Curtis (1907–1930, 9). Other published linguistic sources include Krauss (1973, 1979) and Krauss and Leer (1981).

Chinookans of the Lower Columbia

MICHAEL SILVERSTEIN

Language and Territory

The name Chinookan (chĭ'nōōkən) refers to the people living on the Pacific shore from Willapa Bay to Tillamook Head, along both banks of the Columbia River from its mouth to a short distance above The Dalles, on the Willamette River to its falls, and on the Clackamas River, who spoke languages of the Chinookan family. This family consisted of two quite distinct branches, Lower Chinookan (or Chinook proper) and Upper Chinookan, a dialect chain of languages including Cathlamet, Multnomah, and Kiksht.* Kiksht (kĭkšt) was spoken by the Clackamas, treated here, and by groups farther upriver in the Plateau. The Chinookans treated here are those who lived from the coast to a point above the Willamette River. Those living from the Cascades eastward are treated in volume 12. When referring to people the term Chinook (chĭ'nōōk, sometimes shĭ'nōōk) will be used in its historic sense, for the Chinookans on the north shore of the mouth of the Columbia only.

It is likely that the Chinookan linguistic family as a whole is ultimately an independent branch of Sapir's (1929) Penutian phylum of languages (Hymes 1957, 1964; Silverstein 1965, 1973). The areal connections to Salishan languages of the coast are very strong and structurally important (Silverstein 1974). Boas (1911a) outlined Chinookan grammar. The Chinookan languages are not to be confused with Chinook Jargon, frequently referred to as Chinook or Oregon Trade Language, a trade lingua franca used on the Northwest Coast.

Divisions

Several divisions, both cultural-geographical and linguistic, can be distinguished for the early nineteenth century (fig. 1).

Lower Chinookans

On Willapa (formerly Shoalwater) Bay the Shoalwater Chinook, who spoke Chinook proper, lived in several permanent or winter villages. Several temporary camps, for seasonal activities such as gathering clams, were also maintained. To the north and east were Salishan-speaking Lower Chehalis, and to the east up the Willapa River were the Athapaskan-speaking Kwalhioqua. Whether or not the Chinookans actually had longstanding permanent settlements north of the Nemah River in the earliest period is a much disputed point (Curtis 1907–1930, 9:153; Spier 1936:29–31; Ray 1938:36). Evidence indicates that in this region they were successful newcomers, intermarrying with prior residents and moving the line of Chinookan-affiliated villages northward, at a late date.

On the north bank of the Columbia, from Cape Disappointment to Grays Bay, were villages associated with the principal lower-river Chinook village on Baker Bay. These people, the Chinook of the early writers, also spoke Chinook proper, and it is in fact not clear to what extent they should be distinguished, culturally or politically, from the Shoalwater Chinook.

On the south bank of the Columbia, from Youngs Bay to Point Adams, and southward along the coastal plains to Tillamook Head, were villages of the Clatsop ('klătsəp), who must also have spoken Chinook proper (Boas 1894:5). To the south of the Clatsop, on the Pacific coast south of Tillamook Head, lived the Nehalem Tillamooks, a Salishan-speaking group with strong ties to the Chinookans.

Cathlamet

Up the Columbia, the next dialect cluster of villages, from about Grays Bay to Kalama on the present Washington side, from east of Tongue Point to perhaps Rainier on the

---

*The phonemes of Chinook proper, Cathlamet, and Kiksht are as follows: (voiceless stops and affricates) p, t, ƛ, c, č, k, kʷ, q, qʷ, ʔ; (voiced stops and affricates) b, d, g, gʷ, ġ, ġʷ; (glottalized stops and affricates) ṗ, ṭ, ƛ̓, ċ, č̓, k̓, k̓ʷ, q̓, q̓ʷ; (voiceless continuants) ł, s, š, x, xʷ, x̣, x̣ʷ; (voiced continuants) l, m, n, w, y; (vowels) a, i, u; stress (v́).

The majority of Chinookan self-designations are possessive constructions based on place-names or other terms with geographical reference. These expressions have a prefix complex containing g- 'those who', a mark of the gender of the stem (-i-, -a-, or -it-), and a mark of the possessor (-łá- 'their'). There is sometimes a difference of form in the names of groups in the historical records depending on whether the name used was from the possessive tribal name or the basic place-name (often prefixed with n- and the gender marker or with wá-); for example, names with the feminine -a- after the first consonant might have variants reflecting initial gałá- versus wá-, or between gałá- and ná-. In upriver names especially, the prefix complex frequently does not appear in the traditional English version.

533

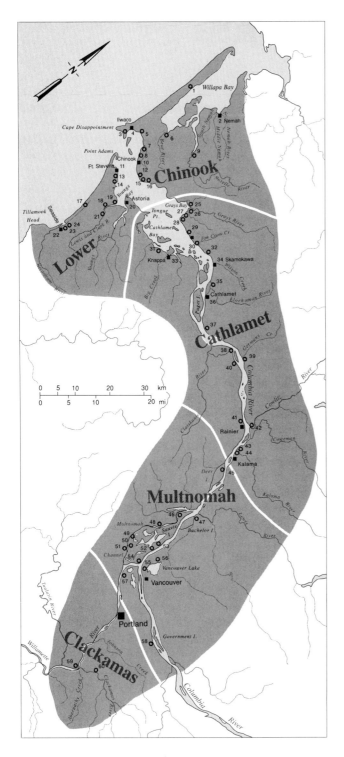

Fig. 1. Chinookan divisions and villages reported, 1792–1850 (Vancouver 1801; Thwaites 1904–1905; Landerholm 1956; Wilkes 1845; Lyman 1900; Minto 1900; Boas 1894, 1901; Curtis 1907–1930; Ray 1938; Strong 1959; and Hodge 1907–1910). Not all villages were occupied at one time. Lower Chinook (Lower River, Shoalwater, Clatsop): 1, *tiápšuyi* 'grassy place'; 2, *nímaxʷ*; 3, *walmĺm* 'rotten wood'; 4, *wíitčutk* 'road coming down'; 5, *wálxat*; 6, *nuʔxʷasʔnł* 'blackberry town'; 7, *qʷacámc*; 8, *waplúcin*; 9, *gitłálilam* 'those of the lake town'; 10, *łáqał* 'their creek'; 11, *niákʰilaki* 'pounded salmon place'; 12, *ucmuyáqxan* 'snails'; 13, *kunupí*; 14, *naiáaqsta* 'at the head'; 15, *qíq̓ayaqilxam* 'middle town'; 16, *qailčíak*; 17, *niákʰiwanqi* 'where there is killing'; 18, Fort Clatsop village; 19, *niʔtl*; 20, *nuʔsmaʔspu;* 21, *sqipanáwunx*; 22, *nakułát*; 23, *nikánikm*; 24, *niakákʷsi* 'where the little pines are'. Cathlamet (Cathlamet, Wakaikam, Qaniak, Skilloots): 25, *kiláwiyuks* 'kingfishers'; 26, *tiaksami* 'where small horns are'; 27, *níqilcł* where it goes down into'; 28, *nakʰáλqʷi*; 29, Waikaikum; 30, *kʷícakasnai*; 31, "Kath-la-mat" Cathlamet main village; 32, *wakatáma*; 33, "Tle-las-qua"; 34, *čaxlkłílxam* 'winter town'; 35, *gałiášgnmaxix* 'those of the place of cedar trees'; 36, *ilóxumin*; 37, *gałámat*; 38, *qániak*; 39, *łá-qałala*; 40, *tiáq̓učui* 'place of bones'; 41, Wiltkwilluk; 42, *qašiamišti* 'those of the place of the beak'; 43, Tlakalama, Kalama village; 44, "Cath la haws". Multnomah: 45, name not recorded; 46, "Clan-nar-min-a-mon"; 47, *gałápuλx* 'those of Lewis River'; 48, *gałáq̓map* 'those of the mound'; 49, "Clak-in-nar-ta"; 50, *gałanakʷaix* 'those of Nakwaix'; 51, "Cath-la-com-mah-cup"; 52, Multnomah; 53, "Clanaquah"; 54, *wáksin* 'dam'; 55, *gałákanasisi* 'those of butterball ducks'; 56, "Shoto"; 57, *nimáłxʷinix*; 58, *ničáqʷli* 'stand of pines'. Clackamas (Clawiwalla, Clackamas): 59, *wálamt*; 60, *niq̓ímašix*.

tribes or nations. They were apparently a series of local groups of one or two villages. In Chinookan terms, there seems not to have been an overall name. In the upriver portion of this string of villages, the Clatskanies and the Lower Cowlitz, who where intermarried with Chinookans (Curtis 1907–1930, 9:172), had settlements on the rivers of those names.

Multnomah

A rather dense stretch of villages was found about the region from the mouth of the Lewis River to Government Island, which includes the Multnomah Channel and Sauvie (Wapato) Island, and the mouth of the Willamette River. These groups must have spoken an Upper Chinookan dialect intermediate between Cathlamet and Clackamas. They include the Cathlapotle, just above Lewis River, the "Shoto" of Lewis and Clark (Thwaites 1904–1905, 4:219) at Lake Vancouver, the Multnomah (məlt'nōmə) of Sauvie Island, together with several smaller groups at other sites on the lower Willamette, and Lewis and Clark's "Nechaco-lee" (Thwaites 1904–1905, 4:236), the easternmost non-Cascades village on the Columbia.

Clackamas

Finally, on the eastern bank of the Willamette near the falls were the Clawiwalla at a site called *wálamt* opposite Oregon City, and extensively along the Clackamas River were the main body of Clackamas ('klǎkəməs), whose dialect is well-documented for the reservation period but whose original village names are unknown. The Clacka-

Oregon side, can all be associated with Cathlamet (kăθ'lămət) speech, named from residents of a village first located by Meriwether Lewis and William Clark (Thwaites 1904–1905, 3:250–252) on the south bank about 10 miles above Tongue Point at Cathlamet Head. Of these peoples, those at Wakaikam in the Pillar Rock area, those at Qaniak just east of Oak Point, and the Skilloots (Lewis and Clark in Thwaites 1904–1905, 3:196, 4:205–207), as well as the Cathlamet, have frequently been referred to as

mas had rather close ties to the other Kiksht speakers from below the Cascades to the Wasco-Wishram.

There was frequent intermarriage with people of the lower Cascades groups; Lewis and Clark even record (Thwaites 1904–1905, 4:259, 261) that the Watlala (*watála*) village of Cascades Chinookans just below Beacon Rock moved to the Willamette Falls for salmon fishing in April. Nevertheless, the Clackamas must have themselves maintained their distinctness from the *sáxlatkš* 'those upriver', Lewis and Clark's Shahalas.

History

The Chinookans, or more particularly the lower-river Chinooks, are first mentioned by Robert Gray and John Boit, captain and mate of the ship *Columbia*, on May 18, 1792 (Greenhow 1845:435; Boit 1921:311), and again on October 21 of the same year by George Vancouver (1801, 3:86–87), whose lieutenant explored the Columbia beyond the Willamette mouth. Lewis and Clark, who descended the river in the autumn of 1805 and wintered at Youngs Bay, give the first extensive account of the place- and tribal names of the riverine area, as well as an outline especially of their material culture, which are confirmed in large part by the fur traders, beginning with Gabriel Franchère, Alexander Ross, Ross Cox, and Alexander Henry in the early period of Astoria, 1811–1814. Before large-scale immigration of Euro-Americans to the Columbia and Willamette regions, contact led principally to incorporating the newcomers into a prior system of trade, re-oriented in part from the native concerns with river products for their own use to facilitating European access to furs. Cohabitation of traders with Chinookan women, both promiscuously and more permanently, and gradual acquisition by Chinookans of more manufactured trade items both had long-term effects.

Euro-Americans, who first entered the Chinookans' economic sphere by maritime trading visits for beaver, sea otter, fox, and other furs, especially for dressed hide garments (traded for furs up north) (Bishop 1967:128; D. Jackson 1978, 2:541), then moved in permanently at Astoria and later at Fort Vancouver. They brought with them goods that, by both their novelty and utility as functional alternatives to those of aboriginal provenance, were sought after and could command high prices.

The European trade items that the Chinookans received were listed by Lewis and Clark as: guns (principally old British or American muskets), powder, balls, and shot; copper and brass kettles; brass teakettles and coffee pots; two-point and three-point blankets; coarse scarlet and blue cloth; plates and strips of sheet copper and brass; large brass wire, knives, beads, and tobacco, with fishhooks, buttons, and some other small articles; and a considerable quantity of sailors' clothes—hats, coats, trousers, and shirts (Thwaites 1904–1905, 3:328).

The acquisition of these items not only accumulated prestige but also gave the downriver groups greater economic independence vis-à-vis the upriver groups in the long trade chains, by freeing them from dependence on items no longer essential. It is no wonder that groups in closest contact with the Astorians, especially the Chinooks under Chief Concomly, sought to prevent or frustrate direct contact of the Whites with their upriver and inland rivals (Ross 1849:76–78).

The settlers, missionaries, and explorers of the period 1830–1855 give an account of the Chinookans that reflects the population decline experienced by these people from smallpox, measles, malaria, and other diseases (Boyd 1985). Most of the earlier sites were abandoned, or with reduced, consolidated populations, particularly the Multnomah and Clackamas Chinookans, who were thoroughly ravaged. Survivors adapted as best they could to the changed conditions, where fur trade was no longer the concern of the larger Euro-American population. By the 1850s, the Multnomah and Clackamas survivors, like their upriver counterparts, were being negotiated onto reservations in exchange for residual fishing rights, many of the treaties for which were never ratified by the United States Senate. The earliest extensive accounts of the Shoalwater Chinook date from late in this period as well, when the oyster and fishing industry was having great consolidating effects on residence and economic patterns, and by which time the Chinookans about Willapa Bay, ancestrally from several Lower Chinook divisions, were heavily intermarried with the Lower Chehalis and the survivors of the Shoalwater Salish. The Chehalis language was adopted fully by the beginning of the twentieth century, Chinook proper passing essentially out of use.

By the very late nineteenth century, Chinookan society as seen by Lewis and Clark was already a memory in most external respects. By 1900 the remnants of the Shoalwater Chinook and the Chinook proper, and, so far as is known, also the lowermost Cathlamet-speaking tribes, had merged residentially and culturally with the remaining Willapa Bay Salishans; many Clatsop had merged with the Tillamooks, adopting their language. They formed an economic fringe in the local industries. Some Multnomah and Clackamas lived on the Grand Ronde Reservation, Oregon, and in the towns of the lower Willamette Valley, and were extensively intermarried with Kalapuya and Molala survivors.

In 1979 the Tchinouk Indians of Klamath Falls, Oregon, and the Chinook Indian Tribe of Chinook, Washington, who both claimed descent from Chinookan signers of the unratified 1851 treaty, independently petitioned the Bureau of Indian Affairs for federal acknowledgment. The former were denied acknowledgment in March 1986, while the latter group's petition was pending in 1988.

Culture

The account here aims to describe the Chinookans in the first half of the nineteenth century.

Chinookan villages and clusters of villages, which may be called tribes, were oriented toward fishing and root-and-berry gathering, with extensive economic and political ties among villages, maintained by exchange of goods and alliance through wives. It appears that these exchanges and alliances were the mechanism, at least among the upper class, for the personal acquisition of wealth in goods and slaves, and prestige. As in the other Northwest Coast societies, social importance accrued to those who not only possessed but also knew how to display the stuff of opulence—food, clothing, high-ranked spouses, slaves, canoes. Before the major epidemics, 1830–1840, with their rapid effects on the social order, Chinookans held economic hegemony on the Columbia and lower Willamette rivers.

Subsistence

The products of fishing and hunting, as well as roots, shoots, and berries, were enjoyed by all the local groups, though the flora and fauna varied over the area. Fishing areas, with many sites, were traditionally controlled by a given group, and they would repair there for the peak fishing seasons. There were different fishing places for the spring chinook salmon run and the fall run, usually; a few distinct sturgeon sites are also recorded. The lower river Chinooks moved from the Columbia, where they had been, with Chehalis visitors, by 1840 (Frost in Pipes 1934:55), for the first salmon run, toward Willapa Bay for the second (Lee and Frost 1844:99); Henry (in Coues 1897, 2:867) mentions Tongue Point as their April sturgeon fishery. The Clatsops were on the Columbia bank above the Wakaikam villages for the first salmon run, and south near the coast, at Neacoxie for the second (Lewis and Clark in Thwaites 1904–1905, 4:107–108, 154–155; Henry in Coues 1897, 2:839; Lee and Frost 1844:275; Frost in Pipes 1934:62, 357). The people in the vicinity of Puget Island apparently fished right in their own area, as did those at the junction of the great rivers. The Clackamas moved to the falls of the Willamette for their heaviest fishing in the spring and summer (Henry in Coues 1897, 2:810–811; Wilkes 1845, 4:346), as apparently did some Chinookans of the mouth of the Willamette, and some from the lower Cascades region (Boyd and Hajda 1987).

Hunting territory can be less well defined, making territorial boundaries away from the water difficult to draw; this undoubtedly reflects the Chinookan point of view. Places for gathering roots such as wapato, particularly in the lakes and swamps about the Columbia-Willamette junction, seem to have been freely accessible to many surrounding groups, who traded these products with groups both downriver and upriver.

In general, it is usufruct rights, rather than ownership, that are recognizable for personal geographical resources such as fishing sites, burial rocks and islands, and perhaps hunting land; ownership was reserved for goods and chattel (Ross 1849:88; Swan 1857:166).

● FISHING The great seasonal runs of salmon (five species), sturgeon, steelhead trout, eulachon, and herring provided both fresh fish and stored, smoke-dried food for the winter. The larger fish were taken in nets (fig. 2) (Lewis and Clark in Thwaites 1904–1905, 3:350–351; Henry in Coues 1897, 2:753), particularly seine near the Columbia mouth, and scoop in natural or artificial small channels in the rivers. Sometimes a spear was used, particularly for steelhead. Another technique, employing a detachable gaff hook on a long line, was the common method for taking sturgeon, a greatly prized delicacy (Swan 1857:245–246), which was steamed in an earth oven (Lewis and Clark in Thwaites 1904–1905, 4:131–132) or smoke-dried for later consumption. Dip-net fishing for summer and fall salmon, from stagings built in the spring, became increasingly important farther upriver, where rocky cliffs and eddies near falls made this practicable (Franchère in Thwaites 1904–1907, 6:249; Wilkes 1845, 4:345, 380). Eulachon were taken in scoop nets or with rakes and smoke-dried in great numbers, skewered transversely, for trade upriver (Ross 1849:94–95; Kane 1857:17; Lewis and Clark in Thwaites 1904–1905, 4:102–103; Henry in Coues 1897, 2:820, 832).

An elaborate preparation, requiring removal of the heart, for separate roasting, and lengthwise cutting of the fish for roasting, or breaking the body into pieces for boiling, characterized the first chinook salmon ceremonies (Franchère in Thwaites 1904–1907, 6:335; Ross 1849:97; Lee and Frost 1844:299–300; Frost in Pipes 1934:

Lib. of Congress: Swan 1857:106.
Fig. 2. Netting salmon with beach seines on Baker Bay, Wash., in the Columbia estuary. The nets were made of twine spun of spruce-root fibers or a grass traded from the north. The floats were cedar sticks, and the sinkers were grooved pebbles. The nets varied from 100 to 600 feet long and 7 to 16 feet deep (Swan 1857:104-107). The Lower Chinook may have relied more heavily on seine fishing than any other Northwest Coast people (Berringer 1982:28-29). Engraving after a sketch by James G. Swan, 1852-1855.

162–163; Wilkes 1845, 4:324, 366, 5:119; Swan 1857:107; Ray 1938:110–111). Other ritual preparation was required for chum and coho salmon (Boas 1894:92–101). By 1855 the ceremonies were attentuated.

Salmon roe was dried for later consumption (Lewis and Clark in Thwaites 1904–1905, 4:164), while pounded dried salmon, from as far upriver as The Dalles, was traded and retraded all the way down the river and to Willapa Bay (Lewis and Clark in Thwaites 1904–1905, 3:182, 343, 362) for winter consumption. Bivalves, in particular clams for drying and trading up the Columbia, were a major food collected in Willapa Bay (Swan 1857:85–86).

Whales, when washed up on shore, as well as seals and sea lions, which were speared (Henry in Coues 1897, 2: 857–858; Swan 1857:83–84), provided sources of meat, blubber, and especially oil, obtained by boiling the blubber and skimming. The Shoalwater Chinooks, the Clatsops, and especially their southern neighbors the Tillamooks procured these items, which formed articles of lively trade with the people upriver. This oil, like that of the salmon, was extensively used with dried foods (Lewis and Clark in Thwaites 1904–1905, 3:309, 329, 338; Swan 1857:29–30; Ray 1938:113–115). Porpoises were taken, by spearing, for their flesh (Lewis and Clark in Thwaites 1904–1905, 4:163).

● HUNTING Particularly at times other than the heaviest fishing season of late spring to summer, Chinookans hunted elk, deer, bear, and other large game, for food, and raccoons, squirrels, beavers, rabbits, otters, and other small animals, for food and skins out of which robes were fashioned. By 1805 (Thwaites 1904–1905, 3:346), the people of the lower Columbia had muskets that they could employ for hunting (as well as taking seals); indeed, in 1795 Bishop (1967:118–119) reports these as novelties among the lower river Chinook. Various deadfall and pit traps, snares, spears, and the bow and arrow were the older means of procuring game. Fowl, including ducks, swans, and geese, were eaten and traded (Henry in Coues 1897, 2:756, 765). It is not clear if the Chinookans themselves hunted the mountain sheep, from which was obtained wool used in blankets for dress and horn for bowls and spoons. These blankets were reportedly traded from non-Chinookan interior peoples (Franchère in Thwaites 1904–1907, 6:360).

● GATHERING Among all the berries, spring shoots, and roots that were gathered and eaten (Ray 1938:119–123), the wapato tuber, found no lower than Cathlamet Head but principally upriver on and around Sauvie Island, is most frequently mentioned as a staple and item of trade among the Chinookans (for example, Lewis and Clark in Thwaites 1904–1905, 3:208, 265, 296–297, 338, 4:95, 200). They were loosened from their underwater attachments with the bare feet and collected in very small canoes (Lewis and Clark in Thwaites 1904–1905, 4:217–218).

Also gathered, with the aid of a digging stick (Thwaites 1904–1905, 4:9), were camas, edible thistle, lupine, bracken fern, horsetail, and cattail roots, for which various recipes are known, the basic preparation being steaming in an earth oven lined with hot stones and fragrant leaves. Shoots of horsetail, salmonberry, cow parsnip, and water parsley ("wild celery") were eaten raw. Berries such as salmonberry, cranberry, strawberry, blue- and huckleberry, salal berry, bearberry, the last three preserved dried or pounded in cakes for winter use (Lewis and Clark in Thwaites 1904–1905, 4:14; Franchère in Thwaites 1904–1907, 6:321–322), were also eaten, as was the wild crabapple (Lewis and Clark in Thwaites 1904–1905, 3:261).

Additionally, fiber for nets and beargrass for basketry, both essential items, were traded into the area from upriver on the Columbia and tributaries (Lewis and Clark in Thwaites 1904–1905,3:180, 353; and Henry in Coues 1897,2:753), the beargrass probably from Sahaptian-speaking peoples ultimately (D. Jackson 1978,2:543). Tobacco, both native and European, was highly prized for smoking (Vancouver 1801, 3:129; Lewis and Clark in Thwaites 1904–1905,3:286, 322; Frost in Pipes 1934:237).

Currency

Dentalium shells (Chinook Jargon *háikwa*), obtained by trade ultimately from Vancouver Island (Ray 1938:100–101), constituted an economic standard for the Chinookans and their neighbors. Strung minimally in fathom-length units, the value depended on the number per fathom, larger shells being more valuable (Ross 1849:95). Their exchange value against other things was subject to market fluctuations, but by comparison they were of very great worth, and were used as ornamentation (Henry in Coues 1897,2:753; Lee and Frost 1844:101). After contact with European traders, the Chinookans acquired blue (and white) China beads as another currency and ornament of great value; they were much in demand from Lewis and Clark (Franchère in Thwaites 1904–1907, 6:326; Thwaites 1904–1905,3:182, 244–245, 278–279, 286, 328). It is clear from Bishop's (1967:128) 1795 account that beaver and sea otter skins were prized before they were valuable in the Euro-American trade; additionally, Ross (1849:95–96) indicates that these too had become standards of measuring the trade value of goods by the time of the founding of Astoria in 1811. Although aboriginally durable goods such as furs, dentalia, and canoes were exchanged for food only in an emergency, this restriction disappeared after contact (Hajda 1984:348–352).

Structures

The winter villages of the Chinookans consisted of oblong, gabled-roof, upright-cedar-plank houses (Ray 1938:124–126), varying in extent from single dwellings to sites

Stark Mus. of Art, Orange, Tex.: 31.78/120,WOP 13.
Fig. 3. Interior of house on the Columbia River, probably near Ft. Vancouver, Oregon Country. A gable-roof house with vertical wall planks, it had a central hearth in an excavated area surrounded by a planked floor covered with mats. Around the walls were bed-platforms built like upper and lower berths (Harper 1971:85), screened on either side by planks and at the end of the house by a large cattail mat, standing against the post holding the ridgepole. The screen on the left is carved with geometric and animal designs, and the central post bears a human face, all in a Chinookan style. Oil painting by Paul Kane, 1846.

with 15–20. One eyewitness put the number in the main Lower River Chinook village at 50 in 1814 (Corney in Barry 1932:357), at the peak of the fishing season there. Henry (in Coues 1897, 2:794–795, 796, 819–820, 832–833) notes of several Columbia and Willamette riverbank villages that the houses were primarily aligned in rows with the river, but this may not have been the case for the entire region of the Chinookans.

Temporary summer villages, particularly at fishing, hunting, and root-gathering camps, consisted of cattail mat sides and perhaps cedar bark roof over a light framework (Kane 1857:19; Ray 1938:126). It is interesting that Lewis and Clark passed only one extensive wapato-gathering and hunting village (of Cascades Chinookans, Thwaites 1904–1905, 3:194, 196, 4:223, 225, 236) in the Multnomah area. It would appear that by and large the lowermost river Chinookans, from the Kalama down, went on shorter, closer-to-home seasonal trips (Boyd and Hajda 1987) in smaller parties (for example, seven Cathlamets in one lodge at a fishing camp on Puget's Island—Thwaites 1904–1905, 4:200–201), or had multiple residences of the sturdier, cedar plank type (for example, Clatsops, Lower River Chinooks). This last condition, in particular, explains the great number of villages recorded both as abandoned and as populated.

A house frame consisted of cedar logs, upright mid-line posts or wide planks for support of the horizontal ridgepole, at a height of perhaps 14–18 feet, rafters sloping on both sides of the ridge-pole to two rows of shorter uprights, supporting two further, horizontal eaves poles at the height of about four to five feet above ground (Lewis and Clark in Thwaites 1904–1905,3:356–357; Swan 1857: 110–111). Such frames made houses ranging from one-family dwellings of about 12 by 20 feet, to extended-family patrifocal dwellings mentioned for some of the chiefly people of 40 by 100 feet. About 50 feet in length, with corresponding width, is an average of those cited.

Over these frames vertical split-cedar planks were lashed with cedar-bark or with cords, to form the low side walls and the pointed gable ends, the center boards of one or both of the latter cut out in an oval for the entrance. The ends were painted in the form of a humanlike face with open mouth, or legs, straddling the doorway, holding up the roof (Vancouver 1801,3:129; Lewis and Clark in Thwaites 1904–1905,4:198–199, 215; Henry in Coues 1897,2:754; Parker 1838:243). Later writers fail to mention this, and it is possible the practice fell into desuetude.

Franchère alone (in Thwaites 1904–1907, 6:328) clearly describes as the general type of wall construction horizontal planks laid between two upright rows of pairs of cedar posts about 10 feet apart. The roofs of Chinookan houses were horizontal or vertical planks, in one shingle-like or two thin layers, finished off with cedar bark particularly upriver, as among the Clackamas and Willamette region people (Vancouver 1801, 3:128; Lewis and Clark in Thwaites 1904–1905, 4:255).

Clark (in Thwaites 1904–1905, 4:240) notes the Nechacolee village-house, which was essentially seven 30-foot square houselike apartments separated by transverse four-foot-wide passageways, but under a single roof; adjacent were the remains of five independent dwellings.

The mat-covered floors of the interior were excavated in most houses to a depth of three to four feet, accessible from the door by a ladder, and the central spaces between each two mid-line supports were further excavated for a foot about eight feet square. This was framed for the nuclear family fireplace, over which was a smokehole (a removable plank) in the roof. Elevated bed platforms, three to four feet off the floor, under and on which goods were stored (or under which there was a second, less desirable row of beds), were on two or three sides of the house, depending on the door arrangements and the number of dwellers (fig. 3). Smoke-drying foods could be hung on rafters over the fire (Lewis and Clark in Thwaites 1904–1905, 3:208, 274, 326; Henry in Coues 1897, 2: 804–805, 820; Wilkes 1845, 4:322–323; Swan 1857:111).

Technology

The aboriginal household items in such dwellings included a variety of carved, woven, and shaped utensils and ornamentations of wood, bone, shell, cedar bark and spruce roots, beargrass, cattail rushes, antler, horn, and other materials (fig. 4). Stone was not so important as a

538

material, except for net-weights and heat radiators for boiling and steaming.

Carved wooden boxes with watertight, inverted covers (Henry in Coues 1897:789–790), troughs for collecting urine for ablution among the Multnomah and Clackamas (Henry in Coues 1897:819; Lewis in Thwaites 1904–1905, 4:220; Jacobs 1958–1959:637–638), extensively carved and painted spirit-power figurines and reliefs on the house framework (Lewis and Clark in Thwaites 1904–1905,4: 198–199, 215; Ross 1849:88–89, 96; Henry in Coues 1897: 805), and elegant bowls and serving pieces, some canoe-shaped trenchers (Lewis and Clark in Thwaites 1904–1905,3:273, 353; Franchère in Thwaites 1904–1907, 6:328–329; Ray 1938:131) were especially noted by early writers.

Baskets of several twined varieties (fig. 5), those of cedar bark watertight, were important for carrying food and for trade or storage of pounded salmon (apparently in large underground caches; see Clark in Thwaites 1904–1905, 3:179). Sewn cattail mats up to six or seven

feet long were extensively used as clean surfaces, as rainwear, for wrapping bodies for burial, and as temporary shelter; many were beautifully ornamented with beargrass designs (Lewis and Clark in Thwaites 1904–1905, 3:354, 4:186; Franchère in Thwaites 1904–1907, 6:325; Swan 1857:161–162).

Hemlock and crabapple wood wedges for splitting wood, chisels made from old European file blades and wooden handles (Lewis in Thwaites 1904–1905, 4:19–20, 32; Franchère in Thwaites 1904–1907, 6:329), needles of bone and wood, and other implements were important for the manufacture of many items.

Clothing

The earliest writers always commented on the dress, or lack of it, of the Chinookans, the men going naked when the weather permitted. The women of the groups below the Cathlapottle on Lewis River wore minimally an above-knee length skirt (fig. 6) of cedar-bark or silk-grass strips

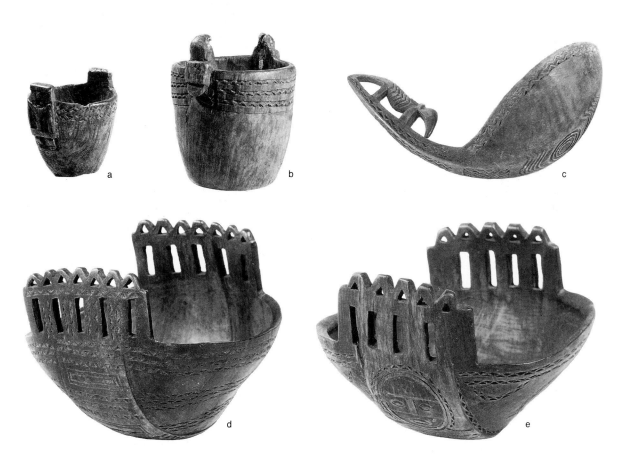

Mus. of the Amer. Ind., Heye Foundation, New York: a, 2/3425, b, 2/3426; Smithsonian, Dept. of Anthr.: c, 701, d, 691, e, 10079.
Fig. 4. Carved utensils. a–b, Wood flat-bottomed cups used to serve oil (Ray 1938:131). Elaborate carving normally designates vessels used in ceremonies. c, Ladle of mountain sheep horn, with an animal carved on the handle. The concentric circles at the bottom and the exposed ribs on the animal are indicative of Columbia River origin. d–e, Bowls of mountain sheep horn, with raised, squared ends characteristic of the Columbia River valley and adjacent western Wash. Bands of incised triangles are the most common geometric elements. Horn was traded to Chinookans from the Columbia Plateau people, and Chinook-made utensils traded back into the interior and north on the coast. a–b, Collected from an island in the Columbia River before 1909; c–e, collected by George Gibbs on the lower Columbia before 1871. Length of ladle bowl c, 15.3 cm; others to same scale.

Fig. 5. Women with shellfish harvesting equipment. Jennie Michel (or Martineau), Clatsop, and Deoso Katata, Tillamook. Their openwork twined baskets of split spruce roots were used to carry clams and mussels, loosened and dug with digging sticks like that held by Katata. Michel wears a mat apron. Photograph by James H. Bratt, 1894.

(Boit 1921:311; Lewis and Clark in Thwaites 1904–1905, 3:208–209, 241–242, 4:186; Franchère in Thwaites 1904–1907, 6:325). The Cathlapottle women, those upriver, and on the Willamette minimally wore a deerskin breechclout (Lewis in Thwaites 1904–1905,4:214; Henry in Coues 1897,2:820; Ross 1849:90–91).

Various robes or capes of fur, sea otter, beaver, raccoon, and wood rat, were worn by both sexes in colder weather, as were vestlike garments (Bishop 1967:126; Lewis in Thwaites 1904–1905,4:214; Henry in Coues 1897, 2:820; Lee and Frost 1844:101). A conical rainproof hat, twined of cedar bark or spruce root and decorated with beargrass, was also a distinctive article of clothing among the lowermost coastal groups (Lewis and Clark in

Fig. 6. Woman's skirt of twined fiber knotted at the ends. Collected near the mouth of the Columbia River about 1806; length 53 cm.

Thwaites 1904–1905,3:359–360; Ross 1849:89; Franchère in Thwaites 1904–1907, 6:325; Scouler 1905:163).

Since European clothing was a lively article of trade to the "chiefs," Lewis and Clark having presented outfits, for example, only to them, these were much in demand. Euro-American "civilizing" pressures, too, must have been at work; by the 1850s only the oldest women wore traditional bark skirts among the Shoalwater Chinook (Swan 1857: 112–113, 154–155).

Personal ornaments, on wrists and ankles, suspended from multiply-pierced ears and nasal septum, and around the neck, were of bone, dentalium and other shells, feathers, and beads. Head flattening was practiced (fig. 7).

Transport

Perhaps the most important chattels were canoes, of which writers distinguish six types among the Chinookans, each functionally specialized. They were skillfully fashioned from a single cedar log by splitting, harrowing, heating, and spreading (Swan 1857:80–82), and were polished, painted (outside black and inside red) and studded with shells, and, according to the type, with prow and stern carvings (fig. 8) (Lewis and Clark in Thwaites 1904–1905,4:30–32, 199; Franchère in Thwaites 1904–1907, 6:327; Ross 1849:98; Henry in Coues 1897,2: 750; Gibbs 1877:216; Ray 1938:101–106).

Most frequently commented on are the Columbia River type (called "Chinook" type), with undercut bow tapered to a finlike cutwater and a high prow. These were 20–35 feet in length, carried about a dozen people and goods, and were sturdy enough for rough river and bay use. The 50-foot canoe for 20–30 people (fig. 9), with fin at both ends, and with large carvings bow and stern (for example, Clark in Thwaites 1904–1905,3:198), is attributed particularly to the tidewater people, and perhaps was gotten from the Tillamook (Lewis in Thwaites 1904–1905, 4:32; Henry in Coues 1897, 2:835). Smaller, narrow, vertical-prow, undercut-stern hunting canoes (Henry in Coues 1897,2:783), and wider, doubly-undercut harpoon hunting types were used. Finally, the 15-foot shovel-nose canoe was especially useful in marshy places, such as on wapato-gathering trips.

Crescent-notched ash paddles four or five feet in length were principally used, though Ray (1938:106) reports pointed-blade paddles for use with shovel-nose canoes.

Horses had been adopted marginally down to the Willamette by early 1814 (Henry in Coues 1897,2: 800,804, 890), when Concomly made a special trip (by canoe) to a village there to purchase some. They never became common among the groups closest to the coast.

SILVERSTEIN

Stark Mus. of Art, Orange, Tex.: 31.78/208, WOP 11.
Fig. 7. Clackamas men with face decoration. The individual on lower left shows the results of head flattening. Three had painted faces, and one (upper right) had what may have been a dentalium in his pierced nasal septum. They had been gambling at a hand game when the artist met them at the mouth of the Clackamas River (Harper 1971:96–97). Oil painting by Paul Kane, 1847.

Social and Political Organization

With the pattern of basically stable, local villages, interlinked economically by areal commerce in subsistence and luxury goods, Chinookan society was organized on the distinction between the ascribed status of free person and slave (iɬláitix 'slave', iɬgixíɬtgiuks 'slaves'), between upper class (iɬkanáximst) and commoners, or lower class (gitáq̓atxal, ixíyal 'common person, man', gitáq̓atxalma(x), txláiwima(x) 'common people, men'), between higher, prestigious rank culminating in chiefdom, and lower rank (Ray 1938:48–58; Boas 1911a:603, 609, 610; Jacobs 1958–1959:342, 346, 528). In general, high status, class, and rank were linked to wealth, great chiefs always being reported as owners of great quantities of or distinctive qualities of things, which were exhibited, consumed, or bestowed as befitted the occasion. This linkage with the economy provided the way for enterprising commoners to elevate themselves to the fringes of the upper class. However, chiefly families, and slaves formed a hereditary maximal dichotomy, and basically it was commoners only who, as individuals, regularly were elevated or lowered through personal achievements or reverses.

● CHIEFS The office of chief (Lower Chinook iɬkánax, Upper Chinookan iɬkák̓mana, iɬštámx) seems to have been formally based on hereditary leadership rights and duties in only one village (Franchère in Thwaites 1904–1907, 6:329), but through proper marriage alliances, control of trade, and skillful and effective diplomacy (Lewis and Clark in Thwaites 1904–1905, 3:360; Franchère in Thwaites, 1904–1907, 6:336; Henry in Coues 1897, 2:753, 798–799), an individual chief could exert influence over a wide area. The famed Concomly (qánq̓mli) was a secondary chief among the Chinooks, for example (Bishop 1967:116, 118; Lewis and Clark in Thwaites 1904–1905, 3: 230, 238, 294, 4:89), until he allied himself by trade and marriage of children to the Europeans at Astoria, to his personal gain, but, as it turned out, to political folly for the Chinookans. Ultimately he became known as the epitome of chiefdom in the whole lower Columbia region, far surpassing Taucum (t̓áwkm), whom both Bishop in 1795 and Lewis and Clark in 1805 put as head chief.

This enterprising quality of ingratiation with the Whites was also evident in the Clatsop noble, perhaps a minor chief, Coalpo (q̓úlpu), who with his wife's connections to the young chief Casino (k̓iásnu) from the Multnomah Channel–Lower Willamette area, could get Casino to act as intermediary for the Astorians in settling a score with the Cascades people at wáiaxix, according to regular Chinookan custom (Ross 1849:106; Henry in Coues 1897, 2:793, 797, 798–799, 802). The highest-ranking chief among the Clatsop at that time, who was far more prominent than either Concomly or Coalpo in the early 1800s, was Comowool (Cooniah) (Thwaites 1904–1905, 3:311; Coues 1897, 2:913).

Thus the histories of these chiefly families are intertwined, particularly through marriage. In 1829, one of Coalpo's wives was a daughter of Concomly himself (Parker 1838:245), enhancing his rank, no doubt. From the mid-1830s, the same chief Casino of the Astorian period had become the most important survivor in close contact with the Hudson's Bay Company people at Fort Vancouver and had for some time been married to Concomly's daughter, ex-wife of fur trader Duncan McDougall. The fragility of these alliances is manifest, however, in the fact that at his son's death, Casino suspected shamanistic murder on the part of his wife, whom he wished to kill in revenge (Parker 1838:251; Kane 1857:12, 24).

Normally the office of chief passed from father to eldest or highest-ranking son; Concomly apparently passed on both his authority and his name, changing his own to mátsu, while still alive (Scouler 1905:168). While serving as arbiter of quarrels, supervisor of activities such as distributing a whale (Boas 1894:258–262), provider for his village in times of need (Henry in Coues 1897, 2:912), the chief had many privileges, such as expropriation of foods, goods, or eligible women at whim, with some recompense to the donor (Ross 1849:88; Ray 1938:56–57). The chief was assisted by an orator, who served the role of speaking directly to the low-ranked people, including commoners and slaves, which a chief did not feel he had to do.

Fig. 8. Canoe burials, left, Prow of burial canoe on bank of Columbia River at La Camas Creek, Clark County, Wash. (Bushnell 1938:5). Drawing by George Gibbs, 1850. right, Burial canoe of the daughter of a Chinook chief, Cowlitz River, Wash. The canoe was decorated with domestic articles, all broken, punctured, or torn so as to be useless in this world. Inside, the body was wrapped in mats, decorated with dentalia, beads and rings, and accompanied by weapons and implements. The canoe had a hole in the bottom as a drain for rainwater (Harper 1971:98). Watercolor based on sketch by Paul Kane, probably about March 1847.

In war between villages, which resulted when some affront could not be smoothed over by negotiated payments or arbitrated revenge. The regional system of intergroup diplomacy led to formalized reparations by payment, enslavement, or execution of the offending party, or, if no satisfaction was so obtained from the offender's village, it led to formalized warfare of honor, terminating in payment of wealth to the victors. This regional system included the Tillamook, Lower Chehalis, Lower Cowlitz, Tualatin, and others as well as Chinookan-speaking groups (Franchère in Thwaites 1904–1907, 6: 330–331; Henry in Coues 1897, 2:855, 867, 879–880, 905, 908; Scouler 1905:279; Minto 1900:311; Hajda 1987).

• SLAVES At the other extreme of society, slaves did not have the rights even over their own bodies, since they were articles of property, chattels bought and sold (Ross 1849: 92; Swan 1857:166), cast off into a makeshift grave or into the water when dead (Franchère in Thwaites 1904–1907, 6:324; Ross 1849:97; Henry in Coues 1897, 2:825–826), and destroyed at a burial of the owner (Bishop 1967:127; Parker 1838:245; Lee and Frost 1844:233; Wilkes 1845, 5:

118; Gibbs 1877:189, 204; Minto 1900:300; Curtis 1907–1930, 8:89), like any other property. While it has been reported that slaves were well treated in the household (Lewis and Clark in Thwaites 1904–1905, 4: 120–121; Franchère in Thwaites 1904–1907, 6:324), to them fell the heaviest work, the division of labor being the usual one according to sex. They could be punished for attempting to escape. Their lowermost position in society made their ridicule keenly felt; it was the worst loss of face to be made fun of by the slaves or be publicly called "slave" (Franchère in Thwaites 1904–1907, 6:325; Ray 1938:53; Jacobs 1958–1959:528). The slaves, in distinction to all others, did not have their heads flattened from birth (Ross 1849:99; Lee and Frost 1844:102; Swan 1857:168), symbolizing an inherited status as alien.

The majority of slaves were obtained by multiple sale or trade from the north down the tributaries of the Columbia and also along the coast to Willapa Bay (Scouler 1905:196; Swan 1857:166–167), and from far south (Lewis and Clark in Thwaites 1904–1905, 4: 120–121; Lee and Frost 1844:103; Kane 1857:20; Gibbs

Fig. 9. Model canoe with characteristic crescent-notched paddles. Carvings fore and aft indicate this model represents the large war or traveling canoe (Franchère in Thwaites 1904–1907, 6:246; Lewis 1906:164). Probably collected before 1867; length 58 cm.

SILVERSTEIN

1877:188–189), though Bishop in 1795 (1967:127) records a Chinook slave-gathering expedition of some six years previous, to what seems to be southern interior Oregon.

Slave raiding increased during the maritime fur trade period. Toward the mid-nineteenth century, it appears that the Oregon settlers in the Willamette Valley regularly bought slaves from the Chinookans and kept them for farmwork (Lee and Frost 1844:133; Wilkes 1845, 4:348).

Among the Chinookans themselves, in the early period, display of slaves paddling canoes (obvious from their round head) is noted by Casino, chief of the Multnomah who displayed six; Coalpo, who displayed eight, and Concomly, who outdid them all with 12 (Coues 1897, 2: 797, 794, 838), which was far above the average nobleman's two or three.

Life Cycle

Not only marriages and first births but also all the significant events of the life cycle that involved achieved statuses were marked by display, by gift distribution emphasizing public recognition through acceptance, by feasting, by singing, and by dancing.

Children were kept in cradles, either the flat board or dugout type (fig. 10) until they could walk, and devices were applied to flatten their heads (Kane 1859:180).

Naming of a child at about one year, with an ancestral name of the appropriate rank, took place with accompanying gift distribution (Ray 1938:66–67); new names, reflecting changes in rank, could be acquired at many other points in life. At puberty, girls were secluded under numerous taboos (Swan 1857:171), for a five-month period marked by two such ceremonies (Boas 1894: 244–246; Ray 1938:71–72); taboos on a woman (and her husband) during each menstruation continued (Jacobs 1958–1959:496–497).

Residence within a village was in patrifocal, ideally virilocal, three-generation houses, a man's wives, some sons or blood relations, and their dependents dwelling together (Lewis in Thwaites 1904–1905, 3:360; Ray 1938: 127–128). The highest man in his prime, by class and rank, was the head, or owner, of the house.

A first marriage, always described as exogamous by village, involved a tentative offer of goods (slaves, canoes, blankets, robes, dentalia) by a postpubescent boy's parents to the head of the prospective bride's house, then their going to the bride's village (cf. Boas 1894:248) for a formal feast and elaborate mutual presentation. After a year the bride's family visited the groom's and made as large a presentation of food as they could, and yet a third such presentation to the groom's family accompanied the bride and her family after the first child was born, preferably back in the bride's village (Lewis and Clark in Thwaites 1904–1905, 4:176; Franchère in Thwaites 1904–1907, 6: 332; Lee and Frost 1844:103; Boas 1894:248–251; Ray

Harvard U. Peabody Mus.: 88–51–10/50695.
Fig. 10. Cedar dugout cradle, which used 2 basketry pads filled with thin cedar bark for head flattening. These were bound in place with thongs. The inside of the dugout was lined with finely shredded cedar bark, bird down, and fur. Square hoods of matting were often provided (Swan 1857:167). Probably collected by Lewis and Clark, 1806; length 66.7 cm.

1938:72–73).

Established men, especially those described as chiefs, arranged for the payment for their own subsequent wives with a presentation to the bride's father or responsible relative (Bishop 1967:126). Degree of polygyny, in the number and rank of wives, was an important symbol of rank. A levirate, sororate, or other continuing marital bond with the survivor of a marriage was always the absolute right of his or her sometime affines. Marriage was of course linked to the class and rank system, propertyless men being able to elevate themselves this way (with uxorilocal residence and service to the househead; cf. Boas 1894:250), with no loss, but rather gain of prestige. Younger people of both sexes were frequently married to older people for all these reasons (not for "experience," Swan 1857:170), though it is clear from jokes and such, recorded at a later date among the Clackamas on Grand Ronde Reservation (for example, Jacobs 1958–1959:530), that in such survivors of upriver groups, with less emphasis on social climbing, marked age differences of spouses was not understood in the same way.

But though marriage was obviously a union, personal property of both spouses, including the trappings of rank, was distinct, and in general there was emphasis on the distinction between one's relatives by blood and one's in-laws. This also appears in the bifurcate, non-merging (bilateral) referential kinship terminology (Boas 1901, 1904:134–135; Jacobs 1958–1959), which keeps blood relations strictly distinct from affines. The terms show distinctions of relatives through elder versus younger, through male versus female, through father versus mother.

Richly decorated canoes elevated on posts (fig. 8) or trees, with another canoe inverted inside, were used for burial among the lowermost Chinookans (Vancouver

1801, 3:89; Lewis and Clark in Thwaites 1904–1905, 3: 252, 260, 4:198; Franchère in Thwaites 1904-1907, 6:333; Ross 1849:97; Boas 1894:253).

An alternative burial method, in elevated carved boxes, is reported among the Clatsop and Lower River Chinook at the earliest period by Vancouver (1801, 3:89) and Bishop (1967:127), though for the Shoalwater Chinook, Swan (1857:186, 192) reports reburial of bones in a box after one year.

Ceremonies and Spirit Powers

Perhaps the most elaborate ceremonialism in Chinookan life was related to the acquisition and display of guardian spirit powers, sought on a prepubescent quest alone at night, and encountered in the form of some animal, bird, or natural formation that "adopted" the seeker (Swan 1857:172–176; Boas 1894:210; Ray 1938:78–80; Jacobs 1958–1959:508). Having such spirit power or powers entailed knowledge of power songs and dances, and possession of specific items, including the carved spirit-power figures noted in Chinookan houses by early writers, such figures dancing under invocation (Boas 1901: 202–204). Spirit powers caused specific behavioral and mental attributes in their possessors.

This constituted a system of psychodynamic explanation for social relations, as shamans or ghosts could use their particularly strong powers at will or more importantly for hire to inflict damage or death upon people by intrusion or soul loss (Scouler 1905:279; Wilkes 1845, 4: 325; Boas 1894:196–205; Ray 1938:86; Jacobs 1958–1959: 508, 521–522), or to cure such calamities bred of jealousy, envy, and so forth. Several early writers described curing ceremonies (Franchère in Thwaites 1904–1907, 6:333; Ross 1849:96–97; Lee and Frost 1844:236–238; Frost in Pipes 1934:56; Swan 1857:177, 181–184; Kane 1857: 26–27), and Jacobs (1958–1959:510–520, 523–526) recorded their vitality as well up to the twentieth century among the Grand Ronde Reservation Clackamas. Avenge for murders shamanistically perpetrated was apparently a major cause of formalized village strife (Scouler 1905: 166).

Ray (1938:89–92) indicates that a Chinookanized form of secret society existed among the groups farthest downriver and on Willapa Bay, the members being upperclass people with special spirit powers, who underwent an initiation and performed spirit-power feats and dramas for restricted audiences.

It was during the winter season, when spirit power ceremonialism was most prominent among Chinookans, that myths and prehistoric narratives were told, the character of which two genres is basically didactic (Jacobs 1959, 1960; Hymes 1968). The myth-age actors in the first, the ancestral actors in the second class of literature, exemplify conduct and attitudes that seem to accrue to

spirit powers, and to various social types. Also during this season, displays of spirit-power songs, dances, and feats, and public recognition ceremonials for new shamans, all managed with appropriate feasts and distributions, marked this sacred period of spiritual preparation and renewal for the return of spring economic pursuits.

Synonymy

The term Chinook was early generalized by traders, explorers, and especially ethnologists, from the Lower Chehalis name *činúk* (Boas 1911a:563) for the inhabitants and a village site on Baker Bay, to apply to all the linguistically related people of the area, though the literature through the first part of the nineteenth century frequently preserved the distinction of the several names for smaller ethnic and political units. Although the name Chinook is of Salishan origin, it must have been used by Chinook speakers in talking to Euro-American traders (Ray 1938:35–36). Variant spellings are listed by Hodge (1907–1910, 1:273). The general terms Columbians and Flatheads (from the practice of head-flattening) have also been used for the whole population of the lower Columbia. The Chinook of early writers were strictly the people of the Baker Bay village.

Subgroups

Cathlamet. The group and dialect name Cathlamet is from *gałámat*, the designation of the people of the village at Cathlamet Head. Spellings in Lewis and Clark include Cathlahmah, Calt-har-mar, and Kath-la-mat (Thwaites 1904–1905, 3:250–252, 4:200). Other variants are Cathlamat, Cuthlamuks, Kathlamet, Katlāmat, and others in Hodge (1907–1910, 1:216–217); Kwillúchinł, given there as the Lower River Chinook name, is actually Lower Chehalis *q*ʷ*lúʔičinł*, probably 'bearberry' (Curtis 1907–1930, 9:186), which must be a recent usage reflecting the switch of languages in the Willapa Bay area from Chinookan to Salishan. The Cathlamet were called Lower Chinook by Ray (1938).

Cathlapottle. Cathlapottle is *gáłapuλx* 'those of Lewis River'; the river name is *nápuλx*. Spellings in Lewis and Clark include Cath-lah-poh-tle, Quathlahphotle, and Quathlapohtle (Thwaites 1904–1905, 4:68, 212, 214); other nineteenth-century spellings are in Hodge (1907–1910, 1:217).

Clackamas. The name Clackamas is from *gitłáqimaš* (also *giłáqimaš*) 'those of Clackamas River', a name based on *niqímašix* 'Clackamas River'. Lewis and Clark recorded the name as Clark-á-mus and Clarkamos (Thwaites 1904–1905, 4:242, 255); variants are Clackama, Klackamas, Thlakeimas, and others listed by Hodge (1907–1910, 1:302). Hodge also gives early recordings of names for the Clackamas in neighboring Indian languages: ákimmash

(Tualatin Kalapuyan); nsekaús and nstiwat (Nestucca Tillamook); túhu tane (Upper Umpqua). Wasco-Wishram Chinookans humorously refer to the Clackamas and other related Chinookans from below the Cascades as qáštxukš 'the qáštxu ones' ('those who say qáštxu 'thus' instead of qídau'). This name was recorded by Lewis and Clark as Cash-hooks and Cush-hooks (Thwaites 1904–1905, 4:233, 241), whence it has entered the literature as Cushook (Hodge 1907–1910, 1:650; Sapir in Spier 1936:23). The name of the village wálamt is the source of the word Willamette.

Clatsop. English Clatsop is from tɬáċəp (also ɬáċp) 'those who have pounded salmon'. Lewis and Clark recorded Clap-sott, Clất·sop's, and Clotsop (Thwaites 1904–1905, 3:238, 244, 6:117); variants include Cladsaps, Clatsaps, Clatsup, Klatsops, Latsop, and others listed by Hodge (1907–1910, 1:305). The Lower River Chinook and the Cathlamet applied to the Clatsop a name of equivalent meaning, tɬák̓ilak (also ɬák̓ilak), referring to the main village as niák̓ilaki (or tiák̓ilaki) 'where there is pounded salmon', a name that appears as Ne-ah-keluc (Lyman 1900:321).

Clawiwalla. The name Clawiwalla is from tɬáwiwala (also ɬáwiwala), recorded as Clough-e-wall-hah, Clow-we-wal-la, Tla-we-wul-lo, and in other ways listed by Hodge (1907–1910, 1:313). Hodge also gives the designations Willamette Falls Indians and Willamette Tum-water band (with Chinook Jargon tumwater 'falls'), as well as the shortened versions Fall Indians and Tumwater.

Kalama. Kalama is from gaɬák̓alama 'those of the rock'. Variants are Tlakalama and Klakalama.

Multnomah. Multnomah is from máɬnumax 'those towards the water' ('those closer to the Columbia River'). The spelling Mult-no-mah appears already in Lewis and Clark (Thwaites 1904–1905, 4:219); variants include Maltnabah, Mathlanobes, and others in Hodge (1907–1910, 1:956). The Sauvie Island peoples were also referred to as the Wapato Indians, based on the early name Wapato Island.

Qaniak. Qaniak is based on Boas's recording as qā′niak of the place-name underlying the term giɬáxaniak, used for the people at Oak Point. Recordings include Cooniac, Kahnyak, Ni-co-ni-ac, and others in Hodge (1907–1910, 1:341).

Shoalwater. The Shoalwater Chinook were named after Shoalwater Bay, the former name for Willapa Bay. The use of name Atsmitl for the Shoalwater Chinook (Boas in Hodge 1907–1910, 1:113; Spier 1936:30) is a transference from an earlier application, recorded as Arts milsh (Swan 1857:210), to the Shoalwater Bay Lower Chehalis; these recordings are based on Lower Chehalis ʔácmiɬč 'Willapa Bay', rather than čtʔácmiɬč 'people of Willapa Bay'. (Curtis 1907–1930, 9:6, 8).

Shoto. The village or local band name Shoto (Shotoes) used by Lewis and Clark (Thwaites 1904–1905, 4:219,

221) may be explained by Franchère's (1969:83, in Thwaites 1904–1907, 6:248) reference to Soto as the personal name of a half-blood who lived in the group's village on Lake Vancouver. These were probably the people later referred to as Kanasisi, from gaɬák̓anasisi 'those of the butterball duck', a designation based on the name of Lake Vancouver, wák̓anasisi 'butterball duck'. Variant spellings are given under the name Wakanasisi in Hodge (1907–1910, 2:894).

Skilloots. The name Skilloots used by Lewis and Clark (Thwaites 1904–1905, 3:196, 4:205–207) is perhaps a rendering of squlups 'Cape Horn' (Curtis 1907–1930, 8:110; Sapir in Spier 1936:24). Possibly the early uses by Lewis and Clark, on the downriver journey, were based on a misunderstanding of the expression s(i)k̓əlútk 'look at him!'; this would explain why the name is used over a very large area at first but much less extensively on the return trip (Thwaites 1904–1905, 3:194, 196, 199, 4:205–207, 223–225, 236). The synonymy in Hodge (1907–1910, 2:591) also includes variants of Calooit and Kreluits, which are renderings of (i)ɬxlúit 'they are strange, different', an expression applied to non-Chinookan peoples; the term Hul-loo-et-tell (Lewis and Clark in Thwaites 1904–1905, 4:206, 208) is a rendering of xluit íl 'strange, different country', which is based on the same root.

Wakaikam. The name Wakaikam is a place-name wáqaiqam (cf. qáiqamix 'region downriver'); spellings include Wahkiakum, Warciacoms, Warkiacom, and others listed in Hodge (1907–1910, 2:890).

Sources

Besides the earliest sketchy accounts of contact between Chinookans and Euro-American exploring and trading vessels (Boit 1921; Gray in Greenhow 1845), Bishop (1967) and Vancouver (1801) give some useful material about villages and goods. The most extensive account of the early nineteenth century, including rich data on how the Chinookans dealt with the newcomers, is in Lewis and Clark's original journals and maps (Thwaites 1904–1905, 3, 4, 6, 7) and in the supplementary material of the expedition (D. Jackson 1978). Franchère (in Thwaites 1904–1907, 6), Ross (1849), Cox (1957), and Henry (in Coues 1897) add great amounts of data on the incorporation of the Astorian fur traders into the sociopolitical system, changing it in many important respects.

By the period of explorers, missionaries, and settlers, there are journal accounts reprinted by historical societies or published then as tracts to encourage more settlers and missionaries. Principal among these are D. Douglas (1904), Scouler (1905), Frost (in Pipes 1934), Lee and Frost (1844), Parker (1838), and Blanchet and Demers (in Landerholm 1956).

The results of the United States Exploring Expedition (Wilkes 1845), contain valuable data, as does George

Gibbs's (1877) work. The earliest valuable account of the Shoalwater Chinook (Swan 1857) also dates from the period of increased settlement by Whites.

Boas's mythological and ethnographic interviewing (1894, 1901, 1904, 1911a) and Curtis's ethnographic interviewing and photography (1907–1930, 7, 8, 9) straddle the turn of the twentieth century. They are "memory" ethnography to an extent, of the mid-nineteenth century, but all the richer for the obvious excellence of minute detail, with linguistic control. Jacobs's Clackamas materials from 1929–1930, both traditional winter texts and ethnographic observations in the language (1958–1959), together with his interpretations (1959, 1960) form the sole basis for making intelligible the fleeting references in the earlier literature to the Clackamas and Multnomah Chinookans, though they reflect the middle-to-late nineteenth century, during the reservation period.

Ray's (1938) ethnographic notes are to be used in conjunction with the other sources, as his principal informant documents a stage at which the lowermost Chinookan populations had already merged with lesser-known Salishan groups (her father and mother had served as informants for Shoalwater and Lower Cowlitz Salishan groups, Curtis 1907–1930, 9:172, 173). The name Chinook for the people consolidated in the Willapa Bay region after the turn of the century was probably influenced both by federal government assignment of "Lower Chinook" claims, for those of partial Chinookan ancestry, and by the view that regardless of linguistic affiliation, "the Shoalwater Bay people . . . are usually considered as Chenooks" (Swan 1857:210).

Spier's tribal distribution for Washington (1936) and Berreman's for Oregon (1937) attempt historical reconstruction of sites and territories for these areas, from narrative source material and various twentieth-century ethnographers, but without apparent linguistic control. Strong (1959) plots the distribution of presumably Chinookan prehistoric sites along the Columbia River. This excellent account is profusely illustrated with artifacts, many of which are in private collections.

Hajda (1984) discusses social organization in the greater Lower Columbia region between 1792 and 1830. Ruby and Brown (1976:247–251, 1986:23–25) cover Chinookan history from early contact to the Indian Claims Commission's $48,692.05 final award to the Chinook Tribe and Bands of Indians in 1971 (Indian Claims Commission 1974).

Kalapuyans

HENRY B. ZENK

Language and Territory

The name Kalapuya (ˌkălə'pōōyu) is applied to the people who spoke Kalapuyan languages, which comprise a family (or a subfamily in Swadesh's 1965 proposed Takelman family) within the putative Penutian phylum.

There were perhaps 13 Kalapuyan divisions or "tribes," each of which is supposed to have been dialectally distinct, but the exact number is not known. The dialects fell into three languages, which while closely related were mutually unintelligible: a northern language, Tualatin-Yamhill (Gatschet 1877a, 1877k, 1877), consisting of at least two dialects (Tualatin and Yamhill); a central language, Central (Gatschet 1877e) (also called Santiam), consisting of six to 10 or more almost insignificantly variant dialects (of which two are linguistically well documented: Santiam and Mary's River); and a southern language, Yoncalla, probably consisting of more than one dialect (Frachtenberg 1915a:89; Jacobs 1930, 1945:7–8, 145–146).*

The Kalapuyans were wholly an inland people. Their territory included the greater portion of the Willamette Valley along with a portion of the Umpqua River drainage immediately to the south of the upper Willamette Valley (fig. 1).

Environment

The banks of the Willamette River and its main tributaries were mostly densely timbered. Away from these belts of timber much of the valley consisted of prairie and oak savanna, diversified by oak and Douglas fir woodlands.

Low-lying areas were seasonally flooded, and there were many marshes and small lakes. The higher hills and surrounding mountains were mostly heavily timbered, with oak forests predominating at lower elevations and coniferous forests at higher elevations. The area was reputedly exceptionally rich in game and vegetable resources (Habeck 1961; Thilenius 1968; Johannessen et al. 1971; Henry in Coues 1897, 2:815–817; D. Douglas 1914:140–142, 213–220; J. Palmer 1847:88–99; Clyman 1960:117–126, 131–147, 152–158). The open character of the Willamette Valley was a direct result of aboriginal occupancy. At the close of each summer, Kalapuyans burned over much of the valley floor (Boyd 1986).

Reports that salmon did not ascend Willamette Falls (Farrand 1907b:645) are incorrect. However, the extent of the aboriginal salmon resource above the falls is uncertain (Zenk 1976:69–74).

Culture

This sketch describes Kalapuya life in the first half of the nineteenth century. It is a synthesis of information from largely manuscript sources, generally referred to simply by the name of the recorder: for Tualatin-Yamhill, Gatschet (1877a, 1877k, 1877), Frachtenberg (1913–1914, 1913–1914b, 1915), and Jacobs (1936, 1936b); for Central, Gatschet (1877e), Frachtenberg (1913–1914a, 1913–1914b, 1914a), and Jacobs (1936a, 1928–1936, 1936, 1945:17–81, 154, 336–350); and for Yoncalla, Frachtenberg (1914b) and Jacobs (1928).

Subsistence

Apparently, vegetable resources accounted for the major portion of Kalapuyan subsistence. Camas, which was remarkably abundant in the Willamette Valley, was the single most important such resource. It was pit-oven roasted, dried, and often pressed into cakes, which were important trade articles. Also much used were wapato; tarweed seeds harvested on burned-over prairies, later parched for storage; hazel nuts; and various kinds of berries. Acorns were of only secondary importance in Kalapuyan subsistence.

The game resource of the valley was varied, with birds,

---

*Tualatin-Yamhill and Central forms cited in italics are in a normalized, tentative phonemic transcription. This transcription uses the following phonemes: (plain stops) $p, t, k, k^w, ?$; (aspirated stops and affricate) $p^h, t^h, č^h, k^h, k^{wh}$; (glottalized stops and affricate) $p̓, t̓, č̓, k̓, k̓^w$; (voiceless continuants) $f [f, \phi], ł, š, x, h$; (voiced continuants) l, m, n, w, y; (short vowels) i, e, a, o, u; (long vowels) $i·, e·, a·, o·, u·$; (stress) $v́$. There are diphthongs ai, au, ui, and (in Tualatin) ei. Forms that could not be phonemicized have been normalized to conform to the Handbook technical alphabet and are not italicized.

The phonemic analysis and the transcriptions used follow Jacobs (1945:13–15, 151–153, 204) and Howard Berman (personal communication 1987); this differs in some respects from the analysis of the Mary's River dialect by Hajda (1976).

547

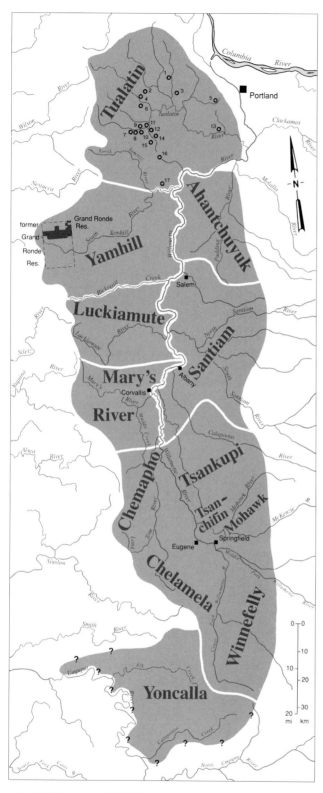

Fig. 1. Kalapuyan tribal divisions during the early 19th century, with emendations showing Grand Ronde Reservation (established 1856), and Tualatin winter villages: 1, čʰapánaxtin; 2, čʰatámnei; 3, čʰakútpalyu; 4, čʰačókʷił; 5, čʰakéipi 'beaver place'; 6, čʰačmé·wa; 7, čʰapékli 'steep hill place'; 8, čʰawayé·t; 9, čʰatákšiš; 10, čʰapúnkatpi; 11, čʰalá·l 'thread grass place'; 12, čʰaláʔwai; 13, čʰačʰimahíyuk 'place in front of híyuk (an aromatic herb growing in marshy places)'; 14, čʰamámpitʰ 'creek place'; 15, čʰatákił 'fir bark place'; 16, čʰahé·ʔlim 'place out, outside'; 17, čʰatílkʷei.

small mammals, black-tailed and white-tailed deer, elk, and black bear (but not grizzlies, which like coyotes were hunted but not eaten) among the animals taken for food by Kalapuyans. Among other foods were: lampreys, grasshoppers (a delicacy, gathered on burned-over prairies), and a type of caterpillar (another delicacy, boiled or pit-oven roasted in quantity). Kalapuyans cultivated tobacco (*Nicotiana multivalvus*), planting the seeds on small plots fertilized by ash.

Clothing and Adornment

Summer and winter dress was notably distinct. In the summer, men often wore little or no clothing. Men's apparel for travel and chilly weather included leggings and moccasins, cloaks, and fur caps made from the intact skins of small animals or from the head-skins of larger animals such as deer, cougar, and a gray fox (fig. 2). Women always wore at least an apron or skirt, made of dressed skin, rush or grass, or shredded cedar bark. In the winter, both men and women might wear thick elk-hide leggings and moccasins, hats (fur for men, and perhaps for women only, tight-fitting basketry caps), and single-piece or interlaced fur cloaks. Winter wear included fringed buckskin shirts and trousers for men and buckskin gowns for women.

Decoration of apparel reflected social position. Wealthy persons' attire was typically ornamented with dentalium shells, porcupine quills, trade and bone beads, and shells and feathers. The same materials were used in nose and ear ornaments, necklaces, and arm and wrist bands.

Tattooed designs were often to be seen on the arms and legs of both men and women. Facial tattooing, of women only, is known from the Central area, but this practice did not extend to the Tualatins. Wealthy men gauged the values of bead and dentalium-shell string lengths with reference to tattooed horizontal lines on their upper arms.

The Tualatins, in common with their Chinookan and northern Oregon coastal neighbors, flattened the heads of all free-born infants. Flattening has also been reported from the Central area but was not in universal practice there.

Settlements

Kalapuyans occupied permanent villages during the winter months, but during the drier part of the year lived in transitory camps. According to Gatschet, Tualatins lived about half the year in such camps, from April or May up to about November. In the summertime, camps were often little more than the shelter of a grove of trees or a brush windbreak. With the major harvests complete and the fall rains imminent, the winter houses were refurbished and re-occupied.

ZENK

Smithsonian Lib.: Wilkes 1845:223.
Fig. 2. A hunter from the southern Willamette Valley. The artist reported that he wore moccasins, an elkskin dress, cap of foxskin, and quiver of sealskin (C. Pickering 1863:32). Engraving after a drawing by Alfred T. Agate, 1841.

Multifamily winter houses were built, but these have not been well described. The basic type seems to have been rectangular, constructed of bark, planks, or both, laid upon either a shed or a gable structural framework. The walls were banked outside with dirt, and the house floor was excavated to a depth of two or three feet. Each family was partitioned off, mats lined walls and served as mattresses, and there was a single central fireplace. Apparently, the Tualatins and other northerners also built gabled cedar-plank houses, on the pattern of their Chinookan neighbors' dwellings. A few further details on Tualatin settlements are provided by Gatschet: houses were sometimes joined together in long house rows; inside, there were bed and storage platforms; each house had two or three low doors; a village might have a large "council hall."

Besides winter houses, a Kalapuyan village invariably had sweathouses of the dome type, heated by steam. Both men and women sweated, recreationally or for self-purification, following with a plunge into cold water.

Technology

Manufactured items included: cattail mats; sewn bark containers (fig. 3); stone mortars and pestles for mashing and mixing foods; antler, bone, wood, and shell implements; and basketry, often decorated. River canoes were hollowed out from cedar, fir, or cottonwood logs.

British Mus., Mus. of Mankind, London: 1900.142.
Fig. 3. Ash-bark parching tray. Coals were placed with seeds in the tray, which was shaken over the fire until the seeds were parched. Collected by S.C. Freer before 1900; length 48 cm.

Political Organization

The treaty-signing Kalapuyan "bands" represent remnants of earlier tribal divisions. Information on those of the southern Willamette Valley is especially scant, and the identification of groups there is less certain. The information on the Tualatin, while by no means adequate, may provide a clue as to the aboriginal nature of these entities. During the first quarter of the nineteenth century, there were about 17 Tualatin winter-village groups (fig. 1). This collectivity of "Tualatin" local groups was recognized and named as such by Natives. Moreover, it seems to have had some degree of economic unity: all member villages shared access to certain tribal hunting territories (while in contrast, each village had its own tarweed-producing areas, within which individuals had their own plots); and it is indicated that the entire tribe participated communally in the annual wapato harvest at Wapato Lake.

The villages of this and the other Kalapuyan tribes were apparently politically basically autonomous. Treaty documents, and some ethnographic sources, furthermore suggest that the tribes themselves were political entities, headed by tribal chiefs. However, it may also be that tribal chieftainship was a historical development, the result of population consolidations and government agents' demands to deal with authoritative representatives of tribes.

There is no evidence that Kalapuyan society had any sort of corporate kin group. One or more patrilocal extended families, occupying a winter-village site, defined the autonomous local group. Political authority was apparently identified with this village group as such, in the person of a 'chief' (Tualatin-Yamhill $a\check{c}ampak^h$, Central $an\check{c}^h\acute{a}mpe\cdot k^h$) (or perhaps, in larger villages, two or three ranked chiefs). A chief adjudicated intravillage disputes and was expected to assist fellow villagers in need. He was invariably wealthy in comparison to his fellow villagers (indeed, the word for 'chief' also strongly connotes 'wealthy'). Gatschet emphasizes that chiefly status per se was not inherited: while chieftainship generally passed from father to son, it did so only as a concomitant of inherited wealth. On the other hand, Frachtenberg has it that Mary's River women might become chiefs, possibly indicating that chiefly succession was hereditary, at least on occasion. Chieftainship could have been inherited as among the Coosans, who selected a female relative when a male relative was not available.

Social Organization

Alongside the neighboring Chinookan system, with its strong emphasis on rank, Kalapuyan society seems less differentiated. Chiefs and their immediate families stood apart at one extreme of social evaluation, slaves (Tualatin-Yamhill awák, Central awáʔkaʔ 'slave') stood well apart at the other. Probably, there was another, less pronounced gradation in between, setting off more respectable "commoners" from a few exceptionally poor people. While slaves comprised the most distinct social stratum, this was evidently not strictly equivalent to the slave caste of Chinookan society. Marriage between slaves and free persons, while probably uncommon, was not unknown, Gatschet noting that such a marriage secured the freedom of the marrying slave.

Most slaves were captives or descendents of captives, originally taken from distant peoples and often traded widely through the area (Ray 1938:51–53; Gibbs 1877:188–189; Spier and Sapir 1930:222–223). There is also reference, from the southern part of the area only, to the selling of free persons, for example, orphaned children, into slavery by others (adoptive kin) for debt payment. While Central and southern Kalapuyans probably kept but few slaves, Tualatins and other northerners were active slave traders. Central and southern Kalapuyans were reportedly notably victimized by slave raiders, including Tualatins and Molalas.

The Tualatin, Mary's River, and Santiam sources all suggest that virilocal residence and local exogamy (related to strong incest avoidance involving all recognized degrees of blood relationship) were the rule, though it is unclear how rigidly so. Men who could afford to be so preferred to be polygynous. The marriage transaction involved reciprocal payments between families, but the groom's family paid a substantially larger sum than did the bride's. Indeed, according to Jacobs, a man with many daughters could expect to become wealthy. Adultery and breaches of levirate rule (as when a nonrelative consorted with a widow without properly "buying" her from the relatives of the deceased) were taken seriously, although here, as in most matters, a wealthy man could resolve difficulties with adequate payment.

The marriage ceremony itself involved the two families in a formalized meeting and exchange, with valuables being transferred to the bride's relatives and the bride being surrendered to the groom and his relatives (Jacobs 1945:44–46, 191–192; cf. Lyman 1900a:175–176).

Religious Life and Shamans

Religious ceremonialism was centered upon so-called guardian-spirit powers (Tualatin-Yamhill ayúɫmei, ayúɫmiˑ, Central ayúˑɫma '[supernatural] power'). A variety of such powers, associated with animals, natural phenomena, inanimate things, and supernatural beings was available, and there was a correspondingly great variation in the strength and good and bad effects of such powers. Evidently, Kalapuyans considered socially significant achievement of any kind to be intimately tied to the possession of such powers. All individuals, men and women, slaves and free, could obtain or receive them.

Individuals, especially young people around the age of puberty, sought powers during solitary five-night quests at known power places. During a quest, an aspirant fasted and worked all night—typically, by swimming, keeping up a fire, and piling up rock, brush, or earth at the power place. A power, if it came, usually appeared in human likeness, during a dream following the vigil.

Most people had their own power songs, which they sang during special winter dances. Such dances were held by individuals, especially shamans, to master or intensify their own powers. Other dancers were paid for attending, since their participation helped the sponsor to heighten his or her own power. Regalia and accouterments used on such occasions included: shamans' otter-skin ceremonial sashes, decorated with feathers, shells, beads, and human hair; carved hand-held shamanistic figures representing powers; hide drums, hollow rattles, and rattle drums; feathered headdresses and feathered dance shirts. Dancers also commonly painted their faces.

Shamanistic status, obtainable by women or men (Tualatin-Yamhill apʰáˑlakʰ, Central ampʰáˑlakʰya 'shaman') was usually achieved only later in life. The occupation was evidently a risky one, since shamans were often suspected of causing death through uncontrolled or deliberate misuse of their powers. Even though a shaman might forestall vengeance by making adequate blood-money payment to the relatives of a supposed victim, repeated incidents might mark him for assassination.

See Jacobs (1945:56–72, 179–185, 338–342, 345–348) for much detail on powers and shamanism, Du Bois (1939) on the Ghost Dance, and Beckham, Toepel, and Minor (1984) on postcontact religious movements.

Life Cycle

Ceremonial occasions accompanied events in the life cycles of individuals, such as the initiation of the career of a shaman, the naming of a child, the first menses of a girl. According to Frachtenberg, such ceremonial occasions often included distribution of presents to those attending.

The dead were customarily buried, though cremation (of the poor?) is also recorded. Things that a person had used during life were either buried with the corpse or burned or otherwise destroyed. Wealthy people were wrapped in valuable blankets and buried with some of their valuables. Certain items, such as perforated baskets and buckets, were placed about the grave. After horses were introduced among the Tualatin-Yamhill, a horse (according to Gatschet, the one that had borne the corpse) was killed and left at the grave. The deceased's house was at least ritually purified; it might be burned entirely. Slaves and "money" (mainly dentalium shells and valuable beads) were divided among the nearest relatives, with other property going to relatives or nonrelatives, in exchange for smaller return gifts (see Jacobs 1945:74–76, 196–198).

History

The first definitely recorded contact between Whites and Kalapuyans occurred in 1812, when a party of Pacific Fur Company traders under Donald McKenzie penetrated the Willamette Valley (Stuart 1935:31–33; Rees 1880:22). From 1812 into the 1840s, Kalapuyans had many contacts with fur traders, and in the 1830s the first settlers and missionaries became established in the Willamette Valley. However, only a few passing references and observations concerning Kalapuyans have come from this period.

Kalapuyan populations suffered catastrophic declines during early historical times, the most dramatic single decrease probably occurring during 1830 to 1833, when malaria swept the Willamette and lower Columbia areas (Boyd 1975). There are no reliable data on how large Kalapuyan populations were before this disastrous event. Lewis and Clark (in Thwaites 1904–1905, 6:118) gave a figure of 2,000 about 1806, the figure from which Mooney (1928:18) projected a population of 3,000 for all the Kalapuyans about 1780. However, these estimates are complicated by the fact that Lewis and Clark also located 10,600 other inhabitants on the Willamette River of whom 7,600 (excluding 3,000 possible Molalas) were presumably, or presumably included, upriver Kalapuyans.

Efforts to negotiate treaties, beginning in 1851 (fig. 4), revealed opposition on the part of surviving Kalapuyans toward government intentions to remove western Oregon Native peoples to the east side of the Cascade Range (United States Unratified Treaties 1851, reproduced in Mackey 1974:90–125). Treaties embracing all the Kalapuyans were ratified in 1855 (Kappler 1904–1941, 2: 657–660, 665–669). In 1856, the few remaining Kalapuyans were taken to Grand Ronde Reservation, Oregon, where they were consolidated with survivors from other interior western Oregon groups (Clackamas, Molala, Upper Umpqua, Takelma, and Shasta). The fate of

Smithsonian, NAA: 2854-f-9.

Fig. 4. Joseph Hudson (*yálkʰama*), or Jo Hutchins, Santiam spokesman. This man, who according to Jacobs's (1928–1936:84, 86) information had a Tualatin father and an Ahantchuyuk mother, played prominent roles in the negotiations for the 1851 unratified treaty and the ratified treaty of 1855, and as a spokesman for his people during the early reservation period. A few of his speeches, perhaps translations of Chinook Jargon originals, are recorded from councils at Grand Ronde Reservation (Brunot in ARCIA 1872: 148–151; Meacham 1875:117–119; Ramsey 1977:120–121). Sketched, probably at treaty negotiations (Bushnell 1938:10), by George Gibbs, Champoeg, Oreg., 1851.

Kalapuyan tribal identities in this heterogeneous yet closely knit reservation community parallels the fate of the Kalapuyan languages there. Chinook Jargon, the lingua franca of the early community, became the symbolic as well as functional community "Indian language." As such, it continued in daily use into the time of widespread English competency and well beyond the effective demise of all the community's tribal languages.

While Grand Ronde people on the whole readily adopted Euro-American dress, housing, and occupational skills (fig. 5), it is equally evident that Native ideological culture and ceremonialism carried on vigorously at Grand Ronde throughout the era of reservation segregation. This is most dramatically apparent with respect to shamanistic ceremonialism, which persisted into the early twentieth century on the half of the reservation dominated by intermarried Kalapuyan, Chinookan, and Molala survivors (Zenk 1988). In 1956 both Grand Ronde Reservation and the tribes resident were terminated by the federal government. In 1974 the Grand Ronde tribes reorganized as The Confederated Tribes of Grand Ronde; the following year they incorporated as a nonprofit organization, *551*

Henry Zenk, Portland, Oreg.

Fig. 5. Mose Hudson's blacksmith shop, Grand Ronde Reservation, Oreg. left to right, Frank Norwest (Iroquois-Kalapuyan), John B. ("Mose") Hudson (Santiam-Yoncalla), Henry Petite (French-Clackamas) holding bear trap, and unidentified White man. Photographed in 1909, cropped.

and they were restored to federal status in 1983. Total tribal membership was estimated at 1,044 in 1987 (U.S. Bureau of Indian Affairs. Financial Management Office 1987:20).

Synonymy

The name Kalapuya is from the Chinookan designations for the speakers of the Kalapuyan languages, Upriver Kiksht *itgalapúywiyukš*, Clackamas *itk̓alapúyawaykš*; the stem *-galapúywi-* or *-k̓alapúywa-* is apparently not originally Chinookan and is of unknown origin (Michael Silverstein, personal communication 1975 and communication to editors 1974; Jacobs 1929–1930). The linguistic family name was coined by Powell (1891:81) as Kalapooian, who was followed by Hodge (1907–1910, 1:645–646). The name Kalapuya has sometimes been applied narrowly to the tribes speaking Central Kalapuyan, or to a subset of them; variants used this way are: Calapooia band of Calapooias, for the Ahantchuyuk, 1855 (Kappler 1904–1941, 2:665); Calapooia proper, for the Mary's River tribe (Frachtenberg 1915a:89); Santiam *k̓alapʰúya*, for the Central groups with or without the Santiam (Jacobs 1928–1936, 46:15, 78); Calapooya (Hodge 1907–1910, 1:187–188). Spellings in early sources include: Cal-lar-po-e-wah and Cal-lah-po-e-wah (Lewis and Clark in Thwaites 1904–1905, 4:241–242, 255), Cathlapoo-yays (Stuart 1935:33), Calipuyowes (Henry in Coues 1897, 2: 814, 879), Calapooie and Calapooya (D. Douglas 1914:59, 237, 238), Kallapooyahs (Slacum 1837:15), Kalapuya (Hale 1846:564–566), Col-lap-poh-yea-ass (Ross 1849: 235, 236), Calipoa (ARCIA 1850:130), Callapooahs

(Hines 1851:100), Call-law-poh-yea-as (Ross 1855:108), Kallapūia (Gibbs 1877:212).

Names for the Kalapuyans in other Indian languages are: Molala mú·khaya (Jacobs 1928), Salmon River Tillamook sqʰulú·tʰwəš 'valley people' (Harrington 1942); Siuslaw qʰáiχqʰa·χhí·čʰ and ʔáučʰhí·čʰ (Harrington 1942); Alsea k̓í·čʌtšlʌm (Harrington 1942). Hodge (1907–1910, 1:188) wrongly gives the local group name tsänh-alokual as applying to a larger grouping. A few early sources refer to the Kalapuyans and other Indians of interior western Oregon as Shoshones (Lewis and Clark in Thwaites 1904–1905, 6:118–119; Stuart 1935:48; Henry in Coues 1897, 2:794).

Tribes

Of the tribes, the political status of those in the southern Willamette valley is uncertain.

Ahantchuyuk. The spelling was established by Hodge (1907–1910, 1:28), for Central *anhánčiyukʰ*, literally 'the ones belonging behind, away'. Historical variants are Hanchoiks and Hanshoke, and local terms are French Prairie Indians and Pudding River Indians.

Chelamela. The name (Hodge 1907–1910, 1:242) is from the Tualatin-Yamhill place-name čʰalámali·, the people of which were alámali· (Gatschet; Frachtenberg). Variants are Lamali, La-malle, and names based on early names for the Long Tom River: Lum Tumbles (Spalding 1853), Long-tongue-buff (Ross 1849:236), Laptambif (Hodge 1907–1910, 1:760).

Chemapho. Hodge's (1907–1910, 1:242) name is Central čʰamé·fuʔ, literally 'mountain place'; they were also referred to as the Maddy Band or Muddy Creek.

Luckiamute ('lukēə,myōot). The name, whose spelling follows that of the river rather than Hodge's (1907–1910, 1:754) Lakmiut, is ultimately from Central alá·k̓mayokʰ, Central and Tualatin-Yamhill alá·k̓mayutʰ. Other variants include Che-luk-i-ma-uke, Lakmayuk, Lakmiuk, Luckamukes, Luckamutes, Luckimute, and Luk-a-mai-yuk.

Mary's River. Named from the English place-name; Hodge's (1907–1910, 1:244) Chepenafa and its variants Chep-en-a-pho and Pineifu are from the place-name corresponding to Central ampí·nefu. Also referred to as Marysville.

Mohawk River. This was apparently the group referred to as Peeyou by Ross (1849:236).

Santiam (ˌsäntē'yăm). This name (Hodge 1907–1910, 2: 461) is based on a term of uncertain status recorded as santyám in Tualatin-Yamhill (Gatschet) and Central (Jacobs). Their Central name anhálpam, literally 'the upland people' or 'the upriver people', also appears as Ahalpam. Santainas and Santaims are also found.

Tsanchifin. The name Tsanchifin (Hodge 1907–1910, 2:821) is an adaptation of a recording by Gatschet of

Central čʰančʰífin; the group was also referred to as Chafan, in the 1855 Dayton treaty, and Lower McKenzie.

Tsankupi. This is Hodge's (1907–1910, 2:821) name, based on Central čʰantʰk̓úpiʔ: variants are Coupé and Tekopa.

Tualatin ('twälətən). This name and Hodge's (1907–1910, 1:108) Atfalati reflect Tualatin-Yamhill atʰfálaȉi, Central antʰwálaȉi; historical spellings include Faladin, Fallatrahs, Follaties, Tualati, Tualaty, Tuhwala-ti, and Twalaty. The group has also been referred to as the Wapato Lake Indians, or Wapato, variously spelled.

Winnefelly. This group, whose name appears in the Dayton treaty of 1855 (Hodge 1907–1910, 2:962), is possibly the same as the Ampishtna (Hodge 1907–1910, 1:50), whose name corresponds to Central čʰampéʔšna.

Yamhill ('yăm,hĭl). This name, for which Hodge (1907–1910, 2:987) used Yamel, reflects Tualatin-Yamhill ayámhil, Central ayámhala. Spelling variants include Yamhelas, Yamil, Yamstills, and Si-yam-il.

Yoncalla (,yäŋ'kälu). This name, Hodge's (1907–1910, 2:1000) Yonkalla, is from Central (and apparently Yoncalla) yánkalatʰ, Tualatin-Yamhill ayanké·lt, the latter name meaning 'high houses' according to Frachtenberg. Spellings include Ayankēld, Yamkallie, Yangoler, Yon-colla, and Jamkallie. The Yoncalla have also been called the Umpqua Kalapuya.

Sources

Only a few direct observations of Kalapuyan life are available from the period of this culture sketch. A number of these, with early government documents and other items, have been published by Mackey (1974).

The results of Gatschet's, Frachtenberg's, and Jacobs's fieldwork are mostly in manuscript. Gatschet's Tualatin texts and Frachtenberg's Mary's River texts (the latter including the best collection of Kalapuyan myths), both reworked and corrected by Jacobs, as well as Jacobs's own Santiam ethnographic and myth texts, have been published by Jacobs (1945).

Aside from myth texts, very little has been preserved of the expressive side of Kalapuyan culture. Music is represented by some Tualatin song texts in Gatschet (1877m), a recording from Frachtenberg (1914a), and recordings with ethnographic notes from Jacobs (1929–1930, 1933). For a guide to Jacobs's ethnographic notes and recordings see Seaburg (1982).

See "Prehistory of the Lower Columbia and Willamette Valley," this volume, for a review of archeological sources and findings. Ethnohistorical surveys include L.R. Collins (1951), Peterson (1975), Beckham (1977:43–55), Minor et al. (1980:51–62), Beckham, Minor, and Toepel (1981:49–82), and Beckham, Toepel, and Minor (1982:118–142, 1984:59–80).

Prehistory of the Oregon Coast

RICHARD E. ROSS

Culturally the Oregon coast has been separated into three sections: the north portion from the Columbia River to the Siletz River, the central portion from the Siletz River south to the Coquille, and the south portion from the Coquille River to the California border. Roughly, the division between the south and central portions corresponds to the geological division between the Coast Range and the Klamath Mountains.

Archeological information from the entire coast consists of site locations (fig. 1), data from several sites that have been systematically tested, and data from the very few intensively excavated sites. The most visible sites are shell middens found on the coastline adjacent to onshore rocks and in the river valleys and estuaries where shellfish were available. These sites range from very small to once-huge mounds of shells. Few of the really large shell mounds are intact. Many coastal sites have been impacted heavily, if not totally destroyed, by erosion. Much more severe has been the human impact; by the 1980s roads and other construction had destroyed probably 60–70 percent of the sites recorded in the 1950s (R.E. Ross 1983).

Too much is known about the area archeologically to consider it merely a southern extension of the Northwest Coast culture area, but not enough to have easily recognizable and well formulated archeological cultures. The limited data available in the form of radiocarbon dates and excavation reports have not been well synthesized.

Excavation of the Lone Ranch site in 1936 was the first systematic investigation of an archeological site anywhere along the Oregon coast (Berreman 1944). The Bullards Beach site and Schwenn site (Leatherman and Krieger 1940) were excavated next. A survey of the northern and central portions of the coast (F.R. Collins 1953) and work on the Coquille River (Cressman 1953, 1953a), Flores Lake, and on the north coast near Tillamook (T.M. Newman 1959) followed.

In the 1960s only two small surveys were undertaken (D.L. Cole 1965; Cole and Davis 1963), and an attempt was made to salvage information from a large site destroyed by Coast Highway 101 (Heflin 1966).

Early in the 1970s a research effort was initiated by Oregon State University. Since that time a number of sites have been intensively sampled (Barner 1981; Brauner

1976a; W.A. Davis 1968; Draper 1980, 1981, 1982; Draper and Hartmann 1979; B.F. Harrison 1978; Hartmann 1978, 1978a; Pullen 1982; R.E. Ross 1975, 1975a, 1976, 1977, 1985; Ross and Snyder 1979, 1985; S.L. Snyder 1978; Snyder and Ross 1980; Zontek 1978, 1983). A few other sites have been tested (Minor, Beckham, and Greenspan 1980; Phebus and Drucker 1979; Stubbs 1973).

Most of the archeological investigations have been conducted primarily on shell middens, an emphasis influenced strongly by the visibility and vulnerability of the site type. Due to the alkaline pH of the shell midden matrix, preservation of bone material is excellent, providing a much more diversified inventory than is typical for most other sites. Cultural differences at these sites can be detected through space and time, but the assemblages and associated faunal material indicate an interesting balance of marine, riverine, and terrestrial resources used from the different locales through time.

Pre-Marine Cultures

There is little information about human adaptations to marine resources along the Oregon coast. However, R.E. Ross (1985) postulates that several sites on the southern coast containing "early" projectile point styles are sites that were used by interior or terrestrially oriented rather than marine or riverine-oriented peoples. Southern coast sites also show strong relationships to interior valley sites that are dated considerably earlier: interior sites are dating from 2000 to 9000 B.C. (Ross and Schreindorfer 1985), while sites showing similar stone artifact assemblages on the coast are dating roughly 1–1000 B.C. It is certainly possible that the coast was inhabited earlier than this 1000 B.C. date by people with an interior orientation, but the evidence is inconclusive.

There has been an attempt to establish a chronology of south coast sites using projectile points as the distinguishing criteria (Pullen 1982). For the Early period (1000 B.C.–A.D. 500) there is no evidence of large permanent or semipermanent occupation sites on coastal headlands or near the mouths of the rivers. This early period is characterized by a reliance on upland resources, with marine resources playing a minor role or not being used at all. Thus Pullen's Early period appears to fit into what has

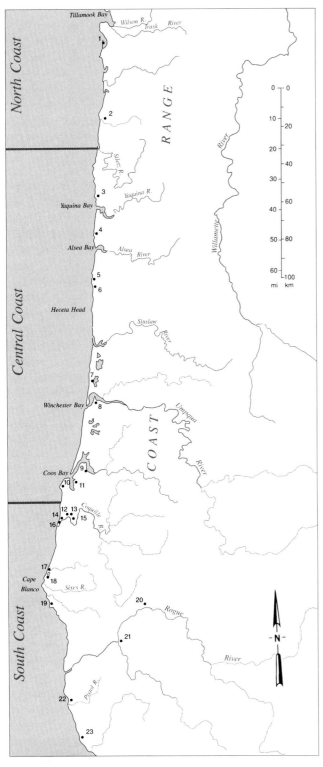

Fig. 1. Archeological sites along the southern Oregon coast: 1, Netarts Spit; 2, Three Rox; 3, Yaquina; 4, Seal Rock; 5, Cape Perpetua; 6, Neptune; 7, Takenitch Lake; 8, Umpqua/Eden; 9, Catching Slough; 10, Cape Arago; 11, Indian Bay; 12, Philpott; 13, Schwenn; 14, Bullards Beach; 15, 35CS23; 16, Bandon Lighthouse; 17, Strain; 18, Blacklock; 19, Port Orford Head and Blundon; 20, Marial; 21, Tlegetlinten; 22, Pistol River and Meyers Creek; 23, Lone Ranch.

here been designated as a pre-marine period.

Diagnostic artifacts for this period consist primarily of stone objects and include ground stone implements for the processing of vegetal resources, and hunting and butchering items such as scrapers, blades, knives, and a wide range of projectile points manufactured from cryptocrystalline and obsidian materials. Projectile points are generally leaf-shaped, expanded stem, contracting stem, and side-notched. There is little information about pre-marine period occupation in the central and northern sections of the coast. Umpqua/Eden in the central section yielded a projectile point and a knife that appear to predate the base of the shell midden, which is dated to 1010 B.C. (table 1). A date of 6350 B.C. came from beneath the shell midden at the Neptune site, but no well established association of artifacts was noted.

Early Marine and Riverine Cultures, 3000 B.C.–A.D. 500

One of the earliest and best components of early human adaptation to coastal environments comes from the Umpqua/Eden site, on the Umpqua River estuary. A carbon-14 date of 1010 ± 45 B.C. (Dicarb 1174) is associated with this early component of relatively thin, sometimes discontinuous layer of shells lying on a clay stratum. The midden was composed predominantly of bay mussels but also included cockles, bent-nose clams, horse mussels, and butter clams. The artifacts show an orientation to marine and riverine foods. Bone harpoons are the most conspicuous, with unilateral barbs, unilateral and bilateral hinge guards, and flat to slightly rounded bases. Other bone tools included antler-tine flake tools and wedges. The variety of bone artifacts in this early component was not so high as that recovered from later middens.

Stone tools were practically nonexistent: a few small lanceolate projectile points (fig. 2) and scrapers, almost all occurring in the late part of the Early Marine.

Harbor seals apparently were the most used species, with a large percentage of infants as well as adults represented. Steller sea lions were represented in smaller quantities, but these relative amounts may be more indicative of the site location than resource preference. Sea and river otter remains were also represented. Land animals were represented by black-tailed deer, beaver, and a few bear and raccoon. As would be expected in an estuarine environment, waterfowl were well represented; almost 85 percent of the bird bones were of various kinds of ducks, with herons and cranes present in much lesser quantities (Ross and Snyder 1985).

Bones of flounder and other flat fish, salmon (chinook and coho), sturgeon, rockfish, greenling, seaperch, buffalo sculpin, and herring were all recovered.

Umpqua/Eden represents only a limited facet of early marine and riverine exploitation of the Oregon coast at this date. People were probably drawn to the site on the basis of resources available from the immediate area—an *555*

Table 1. Prehistoric Sites on the Oregon Coast

Site Name and Number	Dates
North Coast	
Netarts Spit 35TL1	A.D. 1400 ± 150
	A.D. 1670 ± 150
Three Rox 35LNC33	A.D. 1070 ± 70
35LNC59	A.D. 1020 ± 80
Central Coast	
Yaquina 35LNC50	A.D. 800 ± 50
Seal Rock 35LNC14	A.D. 1575 ± 70
	A.D. 1790 ± 80
Neptune 35LN3	A.D. 1630 ± 45
Takenitch Lake 35DO130	
Umpqua/Eden 35DO83	about A.D. 500
	about A.D. 1500
	1010 B.C. ± 45
Catching Slough 35CS42	A.D. 800 ± 55
(Ross)	
Indian Bay 35CS30	A.D. 1700 ± 80
Cape Arago 35CS11	A.D. 410 ± 50
Cape Perpetua 35LN26c	A.D. 600 ± 70
35LN26b	A.D. 480 ± 75
South Coast	
Philpott 35CS1	A.D. 1380 ± 50
	A.D. 1700 ± 40
Bullards Beach 35CS3	about A.D. 1800
Bandon Lighthouse 35CS5	about A.D. 1800
unnamed 35CS23	A.D. 1300 ± 150
	A.D. 1600 ± 150
Port Orford Head 35CU9	about A.D. 1000
Blundon 35CU106	A.D. 1300
	100 B.C. ± 80
Pistol River 35CU61	ca. A.D. 1700
Meyers Creek 35CU62	1050 ± 90 B.C.
Blacklock 35CU75	800 ± 55 B.C.
Lone Ranch 35CU37	ca. A.D. 1400
Marial 35CU84	860 ± 50 B.C.
	3900 B.C. ± 120
	4535 B.C. ± 80
	6610 B.C. ± 190
Schwenn 35CS16	ca. 500 B.C.
Tlegetlinten 35CU59	ca. 4000 B.C.
Strain 35CU47	ca. A.D. 1700

estuarine habitat—and this certainly does not represent the total range of resources available along the coast.

Whether or not adaptation to marine environments had taken place all along the coast 3,000 years ago is not known. However, at the (Meyers Creek site, a carbon sample reportedly from the roof beam of a house was associated with a shell midden dated to 1050 B.C. ± 90 (Cressman 1977). No other information is available since most of the site was destroyed by road construction prior to collection of the sample.

Late Marine Cultures, A.D. 500–1856

Pullen (1982) proposed a Late period (A.D. 500–1856), for the southern coast, which is relatively similar to conditions on the central and northern sections. This was a period of changing culture patterns when most of the villages and campsites were located on or very close to the coast so that marine, riverine, and estuarine resources could be used while terrestrial resources continued to be a part of the resource base.

Distinguishing criteria for this Late Marine period are considerably different than those for the Pre-Marine and Early Marine periods. Not only are patterns of settlement and resource use different, but also the artifact assemblages show little similarity. Because the use of marine resources had become more firmly entrenched, there are sites that contain large quantities of shells.

The major projectile point styles are concave base, triangular, and tanged (fig. 3a-i), which are considerably different from those associated with Early Marine period sites. The tanged (barbed) points, identified as Gunther Barbed (fig. 3f-g) (Leonhardy 1967; Treganza 1958), are common in the Late period sites of interior and coastal sites of southwestern Oregon and northwestern California (Draper 1980). It is a distinct possibility that the introduction of the bow and arrow at around A.D. 500 (Heizer and Hester 1978:10) may be the major factor in changing projectile point styles. Two factors are evident during the period A.D. 500–900: projectile point styles changed a great deal, and there was a drastic change in the use of resources on the south coast, a change followed by cultural stability until White contact.

In addition to the projectile points, stone items include drills, gravers, hammerstones, pestles, scrapers, heavy choppers, netsinkers, bifaces, pipes, bowls. Sites of the Late Marine period do not yield either the range of stone tools found in Pre-Marine sites nor do they yield the overall quantity of finished artifacts or debitage. On the other hand, bone artifacts are generally quite plentiful and represent a wide range of activities. Some of the most common items include antler wedges, flaking tools, chisels, bone needles, awls, fishhooks (composite and single element), bipoints, pendants, fish lures, composite harpoon heads, and gaming pieces. Many of the items found in the Late Marine period as represented in the southern Oregon coast sites show strong cultural affiliations with sites of similar vintage on the northern coast of California (Berreman 1944; Draper 1980; Pullen 1982).

Problems of Interpretation

Marine-oriented sites take two configurations: those in environmental situations where other activities besides the collecting of shellfish were predominant, in which case the decay of organic material is rapid and comparison of

Oreg. State U., Horner Mus., Corvallis: a, N98 E93 9–430; b, STEN TNP-4; c, N100 98E 7–61; d, STEN TNP-1; e, N98 E92 10–100; f, N102 E94 8–17; g, N100 E92 SNM 9-2; h, STEN 1VSM-4; i, STEN T2–4; j, N102 E92 2–45; k, N98 E93 9–315; l, N104 E94 6–10; m, STEN 108–17; n, N100 E93 8–29; o, N98 E93 16-3; p, N98 E92 8–71; q, N98 E94 10–78.

Fig. 2. Artifacts of the Early Marine period: a, antler wedge; b-c, lanceolate projectile points; d, knife; e, grooved sandstone line sinker; f, sandstone pipe bowl; g, baked clay disk; h-i, single component harpoon head bases with bilateral hinge guards; j, unilaterally barbed single component harpoon head; k, cut and smoothed bone fragment; l-o, bone wedges; p, ground wedge-shaped bone section; q, smoothed antler tip. Artifacts not to scale.

artifact assemblages must rest on the lithic collection (Draper 1980); and those where the collecting of shellfish played a role strong enough that the shells formed distinct units themselves in the form of shell middens, in which case organic material is well preserved when in association with the shell. The tool inventory, as well as information about diet, is enhanced tremendously by the presence of shell. The tool inventory of the late sites includes a wide variety of bone items that would probably be absent from a non-shell-midden site either because of poor preservation or because of different activities where those bone tools were not used.

On the basis of preliminary analysis, there does not appear to be a major difference in the kind of resources exploited from early to late occupations but a possible difference appears in how heavily certain resources were utilized at different times.

The south coast is the best known section of the coast. In this area there are sites that correspond to Pre-Marine, Early Marine, and Late Marine periods. In fact, much understanding of coastal adaptations has been generated with evidence from this section. Most data supporting a Pre-Marine period come from the south coast, and this period appears to have close similarities to the interior valleys of Oregon and northern California.

An alternate view of sequential occupation and adaptation (Minor and Toepel 1983) uses the same time periods

as used here (Historic period A.D. 1792; Late Prehistoric, A.D. 500–1792; Middle Prehistoric, 1000 B.C.–A.D. 500) with some of the same criteria but without a Pre-Marine adaptation on the south coast. Rather, the sites showing no marine adaptation are thought to be sites that were used for different functions within an overall marine adaptation.

The Early Marine period has not been well identified here, but there are certainly indications that it existed at least by 1000 B.C., as indicated on the central and north coast.

The Late Marine is well represented and shows interesting connections with the northern California coast and some of the interior valleys.

The central section of the coast has a somewhat different archeological background and orientation from the southern section. First, there is only a thin scattering of evidence suggesting a pre-marine or riverine-oriented occupation. Second, the oldest well-documented marine-oriented site, Umpqua/Eden, is found there. Finally, the central coast cultures do not appear to be so similar to the California cultures as the southern Oregon coast cultures do, maybe because of distance but quite possibly because of other mitigating influences such as different environments (out of acorn country?), more influences from the interior (Kalapuya) valley, and possibly more influence from the Columbia River region. On the north coast a

557

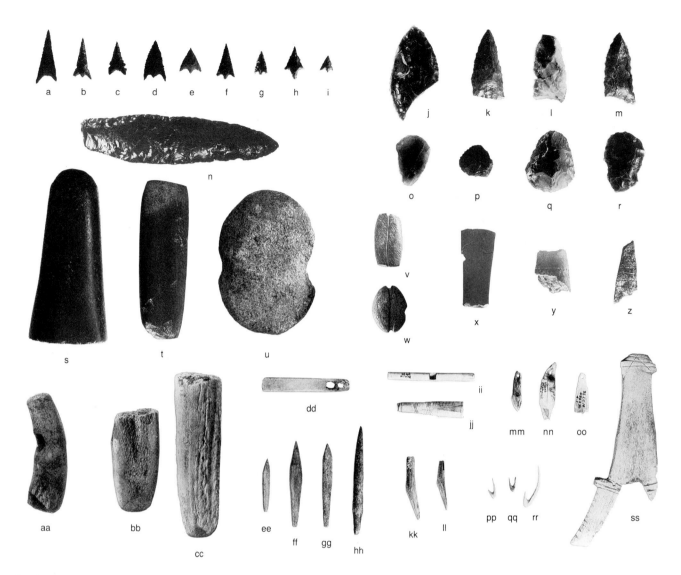

Oreg. State U., Horner Mus., Corvallis: a, N104 E96 1–31; b, N102 E96 4–16; c, N100 E15 5–94; d, N106 E92 6-3; e, N98 2–10; f, N108 E98 3–212; g, N92 E96 1–6; h, N104 E96 3–306; i, N112 E98 3–62; j, N104 E92 8-1; k, N48 E30 8–11C; l, N58 E26 F2 4.11; m, N58 E28 7.1A; n, OH-1C; o, 100N 94E 4–14; p, TB-8-3-68; q, 98N 98E 4–8; r, 98N 98E 3–160; s, 102N 96E 5–8; t, P1-1972; u, PU-1; v, N102 E92 5–8; w, N98 E94 1–22; x, 111 E92 4; y, N88 E125 0–5; z, N160 E94 4-3F; aa, N100 98E 3–7; bb, STEN H-4; cc, 94N 96.85E 2-1; dd, N98 E98 2–17; ee, N104 E94 4–74; ff, N104 E92 2–10; gg, N106 E92 2–91; hh, N100 E92 2–14; ii, 50/30 3–12; jj, N110 E92 3–64; kk, N100 E90 3–174; ll, N100 E90 3–68; mm, 100N 194E 4–13; nn, N98 E94 OM3-2; oo, N50 E30 4-1; pp, N108 E92 3–432; qq, N108 E92 3–431; rr, N110 E92 3–296; ss, 102N 196E 4–9.

Fig. 3. Artifacts of the Late Marine period: a, triangular, concave-base projectile point; b-c, side-notched projectile points; d-i, corner-notched projectile points (f-g, Gunther-barbed type); j, knife; k-m, probable projectile points; n, large obsidian knife; o-r, scrapers; s, pestle fragment; t, unfinished adz; u, large notched basalt cobble; v, shaped and grooved stone sinker; w, small notched and ground rock; x-y, clay pipe bowls; z, clay figurine; aa, bone handle for a drill; bb-cc, antler wedges; dd, bone fid; ee-hh, bone points for a composite harpoon; ii, bird bone whistle; jj, bird bone section with incised decoration; kk-ll, antler valves for a composite harpoon head; mm, perforated elk tooth; nn, perforated canine; oo, perforated bone pendant; pp-rr, single element bone fishhooks; ss, carved bone figurine with incised decoration. Artifacts not to scale.

situation similar to the central coast is found: no good evidence of early pre-marine adapted peoples, and only one early site with a well-developed marine and riverine adaptation.

All sites investigated so far along the central and north coasts show a well-integrated marine and riverine pattern from the oldest known sites at Umpqua/Eden and Palmrose to the contact period sites; however, there is certainly a difference in artifact inventory from the earliest to the later components, that is, different styles of stone projectile points, changes in bone harpoons, and a wider range of decorative items in later sites.

Conclusions

There appear to be at least three distinct cultural periods along most of the Oregon coast. The Pre-Marine period has an undetermined beginning, probably with interior origins and connections, and lasts until at least 500 B.C. and possibly a little later. This period is characterized by people inhabiting the coast line, river valleys, and western foothills but not using the marine resources to any great extent if at all. The sites are primarily open sites without the mitigating soil-changing presence of shells and thus yield only lithic items.

558

Overlapping with at least the end of the Pre-Marine is the Early Marine period, well established and in place all along the coast by at least 1000 B.C. This period signifies the beginning of adjustments to the variety of marine and river resources along the coast. It has not been established satisfactorily whether this was an indigenous adaptation or an adaptation begun elsewhere on the coast of North America and subsequently spread to the Oregon coast. It is readily discernible that the advent of marine exploitation fostered the use of bone tools while the use of lithic tools dropped dramatically. Various riverine resources including fish, waterfowl, shellfish, and small mammals as well as various marine resources, including rockfish, shellfish, and sea mammals were used.

The Early Marine ends at about A.D. 500 and is replaced by the Late Marine. The division between the two is arbitrary rather than an easily discernible change. The Late Marine is a full-fledged marine and riverine adaptation. A proliferation of sites, including large shell middens along the coast line and in the estuaries, indicates a population increase. Terrestrial resources are represented, but the emphasis is on marine and riverine resources. The lithic items are scarce, and stylistically the projectile points change dramatically from the earliest period; however, the emphasis is on a variety of bone tools.

The north coast appears to have been heavily influenced by cultures of the Columbia River area, which in turn implies some influences from farther north along the coast. The central coast seems to be a transition zone between the north and south coasts. It was influenced heavily by the cultures of the Willamette Valley. The south coast was obviously influenced by coastal cultures in northern California and by cultures of the interior valleys of southern Oregon and northern California. The Oregon section of the Northwest Coast of North America was not just a southern extension of the classic Northwest Coast cultures but an area revealing a surprising number of influences from other areas resulting in a culturally heterogeneous area.

Tillamook

WILLIAM R. SEABURG AND JAY MILLER

Language and Territory

The Tillamook ('tĭlə,mōōk) spoke the southernmost language of the Salishan language family. As a single-language subdivision of Salishan, Tillamook is more closely related to the Central Salish than to any other branch of the language family. The exact number of (probably) mildly differentiated dialects is not known but included Nehalem, Nestucca, Salmon River, and Siletz. Siletz is considered to be the most divergent of the dialects.*

The Tillamook occupied the Pacific coastal strip from approximately Tillamook Head in Clatsop County to the Siletz River in Lincoln County, Oregon. They built their villages near the mouths of the principal rivers that flow westward from the mountains of the Pacific Coast Range into the tidewaters of the Nehalem, Tillamook, Netarts, and Nestucca bays as well as near the mouths of the Salmon and Siletz rivers. The number and exact location of individual Tillamook-speaking communities and their populations are not known, but locations of historically attested villages are shown in figure 1.

External Relations

Data on relations between the Tillamook and neighboring Indian groups are not extensive. Lewis and Clark (in Thwaites 1904–1905, 3:338) describe a lively trade network across the whole region. E.D. Jacobs (1976) indicates that tanned beaver hides, canoes, and baskets were taken to the Columbia River to trade for abalone shell, dentalia, buffalo hides and buffalo horn dishes, and a dried, non-smoke-cured Columbia River salmon. Lewis and Clark (in Thwaites 1904–1905, 3:325) report that the

Tillamook traveled east of the Coast Range to Sauvie Island in the Columbia River to purchase wapato roots and other items. Gatschet (1877j; Zenk 1976:49) notes that the Tualatin Kalapuya traveled to Tillamook country to trade and to intermarry with the Tillamook. Slaves, too, played a part in the trading pattern since they were valued primarily for their sale price in Lower Chinook villages. Lewis and Clark (in Thwaites 1904–1905, 4:120) noted that a Clatsop man's young slave had been taken prisoner by the Tillamook from a large "nation" far to the south. Lee and Frost (1844:103) also report that the Tillamook raided their southern neighbors, taking prisoners to the north where they sold them to the Clatsop or the Chehalis.

Lewis and Clark (in Thwaites 1904–1905, 3:313, 320) report a village composed of both Clatsop and Tillamook families near present-day Seaside, Oregon. Boas (1894:5) found a small band of Clatsop Indians at Seaside in 1890 who had all adopted the Nehalem language as the result of marriages with Nehalem speakers. Hajda (1984:327–330) notes marriages between the Nehalem Tillamook and the Alsea and between the Nehalem and the Clatsop. Doubtless there were marriages between the Nehalem and the other Lower Chinookan groups and probably the Clatskanie as well. Such alliances required periodic visits to and gift exchanges with in-laws.

Little is known about conflicts between the Tillamook and their neighbors. In war, elkhide armor was worn, and war paint in stripes of red and black. Franchère (1967:117) recalled seeing Chinookans battling Tillamooks, and Gatschet reported stories of Tillamook warriors invading Tualatin Kalapuyan country (Mallery 1886:26). War expeditions may have been primarily for slave raiding purposes.

History

The first recorded encounter of Europeans with the Tillamook was by Robert Haswell, a member of the crew of Robert Gray's sloop *Lady Washington*, on August 10, 1788. Haswell noted that the natives possessed iron knives and that some were scarred from smallpox (T.C. Elliott 1928:170–171). Lewis and Clark (in Thwaites 1904–1905, 3, 4) were the next Whites to describe the Tillamook during their stay on Clatsop Plains in the winter of

*The phonemes of Nehalem Tillamook are: (plain stops and affricates) *t, c, č, k, q, kʷ, qʷ, ʔ*; (voiced lenis stops) *d, g, ġ, gʷ, ġʷ*; (glottalized stops and affricates) *ƚ, X̣, c̓, č̓, k̓, q̓, k̓ʷ, q̓ʷ*; (voiceless continuants) *ł, s, š, x, x̣, xʷ, x̣ʷ, h*; (plain resonants) *n, l, y, w*; (glottalized resonants) *ṅ, ḷ, ẏ, ẇ*; (vowels) *i, e, ə, a, u*; (stresses) primary (v́), secondary (v̀), weak (unmarked).

Information on Tillamook phonology is from Thompson and Thompson (1966, 1985).

The Tillamook words cited from Jacobs (1933b), E.D. Jacobs (1976), and Harrington (1942–1943) have been normalized but are not phonemicized; those from Thompson and Thompson (1965–1970) are in their phonemic transcription.

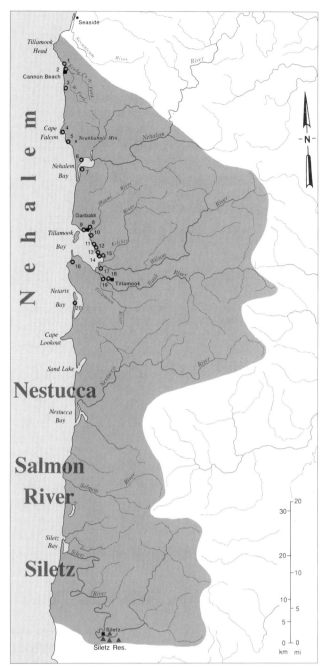

Fig. 1. Mid-19th-century territory and divisions of the Tillamook. Nehalem villages were given, but the village names and locations for Nestucca, Salmon River, and Siletz Tillamook Indians are not available: 1, dəhontəc; 2, No-cost; 3, Nat-ti; 4, kstəlu·ł; 5, nɪsyɛˀyɛ·kł; 6, dəsthkɪ·chən; 7, dɪsliyəqs; 8, Kil-har-hurst; 9, nəsxəwəqhən; 10, nəsga·ga·ł; 11, nəsxenus; 12, dɪstənəqs; 13, cohələˀəqs; 14, Kil-harnar; 15, nəxeɪnəgɪ; 16, skənəyɪwəs; 17, Chish-ucks; 18, thu·qa·tən; 19, Chuck-tins; 20, ni·ta·c.

1805–1806. Other early explorers who encountered the Tillamook include Alexander Henry in 1814, the naturalist David Douglas in 1824, and John K. Townsend in 1834–1836 (Taylor 1974a:49–50).

Lewis and Clark (in Thwaites 1904–1905, 6:117) estimated the number of Tillamooks to be 1,000 in

1805–1806. A Hudson's Bay Company census of about 1838 (Taylor 1974a:59) that recorded the figure of 1,500 included some Alseans and Siuslawans. Wilkes (1845:141) gave 400 as the population of the Tillamook while Lane in 1849 recorded a figure of 200 (Hodge 1907–1910, 2:751). Decline in Tillamook numbers was due more to epidemics of malaria and other diseases in the 1830s (Boyd 1975, 1985) than to warfare with invading White settlers in the 1840s and 1850s. Conflict with Whites following the Oregon Donation Land Act of 1850 and the ceding of Indian lands by the unratified treaties of 1851 with Oregon Superintendent of Indian Affairs Anson Dart was minimized by the peacekeeping efforts of Tillamook headman Kilchis (Vaughn 1851). For the most part the Tillamook were not removed to the Siletz Reservation, established in 1855, or to the Grand Ronde Reservation, established in 1857. Land claim cases by the Tillamook were disposed of by Congress in 1897 and 1912 and by the courts in 1945 (Zucker, Hummel, and Høgfoss 1983). In 1958 and 1962 Tillamooks received awards from the Indian Claims Commission (1974a).

Culture

Structures

Tillamook villages consisted of several permanent dwelling houses, at least one work-and-menstrual hut for women, sweathouses, and a graveyard for raised canoe burials. Villages were probably proportional to the size of the river or stream mouth at which they were often located. Houses occupied by four families were best remembered by E.D. Jacobs's (1976) informant. The Tillamook built rectangular houses of horizontal cedar planks, adzed to a width of about three or four feet and a thickness of about two or three inches, charred, and tied together with peeled and steamed spruce roots. Each had several fires down the middle of the floor pit and platforms for resting and sleeping along the sides. These houses were in two styles, one above-ground and another semisubterranean. Both had a horizontal row of four large center roof support posts, center ridgepoles, and a gabled roof of overlapping planks. At each end of the above-ground house was a cedar board door hung from the top of the board. The semisubterranean house had a door in one end of the roof; one entered by means of a ladder made of a plank into which holes had been cut. Two families shared the same fire, their respective sleeping platforms located on either side of it; mat partitions separated families and multiple wives. The platforms had headboards, rolled mat pillows, and a shelf above them for personal belongings. Some platforms were made into cubicles enclosed by cedar planks. The house floor was covered with a heavy layer of ferns and rush mat coverings. Extra light was provided by pitch torches or by burning fishheads or whale oil. Wood was stored in a small, grass-covered storage shed. Food was stored in baskets, and roots were kept in subfloor pits.

Canoes

Canoes of several sizes and shapes were the vital mode of transportation for travel between villages and for subsistence activities. The large Columbia River or "Chinook style" canoes held up to 12 people, according to E.D. Jacobs (1976). Lewis and Clark (in Thwaites 1904–1905, 4:34) reported large sea-going canoes that held 20–30 people. Canoes were hewn from a single log. They were painted black on the outside with a mixture of soot and elk fat and red on the inside with red clay and elk fat or other oil before they were coated with pitch. The bow and stern pieces were removable. During a war expedition the bow piece was replaced by one in the design of some kind of a "sea serpent" and the paddles were painted in black and red stripes. Two paddle styles were used, one with the end notched to resemble a spread letter w, used by men only, and the other, with a pointed blade, used by both sexes. Both paddles had crossbar handles.

Technology

Awl and needles were fashioned from bone. The shuttle to make nets was of elk antler and wood. Carrying baskets were conical, done in openwork. Basket patterns were done in three colors (Crawford 1983).

Clothing and Adornment

Capes of beaver or painted buckskin were worn, as were blankets of sewed rabbit, bobcat, or sea otter fur. Women wore a large back apron of grass, tule rush, or shredded bark, a small front apron, and short buckskin leggings. They had caps of basketry or animal fur.

Men wore breechclouts, buckskin shirts, and loose skin trousers. A one-piece moccasin was worn. In snow, a circular-type snowshoe was used.

Both sexes painted their central hair part red. Women wore two braids; men, one. Women's legs and arms were tattooed decoratively. Men had one arm tattooed to measure dentalium. Both sexes wore ear pendants; only men wore nose pendants (E.D. Jacobs 1933–1934, 1976; Jacobs 1933–1934; Sauter and Johnson 1974).

Life Cycle

● BIRTH Only women should be present to assist the birth and those assisting might include a midwife and female shaman. Anciently the Tillamook employed a birth rack; later, they utilized a board seat with a horizontal wooden gripping bar. A vertical grasping pole was also sometimes used, but it could be injurious to the newborn.

Tillamook Co. Pioneer Mus., Tillamook, Oreg.: 1319.
Fig. 2. Basket in wrapped twining. Materials are tan and black raffia, but the design is typical of Tillamook work. Attributed to Lizzie Adams of Garibaldi, Oreg., it was made in the early 20th century. Diameter at the rim, 15.2 cm.

Following birth, the rack or pole, mother's clothes, and floor matting were thrown away in the woods. The afterbirth was left on a rush mat at the foot of a spruce sapling so the child would grow tall and strong. When the umbilical cord fell off the baby, it was rolled in charcoal, sewn into a small beaded bag stuffed with feathers, and worn by the toddler until five or six years of age. If the bag were lost, the child would become foolish or disobedient.

The baby had a nursing mother as a wet nurse for the first three days of life because its own mother's milk was considered harmful. The mother remained in confinement for about 15 days. Her breasts were washed in warm water and rubbed with marrow. Her hips were steamed through a hole in her bed matting. For the first five days the woman stayed awake pressing on her abdomen to ensure all the blood was expelled. The father spent 10 nights without sleep. After approximately 10 days the child was bound in a cradle with a head presser to deform the front of his head if he were freeborn.

● CHILDHOOD Infants, who were fed on demand, were given pacifiers of elk sinew, a piece of tough meat or clam, and allowed a little broth. They were denied lamprey or steelhead as too supernaturally powerful for them. Children were given toy versions of the tools they would later use as adults, played at adult tasks or swam during the day, and ate when hungry. Children had to be inside and fed before dark because the red sky of sunset marked a time identified with the feared Wild Woman.

The child was named at an ear piercing ceremony, when girls had their ears pierced and boys had both their ears and nasal septum pierced. Only adults attended the ceremony and the piercing was always performed by a man, usually a shaman, using a bone needle and elk sinew.

Fig. 3. left to right, Minnie Adams Scovell, her mother Emma Adams, Jane Adams, and her daughter Mabel Adams Burns. The older women were noted basketmakers, and all four worked with linguists to record the Tillamook language. They were descendants of the Tillamook Chief Illga Adams and his Clatsop wife, Maggie Adams (Crawford 1983:13–14). Photographed in the Kilchis area, Ore., 1909.

The ceremony included feasting and dancing but its magnitude varied with the status of the parents. Children were often given the names of relatives who had been deceased for several years since there was a taboo on names identical or similar to those of the recently dead. If someone had the name of someone recently deceased, he substituted another name for several years.

Tiny babies were carried in a rectangular cradle, at six months transferred to a canoe-shaped cradle, and slightly older children were carried in a pack basket. Children were not toilet trained until after they were verbal. As baby teeth loosened they were pulled out with fingers and placed on a stake beside a young spruce tree so that the secondary teeth would grow straight and healthy. Only rarely was a misbehaving child whipped by its father; the usual practice was a lecture by a parent or other elder.

• PUBERTY A boy's first kill and a girl's first food gathering were reserved as a gift of respect for the elderly in the community. At puberty a girl was secluded by rush mats hung around her bed platform. The girl fasted four to five days, used a body scratcher, had an already prepared supply of cedar bark menstrual pads, and spent her time being extremely still. She wore red paint on her face, hands, forearms, and lower legs on the first day. On the fourth or fifth evening her old woman attendant, perhaps

a shaman, dressed her in a blanket decorated with beads and dentalium, a beaded halter, a basket cap and gave her a cane before she was sent alone into the woods, keeping a vigil until dawn for a vision of a guardian spirit. During the vigil she repeatedly bathed in a cold stream. She returned before sunrise in order to have her first meal. Any guardian acquired would remain inactive until the girl was middle aged. Boas (1923:6–7) reported that the girl might cook for herself and dance during the evenings of her seclusion but this may represent Alsea influence among the Salmon River or Siletz Tillamook communities. The Nehalem Tillamook girl remained in seclusion about 15 days, rising early each morning to bathe, using her own dishes and wooden fork for another 60 days, and maintaining food taboos on steelhead, eel, crab, and red berries for a year. She had to stay away from the sick, women giving birth, and hunting or fishing equipment. She returned monthly to the communal menstrual house in each village, accompanied by an older woman attendant, perhaps until she was married.

A boy was sent to fast and acquire a guardian spirit when his voice began changing. In the woods, he would frequently bathe in a stream. He might stay five days and nights, but the vision seems to have been expected on the third night. His power was equated with the song he obtained. Rarely, a guardian spirit sought out a boy without benefit of a quest. A shaman directed his or her novice on a more formalized quest. Boys did not activate their spirit powers until middle age.

• MARRIAGE Village exogamy was preferred. Parents and male go-betweens arranged marriages, but the opinions of potential partners seem to have been consulted and valued. The Tillamook recognized two marriage ceremonials: special and common. The special marriage required that at least one parent have a strong power, that the bride be childless even if she had been married previously, and that it be the first marriage of the groom. The special marriage was an elaborate affair involving so many guests that it was held out of doors. It included the lavish display and giving of dentalia, other valuables, and clothing, and a large feast. The common marriage involved a speech by a "good talker" and the delivery of the bride to the husband's home, return gifts, and a feast. A bride price, sčá·wə́šu, representing claims to the children the woman would bear, was paid commensurate with her status. A reciprocal groom price was paid. The groom appeared to have done bride service for five days before he and his bride took up residence with his parents or in his village. Later the couple would consider their options and choose a residence where they felt most comfortable, were due to inherit, or could be of help to kinfolk. A couple probably did not have intercourse until several nights after the wedding, the groom having been cautioned to be kind and careful. A special foreplay technique, x̣á·px̣ap, was used when the bride was a virgin. When a couple had had intercourse during the night, they arose to bathe especially early the next morning.

High status or high class men were polygynous. The levirate was practiced but the sororate was less likely because the widower preferred to broaden his marital alliances. Senior and child-producing wives had authority over younger, or childless co-wives. Jealousy between co-wives or a husband and an unfaithful wife raised the emotions, sometimes with fatal consequences. If matters became unbearable, a wife might leave with her children. The deserted husband might demand a return of the bride price, hire a poison doctor to get revenge, or take matters into his own hands. Illegitimate births were a great disgrace and unless a marriage could be effected, infanticide was likely.

● DEATH When a Tillamook approached death, a shaman was usually present and doctoring. When death was imminent, a man might be concerned with the disposition of his wife, his possessions, and the readying of his burial canoe. At death the body was washed, the eyes closed and bandaged, the face painted solid red, the body dressed, wrapped in a blanket, and bound with overlapping strips of cedar bark. There was a two- or three-day wake while mourners gathered, bringing grave goods. The body rested on its platform bed in the deserted house, attended by several people who kept each other awake so their souls would not be taken away by the deceased. A shaman sang in the early evening in the house of the wake. The body was placed in its canoe and the canoe was removed through a corner of the house. The canoe was placed on supports in the burial ground during the morning hours when the other dead were still asleep. Another canoe was inverted over the burial canoe and grave goods were hung onto, or suspended on a stick over, the canoe. No food was placed with the dead for fear that all similar foods would become spoiled for the living. In wealthy families the canoe might be reopened approximately one year later, the bones cleaned, and grave goods renewed to honor the deceased.

Those who handled the dead had to fast and bathe in a stream in the woods for five days, rubbing themselves with fir needles. Each night they rushed the house of the deceased blowing shrilly on small whistles and pretending to shoot at something outside the house with tiny bows and arrows. A shaman sang each night during this ritual and fed the men cooked camas on the fifth night. After the purification, all the clothes and paraphernalia used by the men were deposited in the woods. Murderers and those who killed in battle underwent this same ritual but for a 10-day period. When a family reached extinction, all its burial canoes might be placed together in the house of the last of the family to die. Close relatives mourned intensely for 15 days and then less actively for the rest of the year. The dead went first to the afterworld of the recently dead, ahá?ɪ; years later they passed to the land of the ancestral dead, áłʒá?aɪ. Apparently, denizens of both lands could sometimes return to trouble the living.

Subsistence

The Tillamook year was divided between the economic summer activities and the religious winter ones. The seasons were named for important fish, roots, and berries; and ritual ceremonies accompanied their first consumption. Spring began with the gathering of salmonberry sprouts around April and progressed through the harvest of the salmonberries in May and June, camas and lamprey harvests in June and July, the salalberry, huckleberry, and strawberry harvest in July and August, the chinook salmon runs in August and September, the coho salmon season in October, fall elk hunting, chum salmon runs in November, the collection of fern and a lily root, yícqa, and kinnickinnick berries in December, and the winter steelhead runs between December and April. Beaver, muskrat, bear, and other mammals were eaten in season. Among the Nehalem, animals were hunted communally, with dogs. Game was lured by calls, driven into enclosures or over cliffs; and deadfalls were used.

Whales, sea lions, seals, and shellfish were taken from the sea. From the rivers, fish were caught in weirs, traps, and seine and gill nets. They could also be speared or clubbed.

Food preparation was by steam cooking in an earth oven, stone-boiling in baskets or bowls, and drying on a rack. Serving dishes were of wood. Spoons were made of wood, mussel shell, or elk antler. Sources for Nehalem subsistence are E.D. Jacobs (1933–1934), Jacobs (1933–1934), and Sauter and Johnson (1974).

Winter Ceremonials

The first salmon ceremony was held on the occasion of the ritual spearing and roasting of the first steelhead of the season. The Tillamook believed that spirits were more active and closer to humans during the winter. Sometime about January or February, each shaman renewed his or her power, (s)xí·tsxɛc, by sponsoring a winter dance. The spirit partner or 'kin' of the shaman returned to make him very ill for about a week. Upon recovery, a dance was held in a large house beginning after supper and lasting until about midnight. The sponsoring shaman began by singing his power song and throughout the dance other "knowers" (those with a guardian spirit) sang their songs. The shaman gave lavishly of food and presents to the guests. The dance could last 5–10 evenings depending on the ability of the shaman to maintain his fast. Only a spirit doctor's singing was privileged to be accompanied by an elkhide drum. Others used a log drum. The winter dance series was the most elaborate Tillamook ceremony. Since all "knowers" invoked their supernatural powers and these were quite diverse, the winter dance period can be viewed as a period of cosmic or world renewal.

Political Organization

Tillamook society was divided into a large class of freeborn individuals and a much smaller class of slaves. A similar but not coterminous division was between the majority of Tillamook who had acquired a guardian spirit and those pitied few without guardians. Occasionally, a slave might acquire a guardian spirit, such as a hunting power, and he might be accorded more respect than a freeman with no spirit power, but he remained a slave nevertheless.

Boas (1923:4–5) reported two chiefs per river drainage for the southern Tillamook while E.D. Jacobs (1976) presented a more dynamic and fluid leadership pattern in her depiction of Tillamook groups led by different task leaders as various activities were planned or executed. Such task leaders included shamans, headmen, and warriors, each sanctioned by his particular spirit vision and continued success. The experts in doctoring, wealth, war, and hunting powers comprised the high-class or elite, šέ·ċən. Women received their status from their own weaker guardians or from the prestige accorded their parents, husband, or other close kinsmen. Postmenopausal women had higher status and considerably more sexual license than younger women.

Those with 'warrior power', tú·naqá·yu, led slaving raids, usually to the south among the Alseans but sometimes to the north above the Columbia River. Hunting and fishing ventures might be led by those with appropriate supernaturals. Each community seems to have had a headman who served as a general coordinator. Such a leader belonged to the elite, and his authority and bravado were felt to be supernaturally derived. He was expected to be brave, a skilled orator, and an able negotiator who could settle disputes to the satisfaction of both parties or, when negotiations failed, could insure the ensuing hostilities would end in his or his client's favor. A skillful headman was probably not an obtrusive figure when village activities were functioning smoothly.

Most intercommunity disputes were settled by arbitration by means of monetary and other payments. Those who set out to avenge a murder did not necessarily anticipate bloodshed; they expected to obtain money in the form of highly valued seashells such as yí?it, the largest and highest-priced dentalium. Resolution of trouble when the offender was from another village was much the same, usually in the form of monetary payments to the humiliated or aggrieved family or individual.

Shamans

The most prominent and in some sense permanent of the task leaders were the shamans. There were five types of such medico-religious specialists: general healers, poison doctors, spirit doctors, love doctors, and baby diplomats. Only the first three were true shamans, whose insignia included a belt of braided human hair with the ends hanging behind them like a tail. Some shamans had additional paraphernalia. Shamans earned their living by curing or recovering souls. They never became permanently wealthy because they gave away much of their possessions at the winter dance ceremonial. Because the powers of a shaman benefited his community but died with him, the death of a powerful doctor was always a great loss.

Both men and women could be general healers, šIša?šú·n. Usually, only men used the drawing-with-the-hands method of healing. Only female shamans sucked as part of the cure, while both men and women would blow upon and rub the patient. The sucking technique was especially effective for illness of the chest, head, and neck. There were three subtypes of female šIša?šú·n: those who sucked out blood, those who sucked out a black substance, and those who sucked out a white substance. The blood-extracting shaman was considered the most potent. Wild Woman, qϵ· k̓ú (sometimes called si·sə́lIsaI), was the source of power for these powerful female shamans, and they exhibited their power emblem or effigy tattooed on their breasts. Male shamans had their emblems carved or painted on the movable headboards, (das)χϵl, of their platform beds.

The female šIša?šú·n sucked her patient with her lips, rather than with a tube, spit the substance into a wooden cup, asked her spittle if the patient would recover, and then either 'drowned' the substance in a bucket of water or spread it on the hot ashes of a fire. If it was a severe illness she might both drown and burn it. In the course of a cure or during the winter dance season she might demonstrate her powers by turning a bucket of water into blood. At the winter dance she used this bucket of water as her drinking water for the duration of the ceremony. The wife of a male shaman aided her husband by singing during the curing. If possible, the doctoring session was held at night.

Only males could be poison doctors, shuté·nən, shamans who specialized in sending and extracting magical poisons sent by other shamans. This type of shaman employed elaborate ritual paraphernalia:doctoring poles, g̓álg̓á?lúxtən, with carved human faces, hair, and abalone shell eyes; a headdress of fringed cedar bark or red male hummingbird scalps; miniature bone human dolls representing poison sent from someone who could be identified; miniature bone fish representing sickness sent from an outsider; a deerhoof rattle and a dance stick layered with eagle feathers used during the winter dance; and most important, their movable headboard with its guardian spirit emblems displayed during "cures" and during the winter dance. Like the male šIša?šú·n, a poison doctor utilized the drawing method of extraction. The doctoring session usually lasted five nights.

Spirit doctors, das?ác?á·cχaɪ, always males, journeyed to the spirit world to retrieve the lost spirits of their patients. At the home of the patient the doctor entered a trance that began in the morning and lasted the entire day. A younger spirit doctor or assistant signaled the end of the trance by singing while someone pounded the doctor's power poles against the ceiling. The revived doctor returned the spirit to his patient by passing his hands down the patient from head to foot. A recovered spirit could only be returned to the patient after dark. Occasionally, a spirit doctor might suck something resembling purplish salmon eggs from his patient. Since it was an affliction sent by the dead, only a spirit doctor could effectively remove the substance. Some spirit doctors received their powers during an illness when visited by spirits of the dead.

Love doctors, dáyɛsəgə́nu, were women who had the ability to affect the bonds between people, especially estranged spouses. They apparently could also influence and strengthen the sexual vigor of individuals.

The baby diplomat or baby doctor, daskgú?úkaɬ, was always a man who had the ability to converse with human babies and to foretell future births and events based upon information he learned from dreams or from talking with babies in their special language.

Mythology and Religion

The only appropriate season for Tillamook myth telling was midwinter. Children and younger persons were required to recline on mats; to sit during a story-telling session would cause them to grow hunchbacked. While tales were not considered private property, stories told by one raconteur should not be recited by another teller during the same season (E.D. Jacobs 1959:vi–vii).

One stylistic feature of Tillamook oral literature unique in the Northwest Coast was the use of one pattern number, four, for purposes of reference to plural female characters or their actions, and another number, five, for male characters or actions.

There is no record of a creation myth for the Tillamook. The earliest time period in Tillamook mythology was the myth age, ƛétin, in which the myth character named Ice, gećɬá, played a prominent role. While not a true trickster-transformer figure, Ice nevertheless modified various features of the myth age. The myth character South Wind, as?á·yáhaɬ, ushered in the transformation era, preparing the world for the arrival of humans.

The Tillamook recognized no deities as such. The Earth itself was personified as omniscient and judgmental of the actions of people, but it was in no sense worshipped.

The mythic personages who inhabited the myth age and transformation era were important to the historical Tillamook because an individual's status and merit was believed to be largely determined by his ability to acquire a life-long partnership with one or more of these 'guardian spirits'. Indeed, for the Tillamook humanlike feelings and attributes characterized the flora, fauna, and weather phenomena as well as myth age figures. All such supernaturals can be thought of as "special kinds of human-like relatives by adoption" (E.D. Jacobs 1958).

A Tillamook was believed to begin existence in Babyland, was born into this world to grow up, to quest for a guardian spirit, to marry and to die before passing first to the afterworld.

Babyland, ánšsgu?úkaɬ, was located somewhere on the earth on the shores of a big blue lake. Babies there wore no clothes, had houses, their own language, and they married. When a baby decided to be born to human parents, the other babies threw mud on him or her in anger and, if he or she were married, the spouse might decide to be born to another set of parents so they could be reunited in marriage as adults. If a baby died before learning human speech it returned to Babyland rather than going to the afterworld. When such a preverbal infant died, its ears were marked and its thumbs and big toes broken by the mother so its possible rebirth in the village would be evidenced by the child's doublejointedness.

Synonymy

The name Tillamook derives from Chinookan *t?ilimuks* 'those of *ni?ilim*'; the etymology of the place-name (Chinookan stem variants -?ilim and -qilim) is unknown (Michael Silverstein, personal communication 1977; Boas 1923:3). Spelling variants include Ca-la-mox, Callamucks, Kil á mox, and Killamuck (Lewis and Clark in Thwaites 1904–1905, 3:295, 308, 4:9); Killimoucks and Killimous (Duflot de Mofras 1844, 2:349, 357); Klemook (Franchère 1854:126); and others listed in Hodge (1907–1910,2:751). The Tillamook name for their language is *chutyéyu* (Thompson and Thompson 1965–1970), given as hutyǽyu by Edel (1939:2).

Names for the Tillamook in the Tillamook dialects and in neighboring languages include Nestucca: Higgaháldshu (Gatschet 1877c), hɪgáha?lčɪu (Jacobs 1933b), hígə́hâ·lə́čU (Harrington 1942–1943); Salmon River (?): Nsietshawus and misprinted Usietshawus (Hale 1846:211, 218), syetčʰə́·wš 'coast Indian' (Harrington 1942–1943); Alsea: Kyaukw (Dorsey 1884a), kʸe?kʷ (Jacobs 1935c), kʸǽ?kU (Harrington 1942–1943), and Coquille Athapaskan: Si ní-tĕ-lĭ 'flatheads', nickname given by the Upper Coquille to the Alsea, Nestucca, and Tillamook (Dorsey 1884b).

Nehalem (ne'hāləm). The Nehalem word for themselves was nə?î·ləm (Harrington 1942–1943). Their language was called níškaзá·ɬaɬ (Jacobs 1933b). See Hodge (1907–1910, 2:53).

Nestucca (nes'tukə). The Nestucca people were called (ks)tá·gáhwəš (Jacobs 1933b), *ksta^ʔg^wəhwəš* 'Nestucca (River) people' (Thompson and Thompson 1965–1970). Synonyms include Salmon River: nəst^həggəwš 'Nestucca person' (Harrington 1942–1943); Alsea: ƛahálču 'Nestucca country' (Jacobs 1935c), ƛə́hâ·lču· 'Nestucca River' (Harrington 1942–1943). See Hodge (1907–1910, 2:57).

Salmon River. The Nehalem called the Salmon River nə·dzí·sni· (Harrington 1942–1943), compare Nat-chies, the name of a tribe on the sea coast south of the "Killamuck" (Lewis and Clark in Thwaites 1904–1905, 3: 341), Ni-ches-ni, a stream south of the "Nes-tug-ga" (Gibbs 1863b:21). Other synonyms include Alsea: Cí-cĭn-xaú (Dorsey 1884a), ší·šənqau 'Salmon River country' (Jacobs 1935c), ší·šnəqə·w 'Salmon River Indians' (Harrington 1942–1943). See Hodge (1907–1910, 2:418).

Siletz (sĭ'lets). The Siletz people were called (ks)tílałx̣énwəš (Jacobs 1933b), *stilełx̣éńwəš* 'Siletz (River) people' (Thompson and Thompson 1965–1970). The etymology of the name Siletz is unknown but it may be a Salmon River Tillamook form; compare nš(ə)lǽč stiwə̀·t 'the Siletz Indians' (Harrington 1942–1943). Synonyms include Alsea: ta^ʔáha, also ná^ʔtkĬčłu 'Siletz country' (Jacobs 1935c); Lower Umpqua: t^hə^ʔáhmí (Harrington 1942–1943); and Miluk Coos: šílε·čič (Jacobs 1939:106), šilæ̀·čič^h (Harrington 1942–1943). See Hodge (1907–1910, 2:572) for other variants.

Sources

Hale (1846) was the first to describe and classify the Tillamook language. Gatschet (1877j) compiled a vocabulary for the Nestucca dialect. Boas (1890e, 1890d, 1890c, 1900) recorded linguistic notes and texts in the Nehalem and Siletz dialects during a brief visit to the Siletz Reservation in 1890. Frachtenberg (1917) recorded a Siletz vocabulary in 1910. In 1931 a Boas student, Edel (1931, 1935), transcribed texts and grammatical and lexical data from speakers of several Tillamook dialects. Her grammar (1939) is the only extensive published account of the language. At Boas's request, Jacobs (1933b) supplemented Edel's recordings with two months' linguistic fieldwork. Harrington (1942–1943) recorded place-names, vocabulary, and grammatical notes; and Metcalf (1951) tape-recorded texts and vocabulary. Thompson and Thompson (1965–1970, 1966, 1985) documented the Tillamook language.

Boas (1890e, 1898a, 1900) transcribed folklore texts and translations. Edel's (1931, 1944) corpus of folklore texts and translations remains largely unpublished. E.D. Jacobs (1959) recorded folklore texts in English translation. Jacobs (1933–1934a), J.P. Marr (1941), and Metcalf (1951) made sound recordings of Tillamook texts and music.

Lewis and Clark (in Thwaites 1904–1905) were the first to describe aspects of Tillamook culture, although it is not clear whether they consistently differentiated between the Tillamook and their Chinookan neighbors. Some few ethnographic observations may be found in Lee and Frost (1844) and Vaughn (1851). Boas (1923) and Barnett (1937) are the most important published sources. E.D. Jacobs's fieldnotes (1933–1934) and manuscripts (1958, 1976) contain the most comprehensive treatment of Tillamook ethnography. Additional notes are found in Edel (1931), Harrington (1942–1943), and Jacobs (1933–1934a, 1958). Crawford (1983) treats Tillamook basketry. The ethnohistorical sources are best summarized in Taylor (1974a) and Hajda (1984). Sauter and Johnson (1974) is based primarily on secondary sources, without benefit of scholarly apparatus. Museums with Tillamook artifacts include the Tillamook County Pioneer Museum, Tillamook, Oregon, and the Oregon State University Museum of Natural History, Corvallis.

Alseans

HENRY B. ZENK

The Alsean (ăl'sēən) people were the speakers of Alsea ('ăl͵sē, ͵ăl'sē in mid-twentieth century local English but historically ͵ăl'sēyu), a language isolate once spoken in two dialects, Yaquina (yə'kwĭnu), on Yaquina Bay and River and the adjacent ocean shores, and Alsea proper, on Alsea Bay and River and along the ocean shore for some distance to the north and south* (fig. 1).

While extensive linguistic records exist for the Alsea proper dialect, Yaquina is poorly documented. Consequently, there has been doubt as to whether the two were dialects or distinct languages. Gatschet (1882:256–257 and in Powell 1891:133–135) believed them distinct enough to be separate languages. The classification as dialects, adopted here, is Frachtenberg's (1918:7–8), based upon lexical comparisons of Alsea proper data collected by himself with Yaquina data collected in 1884 and 1900. Informants' statements (Frachtenberg 1910; Harrington 1942) point to the same conclusion.

In common with other Oregon coastal peoples who occupied a similarly mountainous topography, Alseans lived primarily along the estuaries of their small rivers and along the open coastline. These narrow strips of coastline and river frontage supplied the Alseans with the intertidal, estuarine, and marine resources upon which they depended for their main subsistence.

External Relations

Alseans' closest ties (reflected in intermarriage, bilingualism, and trade) were to the neighboring Tillamooks and Siuslawans (Talbot 1850:112; Farrand 1901:242; Frachtenberg 1910; Harrington 1942). There were also some inland contacts. For example, Alsea River was navigable by canoe upstream to Alsea Valley, near the townsite of

Alsea; there, Alseans sometimes met Willamette Valley Kalapuyans (Frachtenberg 1910; Santee and Warfield 1943:60). It was inland, upriver, that the Alseans had their summer camps.

Alseans, together with Tillamooks and Chinookans, were participants in a network of economic and sociopolitical relationships centered on the lower Columbia River. The most obvious mark of direct participation in this network was flatheadedness as the invariable sign of free birth (Hajda 1984:151–160), a trait that characterized the Alseans but not the Siuslawans to the south (Gibbs 1857d: 4; Farrand 1900; S.B. Smith 1901:255; Jacobs 1935a, folders 63.17, 65.20; Barnett 1937:173). Alseans purchased roundheaded slaves (and probably, if less frequently, conducted slave raids) among coastal peoples to the south, in turn taking or trading their slaves northward to the Columbia River (Talbot 1850:112). Alseans themselves traveled north at least as far as the mouth of the Columbia River to participate in the early trade with European and American ships (Lewis and Clark in Thwaites 1904–1905, 3:340–341).

Alseans had much in common culturally with the Tillamook (Barnett 1937:158, 201–202). This was notable in mortuary practices, the Alseans being the southernmost people to have set their dead above the ground, in canoes or charnel houses. At the same time, there are also definite similarities to their southern neighbors. For example, there are a considerable number of Alsea-Siuslaw lexical resemblances (notably manifest in the kinship terminologies), evidently the result of borrowing in one or both directions; the sibling-cousin terminology (Iroquois in type, according to Hajda 1977), which resembles that of Siuslaw and Coosan; the shamanistic complex, which in its distinction between doctoring and priestly shamanistic functions evidently more resembled the Siuslawan-Coosan complex than it did the Tillamook; and the mythology, which in certain respects closely parallels Coosan mythology.

Culture

The Alseans are not so well described as other Oregon coastal peoples whom they resembled in cultural type. The following sketch applies to the mid-nineteenth century.

*Alsea linguistic forms cited in italics in the *Handbook* are written in a normalized phonemic transcription based on the analysis of Alsea phonology by Jacobs (1935b). The units treated as phonemes are: (voiceless lenis stops and affricate) *p, t, č, kʸ, k, kʷ, q, qʷ, ʔ*; (glottalized stops and affricates) *ṗ, ṫ, c̣, ƛ̓, k̓ʸ, k̓, k̓ʷ, q̓, q̓ʷ*; (voiceless continuants) *š, ɬ, xʸ, x, xʷ, x̣, x̣ʷ, h, hʷ*; (voiced continuants) *m, n, w, l, y*; (short vowels) *i, e, a, u, ə*; (long vowels) *i·, e·, a·, u·*; nasalized vowels corresponding to some or all of the nonnasalized vowels; stress (v́). Glottalization is weak and was often missed by recorders; in the marking of glottalization and back velars and in other respects the transcriptions should be considered tentative.

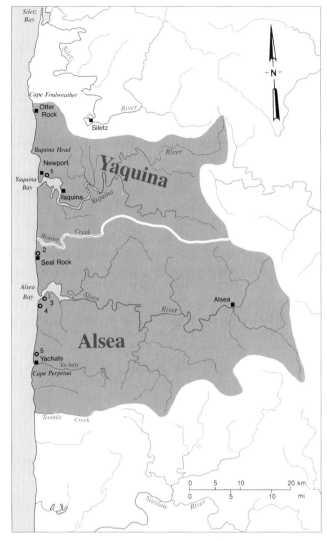

Fig. 1. Selected villages of the Alseans. 1, *mi(·)čú·lštik*[y]; 2, *qtáu*; 3, *łkú·huyu·*, 'where one goes down to the beach', reservation period town; 4, *č í · k*[y]; 5, *yáxaik*[y]; (Dorsey 1884d:183; Frachtenberg 1910; Drucker 1939:82; Harrington 1942). Dorsey (1890) listed 56 Yaquinna and Alsea "villages," but many may have been only camps or place-names (Drucker 1939:82).

Technology

Little record survives of the Alsean woodworking art, but Alseans were remembered by later-day Siuslawan and Coosan informants for their skillfully made and nicely finished wood artifacts (Harrington 1942). In particular, Siuslawans and Coosans obtained prized Columbia River canoes from Alseans. Contrary to Drucker's information (1939:86), these were widely recognized to have been an Alsean product (Gibbs 1857d:4; Jacobs 1935a, folder 65.20; Harrington 1942). While this seems historically to have been the dominant Alsean canoe type, Alseans (and southern Tillamooks) also manufactured the double-ended type more especially associated with Siuslawan and Coosan manufacture (flat-bottomed but with both ends identically tapered, vertical, and slightly raised). Western

red cedar was the usual building material; redwood drift logs, occasionally washed ashore from far to the south, were also used. Reportedly, Alseans, in common with Tillamooks, were proficient handlers of sea-going canoes.

Structures

The Alseans built rectangular multifamily cedar-plank winter houses, similar to those built by Tillamooks and Coosans (roof gabled, floor sunk three to six feet into the ground, furnished inside with bed platforms, mats, and a separate hearth for each family) (Dorsey 1884a; Frachtenberg 1910; Drucker 1939:85–86). A feature that has so far been noted only for Alsean houses is the presence of an adjustable peak, which could be either closed tightly or left slightly open (one side overlapping) for smoke to escape.

Social Organization

Alsean social organization was identical in general type to that noted throughout most of western Oregon. The basic social and political unit was the autonomous winter-village group, consisting of one or more residence groups of paternally related kin. The residence group itself, so far as is known, had no corporate identity. Political authority apparently resided in the village, in the person of its chief; or, in the largest villages, in two or perhaps three chiefs (*k*[y]*éuč* 'wealthy person, chief'; *miłaná·čtiyu* 'leader, chief').

Marriage represented an important bond between families, secured initially by the transaction of a bride price and return payment (not fixed, in contrast to the bride price, but that paid by a wealthy family would nearly equal the bride price), and maintained through subsequent exchanges of wealth (for example, upon the birth of a first child) and continuing obligations (as reflected in the levirate and sororate, and in indemnities incurred by one or the other family in case of infidelity, separation, or death of a child). Wealthy men were often polygamous (fig. 2) and preferred to seek their wives from distant villages or foreign neighbors.

Grievances were customarily redressed through indemnities paid by the offending party. However, serious matters sometimes resulted in feuds.

Shamanism

Shamans were of two principal types. One, called *tú·mšau*, is very little described, apparently also having been much the less numerous. This was identical to the Coosan priestly-type (or *miťé·dən*) shaman. Later-day Alsean informants knew almost nothing of the special duties and powers of these shamans, recalling only their minor curing powers and their sinister reputation for

569

sorcery (Drucker 1939:100–101; cf. Barnett 1937:190).

The other type of shaman (*čuyá²ɫi·słu* or *pá·lqa*), in contrast, excelled at curing serious illness (the result of intrusion or soul-loss) and (unlike the *ɬú·mšau*, as far as informants knew) initiated his or her career at a public ceremonial involving gift distribution and shamanistic displays and dancing. The powers of these shamans were supposed to reside in their guardian spirits (*šú·lheᵏʸiyu*, associated with a variety of supernatural agencies corresponding to animals, natural phenomena, and so on), acquired during a long and arduous training usually beginning at or before puberty. Evidently, guardian spirits were sought or encountered only irregularly by nonshamans.

History

In 1788 the American ship *Columbia*, off the Oregon coast at 44° 20′ north latitude, sent a boat in to investigate the shoreline. There, in what is apparently the first definitely recorded contact between Whites and Alseans, the crew observed a large group of hostile warriors armed with long spears, bows and arrows, and some sort of hide armor (Haswell 1969:32).

Isolated geographically from the main centers of early White settlement, the Alseans receive very little mention from that period. Epidemic diseases, especially smallpox (Gibbs 1857d:5–6; Dorsey 1884a; Harrington 1942), reduced Alsean populations by an undetermined amount. The earliest estimate of Alsean population, in 1806 (Lewis and Clark in Thwaites 1904–1905, 6:117), is based upon secondhand information gathered at the mouth of the Columbia River. The reading of those data adopted here yields an estimate of 1,700 for all Alseans.

In 1856 the original Coast Reservation was established, encompassing the homelands of both the Alseas proper and the Yaquinas. By this time Yaquina populations had been very reduced. As a result, the entire linguistic and ethnographic record on the Alseans, with the exception of a few items collected by Dorsey (1884a), derives from Alsea proper informants. The Alseas proper themselves continued to reside on Alsea Bay, in minimal contact with Whites and with little apparent inclination to alter aboriginal patterns. After the Coast Reservation was split in 1865, they became residents of the remote Alsea Reservation. Records for the year of the closing of Alsea Agency in 1875 show 118 Alseans there (ARCIA 1875: 175), all of whom were presumably removed to Siletz Reservation. The confederated tribes of Siletz were terminated in 1956 and restored in 1977 (Zucker, Hummel, and Høgfoss 1983:112-126).

Synonymy

570   The English name Alsea is a borrowing of a name for the

Lib. of Congress: Nash 1878: opp. p. 170.
Fig. 2. Kaseeah, identified by the artist as an Alsea chief, with his son and two wives at Yaquina Bay, Oreg. The traditional lands of the Alseas and Yaquinas were no longer part of reservation territory by this time, but the proximity of Yaquina Bay to Siletz Agency made it a convenient location for reservation Indians to fish and gather. The family had dressed up for the artist. The man's dress included a beaded headdress with white and magenta feathers, plumes on the arms and in the hands, and black and vermilion paint. The women wore blue and white necklaces (W. Nash 1878:169–170). Engraving after original drawing by Wallis Nash, 1877.

Alsea proper that appears as (Mary's River Kalapuyan and Coosan) *alsí(·)* and Coosan and Tillamook *alsí·ya*. Historical priority evidently goes to *alsí·ya*, which is recorded as Ul-se-âh's (Lewis and Clark in Thwaites 1904–1905, 6:117); Alciyieh (McLeod 1961:161); and Alsiya, Alseya (Milhau 1856d). The Alseans' own name for the Alsea Bay and River region was *wuší!²*, and they called themselves *wuší̜t-šlǝm* 'people of *wuší²*'. Dorsey (1890:229) gives Äl-sí as the self-designation of the Alseas proper, but this is evidently merely the English placename.

Yaquina. The name Yaquina is a variant of *yaqú·na*, *yuqú·na*, the Alseans' own name for the Yaquina Bay and River region (hence, *yaqú·nat-šlǝm* 'people of Yaquina'). Powell's (1891:137) information that the name means 'spirit' evidently reflects a coincidental resemblance of the name to a Chinook Jargon word (i-kon, e-cone 'good spirit', as given in Johnson 1978:420). Dorsey (1890:229) gives the English place-name as the Yaquina self-designation (his Yû-kwĭn´-ă). Variants include: You-cone, Yorick-cone's (Lewis and Clark in Thwaites 1904–1905, 3: 341, 6:117); Econne, Yeaconne (McLeod 1961:157, 172); Yakones, Iakon, Jakon (Hale 1846:218, 221); Yacona (Talbot 1850:112); Yah-quo-nah (U.S. Congress. Senate 1893:8); Yakonah (Gibbs 1857d:2); Ya-kúna (Gibbs 1863b:21); Acona (Lyman 1900:320); and yaqʷoná (Drucker 1939:82).

ZENK

In some early sources the Alseans' close ties to their Tillamook neighbors are reflected in their being classified as Tillamooks. In 1806 Lewis and Clark (Thwaites 1904–1905, 6:117) were under the impression that Alseans (and Siuslawans) were Tillamook speakers (Kila-mucks, Kil-la-mucks, in their spelling). Hale (1846:211–212, 218) referred to the Alseans as the Southern Killamucks, noting that they differed from the Tillamook proper "merely in language." In the unratified treaty of 1855 (U.S. Congress. Senate 1893:8) both the Alsea proper and the Yaquina are identified as Tillamook bands. Hale also referred to the Alseans under variant forms of the name of the Yaquina division. This precedent was followed by Powell (1891:133–135), who adopted the name Yakonan for his linguistic family (now discarded) embracing the Alsea and Siuslaw language isolates. The usage "Alsean" reflects the fact that the Alsea proper are much the better documented of the two Alsea-speaking divisions. Names in other Indian languages applied to the Alseans include: Tillamook *kɬ-q̇əluʔucínu* (Jacobs, as normalized by Lau-rence Thompson, personal communication 1978), tʌhʌʔíyʌsʔáˑɬuwəš 'furtherbeach people' (Harrington 1942); Siuslaw *qpáˑyaˑx* 'northerners' (Harrington 1942), and *haníˑs-híˑč* 'haníˑs people' (Harrington 1942), perhaps more properly a name of the Alsea proper (not the same as *háˑnis*, the Hanis Coosans' self-designation).

Sources

See Drucker (1939) and Farrand (1901) for greater detail on aspects of Alsean life. Barnett (1937) lists Alsean culture traits, extracted from Drucker's fieldnotes. Alsean mythology is represented by two collections, Farrand's from 1900 and Frachtenberg's from 1910 and 1913; both have been published by Frachtenberg (1917a, 1920b). An unpublished corpus of Alsea linguistic data has been preserved, including contributions from Dorsey (1884d, 1884c), Frachtenberg (1918), Jacobs (1935), and Harrington (1942). Beckham (1977) discusses Alsea history along with that of other western Oregon tribes.

Siuslawans and Coosans

HENRY B. ZENK

The Indians referred to as Siuslawan (ˌsī'yōōsləwun) were speakers of the Siuslaw ('sīyōōslä, ˌsī'yōōslä) language isolate, which consisted of two principal dialects: Siuslaw proper, spoken on the Siuslaw River and adjacent ocean coast, and Lower Umpqua ('umpkwä) (not to be confused with Upper Umpqua, an Athapaskan language), spoken on the Umpqua River below the head of tidewater, and along adjacent ocean coast. Those called Coosan ('kōōsun) were speakers of the two languages of the Coosan language family: Hanis ('hănĭs), spoken around the main part of Coos Bay and northward to Lower Umpqua territory, and Miluk ('mĭluk), spoken on the lower Coquille (kō'kēl, historically, kō'kwĕl) River, on the coastline between Coquille River and Coos Bay, and around South Slough on Coos Bay. Both Coosan languages had minor dialectal variations, which have not been specifically documented.*

The histories of the Siuslawans and Coosans following Euro-American contact are considerably intertwined, but the record on the former is especially fragmentary. Barnett (1937:158) indicates close cultural kinship between the two.

Territory and Environment

Each tribe was a collection of like-speaking villages, sharing some rights of access to resources within a common territory, but lacking institutionalized political unity. Definite boundaries have been described where tribal territories adjoined the immediate coastline (Harrington 1942; R.L Hall 1978a:25–26, 36). While access rights to favorable hunting and other resource areas in the interior were clearly recognized, exact boundaries probably were not.

Siuslawan winter villages were evidently all within a few miles of the ocean shore. Their exact number is unclear. Dorsey (1890:230–231) reported 34 Siuslaw proper and 14 Lower Umpqua sites. Harrington (1942) found surviving Siuslaw speakers able to identify most of Dorsey's downstream sites, but they knew very little about his upstream sites (fig. 1) (Dorsey 1884e), which were probably mostly seasonal camps.

Names of 71 Coosan villages were recorded by Jacobs (1931–1934, notebook 92:150–152, 1935a: folders 65.8 and 65.9) and 34 by Harrington (1942). The two lists complement one another; Jacobs's is richer in ethnographic detail, while Harrington's includes a good deal of information on site locations.

The coastal habitat that the Siuslawans and Coosans occupied is characterized by generally mild year-round temperatures and abundant seasonal rainfall. The immediate coastline is ruggedly mountainous at the northern extreme of the area and to the immediate south of Coos Bay, but elsewhere it consists of a narrow zone of relatively level topography (notable for its extensive sandy beaches and dune sheets), bounded to the landward by freshwater lakes and the steep, densely timbered western hills of the Coast Range. The entire area, except for the dune sheets, is covered by dense vegetation, dominated by Sitka spruce toward the ocean and by western hemlock, Douglas fir, and western red cedar inland.

External Relations

External contacts seem to have been confined primarily to immediate neighbors. These included some close ties (evident in intermarriages and bilingualism) between the Siuslaws proper and their Alsea neighbors to the north, and between Miluk Coosans and their Upper Coquille Athapaskan-speaking neighbors. There are also some references to inland contacts: trade with neighboring Kalapuyans and Upper Umpqua Athapaskans, and instances of intermarriage (involving Coosans and Lower Umpquas, at least) with the latter.

---

*The Coosan and Siuslawan forms cited in italics are tentative normalizations of the transcriptions by Jacobs (1931–1934, 1935a) and Harrington (1942), following available treatments (Jacobs 1939:11–18; Hymes 1966; J.E. Pierce 1971). For Coosan these spellings probably correspond well to the phonemic system, for which the following elements are assumed: (aspirated stops and affricates) *p, t, c, č, ƛ, k, q, ʔ*; (unaspirated, optionally voiced stops and affricates) *b, d, ʒ, ǯ, λ, g, ġ*; (glottalized stops and affricates) *p̓, t̓, c̓, č̓, ƛ̓, k̓, q̓*; (voiceless continuants) *s, š, ł, x, x̣, h*; (voiced continuants) *m, n, l, γ, w, y*; (short vowels) *i, e, a, u, ə*; (long vowels) *i·, e·, a·, u·*; (stress) *v́*. In Siuslawan there was the same range of phonetic entities, without *γ, e,* or *e·*, but phonemically there was probably a single plain series corresponding to the aspirated and unaspirated series of Coosan. Phonetic labialized consonants and diphthongs are written with sequences of symbols. The transcriptions should be considered tentative.

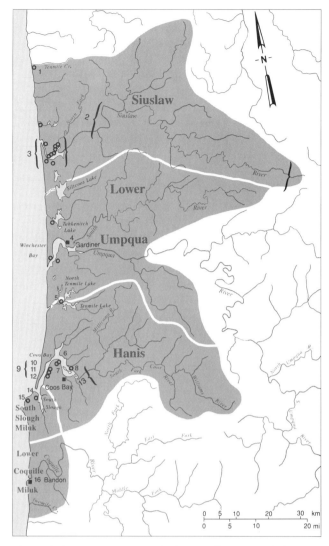

Fig. 1. Siuslawan and Coosan territories and villages about 1830. Siuslawan villages: 1, *ciʔimá·* 'at white clay', a summer village with some permanent inhabitants; 2, *tqáwi·či·č* 'upstream', seasonal use sites; 3, *qáyu·či·č* 'downstream', village complex; 4, *čá·lila·*. Coosan villages: 5, *cgé·ič*, a summer village with some permanent inhabitants; 6, *gáhák̓ič*; 7, *dá·ʔnis*; 8, *wuʔléʔnč* 'fine weather'; 9, *gédíč-ha·nis* 'downstream-Hanis' village complex, including 10–12 and associated smaller villages; 10, *waʔóʔlač*; 11, *ntí·seʔič*; 12, *há·nisi·č*; 13, *dagáič-ha·nis* 'upstream-Hanis' villages; 14, *mílúgwič*; 15, *báldí·mis* 'ocean'; 16, *gúgwis* 'south'.

Culture

The following sketch is of Coosan culture about 1850, supplemented with material on the Siuslawans (Jacobs 1931–1934, 1935a).

Subsistence

The most important resource of the area was salmon, which were taken from canoes in deep water, dipnetted, harpooned, clubbed, and trapped at upriver weirs or in rapids and shallow water. Additionally, the estuaries and rivers supported major runs of herring, smelt, lampreys, and less seasonally limited supplies of various saltwater and freshwater fish.

Other notable resources included shellfish, seals, sea lions, deer, and elk. Stranded whales provided a particularly prized source of meat and oil. Various roots, shoots, and berries completed the diet. These included camas, fern and (immature) skunk-cabbage roots, and wapato (gathered by Hanis Coosans at Tenmile Lake). The only plant cultivated by Siuslawans and Coosans was tobacco.

Most Siuslaws passed the winter season along the lowermost part of Siuslaw River, moving to upriver villages during peak salmon fishing times or to camps for lamprey fishing, hunting, and trapping. The Lower Umpquas probably had a similar seasonal pattern of extended downstream-upstream mobility, as did the Hanis speakers of Coos Bay, but, apparently, not the majority of Miluk speakers, whose fishing and hunting areas were in close proximity to winter bases. The Lower Coquille Miluks are little documented.

Clothing and Adornment

Clothing was made by women from dressed skins and various fibers. The dress of both sexes generally included dressed-hide leggings and moccasins for travel and cold weather, dressed-hide or fiber headbands, and fur or fiber water-shedding capes. Men and boys minimally wore buckskin breechclouts or short trousers. They usually also wore buckskin shirts, belted at the waist, and caps made from the intact skins of small furbearers or sea birds. Women wore dressed-hide or fiber upper garments and knee-to-ankle length skirts, or one-piece dressed-hide sleeveless dresses. Women's woven hats came in two basic types: a flat-topped type, worn around Coos Bay and probably northward (fig. 2); and the half-sphere or northwestern California type, worn by the Lower Coquilles.

Decoration of clothing and jewelry characterized the dress of the wealthy. Specialized attire included various kinds of ornamented dance apparel, such as headdresses made of pileated woodpecker heads, and shaman's decorated belts and headbands.

Men and women had lines tattooed on one or both arms, for measuring strings of dentalia. Women had simple wrist tattoos and, often, more elaborate lower-leg tattoos. Some individuals, perhaps only Lower Coquille women, had facial tattoos. Some Siuslawans had flattened foreheads, but the practice was not universal.

Technology

Technology conformed to general regional type (see Barnett 1937:167–174). Women made tule and cattail mats and a variety of twined, decorated baskets, while men were responsible for the manufacture of weapons and

573

Fig. 2. Clothing. left, Coos Bay Indian children posed wearing traditional rain capes of cattail or shredded bark. The older girl wears dentalium shell necklaces and headband. The younger girl wears a flat-topped basketry hat. Photographed about 1900–1920. right, Chief Jackson (*da·lú·s*) with Mrs. Jackson (center) and daughters, including Lottie Evanoff at left. A hereditary Hanis village chief, Jackson was a signer of the 1855 unratified treaty and remained a leader of the Coosans on Coos Bay until his death in 1907. Evanoff was one of John P. Harrington's main informants in the 1940s (J. Thornton 1978). Jackson wears a feathered headdress, and his wife wears a beaded collar as well as bead and dentalium necklaces. Photographed about 1890s; cropped.

hunting and fishing gear. Wood (notably red cedar, maple, and alder), plant fibers, shell, and bone and antler provided the basic materials. The only adequately documented Coosan craft is basketry, which is represented by some finely worked and decorated examples, as well as by more utilitarian ware, in collections at the Oregon Museum of Natural History, Eugene, and the Lowie Museum, University of California, Berkeley (fig. 3).

Structures

A typical permanent house was 20 to 50 or more feet long and about half as wide and was excavated from three to six feet deep. Two or more center posts supported a single ridgepole from which rafter poles sloped down on either side to the ground or to side supports. Cedar planks were lashed horizontally to the framework to form the walls and gabled roof (fig. 4) (Zucker, Hummel, and Høgfoss 1983:36–37). Inside, the walls were completely lined with tule mats, and mat partitions divided separate families. Mats or hides were laid on the hard dirt floor; there were bed platforms or mat beds.

Sheds (unexcavated, generally thatched-grass, with gabled or one-pitch roofs) provided living quarters at camps and served specific functions at villages, such as work areas and sleeping quarters for adolescents or the "hired men" attached to chiefly households.

Two types of sweathouse are recorded. The men and adolescent boys of a village or of a number of neighboring houses shared a large structure that also served as a "clubhouse" and boys' dormitory. It was square, deeply excavated, plank-walled, and covered by planks and dirt. Trenches provided access to the door and ventilated the fire pit. Sweating was by direct heat. The other type of sweathouse was the familiar "beehive" type, heated by steam and resorted to by either men or women for recreation and self-purification.

Canoes

Three principal canoe types are described for the area. The one commonly made, called *łqwa·* (Lower Umpqua) or *ʔíx* (Hanis 'canoe'), was usually 15 to 20 feet long and flat-bottomed, with both ends vertical, sharp, and slightly raised. A larger type, called *alú·daq* (Lower Umpqua and Hanis, cf. Nehalem Tillamook *alútəq* 'large war canoe') was commonly obtained in trade from the north, especially the Alsea, but may have occasionally been made locally. This was the Columbia River type, favored for ocean fishing. It was flat-bottomed, with stern resembling the ends of the Siuslawan-Coosan type, but with undercut sharp bow and affixed pointed prow (often carved in representations of birds or animals). The third type was the shovelnose, called *má·xmax* (Hanis and Miluk), made

574

ZENK

U. of Calif., Lowie Mus., Berkeley: a, 13241; b, 13739; c. 13238; d, 13225; e, 13224; f, 13203; g, 13249.

Fig. 3. Coosan basketry. a, Close twined, flexible bowl with simple horizontal band and triangle design; b, twined woman's hat decorated with stripes; c, twined carrying basket with handle; d, twined oval bowl with braided rim and wrapped handles; c-d are typical of the reservation period when Coosan basket makers were producing for White consumption. e, Twined cradle with wrapped rim; buckskin thongs held the baby and, passing over the mother's forehead, supported the cradle on the mother's back. Two strands of dentalia and beads carried across the top of the cradle amused the baby. f, Openwork burden basket, with braided carrying straps; g, twined storage basket, elaborately decorated. a, Collected before 1879; b-f, collected before 1929; g, collected about 1869. Diameter of a 30.5 cm; rest to same scale.

in all sizes but used mainly for bay and river travel. At least the larger such models were identified especially with coastal Athapaskan manufacture.

Most canoes were made of red cedar. Port Orford cedar was also used from Coos Bay southward. Better canoes might be ornamented with shells and painted stripes.

Political Organization

The basic political unit of Siuslawan and Coosan society

Fig. 4. Winter plank house near Ft. Umpqua, Oreg. Terr., made of split cedar and lumber; the roof is probably of milled lumber. A plank windbreak is in the foreground. Photograph by Edward Perry Vollum or Lorenzo Lorain, 1857–1858.

was the winter village group, consisting as elsewhere in western Oregon of one or more loosely delimited groups of paternally related males with their wives and children. Also following regional pattern, villages were probably often effectively exogamous.

In general, each major village center (but not each small hamlet) had a principal chief. Ordinarily, he was assisted by a second chief, who functioned as his representative and liaison. Both functionaries were addressed as 'chief' (Hanis, Miluk *hethé·de*, Lower Umpqua *łəná?wa·* 'chief, very wealthy one'; Hanis *sikínxem*, Miluk *sikínen*, Lower Umpqua *ma?á·ti·* 'chief, leader'). Chiefs were furthermore advised and assisted, at least on matters on vital collective importance such as war, by the village's socially respectable or "good" men and women.

Among the Coosans at least, chiefly succession was basically hereditary. Chieftainship ordinarily passed to the son of a deceased or retired principal chief, or lacking a son, to the closest (paternal) male blood relation. However, were there no suitable male heir, a close female blood relation might succeed. Only upon the lack of any suitable successor would someone from outside a chiefly family become a principal chief (apparently, by general consent of the village's "good" people). Even when chiefs were removed succession was generally kept within the chiefly family.

The chief functioned as village arbiter in settling quarrels and imposing indemnities, and as supervisor of communal activities. He was furthermore expected to be generally responsible for the welfare of his fellow villagers, ensuring that no one in the village went hungry, and helping villagers who could not pay indemnities. Villagers reciprocated by contributing a substantial portion of all harvests to the chiefly households.

Social Stratification

Coosan society had four levels of social evaluation: the chiefly and wealthy families; the socially respectable majority of the population; exceptionally poor people; and the very few slaves, kept by wealthy families only. Slaves originated from foreign people through trade or possibly capture. Their children were slaves.

Actual level of subsistence counted for little in Coosan social evaluation. Even the poor had adequate access to basic subsistence requirements. The obligations linking chiefs to their less wealthy fellow villagers helped ensure this. Other mechanisms contributed to the same end: all hauls taken from the major fish runs and communal elk drives were distributed freely to all in the village; and the poor were specifically provided for in the institution of the "begging social call," or formalized mealtime visit to a wealthy household.

Parents sought to arrange marriages for their offspring into families of at least roughly equivalent socioeconomic level. A marriage was contracted by the groom's family upon payment of a bride price. The bond between the families was further cemented by a subsequent return payment, repeated mutual visiting and gift-giving, and the assumption of various obligations (including the levirate and sororate, and responsibility to provide compensation in the event of an unsuccessful marriage, financially or by means of an appropriate arranged remarriage).

Kinship terms were not fully recorded, but it appears that the Siuslawan system was either bifurcate collateral or bifurcate· merging in the parents' generation, while the Coosan system was clearly bifurcate collateral, and both systems may have been of the Iroquois type in the speaker's generation.

Religious Life and Shamans

Intense involvement with the supernatural was primarily the concern of shamans. The pursuit of wealth constituted the primary outlet for Coosan individual aspiration, and the only general focus of interest in the supernatural was centered upon certain usually transitory powers (Hanis *łxí?nex*) believed to ensure luck in gaining wealth. Individuals acquired these in chance encounters with supernaturally charged manifestations (for example, unusual objects kept as charms), or through dreaming or deliberate solitary quests (Jacobs 1939:32–33, 41–42, 68, 98–99).

Coosan shamans were of two principal types. One, called (Hanis) *ilxǵáin*, was much more numerous. An *ilxǵáin* shaman obtained his or her power as the result of an arduous training period (usually beginning at or before puberty) involving repeated dreaming, fasting, and solitary quests at certain locations. He publicly initiated his career with a formal new shaman's dance and a few cures conducted free of charge. His primary function was to cure serious illness, caused by intrusion (of some minute disease-causing object, usually sent by a hostile shaman), or, more rarely, soul-loss.

The duties of the other type of shaman (Hanis, Miluk), *miłé·dən*, were more properly priestly or ritualistic than shamanistic, although these shamans possessed less developed curative powers. Most *miłé·dən*s were men who acquired their shamanistic status relatively late in life. Probably, *miłé·dən* status, more frequently then *ilx̣q̓áin* status, followed membership in certain family lines. In addition to ritual duties, a *miłé·dən* was consulted to find thieves and to wreak supernatural vengeance. Although both types of shaman were considered potentially dangerous (prone to misusing their supernatural powers), the *miłé·dən* especially was feared.

Many ceremonially recognized events of individual life included the participation of the *miłé·dən*. The eating of fresh food was taboo for a girl following her first menstruation, for a woman who had given birth, for anyone who had handled a corpse, or for anyone who had killed a person for any reason. Only the *miłé·dən*, with recitations of appropriate ritual formulae, could lift this taboo, by ritually offering samples of fresh food to the individual concerned. Additionally, the *miłé·dən* conducted rituals included in the important and elaborate girl's puberty ceremonial (for example, the ritual bathing following the first of the two consecutive five-day isolation periods, and the rituals involved in "raising" a girl from her two seclusions), and he was also responsible for many aspects of purification associated with death, burial, and mourning.

Other Ceremonies

Large-scale ceremonials involving feasting, games and gambling, and dancing were regularly held. Some provided occasions for artistic expression, especially in the performance of competitive pantomime-dances, presented by groups of costumed dancers supported by the singing of the audience. Relatively unelaborate ceremonies marked the first salmon caught and the first elk killed each season.

Siuslawans and Coosans buried their dead. Goods and valuables (all broken or otherwise rendered functionless) were placed in and over a grave.

Mythology

Coosan mythology included tales of two main types, those concerning the "first people" (who, in the course of various incidents, came to assume the forms of present animals), and those describing incidents thought to have occurred after the world had already attained its present form. Notable among the former are the stories concerning actors called (Hanis, Miluk) *ċmí·xwn* 'trickster',

believed chiefly responsible for the present world order. In one version (Jacobs 1940:184–222), these stories form a cycle following the careers of five successive generations of tricksters. The fifth of these was tricked by his father (the fourth) into ascending to the sky-world, where he became 'the people's father', a kind of remote deity, and he in turn transformed his father into the coyote, also an important myth character. The trickster cycle was told only once a year, always in the winter.

The sky-world occupied by the 'father' was also the land of the dead, which lay across a river at the end of the Milky Way, the road taken by the souls of the dead. This was believed to be a lovely, treeless land in which life was wholly good.

Coosan folklore, including many stories of the legendary-historical genre, as well as references to many "supernatural" beings of forest and water, is relatively richly recorded (Frachtenberg 1913; Jacobs 1939; R.L. Hall 1978a).

History

In 1792, while offshore from Umpqua River, the American ship *Columbia* was visited by Natives paddling canoes laden with goods for trade (Boit 1969:391–392). Sometime in the same year, the British ship *Jenny* entered the mouth of Umpqua River and spent some days there trading with Natives, who, it was observed, were "numerous" and of a "savage disposition" (Howay and Elliott 1929:201; Bishop 1967:xxv, 53–54). By the 1830s (McLeod 1961:141–219), White fur traders had established contacts from the interior, generally via the Umpqua River.

Except for the massacre perpetrated in 1828 by the Lower Umpquas upon the Jedediah Smith party (Morgan 1953:266–269, 274–279), early Native-White relations in the area were generally peaceful. Tensions increased with major influxes of American miners and settlers in the early 1850s. Although only the Lower Coquilles participated in the hostilities that engulfed southwestern Oregon, climaxing on the coast in late 1855 and early 1856 (Beckham 1971:47–72, 131–145, 169–191), the rest of the Coosans as well as the Siuslawans suffered from these events. In summer 1855, a treaty was concluded with most of the Oregon coastal peoples, including the Siuslawans and Coosans (U.S. Congress. Senate 1893:8–15). However, Senate action on the treaty was delayed, in part due to the outbreak of hostilities later in the year, and the treaty was never ratified. In 1856, all the Coos Bay Coosans were removed to the lower Umpqua River, while the Lower Coquilles were taken, along with other defeated southern Oregon hostiles, to Siletz Agency on the newly created Coast Reservation. In 1860, the Lower Umpquas and Coos Bay Coosans were marched together to the same reservation, locating at Yachats under the Alsea Agency. Only the Siuslaws, whose homeland lay in the original

577

Stephen Dow Beckham, Portland, Oreg.

Fig. 5. Tribal Hall, Coos Bay, Oregon. In 1937 the Bureau of Indian Affairs had this structure built for the use of the Coos–Lower Umpqua–Siuslaw tribes, but they were not recognized. In the 1960s and 1970s the hall was used as a center for administering publicly funded community service programs, for meetings of the Coos–Lower Umpqua tribe and other Indian organizations, and as a museum of the arts and artifacts of coastal Oregon Native people (Beckham 1977: 182–184, 194–199; Zucker, Hummel, and Høgfoss 1983:112–115). The repainting is the work of Paul Trinidad, an Apache who worked at Coos Bay through the CETA manpower program and Doug Stutzman, a Choctaw. Photograph by Jim Thornton, 1977.

Coast Reservation, never experienced the trauma of removal (Beckham 1977:129–145, 154–156).

The Coosans and Lower Umpquas continued to reside at Yachats on the Alsea Reservation until 1875, suffering much privation due to the primitive conditions there. With the closing of the Alsea Reservation in that year, these people refused to submit to removal to Siletz Agency. Many, both Lower Umpquas and Coosans, subsequently joined the Siuslaws on Siuslaw River, while others returned to their original homelands (Frachtenberg 1909; Harrington 1942; Beckham 1977:161–164).

The dream dance, a local manifestation of the messianic Ghost Dance movement, was introduced in the area in the 1870s (DuBois 1939:25–37).

The earliest population estimates, secured secondhand from Natives at the mouth of the Columbia River, give, in 1806, about 900 Siuslaws (proper), either 500 or 1,700 Lower Umpquas, and 1,500 Coosans (presumably only Coos Bay Coosans) (Lewis and Clark in Thwaites 1904–1905, 6:117). In 1867 there reportedly survived 140 Coosans (excluding Lower Coquilles), 88 Lower Coquilles at Siletz Agency, 133 Siuslaws (proper), and 102 Lower Umpquas (ARCIA 1868:62).

Lacking either ratified treaty or reservation affiliation, the Siuslawans and Coosans endured an especially difficult and litigious relationship with the federal government (Beckham 1977:179–203; Zucker, Hummel, and Høgfoss 1983:112–139; Jeff Zucker, personal communication 1987). In 1917, the majority of Siuslawans and Coosans constituted the Coos–Lower Umpqua–Siuslaw tribal government. Full federal recognition was a fact in 1984. In 1988 the Confederated Tribes of Coos, Lower Umpqua and Siuslaw Indians had a tribal membership of 336 (Carolyn Slyter, communication to editors 1988). There was also a group organized as the Coquille Tribe, composed of people of Miluk Coosan and Upper Coquille Athapaskan ancestry.

Synonymy†

Siuslaw. The name Siuslaw is from Siuslaw šáʔyú·šλa·, the name of the Siuslaw River region; other Indian languages have (Coosan) šeʔyúsλe and (Garibaldi Tillamook) šaʔístq̇əl. Variants in historical sources include: Saiústkla, Sayousla, Sayúskla, She-a-stuck-kle, Siouslaw, Siuselaws, Syouslaws (Hodge 1907–1910, 2:584; Lewis and Clark in Thwaites 1905–1905, 6:117; U.S. Congress. Senate 1893:8–9). The linguistic family name Siuslawan was coined by Frachtenberg (1922).

Lower Umpqua. The Lower Umpqua are named for their location on the lower Umpqua River; they are distinct from the Athapaskan Upper Umpqua. A variant is Omp quch (Dale 1941:247). They are called Kuitsh by Hodge (1907–1910, 1:732), from Lower Umpqua qú·í·č 'southern region' (Frachtenberg 1922:442). Historical sources have variants of Kalawatset (Milhau 1856d; also Kil-la-wats, Kiliwátshat, Kal-a-wot-set), a name related to Tillamook q̇álwəc 'Siuslawan region' (Harrington 1942), but Hodge (1907–1910, 1:646) wrongly implies that the broader use of this name, to include the Siuslaw and the Coosans, was the norm. Neighboring languages have (Alsea) tkulmaʔkʸ and (Hanis) bilx̌í·yəx, literally 'northern Indians' (Frachtenberg 1922:442).

Coosan, Coos. The linguistic family name Coosan was coined in the form Kusan by Powell (1891:89) on the basis of the ethnic name Coos. The name Coos reflects that of Coos Bay and the surrounding region, which has been explained as a Southwestern Oregon Athapaskan word

†This synonymy was written by Henry Zenk and Ives Goddard.

578

ku·s 'bay' (Milhau in Powell 1891:89; E.D. Jacobs 1934; Dorsey in Hodge 1907–1910, 1:342) and as a Hanis element meaning 'south' in, for example, *gusimíǯi·č* 'southwards' (Frachtenberg 1922a:305). The Siuslaw name for the Coos is *qú·ya·x* 'southerners'; Alsea *qu·ʔúš*, *qu·quʔúš* and similar Tillamook forms match the early recordings Cook-koo-oose, Co-ose, and kwokwoōs (Hodge 1907–1910, 1:342).

Hanis. The name Hanis is from the Hanis self-designation *há·nis*, used narrowly for the people of *há·nisi·č* village (Anasitch).

Miluk. The name Miluk is from the Miluk self-designation *míluk*, which appears with narrower reference in the name of *milúgwič* village (Melukitz); this is Dorsey's (1890:231) Mûl′luk, whose reference is wrongly narrowed by Hodge (1907–1910, 1:955). The Miluk have also been referred to as the Lower Coquille, from the location of their southernmost villages, or simply Coquille (Hodge 1907–1910, 1:955, 2:34); Frachtenberg (1922a: 305) reported that they were "commonly called Lower Coquelle," a spelling that reflects the older local pronunciation. The name Nas-o-mah appears in the 1855 treaty (U.S. Congress. Senate 1893:9); variants are in Hodge (1907–1910, 2:34). The Coquille Athapaskans called the Miluk language *dəlmé·ši* (E.D. Jacobs 1934); Delmash and other historical spellings are given by Hodge (1907–1910, 1:955).

Sources

Jacobs's Hanis and Miluk texts, including myths and ethnographic description, have been published (Jacobs 1939, 1940), but the bulk of his work remains in manuscript (Jacobs 1931–1934, 1935a). The other principal sources are: Frachtenberg (1909, 1913, 1914), Barnett (1937), and Harrington (1942). Additional ethnographic information, valuable primarily in conjunction with the main sources, is supplied by Gibbs (1857d), St. Clair (1909:25–27), and Drucker (1934). The first major linguistic research in the area was done by Dorsey, who collected short vocabularies of Siuslaw proper (1884e), Lower Umpqua (1884d), and Miluk (in Frachtenberg 1914:142–144). The major systematic linguistic contribution remains Frachtenberg's grammatical sketches of Hanis (1922a) and the Lower Umpqua dialect of Siuslaw (1922). Other linguistic data are from Harrington (1942), Swadesh (1954:132–133), and Hymes (1966).

The observations on Indians available from historical sources are few and scattered. Beckham (1977:95–203) treats the history of contact between Euro-Americans and the Indian populations of western Oregon. See also Beckham, Minor, and Toepel, (1981) and Beckham, Toepel, and Minor (1982:89–117, 1984:35–58).

Athapaskans of Southwestern Oregon

JAY MILLER AND WILLIAM R. SEABURG

Language and Territory

The Athapaskans of southwestern Oregon are the speakers of the Upper Umpqua ('ump͵kwä), Tututni (tōō'tōōtnē), and Galice-Applegate (gă'lēs'ăpəl͵gāt) languages and the Chetco ('chĕt͵ko) dialect of the Tolowa language (vol. 8: 128), all members of the Pacific branch of the Athapaskan family.* Tututni was a chain of dialects, the speakers of which were identified as the Upper Coquille (͵kō'kwĕl, ͵kō'kēl), Tututni, and Chasta Costa (͵shăstə 'kŏstə). The Athapaskans' aboriginal territory included the shores of the Pacific between a point a few miles south of the mouth of the Coquille River and the mouth of the Winchuck River, and inland it included portions of the drainage of the Umpqua, Coquille, and Rogue rivers (fig. 1).

Environment

This is a mountainous region with a straight coastline broken only by the mouths of its many streams. Between the mouth of the Coquille and Port Orford the coast is low with a number of small lakes; south of Port Orford it is generally high and beaches are less common. Rainfall is highest along the coast (over 80 inches a year at the mouth of the Rogue River) and lowest in the Upper Umpqua valley (around 30 inches at Roseburg); and the range of temperature is least on the coast and greatest in the inland valleys (Sternes 1960). The vegetation along the coast is spruce-cedar-hemlock forest, inland there is a belt in which Douglas fir replaces Sitka spruce, and still farther inland there are areas of mixed deciduous trees, with oakwoods, and grasslands in the Upper Umpqua and Upper Rogue valleys (Küchler 1964).

External Relations

A wide trade network, possibly fostered by dugout travel and overland trails, brought camas and hides from the interior and marine products from the coast. Dentalia shells from Vancouver Island and projectile points (Gray 1987:52) from the south were important wealth items. Athapaskans participated in the wealth and ritual complexes of this region as well as in feuds, raids, and warfare.

Culture

Subsistence

Beginning in June, Upper Coquille women dug roots, such as camas and wild carrots, and collected strawberries, raspberries, and salmonberries. The camas was steamed in a large pit holding the separate piles of several women. These wild crops were prepared for storing, except for salmonberries, which were eaten fresh. In July men got trout and lamprey. Men and women gathered plant weaving materials. Through August the old stayed in the village, while the younger people built brush houses in the mountains and hunted the fattened elk and deer, which the women processed on drying racks.

In September and October people moved to fish camps to obtain salmon with toggle harpoons, dip nets, clubs, and salmon fences. Only two species—chinook and coho—were available (Atkinson, Rose, and Duncan 1967: 82–84). The chief directed a move to sandbar camps where men fished and women collected hazelnuts, acorns, tarweed, and roots. The first 5 or 10 Chinook salmon were ritually eaten by everyone. When the men were up all night at the traps, they slept during the day while boys tended the traps. Salmon eggs were smoked. In the fall after the berries were collected, the patches were burned over. Hunting areas were burned over every five years.

People settled in the winter villages for a period of visiting and rituals. Sometimes a hunter was able to drown

---

*The phonemes of the Tututni dialect of Tututni are: (unaspirated stops and affricates) *b, d, ǯ, g, gʷ, ʔ*; (aspirated stop and affricate) *t, č*; (glottalized stops and affricates) *ṭ, λ̓, c̓, c̣̓, ḳ, ḳʷ*; (voiceless continuants) *ł, s, ṣ, š, x, xʷ, h*; (voiced continuants) *l, y, γ, γʷ*: (nasals) *m, n*; (vowels) *i, e, a, o, ə*. The flat apicals (*c̣, ṣ*) are slightly retroflexed with some lip rounding. Information on Tututni phonology and the phonemic transcription of Tututni words is from Golla (1976:218–220) and Victor Golla (communication to editors 1988).

The phonemes of Galice are: (voiceless lenis stops and affricates) *b, d, ʒ, ǯ, g, gʷ, ʔ*; (voiceless fortis stops and affricate) *t, č, k, kʷ*; (glottalized stops and affricates) *ṭ, λ̓, c̓, č̓, ḳ, ḳʷ*; (voiceless continuants) *W, ł, s, š, h*; (voiced continuants) *w, l, z, y*; (nasals) *m, n*; (short oral vowels) *i, e, a, o*; (short nasalized vowels) *i·, ą, ǫ*; (long oral vowels) *i·, e·, a·, o·*; (long nasalized vowels) *i·, ą·, ǫ·*. Information on Galice phonology is from Hoijer (1966:320).

There is no available phonemic analysis of Upper Umpqua. The phonology of the Smith River dialect of Tolowa has been described by Bright (1964).

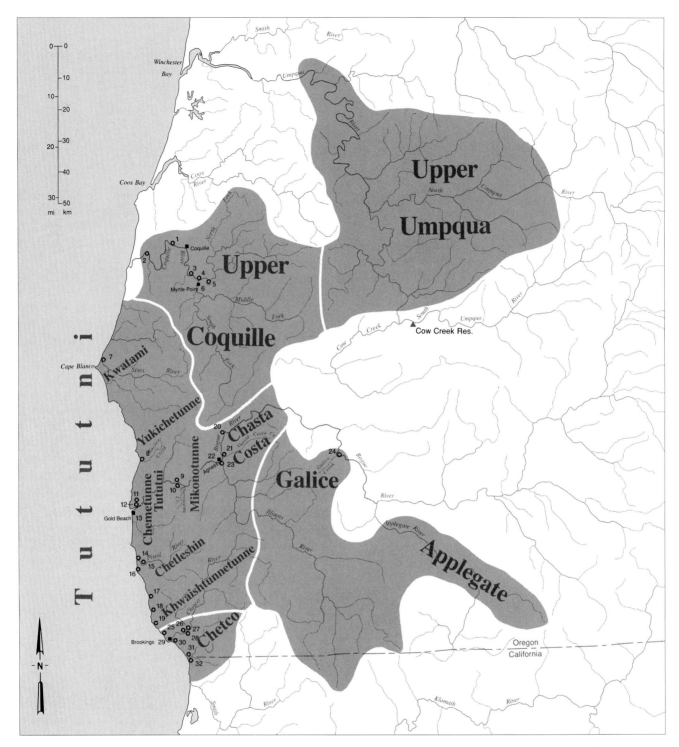

Fig. 1. Mid-19th-century territory, divisions, and primary villages of the Athapaskans of southwest Oreg. Upper Coquille, Tututni, Chasta Costa, Galice, and Chetco villages are given, but the village names and locations for Upper Umpqua and Applegate Athapaskans are not available. Upper Coquille: 1, łənxašdən; 2, xʷešdən; 3, łćəsmeʔ 'in the sand'; 4, čaɣilidən 'place where water flows apart'; 5, čən čaɨahdən; 6, ɨasən ćeɣiłʔadən 'pepperwood-point place'. Tututni: 7, kusume; 8, gʷəsaʔlxəndən 'place of tasty mussels'; 9, mikʷʷənodən 'white clover place'; 10, gwəsetən 'yew place'; 11, žeme; 12, dotodən 'lagoon place'; 13, nagət-xetən; 14, čəλəščəndən 'at the base of the crags'; 15, aʔenetən; 16, enasət; 17, xustenetən 'gravel place'; 18, xainəngintetən 'people all departed'; 19, nałteneten. Chasta Costa: 20, se-ełtaniču 'among large rocks'; 21, yəčigʷəd or dəčigʷəd 'its tailbone'; 22, sełxəddən 'slippery rock place'; 23, tłegət-tłintən 'at the confluence'. Galice: 24, ta·ldašdan. Chetco: 25, kalukwət 'on a baby basket'; 26, łəšxaslidən 'place of clay banks'; 27, tunestən; 28, ɨašuntanšutletən 'where pepperwood nuts drift in under something'; 29, nagət-xetən; 30, ćidxu 'Chetco'; 31, ḳosantanišutša; 32, kosantən 'evening'. These names are a synthesis of Dorsey (1890), Goddard (1903-1904), Waterman (1925), E.D. Jacobs (1935b), Harrington (1942b), and Victor Golla (communication to editors 1988); nonphonemic forms are normalized.

ATHAPASKANS OF SOUTHWESTERN OREGON

an elk swimming in the water during the winter. In late winter, with provisions low or exhausted, women made soup from elk and deer bones that had been saved. They would also boil together dried salmon heads and rotten salmon eggs, which were said to taste good. During the spring, people ate seagull eggs and yellowjacket grubs. About March, men hunted bear, which had to be eaten at a feast as soon as it was butchered. With luck, they might find a beached whale.

This subsistence round was repeated by all the Athapaskan tribes, with some variations. The Upper Umpqua ate grasshoppers. The Tututni ate sugar pine nuts, skunk cabbage flowers, octopus, seaweed, laurel berries, and myrtle nuts. Such food differences, based on local availability, were somewhat leveled out by trade and travel. Among the Tututni, Galice, and Upper Coquille, old men would burn over and fence an area in which they grew tobacco. The Upper Coquille hunted elk with hunting dogs which they bought from the Nestucca Tillamook. Hunters would drink the blood of slain elk. Galice men held target practice before hunting, wore deer head disguises, and built brush deer fences with a circumference of about a mile with snares placed in about 20 openings. The men would stab the snared deer with a bone dagger. Galice hunted grizzlies with dogs and traps. The Applegate camped in brush houses in the mountains to snare deer during September.

Division of Labor

The Tututni daily cycle began before dawn. The men slept together in a sweathouse. They would awaken, sweat, and swim in a nearby stream. They would then go to their houses, where mothers or wives would have prepared a meal. Women and young children lived in these houses. During the day, women would gather firewood, make baskets, prepare foods, cook, collect plants, and carry water. Men fished, hunted, and tanned hides with a mixture of elk brains, tree moss, and starfish. They also made nets, planks, canoes, and tended tobacco. At sundown, a second meal was eaten in the homes before the men and boys returned to the sweathouse to sleep.

Clothing and Adornment

Women wore buckskin aprons. Girls wore aprons of maple bark. Rich women had shells or other ornamentation applied to their apron fronts (fig. 2), with a back apron extending to midcalf. Generally, only the front apron was worn around the house. Women also wore a cape of tule, deerskin, elkskin, or woven rabbit fur strips and a basketry cap (fig. 3). Men and women were usually barefoot, although men wore moccasins when venturing into the brush. Fancy dress for a rich man included a buckskin cap covered with feathers.

Women's hair was parted in the center, with two shoulder strands. Men were often naked or wore a front apron. The male ideal of beauty was long hair, which was tied in the back. Facial hair was plucked out. Face and hair were coated with elk or deer grease.

Structures

Temporary brush shelters, windbreaks on beaches, sheds, sweathouses, and plank winter houses were built. An Upper Coquille sweathouse was excavated about three feet. One could stand in the center or sit up at the sides. The sweathouse included a central fire, board roof, round construction covered with dirt, drafthole, and entrance that was less than a yard in diameter. Each village had at least one sweathouse, and larger towns had more.

The size of a house was proportional to the status of its residents. A house of a wealthy family was 20 by 30 feet with three inside fires, fern and grass wall mats, and rafters for drying fish and meat in the smoky interior. The

Lincoln Co. Histl. Soc., Newport, Oreg.

Fig. 2. Molly Carmichael (left) and her mother Yannah Catfish, Tututni. They wear basketry hats, shell, bead, and dentalium necklaces, and aprons made from buckskin decorated with beads, pine nuts, thimble tinklers, and fringe. They hold feather wands. Photographed about 1909.

582

Fig. 3. Woman's basketry cap, decorated in geometric designs of dark red and maidenhair fern. Collected about 1894, Rogue River, Oreg., diameter, 18 cm.

house had a log ladder with two or three rungs. A smaller home was 10 by 15 feet. Tututni homes had a narrow anteroom and paved porch area.

Technology

Tools and manufactures were largely similar throughout the area. They can be listed by the raw materials used. Wood utensils included: acorn stirrers, spoons, paddles, drying racks, foot-long needles, board drums, dibble, canoes with foot knobs as braces, arrows, bows, spears, traps, clappers for the Make-Doctor Dance, fire tongs, pitch torches, fire drills, planks, gaffs, bowls, a stool for the chief, pipes, and brushes. From hide people fashioned: blankets, aprons, capes, skullcaps, hoop drums (after these were introduced from the Columbia River), sea otter skin quivers, deerskin tobacco pouches, and elkskin armor. Stone tools included: projectile points, obsidian blades, flat round stones for holding fire in canoes while traveling, hammers, pestles, and adz blades. There were also bone whistles for the war dance; elk antler spoons for men, especially for the chief (women used fingers or musselshell spoons), deer-hoof rattles (fig. 4), and antler treasure boxes (fig. 5).

In textiles Oregon Athapaskans manufactured iris fiber nets, maple bark string, sewed tule mats for walls and bedding, and snares. Baskets were used for storage, carrying, sifting, cradles, hoppers, cooking, hats, dippers, and platters. The Tututni made a girl's puberty basket.

Social Organization

Each of these tribal congeries recognized the virtue of wealth and made social distinctions based on it. Each village had a chief who received a portion of all food gathered and processed by his townspeople. He had

Fig. 4. Deer-hoof rattle, the hooves strung on plaited fiber cord. Collected on the Rogue River, Oreg., before 1900; length 33 cm.

several wives and slaves working for him. Other townspeople were distinguished as rich (Tututni xəšxe), moderate, or poor (Tututni dudete). There does not seem to have been a rigid line between slaves and commoners. Among the Upper Coquille all slaves, no matter who their owners, were attached to the household of a chief, where the male slaves were supervised by the chief's son and the female slaves by the chief's daughter. Male slaves slept in the sweathouse. After a period of modest and devoted service, a slave "got to be a person, not a slave anymore." A chief could enslave any of his townspeople who did not behave and sell them away for several hundred dollars (E.D. Jacobs 1935).

A chief might lead a slave raid, receive the son or daughter of someone in debt to him, or purchase a slave from another tribe. The hallmark of a chief seems to have been that he was involved in all financial transactions as the donor of treasure, as an arbitrator, and as the recipient in a division of any acquired wealth. The chieftainship was inherited patrilineally, subject to village consensus on the wealth reserves and personality of the heir. Only the Tututni seem to have been willing to consider lineal female heirs in the absence of males; other tribes preferred to turn to collateral male heirs.

On the whole, except for the position of chief, these social ranks seem less rigid than those among the northernmost Northwest Coast tribes. The rich were expected to look out for the poor: to give them food, to provide treasure for their bride prices, and to share the sweathouse with them.

Shamans

A Galice shaman (di·nan) was gifted by guardian spirits such as Lightning, Snakebite, Yellowjacket sting, and Eagle. Throughout the area, most shamans were women. The object of their medical treatment was the removal of a 'pain': a tiny living object sharply pointed at both ends and holding in its midsection the blood it had sucked from the patient. It was said to be like a blood-filled splinter or hair. The Tututni distinguished sucking shamans, who danced and sucked out the pain, from common shamans, who sat

Fig. 5. Elk antler dentalium purses. Hide or sinew wraps around the slot held the currency securely. Both are carved and show polish from years of use. Collected at the mouth of the Rogue River, Oreg., before 1929. Length of top, 15 cm; other to scale.

and sang, blew smoke over the patient, and waved bunches of flicker (yellowhammer) tail feathers over him. From Port Orford south, shamans blew water over the patient and had the ability to send a 'poison' against a thief, causing sores to erupt. Cures were always held in homes.

If cures were not effective, a shaman might name another shaman as the cause of the illness, and the family of the patient might then kill the accused. The subsequent recovery of the patient would prove the guilt of this shaman, and the murder payment would therefore be much smaller than usual. If the patient died, the curing shaman returned her fee and the relative had to pay the full murder compensation for the other shaman. For fear of such accusations, a respected shaman was always guarded by her village chief, never went out after dark, and never traveled alone. If a shaman was believed to have inadvertently caused harm or death, through letting her power get out of control, she was exorcised by another shaman. The exorcising shaman beat the accused, removed the offending "pain" and drowned it in cold water, and then spared her life.

The fee of a female shaman was paid to her husband. A chief received the pay for a shaman who cured in another village or area.

An Upper Coquille shaman might receive power from Eel, Big Snake, Dog, Knife, Bullet, Otter, or birds (Hawk, Flicker, Hummingbird). Coyote was the best power and Grizzly Bear the most dangerous. A person might have shamanistic powers for years before they finally made him ill. The cure involved a diagnosis of the powers as the source for the illness and led to a Make-Doctor Dance in which a distinguished shaman announced the approach of a power armed with bow and arrow. The new shaman was asked to identify the power as it stood on the roof ready to shoot. If it was Grizzly Bear, the new shaman was told to send it away or it would eventually get out of control and kill the shaman. Other powers were approved and thus permitted to 'shoot' the new shaman. This happened each night for 10 nights, resulting in 10 powers. A powerful shaman should have 100 songs. These encounters also taught the shaman whether to paint her face and forearms black or red when curing. An Upper Coquille shaman wore a coyote pelt over the head and back.

Other people were gifted with specific shamanistic abilities by their guardian spirits. These include the ability to cure dog bites and rattlesnake bites and to talk to medicines and herbs for remedies and love-charming. People gifted to know Knife and Bullet cured war wounds. An old woman might be able to call South Wind and an old man to marshall war power as he tended the outside fire at a war dance. Nightwalkers (Upper Coquille ƛiʔnaɣa) were given evil power from grizzlies and cougars, which enabled them to travel very fast and poison people.

The Upper Coquille, Galice, and Tututni also recognized a specialist with the power of the spoken word or spell, sometimes called a formulist (Galice čołči·da). These spells were inherited patrilineally but might also be purchased. An Upper Coquille formulist prepared the first fresh lamprey or deer for a family after the period of mourning. A Galice formulist had two grizzly bears that did his biding and a rattlesnake who aided him in getting public confessions of thievery. A formulist could also find lost objects.

Life Cycle

Birth was aided by a midwife or female shaman. The midwife took the baby, cut the cord with an heirloom flint knife, and washed the baby using a deer tail and warm water. The afterbirth was put into a split sapling. On the fifth morning after, the mother swam. For the baby of a rich family, dentalia was put around the ankles and basket cradle handle. Parents preferred baby girls because they brought bride price wealth into the family. During the five-day seclusion after birth, Tututni parents ate no fresh food. The mother was fed dried acorn and salmon soup to stimulate her milk. Among the Upper Coquille, a man pierced the nasal septum and each ear in three places when the baby was a week old.

After the five-day seclusion, an Upper Coquille baby received a nickname, but at 10 he received a 'good name', that of a paternal relative of the same sex who had been dead over a year. Sometimes a dying person would bequeath his name. A father usually gave his name to his eldest son. A nonrelative could pay for a particular name with 20–30 dentalia.

The first kill of a boy was distributed to every house in

the village. The first acorns and berries gathered by a girl were also given to everyone. At puberty a girl was secluded. An Upper Coquille girl was secluded 10 days on her bed platform. She wore her finery, used moss menstrual pads, a shell scratcher attached to her wrist to avoid touching her hair and skin, and ate only dry food for a year afterward. She swam early and late each day. Her father could not gamble, hunt, or fish at this time. A Tututni girl wore a tiny basket around her neck that held flicker feathers, pigments, and an obsidian flake to slash her body to encourage the blood to flow. Her body but not her limbs was painted red. She wore flicker wing feathers in her nasal septum during the day, and flicker tail feathers there at meals. When she left the house, a deerskin was placed over her head. On the last day, the Tututni girl dashed from the house and swam 10 times before daybreak. The rite was repeated for her second and third menstruation. Thereafter, she was a woman. The Galice held a round dance of alternating men and women for 5 or 10 nights when a girl reached puberty.

To be respectable a woman had to be purchased in marriage. A rich bride usually cost 100 long dentalia. Children were illegitimate if their mother was not paid for. Children were worth the bride price of their mother. The chief oversaw all transactions and usually received one-half the payment. The parents arranged marriages. If the parents, the chief, and a man 'who knew dentalia' approved, the bride with her family and chief went to the groom's village after five days, gave half the bride price to the groom's father, and held a feast with acorn soup. The bride gave her mother-in-law a fine buckskin dress decorated with shell beads. The bride slept in the home and the groom in the sweathouse. Both sets of parents exchanged gifts and foods. The male members of the families of the groom and bride exchanged their weapons and clothes. The next night the bride and groom slept together in a corner bed platform of the house on a bearskin.

The Upper Coquille wife helped her father-in-law, and the husband could mildly joke with his mother-in-law. A first wife became the head wife in a polygynous family, unless one of the other wives was a shaman or the daughter of a chief. The husband returned from the sweathouse at night to have sex with his wife, after which they swam separately. Marriage alternatives include the levirate, sororate, and a rich couple purchasing a husband to live with their daughter in her own home village. In the event of a divorce, the bride price was returned with adjustments made for each living child. Tututni reasons for divorce were jealousy, meanness, and barrenness. Upper Coquille wives were sometimes driven to suicide by their husbands, who then had to pay fines. After a divorce Tututni and Upper Coquille older children went with the father and younger ones with the mother. Sometimes parents would buy back their daughter, who then had

considerable freedom and could take young men as lovers without censure.

The Galice signaled a death with a high monotone cry. If someone died far away from his village, the Galice cremated the body and returned with the ashes. A dying Upper Coquille would confess any wrongs on the death bed; if he then recovered the family had to pay any resulting fines. The face of the corpse was covered with a skin; then the body was placed in a basket, and removed through a hole made in the west side of the house. Ashes were then put around the hole to deter ghosts. After it had been bathed in warm water and dressed in dentalia and finery, a Tututni corpse was placed on a deerskin held by four men at the corners and carried to the graveyard through the side wall of the house. The corpse was extended, wrapped, and lashed in a skin. The Tututni and Upper Coquille had specialized gravediggers and grave-yards divided into family areas. Tututni gravediggers stuffed grass in their mouths to keep away sickness, faced only in one direction, dug the grave to the height of their breasts, and afterward threw away their clothes. Mourn-ers cut their hair—the closer the kinship relation, the nearer to the scalp. Close Galice relatives put ashes and pitch on heads and faces. A spouse wore pitch for a year. A man might mourn his close kin by rolling on the ground and wailing. At the grave, everyone cried loudly. The chief or a speaker addressed the crowd. As the corpse was raised and lowered five times into the grave, an old man talked in its ear. Treasures were put in the grave. The grave was filled with two inches of river sand placed on top.

If it appeared that the kin would need more time to attend the funeral, the Upper Coquille might keep the body for up to 10 days in a shanty with two men and fire. Neither these two men nor the gravedigger was paid. The Upper Coquille said the soul remained in the grave for five days before it crossed the ocean. The ghost emerged from the skin and bones of the corpse. There was a taboo on the name of the dead for at least one year.

Ceremonies

Aboriginal rites included feasts and gift-giving at birth, naming, first kills, puberty, war, and death as well as in celebration of the Make-Doctor Dance for new shamans.

The Tututni held the Ten Night Dance in the home of the chief at his request in order to forget the dead. Men and women danced alternately. Women wore all their wealth. Recent mourners were paid from a general collection to permit the dance to be held. The bereaved then gave permission for the dance. Small groups of men with a back line of women danced while married men called 'jumpers' took turns with one or two women on the dance floor. The dance "boss" was in the corner near the door. The different dances imitated animals such as deer, *585* woodpeckers, buzzards, and, at the end, comic figures. A good female dancer commanded a substantially higher bride price. The participants slept during the day, eating one meal at noon. For the deer dance, the jumpers wore a basket hat with antlers and an otter-skin quiver with arrows. Men and women wore red and white face stripes.

After killing an enemy or a prisoner the Upper Coquille performed a Murder Dance, involving two men and a woman dancing around an outdoor fire. The crux of the rite was the insulting of the victim name, which would otherwise cost them a fine. A Lamprey Dance was held when the first lampreys were caught. The Brush Dance was a historic introduction to Siletz Reservation derived from the more general Ghost Dance and the foreign use of a hide drum.

Warfare

The Tututni preferred surprise attacks at night; the Upper Coquille killed a warrior if he was seriously wounded and cremated the body if there was time. A man might pay 10 dentalia to a man with the power to mystically 'warm up' or poison his arrows to guarantee that the victim would die. The Upper Coquille were also careful not to kill too many of the enemy so that they would have enough wealth to pay for the slain. Before the battle, they had a war dance around an outside fire. A row of men yelled and whistled, and two women were selected to throw ashes on the faces of the warriors. To settle the battle indemnity, both tribes or villages selected five neutral arbitrators. If the claimants were not satisified with the settlement, one of them kicked the fire to signal the start of a fight between the sides. They fought until the arbitrators stopped it and negotiated the amount of treasure each side had to supply. When the settlement came, each side danced through the other five times delivering blows with the flat side of knives. If a battle developed, the sides separated when the first person was killed. The killer returned to his village, ate only dried fish and meat, and had inch-wide black stripes painted from ear to chin. Afterward, the formulist provided him with fresh fish and meat.

Upper Coquille boys held target practice, and men practiced dodging projectiles while wearing elkskin armor. A warrior had to be at least 20 years old. Warriors always traveled on foot as they were too vulnerable in canoes.

History

Robert Gray traded with some Athapaskan people in April 1792 after having viewed populous coast villages as early as 1788. The botanist David Douglas (1959) encountered the Upper Umpqua in 1826, and Fort Umpqua (Schlesser 1973) was in their territory. Athapaskans and neighboring tribes were shattered by the local gold rush and ravaged by the

Rogue River War of 1855–1856 and previous hostilities. The survivors and neutral tribes such as the Upper Coquilles were shipped up the coast to Portland and then up the Willamette River before being settled on the Grand Ronde and Siletz reservations.

The Ghost Dance was introduced to the Siletz and Grand Ronde reservations via the Shasta in 1871; a variant, the Earth Lodge cult—known locally as the Warm House Dance—was introduced in 1873. At least three Warm House Dance houses were built at Siletz. A modified version of the Siletz Warm House was carried to the Alsea, Siuslaw, and Coos by Coquille Thompson (fig. 7) and Depot Charlie around 1878 (Du Bois 1939).

In 1988 there was a Coquille Tribe consisting of descendants of the Miluk Coosans and Upper Coquille (Ruby and Brown 1986). This entity is in part the product of a claims settlement against the federal government (R.L. Hall 1984).

Synonymy

Upper Umpqua. The Upper Umpqua self-designation was etnémitane, etnémi-tenéyu (Gatschet 1877g). Synonyms include Tututni ʔakʷa (Sapir 1914a:273); Takelma ya·kalàʔ (Sapir 1907a:253); Galice ƛoh-dade· literally 'grass people' (Hoijer 1973a:62); and Hanis Coos diné·yu (Harrington 1942b), probably a borrowing from Athapaskan. See Hodge (1907–1910, 2:866) for additional variants.

Tututni–Chasta Costa–Upper Coquille. The Tututni name for themselves was dotodəni, from doto, a village place-name, and dəni 'people (of that place)' (Golla 1976: 217). Synonyms include Hanis Coos gusiyáʔme· 'Rogue River Indians', literally 'south people' (Harrington 1942b), gení·ʔmis 'southwestern Oregon Athapaskan' (Jacobs 1932–1934); and Tolowa yąsu (ʔ) čid 'Gold Beach (Rogue River) Indians' (Seaburg 1976–1982), literally 'beyond the Chetco River'. Klamath wa·lamkskni· was applied by some speakers to the Latkawa Takelma and by others to the Indians on the Rogue River (Barker 1963: 436). See Hodge (1907–1910, 2:857–858). Berreman (1937:32–33), largely following Schumacher (1877), distinguished seven groups of Tututni: Kwatami or Sixes, Yukichetunne or Euchre Creek, Chemetunne or Joshua, Tututni proper, Mikonotunne, Chetleshin or Pistol River, and Khwaishtunnetunne.

The Chasta Costa name for themselves was šista qʷə́sta (Sapir 1914a:274).

The Upper Coquille self-designation was mišixʷədme·dəneʔ 'people who dwell on the stream called miši' (Harrington 1942b, normalized; Dorsey 1890:232). A rendering of this as Mishikhwutmetunne was used by Hodge (1907–1910, 1:870–871), who gives additional names.

Galice-Applegate. The Galice name for themselves was

Fig. 6. Baldwin Fairchild (b. 1856), Chetco, dressed in an elaborate costume made of red-tailed hawk feathers. He was about to participate in a July 4 celebration. Fairchild was an important linguistic informant for James Owen Dorsey in 1884 (Pilling 1892). Photograph by E.E. Wilson, Siletz Reservation, Oreg., 1910.

ta·ldaš 'Galice Indians', or *ta·ldašdani·* 'people of the Galice tribe' (Hoijer 1973a:54). Synonyms include Upper Coquille galisgʷi (E.D. Jacobs 1935). See Hodge (1907–1910, 2:679–680).

The Galice name for the Applegate Creek Indians was *daʔkoh* (Hoijer 1973a:53), *dáʔkohbeʔ dade·* 'Applegate River person' (Jacobs 1935, 1938–1939a, phonemicized). A rendering of this as Dakubetede was used by Hodge (1907–1910, 1:380), who gives other designations.

Chetco. The Chetco referred to themselves as čedi

Fig. 7. Coquille Thompson (b. 1842, d. 1946), Upper Coquille, and his wife Agnes (b. 1880). He served as an informant to numerous anthropologists including James Owen Dorsey in 1884 (Pilling 1892), Philip Drucker in 1934 (Drucker 1933–1954), Cora Du Bois in 1934 (Du Bois 1939), Melville and Elizabeth D. Jacobs in 1935 (E.D. Jacobs 1935; Jacobs and Jacobs 1935; Jacobs 1936c), John P. Marr in 1941 (J.P. Marr 1941b) and John P. Harrington in 1942 (Mills 1981). Photographed in 1945.

(perhaps the name of their village), or čedi dəne (Dorsey 1890:236, normalized). Synonyms include Tolowa *čid* (Seaburg 1976–1982). See Hodge (1907–1910, 1:249).

Sources

Krauss (1973, 1979) surveys Oregon Athapaskan linguistic research. Published studies include Hale (1846), Sapir (1914a), Curtis (1907–1930, 13), Hoijer (1960, 1966, 1973a), Golla (1976), and Landar (1977). Guides to extensive unpublished materials include Pilling (1892), *587*

Parr (1974), and Mills (1981) for the important Harrington papers, and Seaburg (1982), especially for M. and E.D. Jacobs's research. Sound recordings, including music, were generated by Frachtenberg (1915b, 1915c, 1915d), Jacobs (1935, 1938–1939), Jacobs and Jacobs (1935), J.P. Marr (1941, 1941a, 1941b), Swadesh (1953b, 1953c), Metcalf (1955), Hoijer (1956), J.E. Pierce (1962, 1962a), and Golla (1962).

Jacobs (1962, 1967) summarizes folklore research; Parr (1974) provides additional references. There are few published tests and even fewer textual analyses: Sapir (1914a), Farrand and Frachtenberg (1915), E.D. Jacobs (1968, 1977), Jacobs (1968), and Ramsey (1983). Unpublished text collections were recorded by Goddard (1903–1904), E.D. Jacobs (1935, 1935a, 1976a), Jacobs (1935, 1938–1939a), and J.P. Marr (1941, 1941a, 1941b).

The ethnographic data are fragmentary and largely unpublished. The primary published sources are Barnett's (1937) culture trait list and Drucker (1937), supplemented by Dorsey (1889, 1890), Du Bois (1936), and R.L. Hall (1984). Gray (1987) provides a synthesis for the upper Rogue River area. Important manuscript notes are contained in Dorsey (1884), Du Bois (1934), E.D. Jacobs (1935), and Drucker (1933–1954). Additional ethnographic notes may be gleaned from Goddard (1903–1904), E.D. Jacobs (1935a), Jacobs (1935, 1938–1939a), and Harrington (1940–1942, 1940–1942a, 1942b). Especially valuable for ethnogeographical data are Dorsey (1890), Waterman (1921, 1925), Curtis (1907–1930, 13), and Harrington (1940–1942, 1940–1942a, 1942b). Du Bois (1939), Sackett (1973), and Beckham, Toepel, and Minor (1984) treat postcontact religious movements at the Siletz Reservation. Indian-White contact until the Rogue River War is the subject of Beckham (1971); Harger (1972) and Kent (1977) describe the early years of the Siletz Reservation. Beckham (1977) provides an introductory account of western Oregon Indian history and culture.

Takelma

DAYTHAL L. KENDALL

The Takelma (tə'kelmə) language is a member of the Penutian phylum, within which its closest relatives are the Kalapuyan languages.* The Takelma occupied portions of the drainages of the Umpqua and Rogue rivers in southwestern Oregon. In the Umpqua drainage Takelma territory included at least upper Cow Creek (Sapir 1907a: 252), possibly the whole of Cow Creek, Myrtle Creek, and a portion of the main stem of the South Umpqua (Riddle 1920:34–35; Henry Zenk, personal communication 1986). In the Rogue drainage, Takelma territory included at least the Rogue and its northern tributaries from Grave Creek to Table Rock, possibly the whole drainage from the middle Illinois River to Big Butte Creek, excluding Athapaskan territory on Galice Creek and the Applegate River (fig. 1).

Component Groups

Anthropologists (Sapir 1910a, 1910, 1922; Barry 1927; Spier 1927) have divided the Takelma into two groups: the Takelma proper, who occupied most of the area, and the Latkawa, said to have occupied "the poorer land of the Upper Rogue, east, say, of Table Rock toward the Cascades and in the neighborhood of the present town of Jacksonville" (Sapir 1907a:252).

Dialectal differences constituted one of the primary distinguishing characteristics. However, an examination (Kendall 1976) of Takelma data (Hazen 1857a; Barnhardt 1859; Dorsey 1884; St. Clair 1903–1904, 1903–1904a; Sapir 1906, 1909; Harrington 1933) has shown a twofold division to be insufficient. The linguistic data probably represent four dialects: Lower Takelma, Latkawa, Takelma B, and Takelma H. Other information possibly indicates a fifth dialect, Hanesak (Spier 1927:358), spoken east of Table Rock and probably more closely related to Latkawa than to the other dialects.

*The phonemes of Takelma are: (unaspirated stops) p, t, 'k, kʷ, ʔ; (aspirated stops) pʰ, tʰ, kʰ, kʷʰ; (glottalized stops and affricate) ṗ, ṭ, c̓, k̓; (fricatives) s, x, h; (nasals) m, n; (lateral) l; (semivowels) w, y; (short vowels) i, e, a, o, ü; (long vowels) iˑ, eˑ, aˑ, oˑ, üˑ; (raised or rising pitch) v́, (falling pitch) v̀, (unaccented) v. The unaspirated series is written for phonetically aspirated segments in environments in which the contrast with the aspirated series is neutralized. This phonemic analysis follows that in Kendall (1977), transcribed into the *Handbook* technical alphabet.

External Relations

There are questions about territorial relations with the Athapaskans in the west and the Shasta in the east. Sapir (1907a), Berreman (1937:27–28, 57), and others supposed the Takelma to have been in the upper Illinois drainage, the upper Applegate drainage, and northward to the Rogue, making the Galice and Applegate groups two Athapaskan enclaves within Takelma territory. However, Gray (1987:20–24) concludes that the whole Illinois drainage was Athapaskan, making the Galice and Applegate groups simply the easternmost members of an Athapaskan continuum. There were Shasta groups in the upper Rogue drainage, perhaps mainly on Bear Creek (formerly the Stewart River), during the "wars" of the 1850s (Heizer and Hester 1970:138–144; Beckham 1971: 9), but it is not clear how long they had been there. Earlier apparent identification of the inhabitants of the Rogue River as Shastas, as in Hale (1846:map between 196 and 197), reflects the confusion of the Rogue and Klamath rivers under the name Shaste River. Dixon's (1907:386) Shasta informants asserted a Shasta claim to an area extending to Table Rock and Mount McLaughlin (formerly Mount Pitt). On the other hand, Klamath (Spier 1927:364) and Takelma (Harrington 1933) informants stated that the Latkawa had always lived in this region, the Takelma informant asserting that the Shasta had come during the wars. Heizer and Hester (1970) accept the Shasta claim, suggesting that the Takelma may have moved into the region after the Shasta were driven out by the wars. In the *California* volume of the Handbook (vol. 8:211) the Shasta claim is accepted to the exclusion of the Takelma. But Takelma traditions, village names, and the diversity of Takelma dialects within the disputed region point to a long Takelma occupation. Gray's (1987:17–18) suggestion that Shasta territory extended into the Bear Creek valley only as far as Ashland seems plausible, although Shasta may have remained south of the Siskiyous (Spier 1927:360). It is also possible that the Shasta and Latkawa were intermarried and jointly used some of this region.

Little is known of relations between the Takelma and other groups before the Whites came. They traded, intermarried, and fought with the Shasta (Sapir 1907a,

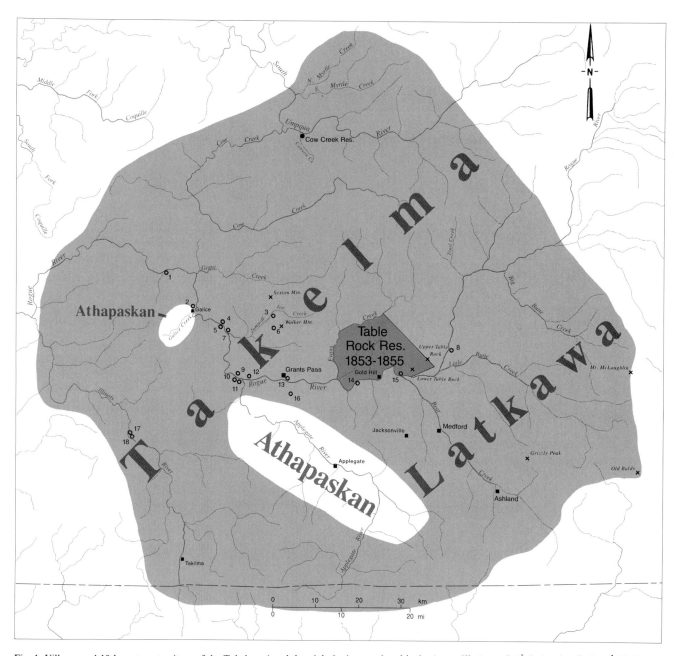

Fig. 1. Villages and 19th-century territory of the Takelma: 1, *taktkamí·k*; 2, skastan; 3, *takĉasín*; 4, *somólk*; 5, yawà·kʰaʔ; 6, *taltaník*; 7, tak̓aláksi; 8, hane·sak; 9, tatmelmal; 10, talkwalk; 11, *salwaxkán*; 12, *kelyálk*; 13, *ti·talám*; 14, *tiʔlo·mí·*; 15, *kʷenpónk*; 16, temeʔhawán; 17, hatka·püsü·ta; 18, ti·wi·k.

1910a). They also fought with the Klamath (Spier 1927) and the Galice Creek Indians (Harrington 1933). The Latkawa found subsistence more difficult than the Lower Takelma and often raided them for food and for slaves to sell to the Klamath (Sapir 1907a, 1910a, 1910). The Takelma allied with neighboring groups against the Whites and probably exercised considerable control over their allies.

Culture

The Takelma have sometimes been identified as culturally a part of the (northern) California area (Sapir 1907a:251). However, location, topography, and linguistic relationships within Oregon Penutian are the reasons for classification as Northwest Coast. The primary food was the acorn; other commonly used vegetables were camas bulbs and various seeds and berries. Their diet also included deer, salmon, and other fish. The only cultivated crop was tobacco. There were a variety of twined baskets for carrying, storing, cooking, eating, and drinking. They used stone primarily for grinding implements and projectile points. Other implements, such as diggers, spoons, and needles, were made of wood, horn, and bone. It seems likely that the Lower Takelma used canoes, Since they considered the Latkawa inferior for using rafts rather than canoes and since canoes are mentioned frequently in the Lower Takelma myths.

Winter houses were rectangular with a tamped earthen floor as much as two feet below ground level, the door above ground level, walls of vertically set sugarpine boards, and a gable roof. Summer houses were roofless brush shelters. The village sweathouse, a rectangular, earth-covered structure usually large enough for six men, was owned by one of the wealthier men. Women, denied access to the men's sweathouse, used a temporary structure of sticks and blankets.

Men wore buckskin shirts, trousers, and moccasins, and bear or deer hide hats. Women wore knee-length buckskin dresses and basketry hats obtained from the Shasta (fig. 2). Ornamentation consisted of red-headed woodpecker scalps, strips of otter skin, porcupine quills,

Fig. 2. Oscharwasha, also known as Jennie, wearing the dress that she made as a burial garment. Made of buckskin ornamented with shell and glass beads, dentalia, and coins, the dress has a Plains-type appliqué sewn onto the back (A.C. Miller 1976:99). She wears a basketry hat and has vertical lines tattooed on her chin. Photograph by Peter Britt, before 1893.

strings of shells, and facial paint. Girls were generally tattooed with three vertical stripes on the chin; tattooing in men was usually limited to marks on the left arm for measuring dentalium strings.

On the basis of the available data (Sapir 1907a: 268–269), it seems that kinship was reckoned bilaterally. In ego's generation, the terms are Iroquois in type with bilaterally symmetrical modifications. In the first ascending generation, the terms are bifurcate collateral; however, father's brother and mother's sister are classed with father's sister's son and mother's brother's daughter, respectively. Cousin marriage and the marriage of a man to his brother's wife's sister were forbidden. A marriage was usually arranged between families in different villages with the woman coming to live with her husband's people. Marriage was by purchase of the bride, with an additional payment due upon the birth of the first child. The amount paid for the wife determined the status of her children. A man might have more than one wife either because of his wealth or because of the obligation to marry his deceased brother's wife.

There seem to have been three levels of society: rich or chief, ordinary free persons, and slaves. In addition to the bride price paid for one's mother, marks of wealth and social status included quality of dress and house, number of wives and servants, strings of dentalium shells, and the quantity and quality of other possessions. Wealth was also used in payment of compensation for injuries and killings and in payment to the go-between who interceded on behalf of the injured party.

The political organization of the Takelma was relatively simple: there seems to have been no firmly established unit larger than the village. Any relatively wealthy man could be called a chief, and there probably were no head chiefs. The Takelma probably developed a greater political unity and a stronger chieftaincy in response to the Whites: among the motivating factors would be self-defense and the Whites' insistence on dealing with a few people in positions of authority.

The only known regular periodic ceremonies were at the first appearance of salmon and of acorns. Dancing (always without drum) was limited to preparation for war, puberty rites for girls, and shamanistic performances. Shamans, male or female, exercised great influence and could both cure and cause illness. Only shamans had access to guardian spirits, of which a shaman would have one or more. These supernatural beings were usually associated with animals or topographical features. Medicine Rock (*tan molokól* 'Rock Old Woman'), probably located on Sexton Mountain, was believed to be an enemy of evil shamans and offerings of food were often placed on the rock to obtain relief from illness.

History

The opening of the Applegate Trail in 1846 and the discovery of gold in 1851–1852 brought increasing numbers of Whites into the valley and into conflict with the Takelma and their Athapaskan and Shasta neighbors. The Whites referred to the groups collectively as The Rogues and the conflicts, in which many natives were massacred, as the Rogue River War. After conclusion of a treaty with the Whites in 1853, most of the Takelma were on the Table Rock Reservation. In 1856, after cessation of hostilities, they were among the numerous tribes moved to the Grand Ronde Reservation and, later, some also to the Siletz Reservation. Interspersion among people of other tribes was a major factor in the destruction of the Takelma as a people and in the loss of their culture.

Mooney (1928) estimated the Takelma population in 1780 at 500, which is probably too low. The censuses for 1852 and 1853 cited by Robison (1943) reporting 1,000–1,100 people possibly included some non-Takelma and, therefore, would be too high. Powell (1891) reported that the Takelma numbered only 27 in 1884. By 1906, there were perhaps six speakers of the language (Sapir 1907a). By the 1970s, there were no Takelma speakers; those people who were of Takelma descent remembered their ancestry as "Rogue Rivers" or "Cow Creeks."

Synonymy

The variant spelling Takilma of Powell's (1891) Takilman stock was superseded by Takelma, which more nearly approximates their name for themselves: *ta·kelmàʔn* 'person (people) from Rogue River' (*ta·kelám* 'Rogue River' [*ta·*- 'along, beside' and *kelám* 'river'] plus *-àʔn* 'person (people) from a particular place') (Sapir 1922:223, 1909:244). The term Rogue Rivers occasionally refers specifically to the Takelma, but more often it includes all the tribes of the Rogue River valley and their allies against the Whites. The indiscriminate use of "Rogue Rivers" in publications (Bancroft 1886b; Walling 1884; late-nine-teenth-century newspapers) and the incorrect use of Tututunne as a synonym for Rogue River Indians (Bancroft 1886b) are the sources of much confusion in modern popular usage of the terms.

The name of the Latkawa, or Upper Takelma, is Takelma *latka·wàʔ* 'person (people) from the village *latká·w*' (Sapir 1922:222, 1909:114–115, 192–293). They were also referred to as *wúlx* 'enemy', a term ordinarily applied to the Shasta (Sapir 1907a:252, 1909:188–189).

Sources

For detailed discussions of religion and other aspects of culture, see Sapir (1907a, 1907, 1910a, 1910). Drucker (1937:294–296) gives additional material on the Latkawa. Gray (1987) gives a synthesis of published and unpublished ethnographic data, with special attention to territory and village sites.

Bancroft (1886b) does not distinguish the Takelma but lumps them into the Rogue River Indians in his discussion of physical and cultural traits. Walling (1884) relies heavily on Bancroft (1886b) for information about the Indians and, like Bancroft, should be used with caution. Beckham (1971) and Robison (1943) discuss relations between the Rogue River Indians (including the Takelma) and the Whites; both contain extensive bibliographies. Barry (1927), Berreman (1937), Dorsey (1890), Sapir (1907a, 1907), and Spier (1927) discuss the geographical distribution of the Takelma. Myths in the Takelma language with English translation and a descriptive grammar of Takelma are available in Sapir (1906, 1909, 1922). A syntactic analysis of the language is found in Kendall (1977). For further discussion of the language, see Frachtenberg (1918a), Gatschet (1882), Hymes (1957), Sapir (1921a), Sapir and Swadesh (1946, 1953), Shipley (1969), Swanton (1952:469–470), and Swadesh (1965). Harrington (1933) gives Takelma names of villages and other places in Lower Takelma, in Latkawa, and a few in both.

Mythology

DELL HYMES

For the Indian peoples of the Northwest Coast, narratives of the past have been central to their ways of life. In them imaginative thought addresses the nature and development of the world; fundamental values are enacted; verbal artistry finds satisfying form.

A distinction between myths and historical tales appears to exist throughout the Northwest Coast, for example, Yakutat Tlingit *λa·gú* 'myth', *š kałni·k* 'historical tale', Tsimshian *ʔatáwx* and *mátəsk*, Cathlamet Chinook *ikʼánam* and *iqíxikałx*, Miluk Coos *bá·saq̓* and *laǵáwiyátas* (Boas 1916). Historical tales take place in the established world in which the people themselves live. Myths tell of an earlier, different time, when some people did not know how to mate or pack wood or were afraid of certain foods, fish were hoarded by a few, and even the sun was kept in a box. Sometimes myths tell of how unfortunate things—mosquitoes, permanent death— came to be part of the established world, but mostly they tell a providential story. The earlier time was not a golden age from which the present has declined but a strange age to be set right for the people who are here now.

Within the myth period further distinctions may be made: stories that are the source of names for individual families (Bella Coola *smayusta*) as against stories generally told; a myth age proper, followed by a period of transformation (Tillamook).

It would be a mistake to think of a strict linear sequence, one age wholly replacing another. It would be more useful to think of a center and a periphery. There is indeed the great divide of transformation, when beings that were humanlike in voice and action became entirely animal, being overcome and diminished or simply choosing to take on their later characteristics and habitats; such as frogs not to hoard fish and water, but to live on the riverbank. Sometimes councils or contests decide things such as the alternations of day and night or the seasons. But some figures of the earlier period continue into the later and even into the present age. Beings that are usually ordinary creatures may still be encountered in extraordinary form. The established world is a center, which the events and beings of the narratives encircle at a distance. One can go out to that periphery, as on a quest for spiritual power (Elmendorf 1984:290). The periphery can come closer, as in the winter sacred season, when power may be displayed in dramatic dance and song, and myths brought to life in words. Especially when the myths are travels of a trickster or transformer, they bring within the confines of the winter house origins in a world of summer.

The Place of Myths

In Oregon and southern Washington, myths are performed only in winter, sometimes just once a winter (Coos), unless to teach them to children (Tillamook). Punishment will befall a person who violates the rule. Myths are knowledge, knowledge accrues with age, and older persons are typically the tellers. Sometimes narratives would be exchanged in a sort of contest; a gifted or enthusiastic older visitor might sometimes go on and on, but typically some formal pattern surrounded the essential task of telling myths to children. Such a telling might be recompensed by a gift of food; or by requiring children, especially children who fell asleep, to cut through ice to bathe in a river. The audience would respond at intervals, perhaps at the end of each segment (as in Clackamas). Sometimes children would be required to repeat each sentence in turn (as in Tillamook, Coos). A story would not just end, but end formally. A summary conclusion might state the outcome of the action, an epilogue might tell what becomes of the actors (especially whether they are transformed and henceforth have certain traits), and a conventional phrase might mark *finis* (Upper Chehalis *kʷalalé··i*). Another formula might state or imply the end of winter and return of good weather and fresh roots, fruits, and fish (Hymes 1981a:322ff.). There are three outcomes, in short: one for the action, one for the nature of the world, and one for the participants and the world of the telling.

Myths were told on winter nights as a kind of world-renewal rite, yet they were present in the lives of people year-round. What could not be performed in full could be quoted or reflected upon. In narrative people both explained and explored the nature of the world. One traveled in a landscape stippled with names, many of them linked to myth. Witty remarks, moral admonitions, and apt proverbs were based upon myth and legend; myth and legend entered as background into speeches, songs, dances, and plastic arts (De Laguna 1972, 2:839). Ironic conversational routines might invoke myths, and myths draw upon such routines (Hymes 1985). Studies of the masterful carving and weaving of the more northern peoples, the rattles, headdresses, masks, hats, baskets, blankets, chests, bowls, and spoons, coppers, pipes, and totem poles necessarily invoke the mythology that informs them (Gunther 1966; Hawthorn 1979; Holm 1983b; Jonaitis 1986). Barbeau's (1950, 1953), studies of totem poles and carving document myths at length, and Lévi-Strauss (1975) structurally analyzes Central Coast Salish and Kwakiutl masks and myths together.

For the socially more stratified peoples in the north, social positions and possessions were legitimated by a myth of origin, the telling of which was an exclusive privilege. This underlies the exuberant diversification of Kwakiutl mythology, as of other groups, a multiplicity of stories of descent having a similar pattern (Boas 1932:viii, 1914). This underlies also a deliberate incompleteness of telling among the Bella Coola (McIlwraith 1948). At the investiture of someone inheriting a privilege validated by a myth, the public would be kept outside and told just enough of the myth to demonstrate the validation, but not so much as to give the myth away.

Kinds of Myths

Perhaps everywhere there was a sense that stories with a personal or family relevance were not open to others to use. Everywhere also there were myths common to the community as a whole, especially stories of one or more myth-age tricksters and transformers. In the north Raven is the gluttonous, lecherous trickster-transformer, center of very extensive cycles of stories among the Tlingit, Haida (fig. 1), and Tsimshian. From the Bella Bella southward as far as the Quileute and the Southern Coast Salish, Raven is a gluttonous trickster but not a transformer, and Mink is Raven's rival in lechery. Among the Southwestern Coast Salish and Chinookans the trickster-buffoon is Bluejay. From the Bella Bella southward to the Oregon coast there is a transformer (a translation of the name in several Coast Salish languages), a serious culture-bringer who does not engage in trickster activity. Coyote is a trickster-transformer on the Lower Columbia (Chinookans), in the inland valleys of western Oregon (Kalapuyans, Takelma), and on a part of the Oregon coast (Alseans). Among the Tillamook the trickster is Ice.

The character of the trickster-transformer is complex (Boas 1898b); he is responsible for so much of the established world, sometimes foresightful and benevolent, yet often selfish, greedy, foolish, obscene. The two characterological poles are managed in a diversity of ways. Tricksters are sometimes shown as less powerful than other figures, such as Eagle and Salmon. Songs are embodiments of power, and tricksters lack a song, or cannot remember, or learn one right. Sometimes the

U. of B.C., Mus. of Anthr., Vancouver: Nbl.481.

Fig. 1. *The Raven and the First Humans*, a sculpture by Bill Reid, of Haida descent. Raven, the trickster and creator, stands atop a clamshell enclosing little creatures that he would transform into the first Haida. As told by Reid (Duffek 1986:44), Raven, upon retreat of the waters of the great flood that once covered the earth, finds a clamshell full of terrified little creatures. These he coerces to leave their shell and explore their new world. Finding that they have no females among them, Raven decides to improve his game, and flies the creatures to North Island, where he induces a sexual experience between these creatures and chitons. Later, the chitons give birth to brown-skinned, black-haired men and women, the original Haidas. These Reid describes as children of the wild coast, born between the sea and the land, who would challenge the strength of the ocean and wrest from it a rich livelihood. Carved from a laminated block of 106 pieces of yellow cedar by Bill Reid and three assistants, 1977–1980.

trickster figure is differentiated by different names (Clackamas) or generations (Alsea, Coos), only one of which embodies trickster nature per se. From the Bella Coola south, benevolent transformations are the work of a separate transformer or set of transformers (Boas 1898b: 11, 1916:618–620). Sometimes both poles simply coexist within the same figure, but myth itself may sort out the two roles. In Kalapuya William Hartless told one Coyote sequence elaborating sheer pleasure in going along, and another exploring Coyote's nature in a series of five adventures. When Coyote's own appetite or need coincides with public good, he succeeds; when it does not, he fails (Hymes 1987a). That may indicate why the two poles of character are so persistently and widely held in tension together. It is understood that the world does not come about by ignoring personal appetite or need, but by harnessing it.

Figures other than the trickster attract attention and stories. In the north, Otter is a constant menace, ready to steal the souls of drowned persons. Salmon is prominent among the Columbia River peoples. The trickster could be a buffoon, a mocker of chiefs, sometimes vain, sometimes pathetic, as Bluejay. There was also a female ogress, a stealer of children, with whom one could frighten children. Among the Kwakiutl this figure, the pendulous-breasted ʒúnuq̇ʷa, is also a source of wealth. Among the Chinook such a figure, Ut'onaqan, is frightening in one visage, a source of invulnerable power in another. Perhaps everywhere there was at least one myth-frame to bring on stage any and all of the beings of the world: a winter dance in which one after another sings its characterizing song, a contest as to who is to be the sun or to wear the antlers of the elk. Throughout the region violation of a taboo brings winter all year round to a village, which discovers its unique plight when a bird drops a fresh berry. Men find themselves with animal wives, women with animal husbands, leading to knowledge and control of animals, of bears, say, among the Haida (fig. 2), or dog-children, who start another story. Offending children are abandoned to starve, but they prosper, so that those who deserted them become dependent on them for food instead (among the Chinookan peoples one or more of the deserters is killed in revenge, but among the rank-conscious Bella Bella, the son accepts chieftainship instead). A young man enters an enemy house disguised as a woman to revenge his sister or rescue his father. A young man travels to the sky and survives horrendous tests from a prospective father-in-law. A group of men travel far and survive deathly contests in another village. An old man has his son go up a tree, then causes the tree to stretch farther and farther upward, so that he can appropriate the young man's wives. A small bird kills a large animal for food by flying inside it. A host provides food by cutting if off himself or his wife, or killing a child, but without harm, whereupon a would-be imitator tries the same and fails. One jealous wife kills another, whereupon the children of the latter slay the children of the former and escape. Two animal actors are partners, such that one tricks the other as to food, or as to a woman who has come to marry the better of them. The youngest sibling is smartest, perceiving the truth of a situation, or meanest, causing trouble.

In practice a community, and individuals, have foci of concern, local cycles, favored figures and formats. Widespread elements and types of story may be given new meaning through structural context and expressive form.

Purposes of Myths

No one purpose explains the stories. Some do account for general features of nature (the sun, moon, stars, winds, fire), why fur of animals is darker above than below, why

Smithsonian, Dept. of Anthr.: 73117.

Fig. 2. *Bear-Mother*, a slate sculpture. Bears were held to be men who had assumed animal shapes. Women and children who came across bear tracks in the woods customarily uttered lavish compliments about bears and about that individual in particular in an effort to ward off an attack (Niblack 1890:301). This figure represents the Haida version of a popular bear legend of abduction. A number of women were in the woods gathering berries when one of them, a chief's daughter, angered the bears by ridiculing the bear species. The bears descended on them and killed all but that woman, whom the bear chief took as his wife. As a result of this union, she bore a half-human, half-bear child. The carving shows the agony of the mother at suckling this rough offspring. In the legend, the woman was later freed from her bondage by a group of Haida bear hunters and taken home, where she became the progenitor of the Haida of the bear totem. Carved by Haida artist Skaowskeay, and finished by the Haida Johnny Kit Elswa, an assistant to James G. Swan. Collected by Swan at Skidegate, Queen Charlotte, Is., B.C., 1883; length 15 cm.

some animals are red, or striped, or have no tails, and why some woods burn well and others not (Waterman 1914). Others account for local phenomena, such as mountains, eddies, which streams have fish, which bogs berries. But myths also invest the natural world with enriched meaning: here the trickster met the old man with a penis wrapped around his waist, these stone pillars were once transformers, there is a whirlpool at the edge of the world. And explicit explanatory elements, the stripes on a chipmunk and the like, are secondary to the plots they follow. The same element will occur with other plots, the same plot with other elements. As narratives, myths explain in a far more pervasive way. They explain by creating, imbuing, and exploring a world. They both teach and discover the consequences of motive, relationship, or act. They can be abstract calculi of human action. In this they may reflect the life around them, but also may compensate for it, imaging what is forbidden, feared or hoped. The marriages and households of myths may not be those of daily life, but ones that allow tensions to be highlighted or contradictions to be overcome.

In principle the world of myth is open, any ingredient of the world may enter it; if such a myth is not known to one person, it may be to another. Myth, and narrative generally, close the world, not through content but through form. The sequence of actions is simultaneously a sequence of lines, and groups of lines, enacting formal patterns of anticipation and outcome over and over again. Such patterns give shape. In communities in which experience takes narrative form their pervasiveness may induce a sense that experience has shape as well. Just as vocabularies and grammars pick out and organize some features of experience rather than others, making them easy to name, remember, and connect, as if language merely mirrored what is there, so narrative form may seem to express a coherence already inherent in life (Hymes 1982).

Whatever other purpose myths may serve, connected with ecology, social structure, cosmology, or personal life, they serve the purpose of enjoyment. Any adequate explanation of the myths must not overlook the fact that in performance they have suspense, humor, and imaginative life.

Performance and Diversity

In the late twentieth century myths are often read, but originally they were heard. The voice of the narrator, and the voices he or she enacts, are central. The appearance of the natural world and cultural setting is taken for granted; details are mentioned when they figure in what happens. Action is likely to culminate in what someone says, or to be what actors say to each other. A text in which no one speaks is almost certainly just a report of how a story goes, not an actual telling of it (Hymes 1981a:79–141, 200–259).

Tradition itself may provide for certain actors in stories to be linguistically marked. In Kwakiutl, the trickster Mink always speaks like a young child (Boas and Hunt 1906:82–154), substituting sibilants (*s, c, ʒ, c̓*) for palatal and lateral consonants (*x, k, g, k̓; ł, λ, ƛ, ƛ̓*). In Nootka

Deer and Mink substitute laterals for sibilants (*ł* for *s* and *λ* for *c* and *č*, *ƛ̓* for *c̓* and *c̓*) (Sapir 1915b). Elk talks through his nose and Raven inserts *x* (Sapir 1915b), or *š* in the Ahousat dialect (Hess 1982), after the first vowel of words. In Lushootseed Salish it is Raven who talks through his nose. For other actors, substitution of labials indicates incompetence; of nasals, endearment; palatalization, childish behavior (Hess 1982). In Takelma *ł-* or palatized *s-* may be put before the words of an actor in myth. Both seem to mock the speech of other people, *ł-* that of neighboring Athapaskans (Sapir 1909), palatalized *s* that of the more distant Siuslaw (Hymes 1981a:65–76). The two sounds do not simply stereotype Bear and Coyote, as stated by Sapir. Only Bears use *ł*, but not all do; Coyote uses palatalized *s*, but only at certain times, and Bears may use it as well. There is a contrast in expressive meaning independent of particular actors. Both express condescension, but *ł* also deprecation, palatized *s* sympathy, even affection; the use of either depends on context. When the ogress Grizzly Woman runs toward laughter she thinks comes from her children, the audience knowing that she is deceived and the children dead, she uses *s*. Such expressive features may be used not only stereotypically, but also selectively, in other languages as well.

Figures may be characterized verbally in other ways, sometimes ways specific to a story or performance. Kinship relationships offer choices. Thus several Clackamas Chinook myths of Victoria Howard are framed by a trio of sister, brother, sister's daughter. Of course the sister is also a mother, the daughter a niece, the brother an uncle. In Seal and Her Younger Brother Lived There the sister-brother relationship of the title becomes in the telling focused on the daughter. Each act is framed by speech of the mother and daughter; when they refer to the man, it is by his relationship to the daughter, that is, as 'uncle'. A myth whose moral is the consequence of acting as does the mother, Seal, becomes in the telling the experience of the daughter. (The daughter warns the mother that the wife who has come to her uncle may be a man; the mother shushes the child, maintaining propriety at the expense of response to empirical experience; something drips on the daughter in a bed beneath that of her uncle, she lights a torch, and finds blood, the uncle dead, his head severed).

This myth illustrates other ways in which verbal detail may shape meaning. When mother and daughter speak in the first two acts, they speak to each other, as shown by the narrator's use of the verb stem *-lxam* 'to tell'. This stem can be used only when someone is being directly addressed. When the mother and daughter speak in the third act, after the uncle is dead, the narrator uses the verb stem *-kim* 'to say'. This stem cannot be used when someone is being directly addressed. The relationship has been broken; the girl is on her own.

Languages have each their own ways of indicating that

a certain character is the one to watch, the one with whose fate the telling is most concerned. In Clackamas many nouns have an initial prefix *i*- or *a*-, showing them to be singular and also masculine or feminine in grammatical gender. A few nouns have *wi*- or *wa*- instead. The *w*- may have an honorific connotation. In her performance of myths Howard adds *w*- to nouns that do not have it grammatically to show that what is designated by the noun will be vital to the outcome. In the myth just discussed, *w*- is added expressively to the term for the girl and for her uncle. Other languages may select an alternative form of pronoun, or elaborate with additional words the introduction of a figure who is to be in focus.

Imagery is effective, yet little noticed, because it is a selection of naturally occurring details. Nothing could be more common than not to be able to see the sun early in the morning on the coast, yet in the Cathlamet Sun myth it signifies that the chief who seeks it lacks the knowledge to control it (Halpin 1981a). In the Clackamas myth of Seal, the story begins at evening, continues in the night, and ends with the daughter raising light (a torch). Likewise the daughter first hears her uncle's "wife" urinate like a man, then feels blood dripping on her face, then produces tears. Both sequences of natural image can go unnoticed, yet sum up the story and its identification with the experience of the girl.

Such imagery may be part of the creative diversification of myths through performance. A hearer may later retell what is in part due to his or her own visual imagination. Remembered words may be from the narrator; remembered picturing cannot be; yet both may seem inseparable.

The paradox of the myths, indeed, is that they vary so much, yet in principle are passed on unchanged. No one claims to make up a myth. The narrator is not an author in that sense but one whose authority is that of a transmitter of knowledge; yet change occurs. Indeed, the diversity of North American Indian narratives is striking in contrast to the relative uniformity of types of traditional tales across much of Europe, from Ireland indeed to India. Many elements are widespread, but crystallized combinations seem not to be (Boas 1916:878; S. Thompson 1946: 390). In important part this may be because North American Indian narratives have developed in communities with little or no supervening political or cultural hegemony. They have been the central verbal form of communities, indeed, families that are culturally autonomous. Literary authority has been local. Invention does occur, linking and extending stories, reallocating roles, substituting actors and details, reversing points of view, but in important part the creativity that mediates change is in selection and grouping. A narrator can use a range of expressive means to give new meaning to a common story. Any one text results from interaction between a sequence of incidents, making it a certain story and not some other, and a weighting and shaping given the incidents on the

Table 1. Part of Soaban, a Coast Tsimshian Myth

ata łúʔutkat łakikét siwá·tkatł skínsmc̀mmú·		And in those days they prized ear wax
atat amaní·sti łakikét siwá·tkatł kímst		And in those days they treasured cedar cotton
ata kikc̀ápa qanqán maq̇ópsx̩n sm wil mikmó·ntka náʔasikí·k		And they used to make pairs of long matches out of hemlock
ata niňí ła tm uksłákt		And with these things they would make campfire.
ata wilt sikéłkata ḱó·ltini skínsimú·t	5	And then one of the men took some ear wax
atat wil txałwáʔalt a qán		And then he put it on the matches
atat wil wilí·lt a anʔónt		And then he rubbed them together in his hands
ata wil txalwilí·ta siwátkatł kíms		And then he rubbed them against the cedar cotton
ata wil haw kʷaʔa łaʔám sx̩aňákat		And then in a while he began to cry out,
c̀í·c, c̀í·c, teya kʷáʔa	10	"Grandmother! Grandmother!" he said nearby,
ata wil luʔaṁámqaqó·t tipkʷáʔa		And then they were happy nearby,
a máłiła c̀ic̀íksakt		that he said his grandmothers.
łatm kʷálkt		It was about to burn,
wá·lt ła sisiṗiyá·nt		He had made it start smoking,
ta wil swánt	15	And then he blew,
ła yá·kʷa kʷánta tipkʷáʔa		and the flames appeared nearby.
ta saʔuks níʔicka két a kiyá·ks		And something caused one of the men to look to sea,
n ławil képn hakʷiló·a		a sea-monster had surfaced,
li łá·s wá·l likikó·l nlax̩ʔót		there were furry things swarming on its back,
ta wil łuwantwánt qaqó·t tipkʷáʔa	20	and then their hearts became troubled nearby.

SOURCE: J.A. Dunn 1984b:288–290.

particular occasion. What is elaborated, what foreshortened; what repeated, what not; what put in focus, what not; who in the story is given voice; where expressive detail is concentrated—all shape meaning. In the Clackamas myth the ostensible moral is the consequence of acting as does the mother, Seal, who figures first in the title. Expressive detail takes the point of view of the daughter, thrust into self-assumed maturity because the responsible adult fails (Hymes 1981a:274–341).

Narrators may differ in their titling of myths, their favored closing formula, their preference for length or terseness, the actors with which they most identify. Such things must be assessed against what can be discerned of community norms. The myths do vary strikingly from group to group, even from person to person within a group, and from performance to performance by the same person (for example, Hymes 1985a). Of course a narrator may have characteristic traits, such as his or her own closing formula (as in Alsea). Boas denied the presence of a single system in Kwakiutl mythology (1933) or the Raven cycle (1916:582) and called attention to the great diversity in origin myths among the Bella Coola (1898: 125–126). Both he and McIlwraith (1948:294) pointed out that traditions are preserved in the family, where conceptual consistence may prevail, not in the community as a whole. When what one person has told is discussed in the name of a tribe, it obscures the complexity of tradition in the group and ignores personal creativity and situation. The contributions of William Beynon (Halpin 1978), Henry Tate (Maud 1989), and George Hunt (Berman 1983) have been explored. What is common to a group, or a region, are resources of content and form, and principles of style, from which emerge novel configurations.

Presentational Form

When one can hear the texts, very likely the rise and fall of the voice makes clear how the narrator shapes the story. One can hear intonational contours, or tone groups, presenting what is said in a series of lines. Audience responses may mark these. Where only the written text is available, much can still be learned. Sometimes a narrative tradition puts markers at the beginning or end of almost every line or verse.

Such is the case with much of a Coast Tsimshian text from Kitkatla, narrated by Dorothy Brown (J.A. Dunn 1984b). Conjunctions translated as 'and' or 'and then' appear at the beginning of many lines; a term meaning 'here by me' (translated here as 'nearby') occurs at the end of a number of lines. The story is a migratory legend, concerning the first encounter of the Kitkatla people with Europeans. When the men, under the leadership of their chief, Soaban ('Leaps out of the Water'), see a ship for the first time off shore, they take it to be a sea monster and the sailors to be hairy beings. Table 1 gives the four verses of

the fourth stanza, and the first of the fifth. Dunn's translation has been revised to bring out the presence of the markers meaning 'and (then)' and 'nearby' in the Tsimshian text.

A similar fourfold patterning is used in Nootka, where a quotative ('they say') also occurs. Table 2 gives the opening of Hamilton George's version of a popular story. Notice that after a brief introduction of the initial set of actors, expressions concerning time introduce each of the remaining three stanzas of the scene: 'four days now', 'It became night again', 'she watches for night now to fall' (4, 8, 18). The repetition in the second and fourth lines (30, 32) of the last stanza both underscores the nature of the discovery and reinforces a sense of culmination at this point. The quotative marker -we?in points up consequential news—the actors (1), a death of a child with a hole in its side (4), the mother's discovery (20, 29).

A profile of these four stanzas of the first act helps to show their organization.

Stanza	Verses	Lines	Features
A	a, b	1, 2–3	'they say', 'And then'
B		4–7	'they say'
C	a	8–10	'again' (3 times)
	b	11–12	'Now . . .'
	c	13–15	
	d	16–17	'And then' (d parallel b)
D	a	18–19	'And then'
	b	20–24	'And then', 'they say'; 5 lines
	c	25–28	'see now', 'find out now'
	d	29–32	'Indeed', 'they say', 30–32

The patterning of action is in terms of four, as the four days of line 4 indicate. In the myth as a whole there are four parts, or acts—discovery of the nature of the boy; disclosure to the mother's father, the chief, and the warriors; pursuit of the boy by the warriors; the compassing of his death and the creation of mosquitoes. Within a larger unit pairing is frequent. The first two acts focus on discovery and disclosure; the second two acts focus on pursuit and resolution. Within the third act the first two scenes are pursuits (on the beach, in a house) that fail; they end with the boy saying, 'You cannot cause me to die, I am a different being'. The next two scenes enact a pursuit (over the mountains) that succeeds; the third leads to the boy being detected when loons are heard (it turns out that they drink his blood), and to his telling the pursuers he will tell them how to kill him. (Thus the boy speaks at the end of the second and the fourth stanzas of the act.) In the first two stanzas of the fourth act the boy tells two young men what to do—to gather wood, and to throw him into the fire; in the next two stanzas mosquitoes arise: when the two young men throw the boy into the fire, the ashes that blow up turn into mosquitoes; that is why mosquitoes are fond of blood, being made out of one fond of blood.

Table 2. The Opening of What Mosquitoes Are Made Of, a Nootka Myth

ḥawit̓itweʔin iananak ḥa·kʷa·ƛuk.	There was a chief, they say, who had as child a daughter.
ʔu·caḥtaksa ticwisa, naẏaqnakši?aƛ meʔiƛqacʔisuk.	And then (she) became pregnant, gave birth now to a little boy.
mu·či·tnakḥʔaƛweʔin, qaḥna·k̓aƛ kʷi·kʷi·sitḥinʔasʔi, 5 ʔusu·ƛ ma·mi·qsuʔi ku·kuḥinqit̓. haya·ʔak̓at qʷiẏi·ḥawu·si.	In four days now, they say, someone died now at the other end of the village, the oldest (child) died with a hole in its side, it was not known what made him die.
ʔa·tḥšiƛƛa· qaḥna·k̓aƛƛa· ƛaʔuktaqimẏasʔi ʔusawiʔaƛƛa· ma·mi·qsuseʔi. 10 ƛaḥʔaƛ maʔasʔi haya·ʔakšiʔaƛ qʷisa·ḥiwu·si qa·ḥkʷačiƛ. ʔuyuʔat̓ʔaƛ tu·csmeʔi ƛa·ḥmat̓ʔi naẏaqak ʔani ḥiḥiẏaqƛwat čat̓ca, naẏaqakšiƛukʔi. 15 ʔu·caḥtaksa ču·šukʷiƛ ʔuyi ʔuḥqu· qa·ḥkʷaʔap.	It became night again, someone died now again in the next house, the very oldest died off now again. Now the village did not know now what was causing people to die. The woman caught sight now of the newborn baby, that his fingers were bloody under the nails, the baby she had given birth to. And then she began to suspect whether it was he causing (people) to die.
ʔu·caḥtaksa nana·či·ḥšiƛ ʔa·tḥšiʔaƛʔitq we·ʔičti·ʔitšiʔaƛ.	And then (she) watches for night now to fall, pretending to be asleep now.
ʔu·caḥtaksa naču?at ya·twe·ʔin 20 či·waḥsut̓ʔap čimca·sʔatʔi kʷikʷinksu, čaqʔatap ʔa·čsa·t̓imʔakʔi, hitakʷiscaƛ naẏaqp̓atakʔi, hini·ʔasʔaƛ.	And then (she) discovers over there, they say, (he) pulls out his right hand, pushes off his head-flattener, gets out now of his baby-basket, goes out now.
na·csa·ƛ tu·csmeʔi qʷa·ʔakʔitq meʔiƛqac, 25 ḥamatsap̓aƛ ʔani ʔuḥqa· qa·ḥqa·ḥa yaqčiʔatḥitq. ʔatwe·ʔinc̓aˤaš qʷa·,	The woman sees now her boy is that way, finds out now it is he who is always killing those who live as his neighbors. Indeed, they say, evidently it was he who was that way,
ḥi·ẏi·ḥ, 30 ku·ḥsinqint̓ʔap, ḥi·ẏi·ḥ.	is after blood, always causes a hole in the side, is after blood.

SOURCE: Sapir and Swadesh 1939:14–15.

Quite a different primary patterning appears among the peoples of the Columbia River region (Chinookan, Chehalis and Cowlitz Salish, Kalapuya, and Klikitat of the Plateau) (Kinkade 1983, 1984, 1985, 1987). The principal pattern number is five. If a series of brothers sets out to rescue a sister, there will be five of them, and so on. In one Upper Chehalis (Southwestern Coast Salish) story Wren challenges Elk. The small bird will kill the large mammal, and get his meat for food, by slipping inside him. The story starts with Wren rejecting five other animals in a row. Each of the five encounters itself has five elements (technically, the first has five scenes, each a stanza with five verses). Table 3 records the beginning of the performance by Silas Heck. After Bobcat and Deer the pattern is repeated with Mouse, Rabbit, and Black Bear.

Patterns of this kind have also been discerned in Alsea (Hymes 1971–1988), Bella Coola (Hymes 1983b). Chinook proper (Hymes 1983), Clackamas Chinook (Hymes 1981a, 1983a, 1985), Coos (Hymes 1971–1988), Kalapuya (Hymes 1981, 1987a), Cathlamet Chinook (Hymes 1985a), Kwakiutl (Berman 1982, 1983, 1986), Takelma (Hymes 1979), Tillamook (Hymes 1971–1988), and Tlingit (Hymes 1971–1988). Myths told in Chinook Jargon show such patterns as well; the type of pattern corresponds to the type of the narrator's first language, five- and three-part patterning for speakers of Chinookan, Kalapuya, and Tututni compared with four- and two-part patterning for speakers of northern Salish languages, Northern Straits Salish, and Lushootseed (Zenk and Moore 1983; Hymes and Zenk 1987; Hymes 1987).

599

Structural Analysis

The most striking and important work on the structural analysis of myths is that of Claude Lévi-Strauss. His analysis of a Tsimshian myth (1958) discussed by Boas became a focus of discussions of his method (M. Douglas 1967; Adams 1974; C. Ackerman 1982; Thomas, Kronenfeld, and Kronenfeld 1976). The four volumes of his *Mythologiques* begin with South American Indian myths and end on the Northwest Coast (1968, 1971). Lévi-Strauss contends that all American Indian myths are part of an ancient system and that the Northwest Coast and parts of South America show special affinities. Myths are related not only to the degree that they have the same elements or same sequences but also, fundamentally, in virtue of systematic correspondences between elements and sequences that may be themselves quite different, or be transformations or inversions of each other. A given myth is itself a system of correspondences and oppositions, especially binary oppositions. Myths change through operations on such oppositions.

Lévi-Strauss is correct that structural relations can be found between Northwest Coast and South American myths (Urban 1984). He is correct that myths can be related not only in terms of likeness but also in terms of systematic difference (C. Ackerman 1982). This discovery is fundamental. However, when he discusses the Northwest Coast (especially Lévi-Strauss 1971), his analyses have changed character. The South American analyses were worked out carefully, point by point, in terms of entire myths. Northwest Coast analyses are often only of extracts from myths, often rechristened and sometimes misunderstood (Hymes 1987a). The material is sometimes fitted into a model imposed from without. This is the antithesis of a structural perspective. And the analyses, while adapting linguistic principles, abstract from the material basis of narrative, language. The analyses rely on translations, and summaries of these, recoding the myths in terms of content alone. Their shape and point rhetorically—expressively—is lost. But verbal shape and point may differ significantly, independently of content, from one telling to another of the same myth (Hymes 1985a). In general, myths may have revealing similarities and differences along dimensions in addition to that examined by Lévi-Strauss, dimensions that require recognition of the presence of literary art and personal voice (Hymes 1981a: 238–242).

Table 3. Beginning of Wren and Elk, an Upper Chehalis Myth

"čé··sa, čé··sa qíl–qílitn.		"Come! Come, Elk!
čé···sa, čé··sa qíl–qílitn.		Come! Come, Elk!
?il–?iláxʷiyaq̓atwàlastàwt."		Let's lock horns."
X̌púw! X̌pé·! X̌púw! X̌pé·!		Crash! Bang! Crash! Bang!
tu cáx̌ʷsmitn tu ?acálstip,	5	Then it appears from the woods,
k̓ʷa x̌iwó?s.		it turns out to be Bobcat.
"míɬtaws nə́wi t sq̓íwtsminš		"It isn't you that I want
tit x̌əs. . . ?acx̌ə́cu?s.		with your ugly face.
wáksa?!		Go on!
ʔanək̓ʷá·la?."	10	Go back where you came from."
wáksn,		He goes,
níɬuq̓ʷas t x̌íwó?s		Bobcat cries
swins ?it tók̓ʷmism.		from being hated.
húy, ʔaɬúnaqimaln t sk̓ʷimó·ms,		And then Wren sings his power song again,
"čé···sa, čé··sa qíl–qílitn.	15	Come! Come, Elk!
c?il–?iláxʷiyàq̓atwàlastàwt."		Let's lock horns."
X̌púw! X̌pé·! X̌púw!		Crash! Bang! Crash!
?ítu, čisóɬaqn.		Then he hears a noise approaching.
X̌púw! X̌pé·! X̌púw!		Crash! Bang! Crash!
cáx̌ʷsmitn,	20	It appears,
k̓ʷa sX̌aláš.̌		it turns out to be Deer.
"mé··ɬtaʷs nə́wi n sqínmisanš,̌		"It isn't you that I'm wanting,
q̓íwtasanš.̌		that I'm calling.
wáksa?!		Go on!
ʔanək̓ʷá·la?,	25	Go back where you came from,
míɬta nsqínmici."		I don't want you."
ʔawáksn sX̌aláš,̌		Deer goes back,
níɬuq̓ʷa.		crying.
míɬta t sqínmist.		He wasn't wanted.

Source: Kinkade 1985.

Continued Vitality

There is a temptation to think of the mythology as a relic of the past. Yet narrative creativity did not end with the arrival of outsiders. Stories have predicted the arrival of the Whites, joined Jesus and the trickster, and sent Coyote out over the ocean in an airplane. Of course the ways of life with which the myths were once interwoven have changed greatly; older Indian people may wonder if younger people, who do not experience those ways of life, can understand the meanings implicit in the stories. Once children had to hear the stories, and life was unintelligible without knowledge of them. The world now is given sense by other sources, schools, churches, media; occasions and audiences for traditional myths are rare. Some of the languages are no longer spoken, and for others there may be no one or only a few who can perform the stories in them.

Certainly authentic oral performance in the Indian language is the root of knowledge. Whatever can still be done to sustain or record such is invaluable. Yet it would be a mistake to dismiss whatever falls short of such a standard. On the one hand, many early texts, though dictated or written out, show patterns of performance. Such texts can be put on the page anew in ways that bring their meanings more fully to life. On the other hand, absence or loss of Indian language need not mean loss of narrative tradition. Myths and tales may be kept alive through the medium of English, for example, Coos traditions passed on in English in the Wasson family (Toelken 1979:164, 192). They may even be provided children to use for a high school assignment. So long as such traditions are kept alive, whatever the language or circumstance, they and what they have come to mean today are part of the continuity of the tradition. And because so much of a once broad river of narrative has been lost, any rivulet may add evidence and insight.

Concern to preserve and know as much as one can leads to revaluation of less polished or precise efforts. All sources that contribute something, not just the linguistically exact, need to be included in the history and future of the traditions. What is obscure in a text dictated to a scholar may be clear in one recorded by an amateur. Something of performance pattern may inform English versions (see Hymes 1981 a:200–259). The fullest version of a myth, including accurately remembered Indian phrases, may have been transmitted in the family of an early White settler (Attwell 1973). What is essential is for non-Indians not to obscure or distort the original form, as some anthologies do, for example, changing both Raven and the Kwakiutl transformer into Coyote, giving Coyote and Frog dialogue the Kalapuya narrator did not, and failing to acknowledge the Indian source at all (cf. Hymes 1987a in regard to Lopez 1977).

The myth figure who persists most vitally in imagination among Indian and non-Indian people alike is that of the trickster. Raven attracts new stories, jokes, and poems among people who live in the northern part of the region, and among some elsewhere who read of him, Coyote in the southern part of the region, as in much of the western United States (cf. Koller et al. 1982; G. Snyder 1977). The mythology as a whole informs the work of the poet Duane Niatum (1975, 1981) and of Agnes Pratt (Dodge and McCullough 1974:63–67, 84–85). There are poets whose Indian descent is from outside the Northwest Coast, but who were born or grew up there, for example, Ed Edmo (1985) and W.M. Ransom (Niatum 1975:184–202). All this is part of a continent-wide renaissance and continuation of literary creativity on the part of Indian people (Bruchac 1983; Hobson 1979; Lincoln 1983). The mythology has been important to well-known poets not of Indian descent, such as Gary Snyder (1960, 1979), William Stafford (1982, 1977:131, 136, 235), and David Wagoner (1978), as well as to others (for example, Hymes 1981b, 1982a; Castro 1983). Songs may occur in myths, or refer to them, and the task of fresh translation attracts poets to both. Thus, it is worth noting that the work of Swann (1985) includes reworked translations from the Haida, Nootka, southern Coast Salish, Takelma, Tlingit, and Tsimshian. Some of the most active interest in the poetic significance of Northwest Coast and other cultures ranges across genres, taking up narrative, song, ritual event (Rothenberg 1985, 1986). An annotated bibliography of Northwest Coast Indian folklore and mythology is in Clements and Malpezzi (1984:176–195); Maud (1982) presents a history of myth collecting in British Columbia and a survey of the corresponding literature.

Figures of Northwest Coast mythology live also in the repertoires of many who take part in the revitalization of story-telling in the United States and Canada. Composers and graphic artists show the inspiration of such figures as well. The mythologies of Indian peoples of the Northwest Coast are the source of a lasting contribution to the imaginative life of all for whom its landscape and history come to have meaning.

Art

BILL HOLM

Although Northwest Coast culture area stretches for 1,500 miles, the art traditions developed and practiced by its native inhabitants exhibited a degree of continuity of concept and and materials. No doubt the relative similarities of climate and natural resources the length of the coast were in part responsible, accentuated by the effects of the formidable mountain barrier that imposed natural restrictions on trade and other contacts with the interior over much of its length and channeled most of this intercourse along the coast. In the few places where major rivers, such as the Chilkat and the Skeena in the north and the Fraser and the Columbia in the south, pierced the barrier and allowed travel and commerce beyond the mountains, the coastal art traditions influenced and were influenced by those of the interior people.

The formal and conceptual relationships shared by the arts of the long coast did not preclude the development of distinctive traditions within the larger, general context. In the nineteenth century these could be seen to fall into three major stylistic and conceptual divisions. The northern province includes the arts of the Tlingit, Haida, Tsimshian, Haisla, Haihais, and Bella Bella; the central province is exemplified by the arts of the Kwakiutl and the Nootkans; the southern province includes the arts of the Coast Salish, Chinookans, and peoples of the Oregon coast. No hard and fast boundaries can be drawn among the three broad stylistic areas; and where they come together, as in the region of the Bella Bella, the arts show relationships to both adjacent traditions. Within these larger boundaries distinctive tribal styles developed and even the works of individual artists are recognizable (Holm 1981, 1983).

Prehistory

Until the 1950s the prehistory of the Northwest Coast was little understood, but in the next 30 years enormous strides were made by archeologists, so that by the 1980s many of the gaps in the knowledge of precontact cultures of the area had been narrowed. The development of wet-site archeology in this period and the discovery and excavation of rich wet sites on various parts of the coast produced evidence of early art production in materials such as wood and plant fibers that had long been thought to have entirely disappeared in the region's rot-inducing environ-

ment (Croes 1976). Bone, antler, and stone artifacts recovered in profusion from early sites have also contributed to the understanding of the art traditions that preceded those of the historic period.

Although some parts of the region have been inhabited for an estimated 13,000 years, very little evidence of the character of art production has been identified before the Middle period of 5,500 to 1,500 years ago (Carlson 1983: 22–28). The richest assemblages of Middle period artifacts that can be regarded as art objects are probably those recovered from the Locarno Beach phase and Marpole phase sites, 1200 B.C.–A.D. 400 (Borden 1983:135–156) ("Prehistory of the Coasts of Southern British Columbia and Northern Washington," figs. 2t, w, aa-bb and 3y-aa, cc-dd, this vol.), establishing the area around the mouth of the Fraser River and the adjacent waterways as very productive of art at least 2,000 years ago. Work in sites on the northern and central coast has established that art production in those areas of the coast roughly paralleled the Fraser River activity in materials, types of artifacts, and many stylistic characteristics at about the same time (Carlson 1983a; MacDonald 1983a:100–120). Material of the same general period from the lower Columbia River indicates similar artistic activity in that area, but differing somewhat stylistically, apparently because of influence from the Plateau culture area. Art objects from the Five Mile Rapids sites, actually in the Plateau region, show close relationships to those recovered from sites below the mouth of the Willamette River and on the northern Oregon coast.

The earliest archeological material from the Northwest Coast consists of utilitarian objects, primarily tools. However, there is simple geometric decoration on artifacts of bone, antler, and soft stone from the Lower Fraser region that have been dated to around 3000 B.C. (Borden 1983:132). Most of these are fragmentary and are of unknown use. As early as 1500 B.C. a few decorated tools and pendants appear in the archeological record in the northern province; and in the period between 1100 B.C. and A.D. 350 decorated tools, weapons, and ornaments began to appear in profusion throughout the coast. In this period anthropomorphic and zoomorphic representation grew to dominate the arts of the coast, although geometric and nonrepresentational design retained a place in all the coastal art traditions throughout the ensuing prehistoric and historic periods.

Many features of representation that characterize the historic arts of the Northwest Coast appear very early in the archeological record. Among the characteristics of early representational art that persisted into the historic period were exaggeration of the size of the heads of both animal and human figures, limbs often flexed in a crouching position, and emphasis of facial features, especially eyes and mouths. In both sculpture (in bone, antler, wood, and stone) and in flat representation, humans were typically rendered frontally, while animals were more often shown in profile, choices almost certainly derived from their normal appearance to the artist in nature and calculated to express most efficiently their salient recognition features. Many of the surviving examples of representational art are on tools and utensils, but some seem to be decorative or ritual objects such as pendants or amulets (Borden 1983; Carlson 1983, 1983a; MacDonald 1983a).

Design details that are commonly recognized as typical of Northwest Coast art, such as the round or ovoid eye with pointed lids, and skeletal details (especially ribs and joints) represented as in an X-ray image, occur on carvings from various parts of the area dating from 500 to 700 B.C. (MacDonald 1983a:fig.6:22; Borden 1983:fig.8: 10c). By the end of the first millennium A.D. figures were being produced that are nearly indistinguishable from pieces made 1,000 years later, as exemplified by a bone comb bearing the representation of a wolf from the Prince Rupert area dated to around A.D. 800 ("Prehistory of the Northern Coast of British Columbia," fig.6b, this vol.).

Particularly intriguing evidence for what appears to be very early use of the concept of defining perceived positive forms by small crescentic and T-shaped incisions is found in artifacts from sites scattered along the coast from Washington to northern British Columbia (Carlson 1983a:fig.7:3a, b, 1983b:fig.11:7; MacDonald 1983a:figs. 6:13c, 6:33). The principle of outlining the positive features of a figure by incising or by cutting away the surface of the surrounding material is universal in relief carving, but the use of these particular stylized negative elements to define positive forms is unique to the Northwest Coast and clearly presages the complex two-dimensional design system of the historic Central Coast Salish and the even more formalized flat art tradition of the northern province. These two systems were fully developed and functional at the beginning of the historic period in the late eighteenth century.

Petroglyphs

The Northwest Coast is very rich in petroglyphic art. By the 1980s there were known to be thousands of glyphs in over 600 sites (Lundy 1983:89) including those at The Dalles on the Columbia River, just inside the boundary of the Plateau culture area. The figures range from extremely simple representations of faces formed of two or three pits, sometimes enclosed in a circle, to elaborate representations of natural or supernatural creatures, some of them rendered in the formline style exemplified by historic two-dimensional art of the northern coast ("Prehistory of the Central Coast of British Columbia," figs. 3–4, this vol.). (Lundy 1983; Hill and Hill 1974). Dating of rock art has been difficult, but the wide distribution of what Lundy terms Basic Conventionalized Rock Art Style and its similarity to other early dated art suggests considerable antiquity for some of it. Other examples are clearly from the historic period, some representing sailing ships and even steamships, the first one of which appeared on the Northwest Coast in 1836.

Petroglyphs seem to have been produced for a variety of purposes. Some were certainly made to pass the time (Leechman 1952:266), some were commemorative (Boas 1897:439), and probably many were associated in some way with the acquisition of supernatural power. Many petroglyphs are associated with resource utilization sites, especially salmon-fishing locations, and may have been intended to influence the return of the salmon as well as to identify the site.

The Historic Period

When Europeans reached the Northwest Coast in the late eighteenth century they found distinctive art traditions operating among the various groups. These traditions were in a continuing state of development, influencing one another and adjusting to changing circumstances. The changes were generally gradual, and objects collected at the beginning of the historic period are stylistically and conceptually related to those from the same groups at the end of the nineteenth century, when social and economic changes were forcing the destruction of many of those art traditions.

Tools

Woodworking tools were essential to the production of art on the Northwest Coast. Before contact with European traders most tool bits were of stone, bone, shell, and teeth, especially beaver incisors. However, early explorers found Northwest Coast carvers in possession of a few iron and steel blades (King 1981:pl. 85, nos. 123, 124) and traces of some others have been found in precontact archeological sites. The sources of this metal are not known with certainty. Intertribal trade across the continent probably accounted for some of it, and some may have been salvaged from drift wreckage from Asia (MacDonald 1984a:74–76; G.I. Quimby 1985). In any case, Northwest Coast carvers were familiar with iron tools when the first

Europeans arrived and quickly acquired enough more to completely supplant carving-tool bits of other materials. Wedges for splitting planks continued to be made of hard wood or antler through the nineteenth century and were used with stone mauls, hafted in the northern province and of tapered, pestle shape in the southern province.

Woodworking tools consisted of adzes, chisels, knives, wedges, mauls, and drills. For the most part, iron and steel bits followed the forms of their precontact prototypes. Adzes were of three main types ("Introduction," fig. 1, this vol.): the elbow adz with a haft of hard wood formed of a branch for the handle with an attached section of flattened trunk for the seat of the bit, common in the northern and central provinces; the D or hand adz with the bit lashed to a closed handle, common to the central and adjacent regions of the southern province ("Southwestern Coast Salish," fig. 8, this vol.); and the straight adz with the bit lashed to a extension of the grip, usually of antler, and with a knuckle guard either integral with the grip or added to it, common to the southern province. An elbow adz with a very short, flaring grip was unique to the Puget Sound region. Other specialized types were developed, including adzes with lipped or hollowed blades and those with acutely angled elbows and thin, springy handles designed to produce the regularly spaced pattern of adz marks characteristic of central and northern province sculpture. Chisels were simply bits hafted with wood or antler and designed to be driven by a maul ("Introduction," fig. 1, this vol.).

The beaver-tooth knife, or perhaps more properly chisel, was the common fine-finishing tool of precontact times. Upon widespread availability of steel blades, knives with wooden or antler handles supplanted the beaver tooth tools. The crooked knife, a variant on the curved-bladed man's knife of northern North America and northeastern Asia (Mason 1899) became the standard fine carving tool of the Northwest Coast ("Introduction," fig. 1, this vol.). It was held palm-up with the blade adjacent to the little finger and characteristically drawn toward the carver, although many Northwest Coast crooked knives are at least partially double-edged and were pushed as well as drawn in use. Blades with various degrees of curve from straight to sharply hooked were used.

Typically Northwest Coast objects in wood were finished with the tool, but some were smoothed with abrasives such as dogfish skin or dried stalks of the horsetail (Equisetum). Paint was applied with brushes that were commonly made, at least in the central and northern provinces, of the guard hair of the porcupine set in a slit in a wooden handle and secured with a lashing, usually of split spruce root ("Haida: Traditional Culture," fig. 8, this vol.). Smoothly pointed sticks were also used as paint applicators for fine lines, specifically for the patterns of lines painted around gambling sticks in the northern province.

Materials other than wood—such as horn, antler, ivory, bone, and soft stones like steatite and argillite—were shaped with woodworking tools or appropriately modified versions of them. Metal engraving, as on silver, gold, and copper jewelry, was begun in the early nineteenth century and followed European techniques except that Indian engravers typically drew their gravers toward themselves, necessitating a modification of the form of the handle and edge of the tool. Harder stones, such as those used for mauls and mortars, were shaped by the techniques of pecking and grinding. Most extant objects made by these techniques were manufactured in precontact times. Their durability and the introduction of substitute trade goods made their continued manufacture unnecessary.

Cultural Provinces

Northern Province

The northernmost of the three loosely defined cultural subareas of the coast is composed of the Tlingit, Haida, Tsimshian, and the northernmost Wakashan-speaking tribes, the Haihais and Haisla. This area was the seat of the development of the sophisticated art tradition that has dominated the common perception of Northwest Coast Indian art since the time of first European contact. It was here that the sophisticated formline design system originated and was practiced almost to the exclusion of any other manner of graphic art. Differences in art among the three major groups of the northern province, the Tsimshian, Haida, and Tlingit, were slight, but there were stylistic and conceptual differences, especially in sculpture, which are discernible.

In the northern province the two primary motives for art, social and religious, were closely intertwined. The social structures of the tribes were rigidly organized and the resulting hierarchy fostered the development of a system of crests and a protocol for their display. The crests and their combinations functioned as a kind of historical record by which the complexities of the clan relationships were made visible. The needs for representations of crests and the illustration of lineage myths, powerful stimuluses to art, clearly were the principal forces in the development of the remarkably sophisticated arts of the northern province.

There was a religious component in the secular arts of the northern tribes, as elsewhere on the coast, in the concept that man related to the spiritual and powerful forces permeating the world about him, and these forces were embodied to a degree in the crests. More obviously religious in motivation and character was the art of the shaman, by which the supernatural world was made manifest. Shamans' art differed from crest art primarily in its individuality and in the choice of subject, issuing from the shamans' personal supernatural experiences rather than from conventional requirements of crest representation. There was a considerable body of art that was neither crest nor shamanic but was essentially embellishment, as the designs on tools, baskets, and bowls, but even in these there was often a magic or symbolic component. The carvings on Tlingit halibut hooks, for example, surely represented the attempt to influence the fish to take the hook by supernatural means, and the ubiquitous fat seal bowls must represent the richness of the oil they contained.

The arrival of European and American fur traders on the northern coast at the close of the eighteenth century was the beginning of an artistic and cultural explosion that lasted nearly a century. Although the artistic traditions of the northern province were well established before the arrival of the traders, the enormous increase in wealth and material goods engendered by the fur trade fostered artistic activity, which was furthered by the readily available steel blades. Even the tragic depletion of the native population through devastating disease had a short-term positive effect on display art on some parts of the coast by encouraging potlatching on the part of rivals for empty positions.

Tlingit artists fulfilled the needs of chiefs to proclaim their nobility and shamans to make visible the powerful forces at their control. The Tlingits stood at the peak of intensity in the cultures of the northern province of the Northwest Coast, where inherited position and the complex relationships of clan and lineage were all-engrossing. As late as the 1980s intense confrontations occurred concerning the ownership of crest objects and the definitions of their appropriate functions. This intensity spawned art, and some of the world's great masterpieces were the result.

Haida artists worked in every medium available on their islands as well as those they were obliged to import, and their production was widely admired and desired. They built the most monumental houses, the largest and the greatest numbers of totem poles, the grandest canoes, as well as some of the most elegant and refined bowls, chests, and masks. It is a wonder that this prodigious production was stopped and almost literally wiped out by the end of the nineteenth century. The destruction of Haida social structure, at least the artistic manifestations of it, by disease and the efforts of missionaries and government was nearly complete. Fortunately, new life was breathed into Haida art in the general Northwest Coast cultural revitalization, and in the 1970s and 1980s there were works of Haida art produced rivaling the best of the old pieces in quality and spirit.

The arts of all the Tsimshian-speaking people, including the Gitksan and the Nishga, were closely related and formed a stylistically discrete body of work. Contact with the Tlingit, Haida, and Northern Wakashan people resulted in some shading of the boundaries of the style, but it appears that more influence was exerted by Tsimshian arts on the others than by them on the Tsimshian. Some scholars have suggested them to have been the main motivators of the development of northern Northwest Coast art, and no doubt they had a considerable influence on it.

Central Province

The central province of the Northwest Coast includes tribes that emphasize the ownership of inherited privileges that were dramatized in elaborate, theatrical rituals and personified in carved masks and figures. Motivation for art production is implicit in the concept of privilege on the Northwest Coast, and the tribes of the central province, Bella Bella, Oowekeeno, Bella Coola, Kwakiutl, and Nootkans, all produced graphic art in quantity, setting them somewhat apart from the people of the southern province.

The Bella Bella occupied with the Bella Coola a transitional position between the central and northern sectors. In their ceremonial life and much of their sculpture they resembled the Kwakiutl, but in some aspects of social organization and in their two-dimensional art, they fit more appropriately in the northern sector. Many of the most striking aspects of Kwakiutl mythology and drama were acquired from the Bella Bella and the Oowekeeno by marriage and capture, so it is not unexpected that there would be similarities in the arts. The other Northern Waskashan speakers, Haisla and Haihais, fit quite clearly in the northern sector.

The Bella Coola, although making up only a small part of the central province, developed such a distinctive variant on the art that they deserve separate consideration. Among them were prolific and imaginative artists, and the complex Bella Coola mythology (Boas 1898) furnished endless inspiration for sculpture and painting.

The Kwakiutl are renowned for their development of the dramatic arts in conjunction with the potlatch and winter ceremonials. Spectacular graphic art production was motivated by the striving of nobles to display crests and inherited dance privileges. The Kwakiutl have had a long contact with the northern Nootkan people, and the mutual influences on the arts of the two groups are apparent. In the late nineteenth century the differences between their arts were increased by a growing tendency toward surface elaboration on the part of Kwakiutl artists, perhaps attributable to their greater contact with northern art and its resulting influence.

The Nootkan cultural continuum extends southward from the Brooks Peninsula on Vancouver Island to the Hoh River on the Olympic Peninsula coast. Nootkan art is recognizable as a distinct tradition, with the usual variations characteristic of a broad geographic range and the influences of adjacent art styles.

Southern Province

The region from Vancouver Island to the California border, which has been designated the southern province, is the largest and the least homogeneous of the three areas of Northwest art traditions. Historically, less art was produced in the south than in the two other provinces, with the possible exception of basketry, which made up a much larger proportion of the total body of creative work in the south than in the north. The reasons for these differences in production are complex and little understood. An abundance of resources and the relative ease of utilizing them with the resulting leisure time seemingly characteristic of the southern Northwest Coast does not necessarily promote the development of art, as shown by the relatively greater productivity in the harsher environment of the north. Another variable is emphasis on rank and inherited privilege, which were accorded much more importance in the northern and central provinces than in the southern, and this may have been an important reason for the phenomenal development of the arts in those provinces in relation to their relatively lower development in the south.

The art of the Northern Coast Salish, especially that of the Comox, in several respects strongly resembles that of the Kwakiutl and in others resembles that of the Central Coast Salish. Between the arts of the Central and Southern Coast Salish no sharp boundary can be drawn. Art was progressively less elaborate and stylized toward the south, but many of the basic premises of design and structure held for the entire Coast Salish area.

The arts of the Southern Coast Salish more clearly conform to the stylistic features of the southern province of Northwest Coast Indian art. Basketry held a predominant place in artistic production, and the main motivating force for representational art was religion. As might be expected, the art of the Southwestern Salish people shared much with that of their Chinookan neighbors.

The Lower Columbia River, the 200-mile stretch from the river mouth to Celilo Falls, can be considered part of the southern province continuum in that the considerable contact and trade among the Chinookan speakers of the coast and the tidewater river and their Plateau Wasco and Wishram linguistic relatives at The Dalles and Celilo resulted in many shared cultural and artistic concepts.

Dislocation of the Oregon coastal tribes took place early in the nineteenth century, and little is known of their aboriginal cultures. In the 1850s many southeastern Oregon and northwestern California Indians were relocated to the Siletz Reservation, where they continued some of their southern arts, particularly basketry, but necessarily modified by their new environment and their proximity to the northwestern Oregon Salish.

Extra-Areal Influences

Like the Columbia River, the Fraser River was an important conduit of trade, in this instance between the Salish of the Fraser valley and the Plateau people above the Fraser Canyon, the Thompson and the Lillooet. At the headwaters of the Skeena River the proximity of the Gitksan and the Subarctic Carrier resulted in exchange of culture features, including the adoption by the Bulkley River Carrier of the upriver Tsimshian art style and ceremonial activities with attendant paraphernalia. The Tahltan were also influenced by the coastal culture, in this case by the Tlingit. Vestiges of Tlingit art style extended into the Pacific Eskimo area as far west as Kodiak Island. Baskets closely related to Tlingit examples in material, technique, and decoration have been collected among the Pacific Eskimo (M. Lee 1981); and many woven spruce-root hats with Tlingit-like painting were made in the Pacific Eskimo region (Collins et al. 1973:fig. 252) (vol. 5: 195). Decorated horn spoons and wooden bowls related in design to Tlingit examples were also made by Pacific Eskimo. Most of these Eskimo pieces can be distinguished from Tlingit objects by their geometricization and inconsistent application of formline design.

Two-Dimensional Art

Since the flat art traditions of all the tribal groups of the northern province were based on the same set of principles, their differences being essentially those of individual styles or emphases, they can be discussed together. The formline system of design, founded on the simple principle that creatures could be represented by delineating their parts, probably began as a naively representational, painted art practiced over much of the coast. The T and crescent incisions in ancient carved objects recovered from widely separated sites give evidence of the early conventionalization of this basic representational system (Carlson 1983a:fig. 7:3, 1983b:fig. 11:7; MacDonald 1983a:fig.6:33). These incisions are the resultant spaces between adjacent positive forms or outlines, and their rather uniform shapes show them to have been systematized in the direction of the later formline system.

The Formline System

In its fully developed form, the design system was based on a set of explicit, formal rules (Holm 1965) that were followed with astounding uniformity throughout the northern province during the protohistoric and historic periods. In essence the system provided that creatures be portrayed by representing their body parts and details with varyingly broad "formlines" which always joined to present an uninterrupted grid over the designed area (fig.

1). The body parts were stylized in forms consistent with the semi-angular, symmetrical, nonconcentric qualities of formlines. Certain uniform shapes resulted, the most obvious and recognizable being ovoids and U forms of different sizes and proportions. Formlines joined one another in a limited number of juncture types, which were designed to permit smooth transitions from one formline to another and to avoid the increase of design weight at the junctures.

The formline design system was first and primarily a painted art. The colors used were the typical black and red, with blue or green as a third, but less important, color. The primary formlines, which delineated the main body parts and formed the uninterrupted grid, were usually black, and the elaborations of the resulting spaces were in red, secondary, formlines. These colors were, on occasion, reversed. The third class of design, tertiary, consisted of resultant spaces within Us and ovoids and, if painted, was always blue. If the painting was then carved in relief, the negative slits, tertiary areas, and background were recessed. The whole design could be produced without painting, for example in horn, silver, argillite or ivory, but the principles remained the same. Many once-painted objects, especially bowls, have lost their paint, but the engraved designs remain undiminished.

Represented creatures could be shown quite naturalistically, with recognizable silhouettes and anatomical features. Using the same design rules, a creature could be rendered in such an abstract form that interpretation, if possible at all, depended on the inclusion of standard recognition features. The more distinctive animals, among them beaver, raven, eagle, and killerwhale (orca), have anatomical features easily represented in formline design that have been frequently described and illustrated (Boas 1927; Feder and Malin 1962; Holm 1967; Inverarity 1950). However, there were many animals, geographical features, plants, and natural phenomena that cannot be recognized without special knowledge of their identities.

Formlines were used to delineate the details of wings, joints, and other features of sculptured figures; and flat designs were often made more three-dimensional by the inclusion of protruding beaks or snouts. The two design concepts, two-dimensional and three-dimensional, cannot be separated in northern art. The formline system had a profound influence on the actual form of northern sculptural art as well, shaping eyesockets and limbs according to its principles. Haida sculpture furnishes the clearest examples.

Tlingit

Some of the most elaborate Tlingit works were great heraldic screens erected on the rear platforms of lineage houses as ceremonial partitions to the house chiefs' apartments. The most famous, and probably the finest of

left, Royal B.C. Mus., Victoria: 15722 R; top right, Amer. Mus. of Nat. Hist., New York: 19/477; center right, McMichael Canadian Coll., Kleinberg, Ont.; bottom right, Natl. Mus. of Canada, Ottawa: GbTo-34-1805.
Fig. 1. Carved formline designs. left, Haida argillite totem pole. Height 53.5 cm; collected before 1978. top right, Tlingit shaman's ivory charm. Length 14.5 cm; collected by G.T. Emmons at Yakutat, Alaska, 1869. center right, Haida silver bracelet carved by Charles Edenshaw about 1910. Circumference 19.1 cm. bottom right, Tsimshian carved bone comb. Length 9 cm; collected at the Kitanbach site at Prince Rupert Harbour, B.C., by George MacDonald in 1972.

these screens, the Rain Screen of the Klukwan Whale House, was said to have been carved in the early part of the nineteenth century (fig. 2). Some claimed it was the work of a Tsimshian carver (Emmons 1916:24), but stylistically it is solidly Tlingit and may have been the work of the artist of the ancient house posts of the Shakes house at Wrangell. Every tenet of the classic formline art was followed assiduously by the artist, whatever his origin. The screen shares many features with other well documented early Tlingit pieces, such as massive, angular formlines, minimum ground, very narrow relief slits and the style of recessing the tertiary areas. These characteristics may have more significance as an indicator of age than of tribal origin. The Tlingits, like all other Northwest Coast people, often acquired objects in trade from others, making it difficult to be certain of the origin of a particular piece unless it is clearly within a known tribal style or object type, or specific information about its history is available. An example is a carved chest collected by George Emmons from the Klukwan Whale House, which he was told had been acquired from the Haida. There is nothing about the chest to clearly establish it to be of Haida, rather than Tlingit, origin, but the information was freely given and was probably accurate. Many boxes, chests, and bowls in the formline tradition were made by Tlingit artists, and unless they incorporate three-dimensional details, such as faces with their Tlingit sculptural characteristics, they would be difficult to identify on the basis of style.

Metalwork has a long tradition in Tlingit art. Native copper obtained in trade was worked in precontact times, although engraving in the European manner apparently was begun in the middle of the nineteenth century. Daggers were said to have been made from native copper, and also from meteoric iron and iron salvaged from drift wreckage before Europeans arrived in the Tlingit country (Veniaminov 1840:80; Shotridge 1920; Holm 1983:98). Many of these weapons were beautifully crafted ("Tlingit," fig. 12, this vol.), and although none of their details would be impossible to produce with simple tools and techniques, they would have been very difficult to make; and their perfection of workmanship and design excites admiration.

Most of the Northwest Coast armor in museum

Fig. 2. Interior of the Whale House of the Raven ǧa·naxte·dí, a Tlingit Raven clan, Klukwan, Alaska. The carved and painted Rain Screen or Raven Screen (Jonaitis 1986) is flanked by the houseposts Woodworm and Raven (Emmons 1916; Holm and Reid 1975:20–22). Carved and painted wooden storage boxes, a large wooden head, a long feast bowl, the Woodworm Dish (top level), and a large basket with handles, the Mother Basket (bottom level), are shown. Clan members are dressed in dance tunics, aprons, furs, spruce-root hats, wooden helmets, and other ceremonial items. Photograph by Lloyd L. Winter and Edwin P. Pond, 1895.

collections is Tlingit. It is of heavy hide or hardwood slats and rods twined together with fine, braided sinew or human hair. Both types were painted with designs that were apparently of crests. On the wooden slat armor, panels were left bare of twining for the designs, while on hide armor, the whole tunic could be covered with painting. Painting on leather was also practiced on robes of tanned moose or caribou hides and on skin dancing aprons. Many of these were used by shamans in their practice, and they were painted with unusual figures common to Tlingit shamans' art and derived from the shamans' personal encounters with the spirit world.

The shaman's work was suffused with art. Paintings and carvings in every material brought his powerful spirit associates to physical life. Many of these manifestations of supernatural power were probably made by the shaman himself, but he could direct others, perhaps professional artists, to make them for him (Emmons 1945). The amulets were made of different hard materials, the favorites being ivory, canine teeth of bears and sea lions, antler, and bone. Sperm whale teeth furnished the finest ivory and many beautiful amulets were carved of it. Antler, with its branched tines, furnished the potential for carvings with extended fins. Amulets frequently were made as deeply carved formline designs. The figures were enigmatic, reflections of the owner's experience in the spirit world. Animals with strange combinations of attributes, or combining parts of different creatures, were common. Otters, octopus, wolves, killerwhales, and other animals with special association with shamans' work were frequently the subject of this complex and mysterious art ("Tlingit," fig. 14, this vol.).

Haida

Haida artists worked within the tenets of the formline system of design, but many different stylistic variations are recognizable. Some of these were changes of fashion over time, while others represent individual artists' response to the aesthetic problems. Documented eighteenth-century Haida examples utilize massive, compact formlines similar to those on Tlingit work of the same era, while some examples from the 1830s have narrow, rounded formlines with wide reliefs and open ground. To what extent these differences represent individual artists' styles or changes of the general tradition over the intervening half-century is not clear. In the late nineteenth century and early twentieth century a number of Haida artists, contemporaries of one another, produced work that was demonstrably different from one another in style, and changes in some of their styles over a period of years are discernable (Holm 1981).

About 1820 Haida artists began to carve small, salable objects in argillite for the seamen visiting the islands (Wright 1985). The first production was in pipes, suitable for smoking, but as the argillite trade developed it became apparent that the objects were not purchased for use, but as decorative souvenirs ("Haida: Traditional Culture," fig. 17, this vol.). Platters, bowls, chests, figures and eventually model totem poles were carved to satisfy the changing market (Macnair and Hoover 1984). Some of these carvings were roughly made or poorly designed, but there are many that stand among the masterpieces of Haida art. Attempts have been made to identify some of the early carvers by name (Barbeau 1957), but success seems more likely in identifying the bodies of work of individual artists, regardless of name (Wright 1985). Most of these argillite objects combine two-dimensional design with sculpture, and it is in this formline detail that individual differences in artists' styles are most apparent.

Another art that developed in response to the Euro-American presence was that of silver engraving. Early in the second half of the nineteenth century northern artists began making jewelry, primarily bracelets, of silver derived from coins. The technique of decorating the silver was engraving, following the European mode, but drawing the graver toward the artist rather than pushing it away. Early designs were also European-inspired, but shortly traditional crest figures began to appear. Silver work was produced over much of the coast, but northern artists, and especially the Haida, excelled. The best examples followed the formline principles of design and can be attributed to individual artists by style. Haida engravers applied their skills to copper as well when that metal was used for jewelry or for other purposes, such as the prestigious coppers (fig. 3).

Tsimshian

Tsimshian, Gitksan, and Nishga artists all adhered to the principles of the formline system. Extremely elaborate paintings on house fronts ("Tsimshian Peoples: Southern Tsimshian, Coast Tsimshian, Nishga, and Gitksan," figs. 6–7, this vol.) and screens have been recorded, and many painted boxes and carved chests have been attributed to the Tsimshian (fig. 4). Lightweight formlines were frequently used, but whether this is a Tsimshian trait or one representing a style widely current in the nineteenth century at the time of the collection of existing artifacts is not certain. In any case there was a great deal of sensitive formline painting of high craftsmanship produced by Tsimshian artists.

Bella Bella

The highly conventionalized, formline system of design organization and style perfected on the northern coast and ubiquitous there throughout the historic period was employed by Bella Bella artists for much of their painting and relief carving. Well-documented boxes painted within the tenets of this system show characteristics that suggest a distinctive Bella Bella style (fig. 5). All the northern province tribes made bent-corner boxes and painted them with symmetrical formline designs, almost all of which fell within a surprisingly limited number of compositional arrangements (Holm 1974:22–23). Bella Bella box painters worked within these limits, and in fact preferred an even more restricted repertoire of compositions. The uniqueness of Bella Bella painting was derived in part from the use of consistently thin formlines, extreme nonconcentricity of the very small, inner ovoids, the use of unidirectional hatching in some secondary and subsecondary U forms and the very consistent choice of certain design units and relationships.

Some Bella Bella painting, especially that on masks, resembled that of the Bella Coola or the Kwakiutl, further illustrating the intertwined relationships of those people and pointing up the occasional difficulty in identifying their works.

Fig. 3. Haida copper with beaver design. Collected by C.F. Newcombe from James Watson, village chief of Chaatl, at Skidegate, B.C., in 1911. It had previously belonged to the chief of Skedans. Height 95 cm.

Bella Coola

The Bella Coola occupied the zone of transition between the central and the northern provinces. Their two-dimensional art, at least in the second half of the nineteenth century, was northern in concept and detail, but with a freedom and flair that is to be expected for the work of artists on the edge of the flamboyant Kwakiutl and Bella Bella area. Elaborately painted housefronts were in the northern formline style ("Bella Coola," fig. 4, this vol.) whereas painting on masks and carved poles ranged from true formline to free, expressionistic stripes and spots of color. The most distinctive of Bella Coola painting styles was that most frequently used on masks in which usually blue lobes or U forms cover much of the surface, crossing the strong, sculptural forms of the face almost as if they were a flat ground and delineated by T-shaped reliefs and ground areas in unpainted wood or occasionally in vermilion. Although similar design and color use by Bella Bella, Haihais, and Haisla artists was not unknown, it was so characteristic of Bella Coola painting that it can be considered a primary recognition feature.

Kwakiutl

Kwakiutl painting was noted for its exuberance and flamboyance. Prior to the influx of northern design concepts in the mid-nineteenth century it was probably more straightforwardly representational, showing its relationship to Nootkan painting. Kwakiutl material from the early contact period is uncommon in collections, as the Kwakiutl had little direct contact with the shipborne explorers and traders who preserved most of the extant examples. After 1849, when the Hudson's Bay Company trading post, Fort Rupert, was established in their country, many examples of Kwakiutl art were collected.

Among the many prestigious privileges claimed by the Kwakiutl nobility were painted housefronts depicting creatures of mythology. An explorer observed painted housefronts in a village at the mouth of the Nimpkish River in 1792 that he suspected of having "meaning... too remote, or hieroglyphical, for our understanding" (Vancouver 1798, 1:346) ("Kwakiutl: Traditional Culture," fig. 3 top left, this vol.). One of the earliest housefront paintings to be photographed, in the 1880s, was a representation of a raven flanked by bears that was said to have been painted by a Bella Bella artist brought to Fort Rupert for the purpose (Barbeau 1950, 2:778; Mungo Martin, personal communication 1956). It was a classic northern painting in every respect and no doubt influenced the Kwakiutl artists who were familiar with it. These artists were quick to borrow ideas that appealed to them, but always with the freedom to interpret and modify, and without the obligation, which the northern artists clearly felt, to follow the complex structural rules of the formline system. Kwakiutl painting often looks superficially like northern painting, but it is distinguishable from it by its individuality and freedom of form and structure.

Flat painting was done on almost any suitable surface, such as those of boxes, chests, canoes, paddles, screens, and housefronts. In common with painting everywhere on the Northwest Coast the principal colors were black and red. If any one other color was used it was usually green or blue. Toward the end of the nineteenth century Kwakiutl artists began to favor painting on a white ground, or at least accenting the background areas with white. Other colors, such as yellow and orange, began to be freely used in the early twentieth century, but black, red, and green remained the colors of choice for most paintings, both on flat surfaces and on sculpture. In the 1920s some Kwakiutl painters, notably the Blunden Harbor artists Willie Seaweed and Charley George, Sr., began to use commercial oil enamel (Holm 1983).

Nootkans

Painting as an art form was much more important in the central province than in the southern, and it was highly developed by the Nootkan artists in the historic period. Artifacts recovered from the precontact wet site village at Ozette illustrate both painting and shallow relief carving, which on the Northwest Coast should be considered to be in the category of two-dimensional art. The Hoko River site produced a carved wooden object (originally identified as a mat creaser but more likely the handle of an ulu-type knife) with both painting and relief carving, in deposits dating to earlier than 500 B.C. (Carlson 1983b:fig. 11:9). There is very little painting extant from before the historic period, when many examples of Nootkan two-dimensional art and decoration on sculpture were recorded and collected.

Historic Nootkan painting was for the most part of two sorts, fairly naturalistic, representational painting depicting mythical beings and incidents, and abstract angular and curvilinear designs that may or may not have had symbolic meaning. The abstract work usually appeared as surface embellishment on various objects such as paddles and canoes and as elaborations on the representational paintings. Spirals, U or featherlike forms, rectangular blocks, circles and ovals, rows of dots, T reliefs and positive-negative reversals all appear on Nootkan paintings.

The painted screens associated with potlatches and ceremonial performances, originally on wooden panels but since the nineteenth century more commonly painted on muslin or canvas, were the most spectacular examples of Nootkan representational painting ("Nootkans of Vancouver Island," fig. 11, this vol.). They very frequently depicted thunderbirds and whales, lightning serpents,

and wolves, although other beings also appeared. The figures represented the characters of myths that accounted for the origin of ceremonies and inherited privileges. Many of the paintings were somewhat narrative in form, graphically illustrating the stories. In style they were bold and naturalistic, with strongly outlined features arranged freely and dynamically within the limits of the screen. Great freedom and inventiveness were displayed by the artists. In the late nineteenth century the influence of the northern formline style was felt as far south as Vancouver Island and many artists incorporated some of its elements and structure, but in a free and individualistic way. These are much more highly structured than earlier, and more typical Nootkan painting, and the figures are less naturalistic. Details of design on many of the flat-sided, constructed dance headdresses made by Nootkan artists in the same period reflect the influence of the northern style (fig. 6). These represented wolves, lightning serpents, and thunderbirds, important figures in the Winter ceremonies.

Nootkan relief carving is related to that of the Central Coast Salish and is best exemplified by the carvings on the pommels of whale bone warclubs. The clubs were heavy, about one-half meter long and up to 10 centimeters broad, with elliptical blades and rounded grips. Characteristic of whalebone clubs was a pommel carved to represent the bold silhouette of the head of a hook-beaked bird, probably a thunderbird, surmounted by the head of a secondary creature somewhat in the manner of a head-dress (King 1981:pl. 47) ("Nootkans of Vancouver Island," fig. 6, this vol.). Their features were delineated by crescent and T shaped grooves, much like the carving on Salish spindle whorls ("Central Coast Salish," fig. 5a–e, this vol.). The median line of the blade was usually detailed with similar elements, also conforming to the widespread principle of implying positive forms by partially defining them with negative recesses.

Central Coast Salish

The earliest collection date for an example of the distinctive two-dimensional relief carved art of the Strait of Georgia Salish is 1778, the year of Capt. James Cook's visit to Nootka Sound. There a member of the expedition collected a ceremonial rattle shaped and carved of mountain sheep horn (Collins et al. 1973:fig. 341). Although collected in Nootkan territory, the form of the rattle and the designs engraved on it conform exactly to the characteristics of documented sheep horn rattles used by and collected from the Cowichan and other Halkomelem speakers. A number of other horn and wood carvings collected at the end of the eighteenth and the beginning of the nineteenth century illustrate this same style and serve to confirm it as distinctive of the Halkomelem area and well established by the beginning of the historic period.

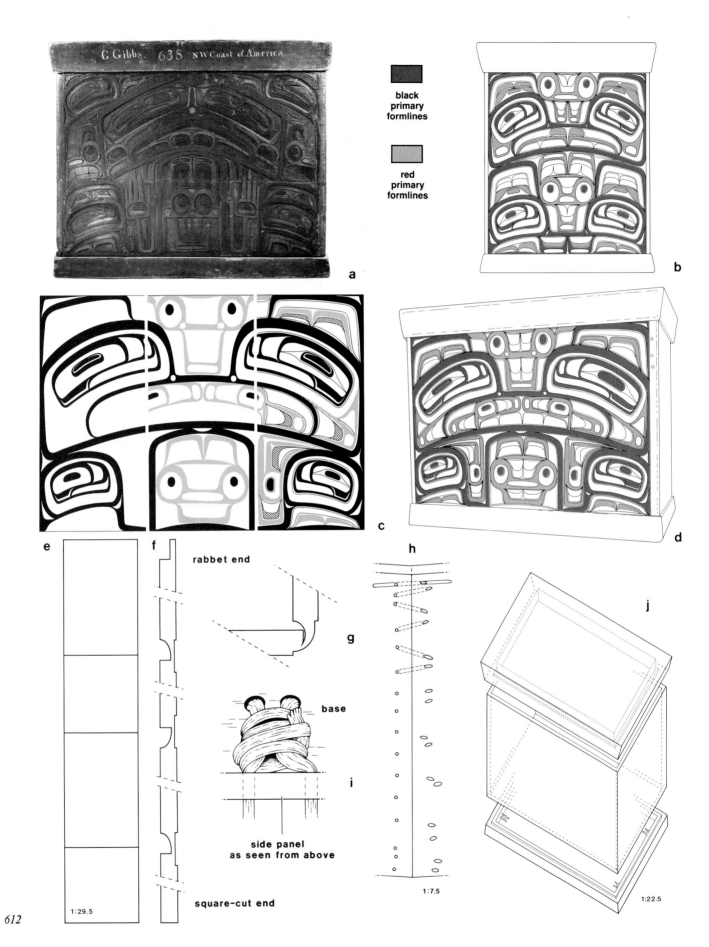

black
primary
formlines

red
primary
formlines

a

b

c

d

e

f

rabbet end

g

h

base

i

side panel
as seen from above

square-cut end

j

1:29.5

1:7.5

1:22.5

G.Gibbs. 638 NW Coast of America

Fig. 4. Tsimshian wooden chest with ornamental formline design. a, b, and d, Front, side, and three-quarter views. Designs on front and back panels were carved in low relief and painted; designs on side panels were painted only. c, Progression of formline design: in the left panel of the diagram, the black primary formlines show the major outlines of the design; the center panel shows the addition of red, used for formlines of secondary importance. True lines and tertiary elements are shown in the right panel. The sides of the chest were formed from a single wood plank. e-f, Placement of kerfs, which are cuts made into the plank to facilitate bending corners. g, Detail of kerf showing how it was bent. To soften the kerfs so a plank could be bent, the plank was placed over a steam pit. h, The rabbet end of the plank was joined to the square-cut end by means of diagonally placed pegs. i, Cedar tie used to fasten the base to the sides. j, Exploded isometric view of the chest. Collected by George Gibbs, Ft. Simpson, B.C., 1862; length 96 cm.

Carving details illustrating some of the most important principles of the design system appear on objects from archeological sites in the same area dating to A.D. 100 (Carlson 1983b:fig.11:7).

This sophisticated system of design organization and form is based on the concept of representing creatures in shallow relief by excising the background around the figure and by defining the positive forms of body parts by negative, carved relief slits in crescent and T or wedge shapes. In its most developed form the spaces between these reliefs were given a substantial and rather uniform width so that they had the effect of a positive, raised design forming a grid over the decorated area. A recessed U shape usually split from the open end by a wedge, was often used within feathers or fins. Circles or ovals, sometimes enclosed in a constricted ellipse as an eyelid, completed the repertoire of design elements used by the Salish artist. With these shapes he was able to represent any of the creatures of mythology in spaces as varied as circular spindle whorls, sheephorn rattles, or fish clubs (Feder 1983; Suttles 1983; Kew 1980). At the same time he organized the decorated space into a dynamic and visually satisfying design. Most of the objects carved in this style are representational, but some, in particular tapered bracelets of mountain goat horn, appear to be carved with purely decorative arrangements of the design elements (Feder 1983:fig. 13). Because of its clear conceptual relationship to the highly conventionalized northern formline system of design this Halkomelem tradition could be called the Salish formline system. This is not to suggest that was derived from northern art, but that the two traditions evolved from what must have been a common body of concepts.

Southern Coast Salish

The motivation for men's art among the Southern Coast Salish was primarily religious. Designs were usually representational, although often highly abstracted. The media included stone, worked by pecking as in petroglyphs or incising on mudstone concretions, bone, and antler, and painting and shallow relief carving on hide and wood. Representations of supernatural beings and their attributes, often dictated in form by the instructions of the beings themselves, were applied to objects that were used in ceremonial acts involving the power of spirit helpers, or that represented the owner's power, such as his house posts. Among the most elaborately painted objects of central Puget Sound were the boards used in the Spirit Canoe ceremony, one of the soul-recovery ceremonies (Dorsey 1902; Waterman 1930; Wingert 1949). The figures represented the supernatural powers associated with the shamans who performed the ceremony for the

Fig. 5. Bella Bella box. Collected by Erna Gunther before 1930; height 54.5 cm.

Fig. 6. Clayoquot wolf mask of wood. Collected by Karl von den Steinen, 1897; length 65 cm.

613

ART

recovery of souls that had been taken to the underground spirit world. The boards themselves had the silhouette of a creature with projecting snout, while the paintings on their surfaces took the forms of birds, animals, anthropomorphic beings, and various power symbols ("Southern Coast Salish," fig. 11, this vol.). Each painting could only be interpreted by its owner, although certain abstract symbols seem to have had relatively fixed meanings, such as rows of dots issuing from a figure's mouth to represent songs. Typical colors were red and black, and occasionally blue, applied on a white ground. Stylistically they were simple, straightforward representations, emphasizing important attributes of the power figures. Very few of these boards have been preserved in museum collections.

Painting and incising on utilitarian objects such as spoons, canoe paddles, boxes, gambling bones, and tool handles were generally decorative and often geometric, although sometimes power figures were applied to these things as well.

Lower Columbia Region

As in all Northwest Coast art traditions, two-dimensional and sculptural arts of the Lower Columbia are hardly separable. There was a very strong geometric tendency in the shallow relief carving used to delineate animal and humanoid figures in bone, wood, antler, and stone. Circles, crescents, zigzags, and chevrons, often in interlocked or concentric groups, characterize surface detailing of three-dimensional objects and figures. The mountain sheep horn bowls and ladles of the upriver Dalles area are good examples of this geometric tradition ("Chinookans of the Lower Columbia," fig. 4, this vol.), with rows of incised triangles forming zigzag ridges, interspersed with concentric circles or rectangles and geometricized human figures. Similar carvings in antler and wood from the Portland Basin are conceptually related.

Sculpture

Tlingit

The sculpture of the northern province was more distinctive tribally than its two-dimensional art. Although certain principles of organization and form were universally followed throughout the area, there were differences that could be recognized and described.

Much of Tlingit sculpture was naturalistic, with the details of anatomy suggested or rendered accurately. Shamans' masks and headdress maskettes, for example, frequently had a portraitlike quality and often represented the souls of humans (fig. 7). Typical Tlingit sculptural characteristics on humanoid faces were rounded features, large eyes with unconstricted lids on rounded orbs, and broad lips, usually open and formed of a continuous band.

Smithsonian, Dept. of Anthr.: 274245.
Fig. 7. Tlingit shaman's mask. Collected before 1912; height 23 cm.

Frequently the upper cheek plane sloped uninterrupted from the eye to the raised lip-band. There were many individual styles represented, but most can be identified as Tlingit by the combination of sculptural characteristics and subject. The painting on shamans' masks often referred to the identity or characteristics of the spirit, and usually could not be identified without information from the owner. Crest masks, on the other hand, were carved in the forms of the creatures of mythology and were ordinarily recognizable. Other materials were frequently combined with the wood (usually alder) such as copper on lips or eyebrows, opercula or teeth in the mouth, and human hair pegged in locks along the forehead and inset on the lip and chin for moustache and beard.

Warriors' helmets were carved as the heads of ferocious beasts or fearsome humans. They share the naturalistic emphasis of shamans' masks, with hair and teeth often added. Weapons and war regalia resembled shamans' implements in many ways, and perhaps the concept of utilizing supernatural power in the shaman's contest with malevolent spirits carried over to human conflict.

All the paraphernalia of nobility was subjected to the artist's skill and imagination. Dancing headdresses, crest hats and staffs, rattles, spoons, bowls, pipes, and carved house posts portrayed the lineage and clan emblems. The same sculptural characteristics evident on masks were seen in these carvings, irrespective of scale. Monumental sculpture of the Tlingit was concentrated on the interior houseposts, especially in the northern villages, where freestanding exterior poles were rarely seen. The house posts, usually four in number, were emblazoned with figures from the lineage myths. Some, like the Dog Salmon posts from the Whale House or the Grizzly Bear posts from the Killer Whale's Long Dorsal Fin House at

614

Klukwan (Jonaitis 1986:figs. 15,16), were true formline designs on flat planks, while others were fully sculptured figures in the distinctive Tlingit style. The Frog Posts from Klukwan combined the two concepts (Jonaitis 1986: figs. 10–11). All these house posts were made as shells fronting the plain, structural posts, making it possible to move them when a house was rebuilt or abandoned and preserving them from the usual destruction by rot suffered from posts permanently set in the ground.

Shamans' amulets were among the many works of Tlingit artists that joined two-dimensional art and sculpture. In many of them the concept was of a flat, formline representation carved on a rounded form, with a sculptural result. Others were carved in the round.

Haida

Haida sculpture is epitomized by the gigantic totem poles that towered over the Queen Charlotte Island village beaches in the nineteenth century (MacDonald 1983) and that continue to be made in the twentieth century (fig. 8). Lifting formlines to a state of monumentality, these great images equaled the power of any of the world's sculpture ("Haida: Traditional Culture," fig. 2, this vol.). Their function was to proclaim the rank and social affiliation of the house owner and his wife, or to memorialize a deceased predecessor. The figures were crests or figures in the mythical adventures of lineage ancestors. The act of raising the pole was both a responsibility of nobility and an affirmation of that nobility. The act was very expensive, involving not only the carver's fee but also payment to those who raised the pole and the witnesses to it. There is only a sparse record of monumental, carved poles in the journals of the earliest explorers on the Northwest Coast, but it is enough to establish the historical fact of their presence (Duff 1964a:84–94). Sculpture on the scale of nineteenth-century Haida poles would have been very difficult and slow without metal tools, but as soon as they became readily available, totem pole carving burgeoned. By the middle of the nineteenth century northern Northwest Coast villages, especially those of the Haida, bristled with elaborately carved monuments, some of them over 15 meters high and one and one-half meters wide.

The carving on Haida totem poles of the nineteenth century was characterized by the qualities of monumentality, compactness, and stability. They had none of the feeling of action or the outward thrust of Kwakiutl totem pole sculpture. Each figure fit just within the cylindrical limits of the pole. The beak of a major figure might jut out, joined to the pole by a sturdy tenon, or a naturalistic creature might perch on the top. But ordinarily beaks and snouts turned down, or were flattened within the confines of the rounded surface. The principle is one of applying a massive, compact formline design to the cylinder (or half cylinder in the case of house frontal poles) and carving it

Fig. 8. Totem poles carved by Robert Davidson, Haida, in 1986. Photograph by Ulli Steltzer, Purchase, N.Y., 1986. Height of pole on the left, 11.9 m.

in relief (Holm 1967). The faces of the principal figures were carved with defined, ovoid eyesockets, and the eyelids were outlined with flat rims, analogous to the tertiary lines of the formline system. To fill the width of the pole, heads were as wide as shoulders, and comparably high. Since the figures usually squatted, with legs and arms drawn close to the body, those heads made up nearly half of each creature's height. Figures interlocked, one biting another, grasping a fin, or squatting between the ears, unlike the poles of almost all the other totem-pole-carving tribes, which tend to be stacked with each figure discrete. Details of wings and fins were formlines. Paint was applied according to formline rules, with little thought of naturalism.

Argillite model totem poles were usually more freely sculptural then the full-size carvings, probably because they were carved from a blank sawed from the rough stone, with none of the physical or conceptual limits of the cedar tree. Haida model wooden poles show both tendencies, with most conforming to the traditional, cylindrical log-form.

Haida sculpture of other sorts—headdress frontlets, rattles, bowls (fig. 9) ("Haida: Traditional Culture," fig. 9, this vol.), weapons, spoon handles—often mirrored the characteristics of the great poles. Strongly influenced by formlines, they retained the tightly organized, crisp

615

Royal B.C. Mus., Victoria: 410.
Fig. 9. Haida soapberry dish. Collected before 1893; length, 34 cm.

delineation of that design system. The variations of individual styles make it impossible to lay out rigid rules of recognition for all Haida art, but those articles that most closely resemble the Haida totem poles in style are almost surely from the same heritage. Stone tobacco mortars made probably by a combination of pecking and grinding illustrate the Haida penchant for massive, compact design very well.

Portraiture, or at least naturalistic representation of human faces, was practiced by sculptors on many parts of the coast, but Haida artists produced some of the finest examples. From the first decades of the nineteenth century northern artists made masks for sale to the visiting Euro-American seamen. No doubt the preponderance of masks made for sale and representing women wearing labrets was due in part to the fascination the sailors had for the custom, often mentioned in their journals. Toward the end of the nineteenth century some Haida artists turned again to making realistic portrait masks for sale, often with detailed hairstyles and movable eyes and lips (Holm 1981:179–181). The masks that Haida carvers made for their own use ranged from portraitlike naturalism to fanciful and stylized forms with copper teeth or eyebrows, movable jaws, and other imaginative features.

Tsimshian

Tsimshian totem poles, in their function of crest display, reflect the bewildering array of Tsimshian crests including plants, ceremonial regalia and other cultural objects, and natural phenomena. They share some of the narrative qualities of Tsimshian button blankets. Although it is unsafe to generalize, it can be said that Tsimshian sculpture itself was spare and uncluttered, with the tendency to represent figures more naturalistically than Haida or Tlingit sculpture. Limbs on carved figures, especially on large totem poles, were rounded and relatively natural in their proportions, and human figures especially were often depicted standing, rather than squatting, giving them a less compacted look. The

sculpture of human faces was often sensitively done, achieving the effect of skin tautly stretched over an underlying anatomical structure. Eyes were large, on wide, smoothly rounded orbs, and the eyelids were often sharply incised, rather than defined by a flat line as was common elsewhere on the northern coast. A distinctive cheek structure—in which the side, upper, and forecheek planes merged in a more or less sharply defined pyramid—was common.

Small carvings, such as the richly ornamented headdress frontlets (fig. 10), were finely finished and often with the face unpainted, enhancing the effect of living skin. Some Tsimshian artists were said to have specialized in the making of these headdresses, and many of Tsimshian origin have been collected from different tribes. Another elegant object frequently made by Tsimshian artists, for whom it was said to be a specialty, was the raven rattle (fig. 11). Certainly many were made by Tsimshian artists, although they were also carved thoughout the northern province. The finest of these were among the most successful amalgamations of sculpture and flat design. Their use in dancing was, along with the headdress frontlet, both a prerogative and a responsibility of chiefs.

Masks and other ceremonial objects afforded Tsimshian artists the opportunity to exercise their imagination and sculptural skills. The most numerous masks used in the Tsimshian area were those used to dramatize the appearance of spirits called Naxnox (Halpin 1984). They represented animals and people, often foreigners or those with unusual physical or personality traits. Carvers were free to interpret these characteristics in sculpture and often produced remarkably dramatic images, some of which were articulated to enable them to change expression or form. The same artists, who were members of a secret and powerful group called Gitsontk, made puppets and other stage properties with which to dramatize the supernatural world (Shane 1984).

Haisla, Haihais, and Bella Bella

The Haisla and Haihais artists produced sculpture that is often nearly indistinguishable from that of the neighboring Coast Tsimshian or the Haida of the Queen Charlotte Islands with which some Coast Tsimshian had close trading and social relationships. Some of their masks were extremely sensitively modeled, seminaturalistic faces with delicate formline painting. Very naturalistic masks are difficult to attribute accurately because the characteristics of tribal carving style are minimized. A distinctive style of mask, of which there are a number of examples in collections, incorporated some of the forms and sharp definition of planes seen in typical Bella Bella masks but are otherwise quite different. Sawyer (1983) tentatively attributed them to the Haihais or Haisla.

Bella Bella monumental sculpture particularly was

The British Mus., Mus. of Mankind, London: 2233.
Fig. 11. Tsimshian raven rattle. Collected before 1865; length 32 cm.

Nat. Mus. of Canada, Ottawa: V11-C-87.
Fig. 10. Tsimshian frontlet. Collected by I.W. Powell at Metlakatla, B.C., 1879; height 19 cm.

very much like that of the Kwakiutl in its naturalism, but it tended to be somewhat more restrained, reflecting the northern influence that effected Bella Bella society so strongly during the historic period. On the other hand, imaginative Bella Bella artists were known for the fantastic figures of men and animals that they carved on staffs and rattles and, in the late nineteenth century, produced for sale to non-Indians. Many of these had a decided Bella Coola appearance in both form and painted decoration, but they could usually be distinguished by the facial features. The characteristic Bella Bella eye structure was based on a relatively flat and large orb, with the surrounding defining planes of the upper cheek and under brow rather narrow and sharply defined. Lips were less likely to be open in the typical "diamond" configuration of Bella Coola human representation and the cheekbone area lacked the familiar "Bella Coola bulge."

Bella Coola

The overall impression of Bella Coola sculpture is one of bold planes and the strong juxtaposition of convex and concave forms. It is best seen in the treatment of the human face. Basically Bella Coola sculptured faces were naturalistic in the forms of the features and their relationship to each other, but those forms were stylized in a distinctive way. Typically human face representations were sloped back from the nose in all directions, giving the face something of a receding forehead and chin. The orb of the eye was pronounced and somewhat of a truncated cone. It was bounded by a distinctly carved underbrow plane that characteristically sloped down on the outer side of the eye to meet the upper cheek plane in a sharp intersection at the outer corner of the orb. The cheek itself was characterized by a distinct bulge, corresponding to the zygomatic arch of anatomy. This distinctive eye/eyesocket structure was typical of the interplay of planes in the rest of the face. The lips, on a strong projection, were nearly always open and rather naturalistically modeled (Boas 1898:pls. 7–12).

The many different mythical beings represented in the sculpture required a great many variations on the basic forms of the face, but the Bella Coola character was almost always present. A few special types, such as the graphite-painted Thunder mask with its heavy hooked nose, lipless mouth, and grossly protruding forehead and chin, lacked most recognition features, but the eye configuration and strong planar structure were consistent with the Bella Coola style ("Bella Coola," fig. 12, this vol.).

Animals and birds were frequent subjects for Bella Coola sculptors, with facial planes and forms like those of humanoid representation, allowing for the differences in basic form. Heavy, downward slating brows; flaring, rounded nostrils; and eye structure were similar. On many bird representations, for example, in the elaborately carved and shell-inlaid headdress frontlets, beaks thrust aggressively upward, imparting a sense of power and movement.

The imaginative genius of Bella Coola sculptors was put to work inventing articulated masks and figures to dramatize family myths in the ceremonial complexes. In this they rivaled Kwakiutl carvers. They also produced monumental sculpture such as house frontal poles with the entrance through a gaping mouth ("Bella Coola," fig. 5, this vol.) or a housepost with enormously outstretched arms that seemed to support the eave beams of the roof (Barbeau 1950, 2:fig. 393). Apparently they never carved tall, fully sculptured poles.

Kwakiutl

Kwakiutl artists were prolific sculptors. They had the motivation to produce sculpture for the active ceremonial life of their tribes, and rich mythology for subject matter. Although early historic Kwakiutl sculpture was somewhat less flamboyant than late nineteenth and twentieth-century examples, it was free in concept and bold in execution. Kwakiutl artists carved massive, functional house posts representing the owners' ancestors or the creatures with which they interacted, and freestanding figures as memorial monuments, as commemorations of the size of a pile of blankets used in the purchase of a copper, or for other purposes related to rank and privilege display. Typically of those northern and central tribes with well developed concepts of rank and crests, Kwakiutl artists were trained and acted as professionals, accepting commissions from chiefs to produce art as manifestations of the prerogatives of inheritance and rank. Their art was straightforwardly illustrative. Humans were naturalistically proportioned, except for the exaggerated size of the head, especially on house posts. The function of supporting the massive roof beams provided both practical and psychological reasons for not radically reducing the diameter of the post. Figures were commonly carved in full sculptural form rather than in high relief as many Salish posts were. Arms of humans and wings, fins, beaks, and snouts of animals and birds were frequently carved separately and attached to the figures to extend them and to express their action and power.

The earliest recorded freestanding Kwakiutl totem poles were tall masts surmounted by single, naturalistic figures of men or birds. Photographs taken in 1873 at Tsawadi village at the head of Knight Inlet furnish the earliest datable record of large, fully sculptured, freestanding Kwakiutl totem poles, which were almost certainly another example of the nineteenth-century influence of northern art on the Kwakiutl. By 1900 many villages had large poles attached to or standing before the houses. A famous example, the earliest large pole in Alert Bay, was the Raven Pole of chief Wakiash. Epitomizing the flamboyant Kwakiutl totem pole, the figures were deeply carved, with extended wings, beaks, and snouts, while the wings, tail, and feet of the great raven at the base was painted on the facade of the house in Kwakiutl style formlines. The raven's beak, extending over three meters from the pole, was hollow and the mandible hinged so that on ceremonial occasions the mouth opened and Chief Wakiash's guests entered the house through the raven's voracious maw.

Kwakiutl sculpture of faces, animal and human, shares with that of the nothern tribes an important and easily discernable feature that readily distinguishes it from the work of most Salish and Nootkan sculptors. The eyes are represented as orbs, underlying and pushing against the eyelids, rather than outlined or incised into the flattened cheek plane, the usual form to the south. This orb, or eye bulge, is a characteristic of sculpture from the Kwakiutl northward, and the lack of it is the norm to the west and south. In keeping with this convex orb, Kwakiutl facial sculpture tended to be bold, with well-defined planes forming the features. Mouths projected, defined by strong cheek lines, and teeth were often bared, giving the represented creature an air of menace.

Poles of the late nineteenth and early twentieth century became progressively more elaborate, with attached parts and contrasting, complex painting on a white ground. This direction continued into the mid-century, when a sort of reaction to the flamboyance led some artists to return to what was perceived as a purer Kwakiutl expression, with unpainted background and less complex detail. By the 1980s many artists were shaking off this inhibition and becoming comfortable again with the freedom that their early twentieth-century predecessors had.

Kwakiutl theatricality in sculpture and painting found an outlet in the masks that were used to make manifest the creatures of myth in dramatic recreations of ancestors' adventures, the basis of privilege. Masks took many forms. Some covered the face, others were worn on the forehead, and still others were carried on the back, covering the dancer's torso (fig. 12). Many of these were articulated; jaws snapped, fins and tails undulated and arched. A specialty of Kwakiutl maskmakers was the transformation mask, in which the mask split or altered itself to reveal another, inner or alter image. The vivid imagination of Kwakiutl carvers, fueled by rich and evocative mythology, was given full play in the design and production of masks. Some were powerful, seemingly naturalistic images of fearsome monsters like the Woodman (fig. 13), while others were fantastic figures depending on their size and striking contours, and the dramatic skills of the wearer, to make them believeable. Rattles, staffs, dancing headdresses, feast dishes, and every other suitable object were carved and decorated in the distinctive Kwakiutl mode. The motivation for most of this art was social—the display of ancestral rights—rather than religious, although there is a current of religion running through the ceremonial context of the objects.

Nootkans

Nootkan sculpture was related to the two-dimensional art of the area in its boldness and naturalism. Anthropomorphic carvings such as commemorative figures ordinarily were rendered with natural proportions and realistic modeling of their musculature. House posts, possibly because of their structural function, were more often stocky and stylized in their representation. Powerfully naturalistic and portraitlike masks were made by Nootkan

618

Denver Art Mus., Colo.: 1953.404.
Fig. 12. Kwakiutl articulated mask. The jaw, flippers, dorsal fin, and flukes can be made to move, used as *λaʔsəla* privilege. Made about 1900; length 1.7 m.

artists, but these often retained stylization of the features common to the regional sculpture. They were much more strongly modeled than humanoid faces on Salish sculpture, with almost none of their flat frontality. Typically the under-brow plane was long and slanted inward, rather than sharply stepped back as in the Salish facial carvings. Eyes were large and round, with long, pointed eyelids, and they were usually rendered flat on the cheek plane, with little or no projection of the orb. Many of these masks and carvings were strikingly lifelike, and some were fitted with rolling eyes that could be made to open and close. Human hair was sometimes attached for hair, moustache and beard for added realism. Southern Nootkan anthropomorphic faces were often based on a deep prismatic form, with the two sides of the face flattened, presenting a bold profile. The long, slanting under-brow plane and large eye on the cheek plane conformed to the Nootkan sculptural conventions. Painting on masks was usually bold, geometric, and often asymmetrical, crossing the facial planes with broad stripes and feather-form Us. The typical colors were black, red, and blue, but, especially in the twentieth century, color use expanded to oranges, yellows, and other hues. Some painted designs were surely symbolic, but the artists apparently had great freedom to invent and experiment.

Animals and birds, particularly wolves and thunderbirds, were also represented in Nootkan sculpture. Monumental carvings and house posts, rattles, clubs, and masks were all carved in the likenesses of creatures of mythology. A smoothly streamlined form was characteristic of many of these sculptures. Wolf headdresses, for example, had long, constricted snouts, narrow, drawn back lips with many teeth, slanted ears and the large eyes with the

pointed lids typical of Nootkan art. Bird rattles were elegantly rendered, the body in globular form with a narrow, extended neck and small head (fig. 14). They were often sparsely decorated, depending on proportion and form for their effect.

Central Coast Salish

Sculpture of the Central Coast Salish exhibited the straightforward, representational style of more southerly Salish carving with, in the nineteenth century, more modeling and detail. Figures of men, animals, and birds were rendered in recognizable form and relatively naturalistic proportions. Typical Salish frontality prevailed for anthropomorphic figures, with the faces constructed on a flat oval principal form, with small eyes on the cheek plane and minimal mouth projection (fig. 15). The features were more rounded than was typical in more southerly sculpture, and some had considerable modeling of the mouth and chin, defined by carved cheek lines. The fingers and the musculature of the limbs were often naturalistically portrayed, along with details of clothing and adornment.

Birds and animals were carved quite naturalistically, with smooth, rounded contours, and with the facial features and other details often rendered in the distinctive two-dimensional style of the area. Short-legged, long-tailed quadrupeds, which probably represented fishers, an animal associated with supernatural power, were frequent themes on house posts and grave monuments (Suttles 1982:65). Fully sculptured figures were commonly carved so as to stand out in high relief from the massive plank of the house post ("Central Coast Salish," fig. 7, this vol.). *619*

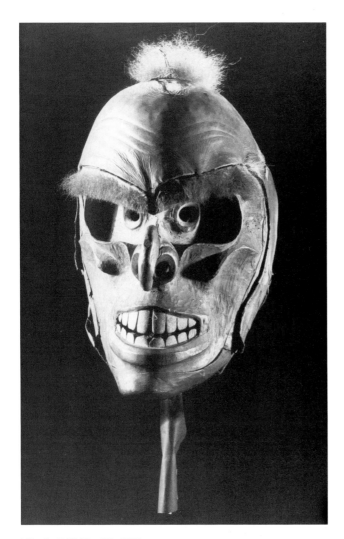

Fig. 13. Kwakiutl Woodman mask. Collected by S.A. Barrett at Ft. Rupert, B.C., 1915; height 29 cm.

Fig. 14. Makah rattle. Collected at Cape Flattery, Wash., before 1915; length 32 cm.

Spinning and weaving equipment such as loom posts and wool bearing swords, as well as other tools and weapons, were frequently embellished with sculptural representations of men and animals. It seems possible that these were indicative of associated supernatural power, but little is known about them. Similar carvings on the rattle staffs of spirit dancers were likely derived from the supernatural experiences of the owners.

Small sculptures in soft stone, often in the form of bowls, have been found in scattered sites in southwestern British Columbia and northwestern Washington. Many of them incorporate sculptural characteristics unlike those of nineteenth-century sculpture of the area. The most distinctive of these are the "seated human figure bowls" carved in the likeness of a seated, anthropomorphic figure holding a shallow bowl between the legs (Duff 1956a). Some of these figures, apparently all from the precontact period, have a sculptural treatment of the face that is much more like the historic sculpture of the northern Northwest Coast than it is like that of the nineteenth-century Salish (Duff 1975:figs.31–57). Their faces are deeply rounded, and instead of the flat, oval face with eyes on the cheek plane, they often exhibit pronounced orbs with defined eyelids, flaring nostrils, bulging cheeks and a large projecting mouth. The bowls were ritual objects, but their specific use is not known.

One manifestation of Central Coast Salish sculpture that continued in use into the 1980s was the sxwayxwey mask (fig. 16). The mythology of the mask and its ritual context are better known than those of many other sculptural objects of the Salish (Barnett 1955:156–159; Duff 1952a:123–126; Jenness 1955:11, 91–92; Suttles 1982). Jutting, cylindrical eyes, two bird or animal heads protruding from the upper corners of the mask, a long and broad projection likened to a tongue drooping from the bottom, and often a creature's head in place of a nose give the mask its distinctive appearance. On the surface of the face the body of the creature represented by the nose, or by the upstanding heads, was often depicted in Salish formline design. The complete mask and dress of the dancer was very elaborate, incorporating many feathers in a ruff under the mask, waving above it, and covering the dancer's tunic. Birdskin leggings and deer hoof rattles covered his lower legs, and he carried a clashing rattle of strung scallop shells ("Central Coast Salish," fig. 11, this vol.).

The form of the sxwayxwey mask remained remarkably stable for the century following the collection of the earliest documented example in 1868 (Suttles 1982:fig. 12). The revival of interest in Salish art in the 1970s resulted in the production of a number of traditional sxwayxwey masks in the years following.

Southern Coast Salish

Of necessity every Salish man carved wood, but certain carvers excelled and often specialized in the production of specific kinds of objects. Canoe makers were specialists, for example, although very likely every man could make a canoe. In the Puget Sound area there were men who were recognized as more skilled as sculptors than others,

Royal B.C. Mus., Victoria: 5707.
Fig. 15. One of 5 Cowichan house posts collected from a house at Quamichan Reserve, B.C., before 1944. These posts originally stood inside a plank house to support the beams. They were later set outside against the wall of a house made of milled lumber, where they had no structural function. Height 2.8 m.

Royal B.C. Mus., Victoria: PN 10851.
Fig. 16. Central Coast Salish sxwayxwey mask of raven type. Collected by G.T. Emmons at Nanaimo, B.C., 1903; height 41 cm.

although most men probably did what little representational wood carving they required themselves.

The most striking examples of wood sculpture in the Puget Sound region were power figures in the shape of anthropomorphic beings (Wingert 1949:pls. 8–15, 17–21). These were made by shamans of the central Puget Sound tribes and were part of the equipment of the Spirit Canoe ceremony. Each one was the property of a shaman whose power enabled him to journey to the land of the dead on a soul-recovery mission. The form of each figure was dictated by the shaman's supernatural helper, of whom the carving was considered a portrait. The figures were boldly carved of red cedar, with strong angles and volumes, as legless torsos with oval heads flattened on the frontal plane. Arms, if they were represented at all, were usually painted on the chest, with bent elbows and spread fingers. Some have the arms carved in relief, occasionally in considerable detail (fig.17). The faces conformed to the southern tenets of sculpture: a flat-oval principal form cut sharply back under the brow; long, narrow nose extending from brow level; and small eyes incised, painted or inlaid on the cheek plane. Spirit Canoe figures often retained the flat facial plane from the forehead, around the rim and across the chin, with the cheek planes deeply concave. Some examples have the features merely painted on the face plane. In place of legs the figures each have a heavy, pointed stake that was set in the ground to hold the carving upright during the ceremony. Painting in red and black, often on a white ground, followed the instructions of the spirit helper. The figures were kept hidden in the forest, and the painting was renewed on each occasion of use.

A very few masks were made and used by the Southern Coast Salish, but they all appear to have been introduced from others and perhaps only since the late nineteenth century (Eells 1985:385–388). Some other ceremonial objects, such as the staffs on which dancers kept their deeerhoof rattles, were carved with power representations, but for the most part the carvers' art was confined to the production of functional objects. Many of these, such as spoons, bailers, adz handles, and canoes, were sculptural in themselves although not ornamented beyond their elegant flare and finish.

Southwestern Coast Salish

The art of the Quinault is best known for a number of carved figures representing supernatural helping spirits used by shamans in their practice. The carvings are said to have been true representations of the appearance of the spirit beings. They range in size from about 10 centimeters in height, carved as a finial on a staff, through figures 30–40 centimeters in height with a cylindrical handle

621

U. of Nebr. State Mus., Lincoln: A 23036.
Fig. 17. Southern Coast Salish spirit canoe figure. Collected in 1892; height 1.4 m.

protruding from the base, to nearly life size (Wingert 1949:pl.1–6). All are standing humanoid figures exhibiting the southern Northwest Coast frontal emphasis. The arms, held straight down along the sides of the torso, were usually separated from it by carved, elliptical openings. The whole figure is angular, in keeping with the geometricity of much southern province sculpture. Ribs were sometimes carved on the chest, but otherwise they were less skeletal than carving from the Lower Columbia region. Clusters of deer hooves, hung from the necks or chest of some figures to serve as rattles, were referred to as the "bones" of the being (Willoughby 1889:278).

The form of the faces of the Quinault figures exemplifies the southern sculptural tradition. Composed within a flat oval, the face was divided horizontally into two distinct steps (the forehead plane and the face plane) by the sharp cut under the brow, or into three steps by another cut defining the lower edge of the cheek plane. The face was cut back to the depth of these cuts, leaving a narrow nose protruding at the level of the forehead plane. The eyes and mouth were small recesses cut into the cheek and chin planes respectively. The principle of representing the face on a frontally oriented, flat plane by cutting away under the brow and the cheeks, leaving the nose protruding, and carving the eyes and mouth into those planes with little modeling, was typical of sculptural representation from the Columbial River to the southern part of Vancouver Island.

622   A variant on the fully sculptured power figures of the

Quinault was a similar figure carved in relief on a broad plank (Wingert 1949:pl.7) ("Southwestern Coast Salish," fig.10, this vol.). All these figures were painted, usually in red and black, and the eyes and sometimes the teeth were represented by shell inlay. Human hair, or in some cases horse hair, was attached to the head. Accounts of the meaning and use of some of these figures in the work of shamans were obtained from their owners (Willoughby 1889:278; Olson 1936:146), and it is on the basis of this information that the similar precontact figures from the Columbia River have been interpreted.

Lower Columbia Region

The Lower Columbia region shared a tradition of sculpture with other areas of the Northwest Coast. Stone, wood, bone, antler, and mountain sheep horn were the media utilized to produce decorated utilitarian and ceremonial objects. As in the basketry of the region, geometricized anthropomorphic and zoomorphic representation was common, along with purely geometric elaboration. Many of the extant sculptural objects were recovered from archeological sites, and their meanings and use are conjectural.

The frontal human figure was a favorite theme in art, either as a discrete carving or as a relief representation on a utilitarian object. A number of bone or antler figures, some fragmentary, have been recovered from cremation sites near The Dalles, suggesting that they had a religious function. They are very small (around 10 centimeters high) and minutely detailed with incised carving. Facial features, skeletal structure, and details of hair, headdresses, and kilts were rendered by carving away the background in crescents, chevrons, and triangles. The face was typically an elongated, flat oval, with almond eyes bounded by arched brows, a long nose, and cheek ridges. Frequently the mouth was shown as smiling, with a rectangular tongue in its center. A striking feature of these figures, and others related to them, is the depiction of the ribs, defined by incised crescents or chevrons (fig.18). They resemble the human figures on twined baskets from the same region in proportion and detail. Similar figures were carved in relief on the upright flanges of the deep wooden mortars used for pulverizing dried salmon and on the small, round bowls made of mountain sheep horn that have been collected in many parts of the northwest but that probably were made in the Wasco-Wishram area of the Plateau. These mortars, bowls, and related horn ladles were further decorated with geometric designs made by excising small triangles in interlocking rows to form bands of zigzag lines, as well as by incised concentric squares and circles. Few if any of these horn bowls and ladles were made after the middle of the nineteenth century.

Larger human figures were carved in wood, incorporating many of the stylistic features of the small bone carvings. Some of these have stafflike bases, suggesting that they were set upright in the ground (like Puget Sound Spirit Canoe figures) or used as rattles or wands (like some Quinault spirit figures). These figures range from 25 centimeters to one meter in height. In 1805 explorers saw a canoe with life-sized wooden figures of a bear and a man attached to the bow and the stern (Lewis and Clark in Biddle 1814, 2:68). Apparently even larger figures were once carved. Paul Kane's 1846 watercolor painting of the interior of a Chinookan house shows a house post in the form of a human figure carved in the Lower Columbia style as well as typical geometric relief carving on a partition plank ("Chinookans of the Lower Columbia," fig.3, this vol.).

Represetations of animals and birds were also part of the repertoire of the Lower Columbia artists. Sculptured figures typically stood atop the handles of horn and wooden spoons and on the butts of antler adz handles. Like the human figures, they were relatively naturalistic in their proportions and detailed with geometric renditions of their skeletal structure and anatomical features.

There is little if any evidence of the existence of a crest system in the region, and it is usually surmised that the representational sculpture of the Lower Columbia was related to a belief in guardian spirits. The use of similar carved figures as representations of powerful supernatural beings by the Quinault and Southern Coast Salish in historic times tends to corroborate that assumption.

Basketry

Tlingit

Baskets had an honored place in Tlingit culture. One of the most treasured relics of the Klukwan Whale House was an enormous, twined spruce root basket, called the Mother Basket (fig.2) (Emmons 1916; Oberg 1973:44-45). Like most Chilkat baskets it was undecorated except for self-patterning in the weave, but many Tlingit baskets were more or less elaborately patterned with a combination of self-designs produced by variations in the twining, dyed weft, and false embroidery with colored grasses in geometric bands (Emmons 1903). A vast array of elaborate, repeat patterns was possible to achieve using combinations of only a few basic elements. Most of the designs had names, which were essentially descriptive rather than symbolic. Baskets were made in all sizes and a number of different forms according to the use to which a basket would be put. Even the cradle was of basketry. It was not woven as such but reassembled from a large basket that was cut apart for the purpose. Some of the most beautifully made Tlingit baskets were pairs of small, slightly tapered cylinders, made so that one slid firmly over the other, completely sealing the contents. Shot for muzzle-loading guns was sometimes carried in such

telescoping baskets, while larger examples held ritual materials such as the eagle down spread over the heads of the participants in ceremonies. These baskets were often completely covered with bands of fine false embroidery. The women of some villages were renowned for their skill in weaving baskets, and many of them produced baskets for sale to Euro-Americans in the late nineteenth and early twentieth centuries. Some basket types and decorations were developed for this trade, and they were often beautifully made, with extremely fine and regular weave. Many of the baskets in museum collections were made for sale and never had native use.

Conical hats twined of spruce root were both utilitarian wear and the most prestigious of crest objects. Tlingit hats were of the northern type, with flaring brims and flat tops. The lower, flaring half was skip-stitch twined with zigzag or concentric diamond self-patterns, while the top half was typically made with fine three-strand twining that left a smooth surface on which to paint. Hats for ordinary use were unpainted, while dress hats were embellished with formline paintings of animals, probably crests. The finest hats were those worn by chiefs to display crest paintings (fig.19). Some of them achieved the high status of crests in themselves. Many were surmounted by stacks of basketry cylinders, woven in very fine three-strand twining around hollow cores of light wood. The whole stack was made as a single unit. Although often described as representing the number of potlatches given by the owner, in fact the significance of the number of cylinders is not clear. It

U. of Wash., Thomas Burke Memorial, Wash. State Mus., Seattle: 2-3844.
Fig. 18. Carved elk antler figure. Found on Sauvie I., Oreg., in Chinookan territory, before 1955; height 19 cm.

seems to have been fixed for specific hats, rather than variable. In any case, a tall stack was prestigious and spectacular. Basketry hat cylinders were also attached to carved wooden crest hats.

Haida

Haida basketry production was almost entirely of twined spruce root; it primarily took the form of cylindrical storage and gathering baskets and flaring hats ("Haida: Traditional Culture," fig.11, this vol.). Haida baskets depend for their artistic qualities on elegant proportion, regular workmanship, understated bands of black dyed weft, and textural detailing of the upper border through the use of multi-strand and skip-stitch twining. Some Haida basketmakers, especially those of Alaska with closer contact to their Tlingit counterparts, used false embroidery decorations, but it was unusual. Haida basketry artists excelled at hats, making many for their own use as well as to trade to tribes on the mainland. They were never decorated by the maker, beyond self-patterns in skip-stitch twining on the brim and the textural change accomplished by weaving the crown with three-strand twining. Decoration of Haida hats was by painting, applied by male artists who, at least in some instances, were the husbands of the makers.

Amer. Mus. of Nat. Hist., New York: 19/1000.
Fig. 19. Chilkat basketry hat painted with a raven. Collected by G.T. Emmons at Chilkat, Alaska, 1869; height 31 cm.

Tsimshian

Basketry was not so important an art among the Tsimshian as among the Haida and Tlingit. Twining was the technique used, with spruce root the material. Probably many of the typical northern style twined hats in collections of Tsimshian material were woven by Tsimshian women. In the late nineteenth and twentieth century twined baskets of cedar bark, with designs in grass false embroidery, were made by weavers at Metlakatla, Alaska. Another very interesting Tsimshian basketry type, utilizing some details of form and technique otherwise found only in some Southern Coast Salish baskets and perhaps introduced from elsewhere, is represented in a small group of baskets from the Gitksan (Weber 1982:26-30). Tsimshian weavers also produced checker weave utility baskets and mats (Laforet 1984). The upper Skeena River Gitksan made and used containers of the same type as those made by Carrier Indians. These were made of birchbark sewn with spruce root and decorated by scraping away the dark surface layer of the bark in abstract foliate or geometric patterns.

Northern Wakashan and Bella Coola

Basketry was a minor art among the Haisla, Haihais, Bella Bella, Oowekeeno, Bella Coola, and Kwakiutl. Almost no elaborately decorated basketry was made, the production confined nearly entirely to utilitarian burden and storage baskets. These were either wrap-twined, openwork burden baskets or plaited cedar bark containers. The workmanship was often fine, but with very little surface decoration other than that resulting from the patterns of the weaving or the use of black-dyed strands. Basketry and weaving filled utilitarian functions, with materials and techniques essentially identical among all these neighboring tribes.

Twined, spruce root hats of the northern type were apparently made by Bella Bella and Kwakiutl weavers. Several large examples, up to a meter in diameter, are known. They apparently refer to a mythical hat that acquired the status of a crest. Work in cedar bark was elevated to the level of art in some of the elaborate red-dyed bark regalia used in the Winter ceremonies. Fine red cedar bark cord was braided, wrapped, and combined in complex constructions to form ceremonial head and neck rings. A kind of soft sculpture resulted from the use of fringes, bundles, knots, and tassels of shredded, dyed cedar bark to embellish masks and other regalia.

Nootkans

Red cedar bark and spruce root were the principal basketry materials of the Nootkan people. The techniques used included many varieties of twining, along with square and diagonal plaiting and twilling in cedar bark, especially for mats and utilitarian baskets. Wet-site archeology, the richest Northwest Coast example of which is the Ozette site on the Washington coast, has produced many examples of basketry illustrating techniques that have been practiced continually from precontact times into the twentieth century ("Prehistory of the Ocean Coast of Washington," figs. 3-4, 6, this vol.). A much older site in the same general area, Hoko River, abounds in plain and wrap-twined basketry dated to about 500 B.C., establishing the fact that twined basketry is a longstanding tradition in the region.

The best known historic examples of Nootkan basketry art are conical hats surmounted by onion-shaped bulbs and decorated with geometric designs and scenes of whales and whaling canoes or thunderbirds and lightning serpents. Only a few of these have been collected, all in the early historic period (fig.20) ("Nootkans of Vancouver Island," fig. 5, this vol.). Artists on the first European ships to visit the Nootkan tribes pictured them, and they were recorded as far south as the Columbia River (Lewis and Clark in Biddle 1814, 2:133). Details of materials and construction were apparently unique to the whalers' hats. Typical of Nootkan basketry hats, they were double, with the inner cedarbark lining joined to the outer shell in the last few rows of twining at the rim. The warp was of split spruce root. The tip of the bulb, the neck, and the rim were twined with spruce root weft, while the body of bulb and hat were twined with black-dyed cedar bark. An overlay of the chalk-white spires of the surf grass (*Phyllospadix torreyi*) formed the white background and details of the designs. Whales, canoes, whalers, and thunderbirds were geometrically stylized, in part due to the limits imposed by the basketry technique, although the heads of the lightning serpents and thunderbirds show that the weavers were capable of reproducing the character of the painted figures.

Late in the nineteenth century Nootkan weavers began working in the wrap-twining technique in the manufacture of elaborately decorated baskets, often made for sale. Wrap-twining had been long used for utility baskets, especially large, openwork burden baskets of spruce root. Specimens have been recovered from the Hoko River site, and drawings by John Webber show wrap-twined burden baskets in use and piled about the houses of Yuquot village, Nootka Sound, in 1778 ("Nootkans of Vancouver Island," fig. 4, bottom left, this vol.). The later, decorated baskets were made with split cedar bark for the warp and inner weft, with grass as the twining element. The grasses were dyed and the different colored wefts introduced to form the patterns. Bands of geometric designs were common, as were swimming birds, whales, and canoes. Many later baskets were lidded and were popular as trinket baskets in the non-native market. Although most were made for sale the quality was often very good, many of them among the finest examples of the basketmaker's

The British Mus., Mus. of Mankind, London: AM 22.229.
Fig. 20. Nootkan whaler's hat. Part of Oldman Collection attributed to Capt. James Cook, 1778; height 28.5 cm.

art. They were still being produced in some quantity in the 1980s. Some weavers in the twentieth century made bulb-top hats in imitation of the rare whaler's hats, but they have all been made using the wrap-twining technique rather than the overlayed plain twining of the early examples.

Northern and Central Coast Salish

The most distinctive baskets of the Northern and Central Coast Salish area were hard coiled baskets of cedar root using techniques, materials, and designs similar to those used throughout the Coast Salish region and into the Plateau. Many of them were undecorated, or very sparsely detailed with imbrication, a process of applying a strip of material (usually bear grass, horsetail root bark, or cherry bark) to the surface by tucking it under succeeding stitches of the sewing strand of cedar root ("Northern Coast Salish," fig. 4, this vol.). Geometric designs were produced by changing the imbrication material at each color change. Imbrication was sometimes combined with beading, a technique by which a strip of grass was laid parallel to the split-root coil while the sewing strand alternately was sewn over and under it.

Many plain, utilitarian baskets, tightly and regularly constructed, had the intrinsic beauty of subtle color, 625 texture, and fine craftsmanship. They were often used for cooking, carrying, or gathering. But even these utilitarian coiled baskets were frequently elaborately imbricated. Basketmakers often left an area of cedar root sewing uncovered, as part of the design.

Very large, covered, hamper-style baskets as well as other introduced forms catering to the non-Indian market were made by Northern and Central Coast Salish women beginning in the late nineteenth century. As elsewhere on the Northwest Coast, basketry became an important source of money in the period of adjustment to the cash economy, and Indian basketmakers of northern Washington and southern British Columbia responded to the new market. Basketry production fell off rapidly in the second quarter of the twentieth century, and by mid-century only a few baskets were being produced. Increase in interest on the part of collectors with the resultant rise in basket prices in the 1970s, as well as a developing pride in native traditions, encouraged the teaching of basketmaking and resulted in something of a revival.

Southern Coast Salish

Almost all the basketry techniques known on the Northwest Coast were practiced in one form or another by Southern Coast Salish women. Coiled cedar root hard baskets held a place in the local culture analogous to that of the bent-corner box in the central and northern Northwest Coast. Patterns were geometric, often great chevrons similar to those of the Plateau baskets. Step patterns and elaborated vertical stripes were also common (Haeberlin, Teit, and Roberts 1928; Thompson and Marr 1983).

Puget Sound hard baskets were characteristically of flaring, slightly convex form with oval cross section, but other shapes were produced, especially toward the end of the nineteenth century, when basketry became one of the chief sources of income in the economy resulting from Euro-American settlement of the region. Producing enormous numbers of baskets of all sizes for sale, Indian women were quick to respond to the demand for highly decorated baskets as well as for new forms, such as laundry hampers, fishing creels, and other introduced shapes. Lidded baskets, some of globular form, were popular. Most were heavily imbricated, and some of the finest examples of Puget Sound basketmakers' art were produced for sale from 1890 to the 1920s. The decline of basketmaking had already begun by that time, and very little traditional basketry was produced during the middle decades of the twentieth century. By the 1980s very few coiled cedar root baskets were being made by the Southern Coast Salish.

The other outstanding basketry tradition was that of the Twana. Although they also made hard coiled cedar root baskets and were not the only group to make soft twined baskets, their outstanding contribution to the art of basketry was a soft twined basket of sedge or cattail leaves decorated with overlay of bear grass and dyed cedar bark. Bold, geometric patterns, often of large zigzags or complex vertical stripes were produced by substituting cedar bark dyed black or dark red for the tan-gold bear grass overlay. Just below the rim, which was often embellished with a series of loops, a narrow band featuring a row of small animal or bird figures was woven. Although a nearly identical band appears on some other Southern Coast Salish baskets and was a common feature of Chehalis and Chinookan wrapped-twined baskets, it has come to be considered one of the recognition marks of a Twana basket. Twana soft twined baskets were prized by non-Indian residents of the area and many were produced for sale in the early twentieth century.

Southwestern Coast Salish

Chehalis and Quinault basketry was predominantly twined. Both groups practiced variants on the techniques of wrap-twining and plain twining, with the plain favored by the Quinault. Their plain twined baskets were of split spruce root, a superb basketry material, decorated with bear grass overlay often in patterns of narrow vertical lines or rectalinear meanders. The Quinault maintained trading relations with the Twana, and their baskets were similar in form and technique but much stiffer than Twana baskets due to the use of spruce root rather than cattail leaves for the structural elements (Marr 1984:46–47).

Lower Columbia Region

Basketry was a women's art, from the gathering and preparation of the materials, through the designing and construction of the basket, to its final function in gathering, cooking, and storage. Hard baskets, made of split cedar root in a coiling technique, were used in gathering roots and berries, for storage, and for cooking by the stone-boiling method. Those produced upriver, especially by the Klikitat, were usually in the form of a truncated cone, while those west of the Cascades were oval in cross-section with convex sides. These characteristics reflect the differences between coiled baskets of the Southern Coast Salish and of the Columbia Plateau generally. Some early Cowlitz baskets have a long, oval cross section (Marr 1984:fig. 10). Coiled, imbricated, cedar root basketry was produced throughout the Coast Salish area, and the technique may have been introduced to the Plateau through marriage and trade, probably between the Klikitat and the Upper Cowlitz (Haeberlin, Teit, and Roberts 1928:136–137). In both regions the design patterns were geometric, often of a series of large, vertical chevrons encircling the basket. The patterns frequently were named, but apparently without symbolic significance.

Several twining techniques were practiced in the Lower Columbia region. The most distinctive was a form of full-twist twining utilizing two colors of weft, one dyed dark brown and the other natural, to form the patterns. Soft, cylindrical baskets using this technique were made by the Wasco and Wishram, and perhaps some of their neighbors, in The Dalles area of the Plateau. The technique is related to wrap-twining, but the designs were made by switching the functions of the two colored wefts from wrapping to inner, nonwrapping weft, rather than by changing the weft itself. Designs were often representational; rows of hexagonal human heads or angular human figures and, apparently beginning in the late nineteenth century, birds, mammals, and fish. These figures were geometric and closely resembled the representational art of the Lower Columbia in other media.

The Lower Chinookans and their Salish neighbors, the Lower Chehalis and Tillamook, made soft baskets in the wrap-twining technique using bear grass weft over rush warp. Designs typically were in horizontal bands of geometric figures, often with a band of animals or birds at the rim (Marr 1984:49–51). Some baskets featured rows of animal or human figures, much smaller and less detailed than those used on the Upper Chinookan soft baskets. These southern wrapped-twined baskets differ from those of the Quileute, Makah, and Nootka in materials and design arrangement, but most obviously in the pitch of the twining (Z rather than S), which imparts a surface texture diagonally up to the right, rather than up to the left as in Nootkan wrap-twining.

Oregon Coast

The people of the northern Oregon coast shared many of the cultural features of the Chinookan tribes at the mouth of the Columbia River. Basketry was the principal medium of art expression. The Tillamook produced basketry that was almost indistinguishable from the wrap-twined work of the Chinookans and the Lower Chehalis. Plain twining was the technique usually employed on the central Oregon coast, generally in spruce root on a warp of hazel shoots, woven entirely of spruce root in fine, close twining. Designs were produced by the use of dyed weft, with details in overlay of dyed bear grass. Openwork twining was also employed for burden or clam baskets, as it was along much of the Northwest Coast.

Textiles

Tlingit

The most elaborate and prized textile of the Northwest Coast, the Chilkat blanket, was almost exclusively the product of Tlingit weavers. The blanket in its classic form

apparently dates only to the beginning of the historic period. The earliest known pictorial record is a drawing by the Russian artist Pavel Mikhailov, dated 1828, and an extremely well woven robe of unique but classic design reached the Peabody Museum in Salem, Massachusetts, in 1832 (fig. 21). Chilkat weaving was a triumph of technical innovation ("Tlingit," fig. 10, this vol). (Samuel 1982). The object was to render the subtle shapes of formline design in twining, an ambitious goal that required the invention of new techniques in a repertoire of twining stitches already in use in basketry and in the weaving of geometrically patterned ceremonial robes of mountain goat wool (fig. 22). The patterns were formed by a variety of techniques, among them full-wrap twining using two colors of weft and the insertion of extra colored wefts between twining rows of undyed wefts.

Tlingit weavers also produced shirts, aprons, leggings, and some shot pouches in classic Chilkat technique. Other examples of these objects were made by assembling pieces of Chilkat blankets that had been cut and distributed in potlatches.

Woolen blankets and flannels manufactured in Europe and the United States were introduced early in the historic period and quickly became the standard of apparel. For ceremonial use these blankets, usually of navy blue color, were decorated with appliquéd borders of red trade flannel demarcated by a row of mother-of-pearl buttons. Frequently the robes featured a crest figure in the center, worked in red cloth and buttons. The earliest record of a button blanket is a drawing by I.G. Voznesenskiĭ of the funeral of a Tlingit chief at Sitka in 1844 (Blomkvist 1972) in which three of the participants wear the blankets. They became the principal ceremonial robe.

Other ceremonial garments such as jackets, aprons, leggings, and headdresses were made of trade cloth

Peabody Mus. of Salem, Mass.: E3648.
Fig. 21. Chilkat blanket. Collected before 1832; width 1.62 m.

627

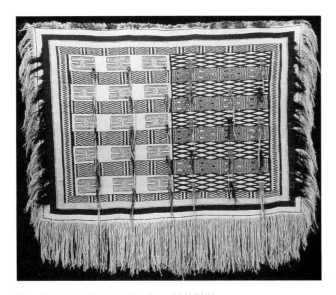

Harvard U., Peabody Mus., Cambridge, Mass.: 9-8-10/76401.
Fig. 22. Twined ceremonial robe of mountain goat wool, probably Tlingit. Collected by Capt. Benjamin Swift, southeastern Alaska, about 1800; length 1.79 m.

decorated with cloth appliqué, buttons, dentalium and abalone shells, or beads. Beadwork was not a major technique of decoration on the Northwest Coast, but wherever it was practiced, outstanding work was produced. Tlingit beadwork may have been derived from Athapaskan prototypes, but it took its own direction, utilizing totemic designs in a modified formline style and abstract foliate figures. Porcupine quillwork was also produced by the Tlingit. The designs were either geometric patterns on aprons and shamans' hats, worked in bands of wrapped quillwork, or formline patterns in which the quills were sewn directly over painted designs.

Haida

In the nineteenth century there may have been some Chilkat robes woven by Haida weavers, but for the most part these were imported from the north. However, it seems probable that some of the elegant geometric blankets first seen by Spanish explorers near the north end of the Queen Charlottes in 1794 were of Haida manufacture. They also wove yellow cedar bark blankets and capes, probably similar to those made by Nootkan and Kwakiutl weavers well into the nineteenth century. Button blankets became popular in the middle of the century and became the usual ceremonial robe. Many of them, as well as appliquéd tunics ("Haida: Traditional Culture," fig. 7 right, this vol.), utilized classic formline designs in red cloth, button, or dentalium appliqué.

Tsimshian

The Tsimshian have been credited with the invention and perfection of the technique called Chilkat weaving, named

for the Tlingit people who produced much of that style of work in the late nineteenth century (Emmons 1907:329). They may well have been among those who perfected the techniques needed to translate formline designs into twined tapestry, and they probably did weave blankets in the early historic period, but by the middle of the nineteenth century the Tsimshian had ceased producing woven dance blankets. They were quick to adopt the button blanket, and Tsimshian button blankets were particularly innovative and handsome. Many of them incorporated true formline patterns into the appliqué design of red cloth on navy blue trade blanket. Tsimshian button blanket designs tended to be more narrative in content than those of other tribes. Often several incidents in the same story were illustrated on the robe. Buttons were used conservatively, unlike their ostentatious elaboration on the blankets of some other tribes, especially the Kwakiutl. Although the Chilkat blanket was highly regarded and considered the special prerogative of chiefs, button blankets had a high status with the Tsimshian, perhaps because of their potential for very specific crest display.

Bella Coola

Bella Coola weaving consisted primarily of robes twined of yellow cedar bark or of mountain goat wool yarn. Some Bella Coola woolen robes from the late nineteenth century were embroidered with elaborate designs in colored yarns on the white background. Bella Coola were masters at working with shredded red cedar bark, and their ceremonial regalia in that material—head and neck rings, embellishment on masks and other paraphernalia—was spectacular. After the development of the appliquéd ceremonial blanket of trade cloth and buttons in the mid-nineteenth century, Bella Coola artists also produced such blankets.

Kwakiutl

The twined robe of yellow cedar bark was the principal textile produced by Kwakiutl weavers. Mountain goat wool yarn was also used for twined robes and capes, and after the advent of the woolen trade blanket, raveled yarn was sometimes substituted for the native materials, producing robes with decorative, colored, vertical stripes. The Kwakiutl were also noted for their button blankets, which were distinctive for their broad, red borders heavily decorated with geometric designs in button appliqué. As usual for button blankets, crest designs appliquéd in red cloth and buttons were centered on the usually navy blue, but sometimes green, field of the robe.

Kwakiutl women excelled in the production of twilled cedar bark mats, which were typically plaited on the diagonal so that there was no discrete warp and weft.

Nootkans

Nootkan women wove blankets of both wool and yellow cedar bark. Typically these were twined rather than twilled, some of the finest bark blankets exhibiting elegant texturing through spacing of the twining rows and some with lower borders of zigzag pattern twining using woolen wefts dyed yellow and brown. Some were painted with designs of mythical beings ("Nootkans of Vancouver Island," fig. 5c, this vol.), as were late nineteenth-century dance blankets made of muslin and canvas.

Central Coast Salish

Mountain goat wool and dog wool blankets were the main products of Central Coast Salish looms at the time of Europeans' arrival on the Northwest Coast and continued to be until the early years of the twentieth century. Most of these were relatively plain, with twill-weave self-designs and simple stripes of colored wool sometimes crossing to form a sort of plaid. Later, strips torn from commercial blankets or fabrics were used for the stripes. Much more spectacular blankets, with complex, geometrically patterned borders or entirely covered with elaborate designs composed of rectangles, triangles, and diamonds were being woven in the early years of European contact (Kissell 1929; Willoughby 1910; W.C. Orchard 1926). There is no good evidence of their having been made in precontact times, and they may be a product of the availability of commercial yarn or raveled cloth. However, the techniques used to produce them—spinning woolen yarn, twining, twilling, and plain or tabby weave—were all present in prehistoric times. Several such blankets and related woven bands were collected by the United States Exploring Expedition in 1841 and recorded in 1847 ("Central Coast Salish," fig. 5, this vol.)

The weaving of elaborately pattern-twined blankets ceased in the late nineteenth century, and only a few have survived. In the early 1960s two Central Coast Salish women, Adeleine Lorenzetto and Mary Peters, began to experiment with blanket weaving techniques, and, encouraged by Oliver Wells, a local non-Indian interested in the native cultures, they and others began weaving patterned blankets. By the 1980s the art had been revived, and a number of Salish weavers were experimenting with traditional designs and new directions in pattern-twining (Wells 1966; P. Gustafson 1980:103–117; Johnson and Bernick 1986).

Southern Coast Salish

The principal textiles produced by Puget Sound women were mats of cattail leaves, tunics and kilts of shredded red cedar bark, and blankets woven of yarn spun of mountain goat wool or the wool of dogs, sometimes with the addition of other materials such as duck feathers and fireweed down. Use of wool shorn from dogs bred and raised for the purpose was mentioned by early explorers (Vancouver 1798, 1:266), and many blankets have been described as having been made of dog wool, but the fibers have not been identified with any certainty. These blankets were all primarily utilitarian and undecorated. The woolen blankets were finger-woven on a two-roller weaving frame, which allowed the weaver to produce a selvage on all four edges through the technique of looping both ends of the warp over a single rod or stretched cord. The surface of the textile was patterned using various twill weaves to form zigzags or concentric diamonds. Stripes of color were often added by introducing dyed warps and wefts. In the late nineteenth century these were often of strips torn from commercial cloth. Elaborately patterned blankets were not commonly made by the Southern Coast Salish, but tumplines of complex designs were twined, often using commercial yarns or raveled cloth over warps of Indian hemp.

The Twentieth Century

The closing years of the nineteenth century saw the art traditions of many of the Northwest Coast peoples at a low ebb. Heavy losses in population, changing economic climate, and the efforts of missionaries and government had eroded the motivations for art. In some groups almost no art was produced, and what was done had little resemblance to what had preceded it. On the other hand, some art traditions continued unabated, that of the Kwakiutl being the best example.

In the mid-twentieth century the situation began to change. Traditional Northwest Coast Indian art began to be discovered by artists and critics in the 1940s (Carpenter 1975; Jonaitis 1981a). Exhibitions of Native American material in prestigious museums honored as "art" what had been denounced by the authorities for a century as backward and debased. Lavishly illustrated books and catalogues were published, featuring the masks, rattles, and boxes that had long been characterized as grotesque and curious.

In the 1960s and 1970s an awakening of pride in Native identity began among Indians generally, and talented young people worked to recover their own heritages. In many cases that meant reading the books and searching the museum collections in order to revive the structure of art traditions that had nearly been destroyed.

Although Tlingit art suffered many of the same setbacks to which the arts of other tribes were subjected in the later years of the nineteenth century, the social structure, and hence the awareness of prerogative and clan emblems remained strong, and many clan emblems and items of chiefly paraphernalia were retained. For this reason it has been possible for some aspects of traditional

Tlingit ceremonial activity to continue, but it may also be that because there was still a fair amount of old ceremonial material available for use during the period of the revitalization of art elsewhere on the coast, the urgency of the revival was not felt so strongly in southeastern Alaska.

In the early 1960s a training program was instituted in Port Chilkoot, Alaska, by Carl Heinmiller, a community leader interested in traditional art. A number of the more successful contemporary Tlingit artists were associated with that program as students and instructors, and some of them, notably Nathan Jackson, produced fine traditional art in all media and forms and continued the training of Indian artists.

Haida art activity was at a very low ebb at the beginning of the twentieth century. A few old and very talented men carried it on for a few years, but in the intervening time until the surge of activity began again in the 1960s the only art produced was a shadow of the past. That lamentable situation was turned around, and in the following decades Haida artists produced pieces that reflected the power of the Haida tradition. The art of Bill Reid was the first of the era to raise awareness in the public to Haida art ("Mythology," fig. 1, this vol.) (Shadbolt 1986). In 1969 Robert Davidson carved and raised the first totem pole in Massett in nearly a century. He created others that are unsurpassed by the poles of the old villages (figs. 8, 23). Other Haida artists have picked up the frazzled ends of the old tradition and carried it forward to every medium.

In the case of the northern two-dimensional formline system, the turning point can, to a large degree, be dated to the publication of *Northwest Coast Indian Art: an Analysis of Form* (Holm 1965), which became a primer for the artists struggling for an understanding of their ancestors' art. Silver and gold engraving and serigraph prints (H. Stewart 1979; Blackman, Hall, and Rickard 1981) led the activity, and exciting variations on Haida art began to appear. Many times more silver bracelets were engraved in the 20 years following the beginning of this revitalization than had been made in the previous century, and many of them were the equal of the best of their predecessors. Boxes, chests, bowls, and other kinds of formline-detailed objects were produced.

The understanding of traditional art principles essentially disappeared in all Tsimshian groups by the early twentieth century, although a few artists continued to work in a much modified style (Garfield 1955, 1955a). In the 1960s a training program for artists was instituted at Hazleton, in Gitksan territory. This program, under the name 'Ksan, brought artists and teachers from other tribes as well as non-native Northwest Coast art scholars to attempt to reestablish traditional art principles in the area. Many of the best Native artists of the late twentieth century received at least part of their training there. They made enormous strides in reinstituting the Tsimshian

sculptural tradition. Many masks, rattles, and frontlets were carved, as well as totem poles, some of which were made as traditional memorials. Others, such as monumental "Big Beaver" pole by the Nishga artist Norman Tait, raised in front of the Field Museum of Natural History, Chicago, in 1982 to mark the opening of an exhibit of Northwest Coast and Arctic cultures, were statements of Indian involvement and ethnicity.

Although by the 1980s Bella Coola art had not experienced the strong revival felt by the art traditions of some other areas, the art itself has had a major influence on the work of artists from other tribes. Many of them admired the strengths and subtleties of Bella Coola sculpture and painting and experimented with the forms.

The revitalization of art had a less dramatic effect on the Kwakiutl than on many other Northwest Coast groups because their production of carvings and paintings for ceremonial use had never ceased. Artists like Mungo Martin (fig. 23) and Willie Seaweed (fig. 24) who had been producing art for traditional use since the early years of the twentieth century, were still working in the 1950s; and their children were continuing in their footsteps (Holm 1983). Despite the official prohibition of ceremonial activity, potlatching and dancing continued almost unabated, with the consequent privilege display and its necessary art. The burgeoning market for Native art motivated a great increase in activity in the 1960s and many young Kwakiutl artists participated in it. Serigraph prints of crest figures and mythical creatures became very popular (Blackman, Hall, and Rickard 1981). The first significant examples in terms of the non-native market were commercially reproduced serigraphs of the paintings of Henry Speck. One of the first artists to produce silkscreen prints was Tony Hunt, the grandson and apprentice of Mungo Martin. The increase in potlatching in the 1960s and 1970s and the subsequent greater involvement by artists in ceremonial activities motivated the designing and making of the traditional dancing robe, the button blanket (fig. 25); and in the 1980s many new ones were produced.

Kwakiutl sculpture continued almost unabated during the early twentieth century years when it had nearly ceased over much of the coast. From the mid-1930s until the late 1950s, no memorial poles were erected. In the 1960s it again became customary to raise a large memorial pole at a potlatch commemorating a deceased chief. Fine masks were being made in the 1980s, some of them for traditional use and some for sale in the Indian art market. Many of the same artists who were widely recognized for their prints were also producing sculpture.

Nootkan two-dimensional art was produced continually from the prehistoric period onward, but it gradually diminished in quality and power in the twentieth century until the 1970s, when a remarkable reassertion of the tradition was launched by Nootkan artists who had

Fig. 23. Selected 20th-century Northwest Coast artists. top, Doug Cranmer, (b. 1927), a Nimpkish Kwakiutl, and Donna Ambers (b. 1953). Cranmer taught at 'Ksan, the Vancouver Museum, and Alert Bay (Macnair, Hoover, and Neary 1980:179). Photograph by Vicki Jensen, Alert Bay, B.C., 1978. bottom left, Artist Bill Reid of Haida descent (b. 1920) in his studio in Vancouver, B.C. bottom center, Robert Davidson (b. 1946) working on a totem pole at his studio in Whiterock, B.C. bottom left and center, Photographs by Ulli Steltzer, 1986. bottom right, Mungo Martin, a Kwakiutl from Ft. Rupert (b. about 1881, d. 1962). Having learned carving from his stepfather Charlie James, he became one of the most important transmitters of the art, as the teacher of his son-in-law Henry Hunt and his grandson Tony Hunt, Doug Cranmer, and others. He oversaw the restoration of totem poles under the auspices of the U. of B.C. and helped replicate old poles on display in the museum park (De Laguna 1963; Macnair, Hoover, and Neary 1980:185). Photograph by Peter Holburn, 1951.

become aware of the strengths of their ancient art heritage and set out to reestablish it as a living entity. Foremost among them were Joe David of Clayoquot, Ron Hamilton of Alberni, and Art Thompson of Nitinaat; many others were a part of the movement (Blackman, Hall, and Rickard 1981). These artists produced both for traditional use and for the art market. Much of their two-dimensional production was in the form of serigraphs, but they also painted screens, dance robes, and drums.

Many of the same artists who revitalized Nootkan two-

Fig. 24. Willie Seaweed (b. 1873, d. 1967), Kwakiutl, and the last hamatsa mask he made, in 1954. left, Crooked beak mask painted with oil enamels. Length 105 cm. right, Seaweed holding an elbow adz. Photograph by Sidney Gerber, Blunden Harbour, B.C., 1954.

dimensional art in the 1970s and 1980s were also sculptors, and their work often expressed extraordinary imagination and power. They produced memorial poles, masks, rattles, and every kind of traditional sculptural object, both for Indian use and for sale. These artists were also deeply involved in the revitalization of traditional ceremonial activities, many of which had nearly disappeared in the early twentieth century.

The long period of development and refinement of Coast Salish art came to an end in the nineteenth century, and it lay dormant until the late 1970s and early 1980s, when several published articles and exhibitions dealing with Central Coast Salish art revived an interest on the part of Salish artists. A number of them began to experiment with and work in this style in wood carving and other media, in particular serigraph prints, as exemplified by the work of the Musqueam artist Susan Point.

Since the 1950s a number of non-Indian artists and artists of Indian ancestry other than Northwest Coast have been involved in the production of art in the Northwest Coast traditions. Some of them have been closely associated with Northwest Coast Indian people in training artists, in ceremonial activities, and producing masks and other material for Indian ceremonial use. Among those are Steve Brown, Bill Holm, John Livingston, Duane Pasco, and the Cherokee artist Lelooska

Fig. 25. Kwakiutl button blanket. Collected before 1966 at Ft. Rupert, B.C.; width 180 cm.

(Falk 1976). Opinions as to the propriety of non-Northwest Coast natives working in the art traditions vary widely, among both Indians and non-Indians, but without any question the influence of some of these artists on the remarkable revival of Northwest Coast art has been a major one.

632

The Indian Shaker Church

PAMELA T. AMOSS

The Indian Shaker Church of the Northwest is an indigenous Native American religious movement. Shakers believe that their religion was a new instrument provided by God to Indian people in their time of great need. In the closing decades of the nineteenth century Puget Sound Indians had seen profound changes in their way of life since the hastily negotiated treaties of the 1850s and the Indian revolt that followed. Indians continued to die in large numbers from diseases introduced in the eighteenth century. A flood of settlers had preempted traditional Indian fishing, hunting, and gathering sites. Indians themselves were being moved to reservations where an alien economic and political system replaced Indian institutions. Christian missionaries daily challenged the old beliefs with new concepts of supernatural power. Although some Indians adjusted successfully to the new order, many could not. Alcohol addiction and symptoms of social disorganization were widespread.

Origins and History

In 1882 a Southern Coast Salish Indian, *səqʷsáq̓tən*, known as John Slocum (fig. 1), reported receiving an extraordinary revelation (Castile 1982:165). At this time Slocum, who was from the Squaxin group (Ballard 1920; Eells 1985; M.W. Smith 1936–1939; Colson 1965), was living on Hammersley Inlet at the southern end of Puget Sound. Shaker traditions report that Slocum, then about 40, fell ill and died (Barnett 1957; Eells 1886; Gunther 1949; Mooney 1896). But while his kinsmen were still making funeral arrangements, he revived, announcing salvation to Indians who would repudiate gambling, drinking, and smoking and reject the ministrations of native shamans. Slocum also said that God had promised a medicine for the faithful that would eclipse the power of the old shamans (Barnett 1957:22). At Slocum's request his relatives built a church for him on Shaker Point opposite Squaxin Island (Harris Teo, personal communication 1988). There he preached his message to the many Indians attracted by news of his miraculous return from the dead.

A year later Slocum again fell sick (according to some traditions because he had succumbed to a temptation to gamble). This time his relatives were sure he would die. In

desperation, they called in a shaman. Slocum's wife, *xʷbúliča*, or Mary, whose faith in his vision was strong, left the house in protest. As she wept and prayed she was overcome by an uncontrollable shaking. Still shaking, she reentered the house and prayed over her husband. Her ministrations restored him and her shaking was hailed as the medicine God had promised.

The news of Slocum's second escape from death through the "shake," as Mary's involuntary trembling was called, spread throughout the southern Puget Sound region. When Slocum called a meeting at his church in summer 1883, Indians abandoned their regular activities to hear the prophet's message. Many experienced the same shaking power that had overcome Mary. This meeting marked the beginning of the movement's explosive growth. On the nearby Skokomish reservation the followers of a local prophet, Big Bill, took up Slocum's message (Eells 1886:161). Other early converts to have great influence later were *yáwələx*, known as Louis Yowaluck (fig. 1) or Mud Bay Louis and his brother *sáwəckət*, called Mud Bay Sam (M.W. Smith 1936–1939).

Most Indian agents and missionaries to Southern Coast Salish tried to suppress Shakerism when they became aware of it. A notable exception was the Presbyterian missionary Matthew G. Mann, who endeavored to bring Shakers into his fold. But efforts to extirpate or incorporate failed to staunch Shaker enthusiasm. Shakers defied or evaded restrictions. For example, when the Indian agent on the Skokomish reservation forbade public Shaker services, the believers held clandestine services off the reservation.

A turning point for Shakers came in 1887 when Congress passed the Dawes Severalty Act providing that Indians who received allotments, or who left the reservation and adopted "the habits of civilized life," were to be accorded full citizenship status. Shaker leaders sought advice from a non-Indian, a lawyer named James Wickersham, who told them the act guaranteed them freedom of worship. He advised them to seek legal recognition as a church to secure their rights. In 1892, the Shakers legally constituted themselves as a church. Mud Bay Louis was chosen "headman" and John Slocum, though still the acknowledged founder, became one of the several "elders" of the church. John Slocum died in 1897 and Louis died in

633

Fig. 1. Shaker Church leaders John Slocum (left) and Louis Yowaluck. Photographed 1883–1892.

1905. In 1907 Mud Bay Sam was elected headman.

In 1910 the Shakers turned to another non-Indian, Milton Giles, justice of the peace at Olympia, to help them incorporate under Washington state law. At his suggestion they created a formal leadership structure modeled on Protestant churches of the period. There was a bishop and a board of elders to be elected every four years at the church convention. The bishop was to appoint ministers for the local churches and traveling missionaries. The first bishop elected under the new laws was Mud Bay Sam. The 1910 organization survived into the 1980s with only minor modifications.

Assured of legal protection, the church expanded steadily until the 1930s. Early growth among Skokomish and Squaxin was rapid; subsequent expansion to other areas was slower. Ties of blood and marriage between communities were the primary links for the dissemination of new ideas, but it was the Shakers who traveled to help the sick who made the dramatic appeal to converts. People the Shakers cured often embraced the faith immediately, bringing their relatives along, but converted or not, they became living witnesses to the power of God in the Shaker faith.

The first expansion beyond the vicinity of Southern Lushootseed and Twana was south to the Chehalis (Southwestern Coast Salish) at Oakville in 1883 (fig. 2). Shortly afterward, two Quinaults, converted during a visit to Puget Sound, successfully proselytized among the Quinault, the Queets, and the Lower Chehalis at Gray's Harbor (Olson 1936:170). About the same time a Cowlitz heard the Shaker message from relatives in Chehalis, and in 1890 Shakers from the Cowlitz area took the word east to the Yakimas (Barnett 1957:70). The Yakima church was soon to become one of the most active in the state, spreading the word into Oregon and California. Shakerism came to the Colville Reservation in 1914 but had little impact until the 1940s (Schultz and Walker 1967:168).

Generally, the eastward movement of Shakerism was slowed by the resistance of entrenched Christian missionaries or local prophet movements (Du Bois 1939).

The Shaker faith spread to British Columbia through the Clallam community at Jamestown, which was converted around 1885 (Langness 1959). Before 1900 Clallams from Jamestown carried Shakerism across the Strait of Juan de Fuca to Clallam and Songhees communities on southeastern Vancouver Island. In 1903 Shakerism also spread to the Makah (Colson 1953:238). A Musqueam woman, converted on Vancouver Island, brought the word home to her reserve adjacent to the city of Vancouver (Kew 1970:240). After initial successes, Shakerism grew more slowly in British Columbia, and in the 1980s its influence was restricted to the Salishan peoples of southern Vancouver Island and the mainland opposite.

Shakerism moved to the Warm Springs Reservation, Oregon, and then to the Klamath (Stern 1966:223). Yakima Shakers took the word to Indians at Siletz around 1923. In 1926 Shakerism was carried from Siletz to the Yurok at Requa in northern California and from them to the Tolowa at Smith River. Hupas first joined the movement in the early 1930s. In the 1970s the Smith River Church was the hub of California Shakerism, the site of the annual August gatherings celebrating the coming of the faith to California (Sackett 1973:123).

In response to sporadic pressure for greater regional autonomy, there were at one time separate bishops for California, British Columbia, and Washington. Although this practice was abandoned, in the 1970s church laws were amended to provide for elders elected from British Columbia, Oregon, and California. Nevertheless, regionalism has never been a serious problem for the church (Gunther 1949:66; Currie 1958).

In the beginning, the paramount problem facing the church was the opposition of missionaries and Indian agents, obstacles Shakers overcame when they learned to use the law to protect their religious freedom. Since then dissension among Shakers themselves has posed the gravest threat to church survival. Shaker respect for individual inspiration and distaste for institutionalized authority engenders a continual tension between the demands of autonomy and unanimity. Disagreements over ritual and doctrine surface often. Even in the early church, differences between John Slocum's closest disciples, Mary Slocum and Mud Bay Louis, threatened the solidarity of the group (Barnett 1957:227).

The most damaging schism in Shaker history divided those who wanted to bring the church closer to Protestant Christianity from those who wanted its unique tradition preserved unchanged. Those favoring a Protestant model for Shaker ritual read from the Bible in services. The opposition claimed that Shakers have no need for written Scripture because they receive inspiration directly "in the Spirit." The Bible, thus, became the major symbol of the

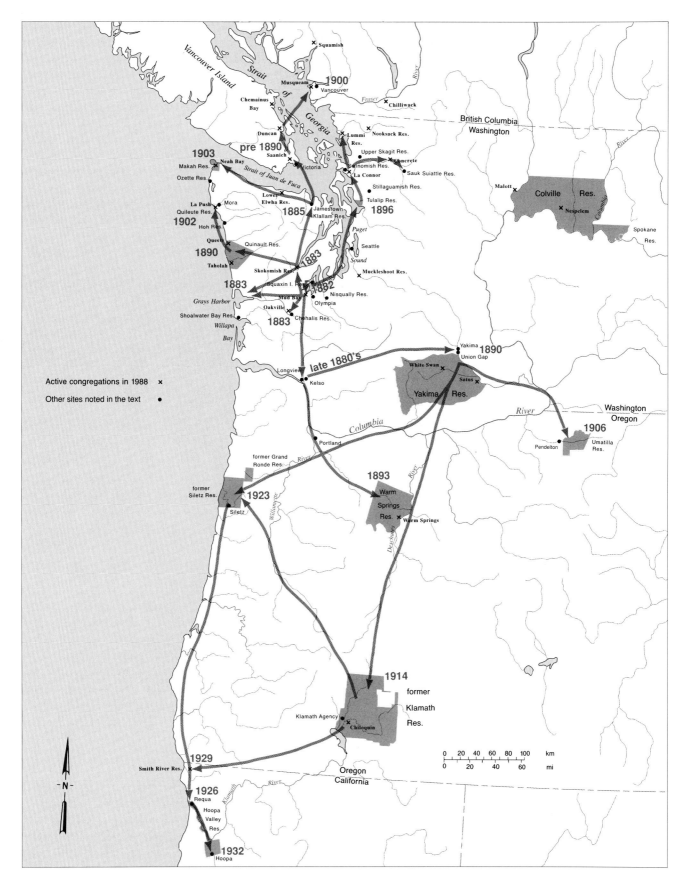

Fig. 2. Diffusion of the Indian Shaker Church with probable dispersal routes, dates of entry, and congregations active in 1988 (Barnett 1957; Kew 1970; Stern 1966; Harris Teo, personal communication 1988).

Active congregations in 1988 x
Other sites noted in the text •

dispute. In 1927 the differences surfaced in competition for the office of bishop. When the pro-Bible group elected William Kitsap from Tulalip, the conservative incumbent, Peter Heck, refused to step down (Indian Shaker Church of Washington and the Northwest for 1942; Barnett 1957: 114; Gunther 1949:66; Pettitt 1950:101; Richen 1974a). For years some Shaker communities were divided between supporters of Bishop Heck and adherents of Bishop Kitsap. In 1945, after a series of legal confrontations, the Snohomish County superior court imposed a solution that created two separate churches. Bishop Heck's supporters retained the title Indian Shaker Church and Bishop Kitsap's group incorporated as the Indian Full Gospel Church (Pettitt 1950:102; Richen 1974a:31ff.). The court decreed that although individual congregations might affiliate with either organization, all church property belonged to the Indian Shaker Church. The formal separation persisted in the 1980s.

There are other independent Shaker groups. Dissensions at Yakima gave birth in 1953 to the Independent Shaker Church, which advocates use of the Bible in ritual but is otherwise conservative. There are two small Shaker churches, one in California at Hupa and one in Pendleton, Oregon, which were chartered separately to avoid involvement in the schismatic disputes (Richen 1974a:ix).

There is one small group, the Annie Lee Shakers in Chiloquin, Oregon, affiliated with the Indian Full Gospel Church, whose name suggests a historical connection with a nineteenth-century Christian sect. The name was supplied by a Methodist missionary who saw similarities between Indian Shakers and the United Society of Believers, popularly known as Shakers (Gunther 1949:68). Founded in England in 1947 by Anne Lee, the Society had communities in the northeastern United States in the nineteenth century. Despite some parallels in ritual, there is no evidence of any connection between the United Society of Believers and any Indian Shaker group (Barnett 1957:333).

Some members of the Full Gospel Church attend Indian Shaker Church conventions, and many younger Shakers feel free to worship with any faction. Some congregations change affiliation when membership changes. Although the schism seems to have had little effect on the spread of Shakerism in British Columbia (Currie 1958), it may have impeded the growth of the new churches in Oregon and California and sapped the strength of some well-established churches in western Washington (Sackett 1973:124; Pettitt 1950:101).

Beliefs and Practices

According to historians of the Shaker movement, both Christian and aboriginal Indian ideas contributed to Shaker doctrine and practice (Spier 1935:50; Gunther 1949:60; Barnett 1957:285). It is also possible that the ultimate source of many Christian-like elements was the pre-Christian Plateau revitalization movement known as the Prophet Dance (Spier 1935:49; Suttles 1957:389). During the half-century preceding Slocum's revelations Indian society in the Northwest was alive with ideological and political activity. Slocum and his close associates were surely influenced by this intellectual climate, but it is difficult to establish a direct connection between Shakerism and any earlier prophets, other than Big Bill. Although Shakerism was seen as a totally new message, its early adherents did not abandon all the teachings they had received from their own traditions, so there are elements from the aboriginal Puget Sound guardian spirit religion that appear transformed in the Shaker system.

The distinctive Shaker sign of the cross, repeated three times, which opens and closes every Shaker prayer, follows the Roman Catholic form. Some Puget Sound Shakers still say the words accompanying the sign in the Lushootseed language, as do some Shaker communities even in Oregon and California. In British Columbia the words are in Squamish (Wayne Suttles, personal communication 1975), Halkomelem, or Northern Straits, and in the Yakima area people use Sahaptin words. Although Yakima Shakers commonly preach and testify in their native Sahaptin language, for many congregations the sign of the cross is all that remains of the aboriginal languages in ritual.

Shakers believe in an all-powerful God, in His Son, Jesus, and in the "Spirit of God" that comes to them when they receive the "shake." It is the Spirit who gives them the power to heal, prophesy, and exorcise evil. Like the old guardian spirits, the Shaker Spirit comes to a person in a trance experience but is always present in a less obvious form. Unlike the guardian spirits, who left their owners before death, the Shaker Spirit stays with the believer when death comes and takes him "home" to heaven (J.M. Collins 1950:408). All Shakers are expected to receive the "shake" when they join. The stronger the trance manifestations that accompany the involuntary trembling, the stronger the contact with divine power. Thereafter, a person may experience the trance and trembling whenever he attends a shake, or only occasionally, depending on the prompting of his individual inspiration. Shakers believe that all sins, especially the sins of drinking, smoking, and gambling, interfere with a person's ability to receive the power of the spirit. They believe that a soul polluted by sin will express itself in a sick body. Sickness can also be caused by sorrow or by supernatural accidents such as soul loss or assaults by ghosts or malicious shamans.

Shaker respect for individual autonomy fosters and protects variation. Furthermore, in Indian tradition, people learn from observation, not exposition. The young are expected to watch carefully and imitate closely. Whether raised in the religion or converted as adults, Shakers learn rituals through participation and dogmas from testimonies and sermons. It is assumed that each person will come to understand the rules by which the Spirit operates from interpretations of illness and from stories of miraculous cures. Close conformity in belief is neither enforced nor valued.

Early Shakers saw themselves locked in mortal combat with the powers of shamans. They mobilized the spirit of God to protect the community against those dangerous forces. However, in some Shaker communities, people believed that the spirit guardian of a convert to Shakerism would also be converted to the service of God (J.M. Collins 1950:403, 1974:172). In the 1980s some Shakers in western Washington and southwestern British Columbia saw the revitalized tradition of aboriginal spirit dancing as a special form of help that Shakers could bring into harmony with the power of God for their own good and the good of the community at large (Amoss 1978; Currie 1958; Kew 1970). On the other hand, there were many Shakers, especially those from Yakima, who believed that a Shaker must make an exclusive commitment to the Church (Darleene A. Fitzpatrick, personal communication 1975).

Churches and Gatherings

Churches are usually rectangular wooden structures with modest bell towers. In most cases the entrances face west and the altar, or prayer table, is set in an alcove on the eastern wall (Barnett 1957:218). The church is usually painted white inside, and Shakers believe it should be kept spotlessly clean. On the prayer table are candles, bells, and a plain cross. There are usually candle sconces along the

walls and candelabra hanging from the ceiling. Although most churches have electric wiring, only candles are used for services because the candle flame itself is believed to have power to cleanse and heal. Hand bells are the only Shaker musical instruments (fig. 3). Seating is provided on benches around three sides of the room, but the center is always left open except when a few chairs may be put out to accommodate sick people seeking help. Men sit on the benches to the left of the entry, women on the right.

If a congregation has no church, members hold services in their homes; a prayer table occupies a prominent place in the living room of every devout Shaker (fig. 4). Although most congregations have a minister, any experienced Shaker can lead the meeting, and many services are conducted without a minister present. In the 1980s ministers were elected by their congregations and confirmed by the bishop. The crucial qualifications were good moral character, strong commitment to the Shaker way, and a willingness to serve.

In the early 1970s under the leadership of Bishop William Martin, several congregations began raising money to replace or repair old churches. The new building on the site of the early church at Mud Bay, known as the mother church, was built through donations from the entire Shaker group and from outsiders.

Formal Shaker rituals include regularly scheduled Sunday meetings, "shakes," funerals, weddings, and dedications. In some parts of the region, shakes are scheduled regularly on Fridays or Saturdays and rotate from community to community during the year (Barnett 1957:79; Kew 1970:244). They may also be held whenever needed to help the sick or bring in a convert. Curing

left, U. of Wash. Lib., Special Coll., Seattle: NA 1121; right, Smithsonian, NAA: 86-11561.
Fig. 3. Interiors of Shaker churches. left, Rectangular wooden building with Clallam participants behind the prayer table where 3 bells of the type used in the service are displayed. Second from left is Susie Sampson Peter, a well-known Upper Skagit story teller. Photograph by Albert Henry Barnes, possibly Jamestown, Wash., 1895–1910. right, Drawing of a service, showing people "getting the power" and transmitting it to 2 men in the center. On the left 2 Shakers are brushing evil off the man facing the prayer table and one woman is helping the man on the right. Here a man is seated on the bench at the right; in the 1970s and 1980s only women occupied the benches on the right. Drawing by an unidentified student at the Quileute Day School, Mora, Wash., 1906–1907.

THE INDIAN SHAKER CHURCH

Fig. 4. Prayer table in the house of Daniel Dan, a minister of the Indian Shaker church. The table contains crosses (an essential symbol in the church), bells (rung during services to accompany the singing), candles, and a copy of Barnett's (1957) book on the Shaker church, an expression of the family's interest in the history of their faith. On the wall are a crucifix, pictures of Jesus, and a license, showing that Dan has the right to function as a Shaker minister. Licenses issued to Shaker ministers and missionaries in the early 20th century showed that the church was recognized by the state of Washington and gave ministers some protection from persecution. Photograph by Wayne Suttles, Musqueam Indian Reserve, Vancouver, B.C., 1963.

sessions usually continue for a series of three (in British Columbia, four) nights, or until the patient recovers. The same pattern is followed when a new member is initiated.

Sunday services, the most formal of Shaker ceremonies, include four elements: first, the minister or surrogate opens with a prayer; second, the minister gives a sermon; third, the whole congregation sings to the rhythm of the handbells and forms a procession moving counterclockwise three times around the church; fourth, beginning with the women every member of the congregation circles the church in a set pattern touching hands with everyone else (Barnett 1957:247ff.). At Sunday services or at any Shaker gathering, as people first enter, each goes around the room shaking hands with everyone there. For Sunday services Shakers may wear the long white robe with a blue ribbon cross appliquéd on the front that every Shaker receives when he joins the church. A tradition begun in Slocum's generation, this robe, called a "garment," symbolizes both the purity of the Shaker faith and the protection it offers the believer. Although the robes are worn only on Sundays, many Shakers wear white or pastel outfits to all church gatherings.

At shakes the invocation and sermon are often omitted or greatly abbreviated; the procession and period of prayer and singing are expanded to encompass healing the sick or initiating new members. As people circle the room or march in place to the rhythm set by the bells, some of them begin to "get the power," manifested by a rapid trembling of hands and body (fig. 3). Converts and sick or troubled people seeking help stand or sit in the open center of the room. Shakers inspired to help particular patients "brush" the sufferers with their hands to remove the evil

causing the illness (Barnett 1957:164ff.). A healer may pass a lighted candle lightly over the patient's body or raise his bells and direct the sound at a person he wants to "bless." Before the meeting disbands, Shakers who have received an insight into a patient's troubles often stand up and explain the cause or suggest a remedy.

Other than a minister, there are no formal roles within the structure of Shaker ritual. People of either sex or any age are free to participate as fully or as little as they like. Some are known to have special gifts that operate when they shake: healing, foretelling the future, sensing who is troubled and unhappy, finding a lost soul, divining the source of illness and the solution for it. Although everyone is free to follow his own inspiration, Shakers believe it is the united efforts that mobilize the power of the Spirit. Conversely, they attribute failures to lack of group harmony.

Shakers have a distinctive way of living. Although moral and ethical behavior is considered a matter of the individual's conscience, the prohibitions on drinking, smoking, and gambling instituted by John Slocum remain an essential part of Shaker practice. Most Shakers light candles on the home prayer table and ring their bells when they pray morning and evening, and when they ask a blessing before and after every meal.

The general Christian admonition to practice charity has a deeper meaning to Shakers because a failure of charity within the congregation or the family will spoil the harmony that mobilizes the Spirit to cure the sick. Furthermore, Shakers teach that they must always be ready to minister to the sick or troubled. They do not restrict their help to church members but offer it freely to anyone who asks. So important is this tradition that active Shakers travel almost every weekend. Whether the cure is successful or not, the helpers must not accept any pay. This practice, instituted by Slocum, sharply differentiated them from shamans, who always expected payment. The only obligation on those who call the Shakers is to offer the best hospitality their means allow.

Shakerism affirms a life after death, but the overwhelming emphasis is on living this life well. By avoiding the contamination of sin and the disrupting effects of anger, a Shaker hopes to be always ready to receive the power of God. By participating actively in the "shake" Shakers continually renew contact with the power and extend its influence to others. By testifying publicly about their own conversions, Shakers encourage others and strengthen their own convictions. By explaining the source of illness or trouble afflicting a sick person, they help the victim respond to the Spirit. An observer remarked on the fruits of the Shaker way: "inwardly they are filled with kindly feelings which cannot be mistaken, for it actually radiates from their faces" (Waterman 1924: 507).

For many years Shakers had been successful helping

people overcome dependence on alcohol or tobacco. In the 1970s they began helping people addicted to illegal drugs as well. In an effort to reach Indians in institutions, in 1975 Bishop Harris Teo began holding services at MacNeil Island Federal Penitentiary, Washington, and in Bureau of Indian Affairs residential schools.

It is almost impossible to determine the total number of Indians who consider themselves members of the Shaker Church in the 1980s because few of the local churches keep membership rolls, and it is not clear who should be counted as a member—only those currently active, or anyone who has ever joined? Nevertheless, it is clear that even under the more inclusive definition, the total number has never been very large. In the 1970s there were estimated to be fewer than 1,000 active Shakers in all branches of the church (Richen 1974a:13).

Numbers, however, do not adequately represent the influence of the church on Native Americans. The teachings of the Shaker Church are well known to local Indians who respect Shakers for their generosity, sobriety, and power to heal. The position of the church in local Indian history is unique. It was the first fully Indian institution to achieve legal respectability in the eyes of the dominant society at a time when other forms of Indian spiritual expression were actively suppressed. Furthermore, when Indian society was racked by hostilities and fears generated by the pressures of alien political and economic control, Shakerism affirmed the principle of Indians working together to help each other against the specters of illness and sin.

Shaker belief provides, as any religious system must, an explanation for suffering and a hope of overcoming it. But, in addition, Shaker belief continues to offer a way for Indians to incorporate the principal religious symbols of a dominant alien culture into their traditional understanding of the relationship between human beings and the supernatural.

Sources

There are few published contemporary accounts of Shaker origins. The Congregational missionary Myron Eells (1886, 1892, 1985), resident at Skokomish from 1874 to 1907, was an observer of the Shaker movement from its inception. Mooney (1896) devotes a chapter to Shakerism drawing on information supplied by Eells and Wickersham. Shorter accounts by other contemporaries of the first generation of Shakers are: Hazeltine (1895), L.W. Quimby (1902), Reagan (1909, 1911a, 1927), and Ober (1910).

The most complete coverage of Shaker Church history, ritual, and social role is Barnett (1957). Gunther (1949) and Waterman (1924) tapped other sources of oral tradition and present different pictures of Shaker history. Du Bois (1938), Rhodes (1960), Spier (1935), and Suttles (1957) set Shakerism in the context of earlier native religious movements.

Shorter works on one or more aspects of the Shaker church include: Amoss (1978, 1982), Castile (1982), J.M. Collins (1950), Gould and Furukawa (1964), Harmon (1971), Richen (1974), Sackett (1973), Schultz and Walker (1967), M.W. Smith (1954), Stern (1929), and Valory (1966).

Works on other topics include significant information on Shakers or their antecedents: J.M. Collins (1974), Colson (1953), Duff (1964), Elmendorf (1960), Hawthorn Belsharo, and Jamieson (1958), Olson (1936), Pettitt (1950), Sampson (1972), M.W. Smith (1959), Stern (1966), and Whitehead (1981).

Valuable material is to be found in theses, dissertations, manuscripts, field notes, and court records (Ballard 1920; J.M. Collins 1946; Colson 1965; Currie 1958; Fitzpatrick 1968; Kew 1970; Langness 1959; Pope 1953; Richen 1974a; M.W. Smith 1936–1939; Sneddon 1960; Wike 1941; B.J. Zakoji 1953). The Records of the Indian Shaker Church in the Washington State Archives, Olympia, Washington, is unique because it presents accounts recorded and translated by Shakers themselves.

Contributors

This list gives the academic affiliations of authors at the time this volume went to press. Parenthetical tribal names identify Indian authors. The dates following the entries indicate when each manuscript was (1) first received in the General Editor's office; (2) accepted by the General Editor's office; and (3) sent to the author (or, if deceased, a substitute) for final approval after revisions and editorial work.

AMES, KENNETH M., Department of Anthropology, Portland State University, Oregon. Prehistory of the Northern Coast of British Columbia: 12/17/76; 7/11/86; 6/27/86.

AMOSS, PAMELA T., Leavenworth, Washington. The Indian Shaker Church: 1/25/74; 2/10/88; 4/20/88.

ARIMA, EUGENE, Historical Research Division, National Historic Parks and Sites Branch, Parks Canada, Ottawa, Ontario. Nootkans of Vancouver Island: 6/27/77; 4/18/86; 11/19/86.

BECKHAM, STEPHEN DOW, Department of History, Lewis and Clark College, Portland, Oregon. History of Western Oregon Since 1846: 9/14/75; 12/20/88; 2/7/89.

BLACKMAN, MARGARET B., Department of Anthropology, State University College at Brockport, New York. Haida: Traditional Culture: 11/3/77; 6/18/86; 9/26/86.

BOOTH, ARNOLD (Tsimshian), Metlakatla, Alaska. Tsimshian of Metlakatla, Alaska: 4/23/73; 3/24/86; 7/28/86.

BOUCHARD, RANDALL T., British Columbia Indian Language Project, Victoria. Bella Coola: 1/11/77; 3/3/86; 10/23/86. Northern Coast Salish: 7/18/77; 3/15/88; 4/20/88.

BOYD, ROBERT T., Northwest Ethnohistorical Research Associates, Portland, Oregon. Demographic History, 1774–1874: 7/30/84; 10/28/88; 11/10/88.

CARLSON, ROY L., Department of Archeology, Simon Fraser University, Burnaby, British Columbia. Cultural Antecedents: 1/26/86; 10/3/88; 10/17/88. History of Research in Archeology: 2/13/79; 10/14/88; 10/31/88.

CODERE, HELEN (emerita), Department of Anthropology, Brandeis University, Waltham, Massachusetts. Kwakiutl: Traditional Culture: 8/5/72; 6/18/86; 11/7/86.

COLE, DOUGLAS, Department of History, Simon Fraser University, Burnaby, British Columbia. History of the Early Period: 3/8/85; 9/26/88; 11/3/88.

CYBULSKI, JEROME S., Archeological Survey of Canada, Canadian Museum of Civilization, Ottawa, Ontario. Human Biology: 3/12/73; 9/14/88; 10/04/88. History of Research in Physical Anthropology: 3/12/73; 7/02/85; 7/26/88.

DARLING, DAVID, Department of History, St. George's School, Vancouver, British Columbia. History of the Early Period: 3/8/85; 9/26/88; 11/3/88.

DAVIS, STANLEY D., Forest Service, United States Department of Agriculture, Sitka, Alaska. Prehistory of Southeastern Alaska: 9/4/85; 12/11/85; 7/29/86.

DE LAGUNA, FREDERICA (emerita), Department of Anthropology, Bryn Mawr College, Pennsylvania. Eyak: 7/7/72; 6/21/85; 6/24/86. Tlingit: 5/12/76; 7/1/85; 1/14/87.

DEWHIRST, JOHN, Archeo Tech Associates, Victoria, British Columbia. Nootkans of Vancouver Island: 6/27/77; 4/18/86; 11/19/86.

DUNN, JOHN A., Department of Modern Language, Literature, and Linguistics, University of Oklahoma, Norman. Tsimshian of Metlakatla, Alaska: 4/23/73; 3/24/86; 7/28/86.

ELMENDORF, WILLIAM W., Department of Anthropology, University of California, Davis. Chemakum: 10/31/73; 6/21/85; 9/26/86.

FLADMARK, KNUT R., Department of Archeology, Simon Fraser University, Burnaby, British Columbia. Prehistory of the Northern Coast of British Columbia: 12/17/76; 7/11/86; 6/27/86.

GUNTHER, ERNA (deceased), Seattle, Washington. Makah: 8/28/86; 11/13/86; 11/24/86.

HAJDA, YVONNE, Northwest Ethnohistorical Research Associates, Portland, Oregon. Southwestern Coast Salish: 2/20/86; 3/15/88; 6/22/88.

HALPIN, MARJORIE M., Museum of Anthropology, University of British Columbia, Vancouver. Tsimshian Peoples: Southern Tsimshian, Coast Tsimshian, Nishga, and Gitksan: 5/31/74; 2/13/86; 8/12/86.

HAMORI-TOROK, CHARLES, Department of Anthropology, Trent University, Peterborough, Ontario. Haisla: 3/1/77; 6/10/86; 7/28/86.

HILTON, SUSANNE F., Department of Anthropology, University of Western Ontario, London. Haihais, Bella Bella, and Oowekeeno: 8/9/85; 2/14/86; 8/11/86.

HOBLER, PHILIP M., Department of Archeology, Simon Fraser University, Burnaby, British Columbia. Prehistory of the Central Coast of British Columbia: 2/24/75; 5/8/86; 6/27/86.

HOLM, BILL (emeritus), Thomas Burke Memorial Washington State Museum, University of Washington, Seattle. Kwakiutl: Winter Ceremonies: 4/5/77; 6/10/86; 10/22/86. Art: 6/3/86; 5/5/88; 7/1/88.

HUDSON, DOUGLAS R., Fraser Valley College, Abbotsford, British Columbia. Tsimshian of British Columbia Since 1900: 2/26/86; 6/18/86; 9/5/86.

HYMES, DELL, Department of Anthropology, University of Virginia, Charlottesville. Mythology: 1/5/87; 5/5/88; 7/21/88.

INGLIS, GORDON B., Department of Anthropology, Memorial University of Newfoundland, St. Johns. Tsimshian of British Columbia Since 1900: 2/26/86; 6/18/86; 9/5/86.

JONAITIS, ALDONA C., Department of Art, State University of New York, Stony Brook. History of Research in Ethnology: 12/7/88; 2/27/89; 3/28/89.

KENDALL, DAYTHAL L., Glenside, Pennsylvania. Takelma: 12/30/75; 5/11/88; 6/20/88.

KENNEDY, DOROTHY I.D., British Columbia Indian Language Project, Victoria. Bella Coola: 1/11/77; 3/3/86; 10/23/86. Northern Coast Salish: 7/18/77; 3/15/88; 4/20/88.

KEW, J.E. MICHAEL, Department of Anthropology and Sociology, University of British Columbia, Vancouver. History of Coastal British Columbia Since 1849: 6/16/77; 1/9/89; 1/26/89. Central and Southern Coast Salish Ceremonies Since 1900: 2/3/87; 3/15/88; 4/22/88.

KINKADE, M. DALE, Department of Linguistics, University of British Columbia, Vancouver. Languages: 1/25/74; 8/3/88; 9/12/88. History of Research in Linguistics: 1/24/77; 8/10/88; 8/23/88.

KRAUSS, MICHAEL E., Alaska Native Language Center, University of Alaska, Fairbanks. Kwalhioqua and Clatskanie: 8/6/87; 3/15/88; 7/19/88.

LANE, BARBARA, Department of Anthropology, University of Washington, Seattle. Southern Coast Salish: 2/3/87; 5/5/88; 5/23/88.

LOHSE, E.S., Department of Sociology, Anthropology, and Social Work, Idaho State University, Pocatello. History of Research: Museum Collections: 8/8/88; 1/23/89; 3/29/89.

MARINO, CESARE, Handbook of North American Indians, Smithsonian Institution, Washington, D.C. History of Western Washington Since 1846: 8/3/88; 8/22/88; 1/10/89.

MILLER, JAY, D'Arcy McNickle Center for the History of the American Indian, Newberry Library, Chicago, Illinois. Tillamook: 8/29/77; 3/15/88; 3/9/88. Athapaskans of Southwestern Oregon: 8/11/86; 7/11/88; 7/26/88.

MITCHELL, DONALD, Department of Anthropology, University of Victoria, British Columbia. Prehistory of the Coasts of Southern British Columbia and Northern Washington: 6/4/73; 4/2/86; 7/9/86.

NELSON, CHARLES M., Department of Anthropology, University of Massachusetts, Boston. Prehistory of the Puget Sound Region: 5/4/72; 3/28/88; 5/23/88.

PETTIGREW, RICHARD M., INFOTEC Research Inc., Eugene, Oregon. Prehistory of the Lower Columbia and Willamette Valley: 1/6/84; 3/15/88; 4/26/88.

POWELL, JAMES V., Department of Anthropology and Sociology, University of British Columbia, Vancouver. Quileute: 4/4/77; 3/7/86; 9/26/86.

RENKER, ANN M., Makah Cultural and Research Center, Neah Bay, Washington. Makah: 8/28/86; 11/13/86; 11/24/86.

RIGSBY, BARBARA K., Department of Anthropology and Sociology, University of Queensland, Saint Lucia, Australia. Tsimshian of British Columbia Since 1900: 2/26/86; 6/18/86; 9/5/86.

RIGSBY, BRUCE, Department of Anthropology and Sociology, University of Queensland, Saint Lucia, Australia. Tsimshian of British Columbia Since 1900: 2/26/86; 6/18/86; 9/5/86.

ROSS, RICHARD E., Department of Anthropology, Oregon State University, Corvallis. Prehistory of the Oregon Coast: 10/4/85; 5/5/88; 6/9/88.

SEABURG, WILLIAM R., Department of Anthropology, University of Washington, Seattle. Tillamook: 8/29/77; 3/15/88; 3/9/88. Athapaskans of Southwestern Oregon: 8/11/86; 7/11/88; 7/26/88.

SEGUIN, MARGARET, Department of Anthropology, University of Western Ontario, London. Tsimshian Peoples: Southern Tsimshian, Coast Tsimshian, Nishga, and Gitksan: 5/31/74; 2/13/86; 8/12/86.

SILVERSTEIN, MICHAEL, Department of Anthropology, University of Chicago. Chinookans of the Lower Columbia: 10/8/74; 1/7/87; 3/28/88.

STEARNS, MARY LEE, Department of Sociology and Anthropology, Simon Fraser University, Burnaby, British Columbia. Haida Since 1960: 5/1/72; 6/10/86; 7/11/86.

SUNDT, FRANCES, Washington, D.C. History of Research: Museum Collections: 8/8/88; 1/23/89; 3/29/89.

SUTHERLAND, PATRICIA D., Archeological Survey of Canada, Canadian Museum of Civilization, Ottawa, Ontario. Prehistory of the Northern Coast of British Columbia: 12/17/76; 7/11/86; 6/27/86.

SUTTLES, WAYNE (emeritus), Department of Anthropology, Portland State University, Oregon. Introduction: 3/10/89; 3/14/89; 4/11/89. Environment: 11/21/88; 2/16/89; 2/24/89. History of Research: Early Sources: 4/26/89; 4/27/89; 4/28/89. History of Research in Ethnology: 12/7/88; 2/27/89; 3/28/89. Central Coast Salish: 7/17/87; 3/15/88; 7/5/88. Southern Coast Salish: 2/3/87; 5/5/88; 5/23/88.

THOMPSON, LAURENCE C. (emeritus), Department of Linguistics, University of Hawaii, Honolulu. Languages: 1/25/74; 8/3/88; 9/12/88.

WEBSTER, GLORIA CRANMER (Nimpkish Kwakiutl), U'mista Cultural Centre, Alert Bay, British Columbia. Kwakiutl Since 1980: 7/22/85; 6/18/86; 10/31/86.

WESSEN, GARY, Makah Cultural and Research Center, Neah Bay, Washington. Prehistory of the Ocean Coast of Washington: 3/1/84; 12/11/85; 7/30/86.

WORL, ROSITA (Tlingit), Chilkat Institute, Anchorage, Alaska. History of Southeastern Alaska Since 1867: 3/11/86; 11/4/88; 12/7/88.

ZENK, HENRY B., Northwest Ethnohistorical Research Associates, Portland, Oregon. Kalapuyans: 8/9/76; 3/15/88; 4/22/88. Alseans: 2/28/86; 3/15/88; 3/18/88. Siuslawans and Coosans: 2/6/78; 3/15/88; 4/22/88.

List of Illustrations

This list identifies the subjects of all illustrations, organized by chapter. All artists, photographers, and some individuals depicted (but not collectors) are included. Every identified individual depicted is found in the index, but not the photographers. Tables are not listed here.

643

LIST OF ILLUSTRATIONS

647

LIST OF ILLUSTRATIONS

Bibliography

This list includes all references cited in the volume, arranged in alphabetical order according to the names of the authors as they appear in the citations in the text. Multiple works by the same author are arranged chronologically; second and subsequent titles by the same author in the same year are differentiated by letters added to the dates. Where more than one author with the same surname is cited, one has been arbitrarily selected for text citation by surname alone throughout the volume, while the others are always cited with added initials; the combination of surname with date in text citations should avoid confusion. Where a publication date is different from the series date (as in some annual reports and the like), the former is used. Dates, authors, and titles that do not appear on the original works are enclosed by brackets. For manuscripts, dates refer to time of composition. For publications reprinted or first published many years after original composition, a bracketed date after the title refers to the time of composition or the date of original publication.

ARCIA = Commissioner of Indian Affairs
1849– Annual Reports to the Secretary of the Interior. Washington: U.S. Government Printing Office. (Reprinted: AMS Press, New York, 1976–1977.)

Abbott, G.H.
1858 Coquille Vocabulary. (Manuscript No. 125 in National Anthropological Archives, Smithsonian Institution, Washington.)

Abbott, Donald N.
1972 The Utility of the Concept of Phase in the Archaeology of the Southern Northwest Coast. *Syesis* 5:267–278. Victoria, B.C.

Abercrombie, William R.
1900 Report of a Supplementary Expedition into the Copper River Valley, Alaska, 1884. Pp. 381–408 in Compilation of Narratives of Explorations in Alaska, 1900. Washington: U.S. Government Printing Office.

Aberle, David F.
1959 The Prophet Dance and Reactions to White Contact. *Southwestern Journal of Anthropology* 15(1):74–83.

Ackerman, Charles
1975 A Tsimshian Oedipus. Pp. 65–85 in Vol. 1 of Proceedings of the 2d Congress of the Canadian Ethnology Society. Jim Freedman and Jerome H. Barkow, eds. *Canada. National Museum of Man. Mercury Series. Ethnology Service Papers* 28. Ottawa.

1982 A Small Problem of Fish Bones. Pp. 113–126 in The Logic of Culture: Advances in Structural Theory and Methods, by Ino Rossi and Contributors. South Hadley, Mass.: J.F. Bergin.

Ackerman, Robert E.
1964 Archeological Survey, Glacier Bay National Monument, Southeastern Alaska. Pt. 1. *Washington State University. Laboratory of Anthropology. Reports of Investigations* 28. Pullman.

1965 Archeological Survey, Glacier Bay National Monument, Southeastern Alaska. Pt. 2. *Washington State University. Laboratory of Anthropology. Reports of Investigations* 36. Pullman.

1968 The Archeology of the Glacier Bay Region, Southeastern Alaska; Final Report of the Archeological Survey of the Glacier Bay National Monument. *Washington State University. Laboratory of Anthropology. Reports of Investigations* 44. Pullman.

1974 Post-Pleistocene Cultural Adaptations on the Northern Northwest Coast. Pp. 1–20 in Proceedings of the International Conference on the Prehistory and Paleoecology of the Western Arctic and Sub-arctic. Calgary, Alta.: University of Calgary Archeological Association.

Ackerman, Robert E., Thomas D. Hamilton, and Robert Stuckenrath
1979 Early Cultural Complexes of the Northern Northwest Coast. *Canadian Journal of Archaeology* 3:195–209.

Ackerman, Robert E., K.C. Reid, J.D. Gallison, and M.E. Roe
1985 Archaeology of Heceta Island: A Survey of 16 Timber Harvest Units in the Tongass National Forest, Southeastern Alaska. *Washington State University. Center for Northwest Anthropology. Project Reports* 3. Pullman.

Adam, Leonhard von
[1923] Nordwest-amerikanische Indianerkunst. Berlin: E. Wasmuth.

1931 Das Problem der asiatisch-altamerikanischen Kulturbeziehungen mit besonderer Berücksichtigung der Kunst. *Wiener Beiträge zur Kunst- und Kulturgeschichte Asiens* 5:40–64. Vienna.

1936 North-west American Indian Art and Its Early Chinese Parallels. *Man: The Journal of the Royal Anthropological Institute* 36(January):8–11. London.

Adams, Jill
1961 Linguistic Notes Concerning Mainland Comox. (Unpublished manuscripts in Wayne Suttles's possession.)

Adams, John W.
1973 The Gitksan Potlatch: Population Flux, Resource Ownership and Reciprocity. Toronto: Holt, Rinehart and Winston of Canada.

1974 Dialectics and Contingency in "The Story of Asdiwal:" An Ethnographic Note. Pp. 170–178 in The Unconscious in Culture: The Structuralism of Claude Lévi-Strauss in Perspective. Ino Rossi, ed. New York: E.P. Dutton.

1981 Recent Ethnology of the Northwest Coast. *Annual Review of Anthropology* 10:361–392. Palo Alto, Calif.

Adamson, Thelma
1926–1927 [Unarranged Sources of Chehalis Ethnology.] (Manuscript in Box 77, Melville Jacobs Collection, University of Washington Libraries, Seattle.)
————, coll. and ed.
1934 Folk-tales of the Coast Salish. *Memoirs of the American Folk-Lore Society* 27. New York. (Reprinted: Kraus Reprint, New York, 1969.)

Adler, Fred W.
1961 A Bibliographical Checklist of Chimakuan, Kutenai, Ritwan, Salish, and Wakashan Linguistics. *International Journal of American Linguistics* 27(3):198–210.

Alekseev, Aleksandr I.
1987 The Odyssey of a Russian Scientist: I.G. Voznesenskiĭ in Alaska, California and Siberia, 1839–1849. Wilma C. Follette, trans. Richard A. Pierce, ed. (*Alaska History* 30) Kingston, Ont.: The Limestone Press.

Alfred, Braxton M., T.D. Stout, John Birkbeck, Melvin Lee, and Nicholas L. Petrakis
1969 Blood Groups, Red Cell Enzymes, and Cerumen Types of the Ahousat (Nootka) Indians. *American Journal of Physical Anthropology* 31(3):391–398.

Allaire, Louis
1978 L'Archéologie des Kitselas d'après le site stratifié de Gitaus (GdTc:2) sur la rivière Skeena en Colombie Britannique.

Canada. National Museum of Man. Mercury Series. Archaeological Survey Papers 72. Ottawa.

1979   The Cultural Sequence at Gitans: A Case of Prehistoric Acculturation. Pp. 18–52 in Skeena River Prehistory. G.F. MacDonald and R.I. Inglis, eds. *Canada. National Museum of Man. Mercury Series. Archaeological Survey Papers* 89. Ottawa.

1984   A Native Mental Map of Coast Tsimshian Villages. Pp. 82–98 in The Tsimshian: Images of the Past, Views for the Present. Margaret Seguin, ed. Vancouver: University of British Columbia Press.

Allen, Henry T.
1887   Report of an Expedition to the Copper, Tananá, and Kóyukuk Rivers, in the Territory of Alaska, in the Year 1885. Washington: U.S. Government Printing Office.

Allen, Rosemary A.
1954   Patterns of Preferential Marriage Among the Alaskan Haidas. *Anthropological Papers of the University of Alaska* 2(2):195–201. College.

1955   Changing Social Organization and Kinship Among the Alaskan Haidas. *Anthropological Papers of the University of Alaska* 4(1):5–11. College.

Allison, Marvin J., Enrique Gerszten, Juan Munizaga, and Calogero Santoro
1980   Metastatic Tumor of Bone in a Tiahuanaco Female. *Bulletin of the New York Academy of Medicine* 56:581–587.

Alsop, Richard *see* Jewitt, John R.

Altman, George J.
1947   Guardian-spirit Dances of the Salish. *The Masterkey* 21(5):155–160.

Ambrose, George
1856   Journal of Removal of Rogue River Tribe of Indians. (Manuscript, 1856–165, Microcopy 2, Roll 14, Records of the Oregon Superintendency, in Record Group 75, National Archives, Washington.)

American Friends Service Committee *see* Friends, Society of

American Indian Policy Review Commission
1976   Transcript of Proceedings, Task Force on Terminated and Nonfederally Recognized Indian Tribes, March 13. (Manuscript, in possession of Stephen D. Beckham, Lake Oswego, Oreg.)

Ames, Kenneth M.
1973   Recent Archaeological Research in the Middle Skeena Valley, British Columbia. *The Midden: Publication of the Archaeological Society of British Columbia* 5(1):3–9. Vancouver.

1976   The Bone Tool Assemblage from the Garden Island Site, Prince Rupert Harbor, British Columbia: An Analysis of Assemblage Variation Through Time. (Unpublished Ph.D. Dissertation in Anthropology, Washington State University, Pullman.)

1979   Report of Excavations at GhSv2, Hagwilget Canyon. Pp. 181–218 in Skeena River Prehistory. G.F. MacDonald and R.I. Inglis, eds. *Canada. National Museum of Man. Mercury Series. Archaeological Survey Papers* 87. Ottawa.

1981   The Evolution of Social Ranking on the Northwest Coast of North America. *American Antiquity* 46(4):789–805.

1983   Towards a General Model of the Evolution of Ranking Among Foragers. Pp. 173–184 in The Evolution of Maritime Cultures on the Northeast and the Northwest Coasts of America. Ronald J. Nash, ed. *Simon Fraser University. Department of Archaeology Publications* 11. Burnaby, B.C.

1984   Pithouse Variability in the Intermontane West. (Paper presented to the 19th Great Basin Anthropological Conference, Boise, Idaho.)

1984a   Second Progress Report: Analysis and Comparisons of the Artifact Assemblages from GbTo:31, GbTo:33 and GbTo:23, Prince Rupert Harbour, British Columbia. (Report on file at the Archaeological Survey of Canada, Ottawa.)

1985   Hierarchies, Stress and Logistical Strategies Among Hunter-gatherers in Northwestern North America. Pp. 155–190 in Prehistoric Hunter-gatherers: The Emergence of Cultural Complexity. T. Douglas Price and James A. Brown, ed. Orlando, Fla.: Academic Press.

Ames, Michael
1986   How Anthropologists Help to Fabricate the Cultures They Study. Pp. 48–58 in Museums, the Public and Anthropology: A Study in the Anthropology of Anthropology, by Michael Ames. (*Ranchi Anthropology Series* 9) Vancouver: University of British Columbia Press.

Amoss, Pamela T.
1972   The Persistence of Aboriginal Beliefs and Practices Among the Nooksack Coast Salish. (Unpublished Ph.D. Dissertation in Anthropology, University of Washington, Seattle.)

1978   Symbolic Substitution in the Indian Shaker Church. *Ethnohistory* 25(3):225–249.

1978a   Coast Salish Spirit Dancing: The Survival of an Ancestral Religion. Seattle: University of Washington Press.

1982   Resurrection, Healing, and "the Shake:" The Story of John and Mary Slocum. Pp. 87–109 in Charisma and Sacred Biography. Michael A. Williams, ed. *Journal of the American Academy of Religion. Thematic Studies* 48(3–4).

1987   The Fish God Gave Us: The First Salmon Ceremony Revived. *Arctic Anthropology* 24(1):56–66.

Anderson, Alexander C.
[1854]   Vocabularies of the Klatskanai and Tah-cully Indians. (Manuscript HHB[P-C44] in Bancroft Library, University of California, Berkeley.)

1854–1855   'Klatskanai' Vocabulary....Recorded in 1854 or 1855 from Ia-coos, a Part-Tlatskanai Living at Cathlamet. (Manuscript No. 107-a-b-c in National Anthropological Archives, Smithsonian Institution, Washington.)

1856   Vocabulary of the Willopah (Dialect of Tahcully, Athapasca); from an Indian at S.S. Fords. (Manuscript No. 110 in National Anthropological Archives, Smithsonian Institution, Washington.)

1857   Notes on Chinook Jargon. (Manuscript No. 404 in National Anthropological Archives, Smithsonian Institution, Washington.)

1858   Concordance of the Athabaskan Languages. (Manuscript No. 123 in National Anthropological Archives, Smithsonian Institution, Washington.)

1876   Notes on North-western America (Descriptive Matter Intended to Accompany a 'Skeleton Map of North-West America', Prepared by Mr. Anderson to Send to the Philadelphia International Exhibition of 1876). Montreal: Mitchell and Wilson.

Anderson, Bern, ed.
1939   The Vancouver Expedition: Peter Puget's Journal of the Exploration of Puget Sound, May 7–June 11, 1792. *Pacific Northwest Quarterly* 30(2):177–217.

Anderson, Hobson D., and Walter C. Eells
1935   Alaska Natives: A Survey of Their Sociological and Educational Status. Stanford, Calif.: Stanford University Press.

Anderson, Stephen R.
1984   Kwakwala Syntax and the Government-binding Theory. Pp. 21–75 in The Syntax of Native American Languages. Eung-Do Cook and Donna B. Gerdts, eds. (*Syntax and Semantics* 16) Orlando, Fla.: Academic Press.

Andrade, Manuel J.
[1928]   Chemakum Vocabulary. (Manuscript 30 (W3b.5) [Freeman No. 707] in the Library of the American Philosophical Society, Philadelphia.)

———   [1930–1953] Notes on the Relations Between Chemakum and Quileute. Edward Spicer and Morris Swadesh, eds. (Manuscript 30 (W3b.4) [Freeman No. 708] in the Library of the American Philosophical Society, Philadelphia.)

———   1931   Quileute Texts. *Columbia University Contributions to Anthropology* 12. New York. (Reprinted: AMS Press, New York, 1969.)

———   1933   Quileute. (Extract from Handbook of American Indian Languages Vol. 3:151–292, Franz Boas, ed.) New York: Columbia University Press.

———   1953   Notes on the Relations Between Chemakum and Quileute. Morris Swadesh, ed. *International Journal of American Linguistics* 19(3):212–215.

Andreev, Aleksandr I., ed.
1952   Russian Discoveries in the Pacific and in North America in the Eighteenth and Nineteenth Centuries: A Collection of Materials. Carl Ginsburg, trans. (*Russian Translation Project Series* 13) Ann Arbor, Mich.: American Council of Learned Societies.

Andrews, Clarence L.
1953   The Story of Alaska. Caldwell, Idaho: Caxton Printers.

Andrews, H.A. et al.
1943   Bibliography of Franz Boas. *Memoirs of the American Anthropological Association* 61. Menasha, Wis.

Andrews, J.T., and R.M. Retherford
1976   Late Quaternary Sea Levels and Glacial Chronology, Bella Bella - Bella Coola Region, British Columbia: A Reconnaissance. (Unpublished manuscript on file, Institute of Arctic and Alpine Research and Department of Geological Sciences, University of Colorado, Boulder.)

Anker, Daniel
1975   Haida Kinship Semantics: 1900–1974. (Unpublished Ph.D. Dissertation in Anthropology, Duke University, Chapel Hill, N.C.)

Annance, Francis
1824–1825   A Journal of a Voyage from Fort George, Columbia River to Fraser River in the Winter of 1824 and 1825. (Manuscript B 71/a/1 in Hudson's Bay Company Archives, Provincial Archives of Manitoba, Winnipeg, Canada.)

[Anonymous]
1872   Collection Scouler. *Revue d'Anthropologie* 1:335. Paris.

———   1977   We-Gyet Wanders On: Legends of the Northwest. Saanichton, B.C.: Hancock House Publishers.

———   1980   Washington Tribes Fight for Their Fishing Rights on a New Front. *American Indian Journal* 6(3):22–25. Washington.

Apland, Brian
1982   Chipped Stone Assemblages from the Beach Sites of the Central Coast. Pp. 13–64 in Papers on Central Coast Archaeology. Philip M. Hobler, ed. *Simon Fraser University. Department of Archaeology Publications* 10. Burnaby, B.C.

Appleton, F.M.
1970   The Life and Art of Charlie Edensaw. *Canadian Geographical Journal* 81(1):20–25. Ottawa.

Archer, David J.W.
1980   Analysis of Spatial Patterns at a Prehistoric Settlement in the Lower Fraser Canyon, B.C. (Unpublished M.A. Thesis in Anthropology, University of Victoria, Victoria, B.C.)

Archer, David J.W., and Kathryn Bernick
1985   Perishable Artifacts from the Musqueam Northeast Site. (Unpublished manuscript in British Columbia Heritage Trust, Victoria, B.C.)

Archibald, Dale
1984   Blue Lake Park, Multnomah County, Oregon, Archaeological Report. Portland: Oregon Historical Society.

Arctander, John W.
1909   The Apostle of Alaska: The Story of William Duncan of Metlakahtla. New York: Fleming H. Revell.

Arctic Institute of North America
1961–1974   Anthropology of the North: Translations from Russian Sources. 9 vols. Henry N. Michael, ed. Toronto: University of Toronto Press.

Arima, Eugene Y.
1975   A Report on a West Coast Whaling Canoe Reconstructed at Port Renfrew, B.C. *Canada. National Historic Parks and Sites Branch. History and Archaeology* 5. Ottawa.

———   1976   [Notes on the Southern West Coast (Nootka) Natives: Environment and Exploitative Techniques of the PʼaːchiːdaʔatH of Port San Juan.] (Unpublished manuscript in Arima's possession.)

———   1983   [Notes on Nootkan Sea Mammal Hunting.] (Paper presented at the Symposium on Megafauna of the Seas, Large Sea Mammal Hunting and Use Among Native Societies. *Proceedings of the 11th International Congress of Anthropological and Ethnological Sciences*. Vancouver, 20–25 August 1983.)

———   1983a   The West Coast People: The Nootka of Vancouver Island and Cape Flattery. *British Columbia Provincial Museum. Special Publication* 6. Victoria.

Arima, Eugene Y., and E.C. Hunt
1975   Making Masks: Notes on Kwakiutl "Tourist Mask" Carving. Pp. 67–128 in Contributions to Canadian Ethnology, 1975. David B. Carlisle, ed. *Canada. National Museum of Man. Mercury Series. Ethnology Service Papers* 31. Ottawa.

Arkeketa, Susan, and Anita Austin
1986   Washington Tribes Prepare for Trial to Protect Water and Land Claims. *NARF Legal Review* 11(4):1–5. Boulder, Colo.

Armstrong, J.E.
1966   Glacial Studies, Kitimat-terrace Area. P. 50 in Report of Activities, May to October, 1965. S.E. Jenness, ed. *Geological Survey of Canada Papers* 66-1. Ottawa.

Arnold, Robert D.
1976   Alaska Native Land Claims. Anchorage: Alaska Native Foundation.

———, et al.
1978   Alaska Native Land Claims. Rev. ed. Anchorage: Alaska Native Foundation.

Aschmann, Homer
1959   The Central Desert of Baja California: Demography and Ecology. *Ibero-Americana* 42. Berkeley, Calif.

Atkinson, C.E., J.H. Rose, and T.O. Duncan
1967   Salmon on the North Pacific Ocean. Pt. IV: Spawning Populations of North Pacific Salmon. 4. Pacific Salmon in the United States. *Bulletin of the International North Pacific Fisheries Commission* 23:43–223. Vancouver, B.C.

651

Attwell, Jim
1973   Tahmahnaw: The Bridge of the Gods. Chicago: Adams Press.

Autrey John T., and Stanley D. Davis
1984   The Excavation of the Mud Bay Shell Midden Site, 49 SIT 240. (Manuscript on file, U.S. Forest Service, Chatham Area, Tongass National Forest, Sitka, Alaska.)

Averkieva, Yulia P.
1966   Slavery Among the Indians of North America [1941]. G.R. Elliott, trans. Victoria, B.C.: Victoria College.

1971   The Tlingit Indians. Pp. 317–342 in North American Indians in Historical Perspective. Eleanor B. Leacock and Nancy O. Lurie, eds. New York: Random House.

1981   Son-in Law: The Heir of Kwakiutl Indians. Pp. 59–65 in North American Indian Studies: European Contributions. Pieter Hovens, ed. Göttingen, Germany: Edition Herodot.

Backlin-Landman, Hedy, ed.
1969   Art of the Northwest Coast. [Catalog of an Exhibit] January 22 Through March 2, 1969. Princeton, N.J.: The Art Museum, Princeton University.

Badner, Mino
1966   The Protruding Tongue and Related Motifs in the Art Styles of the American North-west Coast, New Zealand and China: Two Studies of Art in the Pacific Area. *Wiener Beiträge zur Kulturgeschichte und Linguistik* 15:5–44. Vienna.

Bagley, Clarence B., ed.
1915–1916 Journal of Occurrences at Nisqually House, 1833. *Washington Historical Quarterly* 6(3):179–197, (4):264–278; 7(1):59–75, (2):144–167.

Bailey, Vernon
1936   The Mammals and Life Zones of Oregon. *U.S. Bureau of Biological Survey. North American Fauna* 55. Washington: [U.S. Government Printing Office.]

Baird, Spencer F.
1875   [Letter to Edward P. Smith, July 19, 1875.] (In Office of Indian Affairs, Letters Received, M234, Roll 53, Record Group 75, National Archives, Washington.)

1876   Appendix to the Report of the Secretary. Pp. 58–71 in *Annual Report of the Smithsonian Institution for the Year 1875.* Washington.

Ballard, Arthur
[1920]   [Ethnographic and Linguistic Fieldnotes on Puget Sound Salish.] (Manuscript in the Smith Collection at the Library of the Royal Anthropological Institute of Great Britain and Ireland, London.)

1927   Some Tales of the Southern Puget Sound Salish. *University of Washington Publications in Anthropology* 2(3):57–81. Seattle.

1929   Mythology of Southern Puget Sound. *University of Washington Publications in Anthropology* 3(2):31–150. Seattle.

1935   Southern Puget Sound Kinship Terms. *American Anthropologist* 37(1):111–116.

1950   Calendric Terms of the Southern Puget Sound Salish. *Southwestern Journal of Anthropology* 6(1):79–99.

1957   The Salmon-weir on Green River in Western Washington. *Davidson Journal of Anthropology* 3:37–53. Seattle.

Bancroft, Hubert H.
1874–1876 The Native Races of the Pacific States of North America. 5 vols. New York: D. Appleton.

1886   History of Alaska, 1730–1885. (*The Works of Hubert Howe Bancroft* 33) San Francisco: The History Company. (Reprinted: Antiquarian Press, New York, 1959.)

1886a   History of the Northwest Coast. 2 vols. (*The Works of Hubert Howe Bancroft* 27, 28) San Francisco: The History Company.

1886b   The Native Races of the Pacific States of North America. 5 vols. San Francisco: A.L. Bancroft.

1890   History of Washington, Idaho, and Montana, 1845–1889. (*The Works of Hubert Howe Bancroft* 31) San Francisco: The History Company.

Bandi, Hans-G.
1958   Einige Gegenstände aus Alaska und Britisch Kolumbien .... von James Cook, 1776–1780. Pp. 214–220 in *Proceedings of the 32d International Congress of Americanists.* Copenhagen, 1956.

Banks, Judith J.
1970   Comparative Biographies of Two British Columbia Anthropologists: Charles Hill-Tout and James A. Teit. (Unpublished M.A. Thesis in Anthropology, University of British Columbia, Vancouver.)

Banks, Richard C., Roy W. McDiarmid, and Alfred L. Gardner, eds.
1987   Checklist of Vertebrates of the United States, the U.S. Territories, and Canada. *U.S. Department of the Interior. Fish and Wildlife Service. Resource Publications* 166. Washington.

Baranov, Aleksandr
1979   Letter, Baranov to Shelikhov, from Chugach Bay, July 24, 1793. Pp. 27–37 in A History of the Russian American Company. Vol. 2: Documents, by P.A. Tikhmenev; Dmitri Krenov, trans.; Richard A. Pierce and Alton S. Donnelly, eds. (*Materials for the Study of Alaska History* 13) Kingston, Ont.: The Limestone Press.

Barbeau, C. Marius
1917   Growth and Federation in the Tsimshian Phratries. Pp. 402–408 in *Proceedings of the 19th International Congress of Americanists.* Washington, 1915.

1917a   [Review of] Tsimshian Mythology ... *American Anthropologist* 19(4):548–563. (Reprinted: Pp. 766–781 in Selected Papers from the American Anthropologist, 1888–1920. Frederica De Laguna, ed., Row, Peterson, Evanston, Ill.)

1928   The Downfall of Temlaham. Toronto: Macmillan Company of Canada.

1929   Totem Poles of the Gitksan, Upper Skeena River, British Columbia. *Anthropological Series* 12, *National Museum of Canada Bulletin* 61. Ottawa.

1930   An Indian Paradise Lost. *Canadian Geographical Journal* 1(2):133–148. Ottawa.

1930a   Totem Poles: A Recent Native Art of the Northwest Coast of America. *Geographical Review* 20(2):258–272. New York. (Reprinted: Pp. 559–570 in *Annual Report of the Smithsonian Institution for the Year 1931*, Washington.)

1944   How the Raven Stole the Sun [Charles Edensaw's Argillite Carvings]. *Transactions of the Royal Society of Canada*, 3d ser., Vol. 38 (sect. 2): 59–69. Ottawa.

1945   The Aleutian Route of Migration into America. *Geographical Review* 35(3):424–443.

[1950]   Totem Poles. 2 vols. *Anthropological Series* 30, *National Museum of Canada Bulletin* 119. Ottawa.

[1951]   Tsimshian Songs. Pp. 97–280 in The Tsimshian: Their Arts and Music. (*Publications of the American Ethnological Society* 18) New York: J.J. Augustin.

1953   Haida Myths Illustrated in Argillite Carvings. *Anthropological Series* 32, *National Museum of Canada Bulletin* 127. Ottawa.

1957   Haida Carvers in Argillite. *Anthropological Series* 38, *National Museum of Canada Bulletin* 139. Ottawa.

1958   Medicine-men of the North Pacific Coast. *Anthropological Series* 42, *National Museum of Canada Bulletin* 152. Ottawa.

1961   Tsimsyan Myths. *Anthropological Series* 51, *National Museum of Canada Bulletin* 174. Ottawa.

Barclay, Forbes
1848   [Letter of March 18.] (Manuscript D.5/21, Folder 541, in Hudson's Bay Company Archives, Provincial Archives of Manitoba, Winnipeg, Canada.)

Barker, John
1987   "At Home with the Bella Coola Indians," by T.F. McIlwraith. John Barker, ann. *BC Studies* 75 (Autumn):43–60. Vancouver.

Barker, "M.A.R."
1963   Klamath Dictionary. *University of California Publications in Linguistics* 31. Berkeley.

Barner, Debra C.
1981   Shell and Archaeology: An Analysis of Shellfish Procurement and Utilization on the Central Oregon Coast. (Unpublished M.A. Thesis in Anthropology, Oregon State University, Corvallis.)

Barnett, Homer G.
1935–1936 [Coast Salish Fieldnotes.] (Manuscripts in Special Collections, University of British Columbia Library, Vancouver.)

1937   Culture Element Distributions, VII: Oregon Coast. *University of California Anthropological Records* 1(3):155–204. Berkeley.

1938   The Nature and Function of the Potlatch. (Unpublished Ph.D. Dissertation in Anthropology, University of California, Berkeley.)

1938a   The Coast Salish of Canada. *American Anthropologist* 40(1):118–141.

1938b   The Nature of the Potlatch. *American Anthropologist* 40(3):349–358.

1939   Culture Element Distributions, IX: Gulf of Georgia Salish. *University of California Anthropological Records* 1(5):221–295. (Reprinted: Kraus Reprint, Millwood, N.Y., 1976.)

1941   Personal Conflicts and Cultural Change. *Social Forces* 20(2):160–171.

1942   Applied Anthropology in 1860. *Applied Anthropology* 1(3):19–32.

1944   Underground Houses on the British Columbia Coast. *American Antiquity* 9(3):265–270.

1955   The Coast Salish of British Columbia. *University of Oregon Monographs. Studies in Anthropology* 4. Eugene. (Reprinted: Greenwood Press, Westport, Conn., 1975.)

1957   Indian Shakers: A Messianic Cult of the Pacific Northwest. Carbondale: Southern Illinois University Press. (Reprinted in 1972.)

1968   The Nature and Function of the Potlatch. Eugene: University of Oregon, Department of Anthropology.

Barnhardt, W.H.
1859   [Comparative Vocabulary of the Languages Spoken by the 'Umpqua,' 'Lower Rogue River' [Takelma] and 'Calapooia' Tribes of Indians.] (Manuscript No. 218 in National Anthropological Archives, Smithsonian Institution, Washington.)

Barnston, Alexander
1864   Report Concerning the Vancouver Island Exploring Expedition. (Manuscript No. 794, Vol. 2, Folder 4 in Provincial Archives of British Columbia, Vancouver.)

Barry, J. Neilson
1927   The Indians of Oregon: Geographic Distribution of Linguistic Families. *Oregon Historical Quarterly* 28(1):49–61.

1932   Peter Corney's Voyages, 1814–17. *Oregon Historical Quarterly* 33(4):355–368.

1979   The Washington Fishing Rights Controversy: An Economic Critique. 2d rev. ed. Seattle: University of Washington, Graduate School of Business Administration.

[Barsh, Russel L., and Dennis Whittlesey, comps.]
[1988]   Treaty Tribes and the Federal Acknowledgment Process: A Briefing Book. [Seattle, Wash.: no publisher.]
———, comps.
[1988a]   Summary and Analysis of the Evidence Regarding Tribal Existence of the Duwamish, Samish, Snohomish, Snoqualmie, and Steilacoom Tribes in *United States v. Washington*: A Briefing Book. [Seattle, Wash.: no publisher.]

Bartlett, John
1925   A Narrative of Events in the Life of John Bartlett of Boston, Massachusetts, in the Years 1790–1793, During Voyages to Canton, the Northwest Coast of North America, and Elsewhere. Pp. 287–343 in The Sea, the Ship, and the Sailor: Tales of Adventure from Log Books and Original Narratives. Elliot Snow, ed. Salem, Mass.: Marine Research Society.

Baugh, Timothy G.
1978   Du Kak Si: The Structural Implications of Matrilineal Cross Cousin Marriage; the Tlingit Case. (Unpublished Ph.D. Dissertation in Anthropology, University of Oklahoma, Norman.)

Baxter, Paul W.
1983   The Colt Timber Sale Project: An Archaeological Investigation of Six Sites in the Upper Middle Fork of the Willamette River Valley; a Report to the Rigdon District of the Willamette National Forest. Eugene: University of Oregon, Department of Anthropology.

1984   The Buck Creek Site (35LA297), a Report to the Willamette National Forest. Eugene: University of Oregon, Department of Anthropology.

Baxter, Paul W., Richard D. Cheatham, Thomas J. Connolly and Judith A. Willig
1983   Rigdon's Horse Pasture Cave: An Upland Hunting Camp in the Western Cascades. *University of Oregon Anthropological Papers* 28. Eugene.

Bayly, William
[1778]   [Journal.] (Manuscript in the Alexander Turnbull Library, Wellington, New Zealand.)

Beaglehole, John C., ed.
1967   The Journals of Captain James Cook on His Voyages of Discovery. 4 vols. Vol. 3: The Voyage of the *Resolution* and

653

Discovery, 1776–1780. 2 Pts. Cambridge, England: Published for the Hakluyt Society at the University Press.

Beardslee, Lester A.
1882   Reports of Captain L.A. Beardslee, U.S. Navy, Relative to Affairs in Alaska, and the Operations of the U.S.S. Jamestown, Under His Command, While in the Waters of That Territory. Washington: U.S. Government Printing Office.

Beattie, Owen B.
1976   Skeletal Pathology of Prehistoric Human Remains from Crescent Beach. Pp. 155–164 in Current Research Reports. Roy L. Carlson, ed. *Simon Fraser University. Department of Archaeology Publications* 3. Burnaby, B.C.

————
1980   An Analysis of Prehistoric Human Skeletal Material from the Gulf of Georgia Region of British Columbia. (Unpublished Ph.D. Dissertation in Archeology, Simon Fraser University, Burnaby, B.C.)

————
1985   A Note on Early Cranial Studies from the Gulf of Georgia Region: Long-heads, Broad-heads and the Myth of Migration. *BC Studies* 66(Summer):28–36. Victoria.

Beaumont, Ronald C.
1973   Sechelt Statives. *Canadian Journal of Linguistics* 18(2):102–112.

————
1985   She Shashishalhem, the Sechelt Language: Language, Stories and Sayings of the Sechelt Indian People of British Columbia. Penticton, B.C.: Theytus Books.

Beaver, Herbert
1959   Reports and Letters, 1836–1838, of Herbert Beaver, Chaplain to the Hudson's Bay Company and Missionary to the Indians at Fort Vancouver. Thomas E. Jessett, ed. [Portland, Oreg.]: Champoeg Press.

Beckham, Stephen D.
1969   George Gibbs, 1815–1873: Historian and Ethnologist. (Unpublished Ph.D. Dissertation in History, University of California, Los Angeles.)

————
1971   Requiem for a People: The Rogue River Indians and the Frontiersmen. Norman: University of Oklahoma Press.

————
1977   The Indians of Western Oregon: This Land Was Theirs. Coos Bay, Oreg.: Arago Books.

————
1984   [Testimony in Support of H.R. 5540 Before the House Subcommittee on Interior and Insular Affairs, June 4.] (Manuscript, in House Subcommittee files, Washington.)

————
1986   The Land of the Umpqua: A History of Douglas County, Oregon. Roseburg, Oreg.: Douglas County Commissioners.

————
1987   Chinook Indian Tribe Petition for Federal Acknowledgment. (Manuscript and 11 vols. of exhibits, in U.S. Bureau of Indian Affairs, Branch of Acknowledgment and Research, Washington.)

Beckham, Stephen D., Rick Minor, and Kathryn A. Toepel
1981   Prehistory and History of BLM Lands in West-central Oregon: A Cultural Resources Overview. *University of Oregon Anthropological Papers* 25. Eugene.

Beckham, Stephen D., Kathryn A. Toepel, and Rick Minor
1982   Cultural Resource Overview of the Siuslaw National Forest, Western Oregon. *Heritage Research Associates Reports* 7(1). Oswego, Oreg.

————
1984   Native American Religious Practices and Uses in Western Oregon. *University of Oregon Anthropological Papers* 31. Eugene.

Begg, Alexander
1894   History of British Columbia from Its Earliest Discovery to the Present Time. Toronto: W. Briggs. (Reprinted: McGraw-Hill Ryerson, Toronto, 1972.)

Belcher, Edward
1843   Narrative of a Voyage Round the World, Performed in Her Majesty's Sulphur, During the Years 1836–1842 . . . .London: H. Colburn.

Belcher, William R.
1985   Shellfish Utilization Among the Puget Sound Salish. *Northwest Anthropological Research Notes* 19(1):83–92. Moscow, Idaho.

Belden, G.
1855   Sketch Map of Oregon Territory, Exhibiting the Locations of the Various Indian Tribes, the Districts of Country Ceded by Them, with the Dates of Purchases and Treaties, and the Reserves of the Umpqua and Rogue River Indians. (Map 234, tube 451, Cartographic Records Division, National Archives, Washington. Redrafted: P. 58 in Executive Document No. 25, 53d Congress, 1st sess., 1893.)

Bell, Edward
1914   A New Vancouver Journal [Edmond S. Meany ed.]. *Washington Historical Quarterly* 5(2):129–137, (3):215–224, (4):300–308; 6(1):50–68.

Benedict, Ruth
1934   Patterns of Culture. Boston: Houghton Mifflin. (Reprinted in 1969.)

Benenson, Abram, ed.
1975   Control of Communicable Disease in Man. Washington: The American Public Health Association.

Bensell, Royal A.
1959   All Quiet on the Yamhill: The Civil War in Oregon; the Journal of Corporal Royal A. Bensell [1862–1864]. Gunter Barth, ed. Eugene: University of Oregon Books.

Beresford, William
1789   A Voyage Around the World: But More Particularly to the North-west Coast of America Performed in 1785, 1786, 1787, and 1788, in the King George and Queen Charlotte . . . .George Dixon, ed. London: George Goulding. (Reprinted: Biblioteca Australiana No. 37, Da Capo Press, New York, 1968.)

Berger, Thomas R.
1981   The Nishga Indians and Aboriginal Rights. Pp. 219–254 in Fragile Freedoms: Human Rights and Dissent in Canada. Toronto: Clarke, Irwin.

Bergey, Robin
1983   Determination of Eligibility for the Bear Shell Midden. (Manuscript on file, U.S. Forest Service, Chatham Area, Tongass National Forest, Sitka, Alaska.)

Bergland, Eric O.
1984   Olympic Archaeological Baseline Study. (Report on file with the Division of Cultural Resources, Pacific Northwest Region, National Park Service, Seattle.)

Berman, Judith
1982   Deictic Auxiliaries and Discourse Marking in Kwakw'ala Narrative. Pp. 355–408 in Working Papers for the 17th International Conference on Salish and Neighboring Languages. Portland, Oreg.: Portland State University.

————
1983   Three Discourse Elements in Boas' Kwakw'ala Texts. Pp. 1–52 in Working Papers for the 18th International Conference on Salish and Neighboring Languages. Seattle: University of Washington.

————
1986   The Seals' Sleeping Cave: Method and Theory in the Interpretation of Boas' Kwakw'ala Texts. (Unpublished manuscript, at Department of Anthropology, University of Pennsylvania, Philadelphia.)

Bernick, Kathryn
1983   A Site Catchment Analysis of the Little Qualicum River Site, DiScl: A Wet Site on the East Coast of Vancouver Island, B.C. *Canada. National Museum of Man. Mercury Series. Archaeological Survey Papers* 118. Ottawa.

1985   Plant Fibre Artifacts from the Hesquiat Harbour Area Sites. (Unpublished manuscript in British Columbia Provincial Museum, Victoria, B.C.)

Berreman, Joel V.
1935   A Preliminary Survey of the Shell Mounds and Other Occupied Sites of the Coast of Southern Oregon and Northern Caiifornia. (Unpublished manuscript in Oregon State Museum of Anthropology, University of Oregon, Eugene.)

1937   Tribal Distribution in Oregon. *Memoirs of the American Anthropological Association* 47. Menasha, Wis.

1944   Checto Archaeology: A Report of the Lone Ranch Creek Shell Mound on the Coast of Southern Oregon. *General Series in Anthropology* 11. Menasha, Wis.

Berringer Patricia A.
1982   Northwest Coast Traditional Salmon Fisheries: Systems of Resource Utilization. (Unpublished M.A. Thesis in Anthropology, University of British Columbia, Vancouver.)

Berry, A. Caroline, and R.J. Berry
1967   Epigenetic Variation in the Human Cranium. *Journal of Anatomy* 101(2):361–379.

Beynon, William
1916   [Kitkatka Field Notebook.] (Manuscript in Canadian Centre for Folk Culture Studies, National Museum of Man, Ottawa.)

1941   Tsimshians of Metlakatla, Alaska. *American Anthropologist* 43(1):83–88.

Biddle, Nicholas
1814   History of the Expedition Under the Command of Captains Lewis and Clark . . . .Performed During the Years 1804–5–6. 2 vols. Philadelphia: Bradford and Inskeep. (Reprinted: AMS Press, New York, 1973.)

Birkbeck, John A., and Melvin Lee
1973   Growth and Skeletal Maturation in British Columbia Indian Populations. *American Journal of Physical Anthropology* 38(3):727–738.

Birkbeck, John A., Melvin Lee, Gordon S. Myers, and Braxton M. Alfred
1971   Nutritional Status of British Columbia Indians, II: Anthropometric Measurements, Physical and Dental Examinations at Ahousat and Anaham. *Canadian Journal of Public Health* 62(5):403–414.

Birket-Smith, Kaj
1953   The Chugach Eskimo. *Nationalmuseets Skrifter, Etnografisk Række* 6. Copenhagen.

1964   An Analysis of the Potlatch Institution of North America. *Folk* 6(2):5–13.

1967   Potlatch and Feasts of Merit. *Studies in Circumpacific Culture Relations* 1. Copenhagen: Munksgaard.

Birket-Smith, Kaj, and Frederica De Laguna
1938   The Eyak Indians of the Copper River Delta, Alaska. Copenhagen: Levin and Munksgaard. (Reprinted: AMS Press, New York, 1976.)

Bishop, Charles
1796   Commercial Journal of the Ship "Ruby;" Voyage to the Northwest Coast of America and China, 1794–96. (Manuscript in the British Columbia Provincial Archives, Victoria.)

1967   The Journal and Letters of Captain Charles Bishop on the North-west Coast of America. Michael Roe, ed. Cambridge, England: The Hakluyt Society.

Bishop, Kathleen L., and Kenneth C. Hansen
1978   The Landless Tribes of Western Washington. *American Indian Journal* 4(5):20–31. Washington.

Bishop, Thomas G.
1915   An Appeal to the Government to Fulfill Sacred Promises Made 61 Years Ago. Tacoma, Wash. (Copy in Pacific Northwest Special Collection, University of Washington Library, Seattle.)

Black, Lydia T.
1989   Studies of Russian America: State of the Art. *Pacifica: Journal of Pacific and Asian Studies* 1(1):27–45. Anchorage, Alaska.

Blackman, Margaret B.
1972   *Neï: wɔns* the "Monster" House of Chief *Wi:ha:* An Exercise in Ethnohistorical, Archaeological, and Ethnological Reasoning. *Syesis* 5:211–225. Victoria, B.C.

1973   Totems to Tombstones: Culture Change as Viewed Through the Haida Mortuary Complex, 1877–1971. *Ethnology* 12(1):47–56.

1976   Blankets, Bracelets, and Boas: The Potlatch in Photographs. *Anthropological Papers of the University of Alaska* 18(2):53–67. Fairbanks.

1976a   Creativity in Acculturation: Art, Architecture and Ceremony from the Northwest Coast. *Ethnohistory* 23(4):387–413.

1977   Ethnohistoric Changes in the Haida Potlatch Complex. *Arctic Anthropology* 14(1):39–53.

1979   Northern Haida Land and Resource Utilization. Pp. 43–55 in Tales from the Queen Charlotte Islands. Senior Citizens of the Queen Charlotte Islands, eds. Cloverdale, B.C.: D.W. Friesen and Sons.

1981   Window on the Past: The Photographic Ethnohistory of the Northern and Kaigani Haida. *Canada. National Museum of Man. Mercury Series. Ethnology Service Papers* 74. Ottawa.

1981a   The Changing Status of Haida Women: An Ethnohistorical and Life History Approach. Pp. 65–77 in The World Is as Sharp as a Knife: An Anthology in Honour of Wilson Duff. Donald B. Abbott, ed. Victoria: British Columbia Provincial Museum.

1982   During My Time: Florence Edenshaw Davidson, a Haida Woman. Seattle: University of Washington Press.

1985   Contemporary Northwest Coast Art for Ceremonial Use. *American Indian Art Magazine* 10(3):24–37.

Blackman, Margaret B., and Edwin S. Hall, Jr.
1986   Snakes and Clowns: Art Thompson and the Westcoast Heritage. *American Indian Art Magazine* 11(2):30–45.

Blackman, Margaret B., Edwin S. Hall, Jr., and Vincent Rickard
1981   Northwest Coast Indian Graphics: An Introduction to Silk Screen Printing. Seattle: University of Washington Press.

[Blaine, David, Guert Gansevoort, and William Heebner]
1956   Seattle's First Taste of Battle, 1856. *Pacific Northwest Quarterly* 47(1):1–8.

Blanchet, Francis N.
1878   Historical Sketches of the Catholic Church in Oregon During the Past Forty Years (1838–1878). Portland, Oreg.: no publisher. (Reprinted: Ye Galleon Press, Fairfield, Wash., 1983.)

Blenkinsop, Geo.
1883 [Report, Kwahkewlth Agency, Beaver Harbor, B.C., 17th July, 1882.] Pp. 64–66 in *Dominion of Canada. Annual Report of the Department of Indian Affairs for the Year 1882.* Ottawa.

Blinman, Eric
1980 Stratigraphy and Depositional Environment. Pp. 64–88 in Hoko River: A 2,500 Year Old Fishing Camp on the Northwest Coast of North America. Dale R. Croes and Eric Blinman, eds. *Hoko River Archaeological Project Contributions* 1; Washington State University. Laboratory of Anthropology. *Reports of Investigations* 58. Pullman.

Blomkvist, E.E.
1972 A Russian Scientific Expedition to California and Alaska, 1839–1849: The Drawings of I.G. Voznesenskiĭ. Basil Dmytryshyn and E.A.P. Crownhart-Vaughan, trans. *Oregon Historical Quarterly* 73(2):101–170.

Blukis-Onat, Astrida R.
1976 Archaeological Excavations at Site 45JE16, Indian Island, Jefferson County, Washington. *Washington State University. Archaeological Research Center Project Reports* 30. Pullman.

1984 The Interaction of Kin, Class, Marriage, Property Ownership, and Residence with Respect to Resource Locations Among the Coast Salish of the Puget Lowland. *Northwest Anthropological Research Notes* 18(1):86–96. Moscow, Idaho.

Blukis-Onat, Astrida R., and Trudy Haversat
1977 Archaeological Excavations at Site 45JE16, Indian Island, Jefferson County, Washington; Burial Report. *Washington State University. Archaeological Research Center Project Reports* 61. Pullman.

Blukis-Onat, Astrida R., and Jan L. Hollenbeck, eds.
1981 Inventory of Native American Religious Use, Practices, Localities and Resources: Study Area on the Mt. Baker-Snoqualmie National Forest, Washington State. Seattle: Institute of Cooperative Research.

Blukis-Onat, Astrida R., Lee A. Bennett, Jan L. Hollenbeck, and Rick Oswald
1979 Skagit River Cultural Resources Reconnaissance; Skagit River: Bibliographic Review and Field Reconnaissance for the Skagit River Levee and Channel Improvement Project. Seattle: Seattle Community College.

Boas, Franz
[1885] [Sisiatl Vocabulary (in Seechelt-German)]. (Manuscript No. 30(S2; 4) [Freeman No. 3232] in American Philosophical Society Library, Philadelphia.)

1886 Kapitän Jacobsens Bella-Coola Indianer. *Berliner Tageblatt* 25. Januar, 1886. Berlin.

1886a Mittheilungen über die Vilxûla-Indianer. Pp. 177–182 in *Mittheilungen aus dem Kaiserlichen Museum für Völkerkunde.* Berlin.

[1886b] ["Pĕnlᴸatc Texts", with Interlinear English Translation.] (Manuscript No. 740 in National Anthropological Archives, Smithsonian Institution, Washington.)

[1886c] ["Çālᴸoltq"-English Vocabulary.] (Manuscript No. 711-b in National Anthropological Archives, Smithsonian Institution, Washington.)

[1886d] [English-"Pĕnlᴸatc" Vocabulary.] (Manuscript No. 711-a in National Anthropological Archives, Smithsonian Institution, Washington.)

1887 Census and Reservations of the Kwakiutl Nation (with map). *Bulletin of the American Geographical Society* 19(3):225–232.

1887a Zur Ethnologie Britisch-Kolumbiens. *Petermanns Geographische Mitteilungen* 33(5):129–133. Gotha, Germany.

1887b Notes on the Ethnology of British Columbia. *Proceedings of the American Philosophical Society* 24(126):422–428. Philadelphia.

1887c The Coast Tribes of British Columbia. *Science* 9(216):288–289.

1888 Myths and Legends of the Catloltq of Vancouver Island. *American Antiquarian and Oriental Journal* 10(4):201–211, (6):366–373.

1888a Indian Skulls from British Columbia. *Transactions of the New York Academy of Sciences* 8:4–6. (Abstract of a Paper Read Before the New York Academy of Sciences, October 8, 1888.)

1888b Gleanings from the Emmons Collection of Ethnological Specimens from Alaska. *Journal of American Folk-Lore* 1(3):215–219.

1889 The Houses of the Kwakiutl Indians, British Columbia. *Proceedings of the United States National Museum for 1888,* Vol. 11:197–312. Washington.

1889a The Indians of British Columbia. *Transactions of the Royal Society of Canada for 1888,* Vol. 6(2):47–57. Montreal.

1889b Preliminary Notes on the Indians of British Columbia. Pp. 236–242 in *58th Report of the British Association for the Advancement of Science for 1888.* London.

1889c Notes on the Snanaimuq. *American Anthropologist* 2(4):321–328.

1889d Deformation of Heads in British Columbia. *Science* 13(327):364–365.

1889e [Letter to Mr. Hale, and Preliminary Notes on the Indians of British Columbia.] Pp. 233–242 in *58th Report of the British Association for the Advancement of Science for 1888.* London.

1889f American Museum of Natural History, New York. *Internationales Archiv für Ethnologie* 2:170–171. Leiden, The Netherlands.

1890 First General Report on the Indians of British Columbia [Tlingit, Haida, Tsimshian, and Kutonaga (Kootanie)]. Pp. 801–893 in *59th Report of the British Association for the Advancement of Science for 1889.* London.

[1890a] Chemakum Materials. (Manuscript 30(W3b.1) [Freeman No. 709] in American Philosophical Society Library, Philadelphia.)

1890b The Use of Masks and Head-ornaments on the Northwest Coast of America. *Internationales Archiv für Ethnographie* 3:7–15. Leiden, The Netherlands.

[1890c] [Fieldnotes on Tillamook and Chinookan Dialects.] (Manuscript No. 30(S4.1), [Freeman No. 724] in American Philosophical Society Library, Philadelphia.)

[1890d] [Fieldnotes on Chinookan and Salishan Languages and Gitamat (Kwakiutl), Molala (Sahaptian) and Masset (Haida).] (Manuscript No. 30(Pn4b.5) [Freeman No. 723] in American Philosophical Society Library, Philadelphia.)

[1890e] [Linguistic Field Notebooks, Lexical Files, and Grammatical Notes from Approximately Three Weeks' Fieldwork

Among the Tillamook Salish, Siletz, Oregon.] (In May M. Edel Papers, University of Washington Libraries, Seattle.)

1890f   Schädelformen von Vancouver Island. *Verhandlungen der Berliner Gesellschaft für Anthropologie, Ethnologie and Urgeschichte* 22:29–31.

1891   Second General Report on the Indians of British Columbia. Pp. 562–715 in *60th Report of the British Association for the Advancement of Science for 1890.* London.

1891a   ["Çalᴸō'ltq Texts" with Interlinear Translation.] (Manuscript No. 719 in National Anthropological Archives, Smithsonian Institution, Washington.)

1891b   Sagen aus Britisch Columbien. *Verhandlungen der Berliner Gesellschaft für Anthropologie, Ethnologie und Urgeschichte* 23:532–576, 628–645.

1891c   Physical Characteristics of the Indians of the North Pacific Coast. *American Anthropologist* 4(1):25–32.

1892   Notes on the Chemakum Language. *American Anthropologist* 5(1):37–44.

1892a   The Bilqula. Pp. 408–424 in *61st Report of the British Association for the Advancement of Science for 1891.* London.

1892b   Sagen der Pᴇ́ntlatc. *Verhandlungen der Berliner Gesellschaft für Anthropologie, Ethnologie und Urgeschichte* 24:65–66.

1892c   Eine Sage der Tlaá́men. *Verhandlungen der Berliner Gesellschaft für Anthropologie, Ethnologie und Urgeschichte* 24:62–63.

1892d   Third Report on the Indians of British Columbia. Pp. 408–447 in *61st Report of the British Association for the Advancement of Science for 1891.* London.

1893   Ethnology at the Exposition. *The Cosmopolitan* 15(5):607–609.

1894   Chinook Texts. *Bureau of American Ethnology Bulletin* 20. Washington.

1894a   Indian Tribes of the Lower Fraser River. Pp. 454–463 in *64th Report of the British Association for the Advancement of Science for 1890.* London.

1895   Indianische Sagen von der nordpacifischen Küste Amerikas. Berlin: A. Asher.

1895a   Salishan Texts. *Proceedings of the American Philosophical Society* 34(147):31–48. Philadelphia.

1895b   Fifth Report on the Indians of British Columbia. Pp. 522–592 in *65th Report of the British Association for the Advancement of Science for 1895.* London.

1896   Sixth Report on the Indians of British Columbia. Pp. 569–591 in *66th Report of the British Association for the Advancement of Science for 1896.* London.

1897   The Social Organization and the Secret Societies of the Kwakiutl Indians. Pp. 311–738 in *Report of the U.S. National Museum for 1895.* Washington. (Reprinted: Johnson Reprint, New York, 1970.)

1897a   The Decorative Art of the Indians of the North Pacific Coast. *Bulletin of the American Museum of Natural History* 9:123–176. New York.

1898   The Mythology of the Bella Coola Indians. *Memoirs of the American Museum of Natural History* 2(1):25–127. New York. (Reprinted: AMS Press, New York, 1975.)

1898a   Traditions of the Tillamook Indians. *Journal of American Folk-Lore* 11(40):23–38, 133–150.

1898b   Introduction to James Teit, "Traditions of the Thompson Indians of British Columbia." Pp. 1–18 in *Memoirs of the American Folk-Lore Society* 6. New York. (Reprinted: Pp. 407–424 in Race, Language and Culture, by Franz Boas, Macmillan, New York, 1940.)

1898c   Facial Paintings of the Indians of Northern British Columbia. *Publications of the Jesup North Pacific Expedition* 1; *Memoirs of the American Museum of Natural History* 2:13–24. New York.

1899   The Social Organisation of the Haida. Pp. 648–654 in *68th Report of the British Association for the Advancement of Science for 1898.* London.

1899a   Summary of the Work of the Committee in British Columbia. Pp. 667–682 in *68th Report of the British Association for the Advancement of Science for 1898.* London.

[1900] [Tillamook and Siletz Folkloristic Texts.] (Manuscript No. 30(S4.2), [Freeman No. 3745] in American Philosophical Society Library, Philadelphia.)

1900a   Facial Paintings of the Indians of Northern British Columbia. *Publications of the Jesup North Pacific Expedition* 1(Pt.1); *Memoirs of the American Museum of Natural History* 1(1). New York. (Reprinted: AMS Press, New York, 1975).

1901   Kathlamet Texts. *Bureau of American Ethnology Bulletin* 26. Washington. (Reprinted: Scholarly Press, St. Clair Shores, Mich., 1977.)

1902   Tsimshian Texts [Nass River Dialect]. *Bureau of American Ethnology Bulletin* 27. Washington.

1903   The Jesup North Pacific Expedition. *The American Museum Journal* 3(5):73–119. Nw York.

1904   The Vocabulary of the Chinook Language. *American Anthropologist* n.s. 6(1):118–147.

1905   The Jesup North Pacific Expedition. Pp. 91–100 in *Proceedings of the 13th International Congress of Americanists.* New York, 1902.

1909   The Kwakiutl of Vancouver Island. *Publications of the Jesup North Pacific Expedition* 5(2):301–522; *Memoirs of the American Museum of Natural History* 8(2). New York. (Reprinted: AMS Press, New York, 1975.)

1910   Kwakiutl Tales. *Columbia University Contributions to Anthropology* 2. New York.

1910a   Die Resultate der Jesup-Expedition. Pp. 3–18 in Vol. 1 of *Proceedings of the 16th International Congress of Americanists.* Vienna, 1908.

1911   Anthropology. Pp. 132–134 in A Cyclopedia of Education. Paul Monroe, ed. 5 vols. New York: Macmillan.

1911a   Chinook. Pp. 559–677 in Vol. 1 of Handbook of American Indian Languages. 2 vols. *Bureau of American Ethnology Bulletin* 40. Washington. (Reprinted: Scholarly Press, St. Clair Shores, Mich., 1976.)

1911b   Tsimshian. Pp. 283–422 in Vol. 1 of Handbook of American Indian Languages. 2 vols. *Bureau of American Ethnology Bulletin* 40. Washington. (Reprinted: Scholarly Press, St. Clair Shores, Mich., 1976.)

1911c   Kwakiutl. Pp. 423–557 in Vol. 1 of Handbook of American Indian Languages. 2 vols. *Bureau of American Ethnology Bulletin* 40. Washington. (Reprinted: Scholarly Press, St. Clair Shores, Mich., 1976.)

1911d   Introduction. Pp. 5–83 in Vol. 1 of Handbook of American Indian Languages. 2 vols. *Bureau of American Ethnology Bulletin* 40. Washington. (Reprinted: Scholarly Press, St. Clair Shores, Mich., 1976.)

1912   Tsimshian Texts (New Series). *Publications of the American Ethnological Society* 3:65–285. Leyden, The Netherlands: E.J. Brill.

1914   Mythology and Folk-tales of the North American Indians. *Journal of American Folk-Lore* 27(106):374–410. (Reprinted: Pp. 451–490 in Race, Language and Culture, by Franz Boas, Macmillan, New York, 1940.)

1916   Tsimshian Mythology. Based on Texts Recorded by Henry W. Tate. Pp. 29–1037 in *31st Annual Report of the Bureau of American Ethnology for the Years 1909–1910*. Washington.

1920   The Social Organization of the Kwakiutl. *American Anthropologist* 22(2):111–126. (Reprinted: Pp. 356–369 in Race, Language and Culture. Franz Boas, ed., Macmillan, New York, 1940.)

1920a   The Classification of American Languages. *American Anthropologist* 22(4):367–376.

1921   Ethnology of the Kwakiutl (Based on Data Collected by George Hunt). 2 Pts. Pp. 43–1481 in *35th Annual Report of the Bureau of American Ethnology for the Years 1913–1914*. Washington.

1923   Notes on the Tillamook. *University of California Publications in American Archaeology and Ethnology* 20(1):3–16. Berkeley. (Reprinted: Kraus Reprint, New York, 1965.)

1924   The Social Organization of the Tribes of the North Pacific Coast. *American Anthropologist* 26(3):323–332. (Reprinted: Pp. 370–378 in Race, Language and Culture, by Franz Boas, Macmillan, New York, 1940.)

1924a   A Revised List of Kwakiutl Suffixes. *International Journal of American Linguistics* 3(1):117–131.

1925   Contributions to the Ethnology of the Kwakiutl. *Columbia University Contributions to Anthropology* 3. New York.

1927   Primitive Art. Cambridge, Mass.: Harvard University Press. (Reprinted: Dover Publications, New York, 1955.)

1928   Bella Bella Texts. *Columbia University Contributions to Anthropology* 5. New York.

1929   Classification of American Indian Languages. *Language: Journal of the Linguistic Society of America* 5(1):1–7.

1930   The Religion of the Kwakiutl Indians. 2 Pts. *Columbia University Contributions to Anthropology* 10. New York. (Reprinted: AMS Press, New York, 1969.)

1931   Notes on the Kwakiutl Vocabulary. *International Journal of American Linguistics* 6(3–4):163–178.

1932   Bella Bella Tales. *Memoirs of the American Folk-Lore Society* 25. New York.

1933   [Review of] The Serpent in Kwakiutl Religion: A Study in Primitive Culture, by G.W. Locher. *Journal of American Folk-Lore* 46(182):418–421. (Reprinted: Pp. 446–450 in Race, Language, and Culture, by Franz Boas, Macmillan, New York, 1940.)

1934   Geographical Names of the Kwakiutl Indians. *Columbia University Contributions to Anthropology* 20. New York.

1934a   A Chehalis Text. *International Journal of American Linguistics* 8(2):103–110.

1935   Kwakiutl Culture as Reflected in Mythology. *Memoirs of the American Folk-Lore Society* 28. New York. (Reprinted: Kraus Reprint, New York, 1969.)

1935–1943   Kwakiutl Tales (New Series). 2 Pts. *Columbia University Contributions to Anthropology* 26. New York. (Reprinted: AMS Press, New York, 1969.)

1938   Methods of Research. Pp. 666–686 in General Anthropology. Franz Boas, ed. Boston: D.C. Heath. (Reprinted: Johnson Reprint Corporation, New York, 1965.)

1940   Race, Language, and Culture. New York: Macmillan.

1947   Kwakiutl Grammar, with a Glossary of the Suffixes. Helene Boas Yampolsky and Zellig S. Harris, eds. *Transactions of the American Philosophical Society* 37(3):201–377. Philadelphia.

[1948]   Kwakiutl Dictionary. Helene Boas Yampolsky, ed. (Manuscript 30(W1a.21) [Freeman No. 1937] in the American Philosophical Society Library, Philadelphia.)

1966   Kwakiutl Ethnography. Helen Codere, ed. Chicago: University of Chicago Press.

Boas, Franz, and Livingston Farrand
1899   Physical Characteristics of the Tribes of British Columbia. Pp. 628–644 in *68th Report of the British Association for the Advancement of Science for 1898*. London.

Boas, Franz, and Pliny E. Goddard
1924   Vocabulary of an Athapaskan Dialect of the State of Washington. *International Journal of American Linguistics* 3(1):39–45.

Boas, Franz, and Hermann Haeberlin
1927   Sound Shifts in Salishan Dialects. *International Journal of American Linguistics* 4(2–4):117–136.

Boas, Franz, and George Hunt
1902–1905   Kwakiutl Texts. *Publications of the Jesup North Pacific Expedition* 3(1–3); *Memoirs of the American Museum of Natural History* 5(1–3). New York. (Reprinted: AMS Press, New York, 1975.)

1906   Kwakiutl Texts (Second Series). *Publications of the Jesup North Pacific Expeditions* 10(1); *Memoirs of the American Museum of Natural History* 14(1):1–269. New York. (Reprinted: AMS Press, New York, 1975.)

Boas, Franz, Pliny E. Goddard, Edward Sapir, and Alfred L. Kroeber
1916   Phonetic Transcription of Indian Languages: Report of the Committee of the American Anthropological Association. *Smithsonian Miscellaneous Collections* 66(6). Washington.

Boehm, S.G.
1973   Cultural and Non-cultural Variation in the Artifact and Faunal Samples from St. Mungo Cannery Site, B.C., DgRr

2. (Unpublished M.A. Thesis in Anthropology, University of Victoria, Victoria, B.C.)

Boelscher, Marianne
1985 The Curtain within: The Management of Social and Symbolic Classification Among the Masset Haida. (Unpublished Ph.D. Dissertation in Anthropology, Simon Fraser University, Burnaby, B.C.)

Boit, John
1921 [Reprint of] Boit's Log of the Columbia, 1790–1793. F.W. Howay and T.C. Elliott, ann. *Oregon Historical Society Quarterly* 22(4):265–356.

1969 Remarks on the Ship Columbia's Voyage from Boston, (on a Voyage Round the Globe) [1790–1793]. Pp. 363–431 in Voyages of the "Columbia" to the Northwest Coast, 1787–1790 and 1790–1793. F.W. Howay, ed. New York: Da Capo Press. (Originally published in 1941 by Massachusetts Historical Society.)

Bolduc, Jean Baptiste
1979 Journal, Cowlitz, February 15, 1844. Pp. 103–121 in Mission of the Columbia. Edward Kowrach trans. Fairfield, Wash.: Ye Galleon.

Borden, Charles E.
1950 Preliminary Report on Archaeological Investigations in the Fraser Delta Region. *Anthropology in British Columbia* 1:13–27. Victoria.

1950a Notes on the Pre-history of the Southern Coast. *British Columbia Historical Quarterly* 14(4):241–246. Victoria.

1951 Facts and Problems of Northwest Coast Prehistory. *Anthropology in British Columbia* 2:35–52. Victoria.

1960 DjRi3, an Early Site in the Fraser Canyon, British Columbia. Pp. 101–118 in Contributions to Anthropology 1957. *Anthropological Series* 45, *National Museum of Canada Bulletin* 162. Ottawa.

1961 Fraser River Archaeological Project: Progress Report. *National Museum of Canada Anthropological Papers* 1. Ottawa.

1962 West Coast Crossties with Alaska. Pp. 9–19 in Prehistoric Cultural Relations Between the Arctic and Temperate Zones of North America. John M. Campbell, ed. *Arctic Institute of North America, Technical Papers* 11. Montreal. (Reprinted: Johnson Reprint, New York, 1972.)

1968 Prehistory of the Lower Mainland. Pp. 9–26 in Lower Fraser Valley: Evolution of a Cultural Landscape. Alfred H. Siemens, ed. *University of British Columbia Geographical Series* 9. Vancouver.

1968a The Skagit River Atlatl: A Reappraisal. *BC Studies* 1(Winter):13–19. Vancouver.

1968b A Late Pleistocene Pebble Tool Industry of Southwestern British Columbia. Pp. 55–69 in Early Man in Western North America, by C. Irwin-Williams. *Eastern New Mexico University. Contributions in Anthropology* 1(4).

1969 Early Population Movements from Asia into Western North America. *Syesis* 2(1–2):1–13. Victoria, B.C.

1970 Cultural History of the Fraser-Delta Region: An Outline. Pp. 95–112 in Archaeology in British Columbia, New Discoveries. Roy L. Carlson, ed. *BC Studies* 6–7(Fall-Winter). Vancouver.

1975 Origins and Development of Early Northwest Coast Culture, to About 3000 B.C. *Canada. National Museum of Man. Mercury Series. Archaeological Survey Papers* 45. Ottawa.

1976 A Water-saturated Site on the Southern Mainland Coast of British Columbia. Pp. 233–260 in The Excavation of Water-saturated Archaeological Sites (Wet Sites) on the Northwest Coast of North America. Dale R. Croes, ed. *Canada. National Museum of Man. Mercury Series. Archaeological Survey Papers* 50. Ottawa.

1979 Peopling and Early Cultures of the Pacific Northwest: A View from British Columbia, Canada. *Science* 203(4384):963–971.

1983 Prehistoric Art of the Lower Fraser Region. Pp. 131–165 in Indian Art Traditions of the Northwest Coast. Roy L. Carlson, ed. Burnaby, B.C.: Simon Fraser University, Archaeology Press.

Bork-Feltkamp, A.J. van
1960 Some Remarks on Skulls and Skull Fragments of the Fraser Middens (British Columbia). Amsterdam: Nederlandsch Museum voor Anthropologie.

Borrelly, Maurice A.
1971 A Memorial to Mungo Martin. *Beautiful British Columbia* 12(4):30–35. Victoria.

Bosse, Jean
[1977] Mémoires d'un grand Brainois: Monseigneur Adrien Croquet, le "Saint de l'Orégon." [Braine-l'Alleud, Belgium]: Association du Musée de Braine-l'Alleud.

Bouchard, Randy
[1971–1977] [Ethnographic and Linguistic Notes from Fieldwork Among the Bella Coola Indians, British Columbia.] (Manuscript in British Columbia Indian Language Project, Victoria.)

1971–1981 [Ethnographic and Linguistic Notes on Northern Strait of Georgia Coast Salish. British Columbia Indian Language Project, Victoria.] (Manuscripts in Bouchard's possession.)

Bouchard, Randy, Louis Miranda, and Dorothy I.D. Kennedy
1975 The Squamish Indian People. Victoria: British Columbia Indian Language Project.

Boucher, Nicole
1976 Prehistoric Subsistence at the Helen Point Site. (Unpublished M.A. Thesis in Archaeology, Simon Fraser University, Burnaby, B.C.)

Boxberger, Daniel L.
1980 The Lummi Island Reef-nets. *The Indian Historian* 13(4):48–54.

1986 Resource Allocation and Control on the Lummi Indian Reservation: A Century of Conflict and Change in the Salmon Fishery. (Unpublished Ph.D. Dissertation in Anthropology, University of British Columbia, Vancouver.)

1988 In and Out of the Labor Force: The Lummi Indians and the Development of Commercial Salmon Fishery of North Puget Sound, 1880–1900. *Ethnohistory* 35(2):161–190.

Boyd, Mark F.
1941 An Historical Sketch of the Prevalence of Malaria in North America. *American Journal of Tropical Medicine* 21:223–244. Baltimore, Md.

Boyd, Robert T.
1975 Another Look at the "Fever and Ague" of Western Oregon. *Ethnohistory* 22(2):135–154.

1985 The Introduction of Infectious Diseases Among the Indians of the Pacific Northwest, 1774–1874. (Unpublished Ph.D. Dissertation in Anthropology, University of Washington, Seattle.)

1986   Strategies of Indian Burning in the Willamette Valley. *Canadian Journal of Anthropology* 5(1):65–86.

Boyd, Robert T., and Yvonne P. Hajda
1987   Seasonal Population Movement Along the Lower Columbia River: The Social and Ecological Context. *American Ethnologist* 14(2):309–326.

Brabant, Augustin J.
1900   Vancouver Island and Its Missions, 1874–1900: Reminiscences of the Rev. A.J. Brabant. New York: Messenger of the Sacred Heart Press.

———
[1900a]   [Historical Notes.] (Unpublished manuscript in Sisters of St. Ann Archives, Victoria, B.C.)

———
1911   Dictionary of the Hesquiat or Nootkan Language. (Manuscript No. 983–165 in the Archives of the Diocese of Victoria, B.C.)

———
[1911a]   A Few Remarks About the Language of the Hesquiats. (Manuscript No. 983–165[a] in the Archives of the Diocese of Victoria, B.C.)

———
[1911b]   Dictionary of the Hesquiat or Nootka Language; After the Dictionary of the Kalispel Indian Language by the Missionaries of the Society of Jesus. (Manuscript No. 983–165[b] in the Archives of the Diocese of Victoria, B.C.)

———
[1911c]   Dictionary of the Nootka Language. (Manuscript No. 983–165[c] in the Archives of the Diocese of Victoria, B.C.)

———
1926   Vancouver Island and Its Missions, 1900. Pp. 9–131 in Reminiscences of the West Coast of Vancouver Island, by Charles Moser, Kakawis, B.C. [Victoria, B.C.: Acme Press.]

———
1972   Mission to Nootka, 1874–1900: Reminiscences of the West Coast of Vancouver Island. Charles Lillard, ed. Sidney, B.C.: Gray's Publishing.

Brathwaite, Jean, and W.J. Folan
1972   The Taking of the Ship *Boston*: An Ethnohistoric Study of Nootkan-European Conflict. *Syesis* 5:259–266.

Braun, Judy E.
1975   The North American Indian Exhibits at the 1876 and 1893 World Expositions: The Influence of Scientific Thought on Popular Attitudes. (Unpublished M.A. Thesis in American Civilization, George Washington University, Washington.)

Brauner, David R.
1976   Alpowai: The Culture History of the Alpowa Locality. (Unpublished Ph.D. Dissertation in Anthropology, Washington State University, Pullman.)

———
1976a   The Archaeological Reconnaissance of the Proposed Newport to Waldport to Yachats Sewer System, Lincoln County, Oregon. (Report to Jones and Stokes Associates, and the Oregon State Historic Preservation Office, Salem.) Corvallis: Oregon State University. Department of Anthropology.

Bright, Jane O.
1964   The Phonology of Smith River Athapaskan (Tolowa). *International Journal of American Linguistics* 30(2):101–107.

Brink, Jacob H. van den
1974   The Haida Indians: Cultural Changes Mainly Between 1876–1970. (*Monographs and Theoretical Studies in Sociology and Anthropology in Honour of Nels Anderson, Publication* 8.) Leiden, The Netherlands: E.J. Brill.

The British Colonist
1862   [Articles on Smallpox, March Through December.] Victoria, B.C. (Available from the National Library of Canada, Ottawa.)

British Columbia
1875   [Trutch to Seymour, 1867.] In Papers Connected with the Indian Land Question, 1850–1875. Victoria: Richard Wolfenden.

———
1888   Papers Relating to the Commission Appointed to Enquire into the Condition of the Indians of the North-west Coast. Victoria: Richard Wolfenden.

———
1984   Vital Statistics of the Province of British Columbia. *98th Report of the Department of Health Services and Hospital Insurance for 1969*. Victoria.

British Columbia. Department of Education. Division of Curriculum, and Provincial Archives. Provincial Museum
1951   Introduction to Our Native Peoples. *British Columbia Heritage Series* 1. *Our Native Peoples* 1. Victoria: Don McDiarmid, King's Printer.

———
1952   Coast Salish. *British Columbia Heritage Series* 1. *Our Native Peoples* 2. Victoria: Don McDiarmid, Queen's Printer.

———
1952a   Haida. *British Columbia Heritage Series* 1. *Our Native Peoples* 4. Victoria: Don McDiarmid, Queen's Printer.

———
1952b   Nootka. *British Columbia Heritage Series* 1. *Our Native Peoples* 5. Victoria: Don McDiarmid, Queen's Printer.

———
1952c   Tsimshian. *British Columbia Heritage Series* 1. *Our Native Peoples* 6. Victoria: Don McDiarmid, Queen's Printer.

———
1953   Kwakiutl. *British Columbia Heritage Series* 1. *Our Native Peoples* 7. Victoria: Don McDiarmid, Queen's Printer.

———
1953a   Bella Coola. *British Columbia Heritage Series* 1. *Our Native Peoples* 10. Victoria: Don McDiarmid, Queen's Printer.

British Columbia. Royal Commission on Indian Affairs *see* Canada. Royal Commission on Indian Affairs for the Province of British Columbia

Broderson, Paul, and C.J. Hopkins
1939   Pelagic Seal Hunting as Carried on by the Makah and Quileute Indians of Washington. *Indians at Work* 6(7):12–16. Washington.

Brooks, C.W.
1876   Report of Japanese Vessels Wrecked in the North Pacific Ocean from the Earliest Records to the Present Time. *Proceedings of the California Academy of Sciences for 1875*, Vol. 6:50–66. San Francisco.

Browman, David L., and David A. Munsell
1969   Columbia Plateau Prehistory: Cultural Development and Impinging Influences. *American Antiquity* 34(3):249–264.

Brown, Robert
1864   Vancouver Island Exploration, 1864. Victoria, B.C.: Printed by Authority of the Government by Harries and Company.

———
1868   On the Vegetable Products, Used by the Northwest American Indians as Food and Medicine, in the Arts, and in Superstitious Rites. *Transactions of the Edinburgh Botanical Society* 9:378–396.

———
1873–1876   The Races of Mankind: Being a Popular Description of the Characteristics, Manners and Customs of the Principal Varieties of the Human Family. 4 vols. London: Cassell, Petter, and Galpin.

Brown, Steve
1987   From Taquan to Klukwan: Tracing the Work of an Early Tlingit Master Artist. Pp. 157–175 in Faces, Voices, Dreams: A Celebration of the Centennial of the Sheldon Jackson Museum, Sitka, Alaska 1888–1988. Peter L. Corey, ed. Juneau: Division of Alaska State Museums.

Bruchac, Joseph, ed.
1983   Songs from this Earth on Turtle's Back: Contemporary American Indian Poetry. Greenfield Center, N.Y.: The Greenfield Review Press.

Bruseth, Nels
[1949]   Indian Stories and Legends of the Stillaguamish, Sauks, and Allied Tribes. 2d ed. Arlington, Wash.: Arlington Times Press. (Reprinted: Ye Galleon Press, Fairfield, Wash., 1972.)

Bryan, Alan L.
1955   An Intensive Archaeological Reconnaissance in the Northern Puget Sound Region. (Unpublished M.A. Thesis in Anthropology, University of Washington, Seattle.)

1957   Results and Interpretations of Recent Archaeological Research in Western Washington with Circum-boreal Implications. *Davidson Journal of Anthropology* 3(1):1–16. Seattle.

1963   An Archaeological Survey of Northern Puget Sound. *Occasional Papers of the Idaho State University Museum* 11. Pocatello.

Bryant, Charles
1870   Report of Captain C. Bryant, Late Special Agent of the Treasury Department for Alaska, 1869. Pp. 1–24 in *41st Cong., 2d sess. Senate Executive Document* No. 32 (Serial No. 1405). Washington.

Buchanan, Charles M.
1915   Rights of the Puget Sound Indians to Game and Fish. *Washington Historical Quarterly* 6(2):109–118. Seattle.

Buikstra, Jane E., ed.
1981   Prehistoric Tuberculosis in the Americas. *Northwestern University Archeological Program. Scientific Papers* 5. Evanston, Ill.

Burley, David V.
1979   Marpole: Anthropological Reconstructions of a Prehistoric Northwest Coast Culture Type. (Ph.D. Dissertation in Archeology, Simon Fraser University, Burnaby, B.C.)

1980   Marpole: Anthropological Reconstructions of a Prehistoric Northwest Coast Culture Type. *Simon Fraser University. Department of Archaeology Publications* 8. Burnaby, B.C.

Bushnell, David I., Jr.
1938   Drawings by George Gibbs in the Far Northwest, 1849–1851. *Smithsonian Miscellaneous Collections* 97(8). Washington.

Butler, B. Robert
1961   The Old Cordilleran Culture in the Pacific Northwest. *Occasional Papers of the Idaho State University Museum* 5. Pocatello.

Butler, Virginia L.
1983   Fish Remains from the Black River Sites (45KI59 and 45KI51-D). (Unpublished M.A. Thesis in Anthropology, University of Washington, Seattle.)

Buttle, John
1865   Journal of the Proceedings of the Vancouver Island Exploring Expedition. (Typescript, No. G/V27/B97A in Provincial Archives of British Columbia, Victoria.)

CASA = Community and Systems Analysis
1983   Hydaburg and Haida in Change: A Social Impact Assessment of the Hydaburg-Natzuhini Road Connection of the Community of Hydaburg, Alaska. Bainbridge Island, Wash. (Unpublished report in Mary Lee Stearn's possession.)

Caamaño, Jacinto
1938   The Journal of Jacinto Caamaño [1792]. Henry R. Wagner and W.A. Newcombe, eds. Harold Grenfell, trans. *British Columbia Historical Quarterly* 2(3):189–222, (4):265–301. Victoria.

Cabello, Paz
1983   Coleccionismo americano y expediciones científicas del S. XVIII en la museología española. *Archivio per l'Antropologia e la Etnologia* 113:115–135. Firenze.

Cail, Robert E.
1974   Land, Man, and the Law: The Disposal of Crown Lands in British Columbia, 1871–1913. Vancouver: University of British Columbia Press.

Calder, James A., and Roy L. Taylor
1968   Flora of the Queen Charlotte Islands. Pt. 1. *Canada. Department of Agriculture, Research Branch Monographs* 4. Ottawa.

Calvert, Sheila Gay
1968   The Co-op Site: A Prehistoric Midden on the Northern Northwest Coast. (Unpublished manuscript on file at Laboratory of Archaeology, University of British Columbia, Vancouver.)

1970   The St. Mungo Cannery Site: A Preliminary Report. Pp. 54–76 in Archaeology in British Columbia, New Discoveries. Roy L. Carlson, ed. *BC Studies* 6–7. Vancouver.

1980   A Cultural Analysis of Faunal Remains from Three Archaeological Sites in Hesquiat Harbour, B.C. (Unpublished Ph.D. Dissertation in Archaeology, University of British Columbia, Vancouver.)

Cambon, Kenneth, J.D. Galbraith, and G. Kong
1965   Middle Ear Disease in the Indians of the Mount Currie Reservation, British Columbia. *Canadian Medical Association Journal* 93:1301–1305. Toronto.

Campa y Cos, Miguel de la
1964   A Journal of Explorations Northward Along the Coast from Monterey in the Year 1775. John Galvin, ed. San Francisco: John Howell.

Campbell, Brad C.
1975   The Shining Youth in Tsimshian Mythology. Pp. 86–109 in Vol. 1 of Proceedings of the Second Congress of the Canadian Ethnology Society. 2 vols. *Canada. National Museum of Man. Mercury Series. Ethnology Service Papers* 28. Ottawa.

Campbell, Ken
1984   Hartley Bay, B.C.: A History. Pp. 3–26 in The Tsimshian: Images of the Past, Views for the Present. Margaret Seguin, ed. Vancouver: University of British Columbia Press.

Campbell, Sarah K.
1981   The Duwamish No. 1 Site: A Lower Puget Sound Shell Midden. *University of Washington. Office of Public Archaeology. Institute for Environmental Studies Research Reports* 1. Seattle.

Canada
1901   Census of Canada. Ottawa: Statistics Canada.

1927   The Revised Statutes of Canada. Chapter 98: The Indian Act, sect. 141. Ottawa: F.A. Acland.

1927a   Report and Evidence of Special Joint Committee Appointed to Enquire into the Claims of the Allied Indian Tribes of British Columbia. Ottawa.

[1972]   Schedule of Indian Reserves and Settlements. Ottawa: Department of Indian Affairs and Northern Development.

1981   In All Fairness: A Native Claims Policy. Ottawa: Department of Indian Affairs and Northern Development.

1982   Medical Services Annual Report: Pacific Region. Vancouver: Health and Welfare Canada.

1984   Registered Indian Population by Sex and Residence. Ottawa: Department of Indian and Northern Affairs.

Canada. Department of Citizenship and Immigration. Indian Affairs Branch
1950   Census of Indians in Canada, 1949. Ottawa: Edmond Cloutier.

1955   Census of Indians in Canada, 1954. Ottawa: Edmond Cloutier.

1961   Census of Indians in Canada, 1959. Ottawa: [Edmond Cloutier.]

1963   Traditional Linguistic and Cultural Affiliations of Canadian Indian Bands. Mimeo. [Ottawa.]

Canada. Department of Energy, Mines and Resources. National Geographical Mapping Division
1980   Canada: Indian and Inuit Communities and Languages. Map, in The National Atlas of Canada. 5th ed. Ottawa.

Canada. Department of Indian Affairs and Northern Development
1975   Registered Indian Population by Sex and Residence, 1974. Ottawa.

1978   Registered Indian Population by Sex and Residence, 1977. Ottawa.

1981   Annual Report for the Years 1980–1981. Ottawa: Indian and Northern Affairs Canada.

1982   Registered Indian Population by Sex and Residence, 1980. Ottawa.

1985   Registered Indian Population by Sex and Residence, 1984. Ottawa.

1987   Indian Register, Population by Sex and Residence, 1987. Ottawa: Queen's Printer.

Canada. Department of Indian Affairs and Northern Development. Indian Affairs Branch
1967   Linguistic and Cultural Affiliations of Canadian Indian Bands. Ottawa: Queen's Printer.

1970   Linguistic and Cultural Affiliations of Canadian Indian Bands. G.W. Neville, ed. and comp. Ottawa: Queen's Printer.

Canada. Department of Indian Affairs and Northern Development. Indian and Inuit Affairs Program
1980   Linguistic and Cultural Affiliations of Canadian Indian Bands. Ottawa.

1984   Registered Indian Population by Sex and Residence for Bands, Responsibility Centres, Regions and Canada, December 31, 1983. Ottawa.

Canada. Department of Mines and Resources. Indian Affairs Branch
1945   Census of Indians in Canada, 1944. Ottawa: Edmond Cloutier.

Canada. Department of Transportation
1968   Climatic Normals. Vol. II: Precipitation. Toronto: Queen's Printer.

Canada, Dominion of
1872   Report of the Indian Branch [for 1871–1872]. Ottawa.

1873   Annual Report on Indian Affairs for the Year 1872. Ottawa.

1882   Annual Report of the Department of Indian Affairs for the Year 1881. Ottawa: MacLean, Roger.

1883   Annual Report of the Department of Indian Affairs for the Year 1882. Ottawa: MacLean Roger.

1887   Annual Report of the Department of Indian Affairs for the Year 1886. Ottawa: MacLean, Roger.

1889   Annual Report of the Department of Indian Affairs for the Year 1888. Ottawa: Queen's Printer.

1890   Annual Report of the Department of Indian Affairs for the Year 1889. Ottawa: Queen's Printer.

1891   Annual Report of the Department of Indian Affairs for the Year 1890. Ottawa: Queen's Printer.

1893   Annual Report of the Department of Indian Affairs for the Year 1892. Ottawa: S.E. Dawson.

1894   Census of the Indians of Canada. In Annual Report of the Department of Indian Affairs for the Year 1893. Ottawa: S.E. Dawson.

1895   Annual Report of the Department of Indian Affairs for the Year 1894. Ottawa: S.E. Dawson.

1899   Annual Report of the Department of Indian Affairs for the Year 1898. Ottawa: S.E. Dawson.

1900   Annual Report of the Department of Indian Affairs for the Year 1899. Ottawa: S.E. Dawson.

1901   Annual Report of the Department of Indian Affairs for the Year 1900. Ottawa: S.E. Dawson.

1908   Annual Report of the Department of Indian Affairs for the Year 1908. Ottawa: S.E. Dawson.

1915   Annual Report of the Department of Indian Affairs for the Year 1915. Ottawa: J. de L. Taché.

1924   Annual Report of the Department of Indian Affairs for the Year 1924. Ottawa: F.A. Acland.

1930   Annual Report of the Department of Indian Affairs for the Year 1929. Ottawa: F.A. Acland.

1934   Annual Report of the Department of Indian Affairs for the Year 1934. Ottawa: J.O. Patenaude

Canada. National Museum of Man. Archaeology Division
1972   'Ksan, Breath of Our Grandfathers. An Exhibition of 'Ksan Art. Ottawa: National Museums of Canada.

Canada. Royal Commission on Indian Affairs for the Province of British Columbia
1916   Report of the Royal Commission on Indian Affairs for the Province of British Columbia. 4 vols. Victoria: Acme Press.

Canada. Surveys and Mapping Branch. Geography Division
1974   The National Atlas of Canada. 4th rev. ed. Ottawa: Department of Energy, Mines and Resources.

Canadian Hydrographic Service
1951   British Columbia Pilot (Canadian Edition). Vol. 1: Southern Portion of the Coast of British Columbia . . . .5th ed. Ottawa: Department of Mines and Technical Services.

Canizzo, Jeanne
1983   George Hunt and the Invention of Kwakiutl Culture. Canadian Review of Sociology and Anthropology 20(1):44–58.

Cannon, Aubrey
1987   Central Coast Economic Prehistory. (Unpublished manuscript, on file at Department of Archaeology, Simon Fraser University, Burnaby, B.C.)

1988   Radiographic Age Determination of Pacific Salmon: Species and Seasonal Inferences. *Journal of Field Archaeology* 15(1):103–108.

Capes, Katherine H.
1964   Contributions to the Prehistory of Vancouver Island. *Occasional Papers of the Idaho State University Museum* 15. Pocatello.

———
1977   Archaeological Investigations of the Millard Creek Site, Vancouver Island, British Columbia. *Syesis* 10:57–84. Victoria, B.C.

Carbonell, Virginia M.
1963   Variations in the Frequency of Shovel-shaped Incisors in Different Populations. Pp. 211–234 in Dental Anthropology. Don R. Brothwell, ed. *Symposia of the Society for the Study of Human Biology* 5) New York: Pergamon Press.

Carl, G. Clifford
1950   The Amphibians of British Columbia. 2d ed. *British Columbia Provincial Museum Handbook* 2. Victoria.

———
1951   The Reptiles of British Columbia. 2d ed. *British Columbia Provincial Museum Handbook* 3. Victoria.

Carl, G. Clifford, and C.J. Guiguet
1972   Alien Animals in British Columbia. Rev. ed. *British Columbia Provincial Museum Handbook* 14. Victoria.

Carl, G. Clifford, W.A. Clemens, and C.C. Lindsey
1959   The Fresh-water Fishes of British Columbia. 3d rev. ed. *British Columbia Provincial Museum Handbook* 5. Victoria.

Carlson, Catherine
1979   Preliminary Report on Excavations at Bear Cove (Site EeSu 8), Port Hardy, B.C. (Unpublished manuscript in the Heritage Conservation Branch, Victoria, B.C.)

———
1979a   The Early Component at Bear Cove. *Canadian Journal of Archaeology* 3:177–194.

———
1980   Final Report on Excavations at Bear Cove. (Unpublished draft manuscript in Heritage Conservation Branch, Victoria, B.C.)

Carlson, Roy L.
1954   Archaeological Investigations in the San Juan Islands. (Unpublished M.A. Thesis in Anthropology, University of Washington, Seattle.)

———
1960   Chronology and Culture Change in the San Juan Islands, Washington. *American Antiquity* 25(4):562–586.

———
1970   Excavations at Helen Point on Mayne Island. Pp. 113–125 in Archaeology in British Columbia, New Discoveries. Roy L. Carlson, ed. *BC Studies* 6–7 (Fall–Winter). Vancouver.

———
1970a   Archaeology in British Columbia. Pp. 7–17 in Archaeology in British Columbia, New Discoveries. Roy L. Carlson, ed. *BC Studies* 6–7(Fall-Winter). Vancouver.

———
1972   Excavations at Kwatna. Pp. 41–58 in Salvage '71: Reports on Salvage Archaeology Undertaken in British Columbia in 1971. Roy L. Carlson, ed. *Simon Fraser University. Department of Archaeology Publications* 1. Burnaby, B.C.

———
1976   The 1974 Excavations at McNaughton Island. Pp. 99–114 in Current Research Reports. Roy L. Carlson, ed. *Simon Fraser University. Department of Archaeology Publications* 3. Burnaby, B.C.

———
1979   The Early Period on the Central Coast of British Columbia. *Canadian Journal of Archaeology* 3: 211–228.

———
1979a   C.E. Borden's Archaeological Legacy. *BC Studies* 42(Summer):3–12. Vancouver.

———
1983   Prehistory of the Northwest Coast. Pp. 13–32 in Indian Art Traditions of the Northwest Coast. Roy L. Carlson, ed. Burnaby, B.C.: Archaeology Press, Simon Fraser University.

———
1983a   Prehistoric Art of the Central Coast of British Columbia. Pp. 121–129 in Indian Art Traditions of the Northwest Coast. Roy L. Carlson, ed. Burnaby, B.C.: Archaeology Press, Simon Fraser University.

———
1983b   Change and Continuity in Northwest Coast Art. Pp. 199–205 in Indian Art Traditions of the Northwest Coast. Roy L. Carlson, ed. Burnaby, B.C.: Archaeology Press, Simon Fraser University.

———
1983c   The Far West. Pp. 73–96 in Early Man in the New World. Richard Shutler, Jr., ed. Beverly Hills, Calif.: Sage Publications.

———
1984   The Excavation of an Historic Bella Bella House. (Report on file at the B.C. Heritage Conservation Branch, Victoria.)

———
1987   Cultural and Ethnic Continuity on the Pacific Coast of British Columbia. (Paper presented at the 16th Pacific Science Congress, Seoul.)

Carlson, Roy L., and Philip M. Hobler
1976   Archaeological Survey of Seymour Inlet, Quatsino Sound, and Adjacent Localities. Pp. 115–141 in Current Research Reports. Roy L. Carlson, ed. *Simon Fraser University. Department of Archaeology Publications* 3. Burnaby, B.C.

Carnahan, John W., [ed.]
1976   Biographical Sketches of Authors on Russian America and Alaska [by Henry W. Elliott]. *Anchorage Historical and Fine Arts Museum. Occasional Papers* 2.

Carpenter, Edmund
1975   Introduction. Pp. 9–27 in Form and Freedom: A Dialogue on Northwest Coast Indian Art, by Bill Holm and Bill Reid. Houston, Tex.: Rice University, Institute for the Arts.

Carter, Anthony
1971   In Memory of Mungo Martin. *The Beaver*, Outfit 301(Spring):44–45. Winnipeg.

Castile, George P.
1982   The "Half-Catholic" Movement: Edwin and Myron Eells and the Rise of the Indian Shaker Church. *Pacific Northwest Quarterly* 73(4):165–174.

Castro, Michael
1983   Interpreting the Indian: Twentieth-century Poets and the Native American. Albuquerque: University of New Mexico Press.

Cavanagh, Deborah M.
1983   Northwest Coast Whaling: A New Perspective. (Unpublished M.A. Thesis in Anthropology, University of British Columbia, Vancouver.)

Chambers, Scott
1977   Elbridge Warren Merrill. *The Alaska Journal* 7(3):139–145. Juneau.

Chance, David
1973   Influences of the Hudson's Bay Company on the Native Cultures of the Colville District. *Northwest Anthropological Research Notes. Memoirs* 2. Moscow, Idaho.

Chapman, Anne
1965   Mâts totémiques, Amérique du nord, côte nord-ouest objets et mondes. *La Revue du Musée de l'Homme* 5(3):175–196. Paris.

Chapman, Margaret W.
1982   Archaeological Investigations at the O'Connor Site, Port Hardy. Pp. 65–132 in Papers on Central Coast Archaeo-

logy. Philip M. Hobler, ed. *Simon Fraser University. Department of Archaeology Publications* 10. Burnaby, B.C.

Charlton, Arthur S.
1980   The Belcarra Park Site. *Simon Fraser University. Department of Archeology Publications* 9. Burnaby, B.C.

Chatters, James C.
[1974]   Interim Report of Archaeological Excavations at the Schults Marsh Site. Seattle: University of Washington, Department of Anthropology.

———
1985   [Letter to Roy L. Carlson, June 7, 1985.] (In Carlson's possession.)

Chatters, James C., and Gail Thompson
1979   Test Excavations: 45-SN-29, 45-SN-48 and 45-SN-49, Snohomish County, Washington. *University of Washington. Office of Public Archaeology. Institute for Environmental Studies. Reports in Highway Archaeology* 4. Seattle.

Cheatham, Richard D.
1984   The Fern Ridge Lake Archaeological Project, Lane County, Oregon, 1982–1984. Eugene: University of Oregon, Department of Anthropology.

Chinard, Gilbert, ed.
1937   Le Voyage de Lapérouse sur les côtes de l'Alaska et de la Californie (1786) avec une introduction et des notes . . . Baltimore, Md.: Johns Hopkins Press.

Chirouse, Eugene C.
[1880]   A Short Method to learn the Snohomish Indian Language in 14 Lessons. (Manuscript No. HHB [P–1386] in the Bancroft Library, University of California, Berkeley.)

Chisholm, Brian S.
1986   Reconstruction of Prehistoric Diet in British Columbia Using Stable-carbon Isotopic Analyses. (Unpublished Ph.D. Dissertation in Archaeology, Simon Fraser University, Burnaby, B.C.)

Chisholm, Brian S., D. Erle Nelson, and Henry P. Schwarcz
1982   Stable-carbon Isotope Ratios as a Measure of Marine versus Terrestrial Protein in Ancient Diets. *Science* 216(4550):1131–1132.

———
1983   Marine and Terrestrial Protein in Prehistoric Diets on the British Columbia Coast. *Current Anthropology* 24(3):396–398.

Chittenden, Newton H.
1884   Hyda Land and People: Official Report of the Exploration of the Queen Charlotte Islands for the Government of British Columbia. Victoria: n.p.

Chowning, Ann
1962   Raven Myths in Northwestern North America and Northeastern Asia. *Arctic Anthropology* 1(1):1–5.

Church Missionary Society
1869   Metlahkatla: Ten Years' Work Among the Tsimsheean Indians; from the Journals and Letters of William Duncan. London: Church Missionary House.

Clague, John J.
1984   De-glaciation of the Prince Rupert-Kitimat Area, British Columbia. (Unpublished report on file at the Geological Survey of Canada, Vancouver.)

———
1984a   Quaternary Geology and Geomorphology, Smithers-Terrace-Prince Rupert Area, British Columbia. *Canada. Geological Survey Memoirs* 413. Ottawa.

Clark, Ella E., ed.
1955–1956   George Gibbs' Account of Indian Mythology in Oregon and Washington Territories. *Oregon Historical Quarterly* 56(4):293–325; 57(2):125–167.

Clark, Gerald H.
1979   A Brief Preliminary Comparison of Polished Slate from Two Southeast Alaskan Coastal Middens. (Manuscript on file, U.S. Forest Service, Alaska Region, Juneau.)

———
1979a   Archaeological Testing at the Coffman Cove Site, Southeastern Alaska. (Paper presented at the 32d Annual Northwest Anthropological Conference, Eugene, Oreg.)

Clark, Selden N.
1877   Are the Indians Dying Out? Preliminary Observations Relating to Indian Civilization and Education. Washington: U.S. Bureau of Education.

Clarke, Louise R., and Arthur H. Clarke
1975   Mollusk Utilization by Nootka Indians, 2300 B.C. to A.D. 1966. *Bulletin of the American Malacological Union for 1974* (40th Annual Meeting) 15–16. Houston, Tex.

———
1980   Zooarchaeological Analysis of Mollusc Remains from Yuquot, British Columbia. Pp. 37–57 in *The Yuquot Project.* Vol. 2. William J. Folan and John Dewhirst eds. *Canada. National Historic Parks and Sites Branch. History and Archaeology* 43. Ottawa.

Clements, William M., and Frances M. Malpezzi, comps.
1984   Native American Folklore, 1879–1979: An Annotated Bibliography. Athens, Ohio: Swallow Press.

Clutesi, George C.
1967   Son of Raven, Son of Deer; Fables of the Tse-shaht People. Sidney, B.C.: Gray's Publishing. (Reprinted in 1975.)

———
1969   Potlatch. Sidney, B.C.: Gray's Publishing. (Reprinted in 1973.)

Clyman, James
1960   James Clyman, Frontiersman: The Adventures of a Trapper and Covered-wagon Emigrant as Told in His Own Reminiscences and Diaries. Charles L. Camp, ed. Portland, Oreg.: Champoeg Press.

Coan, C.F.
1921   The First Stage of the Federal Indian Policy in the Pacific Northwest, 1849–1852. *Oregon Historical Quarterly* 22(1):46–85.

———
1922   The Adoption of the Reservation Policy in the Pacific Northwest, 1853–1855. *Oregon Historical Quarterly* 23(1):1–38.

Codere, Helen
1949   The Harrison Lake Physical Type. Pp. 175–183 in Indians of the Urban Northwest. Marian W. Smith, ed. *Columbia University Contributions to Anthropology* 36. New York.

———
1950   Fighting with Property: A Study of Kwakiutl Potlatching and Warfare, 1792–1930. (*Monographs of the American Ethnological Society* 18). New York: J.J. Augustin.

———
1956   The Amiable Side of Kwakiutl Life: The Potlatch and the Play Potlatch. *American Anthropologist* 58(2):334–351.

———
1957   Kwakiutl Society: Rank without Class. *American Anthropologist* 59(3):473–486.

———
1961   Kwakiutl. Pp. 431–516 in Perspectives in American Indian Culture Change. Edward H. Spicer, ed. Chicago: University of Chicago Press.

———
1966   Fighting with Property: A Study of Kwakiutl Potlatching and Warfare, 1792–1930. Seattle: University of Washington Press.

Coe, Ralph T.
1972   Asiatic Sources of Northwest Coast Art. Pp. 85–91 in American Indian Art: Form and Tradition. New York: Dutton.

Cohen, Fay G., ed.
1986   Treaties on Trial: The Continuing Controversy Over Northwest Indian Fishing Rights (a Report prepared for the American Friends Service Committee). Seattle: University of Washington Press.

Cohen, Fay G., and Vivian L. Bowden
1988   A Legacy Restored: Another Perspective on the Boldt Decision. *Cultural Survival Quarterly* 12(3):50–54.

Cohen, Mark N.
1981   Pacific Coast Foragers: Affluent or Overcrowded? Pp. 275–295 in Affluent Foragers: Pacific Coasts East and West. Shuzo Koyama and David Hurst Thomas, eds. *National Museum of Ethnology. Senri Ethnological Studies* 9. Osaka.

Colby, Merle E.
1939   A Guide to Alaska, Last American Frontier. New York: Macmillan.

Cole, David L.
1965   Archaeological Survey of the Proposed Oregon Dunes National Seashore. (Report to the National Park Service; on file, Department of Anthropology, University of Oregon, Eugene.)

————
1968   Archaeology of the Fall Creek Dam Reservoir; Revised Report. Eugene: University of Oregon, Museum of Natural History.

Cole, David L., and Wilbur Davis
1963   Report on Investigations of Archaeological Sites at Gardiner, Oregon. (Manuscript on file, Department of Anthropology, University of Oregon, Eugene.)

Cole, Douglas
1973   The Origins of Canadian Anthropology, 1850–1910. *Journal of Canadian Studies* 8(1):33–45. Peterborough, Ont.

————
1980   Sigismund Bacstrom's Northwest Coast Drawings and an Account of His Curious Career. *BC Studies* 46(Summer):61–86. Vancouver.

————
1982   Franz Boas and the Bella Coola in Berlin. *Northwest Anthropological Research Notes* 16(2):115–124. (Originally published as Kapitän Jacobsen's Bella-Coola Indianer. *Berliner Tageblatt* January 25, 1886.)

————
1982a   Tricks of the Trade: Northwest Coast Artifact Collecting, 1875–1925. *Canadian Historical Review* 63(4):439–460. Toronto.

————
1985   Captured Heritage: The Scramble for Northwest Coast Artifacts. Seattle: University of Washington Press.

Collier, Donald, and Harry Tschopik
1954   The Role of Museums in American Anthropology. *American Anthropologist* 56(4):768–779.

Collins, Floyd R.
1953   Archaeological Survey of the Oregon Coast from June 1951 to December 1952. (Manuscript, on file at the Department of Anthropology, University of Oregon, Eugene.)

Collins, Henry B.
1937   Archaeology of St. Lawrence Island, Alaska. *Smithsonian Miscellaneous Collections* 96(1). Washington.

Collins, June McCormick
1946   A Study of Religious Change Among the Skagit Indians of Western Washington. (Unpublished M.A. Thesis in Anthropology, University of Chicago, Chicago.)

————
1949   Distribution of the Chemakum Language. Pp. 147–160 in Indians of the Urban Northwest. Marian W. Smith, ed. *Columbia University Contributions to Anthropology* 36. New York.

————
1949a   John Fornsby: The Personal Document of a Coast Salish Indian. Pp. 285–341 in Indians of the Urban Northwest. Marian W. Smith, ed. *Columbia University Contributions to Anthropology* 36. New York.

————
1949b   The Influence of White Contact on Class Distinctions and Political Authority Among the Indians of Northern Puget Sound. (Ph.D. Dissertation in Anthropology, University of Chicago, Chicago. Published in Coast Salish and Western Washington Indians II [*American Indian Ethnohistory: Indians of the Northwest Coast*] Garland, New York, 1974.)

————
1950   The Indian Shaker Church: A Study of Continuity and Change in Religion. *Southwestern Journal of Anthropology* 6(4):399–411.

————
1974   Valley of the Spirits: The Upper Skagit Indians of Western Washington. *American Ethnological Society Monographs* 56. Seattle: University of Washington Press. (Reprinted in 1980.)

————
1974a   The Influence of White Contact on Class Distinctions and Political Authority Among the Indians of Northern Puget Sound. Pp. 89–204 in Vol. 2 of Coast Salish and Western Washington Indians [1949]. (American Indian Ethnohistory: Indians of the Northwest Coast) New York: Garland.

————
1979   Multilineal Descent: A Coast Salish Strategy. Pp. 243–254 in Currents in Anthropology: Essays in Honor of Sol Tax. Robert Hinshaw, ed. The Hague: Mouton.

Collins, Lloyd R.
1951   The Cultural Position of the Kalapuya in the Pacific Northwest. (Unpublished M.A. Thesis in Anthropology, University of Oregon, Eugene.)

Collison, H.A.
1941   The Oolachan Fishery. *British Columbia Historical Quarterly* 5(1):25–31. Vancouver.

Collison, William H.
1878   [Letter of August 17, 1878.] (On file at Church Missionary Society Archives, London.)

————
1915   In the Wake of the War Canoe: A Stirring Record of Forty Years' Successful Labour, Peril and Adventure Amongst the Savage Indian Tribes of the Pacific Coast, [etc.] London: Seeley, Service.

Colnett, James
1788   [Manuscript] Journal [Aboard the] Prince of Wales, 16 October - 7 November 1788. (Unpublished Crown-copyrighted manuscript, Adm. 55/146 in Public Records Office, London.)

Colson, Elizabeth
1953   The Makah Indians: A Study of an Indian Tribe in Modern American Society. Minneapolis: University of Minnesota Press. (Reprinted: Greenwood Press, Westport, Conn., 1974.)

————
1965   The Shaker Church of the Indians in the Context of Its Times. (Manuscript in Colson's possession.)

————
1979   In Good Years and in Bad: Food Strategies of Self-reliant Societies. *Journal of Anthropological Research* 35(1):18–29.

Columbia University. Department of Art History and Archaeology
1968   Early Chinese Art and the Pacific Basin: A Photographic Exhibition. New York: Intercultural Arts Press.

Colvocoresses, George M.
1855   Four Years in the Government Exploring Expedition; Commanded by Captain Charles Wilkes to the Island of Madeira, Cape Verd Island, Brazil . . . 5th ed. New York: J.M. Fairchild.

Colyer, Vincent
1870   Bombardment of Wrangel, Alaska. Report of the Secretary
            of War, Secretary of the Interior, and Letter to the
            President. Washington: U.S. Board of Indian Commission-
            ers.

Conn, Richard
1979   Native American Art in the Denver Art Museum. Denver:
            Denver Art Museum.

Connolly, Thomas J., and Paul W. Baxter
1983   The Site at Sardine Confluence: An Archaeological Evalua-
            tion; a Report to the Willamette National Forest. *B.C./A.D.
            Report* 1. Eugene.

Conrad, David E.
1978   Emmons of Alaska. *Pacific Northwest Quarterly*
            69(2):49–60.

Cook, James
1784   A Voyage to the Pacific Ocean; Undertaken by the
            Command of His Majesty, for Making Discoveries in the
            Northern Hemisphere ... 3 vols. [Vol. 3 by James King],
            London: Printed by W. and A. Strahan for G. Nicol and T.
            Cadell.

Cook, Sherburne F.
1939   Smallpox in Spanish and Mexican California, 1770–1845.
            Bulletin of the History of Medicine 7(2):153–191. Baltimore,
            Md.

———
1943   The Conflict Between the California Indian and White
            Civilization, I: The Indian versus the Spanish Mission.
            Ibero-Americana 21. Berkeley, Calif.

———
1955   The Epidemic of 1830–33 in California and Oregon.
            *University of California Publications in American Archaeo-
            logy and Ethnology* 43(3):303–326. Berkeley.

Cook, Warren L.
1973   Flood Tide of Empire: Spain and the Pacific Northwest,
            1543–1819. New Haven, Conn.: Yale University Press.

Coontz, Robert E.
1930   From the Mississippi to the Sea. Philadelphia: Dorrance.

Coppock, Henry A.
1969   Interactions Between Russians and Native Americans in
            Alaska, 1741–1840. (Unpublished Ph.D. Dissertation in
            Geography, Michigan State University, East Lansing.)

Corcoran, Patricia A., F.H. Allen, Jr., A.C. Allison, and B.S.
Blumberg
1959   Blood Groups of the Alaskan Indians and Eskimos.
            American Journal of Physical Anthropology n.s.
            17(3):187–193.

Cordell, Linda S.
1975   The Lingo Site. Pp. 273–307 in Archaeological Studies in
            the Willamette Valley, Oregon. C. Melvin Aikens, ed.
            University of Oregon Anthropological Papers 8. Eugene.

Corey, Peter L.
1983   Tlingit Spruce Root Basketry Since 1903. Pp. 137–138 in
            The Box of Daylight: Northwest Coast Indian Art. Bill
            Holm, ed. Seattle: Seattle Art Museum and University of
            Washington Press.

Costa, Raymond L., Jr.
1986   Asymmetry of the Mandibular Condyle in Haida Indians.
            American Journal of Physical Anthropology 70(1):119–123.

Coues, Elliott, ed.
1893   History of the Expedition Under the Command of Lewis
            and Clark; to the Sources of the Missouri River, Thence
            Across the Rocky Mountains and Down the Columbia
            River to the Pacific Ocean, Performed During the Years
            1804–5–6. 4 vols. New York: Francis P. Harper. (Reprint-
            ed: Dover Publications, New York, 1965.)

———, ed.
1897   New Light on the Early History of the Greater Northwest:
            The Manuscript Journals of Alexander Henry, Fur Trader
            of the Northwest Company, and of David Thompson ...
            1799–1814 ....3 vols. New York: Francis P. Harper.
            (Reprinted: Ross and Haines, Minneapolis, 1965.)

Coupland, Gary C.
1985   Prehistoric Cultural Change at Kitselas Canyon. (Unpub-
            lished Ph.D. Dissertation in Anthropology, University of
            British Columbia, Vancouver.)

Covarrubias, Miguel
1954   The Eagle, the Jaguar, and the Serpent: Indian Art of the
            Americas; North America: Alaska, Canada, the United
            States. New York: Alfred A. Knopf.

Cove, John J.
1976   Back to Square One: A Re-examination of Tsimshian Cross-
            cousin Marriage. *Anthropologica* n.s. 18(2):153–178. Otta-
            wa.

———
1978   Survival or Extinction: Reflections on the Problems of
            Famine in Tsimshian and Kaguru Mythology. Pp. 231–244
            in Extinction and Survival in Human Populations. Charles
            D. Laughlin, Jr., and Ivan A. Brady, eds. New York:
            Columbia University Press.

Cowan, Ian McTaggart
1945   The Ecological Relationships of the Food of the Columbian
            Black-tailed Deer, *Odocoileus hemionus columbianus* (Rich-
            ardson), in the Coast Forest Region of Southern Vancouver
            Island, British Columbia. *Ecological Monographs*
            15(2):109–139. Durham, N.C.

Cowan, Ian M. and Charles J. Guiguet
1965   The Mammals of British Columbia. *British Columbia
            Provincial Museum Handbook* 11. Victoria.

———
1973   The Mammals of British Columbia, 5th ed. *British Colum-
            bia Provincial Museum Handbook* 11. Victoria.

Cowling, Elizabeth
1978   The Eskimos, the American Indians, and the Surrealists. *Art
            History* 1(4):485–500.

Cox, Ross
1957   The Columbia River [1831]. Edgar I. Stewart and Jane R.
            Stewart, eds. Norman: University of Oklahoma Press.

Coxe, William
1803   Account of the Russian Discoveries Between Asia and
            America, to Which Are Added the Conquest of Siberia and
            the History of the Transactions and Commerce Between
            Russia and China. 4th enl. ed. London: Cadell and Davies.

Craig, William
1858   [Statement of 1848.] Pp. 25–27 in Indian Affairs in Oregon
            and Washington Territories. *35th Cong., 1st Sess. House
            Executive Document* No. 39. (Serial No. 955) Washington.

Crawford, Ailsa E.
1983   Tillamook Indian Basketry: Continuity and Change as Seen
            in the Adams Collection. (Unpublished M.A. Thesis in
            Anthropology, Portland State University, Portland, Oreg.)

Creel, Herrlee G.
1937   The Birth of China: A Study of the Formative Period of
            Chinese Civilization. New York: F. Ungar.

Crespí, Juan
1927   Fray Juan Crespí, Missionary Explorer on the Pacific
            Coast, 1769–1774. Herbert E. Bolton ed. and trans.
            Berkeley: University of California Press.

Cressman, Luther S.
1947   Further Information on Projectile Points from Oregon.
            American Antiquity 13(2):177–179.

———
1953   Oregon Coast Prehistory. Pp. 256–260 in *American Philo-
            sophical Society Year Book for 1952*. Philadelphia.

1953a   Oregon Coast Prehistory: Problems and Progress. *Oregon Historical Quarterly* 54(4):291–300.

1977   Prehistory of the Far West: Homes of Vanished Peoples. Salt Lake City: University of Utah Press.

Cressman, Luther S., and O. Larsell
1945   A Case of Probable Osteomyelitis in an Indian Skeleton. *Western Journal of Surgery, Obstetrics, and Gynecology* 53(9):332–335.

Cressman, Luther S., and William S. Laughlin
1941   A Probable Association of Mammoth and Artifacts in the Willamette Valley, Oregon. *American Antiquity* 6(4):339–342.

Cressman, Luther S., David L. Cole, Wilbur A. Davis, Thomas M. Newman, and Daniel J. Scheans
1960   Cultural Sequences at The Dalles, Oregon: A Contribution to Pacific Northwest Prehistory. *Transactions of the American Philosophical Society* 50(10). Philadelphia.

Croes, Dale R.
1976   The Excavation of Water-saturated Archaeological Sites (Wet Sites) on the Northwest Coast of North America. *Canada. National Museum of Man. Mercury Series. Archaeological Survey Papers* 50. Ottawa.

1977   Basketry from the Ozette Village Archaeological Site: A Technological, Functional and Comparative Study. (Unpublished Ph.D. Dissertation in Archaeology, Washington State University, Pullman.)

1985   Radiocarbon Dates from the Hoko River Rock Shelter. (Manuscript in Croes's possession.)

Croes, Dale R., and Eric Blinman, eds.
1980   Hoko River: A 2500 Year Old Fishing Camp on the Northwest Coast of North America. *Washington State University. Laboratory of Anthropology. Reports of Investigations* 58. Pullman.

Croes, Dale R., and Steven Hackenberger
1988   Hoko River Archaeological Complex: Modeling Prehistoric Northwest Economic Evolution. In Prehistoric Economies of the Pacific Northwest Coast. Barry L. Isaac, ed. (*Research in Economic Anthropology Supplement* 3) Greenwich, Conn.: JAI Press.

Cronin, Kay
1960   Cross in the Wilderness. Vancouver, B.C.: Mitchell Press.

Crook, George
1858   "Tah-leu-wah" Vocabulary. (Manuscript No. 86 in National Anthropological Archives, Smithsonian Institution, Washington.)

Crosby, Alfred W.
1972   The Columbian Exchange: Biological and Cultural Consequences of 1492. Westport, Conn.: Greenwood.

Crosby, Thomas
1907   Among the An-ko-me-nums; or Flathead Tribes of Indians of the Pacific Coast. Toronto: William Briggs.

1914   Up and Down the North Pacific Coast by Canoe and Mission Ship. Toronto: The Missionary Society of the Methodist Church, the Young People's Forward Movement Department.

Crosby, Thomas, Charles M. Tate, and William H. Barraclough
1898   Indian Methodist Hymn-book; Staylim-Paypa ta Methodist-Ts'hayilth: Hymns Used on the Fraser River Indian Mission . . . .Chilliwack, B.C.: W.H. Barraclough. (Original copy in Harold Campbell Vaughan Memorial Library, Acadia University, Wolfville, N.S.)

Culin, Stewart
1907   Games of the North American Indian. Pp. 3–809 in *24th Annual Report of the Bureau of American Ethnology for the Years 1902–1903.* Washington.

1908   Report on a Collecting Expedition Among the Indians of California and Vancouver Island, May-August 1908, by Stewart Culin. New York: Brooklyn Museum Archives, Culin Archival Collection.

Cumming, Peter A., and Neil H. Mickenberg, eds.
1972   Native Rights in Canada. 2d ed. Toronto: Indian-Eskimo Association of Canada and General Publishing.

Currie, Ian
1958   [Interviews with Shakers.] (Unpublished manuscript in possession of P. Amoss.)

Curtin, A. Joanne
1984   Human Skeletal Remains from Namu (ElSxi): A Descriptive Analysis. (Unpublished M.A. Thesis in Archeology, Simon Fraser University, Burnaby, B.C.)

Curtis, Edward S.
1907–1930   The North American Indian: Being a Series of Volumes Picturing and Describing the Indians of the United States, the Dominion of Canada, and Alaska. Frederick W. Hodge, ed. 20 vols. Norwood, Mass.: Plimpton Press. (Reprinted: Johnson Reprint, New York, 1970.)

Cutler, Ron, and N. Morrison
1971   Sudden Death: A Study of Characteristics of Victims and Events Leading to Sudden Death in British Columbia. Vancouver: The Alcoholism Foundation of British Columbia with Primary Emphasis on Apparent Alcohol Involvement and Indian Sudden Death.

Cutter, Donald C.
1963   Early Spanish Artists on the Northwest Coast. *Pacific Northwest Quarterly* 54(4):150–157.

————, ed.
1969   The California Coast: A Bilingual Edition of Documents from the Sutro Collection. Norman: University of Oklahoma Press.

Cutter, Donald C., and Mercedes Palau de Iglesias
1977   Malaspina's Artists. Pp. 19–27 in The Malaspina Expedition. Santa Fe: Museum of New Mexico Press.

Cybulski, Jerome S.
[1967–1986]   [Notes on: Prince Rupert Harbour Materials in the Canadian Museum of Civilization, Ottawa; Early Historic Materials in the Field Museum of Natural History, Chicago, and the American Museum of Natural History, New York. (Unpublished manuscripts in Cybulski's possession.)]

1972   Analysis of Skeletal Remains from the Prince Rupert Harbour Area of British Columbia. *Bulletin of the Canadian Archaeological Association* 4:87–89. Ottawa.

1973   The Gust Island Burial Shelter: Physical Anthropology. *Canada. National Museum of Man. Mercury Series. Archaeological Survey Papers* 9:60–113. Ottawa.

1973a   Discrete Non-metric Skeletal Variants and Application to the Study of Early Northwest Coast Physical Variation. (Abstract of a paper presented at the 25th Annual Meeting of the Northwest Anthropological Conference, Portland, Oreg., 1972.) *Northwest Anthropological Research Notes* 7(2):220. Moscow, Idaho.

1973b   British Columbia Skeletal Remains. *Bulletin of the Canadian Archaeological Association* 7:126–127. Ottawa.

1974   Tooth Wear and Material Culture: Precontact Patterns in the Tsimshian Area, British Columbia. *Syesis* 7:31–35. Victoria, B.C.

667

1975   Skeletal Variability in British Columbia Coastal Populations: A Descriptive and Comparative Assessment of Cranial Morphology. *Canada. National Museum of Man. Mercury Series. Archaeological Survey Papers* 30. Ottawa.

1975a   Physical Anthropology at Owikeno Lake, 1975. *Bulletin of the Canadian Archaeological Association* 7:201–210. Ottawa.

1977   Cribra Orbitalia, a Possible Sign of Anemia in Early Historic Native Populations of the British Columbia Coast. *American Journal of Physical Anthropology* 47(1):31–40.

1978   Modified Human Bones and Skulls from Prince Rupert Harbour, British Columbia. *Canadian Journal of Archaeology* 2:15–32.

1978a   An Earlier Population of Hesquiat Harbour, British Columbia: A Contribution to Nootkan Osteology and Physical Anthropology. *British Columbia Provincial Museum. Cultural Recovery Papers* 1. Victoria.

1978b   On the Interpretation and Misinterpretation of Trepanation in British Columbia. *Northwest Anthropological Research Notes* 12(1):59. Moscow, Idaho.

1979   The Paleopathology of a Small Group of Skeletons from Dodge Island, British Columbia. (Paper presented at the Sixth Annual Meeting of the Canadian Association for Physical Anthropology, Niagara-on-the-Lake, Ont., Nov. 9–12, 1978.) Abstract in: *Canadian Review of Physical Anthropology/Revue Canadienne d'Anthropologie Physique* 1(2):79.

1980   Skeletal Remains from Lillooet, British Columbia, with Observations for a Possible Diagnosis of Skull Trephination. *Syesis* 13:53–59. Victoria, B.C.

1980a   Osteology of the Human Remains from Yuquot, British Columbia. Pp. 175–193 in The Yuquot Project. Vol. 2. William E. Folan and John Dewhirst, eds. *Canada. National Historic Parks and Sites Branch. History and Archaeology* 43. Ottawa.

1983   Paleopathology in the Northwest. (Unpublished manuscript, No. 86–2631, in Scientific Records Section, Archaeological Survey of Canada, National Museum of Man, Ottawa.)

1985   Further Observations on Cribra Orbitalia in British Columbia Samples. *American Journal of Physical Anthropology* 66(2):161.

Cybulski, Jerome S., and L. Bradley Pett
1981   Bone Changes Suggesting Multiple Myeloma and Metastatic Carcinoma in Two Early Historic Natives of the British Columbia Coast. Pp. 176–186 in Contributions to Physical Anthropology, 1978–1980. J.S. Cybulski, ed. *Canada. National Museum of Man. Mercury Series. Archaeological Survey Papers* 106. Ottawa.

Cybulski, Jerome S., Donald E. Howes, James C. Haggerty, and Morley Eldridge
1981   An Early Human Skeleton from South-central British Columbia: Dating and Bioarchaeological Inference. *Canadian Journal of Archaeology* 5:49–59.

Dalan, Rinita, Steve Wilke, Lee Stilson, and Karen James
1981   Cultural Resource Survey of Two Areas Proposed for Resource Activities within the Olympic National Forest, Washington. (Report on file with the Olympic National Forest, Olympia, Wash.)

Dale, Harrison C., ed.
1941   The Ashley-Smith Explorations and the Discovery of a Central Route to the Pacific, 1822–1829, with the Original Journals. Glendale, Calif.: Arthur H. Clark.

Dall, William H.
1870   Alaska and Its Resources. Boston: Lee and Shepard. (Reprinted: Arno Press, New York, 1970.)

1877   Tribes of the Extreme Northwest. Pp. 1–156 in Vol. 1 of *Contributions to North American Ethnology.* J.W. Powell, ed. 9 vols. Washington: U.S. Geographical and Geological Survey of the Rocky Mountain Region.

1884   On Masks, Labrets, and Certain Aboriginal Customs, with an Inquiry into the Bearing of Their Geographical Distribution. Pp. 67–203 in *3d Annual Report of the Bureau of American Ethnology for the Years 1881–1882.* Washington.

Dally, Frederick
1866   Journal. (Manuscript No. 2443 in Provincial Archives of British Columbia, Victoria.)

Dalquest, Walter W.
1948   Mammals of Washington. *University of Kansas. Museum of Natural History Publications* 2. Lawrence.

Dalzell, Kathleen E.
1968   The Queen Charlotte Islands, 1744–1966. Terrace, B.C.: C.M. Adam.

Damon, P.E., C.W. Ferguson, A. Long, and E.I. Wallick
1974   Dendrochronologic Calibration of the Radiocarbon Time Scale. *American Antiquity* 39(2):350–366.

Dancey, William S.
1969   Archaeological Survey of Mossyrock Reservoir. *University of Washington. Department of Anthropology. Reports in Archaeology* 3. Seattle.

Daniel, Travers
1856   [Letter to I.I. Stevens, 5/24/1856.] (Manuscript in Records of Washington Superintendency of Indian Affairs, 1853–1874, microfilm M5, roll 16, National Archives, Washington.)

Darling, John D.
1955   The Effects of Culture Contact on the Tsimshian System of Land Tenure During the Nineteenth Century. (Unpublished M.A. Thesis in Sociology, University of British Columbia, Victoria.)

Dart, Anson
1851   Articles of a Treaty, Made and Concluded at Tansey Point, Near Clatsop Plains, This 9th Day of August 1851, Between ....the United States ....and the Wheelappa Band of the Chinook Indians. (Microfilm No. M2 [Records of the Oregon Superintendency of Indian Affairs, 1848–1873], roll 28 [copies of Treaty Proceedings ....], in National Archives, Washington.)

1851a   Articles of a Treaty, Made and Concluded at Tansey Point, Near Clatsop Plains, This 9th Day of August 1851, Between ....the United States ....and the Klatskania Band of Chinooks. (Microfilm No. M2 [Records of the Oregon Superintendency of Indian Affairs, 1848–1873], roll 28 [copies of Treaty Proceedings ....] in National Archives, Washington.)

Dauenhauer, Nora Marks, and Richard Dauenhauer
1987   Haa Shuká, Our Ancestors: Tlingit Oral Narratives. (*Classics of Tlingit Oral Literature* 1) Seattle: University of Washington Press.

Daugherty, Richard D.
1948   Survey of the Washington Coast from Cape Flattery to Cape Disappointment. (Manuscript in Department of Anthropology, University of Washington, Seattle.)

[1949]   [Unpublished Fieldnotes Collected at the Hoh Indian Reservation.] (Manuscript in Daugherty's possession.)

1983   Cultural Resource Survey of Portions of the Duckabush, Calawah, and West Fork of the Humptulips Rivers, Washington. (Report on file with the Olympic National Forest, Olympia, Wash.)

Daugherty, Richard D., and Janet Friedman
1983   An Introduction to Ozette Art. Pp. 183–195 in Indian Art Traditions of the Northwest Coast. Roy L. Carlson, ed. Burnaby, B.C.: Archaeology Press, Simon Fraser University.

Daugherty, Richard D., J.J. Flenniken, and J.M. Welch
1987   A Data Recovery Study of Judd Peak Rockshelters (45-LE-222) in Lewis County, Washington. *U.S. Forest Service. Studies in Cultural Resource Management* 8. Portland, Oreg.

Davidson, George
1901   Explanation of an Indian Map of the Rivers, Lakes, Trails and Mountains from the Chilkaht to the Yukon Drawn by the Chilkaht Chief Kohklux in 1869. *Mazama* 2(2):75–82.

Davis, Barbara Starr, and Richard D. Davis
1974   Tongues and Totems: Comparative Arts of the Pacific Basin. Anchorage: Alaska International Art Institute.

Davis, Henry, comp.
1976   English-Tlingit Dictionary: Nouns. Rev. ed. Sitka, Alaska: Sheldon-Jackson College.

Davis, Horace
1872   On the Likelihood of an Admixture of Japanese Blood on Our North-West Coast. *Proceedings of the American Antiquarian Society* 69:65–84. Worcester, Mass.

Davis, John H.
1970   Some Phonological Rules in Mainland Comox. (Unpublished M.A. Thesis in Linguistics, University of Victoria, Victoria, B.C.)

Davis, Philip W., and Ross Saunders
1973   Lexical Suffix Copying in Bella Coola. *Glossa* 7:231–252. Burnaby, B.C.

1975   Bella Coola Nominal Deixis. *Language: Journal of the Linguistic Society of America* 51(4):845–858.

1975a   Bella Coola Deictic Usage. *Rice University Studies* 61(2):13–35. Houston, Texas.

1976   Bella Coola Deictic Roots. *International Journal of American Linguistics* 42(4):319–330.

1978   Bella Coola Syntax. Pp. 37–65 in Linguistic Studies of Native Canada. Eung-Do Cook and Jonathan Kaye, eds. Vancouver: University of British Columbia Press.

1980   Bella Coola Texts. *British Columbia Provincial Museum. Heritage Record* 10. Victoria.

1984   An Expression of Coreference in Bella Coola. Pp. 149–167 in The Syntax of Native American Languages. Eung-Do Cook and Donna B. Gerdts, eds. (*Syntax and Semantics* 16) Orlando, Fla.: Academic Press.

Davis, Robert T.
1949   Native Arts of the Pacific Northwest from the Rasmussen Collection of the Portland Art Museum. *Stanford Art Series* 1. Stanford, Calif.

Davis, Stanley, D.
1980   Hidden Falls: A Multicomponent Site on the Alexander Archipelago on the Northwest Coast. (Paper presented at the 45th Annual Meeting of the Society of American Archaeology, Philadelphia.)

————, comp. and ed.
1984   The Hidden Falls Site, Baranof Island, Alaska. (Manuscript on file, U.S. Forest Service, Chatham Area, Tongass National Forest, Sitka, Alaska.)

1985   Test Excavation of the Starrigavan Site, 49 SIT 229, Baranof Island, Alaska. (Manuscript on file, U.S. Forest Service, Chatham Area, Tongass National Forest, Sitka, Alaska.

1985a   Test Excavations at the Russian Cove Site, 49 sum 018, Port Houghton, Alaska. (Manuscript on file, U.S. Forest Service, Chatham Area, Tongass National Forest, Sitka, Alaska.)

Davis, Wilbur A.
1968   Oregon Coast Survey. (Fieldnotes, on file at Department of Anthropology, Oregon State University, Corvallis.)

1970   Archaeology of Phase I, Little Muddy Creek. Final Report. Corvallis: Oregon State University, Department of Anthropology.

1970a   Scoggin Creek Archaeology, 1969. Final Report. Corvallis: Oregon State University, Department of Anthropology.

Davis, Wilbur A., C. Melvin Aikens, and Otto E. Henrickson
1973   Archaeology of Phase III, Little Muddy Creek, Oregon. Eugene, Oreg.: Northwest Anthropological Research Institute.

Davydov, Gavrila Ivanovich
1810–1812   Dvukratnoe puteshestvīe v Ameriku morskikh ofitserov Khvostova i Davydova, pisannoe sim poslīednim (A Double Voyage to America by the Naval Officers Khvostov and Davydov, Written by the Latter). St. Petersburg: Morskaīa Tipografīīa.

1812   Slovar' narīechi narodov, nazyvaemykh *Kolyuzhami*, obitayushchikh mezhdu zalivom Chugachoyu i Yakutatom. [Dictionary of the Dialects of the Peoples Named Tlingit Inhabiting Between Chugash and Yakutat Bays]. Pp. i–xi in Part 2 of Dvukratnoe puteshestvīev Ameriku morskikh ofitserov Khvostova i Davydova, pisannoe sim poslīednim. St. Petersburg: Morskaīa Tipografīīa. (Reprinted in: Two Voyages to Russian America, 1802–1807. Colin Bearne, trans. Richard A. Pierce, ed., The Limestone Press, Kingston, Ont., 1977.)

Dawson, George M.
1878   Queen Charlotte's Island Cruise. Microfilm. Montreal: McGill University Library.

1880   Report on the Queen Charlotte Islands, 1878. Pp. 1B–239B in *Geological Survey of Canada. Report of Progress for 1878–1879.* Montreal.

1880a   On the Haida Indians of the Queen Charlotte Islands. Pp. 103–175 (App. A) in Report on the Queen Charlotte Islands, 1878. *Geological Survey of Canada. Report of Progress for 1878–1879.* Montreal.

1880b   Vocabulary of the Haida Indians of the Queen Charlotte Islands. Pp. 177B–189B (App. B) in Report on the Queen Charlotte Islands, 1878. *Geological Survey of Canada. Report of Progress for 1878–1879.* Montreal.

1888   Notes and Observations on the Kwakiool People of the Northern Part of Vancouver Island and Adjacent Coasts, Made During the Summer of 1885; with a Vocabulary of About Seven Hundred Words. Montreal: Dawson Brothers. (Originally issued: *Transactions of the Royal Society of Canada* 5(2):63–98, 1887.)

Deans, James
1886   How the Whull-e-mooch Got Fire. *American Antiquarian and Oriental Journal* 8(1):41–43.

1888   The Raven in the Mythology of Northwest America. *American Antiquarian and Oriental Journal* 10(2):109–114.

1891   Burial Mounds of Vancouver Island and Their Relics. *American Antiquarian and Oriental Journal* 13(3):171–172.

1892   The Antiquities of British Columbia. *American Antiquarian and Oriental Journal* 14(1):41–44.

————, coll.
1899   Tales from the Totems of the Hidery. Oscar L. Triggs, ed. Vol. 2. Chicago: Archives of the International Folk-Lore Association.

Deiss, William A.
1980   Spencer F. Baird and His Collectors. *Journal of the Society for the Bibliography of Natural History* 9(4):635–645. London.

De Laguna, Frederica
1937   A Preliminary Sketch of the Eyak Indians, Copper River Delta, Alaska. Pp. 63–75 in Twenty-fifth Anniversary Studies. D.S. Davidson, ed. *Philadelphia Anthropological Society Publications* 1.

1947   The Prehistory of Northern North America as Seen from the Yukon. *Memoirs of the Society for American Archaeology* 3. Menasha, Wis. (Reprinted: AMS Press, New York, 1980.)

1952   Some Dynamic Forces in Tlingit Society. *Southwestern Journal of Anthropology* 8(1):1–12.

1953   Some Problems in the Relationship Between Tlingit Archaeology and Ethnology. *Memoirs of the Society for American Archaeology* 9:53–57. Menasha, Wis.

1954   Tlingit Ideas About the Individual. *Southwestern Journal of Anthropology* 10(2):172–191.

1960   The Story of a Tlingit Community [Angoon]: A Problem in the Relationship Between Archaeological, Ethnological, and Historical Methods. *Bureau of American Ethnology Bulletin* 172. Washington.

1963   Mungo Martin, 1879–1962. *American Anthropologist* 65(4):894–896.

1965   Childhood Among the Yakutat Tlingit. Pp. 3–23 in Context and Meaning in Cultural Anthropology. Melford R. Spiro, ed. New York: Free Press.

1972   Under Mount Saint Elias: The History and Culture of the Yakutat Tlingit. 3 Pts. *Smithsonian Contributions to Anthropology* 7. Washington.

1975   Matrilineal Kin Groups in Northwestern North America. Pp. 17–147 in Vol. 1 of Proceedings: Northern Athapaskan Conference, 1971. A. McFadyen Clark, ed. 2 vols. *Canada. National Museum of Man. Mercury Series. Ethnology Service Papers* 27. Ottawa.

1983   Aboriginal Tlingit Sociopolitical Organization. Pp. 71–85 in The Development of Political Organization in Native North America. Elisabeth Tooker, ed. *Proceedings of the American Ethnological Society, 1979.*

————, ed.
[1990]   The Tlingit Indians, by G.T. Emmons. Seattle: University of Washington Press.

De Laguna, Frederica, and Catharine McClellan
[1954–1960] [Yakutat and Ahtna Fieldnotes.] (Manuscripts in the authors' possession.)

[1954–1968] [Ahtna Fieldnotes.] 20 vols. (Manuscripts in De Laguna's possession; microfilm copy in the American Philosophical Society Library, Philadelphia.)

De Laguna, Frederica, and Francis A. Riddell
1952   Excavations at "Old Town", Knight Island, Yakutat Bay, Alaska. (Preliminary report of fieldwork, June–September, 1952; report in Department of Anthropology, Bryn Mawr College, Bryn Mawr, Pa.)

De Laguna, Frederica, Francis A. Riddell, Donald F. McGeein Kenneth S. Lane, J. Arthur Freed, and Carolyn Osborne
1964   Archeology of the Yakutat Bay Area, Alaska. *Bureau of American Ethnology Bulletin* 192. Washington.

Deloria, Vine, Jr.
1977   Indians of the Pacific Northwest; from the Coming of the White Man to the Present Day. New York: Doubleday.

1978   The Lummi Indian Community: The Fishermen of the Pacific Northwest. Pp. 87–158 in American Indian Economic Development. Sam Stanley, ed. The Hague: Mouton.

Demers, Modeste
1871   Chinook Dictionary, Catechism, Prayers and Hymns. Montreal: n.p.

Densmore, Frances
1927   The Language of the Makah Indians. *American Speech* 2:237.

1939   Nootka and Quileute Music. *Bureau of American Ethnology Bulletin* 124. Washington. (Reprinted: Da Capo Press, New York, 1972.)

Desai, Indrajit D., and Melvin Lee
1971   Nutritional Status of British Columbia Indians, III: Biochemical Studies at Ahousat and Anaham Reserves. *Canadian Journal of Public Health* 62(6):526–536.

Detling, LeRoy E.
1961   The Chaparral Formation of Southwestern Oregon, with Considerations of Its Postglacial History. *Ecology* 42(2):348–357.

Dewhirst, John
1976   Coast Salish Summer Festivals: Rituals for Upgrading Social Identity. *Anthropologica* n.s. 18(2):231–273. Ottawa.

1978   Nootka Sound: A 4,000 Year Perspective. Pp. 1–29 in nu·tka·: The History and Survival of Nootkan Culture. Barbara S. Efrat and W.J. Langlois, eds. *Sound Heritage* 7(2). Victoria.

1980   The Indigenous Archaeology of Yuquot, a Nootkan Outside Village. *The Yuquot Project.* Vol. 1. William J. Folan and John Dewhirst, eds. *Canada. National Historic Parks and Sites Branch. History and Archaeology* 39. Ottawa.

Dexter, Ralph W.
1966   Putnam's Problems Popularizing Anthropology. *American Scientist* 54(3):315–332.

Dickerson, Mary C.
1910   Herculean Task in Museum Exhibition: Foreward Regarding the Ceremonial Canoe Scene in the North Pacific Hall. *American Museum Journal* 10(8):227–228.

Dietrich, Bill
1985   Washington's Indians: A Special Report. *The Seattle Times*, December 24. Seattle, Wash.

Dikov, Nikolaĭ N.
1979   Drevnie kul´tury Severo-Vostochnoĭ Azii [Ancient Cultures of Northeastern Asia]. Moscow: Nauka.

Dillon, Richard H.
1951   Archibald Menzies' Trophies. *British Columbia Historical Quarterly* 15(3–4):151–159. Vancouver.

Dingwall, Eric J.
1931   Artificial Cranial Deformation: A Contribution to the Study of Ethnic Mutilations. London: John Bale, Sons and Danielsson.

Dixon, C.W.
1962   Smallpox. London: J. and A. Churchill.

Dixon, George *see* Beresford, William

Dixon, Roland B.
1907   The Shasta. *Bulletin of the American Museum of Natural History* 17(5):381–498. New York. (Reprinted: AMS Press, New York, 1983.)

1933   Tobacco Chewing on the Northwest Coast. *American Anthropologist* 35(1):146–150.

Dobyns, Henry
1966   Estimating Aboriginal American Population, 1: An Appraisal of Techniques with a New Hemispheric Estimate. *Current Anthropology* 7(4):395–416.

1983   Introduction to Essays on the Historic Epidemiology of Native American Peoples. (Unpublished ·manuscript in Dobyns' possession.)

Dockstader, Frederick J.
1978   North American Indian and Eskimo Art. Norwich, England: University of East Anglia.

Dodge, Ernest S.
1945   Captain Collectors: The Influence of New England Shipping on the Study of Polynesian Material Culture. *Essex Institute Historical Collections* 81(1):27–34. Salem, Mass.

Dodge, Ernest S., and Charles H.P. Copeland
1949   Handbook of the Collections of the Peabody Museum of Salem. Salem, Mass.: Peabody Museum.

Dodge, Robert K., and Joseph B. McCullough, eds.
[1974] Voices from Wah-Kon-Tah: Contemporary Poetry of Native Americans. New York: International Publishers.

Doig, Ivan
1980   Winter Brothers: A Season at the Edge of America. New York: Harcourt, Brace, Jovanovich.

Dominion of Canada *see* Canada, Dominion of

Donald, Leland
1983   Was Nuu-chah-nulth-aht (Nootka) Society Based on Slave Labor? Pp. 108–119 in The Development of Political Organization in Native North America. Elisabeth Tooker, ed. *Proceedings of the American Ethnological Society, 1979.*

1985   On the Possibility of Social Class in Societies Based on Extractive Subsistence. Pp. 237–244 in Status, Structure and Stratification: Current Archaeological Reconstructions. M. Thompson, M.T. Garcia, and F. Kense, eds. Calgary, Alta.: University of Calgary.

Donald, Leland, and Donald H. Mitchell
1975   Some Correlates of Local Group Rank Among the Southern Kwakiutl. *Ethnology* 14(4):325–346.

Donovan, John
1960   The Oakville Massacre. *Cowlitz County Historical Quarterly* 2(1):13. Kelso, Wash.

1963   Kleeshws and Sulachulwulchs. *Cowlitz County Historical Quarterly* 5(3):11. Kelso, Wash.

1964   Spoop. *Cowlitz County Historical Quarterly* 5(4):5. Kelso, Wash.

1966   The Witch Woman of the Upper Chehalis. *Cowlitz County Historical Quarterly* 8(1):20. Kelso, Wash.

Dorpat, Paul
1984   Seattle Now and Then. Seattle, Wash.: Tartu Publications.

Dorsey, George A.
1897   The Geography of the Tsimshian Indians. *American Antiquarian* 19(4):276–282.

1897a   Wormian Bones in Artificially Deformed Kwakiutl Crania. *American Anthropologist* 10(6):169–173.

1897b   The Long Bones of Kwakiutl and Salish Indians. *American Anthropologist* 10(6):174–182.

1897c   Observations on the Scapulae of Northwest Coast Indians. *The American Naturalist* 31(368):736–745.

1900   The Department of Anthropology of the Field Columbian Museum: A Review of Six Years. *American Anthropologist* n.s. 2(2):247–265.

1902   The Duamish Indian Spirit Boat and Its Use. *Bulletin of the Free Museum of Science and Art of the University of Pennsylvania* 3(4):227–238. Philadelphia.

1907   The Anthropological Exhibits at the American Museum of Natural History. *Science* n.s. 25(641):584–589.

Dorsey, James O.
1884   [Dorsey Papers.] (Manuscript No. 4800 in National Anthropological Archives, Smithsonian Institution, Washington.)

1884a   [Alsea and Yaquina Vocabulary and Grammatical Notes, Spoken by the Alsea (Alsi) Tribe . . . .Alsea River, Oregon.] (Manuscript No. 4800 (391), Dorsey Papers, in National Anthropological Archives, Smithsonian Institution, Washington.)

1884b   [Upper Coquille (Mici'qwŭtmê'tûnnĕ) Vocabulary and Grammatical Notes; Siletz Reservation, Oreg.] (Manuscript No. 4800 (375), Dorsey Papers in National Anthropological Archives, Smithsonian Institution, Washington.)

1884c   [Yaquina (Yakwĭñă) Vocabulary.] (Manuscript No. 4800(393), Dorsey Papers, National Anthropological Archives, Smithsonian Institution, Washington.)

1884d   [Lower Umpqua (Ku-ītc') Vocabulary and Grammatical Notes, Spoken by the Yakonan-speaking Indians Formerly Living on Umpqua Bay, Oregon.] (Manuscript No. 4800(395), Dorsey Papers, National Anthropological Archives, Smithsonian Institution, Washington.)

1884e   [Siuslaw Vocabulary, with Sketch Map Showing Villages and Incomplete Key Giving Village Names.] (Manuscript No. 4800(394), Dorsey Papers, National Anthropological Archives, Smithsonian Institution, Washington.)

1889   Indians of Siletz Reservation, Oregon. *American Anthropologist* 2(1):55–60.

1890   The Gentile System of the Siletz Tribes. *Journal of American Folk-Lore* 3(10):227–237.

Douglas, David
1904   Sketch of a Journey to the Northwestern Parts of the Continent of North America, During the Years 1824–25–26–27. *Oregon Historical Quarterly* 5(3):230–271, (4):325–369.

1914   Journal Kept by David Douglas During His Travels in North America, 1823–1827, Together with A Particular Description of Thirty-three Species of American Oaks and Eighteen Species of *Pinus*. London: W. Wesley. (Reprinted: Antiquarian Press, New York, 1959.)

Douglas, Frederic H., and Rene d'Harnoncourt
1941   Indian Art of the United States. New York: Museum of Modern Art.

Douglas, James
1835   Statistics of the North-west Coast of America. (Manuscript B.40:D72.5, folder 138–140 in Provincial Archives of British Columbia, Victoria).

1839   [Letter of May 10 to James Dale.] (Manuscript B223|b|24, vol. 13 in Hudson's Bay Company Archives, Provincial Archives of Manitoba, Winnipeg, Canada.)

1840   Diary of a Trip to the Northwest Coast, April 22–October 2, 1840. (Manuscript A/B/40 D75.2 in Provincial Archives of British Columbia, Victoria.)

1848   [Letter of December 5.] (Manuscript B.223/b/38, folders 59–60 in Hudson's Bay Company Archives, Provincial Archives of Manitoba, Winnipeg, Canada.)

1848a   [Letter of March 16.] (Manuscript D.5/10, folders 474, 479 in Hudson's Bay Company Archives, Provincial Archives of Manitoba, Winnipeg, Canada.)

1853   [Private Papers, 1st and 2d Series.] (Unpublished manuscript in Provincial Archives of British Columbia, Victoria.)

1854   Report of a Canoe Expedition Along the East Coast of Vancouver Island. *Journal of the Royal Geographical Society* 24:245–249. London.

1878   Census of the Indian Population on the N.W. Coast . . . .Transcribed by Ivan Petrov. (Manuscript No. H.H.B. [P-C 12–13] in Private Papers, Second Series, Bancroft Library, Berkeley; Microfilm A92 of Original in Suzzallo Library, University of Washington, Seattle.)

1931   Douglas Expeditions, 1840–41. 4 Pts. Herman A. Leader, ed. *Oregon Historical Quarterly* 32(1):1–22, (2):145–164, (3):262–278, (4):350–372.

1941   [James Douglas's Letters, Fort Vancouver, 1838.] Pp. 236–294 in The Letters of John McLoughlin from Fort Vancouver to the Governor and Committee. First Series, 1825–38. E.E. Rich, ed. Toronto: The Champlain Society.

Douglas, Mary
1967   The Meaning of Myth. With Special Reference to 'La Geste d'Asdiwal'. Pp. 49–69 in The Structural Study of Myth and Totemism. Edmund Leach, ed. (*A.S.A. Monographs* 5) London: Tavistock.

Drachman, Gaberell
1969   Twana Phonology. *Ohio State University. Working Papers in Linguistics* 5. Columbus.

Draper, John A.
1980   An Analysis of Lithic Tools and Debitage from 35CS1: A Prehistoric Site on the Southern Oregon Coast. (Unpublished M.A. Thesis in Anthropology, Oregon State University, Corvallis.)

1981   Oregon Coast Prehistory: A Brief Review of Archaeological Investigations on the Oregon Coast. *Northwest Anthropological Research Notes* 15(2):149–161. Moscow, Idaho.

1982   An Analysis of Lithic Tools and Debitage from 35CS1: A Prehistoric Site on the Southern Oregon Coast. *Tebiwa: Journal of the Idaho State University Museum* 19:47–48. Pocatello.

Draper, John A., and Glenn Hartmann
1979   A Cultural Resource Evaluation of the Cape Arago Lighthouse Locality, Gregory Point, Oregon. (Report to U.S. Coast Guard, 13th District, Seattle, Wash.) Corvallis: Oregon State University, Department of Anthropology.

Drew, Edwin P.
1856   [Letter of Sept. 24 to Joel Palmer.] (Manuscript 1856-315, microcopy 2, roll 14, Records of the Oregon Superintendency, in Record Group 75, National Archives, Washington.)

Drew, Leslie, and Douglas Wilson
1980   Argillite: Art of the Haida. North Vancouver, B.C.: Hancock House.

Driver, Harold E.
1961   Indians of North America. Chicago: University of Chicago Press.

1962   The Contribution of A.L. Kroeber to Culture Area Theory and Practice. *Indiana University. Publications in Anthropology and Linguistics. Memoirs* 18. Bloomington.

Driver, Harold E., and James L. Coffin
1975   Classification and Development of North American Indian Cultures: Statistical Analysis of the Driver-Massey Sample. *Transactions of the American Philosophical Society* 65(3):1–120. Philadelphia.

Driver, Harold E., and William C. Massey
1957   Comparative Studies of North American Indians. *Transactions of the American Philosophical Society* 47(2):165–456. Philadelphia.

Drucker, Philip
[1933–1954] [Philip Drucker Papers.] (Manuscript No. 4516 in National Anthropological Archives, Smithsonian Institution, Washington.)

1934   [Coos Ethnographic Fieldnotes (Copy).] (Manuscript, folder 65.22, box 65, in Melville Jacobs Collection, University of Washington Libraries, Seattle.)

1936   Diffusion in Northwest Coast Culture in the Light of Some Distributions. (Unpublished Ph.D. Dissertation in Anthropology, University of California, Berkeley.)

1937   The Tolowa and Their Southwest Oregon Kin. *University of California Publications in American Archaeology and Ethnology* 36(4):221–299. Berkeley. (Reprinted: Kraus, New York, 1965.)

1939   Contributions to Alsea Ethnography. *University of California Publications in American Archaeology and Ethnology* 35(7):81–101. Berkeley. (Reprinted: Kraus, New York, 1965.)

1939a   Rank, Wealth, and Kinship in Northwest Coast Society. *American Anthropologist* 41(1):55–65.

1940   Kwakiutl Dancing Societies. *University of California Anthropological Records* 2(6):201–230. (Reprinted: Kraus Reprint, Millwood, N.Y., 1976.)

1943   Archaeological Survey on the Northern Northwest Coast. *Anthropological Papers* 20, *Bureau of American Ethnology Bulletin* 133. Washington. (Reprinted: Shorey Book Store, Seattle, Wash., 1972.)

1948   The Antiquity of the Northwest Coast Totem Pole. *Journal of the Washington Academy of Sciences* 38(12):389–397.

1950   Culture Element Distributions, XXVI: Northwest Coast. *University of California Anthropological Records* 9(3):157–294. Berkeley.

1951   The Northern and Central Nootkan Tribes. *Bureau of American Ethnology Bulletin* 144. Washington.

1955   Indians of the Northwest Coast. New York: McGraw-Hill for the American Museum of Natural History. (Reprinted in 1963.)

1955a Sources of Northwest Coast Culture. Pp. 59–81 in New Interpretations of Aboriginal American Culture History. Washington: Anthropological Society of Washington. (Reprinted: Cooper Square Publishers, New York, 1972.)

1958 The Native Brotherhoods: Modern Intertribal Organizations on the Northwest Coast. *Bureau of American Ethnology Bulletin* 168. Washington.

1963 Indians of the Northwest Coast. Garden City N.Y.: Natural History Press.

1965 Cultures of the North Pacific Coast. San Francisco: Chandler.

1976 Tlingit and Haida, Inc.: Success Story. (Paper presented at the Northwest Coast Studies Conference, Simon Fraser University, Burnaby, B.C.)

1979 [Review of] The Mouth of Heaven: An Introduction to Kwakiutl Religious Thought, by Irving Goldman. *American Ethnologist* 6(1):158–164.

1983 Ecology and Political Organization on the Northwest Coast of America. Pp. 86–96 in The Development of Political Organization in Native North America. Elisabeth Tooker, ed. (Proceedings of the American Ethnological Society, 1979) New York: J.J. Augustin.

Drucker, Philip, and Robert F. Heizer
1967 To Make My Name Good: A Reexamination of the Southern Kwakiutl Potlatch. Berkeley: University of California Press.

Du Bois, Cora A.
[1934] [Tututni (Rogue River) Fieldnotes.] (In University Archives, Bancroft Library, University of California, Berkeley.)

1936 The Wealth Concept as an Integrative Factor in Tolowa-Tututni Culture. Pp. 49–65 in Essays in Anthropology Presented to A.L. Kroeber in Celebration of His Sixtieth Birthday. Robert H. Lowie, ed. Berkeley: University of California Press.

1938 The Feather Cult of the Middle Columbia. *General Series in Anthropology* 7. Menasha, Wis.

1939 The 1870 Ghost Dance. *University of California Anthropological Records* 3(1). Berkeley. (Reprinted: Kraus Reprint, Millwood, N.Y., 1976.)

Duff, Wilson
1952 Gitskan Totem-poles, 1952. *Anthropology in British Columbia* 3:21–30. Victoria.

1952a The Upper Stalo Indians of the Fraser Valley, British Columbia. *Anthropology in British Columbia. Memoirs* 1. Victoria.

1954 Preserving the Talking Sticks. *Digester* 30(6):10–12.

1956 Unique Stone Artifacts from the Gulf Islands. Pp. D45–D55 in *Provincial Museum of Natural History and Anthropology. Report for the Year 1955.* Victoria, B.C.

1956a Prehistoric Stone Sculpture of the Fraser River and Gulf of Georgia. *Anthropology in British Columbia* 5:15–51. Victoria.

1959 Mungo Martin—Carver of the Century. *Museum News* 1(1):3–8.

[1960] The Southern Kawkiutl. (Manuscript, copies at the British Columbia Provincial Museum, and in possession of Wayne Suttles.)

1964 The Indian History of British Columbia. Vol. 1: The Impact of the White Man. *Anthropology in British Columbia. Memoirs* 5. Victoria.

1964a Contributions of Marius Barbeau to West Coast Ethnology. *Anthropologica* n.s. 6(1):63–96. Ottawa.

1967 Arts of the Raven: Masterworks by the Northwest Coast Indian: An Exhibition. Text by Wilson Duff, Bill Holm, and Bill Reid. Vancouver, B.C.: Vancouver Art Gallery and the University of Washington Press.

1969 The Fort Victoria Treaties. *BC Studies* 3(Fall):3–57. Vancouver.

1975 Images: Stone: B.C.: Thirty Centuries of Northwest Coast Indian Sculpture. Seattle: University of Washington Press.

1981 The Killer Whale: A Chief's Memorial to His Son. Pp. 153–156 in The World Is As Sharp As a Knife . . . .Donald N. Abbott, ed. Victoria: British Columbia Provincial Museum.

1981a The World Is As Sharp As a Knife: Meaning in Northern Northwest Coast Art. Pp. 209–224 in The World Is As Sharp As a Knife . . . .Donald N. Abbott, ed. Victoria: British Columbia Provincial Museum. (Also published 1983 as Pp. 47–66 in Indian Art Traditions of the Northwest Coast, Roy Carlson, ed., Archaeology Press, Simon Fraser University Burnaby, B.C.)

1981b Mungo Martin, Carver of the Century. Pp. 37–40 in The World Is As Sharp As a Knife . . . .Donald N. Abbott, ed. Victoria: British Columbia Provincial Museum.

Duff, Wilson, and Michael Kew
1958 Anthony Island: A Home of the Haidas. Pp. 37–64 in *British Columbia Provincial Museum of Natural History and Anthropology. Report for the Year 1957.* Victoria.

Duffek, Karen
1983 A Guide to Buying Contemporary Northwest Coast Indian Arts. (*Museum Note* 10) Vancouver: University of British Columbia, Museum of Anthropology.

1986 Bill Reid: Beyond the Essential Form. Vancouver: University of British Columbia Press.

Duflot de Mofras, Eugène
1844 Exploration du territoire de l'Orégon, des Californies et de la mer Vermeille, exécutée pendant les années 1840, 1841 et 1842. 2 vols. Paris: A. Bertrand. (Microfilm: University of California, Library Photographic Service, Berkeley, 1984.)

1937 Duflot de Mofras' Travels on the Pacific Coast. Marguerite Wilbur, trans. and ed. Santa Ana, Calif.: Fine Arts Press.

Dumond, Don E.
1969 Toward a Prehistory of the Na-Dene, with a General Comment on Population Movements Among Nomadic Hunters. *American Anthropologist* 71(5):857–863.

1974 Remarks on the Prehistory of the North Pacific: To Lump or not to Lump? Pp. 47–55 in International Conference on the Prehistory and Paleoecology of Western North American Arctic and Subarctic. Scott Raymond and Peter Schledermann, eds. Calgary, Alta.: University of Calgary, Archaeological Association, Department of Archaeology.

Duncan, Mary Ann
1977 Archaeological Investigations at the La Push Village Site (45-CA-23): An Interim Report. (Manuscript on file at

Office of Public Archaeology, University of Washington, Seattle.)

Duncan, William
[1853–1916] [The Duncan William Papers. New Metlakatla, Alaska.] (Microfilm in Special Collections Division, University of British Columbia Library, Vancouver.)

———— 1860 [Letter of October 25.] (Microfilm in William Duncan Papers, University of British Columbia, Vancouver.)

———— 1862 [Journal.] (Microfilm in Special Collections Division, University of British Columbia Library, Vancouver).

———— 1880 Church Manual, Metlakatla. (Printed manual, English and Tsimshian, in British Columbia Provincial Archives, Victoria.)

Dundes, Alan
1979 Heads or Tails: A Psychoanalytic Study of the Potlatch. *Journal of Psychological Anthropology* 2(4):395–424.

Dunmore, John, and Maurice de Brossard
1985 Le Voyage de Lapérouse: 1785–1788. 2 vols. Paris: Impr. Nationale.

Dunn, J.R.
1846 [Journal on H.M.S. Fisgard.] (Manuscript Adm. 101/100/4 XC/A/3930 in the Public Record Office, Kew, Surrey, England.)

Dunn, John
1844 History of the Oregon Territory and British North American Fur Trade; with an Account of the Habits and Customs of the Principal Native Tribes on the Northern Continent. London: Edwards and Hughes.

Dunn, John A.
1970 Coast Tsimshian Phonology. (Unpublished Ph.D. Dissertation in Anthropology, University of New Mexico, Albuquerque.)

———— 1978 A Practical Dictionary of the Coast Tsimshian Language: *Canada. National Museum of Man. Mercury Series. Ethnology Service Papers* 42. Ottawa.

———— 1979 A Reference Grammar for the Coast Tsimshian Language. *Canada. National Museum of Man. Mercury Series. Ethnology Service Papers* 55. Ottawa.

———— 1979a Tsimshian Internal Relations Reconsidered: Southern Tsimshian. Pp. 62–82 in The Victoria Conference on Northwestern Languages (Nov. 4–5, 1976). Barbara S. Efrat, ed. Victoria: British Columbia Provincial Museum.

———— 1984 Tsimshian Grandchildren: Redistributive Mechanisms in Personal Property Inheritance. Pp. 36–57 in The Tsimshian and Their Neighbors of the North Pacific Coast. Jay Miller and Carol M. Eastman, eds. Seattle: University of Washington Press.

———— 1984a International Matri-moieties: The North Maritime Province of the North Pacific Coast. Pp. 99–109 in The Tsimshian: Images of the Past, Views for the Present. Margaret Seguin, ed. Vancouver: University of British Columbia Press.

———— 1984b Some Ethnopoetic Features of Dorothy Brown's Soaban. (*Mid-American Linguistics Conference Papers*) David Rood, ed. Boulder: University of Colorado, Department of Linguistics.

Dunn, John A., and Lucienne Dunn
1972 An Equivalence Cycle for Kitkatla Kin-status Terms. *Anthropological Linguistics* 14(6):240–252.

Dunnell, Robert C., and Charlotte Beck
1979 The Caples Site, 45-SA-5, Skamania County, Washington. *University of Washington. Department of Anthropology. Reports in Archaeology* 6. Seattle.

Dunnell, Robert C., and Sarah K. Campbell
1977 Aboriginal Occupation of Hamilton Island, Washington. *University of Washington. Department of Anthropology. Reports in Archaeology* 4. Seattle.

Dunnell, Robert C., and John W. Fuller
1975 An Archaeological Survey of Everett Harbor and the Lower Snohomish Esturary-delta. Seattle: National Park Service.

Dunnell, Robert C., and Dennis E. Lewarch
1974 Archaeological Remains in Home Valley Park, Skamania County, Washington. Seattle: University of Washington, Department of Anthropology.

Durieu, Paul
1874 [Untitled Manuscript Containing Prayers in Squamish, Sechelt, and Stalo.] (Manuscript HPK5241, D96c 7 in Archives Deschatelets, Ottawa.)

————, trans.
1893 Bible History, Containing the Most Remarkable Events of the Old and New Testament . . . .by Rev. Richard Gilmour. New York: Benziger Brothers.

———— 1899 Chinook Bible History. (Written in Chinook Shorthand by J.M. LeJeune.) Kamloops, B.C.

Durlach, Theresa Mayer
1928 The Relationship Systems of the Tlingit, Haida and Tsimshian. (*Publications of the American Ethnological Society* 11) New York: G.E. Stechert.

Dyen, Isidore, and David F. Aberle
1974 Lexical Reconstruction: The Case of the Proto-Athapaskan Kinship System. New York: Cambridge University Press.

Easton, Norman A.
1985 Underwater Archaeology of Straits Salish Reefnetting. (Unpublished M.A. Thesis in Anthropology, University of Victoria, Victoria, B.C.)

Edel, May M.
[1931] [Linguistic Notes: Field Notebooks, Lexical Files, Folklore Texts, Based on Fieldwork Among the Tillamook Salish, Oregon.] (In May M. Edel Papers, University of Washington Libraries, Seattle.)

———— [1935] [Tillamook Combined Vocabulary.] (Manuscript No. 30(S4.4), Freeman No. 3748, in American Philosophical Society Library, Philadelphia.)

———— 1939 The Tillamook Language. *International Journal of American Linguistics* 10(1):1–57.

———— 1944 Stability in Tillamook Folklore. *Journal of American Folklore* 57(224):116–127.

Edmo, Ed
1985 These Few Words of Mine. *Blue Cloud Quarterly* 31(3). Marvin, S.D.

Edwards, Grant T.
1978 Oolachen Time in Bella Coola. *The Beaver*, Outfit 309 (Autumn):32–37. Winnipeg.

———— 1979 Indian Spaghetti. *The Beaver*, Outfit 310 (Autumn):4–11. Winnipeg.

———— 1980 Bella Coola Indian and European Medicines. *The Beaver*, Outfit 311 (Winter):4–11. Winnipeg.

Eells, Edwin
[1916] [Memoirs of Edwin Eells, Indian Agent.] (Unpublished manuscript in Washington State Historical Society Archives, Tacoma.)

Eells, Myron

1877   The Twana Indians of the Skokomish Reservation in Washington Territory. *U.S. Geological and Geographical Survey of the Territories Bulletin* 3(1):57–114.

1878   Chemakum Vocabulary. (Manuscript No. 272 in National Anthropological Archives, Smithsonian Institution, Washington.)

1878a   Hymns in the Chinook Jargon Language. Portland, Oreg.: G.H. Himes. (Reprinted: 2d ed., rev. and enl., D. Steel, Portland, Oreg., 1889.)

1879   Indian Music. *American Antiquarian and Oriental Journal* 1(4):249–253.

1880   The Chemakum Language. *American Antiquarian and Oriental Journal* 3(1):52–54.

1881   The Twana Language of Washington Territory. *American Antiquarian and Oriental Journal* 3(4):296–303.

1882   History of Indian Missions on the Pacific Coast: Oregon, Washington, and Idaho. Philadelphia: American Sunday-school Union.

1884   Census of the Clallam and Twana Indians of Washington Territory. *American Antiquarian and Oriental Journal* 6(1):35–38.

1886   Ten Years of Missionary Work Among the Indians at Skokomish, Washington Territory, 1874–1884. Boston: Congregational Sunday School and Publishing House. (Reprinted: Shorey Book Store, Seattle, Wash., 1972.)

1886a   The Stone Age of Oregon. Pp. 283–295 in *Annual Report of the Smithsonian Institution for the Year 1885*. Washington.

1886–1888   The Indians of Puget Sound. *American Antiquarian and Oriental Journal* 8(1):40–41; 9(1):1–9,(2):97–104, (4):211–219,271–276; 10(1):26–36,(3):174–178.

1887   Decrease of Population Among the Indians of Puget Sound. *American Antiquarian and Oriental Journal* 95(5):271–276.

1889   The Twana, Chemakum, and Klallam Indians of Washington Territory. Pp. 605–681 in *Annual Report of the Smithsonian Institution for the Year 1887*. Washington.

1892   Shaking Religion. *The American Missionary* 46(5):157–158. New York.

[1893]   A Dictionary of the Chinook-Jargon Language (Includes Grammatical Notes). (Unpublished manuscript in Whitman College Library, Walla Walla, Wash.)

1894   The Chinook Jargon. *American Anthropologist* 7(3):300–312.

1903   The Decrease of the Indians. *American Antiquarian and Oriental Journal* 25(3):145–149.

1985   The Indians of Puget Sound: The Notebooks of Myron Eells. George B. Castile, ed. Seattle: University of Washington Press.

Efrat, Barbara Silverman

1969   A Grammar of Non-particles in Sooke, a Dialect of Straits Coast Salish. (Unpublished Ph.D. Dissertation in Linguistics, University of Pennsylvania, Philadelphia.)

Efrat, Barbara Silverman, and W.J. Langlois

1978   Contemporary Accounts of Nootkan Culture. Pp. 31–61 in nu·tka·: The History and Survival of Nootkan Culture. Barbara S. Efrat and W.J. Langlois, eds. *Sound Heritage* 7(2). Victoria, B.C.

Eldridge, Morley

1982   Archaeological Spatial Analysis of DiRi 14. (Unpublished M.A. Thesis in Anthropology, University of Victoria, Victoria, B.C.)

Eliza, Francisco de

1933   [Extract of the Voyage . . . .1791.] Pp. 141–154 in Spanish Explorations in the Strait of Juan de Fuca. Henry R. Wagner, ed. Santa Ana, Calif.: Fine Arts Press. (Reprinted: AMS Press, New York, 1971.)

Elliott, T.C., ed.

1912   Journal of John Work, November and December, 1824. *Washington Historical Quarterly* 3(3):198–228. Seattle.

1927   The Journal of the Ship Ruby. *Oregon Historical Quarterly* 28(3):258–280.

1928   Captain Robert Gray's First Visit to Oregon. *Oregon Historical Quarterly* 29(2):162–188.

Elliott, Charles P.

1900   Salmon Fishing Grounds and Canneries. Pp. 738–741 in Compilation of Narratives of Explorations in Alaska, 1900. Washington: U.S. Government Printing Office.

Ellis, David W.

1976   The Ethnozoology of the Skidegate Haida: Marine Invertebrates. (Unpublished manuscript in Margaret Blackman's possession).

Ellis, David W., and Luke Swan

1981   Teachings of the Tides: Uses of Marine Invertebrates by the Manhousat People. Nanaimo, B.C.: Theytus Books.

Ellis, David W., and Solomon Wilson

1976   The Knowledge and Usage of Marine Invertebrates by the Skidegate Haida People of the Queen Charlotte Islands. (*Monograph Series* 1) [Skidegate, B.C.]: The Queen Charlotte Islands Museum Society.

Ellis, William

1782   An Authentic Narrative of a Voyage Performed by Captain Cook and Captain Clerke, in His Majesty's Ships Resolution and Discovery, During the Years 1776, 1777, 1778, 1779, and 1780 . . . 2 vols. London: Printed for G. Robinson.

Elmendorf, William W.

1940   Twana Ethnological Narratives. (Unpublished manuscript in Elmendorf's possession.)

1946   Twana Kinship Terminology. *Southwestern Journal of Anthropology* 2(4):420–432.

1948   The Cultural Setting of the Twana Secret Society. *American Anthropologist* 50(4):625–633.

1960   The Structure of Twana Culture. *Washington State University. Research Studies* 28(3), Monographic Supplement 2. Pullman. (Reprinted in: Coast Salish and Western Washington Indians, IV, Garland, New York, 1974.)

1961   Skokomish and Other Coast Salish Tales. 3 Pts. *Washington State University. Research Studies* 29(1):1–37, (2):84–117, (3):119–150. Pullman.

1961a   System Change in Salish Kinship Terminologies. *Southwestern Journal of Anthropology* 17(4):365–382.

1962   Relations of Oregon Salish as Evidenced in Numerical Stems. *Anthropological Linguistics* 4(2):1–16.

1965   Linguistic and Geographic Relations in the Northern Plateau Area. *Southwestern Journal of Anthropology* 21(1):63–78.

1969   Geographic Ordering, Subgrouping, and Olympic Salish. *International Journal of American Linguistics* 35(3):220–225.

1970   Skokomish Sorcery, Ethics, and Society. Pp. 147–182 in Systems of North American Witchcraft and Sorcery. Deward E. Walker, Jr., ed. *Anthropological Monographs of the University of Idaho* 1. Moscow.

1971   Coast Salish Status Ranking and Intergroup Ties. *Southwestern Journal of Anthropology* 27(4):353–380.

1984   Coast Salish Concept of Power, Verbal and Functional Categories. Pp. 281–291 in The Tsimshian and Their Neighbors of the North Pacific Coast. Jay Miller and Carol M. Eastman, eds. Seattle: University of Washington Press.

1985   Afterword; Myron Eells as Ethnographer: An Appraisal. Pp. 449–454 in The Indians of Puget Sound: The Notebooks of Myron Eells. George B. Castile, ed. Seattle: University of Washington Press.

Elmendorf, William W., and Wayne Suttles
1960   Pattern and Change in Halkomelem Salish Dialects. *Anthropological Linguistics* 2(7):1–32.

El-Najjar, Mahmoud Y.
1979   Human Treponematosis and Tuberculosis: Evidence from the New World. *American Journal of Physical Anthropology* 51(4):599–618.

El-Najjar, Mahmoud Y., Dennis J. Ryan, Christy G. Turner II, and Betsy Lozoff
1976   The Etiology of Porotic Hyperostosis Among the Prehistoric and Historic Anasazi Indians of the Southwestern United States. *American Journal of Physical Anthropology* 44(3):477–487.

Emmons, Della G.
1965   Leschi of the Nisquallies. Minneapolis, Minn.: T.S. Denison.

Emmons, George T.
1900   [Letter of April 7 to W.H. Holmes.] (Accession No. 37889 in National Museum of Natural History, Smithsonian Institution, Washington.)

1900a   [Letter of October 9 to W.H. Holmes.] (Accession No. 37889 in National Museum of Natural History, Smithsonian Institution, Washington.)

1903   The Basketry of the Tlingit. *Memoirs of the American Museum of Natural History* 3(2):229–277. New York.

1907   The Chilkat Blanket; with Notes on the Blanket by Franz Boas. *Memoirs of the American Museum of of Natural History* 3(4):329–401. New York.

1908   Copper Neck-rings of Southern Alaska. *American Anthropologist* n.s. 10(4):644–649.

1908a   Petroglyphs in Southeastern Alaska. *American Anthropologist* n.s. 10(2):221–230.

1913   [Letter of July 22 to W.H. Holmes.] (Record Unit 192, box 121, folder 10, file No. 44522 in Smithsonian Institution Archives, Washington.)

1914   [Letter of March 1 to W.H. Holmes.] (Record Unit 192, box 121, folder 10, file No. 44522 in Smithsonian Institution Archives, Washington.)

1914a   Portraiture Among the North Pacific Coast Tribes. *American Anthropologist* 16(1):59–67.

1916   The Whale House of the Chilkat. *Anthropological Papers of the American Museum of Natural History* 19(1):1–33. New York.

1930   The Art of the Northwest Coast Indians: How Ancestral Records Were Preserved in Carvings and Paintings of Mythical or Fabulous Animal Figures. *Natural History* 30(3):282–292. New York. (Reprinted: The Haunted Bookshop, Victoria, B.C., 1971.)

[1945]   The Tlingit Indians. (Unpublished manuscript in the American Museum of Natural History, New York.)

Emmons, George T., and Frederica De Laguna
1945–1985   The Tlingit Indians, by George T. Emmons; edited with additions by Frederica De Laguna and a Biography by Jean Low. (Manuscript, copies in American Museum of Natural History, New York, and Provincial Archives, Victoria, B.C.)

Emmons, Richard V.
1952   An Archaeological Survey in the Lower Nooksack River Valley. *Anthropology in British Columbia* 3:49–56. Victoria.

Enrico, John J.
1980   Masset Haida Phonology. (Unpublished Ph.D. Dissertation in Linguistics, University of California, Berkeley.)

Ermatinger, Frank
1907   Earliest Expedition Against Puget Sound Indians. *Washington Historical Quarterly* 1(2):16–29. Seattle.

Ernst, Alice Henson
1952   The Wolf Ritual of the Northwest Coast. Eugene: University of Oregon Press. (Reprinted in 1980.)

Espinosa y Tello, José
1930   A Spanish Voyage to Vancouver and the Northwest Coast of America; Being the Narrative of the Voyage Made in the Year 1792 by the Schooners Sutil and Mexicana to Explore the Strait of Fuca. Cecil Jane, ed. and trans. London: Argonaut Press. (Reprinted: AMS Press, New York, 1971.)

Everette, Willis E.
1882   Vocabulary of the "Tu-tu-tĕne" and Nine Confederated Tribes, Siletz River, Western Oregon. (Manuscript No. 78 in National Anthropological Archives, Smithsonian Institution, Washington.)

1882a   Comparative Vocabulary of the Älsíä and Klă′măç, or Alsea and Klamath Languages of the Pacific Coast of Western Oregon, with English. [Manuscript No. 1247f, cited in Pilling 1885:941.]

[1884]   North American Anthropology: Study of Indian Languages; Comparative Literal Translations and Comparative Vocabulary of Chinookan and Klingit-Chinook and Chilkat Indian Languages from the Pacific Coast of British America and Alaska. (Manuscript No. 270 in National Anthropological Archives, Smithsonian Institution, Washington.)

Ewers, John C.
1959   A Century of American Indian Exhibits in the Smithsonian Institution. Pp. 513–525 in *Annual Report of the Smithsonian Institution for 1958*. Washington.

Falk, Marvin W.
1983   Alaskan Maps: A Cartobibliography of Alaska to 1900. New York: Garland.

1989   Mapping Alaska: The North Pacific Basin and Russian Cartography, 1790–1867. In Proceedings of the Second International Conference on Russian America, Sitka, Alaska, August 19–22, 1987. Richard A. Pierce, ed. (*Alaska History* 33) Kingston, Ont.: The Limestone Press.

Falk, Randolph
1976   Lelooska. Milbrae, Calif.: Celestial Arts.

Farley, Albert L.
1979   Atlas of British Columbia: People, Environment, and Resource Use. Vancouver: University of British Columbia Press.

Farnham, Thomas J.
1843   Travels in the Great Western Prairies, the Anáhuac and Rocky Mountains, and in the Oregon Territory. 2 vols. New York: Greeley and McElrath. (Reprinted: Vols. 28–29 of Early Western Travels, Reuben G. Thwaites, ed., Arthur H. Clark, Cleveland, Ohio, 1906.)

Farrand, Livingston
[1900]   [The Alsi Indians: General Notes.] (Manuscript No. 2516 in National Anthropological Archives, Smithsonian Institution, Washington.)

1900a   Basketry Designs of the Salish Indians. Memoirs of the American Museum of Natural History 2(5):391–399. New York.

1901   Notes on the Alsea Indians of Oregon. American Anthropologist 3(2):239–247.

1902   Traditions of the Quinault Indians. Memoirs of the American Museum of Natural History 4(3):77–132. New York. (Reprinted: AMS Press, New York, 1975.)

1907   Chimakuan Family and Chimakum. P. 269 in Vol. 1 of Handbook of American Indians North of Mexico. Frederick W. Hodge, ed. 2 vols. Bureau of American Ethnology Bulletin 30. Washington.

1907a   Hoh. P. 556 in Vol. 1 of Handbook of American Indians North of Mexico. Frederick W. Hodge, ed. 2 vols. Bureau of American Ethnology Bulletin 30. Washington.

1907b   Kalapooian Family. Pp. 645–646 in Vol. 1 of Handbook of American Indians North of Mexico. Frederick W. Hodge, ed. 2 vols. Bureau of American Ethnology Bulletin 30. Washington.

1910   Quileute. Pp. 340–341 in Vol. 2 of Handbook of American Indians North of Mexico. Frederick W. Hodge, ed. 2 vols. Bureau of American Ethnology Bulletin 30. Washington.

1915   Shasta and Athapascan Myths from Oregon. Leo J. Frachtenberg, ed. Journal of American Folk-Lore 28(109):207–242.

1916   Myths of the Bellabella. Pp. 883–888 in App. 1: Bellabella and Nootka Tales, of Tsimshian Mythology, by Franz Boas. 31st Annual Report of the Bureau of American Ethnology for the Years 1909–1910. Washington.

1919   Quileute Tales. Theresa Mayer, ed. Journal of American Folk-Lore 32(124):251–279.

Farrand, Livingston, and Leo J. Frachtenberg
1915   Shasta and Athapascan Myths from Oregon. Journal of American Folk-Lore 28(109):207–242.

Farrand, Livingston, and W.S. Kahnweiler
1902   Traditions of the Quinault Indians. Memoirs of the American Museum of Natural History 4(3):77–132. New York. (Reprinted: AMS Press, New York, 1975.)

Fast, Edward G.
1869   Catalogue of Antiquities and Curiosities Collected in the Territory of Alaska. New York: Leavitt, Strebeigh and Company.

Feder, Norman
1971   Two Hundred Years of North American Indian Art. (Catalogue of an Exhibition Held at the Whitney Museum of American Art, New York.) New York: Praeger.

1971a   American Indian Art. New York: Abrams.

1977   The Malaspina Collection. American Indian Art Magazine 2(3):40–51, 80–82.

1983   Incised Relief Carving of the Halkomelem and Straits Salish. American Indian Art Magazine 8(2):46–53.

Feder, Norman, and Edward Malin
1962   Indian Art of the Northwest Coast. Denver, Colo.: Denver Art Museum, Department of Indian Art.

Ferguson, R. Brian
1983   Warfare and Redistributive Exchange on the Northwest Coast. Pp. 133–147 in The Development of Political Organization in Native North America. Elisabeth Tooker, ed. Proceedings of the American Ethnological Society, Vancouver, 1979.

1984   A Reexamination of the Causes of Northwest Coast Warfare. Pp. 267–328 in Warfare, Culture, and Environment. R. Brian Ferguson, ed. New York: Academic Press.

Fetzer, Paul
1951   [The First Draft of Some Preliminary Considerations on the Subject of Territory and Sovereignty Among the Nooksack and Their Neighbors.] (Manuscript, dated 7 March 1951; copy in possession of Wayne Suttles.)

Fields, William O., ed.
1975   Mountain Glaciers of the Northern Hemisphere. 2 vols. Hanover, N.H.: U.S. Army Cold Regions Research and Engineering Laboratory.

Finlayson, Duncan
1848   [Fort Victoria Journal.] (Manuscript B.226/a/1, Hudson's Bay Company Archives, Provincial Archives of Manitoba, Winnipeg, Canada.)

Finlayson, Duncan, and John Work
1834–1838   [Fort Simpson Journal.] (Manuscript B.201/a/3, Hudson's Bay Company Archives, Provincial Archives of Manitoba, Winnipeg, Canada.)

Finnegan, Michael J.
1972   Population Definition on the Northwest Coast by Analysis of Discrete Character Variation. (Unpublished Ph.D. Dissertation in Anthropology, University of Colorado, Boulder.)

1974   A Migration Model for Northwest North America. Pp. 57–73 in International Conference on the Prehistory and Paleoecology of the Western North American Arctic and Subarctic. Scott Raymond and Peter Schledermann, eds. Calgary, Alta.: The University of Calgary Archaeological Association.

Finnegan, Michael J., and A. Marcsik
1980   Anomaly or Pathology: The Stafne Defect as Seen in Archaeological Material and Modern Clinical Practice. Journal of Human Evolution 9(1):19–31. London.

Fisher, Harold D.
1952   The Status of the Harbour Seal in British Columbia, with Particular Reference to the Skeena River. Fisheries Research Board of Canada Bulletins 93. Ottawa.

Fisher, Robin
1971   Joseph Trutch and Indian Land Policy. BC Studies 12(Winter):3–33, Vancouver.

1976   Arms and Men on the Northwest Coast, 1774–1825. BC Studies 29(Spring):3–18. Vancouver.

1977   Contact and Conflict: Indian-European Relations in British Columbia, 1774–1890. Vancouver: University of British Columbia Press.

1977a   Indian Control of Maritime Fur Trade and the Northwest Coast. Pp. 65–86 in Approaches to Native History in Canada: Papers of a Conference Held at the National Museum of Man, October 1975. D.A. Muise, ed. *Canada. National Museum of Man. Mercury Series. History Division Papers* 25. Ottawa.

1979   Cook and the Nootka. Pp. 81–98 in Captain James Cook and His Times. Robin Fisher and Hugh Johnston, eds. Seattle: University of Washington Press.

Fisher, Robin, and J.M. Bumsted, eds.
1982   An Account of a Voyage to the North West Coast of America in 1785 and 1786, by Alexander Walker. Seattle: University of Washington Press.

Fitzhugh, William W.
1988   Baird's Naturalists: Smithsonian Collectors in Alaska. Pp. 89–96 in Crossroads of Continents: Cultures of Siberia and Alaska. William W. Fitzhugh and Aron Crowell, eds. Washington: Smithsonian Institution Press.

Fitzhugh, William W., and Aron Crowell, eds.
1988   Crossroads of Continents: Cultures of Siberia and Alaska. Washington: Smithsonian Institution Press.

Fitzhugh, William W., and Ruth O. Selig
1981   The Smithsonian's Alaska Connection: Nineteenth Century Explorers and Anthropologists. Pp. 193–208 in Alaska Journal: A 1981 Collection. Virginia McKinney, ed. Anchorage: Alaska Northwest Publishing Company.

Fitzpatrick, Darleen A.
1968   The "Shake": The Indian Shaker Curing Ritual Among the Yakima. (Unpublished M.A. Thesis in Anthropology, University of Washington, Seattle.)

1986   We Are Cowlitz: Traditional and Emergent Ethnicity. (Unpublished Ph.D. Dissertation in Anthropology, University of Washington, Seattle.)

Fladmark, Knut R.
1970   A Preliminary Report on Lithic Assemblages from the Queen Charlotte Islands, British Columbia. Pp. 117–136 in Early Man and Environments in Northwest North America. R.A. Smith and J.W. Smith, eds. *Proceedings of the 2d Annual Paleo-environmental Workshops of the University of Calgary.* Calgary, Alta.: Students' Press.

1970a   Preliminary Report on the Archaeology of the Queen Charlotte Islands: 1969 Field Season. Pp.18–45 in Archaeology of British Columbia, New Discoveries. R.L. Carlson, ed. *BC Studies* 6–7(Fall-Winter). Vancouver.

1971   Early Microblade Industries on the Queen Charlotte Islands. (Paper presented at the 4th Annual Conference of the Canadian Archaeological Association, Calgary, Alta.)

1972   Prehistoric Cultural Traditions on the Queen Charlotte Islands. (Paper presented at the 25th Annual Northwest Anthropological Conference, Portland, Oreg.)

1973   The Richardson Ranch Site: A 19th Century Haida House. Pp. 53–95 in Historical Archaeology in Northwestern North America. R.M. Getty and K.R. Fladmark eds. Calgary, Alta.: University of Calgary Archaeological Association.

1975   A Paleoecological Model for Northwest Coast Prehistory. *Canada. National Museum of Man. Mercury Series. Archaeological Survey Papers* 43. Ottawa.

1979   The Early Prehistory of the Queen Charlotte Islands. *Archaeology* 32(2):38–45.

1979a   Routes: Alternate Migration Corridors for Early Man in North America. *American Antiquity* 44(1):55–69.

1983   Times and Places: Environmental Correlates of Mid-to-Late Wisconsinan Human Population Expansion in North America. Pp. 13–41 in Early Man in the New World. Richard Shutler Jr., ed. Beverly Hills, Calif.: Sage Publications.

[1984]   The Native Culture History of the Queen Charlotte Islands. In Proceedings of the International Symposium on the Queen Charlotte Islands. In press.

Fladmark, Knut R., D. Alexander, and J. Driver
1984   Excavations at Charlie Lake Cave (HbRf39), 1983. (Report filed with the Heritage Conservation Branch, Victoria, B.C.)

Fleisher, Mark S.
1981   The Potlatch: A Symbolic and Psychoanalytic View. *Current Anthropology* 22(1):69–71.

Flenniken, J. Jeffrey
1980   Replicative Systems Analysis: A Model Applied to the Vein Quartz Artifacts from the Hoko River Site. (Unpublished Ph.D. Dissertation in Anthropology, Washington State University, Pullman.)

1981   Replicative Systems Analysis: A Model Applied to the Vein Quartz Artifacts from the Hoko River Site. *Washington State University. Laboratory of Anthropology. Reports of Investigations* 59; *Hoko River Archaeological Project Contributions* 2. Pullman.

Fleurieu, Charles Pierre Claret de
1797–1800   Voyage autour du monde, pendant les années 1790, 1791, et 1792, par Etienne Marchand. 6 vols. Paris: De l'Imprimerie de la République.

1801   A Voyage Round the World Performed During the Years 1790, 1791, and 1792, by Etienne Marchand. 2 vols. London: T.N. Longmans and O. Rees. (Reprinted: Da Capo Press, New York, 1970.)

Folan, William J.
1972   The Community, Settlement and Subsistence Pattern of the Nootka Sound Area: A Diachronic Model. (Unpublished Ph.D. Dissertation in Anthropology, Southern Illinois University, Carbondale.)

Follansbee, Julie A.
1975   Archaeological Remains at the Beebe Site (35 LA 216) in the Southeastern Willamette Valley Foothills. Pp. 403–424 in Archaeological Studies in the Willamette Valley, Oregon. C. Melvin Aikens, ed. *University of Oregon Anthropological Papers* 8. Eugene.

————, ed.
1977   Unusual Discoveries in Oregon. *Newsletter of the Association of Oregon Archaeologists* 2(1).

Force, Roland, W., and Maryanne Force
1968   Art and Artifacts of the 18th Century; Objects in the Leverian Museum as Painted by Sarah Stone. Honolulu: Bishop Museum Press.

Ford, Clellan S.
1941   Smoke from Their Fires: The Life of a Kwakiutl Chief. New Haven, Conn.: Yale University Press. (Reprinted: Archon Books, Hamden, Conn., 1971.)

Ford, Giles
1862   [Letters to C.H. Hale, 10/6/1862 and 10/10/1862.] (Manuscript, Records of Washington Superintendency of Indian Affairs, 1853–1874, microfilm M5, roll 15 in National Archives, Washington.)

Foreman, Cam, and David Foreman, eds.
1977   Herzog, 45-CL-11. *Oregon Archaeological Society Reports* 3. Portland.

Foster, J. Bristol
1965   The Evolution of the Mammals of the Queen Charlotte
            Islands, British Columbia. *Occasional Papers of the British
            Columbia Provincial Museum* 14. Victoria.

Fouquet, Léon
1870   Lettre du R.P. Fouquet au T.R.P. Supérieur Général, le 20
            décembre, 1868. *Missions de la Congrégation des Mission-
            naires Oblats de Marie Immaculée* 9(2). Paris.

Fournier, Judith A., and John Dewhirst
1980   Zooarchaeological Analysis of Barnacle Remains from
            Yuquot, British Columbia. Pp. 59–102 in *The Yuquot
            Project*. Vol. 2. William J. Folan and John Dewhirst, eds.
            *Canada. National Historic Parks and Sites Branch. History
            and Archaeology* 43. Ottawa.

Frachtenberg, Leo J.
1909   [Hanis Coosan Ethnographic Notes and Myths in English.]
            (Manuscript No. 330 in National Anthropological Ar-
            chives, Smithsonian Institution, Washington.)

1910   [Alsea: Notes on Ethnology.] (Manuscript No. 2516 in
            National Anthropological Archives, Smithsonian Institu-
            tion, Washington.)

[1910a]   [Semantically Grouped Willopah Vocabulary . . . .Column
            I of Three Columns . . . .] (Manuscript No. 4797 in National
            Anthropological Archives, Smithsonian Institution, Wash-
            ington.)

1913   Coos Texts. *Columbia University Contributions to Anthro-
            pology* 1. New York. (Reprinted: AMS Press, New York,
            1969.)

1913–1914   [Yamhill Notebooks, Grand Ronde Reservation, Oregon,
            Vocabulary and Grammar.] 3 vols. (Manuscript No. 1923-e
            in National Anthropological Archives, Smithsonian Institu-
            tion, Washington.)

1913–1914a [Kalapuya Texts; Kalapuya Grammatical Notes, Mary's
            River Dialect.] (Manuscript Nos. 1923-a, 1923-d in Nation-
            al Anthropological Archives, Smithsonian Institution,
            Washington.)

1913–1914b [Documents Relating to Fieldwork with Kalapuyan Infor-
            mants.] (Manuscripts on Microfilm 32-A, Oregon State
            Library, Salem.)

1914   Lower Umpqua Texts and Notes on the Kusan Dialects.
            Columbia University Contributions to Anthropology 4. New
            York. (Reprinted: AMS Press, New York, 1969.)

[1914a]   [Songs Performed by Louisa Selkeah, a Yamhill Kalapu-
            yan.] (Tape dubbing of original cylinders, tape 11, LWO
            8866, Library of Congress Recording Laboratory, Washing-
            ton.)

1914b   [Yoncalla Notebook, Grand Ronde Reservation, Oregon,
            Vocabulary and Grammar.] (Manuscript No. 1923-f in
            National Anthropological Archives, Smithsonian Institu-
            tion, Washington.)

1915   [Linguistic Re-elicitations and Ethnographic Extracts of
            Gatschet (1877a).] (Red-ink annotations in original Gat-
            schet manuscript, with notes; Manuscript No. 4620 in
            National Anthropological Archives, Smithsonian Institu-
            tion, Washington; and folder 70.10, box 70, Melville Jacobs
            Collection, University of Washington, Seattle.)

1915a   Ethnological Researches Among the Kalapuya Indians.
            Smithsonian Miscellaneous Collections 65(6):85–89. Wash-
            ington.

1915b   [Thirteen Wax Cylinder Recordings of Tututni Athabaskan
            Music, Siletz, Oregon, August 1915.] (In Archive of Folk

Culture, American Folklife Center, Library of Congress,
Washington.)

1915c   [Six Wax Cylinder Recordings of Galice Creek Athabaskan
            Music, from Hoxie Simmons, Siletz, Oregon.] (In Archive
            of Folk Culture, American Folklife Center, Library of
            Congress, Washington.)

1915d   [One Wax Cylinder Recording of Upper Umpqua Athabas-
            kan Music from Jack West, Siletz, Oregon, August 1915.]
            (In Archive of Folk Culture, American Folklife Center,
            Library of Congress, Washington.)

1916   Quileute Ethnology: Lapush, Washington. (Field note-
            books, manuscript No. 30 (W3a5), [Freeman No. 3177] in
            American Philosophical Society Library, Philadelphia.)

1917   A Siletz Vocabulary. *International Journal of American
            Linguistics* 1(1):45–46.

1917a   Myths of the Alsea Indians of Northwestern Oregon.
            International Journal of American Linguistics 1(1):64–75.

1918   [Yakonan (Alsea).] (Unpublished grammatical sketch, fold-
            ers 67.6 and 67.7, in box 67, Melville Jacobs Collection,
            University of Washington, Seattle.)

1918a   Comparative Studies in Takelman, Kalapuyan and Chi-
            nookan Lexicography: A Preliminary Paper. *International
            Journal of American Linguistics* 1(2):175–182.

1920   Eschatology of the Quileute Indians. *American Anthropolo-
            gist* 22(4):330–340.

1920a   Abnormal Types of Speech in Quileute. *International
            Journal of American Linguistics* 1(4):295–299.

1920b   Alsea Texts and Myths. *Bureau of American Ethnology
            Bulletin* 67. Washington.

1921   The Ceremonial Societies of the Quileute Indians. *American
            Anthropologist* 23(3):320–352.

1922   Siuslawan (Lower Umpqua). Pp. 431–629 in Vol. 2 of
            Handbook of American Indian Languages. Franz Boas, ed.
            Bureau of American Ethnology Bulletin 40. Washington.

1922a   Coos. Pp. 297–429 in Vol. 2 of Handbook of American
            Indian Languages. Franz Boas, ed. *Bureau of American
            Ethnology Bulletin* 40. Washington.

Franchère, Gabriel
1820   Relation d'un voyage à la Côte du Nord-ouest de l'Amé-
            rique Septentrionale, dans les années 1810, 11, 12, 13, et 14.
            Montreal: C.B. Pasteur.

1854   Narrative of a Voyage to the Northwest Coast of America in
            the Years 1811, 1812, 1813 and 1814; or, The First
            American Settlement on the Pacific [1820]. J.V.
            Huntington, trans. and ed. New York: Redfield.

1967   Adventure at Astoria, 1810–1814. Hoyt C. Franchère, ed.
            and trans. Norman: University of Oklahoma Press.

1969   Journal of a Voyage on the North West Coast of North
            America During the Years 1811, 1812, 1813, and 1814
            [1820]. W. Kaye Lamb, ed., Wessie Tipping Lamb, trans.
            Toronto: The Champlain Society.

Franklin, Jerry F., and C.T. Dyrness
1973   Natural Vegetation of Oregon and Washington. Portland,
            Oreg.: U.S. Forest Service. Pacific Northwest Forest and
            Range Experiment Station.

679

Fraser, Douglas, ed.
1968   Early Chinese Art and the Pacific Basin: A Photographic Exhibition. New York: Intercultural Arts Press.

Frederick, Richard
1980   Photographer Asahel Curtis, Chronicler of the Northwest. *The American West* 17(6):26–40.

Freed, Stanley A., and Ruth S. Freed
1983   Clark Wissler and the Development of Anthropology in the United States. *American Anthropologist* 85(4):800–825.

Freed, Stanley A., Ruth S. Freed, and Laila Williamson
1988   The American Museum's Jesup North Pacific Expedition. Pp. 97–103 In Crossroads of Continents: Cultures of Siberia and Alaska. William W. Fitzhugh and Aron Crowell, eds. Washington: Smithsonian Institution Press.

Freeman, John F.
1966   A Guide to Manuscripts Relating to the American Indian in the Library of the American Philosophical Society. Philadelphia: American Philosophical Society.

Frenkel, Robert E.
1985   Vegetation. Pp. 58–66 in Atlas of the Pacific Northwest. A. Jon Kimerling and Philip L. Jackson, eds. 7th ed. Corvallis: Oregon State University Press.

Fried, Morton H.
1967   The Evolution of Political Society: An Essay in Political Anthropology. New York: Random House.

Friedlaender, M.F.
1975   Economic Status of Native Indians in British Columbia Fisheries, 1964–1973. *Canada. Department of Fisheries and Oceans. Technical Report Series* PAC/T-75-25. Vancouver.

Friedman, Edward I.
1976   An Archaeological Survey of Makah Territory: A Study in Resource Utilization. (Unpublished Ph.D. Dissertation in Anthropology, Washington State University, Pullman.)

Friedman, Janet
1975   The Prehistoric Uses of Wood at the Ozette Archaeological Site. (Unpublished Ph.D. Dissertation in Anthropology, Washington State University, Pullman.)

Friends, Society of
1970   Uncommon Controversy: Fishing Rights of the Muckleshoot, Puyallup, and Nisqually Indians. Seattle: University of Washington Press.

Frish, Rose E.
1977   Nutrition, Fatness and Fertility: The Effect of Food Intake on Reproductive Ability. Pp. 91–122 in Nutrition and Human Reproduction. W. Henry Mosley, ed. New York: Plenum Press.

Fugro Northwest Incorporated
1980   Cultural Resources Assessment for the Cowlitz Falls Hydroelectric Project. Seattle: Fugro Northwest. Mimeo.

Gaasholt, Øystein, and Fay Cohen
1980   In the Wake of the Boldt Decision: A Sociological Study. *American Indian Journal* 6(11):9–17. Washington.

Gabrielson, Ira N., and Stanley G. Jewett
1970   Birds of the Pacific Northwest. New York: Dover. (An abridged ed. of Birds of Oregon, Oregon State College, Corvallis, 1940.)

Gaines, John P.
1851   [Letter of Sept. 28 to C.M. Conrad.] Pp. 150–153 in *32d Congress, 2d Sess., Senate Executive Document* No. 2 (Serial No. 611). Washington.

Galbraith, J.D., S. Grzybowski, C.L. Law, and J. Rowe
1969   Tuberculosis in Indian Children: Primary Pulmonary Tuberculosis. *Canadian Medical Association Journal* 100(11):497–502. Toronto.

Gallatin, Albert
1836   A Synopsis of the Indian Tribes within the United States East of the Rocky Mountains and the British and Russian Possessions in North America. Pp. 1–422 in *Archaeologia Americana: Transactions and Collections of the American Antiquarian Society* 2. Cambridge, Mass.

———
1848   Hale's Indians of North-west America. *Transactions of the American Ethnological Society* 2:xxiii-clxxxviii, 1–130. New York.

Galloway, Brent D.
1977   A Grammar of Chilliwack Halkomelem. (Unpublished Ph.D. Dissertation in Linguistics, University of California, Berkeley.)

———
1980   The Structure of Upriver Halq'eméylem: A Grammatical Sketch. In Tó:lméls Ye Siyelyólexwa, Wisdom of the Elders. Edna Bobb et al., eds. Sardis, B.C.: Coqualeetza Education Training Centre for the Sto:lo Nation.

———
1982   Upriver Sto:lo Ethnobotany. Sardis, B.C.: Coqualeetza Education Training Centre, Sto:lo Sitel Curriculum.

———
1983   A Look at Nooksack Phonology. Pp. 80–132 in *Working Papers for the 18th International Conference on Salish and Neighboring Languages August 10–12*. Seattle: University of Washington.

———
1985   A Grammar of Chilliwack Halkomelem. *University of California Publications in Linguistics* 96. Berkeley.

———
1986   Some Upriver Halkomelem-speaking Reserves (Reservations) and Villages. Map.

———
1988   The Upriver Halkomelem Language Program at Coqualeetza. *Human Organization* 47(4):291–297.

Garfield, Viola E.
1939   Tsimshian Clan and Society. *University of Washington Publications in Anthropology* 7(3):167–340. Seattle.

———
1945   A Research Problem in Northwest Indian Economics. *American Anthropologist* 47(4):626–630.

———
1947   Historical Aspects of Tlingit Clans in Angoon, Alaska. *American Anthropologist* 49(3):438–452.

———
1955   Making a Box Design. *Davidson Journal of Anthropology* 1(2):165–168. Seattle.

———
1955a   Making a Bird or Chief's Rattle. *Davidson Journal of Anthropology* 1(2):155–164. Seattle.

———
1955b   Possibilities of Genetic Relationship in Northern Pacific Moiety Structure. Pp. 58–61 in Asia and North America: Transpacific Contacts. Marian W. Smith, ed. *Memoirs of the Society for American Archaeology* 9. Salt Lake City.

———
1966   The Tsimshian and Their Neighbors. Pp. 3–70 in The Tsimshian Indians and Their Arts, by Viola E. Garfield and Paul S. Wingert. Seattle: University of Washington Press.

Garfield, Viola E., and Pamela T. Amoss
1984   Erna Gunther (1896–1982). *American Anthropologist* 86(2):394–399.

Garfield, Viola E., and Linn A. Forrest
1948   The Wolf and the Raven. Seattle: University of Washington Press.

Garfield, Viola E., and Paul S. Wingert
1966   The Tsimshian Indians and Their Arts. Seattle: University of Washington Press.

Garfield, Viola E., Paul S. Wingert, and Marius Barbeau
[1951]   The Tsimshian: Their Arts and Music. (*Publications of the American Ethnological Society* 18) New York: J.J. Augustin.

Garner, James C.
1960   A Burial Salvage at a Southern Puget Sound Midden Site. *Washington Archaeologist* 4(6):2–8.

Gass, Patrick
1958   A Journal of the Voyages and Travels of a Corps of Discovery, Under the Command of Capt. Lewis and Capt. Clark, . . . During the Years 1804, 1805 and 1806, ...[1807]. David McKeehan, ed. Minneapolis, Minn.: Ross and Haines.

Gaston, Jennette, and G.F. Grabert
1975   Salvage Archaeology at Birch Bay, Washington. Bellingham: Western Washington State University.

Gaston, Jennette, and J.V. Jermann
1975   Salvage Excavations at Old Man House (45-KP-2), Kitsap County, Washington. *University of Washington. Office of Public Archaeology. Institute for Environmental Studies. Reconnaissance Reports* 4. Seattle.

Gates, R. Ruggles, and George E. Darby
1934   Blood Groups and Physiognomy of British Columbia Coastal Indians. *Journal of the Royal Anthropological Institute of Great Britain and Ireland* 64:23–44. London.

Gatschet, Albert S.
1877   [Yamel (Yamhill/Kalapuya) Vocabulary.] (Vocabulary in Powell's Outline; manuscript No. 474 in National Anthropological Archives, Smithsonian Institution, Washington.)

1877a   [Atfalati (Kalapuya) Materials.] (Manuscript No. 472-a-b-c in National Anthropological Archives, Smithsonian Institution, Washington.)

1877b   [Clackamas Place and Tribal Names, Words (Especially Body Parts), Phrases, and Sentences.] (Manuscript No. 268 in National Anthropological Archives, Smithsonian Institution, Washington.)

1877c   [Comparative Vocabulary of Nestucca, Chinook Jargon, and "Macanossisi Near Fort (?) Vancouver".] (Manuscript No. 727 in National Anthropological Archives, Smithsonian Institution, Washington.)

[1877d]   [Divisions of Time Noticed Among the Atfálati Tribe of the Kalapuya Indians, of Northwestern Oregon.] (Manuscript No. 1385 in National Anthropological Archives, Smithsonian Institution, Washington.)

1877e   [Lakmiut and Ahantchuyuk Vocabulary.] (Manuscript No. 473 in National Anthropological Archives, Smithsonian Institution, Washington.)

1877f   [Three Texts with Interlinear English Translations from Stephen Savage, Grand Ronde Reservation, Oreg.] (Manuscript No. 998 in National Anthropological Archives, Smithsonian Institution, Washington.)

[1877g]   [Umpqua (Athpascan) Vocabulary; Recorded at Grand Ronde Indian Reservation, Oregon.] (Manuscript No. 76 in National Anthropological Archives, Smithsonian Institution, Washington.)

1877h   [Wasco Vocabulary.] (Manuscript No. 401 in National Anthropological Archives, Smithsonian Institution, Washington.)

1877i   [Words, Sentences and Various Texts Collected at the Grand Ronde Agency, Northwestern Oregon.] (Manuscript No. 2029 in National Anthropological Archives, Smithsonian Institution, Washington.)

1877j   [Texts, Sentences and Vocables of the Atfalati Dialect of the Kalapuya Language of Willamet Valley, Northwestern Oregon.] (Manuscript No. 472-a in National Anthropological Archives, Smithsonian Institution, Washington.)

1877k   [Calapooian, Atfalati, Wapatu Lake Indians.] (Vocabulary in Powell's Outline, 1st ed.; Manuscript No. 472-d in National Anthropological Archives, Smithsonian Institution, Washington.)

1882   Indian Languages of the Pacific States and Territories and of the Pueblos of New Mexico. *Magazine of American History* 8(4):253–263.

General Land Office
1892–1901   [Indian Allotments in the Roseburg District.] (Manuscript, Vol. 3, Series 39, General Land Office, in Record Group 49, National Archives Branch Office, Seattle, Washington.)

Gerdts, Donna B.
1977   A Dialect Survey of Halkomelem Salish. (Unpublished M.A. Thesis in Linguistics, University of British Columbia, Vancouver.)

1984   A Relational Analysis of Halkomelem Causals. Pp. 169–204 in The Syntax of Native American Languages. Eung-Do Cook and Donna B. Gerdts, eds. (*Syntax and Semantics* 16) Orlando, Fla.: Academic Press.

1988   Object and Absolutive in Halkomelem Salish. New York: Garland.

Gerlach, Arch C., ed., 1970, *see* U.S. Geological Survey 1970

Gessler, Trisha
1971   A Stylistic Analysis of Twelve Haida Drawings. *Syesis* 4(1–2):245–252. Victoria, B.C.

1981   The Art of Nunstins. [Skidegate, B.C.]: Queen Charlotte Islands Museum.

Gharrett, John T., and John I. Hodges
1950   Salmon Fisheries of the Coastal Rivers of Oregon South of the Columbia. *Oregon Fish Commission Contributions* 13. Portland.

Gibbs, George
1850   Chinook Jargon Vocabulary. [Compiled by George Gibbs, with Additions and Alterations by George Suckley.] (Manuscript No. 197b in National Anthropological Archives, Smithsonian Institution, Washington.)

[1851]   [Notes by Gibbs on the Source of His Salishan Vocabularies . . . Belhoola, Kalapuya, and Molele.] (Manuscript No. 742 in National Anthropological Archives, Smithsonian Institution, Washington.)

1851a   [Yamhill Kalapuyan Vocabulary.] (Manuscript No. 475-a-b in National Anthropological Archives, Smithsonian Institution, Washington.)

1851b   [January: Census of the Chinook Tribe of Indians.] (In Records of the Oregon Superintendency of Indian Affairs, National Archives, Washington.)

[1853]   Chemakum Vocabulary. (Manuscript 30(W3b.3) [Freeman No. 710] in the American Philosophical Society Library, Philadelphia.)

1853a   [Indian Nomenclature of Localities in Washington and Oregon Territories.] (Manuscript No. 714 in National Anthropological Archives, Smithsonian Institution, Washington.)

1854   [Alaskan and Skidegate Haida Vocabularies.] (Manuscript No. 1031 in National Anthropological Archives, Smithsonian Institution, Washington.)

1855   Report . . . .to Captain Mc'Clellan, on the Indian Tribes of the Territory of Washington. Pp. 402–434 in Report of Explorations for a Route . . . .from St. Paul to Puget Sound, by I.I. Stevens. In Vol. 1 of Reports of Explorations and Surveys . . . .from the Mississippi River to the Pacific Ocean . . . .1853–4 [etc.]. *33d Congress, 2d Sess. Senate Executive Document No. 78.* (Serial No. 758) Washington: Beverly Tucker, Printer. (Reprinted: Ye Galleon Press, Fairfield, Wash., 1972.)

1855a   Treaty of Neah Bay [Transcript of Journal Proceedings]. (Microcopy No. T–494, roll 5, Records Relating to the Negotiation of Ratified and Unratified Treaties with Various Tribes of Indians, 1801–1869. In National Archives, Washington.)

1857   [Skidegate [Haida] Vocabulary.] (Manuscript No. 710 in National Anthropological Archives, Smithsonian Institution, Washington.)

1857a   [Skat-wan Dialect of the Stikine Language.] (Manuscript No. 531-a-b in National Anthtropological Archives, Smithsonian Institution, Washington.)

1857b   [Tsimshian Vocabulary.] In Vocabularies of the Tongass or Klinkate [etc.]. (Manuscript No. 281 in National Anthropological Archives, Smithsonian Institution, Washington.)

1857c   [Tsim-si-ann.] (Manuscript No. 282-b in National Anthropological Archives, Smithsonian Institution, Washington.)

[1857d]   [Observations on the Coast Tribes of Oregon.] (Manuscript No. 196-a in National Anthropological Archives, Smithsonian Institution, Washington.)

1859   [Vocabulary of the Hailtzuk or Belbella Language of Millbank's Sound; Obtained at Victoria from 'Capt. Stewart', a Belbella Indian, April 1859.] (Manuscript No. 987 in National Anthropological Archives, Smithsonian Institution, Washington.)

1859a   ["Bel-le-whil-la" or Bel'hoo-la Vocabulary, Victoria.] (Manuscript No. 227 in National Anthropological Archives, Smithsonian Institution, Washington.)

1863   Instructions for Research Relative to the Ethnology and Philology of America. *Smithsonian Miscellaneous Collections* 7(11). Washington.

1863a   Alphabetical Vocabularies of the Clallam and Lummi. (*Shea's Library of American Linguistics* 11) New York: Cramoisy Press.

1863b   Alphabetical Vocabulary of the Chinook Language. (*Shea's Library of American Linguistics* 13) New York: Cramoisy Press. (Reprinted: AMS Press, New York, 1970.)

1863c   A Dictionary of the Chinook Jargon, or Trade Language of Oregon. (*Shea's Library of American Linguistics* 12) New York: Cramoisy Press. (Published also as: *Smithsonian Miscellaneous Collections* 7(10). ·Washington.)

1877   Tribes of Western Washington and Northwestern Oregon. *Contributions to North American Ethnology* 1(2):157–361. John Wesley Powell, ed. Washington: U.S. Geographical and Geological Survey of the Rocky Mountain Region. (Reprinted: Shorey, Seattle, Wash., 1970.)

1955–1956   George Gibbs' Account of Indian Mythology in Oregon and Washington Territories. Ella E. Clark, ed. *Oregon Historical Quarterly* 56(4):293–325; 57(2):125–167.

Gibson, James A.
1964   Quinault Phonemics. (Unpublished M.A. Thesis in Linguistics, University of Washington, Seattle.)

Gibson, James R.
1976   Russian Sources for the Ethnohistory of the Pacific Coast of North America in the Eighteenth and Nineteenth Centuries. *Western Canadian Journal of Anthropology* 6(1):91–115. Edmonton, Alta.

1978   European Dependence Upon American Natives: The Case of Russian America. *Ethnohistory* 25(4):359–385.

1982   Smallpox on the Northwest Coast, 1835–1838. *BC Studies* 56(Winter):61–81. Vancouver.

Giglioli, Enrico H.
1978   Notes on an Ethnographic Collection Made During the Third Voyage of Cook and Preserved Until the End of the Last Century in the Royal Museum of Physics and Natural History in Florence. Denzel Carr and Mildred M. Knowlton, trans. Pp. 75–178 in Cook Voyage Artifacts in Leningrad, Berne, and Florence Museums. Adrienne L. Kaeppler, ed. Honolulu: Bishop Museum Press.

Gill, Steven J.
1983   The Ethnobotany of the Makah and Ozette Peoples. (Unpublished Ph.D. Dissertation in Botany and Anthropology, Washington State University, Pullman.)

1985   Indigenous Food Plants of the Lower Columbia River and Willapa Bay (Washington and Oregon). (Paper presented at the 38th Northwest Anthropological Conference, Ellensburg, Wash., April 18–20.)

Gill, Steven J., and Ann M. Renker
1985   Makah Botanical Nomenclature: An Analysis of Taxonomy and Meaning. Pp. 85–96 in *Papers of the 20th International Salish and Neighboring Languages Conference.* Vancouver, 1985.

[1986]   From Phoneme to Text: An Overview of Makah. *Amérindia: Revue d'Ethno-linguistique Amérindienne Special.* In Press.

Gillis, Alix J.
1974   History of the Neah Bay Agency. Pp. 91–115 in Coast Salish and Western Washington Indians, III. (*American Indian Ethnohistory: Indians of the Northwest*) 5 vols. New York: Garland.

Gjullin, Claude M., and Gaines W. Eddy
1972   The Mosquitoes of the Northwestern United States. *USDA Agricultural Research Service. Technical Bulletins* 1447. Washington.

Gladstone, Percy
1953   Native Indians and the Fishing Industry of British Columbia. *Canadian Journal of Economics and Political Science* 19(1):20–34. Toronto.

Glassley, Ray H.
1972   Indian Wars of the Pacific Northwest. 2d ed. Portland, Oreg.: Binfords and Mort.

Gleeson, Paul F.
1980   Ozette Woodworking Technology. *Washington State University, Laboratory of Archaeology and History, Project Reports* 3. Pullman.

1980a   Ozette Archaeological Project, Interim Final Report, Phase XIII. *Washington Archaeological Research Center. Project Reports* 97. Pullman.

1981   Ozette Project Research Design. (Unpublished manuscript on file at Laboratory of Archaeology and History, Washington State University, Pullman.)

Gleason, Paul F., Mark Fleisher, and Geoffrey Gamble
1979   Economic Roles of Nootkan Intrahouse Ranked Positions. (Paper presented at the 44th Annual Meeting of the Society for American Archaeology in Joint Session with the

Canadian Archaeological Association, 25 April, Vancouver, 1979.)

Glover, Richard, ed.
1962   David Thompson's Narrative, 1784–1812. Toronto: The Champlain Society.

Goddard, Ives
1973   Philological Approaches to the Study of North American Indian Languages: Documents and Documentation. Pp. 727–745 in Current Trends in Linguistics. Vol. 10: Linguistics in North America. Pt. 1. Thomas A. Sebeok, ed. The Hague: Mouton. (Reprinted: Plenum Press, New York, 1976.)

Goddard, Pliny E.
[1902–1903] [Tolowa Field Notes.] (Manuscript No. 30(Na20f.1) [Freeman No. 3764] in American Philosophical Society Library, Philadelphia.)

———   [1903–1904] [Galice Creek Linguistic and Ethnographic Field Notebooks and Texts.] (In Melville Jacobs Collection, University of Washington Libraries, Seattle.)

———   1934   Indians of the Northwest Coast. 2d ed. American Museum of Natural History. Handbook Series 10. New York.

Godfrey, W. Earl
1986   The Birds of Canada. Ottawa: National Museums of Canada.

Goeken, . . . von
1885   Das religiöse Leben der Bella Coola Indianer. Original-Mittheilungen aus der Ethnologischen Abtheilung der Königlichen Museen 1:183–186. Berlin.

Gofton, J.P., H.S. Robinson, and G.E. Trueman
1966   Ankylosing Spondylitis in a Canadian Indian Population. Annals of the Rheumatic Diseases 25(6):525–527.

Gofton, J.P., J.S. Lawrence, P.H. Bennett, and T.A. Burch
1966   Sacro-iliitis in Eight Populations. Annals of the Rheumatic Diseases 25(6):528–533.

Gogol, John M.
1985   Cowlitz Indian Basketry. American Indian Basketry 5(4):4–20.

Goldenweiser, Alexander A.
1915   The Social Organization of the Indians of North America. Pp. 350–378 in Anthropology in North America, by Franz Boas et al., eds. New York: G.E. Stechert.

Golder, Frank A.
1922–1925 Bering's Voyages: An Account of the Efforts of the Russians to Determine the Relation of Asia and America. 2 vols. (American Geographical Society Research Sereis 1–2) New York. (Reprinted: Octagon Press, New York, 1968.)

Goldman, Irving
1937   The Kwakiutl Indians of Vancouver Island. Pp. 180–209 in Cooperation and Competition Among Primitive Peoples. Margaret Mead, ed. New York: McGraw-Hill Book Company. (Reprinted: Beacon Press, Boston, Mass., 1961.)

———   1975   The Mouth of Heaven: An Introduction to Kwakiutl Religious Thought. New York: Wiley.

Goldschmidt, Walter R., ed.
1959   The Anthropology of Franz Boas. Memoirs of the American Anthropological Association 89:1–155. Menasha, Wis.

Goldschmidt, Walter R., and Theodore H. Haas
1946   Possessory Rights of the Natives of Southeastern Alaska: A Detailed Analysis of the Early and Present Territory Used and Occupied by the Natives of Southeastern Alaska, Except the Natives of the Village of Kake (Partially Treated), Hydaburg, and Klawock; a Report to the Commissioner of Indian Affairs. Mimeo.

Golla, Victor
1962   [Tape Recording of Vocabulary in Tututni from Ida Bensell, Siletz, Oreg.] (In Language Laboratory, University of California, Berkeley.)

———   1976   Tututni (Oregon Athapaskan). International Journal of American Linguistics 43(3):217–227.

Golovnin, Vasiliĭ M.
1979   Around the World on the Kamchatka, 1817–1819. Ella Lury Wiswell, ed. and trans. Honolulu: Hawaiian Historical Society.

Good, John B.
1880   A Vocabulary and Outlines of Grammar of the Nitlakapamuk or Thompson Tongue . . . Together with a Phonetic Chinook Dictionary, Adapted for Use in the Province of British Columbia. Victoria, B.C.: St. Paul's Mission Press.

Goodenough, Ward H.
1976   On the Origin of Matrilineal Clans: A "Just So" Story. Proceedings of the American Philosophical Society 120(1):21–36. Philadelphia.

Goodfellow, John C.
[1950]   Historical Information re Various United Churches. (Microfilm reel No. 110A, British Columbia Provincial Archives, Victoria.)

Goodman, Linda J.
1978   This is My Song: The Role of Song as Symbol in Makah Life. (Unpublished Ph.D. Dissertation in Anthropology, Washington State University, Pullman.)

Goodspeed, Charles E.
1945   Nathaniel Hawthorne and the Museum of the East India Marine Society. The American Neptune 5(4):266–285. Salem, Mass..

Gordon, Marjory E.
1974   A Qualitative Analysis of Human Skeletal Remains from DgRw-4, Gabriola Island, British Columbia. (Unpublished M.A. Thesis in Archeology, University of Calgary, Calgary, Alta.)

Gormly, Mary
1971   Tlingits of Bucareli Bay, Alaska (1774–1792). Northwest Anthropological Research Notes 5(2):157–180. Moscow, Idaho.

———   1977   Early Culture Contact on the Northwest Coast, 1774–1795: Analysis of Spanish Source Material. Northwest Anthropological Research Notes 11(1):1–80. Moscow, Idaho.

Gosnell, W[esley] B.
1926   Indian War in Washington Territory [1856]. Washington Historical Quarterly 17(4):289–299. Seattle.

Gough, Barry M.
1984   Gunboat Frontier: British Maritime Authority and Northwest Coast Indians, 1846–90. Vancouver: University of British Columbia Press.

Gould, Richard A.
1981   Comparative Ecology of Food-sharing in Australia and Northwest California. Pp. 422–454 in Omnivorous Primates: Gathering and Hunting in Human Evolution. Robert S.O. Harding and Geza Teleki, eds. New York: Columbia University Press.

Gould, Richard A., and Theodore P. Furukawa
1964   Aspects of Ceremonial Life Among the Indian Shakers of Smith River, California. Kroeber Anthropological Society Papers 31:51–67. Berkeley, Calif.

Grant, John M.
1984   Moon of Wintertime: Missionaries and the Indians of Canada in Encounter Since 1534. Toronto: University of Toronto Press.

Grant, Rena V.
1945   Chinook Jargon. *International Journal of American Linguistics* 11(4):225–233.

Grant, W. Colquhoun
1857   Description of Vancouver Island. *Journal of the Royal Geographical Society* 27:268–320. London.

Gray, Dennis J.
1987   The Takelma and Their Athapascan Neighbors: A New Ethnographic Synthesis for the Upper Rogue River Area of Southwestern Oregon. *University of Oregon Anthropological Papers* 37. Eugene.

Grayson, Donald K.
1975   Recent Archaeological Surveys in the Western Cascades: Prehistory and Conservation Archaeology. Pp. 495–503 in Archaeological Studies in the Willamette Valley, Oregon. C. Melvin Aikens, ed. *University of Oregon Anthropological Papers* 8. Eugene.

Green, David M., and R. Wayne Campbell
1984   The Amphibians of British Columbia. *British Columbia Provincial Museum. Handbook* 45. Victoria.

Green, Jonathan S.
1915   Journal of a Tour on the North West Coast of America in the Year 1829; Containing a Description of a Part of Oregon, California and the North West Coast and the Numbers, Manners and Customs of the Native Tribes. (*Heartman's Historical Series* 10) New York: Chas. Fred. Heartman.

Greengo, Robert E.
1966   Archaeological Excavations at the Marymoor Site (45KI9). (Mimeographed report, at Department of Anthropology, University of Washington, Seattle.)

Greengo, Robert E., and Robert Houston
1970   Excavations at the Marymoor Site. *University of Washington. Department of Anthropology. Reports in Archaeology* 4. Seattle.

Greenhow, Robert
1845   The History of Oregon and California, and the Other Territories of the North-west Coast of North America. 2d ed. Boston: C.C. Little and J. Brown. (Reprint of extract: Pp. 435–438 in Voyages of the "Columbia". F.W. Howay, ed., Da Capo Press, New York, 1969.)

Gregory, Patrick T., and R. Wayne Campbell
1984   The Reptiles of British Columbia. *British Columbia Provincial Museum. Handbook* 44. Victoria.

Grekoff, George
1965   [Sechelt Linguistic Fieldnotes.] (Manuscripts in Grekoff's possession; copy held by British Columbia Indian Language Project, Victoria.)

Griffith, Lela M.
1967   The Intertidal Univalves of British Columbia. *British Columbia Provincial Museum. Handbook* 26. Victoria.

Grinev, A.V.
1986   Ob etnonime Koloshchi. [On the Ethnonym "Kolosh".] *Sovetskaia Ėtnografiia* 1:104–108. Moscow.

1986a   Barter Between the Tlingit and Athapaskan Rocky Mountains Indians in the 19th Century. *Sovetskaia Ėtnografiia* 5:113–122. Moscow.

Grinnell, George B.
1901   The Natives of the Alaska Coast Region. Pp. 137–183 in Vol. 1 of The Harriman Alaska Expedition, 1899. New York: Doubleday, Page .

Grubb, David McC.
1977   A Practical Writing System and Short Dictionary of Kwakw'ala (Kwakiutl). *Canada. National Museum of Man. Mercury Series. Ethnology Service Papers* 34. Ottawa.

Gruber, Jacob W.
1967   Horatio Hale and the Development of American Anthropology. *Proceedings of the American Philosophical Society* 111(1):5–37. Philadelphia.

1970   Ethnographic Salvage and the Shaping of Anthropology. *American Anthropologist* 72(6):1289–1299.

Gruening, Ernest H.
1954   The State of Alaska. New York: Random House. (Rev. ed. in 1968.)

Grumet, Robert S.
1975   Changes in Coast Tsimshian Redistributive Activities in the Fort Simpson Region of British Columbia, 1788–1862. *Ethnohistory* 22(4):294–318.

1979   Native Americans of the Northwest Coast: A Critical Bibliography. Bloomington: Published for the Newberry Library by Indiana University Press.

Gsovski, Vladimir
1950   Russian Administration of Alaska and the Status of the Alaskan Natives. *81st Congress 2d Sess. Senate Document No. 152.* (Serial No. 11401) Washington.

Guédon, Marie-Françoise
1984   Tsimshian Shamanic Images. Pp. 174–211 in The Tsimshian: Images of the Past, Views for the Present. Margaret Seguin, ed. Vancouver: University of British Columbia Press.

1984a   An Introduction to Tsimshian Worldview and Its Practitioners. Pp. 137–159 in The Tsimshian: Images of the Past, Views for the Present. Margaret Seguin, ed. Vancouver: University of British Columbia Press.

Guillod, Harry
1882   [Report on the Tribes of the West Coast of Vancouver Island; Alberni, Barclay Sound, 22d September, 1881.] Pp. 161–165 in *Dominion of Canada. Annual Report of the Department of Indian Affairs for the Year 1881.* Ottawa.

Guinn, Stanley J.
1962   White Rock Village Archaeological Site: A Preliminary Report of Investigations. *Washington State University. Laboratory of Anthropology. Reports of Investigations* 16. Pullman.

1963   A Maritime Village on the Olympic Peninsula of Washington. *Washington State University. Laboratory of Anthropology. Reports of Investigations* 22. Pullman.

Gunther, Erna
1925   Klallam Folk Tales. *University of Washington Publications in Anthropology* 1(4):113–169. Seattle.

1926   Analysis of the First Salmon Ceremony. *American Anthropologist* 28(4):605–617.

1927   Klallam Ethnography. *University of Washington Publications in Anthropology* 1(5):171–314. Seattle.

1928   A Further Analysis of the First Salmon Ceremony. *University of Washington Publications in Anthropology* 2(5):129–173. Seattle.

1936   A Preliminary Report on the Zoological Knowledge of the Makah. Pp. 105–118 in Essays in Anthropology Presented to A.L. Kroeber. Robert Lowie, ed. Berkeley: University of California Press.

1942   Reminiscences of a Whaler's Wife. *Pacific Northwest Quarterly* 3(1):65–69.

1945   Ethnobotany of Western Washington. *University of Washington Publications in Anthropology* 10(1):1–62. Seattle. (Rev. ed. in 1973.)

1949   The Shaker Religion of the Northwest. Pp. 37–76 in Indians of the Urban Northwest. Marian W. Smith, ed. New York: Columbia University Press.

1951   Indians of the Northwest Coast. [Catalog for Exhibition at the Taylor Museum of the Colorado Springs Fine Arts Center and the Seattle Art Museum, Seattle, Wash.]

1953   Viewer's Guide to Primitive Art. Seattle: University of Washington Press.

1956   The Social Disorganization of the Haida as Reflected in Their Slate Carving. *Davidson Journal of Anthropology* 2(2):149–153. Seattle.

1960   Vancouver and the Indians of Puget Sound. *Pacific Northwest Quarterly* 51(1):1–12.

1962   Northwest Coast Indian Art: An Exhibit at the Seattle World's Fair Fine Arts Pavilion, Apr. 21–Oct. 21. Seattle: Century 21 Exposition.

1962a   Makah Marriage Patterns and Population Stability. Pp. 538–545 in *Proceedings of the 34th International Congress of Americanists*. Vienna, July 18–25, 1960.

1966   Art in the Life of the Northwest Coast Indians. With a Catalog of the Rasmussen Collection of Northwest Indian Art at the Portland Art Museum. Portland, Oreg.: Portland Art Museum.

1971   Northwest Coast Indian Art. Pp. 318–340 in Anthropology and Art: Readings in Cross-cultural Aesthetics. Charlotte M. Otten, ed. Garden City, N.Y.: Natural History Press.

1972   Indian Life on the Northwest Coast of North America, as Seen by the Early Explorers and Fur Traders During the Last Decades of the Eighteenth Century. Chicago: University of Chicago Press.

1973   Ethnobotany of Western Washington: The Knowledge and Use of Indigenous Plants by Native Americans. Seattle: University of Washington Press.

Gustafson, Carl E.
1968   Prehistoric Use of Fur Seals: Evidence from the Olympic Coast of Washington. *Science* 161:49–51.

Gustafson, Carl E., and Clare Manis
[1984]   The Manis Mastodon Site: An Adventure in Prehistory. Sequim, Wash.: Manis Enterprises.

Gustafson, Carl E., Delbert W. Gilbow, and Richard D. Daugherty
1979   The Manis Mastodon Site: Early Man on the Olympic Peninsula. *Canadian Journal of Archaeology* 3:157–164.

Gustafson, Paula
1980   Salish Weaving. Seattle: University of Washington Press.

Haas, Mary R.
1969   The Prehistory of Languages. (*Janua Linguarum. Series Minor* 57). The Hague: Mouton.

1969a   Internal Reconstruction of the Nootka-Nitinat Pronominal Suffixes. *International Journal of American Linguistics* 35(2):108–124.

1972   The Structure of Stems and Roots in Nootka-Nitinat. *International Journal of American Linguistics* 38(2):83–92.

Haas, Theodore H.
1947   Ten Years of Tribal Government Under I.R.A. *United States Indian Service. Tribal Relations Pamphlets* 1. Lawrence, Kans.

Habeck, James R.
1961   The Original Vegetation of the Mid-Willamette Valley, Oregon. *Northwest Science* 35(2):66–77. Pullman, Wash.

Haberland, Wolfgang
1979   Donnervogel und Raubwal: Die indianische Kunst der Nordwestküste Nordamerikas. [Exhibit Catalogue.] Hamburg: Hamburgisches Museum für Völkerkunde und Christians Verlag.

Hackett, Cecil J.
1976   Diagnostic Criteria of Syphilis, Yaws and Treponarid (Treponematoses) and of Some Other Diseases in Dry Bones (for Use in Osteo-Archaeology). New York: Springer-Verlag.

Haeberlin, Hermann K.
1918   sbEtEtdaˊq a Shamanistic Performance of the Coast Salish. *American Anthropologist* 20(3):249–257.

1918a   Principles of Esthetic Form in the Art of the North Pacific Coast: A Preliminary Sketch. *American Anthropologist* 20(3):258–264.

1924   Mythology of Puget Sound. *Journal of American Folk-Lore* 37(145–146):371–438.

1974   Distribution of the Salish Substantival [Lexical] Suffixes. M. Terry Thompson, ed. *Anthropological Linguistics* 16(6):219–350.

Haeberlin, Hermann K., and Erna Gunther
1924   Ethnographische Notizen über die Indianerstämme des Puget-Sundes. *Zeitschrift für Ethnologie* 56(1–4):1–74. Berlin.

1930   The Indians of Puget Sound. *University of Washington Publications in Anthropology* 4(1):1–83. Seattle.

Haeberlin, Hermann K., James A. Teit, and Helen H. Roberts
1928   Coiled Basketry in British Columbia and Surrounding Region. Pp. 119–484 in *41st Annual Report of the Bureau of American Ethnology for the Years 1919–1924*. Washington.

Haegart, Dorothy
1983   Children of the First People. Vancouver, B.C.: Tillacum Library.

Haekel, Josef
1954   Initiationen und Geheimbünde an der Nordwestküste Nordamerikas. *Mitteilungen der Anthropologischen Gesellschaft in Wien* 83(3):167–190. Vienna.

1958   Kosmischer Baum und Pfahl in Mythus und Kult der Stämme Nordwestamerikas. *Wiener völkerkundliche Mitteilungen* ser. 6, Vol. 1 (1–4):33–81. Vienna.

Hagège, Claude
1981   Le comox lhaamen de Colombie Britannique: Présentation d'une langue amérindienne. *Amérindia: Revue d'Ethnolinguistique Amérindienne. Special Number* 2. Paris.

Haggarty, James C.
1971   A Dermatoglyphic Analysis of Four Indian Populations in British Columbia. (Unpublished M.A. Thesis in Anthropology and Sociology, University of Victoria, Victoria, B.C.)

1982   The Archeology of Hesquiat Harbour: The Archeological Utility of an Ethnographically Defined Social Unit. (Unpublished Ph.D. Dissertation in Archeology, Washington State University, Pullman.)

Hajda, Yvonne P.
1976   Mary's River Kalapuyan: A Descriptive Phonology. (Unpublished M.A. Thesis in Anthropology, Portland State University, Portland, Oreg.)

1977   Western Oregon Kinship Systems: Alsea, Siuslaw, Coos. (Manuscript in Hajda's possession.)

1984 Regional Social Organization in the Greater Lower Columbia, 1792–1830. (Unpublished Ph.D. Dissertation in Anthropology, University of Washington, Seattle.)

1987 Exchange Spheres on the Greater Lower Columbia. (Paper read at the 86th Annual Meeting of the American Anthropological Association, Chicago.)

1987a Creating Tribes. *Anthropology Newsletter* 28(7):2. Washington.

Hajda, Yvonne, and Russel Barsh
1988 [Anthropologists and BIA Decisions: Appearance of Unfairness?] *Anthropology Newsletter* 29(3):2. Washington.

Hale, Horatio
1846 Ethnography and Philology. Vol. 6 of United States Exploring Expedition During the Years 1838, 1839, 1840, 1841, 1842. Philadelphia: Lea and Blanchard. (Reprinted: Gregg Press, Ridgewood, N.J., 1968.)

Haley, Shawn D.
1983 The South Yale Site: Yet Another Point. *The Midden: Publication of the Archaeological Society of British Columbia* 15(5):3–5. Vancouver.

Hall, Alfred J.
1889 A Grammar of the Kwagiutl Language. *Transactions of the Royal Society of Canada for 1888*, Vol. 6(2):59–106. Montreal.

Hall, Carl
1983 Makah Indian Reservation Statistical Information Guide. (Manuscript in Makah Tribal Council Planning Department, Neah Bay, Wash.)

Hall, Edwin S., Jr., Margaret B. Blackman, and Vincent Rickard
1981 Northwest Coast Indian Graphics: An Introduction to Silk Screen Prints. Seattle: University of Washington Press.

Hall, E. [ugene] Raymond
1981 The Mammals of North America. 2d ed. New York: John Wiley and Sons.

Hall, John L.
1968 A Statistical Determination of Components Represented in the Excavated Material from the Helen Point Midden, DfRu 8. (Unpublished B.A. Honors Essay in Anthropology, University of Victoria, Victoria, B.C.)

Hall, Roberta L.
1976 Functional Relationships Between Dental Attrition and the Helicoidal Plane. *American Journal of Physical Anthropology* 45(1):69–76.

1978 Sexual Dimorphism for Size in Seven Nineteenth Century Northwest Coast Populations. *Human Biology* 50(2):159–171.

1978a Oral Traditions of the Coquille Indians, 1978. Corvallis: Oregon State University, Department of Anthropology.

1984 The Coquille Indians: Yesterday, Today and Tomorrow. Lake Oswego, Oreg.: Smith, Smith and Smith Publishing Company.

Hall, Roberta L., and Thomas German
1975 Dental Pathology, Attrition, and Occlusal Surface Form in a Prehistoric Sample from British Columbia. *Syesis* 8:275–289. Vancouver.

Hall, Roberta L., and James C. Haggarty
1981 Human Skeletal Remains and Associated Cultural Material from the Hill Site, DfRu 4, Saltspring Island, British Columbia. Pp. 64–106 in Contributions to Physical Anthropology, 1978–1980. J.S. Cybulski, ed. *Canada. National Museum of Man. Mercury Series. Archaeological Survey Papers* 106. Ottawa.

Hall, Roberta L., and Peter L. Macnair
1972 Multivariate Analysis of Anthropometric Data and Classifications of British Columbian Natives. *American Journal of Physical Anthropology* 37(3):401–409.

Halliday, William M.
1935 Potlatch and Totem, and the Recollections of an Indian Agent. London: J.M. Dent and Sons.

Halpern, Ida, and David Duke
1978 "... A Very Agreeable Harmony." Impressions of Nootkan Music. Pp. 63–70 in nu·tka·: Captain Cook and the Spanish Explorers on the Coast. Barbara S. Efrat and W.J. Langlois, eds. *Sound Heritage* 7(1). Victoria, B.C.

Halpin, Marjorie M.
1973 The Tsimshian Crest System: A Study Based on Museum Specimens and the Marius Barbeau and William Beynon Field Notes. (Unpublished Ph.D. Dissertation in Anthropology, University of British Columbia, Vancouver.)

1978 William Beynon, Ethnographer, 1888–1958. Pp. 141–156 in American Indian Intellectuals. Margot Liberty, ed. *Proceedings of the American Ethnological Society*, 1976. St. Paul, Minn.: West Publishing.

1981 The Tsimshian Monkey Mask and the Sasquatch. Pp. 211–228 in Manlike Monsters on Trial: Early Records and Modern Evidence. Marjorie M. Halpin and Michael M. Ames, eds. Vancouver: University of British Columbia Press.

1981a 'Seeing' in Stone: Tsimshian Masking and the Twin Stone Masks. Pp. 269–288 in The World Is as Sharp as a Knife: An Anthology in Honour of Wilson Duff. D.N. Abbott, ed. Victoria: British Columbia Provincial Museum.

1981b Totem Poles: An Illustrated Guide. Vancouver: University of British Columbia Press.

1984 The Structure of Tsimshian Totemism. Pp. 16–35 in The Tsimshian and Their Neighbors of the North Pacific Coast. Jay Miller and Carol M. Eastman, eds. Seattle: University of Washington Press.

1984a Feast Names at Hartley Bay. Pp. 57–64 in The Tsimshian: Images of the Past, Views for the Present. Margaret Seguin, ed. Vancouver: University of British Columbia Press.

1984b Seeing in Stone: Tsimshian Masking and the Twin Stone Masks. Pp. 281–307 in The Tsimshian: Images of the Past, Views for the Present. Margaret Seguin, ed. Vancouver: University of British Columbia Press.

Ham, Leonard C.
1980 A Preliminary Survey of Nimpkish Heritage Sites. (Unpublished manuscript in Heritage Conservation Branch, Parliament Buildings, Victoria, B.C.)

1983 Seasonality, Shell Midden Layers, and Coast Salish Subsistence Activities at the Crescent Beach Site, DgRr 1. (Unpublished Ph.D. Dissertation in Archeology, University of British Columbia, Vancouver.)

1988 An Archaeological Impact Assessment of the Cohoe Creek Site (FuUb 10), Port Clements, Queen Charlotte Islands, British Columbia. (Manuscript in Heritage Conservation Branch, Parliament Buildings, Victoria, B.C.)

Hamilton, Alexander S.
1856 Haynargger Vocabulary, Smith River, California. (Manuscript No. 87 in National Anthropological Archives, Smithsonian Institution, Washington.)

Hamori-Torok, Charles *see* Torok, Charles H.

Hancock, Samuel
1927   The Narrative of Samuel Hancock, 1845–1860. New York: Robert McBride.

Hanson, Gordon W.
1973   The Katz Site: A Prehistoric Pithouse Settlement in the Lower Fraser Valley, British Columbia. (Unpublished M.A. Thesis in Anthropology, University of British Columbia, Vancouver.)

Harger, Jane M.
1972   The History of the Siletz Reservation, 1856–1877. (Unpublished M.A. Thesis in History, University of Oregon, Eugene.)

Harmon, Ray
1971   Indian Shaker Church of The Dalles. *Oregon Historical Quarterly* 72(2):148–158.

Harner, Michael J., and Albert B. Elsasser
1965   Art of the Northwest Coast. Berkeley: University of California Press.

Harper, J. Russell, ed.
1971   Paul Kane's Frontier, Including Wanderings of an Artist Among the Indians of North America. Austin: University of Texas.

Harrington, John P.
1933   [Takelma: Linguistic, Ethnographic, and Biographical Notes; Records of Placename Trips.] (Microfilm, reel No. 028, John Peabody Harrington Papers, Alaska/Northwest Coast, in National Anthropological Archives, Smithsonian Institution, Washington.)

———— [1940–1942] [Galice/Applegate.] (Microfilm, reel No. 028, John Peabody Harrington Papers, Alaska/Northwest Coast, in National Anthropological Archives, Smithsonian Institution, Washington.)

———— [Kwalhioqua-Tlatskanai.] (Microfilm, reel Nos. 021–024, John Peabody Harrington Papers, Alaska/Northwest Coast, in National Anthropological Archives, Smithsonian Institution, Washington.)

———— 1942   [Alsea, Siuslaw, Coos: Vocabularies, Linguistic Notes, Ethnographic and Historical Notes.] (Microfilm, reel Nos. 021–024, John Peabody Harrington Papers, Alaska/Northwest Coast, in National Anthropological Archives, Smithsonian Institution, Washington.)

———— 1942a   [Lower Chehalis, Upper Chehalis, and Cowlitz Fieldnotes.] (Microfilm, reel No. 017, John Peabody Harrington Papers, Alaska/Northwest Coast, in National Anthropological Archives, Smithsonian Institution, Washington.)

———— [1942b]   [Southwest Oregon Athabascan.] (Microfilm, reel Nos. 025–027, John Peabody Harrington Papers, Alaska/Northwest Coast, in National Anthropological Archives, Smithsonian Institution, Washington.)

———— [1942–1943]   [Tillamook Fieldnotes: Vocabulary, Texts, Grammatical Notes, from Bay Center, Washington and Siletz, Oregon.] (Microfilm, reel No. 020, John P. Harrington Papers, Alaska/Northwest Coast, National Anthropological Archives, Smithsonian Institution, Washington.)

———— 1942–1943a   [Miscellaneous Notes on Quinault.] (Microfilm, reel No. 017, John Peabody Harrington Papers, Alaska/Northwest Coast, National Anthropological Archives, Smithsonian Institution, Washington.)

Harrington, Mark R.
1912   The Northwest Coast Collection. *The Museum Journal* 3(1):10–15. Philadelphia.

Harriott, J.F.
1907   Letter of February 25, 1831 to John McLeod. *Washington Historical Quarterly* 1(1):260–261. Seattle.

Harris, Barbara P.
1983   Handsaw or Harlot? Some Problem Etymologies in the Lexicon of Chinook Jargon. *Canadian Journal of Linguistics* 28(1):25–32.

———— 1985   Klakowiam Mr Smis: Context of Culture as a Factor in the Interpretation of a Chinook Jargon Text. *Anthropological Linguistics* 27(3):303–317.

Harris, Herbert
1977   A Grammatical Sketch of Comox. (Unpublished Ph.D. Dissertation in Linguistics, University of Kansas, Lawrence.)

Harris, Kenneth B.
1974   Visitors Who Never Left: The Origin of the People of Damelahamid. Vancouver: University of British Columbia Press.

Harrison, Brian F.
1978   [Report on a Burial Excavation at Bob Creek (35 LA 10), Lane County, Oregon.] (Report on file, Department of Anthropology, Oregon State University, Corvallis.)

Harrison, Charles
1895   Haida Grammar. Alexander F. Chamberlain, ed. *Transactions of the Royal Society of Canada for 1895, 2d ser.*, Vol. 1(2):123–226. Ottawa.

———— [1900]   Haida Vocabulary. (Manuscript in British Columbia Provincial Archives, Victoria.)

———— 1911–1913   History of the Queen Charlotte Islands: The Haida and Their Legends. *Queen Charlotte Islander* 1(11:November 6, 1911); 2 (34: April 28, 1913). Queen Charlotte City, B.C.

———— 1925   Ancient Warriors of the North Pacific: The Haidas, Their Laws, Customs and Legends, with Some Historical Account of the Queen Charlotte Islands. London: H.F. and G. Witherby.

Harrison, Gordon
1971   Tlingit-Haida Settlement Intensive Look at History of T-H Award. *Tundra Times*, December 17:28. Fairbanks, Alas.

Hartman, Charles W., and Philip R. Johnson
1984   Environmental Atlas of Alaska. 2d rev. ed. Fairbanks: University of Alaska. Institute of Water Resources/Engineering Experiment Station.

Hartmann, Glenn
1978   [An Archaeological Survey of the Proposed Idaho Point Water Line Extension Project, Lincoln County, Oregon.] (Report to Seal Rock Water District, Seal Rock, Oreg.)

———— 1978a   [An Archaeological Evaluation of the Tahkenitch Lake Site, 35 DO 175, Douglas County, Oregon.] (Report to U.S. Department of Agriculture, Forest Service, Siuslaw National Forest, Oregon Dunes Recreation Area, Corvallis.)

Hassrick, Royal B., and Cile M. Bach
1960   Indian Art of the Americas. *Denver Art Museum Quarterly* (Winter).

Haswell, Robert
1969   Robert Haswell's Log of the First Voyage of the "Columbia" [1787–1789]. Pp. 3–107 in Voyages of the "Columbia" to the Northwest Coast, 1787–1790 and 1790–1793. F.W. Howay, ed. New York: Da Capo Press. (Original: Massachusetts Historical Society, 1941.)

Hawthorn, Audrey
1956   People of the Potlatch: Native Arts and Culture of the Pacific Northwest Coast. Vancouver: Vancouver Art Gallery and University of British Columbia.

1964   Mungo Martin, Artist and Craftsman. *The Beaver*, Outfit 295(Summer):18–23. Winnipeg.

1967   Art of the Kwakiutl Indians and Other Northwest Coast Tribes. Seattle: University of Washington Press.

1979   Kwakiutl Art. Seattle: University of Washington Press.

Hawthorn, Harry B.
1961   The Artist in Tribal Society: The Northwest Coast. Pp. 59–70 in The Artist in Tribal Society: Proceedings of a Symposium Held at the Royal Anthropological Institute, London 1957. Marian W. Smith, ed. New York: The Free Press of Glencoe.
————, ed.
1968   A Survey of the Contemporary Indians of Canada: A Report on Economic, Political, Educational Needs and Policies. 2 vols. Ottawa: Indian Affairs Branch.

Hawthorn, Harry B., C.S. Belshaw, and S.M. Jamieson
1958   The Indians of British Columbia: A Study of Contemporary Social Adjustment. Berkeley: University of California Press.

Hayden, Brian
1975   The Carrying Capacity Dilemma: An Alternate Approach. Pp. 11–12 in Population Studies in Archaeology and Biological Anthropology: A Symposium. Alan C. Swedlund, ed. *Memoirs of the Society for American Archaeology* 30. Washington.

Haynes, C. Vance, D.J. Donahue, A.J.T. Jull, and T.H. Zabel
1984   Application of Accelerator Dating to Fluted Point Paleoindian Sites. Pp. 184–191 in New Experiments Upon the Record of Eastern Palaeo-Indian Cultures. R.M. Gramly, ed. *Archaeology of Eastern North America* 12.

Hazard, Joseph T.
1952   Companion of Adventure: A Biography of Isaac Ingalls Stevens, First Governor of Washington Territory. Portland, Oreg.: Binfords and Mort.

Hazeltine, F.A.
1895   Indian Shaker Religion. *South Bend Washington Journal*, 29 November 1895. (Reprinted in: Rolls of Certain Indian Tribes. Glen Adams, ed., Galleon Press, Fairfield, Wash.)

Hazeltine, Jean
1956   The Historical and Regional Geography of the Willapa Bay Area. 2 vols. (Unpublished Ph.D. Dissertation in Geography, Ohio State University, Columbus.)

Hazen, William B.
1857   Letter to George Gibbs, Transmitting Three "Upper Rogue River" Vocabularies; Comparative Vocabulary of Applegate, Ta-kil-ma, and Uppa (Shasta); Individual Applegate Creek and Ta-kil-ma Vocabularies. [Copies by George Gibbs.] (Manuscript No. 154 in National Anthropological Archives, Smithsonian Institution, Washington.)

[1857a]   [Takelma Vocabulary.] (In Manuscript No. 1655 in National Anthropological Archives, Smithsonian Institution, Washington.)

Healey, Elizabeth, comp.
[1958]   History of Alert Bay District. Vancouver: J.M. Bow for the Alert Bay Centennial Committee.

Heath, Joseph
1979   Memoirs of Nisqually. Lucille McDonald, ed. Fairfield, Wash.: Ye Galleon Press.

Hebda, Richard J., and Rolf W. Mathewes
1984   Postglacial History of Cedar and Evolution of Northwest Coast Native Cultures. (Paper presented at the 35th Annual Northwest Anthropological Conference, Simon Fraser University, Burnaby, B.C.)

1984a   Holocene History of Cedar and Native Indian Cultures of the North American Pacific Coast. *Science* 225(4663):711–713.

Heflin, Eugene
1966   The Pistol River Site of Southwest Oregon. *University of California Archaeological Survey Reports* 67:151–206. Berkeley.

Heglar, Rodger
1958   An Analysis of Indian Skeletal Remains from the Marpole Midden. A Report on Indian Skeletal Material from Locarno Beach Site (DhRt:6). Indian Skeletal Remains from the Whalen Site, Pt. Roberts, Washington. (Unpublished manuscripts in Laboratory of Anthropology, University of British Columbia, Vancouver.)

Heizer, Robert F.
1940   The Introduction of Monterey Shells to the Indians of the Northwest Coast. *Pacific Northwest Quarterly* 31(4):399–402.

1940a   The Botanical Identification of Northwest Coast Tobacco. *American Anthropologist* 42(4):704–706.

1942   Walla Walla Indian Expeditions to the Sacramento Valley. *California Hiatorical Society Quarterly* 21(1):1–7. San Francisco.

1943   Aconite Poison Whaling in Asia and America: An Aleutian Transfer to the New World. *Anthropological Papers* 24, *Bureau of American Ethnology Bulletin* 133. Washington.
————, ed.
1975   Narrative of the Adventures and Sufferings of John R. Jewitt, While Held as a Captive of the Nootka Indians of Vancouver Island, 1803 to 1805. (Edited and annotated by Robert F. Heizer from the 1920 ed.) *Ballena Press Publications in Archaeology, Ethnology and History* 5. Ramona, Calif.

Heizer, Robert F., and Thomas R. Hester
1970   Shasta Villages and Territory. *University of California. Archaeological Research Facility Contributions* 9(6):119–138. Berkeley.

1978   Great Basin Projectile Points: Forms and Chronology. *Ballena Press Publications in Archaeology, Ethnology, and History* 10. Socorro, N.M.

Hemphill, Colleen, and Bob Hemphill
1984   Gega qǝnc ǧaǧoƛe x̌a Liǧwale! Campbell River, B.C.: School District No. 72.

Henderson, John R.
1974   Missionary Influences on the Haida Settlement and Subsistence Patterns, 1876–1920. *Ethnohistory* 21(4):303–316.

Henking, Karl H.
1978   A Description of the Webber Collection [1957]. Pp. 25–70 in Cook Voyage Artifacts in Leningrad, Berne, and Florence Museums. Adrienne L. Kaeppler, ed. Honolulu: Bishop Museum Press.

Henn, Winfield
1975   The Indian Ridge Site, Lane County, Oregon. Pp. 455–468 in Archaeological Studies in the Willamette Valley, Oregon. C. Melvin Aikens, ed. *University of Oregon Anthropological Papers* 8. Eugene.

Henry, Alexander *see* Coues 1897

Henry, John F.
1984   Early Maritime Artists of the Pacific Northwest Coast, 1741–1841. Seattle: University of Washington Press.

Hentze, Carl
1936   Objets rituels, croyances et dieux de la Chine antique et de l'Amérique. Antwerp, Belgium: Editions "De Sikkel."

688

Herskovits, Melville J.
1952   Economic Anthropology: A Study in Comparative Eco-
            nomics. New York: Alfred A. Knopf.

Herzog, George, Stanley Newman, Edward Sapir, Mary Haas
Swadesh, Morris Swadesh, and Charles F. Voegelin
1934   Some Orthographic Recommendations. *American Anthro-
            pologist* 36(4):629–631.

Hess, Thomas M. [Thom]
1967   Snohomish Grammatical Structure. (Unpublished Ph.D.
            Dissertation in Linguistics, University of Washington,
            Seattle.)

1976   A Dictionary of Puget Salish. Seattle: University of
            Washington Press.

1982   Traces of 'Abnormal' Speech in Lushootseed. Pp. 89–97 in
            Working Papers for the 17th International Conference on
            Salish and Neighboring Languages. Portland, Oreg.:
            Portland State University.

Hess, Thomas M., and Vi Hilbert (Taqᵂ šəblu)
1980   Lushootseed: The Language of the Skagit, Nisqually, and
            Other Tribes of Puget Sound. 2 vols. Seattle, Wash.:
            Daybreak Star Press.

Hester, James J.
1969   Prehistory of the Bella Bella Region, British Columbia.
            Colorado Anthropologist 2(1):29–38.

Hester, James J., and Sarah M. Nelson, eds.
1978   Studies in Bella Bella Prehistory. *Simon Fraser University.
            Department of Archaeology Publications* 5. Burnaby, B.C.

Heusser, Calvin J.
1960   Late-Pleistocene Environments of North Pacific North
            America: An Elaboration of Late-glacial and Postglacial
            Climatic, Physiographic, and Biotic Changes. *American
            Geographical Society Special Publication* 35.

Hewes, Gordon W.
1947   Aboriginal Use of Fishery Resources in Northwestern
            North America. (Unpublished Ph.D. Dissertation in An-
            thropology, University of California, Berkeley.)

1973   Indian Fisheries Productivity in Pre-contact Times in the
            Pacific Salmon Area. *Northwest Anthropological Research
            Notes* 7(2):133–155. Moscow, Idaho.

Hewitt, George G.
[1891]   Catalogue of the George Goodman Hewitt Collection
            Formed on the Voyage of Captain Vancouver [1790–1795].
            (Ethnological document No. 1126, British Museum, Lon-
            don.)

Hilbert, Vi (Taqᵂ šəblu), ed. and trans.
1985   Haboo: Native American Stories from Puget Sound. Seattle:
            University of Washington Press.

Hilbert, Vi (Taqᵂ šəblu), and Thomas M. Hess
1977   Lushootseed. Pp. 4–32 in Northwest Coast Texts. Barry F.
            Carlson, ed. *Native American Text Series* 2(3). Chicago.

Hill, Beth, and Ray Hill
1974   Indian Petroglyphs of the Pacific Northwest. Seattle:
            University of Washington Press.

Hill, Edward E.
1974   The Office of Indian Affairs, 1824–1880: Historical
            Sketches. New York: Clearwater.

Hill, Robert H., and H.S. Robinson
1969   Rheumatoid Arthritis and Ankylosing Spondylitis in Brit-
            ish Columbia Indians: Their Prevalence and the Challenge
            of Management. *Canadian Medical Association Journal*
            100(11):509–511. Toronto.

Hill, Robert H., and K. Walters
1969   Juvenile Rheumatoid Arthritis: A Medical and Social
            Profile of Non-Indian and Indian Children. *Canadian
            Medical Association Journal* 100(10):458–464. Toronto.

Hills, George
1863   Extracts from the Journal of the Bishop of Columbia, 1862
            and 1863. In *Fourth Annual Report of the Columbia Mission
            for the Year 1862.* London: Rivington's.

Hills, William H.
1853   Journal on Board H.M.S. Portland and H.M.S. Virago.
            (Manuscript, microfilm No. AW1 R5028:2, in Microform
            Division, Main Library, University of British Columbia,
            Vancouver.)

Hill-Tout, Charles
1895   Later Prehistoric Man in British Columbia. *Transactions of
            the Royal Society of Canada*, 2d ser., Vol. 1(2):103–122.
            Ottawa.

1897   Notes on the Cosmogony and History of the Squamish
            Indians of British Columbia. *Transactions of the Royal
            Society of Canada, 2d ser.*, Vol. 3(2):85–90. Ottawa.

1900   Notes on the Sk·qŏ́mic of British Columbia, a Branch of
            the Great Salish Stock of North America. Pp. 472–549
            (Appendix II) in *70th Report of the British Association for
            the Advancement of Science for 1900.* London.

1903   Ethnological Studies of the Mainland Halkŏmēʹlem, a
            Division of the Salish of British Columbia. Pp. 355–449 in
            *72d Report of the British Association for the Advancement of
            Science for 1902.* London.

1904   Report on the Ethnology of the Siciàtl of British Columbia,
            a Coast Division of the Salish Stock. *Journal of the
            Anthropological Institute of Great Britain and Ireland*
            34:20–91. London.

1904a   Ethnological Report on the Stseēlis and Sk·aúlits Tribes of
            the Halkŏmēʹlem Division of the Salish of British Columbia.
            *Journal of the Anthropological Institute of Great Britain and
            Ireland* 34:311–376. London.

1905   Some Features of the Language and Culture of the Salish.
            American Anthropologist 7(4):674–687.

1907   British North America, 1: The Far West. the Home of the
            Salish and Dene. (*The Native Races of the British Empire*)
            London: Archibald Constable.

1907a   Report on the Ethnology of the South-eastern Tribes of
            Vancouver Island, British Columbia. *Journal of the Royal
            Anthropological Institute of Great Britian and Ireland*
            37:306–374. London.

1932   British Columbian Ancestors of the Eskimo? *Illustrated
            London News* (January):90–92.

1948   The Great Fraser Midden. Pp. 8–15 in The Great Fraser
            Midden. Vancouver, B.C.: Vancouver Art, Historical and
            Scientific Association.

Hilton, Susanne
[1968–1969] [Ethnographic Notes from 4 Months' Fieldwork Among the
            Haihais, Bella Bella, and Oowekeeno, B.C.] (Notes in
            Hilton's possession.)

1971   An Investigation of Bella Bella Tribes, Village Sites, and
            Population Movement to 1900: A Preliminary Survey of the
            Written Record. (Unpublished manuscript in Hilton's
            possession.)

[1973–1975] [Ethnographic Notes from Approximately 9 Months' Field-
            work Among the Bella-Bella.] (Unpublished manuscripts in
            Hilton's possession.)

Hilton, Susanne, John C. Rath, and Evelyn W. Windsor, eds.
1982   Oowekeeno Oral Traditions as Told by the Late Chief Simon Walkus, Sr. *Canada. National Museum of Man. Mercury Series. Ethnology Service Papers* 84. Ottawa.

Hinckley, Ted. C.
1972   The Americanization of Alaska, 1867–1897. Palo Alto, Calif.: Pacific Books Publishers.

Hindle, Lonnie, and Bruce Rigsby
1973   A Short Practical Dictionary of the Gitksan Language. *Northwest Anthropological Research Notes* 7(1):1–60. Moscow, Idaho.

Hinds, Richard
1839   Journal. (Manuscript No. 1524 in Oregon Historical Society, Portland.)

Hines, Gustavus
1851   Oregon: Its History, Condition and Prospects . . . .Auburn, N.Y.: Derby and Miller.

Hinsley, Curtis M., and Bill Holm
1976   A Cannibal in the National Museum: The Early Career of Franz Boas in America. *American Anthropologist* 78(2):306–316.

Hitchcock, C. Leo, and Arthur Cronquist
1973   Flora of the Pacific Northwest: An Illustrated Manual. Seattle: University of Washington Press.

Hobler, Philip M.
1970   Archaeological Investigations Carried Out at FaSul, Kwatna Bay. (Manuscript on file, Department of Archaeology, Simon Fraser University, Burnaby, B.C.)

1970a   Archaeological Survey and Excavations in the Vicinity of Bella Coola. Pp. 77–94 in Archaeology in British Columbia, New Discoveries. R.L. Carlson, ed. *BC Studies* 6–7(Fall-Winter). Vancouver.

1972   Archaeological Work at Kimsquit: 1971. Pp. 85–106 in Salvage '71: Reports on Salvage Archaeology Undertaken in British Columbia in 1971. Roy L. Carlson, ed. *Simon Fraser University. Department of Archaeology Publications* 1. Burnaby, B.C.

1975   The Red Dot Rock Art Sites. (Paper presented at the Annual Meeting of the Canadian Rock Art Research Associates, Victoria, B.C.)

1976   Wet Site Archaeology at Kwatna. Pp. 146–157 in The Excavation of Water-saturated Archaeological Sites (Wet Sites) on the Northwest Coast of North America. Dale R. Croes, ed. *Canada. National Museum of Man. Mercury Series. Archaeological Survey Papers* 50. Ottawa.

1978   The Relationship of Archaeological Sites to Sea Levels on Moresby Island, Queen Charlotte Islands. *Canadian Journal of Archaeology* 2:1–13.

1979   Some Early Sites on the Central Coast of British Columbia. (Paper presented at the Pacific Science Congress, Khabarovsk, U.S.S.R.)

1981   Archaeological Sites and Site Clusters on the Central Coast of British Columbia. (Paper presented at the Annual Meeting of the Canadian Archaeological Association, Edmonton, Alta.)
          , ed.
1982   Papers on Central Coast Archaeology. *Simon Fraser University. Department of Archaeology Publications* 10. Burnaby, B.C.

1983   Archaeological Survey of Alexander Mackenzie Provincial Park and Environs, British Columbia. (Report on file, British Columbia Heritage Conservation Branch, Victoria, B.C.)

1983a   Settlement Location Determinants: An Exploration of Some Northwest Coast Data. Pp. 149–156 in The Evolution of Maritime Cultures on the Northeast and the Northwest Coasts of America. R.J. Nash, ed. *Simon Fraser University. Department of Archaeology Publications* 11. Burnaby, B.C.

1984   Measures of the Acculturative Response to Trade on the Central Coast. (Paper read at the Fur Trade Conference, University of British Columbia, Vancouver.)

Hobson, Gary, ed.
1979   The Remembered Earth: An Anthology of Contemporary Native American Literature. Albuquerque: Red Earth Press.

Hobucket, Harry
1934   Quillayute Indian Traditions. *Washington Historical Quarterly* 25(1):49–59. Seattle.

Hodge, Frederick W., ed.
1907–1910   Handbook of American Indians North of Mexico. 2 vols. *Bureau of American Ethnology Bulletin* 30. Washington. (Reprinted: Rowman and Littlefield, New York, 1979.)

Hodge, Robert P.
1976   Amphibians and Reptiles of Alaska, the Yukon and Northwest Territories. Anchorage: Alaska Northwest Publishing Company.

Hodgson, Edward R.
1957   The Epidemic on the Lower Columbia. *The Pacific Northwesterner* 1(4):1–8. Spokane, Wash.

Hoijer, Harry
[1956]   Galice Athapaskan Stems. (Typescript, Partially Published in Hoijer (1973), in Melville Jacobs Collection, University of Washington Libraries, Seattle.)

1960   Athapaskan Languages of the Pacific Coast. Pp. 960–976 in Culture in History: Essays in Honor of Paul Radin. Stanley Diamond, ed. New York: Columbia University Press. (Reprinted: Octagon Books, New York, 1981.)

1966   Galice Athapaskan: A Grammatical Sketch. *International Journal of American Linguistics* 32(4):320–327.

1973   History of American Indian Linguistics. Pp. 657–676 in *Current Trends in Linguistics*. Vol. 10: Linguistics in North America. Thomas A. Sebeok, ed. The Hague: Mouton.

1973a   Galice Noun and Verb Stems. *Linguistics: An International Review* 104:49–73. The Hague.

Holloway, Richard G.
1982   Pollen Analysis of Five Samples from Lake Eva, Alaska. (Unpublished manuscript on file, Texas A & M University, College Station, Texas.)

Holm, Bill
1956–1976   [Ethnographic Notes from Fieldwork Among the Kwakiutl, British Columbia.] (Unpublished manuscript in Holm's possession.)

1965   Northwest Coast Indian Art: An Analysis of Form. (*Thomas Burke Memorial Washington State Museum. Monographs* 1) Seattle: University of Washington Press. (Reprinted in 1970.)

1967   The Northern Style: A Form Analysis. In Arts of the Raven. Vancouver, B.C.: Vancouver Art Gallery.

1972   Heraldic Carving Styles of the Northwest Coast. Pp. 77–83 in American Indian Art: Form and Tradition. (An exhibition organized by [the] Walker Art Center, Indian Art Association, and the Minneapolis Institute of Arts, 22 October–31 December 1972) Minneapolis: Walker Art Center and the Minneapolis Institute of Arts.

1972a   Crooked Beak of Heaven: Masks and Other Ceremonial Art of the Northwest Coast. Seattle: University of Washington Press.

1974   Structure and Design. Pp. 20–32 in Boxes and Bowls: Decorated Containers by Nineteenth-century Haida, Tlingit, Bella Bella, and Tsimshian Indian Artists. Washington: Smithsonian Institution Press.

1974a   The Art of Willie Seaweed: A Kwakiutl Master. Pp. 59–90 in The Human Mirror: Material and Spatial Images of Man. Miles Richardson, ed. Baton Rouge: Louisiana State University Press.

1976   [Review of] The Mouth of Heaven: An Introduction to Kwakiutl Religious Thought, by Irving Goldman. *Ethnohistory* 23(1):72–74.

1977   Traditional and Contemporary Southern Kwakiutl Winter Dance. *Arctic Anthropology* 14(1):5–24.

1981   Will the Real Charles Edensaw Please Stand Up? The Problem of Attribution in Northwest Coast Indian Art. Pp. 175–200 in The World is As Sharp As a Knife: An Anthology in Honour of Wilson Duff. D.N. Abbott, ed. Victoria: British Columbia Provincial Museum.

1982   A Wooling Mantle Neatly Wrought: The Early Historic Record of Northwest Coast Pattern-twined Textiles, 1744–1850. *American Indian Art Magazine* 8(1):34–47.

1983   Smoky-Top: The Art and Times of Willy Seaweed. (*Thomas Burke Memorial Washington State Museum. Monographs* 3) Seattle: University of Washington Press.

1983a   Form in Northwest Coast Art. Pp. 33–45 in Indian Art Traditions of the Northwest Coast. Roy L. Carlson, ed. Burnaby, B.C.: Archaeology Press, Simon Fraser University.

1983b   The Box of Daylight: Northwest Coast Indian Art. Seattle: Seattle Art Museum and University of Washington Press.

1986   The Dancing Headdress Frontlet: Aesthetic Context on the Northwest Coast. Pp. 132–140 in The Arts of the North American Indian: Native Traditions in Evolution. Edwin L. Wade, ed. New York: Hudson Hills Press.

1987   Spirit and Ancestor: A Century of Northwest Coast Indian Art at the Burke Museum. (*Thomas Burke Memorial Washington State Museum. Monographs* 4) Seattle: University of Washington Press.

Holm, Bill, and George I. Quimby
1980   Edward S. Curtis in the Land of the War Canoes: A Pioneer Cinematographer in the Pacific Northwest. Seattle: University of Washington Press.

Holm, Bill, and Bill Reid
1975   Indian Art of the Northwest Coast: A Dialogue on Craftsmanship and Aesthetics. Seattle: University of Washington Press. (Originally published as Form and Freedom: A Dialogue on Northwest Coast Indian Art, Rice University Press, Houston, Texas.)

Holmberg, Henrik Johan von
1855–1863   Ethnographische Skizzen über die Völker des russischen Amerika. 2 vols. Helsinki: H.C. Friis.

1873   Wörterbuch der Thlinkith Sprache. (Manuscript in Leopold F. Radloff Collection, Archives of the Academy of Sciences of the USSR, Leningrad.)

1985   Holmberg's Ethnographic Sketches. Marvin W. Falk, ed. Fritz Jaensch, trans. (*The Rasmuson Library Historical Translation Series* 1) Fairbanks: University of Alaska Press.

Holmes, William H.
1903   The Exhibit of the Department of Anthropology. Pp. 200–218 in *Annual Report of the U.S. National Museum for 1901*. Washington.

Hoover, Alan L.
1983   Charles Edensaw and the Creation of Human Beings. *American Indian Art Magazine* 8(3):62–67, 80.

Hopkins, David M.
1979   Landscape and Climate of Beringia During Late Pleistocene and Holocene Time. Pp. 15–41 in The First Americans: Origins, Affinities and Adaptations. William S. Laughlin and Albert B. Harper, eds. New York: Gustav Fischer.

Horetzky, Charles
1874   Canada on the Pacific, Being an Account of a Journey from Edmonton to the Pacific by the Peace River Valley; and of a Winter Voyage Along the Western Coast of the Dominion; with Remarks on the Physical Features of the Pacific Railway Route and Notice of the Indian Tribes of British Columbia. Montreal: Dawson Brothers.

1874a   Report of Progress on the Explorations and Surveys up to January 1874. Ottawa: Maclean, Roger.

Hoskins, John B.
1941   The Narrative of a Voyage to the North West Coast of America and China on Trade and Discoveries by John Hoskins Performed in the Ship Columbia Rediviva, 1790, 1791, 1792, and 1793. Pp. 161–289 in Voyages of the "Columbia" to the Northwest Coast, 1787–1790 and 1790–1793. F.W. Howay, ed. *Massachusetts Historical Society Collections* 79. Boston. (Reprinted: Da Capo Press, New York, 1969.)

Hough, Walter
1895   Primitive American Armor. Pp. 627–651 in *Annual Report of the U.S. National Museum for 1893*. Washington.

Howay, F.W.
1918   The Dog's Hair Blankets of the Coast Salish. *Washington Historical Quarterly* 9(2):83–92. Seattle.

1922   The Loss of the *Tonquin*. *Washington Historical Quarterly* 13(2):83–92. Seattle.

1925   Indian Attacks Upon Maritime Traders of the North-west Coast, 1785–1805. *Canadian Historical Review* 6(4):287–309. Toronto.

1926   An Early Account of the Loss of the Boston in 1803. *Washington Historical Quarterly* 17(4):280–288. Seattle.

1930   The Ship Margaret: Her History and Historian. Pp. 34–40 in *38th Annual Report of the Hawaiian Historical Society for the Year 1929*. Honolulu.

1932   An Outline Sketch of the Maritime Fur Trade. Pp. 5–14 in *Canadian Historical Association. Report of the Annual Meeting for 1932*. Ottawa.

———, ed.
1940   The Journal of Captain James Colnett Aboard the "Argonaut" from April 26, 1789 to November 3, 1791. Toronto: The Champlain Society.

———, ed.
1941   Voyages of the "Columbia" to the Northwest Coast, 1787–1790 and 1790–1793. *Massachusetts Historical Society Collections* 79. Boston. (Reprinted: Da Capo Press, New York, 1969.)

———, ed.
1969   Boit's Log of the Second Voyage of the Columbia. Pp. 363–431 in Voyages of the Columbia to the Northwest

Coast, 1787–1790 and 1790–1793. New York: Da Capo Press.

———, ed.
1969a   The Dixon-Meares Controversy. Amsterdam: N. Israel/ New York: Da Capo Press.

1973   A List of Trading Vessels in the Maritime Fur Trade, 1785–1825 [1930–1934]. Richard A. Pierce, ed. (*Materials for the Study of Alaskan History* 2) Kingston, Ont.: The Limestone Press.

Howay, F.W., and T.C. Elliott
1929   Voyages of the "Jenny" to Oregon, 1792–94. *Oregon Historical Quarterly* 30(3):197–206.

Hrdlička, Aleš
1909   Tuberculosis Among Certain Indian Tribes. *Bureau of American Ethnology Bulletin* 42. Washington.

1924   Catalogue of Human Crania in the United States National Museum Collections. (Eskimo, Alaska and Related Indians, Mongols.) *Proceedings of the U.S. National Museum* 63:1–51. Washington.

1927   Catalogue of Human Crania in the United States National Museum Collections. (Algonkins and Iroquois, Siouan, Caddoan Tribes, Salish and Sahaptin, Shoshoneans and Californians.) *Proceedings of the U.S. National Museum* 69:1–127. Washington.

1944   Catalogue of Human Crania in the United States National Museum Collections. (Non-Eskimo People of the Northwest Coast, Alaska and Siberia). *Proceedings of the U.S. National Museum* 94:1–172. Washington.

Hudson's Bay Company
1834–1838 [Fort Simpson Journal.] (Manuscript B 201/a/3 in Hudson's Bay Company Archives, Provincial Archives of Manitoba, Winnipeg, Canada.)

Huelsbeck, David R.
1980   Analysis of the Fish Remains. Pp. 104–111 in Hoko River: A 2,500 Year Old Fishing Camp on the Northwest Coast of North America. Dale R. Croes and Eric Blinman, eds. *Hoko River Archaeological Project Contributions* 1, University Laboratory of Anthropology. Reports of Investigation 58. Pullman.

1983   Mammals and Fish in the Subsistence Economy of Ozette. (Unpublished Ph.D. Dissertation in Anthropology, Washington State University, Pullman.)

1988   The Surplus Economy of the Central Northwest Coast. Pt. 3 in Prehistoric Economies of the Pacific Northwest Coast. Barry L. Isaac, ed. (*Research in Economic Anthropology Supplement* 3) Greenwich, Conn.: JAI Press.

1988a   Whaling in the Precontact Economy of the Central Northwest Coast. *Arctic Anthropology* 25(1):1–15.

Hukari, Thomas E., Ruby Peter, and Ellen White
1977   Halkomelem. Pp. 33–68 in Northwest Coast Texts. Barry F. Carlson, ed. *Native American Text Series* 2(3). Chicago.

Hulley, Clarence C.
[1953]   Alaska, 1741–1953. Portland, Oreg.: Binfords and Mort.

Hulse, Frederick S.
1955   Blood-types and Mating Patterns Among Northwest Coast Indians. *Southwestern Journal of Anthropology* 11(2):93–104.

1957   Linguistic Barriers to Gene Flow: The Blood Groups of the Yakima, Okanagon, and Swinomish Indians. *American Journal of Physical Anthropology* 15(2):235–246.

Hulse, Frederick S., and M. Firestone
1961   Blood-type Frequencies Among the Quinault Reservation Indians. Pp. E32–E33 in Abstracts of Papers Presented at the Second International Conference of Human Genetics, Rome. *Excerpta Medica. International Congress Series* 32. Amsterdam.

Hulten, Eric
1968   Flora of Alaska and Neighboring Territories: A Manual of the Vascular Plants. Stanford, Calif.: Stanford University Press.

Hunn, Eugene S., and Helen H. Norton
1984   Impact of Mt. St. Helens Ashfall on Fruit Yield of Mountain Huckleberry, *Vaccinium membranaceum*, Important Native American Food. *Economic Botany* 38(1):121–127.

Hymes, Dell H.
1955   The Language of the Kathlamet Chinook. (Unpublished Ph.D. Dissertation in Linguistics, Indiana University, Bloomington.)

1956   Na-Déné and Positional Analysis of Categories. *American Anthropologist* 58(4):624–638.

1957   Some Penutian Elements and the Penutian Hypothesis. *Southwestern Journal of Anthropology* 13(1):69–87.

1964   Evidence for Penutian in Lexical Sets with Initial *C- and *S-. *International Journal of American Linguistics* 30(3):213–242.

1965   The Methods and Tasks of Anthropological Philology (Illustrated with Clackamas Chinook). *Romance Philology* 19(2):325–340. Berkeley, Calif.

1966   Some Points of Siuslaw Phonology. *International Journal of American Linguistics* 32(4):328–342.

1968   The 'Wife' Who 'Goes Out' Like a Man: Reinterpretation of a Clackamas Chinook Myth. *Social Science Information/ Information sur les Sciences Sociales* 7(3):173–199.

[1971–1988] [Unpublished Ethnopoetic Analyses.] (Manuscripts in Hymes' possession.)

1979   Myth as Verse in Three Native American Languages: Takelma, Tonkawa, Kathlamet. Philadelphia: University of Pennsylvania, Department of Folklore, Archives.

1981   Comment on Karl Kroeber, 'Scarface vs. Scar-face: The Problem of Versions'. *Journal of the Folklore Institute* 18(2–3):144–150.

1981a   "In Vain I Tried to Tell You:" Essays in Native American Ethnopoetics. Philadelphia: University of Pennsylvania Press.

1981b   Spearfish Sequence. Cambridge, Mass.: Corvine Press.

1982   Narrative Form as a "Grammar" of Experience: Native Americans and a Glimpse of English. *Journal of Education* 164(2):121–142. Boston.

1982a   5-Fold Fanfare for Coyote. Pp. 82–83 in Coyote's Journal. James Koller, 'Gogisgi' Carroll Arnett, Steve Nemirow, and Peter Blue Cloud, eds. Berkeley, Calif.: Wingbow.

1983   Poetic Structure of a Chinook Text. Pp. 507–525 in Essays in Honor of Charles F. Hockett. Frederick B. Agard, Gerald Kelley, Adam Makkai, and Valerie Beeker Makkai, eds. Leiden, The Netherlands: E.J. Brill.

1983a   Victoria Howard's "Gitskux and His Older Brother": A Clackamas Chinook Myth. Pp. 129–170 in Smoothing the

Ground: Essays on Native American Oral Literature. Brian Swann, ed., Berkeley: University of California Press.

1983b   Agnes Edgar's Sun Child: Verse Analysis of a Bella Coola Text. Pp. 239–312 in Working Papers for the 18th International Conference on Salish and Neighboring Languages. Seattle: University of Washington, Department of Anthropology.

1984   The Earliest Clackamas Text. *International Journal of American Linguistics* 50(4):358–383.

1985   A Pattern of Verbal Irony in Chinookan. Pp. 113–168 in Working Papers for the 20th International Conference on Salish and Neighboring Languages. Vancouver, B.C.

1985a   Language, Memory and Selective Performance: Cultee's "Salmon's Myth" as Twice-told to Boas. *Journal of American Folklore* 98(390):391–434.

1987   Narrative Form in Chinook Jargon, Hawaiian Pidgin English, Australian Kriol. Working Papers for the 21st International Conference on Salish and Neighboring Languages. Victoria, B.C.

1987a   Anthologies and Narrators: Recovering the Word: Essays on Native American Literature. Brian Swann and Arnold Krupat, eds. Berkeley: University of California Press.

Hymes, Dell and Henry Zenk
1987   Narrative Structure in Chinook Jargon. Pp. 445–465 in Pidgin and Creole Languages: Essays in Memory of John E. Reinecke. Glenn G. Gilbert, ed. Honolulu: University of Hawaii Press.

Idiens, Dale
1983   Catalogue of the Ethnographic Collection: Oceania, America, Africa. Perth, Australia: Perth Museum and Art Gallery.

1987   Northwest Coast Artifacts in the Perth Museum and Art Gallery: The Colin Robertson Collection. *American Indian Art Magazine* 13(1):46–53.

Indian Claims Commission
1974   Commission Findings: The Chinook Tribe and Bands of Indians, Petitioner, vs. The United States of America, Defendant. Decided April 16, 1958. Findings of Fact and Opinion of the Commission. Pp. 257–311 in Oregon Indians, I. (*American Indian Ethnohistory: Indians of the Northwest*) New York: Garland.

1974a   Commission Findings: Tillamook Band of Tillamooks, et al., Plaintiffs, v. The United States of America, Defendant, Decided June 10, 1955. Findings of Fact and Opinion of the Commission. Pp. 313–326 in Oregon Indians, I. (American Indian Ethnohistory: Indians of the Northwest) New York: Garland.

1979   United States Indian Claims Commission, August 13–September 30, 1978: Final Report. Washington: U.S. Government Printing Office.

1980   Final Report, 1979. *96 Congress, 2d Sess., House Document No. 96–383.* (Serial No. 13354) Washington: U.S. Government Printing Office.

Indian Shaker Church of Washington and the Northwest
1892–1945 [Records.] (Microfilm in the Library of the State of Washington, Olympia.)

Ingles, Lloyd G.
1965   Mammals of the Pacific States: California, Oregon and Washington. Stanford, Calif.: Stanford University Press.

Inglis, Gordon B.
1970   Northwest American Matriliny: The Problem of Origins. *Ethnology* 9(2):149–159.

Inglis, Joy
1964   The Interaction of Myth and Social Context in the Village of Cape Mudge. (Unpublished M.A. Thesis in Anthropology, University of British Columbia, Vancouver.)

Inglis, Richard I.
1973   [Archaeological Project in the Prince Rupert Harbour, 1972.] Pp. 19–22 in Archaeological Survey of Canada Annual Review, 1972. George F. McDonald, ed. *Canada. National Museum of Man. Mercury Series. Archaeological Survey Papers* 10. Ottawa.

1973a   Contract Salvage 1973: A Preliminary Report on the Salvage Excavations of Two Shell Middens in the Prince Rupert Harbour, B.C. (GbTo-33/36). *Bulletin of the Canadian Archaeological Association* 5:140–144. Toronto.

Inglis, Richard I., and James C. Haggerty
1983   Provisions of Prestige: A Re-evaluation of the Economic Importance of Nootka Whaling. (Paper presented at the Symposium on Megafauna of the Seas. 11th International Congress of Anthropological and Ethnological Sciences, Vancouver, 20–25 August 1983.)

1986   Pacific Rim National Park Ethnographic History. (Manuscript on file, Parks Canada, Western Region, Environment Canada, Calgary, Alta.)

Inglis, Robin
1986   The Lost Voyage of Lapérouse. [Companion Booklet to an Exhibition . . . .] [Vancouver, B.C.]: Vancouver Maritime Museum.

Inglis, Stephen
1979   Cultural Readjustment: A Canadian Case Study. *Canadian Museums Association Gazette* 12(3):26–30. Ottawa.

Inverarity, Robert B.
1941   Moveable Masks and Figures of the North Pacific Coast. Bloomfield Hills, Mich.: Cranbrook Institute of Science.

1946   Northwest Coast Indian Art: A Brief Survey. *Washington (State) Museum Series* 1.

1950   Art of the Northwest Coast Indians. Berkeley: University of California Press.

Irvin, Terry T.
1977   The Northwest Coast Potlatch Since Boas, 1897–1972. *Anthropology* 1(1):65–77.

Irvine, Albert
1921   How the Makah Obtained Possession of Cape Flattery. Luke Markiston, trans. *Museum of the American Indian. Heye Foundation. Indian Notes and Monographs. Miscellaneous Publications* 6. New York.

Irving, Washington
[1951]   Astoria; or Anecdotes of an Enterprise Beyond the Rocky Mountains [1838]. Portland, Oreg.: Binfords and Mort.

Irwin, Judith
1979   The Cowlitz Way: A Round of Life. *Cowlitz Historical Quarterly* 21(1):5–24. Kelso, Wash.

1987   The Cowlitz People of Southwest Washington: A Humanistic Study. (Manuscript in Irwin's possession.)

Isaac, Barry L., ed.
1988   Prehistoric Economies of the Pacific Northwest Coast. *Research in Economic Anthropology. Supplement* 3. Greenwich, Conn.: JAI Press.

Ivashintsov, N[ikolai] A.
1980   Russian Round-the World Voyages, 1803–1849; with a Summary of Later Voyages to 1867. Glynn R. Barratt,

trans. Richard A. Pierce, ed. (*Materials for the Study of Alaska History* 14) Kingston, Ont.: The Limestone Press.

Izmaĭlov, Gerasim G., and Dimitriĭ I. Bocharov
1981 The Voyage of Izmailov and Bocharov Concerning the Galiot *Three Saints*, Dispatched in 1788 Under the Command of the Two Navigators. Pp. 83–110 in A Voyage to America, 1783–1786, by Grigoriĭ I. Shelikhov. Richard A. Pierce, ed.; Marina Ramsay, trans. (*Materials for the Study of Alaska History* 19) Kingston, Ont.: The Limestone Press.

Jacknis, Ira S.
1974 Functions of the Containers. Pp. 16–19 in Boxes and Bowls: Decorated Containers by Nineteenth Century Haida, Tlingit, Bella Bella, and Tsimshian Indian Artists. Washington: Smithsonian Institution Press.

1984 Franz Boas and Photography. *Studies in Visual Communication* 10(1):2–60. Philadelphia.

1985 Franz Boas and Exhibits: On the Limitations of the Museum Method of Anthropology. Pp. 75–111 in Objects and Others: Essays on Museums and Material Culture. George W. Stocking, Jr., ed. (*History of Anthropology* 3) Madison: University of Wisconsin Press.

Jackson, Donald D., ed.
1978 Letters of the Lewis and Clark Expedition with Related Documents, 1783–1854. 2d ed. 2 vols. Urbana: University of Illinois Press.

Jackson, Philip L.
1985 Climate. Pp. 48–57 in Atlas of the Pacific Northwest. A. Jon Kimerling, and Philip L. Jackson, eds. 7th ed. Corvallis: Oregon State University Press.

Jackson, Sheldon
1880 Alaska, and Missions on the North Pacific Coast. New York: Dodd, Mead.

1908 [Letter to the Chief of the Division, Bureau of Education, dated January 17, 1908.] (Manuscript in Alaska Division, Kasaan, Record Group 75, National Archives, Washington.)

Jacobs, Elizabeth D.
[1933–1934] [Ethnographic Notes: Field Notebooks, Folklore, and Ethnography, Based on Three Months' Fieldwork Among the Tillamook Salish, Garibaldi, Oreg.] (Manuscripts in Melville Jacobs Collection, University of Washington Libraries, Seattle.)

[1934] [Upper Coquille Athapaskan Linguistic and Ethnographic Data.] (Manuscripts, fieldnotebook 104, box 58, and folder 75.3, box 75, Melville Jacobs Collection, University of Washington Libraries, Seattle.)

[1935] [Upper Coquille Linguistic and Ethnographic Notes, Folklore Texts (in English) from Fieldwork with Coquille Thompson, Siletz, Oreg.] (In Melville Jacobs Collection, University of Washington Libraries, Seattle.)

[1935a] [Chetco Linguistic Field Notebooks: Notes and Texts from Approximately 10 Days' Fieldwork with Billy Metcalf, Siletz, Oreg.] (In Melville Jacobs Collection, University of Washington Libraries, Seattle.)

[1935b] [Galice Creek Linguistic Notebook, Notes from Approximately 6 Days' Fieldwork with Hoxie Simmons and Nettie West, Logsden, Oreg.] (In Melville Jacobs Collection, University of Washington Libraries, Seattle.)

[1958] [Introduction to Proposed Popular Edition of Elizabeth D. Jacobs' *Nehalem Tillamook Tales.*] (In Melville Jacobs Collection, University of Washington Libraries, Seattle.)

1959 Nehalem Tillamook Tales. [Dictated in English by Clara Pearson.] Melville Jacobs, ed. *University of Oregon Monographs. Studies in Anthropology* 5. Eugene.

1968 A Chetco Athabaskan Myth Text from Southwestern Oregon. *International Journal of American Linguistics* 34(3):192–193.

[1976] [Nehalem Tillamook Ethnographic Notes.] William R. Seaburg, ed. (Unpublished manuscript in Seaburg's possession.)

[1976a] [Upper Coquille Athabaskan Folklore.] William R. Seaburg, ed. (Unpublished manuscript in Seaburg's possession.)

1977 A Chetco Athapaskan Text and Translation. *International Journal of American Linguistics* 43(4):269–273.

Jacobs, Mark, Jr., and Mark Jacobs, Sr.
1982 Southeast Alaska Native Foods. Pp. 112–130 in Raven's Bones. Andrew Hope, III, ed. Sitka, Alas.: Sitka Community Association.

Jacobs, Melville
[1928] [Yoncalla Kalapuyan: Vocabulary, Grammatical and Ethnologic Notes.] (Field notebook No. 45 in box 51, Melville Jacobs Collection, University of Washington Libraries, Seattle.)

1928–1936 [Santiam Kalapuyan: Texts, Vocabulary, Grammatical and Ethnologic Notes.] (Field notebooks Nos. 33–37, 46–47, 76–90, in boxes 50, 52, 55, 56, Melville Jacobs Collection, University of Washington Libraries, Seattle.)

1929–1930 [Songs Performed by Victoria Howard, a Clackamas Chinookan.] (Tape dubbings of original cylinders, tapes 9 and 11 in boxes 7 and 8, Melville Jacobs Collection, University of Washington Libraries, Seattle.)

[1930] [Notes for a Grammatical Sketch of Kalapuyan.] (Manuscripts, folder 70.2 in box 70, Melville Jacobs Collection, University of Washington Libraries, Seattle.)

1931 A Sketch of Northern Sahaptin Grammar. *University of Washington Publications in Anthropology* 4(2):85–292. Seattle.

1931–1934 [Hanis and Miluk Coosan Texts and Linguistic and Ethnographic Data.] (Field notebooks Nos. 91–104, boxes 56, 57, and 58, Melville Jacobs Collection, University of Washington Libraries, Seattle.)

1932 Notes on the Structure of Chinook Jargon. *Language: Journal of the Linguistic Society of America* 8(1):27–50.

[1932–1934] [Linguistic and Ethnographic Notes from Fieldwork Among the Hanis and Miluk Coos, Florence and Charleston, Oregon.] (In Melville Jacobs Collection, University of Washington Libraries, Seattle.)

1933 [Northwest Oregon Song Collection; Song Texts and Organized Ethnographic Notes.] (Manuscript, folder 66.1 in box 66, Melville Jacobs Collection, University of Washington Libraries, Seattle.)

1933a [Tillamook Fieldnotes.] (Manuscript in Melville Jacobs Collection, University of Washington Libraries, Seattle.)

[1933b] [Linguistic Notes, from Approximately 35 Days' Fieldwork Among the Tillamook Salish, Garibaldi, Oreg.] (In Melville Jacobs Collection, University of Washington Libraries, Seattle.)

[1933–1934] [Klimek-Kroeber-Gifford Tribal Trait Analysis for Nehalem Tillamook and for Coos.] (In Melville Jacobs Collection, University of Washington Libraries, Seattle.)

——— [2 Wax Cylinder and 10 Acetate Disc Recordings of Texts and Music in Garibaldi and Nehalem Tillamook Salish, from Ellen Center and Clara Pearson, Garibaldi, Oreg.] (In Melville Jacobs Collection, University of Washington Libraries, Seattle.)

1934 Northwest Sahaptin Texts. 2 vols. *Columbia University Contributions to Anthropology* 19. New York. (Reprinted: AMS Press, New York, 1969.)

1935 [Alsea Linguistic Slip Files.] (In boxes 45 and 46, Melville Jacobs Collection, University of Washington Libraries, Seattle.)

1935a [Organized Coosan Ethnographic Notes.] (Manuscripts in boxes 63, 64, 65, Melville Jacobs Collection, University of Washington Libraries, Seattle.)

[1935b] [The Phonemes of Alsea, a Coastal Oregon Language.] (Manuscript in folder 67.3, box 67, Melville Jacobs Collection, University of Washington Libraries, Seattle.)

[1935c] [Alsea Linguistic Notes from Approximately Two Months' Fieldwork with John Albert, Oakville, Wash.] (In Melville Jacobs Collection, University of Washington Libraries, Seattle.)

[1935, [16 Acetate Disc Recordings of Galice Creek Athabaskan
1938–1939] Texts, a Word List, and Music from Hoxie Simmons at Siletz (Logsden), Oreg.] (In Melville Jacobs Collection, University of Washington Libraries, Seattle.)

[1935, [Galice Creek Linguistic Field Notebooks, Lexical File,
1938–1939a] Folklore Texts, Based on Fieldwork with Hoxie Simmons, Logsden, Oreg.] (In Melville Jacobs Collection, University of Washington Libraries, Seattle.)

1936 [Kalapuya Element List; Typed Copy of Original Received by A.L. Kroeber in 1936.] (Manuscript, folder 70.5 in box 70, Melville Jacobs Collection, University of Washington Libraries, Seattle.)

[1936a] [Santiam Kalapuyan Text Translations and Organized Ethnographic Notes.] (Manuscripts, folder 70.4 in box 70, Melville Jacobs Collection, University of Washington Libraries, Seattle.)

[1936b] [Tualatin Kalapuyan Linguistic and Ethnographic Data.] (Texts by Jacobs, with Reelicitations of Linguistic Data Originally Collected by Jaime De Angulo and Lucy S. Freeland. Manuscripts, folders 71.1, 71.3 in box 71, Melville Jacobs Collection, University of Washington Libraries, Seattle.)

1936c Texts in Chinook Jargon. *University of Washington Publications in Anthropology* 7(1):1–27. Seattle.

1937 Historic Perspectives in Indian Languages of Oregon and Washington. *Pacific Northwest Quarterly* 28(1):55–74.

1939 Coos Narrative and Ethnologic Texts. *University of Washington Publications in Anthropology* 8(1):1–125. Seattle.

1940 Coos Myth Texts. *University of Washington Publications in Anthropology* 8(2):127–259. Seattle.

1945 Kalapuya Texts. (Pt. 1: Santiam Kalapuya Ethnologic Texts, by M. Jacobs. Pt. 2: Santiam Kalapuya Myth Texts, by M. Jacobs. Pt. 3: Kalapuya Texts, by A.S. Gatschet, L.J.

Frachtenberg, and M. Jacobs.) *University of Washington Publications in Anthropology* 11. Seattle.

1954 The Areal Spread of Sound Features in the Languages North of California. Pp. 46–56 in Papers from the Symposium on American Indian Linguistics, Held at Berkeley, July 7, 1951. *University of California Publications in Linguistics* 10. Berkeley.

1958 The Romantic Role of Older Women in a Culture of the Pacific Northwest Coast. *Kroeber Anthropological Society Papers* 18(Spring):79–85. Berkeley, Calif.

1958–1959 Clackamas Chinook Texts. 2 vols. *Indiana University. Research Center in Anthropology, Folklore and Linguistics Publications* 8(11). Bloomington.

1959 The Content and Style of an Oral Literature. *Viking Fund Publications in Anthropology* 26. New York.

1959a Folklore. Pp. 119–138 in The Anthropology of Franz Boas: Essays on the Centennial of His Birth. Walter Goldschmidt, ed. *Memoirs of the American Anthropological Association* 89. Menasha, Wis.

1960 The People Are Coming Soon: Analyses of Clackamas Chinook Myths and Texts. Seattle: University of Washington Press.

1962 The Fate of Indian Oral Literatures in Oregon. *Northwest Review* 5:90–99.

1967 Our Knowledge of Pacific Northwest Indian Folklores. *Northwest Folklore* 2(2):14–21.

1968 An Historical Event Text from a Galice Athabaskan in Southwestern Oregon. *International Journal of American Linguistics* 34(3):183–191.

Jacobs, Melville, and Elizabeth D. Jacobs
[1935] [16 Acetate Disc Recordings of Upper Coquille Athabaskan Music and One Text from Coquille Thompson at Siletz, Oreg.] (In Melville Jacobs Collection, University of Washington Libraries, Seattle.)

Jacobs, Melville, and Bernhard J. Stern
1947 Outlines of Anthropology. New York: Barnes and Noble.

Jacobsen, Philipp B.
1891 Reiseberichte aus unbekannten Teilen British-Columbiens. *Das Ausland: Wochenschrift für Erd- und Völkerkunde* 64(47):922–928. Stuttgart, Germany.

1895 Sissauch-dansen. Beskrifning på Sissauch-dansarna hos Bella Colla-stammen och andra indianstammar af samma språk, såsom Kimskwit och Tallio. [The Sissauch Dance. Description of the Sissauch Dances Among the Bella Coola Tribe and Other Indian Tribes of the Same Language, Such as the Kimskwit and Tallio.] *Ymer: Tidskrift Utgifven af Svenska Sällskapet för Autropologi och Geografi* 15:1–23. Stockholm.

1895a Indianska Sagor [Indian Tales]. *Ymer: Tidskrift Utgifven af Svenska Sällskapet för Anthropologi och Geografi* 14. Stockholm.

Jacobsen, Johan Adrian
1884 Capitain Jacobsen's Reise an der Nordwestküste Amerikas, 1881–1883, zum Zwecke ethnologischer Sammlungen und Erkundigungen, nebst Beschreibung persönlicher Erlebnisse, für den deutchen Leserkreis. A. Woldt ed. Leipzig, Germany: M. Spohr.

1890 Bella-Coola-Sagen. *Das Ausland: Wochenschrift für Erd- und Völkerkunde* 63(18):352–354. Stuttgart, Germany.

695

1891   Geheimbünde der Küstenbewohner Nordwest-Amerika's. Pp. 383–395 in Verhandlungen der Berliner Gesellschaft für Anthropologie, Ethnologie und Urgeschichte, 1891. *Zeitschrift für Ethnologie* 23. Berlin.

1892   Der Kosiyut-Bund der Bella-Coola-Indianer. *Das Ausland: Wochenschrift für Erd- und Völkerkunde* 65:437–441. Stuttgart, Germany.

1977   Alaskan Voyage, 1881–1883: An Expedition to the Northwest Coast of America. Erna Gunther, trans. Chicago: University of Chicago Press.

Jacobsen, William H., Jr.
1969   Origin of the Nootka Pharyngeals. *International Journal of American Linguistics* 35(2):125–153.

1979   Wakashan Comparative Studies. Pp. 766–791 in The Languages of Native America: Historical and Comparative Assessment. Lyle Campbell and Marianne Mithun, eds. Austin: University of Texas Press.

1979a   Chimakuan Comparative Studies. Pp. 792–802 in The Languages of North America: Historical and Comparative Assessment. Lyle Campbell and Marianne Mithun, eds. Austin: University of Texas Press.

1979b   First Lessons in Makah. Forks, Wash.: Olympic Graphic Arts.

1979c   Noun and Verb in Nootkan. Pp. 83–155 in The Victoria Conference on Northwestern Languages, Victoria, British Columbia, November 4–5, 1976. Barbara S. Efrat, ed. *British Columbia Provincial Museum. Heritage Record* 4. Victoria.

James, M.D.
1984   Historic and Present Native Participation in Pacific Coast Commercial Fisheries. *Canada. Department of Fisheries and Oceans. Manuscript Report of Fisheries and Aquatic Sciences* 1786. Vancouver.

Jamieson, Stuart, and Percy Gladstone
1950   Unionism in the Fishing Industry of British Columbia. *Canadian Journal of Economics and Political Science* 16(1):1–11, (2):146–171. Toronto.

Jane, Cecil *see* Espinosa y Tello, José

Jenness, Diamond
1934   The Indians of Canada. 2d ed. *Anthropological Series* 15, *National Museum of Canada Bulletin* 65. Ottawa.

1934a   [Unpublished Fieldnotes.] (Manuscripts in Ethnology Division, National Museum of Man, Ottawa.)

[1934–1935] The Saanich Indians of Vancouver Island. (Manuscript [No. VII-G-8M] in Canadian Ethnology Service Archives, National Museum of Civilization, Ottawa.)

1943   The Carrier Indians of Bulkley River, Their Social and Religious Life. *Anthropological Papers* 25, *Bureau of American Ethnology Bulletin* 133. Washington.

1955   The Faith of a Coast Salish Indian. *Anthropology in British Columbia. Memoirs* 3. Victoria.

Jenson, Vickie, and Carol McLaren
1976   Quileute for Kids, I-III. La Push, Wash.: Quileute Tribe.

Jermann, Jerry V., Dennis E. Lewarch, and Sarah K. Campbell
1975   Salvage Excavations at the Kersting Site (45-CL-21): A Preliminary Report. *University of Washington. Office of Public Archaeology. Reports in Highway Archaeology* 2. Seattle.

Jewett, Stanley G., Walter P. Taylor, William T. Shaw, and John W. Aldrich
1953   Birds of Washington State. Seattle: University of Washington Press.

Jewitt, John R.
1807   A Journal Kept at Nootka Sound, by John R. Jewitt. One of the Surviving Crew of the Ship Boston, of Boston; John Salter, Commander Who Was Massacred on 22d of March, 1803. Interspersed with Some Account of the Natives, Their Manners and Customs. Boston: Printed for the author.

1815   A Narrative of the Adventures and Sufferings of John R. Jewitt; Only Survivor of the Crew of the Ship Boston, During a Captivity of Nearly Three Years Among the Savages of Nootka Sound [etc.]. Middletown, Conn.: Seth Richards.

1931   A Journal Kept at Nootka Sound . . . .[1807]. Norman L. Dodge, ed. Boston: C.E. Goodspeed.

1967   A Narrative of the Adventures and Sufferings of John R. Jewitt; Only Survivor of the Crew of the Ship Boston [1815]. Fairfield, Wash.: Ye Galleon Press.

1974   The Adventures and Sufferings of John R. Jewitt, Captive Among the Nootka, 1803–1805. Derek G. Smith, ed. Toronto: McClelland and Stewart.

1975   Narrative of the Adventures and Sufferings of John R. Jewitt While Held as a Captive of the Nootka Indians of Vancouver Island 1803 to 1805. Robert Heizer, ed. Ramona, Calif.: Ballena Press.

1976   A Journal, Kept at Nootka Sound. (Facsimile of 1807 ed., Boston.); A Narrative of the Adventures and Sufferings of John R. Jewitt. (Facsimile of 1815, ed., Middletown, Conn.) (*Garland Library of Narratives of North American Indian Captivities* 28) New York: Garland.

Jilek, Wolfgang G.
1974   Salish Indian Mental Health and Culture Change: Psychohygienic and Therapeutic Aspects of the Guardian Spirit Ceremonial. Toronto: Holt, Rinehart and Winston of Canada.

1982   Indian Healing: Shamanic Ceremonialism in the Pacific Northwest Today. Surrey, B.C.: Hancock House.

Jilek, Wolfgang G., and Norman Todd
1974   Witchdoctors Succeed Where Doctors Fail: Psychotherapy Among Coast Salish Indians. *Canadian Psychiatric Association Journal* 19(4):351–356.

Johannessen, Carl L., William A. Davenport, Artimus Millet, and Steven McWilliams
1971   The Vegetation of the Willamette Valley. *Annals of the Association of American Geographers* 61(2):286–302. Lawrence, Kansas.

Johansen, Dorothy O.
1946   McLoughlin and the Indians. *The Beaver*, Outfit 277(June):18–21. Winnipeg.

1957   The Roll of Land Laws in the Settlement of Oregon. Pp. iii–viii in Genealogical Material in Oregon Donation Land Claims. Vol. 1. Portland, Oreg.: Genealogical Forum of Portland.

Johansen, Uwe von
1963   Versuch einer Analyse dokumentarischen Materials über die Identitätsfrage und die kulturelle Position der Eyak-Indianer Alaskas. *Anthropos* 58(5–6):868–896.

Johnson, Elizabeth L., and Kathryn Bernick
1986   Hands of Our Ancestors: The Revival of Salish Weaving at Musqueam. *University of British Columbia. Museum of Anthropology Notes* 16. Vancouver.

Johnson, LeRoy
1972   Problems in "Avant-Garde" Archaeology. *American Anthropologist* 74(3):366–377.

Johnson, Ronald
[1973]   The Art of the Shaman. Catalog of the Exhibit, January 18 through February 25, 1973. Iowa City: University of Iowa Museum.

Johnson, Samuel V.
1978   Chinook Jargon: A Computer Assisted Analysis of Variation in an American Indian Pidgin. (Unpublished Ph.D. Dissertation in Anthropology, University of Kansas, Lawrence.)

Jonaitis, Aldona
1978   Land Otters and Shamans: Some Interpretations of Tlingit Charms. *American Indian Art Magazine* 4(1):62–66.

1980   The Devilfish in Tlingit Sacred Art. *American Indian Art Magazine* 5(3):42–47.

1981   Tlingit Halibut Hooks: An Analysis of the Visual Symbols of a Rite of Passage. *Anthropological Papers of the Museum of Natural History* 57(1). New York.

1981a   Creations of Mystics and Philosophers: The White Man's Perceptions of Northwest Coast Indian Art from the 1930's to the Present. *American Indian Culture and Research Journal* 5(1):1–45.

1982   Sacred Art and Spiritual Power: An Analysis of Tlingit Shamans' Masks. Pp. 119–136 in Native North American Art History: Selected Readings. Z. Mathews and A. Jonaitis, eds. Palo Alto, Calif.: Peek Publications.

1986   Art of the Northern Tlingit. Seattle: University of Washington Press.

1988   From the Land of the Totem Poles: The Northwest Coast Indian Art Collection at the American Museum of Natural History. New York: The American Museum of Natural History.

1988a   Women, Marriage, Mouths, and Feasting: The Symbolism of the Tlingit Labrets. Pp. 191–205 in Marks of Civilization: Artistic Transformations of the Human Body. Arnold Rubin, ed. Los Angeles: University of California, Museum of Cultural History.

Jones, DeL. Floyd
1857   [Report of First Lieutenant DeL. Floyd Jones, September 1, 1853.] Pp. 4–10 in Indian Affairs on the Pacific [etc.] *34th Congress 3d Sess., House Executive Document* No. 76. (Serial No. 906) Washington.

Jones, George T., Sarah Campbell, and Sarah Studenmund
1978   An Archaeological Reconnaissance of Urban Levee Alignments in the Centralia-Chehalis Area, Lewis County, Washington. *University of Washington. Office of Public Archaeology. Reconnaissance Reports* 17. Seattle.

Jones, Joan M.
1968   Northwest Coast Basketry and Culture Change. *Thomas Burke Memorial Washington State Museum. Research Reports* 1. Seattle.

Jones, Livingston F.
1914   A Study of the Thlingets of Alaska. New York: Fleming H. Revell. (Reprinted: Johnson Reprint Corporation, New York, 1970.)

Jones, Roy
1972   Wappato Indians of the Lower Columbia River Valley: Their History and Prehistory. Portland, Oreg.: Privately printed.

Joppien, Rüdiger, and Bernard Smith
1985–1988   The Art of Captain Cook's Voyages. 4 vols. New Haven, Conn.: Yale University Press.

Jorgensen, Joseph G.
1969   Salish Language and Culture: A Statistical Analysis of Internal Relationships, History, and Evolution. (*Language Science Monographs* 3) Bloomington: Indiana University.

1980   Western Indians: Comparative Environments, Languages, and Cultures of 172 Western American Indian Tribes. San Francisco: W.H. Freeman.

Josephy, Alvin M., Jr.
1984   The Great Northwest Fishing War. Pp. 177–211, 282–286 in Now That the Buffalo's Gone: A Study of Today's American Indians. Norman: University of Oklahoma Press.

Kaeppler, Adrienne L., ed.
1978   Cook Voyage Artifacts in Leningrad, Berne and Florence Museums. Honolulu: Bishop Museum Press.

Kaiper, Dan, and Nan Kaiper
1978   Tlingit: Their Art, Culture, and Legends. Saanichten, B.C.: Hancock House.

Kaiser, Rudolf
1987   Chief Seattle's Speech(es): American Origins and European Reception. Pp. 497–536 in Recovering the Word: Essays on Native American Literature. Brian Swann and Arnold Krupat, eds. Berkeley: University of California Press.

Kamenskiĭ, Archimandrite Anatoliĭ
1985   Tlingit Indians of Alaska. Sergei Kan, trans. Fairbanks: University of Alaska Press.

Kan, Sergei
1983   Words That Heal the Soul: An Analysis of the Tlingit Potlatch Oratory. *Arctic Anthropology* 20(2):47–59.

1985   Russian Orthodox Brotherhoods Among the Tlingit: Missionary Goals and Native Response. *Ethnohistory* 32(3):196–222.

1987   Memory Eternal: Russian Orthodox Christianity and the Tlingit Mortuary Complex. *Arctic Anthropology* 24(1):32–55.

Kane, Paul
1857   The Chinook Indians. *Canadian Journal of Industry, Science and Art* n.s. 7:11–30. Toronto.

1859   Wanderings of an Artist Among the Indians of North America, from Canada to Vancouver's Island and Oregon ....London: Longmans, Brown, Green, Longmans, and Roberts. (Reprinted: C.E. Tuttle, Rutland, Vt., 1967.)

Kaplan, Susan A., and Kristin J. Barsness
1986   Raven's Journey: The World of Alaska's Native People. Philadelphia: University of Pennsylvania, University Museum.

Kaplanoff, Mark D., ed.
1971   Joseph Ingraham's Journal of the Brigantine Hope on a Voyage to the Northwest Coast of North America, 1790–1792. Barre, Mass.: Imprint Society.

Kappler, Charles J., comp.
1904–1941   Indian Affairs: Laws and Treaties. 5 vols. Washington: U.S. Government Printing Office. (Reprinted: AMS Press, New York, 1971.)

Kari, James, comp.
1977   Dena'ina Noun Dictionary. Fairbanks: University of Alaska, Native Language Center.

Kari, James, and Mildred Buck, comps.
1975   Ahtna Noun Dictionary. Fairbanks: University of Alaska, Native Language Center.

697

Kasakoff, Alice Bee

1974 Lévi-Strauss' Idea of the Social Unconscious: The Problem of Elementary and Complex Structures in Gitksan Marriage Choice. Pp. 143–169 in The Unconscious in Culture: The Structuralism of Claude Lévi-Strauss in Perspective. Ino Rossi, ed. New York: E.P. Dutton.

1984 Gitksan Kin Term Usage. Pp. 69–108 in The Tsimshian and Their Neighbors of the North Pacific Coast. Jay Miller and Carol M. Eastman, eds. Seattle: University of Washington Press.

Kaufmann, Carole N.

1969 Changes in Haida Indian Argillite Carvings, 1820 to 1910. (Unpublished Ph.D. Dissertation in Art History, University of California, Los Angeles.)

1976 Functional Aspects of Haida Argillite Carvings. Pp. 56–69 in Ethnic and Tourist Arts: Cultural Expressions from the Fourth World. Nelson H.H. Graburn, ed. Berkeley: University of California Press.

Kautz, August V.

1855 English-"Tou-tout-en" Vocabulary of About 70 Words. (Manuscript No. 199 in National Anthropological Archives, Smithsonian Institution, Washington.)

1855a Vocabulary of the Indian Languages of the Tou-tout-en Tribe. (Manuscript No. 198 in National Anthropological Archives, Smithsonian Institution, Washington.)

Keddie, Grant R.

1981 The Use and Distribution of Labrets on the North Pacific Rim. Syesis 14:59–80. Victoria, B.C.

Keely, Patrick B., Charlene S. Martinsen, Eugene S. Hunn, and Helen H. Norton

1982 Composition of Native American Fruits in the Pacific Northwest. Journal of the Dietetic Association 81(5):568–572.

Keen, John H.

1906 A Grammar of the Haida Language. London: Society for Promoting Christian Knowledge.

Keen, Sharon D.

[1975] The Growth of Clam Shells from Two Pentlatch Middens as Indicators of Seasonal Gathering. British Columbia. Heritage Conservation Branch. Occasional Papers 3. Victoria.

Keithan, Edward L.

1940 The Petroglyphs of Southeastern Alaska. American Antiquity 6(2):123–132.

1954 Human Hair as a Decorative Feature in Tlingit Ceremonial Paraphernalia. University of Alaska Anthropological Papers 3(1):17–20. College.

1962 Stone Artifacts of Southeastern Alaska. American Antiquity 28(1):66–77.

1963 Monuments in Cedar: The Authentic Story of the Totem Pole. Rev. ed. Seattle: Superior Publishing Company.

1964 Origin of the "Chief's Copper" or "Tinneh". University of Alaska Anthropological Papers 12(2):59–78. College.

1981 The Authentic History of the Shakes Island and Clan. Wrangell, Alas.: Wrangell Historical Society. (Reprinted from the Wrangell Sentinel, 1940.)

Kelly, William A., and Frances H. Willard

1906 Grammar and Vocabulary of the Hlingit Language of Southeastern Alaska. Pp. 715–766 in U.S. Bureau of Education. Report of the Commissioner of Education for 1903–1904. Washington. (Reprinted: Shorey Book Store, Seattle, 1971.)

Kendall, Daythal L.

1976 Takelma and Takelman. (Paper presented before the Meeting of the American Anthropological Association, Washington.)

1977 A Syntactic Analysis of Takelma Texts. (Unpublished Ph.D. Dissertation in Linguistics, University of Pennsylvania, Philadelphia.)

Kendrew, Wilfrid G., and Donald Kerr

1955 The Climate of British Columbia and the Yukon Territory. Ottawa: E. Cloutier, Queen's Printer.

Kennedy, F.

1877 [Letter to C. Jones at Bella Bella, Dated Bella Coola, B.C., October 24, 1877, re Supplies for Hudson's Bay Company Post.] (Manuscript in British Columbia Provincial Archives, Victoria.)

Kennedy, Alexander

1824–1825 [Fort George District, Columbia Department Report.] (Manuscript B.7/b/e, in Hudson's Bay Company Archives, Provincial Archives of Manitoba, Winnipeg, Canada.)

Kennedy, Dorothy I.D.

[1971–1977] [Ethnographic Notes from Fieldwork Among the Bella Coola Indians, British Columbia.] (Manuscripts in British Columbia Indian Language Project, Victoria.)

1971–1981 [Ethnographic Notes Pertaining to the Northern Strait of Georgia Coast Salish.] (Manuscript in Kennedy's possession; copy held by British Columbia Indian Language Project, Victoria.)

Kennedy, Dorothy I.D., and Randy Bouchard

[1976] Ethnobotany of the Squamish Indian People of British Columbia. Victoria: British Columbia Indian Language Project.

[1976a] Utilization of Fish, Beach Foods, and Marine Mammals by the Squamish Indian People of British Columbia. Victoria: British Columbia Indian Language Project.

1983 Sliammon Life, Sliammon Lands. Vancouver, B.C.: Talonbooks.

1985 Bella Coola. P. 161 in The Canadian Encyclopedia. 3 vols. Edmonton, Alta.: Hurtig.

Kennelly, Anthea

1985 Nutrient Composition of Bella Coola Salmon. (Unpublished M.A. Thesis in Human Nutrition, University of British Columbia, Vancouver.)

Kent, William E.

1977 The Siletz Indian Reservation, 1855–1900. Newport, Oreg.: Lincoln County Historical Society.

Kenyon, Susan M.

1973 The Indians of the West Coast of Vancouver Island (the Nootka). (Report on file at the Canadian Ethnology Service, National Museum of Man, Ottawa.)

1975 Rank and Property Among the Nootka: Ethnographic Research on the West Coast of Vancouver Island. (Manuscript on file at the Canadian Ethnology Service, National Museum of Man, Ottawa.)

1976 The Nature of the Nootkan Local Group: Kinship and Descent on the West Coast of Vancouver Island. (Manuscript in Kenyon's possession.)

1977 Traditional Trends in Modern Nootka Ceremonies. Arctic Anthropology 14(1):25–38.

[Kermode, Francis]

1916 Anthropology: [Descriptive List of Northwest Collections, 1915]. Pp. N10–N11 in British Columbia Provincial Museum Report for the Year 1915. Victoria.

1917 Anthropology: Accessions, 1916: [Annotated List of Collections from the Northwest]. Pp. Q10–Q12 in *British Columbia Provincial Museum Report for the Year 1916.* Victoria.

Kerr, Robert
1953 For the Royal Scottish Museum. *The Beaver,* Outfit 284 (June):32–35. Winnipeg.

Ketz, John, and John F.C. Johnson
1985 Chugach Archaeological Inventory of Controller Bay, Alaska, June 1983. Anchorage: Chugach Alaska Corporation. Mimeo.

Kew, J.E. Michael
1970 Coast Salish Ceremonial Life: Status and Identity in a Modern Village. (Unpublished Ph.D. Dissertation in Anthropology, University of Washington, Seattle.)

1976 Salmon Abundance, Technology, and Human Populations on the Fraser River Watershed. (Unpublished manuscript in Department of Anthropology and Sociology, University of British Columbia, Vancouver.)

1980 Sculpture and Engraving of the Central Coast Salish Indians. *University of British Columbia. Museum of Anthropology Notes* 9. Vancouver.

1988 Salmon Availability, Technology, and Cultural Adaptation on the Fraser River Watershed. (Manuscript in Kew's possession.)

Kew, J.E. Michael, and Della Kew
1981 "People Need Friends, It Makes Their Minds Strong:" A Coast Salish Curing Rite. Pp. 29–35 in The World Is As Sharp As a Knife: An Anthology in Honour of Wilson Duff. Donald N. Abbott, ed. Victoria: British Columbia Provincial Museum.

Khlebnikov, Kyrill T.
1976 Colonial Russian America: Kyril T. Khlebnikov's Reports, 1817–1832. B. Dmytryshyn and E.A.P. Crownhart-Vaughan, trans. Portland: Oregon Historical Society.

1985 Russkaiả Amerika v "zapiskakh" Kirila Khlebnikova: Novo-Arkhangel'sk [Russian America in "The Notes" of Kiril Khlebnikov: Novo-Arkhangel'sk (Sitka)]. S.G. Federova and V.A. Aleksandrov, eds. Moscow: Nauka.

Kickingbird, Kirke, and Karen Duchencaux
1973 A Beleaguered Little Band: The Nisquallys of Washington State. Pp. 179–195 in One Hundred Million Acres, by Kirke Kickingbird and Karen Duchencaux. New York: Macmillan.

Kidd, George E.
1930 A Case of Primitive Trephining. *Museum and Art Notes* 5(3):85–87. Vancouver, B.C.

1933 Report on Collection of B.C. Indian Skulls in the Vancouver City Museum. *Museum and Art Notes* 7 (Supplement 4):1–8. Vancouver, B.C.

1946 Trepanation Among the Early Indians of British Columbia. Arthritis Among the Early Indians of British Columbia. Artificial Deformation of the Skull Among the Early Indians of British Columbia. *Canadian Medical Association Journal* 55(5):513–516. Toronto.

Kidd, George E., and George E. Darby
1933 The Teeth of the Pacific Coast Indian. Vancouver, B.C.: City Museum and Art Gallery.

Kidd, Robert S.
1964 A Synthesis of Western Washington Prehistory from the Perspective of Three Occupational Sites. (Unpublished M.A. Thesis in Anthropology, University of Washington, Seattle.)

1966 The Archaeology of the Puget Sound Area, Washington. (Manuscript on file at Department of Anthropology, University of Alberta, Edmonton.)

1967 The Martin Site, Southwestern Washington. *Tebiwa: Journal of the Idaho State University Museum* 10(2):13–38. Pocatello.

King, Arden R.
1950 Cattle Point, a Stratified Site on the Southern Northwest Coast. *Memoirs of the Society for American Archaeology* 7. Menasha, Wis. (Reprinted: Kraus Reprint, Millwood, N.Y., 1974.)

King, James
1967 [Extract from Journal, 1777–1778.] Pp. 1361–1455 in Pt. 2 of The Journals of Captain James Cook on His Voyages of Discovery. J.C. Beaglehole, ed. Cambridge, Mass.: Published for the Hakluyt Society at the University Press. (Reprinted: Kraus Reprint, Millwood, N.Y., 1988.)

King, Jonathan C.H.
1979 Portrait Masks from the Northwest Coast of America. New York: Thames and Hudson.

1981 Artificial Curiosities from the Northwest Coast of America: Native American Artefacts in the British Museum Collected on the Third Voyage of Captain James Cook and Acquired Through Sir Joseph Banks. London: British Museum Publications.

Kinkade, M. Dale
1963–1964 Phonology and Morphology of Upper Chehalis. *International Journal of American Linguistics* 29(3):181–195, (4):345–356; 30(1):32–61, 251–260.

1976 The Salishan Languages. (Unpublished paper presented at the Northwest Coast Studies Conference, Burnaby, B.C.)

1983 "Daughters of Fire": Narrative Verse Analysis of an Upper Chehalis Folktale. Pp. 267–278 in North American Indians: Humanistic Perspectives. James S. Thayer, ed. *University of Oklahoma. Department of Anthropology. Papers in Anthropology* 24(2). Norman.

1983a Salish Evidence Against the Universality of 'Noun' and 'Verb'. *Lingua: International Review of General Linguistics* 60(1):25–39.

1984 "Bear and Bee": Narrative Verse Analysis of an Upper Chehalis Folktale. Pp. 246–261 in 1983 Mid-America Linguistics Conference Papers. David S. Rood, ed. Boulder: University of Colorado, Department of Linguistics.

1985 The Line in Upper Chehalis Narrative: Wren and Elk. (Paper presented at the Annual Meeting of the American Anthropological Association, Washington.)

1985a More on Nasal Loss on the Northwest Coast. *International Journal of American Linguistics* 51(4):478–480.

1987 Bluejay and His Sister. Pp. 255–296 in Recovering the Word: Essays on Native American Literature. Brian Swann and Arnold Krupat, eds. Berkeley: University of California Press.

Kinkade, M. Dale, and J.V. Powell
1976 Language and the Prehistory of North America. *World Archaeology* 8(1):83–100.

Kinkade, M. Dale, and Wayne Suttles
1987 New Caledonia and Columbia. Map. Plate 66 in Historical Atlas of Canada. Vol. 1. R. Cole Harris and Geoffrey J. Matthews, cart. Toronto: University of Toronto Press.

699

Kinkade, M. Dale, and Laurence C. Thompson
1974   Proto-Salish *r. *International Journal of American Linguistics* 40(1):22–28.

Kinney, Jay P.
1937   A Continent Lost - A Civilization Won: Indian Land Tenure in America. Baltimore, Md.: Johns Hopkins Press. (Reprinted: Octagon Books, New York, 1975.)

Kirk, Ruth
1974   Hunters of the Whale. New York: Harcourt, Brace and Jovanovich.

Kissell, Mary L.
1916   A New Type of Spinning in North America. *American Anthropologist* 18(2):264–270.

————   1928   The Early Geometric Patterned Chilkat. *American Anthropologist* 30(1):116–120.

————   1929   Organized Salish Blanket Pattern. *American Anthropologist* 31(1):85–88.

Klatsky, Meyer
1948   Studies in the Dietaries of Contemporary Primitive Peoples. *Journal of the American Dental Association* 36(4–5):385–391. Chicago.

Klein, Laura F.
1975   Tlingit Women and Town Politics. (Unpublished Ph.D. Dissertation in Anthropology, New York University, New York.)

————   1976   "She's One of Us, You Know": The Public Life of Tlingit Women; Traditional, Historical, and Contemporary Perspectives. *Western Canadian Journal of Anthropology* 6(3):164–183.

Knapp, Frances, and Rheta Louise Childe
1896   The Thlinkets of Southeastern Alaska. Chicago: Stone and Kimball.

Knight, Rolf
1978   Indians at Work: An Informal History of Native Indian Labour in British Columbia, 1858–1930. Vancouver, B.C.: New Star Books.

[Knipe, Christopher]
1868   Some Account of the Takaht Language, as Spoken by Several Tribes on the Western Coast of Vancouver Island. London: Hatchard.

Knutson, Peter
1987   The Unintended Consequences of the Boldt Decision. *Cultural Survival Quarterly* 11(2):43–47.

Kobrinsky, Vernon
1975   Dynamics of the Fort Rupert Class Struggle: Fighting with Property Vertically Revisited. Pp. 32–59 in Papers in Honour of Harry Hawthorn. Vernon C. Serl and Herbert C. Taylor, Jr., eds. Bellingham, Wash.: Northwest Scientific Association.

Koller, James, 'Gogisgi' Carroll Arnett, Steve Nemirow, and Peter Blue Cloud, eds.
1982   Coyote's Journal. Berkeley, Calif.: Wingbow.

Kolstee, Anton F.
1982   Bella Coola Indian Music: A Study of the Interaction Between Northwest Coast Indian Structures and Their Functional Context. *Canada. National Museum of Man. Mercury Series. Ethnology Service Papers* 83. Ottawa.

Kool, Richard
1982   Northwest Coast Indian Whaling: New Considerations. *Canadian Journal of Anthropology* 3(1):31–43.

Kopas, Cliff
1970   Bella Coola. Vancouver, B.C.: Mitchell Press. (Reprinted: Douglass and McIntyre, Vancouver, B.C., 1980.)

Koppert, Vincent A.
1928   Some Myths of the Nootka Indians. (Manuscript No. 1095 in Catholic University of America Library, Washington.)

————   1930   The Nootka Family. *Primitive Man* 3(3–4):49–55.

————   1930a   Contributions to Clayoquot Ethnology. *Catholic University of America. Anthropological Series* 1:1–130. Washington.

Korey, Kenneth A.
1980   The Incidence of Bilateral Nonmetric Skeletal Traits: A Reanalysis of Sampling Procedures. *American Journal of Physical Anthropology* 53(1):19–23.

Kotzebue, Otto von
1830   A New Voyage Round the World, in the Years 1823, 24, 25, and 26. 2 vols. (Translation of Puteshestvïe vokrug svïeta) London: H. Colburn and R. Bentley. (Reprinted: Da Capo Press, New York, 1967.)

————   1967   A Voyage of Discovery into the South Sea and Bering Strait . . . in the Years 1815–1818. H.E. Lloyd, trans. 3 vols. (*Bibliotheca Australiana* 17–19) New York: Da Capo Press.

Kozloff, Eugene N.
1983   Seashore Life of the Northern Pacific Coast: An Illustrated Guide to Northern California, Oregon, Washington, and British Columbia. Seattle: University of Washington Press.

Krajina, Vladimir J.
1970   Ecology of Forest Trees in British Columbia. Pp. 1–146 in *Ecology of Western North America* 2(1). V.J. Krajina and R.C. Brooke, eds. Vancouver: University of British Columbia, Department of Botany.

Krause, Aurel
1885   Die Tlingit-Indianer: Ergebnisse einer Reise nach der Nordwestküste von Amerika . . . in den Jahren 1880–1881. Jena, Germany: Hermann Costenoble.

————   1956   The Tlingit Indians: Results of a Trip to the Northwest Coast of America and Bering Straits. Erna Gunther, trans. (*Monographs of the American Ethnological Society* 26) Seattle: University of Washington Press.

————   1981   Journey to the Tlingits, by Aurel and Arthur Krause, 1881/82. Margot Krause McCaffrey, trans. Haines, Alaska: Centennial Commission, Alaska.

Krauss, Michael E.
1963–1970 Eyak Texts. Fairbanks: University of Alaska and Massachusetts Institute of Technology. Mimeo.

————   1963–1988 [Kwalhioqua and Clatskanie (Athapaskan) Linguistic Material.] (Manuscripts in Alaska Native Language Center, University of Alaska, Fairbanks.)

————   1964   Proto-Athapaskan-Eyak and the Problem of Na-Dene: The Phonology. *International Journal of American Linguistics* 30(2):118–131.

————   1965   Eyak: A Preliminary Report. *Canadian Journal of Linguistics* 10(2–3):167–187.

————   1970   Eyak Dictionary. College: University of Alaska.

————   1970a   Eyak Texts. College: University of Alaska and Massachusetts Institute of Technology. Mimeo.

————   1973   Na-Dene. Pp. 903–978 in *Current Trends in Linguistics*. Vol. 10: Linguistics in North America. Thomas A. Sebeok, ed. The Hague: Mouton. (Reprinted: Plenum Press, New York, 1976.)

————   1974   Minto-Nenana Athabaskan Dictionary. Preliminary Version. Fairbanks: University of Alaska, Native Language Center.

700

1979   Na-Dene and Eskimo-Aleut. Pp. 803–901 in The Languages of Native America: Historical and Comparative Assessment. Lyle Campbell and Marianne Mithun, eds. Austin: University of Texas Press.

1982   In Honor of Eyak: The Art of Anna Nelson Harry. Fairbanks: Alaska Native Language Center.

Krauss, Michael E., and Jeff Leer
1981   Athabascan, Eyak, and Tlingit Sonorants. *Alaska Native Language Center Research Papers* 5. Fairbanks.

Krauss, Michael E., and Mary Jane McGary
1980   Alaska Native Languages: A Bibliographical Catalogue. Pt. 1: Indian Languages. *Alaska Native Language Center Research Papers* 3. Fairbanks.

Krech, Shepard, III
1981   "Throwing Bad Medicine:" Sorcery, Disease, and the Fur Trade Among the Kutchin and Other Northern Athapascans. Pp. 73–108 in Indians, Animals and the Fur Trade: A Critique of Keepers of the Game. Shepard Krech, III, ed. Athens: University of Georgia Press.

Krieger, Alex D.
1944   [Review of] Archaeological Researches in the Northern Great Basin, by L.S. Cressman et al. (*Carnegie Institution of Washington Publication* 538) *American Antiquity* 9(3):351–359.

Krieger, Herbert W.
1926   Some Aspects of Northwest Coast Indian Art. *Scientific Monthly* 23(September):210–219.

1928   Indian Villages of Southeast Alaska. Pp. 467–494 in *Annual Report of the Smithsonian Institution for the Year 1927.* Washington.

Kroeber, Alfred L.
1904   Types of Indian Culture in California. *University of California Publications in American Archaeology and Ethnology* 2(3):81–103. Berkeley.

1923   American Culture and the Northwest Coast. *American Anthropologist* 25(1):1–20.

1923a   Anthropology. New York: Harcourt, Brace.

1925   Handbook of the Indians of California. *Bureau of American Ethnology Bulletin* 78. Washington. (Reprinted: Book Company, Berkeley, Calif., 1953.)

1936   Culture Element Distributions, III: Area and Climax. *University of California Publications in American Archaeology and Ethnology* 37(3):101–116. Berkeley.

1939   Cultural and Natural Areas of North America. *University of California Publications in American Archaeology and Ethnology* 38. Berkeley.

1948   Anthropology: Race, Language, Culture, Psychology, Prehistory. Rev. ed. New York: Harcourt, Brace.

Kroeber, Alfred L., et al.
1943   Franz Boas, 1858–1942. *Memoirs of the American Anthropological Association* 61. (Reprinted: Kraus Reprint, New York, 1969.)

Kruzenshtern, Ivan Fedorovich
1813   Wörtersammlungen aus den Sprachen einiger Völker des östlichen Asiens und der Nordwest-Küste von Amerika. St. Petersburg: Gedruckt in der Druckerey der Admiralität.

'Ksan Book Builders, comps.
1977   We-Gyet Wanders On: Legends of the Northwest. Texts in English and Tsimshian. Saanichton, B.C.: Hancock House.

Küchler, August W.
1964   Potential Natural Vegetation of the Coterminous United States, *American Geographical Society Special Publications* 36. New York.

Kuhnlein, Harriet V.
1984   Traditional and Contemporary Nuxalk Foods. *Nutrition Research* 4:789–809.

Kuhnlein, Harriet V., N.J. Turner, and P.D. Kluckner
1982   Nutritional Significance of Two Important Root Foods (Springbank Clover and Pacific Silverweed) Used by Native People on the Coast of British Columbia. *Ecology of Food and Nutrition* 12:89–95.

Kuhnlein, Harriet V., Alvin C. Chan, J. Neville Thompson, and Shuryo Nakai
1982   *Ooligan* Grease: A Nutritious Fat Used by Native People of Coastal British Columbia. *Journal of Ethnobiology* 2(2):154–161.

Kuipers, Aert H.
1967–1969 The Squamish Language. 2 Pts. The Hague: Mouton.

1970   Towards a Salish Etymological Dictionary. *Lingua: International Review of General Linguistics* 26(1):46–72. Amsterdam, The Netherlands.

1978   On the Phonological Typology of Proto-Salish. *Proceedings of the 42d International Congress of Americanists,* Vol. 4:607–621. Paris.

1981   On Reconstructing the Proto-Salish Sound System. *International Journal of American Linguistics* 47(4):323–335.

1982   Towards a Salish Etymological Dictionary II. *Lingua: International Review of General Linguistics* 57(1):71–92.

Laforet, Andrea
1984   Tsimshian Basketry. Pp. 215–280 in The Tsimshian: Images of the Past, Views for the Present. Margaret Seguin, ed. Vancouver: University of British Columbia Press.

La Grasserie, Raoul de
1902   Cinq langues de la Colombia Brittanique: Haida, Tshimshian, Kwaqiutl, Nootka, et Tlinkit. (*Bibliothèque Linguistique Américaine* 24) Paris: J. Maisonneuve.

Lamb, W. Kaye, ed.
1960   The Letters and Journals of Simon Fraser, 1806–1808. Toronto: Macmillan of Canada.

1970   The Journals and Letters of Sir Alexander Mackenzie. Toronto: Macmillan of Canada.

————, ed.
1984   A Voyage of Discovery to the North Pacific Ocean and Round the World, 1791–1795; with an Introduction and Appendices. 4 vols. London: Hakluyt Society.

Landar, Herbert
1977   Three Rogue River Athapaskan Vocabularies. *International Journal of American Linguistics* 43(4):289–301.

Lane, Barbara S.
1951   The Cowichan Knitting Industry. *Anthropology in British Columbia* 2:14–27. Victoria

1953   A Comparative and Analytic Study of Some Aspects of Northwest Coast Religion. (Unpublished Ph.D. Dissertation in Anthropology, University of Washington, Seattle.)

1973   Political and Economic Aspects of Indian-White Culture Contact in Western Washington in the Mid-19th Century. (Unpublished report in Lane's possession.)

1977   Background of Treaty Making in Western Washington. *American Indian Journal* 3(4):2–11. Washington.

701

Lane, Joseph
1878   Autobiography. (Manuscript P-A 43 in Bancroft Library, University of California, Berkeley.)

Lang, Janet, and Nigel Meeks
1981   Report on the Examination of Two Iron Knives from the Northwest Coast of America. App. 5 in Artificial Curiosities from the Northwest Coast of America. J.C.H. King, ed. London: British Museum Publications.

Langdon, Steven
1976   The Development of the Nootkan Cultural System. (Unpublished manuscript in Langdon's possession.)

1977   Technology, Ecology, and Economy: Fishing Systems in Southeast Alaska. (Unpublished Ph.D. Dissertation in Anthropology, Stanford University, Palo Alto, Calif.)

1979   Comparative Tlingit and Haida Adaptation to the West Coast of the Prince of Wales Archipelago. *Ethnology* 18(2):101–119.

Langness, Lewis L.
1959   A Case of Post-contact Reform Among the Clallam. (Unpublished M.A. Thesis in Anthropology, University of Washington, Seattle.)

Langsdorf, George H. von
1813–1814 Voyages and Travels in Various Parts of the World During the Years 1803–1807. 2 vols. London: H. Colburn. (Reprinted: Da Capo Press, New York, 1968.)

Lantis, Margaret
1938   The Alaskan Whale Cult and Its Affinities. *American Anthropologist* 40(3):438–464.

La Pérouse, Jean François Galaup, Comte de
1797   Voyage de La Pérouse autour du Monde. 4 vols. M.L.A. Milet-Mureau, ed. Paris: L'Imprimerie de la République.

1797–1799 A Voyage Round the World Performed in the Years 1785, 1786, 1787, 1788, by Boussole and Astrolabe....2 vols. London: G.G. and J. Robinson.

La Potin, Armand S., ed.
1987   Native American Voluntary Organizations. Westport, Conn.: Greenwood Press.

Large, Richard G.
1957   The Skeena, River of Destiny. Vancouver: Mitchell Press. (Reprinted: Gray's Publishing, Sidney, B.C., 1981.)

1968   Drums and Scalpel: From Native Healers to Physicians on the North Pacific Coast. Vancouver: Mitchell Press.

Larrison, Earl J.
1981   Birds of the Pacific Northwest: Washington, Oregon, Idaho and British Columbia. Moscow: University Press of Idaho.

Larsell, Olof
1947   The Doctor in Oregon: A Medical History. Portland, Oreg.: Binfords and Mort for the Oregon Historical Society.

Latham, Robert G.
1862   Elements of Comparative Philology. London: Walton and Maberly.

LaViolette, Forrest E.
1961   The Struggle for Survival: Indian Cultures and the Protestant Ethic in British Columbia. Toronto: University of Toronto Press. (Rev. ed. in 1973.)

Lawhead, Stephen
1980   Salvage Archaeology Project, May - September, 1979: A Report on the Investigations of the Mobile Salvage Crew. (Unpublished manuscript in Heritage Conservation Branch, Victoria, B.C.)

Lawrence, Donald, and Elisabeth Lawrence
1958   Bridge of the Gods Legend: Its Origin, History and Dating. *Mazama* 40(13):33–41. Portland, Oreg.

Lawrence, Erma, comp.
1977   Haida Dictionary. Fairbanks: Society for the Preservation of Haida Language and Literature, and the University of Alaska, Alaska Native Language Center.

Lazenby, Richard A., and Peter McCormack
1985   Salmon and Malnutrition on the Northwest Coast. *Current Anthropology* 26(3):379–384.

Leatherman, Kenneth E., and Alex D. Krieger
1940   Contributions to Oregon Coast Prehistory. *American Antiquity* 6(1):19–28.

LeClair, Ronald
1976   Investigations at the Maurer Site Near Agassiz. Pp. 33–42 in Current Research Reports. Roy L. Carlson, ed. *Simon Fraser University. Department of Archaeology Publications* 3. Burnaby, B.C.

Ledyard, John
1964   Journal of Captain Cook's Last Voyage [1783]. James K. Munford, ed. Corvallis: Oregon State University Press.

Lee, Daniel, and Joseph H. Frost
1844   Ten Years in Oregon. New York: Published for the authors by J. Collard. (Reprinted: Ye Galleon Press, Fairfield, Wash., 1968, Arno Press, New York, 1973.)

Lee, Melvin, Rejeanne G. Reyburn, and Anne Carrow
1971   Nutritional Status of British Columbia Indians. I: Dietary Studies at Ahousat and Anaham Reserves. *Canadian Journal of Public Health* 62(July-August):285–296.

Lee, Melvin, Braxton M. Alfred, John A. Birkbeck, Indrajit D. Desai, Gordon S. Myers, Rejeanne G. Reyburn, and Anne Carrow
1971   Nutritional Status of British Columbia Indian Populations, I: Ahousat and Anaham Reserves. Vancouver: University of British Columbia, School of Home Economics, Division of Human Nutrition.

Lee, Molly
1981   Pacific Eskimo Spruce Root Baskets. *American Indian Art Magazine* 6(2):66–73.

Lee, Richard
1963   A Collection of Artifacts from the Alexander Lee Farm on the North Fork of the Skagit River. *Washington Archaeologist* 7(3):21–23.

1972   Population Growth and the Beginnings of Sedentary Life Among the ng Bushmen. Pp. 329–342 in Population Growth: Anthropological Implications. Brian Spooner, ed. Cambridge, Mass.: MIT Press.

Leechman, Douglas
1928   Native Canadian Art of the West Coast. *Studio* 96(November):331–333.

1944   Trephined Skulls from British Columbia. *Transactions of the Royal Society of Canada 3d ser. Vol.* 38(Sect. 2):99–102. Ottawa.

1952   The Nanaimo Petroglyph. *Canadian Geographical Journal* 44(6):266–267. Ottawa.

Legros, Dominique
1984   Commerce entre Tlingits et Athapaskans Tutchones au XIX Siècle. *Recherches Amérindiennes au Québec* 14(2):11–24.

Le Jeune, Jean-Marie R.
1886   Practical Chinook Vocabulary, Comprising All & the Only Usual Words of That Wonderful Language....Kamloops, B.C.: St. Louis Mission.

1891–1905 Kamloops Wawa. Kamloops, B.C.: [St. Louis Mission.]

1892   Chinook Primer: By Which the Natives of British Columbia ... Are Taught to Read and Write Chinook in Shorthand in the Space of Few Hours. Kamloops, B.C.: Mimeographed at St. Louis Mission.

1896   Sheshel Manual; or, Prayers, Hymns and Catechism in the Sheshel Language. Kamloops, B.C.: [St. Louis Mission.] (Microfiche in Canadian Institute for Historical Micro-reproductions, Ottawa, 1982.)

1896a   The Wawa Shorthand Instructor. Kamloops, B.C.: [St. Louis Mission.]

1896–1897   Polyglott Manual. Kamloops, B.C.: [St. Louis Mission.]

1898   Chinook and Shorthand Rudiments. Kamloops, B.C.: [St. Louis Mission.]

Lemert, Edwin
1954   The Life and Death of an Indian State. *Human Organization* 13(3):23–27.

Lemmens, John N.
1888   Nootka (or Clayoquot Sound) Vocabulary. (Manuscript No. 1041 in National Anthropological Archives, Smithsonian Institution, Washington.)

[1889]   A Vocabulary of the West Coast Indian Language; Chiefly Barclay Sound Dialect. (Manuscript in the Archives of the Diocese of Victoria, B.C.)

Lemmens, John N., and Louis Enssen
1888   A Vocabulary of the Clayoquot Sound Language. (Manuscript cited in Pilling 1894:42 [under Lemmens, T.N., and Enssen, F.].)

Leonhardy, Frank
1967   The Archaeology of a Late Prehistoric Village in Northwestern California. *University of Oregon. Museum of Natural History Bulletins* 4. Eugene.

Leonhardy, Frank C., and David G. Rice
1970   A Proposed Culture Typology for the Lower Snake River Region. *Northwest Anthropological Research Notes* 4(1):1–29. Moscow, Idaho.

Lepofsky, Dana
1985   Bella Coola Settlement Patterns. (Unpublished M.A. Thesis in Anthropology, University of British Columbia, Vancouver.)

Lepofsky, Dana, Nancy J. Turner, and Harriet V. Kuhnlein
1985   Determining the Availability of Traditional Wild Plant Foods: An Example of Nuxalk Foods, Bella Coola, British Columbia. *Ecology of Food and Nutrition* 16(3):223–241.

Lerman, Norman, coll.
1976   Legends of the River People. Betty Keller, ed. Vancouver, B.C.: November House.

Leslie, Adrian R.
1979   A Grammar of the Cowichan Dialect of Halkomelem Salish. (Unpublished Ph.D. Dissertation in Linguistics, University of Victoria, Victoria, B.C.)

Levine, Robert D.
1973   Notes on a Haida Text. *The Charlottes: A Journal of the Queen Charlotte Islands* 2:28–32. Queen Charlotte, B.C.

1977   The Skidegate Dialect of Haida. (Unpublished Ph.D. Dissertation in Linguistics, Columbia University, New York City.)

1977a   Kwakwala. Pp. 98–126 in Northwest Coast Texts. Barry F. Carlson, ed. *Native American Text Series* 2(3). Chicago.

1979   Haida and Na-Dene: A New Look at the Evidence. *International Journal of American Linguistics* 45(2):157–170.

1984   Empty Categories, Rules of Grammar, and Kwakwala Complementation. Pp. 215–245 in The Syntax of Native American Languages. Eung-Do Cook and Donna B. Gerdts, eds. (*Syntax and Semantics* 16) Orlando, Fla.: Academic Press.

Levine, Robert D., and Freda Cooper
1976   The Suppression of B.C. Languages: Filling in the Gaps in the Documentary Record. *Sound Heritage* 4(3–4):43–75. Victoria, B.C.

Levine, Victor E.
1951   The Blood Groups of Alaskan Indians. (Abstract). *American Journal of Physical Anthropology* n.s. 9(2):238.

Lévi-Strauss, Claude
1943   The Art of the Northwest Coast at the American Museum of Natural History. *Gazette des Beaux-Arts*, ser. 6, Vol. 24:175–182.

1958   La Geste d'Asdiwal (*Extrait de l'Annuaire, 1958–1959*). *Ecole Prâtique des Hautes Etudes. Section des Sciences Religieuses* 2–43. Paris.

1963–1976   Structural Anthropology. 2 vols. New York: Basic Books.

1967   The Story of Asdiwal. Pp. 1–47 in The Structural Study of Myth and Totemism. Edmund Leach, ed. (*A.S.A. Monographs* 5) London: Tavistock.

1968   L'Origine des manières de table. (*Mythologiques* 3) Paris: Plon. (Translated by John and Doreen Weightman as *The Origin of Table Manners*, Harper and Row, New York, 1978.)

1971   L'Homme nu (*Mythologiques* 4) Paris: Plon. (Translated by John and Doreen Weightman as *The Naked Man*, Harper and Row, New York, 1981.)

1975   La Voie des masques. Geneva, Switzerland: Editions Albert Skira.

1982   The Way of the Masks. Sylvia Modelski, trans. Seattle: University of Washington Press.

Lewarch, Dennis E.
1979   Summary of Cultural Resources Overview of the Cedar and Tolt River Watersheds. *University of Washington. Office of Public Archaeology. Institute for Environmental Studies. Reconnaissance Reports* 24. Seattle.

Lewarch, Dennis E., and Lynn L. Larson
1977   An Archaeological Assessment of Chester Morse Lake and Masonry Dam Pool, Cedar River Watershed, Central Washington Cascades. *University of Washington. Office of Public Archaeology. Institute for Environmental Studies. Reconnaissance Reports* 15. Seattle.

Lewis, T.H.
1864   Vancouver Island Exploring Expedition. (Manuscript No. 794, Vol. 2, folder 6 in Provincial Archives of British Columbia, Victoria.)

Lewis, Albert B.
1906   Tribes of the Columbia Valley and the Coast of Washington and Oregon. *Memoirs of the American Anthropological Association* 1(2):147–209. (Reprinted: Kraus Reprint, Millwood, N.Y., 1983.)

Lewis, Claudia
1970   Indian Families of the Northwest Coast: The Impact of Change. Chicago: University of Chicago Press.

Lewis, Meriwether, and William Clark
1805–1806   [Estimate of the Western Indians.] (Manuscript, [Freeman No. 2441]. Pp. 147–155 in Codex I; Clark's Journal, American Philosophical Society Library, Philadelphia.)

Lewis, Meriwether, and William Clark *see also* Thwaites, Reuben G. 1904–1905

Lightfoot, Ricky R.
1983   Component 2 at the Hidden Falls Archaeological Site, Southeastern Alaska. (Unpublished M.A. Thesis in Anthropology, Washington State University, Pullman.)

Liljeblad, Sven
1962   The People Are Coming Soon: A Review Article. *Midwest Folklore* 12(2):93–103. Bloomington, Ind.

Lincoln, Kenneth
1983   Native American Renaissance. Berkeley: University of California Press.

Lincoln, Neville J., and John C. Rath
1980   North Wakashan Comparative Root List. *Canada. National Museum of Man. Mercury Series. Ethnology Service Papers* 68. Ottawa.

————
1986   Phonology, Dictionary and Listing of Roots and Lexical Derivates of the Haisla Language of Kitlope and Kitimaat, B.C. 2 vols. *Canada. Museum of Civilization. Mercury Series. Canadian Ethnology Service Papers* 103. Ottawa.

Linton, Ralph
1940   The Distinctive Aspects of Acculturation. Pp. 501–520 in Acculturation in Seven American Indian Tribes. Ralph Linton, ed. New York: D. Appleton-Century. (Reprinted: Peter Smith, Gloucester, Mass., 1963.)

————
1955   The Tree of Culture. New York: Knopf. (Reprinted in 1972.)

Lipshits, B.A.
1950   Etnograficheskie materialy po severo-zapadnoĭ Amerike v arkhive I.G. Voznesenskogo [Ethnographic Materials on Northwest America in the I.G. Voznesenskiĭ Archives]. *Izvestiia Vsesoiuznogo Geographicheskogo Obshchestva* 82(4):415–420. Leningrad.

Lisiānskiĭ, IŪriĭ Fedorovich
1812   Puteshestvīe vokrug svīeta v 1803, 4, 5, i 1806 godakh, po povelēnīiū Ego Imperatorskago Velichestva Aleksandra Pervago, na korablīe *Nevīe*. 2 vols. St. Petersburg: Naval Printing Office.

————
1814   A Voyage Round the World in the Years 1803, 4, 5, & 6: Performed by Order of His Imperial Majesty Alexander the First, Emperor of Russia, in the Ship Neva. London: Printed for J. Booth. (Reprinted: Da Capo Press, New York, 1968.)

Litke, Fedor Petrovich
1835–1836   Voyage autour du monde, exécuté par ordre de Sa Majesté l'empereur Nicolas Ier, sur la corvette le Séniavine, dans les années 1826, 1827, 1828 et 1829, par Frédéric Lutké... .Paris: Didot Frères.

————
1987   A Voyage Around the World, 1826–1829. Vol. 1: To Russian America and Siberia. Renée Marshall, [trans.]. Richard A. Pierce, ed. (*Alaska History* 29) Kingston, Ont.: The Limestone Press.

Locher, G.W.
1932   The Serpent in Kwakiutl Religion: A Study in Primitive Culture. Leiden, The Netherlands: E.J. Brill.

Loeb, Edwin M.
1929   Tribal Initiations and Secret Societies. *University of California Publications in American Archaeology and Ethnology* 25(3):249–288. Berkeley.

Loewenberg, Robert J.
1976   Equality on the Oregon Frontier: Jason Lee and the Methodist Mission, 1834–43. Seattle: University of Washington Press.

Lopatin, Ivan A.
1945   Social Life and Religion of the Indians in Kitimat, British Columbia. *University of Southern California. Social Science Series* 26. Los Angeles.

Lopez, Barry H.
1977   Giving Birth to Thunder, Sleeping with His Daughter: Coyote Builds North America. Kansas City: Sheed Andrews and McMeel.

Lord, John K.
1866   The Naturalist in Vancouver Island and British Columbia. 2 vols. London: Richard Bentley.

Loring, Charles G.
1864   Memoir of the Hon. William Sturgis; Prepared Agreeably to a Resolution of the Massachusetts Historical Society. Boston: John Wilson and Son.

Low, Jean
1977   George Thornton Emmons. *The Alaska Journal* 7(1):2–11. Juneau.

Lowie, Robert H.
1908   The Test-theme in North American Mythology. *Journal of American Folk-Lore* 21(81–82):97–148.

————, ed.
1910   Notes Concerning New Collections. *Anthropological Papers of the American Museum of Natural History* 4(2):271–337. New York.

————
1937   The History of Ethnological Theory. New York: Farrar and Rinehart.

————
1948   Social Organization. New York: Rinehart.

————
1956   Boas Once More. *American Anthropologist* 58(1):159–164.

————
1960   Nomenclature and Social Structure. Pp. 128–134 in Lowie's Selected Papers in Anthropology. Cora Du Bois, ed. Berkeley: University of California Press.

Lowry, R.B.
1970   Recurrence Risks for Cleft Lip and Cleft Palate in British Columbia Indians. *The Lancet* 2(7675):727.

————
1970a   Sex-linked Cleft Palate in a British Columbia Indian Family. *Pediatrics* 46(1):123–128.

Lowry, R.B., and D.H.G. Renwick
1969   Incidence of Cleft Lip and Palate in British Columbia Indians. *Journal of Medical Genetics* 6(1):67–69. London.

Loy, William G., Stuart Allen, Clyde P. Patton, and Robert D. Plank
1976   Atlas of Oregon. Eugene: University of Oregon Books.

Lundy, Doris
1974   Rock Art of the Northwest Coast. (Unpublished M.A. Thesis in Archaeology, Simon Fraser University, Burnaby, B.C.)

————
1983   Styles of Coastal Rock Art. Pp. 89–97 in Indian Art Traditions of the Northwest Coast. Roy Carlson, ed. Burnaby, B.C.: Simon Fraser University Archaeology Press.

Lundy, John K.
1981   Spondylolysis of the Lumbar Vertebrae in a Group of Prehistoric Upper Puget Sound Indians at Birch Bay, Washington. Pp. 107–114 in Contributions to Physical Anthropology, 1978–1980. J.S. Cybulski, ed. *Canada. National Museum of Man. Mercury Series. Archaeological Survey Papers* 106. Ottawa.

Lyman, H.S.
1900   Indian Names. *Oregon Historical Society Quarterly* 1(3):316–326.

1900a   Reminiscences of Louis Labonte. *Oregon Historical Society Quarterly* 1(2):169–188.

Lyons, Chester P.
1952   Trees, Shrubs and Flowers to Know in British Columbia. Toronto: J.M. Dent. (Rev. ed. 1965.)

Lyons, Cicely
1969   Salmon, Our Heritage: The Story of a Province and an Industry. Vancouver, B.C.: Mitchell Press.

Lyons, Letitia Mary
1940   Francis Norbert Blanchet and the Founding of the Oregon Missions (1838–1848). *Catholic University of America. Studies in American Church History* 31. Washington. (Reprinted: AMS Press, New York, 1974.)

Maass, John
1976   The Centennial Success Story. Pp. 11–23 in 1876: A Centennial Exhibition. Robert Post, ed. Washington: Smithsonian Institution, National Museum of History and Technology.

McAllister, Nancy M.
1980   Avian Fauna from the Yuquot Excavation. Pp. 103–174 in *The Yuquot Project*. Vol. 2. William J. Folan and John Dewhirst, eds. *Canada. National Historic Parks and Sites Branch. History and Archaeology* 43. Ottawa.

MacCallum, Spencer H.
1969   Art of the Northwest Coast. [Illustrated Catalogue of Exhibit] January 22 Through March 2, 1969, The Art Museum, Princeton University. Princeton, N.J.: Princeton Printing Company.

McChesney, Charles E.
1906   Rolls of Certain Indian Tribes in Oregon and Washington. *59th Congress, 2d Sess., House Document No. 133*. (Serial No. 5151) Washington. (Reprinted: Ye Galleon Press, Fairfield, Wash., 1969.)

McClellan, Catherine
1954   The Interrelations of Social Structure with Northern Tlingit Ceremonialism. *Southwestern Journal of Anthropology* 10(1):75–96.

McCullagh, James B.
1897   Nisga Primer, Pt I: Spelling and Reading. London: Society for Promoting Christian Knowledge.

McCurdy, James G.
1961   Indian Days at Neah Bay; from an Unfinished Manuscript by the Late James G. McCurdy. Gordon Newell, ed. Seattle, Wash.: Superior Publishing Company.

McDonald, Archibald
1830   [Letter of February 25 to the Governor.] (Manuscript D. 4/123, folder 120 in Hudson's Bay Company Archives, Provincial Archives of Manitoba, Winnipeg, Canada.)

MacDonald, George F.
1969   Preliminary Culture Sequence from the Coast Tsimshian Area, British Columbia. *Northwest Anthropological Research Notes* 3(2):240–254. Moscow, Idaho.

1971   Prince Rupert Midden Rebuilt in Ottawa Museum: Report of Activities on the Northern Coast of British Columbia, 1971. *The Midden: Publication of the Archaeological Society of British Columbia* 3(5):2–4. Vancouver.

1973   Haida Burial Practices: Three Archaeological Examples. *Canada. National Museum of Man. Mercury Series. Archaeological Survey Papers* 9:1–59. Ottawa.

1979   Kitwanga Fort National Historic Site, Skeena River, British Columbia: Historical Research and Analysis of Structural Remains. Ottawa: National Museum of Man.

1981   Cosmic Equations in Northwest Coast Indian Art. Pp. 225–238 in The World Is As Sharp As a Knife: An Anthology in Honour of Wilson Duff. Donald Abbott, ed. Victoria: British Columbia Provincial Museum.

1983   Haida Monumental Art: Villages of the Queen Charlotte Islands. Vancouver: University of British Columbia Press.

1983a   Prehistoric Art of the Northern Northwest Coast. Pp. 99–120 in Indian Art Traditions of the Northwest Coast. Roy L. Carlson, ed. Burnaby, B.C.: Simon Fraser University, Archaeology Press.

1984   Painted Houses and Woven Blankets: Symbols of Wealth in Tsimshian Art and Myth. Pp. 109–136 in The Tsimshian and Their Neighbors of the North Pacific Coast. Jay Miller and Carol M. Eastman, eds. Seattle: University of Washington Press.

1984a   The Epic of the Nekt. Pp. 65–81 in The Tsimshian: Images of the Past, Views for the Present. Margaret Seguin, ed. Vancouver: University of British Columbia Press.

MacDonald, George F., and Richard I. Inglis, eds.
1979   Skeena River Prehistory. *Canada. National Museum of Man. Mercury Series. Archaeological Survey Papers* 87. Ottawa.

1981   An Overview of the North Coast Prehistory Project (1966–1980). Pp. 37–63 in Fragments of the Past: British Columbia Archaeology in the 1970s. Knut R. Fladmark, ed. *BC Studies* 48(Winter). Vancouver.

McDonald, James A.
1985   Trying to Make a Life: The Historical Political Economy of Kitsumkalum. (Unpublished Ph.D. Dissertation in Anthropology, University of British Columbia, Vancouver.)

McDonald, Lucile
1972   Swan Among the Indians: Life of James G. Swan, 1818–1900; Based Upon Swan's Hitherto Unpublished Diaries and Journals. Portland, Oreg.: Binfords and Mort.

Macfarlane, Nathalie
1978   Joe David. Vancouver: University of British Columbia, Museum of Anthropology.

McFeat, Tom, ed.
1966   Indians of the North Pacific Coast. Seattle: University of Washington Press.

McGillivray, Simon
1830–1831   [Fort Nez Perces Journal.] (Manuscript B.146/a, in Hudson's Bay Company Archives, Provincial Archives of Manitoba, Winnipeg, Canada.)

McIlwraith, Thomas F.
1922   [Letter to Dr. Haddon, Ontario, Dated 29 August 1922.] (Manuscript in Cambridge University Library, Cambridge, England.)

1922–1924   [Bella Coola Fieldnotes.] (Manuscript, Collection No. 60, University of Toronto Rare Book Collection, Toronto, Ont.)

1923   [Letter to Dr. Edward Sapir, Anthropological Division, Victoria Memorial Museum, Dated 26 December 1923.] (Manuscript in National Museum of Man, Ottawa.)

1925   Certain Beliefs of the Bella Coola Indians Concerning Animals. Pp. 17–27 in App. to the *Annual Archaeological Report to the Ontario Minister of Education for 1924–1925*. Toronto.

1948   The Bella Coola Indians. 2 vols. Toronto: University of Toronto Press.

1964   Facts and Their Recognition Among the Bella Coola. Pp. 183–200 in Fact and Theory in Social Science. W. Count and Gordon T. Bowles, eds. Syracuse, N.Y.: Syracuse University Press.

Mackay, David
1985   In the Wake of Cook: Exploration, Science and Empire, 1780–1801. New York: St. Martin's Press.

McKenna - McBride Commission *see* Canada. Royal Commission on Indian Affairs for the Province of British Columbia

Mackenzie, Sir Alexander
1801   Voyages from Montreal, on the River St. Lawrence, Through the Continent of North America, to the Frozen and Pacific Oceans; in the Years 1789 and 1793. London: Printed for T. Cadell, Jr. (Reprinted: [in] The Journals and Letters of Sir Alexander Mackenzie. W. Kaye Lamb, ed. Cambridge University Press, Cambridge, Mass., 1970.)

McKenzie, Kathleen H.
1974   Ozette Prehistory-prelude. (Unpublished M.A. Thesis in Archaeology, University of Calgary, Calgary, Alta.)

McKervill, Hugh W.
1964   Darby of Bella Bella: Wo-Ya-La. Toronto: Ryerson Press.

Mackey, Harold
1974   The Kalapuyans: A Sourcebook on the Indians of the Willamette Valley. Salem, Oreg.: Mission Mill Museum Association.

Maclachlan, Morag
1983   The Founding of Fort Langley. Pp. 9–28 in The Company on the Coast. E. Blanche Norcross, ed. Nanaimo, B.C.: Nanaimo Historical Society.

McLaren, Carol Sheehan
1978   Moment of Death: Gift of Life. A Reinterpretation of the Northwest Coast Image "Hawk." *Anthropologica* n.s. 20(1–2):65–90. Ottawa.

McLaughlin, S.
1971   The Original Vegetation of Northern Puget Sound. (Manuscript, on file at Laboratory of Archaeology, Department of Anthropology, University of Washington, Seattle.)

McLendon, Sally
1981   Preparing Museum Collections for Use as Primary Data in Ethnographic Research. Pp. 201–227 in The Research Potential of Anthropological Museum Collections. Anne-Marie Cantwell et al., eds. *Annals of the New York Academy of Sciences* 376.

McLeod, Alexander R.
1961   Journal of A.R. McLeod (1826–1827). Pp. 141–219 in Peter Skene Ogden's Snake Country Journal, 1826–27. K.G. Davies, ed. London: The Hudson's Bay Record Society.

MacLeod, William C.
1925   Debtor and Chattel Slavery in Aboriginal North America. *American Anthropologist* 27(3):370–380.

————
1929   On the Diffusion of Central American Culture to Coastal British Columbia and Alaska. *Anthropos* 24(3–4):417–439.

————
1929a   The Origin of Servile Labor Groups. *American Anthropologist* 31(1):89–113.

McLoughlin, John
1941–1944   The Letters of John McLoughlin from Fort Vancouver to the Governor and Committee. 3 vols. E.E. Rich, ed. Toronto: The Champlain Society.

————
1948   Letters of Dr. John McLoughlin, Written at Fort Vancouver in 1829–32. Burt B. Barker, ed. Portland: Binfords and Mort for the Oregon Historical Society.

McMillan, Alan D.
1979   Archaeological Evidence for Aboriginal Tuna Fishing on Western Vancouver Island. *Syesis* 12:117–119. Victoria, B.C.

McMillan, Alan D., and Denis E. St. Claire
1982   Alberni Prehistory: Archaeological and Ethnographic Investigations on Western Vancouver Island. Penticton and Port Alberni: Theytus Books and Alberni Valley Museum.

MacMillan, James, and Archibald McDonald
1827–1830   [Fort Langley Journal, June 27, 1827–July 30, 1830.] (Typescript, transcribed by Winnifreda MacIntosh; in Provincial Archives of British Columbia, Victoria.)

McMurdo, John
1971   Salvage Excavations at the Canal Site, Pender Island. (Unpublished manuscript in Heritage Conservation Branch, Victoria, B.C.)

Macnair, Peter L.
1971   Descriptive Notes on the Kwakiutl Manufacture of Eulachon Oil. *Syesis* 4(1–2):169–177. Victoria, B.C.

————
1973–1974   Inheritance and Innovation: Northwest Coast Artists Today. *Artscanada* (December-January):182–189. Toronto.

————
1982   The Northwest Coast Collections: Legacy of a Living Culture. *Bulletin of the Field Museum of Natural History* 53(4):3–9. Chicago.

Macnair, Peter L., and Alan L. Hoover
1984   The Magic Leaves: A History of Haida Argillite Carving. *British Columbia Provincial Museum. Special Publication* 7. Victoria.

Macnair, Peter L., Alan L. Hoover, and Kevin Neary
1980   The Legacy: Continuing Traditions of Canadian Northwest Coast Indian Art. Victoria: British Columbia Provincial Museum. (Reprinted: University of Washington Press, Seattle, 1984.)

McNeary, Stephen A.
1976   Where Fire Came Down: Social and Economic Life of the Niska. (Unpublished Ph.D. Dissertation in Anthropology, Bryn Mawr College, Bryn Mawr, Pa.)

McNeil, R. William, and George N. Newton
1965   Cranial Base Morphology in Association with Intentional Cranial Vault Deformation. *American Journal of Physical Anthropology* 23(3):241–254.

McNeill, William
1862   [Fort Simpson Journal, Sept. 1859–Dec. 1862.] (Manuscript B.201/a in Hudson's Bay Company Archives, Provincial Archives of Manitoba, Winnipeg, Canada.)

McPhail, J.D., and C.C. Lindsey
1986   Zoogeography of the Freshwater Fishes of Cascadia (the Columbia System and Rivers North to the Stikine). Pp. 615–638 in The Zoogeography of North American Freshwater Fishes. Charles H. Hocutt, and E.O. Wiley, eds. New York: Wiley and Sons.

Majors, Harry M.
1980   The Hezeta and Bodega Voyage of 1775. *Northwest Discovery: The Journal of Northwest History and Natural History* 1(4):208–252. Seattle, Wash.

Makah Cultural and Research Center
1979   Makah Alphabet Book. Forks, Wash.: Olympic Graphic Arts.

Makah Language Program
1981–1986   Makah Public School Curriculum. (Curriculum on file, Makah Archives, Makah Cultural and Research Center, Neah Bay, Wash.)

Malaspina, Alessandro
1791   Appendix: Physical Description of the Coasts of Northwest America Visited by the Corvette. Pp. 198–235 in Politico-Scientific Voyages Around the World . . . .Carl Robinson, trans. (Typescript, at University of British Columbia Library, Vancouver.)

1885   Viaje político-científico alrededor del mundo por las corbetas Descubierta y Atrevida al mando de los capitanes de navío D. Alejandro Malaspina y Don José de Bustamante y Guerra desde 1789 á 1794. Madrid: Impr. de la viuda é hijos de Abienzo.

Malin, Edward
1978   A World of Faces: Masks of the Northwest Coast Indians. Portland, Oreg.: Timber Press.

1986   Totem Poles of the Pacific Northwest Coast. Portland, Oreg.: Timber Press.

Mallery, Garrick
1886   Pictographs of the North American Indians: A Preliminary Paper. Pp. 3–256 in *4th Annual Report of the Bureau of American Ethnology for the Years 1882–1883.* Washington.

Malloy, Mary
1986   Souvenirs of the Fur Trade, 1799–1832: The Northwest Coast Indian Collection of the Salem East Indian Marine Society. *American Indian Art Magazine* 11(4):30–35, 74.

Maranda, Lynn
1984   Coast Salish Gambling Games. *Canada. National Museum of Man. Mercury Series. Ethnology Service Papers* 93. Ottawa.

Marchand, Etienne *see* Fleurieu, Charles P.

Marr, Carolyn J.
1983   Washington Coastal Indian Villages, 1907: The Photographs of Albert Henry Barnes. *Pacific Northwest Quarterly* 74(3):106–113.

1984   Salish Baskets from the Wilkes Expedition. *American Indian Art Magazine* 9(3):44–51.

Marr, Carolyn J., Lloyd Colfax, and Robert D. Monroe
1987   Portrait in Time: Photographs of the Makah by Samuel G. Morse, 1896–1903. [Neah Bay, Wash.]: The Makah Cultural and Research Center in Cooperation with the Washington State Historical Society.

Marr, John P.
[1941]   [Aluminum Disc Recordings of Texts and Music in Galice Creek Athabaskan, from Hoxie Simmons, Siletz, Oreg.] (In John Peabody Harrington Papers, National Anthropological Archives, Smithsonian Institution, Washington.)

[1941a]   [Aluminum Disc Recordings of Vocabulary, Sentences, and Texts in Tututni (Rogue River) Athabaskan, from Lucy Smith, Siletz, Oreg.] (In John Peabody Harrington Papers, National Anthropological Archives, Smithsonian Institution, Washington.)

[1941b]   [Aluminum Disc Recordings of Vocabulary, Texts, and Music in Upper Coquille Athabaskan, from Coquille Thompson, Siletz, Oreg.] (In John Peabody Harrington Papers, National Anthropological Archives, Smithsonian Institution, Washington.)

Martin, Douglas D.
1969   Indian-White Relations on the Pacific Slope, 1850–1890. (Unpublished Ph.D. Dissertation in History, University of Washington, Seattle.)

Martin, Paul S., George I. Quimby, and Donald Collier
1947   Indians Before Columbus: Twenty Thousand Years of North American History Revealed by Archeology. Chicago: University of Chicago Press.

Masmith, Hugh
1970   Pleistocene Geology of the Queen Charlotte Islands and Southern British Columbia. Pp. 5–9 in Early Man and Environments in Northwest North America. R.A. Smith and J.W. Smith, eds. *Proceedings of the 2d Annual Paleo-Environmental Workshop of the University of Calgary.* Calgary, Alta.: Students' Press.

Mason, Otis T.
1875   Ethnological Directions Relative to the Indian Tribes of the United States. Prepared Under the Direction of the Indian Bureau. Washington: U.S. Government Printing Office.

1885   Throwing Sticks in the National Museum. Pp. 279–290 in *Report of the U.S. National Museum for 1884.* Washington.

1894   Summary of Progress in Anthropology. Pp. 601–629 in *Annual Report of the Smithsonian Institution for the Year 1893.* Washington.

1894a   Ethnological Exhibit of the Smithsonian Institution at the World's Columbian Exposition. Pp. 208–216 in Memoirs of the International Congress of Anthropology. C. Staniland Wake, ed. Chicago: Schulte Publishing Company.

1896   Influence of Environment Upon Human Industries or Arts. Pp. 639–665 in *Annual Report of the Smithsonian Institution for the Year 1895.* Washington.

1899   The Man's Knife Among the North American Indians: A Study in Collections of the U.S. National Museum. *Report of the U.S. National Museum for 1897.* Washington.

1901   [Letter of April 5 to W.H. Holmes.] (Accession No. 37889 in National Museum of Natural History, Smithsonian Institution, Washington.)

1904   Aboriginal American Basketry: Studies in a Textile Art without Machinery. *Annual Report of the U.S. National Museum for 1902,* Vol. 1:171–784; Vol. 2:1–248. Washington.

1907   Environment. Pp. 427–430 in Vol. 1 of Handbook of American Indians North of Mexico. Frederick W. Hodge, ed. 2 vols. *Bureau of American Ethnology Bulletin* 30. Washington.

Masson, Louis F.R., ed.
1889–1890   Les Bourgeois de la Compagnie du Nord-ouest. 2 vols. Quebec: A. Coté. (Reprinted: Antiquarian Press, New York, 1960.)

Matson, R.G.
1974   Clustering and Scaling of Gulf of Georgia Sites. *Syesis* 7:101–114. Victoria, B.C.

1976   The Glenrose Cannery Site. *Canada. National Museum of Man. Mercury Series. Archaeological Survey Papers* 52. Ottawa.

1981   Prehistoric Subsistence Patterns in the Fraser Delta: The Evidence from the Glenrose Cannery Site. Pp. 64–85 in Fragments of the Past: British Columbia Archaeology in the 1970s. Knut R. Fladmark, ed. *BC Studies* 48 (Winter).

1983   Intensification and the Development of Cultural Complexity: The Northwest versus the Northeast Coast. Pp. 125–148 in The Evolution of Maritime Cultures on the Northeast and the Northwest Coasts of America. Ronald J. Nash, ed. *Simon Fraser University. Department of Archaeology Publications* 11. Burnaby B.C.

1985   The Relationship Between Sedentism and Status Inequalities Among Hunter-gatherers. Pp. 245–252 in Status, Structure and Stratification: Current Archaeological Reconstructions. Marc Thompson, Maria Teresa Garcia, and François J. Kense, eds. Calgary, Alta.: Archaeological Association of the University of Calgary.

Matthews, Mark A.
1939   Independent Report on the Metlakahtla Case. Pp. 18541–19686 in Survey of Conditions of the Indians in the United States. Pt. 35: Metlakahtla Indians, Alaska. Hearings Before a Subcommittee of the Senate Committee on

Indian Affairs. Washington: U.S. Government Printing Office.

Mattison, David
1981   On the March: Indian Brass Bands, 1866–1915. *B.C. Historical News* 15(1):6–14.

Mattson, John L.
1971   A Contribution to Skagit Prehistory. (Unpublished M.A. Thesis in Anthropology, University of Washington, Seattle.)

Maud, Ralph, ed.
1978   The Salish People: The Local Contribution[s] of Charles Hill-Tout. 4 vols. Vancouver, B.C.: Talonbooks.

————
1982   A Guide to B.C. Indian Myth and Legend: A Short History of Myth-collecting and a Survey of Published Texts. Vancouver, B.C.: Talonbooks.

————
1989   The Henry Tate-Franz Boas Collaboration on Tsimshian Mythology. *American Ethnologist.* In press.

Mauger, Jeffrey E.
1978   Shed Roof Houses at the Ozette Archaeological Site: A Protohistoric Architectural System. *Washington State University. Archaeological Research Center Project Reports* 73. Pullman.
————, comp.
1979   Ozette Archaeological Project, Interim Final Report, Phase XI. Richard D. Daugherty, ed. *Washington State University. Archaeological Research Center Project Reports* 68. Pullman.

————
1982   Ozette Kerfed-corner Boxes. *American Indian Art Magazine* 8(1):72–79.

Mauss, Marcel
1967   The Gift; Forms and Functions of Exchange in Archaic Societies. Ian Cunnison, trans. New York: Norton.

Mauzé, Marie
1984   Enjeux et jeux du prestige des Kwagul méridionaux aux Lekwiltoq (côte nord-ouest du Pacifique). 2 vols. (Thèse pour le doctorat de troisième cycle, Ecole des Hautes Etudes en Sciences Sociales, Paris.)

May, Joyce
1979   Archaeological Investigations at GbTn:19, Ridley Island, a Shell Midden in the Prince Rupert Area. (Manuscript No. 1530, in Archaeological Survey of Canada Archives, Ottawa.)

Mayne, Richard C.
1860   [Letter to Capt. George Richards of H.M.S. Plumper, Dated 15 October 1860.] (In Provincial Archives of British Columbia, Victoria, GR 1372 [Colonial Correspondence], file 1217, microfilm No. B1349.)

————
1862   Four Years in British Columbia and Vancouver Island: An Account of Their Forests, Rivers, Coasts, Gold Fields and Resources for Colonisation. London: J. Murray. (Reprinted: Johnson Reprint Corporation, New York, 1969.)

Meacham, Alfred B.
1875   Wigwam and Warpath; or The Royal Chief in Chains. Boston: J.P. Dale.

Meade, Edward F.
1980   The Biography of Dr. Samuel Campbell, R.N., Surgeon & Surveyor. Including the Naming and History of the Campbell River. [Campbell River, B.C.: E.F. Meade.]

Meany, Edmond S., ed.
1914–1915   A New Vancouver Journal. *Washington Historical Quarterly* 5(2):129–137, (3):215–224, (4):300–308; 6(1):50–68. Seattle.

1925–1926   The Diary of Wilkes in the Northwest. *Washington Historical Quarterly* 16(1):49–61, (2):137–145, (3):206–223, (4):290–301; 17:(1)43–65, (2):129–144, (3):223–229. Seattle.

————
1927   History of the State of Washington. New York: Macmillan.

————
1942   Vancouver's Discovery of Puget Sound: Portraits and Biographies of the Men Honored in the Naming of Geographic Features of Northwestern America. Portland, Oreg.: Binfords and Mort. (Reprinted in 1957.)

Meares, John
1790   Voyages Made in the Years 1788 and 1789 from China to the North West Coast of America: With an Introductory Narrative of a Voyage Performed in 1786, from Bengal, in the Ship Nootka. 2 vols. London: Logographic Press. (Reprinted: Da Capo Press, New York, 1967.)

Meeker, Ezra
1905   Pioneer Reminiscences of Puget Sound: The Tragedy of Leschi. Seattle: Lowman and Hanford.

Meighan, Clement W., ed.
1956   Notes and News. *American Antiquity* 21(4):440–452.

Meilleur, Brien A.
1979   Speculations on the Diffusion of *Nicotiana quadrivalvis* Pursh to the Queen Charlotte Islands and Adjacent Alaskan Mainland. *Syesis* 12:101–104. Victoria, B.C.

Melina, Lois
1986   Politicos, Indians and the Press [The Stevens-Wool Controversy]. Pp. 123–136 in Indians, Superintendents, and Councils: Northwestern Indian Policy, 1850–1855. Clifford E. Trafzer, ed. Lanham, Md.: University Press of America.

Menzies, [Sir] Archibald
1793   [Journal.] (Microfilm No. 27 in Suzzallo Library, University of Washington, Seattle.)

————
[1795]   Memorandum to Banks, Listing Curiosities and Artifacts Brought Home on the *Discovery* from Tahiti, the Sandwich Islands, Nootka, Cross Island, New Georgia, Port Trinidad, and Cook's Inlet. (Manuscript in Sutro Library, San Francisco.)

————
1923   Menzies' Journal of Vancouver's Voyage, April to October, 1792. C.F. Newcombe, ed. *Archives of British Columbia. Memoirs* 5. Victoria.

Merbs, Charles F.
1974   The Effects of Cranial and Caudal Shift in the Vertebral Columns of Northern Populations. *Arctic Anthropology* 11(Supplement):12–19.

Merk, Frederick, ed.
1968   Fur Trade and Empire: George Simpson's Journal . . . 1824–25. Rev. ed. Cambridge, Mass.: Belknap Press of Harvard University Press.

Metcalf, Leon V.
[1951]   [Tape Recording of Texts and Vocabulary in Tillamook Salish, from Mrs. Mabel Adams Burns, Portland, Oreg.] (In Ethnology Archives, Thomas Burke Memorial Washington State Museum. University of Washington, Seattle.)

————
[1955]   [Tape Recording of Galice Creek Athabaskan Music from Hoxie Simmons at Siletz, Oreg.] (In Anthropology Archives, Thomas Burke Memorial Washington State Museum, University of Washington, Seattle.)

Metcalfe, Robert B.
1857   [Census of Sept. 22.] (Manuscript, miscellaneous loose papers, 1850–1873, microcopy 2, roll 30, Records of the Oregon Superintendency, in Record Group 75, National Archives, Washington.)

Methodist Church
1895   Seventy-first Annual Report of the Missionary Society of the Methodist Church. Toronto: Methodist Mission Rooms.

Michie, Peter S.
1901   General McClellan. New York: D. Appleton.

Miles, Don
1972   The Burke Site, 45SN10: A Report of Preliminary Investigations of a Site on the Pilchuck River Above Snohomish, Washington. *Washington Archaeologist* 26(2):1–8.

Milhau, John J.
1856   [Vocabulary of "Umpqua Valley (Proper).")] (Manuscript No. 193-a in National Anthropological Archives, Smithsonian Institution, Washington.)

――――   1856a   ["Alseya and Ya-ko-ner" Vocabulary.] (Manuscript No. 955-a in National Anthropological Archives, Smithsonian Institution, Washington.)

――――   1856b   ["Coose Bay" Language Vocabulary of Two Different Dialects of the Same Language (An-a-stich and Coòs Bay).] ([Part of] Manuscript No. 191-a in National Anthropological Archives, Smithsonian Institution, Washington.)

――――   1856c   Kalawataet or Lower Umpqua Vocabulary. (Manuscript No. 958 in National Anthropological Archives, Smithsonian Institution, Washington.)

――――   1856d   [Letter to George Gibbs, with Short Vocabularies of the Alsea, Siuslaw, Hanis, and Miluk Languages.] ([Part of] Manuscript No. 191-a, in National Anthropological Archives, Smithsonian Institution, Washington.)

Miller, Alan C.
1976   Photographer of a Frontier: The Photographs of Peter Britt. Eureka, Calif.: Interface California.

Miller, Beatrice D.
1952   The Makah in Transition. *Pacific Northwest Quarterly* 43(4):262–272.

Miller, David H.
1981   The Alaska Treaty [1944]. (*Alaska History* 18) Kingston, Ont.: The Limestone Press.

Miller, Floyd E.
1975   The Benjamin Sites (35 LA 41, 42). Pp. 309–347 in Archaeological Studies in the Willamette Valley, Oregon. C. Melvin Aikens, ed. *University of Oregon Anthropological Papers* 8. Eugene.

Miller, Jay
1988   Shamanic Odyssey: The Lushootseed Salish Journey to the Land of the Dead. *Ballena Press Anthropological Papers* 32. Menlo Park, Calif.

Miller, Jay, and Carol M. Eastman, eds.
1984   The Tsimshian and Their Neighbors of the North Pacific Coast. Seattle: University of Washington Press.

Miller, John F.
1857   Census of Indians at the Grand Ronde Reservation, Oregon Territory. (Manuscript 1856-244, microcopy 2, roll 14, Records of the Oregon Superintendency, in Record Group 75, National Archives, Washington.)

Miller, Polly
[1967] Lost Heritage of Alaska: The Adventure and Art of the Alaskan Coastal Indians. Graphics by Leon G. Miller. Cleveland, Ohio: World.

Mills, Elaine L., ed.
1981   The Papers of John Peabody Harrington in the Smithsonian Institution, 1907–1957. Vol. 1: A Guide to the Field Notes; Native American History, Language and Culture of Alaska/Northwest Coast. Millwood, N.Y.: Kraus International Publications.

Minckley, W.L., Dean A. Hendrickson, and Carl E. Bond
1986   Geography of Western North American Freshwater Fishes: Description and Relationships to Intracontinental Tectonism. Pp. 519–614 in The Zoogeography of North American Freshwater Fishes. Charles H. Hocutt and E.O. Wiley, eds., New York: John Wiley and Sons.

Miner, H. Craig
1972   The United States Government Building at the Centennial Exhibition, 1874–1877. *Prologue: The Journal of the National Archives* 4(4):202–218. Washington.

Minor, Rick
1978   Archaeological Testing at the Skamokawa Site (45-WK-5), Wahkiakum County, Washington. *University of Washington. Office of Public Archaeology. Reconnaissance Reports* 19. Seattle.

――――   1980   Further Archaeological Testing at the Skamokawa Site (45-WK-5), Wahkiakum County, Washington. *University of Washington. Office of Public Archaeology. Reconnaissance Reports* 36. Seattle.

――――   1983   Aboriginal Settlement and Subsistence at the Mouth of the Columbia River. (Unpublished Ph.D. Dissertation in Anthropology, University of Oregon, Eugene.)

――――   1984   An Early Complex at the Mouth of the Columbia River. *Northwest Anthropological Research Notes* 18(1):1–22. Moscow, Idaho.

――――   1985   Paleo-Indians in Western Oregon: A Description of Two Fluted Projectile Points. *Northwest Anthropological Research Notes* 19(1):33–40. Moscow, Idaho.

Minor, Rick, and Christine Pickett
1982   Botanical Remains from the Halverson Site, Upper Willamette Valley, Oregon. *Tebiwa: Journal of the Idaho Museum of Natural History* 19(1):15–25. Pocatello.

Minor, Rick, and Kathryn Anne Toepel
1982   The Halverson Site: A Late Prehistoric Campsite in the Upper Willamette Valley, Oregon. *Tebiwa: Journal of the Idaho Museum of Natural History* 19(1):1–14. Pocatello.

――――   1982a   An Archaeological Evaluation of the Tidbits Site (35LIN100), Linn County, Oregon. *Heritage Research Associates Reports* 14. Eugene.

――――   1983   Patterns of Aboriginal Land Use in the Southern Oregon Coastal Region. Pp. 225–253 in Prehistoric Places on the Southern Northwest Coast. Robert E. Greengo, ed. Seattle: University of Washington, Washington State Museum.

Minor, Rick, Stephen D. Beckham, and Ruth L. Greenspan
1980   Archaeology and History of the Port Orford Locality: Investigations at the Blundon Site (35 CU106) and Historic Port Orford. (Report to the State Historical Preservation Office) Salem: Oregon State Department of Transportation.

Minor, Rick, Stephen D. Beckham, Phyllis E. Lancefield-Steeves, and Kathryn Anne Toepel
1980   Cultural Resource Overview of the BLM Salem District, Northwestern Oregon: Archaeology, Ethnography, History. *University of Oregon Anthropological Papers* 20. Eugene.

Minto, John
1900   The Number and Condition of the Native Race in Oregon When First Seen by White Men. *Oregon Historical Quarterly* 1(3):296–315.

Mishra, Sheila
1975   Archaeological Survey in the Kitimat Area. (Report on file, British Columbia Heritage Conservation Branch, Victoria.)

Mitchell, Donald H.
1963   Esilao: A Pithouse Village in the Fraser Canyon. (Unpublished M.A. Thesis in Anthropology, University of British Columbia, Vancouver.)

1968   Excavations at Two Trench Embankments in the Gulf of Georgia Region. *Syesis* 1(1–2):29–46. Victoria, B.C.

1969   Site Survey in the Johnston Strait Region. Pp. 193–216 in Current Archaeological Research on the Northwest Coast - Symposium, by George F. MacDonald, et al. *Northwest Anthropological Research Notes* 3(2):193–263. Moscow, Idaho.

1971   Archaeology of the Gulf of Georgia Area, a Natural Region and Its Culture Types. *Syesis* 4(Supp. 1). Victoria, B.C.

1972   Artifacts from Archaeological Surveys in the Johnstone Strait Region. *Syesis* 5:21–42. Victoria, B.C.

1979   Excavations at the Hopetown Village Site (EfSq 2) in the Knight Inlet Area of British Columbia. Pp. 87–99 in *Annual Report for the Year 1976: Activities of the Provincial Archaeologists Office of British Columbia and Selected Research Reports*. Victoria, B.C.

1980   DcRt 1: A Salvaged Excavation from Southern Vancouver Island. *Syesis* 13:37–51. Victoria, B.C.

1981   Sebassa's Men. Pp. 79–86 in The World Is As Sharp As a Knife: An Anthology in Honour of Wilson Duff. Donald N. Abbott, ed. Victoria: British Columbia Provincial Museum.

1981a   DcRu 78: A Prehistoric Occupation of Fort Rodd Hill National Historic Park. *Syesis* 14:131–150. Victoria, B.C.

1981b   Test Excavations at Randomly Selected Sites in Eastern Queen Charlotte Strait. Pp. 103–123 in Fragments of the Past: British Columbia Archaeology in the 1970s. Knut R. Fladmark, ed. *BC Studies* 48 (Winter). Vancouver.

1983   Seasonal Settlements, Village Aggregations and Political Autonomy on the Central Northwest Coast. Pp. 97–107 in The Development of Political Organization in Native North America. Elisabeth Tooker, ed. *Proceedings of the American Ethnological Society*. Washington, 1979.

1983a   Tribes and Chiefdoms of the Northwest Coast: The Tsimshian Case. Pp. 57–64 in The Evolution of Maritime Cultures on the Northeast and Northwest Coasts of America. Ronald J. Nash, ed. *Simon Fraser University, Department of Archaeology Publications* 11. Burnaby, B.C.

1984   Predatory Warfare, Social Status, and the North Pacific Slave Trade. *Ethnology* 23(1):39–48.

1985   The Baynes Sound Sequence in Gulf of Georgia Prehistory. (Manuscript in Mitchell's possession.)

1985a   Hopetown Village and a Southern Kwakiutl Area Archaeological Sequence. (Manuscript in Mitchell's possession.)

1985b   A Demographic Profile of Northwest Coast Slavery. Pp. 227–236 in Status, Structure and Stratification: Current Archaeological Reconstructions. Marc Thompson, Maria T. Garcia, and François J. Kense, eds. Calgary, Alta.: University of Calgary.

Mitchell, Donald, and Leland Donald
1985   Some Economic Aspects of Tlingit, Haida, and Tsimshian Slavery. Barry L. Isaac, ed. *Research in Economic Anthropology* 7:19–35. Greenwich, Conn.

Mitchell, Marjorie R.
1968   A Dictionary of Songish, a Dialect of Straits Salish. (Unpublished M.A. Thesis in Linguistics, University of Victoria, Victoria, B.C.)

1976   Women, Poverty, and Housing: Some Consequences of Hinterland Status for a Coast Salish Indian Reserve in Metropolitan Canada. (Unpublished Ph.D. Dissertation in Anthropology, University of British Columbia, Vancouver.)

Mobley, Charles M.
1984   An Archaeological Survey of 15 Timber Harvest Units at Naukati Bay on Prince of Wales Island, Tongass National Forest, Alaska. (Report, at U.S. Forest Service, Ketchikan, Alaska.)

Mochanov, Yu. A.
1976   Paleolit Sibiri. [The Palaeolithic of Siberia.] Pp. 540–565 in Beringiĩa v Kaĩnozoe [Beringia in the Cenozoic]. V.L. Kontrimavichus, ed. Vladivostok: Academy of Sciences of the USSR, Far-Eastern Scientific Centre. (English ed.: Beringia in the Cenozoic Era, Oxonian Press, New Delhi, 1984.)

1984   Paleolithic Finds in Siberia (Resume of Studies). Pp. 694–724 in Beringia in the Cenozoic Era. V.L. Kontrimavichus, ed. New Delhi: Oxoniau Press.

Mochon, Marion Johnson
1966   Masks of the Northwest Coast: The Samuel A. Barrett Collection. Robert Ritzenhaler and Lee A. Parsons, eds. *Milwaukee Public Museum. Publications in Primitive Art* 2. Milwaukee, Wis.

Moeller, Beverly B.
1966   Captain James Colnett and the Tsimshian Indians, 1787. *Pacific Northwest Quarterly* 57(1):13–17.

Moeran, J.W.W.
1923   McCullagh of Aiyansh. London: Marshall Brothers.

Mohs, Gordon
1987   Spiritual Sites, Ethnic Significance, and Native Spirituality: The Heritage and Heritage Sites of the Sto:lo Indians of British Columbia. (Unpublished M.A. Thesis in Archaeology, Simon Fraser University, Burnaby, B.C.)

Møller-Christensen, Vilhelm, and R.G. Inkster
1965   Cases of Leprosy and Syphilis in the Osteological Collection of the Department of Anatomy, University of Edinburgh. *Danish Medical Bulletin* 12(1):11–18.

Monks, Gregory G.
1973   Interrelationships of Artifact Classes from the Gulf of Georgia Area. (Unpublished M.A. Thesis in Anthropology, University of Victoria, Victoria, B.C.)

1976   Quantitative Comparison of the Glenrose Components with the Marpole Component from DhRt 3. Pp. 267–280 in The Glenrose Cannery Site. R.G. Matson, ed. *Canada. National Museum of Man. Mercury Series. Archaeological Survey Papers* 52. Ottawa.

1977   An Examination of Relationships Between Artifact Classes and Food Resource Remains at Deep Bay, DiSe 7. (Unpublished Ph.D. Dissertation in Anthropology, University of British Columbia, Vancouver.)

1980   Saltery Bay: A Mainland Archaeological Site in the Northern Strait of Georgia. *Syesis* 13:109–136. Victoria, B.C.

Montler, Timothy R.
1986   An Outline of the Morphology and Phonology of Saanich, North Straits Salish. Rev. ed. *University of Montana. Occasional Papers in Linguistics* 4. Missoula.

Mooney, James
1896   The Ghost-dance Religion and the Sioux Outbreak of 1890. Pp. 641–1136 in Pt. 2 of *14th Annual Report of the Bureau of American Ethnology for the Years 1892–1893*. Washington.

1928   The Aboriginal Population of America North of Mexico. *Smithsonian Miscellaneous Collections* 80(7). Washington.

Mooney, Kathleen
1976   Social Distance and Exchange: The Coast Salish Case. *Ethnology* 15(4):323–346.

———
1978   The Effects of Rank and Wealth on Exchange Among the Coast Salish. *Ethnology* 17(4):391–406.

Moore, Turrall A.
1977   The Emergence of Ethnic Roles and the Beginning of Nootkan Native-overseas European Relations. (Unpublished Ph.D. Dissertation in Anthropology, University of Oregon, Eugene.)

Moret, A., and G. Davy
1926   From Tribe to Empire: Social Organization Among Primitives and in the Ancient East. V.G. Childe, trans. New York: A.A. Knopf. (Reprinted: Cooper Square, New York, 1970.)

Morgan, Dale L.
1953   Jedediah Smith and the Opening of the West. New York: Bobbs-Merrill. (Reprinted: University of Nebraska Press, Lincoln, 1969.)

Morgan, Dale L., and George P. Hammond, eds.
1963   A Guide to the Manuscript Collections of the Bancroft Library. Vol. 1: Pacific and Western Manuscripts. Berkeley: University of California Press.

Morgan, R. Christopher
1981   The Economic Basis of Nootka Polities. *Canberra Anthropology* 4(2):29–44. Canberra, Australia.

Morice, Adrian G.
1910   The History of the Catholic Church in Western Canada, from Lake Superior to the Pacific. Toronto: Musson.

Morris, William G.
1879   Report Upon the Customs District, Public Service, and Resources of Alaska Territory. *45th Congress, 3d Sess. Senate Executive Document* No. 59. (Serial No. 1831) Washington. (Reprinted: Pp. 1–163 in Vol. 4 of Seal and Salmon Fisheries and General Resources of Alaska, *55th Congress, 1st Sess. House Document* No. 92, Washington, 1898.)

Morrison, Samuel E.
1927   New England and the Opening of the Columbia River Salmon Trade, 1830. *Oregon Historical Quarterly* 28(2):111–132.

Morse, Jedidiah
1822   A Report to the Secretary of War of the United States, on Indian Affairs, Comprising a Narrative of a Tour Performed in the Summer of 1820. New Haven, Conn.: S. Converse. (Reprinted: Augustus M. Kelly, New York, 1970; Scholarly Press, St. Clair Shores, Mich., 1972.)

Moser, Charles
1926   Reminiscences of the West Coast of Vancouver Island, by Rev. C. Moser, O.S.B., Kakawis, B.C. Victoria, B.C.: Acme Press.

Moss, Madonna L., and Jon M. Erlondson
1985   [Preliminary Results of Archaeological Investigations on Admiralty Island, Southeast Alaska: 1985 Field Season.] (Unpublished report, on file at the U.S. Forest Service, Admiralty Monument, Juneau, Alas.)

Moulton, Gary E.
1983   Atlas of the Lewis and Clark Expedition. (*The Journals of the Lewis and Clark Expedition*, 1) Lincoln: University of Nebraska Press.

Mourant, Arthur E.
1954   The Distribution of the Human Blood Groups. Oxford, England: Blackwell Scientific Publications.

Moziño Suárez de Figueroa *see* Moziño, José Mariano

Moziño, José Mariano
1970   Noticias de Nutka: An Account of Nootka Sound in 1792. Iris H. Wilson, ed. (*American Ethnological Society Monographs* 50) Seattle: University of Washington Press.

Muir, John
1915   Travels in Alaska. Boston: Houghton Mifflin. (Reprinted in 1979.)

Müller, Werner
1955   Weltbild und Kult der Kwakiutl-Indianer. (*Studien zur Kulturkunde* 15) Wiesbaden, Germany: Franz Steiner Verlag.

Munger, Thornton T.
1940   The Cycle from Douglas Fir to Hemlock. *Ecology* 21(4):451–459.

Munnick, Harriet Duncan, and Stephen D. Beckham, eds.
1987   Catholic Church Records of the Pacific Northwest: Grand Ronde Register I (1860–1885), Grand Ronde Register II (1886–1898), St. Michael the Archangel Parish, Grand Ronde Indian Reservation. Vol. 6. Portland, Oreg.: Binfords and Mort.

Munro, J.A., and I. McT. Cowan
1947   A Review of the Bird Fauna of British Columbia. *British Columbia Provincial Museum. Special Publication* 2. Victoria.

Munsell, David A.
1970   The Wapato Creek Fish Weir Site, 45PI47, Tacoma, Washington. Seattle: U.S. Army Corps of Engineers, Seattle District.

———
1976   Excavation of the Conway Wet Site, 45SK596 Conway, Washington. Pp. 86–121 in The Excavation of Water-saturated Archaeological Sites (Wet Sites) on the Northwest Coast of North America. Dale R. Croes, ed. *Canada. National Museum of Man. Mercury Series. Archaeological Survey Papers* 50. Ottawa.

Murdock, George P.
1934   Kinship and Social Behavior Among the Haida. *American Anthropologist* 36(3):355–385.

———
1934a   The Haidas of British Columbia. Pp. 221–263 in Our Primitive Contemporaries. George P. Murdock, ed. New York: MacMillan.

———
1936   Rank and Potlatch Among the Haida. *Yale University Publications in Anthropology* 13:1–20. New Haven, Conn. (Reprinted: Pp. 262–289 in Culture and Society: Twenty-Four Essays, by G.P. Murdock, University of Pittsburgh Press, Pittsburgh, 1965.)

———
1949   Social Structure. New York: Macmillan.

———
1955   North American Social Organization. *Davidson Journal of Anthropology* 1(2):85–95. Seattle.

Murdock, George P., and Timothy J. O'Leary
1975   Ethnographic Bibliography of North America. 4th ed. 5 vols. New Haven, Conn.: Human Relations Area Files Press.

Murdy, Carson N., and Walter J. Wentz
1975   Artifacts from the Fanning Mound, Willamette Valley, Oregon. Pp. 349–374 in Archaeological Studies in the Willamette Valley, Oregon. C. Melvin Aikens, ed. *University of Oregon Anthropological Papers* 8. Eugene.

Murray, Jeffrey S.
1981   Prehistoric Skeletons from Blue Jackets Creek (F1Ua 4), Queen Charlotte Islands, British Columbia. Pp. 127–175 in Contributions to Physical Anthropology, 1978–1980. J.S. Cybulski, ed., *Canada. National Museum of Man. Mercury Series. Archaeological Survey Papers* 106. Ottawa.

711

Murray, Peter
1985   The Devil and Mr. Duncan. Victoria, B.C.: Sono Nis Press.

Museum of New Mexico
1977   The Malaspina Expedition: "In the Pursuit of Knowledge . . . ." Santa Fe: University of New Mexico Press.

Nabokov, Peter, and Robert Easton
1989   Native American Architecture. New York: Oxford University Press.

Naish, Constance M.
1966   A Syntactic Study of Tlingit. (Unpublished M.A. Thesis in Linguistics, University of London, London.)

Naish, Constance, and Gillian Story
1963   English-Tlingit Dictionary: Nouns. Fairbanks, Alas.: Summer Institute of Linguistics.

Nalty, Bernard C., and Truman R. Strobridge
1964   The Defense of Seattle, 1856: "And Down Came the Indians." *Pacific Northwest Quarterly* 55(3):105–110.

Nash, Ronald J., ed.
1983   The Evolution of Maritime Cultures on the Northwest and the Northeast Coasts of America. *Simon Fraser University. Department of Archaeology Publications* 11. Burnaby, B.C.

Nash, Wallis
1878   Oregon: There and Back in 1877. London: Macmillan. (Reprinted: Oregon State University Press, Corvallis, 1976.)

National Anthropological Archives
1975   Catalog to Manuscripts at the National Anthropological Archives, Department of Anthropology, National Museum of Natural History, Smithsonian Institution, Washington. 4 vols. Boston: G.K. Hall.

Neandross, Sigurd
1910   The Work on the Ceremonial Canoe. *American Museum Journal* 10(8):238–243.

Nelson, J.G.
1962   Drift Voyages Between Eastern Asia and the Americas. *Canadian Geographer* 6(2):54–59.

Nelson, Charles G.
1959   Occurrences of Graphite in Washington. *Washington Archaeologist* 3(10):5–8.

Nelson, Charles M.
1962   The Washington Archaeological Society's Work at 45IS316. *Washington Archaeologist* 6(2):2–15.

1962a   Stone Artifacts from SN100. *Washington Archaeologist* 6(4):2–41.

1969   The Sunset Creek Site (45KT28) and Its Place in Plateau Prehistory. *Washington State University. Laboratory of Anthropology. Reports of Investigations* 47. Pullman.

1976   The Radiocarbon Age of the Biderbost Site (45SN100) and Its Interpretive Significance for the Prehistory of the Puget Sound Basin. *Washington Archaeologist* 20(1):1–17.

Nelson, D.E., J.M. D'Auria, and R.B. Bennett
1975   Characterization of Pacific Northwest Coast Obsidian by X-ray Fluorescence Analysis. *Archaeometry* 17(1):85–97. Oxford, England.

Nelson, D.E., R.G. Korteling, and W.R. Stott
1977   Carbon-14: Direct Detection at Natural Concentrations. *Science* 198(4316):507–508.

Nelson, D.E., J.S. Vogel, and J.R. Southon
1985   Radiocarbon Measurements for DeRt 1 and DeRt 2. In The 1984 Excavations at the Canal Site. (Unpublished manuscript at Archaeology Department, Simon Fraser University, Burnaby, B.C.)

Nesbitt, James K.
1954   Potlatch in the Park. *The Beaver*, Outfit 284 (March):8–11. Winnipeg.

Nesbitt, Paul E.
1969   The Cofchin Ranch Site. *Washington Archaeologist* 13(1):2–14.

Newcombe, Charles F.
1906   [Letter to George Dorsey, Dated November 5, 1906.] (On file at the Field Museum of Natural History, Chicago.)

1909   Guide to the Anthropological Collection in the Provincial Museum. Victoria, B.C.: Richard Wolfenden.

1912   [Interior of House at Mimquimimlees Village Island, B.C.] (In notebook 24-a, on file at Provincial Museum, Victoria, B.C.)

1914   Report [and] List of Specimens Collected, 1913. Pp. G23–G27 in *British Columbia Provincial Museum. Report for the Year 1913*. Victoria.

1915   Report [and] List of Specimens Collected, 1914. Pp. F33–F34, F36-Plates 1–10 in *British Columbia Provincial Museum. Report for the Year 1914*. Victoria.

Newman, Barnett
1946   Northwest Coast Indian Painting. New York: Betty Parsons Gallery.

1947   The Ideographic Picture Show. New York: Betty Parsons Gallery.

Newman, Marshall T.
1976   Aboriginal New World Epidemiology and Medical Care, and the Impact of Old World Disease Imports. *American Journal of Physical Anthropology* 45(3):667–672.

Newman, Philip L.
1957   An Intergroup Collectivity Among the Nootka. (Unpublished M.A. Thesis in Anthropology, University of Washington, Seattle.)

Newman, Stanley
1947   Bella Coola I: Phonology. *International Journal of American Linguistics* 13(3):129–134.

1969   Bella Coola Paradigms. *International Journal of American Linguistics* 35(4):299–306.

1969a   Bella Coola Grammatical Processes and Form Classes. *International Journal of American Linguistics* 35(2):175–179.

1971   Bella Coola Reduplication. *International Journal of American Linguistics* 37(1):34–38.

1976   Salish and Bella Coola Prefixes. *International Journal of American Linguistics* 42(3)228–242.

1979   A History of the Salish Possessive and Subject Forms. *International Journal of American Linguistics* 45(3):207–223.

1979a   The Salish Object Forms. *International Journal of American Linguistics* 45(4):299–308.

1980   Functional Changes in the Salish Pronominal System. *International Journal of American Linguistics* 46(3):155–167.

Newman, Thomas M.
1959   Tillamook Prehistory and Its Relation to the Northwest Coast Culture Area. (Unpublished Ph.D. Dissertation in Anthropology, University of Oregon, Eugene.)

1966   Cascadia Cave. *Occasional Papers of the Idaho State University Museum* 18. Pocatello.

Newman, Thomas S.
1959   Toleak Point: An Archaeological Site on the North Central Washington Coast. *Washington State University. Laboratory of Anthropology. Reports of Investigation* 4. Pullman.

Niatum, Duane, ed.
[1975]   Carriers of the Dream Wheel: Contemporary Native American Poetry. New York: Harper and Row.

1981   Songs for the Harvester of Dreams. Seattle: University of Washington Press.

Niblack, Albert P.
1890   The Coast Indians of Southern Alaska and Northern British Columbia. Pp. 225–386 in *Annual Report of the U.S. National Museum for 1888.* Washington.

Nicolay, Charles G.
1846   The Oregon Territory: A Geographical and Physical Account of That Country and Its Inhabitants, with Outlines of Its History and Discovery. London: Charles Knight.

Nicolaye, Joseph
[1890]   Dictionary of the "West Coast Language." (Manuscript in the Archives of the Diocese of Victoria, B.C.)

Nordquist, Delmar
1960   Open Plaited Basketry from 45SN100. *Washington Archaeologist* 4(11):2–5.

1960a   Basketry from Site 45SN100: General Comments. *Washington Archaeologist* 4(9):2–6.

1961   The Fishing Hook as Found in 45SN100. *Washington Archaeologist* 5(3):10–17.

1961a   Bound Net Weights from 45SN100. *Washington Archaeologist* 5(1):3–6.

1961b   A Fish Weir Fragment from 45SN100. *Washington Archaeologist* 5(8–9):6–9.

Northwest Indian Fisheries Commission [et al.]
1977   Tribal Report to the Presidential Task Force on Treaty Fishing Rights in the Northwest [Comprising Reports Prepared by the Five Inter-tribal Treaty Councils]. [Olympia, Wash.: Northwest Indian Fisheries Commission.]

1980   Treaty Fishing Rights and the Northwest Indian Fisheries Commission. Olympia, Wash.: The Commission.

1986   What Is Cooperative Management? Olympia, Wash.: Northwest Indian Fisheries Commission.

Norton, Helen H.
1979   The Association Between Anthropogenic Prairies and Important Food Plants in Western Washington. *Northwest Anthropological Research Notes* 13(2):175–200. Moscow, Idaho.

1979a   Evidence for Bracken Fern as a Food for Aboriginal Peoples of Western Washington. *Economic Botany* 33(4):384–396.

1981   Plant Use in Kaigani Haida Culture: Correction of an Ethnohistorical Oversight. *Economic Botany* 35(4):434–449.

1985   Women and Resources of the Northwest Coast: Documentation from the 18th and Early 19th Centuries. (Unpublished Ph.D. Dissertation in Anthropology, University of Washington, Seattle.)

Norton, Helen H., E.S. Hunn, C.S. Martinsen, and P.B. Keely
1984   Vegetable Food Products of the Foraging Economies of the Pacific Northwest. *Ecology of Food and Nutrition* 14(3):219–228.

Novo y Colson, Pedro de *see* Malaspina, Alessandro

Nussbaum, Ronald A., Edmund D. Brodie, Jr., and Robert M. Storm
1983   Amphibians and Reptiles of the Pacific Northwest. Moscow: University Press of Idaho.

Nuxalk Food and Nutrition Program
1984   Nuxalk Food and Nutrition Handbook: A Practical Guide to Family Foods and Nutrition Using Native Foods. Bella Coola, B.C.: Nuxalk Food and Nutrition Program.

Nuytten, Phil
1982   The Totem Carvers: Charlie James, Ellen Neel, and Mungo Martin. Vancouver, B.C.: Panorama Publications.

Ober, Sarah Endicott
1910   A New Religion Among the West Coast Indians. *Overland Monthly* 56(6):583–594. San Francisco.

Oberg, Kalervo
1934   Crime and Punishment in Tlingit Society. *American Anthropologist* 36(2):145–156.

1973   The Social Economy of the Tlingit Indians. (*American Ethnological Society Monographs* 55) Seattle: University of Washington Press.

Oetteking, Bruno
1917   Preliminary Remarks on the Skeletal Material Collected by the Jesup Expedition. Pp. 621–624 in *Proceedings of the 19th International Congress of Americanists.* Washington, 1915.

1924   Declination of the Pars Basilaris in Normal and Artifically Deformed Skulls. *Museum of the American Indian. Heye Foundation. Indian Notes and Monographs* 21. New York.

1928   Craniology of the Northwest Coast of North America. Pp. 421–425 in Vol. 1 of *Proceedings of the 22d International Congress of Americanists.* 2 vols. Rome, 1926.

1928a   On Morphological Changes in Artificially Deformed Skulls from the North Pacific Coast. Pp. 25–95 in Vol. 2 of *Proceedings of the 20th International Congress of Americanists.* 2 vols. Rio de Janeiro, 1922.

1930   Craniology of the North Pacific Coast. *Publications of the Jesup North Pacific Expedition* 11(1); *Memoirs of the American Museum of Natural History* 15(1). New York. (Reprinted: AMS Press, New York, 1975.)

Office of Indian Affairs
1899   Statistics of Indian Tribes, Indian Agencies, and Indian Schools of Every Character. Washington: U.S. Government Printing Office.

Ogden, Peter Skene
1933   Traits of American Indian Life and Character [1853]. San Francisco: Grabhorn Press. (Reprinted: AMS Press, New York, 1972.)

Okuń, Semen Benťsionovich
1951   The Russian-American Company. D.B. Grekov, ed. Carl Ginsburg, trans. (*Russian Translation Project Series of the American Council of Learned Societies* 9) Cambridge, Mass.: Harvard University Press.

Olsen, Thomas A.
1975   Baby Rock Shelter. Pp. 469–494 in Archaeological Studies in the Willamette Valley, Oregon. C. Melvin Aikens, ed. *University of Oregon Anthropological Papers* 8. Eugene.

Olson, Ronald L.
1927   Adze, Canoe, and House Types of the Northwest Coast. *University of Washington Publications in Anthropology* 2(1). Seattle.

1929   The Possible Middle American Origin of Northwest Coast Weaving. *American Anthropologist* 31(1):114–121.

713

1933   Clan and Moiety in Native America. *University of California Publications in American Archaeology and Ethnology* 33(4):351–421. Berkeley.

1936   The Quinault Indians. *University of Washington Publications in Anthropology* 6(1):1–190. Seattle.

1936a   Some Trading Customs of the Chilkat Tlingit. Pp. 211–214 in Essays in Anthropology Presented to A.L. Kroeber. Robert L. Lowie, ed. Berkeley: University of California Press.

1940   The Social Organization of the Haisla of British Columbia. *University of California Anthropological Records* 2(5):169–200. Berkeley.

1954   Social Life of the Owikeno Kwakiutl. *University of California Anthropological Records* 14(3):213–259. Berkeley.

1955   Notes on the Bella Bella Kwakiutl. *University of California Anthropological Records* 14(5):319–348. Berkeley.

1956   Channeling of Character in Tlingit Society. Pp. 675–687 in Personal Character and Cultural Milieu: A Collection of Readings. Douglas G. Haring, ed. Syracuse, N.Y.: Syracuse University Press.

1967   Social Structure and Social Life of the Tlingit in Alaska. *University of California Anthropological Records* 26. Berkeley.

Olson, Wallace M.
1983   Tlingit Government in Context. (Paper presented at the Annual Meeting of the Alaska Historical Society in Sitka, November 1983.)

Oman, Mary, and Mike Reagan
1971   Archaeology of Phase II, Little Muddy Creek, Oregon. Corvallis: Oregon State University, Department of Anthropology.

Onat, Astrida R., and Lee A. Bennett
1968   Tokul Creek: A Report on Excavations on the Snoqualmie River by the Seattle Community College. *Occasional Papers of the Washington Archaeological Society* 1. Seattle.

O'Neill, Bryan L.
1987   Archaeological Reconnaissance and Testing in the Noti-Veneta Section of the Florence-Eugene Highway, Lane County, Oregon. (A Report to the Oregon State Highway Division). *University of Oregon. Oregon State Museum of Anthropology [Report]* 87-6. Eugene.

Orans, Martin
1975   Domesticating the Functionalist Dragon: An Analysis of Piddocke's Potlatch. *American Anthropologist* 77(2):312–328.

Orchard, Imbert
1965   [Interview with Clarence Joe, Sechelt, B.C.] (Tape 960:1–2 in Provincial Archives of British Columbia, Sound and Moving Images Division, Victoria.)

Orchard, William C.
1926   A Rare Salish Blanket. *Museum of the American Indian. Heye Foundation. Leaflets* 5. New York.

Oregon Historical Society
1972–   North Pacific Studies Series. Portland: Oregon Historical Society/Western Imprints.

Oregon Legislature
1854   The Statutes of Oregon; Enacted and Continued in Force by the Legislative Assembly, at the Seminar Commencing 5th December, 1853. [Salem]: Asahel Bush, Public Printer.

1866   Acts and Resolutions of the Legislative Assembly of the State of Oregon. Salem: W.A. McPherson, State Printer.

1951   Oregon Laws. Salem: State Printing Department.

Osborn, Henry F.
1911   The American Museum of Natural History: Its Origin, Its History, the Growth of Its Departments to December 31, 1901. New York: Irving Press.

Osborne, Carolyn
1964   The Yakutat Blanket. Pp. 187–199 in Archeology of the Yakutat Bay Area, Alaska, by Frederica De Laguna, F.A. Riddell, D.F. McGeein, K.S. Lane, and T.A. Fried. *Bureau of American Ethnology Bulletin* 192. Washington.

Osborne, Douglas
1956   Evidence of Early Lithic in the Pacific Northwest. *Washington State College. Research Studies* 24(1):38–44. Pullman.

Ossenberg, Nancy S.
1969   Discontinuous Morphological Variation in the Human Cranium. (Unpublished Ph.D. Dissertation in Anatomy, University of Toronto, Toronto, Ont.)

1981   Mandibular Torus: A Synthesis of New and Previously Reported Data and a Discussion of Its Cause. Pp. 1–52 in Contributions to Physical Anthropology, 1978–1980. J.S. Cybulski, ed. *Canada. National Museum of Man. Mercury Series. Archaeological Survey Papers* 106. Ottawa.

Owens, Kenneth N., ed.
1985   The Wreck of the *Sv. Nikolai*: Two Narratives of the First Russian Expedition to the Oregon Country, 1808–1810. Alton S. Donnelly, trans. Portland, Oreg.: Western Imprints.

Paalen, Wolfgang
1943   Totem Art. *Dyn: The Journal of the Durham University Anthropological Society* 4–5:7–39. Durham City, England.

Pacific Fisherman Yearbook
1918   Pacific Fisherman Yearbook. Seattle, Wash.: Miller Freeman.

Paige, George
1863   [Letter to C.H. Hale, 11/18/1863.] (Manuscript in Records of Washington Superintendency of Indian Affairs, 1853–1874, microfilm M5, roll 15, National Archives, Washington.)

Palau de Iglesias, Mercedes
1980   Catálogo de los Dibujos, Aguadas y Acuarelas de la Expedición Malaspina 1789–1794 (donación Carlos Sanz). [Madrid]: Ministerio de Cultura, Dirección General de Bellas Artes, Archivos y Bibliotecas, Patronato Nacional de Museos.

1984   La Expedición Malaspina, 1789–1794: Viaje a América y Oceania de las Corbetas "Descubierta" y "Atrevida." Madrid: Ministerio de Cultura/Ministerio de Defensa.

1988   El Ojo del totem: Arte y cultura de los Indios del noroeste de América. [Madrid]: Comisión Nacional Quinto Centenario.

Palmer, H. Spencer
1863   Report of a Journey of Survey from Victoria to Fort Alexander, via North Bentinck Arm. New Westminster, B.C.: Royal Engineer Press.

Palmer, Joel
1847   Journal of Travels Over the Rocky Mountains, to the Mouth of the Columbia River; Made During the Years 1845 and 1846 . . . . Cincinnati, Ohio: J.A. and U.P. James.

1853   [Diary.] (Manuscript, in Palmer Papers in possession of Sheila Henry, Dayton, Oreg.)

1854   [Letter of July 26.] (Manuscript, evidence item No. 8, docket 240, *Alcea Band of Tillamooks v. United States*, in Record Group 219, National Archives, Washington.)

1856   [Diary.] (Manuscript in Palmer Papers, Oregon Historical Society, Portland.)

Parker, Samuel
1837   Indians on the Northwest Coast. *Missionary Herald* 33(8):348–349. Boston.

1838   Journal of an Exploring Tour Beyond the Rocky Mountains, Under the Direction of the A.B.C.F.M. Performed in the Years 1835, '36, and '37. Ithaca, N.Y.: Published by the author. (Reprinted: Ross and Haines, Minneapolis, 1967.)

1844   Journal of an Exploring Tour Beyond the Rocky Mountains. 4th ed. Ithaca, N.Y.: Andrus, Woodruff and Gauntlett.

1936   [The Report of Rev. Saml. Parker: Tour West of the Rocky Mountains in 1835–7.] Pp. 90–135 in Marcus Whitman, Crusader. Pt. 1: 1802–1839. Archer B. Hulbert and Dorothy P. Hulbert, eds. Denver: The Denver Public Library.

Parmenter, Ross
1966   Explorer, Linguist and Ethnologist: A Descriptive Bibliography of the Published Works of Alphonse Louis Pinart, with Notes on His Life. Los Angeles: Southwest Museum.

Parr, Richard T.
1974   A Bibliography of the Athapaskan Languages. *Canada. National Museum of Man. Mercury Series. Ethnology Service Papers* 14. Ottawa.

Patenaude, Valerie C., ed.
1985   The Pitt River Archaeological Site, DhRq 21: A Coast Salish Seasonal Camp at the Lower Fraser River. *British Columbia. Heritage Conservation Branch. Occasional Papers* 10. Victoria.

Patterson, David K., Jr.
1984   A Diachronic Study of Dental Palaeopathology and Attritional Status of Prehistoric Ontario Pre-Iroquois and Iroquois Populations. *Canada. National Museum of Man. Mercury Series. Archaeological Survey Papers* 122. Ottawa.

Patterson, E. Palmer, II
1982   Mission on the Nass: The Evangelization of the Nishga (1860–1890). Waterloo, Ont.: Eulachon Press.

1982a   Kincolith, B.C.: Leadership Continuity in a Native Christian Village, 1867–1887. *Canadian Journal of Anthropology* 3(1):45–55.

Paul, Frances L.
1944   Spruce Root Basketry of the Alaska Tlingit. Lawrence, Kan.: U.S. Department of the Interior, Bureau of Indian Affairs, Branch of Education. (Reprinted: Arrowhead Press, Sitka, Alaska, 1981.)

Peacock, William B.
1981   The Telep Site: A Late Autumn Fish Camp of the Locarno Beach Culture. (Unpublished manuscript in British Columbia Heritage Conservation Branch, Victoria.)

Pearse, P.H.
1982   Turning the Tide: A New Policy for Canada's Pacific Fisheries. Final Report. Vancouver, B.C.: Commission on Pacific Fisheries.

The People of 'Ksan
1972   'Ksan: Breath of our Grandfathers; an Exhibition of 'Ksan Art. Ottawa: National Museum of Man, Archaeology, Ethnology and Communications Division.

1980   Gathering What the Great Nature Provided: Food Traditions of the Gitksan. Vancouver, B.C.: Douglas and McIntyre.

Percy, Richard C.W.
1974   The Prehistoric Cultural Sequence at Crescent Beach, British Columbia. (Unpublished M.A. Thesis in Archaeology, Simon Fraser University, Burnaby, B.C.)

Perkes, Augustus C.A., ed.
1876   The Display of the United States Government at the Great Exhibition. Philadelphia: George S. Ferguson.

Perkins, Henry
1840   [Letter of September 12 to Daniel Lee.] (Manuscript in University of Puget Sound Archives, Tacoma, Wash.)

Peterson, Jan
1975   A Sketch of Kalapuya Ethnography. Pp. 1–15 in Archaeological Studies in the Willamette Valley, Oregon. C. Melvin Aikens, ed. *University of Oregon Anthropological Papers* 8. Eugene.

Peterson, Lester R.
1958–1963   Index to Map of Sechelt Indian Names. (Manuscript No. 54, Vol. 13, file 22 in Major Matthews Collection, City Archives, Vancouver, B.C.)

[1968]   The Story of the Sechelt Nation. (Unpublished manuscript in Peterson's possession.)

Peterson, Marilyn S.
1978   Prehistoric Mobile Stone Sculpture of the Lower Columbia River Valley: A Preliminary Study in a Southern Northwest Coast Culture Subarea. (Unpublished M.A. Thesis in Anthropology, Portland State University, Portland, Oreg.)

Pethick, Derek
1978   British Columbia Disasters. Langley, B.C.: Stagecoach.

1980   The Nootka Connection: Europe and the Northwest Coast, 1790–1795. Vancouver, B.C.: Douglas and McIntyre.

Petrakis, Nicholas L.
1969   Dry Cerumen - a Prevalent Genetic Trait Among American Indians. *Nature* 222(5198):1080–1081.

Petroff, Ivan *see* U.S. Census Office. 10th Census 1884

Pettigrew, Richard M.
1974   On the Early Prehistory of the Northwest Coast. *University of Oregon Anthropological Papers* 7:37–51. Eugene.

1975   A Comparison of Two Prehistoric Sites in Lane County, Oregon. Pp. 425–454 in Archaeological Studies in the Willamette Valley, Oregon. C. Melvin Aikens, ed. *University of Oregon Anthropological Papers* 8. Eugene.

1977   A Prehistoric Culture Sequence in the Portland Basin of the Lower Columbia Valley. (Ph.D. Dissertation in Anthropology, University of Oregon, Eugene.)

1980   Archaeological Investigations at Hager's Grove, Salem, Oregon. *University of Oregon Anthropological Papers* 19. Eugene.

1981   A Prehistoric Culture Sequence in the Portland Basin of the Lower Columbia Valley. *University of Oregon Anthropological Papers* 22. Eugene.

Pettitt, George A.
1950   The Quileute of La Push, 1775–1945. *University of California Anthropological Records* 14(1). Berkeley. (Reprinted: Kraus Reprint, Millwood, N.Y., 1976.)

Petroff, Ivan
1882   The Limit of the Innuit Tribes on the Alaska Coast. *The American Naturalist* 16(7):567–575.

Phebus, George E., and Robert M. Drucker
1975   Archaeological Investigations of the Northern Oregon Coast: A Brief Summary of the Smithsonian Sponsored Excavations in the Seaside Area with Comments on the Archaeological Resources of Western Clatsop County.

(Manuscript, on file, Department of Anthropology, Smithsonian Institution, Washington.)

1979   Archeological Investigations at Seaside, Oregon. Seaside, Oreg.: Seaside Museum and Historical Society.

Phillips, Earl L.
1960   Climates of the States: Climatography of the United States. Washington: U.S. Department of Commerce, Weather Bureau. (Rev. ed. in 1965.)

Phillips, Earl L., and Wallace Donaldson
1972   Weather and Climate for the Clallam, Gray's Harbor, Jefferson, Pacific and Wahkiakum Counties. (Manuscript No. EM 3708 in Cooperative Extension Service, College of Agriculture, Washington State University, Pullman.)

Philpott, Stuart B.
1963   Trade Unionism and Acculturation: A Comparative Study of Urban Indians and Immigrant Italians. (Unpublished M.A. Thesis in Anthropology, University of British Columbia, Vancouver.)

Phinney, Lloyd A., and Patrick Bucknell
1975   A Catalog of Washington Streams and Salmon Utilization. Vol. 2: Coastal Region. R. Walter Williams, ed. Olympia: Washington Department of Fisheries.

Pickering, Charles
1863   The Races of Man; and Their Geographic Distribution. New Edition to Which is Prefixed, an Analytical Synopsis of the Natural History of Man, by John Charles Hall. London: H.G. Bohn.

Pickering, John
1818   On the Adoption of a Uniform Orthography for the Indian Languages of North America. *Memoirs of the American Academy of Arts and Sciences* 4(2):319–360. Boston. (Reprinted as: An Essay on a Uniform Orthography for the Indian Languages of North America, University Press, Cambridge, Mass., 1820.)

Piddocke, Stuart
1965   The Potlatch System of the Southern Kwakiutl: A New Perspective. *Southwestern Journal of Anthropology* 21(3):244–264.

Pierce, Joe E.
[1962]   [Tape Recordings of Tututni Athabaskan from Ida Bensell at Siletz, Oreg.] (In Department of Anthropology, Portland State University, Portland, Oreg.)

[1962a]   [Tape Recording of Galice Creek Athabaskan Words and Phrases from Hoxie Simmons at Siletz, Oreg.] (In Department of Anthropology, Portland State University, Portland, Oreg.)

1971   Hanis (Coos) Phonemics. *Linguistics: An International Review* 75:31–42. The Hague.

Pierce, Richard A., ed.
1972–   Materials for the Study of Alaska History. (Monographic series, issued as Alaska History after 1980). Kingston, Ont.: The Limestone Press.

1975   Voznesenskiĭ: Scientist in Alaska. *The Alaska Journal* 5(1):11–15. Juneau.

1987   Archival and Bibliographic Materials on Russian America Outside the USSR. Pp. 353–365, 419–420 in Russia's American Colony. S. Frederick Starr, ed. Durham, N.C.: Duke University Press.

————, comp.
1989   Russian America: A Biographical Dictionary. (*Alaska History* 34) Kingston, Ont.: The Limestone Press.

Pierce, William H.
1933   From Potlatch to Pulpit, Being the Autobiography of the Rev. William Henry Pierce. J.P. Hicks, ed. Vancouver, B.C.: The Vancouver Bindery.

Pike, Gordon C., and I.B. MacAskie
1969   Marine Mammals of British Columbia. *Fisheries Research Board of Canada Bulletins* 171. Ottawa.

Pilling, James C.
1885   Proof-sheets of a Bibliography of the Languages of the North American Indians. *Miscellaneous Publications of the Bureau of American Ethnology* 2. Washington.

1892   Bibliography of the Athapascan Languages. *Bureau of American Ethnology Bulletin* 14. Washington.

1893   Bibliography of the Salishan Languages. *Bureau of American Ethnology Bulletin* 16. Washington.

1893a   Bibliography of the Chinookan Languages (Including Chinook Jargon). *Bureau of American Ethnology Bulletin* 15. Washington.

1894   Bibliography of the Wakashan Languages. *Bureau of American Ethnology Bulletin* 19. Washington.

Pinart, Alphonse L.
1849   Dictionnaire du jargon Tchinouk. (Manuscript No. [P-A 171] in Bancroft Library, University of California, Berkeley.)

1876   A List of Words in the Cowitchin Dialect. (Manuscript No. [P-C46(1)] in the Bancroft Library, University of California, Berkeley.)

1880   Religious Texts and List of Words in Cowichan. (Manuscript No. [P-C46(2)] in the Bancroft Library, University of California, Berkeley.)

[1880a]   Vocabulaire de Tchinkîtâné....(Manuscript No. [P-C46(3)] in the Bancroft Library, University of California, Berkeley.)

[1880b]   [Word List in the Language of the Indians of Nootka Sound.] (Manuscript No. [P-C46(4)] in the Bancroft Library, University of California, Berkeley.)

[1880c]   Catechism and Hail Mary [in Cowichan]. (Manuscript No. [P-C46(5)] in the Bancroft Library, University of California, Berkeley.)

Pinkerton, Evelyn
1984   Les Réactions du gouvernement de Colombie-Britannique face aux poursuites judiciaries des Haidas sur la mise en valeur des ressources. Pierre Bérubé et Sylvie Loslier, trans. *Recherches Amérindiennes au Québec* 14(2):47–56.

Pinnow, Heinz-Jürgen
1966   Grundzüge einer historischen Lautlehre des Tlingit: Ein Versuch. Wiesbaden, Germany: Otto Harrassowitz.

1977   Geschichte der Na-Dene-Forschung. *Indiana: Beiträge zur Völker- und Sprachenkunde, Archäologie und Anthropologie des indianischen Amerika. Supp.* 5. Berlin.

Piper, Charles V.
1906   Flora of the State of Washington. *Smithsonian Institution. United States National Museum. Contributions from the United States National Herbarium* 11:1–637. Washington.

Pipes, Nellie B., ed.
1934   Journal of John Frost, 1840–43. *Oregon Historical Quarterly* 35(1):50–73, (2):139–167, (3):235–262, (4):348–375.

Polansky, Patricia
1987   Published Sources on Russian America. Pp. 319–352 in Russia's American Colony. S. Frederick Starr, ed. Durham, N.C.: Duke University Press.

Polesky, H.F., and D.A. Rokala
1967   Serum Albumin Polymorphism in North American Indians. *Nature* 216(5111):184–185.

716

Pomeroy, John A.
1976 Stone Fish Traps of the Bella Bella Region. Pp. 165–173 in Current Research Reports. Roy L. Carlson, ed. *Simon Fraser University, Department of Archaeology Publications* 3. Burnaby, B.C.

1980 Bella Bella Settlement and Subsistence. (Unpublished Ph.D. Dissertation in Archaeology, Simon Fraser University, Burnaby, B.C.)

Poole, Francis
1872 Queen Charlotte Islands: A Narrative of Discovery and Adventure in the North Pacific. John W. Lyndon, ed. London: Hurst and Blackett.

Pope, Richard K.
1953 The Indian Shaker Church and Acculturation at Warm Springs Reservation. (Unpublished B.A. Thesis in Anthropology, Reed College, Portland, Oreg.)

Portlock, Nathaniel
1789 A Voyage Round the World; But More Particularly to the North-west Coast of America: Performed in 1785, 1786, 1787 and 1788, in the King George and Queen Charlotte . . . .London: Printed for J. Stockdale, and G. Goulding. (Reprinted: Da Capo Press, New York, 1968.)

Powell, I.W.
1873 Report of the Superintendent of Indian Affairs for British Columbia for 1872 and 1873. Sessional Paper 23 in *Dominion of Canada. Parliament. Sessional Papers* 6(5). Ottawa.

1876 [Report on Indian Affairs in the Victoria Superintendency.] Pp. 32–36 in *Report of the Deputy Superintendent General of Indian Affairs for 1875–1876.* [Ottawa.]

Powell, J.V.
1972 The Predicate in Chimakum. *University of Hawaii. Working Papers in Linguistics* 4(3):83–112. Honolulu.

1974 Proto-Chimakuan: Materials for a Reconstruction. (Ph.D. Dissertation in Linguistics, University of Hawaii, Honolulu.)

1975 Proto-Chimakuan: Materials for a Reconstruction. *University of Hawaii. Working Papers in Linguitics* 7(2). Honolulu.

1975a Quileute Language: Book I. La Push. Wash.: Quileute Tribe.

1976 Quileute Language: Book 2. La Push, Wash.: Quileute Tribe.

1976a Chimakuan-Wakashan: Evidence of Genetic Relationship. (Paper read at the Northwest Coast Studies Conference, Simon Fraser University, Burnaby, B.C., 1976.)

Powell, J.V., and Vickie Jensen
1976 Quileute: An Introduction to the Indians of La Push. Seattle: University of Washington Press.

Powell, J.V., and Fred Woodruff
1973 Additions to the Quileute Entries. Pp. 51–52 (App.1) in Ethnobotany of Western Washington: The Knowledge and Use of Indigenous Plants by Native Americans, by Erna Gunther. Rev. ed. Seattle: University of Washington Press.

1976 Quileute Dictionary. *Northwest Anthropological Research Notes. Memoirs* 3. Moscow, Idaho.

Powell, J.V., Vickie Jensen, Agnes Cranmer, and Margaret Cook
1981 Learning Kwak'wala Series, Books 1 to 12. Gloria Cramer Webster, series ed. Alert Bay, B.C.: U'mista Cultural Society.

Powell, J.V., William Penn, et al.
1972 Place Names of the Quileute Indians. *Pacific Northwest Quarterly* 63(3):105–112.

Powell, John Wesley
1877 Introduction to the Study of Indian Languages with Words, Phrases and Sentences to Be Collected. Washington: U.S. Government Printing Office. (2d ed. in 1880.)

1891 Indian Linguistic Families of America North of Mexico. Pp. 1–142 in *7th Annual Report of the Bureau of American Ethnology for the Years 1885–1886*. Washington. (Reprinted: University of Nebraska Press, Lincoln, 1966.)

Powell, Joseph M.
1965 Annual and Seasonal Temperature and Precipitation Trends in British Columbia Since 1890. Toronto: Department of Transportation, Meteorological Branch.

Preston, Richard
1980 Reflections on Sapir's Anthropology in Canada. *Canadian Review of Sociology and Anthropology* 17(4):367–375.

Price, Weston A.
1934 Why Dental Caries with Modern Civilizations? VIII: Field Studies of Modernized Indians in Twenty Communities of the Canadian and Alaskan Pacific Coast. *Dental Digest* 40(3):81–84.

Princeton University Art Museum
1969 Art of the Northwest Coast. [Catalogue of Exhibition, Jan. 22–March 2], Hedy Backlin-Landman, ed. Princeton, N.J.: Princeton Printing Company.

Pritchard, John C.
1977 Economic Development and the Disintegration of Traditional Culture Among the Haisla. (Unpublished Ph.D. Dissertation in Anthropology, University of British Columbia, Vancouver.)

Prucha, Francis P.
1984 The Great Father: The United States Government and the American Indians. 2 vols. Lincoln: University of Nebraska Press.

Puget, Peter
1792 [Log of the Discovery, June 12–August 19, 1792.] (Manuscript Admiralty 55/27, Public Record Office, London; Microfilm No. 274 in Suzzallo Library, University of Washington, Seattle.)

1793 [Journal.] (Microfilm No. 635 in Suzzallo Library, University of Washington, Seattle.)

1939 The Vancouver Expedition: Peter Puget's Journal of the Exploration of Puget Sound, May 7–June 11, 1792. Bern Anderson, ed. *Pacific Northwest Quarterly* 30(2):177–217.

Pullen, Reginald J.
1982 The Identification of Early Prehistoric Settlement Patterns Along the Coast of Southwest Oregon: A Survey Based Upon Amateur Artifact Collections. (Unpublished M.A. Thesis in Interdisciplinary Studies, Oregon State University, Corvallis.)

Purtov, Egor, and Demid Kulikalov
1979 Report, Company Employees Egor Purtov and Demid Kulikalov, to Baranov, from Paul's Harbor, August 9, 1794. Pp. 46–52 in A History of the Russian American Company. Vol. 2: Documents, by P.A. Tikhmenev. Dmitri Krenov, trans., Richard A. Pierce and Alton S. Donnelly, eds. (*Materials for the Study of Alaska History* 13) Kingston, Ont.: The Limestone Press.

Puter, Stephen A.D.
1908 Looters of the Public Domain: King of the Oregon Land Fraud Ring, in Collaboration with Horace Stevens Embracing a Complete Exposure of a Fraudulent System of Acquiring Titles to the Public Lands of the United States . . . Portland, Oreg.: Portland Printing House.

Quaife, Milo M., ed.
1916 The Journals of Captain Meriwether Lewis and Sergeant John Ordway Kept on the Expedition of Western Explora-

tion, 1803–1806. Madison: The State Historical Society of Wisconsin. (Reprinted in 1965.)

Quayle, D.B.
1960   The Intertidal Bivalves of British Columbia. *British Columbia Provincial Museum Handbook* 17. Victoria.

Quimby, George I., Jr.
1948   Culture Contact on the Northwest Coast, 1785–1795. *American Anthropologist* 50(2):247–255.

———
1985   Japanese Wrecks, Iron Tools, and Prehistoric Indians of the Northwest Coast. *Arctic Anthropology* 22(2):7–15.

Quimby, Lida W.
1902   Puget Sound Shakers. *The State* 7:188–189. Tacoma, Wash.

Rabich-Campbell, Chris
1984   Preliminary Report Describing Results of a Test Excavation at CRG-164, Sarkar Entrance, Prince of Wales Island, Southeast Alaska. (Paper presented at the 11th Annual Alaskan Anthropological Meetings, March 16–17. Fairbanks, 1984.)

Radloff, Leopold
1858   Über die Sprache der Ugalachmut. *Bulletin de la Classe Historico-Philologiques de l'Académie Impériale des Sciences* 15:25–37, 49–63, 125–139. St. Petersburg.

———
1858a   Einige Nachrichten über die Sprache der Kaiganen. *Bulletin de la Classe Historico-Philologiques de l'Académie Impériale des Sciences* 15:20–22, 305–331. St. Petersburg.

Raffo, Yolanda A.
1972   A Phonology and Morphology of Songish, a Dialect of Straits Salish. (Unpublished Ph.D. Dissertation in Linguistics, University of Kansas, Lawrence.)

Raley, George H.
[1904]   Kitimat Language: Dictionaries, Vocabularies, Grammar, Sermons etc. (Manuscript in the British Columbia Provincial Archives, Victoria.)

———
1948   A Monograph of the Totem Poles in Stanley Park, Vancouver, British Columbia. Vancouver: Lumberman Print.

Ramsey, Jarold W., ed.
1977   Coyote Was Going There: Indian Literature of the Oregon Country. Seattle: University of Washington Press.

———
1983   Creations and Origins. Pp. 1–23 in Reading the Fire: Essays in the Traditional Indian Literatures of the Far West. Jarold Ramsey, ed. Lincoln: University of Nebraska Press.

Rath, John C.
1981   A Practical Heiltsuk-English Dictionary with a Grammatical Introduction. 2 vols. *Canada. National Museum of Man. Mercury Series. Ethnology Service Papers* 75. Ottawa.

Ratzel, Friedrich
1896–1898   The History of Mankind. 3 vols. London: Macmillan.

Raunet, Daniel
1984   Without Surrender without Consent: A History of the Nishga Land Claims. Vancouver, B.C.: Douglas and McIntyre.

Ray, Charles K.
1958   A Program of Education for Alaska Natives: A Research Report. College: University of Alaska.

Ray, Verne F.
1937   The Historical Position of the Lower Chinook in the Native Culture of the Northwest. *Pacific Northwest Quarterly* 28(4):363–372.

———
1938   Lower Chinook Ethnographic Notes. *University of Washington Publications in Anthropology* 7(2):29–165. Seattle.

1955   [Review of] Franz Boas: The Science of Man in the Making, by Melville J. Herskovits. *American Anthropologist* 57(1):138–140.

———
1956   Rejoinder. *American Anthropologist* 58(1):164–170.

———
1973   Evidence Bearing Upon the Makah Quileute Tribal Boundary. (Library of American Indian Affairs [from] the Expert Testimony Before the Indian Claims Commission.) New York: Clearwater.

———
1974   Handbook of Cowlitz Indians. Pp. 245–315 in Coast Salish and Western Washington Indians, III. (*American Indian Ethnohistory: Indians of the Northwest*) New York: Garland.

Read, Charles H.
1892   An Account of a Collection of Ethnographical Specimens Formed During Vancouver's Voyages in the Pacific Ocean. *Journal of the Anthropological Institute of Great Britain and Ireland* 21:99–108. London.

Reagan, Albert B.
1909   The Shake Dance of the Quilente [*sic*] Indians, with Drawings by an Indian Pupil of the Quilente Day School. Pp. 71–74 in *Proceedings of the Indiana Academy of Science for 1908*. Indianapolis.

———
1911   Sketches of Indian Life and Character. *Transactions of the Kansas Academy of Science* 23:141–149. Lawrence.

———
1911a   Notes on the Shaker Church of the Indians. Pp. 115–116 in *Proceedings of the Indiana Academy of Science for 1910*. Indianapolis.

———
1917   Archaeological Notes on Western Washington and Adjacent British Columbia. *Proceedings of the California Academy of Sciences, 4th ser.*, Vol. 7(1). San Francisco.

———
1922   Hunting and Fishing of Various Tribes of Indians. *Transactions of the Kansas Academy of Science* 30:443–448. Lawrence.

———
1925   Whaling of the Olympic Peninsula Indians. *Natural History* 25(1):25–32.

———
1927   The Shaker Church of the Indians. *The Southern Workman* 56(10):447–448. Hampton, Va.

———
1928   Ancient Sites and Burial Grounds in the Vicinity of Queets, Washington. *El Palacio* 25(19):296–299.

———
1929   Traditions of the Hoh and Quillayute Indians. *Washington Historical Quarterly* 20(3):178–189. Seattle.

———
1934   Various Uses of Plants by West Coast Indians. *Washington Historical Quarterly* 25(2):133–137. Seattle.

———
1934a   Some Notes on the Occult and Hypnotic Ceremonies of Indians. *Proceedings of the Utah Academy of Sciences, Arts and Letters* 11:65–71. Provo.

———
1934b   Plants Used by the Hoh and Quileute Indians. *Transactions of the Kansas Academy of Science* 37:55–70. Lawrence.

———
1934c   Some Additional Myths of the Hoh and Quileute Indians. *Proceedings of the Utah Academy of Sciences, Arts and Letters* 11:17–37. Provo.

———
1935   Some Myths of the Hoh and Quillayute Indians. *Transactions of the Kansas Academy of Science* 38:43–85. Lawrence.

Reagan, Albert B., and L.V.W. Walters
1933   Tales from the Hoh and Quileute. *Journal of American Folk-Lore* 46(182):297–346.

Reckendorf, Frank F., and Roger B. Parsons
1966   Soil Development Over a Hearth in the Willamette Valley, Oregon. *Northwest Science* 40(2):46–55. Pullman, Wash.

Rees, Willard H.
1880   Annual Address. Pp. 18–31 in *Transactions of the 7th Annual Re-union of the Oregon Pioneer Association for 1879.* Salem, Oreg.

Reichard, Gladys A.
1938   Social Life. Pp. 409–486 in General Anthropology. Franz Boas, ed. New York: D.C. Heath.

1943   Franz Boas and Folklore. Pp. 52–57 in Franz Boas, 1858–1942. A.L. Kroeber et al., eds. *Memoirs of the American Anthropological Association* 61. (Reprinted: Kraus Reprint, New York, 1969.)

1958–1960 A Comparison of Five Salish Languages. Florence M. Voegelin, ed. *International Journal of American Linguistics* 24(4):293–300; 25(1):8–15, (2)90–96, (3):154–167, (4):239–253; 26(1):50–61.

Reid, Alfred
1987   An Ecological Perspective of the Intergroup Relations of an Inland Coast Salish Group: The Nooksack Peoples. (Unpublished M.A. Thesis in Anthropology, Western Washington University, Bellingham.)

Reid, Bill
1967   The Art: An Appreciation. In Arts of the Raven: Masterworks by Northwest Coast Indians. Wilson Duff, ed. Vancouver, B.C.: Vancouver Art Gallery Catalog.

1971   Out of the Silence. Photos by Adelaide de Menil. New York: Outerbridge and Dienstfrey for Amon Carter Museum, Fort Worth, Texas.

Reid, Martine Jeanne
1981   La Cérémonie hamatsa des Kwagul: Approche structuraliste des rapports mythe-rituel. (Unpublished Ph.D. Dissertation in Anthropology, University of British Columbia, Vancouver.)

1984   Le Mythe de Baxbakwalanuxsiwae: Une affaire de famille. *Recherches Amérindiennes au Québec* 14(2):25–33.

Reid, Susan K.
1973   Fondements de la pensée kwakiutl. *Recherches Amérindiennes au Québec* 3(1–2):117–125.

1976   The Origins of the Tsetseqa in the Baxus: A Study of Kwakiutl Prayers, Myths and Rituals. (Unpublished Ph.D. Dissertation in Anthropology, University of British Columbia, Vancouver.)

1979   The Kwakiutl Man Eater. *Anthropologica* n.s. 21(2):247–275. Ottawa.

Renker, Ann M.
1980   The Makah Language Survey. (Manuscript in Makah Archives, Makah Cultural and Research Center, Neah Bay, Wash.)

[1980–1985] [Ethnographic and Linguistic Fieldnotes from Five Years' Fieldwork in Neah Bay, Wash., with Makah People.] (Manuscripts in Renker's possession.)

1985   The Makah Language Survey, II. (Manuscript in Makah Archives, Makah Cultural and Research Center, Neah Bay, Wash.)

1985a   [The Makah Language Program Proposal.] (Manuscript in Makah Archives, Makah Cultural and Research Center, Neah Bay, Wash.)

Renker, Ann M., and Greig Arnold
1988   Exploring the Role of Education in Cultural Resource Management: The Makah Cultural and Research Center Example. *Human Organization.* 47(4):302–307.

Renker, Ann M., and Steven J. Gill
1985   Salient Features of Makah Zoological Nomenclature. Pp. 325–336 in *Papers of the 20th International Salish and Neighboring Languages Conference.* Vancouver, 1985.

Renker, Ann M., and Helma Ward
1984   The Updated Swan Vocabulary. (Manuscript in Makah Archives, Makah Cultural and Research Center, Neah Bay, Wash.)

The Renwick Gallery
1974   Boxes and Bowls: Decorated Containers by Nineteenth-century Haida, Tlingit, Bella Bella, and Tsimshian Indian Artists. [Exhibition Catalogue.] Washington: Smithsonian Institution Press.

Reynolds, Stephen W.
1938   The Voyage of the New Hazard to the Northwest Coast, Hawaii, and China, 1810–1813, by Stephen Reynolds, a Member of the Crew. F.W. Howay, ed. Salem, Mass.: Peabody Museum.

Rey-Tejerina, Arsenio
1988   The Spanish Exploration of Alaska, 1774–1796: Manuscript Sources. *Alaska History* 3(1):45–61. Anchorage.

Rhodes, Willard
1960   The Christian Hymnology of the North American Indians. Pp. 324–331 in Men and Cultures: Selected Papers of the Fifth International Congress of Anthropological and Ethnological Sciences. Anthony F.C. Wallace, ed. Philadelphia: University of Pennsylvania Press.

Rice, David G.
1964   Test Excavations at Wild Rose Rockshelter: A Site on the Eastern Slope of the Cascades. *Washington Archaeologist* 8(4):2–23.

1964a   Indian Utilization of the Cascade Mountain Range in South Central Washington. *Washington Archaeologist* 8(1):5–20.

1965   Archaeological Test Excavations in Fryingpan Rockshelter, Mount Rainier National Park. *Washington State University. Laboratory of Anthropology. Reports of Investigations* 33. Pullman.

1965a   Commentary on Archaeological Findings at Old Man House on Puget Sound. *Washington Archaeologist* 9(1):2–9.

1966   An Archaeological Reconnaissance of the Wynoochee Dam Reservoir, Grays Harbor County, Washington. (Report on file with the State Office of Archaeology and Historic Preservation, Olympia, Wash.)

1969   Archaeological Reconnaissance: South-central Cascades. *Occasional Papers of the Washington Archaeological Society* 2. Seattle.

1972   The Windust Phase in Lower Snake River Region Prehistory. *Washington State University. Laboratory of Anthropology. Reports of Investigations* 50. Pullman.

Rich, E.E., ed.
1941   The Letters of John McLoughlin from Fort Vancouver to the Governor and Committee. First Series, 1825–1838. Toronto: The Champlain Society.

————, ed.
1943   The Letters of John McLoughlin, from Fort Vancouver to the Governor and Committee: Second Series, 1839–44. Toronto: The Champlain Society.

———, ed.
1944   The Letters of John McLoughlin, from Fort Vancouver to the Governor and Committee: Third Series, 1844–46. Toronto: The Champlain Society.

———, ed.
1947   Part of Dispatch from George Simpson, Esq., Governor of Ruperts Land, to the Governor and Committee of the Hudson's Bay Company, London, March 1, 1829. Continued and Completed March 24 and June 5, 1829. Toronto: The Champlain Society.

1958–1959   A History of the Hudson's Bay Company, 1670–1870. 2 vols. London: Hudson's Bay Record Society.

Richards, Kent D.
1979   Isaac I. Stevens: Young Man in a Hurry. Provo, Utah: Brigham Young University Press.

Richardson, Allan S.
1974   Traditional Fisheries and Traditional Villages, Camps, and Fishing Sites of the Nooksack Indians. Deming, Wash.: Nooksack Tribal Council.

1979   Longhouses to Homesteads: Nooksack Indian Settlement, 1820 to 1895. American Indian Journal 5(8):8–12. Washington.

1982   The Control of Productive Resources on the North Northwest Coast of North America. Pp. 93–112 in Resource Managers: North American and Australian Hunter-gatherers. Nancy M. Williams and Eugene S. Hunn, eds. (AAAS Selected Symposia 67) Boulder, Colo.: Westview Press.

Richardson, Allan S., and Brent Galloway
1986   Nooksack Indian Placenames. Map.

Richen, Marily C.
1974   Authority and Office: Leadership in the Shaker Church. Pp. 1–10 in Collected Papers in Anthropology. James J. McKenna, Richard M. Pettigrew and Victoria A.S. Young, eds. University of Oregon Anthropological Papers 7. Eugene.

1974a   Legitimacy and the Resolution of Conflict in an Indian Church. (Unpublished Ph.D. Dissertation in Anthropology, University of Oregon, Eugene.)

Riches, David
1979   Ecological Variation on the Northwest Coast: Models for the Generation of Cognatic and Matrilineal Descent. Pp. 145–166 in Social and Ecological Systems. P.C. Burnham and R.F. Ellen, eds. (A.S.A. Monograph 8) New York: Academic Press.

Rick, Anne M.
1980   Identification of and Biological Notes on Selected Bone and Tooth Artifacts from Yuquot, British Columbia. Pp. 23–36 in The Yuquot Project. Vol. 2. William J. Folan and John Dewhirst, eds. Canada. National Historic Parks and Sites Branch. History and Archaeology 43. Ottawa.

Rickard, T.A.
1937   Gilbert Malcolm Sproat. British Columbia Historical Quarterly 1(1):21–32. Victoria.

Rickman, John
1781   Journal of Captain Cook's Last Voyage to the Pacific Ocean . . . .London: E. Newbery. (Reprinted: Da Capo Press, New York, 1967.)

Riddle, George W.
1920   History of Early Days in Oregon. Riddle, Oreg.: The Riddle Enterprise.

Ride, Lindsay
1935   Anthropological Studies Amongst North American Indians of British Columbia. Caduceus: Journal of the Hongkong University Medical Society 14(3):205–216. Hong Kong.

Ridley, William
[1895] A Grammar of the Zimshian Language, with Some Observations on the People. (Manuscript No. 1812-b in National Anthropological Archives, Smithsonian Institution, Washington.)

Riesenfeld, Alphonse
1956   Multiple Infraorbital, Ethmoidal, and Mental Foramina in the Races of Man. American Journal of Physical Anthropology 14(1):85–100.

Righter, Elizabeth
1980   Cultural Resource Survey of Six Areas Proposed for Land Exchanges and Timber Sales within the Olympic National Forest, Washington. (Report on file with the Olympic National Forest, Olympia, Wash.)

Rigsby, Bruce
1975   Nass-Gitksan: An Analytic Ergative Syntax. International Journal of American Linguistics 41(4):346–354.

Riley, Carroll L.
1968   The Makah Indians: A Study of Political and Social Organization. Ethnohistory 15(1):57–95.

Ritzenthaler, Robert, and Lee A. Parsons, eds.
1966   Masks of the Northwest Coast. Milwaukee Public Museum. Publications in Primitive Art 2. Milwaukee, Wis.

Rivera, Trinita
1949   Diet of a Food-gathering People, with Chemical Analysis of Salmon and Saskatoons. Pp. 19–36 in Indians of the Urban Northwest. Marian W. Smith, ed. Columbia University Contributions to Anthropology 36. New York.

Roberts, George B.
1878   [Letter of November 28 to Frances Fuller Victor.] (Manuscript HHB[P-A83] in Bancroft Library, University of California, Berkeley.)

1962   The Round Hand of George B. Roberts. Oregon Historical Quarterly 63(2–3):101–241.

Roberts, Helen H., and Hermann K. Haeberlin
1918   Some Songs of the Puget Sound Salish. Journal of American Folk-Lore 31(121):496–520.

Roberts, Helen H., and Morris Swadesh
1955   Songs of the Nootka Indians of Western Vancouver Island. Transactions of the American Philosophical Society n.s. 45(3):199–327. Philadelphia.

Roberts, Larry
1982   Southeastern Archaeology in Light of the Irish Creek Site. (Paper presented at the 9th Annual Alaska Anthropological Association Meetings, April 2–3. Fairbanks, 1982.

Roberts, Natalie A.
1975   A History of the Swinomish Tribal Community. (Unpublished Ph.D. Dissertation in Anthropology, University of Washington, Seattle.)

Robinson, Doane, and Cyrus Thomas
1910   Tamaha. P. 680 in Vol. 2 of Handbook of American Indians North of Mexico. Frederick W. Hodge, ed. 2 vols. Bureau of American Ethnology Bulletin 30. Washington.

Robinson, Ellen W.
1976   Harlan I. Smith, Boas, and the Salish: Unweaving Archaeological Hypotheses. Northwest Anthropological Research Notes 10(2):185–196. Moscow, Idaho.

Robinson, Gordon
1962   Tales of Kitamaat: A Selection of Legends, Folk Stories, and Customs of the Haisla People, ...Kitimat, B.C.: Northern Sentinel Press.

Robinson, Michael P.
1978   Sea Otter Chiefs. Friendly Cove, B.C.: Friendly Cove Press.

Robinson, Sarah A.
1963   Spirit Dancing Among Salish Indians of Vancouver Island and British Columbia. (Unpublished Ph.D. Dissertation in Anthropology, University of Chicago, Chicago.)

Robinson, Stephen W., and Gail Thompson
1981   Radiocarbon Corrections for Marine Shell Dates with Application to Southern Pacific Northwest Coast Prehistory. *Syesis* 14:45–57. Victoria, B.C.

Robinson, H.S., J.P. Gofton, and G.E. Price
1963   A Study of Rheumatic Disease in a Canadian Indian Population. *Annals of the Rheumatic Diseases* 22(4):232–236. London.

Robison, Houston T.
1943   The Rogue River Indians and Their Relations with the Whites. (Unpublished M.A. Thesis in History, University of Oregon, Eugene.)

Rogers, George W.
1960   Alaska in Transition: The Southeast Region. Baltimore, Md.: Johns Hopkins Press.

Rohner, Ronald P.
1967   The People of Gilford: A Contemporary Kwakiutl Village. *Canada. National Museum Bulletin* 225, *Anthropological Series* 83. Ottawa.
————, ed.
1969   The Ethnography of Franz Boas: Letters and Diaries of Franz Boas Written on the Northwest Coast from 1886 to 1931. Chicago: University of Chicago Press.

Rohner, Ronald P., and Evelyn C. Rohner
1970   The Kwakiutl: Indians of British Columbia. New York: Holt, Rinehart and Winston.

Roll, Tom E.
1974   The Archaeology of Minard: A Case Study of a late Prehistoric Northwest Coast Procurement System. (Unpublished Ph.D. Dissertation in Anthropology, Washington State University, Pullman.)

Rollins, David
1972   Materia Medica of the Northwest Coast Indians. (Manuscript filed with British Columbia Indian Language Project, Victoria.)

Romanoff, Steven
1985   Fraser Lillooet Salmon Fishing. *Northwest Anthropological Research Notes* 19(2):119–160. Moscow, Idaho.

Rose, Suzanne M.
1981   Kyuquot Grammar. (Unpublished Ph.D. Dissertation in Linguistics, University of Victoria, Victoria, B.C.)

Rosenfeld, Charles L.
1985   Landforms and Geology. Pp. 40–47 in Atlas of the Pacific Northwest. A.J. Kimerling, and P.L. Jackson, eds. 7th ed. Corvallis: Oregon State University Press.

Rosenstiel, Annette
1983   Red and White: Indian Views of the White Man, 1492–1982. New York: Universe Books.

Rosman, Abraham, and Paula G. Rubel
1971   Feasting with Mine Enemy: Rank and Exchange Among Northwest Coast Societies. New York: Columbia University Press.

1972   The Potlatch: A Structural Analysis. *American Anthropologist* 74(3):658–671.

1986   The Evolution of Central Northwest Coast Societies. *Journal of Anthropological Research* 42:557–572.

Ross, Alexander
1849   Adventures of the First Settlers on the Oregon or Columbia River: Being a Narrative of the Expedition Fitted Out by John Jacob Astor, to Establish the Pacific Fur Company, with an Account of Some Indian Tribes on the Coast of the

Pacific. London: Smith, Elder. (Reprinted: Citadel Press, New York, 1969.)

1855   The Fur Hunters of the Far West. London: Smith, Elder. (Reprinted: Donnelly and Sons, Chicago, 1924.)

1956   The Fur Hunters of the Far West. Kenneth A. Spaulding, ed. Norman: University of Oklahoma Press.

Ross, Richard E.
1975   [Archaeological Survey of Cascade Head Scenic Research Area.] (Report to Siuslaw National Forest, Corvallis, Oreg.)

1975a   Prehistoric Inhabitants at Seal Rock, Oregon. *Geological Society of the Oregon Country. Newsletter* 45(5):38–39. Portland.

1976   Archaeological Survey of State Park Lands Along the Oregon Coast. Salem: Oregon State Parks and Recreation.

1977   Preliminary Archaeological Investigations at 35 CU 9, Port Orford, Oregon. Salem: Oregon State Parks and Recreation.

1983   Archaeological Sites and Surveys on the North and Central Coast of Oregon. Pp. 211–218 in Prehistoric Places on the Southern Northwest Coast. Robert E. Greengo, ed. Seattle: University of Washington, Washington State Museum.

1985   Terrestrial Oriented Sites in a Marine Environment Along the Southern Oregon Coast. *Northwest Anthropological Research Notes* 18(2):241–255. Moscow, Idaho.

Ross, Richard E., and Crystal Schreindorfer
1985   An Early Interior Site in Southwestern Oregon. (Paper presented at the 50th Annual Meeting for the Society for American Archaeology, Denver, Colo.)

Ross, Richard E., and Sandra L. Snyder
1979   Excavations at Umpqua/Eden. Pp. 92–105 in Umpqua River Basin Cultural History, Phase I: Research. Thomas C. Hogg, ed. Report to Douglas County Commissioners, Roseburg, Oregon. Corvallis: Oregon State University, Department of Anthropology.

1985   An Early Estuarine Adaptation Along the Oregon Coast. (Manuscript, on file, Department of Anthropology, Oregon State University, Corvallis.)

Roth, George
1988   [Anthropologists and BIA Decisions: Not So!]

Rothenberg, Jerome, ed.
1985   Technicians of the Sacred: A Range of Poetries from Africa, America, Asia, Europe and Oceania. 2d ed. Berkeley: University of California Press.

1986   Shaking the Pumpkin: Traditional Poetry of the Indian North Americas. Rev. ed. New York: Alfred van der Marck Editions.

Rozen, David L.
1978   The Ethnozoology of the Cowichan Indian People of British Columbia. Vol. 1: Fish, Beach Foods, and Marine Mammals. (Report in Rozen's possession.)

Rozina, L.G.
1978   The James Cook Collection in the Museum of Anthropology and Ethnography, Leningrad. Ella Wiswell, trans. Pp. 3–17 in Cook Voyage Artifacts in Leningrad, Berne, and Florence Museums. Adrienne L. Kaeppler, ed. Honolulu: Bishop Museum Press.

Rubel, Paula G., and Abraham Rosman
1970   Potlatch and Sagali: The Structures of Exchange in Haida and Trobriand Societies. *Transactions of the New York Academy of Sciences* ser. 2, Vol. 32(6):732–742.

721

1971   Potlatch and Hakari: An Analysis of Maori Society in Terms of the Potlatch Model. *Man: The Journal of the Royal Anthropological Institute* 6(4):660–673. London.

1983   The Evolution of Exchange Structures and Ranking: Some Northwest Coast and Athapaskan Examples. *Journal of Anthropological Research* 39(1):1–25.

Ruby, Robert H., and John A. Brown
1976   The Chinook Indians: Traders of the Lower Columbia River. Norman: University of Oklahoma Press.

1976a   Myron Eells and the Puget Sound Indians. Seattle, Wash.: Superior Publishing Company.

1981   Indians of the Pacific Northwest: A History. Norman: University of Oklahoma Press.

1986   A Guide to the Indian Tribes of the Pacific Northwest. Norman: University of Oklahoma Press.

Ruddell, Rosemary
1973   Chiefs and Commoners: Nature's Balance and the Good Life Among the Nootka. Pp. 254–265 in Cultural Ecology: Readings on the Canadian Indians and Eskimos. Bruce A. Cox, ed. Toronto: McClelland and Stewart.

Rüstow, Anna
1939   Die Objekte der Malaspina-Expedition im archäologischen Museum zu Madrid. *Baessler-Archiv* 22(4):172–204. Berlin.

Ruggles, Richard I.
1987   Exploration in the Far Northwest. Plate 67 in Historical Atlas of Canada. R. Cole Harris and Geoffrey J. Matthews, eds. Toronto: University of Toronto Press.

Rumley, Hilary E.
1973   Reactions to Contact and Colonization: An Interpretation of Religious and Social Change Among the Indians of British Columbia. (Unpublished M.A. Thesis in Anthropology, University of British Columbia, Vancouver.)

Russell, Frank
1900   Studies in Cranial Variation. *American Naturalist* 34(405):737–745.

Ruyle, Eugene E.
1973   Slavery, Surplus, and Stratification on the Northwest Coast: The Ethnoenergetics of an Incipient Stratification System. *Current Anthropology* 14(5):603–631.

Ryan, Joan
1973   Squamish Socialization. (Unpublished Ph.D. Dissertation in Anthropology, University of British Columbia, Vancouver.)

Ryan, Joe
1979   Indian Treaties, Indian Fish: The Controversy of Fishing in Common. *American Indian Journal* 5(4):2–10. Washington.

Rydell, Robert W.
1980   All the World's a Fair: America's International Expositions, 1876–1916. (Unpublished Ph.D. Dissertation in History, University of California, Los Angeles.)

1984   All the World's a Fair: Visions of Empire at American International Expositions, 1876–1916. Chicago: University of Chicago Press.

Saavedra, Ramon
1794   Informe de lo ocurrido en Noutka del 7 de Junio de 93 al 15 de Julio de 94. In Official Documents Relating to Spanish and Mexican Voyages of Navigation, Exploration and Discovery Made in North America in the Eighteenth Century. Mary Daylton, trans. and ed. (Typescript in Northwest Collection, Suzzallo Library, University of Washington, Seattle).

Sackett, Lee
1973   The Siletz Indian Shaker Church. *Pacific Northwest Quarterly* 64(3):120–126.

St. Clair, Harry H.
1901   Wasco Text. (Manuscript No. 2048a in National Anthropological Archives, Smithsonian Institution, Washington.)

1903–1904   [Takelma Vocabulary and Myths.] (Manuscript No. 1655 in National Anthropological Archives, Smithsonian Institution, Washington.)

1903–1904a [Coos and Takelma Vocabulary.] (Manuscript No. 1277 in National Anthropological Archives, Smithsonian Institution, Washington.)

1909   Traditions of the Coos Indians of Oregon. Leo J. Frachtenberg, ed. *Journal of American Folk-Lore* 22(83):25–41.

St. Claire, Denis E.
1984   Ahousaht Place Names. (Manuscript on file, British Columbia Provincial Museum, Vancouver.)

1984a   Barkley Sound Tribal Territories. (Manuscript on file, British Columbia Provincial Museum, Vancouver.)

St. John, Lewis H.
1914   The Present Status and Probable Future of the Indians of Puget Sound. *Washington Historical Quarterly* 5(1):12–21. Seattle.

Saleeby, Becky
1983   Zooarchaeological Indicators of Seasonality: Six Portland Basin Sites. Pp. 57–65 in Contributions to the Archaeology of Oregon, 1981–1982. Don E. Dumond, ed. Association of Oregon Archaeologists. Occasional Papers 2. Portland.

Salisbury, Oliver M.
1962   Quoth the Raven: A Little Journey into the Primitive. Seattle, Wash.: Superior Publishing Company.

Sampson, Martin J.
1972   Indians of Skagit County. Mt. Vernon, Wash.: Skagit County Historical Society.

Samuel, Cheryl
1982   The Chilkat Dancing Blanket. Seattle, Wash.: Pacific Search Press.

1984   Northern Geometric Style Robes of the Northwest Coast. (Manuscript in National Museum of Man, Ottawa.)

1987   The Raven's Tail. Vancouver: University of British Columbia Press.

Samuels, Stephan R.
1983   Spatial Patterns and Cultural Processes in Three Northwest Coast Longhouse Floor Middens from Ozette. (Unpublished Ph.D. Dissertation in Anthropology, Washington State University, Pullman.)

Sanders, Douglas
1973   The Nishga Case. *BC Studies* 19(Autumn):3–20.

Sanford, Patricia R.
1975   The Lynch Site (35 LIN 36). Pp. 228–271 in Archaeological Studies in the Willamette Valley, Oregon. C. Melvin Aikens, ed. *University of Oregon Anthropological Papers* 8. Eugene.

Santee, J.F., and F.B. Warfield
1943   Accounts of Early Pioneering in the Alsea Valley. *Oregon Historical Quarterly* 44(1):56–60.

Sapir, Edward
[1906] [Field Notebooks of Takelma Myths, Paradigms, and Other Grammatical Notes.] (In Boas Collection, American Philosophical Society, Philadelphia.)

1907   Religious Ideas of the Takelma Indians of Southwestern Oregon. *Journal of American Folk-Lore* 20(76):33–49.

722

1907a   Notes on the Takelma Indians of Southwestern Oregon. *American Anthropologist* 9(2):251–275.

1909   Takelma Texts. *University of Pennsylvania. University Museum. Anthropological Publications* 2(1):1–267. Philadelphia.

1909a   Wishram Texts. *Publications of the American Ethnological Society* 2. (Reprinted: AMS Press, New York, 1974.)

1910   Upper Takelma. P. 872 in Vol. 2 of Handbook of American Indians North of Mexico. 2 vols. Frederick W. Hodge, ed. *Bureau of American Ethnology Bulletin* 30. Washington.

1910a   Takelma. Pp. 673–674 in Vol. 2 of Handbook of American Indians North of Mexico. 2 vols. Frederick W. Hodge, ed. *Bureau of American Ethnology Bulletin* 30:673–674. Washington.

[1910–1914] Nootka Notes. (Manuscript No. 1237.5–6, on file at Canadian Ethnology Service, National Museum of Man, Ottawa.)

1911   Some Aspects of Nootka Language and Culture. *American Anthropologist* 13(1):15–28.

1914   A Girl's Puberty Ceremony among the Nootka Indians. *Proceedings and Transactions of the Royal Society of Canada for 1913*, 3d. ser., Vol. 7(sect. 2):67–80. Ottawa.

1914a   Notes on Chasta Costa Phonology and Morphology. *University of Pennsylvania. University Museum. Anthropological Publications* 2(2):269–340. Philadelphia.

1915   Noun Reduplication in Comox, a Salish Language of Vancouver Island. *Anthropological Series 6, Geological Survey of Canada Memoir 63.* Ottawa.

1915a   A Sketch of the Social Organization of the Nass River Indians. *Anthropological Series 7, Geological Survey Bulletin 19.* Ottawa.

1915b   Abnormal Types of Speech in Nootka. *Anthropological Series 5, Geological Survey of Canada Memoir 62.* Ottawa. (Reprinted in: Selected Writings of Edward Sapir. David Mandelbaum, ed., University of California Press, Berkeley, 1946, 1986.)

1915c   The Na-dene Languages, a Preliminary Report. *American Anthropologist* 17(4):534–558.

1916   The Social Organization of the West Coast Tribes. *Proceedings and Transactions of the Royal Society of Canada for 1915*, 3d. ser., Vol. 9(sect. 2):355–374. Ottawa.

1916a   Time Perspective in Aboriginal American Culture: A Study in Method. *Anthropological Series 13, Geological Survey of Canada Memoir 40.* Ottawa.

1920   Nass River Terms of Relationship. *American Anthropologist* 22(3):261–271.

1921   The Life of a Nootka Indian. *Queen's Quarterly* 28:232–243, 351–367. (Reprinted as: Sayach'apis, a Nootka Trader. Pp. 297–323 in American Indian Life. Elsie C. Parsons, ed., B.W. Huebsch, New York, 1922.)

1921a   A Characteristic Penutian Form of Stem. *International Journal of American Linguistics* 2(1–2):58–67.

1922   The Takelma Language of Southwestern Oregon. Pp. 1–296 in Vol. 2 of Handbook of American Indian Languages. Franz Boas, ed. 2 vols. *Bureau of American Ethnology Bulletin* 40. Washington.

1924   The Rival Whalers, a Nitinat Story (Nootka Text with Translation and Grammatical Analysis). *International Journal of American Linguistics* 3(1):76–102.

1928   Vancouver Island Indians. Pp. 591–595 in Vol. 12 of Encyclopaedia of Religion and Ethics. James Hastings, ed. 13 vols. New York: Charles Scribner's Sons.

1929   Central and North American Languages. Pp. 138–141 in Vol. 5 of Encyclopaedia Britannica. 14th ed. London and New York: Encyclopaedia Britannica. (Reprinted: Pp. 169–178 in Selected Writings of Edward Sapir in Language, Culture and Personality. David G. Mandelbaum, ed., University of California Press, Berkeley, 1963.)

1938   Glottalized Continuants in Navaho, Nootka, and Kwakiutl (with a Note on Indo-European). *Language: Journal of the Linguistic Society of America* 14(4):248–274.

1939   Songs for a Comox Dancing Mask. Leslie Spier, ed. *Ethnos* 4(2):49–55.

Sapir, Edward, and Morris Swadesh
1939   Nootka Texts: Tales and Ethnological Narratives, with Grammatical Notes and Lexical Material. Philadelphia: University of Pennsylvania, Linguistic Society of America. (Reprinted: AMS Press, New York, 1978.)

1946   American Indian Grammatical Categories. *Word* 2(2):103–112. (Reprinted: Pp. 101–107 in Language in Culture and Society, Dell Hymes, ed., Harper and Row, New York, 1964.)

1953   Coos-Takelma-Penutian Comparisons. *International Journal of American Linguistics* 19(2):132–137.

1955   Native Accounts of Nootka Ethnography. *Indiana University. Research Center in Anthropology, Folklore and Linguistics Publications* 1:1–457. Bloomington. (Reprinted: AMS Press, New York, 1978.)

Sarafian, Winston L.
1977   Smallpox Strikes the Aleuts. *The Alaska Journal* 7(1):46–49. Juneau.

Saunders, Ross, and Philip W. Davis
1975   The Internal Syntax of Lexical Suffixes in Bella Coola. *International Journal of American Linguistics* 41(2):106–113.

1975a   Bella Coola Lexical Suffixes. *Anthropological Linguistics* 17(4):154–189.

1975b   Bella Coola Referential Suffixes. *International Journal of American Linguistics* 41(4):355–368.

Sauter, John, and Bruce Johnson
1974   Tillamook Indians of the Oregon Coast. Portland, Oreg.: Binfords and Mort.

Sawyer, Alan R.
1983   Toward More Precise Northwest Coast Attributions: Two Substyles of Haisla Masks. Pp. 143–147 in The Box of Daylight: Northwest Coast Indian Art, by Bill Holm. Seattle: Seattle Art Museum and University of Washington Press.

Sayachapis, Tom, Frank Williams, William Big Fred, Captain Bill, and Kwishanishm
1985   Legendary Hunters, Mainly Whalers, of the West Coast of Vancouver Island. Pt. 9 of *Nootka Legends and Stories*, Vol. 3 of Nuu-chah-nulth Texts. Eugene Arima, ed. Edward Sapir and Alexander Thomas, colls. John Thomas, Edward Sapir and Morris Swadesh, trans. (Manuscript on file at National Museum of Man, Ottawa.)

Scammon, Charles M.
1874   The Marine Mammals of the Northwestern Coast of North America. San Francisco: John H. Carmany. (Reprinted: Dover Publications, New York, 1968.)

Schalk, Randall F.
1977   The Structure of an Anadromous Fish Resource. Pp. 207–249 in For Theory Building in Archaeology. Lewis R. Binford, ed. New York: Academic Press.

————
1986   Estimating Salmon and Steelhead Usage in the Columbia Basin Before 1850: The Anthropological Perspective. *Northwest Environmental Journal* 2(2):1–29. Seattle, Wash.

Schlesser, Norman D.
1973   Fort Umpqua, Bastion of Empire. Oakland, Oreg.: Oakland Printing Company.

Schneider, Harold K.
1974   Economic Man: The Anthropology of Economics. New York: Free Press.

Schoenberg, Wilfred P.
1987   A History of the Catholic Church in the Pacific Northwest, 1743–1983. Washington: Pastoral Press.

Schoolcraft, Henry R.
1851–1857   Historical and Statistical Information Respecting the History, Condition and Prospects of the Indian Tribes of the United States. 6 vols. Philadelphia: Lippincott, Grambo.

Schrader, Robert F.
1983   The Indian Arts and Crafts Board: An Aspect of New Deal Indian Policy. Albuquerque: University of New Mexico Press.

Schulenburg, Albrecht C. von
1894   Die Sprache der Zimshian-Indianer in Nordwest-America. Braunschweig, Germany: Verlag Richard Sattler. (Reprinted: M. Sändig, Walluf bei Wiesbaden, Germany, 1972.)

Schulte-Tenckhoff, Isabelle
1986   Potlatch: conquête et invention. Lausanne, Switzerland: Editions D'en bas.

Schultz, John L., and Deward Walker, Jr.
1967   Indian Shakers on the Colville Reservation. *Commentary Research Studies* 35(2):167–172.

Schumacher, Paul
1874   Remarks on the Kjökken-Möddings of the Northwest Coast of America. Pp. 354–362 in *Annual Report of the Smithsonian Institution for 1873.* Washington.

————
1877   Researches on the Kjökkenmöddings and Graves of a Former Population of the Coast of Oregon. *Bulletin of the United States Geological and Geographical Survey of the Territories* 3(1):27–35. Washington.

————
1877a   Aboriginal Settlements of the Pacific Coast. *Popular Science Monthly* 10(57):353–356.

Schuster, Carl
1951   Joint-marks: A Possible Index of Cultural Contact Between America, Oceania and the Far East. *Koninklijk Instituut voor de Tropen. Mededeling* 94. *Afdeling Culturele en Physische Anthropologie* 39. Amsterdam.

Schwartz, Maurice L., and Garland F. Grabert
1973   Coastal Processes and Prehistoric Maritime Cultures. Pp. 303–320 in Coastal Geomorphology: A Proceedings Volume of the Third Annual Geomorphology Symposia Series, Held at Binghamton, New York, Sept. 28–30, 1972. Donald R. Coates, ed. Binghamton: State University of New York, Publications in Geomorphology.

Schwatka, Frederick
1900   Report of a Military Reconnaissance Made in Alaska in 1883. Pp. 283–362 in Compilation of Narratives of Explorations in Alaska. Washington: U.S. Government Printing Office.

Scidmore, Eliza
1885   Alaska, Its Southern Coast and the Sitkan Archipelago. Boston: D. Lothrop.

————
1893   Appleton's Guide-book to Alaska and the Northwest Coast. New York: D. Appleton.

Scott, James W., and Roland L. De Lorme
1988   Historical Atlas of Washington. Norman: University of Oklahoma Press.

Scott, Leslie M.
1928   Indian Diseases as Aids to Pacific Northwest Settlement. *Oregon Historical Quarterly* 29(2):144–161.

Scouler, John
1841   Observations on the Indigenous Tribes of the N.W. Coast of America. *Journal of the Royal Geographical Society of London* 11:215–251.

————
1848   On the Indian Tribes Inhabiting the Northwest Coast of America. *Journal of the Ethnological Society of London* 1:228–252.

————
1905   Dr. John Scouler's Journal of a Voyage to N.W. America [1824]. F.G. Young, ed. *Oregon Historical Quarterly* 6(1):54–75, (2):159–205, (3):276–287.

Seaburg, William R.
[1976–1982]   [Linguistic Notes from Fieldwork Among the Tolowa Athabaskan, Smith River and Crescent City, California.] (Manuscripts in Seaburg's possession.)

————
1982   Guide to Pacific Northwest Native American Materials in the Melville Jacobs Collection and in Other Archival Collections in the University of Washington Libraries. Seattle: University of Washington Libraries.

Seeman, Carole
1987   The Treaty and Non-treaty Coastal Indians. Pp. 37–67 in Indians, Superintendents, and Councils: Northwestern Indian Policy, 1850–1855. Clifford E. Trafzer, ed. Lanham, Md.: University Press of America.

Seguin, Margaret, ed.
1984   The Tsimshian: Images of the Past, Views for the Present. Vancouver: University of British Columbia Press.

————
1984a   Tsimshian Basketry: Report on a Field Research Contract. (Manuscript, on file, National Museum of Man, Ottawa.)

————
1985   Interpretive Contexts for Traditional and Current Coast Tsimshian Feasts. *Canada. National Museum of Man. Mercury Series. Ethnology Service Papers* 98. Ottawa.

Sendey, John, comp.
1977   The Nootkan Indian: A Pictorial. Port Alberni, B.C.: Alberni Valley Museum.

Severs, Patricia
1974   A View of Island Prehistory: Archaeological Investigations at Blue Jackets Creek, 1972–73. *The Charlottes: A Journal of the Queen Charlotte Islands* 3:2–12. Queen Charlotte, B.C.

————
1974a   Archaeological Investigations at Blue Jackets Creek, FlUa-4, Queen Charlotte Islands, British Columbia, 1973. *Canadian Archaeological Association Bulletin* 6:163–205.

————
1974b   Salvage Archaeology at the Council Site, GAUb-7, Queen Charlotte Islands. (Manuscript on file, Archaeological Sites Advisory Board of British Columbia, Vancouver.)

————
1975   Recent Research into the Prehistory of the Queen Charlotte Islands. *The Midden: Publication of the Archaeological Society of British Columbia* 7(2):15–17. Vancouver.

Sewid, James *see* Spradley, James P., ed.

Sewid-Smith, Daisy (My-yah-nelth)
1979   Prosecution or Persecution. Cape Mudge, B.C.: Nu-yum-baleess Society.

Shadbolt, Doris
1986   Bill Reid. Seattle: University of Washington Press.

Shane, Audrey P.M.
1984   Power in Their Hands: The Gitsontk. Pp. 160–173 in The Tsimshian: Images of the Past, Views for the Present. Margaret Seguin, ed. Vancouver: University of British Columbia Press.

Shankel, George E.
1945   The Development of Indian Policy in British Columbia. (Unpublished Ph.D. Dissertation in History, University of Washington, Seattle)

Shaw, Earl B.
1965   Fundamentals of Geography. New York: John Wiley.

Shaw, Robert D.
1975   Report of Excavations: The Martin Site (45PC7), 1974. Pullman: Washington State University, Department of Anthropology.

———
1977   Report of Excavations: The Martin Site (45-PC-7), 1974. *Washington Archaeological Society Occasional Paper* 5. Seattle.

Sheehan, Carol
1981   Pipes That Won't Smoke; Coal That Won't Burn: Haida Sculpture in Argillite. Calgary, Alta.: Glenbow Museum. *See also* McLaren, Carol Sheehan

Sheldon Jackson Museum
1976   A Catalogue of the Ethnological Collections in the Sheldon Jackson Museum. [Erna Gunther, comp.] Sitka, Alas.: Sheldon Jackson College.

Shelekhov, Grigoriĭ Ivanovich
1791   Rossiĭskago kupt͡sa Grigor ͡ia Shelekhova stranstvovanīe v 1783 . . . .[Journey of the Russian Merchant Grigoriĭ Shelekhov in 1783 . . . .] St. Petersburg: Johann Zacharias Logan.

———
1793   Schelekov's Reise von Ochotsk nach Amerika, vom Jahr 1783 bis 1787. Pp. 165–249 (Pt. 7) in Vol. 6 of Neue Nordische Beyträge . . . .Peter S. Pallas, ed. St. Petersburg and Leipzig: Johann Zacharias Logan.

———
1981   A Voyage to America, 1783–1786. Marina Ramsay, trans., Richard A. Pierce, ed. (*Materials for the Study of Alaska History* 19) Kingston, Ont.: The Limestone Press.

Shelikhov, Grigor *see* Shelekhov, Grigoriĭ Ivanovich

Sherzer, Joel
1973   Areal Linguistics in North America. Pp. 749–795 in *Current Trends in Linguistics.* Vol. 10: Linguistics in North America. Thomas A. Sebeok, ed. The Hague: Mouton. (Reprinted: Plenum Press, New York, 1976.)

Shipley, William F.
1969   Proto-Takelman. *International Journal of American Linguistics* 35(3):226–230.

———
1970   Proto-Kalapuyan. Pp. 97–106 in Languages and Cultures of Western North America: Essays in Honor of Sven S. Liljeblad. Earl H. Swanson, ed. Pocatello: Idaho State University Press.

———
1973   California. Pp. 1046–1078 in *Current Trends in Linguistics.* Vol. 10: Linguistics in North America. Thomas A. Sebeok, ed. The Hague: Mouton. (Reprinted: Plenum Press, New York, 1976.)

Shoop, Gregg B.
1972   The Participation of the Ohiaht Indians in the Commercial Fisheries of the Bamfield-Barkley Sound Area of British Columbia. (Unpublished M.A. Thesis in Anthropology, University of Victoria, Victoria, B.C.)

Shortess, Robert
1851   [Letter of February 5 to Anson Dart.] (In Records of the Oregon Superintendency of Indian Affairs, Washington.)

Shotridge, Florence
1913   The Life of a Chilkat Indian Girl. *University of Pennsylvania Museum Journal* 4(3):101–103. Philadelphia.

Shotridge, Louis
1917   My Northland Revisited. *University of Pennsylvania Museum Journal* 8(2):105–115. Philadelphia.

———
1919   A Visit to the Tsimshian Indians: The Skeena River (Continued). *University of Pennsylvania Museum Journal* 10(3):117–148. Philadelphia.

———
1919a   War Helmets and Clan Hats of the Tlingit Indians. *University of Pennsylvania Museum Journal* 10(1–2):43–48. Philadelphia.

———
1920   Ghost of Courageous Adventurer. *University of Pennsylvania Museum Journal* 11(1):11–26. Philadelphia.

———
1921   Tlingit Woman's Root Basket. *University of Pennsylvania Museum Journal* 12(3):162–178. Philadelphia.

———
1928   The Emblems of the Tlingit Culture. *University of Pennsylvania Museum Journal* 19(4):350–377. Philadelphia.

———
1929   The Bridge of Tongass: A Study of the Tlingit Marriage Ceremony. *University of Pennsylvania Museum Journal* 20(2):131–156. Philadelphia.

———
1929a   The Kaguanton Shark Helmet. *University of Pennsylvania Museum Journal* 20(3–4):339–343. Philadelphia.

Shotridge, Louis, and Florence Shotridge
1913   Indians of the Northwest. *University of Pennsylvania Museum Journal* 4(3):71–100. Philadelphia.

Shur, Leonid A., and R.A. Pierce
1976   Artists in Russian America: Mikhail Tikhanov, 1818. *The Alaska Journal* 6(1):40–49. Juneau.

Siebert, Erna, and Werner Forman
1967   North American Indian Art. Philippa Hentgès, trans. London: Paul Hamlyn.

Silverstein, Michael
1965   Penutian: The Grammatical Dimensions of Sapir's Hypothesis. (A.B. Honors Thesis, Harvard College, Cambridge, Mass.)

———
1972   Chinook Jargon: Language Contact and the Problem of Multi-level Generative Systems. *Language: Journal of the Linguistic Society of America* 48(2):378–406, (3):596–625.

———
1973   Chinook Person, Number, Gender. (Paper delivered to the 72d Annual Meeting of the American Anthropological Association, and to the 1973 Annual Meeting of the Linguistic Society of America.) (In Silverstein's possession.)

———
1974   Dialectal Developments in Chinookan Tense-aspect Systems: An Areal-historical Analysis. *Indiana University Publications in Anthropology and Linguistics, Memoirs* 29. Bloomington.

———
1976   Time Perspective in Northern and Western Penutian. (Unpublished paper presented at the Northwest Coast Studies Conference, Burnaby, B.C.)

1976a   Hierarchy of Features and Ergativity. Pp. 112–171 in Grammatical Categories in Australian Languages. R.M.W. Dixon, ed. Canberra: Australian Institute of Aboriginal Studies.

1979   Penutian: An Assessment. Pp. 650–691 in The Languages of Native America: Historical and Comparative Assessment. Lyle Campbell and Marianne Mithun, eds. Austin: University of Texas Press.

Simonsen, Bjorn O.
1973   Archaeological Investigations in the Hecate Strait-Milbanke Sound Area of British Columbia. *Canada. National Museum of Man. Mercury Series. Archaeological Survey Papers* 13. Ottawa.

Simpson, Sir George
1847   Narrative of a Journey Round the World, During the Years 1841 and 1842. 2 vols. London: Henry Colburn.

1931   Fur Trade and Empire: George Simpson's Journal . . . 1824–1825 [etc.]. Frederick Merk, ed. Cambridge, Mass.: Harvard University Press. (Reprinted: Belknap Press, Cambridge, Mass., 1968.)

Singh, Ram Raj Prasad
1956   Aboriginal Economic System of the Olympic Peninsula Indians, Western Washington. (Ph.D. Dissertation in Anthropology, University of Washington, Seattle.)

1966   Aboriginal Economic System of the Olympic Peninsula Indians, Western Washington. *Sacramento Anthropological Society Papers* 4. Sacramento.

Sismey, Eric
1961   H'kusam, a Kwakiutl Village. *The Beaver Outfit* 292(Winter):24–27. Winnipeg.

Skinner, S. Alan
1981   Clah-Cleh-Lah: An Archaeological Site at Bonneville Dam, Washington. Dallas, Tex.: Environment Consultants.

Slacum, William A.
1837   Memorial of William A. Slacum: Praying Compensation for His Services in Obtaining Information in Relation to the Settlements on the Oregon River. *25th Congress, 2d Sess., Senate Document* No. 24 (Serial No. 314). Washington.

1972   *Memorial* to the Senate Committee on Foreign Relations, December 18, 1837. Fairfield, Wash.: Ye Galleon Press.

Slocum, Robert G., and Kenneth H. Matsen
1968   Shoto Clay: A Description of Clay Artifacts from the Herzog Site (45-CL-4) in the Lower Columbia Region. *Oregon Archaeological Society Publications* 4. Portland.

Smet, Pierre Jean de
1905   Life, Letters and Travels of Father Pierre-Jean de Smet, S.J., 1801–1873 . . . .Hiram M. Chittenden and Alfred T. Richardson, eds. 4 vols. New York: F.P. Harper.

Smith, Asa B.
1958   [Letter of February 6, 1840.] Pp. 124–144 in The Diaries and Letters of Henry H. Spalding and Asa Bowen Smith Relating to the Nez Perce Mission, 1838–1842. Clifford M. Drury, ed. Glendale, Calif.: Arthur H. Clark.

Smith, Barbara S.
1980   Orthodoxy and Native Americans: The Alaskan Mission. *Orthodox Church in America, Department of History and Archives, Historical Society Occasional Papers* 1. Syosset, N.Y.

Smith, Harlan I.
1903   Shell-heaps of the Lower Fraser River, British Columbia. *Publications of the Jesup North Pacific Expedition* 2(4); *Memoirs of the American Museum of Natural History* 4(4):133–191. New York. (Reprinted: AMS Press, New York, 1975.)

1907   Archaeology of the Gulf of Georgia and Puget Sound. *Publications of the Jesup North Pacific Expedition* 2(6); *Memoirs of the American Museum of Natural History* 4(6):303–441. New York.

1909   Archeological Remains on the Coast of Northern British Columbia and Southern Alaska. *American Anthropologist* n.s. 11(4):595–600.

[1920–1924] [Bella Coola Fieldnotes.] (Manuscript No. 1192. 1A1-1N2, Ethnology Division Archives, National Museum of Man, Ottawa.)

1924   Eagle Snaring Among the Bella Coola. *Canadian Field Naturalist* 38(9):167–168.

1924a   A Bellacoola, Carrier, and Chilcotin Route Time Recorder. *American Anthropologist* 26(2):293.

1924b   Trephined Aboriginal Skulls from British Columbia and Washington. *American Journal of Physical Anthropology* 7(4):447–452.

1925   Sympathetic Magic and Witchcraft Among the Bella Coola. *American Anthropologist* 27(1):116–121.

1925a   Entomology Among the Bellacoola and Carrier Indians. *American Anthropologist* 27(3):436–440.

1928   Restoration of Totem-poles in British Columbia. *National Museum of Canada Bulletin* 50:81–83. Ottawa.

1929   Kitchen-middens of the Pacific Coast of Canada. *National Museum of Canada. Annual Report for 1927, Bulletin* 56:42–46. Ottawa.

1929a   Materia Medica of the Bella Coola and Neighbouring Tribes of British Columbia. *National Museum of Canada. Annual Report for 1927. Bulletin* 56:47–68. Ottawa.

1930   A List of Archaeological Sites Near Prince Rupert, British Columbia. (Manuscript on file at the Archaeological Survey of Canada Archives, Ottawa.)

Smith, Harlan I., and G. Fowke
1901   Cairns of British Columbia and Washington. *Memoirs of the American Museum of Natural History* 4(2). New York.

Smith, Marian W.
[1936–1939] [Ethnographic Notes on the North Coast Salish, Washington and British Columbia.] (Manuscript in the Library of the Royal Anthropological Institute of Great Britain and Ireland, London.)

1940   The Puyallup-Nisqually. *Columbia University Contributions to Anthropology* 32. New York. (Reprinted: AMS Press, New York, 1969.)

1940a   The Puyallup of Washington. Pp. 3–36 in Acculturation in Seven American Indian Tribes. Ralph Linton, ed. New York: D. Appleton-Century.

1941   The Coast Salish of Puget Sound. *American Anthropologist* 43(2):197–211.

1947   House Types of the Middle Fraser River. *American Antiquity* 12(4):255–267.

1949   Indians of the Urban Northwest. *Columbia University Contributions to Anthropology* 36. New York. (Reprinted: AMS Press, New York, 1969.)

1950   Archaeology of the Columbia-Fraser Region. *Memoirs of the Society for American Archaeology* 6. Menasha, Wis.

726

1950a   The Nooksack, the Chilliwack, and the Middle Fraser. *Pacific Northwest Quarterly* 41(4):330–341.

1954   Shamanism in the Shaker Religion of Northwest America. *Man: The Journal of the Royal Anthropological Institute* 54(August):119–122. London.

1959   Towards a Classification of Cult Movements. *Man: The Journal of the Royal Anthropological Institute* 59(January):8–12. London.

Smith, Silas B.
1901   Primitive Customs and Religious Beliefs of the Indians of the Pacific Northwest Coast. *Quarterly of the Oregon Historical Society* 2(3):255–265. Eugene.

Smith, Thomas H.
1856   [Letter of Jan. 8 to Joel Palmer.] (Manuscript 1856-11, Microcopy 2, Roll 14, Records of the Oregon Superintendency, in Record Group 75, National Archives, Washington.)

Smithy, R.A., and J.W. Smithy, eds.
1970   Early Man and Environments in Northwest North America. *Proceedings of the 2d Annual Paleo-environmental Workshop of the University of Calgary Archaeological Association, 1970.* Calgary, Alta.: The Students' Press.

Smyly, John, and Carolyn Smyly
1975   The Totem Poles of Skedans. Seattle: University of Washington Press.

Sneddon, James O.
1960   Out of This World: A Study of the Indian Shakers at the Muckleshoot Reservation. (Unpublished paper in the Northwest Collection of the University of Washington Library, Seattle.)

Sneed, Paul
1971   Of Salmon and Men: An Investigation of Ecological Determinants and Aboriginal Man in the Canadian Plateau. Pp. 229–242 in Aboriginal Man and Environments on the Plateau of Northwest America. Arnold H. Stryd and R.A. Smith, eds. Calgary, Alta.: Student's Press.

Snyder, Gary
1960   Myths and Texts. New York: Totem Press. (Reprinted: New Directions, New York, 1978.)

1977   The Incredible Survival of Coyote. Pp. 67–93 in The Old Ways: Six Essays. San Francisco: City Lights Books.

1979   He Who Hunted Birds in His Father's Village: The Dimensions of a Haida Myth. Bolinas, Calif.: Grey Fox Press.

Snyder, Sally
1964   Skagit Society and Its Existential Basis: An Ethnofolkloristic Reconstruction. (Unpublished Ph.D. Dissertation in Anthropology, University of Washington, Seattle.)

1975   Quest for the Sacred in Northern Puget Sound: An Interpretation of Potlatch. *Ethnology* 14(2):149–161.

Snyder, Sandra L.
1978   An Osteo-archaeological Investigation of Pinniped Remains at Seal Rock, Oregon (35 LNC 14). (Unpublished M.A. Thesis in Anthropology, Oregon State University, Corvallis.)

Snyder, Sandra L., and Richard E. Ross
1980   Excavations at the Yaquina Site, Lincoln County, Oregon. Newport, Oreg.: Lincoln County Commissioners.

Snyder, Warren A.
1956   Archaeological Sampling at "Old Man House" on Puget Sound. *Washington State College Research Studies* 24(1):1–35. Pullman.

1956a   "Old Man House" on Puget Sound. *Washington State University Research Studies* 24:17–37. Pullman.

1968   Southern Puget Sound Salish: Phonology and Morphology. *Sacramento Anthropological Society Papers* 8. Sacramento, Calif.

1968a   Southern Puget Sound Salish: Texts, Place Names and Dictionary. *Sacramento Anthropological Society Papers* 9. Sacramento, Calif.

Société des Amis du Musée de l'Homme
1969   Masterpieces of Indian and Eskimo Art from Canada. [Exhibition Catalog.] Paris: Musée de l'Homme.

Soil Conservation Service
1982   National List of Scientific Plant Names. Vol. 1: List of Plant Names. Washington: U.S. Department of Agriculture.

Sotoca, Maria del Carmen Garcia
[1970]   [Catalogue of Malaspina Drawings.] (Manuscript at Museo Naval, Madrid.)

Sotos Serrano, Carmen
1982   Los Pintores de la expedición de Alejandro Malaspina. 2 vols. Madrid: Real Academia de la Historia.

Spaid, Stanley
1950   Joel Palmer and Indian Affairs in Oregon. (Unpublished Ph.D. Dissertation in History, University of Oregon, Eugene.)

Spalding, Henry H.
[1853]   Statement of Number and Condition of Indian Tribes West of the Cascade Mountains. (Manuscript No. 1201 in Oregon Historical Society, Portland.)

Sparrow, Leona
1976   Work History of a Coast Salish Couple. (Unpublished M.A. Thesis in Anthropology, University of British Columbia, Vancouver.)

Spaulding, Albert C.
1955   Prehistoric Cultural Development in the Eastern United States. Pp. 12–27 in New Interpretations of Aboriginal American Culture History. Washington: Anthropological Society of Washington. (Reprinted: Cooper Square Publishers, New York, 1972.)

Spier, Leslie
1925   The Distribution of Kinship Systems in North America. *University of Washington Publications in Anthropology* 1(2):69–88. Seattle.

1927   Tribal Distribution in Southwestern Oregon. *Oregon Historical Quarterly* 28(4):358–376.

1931   Historical Interrelation of Culture Traits: Franz Boas' Study of Tsimshian Mythology. Pp. 449–457 in Methods in Social Science: A Case Book. Stuart A. Rice, ed. Chicago: University of Chicago Press.

1935   The Prophet Dance of the Northwest and Its Derivatives: The Source of the Ghost Dance. *General Series in Anthropology* 1. Menasha, Wis. (Reprinted: AMS Press, New York, 1979.)

1936   Tribal Distribution in Washington. *General Series in Anthropology* 3. Menasha, Wis.

Spier, Leslie, and Edward Sapir
1930   Wishram Ethnography. *University of Washington Publications in Anthropology* 3(3):151–300. Seattle.

Splawn, Andrew J.
1944   *Ka-mi-akin*: Last Hero of the Yakimas [1917]. 2d ed. Portland: Binfords and Mort, for the Oregon Historical Society.

727

Spradley, James P., ed.
1969   Guests Never Leave Hungry: The Autobiography of James Sewid, a Kwakiutl Indian. New Haven, Conn.: Yale University Press.

Spradley, James P., and David W. McCurdy
1975   Anthropology: The Cultural Perspective. New York: John Wiley.

Spragge, William
1873   Abstract of the Report of J.W. Powell . . . .Indian Superintendent for British Columbia, Dated 11th January, 1873. Pp. 7–12 in [Canada]. *Annual Report on Indian Affairs for the Year 1872.* Ottawa.

Sprague, Roderick
1976   The Submerged Finds from the Prehistoric Component, English Camp, San Juan Island, Washington. Pp. 78–85 in The Excavation of Water-saturated Archaeological Sites (Wet Sites) on the Northwest Coast of North America. Dale R. Croes, ed. *Canada. National Museum of Man. Mercury Series. Archaeological Survey Papers* 50. Ottawa.

Sproat, Gilbert M.
1867   The West Coast Indians in Vancouver Island. *Transactions of the Ethnological Society of London* n.s. 5:243–254.

————
1868   Scenes and Studies of Savage Life. London: Smith, Elder. (Reprinted: Sono-Nis Press, Victoria, B.C., 1987.)

————
1876   [Letter of December 20, to the Minister of the Interior.] (In Record Group 10, Vol. 3611, File 3756-4, Public Archives of Canada, Ottawa.)

————
1880   Letter, Dated 28th October, 1879 from Fort Rupert to the Chief Commissioner of Lands and Works, Victoria. Pp. 145–146 in *Canada. Report of the Deputy Superintendent General of Indian Affairs for 1879.* Ottawa.

Sprot, G.D.
1928   The Early Indian Wildfowler of Vancouver Island. *Canadian Field-Naturalist* 42(6):139–143. Ottawa.

Spuhler, James N.
1979   Genetic Distances, Trees, and Maps of North American Indians. Pp. 135–183 in The First Americans: Origins, Affinities, and Adaptations. William S. Laughlin and Albert B. Harper, eds. New York: Gustav Fischer.

Stafford, William
1977   Stories That Could Be True: New and Collected Poems. New York: Harper and Row.

————
1982   Hearing the Song; Oregon haiku. Pp. 1–2 in Coyote's Journal. James Koller, 'Gogisgi' Carroll Arnett, Steve Nemirow, and Peter Blue Cloud, eds. Berkeley, Calif.: Wingbow.

Stallard, Bruce, and Clayton Denman
1956   Archaeological Site Survey of the Olympic Coast Between the Queets and Ozette Rivers. (Manuscript on file at Olympic National Park, Port Angeles, Wash.)

Stanbury, W.T., and Jay H. Siegel
1975   Success and Failure: Indians in Urban Society. Vancouver: University of British Columbia Press.

Stanbury, W.T., D.B. Fields, and D. Stevenson
1972   B.C. Indians in an Urban Environment: Income, Poverty, Education and Vocational Training. *Manpower Review. Pacific Region* 5(3):11–33. Vancouver, B.C.

————
1972a   Unemployment and Labour Force Participation Rates of B.C. Indians Living Off Reserves. *Manpower Review. Pacific Region* 5(2):21–45. Vancouver, B.C.

Stanford, Martin
1980   Archaeological Investigations of the Disturbances at the Portage Arm Site (49 SIT 123). (Manuscript on file, U.S. Forest Service, Chatham Area, Tongass National Forest, Sitka, Alas.)

Stanford, Martin, and Theresa Thibault
1980   Archaeological Investigation at Traders Island (49 SIT 120) on Catherine Island, Alaska. (Manuscript on file, U.S. Forest Service, Chatham Area, Tongass National Forest, Sitka, Alaska.)

Stanley, George F.G., ed.
1970   Mapping the Frontier: Charles Wilson's Diary of the Survey of the 49th Parallel, 1858–1862, While Secretary of the British Boundary Commission. Toronto: Macmillan of Canada.

Stanley, Golden
1954   [Notes from Noel George, Sliammon.] (Typescript in Powell River Museum, Powell River, B.C.)

————
1968   [Notes on Sliammon Genealogy.] (Manuscript in Powell River Museum, Powell River, B.C.)

Stanton, William R.
1975   The Great United States Exploring Expedition of 1838–1842. Berkeley: University of California Press.

Starling, E.A.
1853   [Letter of December 4 to I.I. Stevens.] (In Records of the Washington Superintendency of Indian Affairs, Washington.)

Starr, Frederick
1893   Anthropology at the World's Fair. *Popular Science Monthly* 43(5):610–621. New York.

Stearns, Mary Lee
1975   Life Cycle Rituals of Modern Haida. Pp. 129–169 in Contributions to Canadian Ethnology, 1975. David B. Carlisle, ed. *Canada. National Museum of Man. Mercury Series. Ethnology Service Papers* 31. Ottawa.

————
1977   The Reorganization of Ceremonial Relations in Haida Society. *Arctic Anthropology* 14(1):54–63.

————
1981   Haida Culture in Custody, the Masset Band. Seattle: University of Washington Press.

————
1984   Succession to Chiefship in Haida Society. Pp. 190–219 in The Tsimshians and Their Neighbors of the North Pacific Coast. Jay Miller and Carol M. Eastman, eds. Seattle: University of Washington Press.

Steele, Harvey
1980   Bachelor Island. *Oregon Archaeological Society Reports* 8. Portland.

Steinbock, R. Ted
1976   Paleopathological Diagnosis and Interpretation: Bone Diseases in Ancient Human Populations. Springfield, Ill.: Charles C. Thomas.

Steller, Georg W.
1988   Journal of a Voyage with Bering, 1741–1742. O.W. Frost, ed. Margritt A. Engel and O.W. Frost, trans. Stanford, Calif.: Stanford University Press.

Steltzer, Ulli
1984   A Haida Potlatch. Seattle: University of Washington Press.

Stenzel, Franz
1975   James Madison Alden: Yankee Artist of the Pacific Coast, 1854–1860. Fort Worth, Texas: Amon Carter Museum.

Stern, Bernhard J.
1929   An Indian Shaker Initiation and Healing Service. *Social Forces* 7(3):432–434.

————
1934   The Lummi Indians of Northwest Washington. New York: Columbia University Press.

Stern, Theodore
1966 The Klamath Tribe: A People and Their Reservation. (*American Ethnological Society Monograph* 41). Seattle: University of Washington Press.

Sternes, Gilbert L.
1960 Climates of the States: Oregon (*Climatography of the United States* 60-35). Washington: U.S. Government Printing Office.

Stevens, Hazard
1901 The Life of Isaac Ingalls Stevens, by His Son. 2 vols. Boston and New York: Houghton Mifflin.

Stevens, Isaac I.
1855 Report of Explorations for a Route for the Pacific Railroad . . . from St. Paul to Puget Sound. In Vol. 1 of Reports of Explorations and Surveys . . . from the Mississippi River to the Pacific Ocean [1853–1854]. Washington: Beverly Tucker, Printer.

Stevenson, David
1980 The Oowekeeno People: A Cultural History. (Unpublished report prepared for the National Museum of Man, Ottawa.)

————
1985 One Large Family: The Ceremonial Names of the Oowekeeno People of Rivers Inlet. (Unpublished report prepared for the National Museum of Man, Ottawa.)

Stevenson, Ian
1966 Twenty Cases Suggestive of Reincarnation. *Proceedings of the American Society for Psychical Research* 26. New York. (Reprinted: University of Virginia, Charlottesville, 1980.)

————
1975 The Belief and Cases Related to Reincarnation Among the Haida. *Journal of Anthropological Research* 31(4):364–375.

Steward, Julian
1940 Native Cultures of the Intermontane (Great Basin) Area. Pp. 445–502 in Essays in Historical Anthropology of North America Published in Honor of John R. Swanton. *Smithsonian Miscellaneous Collections* 100. Washington.

Stewart, Frances L.
1975 The Seasonal Availability of Fish Species Used by the Coast Tsimshians of Northern British Columbia. *Syesis* 8:375–388. Victoria, B.C.

————
[1977] Vertebrate Faunal Remains from the Boardwalk Site (GbTo:31) of Northern British Columbia. (Manuscript No. 1263 on file at the Archaeological Survey of Canada Archives, Ottawa.)

Stewart, Hilary
1977 Indian Fishing: Early Methods on the Northwest Coast. Seattle: University of Washington Press.

————
1979 Robert Davidson: Haida Printmaker. Seattle: University of Washington Press.

————
1979a Looking at Indian Art of the Northwest Coast. Seattle: University of Washington Press.

————
1984 Cedar: Tree of Life to the Northwest Coast Indians. Seattle: University of Washington Press.

Stewart, Susan
1982 Sir George Simpson: Collector. *The Beaver*, Outfit 313(1)4–9. Winnipeg.

Stewart, T. Dale
1958 Stone Age Skull Surgery: A General Review, with Emphasis on the New World. Pp. 469–491 in *Annual Report of the Smithsonian Institution for the Year 1957*. Washington.

Stilson, M. Leland
1972 Fluctuations in Aboriginal Environmental Utilization in Response to Delat Progradation: Three Sites from Skagit County. (Unpublished B.A. Senior Thesis in Anthropology, University of Washington, Seattle.)

Stilson, M. Leland, and James C. Chatters
1981 Excavations at 45-SN-48N and 45-SN-49A, Snohomish County, Washington. *University of Washington. Office of Public Archaeology. Institute for Environmental Studies. Reports in Highway* Archaeology 6. Seattle.

Stirling, M.W.
1943 Report on the Bureau of American Ethnology. Pp. 49–60 (Appendix 5) in *Annual Report of the Smithsonian Institution for the Year 1942*. Washington.

Stocking, George W., Jr.
1974 The Boas Plan for the Study of American Indian Languages. Pp. 454–484 in Studies in the History of Linguistics: Traditions and Paradigms. Dell Hymes, ed. Bloomington: Indiana University Press.

————, ed.
1974a The Shaping of American Anthropology 1883–1911: A Franz Boas Reader. New York: Basic Books.

Stone, William L.
1838 Life of Joseph Brant-Thayendanega: Including the Border Wars of the American Revolution, Sketches of the Indian Campaigns of Generals Harmar, St. Clair, and Wayne . . . 2 vols. New York: George Dearborn.

Storie, Susanne, ed.
1973 Bella Coola Stories. Victoria: British Columbia Indian Advisory Committee.

————, ed.
1973a Oweekano Stories. Victoria: British Columbia Indian Advisory Committee.

Storie, Susanne, and Jennifer Gould, eds.
1973 Bella Bella Stories. Victoria: British Columbia Indian Advisory Committee.

————, eds.
1973a Klemtu Stories. Victoria: British Columbia Indian Advisory Committee.

Story, Gillian L.
1966 A Morphological Study of Tlingit. (Unpublished M.A. Thesis in Linguistics, University of London. London.)

Story, Gillian L., and Constance M. Naish, comps.
1973 Tlingit Verb Dictionary. College: University of Alaska, Native Language Center.

Stott, Margaret A.
1975 Bella Coola Ceremony and Art. *Canada. National Museum of Man. Mercury Series. Ethnology Service Papers* 21. Ottawa.

Strange, James
1929 James Strange's Journal and Narrative of the Commercial Expedition from Bombay to the North-West Coast of America; Together with a Chart Showing the Tract of the Expedition. Introduction by A.V. Venkatarama Ayyar. Madras, India: Government Press. (Reprinted: Shorey Book Store, Seattle, 1972.)

Strathern, Gloria M., comp.
1970 Navigations, Traffiques, & Discoveries, 1774–1848: A Guide to Publications Relating to the Area Now British Columbia. Victoria: University of Victoria. (A Companion Volume to Barbara Lowther's A Bibliography of British Columbia: Laying the Foundations, 1849–1899.)

Strong, Emory M.
1959 Stone Age on the Columbia River. Portland, Oreg.: Binfords and Mort. (Reprinted in 1967.)

Strong, W. Duncan, W. Egbert Schenck, and Julian H. Steward
1930 Archaeology of The Dalles - Deschutes Region. *University of California Publications in American Archaeology and Ethnology* 29(1):1–154. Berkeley.

Stuart, Robert
1935 The Discovery of the Oregon Trail: Robert Stuart's Narratives of His Overland Trip Eastward from Astoria, 1812–13. Philip A. Rollins, ed. New York: Charles Scrib-

ner's Sons. (Translated from Nouvelles Annales des Voyages, Paris, 1821.)

Stuart, Wendy Bross
1972   Gambling Music of the Coast Salish Indians. *Canada. National Museum of Man. Mercury Series. Ethnology Service Papers* 3. Ottawa.

Stubbs, Ron D.
1973   [Preliminary Report on Indian Bay Site (35 CS30).] (Report to Corps of Engineers, Portland, Oregon District.)

Stumpf, Carl
1886   Lieder der Bellakula-Indianer. *Vierteljahres-chrift für Musikwissenschaft* 2:405–426. Leipzig, Germany.

Sturgis, William
[1799] [Journal Kept by William Sturgis, February 13–May 16, 1799.] (Manuscript in Massachusetts Historical Society, Boston.)

Styles, Norla
1976   Preliminary Report on the Burials at Glenrose. Pp. 203–213 in The Glenrose Cannery Site. R.G. Matson, ed. *Canada. National Museum of Man. Mercury Series. Archaeological Survey Papers* 52. Ottawa.

Sucher, David, ed.
1973   The Asahel Curtis Sampler. Seattle, Wash.: Puget Sound Access.

Suckley, George, and James G. Cooper
1860   The Natural History of Washington Territory and Oregon . . . ..New York: Baillière Brothers.

Sullivan, Louis R.
1922   The Frequency and Distribution of Some Anatomical Variations in American Crania. *Anthropological Papers of the American Museum of Natural History* 23(5):203–258. New York.

Sullivan, Mary Louise
1932   Eugene Casimir Chirouse, O.M.I., and the Indians of Washington. (Unpublished M.A. Thesis in Anthropology, University of Washington, Seattle.)

The Suquamish Museum
1985   The Eyes of Chief Seattle. (Exhibition Catalogue) Suquamish, Wash.: The Suquamish Museum.

Suría, Tomás de
1936   Journal of Tomás de Suría of His Voyage with Malaspina to the Northwest Coast of America in 1791. Henry R. Wagner, ed. and trans. *Pacific Historical Review* 5(3):234–276.

Sutherland, Patricia C.
1978   Dodge Island, a Prehistoric Coast Tsimshian Settlement Site in Prince Rupert Harbour, B.C. (Manuscript No. 1343, on file at the Archaeological Survey of Canada Archives, Ottawa.)

———
1980   Understanding Cultural Relationships Across Hecate Strait, Northern British Columbia. (Paper presented at the 13th Annual Meeting, Canadian Archaeological Association, Saskatoon, Sask.)

Suttles, Wayne
[1946–1952] [Straits Ethnographic Fieldnotes.] (Notebooks and manuscripts in Suttles' possession.)

[1947–1952] [Northern Puget Sound Fieldnotes.] (Unpublished manuscript in Suttles's possession.)

1951   Economic Life of the Coast Salish of Haro and Rosario Straits. (Ph.D. Dissertation in Anthropology, University of Washington, Seattle.)

1951a   The Early Diffusion of the Potato Among the Coast Salish. *Southwestern Journal of Anthropology* 7(3):272–288.

1952   Notes on Coast Salish Sea-mammal Hunting. *Anthropology in British Columbia* 3:10–20. Victoria.

[1952–1971] [Halkomelem Ethnographic Fieldnotes.] (Notebooks and manuscripts in Suttles's possession.)

1954   Post-contact Culture Change Among the Lummi Indians. *British Columbia Historical Quarterly* 18(1–2):29–102. Vancouver.

1957   The Plateau Prophet Dance Among the Coast Salish. *Southwestern Journal of Anthropology* 13(4):352–396.

1957a   The "Middle Fraser" and "Foothill" Cultures: A Criticism. *Southwestern Journal of Anthropology* 13(2):156–183.

1958   Private Knowledge, Morality, and Social Classes Among the Coast Salish. *American Anthropologist* 60(3):497–507.

1960   Affinal Ties, Subsistence, and Prestige Among the Coast Salish. *American Anthropologist* 62(2):296–305.

1961   [Ethnographic and Linguistic Fieldnotes Concerning Sliammon and Comox.] (Manuscripts in Suttles's possession.)

1962   Variation in Habitat and Culture on the Northwest Coast. Pp. 522–537 in *Proceedings of the 34th International Congress of Americanists*. Vienna, 1960.

[1962–1963] Musqueam Texts. (Unpublished notes in Suttles's possession.)

1963   The Persistence of Intervillage Ties Among the Coast Salish. *Ethnology* 2(4):512–525.

1968   Coping with Abundance: Subsistence on the Northwest Coast. Pp. 56–68 in Man the Hunter. Richard B. Lee and Irven DeVore, eds. Chicago: Aldine.

1973   [Laichkwiltach (Yuculta) Place Names.] (Manuscript in Suttles's possession.)

1973a   [Comment on] Eugene E. Ruyle's Slavery, Surplus, and Stratification on the Northwest Coast: The Ethnoenergetics of an Incipient Stratification System. *Current Anthropology* 14(5):622–623.

1974   The Economic Life of the Coast Salish of Haro and Rosario Straits. New York: Garland.

———, comp.
1978   Native Languages of the North Pacific Coast of North America. Map. Portland Oregon.

1979   *The Mouth of Heaven* and the Kwakiutl Tongue: A Comment on Walens on Goldman. *American Anthropologist* 81(1):96–98.

1982   The Halkomelem Sxwayxwey. *American Indian Art Magazine* 8(1):56–65.

1983   Productivity and Its Constraints: A Coast Salish Case. Pp. 67–87 in Indian Art Traditions of the Northwest Coast. R.L. Carlson, ed. Burnaby, B.C.: Archaeology Press.

1984   A Reference Grammar of the Musqueam Dialect of the Halkomelem. (Manuscript, on file, British Columbia Provincial Museum, Victoria.)

1987   Spirit Dancing and the Persistence of Native Culture Among the Coast Salish. Pp. 199–208 in Coast Salish Essays. Wayne Suttles, ed. Seattle: University of Washington Press.

1987a   Coast Salish Essays (Compiled and edited with the assistance of Ralph Maud). Seattle: University of Washington Press.

1987b   Northwest Coast Linguistic History—a View from the Coast. Pp. 265–281 in Coast Salish Essays. Wayne Suttles, ed. Vancouver, B.C.: Talonbooks.

1987c   Cultural Diversity within the Coast Salish Continuum. Pp. 243–249 in Ethnicity and Culture. Reginald Auger, Margaret F. Glass, Scott MacEachern, and Peter H. McCartney, eds. Calgary, Alta.: Archaeological Association, University of Calgary.

Suttles, Wayne, and William W. Elmendorf
1963   Linguistic Evidence for Salish Prehistory. Pp. 41–52 in Symposium on Language and Culture. V.E. Garfield, ed. *Proceedings of the 1962 Annual Spring Meeting of the American Ethnological Society.* Seattle, Wash.

Suttles, Wayne, and Cameron Suttles
1985   Native Languages of the Northwest Coast. Portland: Western Inprints, the Press of the Oregon Historical Society.

Swadesh, Mary Haas, and Morris Swadesh
1932   A Visit to the Other World, a Nitinat Text (with Translation and Grammatical Analysis). *International Journal of American Linguistics* 7(3–4):195–208.

Swadesh, Morris
1938   Nootka Internal Syntax. *International Journal of American Linguistics* 9(2–4):77–102.

1948   Motivations in Nootka Warfare. *Southwestern Journal of Anthropology* 4(1):76–93.

1950   Salish Internal Relationships. *International Journal of American Linguistics* 16(4):157–167.

1952   Salish Phonologic Geography. *Language: Journal of the Linguistic Society of America* 28(2):232–248.

1953   Mosan I: A Problem of Remote Common Origin. *International Journal of American Linguistics* 19(1):26–44.

1953a   Mosan II: Comparative Vocabulary. *International Journal of American Linguistics* 19(3):223–236.

[1953b]   [Tape Recording of Dootoodn Athabaskan Words and Phrases from Miller Collins, Ada Collins, and Daisy Collins Fuller at Siletz, Oreg.] (In Archives of Traditional Music, Indiana University, Bloomington.)

[1953c]   [Tape Recording of Galice Creek Athabaskan Words and Phrases from Hoxie Simmons at Siletz, Oreg.] (In Archives of Traditional Music, Indiana University, Bloomington.)

1954   On the Penutian Vocabulary Survey. *International Journal of American Linguistics* 20(2):123–133.

1955   Chemakum Lexicon Compared with Quileute. *International Journal of American Linguistics* 21(1):60–72.

1956   Problems of Long-range Comparison in Penutian. *Language: Journal of the Linguistic Society of America* 32(1):17–41.

1965   Kalapuya and Takelma. *International Journal of American Linguistics* 31(3):237–240.

1971   The Origin and Diversification of Language. Chicago: Aldine-Atherton.

Swan, James G.
1857   The Northwest Coast; Or, Three Years' Residence in Washington Territory. New York: Harper. (Reprinted: University of Washington Press, Seattle, 1972.)

[1859–1866]   [Unpublished Diaries.] (In Manuscript Collection, Suzzallo Library, University of Washington, Seattle.)

1861   A Cruise in the *Sarah Newton* on the Pacific Coast, July 18–August 14, 1861; No. 1 and No. 2. *Washington Standard* 5 October 1861, 12 October 1861. (Reprinted in Almost Out of the World, William A. Katz, ed., Washington State Historical Society, Tacoma, 1971.)

1870   The Indians of Cape Flattery, at the Entrance to the Strait of Fuca, Washington Territory. *Smithsonian Contributions to Knowledge* 16(8):1–106. Washington. (Reprinted: Shorey Publications, Seattle, 1982.)

1875   [Letters of June 17, July 29, August 3, September 30, October 4, November 9, and December 6, 1875 to Spencer F. Baird.] (In James G. Swan Correspondence, 1875–1876, Smithsonian Institution Archives, Record Unit 70, Box 5, Washington.)

1876   The Haidah Indians of Queen Charlotte's Island, British Columbia. With a Brief Description of Their Carvings, Tattoo Designs, etc. *Smithsonian Contributions to Knowledge* 21(4):1–18. Washington.

1876a   [Letters of January 24, March 27, and April 9, 1876 to Spencer F. Baird.] (In Incoming Correspondence 1850–1877, Smithsonian Institution Archives, Record Unit 53, Box 52, Folder 19, Washington.)

1881   The Surf-smelt of the Northwest Coast, and the Method of Taking Them by the Quillehute Indians, West Coast of Washington Territory. *Proceedings of the United States National Museum for 1880.* Vol. 3:43–46. Washington.

1883   Journal of a Trip to Queen Charlotte Islands, B.C. Microfilm. Seattle: University of Washington, Suzallo Library.

1884–1887   The Fur-seal Industry of Cape Flattery and Vicinity. Pp. 393–400 in The Fisheries and Fishery Industries of the United States. George B. Goode, ed. 8 vols. in 7. Washington: U.S. Government Printing Office.

1971   Almost Out of the World; Scenes from Washington Territory, the Strait of Juan de Fuca, 1859–61. William A. Katz, ed. Tacoma: Washington State Historical Society.

Swann, Brian, ed.
1985   Song of the Sky: Versions of Native American Songs and Poems. Ashuelot, N.H.: Four Zoas Night House.

Swanson, Karen S. and Stanley D. Davis
1982   Young Bay Midden Cultural Resource Investigations. (Manuscript on file, U.S. Forest Service, Chatham Area, Tongass National Forest, Sitka, Alaska.)

1982a   Greens Creek Midden Cultural Resource Investigations. (Manuscript on file, U.S. Forest Service, Chatham Area, Tongass National Forest, Sitka, Alaska.)

1983   Archaeological Investigation at Lake Eva, Baranof Island, Alaska. (Manuscript on file, U.S. Forest Service, Chatham Area, Tongass National Forest, Sitka, Alas.)

Swanson, Karen S., and Alexander Dolitsky
1985   [Archaeological Fieldnotes for the Test Excavation at the Poison Cove Site.] (Unpublished notes, on file at the U.S. Forest Service, Chatham Area, Tongass National Forest, Sitka, Alas.)

Swanton, John R.
1900   Morphology of the Chinook Verb. *American Anthropologist* n.s. 2(2):199–237.

1902   Notes on the Haida Language. *American Anthropologist* 4(3):392–403.

1904   The Development of the Clan System and of Secret Societies Among the Northwestern Tribes. *American Anthropologist* n.s. 6(3):477–485. (Reprinted: Pp. 583–593 in Selected Papers from the American Anthropologist, 1888–1920, Frederica De Laguna, ed., Row, Peterson and Company, Evanston, Ill., 1960.)

1905   Contributions to the Ethnology of the Haida. *Publications of the Jesup North Pacific Expedition* 5; *Memoirs of the American Museum of Natural History* 8(1):1–300. New York.

1905a   Haida Texts and Myths, Skidegate Dialect. *Bureau of American Ethnology Bulletin* 29. Washington. (Reprinted: Scholarly Press, St. Clair Shores, Mich., 1976.)

1905b   The Social Organization of American Tribes. *American Anthropologist* 7(4):663–673.

1907   Haida. Pp. 520–523 in Vol. 1 of Handbook of American Indians North of Mexico. 2 vols. Frederick W. Hodge, ed. *Bureau of American Ethnology Bulletin* 30. Washington. (Reprinted: Rowman and Littlefield, New York, 1971.)

1908   Haida Texts, Masset Dialect. *Publications of the Jesup North Pacific Expedition* 10(2); *Memoirs of the American Museum of Natural History* 14(2). New York. (Reprinted: AMS Press, New York, 1975.)

1908a   Social Conditions, Beliefs, and Linguistic Relationships of the Ṭlingit Indians. Pp. 391–485 in *26th Annual Report of the Bureau of American Ethnology for the Years 1904–1905.* Washington.

1909   Tlingit Myths and Texts. *Bureau of American Ethnology Bulletin* 39. Washington. (Reprinted: Scholarly Press, St. Clair Shores, Mich., 1976.)

1911   Tlingit. Pp. 159–204 in Vol. 1 of Handbook of American Indian Languages. Franz Boas, ed. *Bureau of American Ethnology Bulletin* 40. Washington.

1911a   Haida. Pp. 205–282 in Vol. 1 of Handbook of American Indian Languages. Franz Boas, ed. *Bureau of American Ethnology Bulletin* 40. Washington.

1952   The Indian Tribes of North America. *Bureau of American Ethnology Bulletin* 145. Washington. (Reprinted: Smithsonian Institution Press, Washington, 1968.)

[Swindell, Edward G., Jr.]
1942   Report on Source, Nature, and Extent of the Fishing, Hunting, and Miscellaneous Related Rights of Certain Indian Tribes in Washington and Oregon [etc.]. Los Angeles, Calif.: United States Department of the Interior, Office of Indian Affairs, Division of Forestry and Grazing.

Swineford, Alfred P.
1898   Alaska, Its History, Climate and Natural Resources. Chicago and New York: Rand, McNally.

Szathmary, Emöke J.E.
1979   Blood Groups of Siberians, Eskimos, Subarctic and Northwest Coast Indians: The Problem of Origins and Genetic Relationships. Pp. 185–209 in The First Americans: Origins, Affinities, and Adaptations. William S. Laughlin and Albert B. Harper, eds. New York: Gustav Fischer.

Szathmary, Emöke J.E., and Nancy S. Ossenberg
1978   Are the Biological Differences Between North American Indians and Eskimos Truly Profound? *Current Anthropology* 19(4):673–701.

Talbot, Theodore
1850   Lieutenant Theodore Talbot's Report to General Smith. Fort Vancouver, Oregon, Oct. 5, 1849. Pp. 108–116 in Report of the Secretary of War, Communicating Information in Relation to the Geology and Topography of California. *31st Congress, 1st Sess. Senate Executive Document* No. 47. (Serial No. 558) Washington: U.S. Government Printing Office.

Tappan, William
1854   [Annual Report, Southern Indian District, Washington Territory.] (In Records of the Washington Superintendency of Indian Affairs, Washington.)

Tarpent, Marie-Lucie
1983   Morphophonemics of Nisgha Plural Formation: A Step Towards Proto-Tsimshian Reconstruction. *Kansas Working Papers in Linguistics* 8(2):123–214. Lawrence.

1989   A Grammar of the Nisgha Language. (Unpublished Ph.D. Dissertation in Linguistics, University of Victoria, Victoria, B.C.)

Tate, Charles M.
1889   Chinook as Spoken by the Indians of Washington Territory, British Columbia and Alaska; for the Use of Traders, Tourists and Others Who Have Business Intercourse with the Indians. Victoria, B.C.: M.W. Waitt.

Taylor, Herbert C., Jr.
1960   The Fort Nisqually Census of 1838–1839. *Ethnohistory* 7(4):399–409.

1961   The Utilization of Archeological and Ethnohistorical Data in Estimating Aboriginal Population. *Bulletin of the Texas Archeological Society* 32:121–140. Austin.

1963   Aboriginal Populations of the Lower Northwest Coast. *Pacific Northwest Quarterly* 54(4):158–165.

1974   Anthropological Investigation of the Makah Indians Relative to Tribal Identity and Aboriginal Possession of Lands. Pp. 27–89 in Coast Salish and Western Washington Indians, III. (*American Indian Ethnohistory: Indians of the Northwest*) New York: Garland.

1974a   Anthropological Investigations of the Tillamook Indians. Pp. 25–102 in Oregon Indians, I. (*American Indian Ethnohistory: Indians of the Northwest*) New York: Garland.

1974b   Anthropological Investigation of the Medicine Creek Tribes Relative to Tribal Identity and Aboriginal Possession of Lands. Pp. 401–473 in Coast Salish and Western Washington Indians, II. (*American Indian Ethnohistory: Indians of the Northwest*) New York: Garland.

Taylor, Herbert C., Jr., and Wilson Duff
1956   A Post-contact Southward Movement of the Kwakiutl. *Washington State College. Research Studies* 24(1):55–66. Pullman.

Taylor, Herbert C., Jr., and Lester L. Hoaglin, Jr.
1962   The 'Intermittent' Fever Epidemic of the 1830's on the Lower Columbia River. *Ethnohistory* 9(2):160–178.

Taylor, John F.
1977   Sociocultural Effects of Epidemics on the Northern Plains: 1734–1850. *Western Canadian Journal of Anthropology* 7(4):55–81. Edmonton, Alta.

Tebenkov, Mikhail Dmitrievich
1981   Atlas of the Northwest Coasts of America: From Bering Strait to Cape Corrientes and the Aleutian Islands with

Several Sheets on the Northwest Coast of Asia [1852]. Richard A. Pierce, trans. and ed. (*Materials for the Study of Alaska History* 21) Kingston, Ont.: The Limestone Press.

Teichmann, Emil
1963   A Journey to Alaska in the Year 1868: Being a Diary of the Late Emil Teichmann. Oskar Teichmann, ed. New York: Argosy-Antiquarian.

Teit, James A.
1900   The Thompson Indians of British Columbia. Franz Boas, ed. *Memoirs of the American Museum of Natural History* 2(4):163–392. New York.

1906   The Lillooet Indians. *Publications of the Jesup North Pacific Expedition* 2(5); *Memoirs of the American Museum of Natural History* 4(5). New York.

[1910]   [Notes to Willapa-an Athabascan Language.] (Manuscript No. 30 Na 9.2 [Freeman No. 3848] in American Philosophical Society Library, Philadelphia.)

[1910a]   [Willapa Word List. Franz Boas, ed.] (Manuscript No. 30 Na 9.1 [Freeman No. 3847] in American Philosophical Society Library, Philadelphia.)

[1916–1917] Quinault Vocabulary and Paradigms. (Manuscript No. 30(S2a.2) [Freeman No. 3199] in American Philosophical Society Library, Philadelphia.)

1917   Tales from the Lower Fraser River. Pp. 129–134 in Folktales of Salishan and Sahaptin Tribes. Franz Boas, ed. *Memoirs of the American Folk-Lore Society* 11. Lancaster, Pa.

1928   The Middle Columbia Salish. Franz Boas, ed. *University of Washington Publications in Anthropology* 2(4):83–128. Seattle.

1930   The Salishan Tribes of the Western Plateaus. Franz Boas, ed. Pp. 23–396 in *45th Annual Report of the Bureau of American Ethnology for the Years 1927–1928*. Washington. (Reprinted: Shorey Book Store, Seattle, Wash., 1973.)

Tennant, Paul
1982   Native Indian Political Organization in British Columbia, 1900–1969: A Response to Internal Colonialism. *BC Studies* 55(Autumn):3–49. Vancouver.

1983   Native Indian Political Activity in British Columbia, 1969–1983. *BC Studies* 57(Spring):112–136. Vancouver.

Testart, Alain
1982   The Significance of Good Storage Among Hunter-Gatherers: Residence Patterns, Population Densities, and Social Inequalities. *Current Anthropology* 23(5):523–537.

Thilenius, John F.
1968   The *Quercus Garryana* Forests of the Willamette Valley, Oregon. *Ecology* 49(6):1124–1133.

Thomas, J.W., Margaret A. Stuckey, H.S. Robinson, J.P. Gofton, D.O. Anderson, and J.N. Bell
1964   Blood Groups of the Haida Indians. *American Journal of Physical Anthropology* n.s. 22(2):189–192.

Thomas, L.L., J.Z. Kronenfeld, and D.B. Kronenfeld
1976   Asdiwal Crumbles: A Critique of Lévi-Straussian Myth Analysis. *American Ethnologist* 3(1):147–173.

Thomas, W.D.S.
1968   Maternal Mortality in Native British Columbia Indians, a High-risk Group. *Canadian Medical Association Journal* 99(2):64–67. Toronto.

Thomas, Alex, and Eugene Y. Arima
1970   t'a:t'a:qsapa: A Practical Orthography for Nootka. *Canada. National Museum of Man. Publications in Ethnology* 1. Ottawa.

Thomas, Monica E.
1986   The Alaska Native Claims Settlement Act: Conflict and Controversy. *Polar Record* 23(142):27–36. Cambridge, England.

1988   The Alaska Native Land Claims Settlement Act: An Update. *Polar Record* 24(151):328–329. Cambridge, England.

Thomas, Susan J.
1967   The Life and Work of Charles Edenshaw: A Study of Innovation. (Unpublished B.A. Thesis in Anthropology and Sociology, University of British Columbia, Vancouver.)

Thomason, Sarah Grey
1983   Chinook Jargon in Areal and Historical Context. *Language: Journal of the Linguistic Society of America* 59(4):820–870.

Thomason, Sarah Grey, and Terrence Kaufman
1988   Language Contact, Creolization, and Genetic Linguistics. Berkeley: University of California Press.

Thompson, Gail
1978   Prehistoric Settlement Changes in the Southern Northwest Coast: A Functional Approach. *University of Washington Reports in Archaeology* 5. Seattle.

Thompson, Judy
1977   The North American Indian Collection: A Catalogue. Berne, Switzerland: Berne Historical Museum.

Thompson, Laurence C.
1973   The Northwest. Pp. 979–1045 in *Current Trends in Linguistics*. Vol. 10: Linguistics in North America. Thomas A. Sebeok, ed. The Hague: Mouton. (Reprinted: Plenum Press, New York, 1976.)

1979   Salishan and the Northwest. Pp. 692–765 in The Languages of Native North America: Historical and Comparative Assessment. Lyle Campbell and Marianne Mithun, eds. Austin: University of Texas Press.

1985   Control in Salish Grammar. Pp. 391–428 in Relational Typology. Frans Plank, ed. *Trends in Linguistics. Studies and Monographs* 28. Berlin.

Thompson, Laurence C., and M. Terry Thompson
1964   [Sechelt Vocabulary.] (Manuscript in Thompson and Thompson's possession.)

1964a   [Comparative Comox Vocabulary.] (Manuscripts in Thompson and Thompson's possession.)

[1965–1970] [Linguistic Fieldnotes.] (Manuscript in Thompson and Thompson's possession.)

1966   A Fresh Look at Tillamook Phonology. *International Journal of American Linguistics* 32(4):313–319.

1971   Clallam: A Preview. Pp. 251–294 in Studies in American Indian Languages. Jesse Sawyer, ed. *University of California Publications in Linguistics* 65. Berkeley.

1972   Language Universals, Nasals, and the Northwest Coast. Pp. 441–456 in Studies in Linguistics in Honor of George L. Trager. M. Estellie Smith, ed. (*Janua Linguarum. Series Maior* 52) The Hague: Mouton.

1985   A Grassmann's Law for Salish. Pp. 134–147 in For Gordon H. Fairbanks. Veneeta Z. Acson and Richard L. Leed, eds. *Oceanic Linguistics. Special Publication* 20. Honolulu.

Thompson, Laurence C., M. Terry Thompson, and Barbara S. Efrat
1974   Some Phonological Developments in Straits Salish. *International Journal of American Linguistics* 40(3):182–196.

Thompson, Nile
1979   Twana Dictionary (Student Version). Shelton, Wash.: Skokomish Indian Tribe, Twana Language Project.

Thompson, Nile, and Carolyn Marr
1983   Crow's Shells: Artistic Basketry of Puget Sound. Seattle, Wash.: Dushuyay Publications.

Thompson, Nile, Carolyn Marr, and Janda Volkmer
1980   Twined Basketry of the Twana, Chehalis, and Quinault. *American Indian Basketry* 1(3):12–19. Portland, Oreg.

Thompson, Stith
1946   The Folktale. New York: Dryden Press. (Reprinted: University of California Press, Berkeley, 1977.)

Thomson, Jack
1961   Preliminary Archaeological Survey of the Pilchuck River and South Fork of the Stillaguamish River. *Washington Archaeologist* 5(3):4–10.

Thomson, Richard E.
1981   Oceanography of the British Columbia Coast. *Canadian Special Publication of Fisheries and Aquatic Sciences* 56. Ottawa.

Thornton, Jim, comp.
[1978]   The Indians of the Oregon Coast, the Ancient and Original Inhabitants . . . As Recorded in the John P. Harrington Collection of the National Anthropological Archives, Smithsonian Institution. Coos Bay, Oreg.: Coos County Education Service District.

Thornton, Mildred Valley
1966   Indian Lives and Legends. Vancouver, B.C.: Mitchell Press.

Thwaites, Reuben G., ed.
1904–1905   Original Journals of the Lewis and Clark Expedition, 1804–1806. 8 vols. New York: Dodd, Mead.

⸻
1904–1907   Early Western Travels 1748–1846. 38 vols. Cleveland, Ohio: Arthur H. Clark.

⸻
1959   Original Journals of the Lewis and Clark Expedition 1804–1806. 8 vols. New York: Antiquarian Press.

Tichenor, William
1883   Among the Oregon Indians. (Manuscript P-A 84, in Bancroft Library, University of California, Berkeley.)

Tikhmenev, Pëtr Aleksandrovich
1861–1863   Istoricheskoe obozrienie obrazovaniia Rossiisko-Amerikanskoy Kompanii i i drei istviia eia do nastoiashchago vremeni [Historical Survey of the Formation of the Russian-American Company and of Its Activities to the Present Time]. 2 Pts. St. Petersburg: E. Veimar. (Translation by Dmitri Krenov, U.S. Works Progress Administration, Seattle, 1939–1940.)

⸻
1978–1979   A History of the Russian American Company. 2 vols. Richard A. Pierce and Alton S. Donnelly, eds. (*Materials for the Study of Alaska History* 13) Kingston, Ont.: The Limestone Press.

Timmers, Jan A.
1977   A Classified English-Sechelt Word-list. Lisse, The Netherlands: The Peter de Ridder Press.

⸻
1978   Comox Stem-List. Leiden, The Netherlands: n.p.

⸻
1978a   Sechelt Stem-List. Leiden, The Netherlands: n.p.

Tlingit and Haida Indian Tribes of Alaska
1985   A Historical Profile of the Central Council and the Tlingit and Haida People. Mimeo.

Todd, Norman
1975   Fatal Fat Embolism During Ritual Initiation. *Canadian Medical Association Journal* 113(July 26):133–135. Toronto.

Toelken, Barre
1979   The Dynamics of Folklore. Boston: Houghton Mifflin.

Toepel, Kathryn Anne, and Rick Minor
1980   Archaeological Investigations at the Flanagan Site (35LA218): The 1978 Season. Eugene: University of Oregon, Department of Anthropology.

Toepel, Kathryn A. and Robert L. Sappington
1982   Obsidian Use in the Willamette Valley: Trace Element Analysis of Obsidian from the Halverson Site. *Tebiwa: Journal of the Idaho State University Museum* 19(1):27–40. Pocatello.

Tollefson, Kenneth D.
1977   A Structural Change in Tlingit Potlatching. *Western Canadian Journal of Anthropology* 7(3):16–27. Edmonton, Alta.

⸻
1978   From Localized Clans to Regional Corporations: The Acculturation of the Tlingit. *Western Canadian Journal of Anthropology* 8(1):1–20. Edmonton, Alta.

⸻
1982   Northwest Coast Village Adaptations: A Case Study. *Canadian Journal of Anthropology* 3(1):19–30.

⸻
1984   Tlingit Acculturation: An Institutional Perspective. *Ethnology* 23(3):229–427.

Tolmie, William F.
1963   The Journals of William Fraser Tolmie, Physician and Fur Trader. Vancouver, B.C.: Mitchell Press.

Tolmie, William F., and George M. Dawson
1884   Comparative Vocabularies of the Indian Tribes of British Columbia, with a Map Illustrating Distribution. Montreal: Dawson Brothers.

Torok, Charles H.
1951   [Kitimat Fieldnotes.] (Manuscripts in Hamori-Torok's possession.)

⸻
1956   [Kemano Fieldnotes.] (Manuscripts in Hamori-Torok's possession.)

Touchie, Bernice
1977   Report of the Settlement of Whyack Village, Vancouver Island, British Columbia. (Unpublished report on file at National Historic Parks and Sites Branch, Calgary, Alta.)

⸻
1977a   Nitinaht. Pp. 69–97 in Northwest Coast Texts. Barry F. Carlson, ed. *Native American Text Series* 2(3). Chicago.

Townsend, John K.
1978   Narrative of a Journey Across the Rocky Mountains to the Columbia River [1839]. Lincoln: University of Nebraska Press.

Trace, Andrew A.
1981   An Examination of the Locarno Beach Phase as Reported at the Crescent Beach Site, DgRr 1, British Columbia. (Unpublished M.A. Thesis in Archaeology, Simon Fraser University, Burnaby, B.C.)

Trafzer, Clifford E., ed.
1986   Indians, Superintendents, and Councils: Northwestern Indian Policy, 1850–1855. Lanham, Md.: University Press of America.

Treganza, Adan E.
1958   Salvage Archaeology in the Trinity Reservoir Area, Northern California. *University of California Archaeological Survey Reports* 43:1–38. Berkeley.

Trennert, Robert A., Jr.
1974   A Grand Failure: The Centennial Indian Exhibition of 1876. *Prologue: The Journal of the National Archives* 6(2):118–129. Washington.

1975   Alternative to Extinction: Federal Indian Policy and the Beginnings of the Reservation System, 1846–51. Philadelphia: Temple University Press.

Trotter, Mildred, and Goldine C. Gleser
1958   A Re-evaluation of Estimation of Stature Based on Measurements of Stature Taken During Life and of Long Bones After Death. *American Journal of Physical Anthropology* n.s. 16(1):79–123.

Tuohy, Donald R., and Alan L. Bryan
1958–1959   Southwestern Washington Archaeology: An Appraisal. *Tebiwa: Journal of the Idaho State University Museum* 2(1):27–58. Pocatello.

Turner, Christy G., II
1983   Dental Evidence for the Peopling of the Americas. Pp. 147–157 in Early Man in the New World. Richard Shutler Jr., ed. Beverly Hills, Calif.: Sage Publications.

1984   Advances in the Dental Search for Native American Origins. *Acta Anthropogenetica: International Journal of Research in Human Genetics* 8(1–2):23–78. New Delhi.

1986   The First Americans: The Dental Evidence. *National Geographic Research* 2(1):37–46.

Turner, Nancy J.
1972   Haida Plant Names: Skidegate Dialect. (Manuscript in Margaret Blackman's possession.)

1973   The Ethnobotany of the Bella Coola Indians of British Columbia. *Syesis* 6:193–220. Victoria, B.C.

1974   Plant Taxonomic Systems and Ethnobotany of Three Contemporary Indian Groups of the Pacific Northwest (Haida, Bella Coola, and Lillooet). *Syesis* 7(supp. 1):1–104. Victoria, B.C.

1975   Food Plants of British Columbia Indians. Pt. 1: Coastal Peoples. *British Columbia Provincial Museum. Handbook* 34. Victoria.

1977   Economic Importance of Black Tree Lichen (*Bryoria fremontii*) to the Indians of Western North America. *Economic Botany* 31(4):461–470.

1978   Plants of the Nootka Sound Indians as Recorded by Captain Cook. Pp. 78–87 in nu·tka·: Captain Cook and the Spanish Explorers on the Coast. Barbara S. Efrat and W.J. Langlois, eds. *Sound Heritage* 7(1). Victoria.

1979   Plants in British Columbia Indian Technology. *British Columbia Provincial Museum. Handbook* 38. Victoria.

1981   A Gift for the Taking: The Untapped Potential of Some Food Plants of North American Native Peoples. *Canadian Journal of Botany* 59(11):2331–2357. Ottawa.

1982   Traditional Use of Devil's-Club (*Oplopanax horridus*; Araliaceae) by Native Peoples in Western North America. *Journal of Ethnobiology* 2(1):17–38.

Turner, Nancy J., and Marcus A.M. Bell
1971   The Ethnobotany of the Coast Salish Indians of Vancouver Island. *Economic Botany* 25(1):63–104.

1973   The Ethnobotany of the Southern Kwakiutl Indians of British Columbia. *Economic Botany* 27(3):257–310.

Turner, Nancy J., and Barbara S. Efrat
1982   Ethnobotany of the Hesquiat People of the West Coast of Vancouver Island. *British Columbia Provincial Museum. Cultural Recovery Papers* 2. Victoria.

Turner, Nancy J., and Harriet V. Kuhnlein
1982   Two Important "Root" Foods of the Northwest Coast Indians: Springbank Clover (*Trifolium wormskioldii*) and Pacific Silverweed (*Potentilla anserina* ssp. *pacifica*). *Economic Botany* 36(4):411–432.

1983   Camas (*Camassia* spp.) and Riceroot (*Fritillaria* spp.): Two Liliaceous "Root" Foods of the Northwest Coast Indians. *Ecology of Food and Nutrition* 13(4):199–219.

Turner, Nancy J., and Roy L. Taylor
1972   A Review of the Northwest Coast Tobacco Mystery. *Syesis* 5:249–257. Victoria, B.C.

Turner, Nancy J., John Thomas, Barry F. Carlson, and Robert T. Ogilvie
1983   Ethnobotany of the Nitinaht Indians of Vancouver Island. *Occasional Papers of the British Columbia Provincial Museum* 24. Victoria.

Tweddell, Colin E.
1950   The Snoqualmie-Duwamish Dialects of Puget Sound Coast Salish. *University of Washington Publications in Anthropology* 12:1–78. Seattle.

1974   A Historical and Ethnological Study of the Snohomish Indian People: A Report Specifically Covering Their Aboriginal and Continued Existence, and Their Effective Occupation of a Definable Territory. Pp. 475–694 in Coast Salish and Western Washington Indians, II. (*American Indian Ethnohistory: Indians of the Northwest*) New York: Garland.

Ubelaker, Douglas
1976   The Sources and Methodology for Mooney's Estimates of North American Indian Populations. Pp. 243–288 in The Native Population of the Americas in 1492. William Denevan, ed. Madison: University of Wisconsin Press.

1976a   Prehistoric New World Population Size: Historical Review and Current Appraisal of North American Estimates. *American Journal of Physical Anthropology* 45(3):661–665.

U'mista Cultural Society
1975   Potlatch. [Motion picture; 2 reels; 16 mm; sound; color.] Vancouver: Pacifique Cinémathèque.

1983   Box of Treasures. [Motion picture; 1 reel; 16mm; sound; color.] Chicago: Chuck Olin Associates.

Underhill, Ruth
[1944]   Indians of the Pacific Northwest. (*Sherman Pamphlets on Indian Life and Customs* 5) Riverside, Calif.: U.S. Office of Indian Affairs, Education Division.

U.S. Bureau of Indian Affairs
1838–1863   Documents Relating to the Negotiation of Ratified and Unratified Treaties with Various Indian Tribes, 1801–1869. (Manuscripts, microfilm No. T494, rolls 4, 5, 8 in Record Group 75, National Archives, Washington.)

1919   Competency Commission Report, Fourth Section Allottees. (Manuscripts, box 69, decimal files, Grand Ronde-Siletz Agency, in Record Group 75, National Archives Branch Office, Seattle, Wash.)

1977   Indian Fishing Rights in the Pacific Northwest. Washington: Bureau of Indian Affairs. (Revised edition by Northwest Indian Fisheries Commission, Olympia, Wash., 1979.)

1988   Nine Tribes Working on Self-governance Projects. *Indian News* 12(11):3. Washington.

U.S. Bureau of Indian Affairs. Branch of Acknowledgment and Research
1987   Status of Federal Acknowledgment Petitions (as of November 17, 1987). (Computer printout list; copy in *Handbook* files.)

U.S. Bureau of Indian Affairs. Branch of Tribal Relations
1987   Organizational Status of Federally Recognized Indian Entities. (Memorandum; copy in *Handbook* files.)

U.S. Bureau of Indian Affairs. Financial Management Office
1985   Local Estimates of Resident Indian Population and Labor Force Status: January 1985. Washington. Mimeo.

————
1987   Indian Service Population and Labor Force Estimates. Washington: Bureau of Indian Affairs.

U.S. Bureau of the Census. 13th Census
1915   Indian Population of the United States and Alaska. 13th Census: 1915. Washington: U.S. Government Printing Office.

U.S. Census Office. 10th Census
1884   Report on the Population, Industries, and Resources of Alaska, by Ivan Petroff. 10th Census: 1880. Washington: U.S. Government Printing Office.

U.S. Census Office. 11th Census
1893   Report on Population and Resources of Alaska at the Eleventh Census: 1890. Washington: U.S. Government Printing Office.

U.S. Commission on Civil Rights
1981   Fishing in Western Washington–a Treaty Right, a Clash of Cultures. Pp. 61–100 in Indian Tribes, a Continuing Quest for Survival: A Report of the United States Commission on Civil Rights. Washington: U.S. Government Printing Office.

U.S. Congress
1954   Termination of Federal Supervision Over Certain Tribes of Indians. Pt. 3: Western Oregon, February 17. *83d Congress, 2d Sess*: Joint Hearings Before the Subcommittees of the Committees on Interior and Insular Affairs on S. 2746 and H.R. 7317. Washington.

U.S. Congress. Senate
1893   Articles of Agreement and Convention Made and Concluded . . . by Joel Palmer . . . .and the Following Chiefs and Headmen of the Confederate Tribes of Indians . . . August 11, 1855. Pp. 8–15 in Letter from the Secretary of the Interior, Transmitting Copies of Treaties Between the United States and Certain Indians in Oregon [etc]. *53rd Congress, 1st Sess. Senate Executive Document* No. 25. (Serial No. 3144) Washington: U.S. Government Printing Office.

————
1912   Final Settlement with Tillamook Indians for Certain Oregon Lands. *62d Congress, 2d Sess. Senate Report* No. 503 (Serial No. 6121). Washington.

U.S. Congress. Senate. Committee on Military Affairs
1900   Compilation of Narratives of Explorations in Alaska. (Issued also as: *56th Congress, 1st Sess., Senate Report No. 1023*) Washington: U.S. Government Printing Office.

U.S. Congress. Senate. Subcommittee of the Committee on Indian Affairs
1939   Survey of Conditions of the Indians in the United States, Pt 35: Metlakahtla Indians, Alaska. Hearings Before a Subcommittee of the Senate Committee on Indian Affairs. *74th Congress, 2d Sess*. Washington: U.S. Government Printing Office.

United States Court of Claims
1938   Coos (or Kowes) Bay, Lower Umpqua (or Kalawatset), and Siuslaw Indian Tribes v. the United States of America (Records of the U.S. Court of Claims: K-345, RG 123). (Extracts in: Testimony of 1931 Hearings in Court of Claims of the United States. Microfilm reel No. 024- frames 0774–0855, John Peabody Harrington Papers, Alaska/Northwest Coast, in National Anthropological Archives, Smithsonian Institution, Washington.)

————
1962   The Tlingit and Haida Indians of Alaska v. the United States [No. 47900. Decided Oct. 7, 1959]. Pp. 315–439 in Cases Decided in the United States Court of Claims, July 15–Dec. 31, 1959. *Court of Claims Reports* 147. Washington.

U.S. Geological Survey
1970   The National Atlas of the United States of America. Arch C. Gerlach, ed. Washington: U.S. Geological Survey.

The University of Alaska, Elmer E. Rasmuson Library
1985–   The Rasmuson Library Historical Translation Series. Marvin W. Falk, ed. Fairbanks: University of Alaska Press.

University of British Columbia. Museum of Anthropology
1975   Northwest Coast Indian Artifacts from the H.R. MacMillan Collections in the Museum of Anthropology, Univeristy of British Columbia. [Vancouver]: University of British Columbia Press.

————
1975a   Indian Masterpieces from the Walter and Marianne Koerner Collection in the Museum of Anthropology, University of British Columbia. [Vancouver]: University of British Columbia Press.

Urban, Greg
1984   Speech About Speech in Speech About Action. *Journal of American Folklore* 97(385):310–328.

Urquart, M.C., and K.A.H. Buckley, eds.
1965   Historical Statistics of Canada. Toronto: Macmillan.

Usher, Jean
1969   William Duncan of Metlakatla: The Victorian Origins of an Indian Utopia. (Unpublished Ph.D. Dissertation in History, University of British Columbia, Vancouver.)

————
1974   William Duncan of Metlakatla: A Victorian Missionary in British Columbia. *Canada. National Museum of Man. Publications in History* 5. Ottawa.

Utley, Robert M.
1973   Frontier Regulars: The United State Army and the Indian, 1866–1891. New York: Macmillan.

Valle, Rosemary K.
1973   James Ohio Pattie and the 1827–1828 Alta California Measles Epidemic. *California Historical Quarterly* 52(1)28–36. San Francisco.

Valory, Dale
1966   The Focus of Indian Shaker Healing. *Kroeber Anthropological Society Papers* 35:67–112. Berkeley, Calif.

Vancouver Art Gallery
1974   Bill Reid: A Retrospective Exhibition [Nov. 6–Dec. 8]. Vancouver: The Vancouver Art Gallery.

Vancouver, George
1798   A Voyage of Discovery to the North Pacific Ocean, and Round the World; In Which the Coast of North-west America Has Been Carefully Examined and Accurately Surveyed. 3 vols. London: Printed for G.G. and J. Robinson.

————
1801   A Voyage of Discovery to the North Pacific Ocean, and Round the World . . . .New ed. John Vancouver, ed. 6 vols. London: Printed for John Stockdale.

————
1967   A Voyage of Discovery to the North Pacific Ocean, and Round the World [1790–1795]. 3 vols. (*Bibliotheca Australiana* 30–32). New York: Da Capo Press.

Van den Brink, Jacob H. *see* Brink, Jacob H. van den

Van Eijk, Jan P., and Thom Hess
1986   Noun and Verb in Salish. *Lingua: International Review of General Linguistics* 69(4):319–331. Amsterdam, The Netherlands.

Van Kirk, Sylvia
1980   "Many Tender Ties": Women in Fur-trade Society in Western Canada, 1670–1870. Winnipeg, Man.: Watson and

Dwyer. (Reprinted: University of Oklahoma Press, Norman, 1983.)

Vankoughnet, L.
1885   Tabular Statement No. 4: Census Return of Resident and Nomadic Indians in the Dominion of Canada, by Provinces. Pp. 183–190 in Pt. 1 of *Dominion of Canada. Annual Report of the Department of Indian Affairs for the Year 1884.* Ottawa.

Van Stone, James
1979   Ingalik Contact Ecology: An Ethnohistory of the Lower Middle Yukon. *Fieldiana: Anthropology* 71. Chicago.

Van Syckle, Edwin
1982   River Pioneers: Early Days on Grays Harbor. David James, ed. [Aberdeen, Wash.]: Pacific Search Press and Friends of the Aberdeen Public Library.

Van West, John J.
1976   George Mercer Dawson: An Early Canadian Anthropologist. *Anthropological Journal of Canada* 14(4):8–12.

Vastokas, Joan M.
1966   Architecture of the Northwest Coast Indians of America. Ann Arbor, Mich.: University Microfilms.

———
1973   The Shamanic Tree of Life. *Artscanada* 184–187: 125–149. Toronto.

———
1978   Cognitive Aspects of Northwest Coast Art. Pp. 243–259 in Art in Society. M. Greenhalgh and V. Megaw, eds. London: Duckworth.

Vaughan, J. Daniel
1976   Haida Potlatch and Society: Testings of a Structural Analysis. (Paper presented at the Northwest Coast Studies Conference, Simon Fraser University, Burnaby, B.C.)

———
1984   Tsimshian Potlatch and Society: Examining a Structural Analysis. Pp. 58–68 in The Tsimshian and Their Neighbors of the North Pacific Coast. Jay Miller and Carol M. Eastman, eds. Seattle: University of Washington Press.

Vaughan, Thomas, ed.
1971   Paul Kane, the Columbia Wanderer 1846–47: Sketches and Paintings of the Indians and His Lecture, "The Chinooks." Portland: Oregon Historical Society.

Vaughan, Thomas, and Bill Holm
1982   Soft Gold: The Fur Trade and Cultural Exchange on the Northwest Coast of America. Portland: Oregon State Historical Society.

Vaughn, Warren N.
[1851]   Early History of Tillamook. (Manuscript at the Oregon Historical Society, Portland.)

Vayda, Andrew P.
1961   A Re-examination of Northwest Coast Economic Systems. *Transactions of the New York Academy of Sciences*, ser. 2, Vol. 23(7):618–624.

Velten, H.V.
1939   Two Southern Tlingit Tales. *International Journal of American Linguistics* 10(2–3):65–74.

———
1944   Three Tlingit Stories. *International Journal of American Linguistics* 10(4):168–180.

Veniaminov, Ivan Evîeevich Popov, comp.
1840   Zapiski ob ostrovakh Unalashkinskago otdîela [Notes on the Islands of the Unalaska District]. 3 vols. in 2. St. Petersburg: Russian-American Company. (English translation: The Limestone Press, Kingston, Ont., 1985.)

———
1846   Zamîechaniîa o koloshenskom i kad'îakskom îazykakh i otchasti o prochikh rossî îsko-amerikanskikh . . . .[Remarks on the Tlingit and Kodiak Languages, and in Part on Others of Russian America . . . .]. St. Petersburg: Tip. Imp. Akademîa Nauk.

———
1972   The Condition of the Orthodox Church in Russian America. Robert Nichols and Robert Croskey, trans. *Pacific Northwest Quarterly* 63(2):41–54.

———
1984   Notes on the Islands of the Unalashka District [1840]. Lydia T. Black and R.H. Geoghegan, trans. Richard A. Pierce, ed. (*Alaska History* 27) Kingston, Ont.: The Limestone Press.

Vernon, Manfred C., and James W. Scott, eds.
1977   Fisheries in Puget Sound: Public Good and Private Interests. Proceedings of a Conference Held at Western Washington State College, June 18–19, 1976. *Western Washington State College. Center for Pacific Northwest Studies. Occasional Papers* 9. Bellington.

Virchow, Rudolph L.
1886   Die anthropologische Untersuchung der Bella-Coola. Pp. 206–215 in *Verhandlungen der Berliner Gesellschaft für Anthropologie, Ethnologie und Urgeschichte.* Berlin.

Voegelin, Charles F., and Zellig S. Harris
1945   Index to the Franz Boas Collection of Materials for American Linguistics. (*Language Monographs* 22) Baltimore, Md.: Linguistic Society of America.

Von Krogh, G. Henning
1976   The 1974 Katz Salvage Project. Pp. 68–82 in Current Research Reports. Roy L. Carlson, ed. *Simon Fraser University. Department of Archaeology Publications* 3. Burnaby, B.C.

———
1980   Archaeological Investigations at the Flood and Pipeline Sites, Near Hope, British Columbia. *British Columbia. Heritage Conservation Branch. Occasional Papers* 4. Victoria.

Vool, Cathy
1961–1962   [Linguistic Notes on Island and Mainland Comox.] (Manuscripts in Wayne Suttles' possession.)

Wade, Mark S.
1931   The Overlanders of '62. *Archives of British Columbia. Memoirs* 9. Victoria. (Reprinted: Heritage House, Surrey, B.C., 1981.)

Wagner, Henry R.
1931   Apocryphal Voyages to the Northwest Coast of America. *Proceedings of the American Antiquarian Society* 41(1):179–234. Worcester, Mass.

———
1933   Spanish Explorations in the Strait of Juan de Fuca. Santa Ana, Calif.: Fine Arts Press. (Reprinted: AMS Press, New York, 1971.)

———, ed. and trans.
1936   Journal of Tomás de Suría of His Voyage with Malaspina to the Northwest Coast of America in 1791. Glendale, Calif.: Arthur H. Clark. (Originally issued in: *Pacific Historical Review* 5(3):234–276.)

———
1937   The Cartography of the Northwest Coast of America to the Year 1800. 2 vols. Berkeley: University of California Press.

———
1968   The Cartography of the Northwest Coast of America to the Year 1800. Amsterdam: N. Israel.

Wagner, Henry R., and A.J. Baker, eds. and trans.
1930   Fray Benito de la Sierra's Account of the Hezeta Expedition to the Northwest Coast in 1775. *California Historical Quarterly* 9(3):201–242. San Francisco.

Wagoner, David
1978   Who Shall Be the Sun? Poems Based on the Lore, Legends, and Myths of Northwest Coast and Plateau Indians. Bloomington: Indiana University Press.

Waite, Deborah
[1966]   Kwakiutl Transformation Masks. Pp. 266–300 in The Many
          Faces of Primitive Art: A Critical Anthology. Douglas
          Fraser, ed. Englewood Cliffs, N.J.: Prentice-Hall.

Walbran, John T.
1909   British Columbia Coast Names, 1592–1906; To Which Are
          Added a Few Names in Adjacent United States Territory,
          Their Origin and History. Ottawa: Government Printing
          Bureau. (Reprinted: University of Washington Press, Seat-
          tle, 1972.)

Walens, Stanley
1981   Feasting with Cannibals: An Essay on Kwakiutl Cosmolo-
          gy. Princeton, N.J.: Princeton University Press.

Walker, Alexander
1982   An Account of a Voyage to the North West Coast of
          America in 1785 and 1786. Robin Fisher and J.M. Bumsted,
          eds. Vancouver, B.C.: Douglas and McIntyre.

Walker, Elkanah
1976   Nine Years with the Spokane Indians: The Diary,
          1838–1848, of Elkanah Walker. Clifford Drury, ed. Glen-
          dale, Calif.: Arthur H. Clark.

Walker, Phillip L.
1986   Porotic Hyperostosis in a Marine-dependent California
          Indian Population. American Journal of Physical Anthropol-
          ogy 69(3):345–354.

Wallas, James
1981   Kwakiutl Legend as Told to Pamela Whitaker. North
          Vancouver, B.C.: Hancock House Publishers.

Walling, A.G.
1884   History of Southern Oregon, Comprising Jackson,
          Josephine, Douglas, Curry and Coos Counties. Portland,
          Oreg.: Printing and Lithography House of A.G. Walling.

Warbass, U.G.
1857–1858 George Gibbs Correspondence. (Manuscript No. 726 in
          National Anthropological Archives, Smithsonian Institu-
          tion, Washington.)

1858   [Comparative Vocabulary of Cowlitz and Chinook.] (Manu-
          script No. 724 in National Anthropological Archives,
          Smithsonian Institution, Washington.)

Wardwell, Allen
1964   Yakutat South; Indian Art of the Northwest Coast.
          (Illustrated Catalogue of Exhibition, The Art Institute of
          Chicago, March 13–April 26.) Chicago: Hillison and Etten.

1978   Objects of Bright Pride: Northwest Coast Indian Art from
          the American Museum of Natural History. New York: The
          Center for Inter-American Relations, and The American
          Federation of Artists.

Warner, George, and Irene Warner
1975   Trojan III. Oregon Archaeological Society Publications 7.
          Portland.

Warre, Henry J.
1976   Overland to Oregon in 1845: Impressions of a Journey
          Across North America [1845]. Madeleine Major-Frégeau,
          ed. Ottawa: Public Archives of Canada.

[Warre, Henry J., and M. Vavasour]
1909   Documents Relative to Warre and Vavasour's Military
          Reconnoisance in Oregon, 1845–6. Joseph Schafer, ed.
          Oregon Historical Quarterly 10(1):1–99.

Warren, Claude N.
1959   Wenas Creek: A Stratified Site on the Yakima River, Its
          Significance for Plateau Chronology and Cultural Relation-
          ships. (Unpublished M.A. Thesis in Anthropology, Univer-
          sity of Washington, Seattle.)

Waterman, Thomas T.
1914   The Explanatory Element in the Folk-Tales of the North-
          American Indians. Journal of American Folk-Lore
          27(103):1–54.

1920   The Whaling Equipment of the Makah Indians. University
          of Washington Publications in Anthropology 1(2). Seattle.

[1920a]   [Puget Sound Geography.] (Manuscript No. 1864 in Na-
          tional Anthropological Archives, Smithsonian Institution,
          Washington.)

[1921]   [Athapascan Indians of Southwestern Oregon and North-
          western California.] (Manuscript No. 3183 in National
          Anthropological Archives, Smithsonian Institution, Wash-
          ington.)

1923   Some Conundrums in Northwest Coast Art. American
          Anthropologist 25(4):435–451.

1924   The "Shake Religion" of Puget Sound. Pp. 499–507 in
          Annual Report of the Smithsonian Institution for the Year
          1922. Washington.

1925   The Village Sites in Tolowa and Neighboring Areas in
          Northwestern California. American Anthropologist
          27(4):528–543.

1930   The Paraphernalia of the Duwamish "Spirit Canoe" Cere-
          mony. Museum of the American Indian. Heye Foundation.
          Indian Notes 7(2):129–148, (3):295–312, (4):535–561. New
          York.

1973   Notes on the Ethnology of the Indians of Puget Sound.
          Museum of the American Indian. Heye Foundation. Indian
          Notes and Monographs. Miscellaneous Series 59. New York.

Waterman, Thomas T., and Geraldine Coffin
1920   Types of Canoes on Puget Sound. Museum of the American
          Indian. Heye Foundation. Indian Notes and Monographs.
          Miscellaneous Series 5. New York.

Waterman, Thomas T., and Ruth Greiner
1921   Indian Houses of Puget Sound. Museum of the American
          Indian. Heye Foundation. Indian Notes and Monographs.
          Miscellaneous Series 9. New York.

Watt, James
1979   Medical Aspects and Consequences of Cook's Voyages. Pp.
          129–157 in Captain James Cook and His Times. Robin
          Fisher and Hugh Johnston, eds. Seattle: University of
          Washington Press.

Weber, Michael
1976   "In the Pursuit of Knowledge..:" Malaspina Explores the
          Northwest Coast. El Palacio 82(4):4–10.

Weber, Ronald L.
1982   Tsimshian Twined Basketry: Stylistic and Cultural Rela-
          tionships. American Indian Basketry 2(2):26–30.

1985   Photographs as Ethnographic Documents. Arctic Anthro-
          pology 22(1):67–78.

1986   Emmons's Notes on Field Museum's Collection of North-
          west Coast Basketry: Edited with an Ethnoarchaeological
          Analysis. Fieldiana: Anthropology n.s. 9. Chicago.

Webster, Peter S.
1983   As Far As I Know. Campbell River, Queensland: Campbell
          River Museum and Archives.

Weightman, Barbara A.
1976   Indian Social Space: A Case Study of the Musqueam Band
          of Vancouver, British Columbia. The Canadian Geographer
          20(2):171–186. Toronto.

Weinberg, Daniela
1973   Models of Southern Kwakiutl Social Organization. Pp. 227–253 in Cultural Ecology: Readings on the Canadian Indians and Eskimo. Bruce A. Cox, ed. Toronto: McClelland and Stewart.

Welch, Jeanne M.
1983   The Kwalhioqua in the Boistfort Valley of Southwestern Washington. Pp. 153–168 in Prehistoric Places on the Southern Northwest Coast. R.E. Greengo, ed. Seattle: University of Washington.

Weld, Willi
1963   Dentalium: The Money Shell of the Northwest Coast. *Washington Archaeologist* 7(1):4–18.

Wellcome, Henry S.
1887   The Story of Metlakahtla. 2d ed. New York: Saxon.

Wells, Oliver
1966   Return of the Salish Loom. *The Beaver*, Outfit (296):40–45. Winnipeg.

Wertsman, Vladimir, comp. and ed.
1977   The Russians in America, 1727–1975: A Chronology and Fact Book. Dobbs Ferry, N.Y.: Oceana Publications.

Wessen, Gary
1977   An Archaeological Site Survey of the Proposed Coast Guard Station at La Push, Washington. *Washington Archaeological Research Center Project Reports* 49. Pullman.

1978   Archaeological Reconnaissance of River Valleys on the Western Olympic Peninsula, Washington. *Washington Archaeological Research Center Project Reports* 69. Pullman.

1981   Radiocarbon Dates and Stratigraphic Notes from the Tongue Point Site. (Manuscript in Wessen's possession.)

1982   Shell Midden as Cultural Deposits: A Case Study from Ozette. (Unpublished Ph.D. Dissertation in Anthropology, Washington State University, Pullman.)

1984   A Report of Preliminary Archaeological Investigations at 45Ca 201: A 'Second Terrace' Shell Midden Near Sand Point, Olympic National Park, Washington. (Report on file with the Division of Cultural Resources, Pacific Northwest Region, National Park Service, Seattle.)

Wessen, Gary, and Richard D. Daugherty
1983   Archaeological Investigations at Vancouver Lake, Washington. Olympia, Wash.: Western Heritage.

Wessen, Gary, James Gallison, and Jeuel Virden
1985   A Cultural Resource Survey of a Portion of the Upper Canyon Creek Area, Quilcene District, Olympic National Forest. (Report on file with the Olympic National Forest, Olympia, Wash.)

White, J.W.
1868   A Cruise in Alaska [from Official Reports of Captain J.W. White, Commander of the United States Revenue Steamer Wayanda]. *40th Congress, 3d Sess., Senate Executive Document* No. 8. (*Serial No. 1360*) Washington.

White, John R.
1975   The Hurd Site. Pp. 141–225 in Archaeological Studies in the Willamette Valley, Oregon. C. Melvin Aikens, ed. *University of Oregon Anthropological Papers* 8. Eugene.

1975a   A Proposed Typology of Willamette Valley Sites. Pp. 17–140 in Archaeological Studies in the Willamette Valley, Oregon. C. Melvin Aikens, ed. *University of Oregon Anthropological Papers* 8. Eugene.

White, Leslie A.
1963   The Ethnography and Ethnology of Franz Boas. *Bulletin of the Texas Memorial Museum* 6. Austin.

1966   The Social Organization of Ethnological Theory. *Monograph in Cultural Anthropology. Rice University Studies* 52(4). Houston, Texas.

White, Richard
1980   Land Use, Environment, and Social Change: The Shaping of Island County, Washington. Seattle: University of Washington Press.

Whitehead, Margaret
1981   Christianity, a Matter of Choice: The Historic Role of Indian Catechists in Oregon Territory and British Columbia. *Pacific Northwest Quarterly* 72(3):93–106.

Whitehill, Walter M.
1949   The East India Marine Society and the Peabody Museum of Salem: A Sesquicentennial History. Salem, Mass.: Peabody Museum.

Whitlam, Robert
1983   Models of Coastal Adaptation: The Northwest Coast and Maritimes. Pp. 109–124 in The Evolution of Maritime Cultures on the Northeast and the Northwest Coasts of America. Ronald J. Nash, ed. *Simon Fraser University. Department of Archaeology Publications* 11. Burnaby, B.C.

Whitner, Robert L.
1977   Culture Conflict in the Agency School: An Introduction to a Case Study, the Neah Bay Reservation, 1861–1896. (Manuscript in Makah Archives, Makah Cultural and Research Center, Neah Bay, Wash.)

1984   Makah Commercial Sealing, 1860–1897: A Study in Acculturation and Conflict. Pp. 121–130 in Rendezvous: Selected Papers of the Fourth North American Fur Trade Conference, 1981. Thomas C. Buckley, ed. St. Paul, Minn.: North American Fur Trade Conference.

Whymper, Frederick
1868   Travel and Adventure in the Territory of Alaska, ...and in Various Other Parts of the North Pacific. London: J. Murray.

Wickersham, James
1896   Some North-west Burial Customs. *American Antiquarian and Oriental Journal* 18(4):204–206.

1896a   Pueblos of the Northwest Coast. *American Antiquarian and Oriental Journal* 18(1):21–24.

[1898]   [Athapascan Language; Spoken by a Small Band of Tinneh (Tena) at Boistfort, Washington.] (Manuscript in Alaska State Historical Library, Juneau.)

1899   Notes on the Indians of Washington. *American Antiquarian and Oriental Journal* 21(6):369–375.

1900   Some Relics of the Stone Age from Puget Sound. *American Antiquarian and Oriental Journal* 22(5):141–149.

1938   Old Yukon; Tales-Trails-and Trials. Washington: Washington Law Book Company.

Widerspach-Thor, Martine de
1981   The Equation of Copper. Pp. 157–174 in The World Is As Sharp As a Knife . . . .Donald N. Abbott, ed. Victoria: British Columbia Provincial Museum.

Wigen, Rebecca J.S.
1980   A Faunal Analysis of Two Middens on the East Coast of Vancouver Island. (Unpublished M.A. Thesis in Anthropology, University of Victoria, Victoria, B.C.)

Wike, Joyce A.
1945   Modern Spirit Dancing of Northern Puget Sound. (Unpublished M.A. Thesis in Anthropology, University of Washington, Seattle.)

739

1951   The Effect of the Maritime Fur Trade on Northwest Coast Indian Society. (Unpublished Ph.D. Dissertation in Political Science, Columbia University, New York City.)

1952   The Role of the Dead in Northwest Coast Culture. Pp. 97–103 in [Vol. 3 of] *Selected Papers of the 29th International Congress of Americanists.* (Indian Tribes of Aboriginal America) Sol Tax, ed. Chicago: University of Chicago Press.

1958   Social Stratification Among the Nootka. *Ethnohistory* 5(3):219–241.

Wilkes, Charles
1845   Narrative of the United States Exploring Expedition. During the Years 1838, 1839, 1840, 1841, 1842. 5 vols. and Atlas. Philadelphia: Lea and Blanchard.

1925–1926   Diary of Wilkes in the Northwest. Edmond Meany, ed. *Washington Historical Quarterly* 16(1):49–61, (2):137–145, (3):206–223, (4):290–301; 17(1):43–65, (2):129–144, (3):223–229. Seattle.

Willard, Caroline McCoy
1884   Life in Alaska: Letters of Mrs. Eugene S. Willard. Eva McClintock, ed. Philadelphia: Presbyterian Board of Publication.

Willey, Gordon W., and Philip Phillips
1958   Method and Theory in American Archaeology. Chicago: University of Chicago Press.

Williams, Frank, and Emma Williams
1978   Tongass Texts. Jeff Lear, ed. Fairbanks: University of Alaska Native Language Center.

Williams, Melvin D.
1979   The Harvesting of "Sluckus" (*Porphyra perforata*) by the Straits Salish Indians of Vancouver Island, British Columbia. *Syesis* 12:63–69. Victoria, B.C.

Willmott, Jill
1961   [Sechelt Linguistic Notebook.] (Manuscript in Wayne Suttles' possession.)

Willoughby, Charles C.
1889   Indians of the Quinaielt Agency. Pp. 267–282 in *Annual Report of the Smithsonian Institution for the Year 1886.* Washington. (Reprinted: Shorey Book Store, Seattle, Wash., 1969.)

1910   A New Type of Ceremonial Blanket from the Northwest Coast. *American Anthropologist* 12(1):1–10.

Wilson, Charles W.
1866   Report on the Indian Tribes Inhabiting the Country in the Vicinity of the 49th Parallel of North Latitude. *Transactions of the Ethnological Society of London* n.s. 4:275–332.

1970   Mapping the Frontier: Charles Wilson's Diary of the Survey of the 49th Parallel, 1858–1862. George F.G. Stanley, ed. Toronto: Macmillan of Canada.

Wilson, Peter, and James Henderson
1980–1981   Kwakwala Language Materials; Including Northwest Coast Culture Lessons, Kwakwala Alphabet, Kwakwala Language Lessons and Advanced Kwakwala Lessons and Stories for Children. Campbell River, B.C.

Wingert, Paul S.
1949   American Indian Sculpture: A Study of the Northwest Coast. New York: J.J. Augustin.

1949a   Coast Salish Painting. Pp. 77–91 in Indians of the Urban Northwest. Marian W. Smith, ed. New York: Columbia University Press. (Reprinted: AMS Press, New York, 1969.)

[1951]   Tsimshian Sculpture. Pp. 73–94 in The Tsimshian: Their Arts and Music. Viola E. Garfield, Paul D. Wingert, and Marius Barbeau, eds. New York: J.J. Augustin.

1952   Prehistoric Stone Sculptures of the Pacific Northwest. Portland, Oreg.: Portland Art Museum.

Wintemberg, W.J.
1940   Harlan Ingersoll Smith. *American Antiquity* 6(1):63–64.

Winthrop, Theodore
1913   The Canoe and the Saddle; or, Klalam and Klickatat, ...To Which Are Now First Added His Western Letters and Journals. John H. Williams, ed. Tacoma, Wash.: John H. Williams.

Wissler, Clark
1914   Material Cultures of the North American Indians. *American Anthropologist* 16(3):447–505.

1917   The American Indian: An Introduction to the Anthropology of the New World. New York: Douglas C. McMurtrie.

Wollcott, Harry F.
1967   A Kwakiutl Village and School. New York: Holt, Rinehart and Winston. (Reprinted: Waveland Press, Prospect, Ill., 1984.)

Wolverton, Anne L.
1978   Human Osteological Analysis; 1977 Excavations. Appendix I in Prehistoric Archaeology at 45WH17, by G.F. Grabert, J.A. Cressman, and A. Wolverton. *Western Washington University. Department of Anthropology. Reports in Anthropology* 8. Bellingham.

Wood, Corinne S.
1979   Human Sickness and Health: A Biocultural View. Palo Alto, Calif.: Mayfield.

Woodward, John A.
1972   The Geertz Site: An Early Campsite in Western Oregon. *Tebiwa: Journal of the Idaho State University Museum* 15(2):55–62. Pocatello.

1974   Salmon, Slaves, and Grizzly Bears: The Prehistoric Antecedents and Ethnohistory of Clackamas Indian Culture. (Unpublished Ph.D. Dissertation in Anthropology, University of Oregon, Eugene.)

1977   An Early Ceramic Tradition on the Pacific Coast. *The Masterkey* 51(2):66–72.

Woodward, John A., Carson N. Murdy, and Franklin Young
1975   Artifacts from the Fuller Mound, Willamette Valley, Oregon. Pp. 375–402 in Archaeological Studies in the Willamette Valley, Oregon. C. Melvin Aikens, ed. *University of Oregon Anthropological Papers* 8. Eugene.

Work, John
1824–1825   [Journal, April 15–November 17 and November 18–November 25, 1824.] (Manuscript No. 219 in Oregon Historical Society, Portland.)

1829   [Answers to Queries on Natural History, April 1, 1829, Fort Colvile.] (Manuscript B.45/e/2 in Hudson's Bay Company Archives, Provincial Archives of Manitoba, Winnipeg, Canada.)

1838   [Letter of October 20 to James Douglas.] (Manuscript B.223/c/1 #25, folder 113 in Hudson's Bay Company Archives, Provincial Archives of Manitoba, Winnipeg, Canada.)

1848   [Letter of February 10.] (Manuscript A.11/67, folders 5–6 in Hudson's Bay Company Archives, Provincial Archives of Manitoba, Winnipeg, Canada.)

1945 The Journal of John Work, January to October, 1835. *Archives of British Columbia. Memoirs* 10. Victoria.

1945a Fur Brigade to the Bonaventura: John Work's California Expedition, 1832–1833 . . . . Alice B. Maloney, ed. San Francisco: California Historical Society.

Worl, Rosita
1980 Ethnohistory of Southeastern Alaska Indians: Tlingit, Haida and Tsimshian. (Unpublished paper in Worl's possession.)

Wrangell, Ferdinand Petrovich von
1839 Obitateli sîevero-zapadnykh beregov Ameriki [The Inhabitants of the Northwest Coasts of America]. *Syn Otechestva* 7(3):51–82. St. Petersburg.

1839a Statistische und etnographische Nachrichten über die russischen Besitzungen an der Nordwestküste von Amerika. K.E. von Baer, ed. St. Petersburg: Buchdruckerei der Kaiserlichen Akademie der Wissenschaften.

1970 The Inhabitants of the Northwest Coast of America [1839]. James W. VanStone, trans. *Arctic Anthropology* 6(2):5–20.

1980 Russian America: Statistical and Ethnographic Information. Translated from the German ed. of 1839 by Mary Sandouski. Richard A. Pierce, ed. (*Materials for the Study of Alaska History* 15) Kingston, Ont.: The Limestone Press.

Wright, Milton
1988 Coquitlam Lake. (Paper presented at the Canadian Archaeological Association Annual Meeting, Whistler, B.C.)

Wright, Robin K.
1979 Haida Argillite Ship Pipes. *American Indian Art Magazine* 5(1):40–47.

1980 Haida Argillite Pipes: The Influence of Clay Pipes. *American Indian Art Magazine* 5(4):42–47, 88.

1982 Haida Argillite–Made for Sale. *American Indian Art Magazine* 8(1):48–55.

1983 Anonymous Attributions: A Tribute to a Mid-19th Century Haida Argillite Pipe Carver, the Master of the Long Fingers. Pp. 139–142 in The Box of Daylight: Northwest Coast Indian Art. Bill Holm, ed. Seattle: Seattle Art Museum and University of Washington Press.

1985 Nineteenth Century Haida Argillite Pipe Carvers: Stylistic Attribution. (Unpublished Ph.D. Dissertation in Fine Arts, University of Washington, Seattle.)

1986 The Depiction of Women in Nineteenth Century Haida Argillite Carving. *American Indian Art Magazine* 11(4):36–45.

1987 Haida Argillite Carving in the Sheldon Jackson Museum. Pp. 76–199 in Faces, Voices, and Dreams: A Celebration of the Centennial of the Sheldon Jackson Museum, Sitka, Alaska, 1888–1988. Peter L. Corey, ed. Sitka, Alas.: Sheldon Jackson Museum.

Wyatt, Victoria
1984 Shapes of Their Thoughts: Reflections of Culture Contact in Northwest Coast Indian Art. Norman: University of Oklahoma Press.

Yale, J.M.
1838–1839 [Census of Indian Population.] (Manuscript B.223/z/1 in Hudson's Bay Company Archives, Provincial Archives of Manitoba, Winnipeg, Canada.)

Yarmie, Andrew
1968 Smallpox and the British Columbia Indians: Epidemic of 1862. *British Columbia Library Quarterly* 31(3):13–21. Vancouver.

Yesner, David R.
1980 Maritime Hunter-gatherers: Ecology and Prehistory. *Current Anthropology* 21(6):727–750.

Young, Samuel H.
1927 Hall Young of Alaska, "The Mushing Parson:" The Autobiography of S. Hall Young. New York: Fleming H. Revell.

Zaikov, Potap
1979 Journal of Navigator Potap Zaikov, on Ship Sv. Aleksandr Nevskii, July 27–October 22, 1783 (Extract). Pp. 1–6 in A History of the Russian American Company. Vol. 2: Documents, by P.A. Tikhmenev. Dmitri Krenov, trans., Richard A. Pierce and Alton S. Donnelly, eds. (*Materials for the Study of Alaska History* 13) Kingston, Ont.: The Limestone Press.

Zakoji, Hiroto
1953 Klamath Culture Change. (Unpublished M.A. Thesis in Anthropology, University of Oregon, Portland.)

Zenk, Henry B.
1976 Contributions to Tualatin Ethnography: Subsistence and Ethnobiology. (Unpublished M.A. Thesis in Anthropology, Portland State University, Portland, Oreg.)

1984 Chinook Jargon and Native Cultural Persistence in the Grand Ronde Indian Community, 1856–1907: A Special Case of Creolization. (Unpublished Ph.D. Dissertation in Anthropology, University of Oregon, Eugene.)

1988 Chinook Jargon in the Speech Economy of Grand Ronde Reservation, Oregon: An Ethnography-of-speaking Approach to an Historical Case of Creolization in Process. Pp. 107–124 in Sociolinguistics and Pidgin-Creole Studies. John R. Rickford, ed. Joshua A. Fishman, gen. ed. (*International Journal of the Sociology of Language* 71) Amsterdam, The Netherlands: Mouton de Gruyter.

Zenk, Henry, and Robert Moore
1983 "How We Went Up to Steal a Mattress": A Comedy in Three Acts, by Clara Riggs. Pp. 353–398 in *Working Papers for the 18th International Conference on Salish and Neighboring Languages.* Seattle: University of Washington, Department of Anthropology.

Zimmermann, Heinrich
[1930] Zimmermann's Captain Cook: An Account of the Third Voyage of Captain Cook Around the World, 1776–1780. Elsa Michaelis, trans.; F.W. Howay, ed. Toronto, Ont.: Ryerson Press.

Zolotarevskaja, I.A., E.E. Blomkvist, and E.V. Zibert
1956 Ethnographical Material from the Americas in Russian Collections. Pp. 221–231 in *Proceedings of the 32d International Congress of Americanists,* Copenhagen, 1956.

Zontek, Terry
1978 Test Excavation and Cultural Resources Evaluation of the Oceanside Site (35 TI 47). Salem: Oregon State Parks and Recreation.

1983 Aboriginal Fishing at Seal Rock (35-LC-14) and Neptune (35-LA-3): Late-prehistoric Archaeological Sites on the Central Oregon Coast. (Unpublished M.A. Thesis in Anthropology, Oregon State University, Corvallis.)

Zucker, Jeff, Kay Hummel, and Bob Hogfoss
1983 Oregon Indians; Culture History and Current Affairs: An Atlas and Introduction. [Portland, Oreg.]: Western Imprints, The Press of the Oregon Historical Society.

Index

Italic numbers indicate material in a figure; roman numbers, material in the text.

All variant names of groups are indexed, with the occurrences under synonymy discussing the equivalences. Variants of group names that differ from those cited only in their capitalization, hyphenation, or accentuation have generally been omitted; variants that differ only in the presence or absence of one (noninitial) letter or compound element have been collapsed into a single entry with that letter or element in parentheses.

The entry Indian words *indexes, by language, all words appearing in the standard orthographies and some others.*

Specific reservations and reserves are at reservations and reserves.

batons: 380, 381, *401*
Bayly, William: 98
Bays of Akoie people; synonymy: 203
Beach Grove site: 340, 346
beads: 122, 131, *216*, 348, 399, *428*, 463, 505, 508, 540, *541*, 548, 551, *574*, *582*, 628. bone: 202, 233, 237. China: 537. coal: 202. copper: 200. prehistoric: 61, 199, 200, *201*, 202, 233, 234, *236*, 237, 345, *345*, 349, 350, *350*, 351, *351*, 352, 355, 481, 493, 518, 528. seed: *245*, *373*. shale: 346. shell: 29, 61, *201*, 202, 234, *236*, 237, 346, 355. stone: *201*, 202, 234, *351*. tooth: 202, *236*, 237
Bear Cove site: 62–67, 353–354
Beardslee, Lester A.: 150
bears. *See* food; hunting
Bear Shell Midden site: 197, *198*
Beaver: 141, 159
Beaver, Herbert: 72, 131–132
bedding: 191, 219, *398–399*, 459–461, 490, 583
Beebe site: *521*, 526
Belhoola; synonymy: 338
Bella Bella: 9, *10*, 11, 14, 54, 55, 77, 78, 312–322. adornment: 13, 52–53, *124*, 315. art: 247, 300, 316, *316*, 602, 605, 609–610, *613*, 616–617, 624. ceremonies: 253, *318*, 318–319, *319*, 332, 375, 379, 381, 384, 385, 386, 605. clothing: 315. disease: 58, 140, 141, 142, 144, 320. environment: 312, 314. external relations: 306, 314, 323, 360, 605. history: 112, *112*, 161, 319–321, *321*. kinship terminology: 317. Koeye: 312. language: 312. life cycle: 300, 317–318. migration: 314, 321. mythology: 594, 595. orthography: 312. political organization: 314, 316–317. population: 141, 144, 165, 320. prehistory: 108, 110, 111, 112, *112*, 113, 114, 298, 300, 301–302, 303, 304. reserves: 161, 165. settlements: *313*, 320, *320*. social organization: 314, 317, 605. structures: 315, *316*. subsistence: 314–315. synonymy: 311, 321, 376. technology: *124*, 315–316, *316*. territory: 312, *313*, 323. trade: 319–320, 325, 327. transport: 316, 327. Uyalit: 317, 321. warfare: 246, 314, 375. *See also* Indian words
Bella Bella language: 34, 44, 99, 101, 102, 312
Bella Coola: *10–11*, 11, 15, 52, 54, 74, 95–97, 116, 323–339. adornment: 13, 52–53, 326–327. art: 83, 132, *328*, 336, 373, 605, 610, 617, 624, 628, 630. ceremonies: *75*, 78, 84, *329*, 332–335, *333*, *334*, *335*, *337*, *338*. clothing: *75*, 326, 628. cosmology: 81, 330. disease: 140, 141, 143, 144. environment: 323. external relations: 314, 323–325. history: 72, *76*, 112, 125, 159, 161, 336–338. Kimsquit: 34, 36, 159, *326*, 328, 337, 338. kinship terminology: 328. Kwatna: 328, 337, 339. language: 323, 338. lifecycle: 306, 330–332. menstrual practices: 331. music: 336. mythology: 74, 76, 78, 81, 593, 594, 598, 599, 605. orthography: 323. population: 136, 141, 144, 165, 337. prehistory: 111, 112, 113, 114, 298, 301–305, 357. religion: 78.

reserves: 160, 161, 165. settlement pattern: 323, *324–325*. settlements: *324–325*, 327. shamanism: 335. social organization: 4, 13, 328–330. structures: *6*, 327, *327*, *328*. subsistence: 308, 325–326, *326*. synonymy: 15, 338. Tallio: 34, 36, 314, 328, 337, 339. technology: 327. territory: 47, 323, *324–325*. trade: 125, 314, 325, 337. transport: 327. warfare: 325, 335–336, 363, 375. *See also* Indian words
Bella Coola Band Council: 338
Bella Coola language grouping: 15, *32*, 33, 34, 36, 39, 44, 46–47, 48, 98, 99, 105, 282, 323, 338. dialects: 34, 36
Bella Coola United Church Women's Guild: 338
Bellaghchoola; synonymy: 338
Bellichoola; synonymy: 338
bálxʷəlá; synonymy: 338
Benedict: *403*
Benjamin site: *521*
Bering, Vitus: 70, *120*
Bernisches Historisches Museum: 88, 95
bəšáləbš̌; synonymy: 487, 488
Beynon, William: 79, 101–102, 283–284, 598
Biederbost site: *482*, 483
Big Bill: 633, 636
Bilbilla; synonymy: 321
Billichoola; synonymy: 338
Bîlxula; synonymy: 338
Bini: 255
Birch Bay site: 63
Birket-Smith, Kaj: 78
birth: 330–331, 388. abortion: 331. afterbirth: 331, 405, 433, 448, 562, 584. assistance: 217, 253, 277, 433, 448, 465, 562, 584. ceremonies: 194, 433. devices for: 562. infanticide: 331, 564. position at: 433, 447. ritual observances: 193, 210, 216–217, 253, 562. structures: 207, 216–217, 465. taboos: 193, 253, 405, 433, 447, 495, 577, 584. umbilical cord: 433, 562
Bishop, Charles: 72
Bishop, Heber R.: 90
Bishop, Thomas G.: 178
Bishopbrick site: *521*
Bishop Christie Indian Residential School: 410
Blacklock site: *555*, 556
Blanchet, Francis Norbert: 72, 133, 499–500
blankets. *See* button blankets; Chilkat blankets; clothing
Blue Jackets Creek site: 54, 55–56, *56*, 57, 58, 230, *230*, 235, 236, 237
Blue Jay. *See* mythology
Blue Lake site: *521*, 524
Blundon site: *555*, 556
Boardwalk site: 57, 234, *234*, 235
Boas, Franz: 74, *76*, 90, *103*, 337. artifacts collected by: *76*, *374–375*, *395*. on cultural classifications: 5, 12, 77. ethnographic work: 73–87, 377. feast sponsored by: *371*, *382*. influence on anthropology: 77–81, 101. Jesup North Pacific Expedition directorship: 76–77, 90, 107. linguistic material collected by: 36, 37, 40, 41, 44, 45,

74–77, 79, 101, 377, 440. mythological work: 80–81. physical anthropology work: 52–59, 116–117
Bocharov, Dimitrii: *120*
Bodega y Quadra, Juan Francisco de la: 70, *120*, 127, 138, 513
Boit, John: 72, 535
Boldt, George: 176–179, *178*, 501
Bolduc, J.B.: 133, 500
Bolton, Frank: *280*
Borden, Charles E.: 108–109
Bornite phase: 67, 232, 237, 238
Boston: 127, 408
Boston Marine Society: 91
Boston Society of Natural History: 91
Boundary Commission: 73, 100
bows and arrows: 132, 190, 209, 216, 246, 325, *337*, 397, 431, 445, 458, 489, 495, 507, 509, 537, 570, 584. arrows: 121, *326*, 345, 394, *400*, 414, *427*, 583, 586. bows: 24, 126, *400*, 426, *427*, 459, 583. construction and materials: 24, 192, 209, *326*, 433. prehistoric: 416, 523, 528, 529, 556. quivers: *218*, *400*, *427*, *549*, 583, 586
Boxer: 366
boxes and bowls. *See* containers
Brabant, Augustin J.: 100, 409
Bradford, John: *187*
Bradford, Mary: *187*
Bradley-Moen site: *521*, 526
Brainard, Bill: *188*
Bremen Museum: 90
Breton, André: 92
British Association for the Advancement of Science: 75, 101
British Columbia Association of Non-Status Indians: 167
British Columbia Indian Language Project: 49
British Columbia Provincial Museum: 91, 93
British Library: 95
British Museum: 88, 95
Brooklyn Museum: 91, 95
Brown, Anja Streich: *112*
Brown, Charlie: *275*
Brown, Dorothy: 598
Brown, Eliza: *275*
Brown, Robert: 73, 311
Brown, Steve: *385*, 632
Browning, O.H.: 149
Buchanan, Charles M.: 176
Buck Creek site: *521*, 527
Buckley Bay site: 341
Bullards Beach site: 554, *555*, 556
Bureau of American Ethnology: 74, 77, 100–101, 102, 109
Bureau of Indian Affairs: 148, 155, 178, 182–183, 261, *578*. agencies: 171, 172–175, *174*, 183, 185, 187, 363, 428–429, 577, 578. agents: 171, 172–175, 176, 182, 183, 436, 515, 531. agriculture: 427. education: 151, *151*, 183, 427. potlatch policy: 476. removal: 180, 183. superintendencies: 180, 181, 182, 183, 187. tribal recognition: 156, 176, 177–179, 188, 472, 535
burial. *See* death practices

East India Marine Society of Salem: 88
Eayem phase: 67, 348
Echeverria, Anastasio: 71
Echo Bay site: 353–354
Econne; synonymy: 570
economy: 186. loans: 85, 187. prestige: 85. *See also* businesses; employment; trade
Eddy Point site: 519, *521*, 522, 524
Edel, May: 101
Edenshaw, Charles: 76, 83, 90–91, 265, *265*, *607*
Edmo, Ed: 601
education: 112, 172, 182, 266, 387, 409, 427, 472. agricultural: 427. bilingual: 286, 290, 293, 437. boarding schools: *151*, 162, 173, *174*, 176, 183, 195, 224, 286, 363, 388, 410, 427–428, 471. community-based schools: 473, 501. curriculum: *174*, 262, 290, 293, 295, *328*, 388, *388*, 429. day schools: 162, 173, 183, 264, 363, 388, 427, *434–435*. enrollment: 173, *174*. Indian culture: 157–158, *388*, 626. Indian language: 49, *50*, 103, 157, 179, *388*. Indian languages used in: 151, 262. Indian-operated schools: 186, 388, 501. missionary: 133, 151, *151*, 162, 173, 183, 224, 286, 363, 388, 410, 471. Native teachers: 262. postsecondary: 164, 266, 388, 473. public school enrollment: 151, 162, 264, 266, 286. tribal schools: 388, 473, 501. vocational: 151, *151*, 164, *174*, *296–297*, 363, 388
Edward VII: 166
Eeak tella; synonymy: 196
Eeksen; synonymy: 450. *See also* Salish, Northern Coast
Eells, Edwin: 173, 500
Eells, Myron: 74, 100, 107, 173, 471, 500, 639
éeqsen; synonymy: 450
EeSu 5 site: 303
eiksan; synonymy: 450
elderly: *273*, *277*
Eliza y Reventa, Francisco de: 70, *120*, 470
Ellis, William: 98
Elmendorf, William W.: 78
Elswa, Johnny Kit: *75*, *595*
ElTb 10 site: 303
elx̣í´mix; synonymy: 282
Emery phase: 348, 351, 352
Emmons, George Thornton: 74, *75*, 90–91, *274*, *459*, *460–461*, 607
employment: agriculture: 163, 224, 500, 515. canneries: 153, 163, 172, 195, 224, 257, 263, 282, 287, 289, 364, 409, 410, 471. construction: 264, 387. crafts: *152*, *173*, 224, 263, 409, 410, *461*, 629. domestic: *152*, 187. farming and ranching: 286–287, 471, 500. fishing: 162–164, *163*, 166–167, 172, 224, 257, 262, 263, 266, 286–287, 288, 364, 387, 409, 410, 428, 437, 450, 471, 473, 500, 515. hop-picking: 163, 172, *172*, *173*, 187, 409, 410, 450, 471, 515. labor unions: 163. lumber: 163, 187, 262, 263–264, 266, 286–287, 289, 387, 410, 428, 437, 450, 471, 500, 515. mining: 224, 256, 387. railroads: 515. on reservations: 165, 262, 263, 286–287, 387–388, 428. sales: 500. sealing:

409, 428. stevedoring: 163. temporary and part-time: 172, 264, 287. training: 266. trapping: 286, 410. unemployment: 164–165, 188, 266, 287, 387. wage work: 129, 172, 224, 257, 263, 282, 285
ᶜnaʹkǃwax·daᶜxᵘ; synonymy: 376
ᶜnE´mgis; synonymy: 376
English Camp site: 346
engraving. *See* sculpture
environment: 11, 16–29. animal resources: 1, 19–20, 24–29, 135, 190, 205, 229, 241, 269, 289, 312, 314, 325, 341, 345, 346–347, 350, 353–354, 356–357, 364, 393, 412, 418, 419, 422, 431, 456, 481, 518, 530, 547. climate: 1, 17–18, *18*, *19*, 190, 205, 229, 230, 241, 269, 304, 306, 312, 323, 393–394, 412, 422, 431, 438, 444, 456, 485–488, 505, 572, 580, 602. geology: 190, 229. hydrology: 16–17, *18*–20, 190, 229, 269, 312, 323, 348, 364, 391, 393, 408, 412, 413, 414, 416, 419, 421, 422, 431, 438, 455–456, 481, 485, 505, 523–525, 547, 572, 580. prehistoric: 229–230, 237, 304, 481, 518, 519, 523, 554. terrain: 1, 16–17, *17*, *22*, 189–190, 205, 229, 241, 269, 323, 393, 412, 413, 414, 431, 456, 481, 488, 505, 524, 547, 572, 580. tidal cycle: 18–20. vegetation: 1, *20*, 20–24, *22*, 29, 190, 241, 269, 289, 304, 312, 323, 341, 364, 393–394, 412, 422, 431, 444, 456, 481, 488, 505, 523, 530, 547, 572, 580. White impact on: 29
Ernst, Max: 92
Esilao phase: 348, 351
Esilao Village site: *343*, 348, 349, 350, *350*, 351
Eskimo: 5, 78, 89. history: 70, 133. migrations: 56, 81. mythology: 81. physical anthropology: 54, 56, 114. prehistory: 9, 68–69, 107, 114
Eskimo, Bering Strait: 209, 420
Eskimo, Pacific; art: 606. Chugach: 189, 192, 194, *195*, 208, 226. history: 427. Koniag: 127. language: 30. social organization: 4. synonymy: 189, 196. territory: 189. warfare: 195. *See also* Indian words
Esleytok; synonymy: 321
Estedox; synonymy: 321
etnémitane; synonymy: 586
etnémi-tenéyu; synonymy: 586
Etolin, Adolph K.: 88
Euchre Creek; synonymy: 586
Euclataw; synonymy: 377
eulachon. *See* fishing
Evanoff, Lottie: *574*
Everette, Willis Eugene: 101
ʔəẁaʔíƛəla; synonymy: 377
ᶜwálas Kwag·uɫ; synonymy: 376
exploration. *See* history, exploration
Eyak: 5, 14, 78, 189–196, 213. adornment: 191–192. ceremonies: 84, 193, 194, *194*. Chilkat: 189, *190*. clothing: 191, 192, *192*. environment: 189–190, *191*. external relations: 190, 191, 192, 193, 226. Eyak proper: 189, *190*. history: 70, 143, 194–196. kinship: *195*. language: 189, 195, *195*. life cycle: 193–194. migrations: 189, 193.

music: 193, 194, *194*. mythology: 194. orthography: 189. political organization: 193. population: 136, 195, 196. prehistory: 197, 202. settlements: 189, 190, *190*, *191*, 195. shamanism: 194, *195*. social organization: 4, 189, 191, 192–193. structures: 191, *191*, *195*. subsistence: 190–191, *191*, 195. synonymy: 189, 196. technology: 191, 192, *192*. territory: 1, 189, *190*, 193, 203. Tlingitized: 189, *190*, 195, 203. trade: 190, 193, 208. transport: 190, 191, *192*, 208. warfare: 195. Yakatag: 189, *190*, 203. *See also* Indian words
Eyak-Athapaskan language family: 30–31, 34, 45, 48, 68, 69, 104, 189, 203
Eyak Corporation: 195–196
Eyak language: 30–31, *32*, 34, 43, 44, 46–47, 48, 49, 98, 100, 189, 195, *195*
eyəqsən; synonymy: 450

F
Fairchild, Baldwin: *587*
Faladin; synonymy: 553
Fallatrahs; synonymy: 553
Fall Creek site: *521*
Fall Indians; synonymy: 545
False Narrows site: 346
family groups. *See* social organization
famine: 130, 136, 180, 183, 271
Fanning Mound site: *521*, 526
Farlow, Lewis H.: 91
Farrand, Livingston: 76–77, 90, 101
feasts: 84, *247*, 278–279, 285, 286, 331, *371*, *382*, 385, 400, 402, 405, *406*, 469, 476, 513, 544. ceremonies: 291, 379, 380. foods: 245, 271, 493. functions of: 252, 278, 401. grease: 368. intergroup: 485. memorial: 86, 219, 265, 286, 496. occasions for: 217, 252, 253, 254, 400, 401, 496, 497, 543, 585. at potlatches: *389*, 401–402
Feldheimer site: *521*, 524
feuds: 215, 359, 569, 580
Fidalgo, Salvador: 70, *120*
Field Columbian Museum: 90–91
Field Museum of Natural History: 57, 59, 90, *94*, 95, 630
Fife Sound site: 353
figurines and effigies: *250–251*, *256*, 433, 539, 544, 605, 615, 617, 618. postcontact: *129*, *256*, 609. prehistoric: *303*, *344*, 351, 518, *520*, *558*. *See also* sculpture; totem poles
Finlayson, Duncan: 282
firearms: 126–128, 131, 148, 180, 187. impact: 136, 358, 428, 509. introduction of: 499, 535. trade: 120–121, 122, 125, 127, 131, 209, 223, 361, 363, 407–408, 535. types: 126, *255*
firemaking: 212. mythology: 280
Fisher Channel site: 302
fishhooks: 67, 211, *211*, 232, 237, *243*, 244, *302*, 304, 308, 315, 341, 346, 347, *347*, 348, 356, *356*, 357, 394, *396–397*, 416, *419*, *426*, 483, 556, 605
fishing: 4, *22*, 172, 191, 245, 246, 266, 269, 286, 291, 346, 353, 395–397, 418, 419, 420, 422, 425, 472, 484, 510, 515, *558*, 573, 580.

Southwestern Coast

763

35, 183, 572, *573*, 577, 578. social organization: 576. structures: 574, *576*. subsistence: 573. synonymy: 571, 578. technology: 573–574. territory: 572, *573*. trade: 574. transport: 569, 574–575. *See also* Indian words

Siuslaw language: 31, *32*, 35, 38, 42, 43, 45, 46–47, 49, 99, 100–101, 104, 568, 571, 572, 578, 596. dialects: 31, 35, 572. orthography: 572

Siwallace, Margaret: 338

Siwash; synonymy: 51

Sixes; synonymy: 586

Sixes George: 183

Si-yam-il; synonymy: 553

Skagit. *See* Salish, Southern Coast

Skagit, Lower: 141

Skagit, Upper; synonymy: 488. *See also* Salish, Southern Coast

Skagit-Snohomish language: 105

Skagit System Cooperative: 501

Skahakmehu; synonymy: 487

Skaiakos; synonymy: 452. *See also* Salish, Northern Coast

Skaito; synonymy: 259

Skai-wha-mish; synonymy: 487

Skamel culture: 349–353, *350*

Skamokawa site: *521*, 524

Skaowskeay: *595*

Skedans: *242*, 249

Skedans: 240, 241, *241*. synonymy: 259–260

Skee-dans; synonymy: 259

Skeena phase: 237–238

Skeena River sites: 230, *230*, 232, 237–238

Skelakhan: 456

Skidans; synonymy: 259

Skiddan; synonymy: 259

Skid-de-gates; synonymy: 259

Skidegat; synonymy: 259

Skidegate: *242*, 249, 255

Skidegate VI: *242*

Skidegate ; synonymy: 258. *See also* Haida

Skihwamish; synonymy: 487

Skilloots; synonymy: 545. *See also* Chinookans of the Lower Columbia

Skit-e-gates; synonymy: 259

Skittagets; synonymy: 259

Skittegetan language family: 104

S'Klallam; synonymy: 474

Skoglund's Landing site: *61*, 65, *230*, 231, 235, 238

Skokomish; synonymy: 502. *See also* Salish, Southern Coast

Skokomish Tribe: 177

s'ko-mook; synonymy: 450

Skopamish; synonymy: 487. *See* Salish, Southern Coast

Skope-ahmish; synonymy: 487

Skowal: 243

Sk·qŏ́mic; synonymy: 473

Sk-tah-le-jum; synonymy: 487

Sk-tahl-mish; synonymy: 487

Skykomish; synonymy: 501. *See also* Salish, Southern Coast

slaiäman; synonymy: 451

slavery: 4, 87, 130, 369, 399–400, 401, 407, 465, 493, 505, 541, 542–543, 551. abolition: 169, 213, 224, 368, 450. by Americans: 182, 543. Indian raiders: 13, 129, 136–137, 206, 246, 276, 336, 360, 495, 510, 543, 550, 560, 565, 568, 583, 590. trade: 129, 209, 246, 281, 317, 542, 550, 560, 568

slaves: 130, 148, 207. acquisition of: 4, 209, 276, 317, 336, 494, 510, 550, 583. adornment: 463, 465, 493, 510, 542. death practices: 58, 87, 192–193, 219, 255, 512, 542. guardian spirits of: 565. marriage: 4, 276, 510. ownership of: 4, 58, 87, 192, 495, 543. social rank: 4, 213, 252, 276, 308, 317, 330, 423, 432, 465, 494, 510, 512, 542, 550, 565, 576, 583. subsistence activities: 208, 210, 246, 277, 542. Whites as: 435

Sliammon; synonymy: 451. *See also* Salish, Northern Coast

sling and dart: 209–210

Slocum, John: 174, 500, 633, *634*, 638

Slocum, Mary: 500, 633, 634

Smalh-kamish; synonymy: 487

Smalihu; synonymy: 487

Small Tribes Organization of Western Washington: 179

Smart, Henry: *280*

Smith, A.W.: 435, 437

Smith, Celiast: 185

Smith, Frederick M.: 182

Smith, Harlan I.: 76–77, 90, 108, 228, 323, 339

Smith, Jedediah: 577

Smith, Marian W.: 77, 78

Smith, Silas: 185, 532

Smithfield Mound site: *521*

Smithsonian Institution: *38*, 74, 75, *76*, 89–91, *91*, 96–97, 99, 102, 106, 109

Smulkamish; synonymy: 487. *See also* Salish, Southern Coast

Snanaimooh; synonymy: 473

Snanaimuq; synonymy: 473

Snohomish. *See* Salish, Southern Coast

Snohomish Tribe: 179

Snoqualmie. *See* Salish, Southern Coast

Snoqualmie Indian Tribe: 179

Snoqualmoo; synonymy: 439, 487

Snoqualmoo Tribe of Whidbey Island: 179

Snoqualmu; synonymy: 487

snowshoes: 191, *192*, 208, *273*, 280, 308, 327, 397, 463, 492, 562. trade: 444

Snyder, Gary: 601

Snyder, Sally: 78, 81

Snyder, Warren A.: 78, 109

social evolutionism: 77, 80, 86–87

social organization; avoidance relationships: 13, 81, 193, 251. ceremonial privileges: 379, 380–381, 384, 402, 404, 448–449, 464. clans: 86–87, 157, 189, 193, 203, 205–206, 207, 208, 212, 213, *214*, 215, 220, 221, 224, *225*, 226–227, 246, 248, 274, 275, 280, 289, 291, 295, 306, 308, 432, 464, 604–605, *608*, 629. class structure: 4, 87, 128–130, 192–193, 252, 275–276, 308, 317, 329–330, 368, 399–401, 419, 423, 432, 465, 493–494, 510, 550, 565, 583, 591. descent rules: 4,

13, 86–87, 157, 248–249, 251, 274, 276, 288, 289, 291, 295, 309, 317, 325, 329, 332, 367, 391, 399, 402, 423, 464. family groups: 86, 174, 262, 328–329, 399, 432, 447, 464, 493. households: 329, 447, 464, 493, 511. 'houses': 251, 87, 249, 252, 274, 289, 291, 295. joking relationships: 13, 193, 220, 251, 585. lineages: 13, 251, 85, 193, 210, 212, 213, 221, 235, 246, 248–249, 252, 254, 257. local groups: 418, 447, 464. moieties: 13, 191, 192, 193, *194*, 203, 205, 208, 212, 213, *214*, *215*, 217, 219, 220, 224, 246, 248, 249, 252, 253, 254, 274, 280. numayms: 84, 86–87, 317, 359, 366–367, 373, 375, 376, 384. phratries: 13, 246, 291. postcontact: 128–130, 157, 224, 257, 285, 290, 294–295, 308, 368–372, 633. prehistoric: 234, 235, 239. ranking: 4, 5, 77, 85, 87, 210, 213, 217, 219, 220, 234, 235, 239, 243, 245, 246, 251–252, 254, 255, 308, 317, 330, 423, 494, 498, 510, 541, 543, 565, 576, 583, 591, 606, 618. regional networks: 12–14, 15. sublineages: 249, 251, 252. villages: 267, 274, 328–329, 464, 493, 511, 569. *See also* division of labor; kinship; kinship terminology

Société des Amis du Musée de L'Homme: 93

Sokolov, Kharlampii: *224*

s'óksŭn; synonymy: 452

Somass River sites: 67, *68*

Sonese; synonymy: 474

Songhees; synonymy: 474. *See also* Salish, Central Coast

Songish: *10*. synonymy: *11*, 474

songs. *See* music

Sonihat: *254*

Sonora: 127, 435

Sooes site: *413*, 414, 419

Sooke. *See* Salish, Central Coast

sorcery: 335, 497, 512–513, 544, 570. witches: 193, 194, 207, 221, 279, 372. *See also* spells

Soto: 545

Souscitsa: *440*

Southern Kwakiutl: *11*. synonymy: 376

Southern Tsimshian language: 32, 267, 282. orthography: 267

Southern Wakashans; synonymy: 11, 14

South Yale site: *61*, 62, *62*

Spain. *See* history, Spanish period

Sparrow, Sr., Ed: *468*

spears: 121, 394, 414, 583. construction: 24, 209. fishing: 190, 210–211, 445, 457, 489, 507, 531. hunting: 190, 209, 210, 308, 315, 458, 459, 537. war: 209, 216, 495, 509

Speck, Henry: 630

speeches: 380, 385, 402. at burials: 585. ceremonial invitations: 380. by chiefs: 128, 169, *400*, 585. marriage: 405, 563. potlatches: 85, 478. speakers: 400, 541, *551*, 565, 585. *See also* storytelling

spells: 4, 467, 497, 584

Spier, Leslie: 77, 78

spindles: *460–461*, 461, 611, 613

spirit questing: 433, 435

spirits. *See* supernatural beings

Spokane; population: 139

Tomlinson, Robert: 282
Tongass. *See* Tlingit, Coastal
Tongass National Forest: 56, 153, 155
Tongue Point site: *413*, 414
Tonquin: 98, 127, 408
Too a nook; synonymy: 501
tools: *2–3*, 24, 131, 192, 212, *256*, 274, *274*,
    308, 315–316, 425, *426*, 433, 446, 459, 489,
    509, *510*, 583. decoration: 375, 433,
    602–603, 614, 620. postcontact adaptations:
    132, 223, 363, 603–604, 615. prehistoric:
    60–69, *62*, *64*, *65*, 198, 199, 200, *201*, 202,
    231, 232, *232*, 233, *233*, 234, *234*, 235, *235*,
    236, *236*, 237, 238, *302*, 303, *303*, 304, 341,
    344, 345, *345*, 346, 347–348, 349, *349*, 350,
    350, 351, *351*, 352, 353, 354, *354*, *355*, *356*,
    357, 414, 417, *417*, *418*, *420*, 421, 481–484,
    518, 519, *520*, 521–522, 525, 527, 528, 555,
    556, 557, 559, 603–604. *See also* adzes;
    awls; chisels; drills; gravers; grinding
    implements; knives; mauls; scrapers;
    wedges
Toquaht. *See* Nootkans of Vancouver Island
torches: 351, 445, 583
to-tee-heen; synonymy: 226
Totem Park: 93, *94*, 95, *631*
totem poles: 82–83, 89, *93*, 132, 244, 256,
    257, 272–273, *274*, 278, *290*, *320*, 333, 389,
    594, 605, *615*. carving of: 209, *214*, *242*,
    247, 252, 265, 273, 275, 276, 375, 403, *403*,
    409, *491*, *607*, 609, 615, 616, 617, 618, 630.
    function of: 213, 333, 615. location of: 191,
    206, 241, 271, 618. mortuary: *214*, 219,
    241, *242*, 252, 630, 632. naming of: 207.
    painting of: *242*, 610, 618. postcontact: 93,
    94, 265–266, 291, *291*, 630, 632.
    prehistoric: 132. preservation of: 92, 93,
    214, 262, *631*. *See also* death practices,
    grave posts; structures, houseposts
tourism: 83, 109, 288, 291–293, 389, 409, *409*,
    410, *426*, 428, 436–437
Towhaha; synonymy: 487
Tow Hill site: 230, 235, 237
Townsend, John K.: 561
toys: *208*, 388, 446, 562. dolls: 194, 217, 433,
    495
T'Peeksin; synonymy: 487
trade: 206, 209, 364, 418, 425, 427, 456, 539,
    541, 576, 602. European goods: 119–120,
    122, *124*, 128, 131–132, 159, *273*, 281, 336,
    360–361, 427, 463, 470, 482, 508, 535, 604.
    intergroup: 24, 28, 119, 120–121, 122, 129,
    132–133, 190, 193, 208–209, 210, 211, 244,
    246, *247*, 255, 281, 337, 360–361, 394, 432,
    463, 490, 505, 530, 537, 568, 572, 574, 589,
    603, 606, 607, 626. items: 24, 28, 83,
    120–126, *123*, 131–132, 159, 208, 209, 210,
    211, 216, 223, 234, 237, 244, 246, *247*, 255,
    255, 269, 271, 281, 304, 363, 401, 409, 425,
    426, 433, 444, 449, 461, 481, 482, 484, 492,
    506, 518, 528, 536–537, 540, 547, 560, 580,
    608, 624, 627–628. media of exchange: 246,
    505, 537. middlemen: 150, 209, 407–408,
    423, 470, 514. networks: 81, 122, 129, 159,
    407, 418, 484, 535, 560, 580. partners: 208,
    246. prehistoric: 113, 234, 237, 239,
    303–304, 483–484. rates of exchange: 537.
    routes: 190, 208, 269, 281, 394, 514, 539,
    560, 606. with Whites: 209, 255, 336, 337,
    449, 499, 505, 513, 535, 568, 577, 609. *See
    also* fur trade
Traders Island site: 197, 199
trading posts and stores: 70, 119, 125,
    126–128, *127*, 129, 130, 132, 141, 143, 148,
    159, *191*, 223, 255, 319, 337, 363, 376, 409,
    470–471, 499, 514, 535
Training School for Indian Youth: 172, 183
Transitional complex: 235, 238
transitional stage: 198–199
transport; bidarkas: 191, 208. boats: *122*, 153,
    154, *163*, 164, 191, 238, 380, *389*. carrying:
    208. horses: 492, 507, 540. kayaks: *122*,
    191, 208. postcontact: 369, 380, 409, 428.
    prehistoric: 66, 67, 231, 237, 238, 298.
    rafts: 591. sleds and sledges: 191, 208,
    273. tumpline: 208. umiaks: 208. *See also*
    canoes; showshoes
traps. *See* fishing, implements; hunting,
    implements
travel: 17, 20, 208, 453, 505, 511, 602.
    prehistoric: 237. subsistence-related: 223,
    511. trade-related: 190, 223, 505, 560, 568.
    trails: 269, 394, 463, 488, 508, 525, 580. *See
    also* snowshoes; transport
treaties, British Columbia: 159–160, *162*
treaties, Canadian; land: 290
treaties, intertribal: 150
treaties and agreements, United States: 73,
    147, 148, 180–182, 464, 485, 487–488, 503,
    531, 561, 571, *574*, 633. education and
    health services: 182. fishing rights:
    169–172, *171*, 175–179, 181, 501, 535. land:
    186, *186*, 427, 514, 531, 561. land cessions:
    149, 169–172, *170*, *171*, 182. peace: 150,
    180–181. removal: 435, 439, 551, 571, 577,
    579, 592. reservations: 169, 181, 182, 435,
    535. sealing: 428. slavery: 169
Treaties of Fort Victoria: 464
Treaties of Tansey Point: 171, 181
Treaty of Dayton of 1855: 553
Treaty of Medicine Creek: 169, 176, 500
Treaty of Neah Bay: 171, 427
Treaty of Olympia: 514
Treaty of Point Elliott: 169, *171*, 471, 480,
    500
Treaty of Point No Point: 171, 439, 471, 474,
    500
Treaty of Washington: 71, 471, 500, 514
tribal councils. *See* political organization
tricksters. *See* mythology
Trinidad, Paul: *578*
Trojan site: *521*, 524
Trutch, Joseph: 159
Tsable River site: 341, 344, 352
Tsahwawtineuch; synonymy: 377
Tsamosan language grouping. *See* Salishan
    language family
Tsanchifin; synonymy: 552. *See also*
    Kalapuyans
tsänh-alokual; synonymy: 552
Tsankupi; synonymy: 553. *See also*
    Kalapuyans
Tsaumas; synonymy: 474
Tsawatainuk; synonymy: 377. *See also*
    Kwakiutl
Ts'āwatᴇēnôx; synonymy: 377
Tsawwassen. *See* Salish, Central Coast
Tsclallum language: 474
tseashall; synonymy: 452
Tsemakum; synonymy: 440
Tsetsaut: 30, 280, 289
Tsheheilis; synonymy: 516
Tsihaili-Selish language family: 516
Tsihailish; synonymy: 516
Tsihalis, Upper; synonymy: 516
Tsilwak: *250–251*
Tsimpsean; synonymy: 282
Tsimpshean; synonymy: 282, 294
Tsimpshean Committee: 295
Tsimsean; synonymy: 282
Tsimseyans; synonymy: 282
Tsimsheeans; synonymy: 282
Tsimshian: 9, 12, 14, 52–53, 55, 77, *94*,
    95–97, 116–117, 153, *254*, 267–297, *276*,
    280. art: 5, 82–83, *94*, 247, *250–251*, 276,
    292, 373, 602, 604, 605, 606, 607, *607*, 609,
    612–613, 616, *617*, 624, 628, 630.
    ceremonies: 84, 132, 251, 278–279, 386.
    disease: 140, 141, 142, 143, 147.
    environment: 229, 269. external relations:
    213, 280–281. history: 74–75, 80, 153, 156,
    160, 161, 165, 166, 267, 281–282. kinship:
    86, 274–275. kinship terminology: 280, 309.
    life cycle: 277–278. migrations: 9, 81, 233.
    music: 220. mythology: 74, 77, 79, 280,
    594, 600, 601. political organization:
    276–277, 285–286, 294–295. population:
    136, 141, 147, 165, 282, 287, 297.
    prehistory: 9, 45, 69, 110, 113, 114, 115,
    136, 229, 232, 235, 298, 357. religion: 255,
    279. shamanism: 221. social organization:
    13, 78, 213, 235, 248, 251, 274–276,
    294–295. structures: 89, 271–273, *273*, *274*.
    subsistence: 210, 269–271, *270*, 282,
    286–287. synonymy: 14, 282. technology:
    232, 273–274. territory: 210, 267. trade:
    125, 129, 130, 208, 209, 211, 244, *247*.
    transport: *274*. warfare: 136. *See also*
    Indian words
Tsimshian, Coast: *11*, 14, 53, 54, 267–288,
    337. art: 616. ceremonies: 85–86, 253, 278.
    education: 286. environment: 269. external
    relations: 306. Gilutsau: 267, 283.
    Ginadoiks: 267, 283. Ginakangeek: 267,
    283. Gispakloats: 267, 277, 283, 294, 306.
    Gitandau: 267, 283. Gitlan: 267, 283, 294.
    Gitsees: 267, 283. Gitwilgyots: 267, 283.
    Gitwilkseba: 267, 283. Gitzaklalth: 267,
    283. history: 125, 144, 161, 165, 255, 256,
    281, 294–295. kinship: 274–275. Kitselas:
    269, 283, 287, 288, 294. Kitsumkalum: 269,
    271, 277, 283, 284, 287, 288. language: 31,
    32–33, 33, 34, 44, 46, 48, 267, 282, 295.
    mythology: 597, 598. orthography: 267.
    political organization: 276, 286. population:
    136, 144, 267, 269, 282, 287. Port Simpson
    band: 165, 168, 269, 283, 287, 388.
    prehistory: 108, 113, 235. settlements:

776